COMPLETE COURSE IN ISC

HINDI

In accordance with the latest syllabus of Council for the Indian School Certificate Examinations

COMPLETE COURSE IN ISC HINDI

Class XI & XII

Compiled By :

B. R. Sharma
(M.A., B. Ed.)

Dr. Alok Tripathi
(Ph. D.)
Sahyadri School, Pune

OSWAL PUBLISHERS

1/12, Sahitya Kunj, M. G. Road, Agra-282 002

Edition : 2019

Price : ₹ 452·00

ISBN : 978-93-87660-36-6

OSWAL PUBLISHERS

Head office	:	1/12, Sahitya Kunj, M.G. Road, Agra–282 002
Phone	:	(0562) 2527771–4
E-mail	:	contact@oswalpublishers.com,sales@oswalpublishers.com
Website	:	www.oswalpublishers.com
Facebook link	:	https://www.facebook.com/oswalpublishersindia
Also available on	:	Amazon, Flipkart, snapdeal
Printed at	:	Upkar Printing Unit, Agra

Preface

We feel immense pleasure in introducing this new revised edition of Complete Course in ISC Hindi for the students of Indian School Certificate Examination (Class XI & XII).

This book is divided into two sections—Section A and Section B. Section A includes composition, unseen passage and grammar. The main objective to include this section in our book is to create the ability in the students to express themselves in writing. Section B includes literature part of the prescribed books. This section is structured to aid students in properly understanding the subject matter of the prescribed books as it not only contains short summaries on different lessons but also answers to the questions asked in the Board examination.

All the matter presented in the book is strictly according to the syllabus laid down by the Council. We hope that with all these unique features, this book will be a relief for the students from the burdensome task of making notes.

Lastly, we are much grateful for the efforts made by ***B. R. Sharma & Dr. Alok Tripathi*** *who left no stone unturned in the completion of this book.*

Suggestions for the improvement of the book shall be gratefully acknowledged and will be duly incorporated in the next edition.

—THE PUBLISHER

Syllabus

CLASS XI AND XII

There will be one paper of 3 hours duration, which will consist of two sections :

Section A : Language (50 Marks)

Section B : Prescribed Textbooks (50 marks)

1. **Composition :** One composition of 400 words approximately in the language to be written out of a choice of 6 topics set within the experience and mental maturity of the age-group of the candidates. (20 Marks)
2. **Comprehension :** An unseen passage of about 300 words to be set with questions and / or summary (with heading to test the ability to summarise and/or to expand an idea given in the passage.) (20 Marks)
3. **Grammar :** Functional grammar-correction of sentences and using words/idioms in sentences, viz., correct structure with proper agreement of the subject and verb according to the number, gender, case, tense and voice. (10 Marks)

Candidates will be required to answer **four** questions from **at least three** of the prescribed textbooks.

4. **Prescribed Textbooks :** Candidates will be required to answer **four** questions on **any three** of the prescribed textbooks. (50 Marks)
   - Saara Akash
   - Ashadh Ka Ek Din
   - Kavya Manjari
   - Gadya Sankalan

विषय-सूची

Section – A

निबन्ध (Essays)

Section – B

गद्य संकलन (Gadya Sankalan)

निबन्ध

(ESSAYS)

हर चीज आसान होने से पहले कठिन होती है।

अथवा

हर चीज प्रारम्भ में कठिन होती है जिसे अभ्यास और परिश्रम से सरल बना लिया जाता है। इस कथन की सत्यता को सिद्ध कीजिए।

अथवा

''करत-करत अभ्यास ते जड़मति होत सुजान।'' इस कथन की सत्यता सिद्ध कीजिए।

हर चीज आसान होने से पहले कठिन होती है, जिसे आसान करने के लिए कठिन परिश्रम और अभ्यास की आवश्यकता होती है। इसीलिए यह कहा जा सकता है कि अभ्यास मनुष्य को परिपक्व बना देता है। आज मानव इस पृथ्वी का श्रेष्ठ प्राणी है। इस श्रेष्ठता को प्राप्त करने के लिए मनुष्य को वर्षों तक कठिन परिश्रम करना पड़ा। जीवन की इस विकास यात्रा का प्रारम्भिक चरण बड़ा ही कठिन था, जो धीरे-धीरे परिश्रम और अभ्यास से सरल हो गया।

हर चीज जो आज हमें सरल-सी प्रतीत होती है, वह अपने आरम्भिक रूप में हमारे लिए एक चुनौती ही थी। आग का प्रयोग, पहिये के आविष्कार से लेकर आज के आधुनिक आविष्कार, सब में एक चुनौती ही थी। तब से लेकर अब तक आधुनिक काल के इस जीवन में अनेक बदलाव परिलक्षित होते हैं।

आज जब हम किसी को कोई कार्य बड़ी सुगमता से करते हुए देखते हैं तभी हमें यह विचार कर लेना आवश्यक है कि अपने प्रारम्भिक चरण में यह कार्य कठिन रहा होगा। मानव जीवन की विकास यात्रा का ही एक उदाहरण ले सकते हैं। बड़े हो जाने पर मनुष्य का जमीन पर अपने पैरों से चलना कितनी साधारण और सरल-सी बात है, लेकिन जब शैशवावस्था होती है, शिशु अपने पैरों पर खड़ा होने का प्रयास करता है, तो वही कार्य उसके लिए किसी चुनौती से कम नहीं होता। वही चुनौतीपूर्ण कार्य धीरे-धीरे अभ्यास और श्रम से आज सरल बन गया है। इस प्रकार यह स्पष्ट हो जाता है कि हर चीज आसान होने से पहले कठिन होती है।

हमारे पुराणों में इसके अनेक उदाहरण मौजूद हैं। महाभारत में जब गुरु द्रोणाचार्य, एकलव्य को धनुर्विद्या की शिक्षा देने से इंकार कर देते हैं, तो वह जंगल में उनकी प्रतिमा बनाकर उसके समक्ष अभ्यास कर इतना कुशल धनुर्धर बन जाता है कि जिसे देख अर्जुन और गुरु द्रोणाचार्य दोनों ही दंग रह जाते हैं।

उसी प्रकार जल-विद्या में निपुण होने के लिए दुर्योधन घंटों पानी में खड़े रहने का अभ्यास करता है। इसी प्रकार अनेक ऐसे उदाहरण मिलते हैं जो यह स्पष्ट कर देते हैं कि आज हम जिसे सरल समझ रहे हैं उसे सरल बनाने में कितने परिश्रम और अभ्यास की आवश्यकता पड़ी थी।

कबीरदास जी ने यह तक कह दिया कि यदि कोई मूर्ख व्यक्ति भी अभ्यास और परिश्रम करे तो वह ज्ञानवान बन सकता है—

करत-करत अभ्यास ते जड़मति होत सुजान।
रसरी आवत जात ते सिल पर परत निसान।।

अब यदि हम दैनिक जीवन के कार्यों को ही लें तो पता चलता है कि आज हम जिन कार्यों को बड़ी सरलता से कर लेते हैं, वही कार्य प्रारम्भिक चरण में दुष्कर ही नहीं कभी-कभी दुर्लभ भी प्रतीत हुआ करते थे। बच्चों का चलना, बोलना, पढ़ना, लिखना, समझना आदि ऐसी क्रियाएँ हैं जो बहुत ही आसान प्रतीत होती

हैं, परन्तु यही क्रियाएँ अपनी आरम्भिक अवस्था में बहुत ही कठिन थीं। जिसे हमने अपने निरन्तर प्रयास और अभ्यास से सरल बना लिया है।

इस तरह अन्त में निष्कर्ष रूप में यह कहा जा सकता है कि यह कथन पूर्णतया सत्य है कि हर चीज आसान होने से पहले कठिन होती है।

युवाओं और प्रौढ़ों (बुजुर्गों) में से समाज में अधिक महत्वपूर्ण कौन है ?

अथवा

समाज के निर्माण में युवा वर्ग और प्रौढ़ (बुजुर्ग) वर्ग दोनों का ही समान योगदान होता है।'' इस कथन के सन्दर्भ में अपने विचार स्पष्ट कीजिए।

अथवा

युवा वर्ग जहाँ उर्जा का स्त्रोत है, बुजुर्ग अनुभव का खजाना है।'' आप इस कथन से कहाँ तक सहमत हैं ?

व्यक्तियों के समूह से समाज का निर्माण होता है। इस समूह में अनेक आयु-वर्ग के लोग रहते हैं— बालक, युवा और प्रौढ़। समाज के हर आयु-वर्ग के लोगों का सामाजिक संरचना में योगदान होता है। ये आयु-वर्ग एक-दूसरे पर आश्रित भी रहते हैं। एक वर्ग दूसरे वर्ग के लिए प्रेरणा का स्त्रोत बन जाता है।

अब यदि सिर्फ समाज के दो वर्गों की बात की जाये युवा और प्रौढ़ तो इन दोनों वर्गों से समाज को एक विशेष योगदान मिलता है। जहाँ युवा वर्ग जोश, उत्साह और ऊर्जा से भरा है, वहीं बुजुर्ग वर्ग अनुभवों की खान हैं। यदि इनमें से किसी एक के महत्वपूर्ण होने की बात की जाये तो यह दूसरे के साथ अन्याय होगा, क्योंकि सामाजिक संरचना में दोनों का समान योगदान होता है।

यदि हम समाज के प्रौढ़ व्यक्तियों को उपेक्षित कर दें तो हमारे समाज को उनके द्वारा मिलने वाले अनुभवजन्य ज्ञान का लाभ नहीं मिल सकेगा। यही प्रौढ़ वर्ग हमारा शिक्षक और मार्गदर्शक होता है। अपने अनुभवों से युवावर्ग को अवगत कराना ही प्रौढ़ वर्ग का दायित्व है। ये प्रौढ़ वर्ग अपने जीवन की सफलताओं और असफलताओं से अनुभव प्राप्त करता है। ये अनुभव हमें बुजुर्गों द्वारा माता-पिता, दादा-दादी, नाना-नानी आदि अनेक रूपों के अलावा कभी-कभी अन्य रूप में आकर हमें जीवन का अनुभवजन्य ज्ञान देता है।

इन दोनों के महत्व को इमारत के उदाहरण द्वारा बड़ी सुगमता से समझा जा सकता है। जिस प्रकार इमारत के मजबूत होने में नींव का बड़ा योगदान होता है ठीक उसी प्रकार हमारे समाजरूपी इमारत की संरचना में बुजुर्गों की भूमिका उस नींव की ही तरह है जो सम्पूर्ण समाजरूपी इमारत को सुदृढ़ता प्रदान करती है। जिस प्रकार एक सुदृढ़ इमारत में नींव महत्वपूर्ण है, उसी प्रकार समाज में बुजुर्ग भी महत्वपूर्ण हैं। किसी कवि ने सत्य ही कहा है—

''पदचिन्ह अपने पूर्वजों के यत्नपूर्वक खोज लेने चाहिए।''

इस प्रकार बुजुर्ग अपने अनुभवजन्य ज्ञान से युवावर्ग का मार्गदर्शन कर उनका मार्ग प्रशस्त करते हैं। लेकिन सिर्फ नींव को इमारत नहीं कहा जा सकता। इमारत के मजबूत होने के लिए जोश, उत्साह से भरा युवावर्ग भी चाहिए जो इमारत की संरचना को आकार दे सके।

ऐसे समाज की संकल्पना नहीं की जा सकती जिसमें सिर्फ बुजुर्ग ही हों, क्योंकि बिना युवावर्ग के समाज में जोश, उत्साह एवं उर्जा का अभाव रहेगा। प्रौढ़ भविष्य के सपने तो देख सकते हैं, परन्तु उन सपनों को पूरा करने के लिए युवा शक्ति आवश्यक है। इसलिए समाज के समृद्ध होने के लिए युवा व प्रौढ़ दोनों वर्गों की समान आवश्यकता है। किसी एक के बिना समाज की कल्पना नहीं की जा सकती है।

आज का युवा सपनों को साकार करेगा, क्योंकि उसमें ऊर्जा और उत्साह है। लेकिन कुछ वर्षों बाद जब वही युवा प्रौढ़ बन जाता है तो वह मार्गदर्शक बन जाता है। इस तरह एक शृंखला बन जाती है जो अनवरत चलती रहती है।

एक माध्यमिक विद्यालय में कितने विषय पढ़ाने चाहिए ?

अथवा

आधुनिक शिक्षा पद्धति में माध्यमिक विद्यालयों में विषयों की संख्या अधिक होती जा रही है। क्या आप इन विषयों की उपयोगिता व आवश्यकता से सहमत हैं ?

माध्यमिक शिक्षा वह मंजिल है जहाँ पर छात्रों को विज्ञान, मानविकी और सामाजिक विज्ञानों की आधारभूत जानकारियों से परिचित कराया जाना चाहिए। संवैधानिक और नागरिक अधिकारों का समुचित ज्ञान प्रदान किया जाना चाहिए। मुख्यत: इन उद्देश्यों की पूर्ति को ध्यान में रखकर ही शिक्षा-पद्धति का निर्माण किया गया है।

भारतीय शिक्षण प्रक्रिया में सम्पूर्ण शिक्षा को तीन भागों में विभाजित कर दिया गया है—

(1) प्राथमिक शिक्षा, (2) माध्यमिक शिक्षा, (3) उच्च शिक्षा।

माध्यमिक शिक्षा में विकास सर्वाधिक स्थान लेता है और यह उच्च शिक्षा की नींव का निर्माण करता है। शिक्षा पद्धति के चरणों में माध्यमिक शिक्षा का एक विशेष योगदान होता है कक्षा 10 और 12 में आते ही विद्यार्थी को अपना लक्ष्य दिखाई देने लगता है कि उसे किन विषयों को आधार बनाकर उच्च शिक्षा प्राप्त करनी है। इस समय विद्यार्थी का मस्तिष्क विकास की चरम अवस्था पर होता है। ऐसे समय में उस पर कितना दबाव दें, यह जानना आवश्यक हो जाता है।

माध्यमिक शिक्षा के दौरान विषयों की संख्या यह एक महत्वपूर्ण विषय है। विषयों की संख्या के अधिक होने से विद्यार्थियों पर बोझ बढ़ता है। विषयों की संख्या अधिक होने से शिक्षा की गुणवत्ता पर भी प्रभाव पड़ता है। शैक्षिक सत्र की एक सीमित परिधि होती है तथा प्रत्येक विद्यालय प्रशासन को सभी विषयों को पूरा करना अपेक्षित होता है। ऐसी परिस्थिति में विषयों की अधिक संख्या होने से शिक्षण का प्रवाह बढ़ाया जायेगा जिससे विषय का गहनता से अध्ययन नहीं किया जा सकेगा।

विषयों की संख्या अधिक होने से विद्यार्थियों को समय-सूची का निर्माण करना एक बड़ी समस्या हो जाती है। दिन भर में जो समय मिलता है वही विद्यार्थियों के सर्वांगीण विकास के लिए आवश्यक होता है लेकिन जब विषयों की संख्या बढ़ जाती है तो विद्यार्थी को अन्य गतिविधियों में से भी समय निकालकर अध्ययन में लगाना पड़ता है। जबकि वे अन्य गतिविधियाँ जैसे खेलकूद, मनोरंजन आदि भी उतने ही महत्वपूर्ण हैं जितना कि अध्ययन। यह अधिक विषय छात्रों के सर्वांगीण विकास में बाधक होते हैं।

इस प्रकार उपर्युक्त विवेचन से यह स्पष्ट हो जाता है कि माध्यमिक विद्यालय में विषयों की अधिक संख्या किसी भी रूप में छात्रों के हित में नहीं हैं। अब प्रश्न यह उठता है कि विषयों की संख्या को कितना रखा जाये ?

आज इस प्रश्न पर बड़ी गम्भीरता से विचार किया जा रहा है। हमारे शैक्षिक विचारकों और विभिन्न शैक्षिक परिषदों ने इस बात को स्वीकार किया है कि माध्यमिक विद्यालयों में पढ़ाये जाने वाले विषयों की संख्या पर विचार करना आवश्यक है। कुछ राज्य-स्तरीय तथा केन्द्रीय परिषदों ने तो अपने पाठ्यक्रमों में विषयों की संख्या को कम करना भी प्रारम्भ कर दिया है। जो कि विद्यार्थियों के हित की दिशा में लिया गया एक बड़ा कदम है।

विषयों की संख्या उतनी ही हो, जिन्हें विद्यार्थी सुगमता से निर्धारित समय में अन्य आवश्यक गतिविधियों के साथ गुणवत्तापूर्वक पूरा कर सके। इस दिशा में सराहनीय कदम उठाये जा रहे हैं जिनसे आशातीत सफलता मिलने की सम्भावना है।

क्या पर्यटन के अधिक अनावरण से सांस्कृतिक परम्पराएँ नष्ट हो सकती हैं ?

अथवा

अधिक पर्यटन से हमारी सांस्कृतिक धरोहरों को हानि पहुँच सकती है। क्या आप इस कथन से सहमत हैं ? तर्क सहित अपने विचार लिखें।

भारतीय प्राचीन ग्रन्थों में स्पष्ट रूप से मानव के विकास, सुख और शान्ति की सन्तुष्टि व ज्ञान के लिए पर्यटन आवश्यक माना गया है। हमारे देश के ऋषि-मुनियों ने भी पर्यटन को प्रथम महत्व दिया है। कहा गया है कि बिना पर्यटन मानव अंधकार प्रेमी होकर रह जायेगा। पर्यटन आवश्यक है परन्तु पर्यटकों के आने से जहाँ अनेक प्रकार के लाभ होते हैं वहीं पर्यटकों का अधिक आगमन सांस्कृतिक धरोहरों के लिए एक खतरा भी बन चुका है।

अधिक पर्यटन से समाज में अनचाहे परिवर्तन होते हैं जिससे सांस्कृतिक विघटन शुरू हो जाता है। अलग-अलग प्रकार की सभ्यताओं और संस्कृतियों से आने वाले पर्यटकों की वजह से उस स्थान की सांस्कृतिक अस्मिता को खतरा उत्पन्न हो जाता है। जिसका जीता-जागता उदाहरण गोवा है जहाँ पर नशीली दवाइयाँ और वैश्यावृत्ति इस प्रकार बढ़ गयी है कि वहाँ की सांस्कृतिक परम्पराएँ नष्ट होने के कगार पर आ गई हैं।

इस प्रकार पर्यटन के अधिक अनावरण से सांस्कृतिक परम्पराओं के नष्ट होने की सम्भावना बढ़ जाती है। जिस पर्यटन क्षेत्र में पर्यटकों की संख्या बढ़ जाती है उन स्थलों पर स्थानीय लोगों को उतना लाभ नहीं मिल पाता जितना हवाई जहाज, होटल वाले आदि बड़े पूँजीपतियों को मिलता है। इस प्रकार लाभ कम मिलने के कारण लोगों में सामाजिक व सांस्कृतिक असुरक्षा की भावना जाग्रत होती है, जो स्थानीय लोगों की मूल संवेदना को नष्ट कर देती है।

पर्यटकों के अधिक आगमन से उनके रहन-सहन का ढंग अलग होने से अनेक प्रकार की परेशानियाँ होती हैं। पर्यटकों का अधिक आगमन पर्यावरण की दृष्टि से भी उचित नहीं है क्योंकि अधिक पर्यटकों के आने के कारण प्रदूषण बढ़ जाता है। इन प्रदूषण के कारणों से जलवायु पर प्रतिकूल प्रभाव पड़ता है जिसका असर हमारी ऐतिहासिक इमारतों पर भी पड़ता है। जिसके अनेक समाचार समाचार-पत्रों में आते रहते हैं।

इस प्रकार अन्त में यह कहा जा सकता है कि पर्यटन के अधिक अनावरण से सांस्कृतिक परम्पराओं के नष्ट होने का जोखिम अवश्य है। सांस्कृतिक परम्पराओं पर पर्यटन का सकारात्मक और नकारात्मक दोनों रूपों में प्रभाव पड़ता है। जहाँ एक ओर पर्यटकों के आने से सांस्कृतिक आदान-प्रदान होता है जो पर्यटन का सकारात्मक पहलू है। वहीं दूसरी ओर कभी-कभी पर्यटकों की संस्कृति का प्रभाव इतना प्रबल होता है कि पर्यटकों की संस्कृति मेजबानों की संस्कृति से अधिक प्रभावशाली होती है जिसके प्रभाव में आकर उस स्थल की सांस्कृतिक अस्मिता खतरे में पड़ जाती है। इस प्रकार पर्यटन का अधिक अनावरण हमारी सांस्कृतिक परम्पराओं के नष्ट होने का कारण बन जाता है।

मेधावी छात्रों को अलग से पढ़ाया जाना चाहिए। इस कथन से आप कहाँ तक सहमत हैं ?

अथवा

क्या अध्यापन के दौरान छात्रों को उनकी बौद्धिक क्षमता के आधार पर कक्षाओं में बाँटा जाना उचित है ? आपकी दृष्टि में यह कहाँ तक उचित है ?

विद्या स्वर्ण है, परन्तु भूमि की मिट्टी और मलिनता से लथपथ विद्यारूपी स्वर्ण को जब तक प्रयोग की भट्टी में न तपाया जाये, तब तक उस पर कांति और आभा नहीं आती। सच्चा विद्यार्थी वही है जिसके मन में विद्यार्जन के प्रति सच्ची जिज्ञासा और लगन हो। शिक्षा मौलिक अधिकारों में से एक है, शिक्षा पर सभी का समान रूप से अधिकार है।

कक्षा में विद्यार्थियों का एक समूह होता है जिसमें अनेक विद्यार्थी होते हैं। इन विद्यार्थियों की बौद्धिक क्षमताएँ भी अलग-अलग होती हैं। इन्हें जब एक साथ कक्षा में पढ़ाया जाता है तो कुछ विद्यार्थी जिनकी बौद्धिक क्षमता कुछ अधिक होती है, वो विषयवस्तु को बड़ी सहजता से समझ जाते हैं। वहीं कुछ ऐसे विद्यार्थी भी होते हैं जो उस समय समझ नहीं पाते हैं। इस प्रकार विभिन्न मानसिक स्तर वाले विद्यार्थियों को एक साथ पढ़ाना शिक्षक के लिए चुनौतीपूर्ण कार्य बन जाता है। इस प्रकार इस कथन के सम्बन्ध में अपनी सहमति अथवा असहमति देने से पूर्व इनके गुण-दोषों का विवेचन आवश्यक है।

मेधावी छात्रों को सामान्य विद्यार्थियों के साथ रखने पर कुछ लाभ अवश्य होते हैं—

(1) मेधावी छात्र अपने मित्र छात्रों की शंका को निर्मूल करने का कार्य कर सकते हैं।

(2) अध्ययन में अन्य छात्रों का सहयोग करने से उनके अन्दर सहयोग की भावना का विकास होगा।

(3) अन्य छात्र भी मेधावी छात्र के प्रदर्शन से प्रेरित होकर अध्ययन में विशेष ध्यान देते हैं।

मेधावी छात्रों के कक्षा में रहने से कक्षा की कठिनाई कुछ इस प्रकार बढ़ जाती हैं—

(1) मेधावी छात्र बड़ी जल्दी ही कक्षा को अपने नियन्त्रण में कर लेते हैं।

(2) अध्यापक भी मेधावी छात्रों की कुशलता से शीघ्र ही प्रभावित हो जाते हैं, क्योंकि अध्यापक हर उस विद्यार्थी को ज्यादा पसन्द करता है जो कार्य अच्छा और प्रभावशाली तरीके से करता है। जब अध्यापक मेधावी छात्र से प्रभावित हो जाता है तो अध्यापक के व्यवहार में परिवर्तन आ जाता है। जिसके कारण सामान्य विद्यार्थी कक्षा में उपेक्षित महसूस कर सकते हैं।

(3) सामान्य अथवा औसत श्रेणी का विद्यार्थी जब एक-दो बार कक्षा में सामान्य और आसान प्रश्नों को पूछता है तो मेधावी छात्रों के द्वारा कभी-कभी उपहास का पात्र बन जाता है। इस प्रकार औसत विद्यार्थी की कक्षा में भागीदारी धीरे-धीरे कम होती जाती है।

(4) मेधावी छात्र की प्रगति को देखकर अन्य छात्र स्वयं को हीन समझने लगते हैं। जिसके कारण उनका आत्मविश्वास टूटने की सम्भावना बढ़ जाती है।

(5) वहीं दूसरी ओर जब अध्यापक सम्पूर्ण कक्षा के स्तर को ध्यान में रखकर अध्यापन करता है तो कक्षा की चुनौतियाँ मेधावी छात्र को बहुत सरल लगती हैं और उसमें अति आत्मविश्वास का विकास उत्पन्न होने लगता है।

(6) मेधावी छात्र को चुनौतीपूर्ण कार्य न मिलने से उसका शैक्षिक स्तर कम होने की सम्भावना रहती है।

इस प्रकार पूर्णतया यह नहीं कहा जा सकता कि मेधावी छात्रों के कक्षा में रहने से अन्य छात्रों का नुकसान ही होता है। लेकिन यह बात तो तय है कि अन्य छात्रों को लाभ कम मिलता है।

मैं इस कथन से पूरी तरह से सहमत हूँ कि मेधावी छात्रों को अलग से ही पढ़ाया जाना चाहिए। जिससे उन्हें उनकी बौद्धिक क्षमता के अनुरूप कार्यों को करा कर उनकी मेधा का विकास किया जा सके। मेधावी छात्रों के अलग से पढ़ने से कक्षा के कमजोर विद्यार्थियों को उनकी सीखने की गति व आवश्यकता के अनुरूप अध्यापन किया जा सकेगा जिससे सभी विद्यार्थी लाभान्वित होंगे।

जब वरिष्ठ नागरिकों और पूर्ववर्ती पीढ़ी को आभार प्रकट किया जायेगा तब एक सभ्य समाज भी महान बन जायेगा।

अथवा

वरिष्ठ नागरिकों और पूर्ववर्ती पीढ़ी के प्रति आभार प्रकट करने से किस प्रकार एक सभ्य समाज महान बन जाता है ?

अथवा

एक सभ्य समाज के महान होने में वरिष्ठ नागरिकों और पूर्ववर्ती पीढ़ी का क्या योगदान होता है ?

जब बात समाज और सभ्यता की हो, संस्कारों की हो, तो यह जान लेना आवश्यक हो जाता है कि ये संस्कार और ये सभ्यताएँ किस प्रकार हमारे जीवन को प्रभावित करती है और कहाँ से आई हैं ? इनका बीज हमारे भीतर कैसे आरोपित हुआ ?

जब हम इन प्रश्नों पर विचार करने लगते हैं तो यह पता चलता है कि इस सभ्य और सुसंस्कृत समाज का निर्माण एक पीढ़ी या दो पीढ़ियों में नहीं हुआ ये तो सदियों पुरानी परम्पराएँ हैं जिन्हें हमारे पूर्वजों ने विरासत के रूप में हमें दिया है। इस सम्बन्ध में दिनकर जी का यह कथन उल्लेखनीय है—

''हम अपने जीवन में जो संस्कार जमा करते हैं वह भी हमारी संस्कृति का अंग बन जाता है और मरने के बाद हम अन्य वस्तुओं के साथ अपनी संस्कृति की विरासत भी अपने संतानों के लिए छोड़ जाते हैं।''

इस प्रकार आज हम जो भी हैं वह अपने पूर्वजों की वजह से हैं। अनेक शताब्दियों तक हमारे पूर्वज जिस तरह रहते-सहते, धर्म-कर्म करते, राज-काज चलाते हैं, उन्हीं से हमारी संस्कृति उत्पन्न हुई है। आज हम जो कुछ भी करते हैं उसमें हमारी संस्कृति की झलक होती है। इसके निर्माण में हमारे पूर्वजों का हाथ है।

इस प्रकार आज हमारा होना उन्हीं के कारण सम्भव है। इसलिए हमारी जीवन शैली के विकास और प्रगति का प्रथम अध्याय उन्हीं नागरिकों ने लिखा है। इसलिए हमें यह कभी नहीं भूलना चाहिए तथा जब भी अवसर मिले हमें अपने पूर्वजों व वरिष्ठ नागरिकों का आभार व्यक्त करना चाहिए।

यह सभ्य समाज जब अपने पूर्वजों का आभार व्यक्त करता है तो साथ ही सन्देश भी देता है। उन्हें एक बार याद कर लेने से हमें भी यह आभास हो जाता है कि जैसे हमारे पूर्वजों ने हमारे लिए एक उपजाऊ पृष्ठभूमि तैयार की है ठीक उसी प्रकार हमें भी अपने भविष्य के कर्णधारों को ऐसी ही पृष्ठभूमि देनी है जिस पर विकास के असंख्य कमलों को खिलाया जा सके।

इस प्रकार यह स्पष्ट हो जाता है कि जब भी हम पूर्वजों को याद करते हैं हम उनका धन्यवाद करते हैं। हम उनके योगदानों के प्रति अपना आभार व्यक्त करते हैं। जो हमें कृतज्ञता का पाठ सिखाता है और हमारा यह सभ्य समाज महानता पथ पर एक और कदम रख देता है। इस प्रकार हमारा यह सभ्य समाज महान बन जाता है।

बस एक क्लिक दूर

बस एक क्लिक और लो हम जुड़ गये सारी दुनिया से। हाँ ! यह सच है, शत-प्रतिशत। आज बस एक क्लिक से बड़े से बड़े काम हो जाते हैं। इस क्लिक ने मनुष्य के जीवन को अपनी मुट्ठी में कर लिया है। इस क्लिक ने मनुष्य के जीवन के प्रत्येक पहलू पर अपनी गहरी छाप छोड़ी है। आज इस क्लिक के बिना आधुनिकता से परिपूर्ण इस दुनिया में जीना दुर्लभ हो गया है।

इस क्लिक का प्रभाव बड़ा ही व्यापक है। इसकी व्यापकता का अनुमान इसी तरह से लगाया जा सकता है कि इसने मनुष्य के शिक्षा, स्वास्थ्य, सामाजिकता व अर्थव्यवस्था जैसे प्राथमिक क्षेत्रों पर सम्भवतः पूर्णरूपेण अधिकार कर लिया है। इनके अतिरिक्त यह क्लिक मनुष्य की दिनचर्या की आवश्यकता की हद तक पहुँच चुकी हैं। अरे ! यह चमत्कार इंसानों के बनाये, इंसानों की मुट्ठी में रहने वाले उस छोटे से माउस की क्लिक का है।

आज आप अपने घर में बैठकर दुनिया के एक छोर से लेकर दूसरे छोर तक एक क्लिक से जुड़ सकते हैं। आप अपने मित्र के साथ एक-दूसरे को देखते हुए बातचीत कर सकते हैं। इस प्रकार से इस क्लिक ने सिर्फ संचार माध्यम में क्रान्ति नहीं लायी बल्कि इस क्लिक से आप उन स्थानों और लोगों के बारे में जानकारी प्राप्त कर सकते हैं, जहाँ वास्तविकता में पहुँचना स्वप्न से कम नहीं है। आप उनसे मित्रता कर उनके रहन-सहन, खान-पान, संस्कार आदि के बारे में जान सकते हैं। इस प्रकार एक क्लिक से संस्कारों और सभ्यताओं का आदान-प्रदान बड़ी ही सुगमता से सम्भव है। इतना ही नहीं कला और मनोरंजन आदि के क्षेत्र में भी इस क्लिक ने नये आयाम प्रतिस्थापित किये हैं।

शिक्षा के क्षेत्र में भी क्लिक ने नये सोपान निर्मित किये हैं। आज इस क्लिक की सहायता से आप कहीं से भी विशेषज्ञों के माध्यम से व्याख्यान सुन सकते हैं। अमेरिका में दिया गया व्याख्यान यहाँ के छात्रों द्वारा सुना जा सकता है। आप अपने विषय के सन्दर्भ में प्रचुर जानकारी बस एक क्लिक से प्राप्त कर सकते हैं। ज्ञान सिर्फ पुस्तकों और अध्यापकों से ही प्राप्त किया जा सकता है लेकिन इस क्लिक ने उसमें एक नया विकल्प भी जोड़ दिया है, जो हर वर्ग के विद्यार्थियों के लिए सुगम है।

चिकित्सा के क्षेत्र में इस क्लिक ने एक नया अध्याय जोड़ा है। आज एक चिकित्सक दूसरे विशेषज्ञ के लिए कार्य को बस एक क्लिक द्वारा देख और सुन सकता है। औषधियों के सन्दर्भ में जानकारी, रोगों और उनके उपचारों के सम्बन्ध में होने वाली नित नई उपलब्धियों को पलक झपकते ही जान सकते हैं।

इस प्रकार यह क्लिक एक ऐसा जादू है जिसने हमारी दुनिया को पूरी तरह से बदलकर रख दिया है। ये बदलाव कहीं प्रगति का एक पुष्ट सोपान बन जाते हैं, परन्तु जब इनका दुरुपयोग होता है तो सम्पूर्ण मानवता को हानि पहुँचती है। यदि हम इस क्लिक का उपयोग मानवता के विकास के लिए करें तो यह परी के उस जादुई छड़ी की तरह है जो सारी कामनाओं को पूरा कर सकती है।

युवा वर्ग की बदलती हुई मानसिकता

पक्ष—मनुष्य, पशु-पक्षी आदि अपने-अपने समूह में समाज में रहते हैं। सभी एक-दूसरे के सहयोग से काम करते हैं। प्रकृति ने विषमलिंगी जीव पैदा करके साथ रहने के आकर्षण को और अधिक बढ़ा दिया है।

आदिकाल से ही एक-दूसरे के साथ रहने की प्रवृत्ति मनुष्य में है। हर व्यक्ति अपने समान अवस्था वाले साथियों के साथ रहना, खेलना तथा पढ़ना पसन्द करते हैं।

प्राचीनकाल में गुरुकुल में पढ़ाई के लिए अवस्था निर्धारित थी। परिश्रम तथा लगन से पढ़ने वाले छात्र पढ़ाई में बहुत योग्यता हासिल कर लेते थे और न पढ़ने वाले तब भी एक-दूसरे को परेशान करते रहते थे। धर्म, अर्थ, काम और मोक्ष को ध्यान में रखकर शिक्षा की व्यवस्था की गयी थी। कुछ भी हो उस समय मानव में मानवता का विकास हो इस पर विशेष ध्यान दिया जाता था। प्रत्येक व्यक्ति पढ़ाई के साथ-साथ गुरु, गुरु परिवार तथा आगन्तुकों की सेवा गुरुकुलों में बड़े भक्ति भाव से किया करते थे। जिससे उनमें नम्रता, दया, क्षमा आदि गुणों का अनायास ही विकास हो जाता था। खेती और घर के अधिकांश कार्य हाथों द्वारा सम्पादित होते थे तथा मनोरंजन के साधन सीमित थे। अतः मनुष्यों को एक दूसरे के साथ समय बिताने का अवसर मिल जाता था।

आधुनिक युग में विज्ञान के नये-नये आविष्कारों और मनोरंजन के आधुनिक साधनों ने मनुष्य के मन-मस्तिष्क को जरूरत से अधिक सक्रिय बना दिया है। आज की शिक्षा प्रणाली भी अर्थ प्रधान हो गयी है। शिक्षण संस्थाएँ भी व्यापारिक संस्थानों का रूप लेती जा रही हैं। अध्यापक भी विद्यालय में पढ़ाने की अपेक्षा अपने घर ट्यूशन या कोचिंग सेण्टरों पर पढ़ाना अधिक उत्तम मानते हैं। फलतः शिक्षकों की उदासीनता और माँ-बाप की ढील के कारण आज अधिकांश युवक सुविधा मिलने पर भी पढ़ाई में कम ध्यान दे रहे हैं। वे अपना अधिकांश समय अपने साथियों के साथ खेलकूद में या फिर सिनेमा आदि देखने में व्यर्थ गँवा देते हैं।

इन सबका मुख्य कारण है बच्चे का मन। बच्चे का मन दर्पण के समान स्वच्छ और निर्मल होता है। उस समय उसके मन पर जो अंकित हो जाय वही उसकी स्थाई प्रवृत्ति हो जाती है। आज के युग में पति-पत्नी अपने-अपने दफ्तर चले जाते हैं। उनके पास बच्चों में संस्कार उत्पन्न करने का अवसर ही नहीं होता। शिक्षकों का हाल यह है कि आज की महँगाई में वह बच्चों में संस्कार गढ़ने की अपेक्षा अधिक से अधिक पैसा कमाकर अपने परिवार को खुशहाल रखना चाहते हैं। अतः शिक्षा और बालक के विकास की ओर उनका कम ध्यान रहता है।

मानव की गति झरने की भाँति होती है जिस प्रकार उन्नति के पथ पर चलना कष्टों भरा होता है और अवनति का मार्ग सीधा सरल होता है उसी प्रकार झरने का पानी आसानी से नीचे गिरता है, किन्तु ऊपर जाने में

परेशानी होती है इसी प्रकार अवनति के मार्ग पर ले जाने वाले आसानी से मिल जाते हैं। किन्तु कष्टों को झेलते हुए भी मानव यदि सच्ची राह पर चलता है तो उसे अमृत फल मिलता है।

आज दूरदर्शन और चलचित्रों का प्रभाव बच्चों के मन को बरबस अपनी ओर आकर्षित कर लेता है। दिन-रात प्रसारित होने वाले विभिन्न प्रकार के कार्यक्रमों को चटकीला-भड़कीला बनाकर इस तरह पेश किया जाता है कि किशोर उसके सामने से उठना ही नहीं चाहते।

इसका एक मुख्य कारण एकान्त भी है। आज के समय में जब केवल पिता की आय से घर चलाना मुश्किल होता है तब माँ को भी उनका हाथ बँटाने के लिए घर से बाहर काम पर जाना पड़ता है। ऐसी स्थिति में बच्चे घर पर अकेले रह जाते हैं उन पर किसी प्रकार का कोई दवाब नहीं होता। उनके कहीं भी जाने तथा कुछ भी करने पर कोई पाबन्दी नहीं होती। घर का यह वातावरण बच्चों को उद्दण्ड बना देता है। इसके अतिरिक्त कुछ माता-पिता समय होते हुए भी अपने बच्चों को गलत राह पर जाने से नहीं रोक पाते। समाज में बढ़ते हुए भौतिकवाद ने भी इसे बढ़ावा दिया है। आज बच्चे घर पर रहने की अपेक्षा अपने साथियों के साथ घूमना-फिरना व चलचित्र देखना अधिक पसन्द करते हैं।

आर्थिक विकास भी इनमें काफी सहयोगी है। आज मनुष्य अर्थ के बल पर सब कुछ पाना चाहता है। आज के युवा वर्ग में कम काम करके अधिक से अधिक धन कमाने की लालसा उत्पन्न होती जा रही है। विश्वविद्यालयों में पढ़ने वाले छात्र पूरे वर्ष तो पढ़ाई पर ध्यान नहीं देते और परीक्षा का समय निकट आने पर कोचिंग जाकर, ट्यूशन पढ़कर, पेपर आउट करवाकर या फिर मार्कशीट में नम्बर बढ़वाकर उत्तीर्ण होने में विश्वास करते हैं। 'पैसा फेकेंगे तमाशा देखेंगे' मान्यता को जीवन में स्थान देने वाले ये युवा अन्त में पछताते हैं। विद्वानों ने सच्चे मित्र के लक्षण बताये हैं। (जो उन्नति के पथ पर ले जायें, हमारी बुराइयों को बताएँ, विपत्ति में सहायक हों) किन्तु आज के विद्यार्थी में घर-परिवार यह योग्यता पैदा नहीं कर पाता कि वह योग्य मित्र का चुनाव कर सके और यह तो स्वाभाविक है कि हर अवस्था वाला व्यक्ति अपनी अवस्था वालों के साथ ही रहना चाहता है, खेलना चाहता है और पढ़ना चाहता है। बच्चे बच्चों के साथ समय बिताना पसन्द करते हैं, युवक युवकों के साथ और वृद्ध-वृद्धों के साथ। यही नहीं प्रत्येक अवस्था के लोगों के आचार-विचार, क्रिया-कलाप भी भिन्न-भिन्न होते हैं, किन्तु आज के विद्यार्थी में पढ़ने के स्थान पर अपने साथियों के साथ खेलने व चलचित्र आदि देखने का प्रचलन तीव्र गति से बढ़ता जा रहा है। कृत्रिम आडम्बरों से बच्चे में स्वतन्त्र चिन्तन करने की प्रवृत्ति ही उत्पन्न नहीं हो पाती। ●●

वर्तमान शिक्षा प्रणाली

प्रस्तावना—शिक्षा मानव जीवन का एक अभिन्न अंग है। उसका जीवन में महत्वपूर्ण स्थान है। यह मानव को पशु से मानव और देवता बनाने में सक्षम है। यह एक ऐसा साधन है जो मानव के सुप्त संस्कारों को जाग्रत करती है। शिक्षा के स्वरूप पर ही मानव का जीवन एवं भविष्य निर्भर करता है। समाज में रहने वाले सभी लोग अपने बच्चों को यथासम्भव अच्छी-से-अच्छी शिक्षा प्रदान करते हैं। कौन-सी शिक्षा श्रेष्ठ और आदर्श होती है ? इसका उत्तर है, "जो बालक के सुप्त संस्कारों को जाग्रत करके उसे स्वस्थ नैतिक एवं आर्थिक दृष्टि से संस्कारित जीवन की प्रेरणा देती है, जो मानव में सामाजिकता का भाव उत्पन्न कर बालक को एक उपयोगी नागरिक और देशभक्त बनाती है। उसे ही आदर्श और सर्वोत्तम शिक्षा मान सकते हैं।"

शिक्षा पद्धति—वर्तमान शिक्षा प्रणाली पूर्ण रूप से पुस्तकीय ज्ञान पर आधारित है। अध्यापकों द्वारा छात्रों को किसी भी तरह केवल यह पुस्तकीय ज्ञान प्रदान कर दिया जाता है। किन्तु उसे व्यवहारिक तथा दैनिक जीवन की समस्याओं से सम्बन्धित किसी भी प्रकार का कोई ज्ञान प्राप्त नहीं होता है। हमारी वर्तमान शिक्षा प्रणाली पूरी तरह अंग्रेजी शासन से प्रभावित है। उस पर चार्ल्स वुड और लॉर्ड मैकाले का प्रभाव है। तत्कालीन सरकार का उद्देश्य काले गुलाम हिन्दुस्तानी को केवल इतना शिक्षित करना था जो सरकारी कार्यालयों के क्लर्क

का कार्य कर सकें। भारत को स्वतन्त्रता प्राप्त हुए 50 से भी अधिक वर्ष बीत चुके हैं, शिक्षा के क्षेत्र में विकास भी हुआ है, किन्तु आज भी हमारी शिक्षा प्रणाली पूर्ण रूप से विकसित नहीं है जो छात्रों को पुस्तकीय ज्ञान के साथ-साथ व्यवहारिक ज्ञान भी दे सके।

शिक्षा प्रणाली का स्वरूप—दुर्भाग्य की बात है कि स्वतन्त्रता के बाद शिक्षा सुधार की अनेक योजनाएँ बनने के बाद शिक्षित व्यक्तियों की संख्या में तो सुधार हुआ है, किन्तु आज भी उनमें व्यवहारिक ज्ञान का अभाव है। मैं इस विचार के पक्ष में हूँ कि वर्तमान शिक्षा पद्धति छात्रों की भावनाओं और आवश्यकताओं के प्रतिकूल है। अपने विचार के पक्ष में मैं निम्नलिखित तथ्य प्रस्तुत कर रहा हूँ—

(1) वर्तमान शिक्षा पद्धति में सैद्धान्तिक और पुस्तकीय ज्ञान को अधिक महत्व दिया गया है। छोटी-छोटी कक्षाओं में पुस्तकों की संख्या दिन पर दिन बढ़ती जा रही है। पुस्तकों के साथ सहायक पुस्तकें, उनकी उत्तरमाला और नोट्स आदि की संख्या में भी दिन-प्रतिदिन बढ़ोत्तरी हो रही है जिसके कारण छात्रों का बोझा बढ़ता जा रहा है। उम्र एवं कक्षा के साथ पुस्तकों की मोटाई और वजन इतना बढ़ता जाता है कि छात्रों को उन्हें देखने की भी इच्छा नहीं होती।

(2) पारिवारिक स्थिति भी वर्तमान शिक्षा-पद्धति के प्रति छात्र के मन में अरुचि की भावना को जन्म देती है। वर्तमान प्रणाली में शिक्षा अत्यन्त महँगी होती जा रही है। मध्यम व निम्न वर्ग के लोग तो उच्च शिक्षा के विषय में सोचते ही नहीं। शिक्षा प्राप्ति के बाद भी रोजगार न मिलने से माता-पिता उस पर होने वाले व्यय को व्यर्थ ही समझते हैं। शिक्षा का स्वरूप सरल व सुलभ होना चाहिए। जिससे प्रत्येक वर्ग के लोगों को शिक्षा प्राप्ति का अवसर मिल सके।

(3) शिक्षा के स्वरूप में बदलाव का एक कारण यह भी है कि अधिकतर माता-पिता बच्चों का विद्यालय में प्रवेश कराने के बाद इस बात की कोई चिन्ता नहीं करते कि उनका बच्चा क्या कर रहा है ? इसके अतिरिक्त निर्धनता के कारण अधिकतर माता-पिता बच्चों को जल्दी ही किसी न किसी कार्य पर लगा देते हैं। इससे उनकी शिक्षा प्रभावित होती है।

विद्यालय का वातावरण भी शिक्षा के अनुकूल नहीं है। कक्षा में छात्र और अध्यापक का अनुपात अधिकतम 40 और 1 का होना चाहिए, किन्तु वर्तमान में यह अनुपात 80 से भी अधिक देखा जाता है। परिणाम यह होता है कि अध्यापक छात्रों के प्रति व्यक्तिगत रूप से ध्यान नहीं दे पाते। स्वयं को उपेक्षित पाकर छात्र भी कक्षाओं से दिल चुराने लगते हैं। इससे उनमें अनुशासनहीनता की भावना जन्म लेती है।

उपसंहार—अध्यापक भी निजी स्वार्थ एवं राजनीति में लिप्त होने के कारण कक्षाओं में नहीं पढ़ाते। वे राजनीति, गुटबाजी तथा अन्य कार्यों में लिप्त रहकर कक्षाओं में नहीं जाते।

दोषपूर्ण परीक्षा पद्धति भी वर्तमान शिक्षा प्रणाली का एक दुर्भाग्य है। इसमें वर्ष भर की पढ़ाई की जाँच दो या तीन घण्टे में छात्रों द्वारा दिए गए उत्तरों के आधार पर की जाती है। इससे छात्रों के ज्ञान की पूर्ण रूप से परीक्षा नहीं हो सकती।

सरकार की उदासीनता, व्यवहारिक और व्यवसायिक शिक्षा का अभाव, बढ़ती जनसंख्या के लिए विद्यालयों का अभाव आदि शिक्षा पद्धति के अन्य दोष हैं।

●●

युद्ध-समस्या या समाधान

"लौट आओ, माँग के सिन्दूर की सौगन्ध तुमको
नयन का सावन, निमन्त्रण दे रहा है।"

चीन-वियतनाम युद्ध तथा इससे पूर्व हुए युद्धों में वीरगति को प्राप्त हुए सैनिकों की विधवायें आज भी एक दर्दभरी आह भरकर उपरोक्त पंक्तियाँ दुहराने लगती हैं। इन युद्धों का परिणाम अत्यन्त कारुणिक है। मानव

स्वभाव से अत्यन्त स्वार्थी है वह अपने पड़ोसी को सुखी देख उससे ईर्ष्या करता है। इसी प्रकार एक राष्ट्र, दूसरे राष्ट्र की प्रगति एवं उपलब्धियों से ईर्ष्या करता है तथा स्वयं को उससे आगे देखना चाहता है। इसके लिये वह उस राष्ट्र के आन्तरिक मामलों में हस्तक्षेप करके, गृह-युद्ध भड़काकर बाहर से आक्रमण करने की प्रतीक्षा में घात लगाये बैठा रहता है। स्वार्थों का टकराव, अपनी सार्वभौमिकता की रक्षा, नियन्त्रण में रखने की मनोवृत्ति, दूसरों पर अपना प्रभुत्व स्थापित करने का गर्व आदि कारण रूपी तीव्र वायु युद्ध के बादलों को एक जगह लाकर इकट्ठा कर देते हैं।

देवासुर संग्राम सदैव से होते आये हैं। 'वीर भोग्या वसुन्धरा' के आधार पर सदैव से शक्तिशालियों ने अशक्त पर आक्रमण और अत्याचार किये हैं। जर, जोरू और जमीन आदि प्रसंगों पर भी राजाओं में युद्ध होते थे, परन्तु उन युद्धों और आज के युद्धों में जमीन और आसमान का अन्तर है। आमने-सामने की लड़ाई और मल्ल युद्धों का समय जा चुका है। युद्ध-साधनों की व्यापकता इतनी बढ़ गई है कि कुछ कहा नहीं जा सकता कि कब क्या हो जाये ? जल, थल और नभ तीनों प्रकार की युद्धकलाओं के नवीन आविष्कारों ने युद्ध के प्रारूप में आमूल-चूल परिवर्तन उपस्थित कर दिया है।

युद्ध का कल्पनातीत नर-संहार, कितनी माताओं के इकलौते लाड़लों को, कितनी प्रेयसियों के जीवनाधारों को, कितनी सधवाओं के सौभाग्य बिन्दुओं को, कितनी बहिनों की राखियों को अपने क्रूर हाथों से एक साथ ही छीन लेता है। यह विचार भी नहीं किया जा सकता कि कितने बच्चे अनाथ होकर दर-दर की ठोकरें खाने लगते हैं, कितनी विधवाएँ अपने जीवन को सारहीन समझकर आत्महत्या कर लेती हैं, कितने परिवारों का दीपक हमेशा के लिए बुझ जाता है, कितने पिता अपने पुत्र को याद करते-करते अपना प्राणोत्सर्ग कर लेते हैं, कौन जाने ? असंख्य पुरुषों का संहार और नारियों का अवशेष जीवन देश में चरित्रहीनता ला देता है। पुरुषों के अभाव में देश की उन्नति रुक जाती है। वृद्ध रह जाते हैं जो न खेती कर सकते हैं और न कल-कारखानों में काम। देश के कलाकार, शिल्पकार, वीर, विशेषज्ञ, डॉक्टर सभी समय पड़ने पर आपातकालीन स्थिति में युद्ध भूमि में बुला लिये जाते हैं। परिणाम यह होता है कि युद्ध के बाद न तो किसी कला का दक्ष बच पाता है और न ही वीर।

बुभुक्षितः किं न करोति पापम् ?

युद्ध के समय जो कुछ उत्पादन होता है उसका बहुत बड़ा भाग सेना के उपयोग के लिए चला जाता है। चाहे वह अन्न हो, वस्त्र हों, दूध हो या अन्य उपयोगी वस्तुएँ। युद्ध-सामग्री का उत्पादन इतना बढ़ जाता है कि सामान्य उपयोग की वस्तुओं का अभाव हो जाता है। अतः महँगाई बढ़ जाती है। देश में अराजकता और अव्यवस्था फैल जाती है। सरकारी कोष समाप्त होने लगता है जिसके कारण जनता पर युद्ध-कालीन कर बढ़ा दिये जाते हैं। अतः युद्धकालीन तथा युद्धोत्तर दोनों ही स्थितियाँ जनता के लिए अभिशाप बनकर सामने आती हैं।

क्या युद्ध भी वरदान हो सकता है ? इसका प्रत्यक्ष उत्तर उस समय सामने आया जब पड़ोसी देश चीन ने आक्रमण किया। पं. नेहरू की पुकार पर सारा देश सेना लिये खड़ा था। देश रक्षा के लिए अपने प्राण प्रिय नेता नेहरू के संकेत पर सर्वस्व समर्पण! देश की इस अभूतपूर्व भावात्मक एकता तथा जन-जागृति के लिए चीनी आक्रमण एक वरदान के रूप में देश के सामने आया। इसी वरदान की पुनरावृत्ति सितम्बर 1965 और दिसम्बर 1971 में हुई जब पाकिस्तान ने भारत पर अचानक आक्रमण कर दिया।

सृष्टि का निर्माण भी गुण-अवगुण तथा सुख-दुःखों की भित्ति पर हुआ है। युद्ध मानव कल्याण के लिए कम एवं मानव विनाश के लिए अधिक हैं। युद्ध रुक सकते हैं, यदि विश्व भारत द्वारा प्रदर्शित शान्ति मार्ग पर चले। निःशस्त्रीकरण आज के युग में विश्वशान्ति के लिए अनिवार्य है। पर कहते सब हैं, करता कोई नहीं। तात्पर्य यह है कि युद्ध निःसन्देह मानव-मात्र के लिए अभिशाप है, विष भला अमृत कैसे हो सकता है ?

इक्कीसवीं शताब्दी में भारत

प्रस्तावना—आज हम इक्कीसवीं शताब्दी में प्रवेश कर चुके हैं। अभी तो इस सदी का प्रारम्भ हुआ और हम जीवन के प्रत्येक क्षेत्र में प्रगति कर रहे हैं। कल तक जो बातें केवल स्वप्न थीं, अब वह सत्य का रूप लेकर सामने आ रही हैं। इस सदी के आने वाले अनेकानेक वर्षों में भारत कितनी प्रगति करेगा ? संसार के श्रेष्ठ देशों में भारत का क्या स्थान होगा ? यह नयी शताब्दी भारतीयों को किस प्रकार के अनुभव दे जायेगी ? नयी शताब्दी के यह आने वाले दिन तथा वर्ष कैसे होंगे ? अच्छे या पहले से भी बदतर। यह सिर्फ अनुमानित ही किया जा सकता है, अनुभव नहीं।

आगामी वर्षों में भारत का स्वरूप—आज भारत ज्ञान-विज्ञान के क्षेत्रों में निरन्तर नये-नये आविष्कार करते हुए नये-नये उद्योग-धन्धे, कल-कारखाने स्थापित कर तथा व्यवहारपरक खुली नीतियाँ अपनाकर जिस प्रकार विश्व में नई शक्ति के रूप में उभर रहा है उससे प्रतीत होता है कि भारत प्रत्येक क्षेत्र में निरन्तर उन्नति करता रहेगा। भारत की उत्पादन क्षमता बढ़ेगी। बढ़ती हुई जनसंख्या पर व उद्योग-धन्धों का निरन्तर विकास कर बेरोजगारी जैसी समस्याओं पर काबू पा लिया जायेगा। भ्रष्टाचार समूल समाप्त कर शासन-प्रशासन को हर स्तर पर साफ-सुथरा बना लिया जायेगा। कम्प्यूटर का प्रयोग व्यापक रूप से बढ़ता जा रहा है। सभी को हर प्रकार की सुविधा उपलब्ध होगी। अभाव का कहीं नाम नहीं रहेगा।

देश में आकाशवाणी, दूरदर्शन आदि संचार माध्यमों का विकास कम्प्यूटर तकनीकी द्वारा किया जा रहा है। बैंकों में भी कम्प्यूटर का उपयोग युद्ध स्तर पर जारी है। 21वीं सदी के आने वाले वर्षों में सभी सरकारी एवं गैर सरकारी कम्प्यूटरीकृत हो जायेंगे। शिक्षा क्षेत्र, आणविक ऊर्जा, विद्युत उत्पादन में भारत आत्मनिर्भरता की श्रेणी में पहुँच चुका है तथा आगे भी इसी प्रकार लगातार उन्नति करेगा।

भारत की नई शिक्षा नीति रोजगारोन्मुखी होगी, व्यावसायिक शिक्षा का महत्व बढ़ेगा। 21वीं सदी में यहाँ का युवा वर्ग शिक्षित होगा और उसे रोजगार मिलेगा। बेरोजगारी, भ्रष्टाचार, हिंसा, साम्प्रदायिक अराजकता, लूटपाट समाप्त होगी। सभी लोग एक-दूसरे की मानसिकता, आवश्यकता व स्थिति का ध्यान रखकर प्रेम, अहिंसा और भाईचारे से निवास करने वाले होंगे। विद्यालय एवं विश्वविद्यालय एक अनूठा रूप लेंगे।

भारतीय कलाकारों का विदेश में काफी सम्मान हो रहा है। 21वीं सदी में सारा विश्व भारतीय कला का लोहा मानने लगेगा। हम यह कल्पना कर सकते हैं कि 21वीं सदी का भारत एक नई जागृति, नई चेतना और नई आशा का संचार करेगा। हमें आशा रखनी चाहिए कि 21वीं सदी में भारत एक सुखी तथा सम्पन्न देश होगा। जिस प्रकार सिक्के के दो पहलू होते हैं उसी प्रकार आर्थिक उन्नति होने के साथ ही साथ कुछ नयी समस्याएँ भी उत्पन्न होंगी।

भोजन एवं शयन से लेकर भवन-निर्माण, यातायात, शिक्षण सभी कुछ कम्प्यूटर के सहारे होने लगेगा। अगला विश्व युद्ध आणविक अस्त्रों द्वारा अन्तरिक्ष में लड़ा जायेगा और संसार विनाश के पथ पर अग्रसर हो जायेगा। रोटी, कपड़ा, मकान की समस्या भीषण समस्या बन जायेगी। जल स्रोत, ईंधन और ऊर्जा के सारे प्राकृतिक स्रोत घटकर आधे रह जायेंगे। जनजीवन अस्त-व्यस्त हो जायेगा। कुरीतियों और भ्रष्टाचार का बोलबाला होगा जो आदमी को कहीं का नहीं रहने देगा।

भारत एक धनी देश है, परन्तु यहाँ के निवासी निर्धन हैं। यह कहावत 21वीं सदी में पूर्णत: चरितार्थ होगी। वर्तमान युग में आर्थिक संकट बढ़ता जा रहा है। पूँजीवादी व्यवस्था जमाखोरी और तस्करी में वृद्धि की परिचायक साबित हो रही है। पंचवर्षीय योजनाओं के लिए जुटाया गया धन विकास कार्य हेतु कागजों तक सीमित हो जायेगा।

उपसंहार—हमारा विश्वास है कि 21वीं सदी में भारत विकसित देश की भाँति संसार के सभी देशों में अग्रणी होगा। कुल मिलाकर 21वीं सदी का भारत अपनी प्रस्तुत आकांक्षाओं को साकार करने में समर्थ होगा और संसार की अग्रणी शक्ति के रूप में उभरकर आयेगा।

●●

राष्ट्रीय एकता

प्रस्तावना—स्वाधीनता मिलने के 68 वर्ष व्यतीत होने के बाद भी देश में जिस प्रकार विघटनकारी शक्तियों का नग्न नृत्य हो रहा है उसे देखकर देश के प्रबुद्ध नागरिक तथा कुछ राष्ट्रभक्त नेताओं को चिन्ता होने लगी है। इसका कारण है कि राष्ट्र की प्रगति, विकास तथा समृद्धि के लिए राष्ट्र के नागरिकों में एकता परमावश्यक है। इसी भावना के जन्म और विकास से राष्ट्र पर आने वाले संकट के बादल सहज ही हट जाते हैं। राष्ट्रीय एकता की बात करने से पूर्व राष्ट्र, उसका स्वरूप और राष्ट्रीयता के सम्बन्ध में पर्याप्त ज्ञान प्राप्त करना आवश्यक है।

राष्ट्रीय एकता का अर्थ— राष्ट्र शब्द का अर्थ एवं स्वरूप बहुत व्यापक है। इसमें तीन तत्व शामिल हैं—भूमि, जन तथा उनकी संस्कृति। हम इस बात को भली-भाँति जानते हैं कि किसी भी राष्ट्र का निर्माण हवा में नहीं होता। उसके लिए निश्चित भू-भाग की आवश्यकता होती है। यह देश उत्तर में हिमालय से दक्षिण में रामेश्वरम् तथा पूर्व में बंगाल और असम से लेकर पश्चिम में द्वारिका तक व्याप्त है।

एकता का स्वरूप—किसी भू-खण्ड के राष्ट्र कहलाने के लिये जनता का होना आवश्यक है। भारत एक विशाल जनसंख्या वाला राष्ट्र है। वर्तमान में यहाँ की जनसंख्या 1 अरब से अधिक है इसके साथ ही जनसंख्या में आपसी स्नेह और निकटता भी अनिवार्य है। हवा, जल और अन्न का सेवन करके तथा लम्बे समय तक एक साथ रहते-रहते निकटता का भाव उत्पन्न होना स्वाभाविक है। भारत में विभिन्न धर्म और विचारधाराऐं होने पर भी सभी स्वयं के भारतीय कहलाने में गर्व करते हैं। राष्ट्र का तीसरा तत्व है संस्कृति। संस्कृति और सभ्यता विभिन्न धर्म और जाति के लोगों में निकटता और घनिष्ठता का भाव पैदा करती है। संस्कृति किसी भी राष्ट्र की आत्मा है। संस्कृति भी राष्ट्र को वैसे ही जीवन और उत्साह प्रदान करती है जैसे आत्मा शरीर को। भारत की श्रेष्ठता उसकी संस्कृति में है। यहाँ के नागरिक प्रान्तों, भाषा, वेश-भूषा और खान-पान के अलग होने पर भी एक हैं। यहाँ की मूल संस्कृति (हिन्दू) एवं सभ्यता की एकता उसके सोलह संस्कारों में तीर्थाटन में, धार्मिक और आध्यात्मिक भावना में कदम-कदम पर दिखाई देती है। राष्ट्र की जनता में जन्मभूमि के प्रति यह ममत्व की भावना ही राष्ट्रीयता कहलाती है। 'यह भूमि मेरी माँ है, मैं इसका पुत्र हूँ, यहाँ की संस्कृति ही मेरा प्राण है।' इस भावना की सुदृढ़ता ही व्यक्ति को आत्म बलिदान के लिए प्रेरित करती है।

वर्तमान में राष्ट्रीय एकता की परम आवश्यकता है। यहाँ के मूल निवासियों के अतिरिक्त शक, सिदिमन हूण, अरब, तुर्क, अफगान तथा गजनी के आक्रांता आए। कुछ लोग तो मिलकर यहीं के हो गए, किन्तु पृथक् संस्कृति को लेकर आने वाले इस्लाम के समर्थक अपनी अलग संस्कृति और विचार लेकर आये। वे भी यहाँ बस गये। परिणाम यह है कि आज देश में सभी प्रान्तों, भाषा, संस्कृति और धर्म के लोगों के होते हुए भी यहाँ के नागरिकों में भारतीयता की भावना दिखाई देती है।

उपसंहार— आज आवश्यकता इस बात की है कि स्वार्थ भावना को त्यागकर सभी धर्मों को मानने वाले नागरिक, राष्ट्र प्रेम की बात करने के साथ ही उसे आचरण से प्रकट करके दिखाऐं। ऐसा केवल सांस्कृतिक एकता से ही सम्भव है। ●●

बेकारी की समस्या

प्रस्तावना— आज भारत के सामने अनेक समस्याएँ मुँह खोले खड़ी हैं। उनमें सर्वाधिक विकट समस्या है—बेकारी की। इस समस्या के समाधान के अनेक प्रयत्न होने पर भी यह दिन प्रतिदिन सुरसा के मुख के समान विशाल रूप धारण करती जा रही है। भारत में बेकारों के दो वर्ग हैं—एक शिक्षित बेकार और दूसरा अशिक्षित बेकार। इसमें शिक्षित वर्ग की बेरोजगारी का कारण वर्तमान शिक्षा प्रणाली है। शिक्षा की प्रचलित प्रणाली से (जोकि ब्रिटिश राज्य की देन है) छात्रों में न तो कोई स्वतन्त्र चिन्तन शक्ति उत्पन्न होती है और न उन्हें कोई शिल्प या उद्योग का ही ज्ञान प्राप्त होता है।

बेकारी के कारण—विद्यालयों, महाविद्यालयों से प्रतिवर्ष लाखों विद्यार्थी विश्वविद्यालय प्रमाण-पत्र लेकर निकलते हैं सभी यह चाहते है कि उन्हें किसी-न-किसी कार्यालय में नौकरी मिल जाए, किन्तु अधिकांश इस उद्देश्य में विफल रहते है। उन्हें किसी शिल्प, विज्ञान, प्रविधि अथवा कला का ज्ञान तो होता नहीं हाथ से काम करने में लज्जा आती है, परिणामस्वरूप वे बेरोजगार रह जाते हैं। तकनीकी काम जानने वालों में भी सफेदपोशी की यह प्रवृत्ति घर कर रही है। फिर बेकारी न फैले तो क्या हो ? माता-पिता तथा देश दोनों के लिए ऐसे बेकार भार बन जाते हैं।

इधर आरक्षण व्यवस्था भी बेकारों की संख्या बढ़ाने में सहायक हुई। प्रत्येक क्षेत्र में अनुसूचित जातियों और जनजातियों के लिए स्थान सुरक्षित है उनमें योग्य लोग न मिलने पर भी वे स्थान उन्हीं को दिये जाते हैं । चाहे वह व्यक्ति उस पद के योग्य ही न हो।

अशिक्षितों में बेकारी का मुख्य कारण है कुटीर उद्योगों का विनाश। मशीनों के प्रचलन से लाखों मनुष्यों का रोजगार भी छिन गया। एक मशीन बीस आदमियों का काम करती है और उसको चलाने के लिए केवल एक व्यक्ति पर्याप्त होता है इस प्रकार उन्नीस व्यक्ति बेकार हो जाते हैं। कम्प्यूटरीकरण के कारण बेकारी की समस्या और भी भयंकर हो गई है। कारखाने और हाथ की बनी चीज में अन्तर होता है। कुटीर-उद्योग मशीनों के सामने टिक न सके और वे प्रायः लुप्त हो चुके हैं।

बेकारी का एक और बड़ा कारण है—भारत की तीव्रता से बढ़ती हुई जनसंख्या इसके साथ ही सरकार की दोषपूर्ण नीतियाँ भी बेकारी का कारण है।

बेकारी दूर करने के उपाय—बेकारी को दूर करने के लिए हमें बढ़ती जनसंख्या पर नियन्त्रण करना होगा। इसका उपाय है परिवार नियोजन। वर्तमान शिक्षा प्रणाली में आवश्यक परिवर्तन करना होगा। छात्रों को विभिन्न विषयों की शिक्षा के साथ ही कुछ चुने हुए व्यवसायों की भी शिक्षा दी जानी चाहिए। जिससे वे विद्यालयों से शिक्षा समाप्त करने के बाद अपनी जीविका का उपार्जन कर सकें। देश में विभिन्न प्रकार के औद्योगिक प्रशिक्षण स्कूलों की आवश्यकता है। जिनमें छात्र विभिन्न शिल्पों का प्रयोगात्मक शिक्षण ले सकें।

कुटीर तथा लघु उद्योगों की पुनः स्थापना और विकास भारत में बेरोजगारी दूर करने का साधन बनेगा। नमक, साबुन, तेल, जूते, चादरें, पर्दे आदि का उत्पादन लघु उद्योगों की श्रेणी में ही रखनी चाहिए। कुटीर-उद्योगों की उपज को सस्ता बनाने के लिए करों में छूट मिलनी चाहिए। विदेशी माल का आयात बन्द कर देना चाहिए।

भारत में आज भी ऐसी लाखों एकड़ भूमि है जो खाली पड़ी है, जिस पर वृक्ष लगाये जा सकते हैं। पशु पालकों को पशुपालन (गाय, भैंस, बकरी) के लिए प्रेरित किया जाना चाहिए। इससे बेकारी तो दूर होगी ही लोगों को दूध, माँस, ऊन आदि भी पर्याप्त मात्रा में प्राप्त होंगे।

उपसंहार—हमारा विश्वास है कि उपर्युक्त उपायों से देश में बढ़ती हुई बेकारी को दूर किया जा सकता है। यह बात निर्विवाद सत्य है कि जब तक बेकारी की समस्या हल नहीं हो जाती है हमारी उन्नति की सभी बातें विशेषतः समाजवाद लाने की बातें निरर्थक है। अतः जनता व सरकार दोनों को इस दिशा में पूर्ण प्रयत्न कर इसका समाधान करना चाहिए।

●●

निर्धनता की समस्या—कारण तथा समाधान

"निर्धनता वह दशा है जिसमें कोई व्यक्ति अपर्याप्त आमदनी या अविवेकशील खर्चों के कारण ऐसा रहन-सहन का स्तर कायम नहीं रख पाता जिससे उसकी शारीरिक और मानसिक कार्यक्षमता बनी रहे और वह समाज के सदस्य के रूप में उसके स्तर के अनुकूल अपने को और अपने आश्रितों को क्रियाशील रख सके।"

व्यक्तियों की आर्थिक दशा की तुलना करने के लिये धनी तथा निर्धन शब्दों का प्रयोग किया जाता है। जिस मात्रा में कोई व्यक्ति जीवन की आवश्यकताओं, सुविधाओं और आनन्दों का उपभोग कर सकता है, उसी अनुपात में वह धनी व निर्धन होता है।

निर्धनता एक ऐसी दशा है जिसमें साधनों की कमी होने के कारण व्यक्ति अपनी आवश्यकताओं की पूर्ति भली-भाँति नहीं कर पाता। यह दशा व्यक्ति में मानसिक क्षोभ उत्पन्न करती है और वह मानसिक रूप से सदैव अशांत रहता है।

निर्धनता के कारण

शादी-विवाह में अपव्यय, दहेज-प्रथा, मर जाने के उपरान्त प्रीतिभोज का आयोजन करना ये प्रथायें निर्धन को और निर्धन बना देती हैं।

देश में प्रतिवर्ष तरह-तरह के रोग फैलते हैं इन रोगों की रोकथाम के लिये उचित व्यवस्था नहीं है। रोगी के ठीक न होने के पश्चात् उसकी कार्य-शक्ति घट जाती है और उसकी रोजी पर असर पड़ता है। निर्धनता का दूसरा प्रमुख कारण हमारी शिक्षा का सैद्धान्तिक होना है। इसका सम्बन्ध जीवन के व्यवहारिकपक्ष से बहुत कम है। छात्र डिग्री प्राप्त करने के बाद भी बेरोजगार हैं।

भारत एक कृषि प्रधान देश है। यहाँ के अधिकांश लोगों का व्यवसाय कृषि है। कृषि की हीन दशा भारत की अधिकांश जनता की दरिद्रता के लिये उत्तरदायी है। प्रत्येक देश की समृद्धि और सम्पन्नता उसके औद्योगिक विकास पर निर्भर होती है। देश में जितना अधिक उत्पादन होगा उतना ही लोगों को धन मिलेगा और वे आर्थिक दृष्टि से सम्पन्न होंगे। भारत प्राकृतिक साधनों से सम्पन्न होने पर भी उत्पादन की दृष्टि से पिछड़ा है। इसलिये यहाँ की जनता निर्धन है।

प्राचीन समय में भारत में कुटीर उद्योग अत्यधिक विकसित दशा में थे। उनसे लाखों परिवारों की रोजी-रोटी चलती थी। अंग्रेजों ने इन्हें नष्ट कर दिया। इससे देश में निर्धनता बढ़ी है। व्यक्ति की आर्थिक दशा बहुत कुछ अपनी योग्यता और कार्यक्षमता पर निर्भर होती है। शारीरिक रूप से अशक्त, विकलांग या अति दुर्बल होने के कारण जो लोग अधिक कार्य करने में असमर्थ होते हैं। वे अधिक धन नहीं कमा पाते।

आज का युग बुद्धि-बल का युग है। बौद्धिक कार्य करने वालों को शारीरिक कार्य करने वालों की अपेक्षा अधिक वेतन मिलता है। आज के समय में फैलती हुई बीमारियाँ व्यक्ति को दुर्बल बना देती है और वह कार्य करने योग्य नहीं रहता। फलतः आमदनी कम हो जाती है या बिल्कुल बन्द हो जाती है। बीमारी का इलाज कराने में भी पैसा खर्च होता है जिससे पारिवारिक निर्धनता और बढ़ जाती है।

शिक्षा व्यक्ति की कार्यक्षमता बढ़ाती है। कुछ व्यवसाय ऐसे हैं जो शिक्षा के बिना सम्भव नहीं हैं, जैसे—डॉक्टरी, इंजीनियरिंग, अध्यापन, आफिस का काम, वकालत इत्यादि। सभ्य समाज के अधिकांश व्यवसाय शिक्षा पर निर्भर होते हैं। शिक्षा के अभाव में व्यक्ति उनसे वंचित रह जाता है। अतः निर्धनता बढ़ती है।

वृद्धावस्था में कार्य शक्ति क्षीण होने से धनोपार्जन की क्षमता घट जाती है। यदि किसी परिवार में एक ही व्यक्ति कमाने वाला हो और खाने वाले अनेक हों तथा दुर्भाग्य से उसकी मृत्यु हो जाए तो सारा परिवार निर्धनता के गर्त में डूब जाता है। वैश्यागमन, शराबखोरी, जुआ खेलना और अन्य नशे करना आदि ऐसे कार्य होते हैं जिनमें धन का अपव्यय होता है और निर्धनता बढ़ती है।

जिस देश में शक्ति साधनों एवं खनिज-पदार्थों का अभाव होता है, वह देश आर्थिक दृष्टि से दुर्बल होता है। कृषि उत्पादन में कमी भी देश के निर्धन होने का एक प्रमुख कारण है। देश के बहुत से भागों में कृषि के लिये अनुकूल जलवायु नहीं है। बाढ़ के प्रकोप से तथा सूखा पड़ने से मानव-जीवन अस्त-व्यस्त हो जाता है। सिंचाई के साधनों के अभाव में कृषि कार्य तथा उत्पादन पर प्रभाव पड़ता है। जलवायु की विषमता भी लोगों

की निर्धनता का कारण है। भूकम्प का आना, बाढ़ या तूफान आना, सूखा पड़ना, ज्वालामुखी का विस्फोट होना आदि प्राकृतिक विपदायें भी निर्धनता उत्पन्न करती हैं।

इन सभी कारणों के अतिरिक्त जनसंख्या की अतिरिक्त वृद्धि भी निर्धनता का प्रमुख कारण है। सीमित साधन तथा निरन्तर बढ़ती हुई जनसंख्या देश में बढ़ती हुई निर्धनता का प्रमुख कारण है। जनसंख्या बढ़ती ही जा रही है, किन्तु लोगों की आय नहीं बढ़ रही है। इस कारण भी निर्धन और निर्धन होते जा रहे हैं।

राजनीतिक व्यवस्था के दोषपूर्ण होने से देश में धन का सदुपयोग नहीं हो पा रहा है और जनता की निर्धनता बढ़ रही है। देश से निर्धनता की समस्या को दूर करने तथा देशवासियों का जीवन स्तर ऊँचा उठाने के लिए कई नवीन योजनायें आरम्भ की गयी हैं किन्तु इन योजनाओं का भी पूरा लाभ जनता को नहीं मिल पा रहा है। देश के विकास के लिये मिलने वाली रकम का दुरुपयोग होता है।

निर्धनता का समाधान—निर्धनता एक विकट समस्या है। भारत के सामने भी यह समस्या विकट रूप से मुँह खोले खड़ी है। इसका अन्त करके देश में प्रति व्यक्ति वार्षिक आय बढ़ाना तथा राष्ट्र की वार्षिक आय की वृद्धि देश के लिये बहुत आवश्यक है। निर्धनता अभिशाप है और इसके रहते किसी भी राष्ट्र का पूरा विकास सम्भव नहीं है। इसके उन्मूलन के लिये निम्नलिखित उपायों को अपनाया जा सकता है—

(1) अनिवार्य व नि:शुल्क शिक्षा आवश्यक है ताकि सभी नागरिक अपनी प्रतिभा का विकास कर सकें और तरह-तरह के कार्यों को करने की उनमें शक्ति उत्पन्न हो।

(2) सामाजिक शिक्षा के द्वारा कुविचार व कुप्रथाओं का अन्त कर देना आवश्यक है जिससे निर्धनता की समस्या का समाधान हो सके।

(3) पारिवारिक ढाँचे में सुधार करने से भी इस समस्या को हल किया जा सकता है। दहेज प्रथा का अन्त करके परिवार में कमाने वालों की संख्या को बढ़ाया जाये।

(4) व्यावसायिक शिक्षा को केन्द्रित बनाना होगा। छात्रों को उनकी रुचियों तथा योग्यता के अनुसार शिक्षा दी जाये।

(5) सरकार के द्वारा इस प्रकार की प्राकृतिक विपत्तियों से सुरक्षा का प्रबन्ध होना चाहिये, जैसे—बाढ़, सूखा, कीड़े-मकोड़ों का प्रकोप आदि।

(6) निर्धनता के उन्मूलन के लिये उद्योग-धन्धों का विकास भी आवश्यक है।

●●

शिक्षा में खेल-कूद का महत्व

प्रस्तावना—खेल मनुष्य की जन्मजात प्रवृत्ति है। यह प्रवृत्ति बालकों, युवकों और वृद्धों तक में पाई जाती है। जो बालक अपनी बाल्यावस्था में खेलों में भाग नहीं लेता, वह बहुत-सी बातें सीखने से वंचित रह जाता है और उसके व्यक्तित्व का भली प्रकार विकास नहीं हो पाता। हमारे पूर्वजों ने मानव जीवन को 100 वर्ष का माना था। इसमें प्रथम 25 वर्ष विद्याध्ययन एवं शारीरिक पुष्टि के लिए निर्धारित किए गए थे। विद्यार्थी अपने अध्ययन काल में ब्रह्मचर्य का पालन करते हुए शरीर को पुष्ट बनाते थे एवं विद्याध्ययन करते थे।

स्वास्थ्य जीवन की आधार शिला है। स्वस्थ मनुष्य ही अपने जीवन सम्बन्धी कार्यों को भली-भाँति पूर्ण कर सकते हैं। स्वास्थ्य के सम्बन्ध में अनेक लोकोक्तियाँ भी प्रचलित हो गई हैं; जैसे—**'पहला सुख निरोगी काया'**, **'तन्दुरुस्ती हजार नियामत है'**, **'जान है तो जहान है'** आदि। इन सभी लोकोक्तियों का अभिप्राय यही है कि मानव को सबसे पहले अपने स्वास्थ्य का ध्यान रखना चाहिए। तभी भारतेन्दु जी ने कहा था—

दूध पियो कसरत करो, नित्य जपो हरि नाम।
हिम्मत से कारज करो, पूरेंगे सब राम॥

यह स्वास्थ्य हमें व्यायाम अथवा खेल-कूद से प्राप्त होता है।

शिक्षा और खेल का सम्बन्ध—यह निर्विवाद रूप से कहा जा सकता है कि शिक्षा और खेल का गहरा सम्बन्ध है। शिक्षा यदि मनुष्य का सर्वांगीण विकास करती है तो उस विकास का पहला अंग है—शारीरिक विकास। शारीरिक विकास व्यायाम और खेल-कूद के द्वारा ही सम्भव है। इसलिए खेलकूद या क्रीड़ा को अनिवार्य बनाए बिना शिक्षा की प्रक्रिया का सम्पन्न हो पाना सम्भव नहीं है। यही कारण है कि प्रत्येक विद्यालय में पुस्तकीय शिक्षा के साथ-साथ खेल-कूद और व्यायाम की शिक्षा भी अनिवार्य रूप से दी जाती है। विद्यालयों में व्यायाम शिक्षक, स्काउट मास्टर, एन. डी. एस. आई. आदि शिक्षकों की नियुक्ति इसीलिए की जाती है कि प्रत्येक बालक उनके निरीक्षण में अपनी रुचि के अनुसार खेल-कूद में भाग ले सके और अपने स्वास्थ्य को सबल और पुष्ट बना सके।

शरीर को शक्तिशाली, स्फूर्तियुक्त और ओजस्वी तथा मन को प्रसन्न बनाने के लिए जो कार्य किए जाते हैं, उन्हें हम खेल-कूद, क्रीड़ा या व्यायाम कहते हैं। खेलकूद और व्यायाम से शरीर में तीव्र गति से रक्त संचार होता है। अत: दौड़, क्रिकेट, फुटबाल, बैडमिण्टन, टेनिस, हॉकी आदि खेल इसी दृष्टि से खेले जाते हैं।

खेल-कूद का महत्त्व—संकुचित अर्थ में शिक्षा का तात्पर्य पुस्तकीय ज्ञान प्राप्त करना और मानसिक विकास करना ही समझा जाता है, लेकिन व्यापक अर्थ में शिक्षा से तात्पर्य केवल मानसिक विकास से ही नहीं है वरन् शारीरिक, चारित्रिक और आध्यात्मिक विकास अर्थात् सर्वांगीण विकास से है। सर्वांगीण विकास के लिए शारीरिक विकास आवश्यक है और शारीरिक विकास के लिए खेल-कूद और व्यायाम का विशेष महत्त्व है। खेल-कूद से शरीर के विभिन्न अंगों में एक सन्तुलन स्थापित होता है, शरीर में स्फूर्ति उत्पन्न होती है और रक्त-संचार ठीक प्रकार से होता है। स्वस्थ बालक पुस्तकीय ज्ञान को ग्रहण करने की अधिक क्षमता रखता है।

मानसिक विकास की दृष्टि से भी खेल-कूद अत्यन्त महत्त्वपूर्ण हैं। इस सम्बन्ध में एक कहावत भी प्रचलित है कि **'तन स्वस्थ तो मन स्वस्थ'** (*Healthy mind in a healthy body);* अर्थात् स्वस्थ शरीर में ही स्वस्थ मन का वास होता है। शरीर से दुर्बल व्यक्ति विभिन्न रोगों तथा चिन्ताओं से ग्रस्त हो जाता है। वह मानसिक रूप से कमजोर तथा चिड़चिड़ा बन जाता है। वह जो कुछ भी पढ़ता-लिखता है, वह उसे याद नहीं रहता। खेल-कूद से शारीरिक शक्ति में तो वृद्धि होती ही है साथ ही साथ मन में प्रफुल्लता, सरसता और उत्साह भी बना रहता है।

खेल-कूद से शारीरिक एवं मानसिक शक्ति, धैर्य, साहस एवं सद्‌भाव की भावना विकसित होती है। बालक जीवन में घटित होने वाली घटनाओं को खेल-भावना से ग्रहण करने के अभ्यस्त हो जाते हैं तथा शिक्षा-प्राप्ति के मार्ग में आने वाली बाधाओं को हँसते-हँसते पार कर सफलता के सर्वोच्च शिखर पर पहुँच जाते हैं।

जिस प्रकार योगी व्यक्ति सुख-दु:ख, हानि-लाभ अथवा जय-पराजय को समान भाव से देखता है उसी प्रकार खिलाड़ी में भी यह भावना विकसित होती है।

आधुनिक शिक्षाशास्त्रियों के अनुसार यदि बालकों को शिक्षित करने का कार्य खेल-पद्धति के आधार पर किया जाता है तो बालक उसमें अधिक रुचि लेते हैं। अत: खेल के द्वारा दी गई शिक्षा सरल, रोचक और प्रभावपूर्ण होती है। इसी मान्यता के आधार पर ही किण्डरगार्टन, मॉण्टेसरी, प्रोजेक्ट आदि आधुनिक शिक्षण-पद्धतियाँ विकसित हुई हैं।

उपरोक्त विवरण से यह स्पष्ट है कि शिक्षा में व्यायाम और खेलकूद का महत्वपूर्ण स्थान है। किसी भी एक कार्य को निरन्तर ही करते रहना ठीक नहीं है। इस सम्बन्ध में एक अंग्रेज कवि द्वारा निम्नलिखित उद्‌गार प्रकट किए गए हैं—

Work while you work
Play while you play,
That is the way
To be happy and gay.

अर्थात् काम के समय मन लगाकर काम करो और खेलने के समय मन लगाकर खेलो। जीवन में प्रसन्नता प्राप्त करने का यही एकमात्र तरीका है।

अत: हमें पढ़ाई के समय खेलकूद से दूर रहना चाहिए और खेल के समय प्रत्येक दृष्टि से चिन्तारहित होकर केवल खेलना ही चाहिए।

उपसंहार—व्यायाम और खेलकूद से शक्ति का संचार होता है, जीवन में ताजगी और स्फूर्ति मिलती है। आधुनिक शिक्षा-जगत में खेल के महत्त्व को स्वीकार कर लिया गया है। यदि भविष्य में सुयोग्य नागरिक एवं सर्वांगीण विकासयुक्त शिक्षित व्यक्तियों का निर्माण करना है तो शिक्षा में खेलकूद की उपेक्षा न करके उसे व्यवहारिक रूप प्रदान करना होगा।

●●

आरक्षण राष्ट्रीय एकता में बाधक है

प्रस्तावना—स्वतन्त्रता प्राप्ति के पश्चात् देश के संविधान निर्माताओं ने समाज के सभी वर्गों को राष्ट्र के विकास में बराबर का भागीदार बनाने के लिए तथा आर्थिक और शैक्षणिक रूप से पिछड़े वर्गों के लिए संविधान में आरक्षण की व्यवस्था की। इसी आधार पर संविधान में अनुसूचित जातियों तथा जनजातियों के लिए व शैक्षणिक रूप से पिछड़े लोगों के लिए आरक्षण की व्यवस्था की गई। जिससे इन वर्गों के लोग भी आर्थिक रूप से सुदृढ़ होकर राष्ट्र की प्रगति में योगदान कर सकें। आरम्भ में यह व्यवस्था केवल 10 वर्ष के लिए की गयी। बाद में क्षुद्र राजनैतिक स्वार्थ के लिए इन्हें 10 और वर्ष के लिए बढ़ाते हुए तत्कालीन सरकारों द्वारा इन वर्गों में यह भावना बिठायी गयी कि उनका भला आरक्षण में रहने में ही है।

आरक्षण का अर्थ—भारत की अर्थव्यवस्था में रोजगार के अवसर सीमित होने के कारण आरक्षण की व्यवस्था करने के लिए इन वर्गों द्वारा दबाव बढ़ाया गया। इसको देखकर अन्य जातियों ने भी अपने लिए आरक्षण की माँग करना आरम्भ कर दिया। 1979 में तत्कालीन जनता सरकार ने वी. पी. मण्डल की अध्यक्षता में एक आयोग का गठन किया। जिसका कार्य आर्थिक एवं सामाजिक रूप में पिछड़ी जातियों का पता लगाकर सरकार को सूचित करना था। इस आयोग ने सन् 1980 में अपना प्रतिवेदन सरकार को प्रस्तुत किया। दस वर्षों तक इस सम्बन्ध में कुछ न हुआ, किन्तु 7 अगस्त, 1990 को तत्कालीन प्रधानमन्त्री विश्वनाथ प्रताप सिंह ने इस रिपोर्ट के आधार पर पिछड़ी जातियों तथा जनजातियों के लिए सरकारी नौकरियों में 27% आरक्षण लागू कर दिया। इसके पीछे इसका राष्ट्रीय मोर्चे के घोषणा पत्र में शामिल होना था। इस विवादास्पद नीति को लागू करने में की गयी जल्दबाजी की कीमत देश को चुकानी पड़ी।

आरक्षण राष्ट्रीय एकता में बाधक—यह देश का दुर्भाग्य रहा है कि कुछ नेताओं ने अपने व्यक्तिगत स्वार्थ के लिए देश को बार-बार जाति और धर्म के नाम पर बाँटा। आरक्षण का वर्तमान निर्णय स्पष्ट करता है कि राजनैतिक दलों द्वारा ऐसा अपने वोट बैंक को पक्का करने के लिए किया गया। देश में पहले से ही भीषण त्रासदी के अवसर पर भी जातिवाद की इस गाय को दुहने पर तत्पर राजनैतिक दल, पहले ही समस्या बनी बेकारी की प्रथा को बढ़ाने पर आमादा हैं। जनसंख्या बढ़ती जा रही है, जबकि रोजगार के अवसर कम होते जा रहे हैं। वर्तमान समय में कुल आरक्षण का प्रतिशत 49·5% हो गया है। सरकार का यह प्रयास सामाजिक तथा आर्थिक दृष्टि से पिछड़े लोगों को न्याय दिलाने के लिए था। अत: मण्डल आयोग द्वारा जातियों को चिह्नित करने का आधार ही दोषपूर्ण है। संविधान के अनुसार पिछड़ेपन का आधार शैक्षणिक और आर्थिक होना चाहिए, जबकि मण्डल आयोग ने इसे जातिगत आधार पर निश्चित किया। ऐसा नहीं होना चाहिए।

परिणाम—इसका परिणाम यह हुआ है कि शहरों में विभिन्न धन्धों में लगी जातियाँ चाहे वह भूमिपति वर्ग की हो अथवा भूमिहीन वर्ग की, अपना नाम आरक्षण वर्ग में जुड़वाने के लिए उतावली दिखाई देती है। इससे सम्पूर्ण सामाजिक व्यवस्था में बदलाव आ गया है। अब आरक्षण केवल नौकरी पाने का एक साधन मात्र बनकर रह गया है। इससे युवक स्वावलम्बी बनने की अपेक्षा नौकरियों के लिए आरक्षण को महत्व देने लगे हैं।

इसका परिणाम यह हुआ है कि मेधावी लोगों के भविष्य पर प्रश्नचिह्न लग गया है। आज स्थिति यह है कि इंजीनियरिंग कॉलेजों में प्रवेश के लिए 60% से 80% अंकों की आवश्यकता है, जबकि तथाकथित अनुसूचित जातियों के लिए 25% से 40% अंकों की आवश्यकता है।

इससे सामान्य वर्ग के छात्रों में क्षोभ और विद्रोह की भावना उग्र होती जा रही है। इससे आर्थिक आधार पर चलने वाले संघर्ष ने जातिगत संघर्ष का रूप ले लिया है।

स्वतन्त्रता से पूर्व जातीय सम्बन्धों में स्नेह, सहयोग और सौहार्द्र की भावना बढ़ने के स्थान पर घृणा का रूप लेती जा रही है। इससे समाज की एकता और संगठन पर प्रभाव पड़ा है। सन् 1990 में होने वाला पनवारी काण्ड तथा राष्ट्र में जातीय तनाव और संघर्ष का परिणाम पारस्परिक जातीय घृणा के भाव में होने वाली वृद्धि है।

●●

विलास की वस्तुएँ

वर्तमान युग में मनुष्य के जीवन को सुविधाजनक बनाने के अनेक ऐसे साधन उपलब्ध हैं जो मनुष्य को विलासिता पूर्ण जीवन जीने का आदी बना रहे हैं। ऐसे ही कुछ साधन वातानुकूलित यन्त्र, फ्रिज, कक्ष-ताप नियन्त्रक तथा आत्म-नियन्त्रित वाहन आदि हैं।

आधुनिक युग में विज्ञान ने प्रगति के सभी आँकड़े पार कर दिये हैं। जीवन का कोई क्षेत्र, प्रगति का कोई कोना ऐसा नहीं बचा है, जहाँ विज्ञान ने अपने कदम न रखें हों। विज्ञान ने मानव के हर स्वप्न को साकार तथा हर असम्भव को सम्भव करके दिखा दिया है। प्रकृति का परिवर्तन भी इससे अछूता नहीं बचा है। अतः यदि यह कहा जाये कि विज्ञान ने मानव के जीवन को विलास से पूर्ण करके जीवन को स्वर्ग बना दिया है, तो असत्य न होगा।

विज्ञान ने समय और गति सीमा में क्रान्ति पैदा कर दी है। इस क्षेत्र में स्वचालित तीव्रगामी वाहन सड़क, जल और वायुमार्ग पर समय और धन की बचत करते हुए दृष्टिगोचर होते हैं। सड़कों पर दौड़ते हुए वर्तमान अश्व-शक्ति मोपेड से लेकर भारी गाड़ियाँ, सार्वजनिक बसें तथा तीव्रगामी रेल गाड़ियाँ दिन-रात नगरों को परस्पर जोड़ती रहती हैं। इससे समय और धन दोनों की बचत होती है। वायु-मार्ग द्वारा विभिन्न प्रकार के वाहन हमें कुछ ही पलों में विश्व के किसी भी भाग में पहुँचा सकते हैं।

विज्ञान ने जीवन को विलासितापूर्ण बना दिया है। ताप के नियन्त्रण के लिए वायु-ताप नियन्त्रक (कूलर) है ताप को शीतल करने वाला यह यन्त्र शरीर को जलाने वाली गर्मी में पर्वतीय शीतलता का आनन्द दे सकता है। गर्मी में शीतल तथा सर्दी में ऊष्ण जल के कारण मौसम की विषमता से रक्षा हो जाती है। आज हम हर मौसम की सब्जी और फल, हर समय प्राप्त कर सकते हैं। विज्ञान की सहायता से हम अपने अनाज, फल और सब्जियों को सड़ने से बचा सकते हैं।

विज्ञान ने विश्व के हर भाग के दुर्गम स्थलों, काल्पनिक दृश्यों तथा स्थानों को भी दृश्य-श्रव्य साधनों के माध्यम से हम तक पहुँचा दिया है। आज रेडियो, दूरदर्शन आदि ने हर प्रकार की जानकारी को सम्भव बनाकर, प्राचीन एवं दुर्लभ रहस्यों को हल करके हम तक पहुँचा दिया है।

कम्प्यूटर तकनीक के विकास ने सूचना के क्षेत्र में क्रान्ति उत्पन्न कर दी है। आज घर बैठे ही ई-मेल द्वारा सूचना भेज और प्राप्त कर सकते हैं। इस प्रकार सूचना प्रौद्योगिकी के क्षेत्र में भी विज्ञान ने मानव-जीवन को देवताओं के समान विलासिता से पूर्ण बना दिया है। आज कम्प्यूटर बड़े से आँकड़ों की सहायता से हमारा हिसाब समायोजित कर सकता है। सभी महत्वपूर्ण जानकारियों का संग्रह कर उसे सदैव के लिए सुरक्षित रख सकता है।

विज्ञान के आविष्कारों ने जीवन को दीर्घायु और आरामदायक बना दिया है। आज विद्युत हमारे घर की सफाई से लेकर खाना पकाने जैसे छोटे बड़े सभी कार्य कर सकती है। आज विज्ञान के द्वारा हम संजय के समान कमरे में बैठे हुए कुरुक्षेत्र में होने वाले महाभारत युद्ध की आँखों देखी झाँकी का आनन्द प्राप्त कर सकते हैं। चाहे क्रिकेट मैच हो या भूकम्प आपदा, युद्ध के मोर्चे की स्थिति हो या किसी सार्वजनिक कार्य की प्रगति, विज्ञान हमें तुरन्त उसी रूप में यह सम्पूर्ण विवरण प्रस्तुत कर देता है। विज्ञान ने वास्तव में धर्म-शास्त्रों में वर्णित देवताओं के समान हमारे जीवन के हर क्षेत्र को विलासिता से भर दिया है।

चिकित्सा के क्षेत्र में—हम एक्स-रे, सोनोग्राफी तथा कैट-स्कैन जैसी क्रान्तिकारी प्रगति की सहायता से असाध्य रोगों का पता लगाने में सफल हो गए हैं।

अन्त में हम कह सकते हैं कि विज्ञान ने मानव जीवन को हर क्षेत्र में विलासिता से पूर्ण कर दिया है।

●●

विज्ञान की देन

प्रस्तावना—'वर्तमान युग विज्ञान का युग है।' वैज्ञानिक आविष्कारों ने मानव एवं विश्व का परिवेश पूरी तरह बदल दिया है। आज से लगभग 100 वर्ष पूर्व तक जिन बातों की कल्पना भी मानव नहीं कर सकता था, वे साकार रूप में उसके जीवन में सम्भव हो गयीं हैं। आज सैकड़ों वैज्ञानिक आविष्कारों ने हमारे जीवन में क्रान्तिकारी परिवर्तन ला दिये हैं। वैज्ञानिक आविष्कारों से जहाँ जीवन सुखी और समृद्ध हो गया है, वहीं इन आविष्कारों ने विकास की गति तीव्र कर दी है। महाभारत में जिस दिव्य दृष्टि का उल्लेख है, विज्ञान ने आज उसे सम्भव बना दिया है। धृतराष्ट्र को महाभारत के युद्ध का वर्णन सुनाने के लिए श्रीकृष्ण द्वारा संजय को दिव्य दृष्टि प्रदान की गयी थी। आज दूरदर्शन के रूप में यह दृष्टि या योग्यता सम्पूर्ण विश्व के सामान्य मानव को प्राप्त है। विज्ञान के बिना मनुष्य के स्वतन्त्र अस्तित्व की कल्पना भी नहीं की जा सकती। एक समय था जब मनुष्य सृष्टि की प्रत्येक वस्तु को कौतूहलपूर्ण व आश्चर्यजनक समझता था किन्तु आज विज्ञान ने प्रकृति को वश में करके उसे मानव की दासी बना दिया है।

विज्ञान की इस प्रगति का इतिहास 250 वर्ष से अधिक पुराना नहीं है, किन्तु इतने अल्प समय में भी विज्ञान ने मानव के भौतिक सुख-साधनों में उल्लेखनीय वृद्धि की है। विज्ञान के आविष्कारों में लाभप्रद और हानिप्रद, दोनों ही प्रकार के आविष्कार हैं, किन्तु यह स्पष्ट है कि विज्ञान के आविष्कारों की सहायता से मानव ने अपनी सुख-समृद्धि को बढ़ा लिया।

विविध क्षेत्रों में विज्ञान के आविष्कार— विज्ञान की असीमित शक्ति का पता उसके चमत्कारपूर्ण आविष्कारों से लगता है। इसके चमत्कारिक आविष्कारों का सहारा लेकर मानव ने बड़ी-बड़ी समस्याओं का समाधान खोज निकाला है। उसकी वरदायिनी शक्ति मानव को अपरिमित सुख-समृद्धि प्रदान कर रही है। जीवन के प्रत्येक क्षेत्र में वैज्ञानिक आविष्कारों ने प्रभुत्व स्थापित कर लिया है; यथा—

प्राचीनकाल में सन्देशों के आदान-प्रदान में बहुत अधिक समय लग जाता था परन्तु अब टेलीफोन और टेलीग्राफ द्वारा क्षण भर में ही किसी भी प्रकार के सन्देश एवं विचारों का आदान-प्रदान किया जा सकता है। टेलीप्रिण्टर, रेडियो और टेलीविजन द्वारा कोई समाचार अब कुछ ही क्षणों में विश्व भर में प्रसारित किया जा सकता है। विज्ञान ने पृथ्वी और आकाश की सारी दूरी समेट ली है।

आज रेल, मोटर तथा वायुयानों ने लम्बी यात्राएँ अत्यन्त सुगम व सुलभ कर दी हैं। पृथ्वी ही नहीं, आज इन वैज्ञानिक साधनों के द्वारा मनुष्य ने चन्द्रमा पर भी अपने कदमों के निशान बना दिए हैं।

विज्ञान ने मनुष्य के जीवन को समृद्ध किया है। अनेक असाध्य बीमारियों का इलाज विज्ञान द्वारा ही सम्भव हुआ है। आधुनिक चिकित्सा-पद्धति इतनी विकसित हो गई है कि नेत्रहीन को आँखें और विकलांग को अंग मिलना अब असम्भव नहीं लगता। शल्य चिकित्सा, कृत्रिम श्वास एवं विविध प्रकार की जीवनरक्षक औषधियों द्वारा अब मनुष्य को नया जीवन प्रदान किया जाता है। चिकित्सा की नवीन पद्धतियों के आविष्कार ने मनुष्य को दीर्घजीवी बनाया है। ज्ञान के प्रचार एवं प्रसार में विज्ञान ने महत्वपूर्ण योगदान दिया है। मुद्रण यन्त्रों के आविष्कार ने पुस्तक प्रकाशन के क्षेत्र में क्रान्ति उत्पन्न कर दी है। विभिन्न प्रकार के उर्वरकों, बुवाई-कटाई के आधुनिक साधनों, कीटनाशक दवाओं तथा सिंचाई के कृत्रिम साधनों ने खेती को अत्यन्त सुविधापूर्ण एवं सरल बना दिया है। अनाज को सुरक्षित रखने के लिए भी अनेक नवीन कीटनाशक औषधियों का आविष्कार किया गया है। हमारे दैनिक जीवन का प्रत्येक कार्य विज्ञान के आविष्कारों पर ही निर्भर हो गया है। विद्युत हमारे जीवन का महत्वपूर्ण अंग है। बिजली के पंखे, प्रेस, कुकिंग गैस, स्टोव, फ्रिज, सिलाई-मशीन आदि के निर्माण ने मानव को सुविधापूर्ण जीवन दिया है। इन सबके साथ औद्योगिक क्षेत्र में विभिन्न नवीन मशीनों के आविष्कार ने उत्पादन में वृद्धि की है। आज अणुशक्ति द्वारा कृत्रिम बादलों के माध्यम से वर्षा भी की जा सकती है। पृथ्वी और समुद्र से मूल्यवान खनिज प्राप्त किये जा रहे हैं। विज्ञान ने मानव के जीवन को अत्यन्त सरल बना दिया है।

विज्ञान ने मानव के शारीरिक श्रम को भी कम कर दिया है। आज विभिन्न वैज्ञानिक उपकरणों की सहायता से मानव कम-से-कम परिश्रम करके अधिक-से-अधिक कार्य कर सकता है जिससे समय व शक्ति की बचत होती है। इस प्रकार विज्ञान ने विश्व को हर प्रकार से रहने योग्य बना दिया है। आज धरती भी स्वर्ग के समान सुख-समृद्धि के सभी साधनों का आधार बन गयी है। आवश्यकता इस बात की है कि आज मानव आत्म-नियन्त्रण का परिचय देते हुए प्रकृति से डरे तथा उसकी रक्षा का प्रयास करे, अन्यथा विज्ञान का मानव निर्मित विनाशक रूप स्वयं मानव एवं मानव सभ्यता को नष्ट कर देगा। उपर्युक्त विवरण से स्पष्ट है कि विज्ञान विश्व को रहने के लिये अधिक अच्छा निवास-स्थान बना रहा है किन्तु यदि हम विज्ञान का सदुपयोग करें।

वैज्ञानिक आविष्कारों से हानि— वैज्ञानिक आविष्कारों की निरन्तर वृद्धि विश्व को खतरनाक मोड़ पर ले जा रही है। परमाणु तथा हाइड्रोजन बमों का आविष्कार निःसन्देह विश्व-शान्ति के लिये खतरा बन गया है। इन आविष्कारों का गलत प्रयोग किसी भी क्षण सम्पूर्ण विश्व का विनाश कर सकता है। यद्यपि विज्ञान मानव के लिए वरदान है तथा वह मानव-जीवन के प्रत्येक क्षेत्र को समृद्ध कर रहा है। किन्तु विज्ञान का एक दूसरा पहलू भी है। विज्ञान ने मनुष्य के हाथ में बहुत अधिक शक्ति दे दी है, किन्तु उसके प्रयोग पर कोई बन्धन नहीं लगाया है। स्वार्थी मानव इस शक्ति का प्रयोग जितना रचनात्मक कार्यों के लिए कर रहा है उससे अधिक प्रयोग विनाशकारी कार्यों के लिए भी कर रहा है।

सुविधा प्रदान करने वाले उपकरणों ने मनुष्य को आलसी बना दिया है। यन्त्रों के अत्यधिक उपयोग ने देश में बेरोजगारी को जन्म दिया है। परमाणु-अस्त्रों के परीक्षणों ने मानव को भयकम्पित कर दिया है। जापान के नागासाकी और हिरोशिमा नगरों का विनाश विज्ञान की ही देन माना गया है। मनुष्य अपनी पुरानी परम्पराएँ और आस्थाएँ भूलकर भौतिकवादी होता जा रहा है। भौतिकता को अत्यधिक महत्त्व देने के कारण वह स्वार्थी होता जा रहा है तथा उसमें विश्वबन्धुत्व की भावना लुप्त होती जा रही है।

उपसंहार— विज्ञान के विषय में उक्त दोनों दृष्टियों से विचार करने के बाद यह बात पूरी तरह स्पष्ट हो जाती है कि एक ओर विज्ञान हमारे लिए कल्याणकारी है, तो दूसरी ओर विनाश का कारण भी। किन्तु विनाश के लिए विज्ञान को ही उत्तरदायी नहीं ठहराया जा सकता है। विज्ञान तो एक शक्ति है जिसका उपयोग अच्छे

और बुरे दोनों तरह के कार्यों के लिए किया जा सकता है। यह एक तलवार है जिससे शत्रु का भी गला काटा जा सकता है और मूर्खतावश अपना भी। यदि मनुष्य इसका प्रयोग रचनात्मक कार्यों में करे तो विज्ञान एक वरदान है।

विज्ञान का वास्तविक लक्ष्य है—मानव-हित और मानव-कल्याण।

●●

मनोरंजन के आधुनिक साधन

''दो दिन की जिन्दगी में हैं दुःखड़े बेशुमार।
है जिन्दगी उसी की जो हँस-हँस के दे गुजार॥''

प्रस्तावना—मनोरंजन का अर्थ है—मन को प्रसन्न करना। कहा भी गया है कि ''मन चंगा तो कठौती में गंगा।'' अर्थात् यदि मन प्रसन्न है तो हम जोश, खुशी तथा नई उमंग से भर जाते हैं। आज मशीनीकरण की वजह से मानव का जीवन अत्यन्त व्यस्त हो गया है। सुबह से लेकर शाम तक उसे अनेक चिन्ताएँ घेरे रहती हैं। जीवन संघर्ष उसके जीवन को बोझिल बना देते हैं। इन चिन्ताओं तथा संघर्षों से मुक्ति पाने का एकमात्र साधन है मनोरंजन।

प्राचीनकाल एवं मनोरंजन—प्राचीनकाल में ताश, शतरंज, शिकार, नाटक, नौटंकी, ढोला एवं रामलीला मानव के मनोरंजन के प्रमुख साधन थे। गाँव के लोग चौपालों पर बैठकर लोकगीत गाकर अथवा किस्से कहानी सुनाकर अपना मनोरंजन कर लिया करते थे।

आधुनिक युग एवं मनोरंजन—आज विज्ञान का युग है। विज्ञान ने मानव के लिए मनोरंजन के अनेक साधन जुटाए हैं। आज का मानव उपन्यास, कहानी, समाचार-पत्र, दैनिक एवं साप्ताहिक पत्र-पत्रिकाओं के द्वारा अपना मनोरंजन करने लगा हैं।

सर्कस, मेले तथा प्रदर्शनी भी आधुनिक युग के मनोरंजन के प्रमुख साधन हैं। घर की चारदीवारी के अन्दर बच्चे लूडो तथा कैरम के द्वारा भी मनोरंजन करते हैं।

खेल—आधुनिक युग में खेल भी मनोरंजन के प्रमुख साधन बन गये हैं। हॉकी, फुटबॉल, क्रिकेट, टेनिस, बास्केटबॉल तथा कबड्डी भी मनोरंजन के प्रमुख साधन हैं। खेल के मैदान में जहाँ शारीरिक व्यायाम होता है। वहीं मन को भी सन्तुष्टि मिलती है तथा खेल भावना का विकास होता है।

भ्रमण एवं पर्यटन—आज आवागमन के साधनों में वृद्धि होने से सम्पूर्ण विश्व एक घर-आँगन बन गया है। पर्यटन द्वारा मानव का पर्याप्त रूप में मनोरंजन होता है। प्रकृति की हरियाली, नाचते हुए मोर, ऐतिहासिक भवन तथा प्राचीन सभ्यता एवं संस्कृति की धरोहर का यथार्थ ज्ञान उनको निकट से निरीक्षण करने पर ही होता है। भ्रमण पर जाने से दूसरे देश के लोगों के मनोभावों, विचारों तथा भावनाओं का भी परिचय मिलता है।

रेडियो, टेलीविजन एवं सिनेमा—मनोरंजन के आधुनिक साधनों में सर्वाधिक सुगम, सस्ता एवं लोकप्रिय साधन टेलीविजन (टी. वी.) है। टेलीविजन से घर बैठे दूर-दूर के समाचार, चित्रहार, नाटक, खेल तथा पशु-पक्षियों के विषय में जानकारी आदि भी प्राप्त कर सकते हैं और काव्य-गोष्ठी, धार्मिक धारावाहिक, जासूसी नाटक, बच्चों के कार्यक्रम आदि के प्रसारण भी देख सकते हैं। यह साधन बच्चों से लेकर बुजुर्गों तक का प्रिय मनोरंजन का साधन है।

रेडियो, टेप रिकार्डर आदि ध्वनि कार्यक्रमों पर आधारित साधन भी समाज को स्वस्थ मनोरंजन प्रदान करते हैं। इन पर लोकरुचि और स्वरुचि के कार्यक्रम, कर्ण मधुर शास्त्रीय संगीत, गीत, नाटक, काव्य आदि का श्रवण कर मनुष्य मन्त्रमुग्ध होकर, थकान भूलकर प्रफुल्लित हो जाता है।

आज के मनोरंजन का एक अन्य लोकप्रिय साधन सिनेमा है। मित्रों की मण्डली में, घर में तथा बाहर सिनेमा की चर्चा, सिनेमा के ही गाने सुनाई देते हैं। यह मनोरंजन का सस्ता और अच्छा साधन है।

सांस्कृतिक कार्यक्रम—आज के युग में सांस्कृतिक कार्यक्रमों का वृहद् रूप से आयोजन किया जाता है। संगीत, नृत्य, मुशायरा, कवि सम्मेलन, नाटक तथा रामलीला आज भी मनोरंजन के प्रमुख साधन हैं। लोग रात-रात भर जागकर कवि सम्मेलनों, रामलीला एवं रासलीला का आनन्द प्राप्त करते हैं। वृन्दावन की रासलीला में तो न जाने कितने श्रद्धालु पहुँचकर मनोरंजन के साथ-साथ आत्मिक लाभ प्राप्त करते हैं। इन सबके द्वारा जीवन की विभीषिकाओं से ऊबे हुए मानवों को शान्ति तथा आनन्द का अनुभव होता है।

सर्कस तथा खेल तमाशा—सर्कस के अचम्भे से भरे करतबों को देखकर तो मानव विस्मय के सागर में गोते लगाता है। शेर, हाथी, नारी तथा पुरुष इतने आश्चर्यजनक कारनामों का प्रदर्शन करते हैं जो कि अकथनीय है। जोकर अपने हास्यमय अभिनय तथा करतबों से दर्शकों को खिल-खिलाकर हँसने के लिए विवश कर देता है।

उपसंहार—मनोरंजन मन व शरीर को स्वस्थ एवं उल्लासित करने का प्रमुख साधन है। किन्तु हमें मनोरंजन के साधनों का एक सीमा तक ही प्रयोग करना चाहिये, क्योंकि 'अति सर्वत्र वर्जयेत'। मदिरापान तथा जुआ खेलना मनोरंजन के साधन न होकर विनाश के साधन हैं। अत: डटकर काम कीजिए तथा भरपूर मनोरंजन करके अपने मन को प्रसन्न रखिए। प्रसिद्ध है कि—"Laughing thrice a day, keeps a Doctor away".

●●

दैनिक जीवन में बिजली की उपयोगिता

प्रस्तावना—रात का अँधेरा धीरे-धीरे धरती पर उतर रहा था। मैंने तुरन्त ही घर में लगे हुए बटन को दबाया। पलक झपकते ही सारा वातावरण रोशनी से भर गया। अन्धकार किसी पराजित शत्रु के समान सिर पर पैर रख कर भागा। यह विवरण किसी नाटक या उत्सव का नहीं, बल्कि विद्युत क्षेत्र में अपनी मजबूत पकड़ का है। हमारे जीवन का कोई क्षेत्र क्यों न हों, कोई समय या स्थान क्यों न हो, बिजली हमें स्वामिभक्त और एक ईमानदार सेवक के रूप में दिखाई देती है। इसके बिना मानव स्वयं को एक दुर्बल, असहाय, हीन तथा अनिश्चय की भावना से ग्रस्त अनुभव करता है।

विद्युत का आविष्कार—इतनी अधिक महत्त्व की विद्युत शक्ति का आविष्कार अमेरिका के महान वैज्ञानिक डाक्टर थॉमस एल्वा एडीसन ने किया था। उसने वर्षों तक अथक परिश्रम, लगन और उत्साह से रात दिन कार्य किया। उसने सबसे पहले अपने आवास पर बिजली का प्रदर्शन किया। उसने वादा किया कि मैं न्यूयार्क में रात के अन्धेरे को दिन के प्रकाश में बदल दूँगा और अपनी धुन के पक्के इस वैज्ञानिक ने यह भी करके दिखा दिया। उसी दिन से मानव जीवन को सुख-शान्ति और सम्पन्नता से भरने के लिए विज्ञान की यह बहुमूल्य देन बराबर कार्य कर रही है। यह शक्ति मुख्य रूप से तीन प्रकार की होती है—जल विद्युत, ताप विद्युत तथा आणविक विद्युत। आरम्भ में विद्युत का उत्पादन अक्सर नदियों, घाटियों अथवा पर्वतीय प्रदेशों में ऊंचाई से तीव्रगति से नीचे गिरते जल अथवा विभिन्न टरबाइन के द्वारा जल को ऊँचाई से फेंक कर किया जाता था। बाद में ताप-विद्युत कोयले की शक्ति से ऊर्जा पैदा करके उसे प्रयोग में लाया गया। अणु शक्ति से भी बिजली का उत्पादन किया जा रहा है। स्थिति यह हो गई कि बिजली के अभाव में कुछ क्षण भी रह पाना कठिन है।

विद्युत एक शक्ति—आज विद्युत ने एक शक्ति के रूप में मानव जीवन में बहुत महत्त्वपूर्ण स्थान बना लिया है। घर में पानी भरने, पानी ठण्डा करने के लिए बिजली का प्रयोग किया जाता है। घर की सफाई, कमरों को शीतल रखने अथवा वातानुकूलित करने के लिए भी बिजली का ही प्रयोग होता है। घर में तथा बाहर तरकारियों को खराब होने से बचाने के लिए भी बिजली का प्रयोग होता है।

यातायात के क्षेत्र में बिजली या बैटरी की शक्ति से चलने वाली रेलें, बसें तथा अनेक क्षेत्रों में बिजली के प्रयोग से समय और शक्ति की बचत भी हो रही है।

उत्पादन के क्षेत्र में छोटी बड़ी मशीनों के चलने में भी बिजली का प्रयोग होता है। बिजली के प्रयोग से ही बड़े-बड़े पर्वतों को तोड़कर मार्ग को समतल किया जाता है।

मनोरंजन तथा संचार के साधनों के क्षेत्र में रेडियो, टेलीविजन, टेलीप्रिन्टर, समाचार-पत्र तथा बेतार के तारों में भी प्रत्यक्ष या अप्रत्यक्ष रूप में बिजली का प्रयोग किया जाता है।

उपसंहार—इस प्रकार हम कह सकते हैं कि आज बिजली आकाश से उतरकर धरती पर आ गई है। यह आज मानव की दासी बन चुकी है। हमें चाहिए कि हम इसका प्रयोग सावधानी से आवश्यकता के अनुसार करें अन्यथा यह हमारी स्वामिनी बनकर शासन करना प्रारम्भ कर देगी। इसके तार, स्विच बोर्ड आदि बच्चों की पहुँच से दूर होने चाहिए। बिजली के निकट नंगे पैरों या गीले कपड़े पहनकर नहीं जाना चाहिए। बिजली के नंगे तारों को छूना भी नहीं चाहिए। ऐसा करने से यह हमारे जीवन की शत्रु बन उसे समाप्त भी कर सकती है।

●●

आधुनिक समाज में व्याप्त समस्याएँ

प्रस्तावना—प्रत्येक समाज अपने सदस्यों की आकांक्षाओं इच्छाओं की पूर्ति का साधन होता है। समाज के अस्तित्व के लिए यह आवश्यक है कि उसका प्रत्येक सदस्य प्रसन्न हो और समाज के साधनों का उपभोग सभी व्यक्ति समान रूप से कर सकें। इसके लिए समाज कुछ नियम व मान्यताएँ निर्धारित करता है, किन्तु समय के साथ-साथ जब सामाजिक मान्यताएँ नष्ट होने लगती है और कुछ शक्तिशाली व्यक्ति केवल अपने स्वार्थ के लिए समाज के साधनों और सुविधाओं का उपभोग करने लगते हैं, जिससे अधिकांश व्यक्ति साधनहीन हो जाते हैं तो समाज में अनेक प्रकार की समस्याएँ उत्पन्न हो जाती हैं।

हमारा समाज और विविध समस्याएँ—कई वर्षों की परतन्त्रता के कारण हमारे समाज में अनेक प्रकार की कुरीतियों ने जन्म ले लिया। वही कुरीतियाँ आज हमारे सामने चुनौती बनकर खड़ी हैं। आज हमारे देश में अनेक नई आर्थिक, सांस्कृतिक और सामाजिक बुराइयाँ भी उत्पन्न हो गईं।

ईश्वर की दृष्टि में सभी मनुष्य समान हैं, किन्तु हमने अपनी सुविधा के लिए समाज में अनेक वर्गों की रचना कर दी है। हजारों वर्षों पूर्व किए गए इस वर्ग-विभाजन को आज भी हम उसी रूप में मानते चले आ रहे हैं। यदि कोई नीची जाति का युवक आगे बढ़कर कुछ करना चाहता है तो सबसे पहले उसकी जाति उसके मार्ग की बाधा बनती है। इसमें सन्देह नहीं है कि समाज के किसी भी युवक का विकास समाज या राष्ट्र का विकास है। इस प्रकार की संकीर्ण विचारधाराओं के फलस्वरूप पूरा राष्ट्र उस प्रगति से वंचित हो जाता है।

कभी हमारे देश में नारी को पुरुष के समान अधिकार प्राप्त थे, किन्तु मध्य युग में मुगलों के शासन काल में उसे उसके सभी अधिकारों से वंचित कर दिया गया। आज पुरुष उसे सेविका से अधिक नहीं समझता और उस पर अनेक प्रकार के अत्याचार करता है। जिस नारी को त्याग और ममता की प्रतिमूर्ति समझा जाता रहा है, जो पुरुष की जन्मदात्री है, वही नारी आज पुरुषों द्वारा ही शोषण का शिकार हो रही है। यद्यपि भारतीय संविधान में नारी को पुरुषों के समान ही अधिकार प्रदान किए गए हैं किन्तु व्यवहारिक रूप से वह उन अधिकारों से वंचित है और उसे आज भी पुरुष की कृपा पर ही निर्भर रहना पड़ता है।

दहेज प्रथा ने नारी-समाज को असह्य पीड़ा दी है। कितनी ही युवतियाँ प्रतिदिन दहेज की वेदी पर बलि चढ़ाई जा रही हैं, फिर भी हमारी आँखें बन्द हैं। दहेज के इस अभिशाप के कारण सुयोग्य और सुन्दर कन्याओं का विवाह अयोग्य युवकों के साथ कर दिया जाता है।

समाज की आर्थिक समस्याओं के अन्तर्गत भ्रष्टाचार की समस्या सर्वाधिक विशाल है। भ्रष्टाचार का मुख्य कारण रिश्वत है। यद्यपि रिश्वत लेना और देना कानूनी अपराध है, किन्तु फिर भी आज यह 'दस्तूर' के रूप में प्रचलित हो रही है। अपना काम कराने के लिये आप रिश्वत देने को विवश हैं। रिश्वत के कारण भ्रष्टाचार बढ़ता जा रहा है। भ्रष्टाचार का दूसरा रूप है—कालाबाजारी या चोरबाजारी। अधिक लाभ कमाने के लालच में व्यापारी सामान को गोदामों में छिपाकर रख देते हैं और उन वस्तुओं की कमी पैदा करके उसे ऊँचे दामों पर बेचते हैं। इस काले धन का उपयोग पुनः सामाजिक भ्रष्टाचार को बढ़ाने के लिए किया जाता है।

हमारा देश शिक्षित और अशिक्षित दोनों प्रकार की बेकारी से ग्रस्त है। जब योग्य व्यक्ति को इच्छित काम नहीं मिलता है तो अपना पेट भरने के लिए वह चोरी, डकैती और इसी प्रकार के अन्य आर्थिक-सामाजिक अपराधों की ओर अग्रसर होता है वस्तुतः बेरोजगारी की समस्या समाज का सबसे बड़ा अभिशाप है।

हमारी चालीस प्रतिशत से भी अधिक जनसंख्या गरीबी स्तर से नीचे अपना जीवन व्यतीत कर रही है। अधिक लाभ कमाने के लालच में व्यापारी चीजों के दाम बढ़ाते चले जाते हैं। सरकार की नीतियाँ भी महँगाई बढ़ाने में सहायक हो रही हैं। अतः देश के विकास के लिए महँगाई की समस्या पर नियन्त्रण करना आवश्यक है।

इसके अतिरिक्त जनसंख्या-वृद्धि हमारे समाज की ऐसी समस्या है, जिसका निदान हमारे ही हाथ में है; किन्तु अज्ञानवश हम इस ओर ध्यान ही नहीं देते। समाज की सभी समस्याओं का मूल कारण जनसंख्या में वृद्धि होना है। हमारे साधन सीमित हैं किन्तु जनसंख्या दिन-प्रतिदिन बढ़ती ही जा रही है। जिसके फलस्वरूप हम सुविधाओं से वंचित रहते हैं। यदि हमें समाज को समृद्ध बनाना है तो जनसंख्या-वृद्धि को रोकना होगा। सरकार इस समस्या को रोकने का प्रयास कर रही है, किन्तु सामाजिक चेतना के अभाव में इस समस्या से छुटकारा पाना असम्भव-सा प्रतीत होता है।

इन सबके अतिरिक्त मानव-निर्मित समस्याओं में सबसे बड़ी समस्या प्रदूषण की समस्या है। हरे-भरे जंगल काटे जा रहे हैं। कारखानों का धुआँ और कचरा इस प्रदूषण को बढ़ाने में अत्यधिक सहयोग कर रहा है। एक ओर वायु दूषित हो रही है तो दूसरी ओर नदियों का जल भी विषैला होता जा रहा है।

प्रदूषण को रोकने के लिए सरकार व सामाजिक संस्थाएँ निरन्तर प्रयत्न कर रही हैं किन्तु ये प्रयास ऊँट के मुँह में जीरा ही सिद्ध हो रहे हैं।

उपसंहार— यदि हम अपने समाज और राष्ट्र का कल्याण चाहते हैं तो हमारा कर्त्तव्य है कि हम इन सामाजिक बुराइयों को दूर करें।

सामाजिक समस्याओं का निदान केवल कानून बनाकर नहीं हो सकता। इसके लिए आवश्यक है कि समाज की मानसिकता को बदला जाए। जब समाज का प्रत्येक सदस्य इन बुराइयों को दूर करने के लिए कृतसंकल्प हो जाएगा, तभी इनका निदान सम्भव होगा।

●●

विद्यार्थियों में नकल करने की दुष्प्रवृत्ति

प्रस्तावना—विद्यार्थी जब विद्याध्ययन करता है तो उस विद्या को—पढ़े हुए को कितना ....हृदयंगम कर लिया है इसके लिए परीक्षा-पद्धति प्रचलित है। वस्तुतः परीक्षा द्वारा ही छात्र की योग्यता आँकी जाती है। भारत में प्राचीनकाल में यह परीक्षा मौखिक ही होती थी, किन्तु अब सभी देशों में मुख्यतः परीक्षा लिखित रूप में ही ली जाती है।

जीविका के लिए शिक्षा—आज शिक्षा मुख्य रूप से नौकरी या जीविका कमाने के लिए ग्रहण की जाती है। आज के युग में शिक्षा या उपाधि (डिग्री) केवल नौकरी पाने का साधन मात्र रह गई है। अतः विद्यार्थी भी

सोचते हैं कि बड़ी-बड़ी और सम्पूर्ण पुस्तकों को पढ़ने से क्या लाभ है ? वे कुछ महत्वपूर्ण प्रश्नों के उत्तरों को रट लेते हैं और यदि संयोग से वे ही प्रश्न परीक्षा में आ गये तो परीक्षार्थी उत्तर-पुस्तिका में रटे-रटाये उत्तरों को लिखकर समझता है कि उसने दुर्ग जीत लिया।

नकल का सहारा—धीरे-धीरे छात्रों की इस प्रवृत्ति में भी बदलाव आता जा रहा है अब वे कुछ महत्वपूर्ण प्रश्न भी याद नहीं करना चाहते। परीक्षा आने पर उत्तीर्ण होने के लिए वे खुलकर नकल का सहारा लेते हैं।

आज परीक्षार्थी परीक्षा भवन में छोटे-छोटे पर्चों पर उत्तर लिखकर ले जाते हैं, कुन्जियों या पुस्तकों की कतरने ले जाते हैं। इसके अतिरिक्त आस-पास बैठे विद्यार्थियों से पूछकर या उनकी कापी में देखकर भी उत्तर लिख लेते हैं। कुछ तो परीक्षा से पूर्व परीक्षा भवन की दीवारों पर संभावित प्रश्नों के उत्तर लिख लेते हैं। कई छात्र तो शरीर के अंगों पर उत्तर लिखकर ले जाते हैं। आजकल तो कुछ ''विद्यार्थी दादा'' कुन्जियों और गाइडों को साथ ले जाते हैं और चाकू, छुरी या पिस्तौल के बल से भी नकल करते हैं तो कई परीक्षार्थी निरीक्षक को रिश्वत देकर भी नकल करते हैं। बोर्ड की परीक्षाओं में अब ठेके पर नकल होती है। नकल कराने वाले शिक्षक ही होते हैं। कुछ परीक्षार्थियों के मित्र परीक्षा भवन के बाहर से भी प्रश्नों के उत्तर लिखकर किसी प्रकार अन्दर पहुँचा देते हैं। पर इन बुरे कार्यों का परिणाम भी बुरा होता है। परीक्षार्थी नकल करते हुए पकड़े जाते हैं, जिससे उनका भविष्य बिगड़ जाता है। इसलिए नकल की इस बीमारी को रोकना चाहिए, किन्तु नकल की यह प्रवृत्ति कैसे रोकें ?

छात्रों की बढ़ती हुई इस दुष्प्रवृत्ति को रोकने के लिए प्रारम्भिक श्रेणियों से ही नैतिक शिक्षा दी जानी चाहिए, ताकि वे प्रारम्भ से ही सत्य के मार्ग पर चलें। इसके साथ ही नौकरियों का सम्बन्ध उपाधियों (डिग्रियों) से न जोड़ा जाये। योग्यता के आधार पर ही व्यक्ति को सेवा-कार्य में नियुक्त किया जाए।

एक उपाय यह भी हो सकता है कि छात्रों को उन विषयों के कठिन-से-कठिन प्रश्न-पत्र बनाकर दे दिए जाएँ तथा पुस्तकों से ही उत्तर लिखने की छूट दे दी जाए। तब वे नकल करने की स्वाभाविक आदत स्वतः छोड़ देंगे।

पुस्तकों का भार कम हो—आधुनिक शिक्षा पद्धति में विद्यार्थियों पर पुस्तकों का भी अधिक बोझा लादा गया है। छात्र सभी विषयों पर पूर्णतः ध्यान नहीं दे पाते और परीक्षा के दिनों में गाइडों को लेकर प्रश्नों के उत्तर तैयार करना चाहते हैं। कुछ इन्हें याद करना कठिन समझते हैं तो कुन्जियों आदि को ही परीक्षा भवन में ले जाकर नकल करते हैं। कई परीक्षार्थी यह भी नहीं जानते कि प्रश्न-पत्र में आए प्रश्न का उत्तर क्या होगा और उसका कितना अंश लिखना आवश्यक होगा ?

उपसंहार—यदि छात्रों पर विषयों का भार कम कर दिया जाये तो विद्यार्थी विषयों की अच्छी तैयारी कर लेंगे। तब उन्हें नकल जैसी दुष्प्रवृत्ति का आश्रय नहीं लेना पड़ेगा, क्योंकि उनके ज्ञान में अध्ययन के कारण पर्याप्त वृद्धि होगी। छात्रों को अध्ययनकाल में एक या दो तकनीकी विषयों का प्रशिक्षण भी अवश्य दिया जाये, ताकि वे शिक्षा के पश्चात् अपनी जीविका का साधन उसे बना लें। इस प्रकार वे डिग्रियों पर आश्रित नहीं रहेंगे तो नकल करने की आदत स्वतः छूट जाएगी।

●●

समाज-सेवा

भारतीय समाज को ब्राह्मण, क्षत्रिय, वैश्य और शूद्र आदि वर्गों में बाँट दिया गया है। जन्म लेते ही बालक की गिनती समाज में होने लगती है। प्रत्येक समाज के अपने अलग-अलग आचार-विचार होते हैं और प्रत्येक मनुष्य की विचारधारा भी पृथक होती है। समाज के विभिन्न वर्गों में जन्म, विवाह, मृत्यु आदि संस्कार भी अलग-अलग होते हैं। समाज के सारे नियमों का विधि-विधान पूर्वक संचालन हो इसके लिए एक-दूसरे के सहयोग की आवश्यकता होती है।

मनुष्य अपनी प्रत्येक आवश्यकता की पूर्ति समाज में रहकर करता है तथा स्वयं भी समाज का सहयोग करता है। इसी समाज में रहकर ही व्यक्ति विद्या प्राप्त करता है, धन प्राप्त करता है और अपने परिवार का पालन करता है तथा समाज में रहते हुए ही प्रतिष्ठा एवं उच्च पद प्राप्त करने में समर्थ हो सकता है। समाज की उन्नति में ही व्यक्ति की उन्नति सम्मिलित है। समाज में रहने वाले लोग ही समाज में रहने के नियम बनाते हैं और समाज में रहने वाले प्रत्येक व्यक्ति को इन नियमों का पालन करना पड़ता है।

प्राचीनकाल में सामाजिक नियम अत्यन्त कठोर थे। उस समय राजाज्ञा का उल्लंघन हो सकता था किन्तु समाज के नियमों का उल्लंघन करना अक्षम्य अपराध था। अपराधी व्यक्ति के लिए भी समाज ही नियम निर्धारित करता था। इन नियमों में कुछ प्रथाएँ ऐसी थीं जो समाज एवं राष्ट्र के लिए कलंक थीं। इन प्रथाओं को या नियमों को दूर करने के लिए अनेकानेक व्यक्तियों ने महत्त्वपूर्ण कार्य किये और सफलता पाई।

भक्ति-युग में कबीरदास, सूरदास, तुलसीदास आदि ऐसे अनेक कवि हुए जिन्होंने धर्म के नाम पर बिखर रहे समाज को एकता के सूत्र में बाँधा। इन्होंने मनुष्य को इस बात का ज्ञान कराया कि राम-अल्लाह दोनों एक हैं, केवल उनके नाम अलग हैं। इसलिये प्रत्येक व्यक्ति को दूसरे व्यक्ति को अपना भाई समझना चाहिए। प्रत्येक धर्म का एक ही उद्देश्य है मनुष्य को ईश्वर तक पहुँचने का मार्ग दिखाना। ईश्वर तो एक ही है उसके मानने वाले उसे विभिन्न नामों से पुकारते हैं। हमें धर्म के नाम पर एक दूसरे से झगड़ना नहीं चाहिये अपितु एक साथ मिलकर समाज की उन्नति में योगदान देना चाहिये।

इन कवियों ने ज्ञान और भक्ति की नई राह दिखाकर भटकते हुए मानव को एक नया मार्ग दिखाया तथा समाज में प्रचलित छुआछूत, ऊँच-नीच जैसी कुरीतियों को दूर करने का सफल प्रयास किया। इसीलिये कबीर को समाज-सुधारक और तुलसी को 'लोकनायक तुलसीदास' कहा गया। राजा राममोहन राय के कठिन परिश्रम के बल पर सती प्रथा का अन्त हुआ। साथ ही बाल-विवाह आदि कुप्रथाओं को रोका जा सका।

आधुनिक समाज में भी महात्मा गाँधी, लाल बहादुर शास्त्री आदि ऐसे अनेकानेक महापुरुष हुए हैं जिन्होंने ऊँच-नीच, छुआछूत आदि की दीवारों को गिरा दिया। महात्मा गाँधी ने तो अछूतों की बस्ती में रहकर तथा खाना खाकर उन्हें सम्मान दिया तथा अछूतों को 'हरिजन' अर्थात् भगवान के लोग कहकर समाज में उचित स्थान दिलाया।

पहले स्त्री-शिक्षा का बहुत विरोध किया जाता था किन्तु समाज सेवकों के भरसक प्रयासों ने स्त्री-शिक्षा को अनिवार्य करके केवल स्त्रियों को ही नहीं अपितु समाज, देश एवं राष्ट्र को बहुमुखी विकासोन्मुख बना दिया। आज जीवन के प्रत्येक क्षेत्र में स्त्री पुरुषों के साथ कन्धे से कन्धा मिलाकर कार्य कर रही हैं। राजनीति हो, विज्ञान हो या दफ्तर हो या घर सभी जगह स्त्री पुरुषों के समान आगे बढ़ रही है।

जागरूक या समाज-सेवी व्यक्तियों के प्रयास से ही आज बाल-विवाह को बिल्कुल बन्द कर दिया गया है एवं विधवा-विवाह को प्रोत्साहन दिया गया है। इससे सैकड़ों उजड़े हुए घर फिर से फलीभूत होते हुए देखे जा सकते हैं।

प्राचीनकाल से ही समाजसेवी मनुष्यों की कमी नहीं है। समाज के प्रति मनुष्य का यह कर्त्तव्य है कि समाज की जो नीति दुःखदाई या अनीतिपूर्ण हो उसे समाप्त कर नई नीति बनाएँ। प्राचीनकाल से आज तक राम-लक्ष्मण, कृष्ण, युधिष्ठिर, हरिश्चन्द्र, कर्ण, तुलसीदास, कबीर, राजा राममोहन राय, महात्मा गाँधी, इन्दिरा गाँधी, रामधारी सिंह दिनकर आदि ऐसे समाज सुधारक एवं कवि हुए हैं जिन्होंने अपने कार्यों एवं रचनाओं से समाज को लाभान्वित किया तथा यह सिद्ध किया कि समाज-सेवा मानव का कर्त्तव्य है। जिस समाज से उसे सब कुछ मिलता है उसको स्वच्छ रखना अर्थात् उसकी कुरीतियों को दूर करना उसका कर्त्तव्य है क्योंकि मनुष्य से समाज और समाज से देश का निर्माण होता है।

समाज सेवा देश प्रेम की उदात्त भावना को व्यक्त करती है, क्योंकि समाज देश सेवा की एक महत्वपूर्ण कड़ी है। राष्ट्र का निर्माण उसमें रहने वाले व्यक्तियों से होता है। इसकी सेवा तन से भी की जा सकती है धन से भी एवं मन से भी। यदि मनुष्य सोच ले कि मुझे कुछ करना है तो वह कर लेता है अन्यथा स्वार्थ में लिप्त होकर पशुओं की तरह जीवन बिता देता है। सच्चा समाज सेवी सूर्य के समान सबको प्रकाश देता है, मानवता को सच्ची राह दिखाता है और अपनी अपरिमित शक्ति से समाज के बिगड़े ढाँचे को नवीन परिष्कृत रूप प्रदान कर एक आदर्श उपस्थित कर देता है जिस पर चलकर आगामी पीढ़ियाँ लाभान्वित होती हैं।

समाज-सेवा ही सच्ची मानव सेवा और देश सेवा है। प्रत्येक मनुष्य को समाज के प्रचलित नियमों का दृढ़ता से पालन करना चाहिए एवं कुरीतियों को दूर करने का दृढ़ संकल्प लेकर सामाजिक परिवेश को स्वच्छ एवं अनुकरणीय बनाने का सतत् प्रयास करना चाहिए।

●●

युवा वर्ग-फैशन का शिकार

प्रस्तावना—जीवन के चार आश्रमों में ब्रह्मचर्य प्रथम है। इसे ही विद्यार्थी जीवन भी कहा जाता है। विद्यार्थी शब्द का अर्थ है—विद्या प्रगति का अभिलाषी व्यक्ति। विद्यार्थी जीवन विद्याध्ययन, चरित्र निर्माण तथा शारीरिक और मानसिक शक्तियों के विकास के लिए ही होता है।

विद्यार्थी का कर्त्तव्य—छात्र का कर्त्तव्य है कि वह पढ़ने के साथ ही शरीर का भी विकास करे। विद्याध्ययन के काल में भौतिक सुखों की इच्छा विघ्न बनकर आती है। इसीलिए कहा गया है कि—

सुखार्थिनः कुतो विद्या कुतो विद्यार्थिनः सुखम्।

सुखार्थी चेत त्येजेद विद्यां विद्यार्थी चेत त्येजेत सुखम्॥

अर्थात् सुख चाहने वाले को विद्या की चाह नहीं करनी चाहिए और विद्यार्थी को सुख का त्याग कर देना चाहिए। उसे अनेक प्रकार की इच्छाओं, स्वाद, शृंगार, कौतुक, तमाशा आदि से दूर रहना चाहिए। चरित्र निर्माण पर विशेष ध्यान देना चाहिए।

आज के विद्यार्थी—किन्तु खेद से कहना पड़ता है कि आज के अधिकांश विद्यार्थी चरित्र निर्माण और स्वास्थ्य की चिन्ता नहीं करते। आज के विद्यार्थी ज्ञान प्राप्ति के अभिलाषी न होकर, विद्या की अर्थी ढोने वाले हो गये हैं। विद्याध्ययन तो एक कठोर तप है, सतत् साधना है पर वह उनके वश का रह नहीं गया है। दो घण्टे भी जमकर वे पढ़ नहीं सकते। आज उन्हें इस बात की चिन्ता नहीं कि उनका रहन-सहन सरल हो। वे उच्च विचारों वाले हों या लोग उन्हें आदर्श छात्र कहें। वे तो चाहते हैं कि सहपाठी और अन्य व्यक्ति उन्हें सुन्दर और चुस्त (स्मार्ट) कहें। इसके लिए वे फैशन की ओर भागते हैं। वे विद्या के उपासक कम और फैशन उपासक अधिक हो गए हैं।

फैशन की परिभाषा—फैशन क्या है ? यही कि पुरानी वेश-भूषा को त्यागकर नया-सा पहनावा पहनना। नई से नई बातों को अपनाना। बोलचाल, उठना-बैठना आदि में भी कुछ नवीनता, सामान्य से भिन्नता ही फैशन बन रहा है। समाज के समस्त तरुण वर्ग पर फैशन का भूत सवार है।

अपने बालों को नये-नये ढंग से सँवारने की, तरह-तरह के सुगन्धित तेल लगाने की, क्रीम पाउडर व शैम्पू के प्रयोग की, बढ़िया-से-बढ़िया चमकदार और बहुमूल्य वस्त्रों को पहनने की या यूरोपीय वेश-भूषा धारण करने की छात्रों में होड़-सी लगी है। न केवल छात्र अपितु छात्राएँ भी फैशन में पीछे नहीं हैं। वे फैशन की पुतली बनकर ही कॉलेज के अन्दर-बाहर मँडराती फिरती है। देखा जाय तो आज के छात्रों का अधिकांश समय फैशनपरस्ती में ही नष्ट हो रहा है।

फैशन के दुष्परिणाम—छात्रों में बढ़ती हुई इस प्रवृत्ति के अनेक दुष्परिणाम सामने आ रहे हैं। इससे छात्रों में अध्ययन के स्थान पर यौन-आकर्षण बढ़ रहा है। नैतिकता के भाव नष्ट हो रहे हैं और उच्छृंखलता बढ़ रही है। कालेज लॉन में, कॉफी घरों के बाहर, किसी रेस्ट्राँ के पास निरुद्देश्य खड़े होकर गप्पे हाँकते हुए छात्रों का समूह नित्य ही देखने को मिलता है। विद्याध्ययन में निश्चित ही बाधा आ रही है। इसका दुष्परिणाम अनुत्तीर्ण होने या तृतीय श्रेणी में उत्तीर्ण होने के रूप में विद्यार्थियों को ही भोगना पड़ता है, अपितु उनके माता-पिता पर भी बोझ पड़ता है। उनका व्यय-भार अनावश्यक रूप से बढ़ जाता है और फिर उन्हें अनैतिक ढंग से कमाई करनी पड़ती है।

विद्याध्ययन तो एक कठोर तप है। उसके लिए कठिन परिश्रम, त्याग, तपस्या और साधना की आवश्यकता पड़ती है। यदि छात्रों को अपनी इस अवस्था से छुटकारा पाना है तो उन्हें फैशन का मोह छोड़ना पड़ेगा। नये-नये फैशन को प्रचलित करने वाले चलचित्र और पत्र-पत्रिकाओं पर नियन्त्रण करना होगा। छात्र-छात्राओं को सादी और स्वच्छ वेश-भूषा धारण करने के लिए प्रेरित करना होगा। घरों के वातावरण में भी सादगी लानी होगी। तभी छात्र-छात्राएँ फैशन के भूत से बच सकेंगे। नहीं तो पतन निश्चित है।

●●

सड़क दुर्घटना के कारण तथा रोक

प्रस्तावना—यातायात के वर्तमान प्रकारों में सड़कों का सर्वाधिक महत्व है। संसार की जनसंख्या का दवाब बढ़ने के साथ सड़कों पर यातायात का भार बढ़ता जा रहा है। वैज्ञानिक उन्नति के साथ यातायात के साधनों की वृद्धि हुई है। आज साइकिल, रिक्शे तथा पशुओं का उपयोग तो पुरानी बात है। अब तो मोपेड, स्कूटर, मोटरसाइकिल तथा कार जैसे तीव्रगामी वाहन सड़कों पर दौड़ते हुए दिखाई देते हैं। वाहनों की इस अति ने सड़कों की दशा बहुत खराब कर दी है। इसका परिणाम है कि सड़क दुर्घटनाओं की संख्या बढ़ती जा रही है।

संयुक्त राष्ट्र संघ की रिपोर्ट के अनुसार संसार में सड़क दुर्घटनाओं में हजारों मनुष्य प्राणों से हाथ धोते हैं तथा इतनी ही संख्या में व्यक्ति 'अपाहिज' जैसा जीवन व्यतीत करने को बाध्य होते है।

भारत एक विकासशील देश है। यहाँ के क्षेत्रफल को देखते हुए सड़कों का कुल क्षेत्रफल आवश्यकता की तुलना से कम है। आवश्यकता को देखते हुए हमारे साधन सीमित हैं। आज हमारे देश में सड़कें अपर्याप्त हीं नहीं ऊबड़-खाबड़ और असुरक्षित भी हैं। यही कारण है कि प्रायः हम समाचार-पत्रों में सड़क दुर्घटना में मृत और आहत व्यक्तियों के विषय में पढ़ते हैं।

दुर्घटनाओं का कारण—दुर्घटनाओं का सबसे महत्वपूर्ण कारण है स्वयं सड़कें। प्रतिवर्ष नयी सड़कों के निर्माण की योजना बनती है, किन्तु धन के अभाव में पूर्ण नहीं हो पातीं। प्रतिवर्ष बजट के समय सड़कों के निर्माण की अपेक्षा उनकी मरम्मत और सुधार पर धन का व्यय अधिक होता है। इसका परिणाम यह होता है कि कहीं-कहीं तो गड्ढों में गिट्टी भरकर उन पर मिट्टी भरने के बाद उसे अस्थायी रूप से सही किया जाता है। आँधी, पानी तथा यातायात के दबाव के कारण वह गड्ढा फिर से अपने पूर्व रूप में आकर अनेक दुर्घटनाओं का कारण बनता है। इसके लिए आवश्यक है कि गड्ढा होते ही उसको स्थायी रूप से भरने का प्रबन्ध करना चाहिये।

इसके अतिरिक्त टेलीफोन के लिए लाइन डालने, पुरानी लाइन की मरम्मत करने, पानी की नई लाइन डालने, सीवर आदि के निर्माण आदि के कारण सरकारी ठेकेदार सड़क खोदने के बाद अपना काम करते हैं, किन्तु उसके बाद उसी मिट्टी को उल्टे-सीधे ढंग से डालकर गड्ढा भर देते हैं। कुछ समय बाद यातायात के दबाव के कारण वह गड्ढा और गहरापन दुर्घटनाओं को आमन्त्रण देता है।

इस दशा में सरकार का जो विभाग सड़क में तोड़-फोड़ करता है, उसी का यह उत्तरदायित्व होना चाहिए कि वह सड़क की मरम्मत का व्यय वहन करे तथा उसका प्रबन्ध भी करे।

उपसंहार—सड़क दुर्घटनाओं को रोकने के लिए हमें सड़कों की व्यवस्था को सुधारना होगा। जिन सड़कों को सरकार के किसी भी विभाग के कर्मचारियों द्वारा नुकसान पहुँचाया जाता है, उसकी मरम्मत पर व्यय होने वाले रुपयों की व्यवस्था भी उसे ही करनी होगी। जिससे सड़क पर चलने वाले वाहनों तथा यात्रियों को किसी प्रकार की क्षति न पहुँचे।

●●

जीवन में स्वास्थ्य का महत्व

'धर्मार्थकाममोक्षाणाम् आरोग्यंमूलमुत्तमम्।'

महर्षि चरक ने कहा (लिखा) है कि धर्म, अर्थ, काम, मोक्ष, इन चारों का मूल आधार स्वास्थ्य ही है। मानव-जीवन की सफलता धर्म, अर्थ, काम और मोक्ष प्राप्त करने में ही निहित है, परन्तु सबकी आधारशिला मनुष्य का स्वास्थ्य है, उसका निरोग जीवन है। रुग्ण और अस्वस्थ मनुष्य न धर्मचिन्तन कर सकता है, न अर्थोपार्जन कर सकता है, न काम प्राप्ति कर सकता है, न ही मानव-जीवन के सबसे बड़े स्वार्थ मोक्ष की ही उपलब्धि कर सकता है, क्योंकि इन सबका मूल आधार शरीर है, इसलिए महाकवि कालिदास ने कहा है कि—

शरीर माद्यमूखलु धर्मसाधनम्।

अस्वस्थ व्यक्ति न अपना कल्याण कर सकता है, न अपने परिवार का, न अपने समाज और न देश का। देश का निर्माण, देश की उन्नति, बाह्य और आन्तरिक शत्रुओं से रक्षा, देश का समृद्धिशाली होना, वहाँ के नागरिकों पर आधारित होता है। सभ्य और अच्छा नागरिक वही हो सकता है जो तन, मन, धन से स्वस्थ हो। अतः स्वास्थ्य, प्रत्येक दृष्टि से प्राणी के लिए महत्वपूर्ण वस्तु है। अँग्रेजी में कहावत है—

1. "Health is wealth." अर्थात् स्वास्थ्य ही धन है।

2. "Sound mind in a Sound body" अस्वस्थ मन अस्वस्थ विचारों का आश्रय स्थल है जो मनुष्य को अविवेकी, अकर्मण्य, क्रोधी और विचारशून्य कर देता है। तभी तो कहा गया है—

'पहला सुख निरोगी काया'' अर्थात् सबसे बड़ा सुख स्वस्थ शरीर है। स्वास्थ्य का मूल मन्त्र व्यायाम है—

व्यायामान्पुष्ट मात्राणी।

जिस प्रकार किसी मशीन से बहुत समय तक काम न लेने से उसमें जंग लग जाती है और वह उपयोगी नहीं रह जाती, ठीक उसी प्रकार, शरीर रूपी यन्त्र भी काम न लेने पर अनुपयोगी हो जाता है। इस यन्त्र को आजीवन उपयोगी रखने का मुख्य साधन है व्यायाम। व्यायाम नियमित रूप से करना चाहिए। व्यायाम की मात्रा धीरे-धीरे बढ़ानी चाहिए और थकान अनुभव होते ही कम कर देना चाहिए। भोजन के पहले या एकदम बाद भी व्यायाम वर्जित है। ब्रह्ममुहूर्त या प्रातःकाल में शुद्ध और खुली हवा में व्यायाम करना अत्यन्त लाभकारी होता है, व्यायाम के पश्चात् स्नान अनिवार्य है।

स्वच्छता— स्वास्थ्य रक्षा का दूसरा नियम है स्वच्छता। शुद्ध वायु का सेवन, आयुवृद्धि औषधि है। शारीरिक स्वच्छता, परिधानों की (वस्त्रों की) स्वच्छता, घर और आस-पास के वातावरण की स्वच्छता अत्यन्त आवश्यक है।

शुद्ध भोजन—स्वास्थ्य रक्षा का तीसरा नियम है—पौष्टिक, सन्तुलित एवं स्वास्थ्यकर भोजन। भूख लगने पर शारीरिक प्रकृति और ऋतु के अनुसार तथा नियम से ही भोजन करना चाहिए। घी, दूध, फल, सब्जियों आदि का प्रयोग भोजन में पौष्टिकता लाता है। गरिष्ठ, तले हुए पदार्थ, बार-बार भोजन, शराब, अफीम, गाँजा, चरस आदि नशीले द्रव्यों का सेवन व उपयोग नहीं करना चाहिए।

निद्रा—गहरी और शान्त निद्रा से शरीर की थकावट दूर होती है, मस्तिष्क स्वस्थ होता है और चेतना जाग्रत होती है। निद्रा तो स्वास्थ्य की सहचरी है। महाकवि जयशंकर प्रसाद 'निद्रा को अत्यन्त प्यारी वस्तु बताते हैं घोर दुख के समय भी मनुष्य को यही सुख देती है।' शरीर स्वस्थ हो तो काँटों पर भी नींद आ जाती है, वरना फूलों की सेज भी सुख नहीं दे पाती।

ब्रह्मचर्य—पाँचवाँ मूल मन्त्र है ब्रह्मचर्य। अर्थात् मन, वचन और कर्म से समस्त इन्द्रियों का संयम। अथर्ववेद के अनुसार, ब्रह्मचर्य रूपी तपोबल से ही विद्वान लोगों ने मृत्यु को जीता है—

ब्रह्मचर्येण तपसादेवाः मृत्यु मुपाहनत।

जीवन की सफलता स्वास्थ्य पर आधारित है। स्वस्थ व्यक्ति कभी पराश्रित या दुःखी नहीं रह सकता, वह जो काम चाहे कर सकता है। अतः हमारा कर्त्तव्य है कि हम इस स्वास्थ्य रूपी धन को व्यर्थ ही नष्ट न करें, जिससे हमें जीवन भर पश्चाताप की अग्नि में न जलना पड़े। प्राण रूपी पक्षी को शरीर रूपी पिंजड़े में सुरक्षित रखने के लिए स्वास्थ्य रूपी सीकचों (मजबूत) की आवश्यकता है। जीवन में प्रसन्नता के लिए स्वास्थ्य की रक्षा का सदैव ध्यान रखना चाहिए।

●●

समय का सदुपयोग

प्रस्तावना—समय के सम्बन्ध में कहा जाता है कि समय अमूल्य वस्तु है। संसार में ऐसी कोई वस्तु नहीं जिसे देकर हम खोये हुए समय को पुनः प्राप्त कर सकें। समय ही जीवन है हमारे जीवन की सफलता या असफलता समय के सदुपयोग पर निर्भर है। जो व्यक्ति समय के मूल्य को नहीं समझता, वह जीवन में कभी सफल नहीं हो सकता। समय के महत्व को पहचानना ही समय का सदुपयोग है। प्रत्येक व्यक्ति के जीवन में ऐसे विशेष क्षण आते हैं जिन पर उसके भाग्य का बनना या बिगड़ना निर्भर होता है। यदि वह उन क्षणों में जरा भी हिचकिचाया तो जीवन का सब कुछ खो देता है। समय के महत्व के सम्बन्ध में निम्न उदाहरण देखने योग्य है—

एक मूर्तिकार ने एक मूर्ति बनाई और दर्शकों के देखने के लिये उसे बाजार में रख दिया। दर्शकों की भीड़ एकत्र हो गयी। जब मूर्ति के ऊपर से पर्दा हटाया तो लोगों ने देखा कि उसका मुख बालों से ढका है और सिर का पीछे का भाग बिल्कुल गंजा है। जब मूर्तिकार से इसका रहस्य पूछा गया तो उसने बताया कि यह समय की मूर्ति है। यदि व्यक्ति इसके आते ही इसके सामने के बाल पकड़ लेता है तो वह आगे निकल जाता है, पर सिर गंजा होने के कारण यह पीछे से पकड़ा नहीं जा सकता है।

समय का सदुपयोग से अभिप्राय—समय के सदुपयोग से अभिप्राय है कि हम अपने समय को उन्हीं कामों में लगायें जिससे हमारा जीवन उज्ज्वल हो। संसार में जितने भी महापुरुष हुए हैं, उन सभी ने समय का सदुपयोग किया और बड़े-बड़े काम किये। दरिद्र से दरिद्र मनुष्य भी समय का सदुपयोग करके महान बन गये। सब प्रकार के साधनों से हीन, नितान्त दरिद्र समय के सदुपयोग से उच्चकोटि के प्रोफेसर, वकील, इन्जीनियर तथा वैज्ञानिक बन गये। समय का उचित उपयोग ही सफलता की कुंजी है।

नेपोलियन की महती विजय के मूल में समय का ही हाथ था। वह समय के मूल्य को पहचानता था और कभी भी उसे हाथ से नहीं जाने देता था। पाँच मिनट के समय के दुरुपयोग से आस्ट्रिया वाले नेपोलियन से हार गये थे। वाटरलू के युद्ध में नेपोलियन की हार का मुख्य कारण 'पाँच मिनट' ही थे। उसके साथी ग्रूशी के आने में पाँच मिनट की देरी हो गयी थी और विलम्ब ने नेपोलियन को बन्दी बनवा दिया था।

समय किसी के लिये रुकता नहीं, बल्कि समय के अनुसार सबको चलना पड़ता है। इसलिये आज जिस काम को करना है, उसे आज ही कर लेना चाहिये। 'कल' तो कभी आता ही नहीं। कबीरदास ने कहा है—

काल करै सो आज कर, आज करै सो अब।
पल में परलै होएगी, बहुरि करैगो कब॥

मनोरंजन जीवन को प्रसन्न रखने और मन लगाने का बहुत अच्छा साधन है। किन्तु केवल मनोरंजन में ही अपना समय न गँवाकर हम उन कामों को करें जिससे हमारा जीवन उज्ज्वल और सुखमय हो और हमारे जीवन से समाज को लाभ हो।

किसी काम को आगे के लिये स्थगित कर देने का तात्पर्य है उसे सदा के लिये छोड़ देना। कहा भी है—"अषाढ़ का चूका किसान और डाल का चूका बन्दर कहीं का नहीं रहता।" इसीलिये जो व्यक्ति आलस्यवश किसी कार्य से चूक जाते हैं, वे बार-बार उस अवसर को नहीं पा सकते, क्योंकि "गया वक्त फिर वापस नहीं आता।" समय निकल जाने पर पश्चात्ताप करने का कोई औचित्य नहीं होता है।

समय का महत्व न समझने वालों और बाद में पछताने वालों के सम्बन्ध में कई पंक्तियाँ प्रचलित हैं। जैसे—

का वरषा जब कृषि सुखाने।
समय चूकि पुनि का पछताने॥

और

अब पछताय होत का, जब चिड़ियाँ चुग गईं खेत।

उपसंहार—उपर्युक्त उदाहरणों को ध्यान में रखते हुए अभिलाषी व्यक्ति को ठीक समय पर काम में जुट जाना चाहिये। पता नहीं कब समय समाप्त हो जाये और मृत्यु आकर साँसों का अमूल्य खजाना समेट ले जाये। महापुरुषों ने इस तथ्य को भली प्रकार पहचान कर ही एक साँस या पल भी बेकार न गँवाने की बात कही है। समय का सदुपयोग रंक को राजा और समय का दुरुपयोग राजा को भिखारी बना देता है। अत: समय के मूल्य को पहचानना ही जीवन की सबसे बड़ी सफलता है।

समाचार-पत्रों की उपयोगिता

प्रस्तावना—जिज्ञासा मानव की स्वाभाविक प्रवृत्ति है। प्रत्येक व्यक्ति अपने स्वास्थ्य, अपनी समस्याओं के समाधान, व्यवसाय, खेल-कूद तथा देश-विदेश में घटित घटनाओं के बारे में अधिकाधिक जानकारी प्राप्त करना चाहता है। इस दृष्टि से समाचार-पत्र एक सस्ता व सर्वसुलभ साधन है।

समाचार शब्द के अर्थ पर दृष्टि डालने से स्पष्ट होता है कि समाचार अर्थात् सम + आचार = समान आचरण करने वाला पत्र। वास्तव में समाचार-पत्र समान दृष्टिकोण को अपनाने वाला पत्र होता है। यह किसी के भी प्रति अन्यायपूर्ण दृष्टिकोण नहीं अपनाता। इस प्रकार से निष्पक्ष दृष्टिकोण रखने वाला पत्र ही समाचार-पत्र है।

आदि काल से ही मानव की जिज्ञासा रही है कि वह अधिक से अधिक ज्ञान प्राप्त करे। इससे बुद्धि का विकास होता है। वह संसार के सभी जीवधारियों में सर्वाधिक बुद्धिमान है। अपने मस्तिष्क एवं बुद्धि की भूख मिटाने के लिए उसे साहित्य की आवश्यकता है। समाचार-पत्र के माध्यम से हम देश-विदेश के राजनीतिक, धार्मिक, सामाजिक एवं नवीन पद्धतियों के बदलते हुये ढाँचे का ज्ञान प्राप्त करते हैं।

समाचार-पत्रों का समाज में समाचार लेकर उपस्थित होना कोई नई बात नहीं है। प्राचीन काल में समाचारों का आदान-प्रदान सन्देशवाहकों से होता था, चाहे वे सन्देशवाहक मानव हों, या पशु-पक्षी।

समाचार-पत्र का जन्म—सर्वप्रथम समाचार-पत्र का जन्म इटली में हुआ था। इटली के वेनिस प्रान्त में एक स्थान से दूसरे स्थान तक विचारों के आदान-प्रदान के लिये समाचार-पत्र का प्रयोग होने लगा। सत्रहवीं

शताब्दी में ही इस परम्परा से प्रभावित होकर इंग्लैण्ड में भी समाचार-पत्रों का प्रकाशन प्रारम्भ हो गया। इस प्रकार यह प्रक्रिया देश-देशान्तरों में वृद्धि को प्राप्त होने लगी। मुद्रण-कला के विकास के साथ-साथ समाचार-पत्रों का प्रयोग और प्रसार भी बढ़ा।

भारतवर्ष में समाचार-पत्रों का प्रादुर्भाव मुगलकाल में ही हो चुका था। 'अखबारात-ई-मुअल्ले' नामक समाचार-पत्र का उल्लेख मुगल काल में मिलता है। हिन्दी में भी सबसे पहला समाचार-पत्र कलकत्ता से प्रकाशित हुआ था। इस समाचार-पत्र का नाम 'उदन्त-मार्तण्ड' था। समाचार-पत्रों के प्रकाशन को भारतीय समाज-सुधारकों ने समाज के लिये आवश्यक माना। धीरे-धीरे साहित्यिक निबन्ध, कविता, आदि का प्रकाशन भी समाचार-पत्रों में होने लगा। धीरे-धीरे प्रेस के ऊपर से प्रतिबन्ध हटे तो मुद्रण कार्य को कुछ राहत मिली और स्वतन्त्र प्रकाशन होने लगा। इससे समाचार-पत्रों के प्रकाशन का कार्य अब देश के प्रायः सभी प्रान्तों में होने लगा।

समाचार-पत्रों के प्रकार— क्षेत्रीय, जनपदीय, प्रान्तीय एवं राष्ट्रीय विषय की दृष्टि से—साहित्यिक, राजनीतिक, धार्मिक एवं सांस्कृतिक तथा समयावधि की दृष्टि से—दैनिक, साप्ताहिक, पाक्षिक, मासिक, त्रैमासिक, अर्द्धमासिक, वार्षिक आदि सभी प्रकार के समाचार-पत्रों का प्रकाशन हो रहा है।

प्रत्येक प्रबन्धक या सम्पादक अपने समाचार-पत्रों को समयावधि के अनुसार प्रकाशित करता है। इस समयावधि में प्रकाशन के आधार पर ही समाचार-पत्रों के विभिन्न प्रकार दिखाई देते हैं।

उपयोगिता— संसार में होने वाली राजनीतिक, सामाजिक, धार्मिक, आर्थिक, साहित्यिक, नैतिक, सांस्कृतिक, ज्योतिष और मनोरंजन आदि की जानकारी समाचार-पत्रों के द्वारा प्राप्त होती है। वर्तमान समय में रोजगार से सम्बन्धित समाचार-पत्र भी प्रकाशित होता है। इससे हमारे शिक्षित, प्रशिक्षित तथा बेरोजगारों को नौकरी प्राप्त होती है। व्यावसायिक समाचार-पत्र तथा पत्रिकाओं के माध्यम से व्यापार सम्बन्धी-ज्ञान प्राप्त होता है।

समाचार-पत्रों की उपयोगिता उनकी विविधता से है। समाचार-पत्र न केवल किसी एक क्षेत्र विशेष का ही प्रतिनिधित्व करते हैं, अपितु वे प्रत्येक क्षेत्र के साथ-साथ प्रत्येक प्रान्त, तथा अन्तर्राष्ट्रीय स्तर के लिये भी उपयोगी हैं। समाचार-पत्रों के द्वारा हम लोकतन्त्र में विभिन्न प्रकार के सुझाव, सम्मति तथा आलोचनाओं से अपने राजनैतिक, सामाजिक तथा आर्थिक हितों की रक्षा करते हैं तथा जनता जागरूक और योग्य हो जाती है।

समाचार-पत्रों के माध्यम से ही हमें संसार की गतिविधियों की जानकारी होती है। समाचार-पत्रों के माध्यम से हमारी चिन्तन शक्ति में वृद्धि होती है। समाचार-पत्रों का मूल्य कम होने के कारण कोई भी व्यक्ति इन्हें खरीदकर पढ़ सकता है।

कुछ प्रकाशकों एवं सम्पादकों द्वारा अपने अधिकारों का दुरुपयोग, पीत-पत्रकारिता पर आधारित भ्रमित करने वाली, राष्ट्र विरोधी एवं अतिश्योक्तिपूर्ण घटनाओं के प्रकाशन से समाज एवं राष्ट्र को नुकसान पहुँचता है। इस तरह की बातें आज राज्य एवं समाज के लिये एक चुनौती बन गई हैं। असत्य एवं भ्रामक विचारों के प्रकाशन से समाज, राज्य एवं राष्ट्र पर प्रतिकूल प्रभाव पड़ता है। कुछ पत्रों का उद्देश्य केवल धन कमाना होता है। इसके फलस्वरूप राष्ट्रीय एकता को खतरा रहता है, समाज में अनैतिकता का प्रसार होता है और कोई भी जानकारी यथार्थ रूप में नहीं मिल पाती है।

उपसंहार—आज जब सम्पूर्ण विश्व संघर्ष के समय से गुजर रहा है। युद्ध के काले बादल चारों ओर मँडरा रहे हैं। ऐसे समय में समाचार-पत्रों को वह भूमिका निभानी है जिससे मानव में परस्पर सद्भाव और भाईचारे की भावना का विकास हो।

समाचार-पत्रों की भूमिका अत्यन्त महत्त्वपूर्ण है। अनेक दृष्टियों से समाचार-पत्र उपयोगी हैं, परन्तु इनमें विश्वसनीय, जन-हितकारी, ज्ञानवर्द्धक, सामग्री का ही समावेश होना चाहिए।

समाचार प्रकाशन पर पूर्ण नियन्त्रण होना जरूरी है। अश्लील और सस्ते साहित्य के प्रकाशन पर पूर्ण प्रतिबन्ध होना चाहिए। समाचार-पत्रों में ऐसे समाचार प्रकाशित होने चाहिए जो देश की जनता को जागरूक एवं कर्त्तव्यपरायण बनायें।

●●

हमारी सामाजिक रूढ़ियाँ

भारतीय समाज में अनेक ऐसी सामाजिक रूढ़ियाँ हैं। जिनका अन्धानुकरण करता हुआ मनुष्य पीढ़ी-दर-पीढ़ी उन पर विश्वास करता जाता है। इनका कोई मूल साहित्य नहीं फिर भी समाज में ये कुरीतियाँ गेहूँ के खेत में बथुए की तरह फैली हुई है। अशिक्षित ही नहीं अपितु शिक्षित वर्ग भी इन जादू-टोने की मानसिकता में बुरी तरह बद्ध है। सामाजिक विकास के लिए ये कुरीतियाँ बाधक हैं। समाज में प्रचलित कुछ अन्धविश्वास निम्नलिखित हैं—

वशीकरण—एक-दूसरे को वश में करने के लिए तान्त्रिक वशीकरण की क्रिया करते हैं। लोगों का विश्वास है कि इस क्रिया द्वारा जिसे चाहे वश में किया जा सकता है।

सिद्धि मन्त्र—समाज में भूत-प्रेत, रोग-शोक उतारने के अनेक मन्त्र प्रचलित है। ओझा आदि अर्द्ध रात्रि में शमशान भूमि में या पीपल के पेड़ के नीचे बैठकर ऐसे मन्त्र सिद्ध करने की बात बताते हैं जिनसे जो चाहे प्राप्त कर सकते हैं।

भूत-प्रेत सिद्धि—भूत-प्रेत योनियों को अपने वश में करके वांछित फल पाया जा सकता है। रातों-रात अरबपति-खरबपति हुआ जा सकता है। ऐसी भ्रान्तियाँ फैलाने वाले भी जादू-टोने ही है। चौकी रखना, सात गाँठ का धागा खिलाना, मारण विधि आदि ऐसे जादू-टोने हैं जिनको सुनकर ही कमजोर व्यक्ति घबरा जाता है और इनका सहारा लेकर जीविका चलाने वालों के चंगुल में बुरी तरह से फँस जाता है।

शगुन-अपशगुनों की शृंखला में बिल्ली द्वारा रास्ता काटना ऐसा अपशगुन माना जाता है कि यदि आप कहीं जा रहे हैं और बिल्ली रास्ता काट गयी तो आपका कार्य नहीं बनेगा, जीवन को भी खतरा हो सकता है। बाँझ स्त्री का सामने पड़ना, विधवा का रास्ता काटना, तेली, काँणा, उल्लू का बोलना, साँप आदि का सामने आना। दाएँ-बाएँ गधा या सूअर का आना, सूखी डाल पर कौए का बैठे देखना अपशकुन माना जाता है। भरत जिस समय ननिहाल से चले तो अनेक अपशगुन हुए।

"बाएँ काकपा दाएँ खर-सूअर" कहकर स्पष्ट किया है कि कौआ, गधे और सूअर आते समय भरत के रास्ते में पड़े थे जो अपशगुन बता रहे थे।

शगुनों की शृंखला भी बहुत बड़ी है। जब राम सीता स्वयंवर में गये तब कहा—

होहिं शकुन शुभ सुन्दर नाना

इनके अन्तर्गत वाम अंग का फड़कना, पानी का भरा हुआ घड़ा लेकर किसी कन्या या सुहागिन स्त्री का मिलना, नेवले के दर्शन, दही या दूध का बर्तन सामने दिखायी देना, हरी डाली पे तोते आदि पक्षी का दिखायी देना, दवा की शीशी फैल जाना, मुर्दे का सामने पड़ना आदि शुभ-शगुन माने जाते हैं। इनका मूल कारण है अशिक्षा, अन्धानुकरण, अज्ञान, स्वार्थ भावना की प्रधानता, भूत-प्रेतादि से सम्बन्धित साहित्य का समाज में प्रचलन, धैर्य व ज्ञान का अभाव। ये अन्धविश्वास समाज में अनादिकाल से चले आ रहे हैं। सभ्यता के विकास के साथ-साथ इनका भी विकास ही हुआ है, कमी नहीं आयी है। किसी अपशकुन को देखकर लोग अपना कार्य छोड़ देते हैं और बाद में पश्चाताप करते हैं। ऐसी अनेक पुस्तकें समाज में प्रचलित हैं जो मनुष्य के चमत्कारी मस्तिष्क को प्रभावित कर अन्धानुकरण करने वाला बना देती है। मनुष्य में धैर्य का अभाव, शारीरिक और मानसिक कमजोरी इस प्रवृत्ति को और अधिक बढ़ा देती है। आज का शिक्षित समाज इन बातों पर कम

ध्यान देता है। इन रूढ़ियों और इन कुरीतियों को दूर करने के लिए जनसाधारण में शिक्षा का प्रसार-प्रचार आवश्यक है। जीवन में धैर्य के साथ सबके कल्याण की भावना होनी चाहिए, क्योंकि स्वार्थ ही अनेकानेक अनीतिपूर्ण कार्य करवाता है। चोरी छिपे बिक रही भ्रान्ति उत्पन्न करने वाली पुस्तकों पर रोक लगा देनी चाहिए तथा ऐसे व्यक्तियों को दण्डित किया जाना चाहिए, क्योंकि रोचक एवं आकर्षक रूप से छपी इन पुस्तकों को पढ़कर कमजोर मन, मस्तिष्क वाले व्यक्ति गुमराह हो जाते हैं और अपने साथ ही अपने परिवार और समाज के लिए सिरदर्द बन जाते हैं। शगुन-अपशगुन समाज को हानि पहुँचाते हैं। किन्तु जादू-टोना समाज के विकास में कोढ़ है। इनमें फँसकर व्यक्ति शरीर एवं मन से ही नहीं अपितु धन से भी बर्बाद हो जाता है। जादू-टोना करने वाले व्यक्तियों के विरुद्ध भी सख्त कदम उठाने चाहिए। यदि हम अन्धविश्वास फैलाने वाले कारणों को दूर करने का प्रयास करें तो निश्चित ही धीरे-धीरे इनका प्रभाव कम हो जायेगा।

●●

विद्यार्थी व राजनीति

प्रस्तावना—आज का बालक कल का पिता और राष्ट्र का सुयोग्य नागरिक बनता है। नागरिक ऐसा जिस पर सम्पूर्ण राष्ट्र को गर्व हो। जो अपने मन, कर्म और वचन से राष्ट्र का सम्मान बढ़ाए।

मानव-जीवन में छात्र जीवन का विशेष महत्व है। यही सम्पूर्ण जीवन की आधारशिला है। इस जीवन में लगन से अध्ययन करने वाला छात्र ही अपने उज्ज्वल भविष्य का निर्माण करने में सफल होता है।

ज्ञान के साथ-साथ विवेक एवं विनम्रता ही बालक को मनुष्यता के द्वार तक ले जाती है। विद्यार्थी जब गुरु की शरण में जाता है तो ज्ञान के साथ-साथ उसके शिक्षक द्वारा उसमें इन गुणों का विकास करने की भी जिम्मेदारी होती है। बालक संसार में जन्म लेता है तथा अपने परिवार के सदस्यों के आचार-व्यवहार को देखकर स्वयं को सांसारिक गतिविधियों के अनुकूल बनाता है। शिक्षा उसे एक अच्छा नागरिक एवं राष्ट्र की उन्नति में सहायक सदस्य बनाती है। विद्यार्थी जीवन लगन, परिश्रम तथा तपस्या का जीवन है।

आदर्श विद्यार्थी के गुण—आदर्श विद्यार्थी ही आगे चलकर राष्ट्र को उन्नति के पथ पर अग्रसर करते हैं। आदर्श विद्यार्थी में कुछ गुणों का होना आवश्यक माना गया है। संस्कृत का निम्न श्लोक आदर्श विद्यार्थी के गुणों को पूर्ण रूप से प्रदर्शित करने में सक्षम है—

काकचेष्टा, वकोध्यानम्, श्वाननिद्रा, तथैव च।
अल्पाहारी, गृहत्यागी विद्यार्थी पञ्चलक्षणम्॥

अर्थात् काक चेष्टा (कौए जैसा प्रयत्न) वकोध्यानम (बगुले जैसा ध्यान), स्वान-निद्रा (कुत्ते जैसी अत्यधिक सावधानी से पूर्ण नींद), अल्पाहारी (कम खाने वाला), गृहत्यागी (घर छोड़कर आत्मसंयम से पूर्ण जीवन व्यतीत करने वाला) आदि लक्षणों से युक्त छात्र को आदर्श छात्र (विद्यार्थी) माना गया है।

विपक्ष में—समय के बदलने के साथ मानवीय विचारधारा में भी परिवर्तन आया है जिसके फलस्वरूप राजनीति ने मानव-जीवन में गहराई से प्रवेश कर लिया है। छात्र भी इससे प्रभावित हुए हैं उनमें शिष्टता और अनुशासन का अभाव हो गया तथा गुटबाजी और अनुशासनहीनता बढ़ती जा रही है। इन्हीं सब कारणों के फलस्वरूप, विद्यार्थियों का राजनीति में प्रवेश भी बढ़ता जा रहा है। राजनीति के छात्र-जीवन में प्रवेश करते ही अध्ययन-अध्यापन सब कुछ चौपट हो जाता है।

एक सुयोग्य अध्ययनशील विद्यार्थी को अध्ययन के अतिरिक्त अन्य खुराफातों के लिए समय ही नहीं होता है। सफलता योग्य व्यक्ति के पीछे भागती है। नियम है कि पहले योग्यता प्राप्त कीजिए तब महत्वाकांक्षा पैदा कीजिए। जब छात्र राजनीति में भाग लेता है तो उसका मन दो नावों पर सवार व्यक्ति के समान हो जाता है। वह न तो अध्ययन ही कर पाता है और न राजनीति को ही उचित समय दे पाता है। उसकी स्थिति दुविधाग्रस्त हो जाती है।

दो नावों में पैर रखकर कोई भी अपने गंतव्य स्थान तक नहीं पहुँच सकता। वह न तो ज्ञान ही अर्जित कर पाता है और न एक कुशल तथा योग्य नेता ही बन पाता। उसके जीवन में अन्धकार के काले बादल छा जाते हैं तथा उसका पथ दुर्गम हो जाता है। विद्यार्थी समाज का एक आवश्यक अंग है। उनका लक्ष्य केवल विद्या अर्जित करना होना चाहिए। राजनीति विद्यार्थी जीवन में केवल अनुशासनहीनता ही नहीं लाती वरन् विनाश का घना अन्धकार लेकर आती है।

उपसंहार— विद्यार्थी जीवन वह समय है जिसमें व्यक्ति एक सफल गृहस्थ, कुशल समाजसेवी एवं राजनीतिज्ञ के गुण ग्रहण करता है यद्यपि राजनीति में हो रहे परिवर्तन विद्यार्थी जीवन पर गहरा प्रभाव डालते हैं किन्तु फिर भी छात्रों को राजनीति से दूर रहना चाहिए। उन्हें चाहिए कि वे राजनीति में पनप रहे भ्रष्टाचार को दूर करने का संकल्प ले तथा बड़े होकर अपने संकल्पों को मूर्त रूप प्रदान करें।

●●

'पुरुषों की अपेक्षा महिलाएँ अधिक अच्छी राजनीतिज्ञ होती हैं'

प्रस्तावना— आजादी मिलने के पहले से ही भारतीय नारी राजनीतिक जीवन में भाग लेने लगी थी। भारतीय स्त्रियों ने असहयोग आन्दोलन, विदेशी वस्त्र बहिष्कार करने, जेल जाने, सार्वजनिक प्रदर्शन, हड़ताल, जुलूस आदि में भाग लिया। नेताजी सुभाष चन्द्र बोस ने राष्ट्रीय फौज में लक्ष्मीबाई को कैप्टन के पद पर नियुक्त करके स्त्रियों के लिए एक नया रास्ता खोल दिया। आजादी मिलने के पश्चात् वे हर क्षेत्र में कार्य करने लगीं। वे लोकसभा और विधानसभा चुनाव लड़ने लगीं। मन्त्री, प्रधानमन्त्री, विधायिका, अफसर आदि पदों को विभूषित करने लगीं। इस प्रकार उनका राजनीति में सहयोग बढ़ा।

आज की नारी—आधुनिक युग में स्त्रियाँ सामाजिक, धार्मिक, राजनैतिक एवं साहित्यिक सभी क्षेत्रों में पुरुषों के समान कार्य करने लगी हैं। इनमें विजयलक्ष्मी पण्डित, कमला नेहरू, सुचेता कृपलानी, सरोजिनी नायडू, इन्दिरा गाँधी, सुभद्राकुमारी चौहान, महादेवी वर्मा आदि का नाम उल्लेखनीय है।

नारी तुम केवल श्रद्धा हो, विश्वास रजतनग पग तल में।
पीयूष स्रोत सी बहा करो, जीवन के सुन्दर समतल में।।

स्वतन्त्रता प्राप्ति के पश्चात् भारत सरकार ने स्त्रियों की स्थिति सुधारने के लिए अनेक कार्य किये। सरकार ने कानून में सुधार करके नारी और पुरुष को एक समान भूमि पर लाकर खड़ा कर दिया है, लेकिन पाश्चात्य संस्कृति का अन्धानुकरण करके नारी ने अपने आदर्शों को तिलांजलि दे दी है। सामाजिक एवं आर्थिक स्वतन्त्रता ने उसे भोगवाद की ओर प्रेरित कर दिया है। आधुनिकता के मोह में पड़कर नारी आज पतन की ओर जा रही है। नारी ने सुलभ कोमलता, दया, ममता, करुणा की भावना को त्यागकर, राजनीति में फल-फूल का रस लेने वाली तितली का रूप धारण कर लिया है।

विपक्ष में तर्क—राजनीति में स्त्रियों के भाग लेने की प्रवृत्ति को कुछ लोगों ने तो अच्छा समझा है, लेकिन समाज का एक वर्ग ऐसा भी है जिसने इस प्रवृत्ति को शुभ लक्षण नहीं माना। इस पुरातन पन्थीवर्ग का कहना है कि स्त्रियाँ शरीर से पुरुषों की अपेक्षा निर्बल होती हैं। इसलिये वे पुरुषों के समान सभी काम उतनी दक्षता के साथ नहीं कर सकतीं। फिर समाज के असामाजिक तत्व उनके साथ छेड़खानी करते हैं, उनका अपमान करते हैं और उनके सम्मान का ह्रास होता है। इनकी अगली दलील है कि स्त्रियों के पुरुषों के साथ कार्य करने से स्वेच्छाचारिता और अनैतिकता में वृद्धि होती है। इनका तर्क है कि स्त्रियाँ पारिवारिक जीवन की धुरी हैं। यदि वे घर नहीं सँभालती हैं तो बच्चों की शिक्षा भली-भाँति नहीं हो पाती है। उनके पालन-पोषण और देख-रेख में कमी रह जाती है। गृहस्थी अस्त-व्यस्त हो जाती है। इसलिये स्त्रियों के लिये सबसे उपयुक्त स्थान घर ही है। अत: स्त्रियों का राजनीति में भाग लेना अनुचित एवं हानिकारक है।

पक्ष में तर्क—विचार करने पर प्रतीत होता है कि स्त्रियों का राजनीति में प्रवेश लेना सर्वथा संगत एवं वांछनीय है। इसके पक्ष में तर्क दिये जा सकते हैं—

(1) प्राचीनकाल में स्त्रियाँ राजनीति में भाग लेती थीं, उच्च शिक्षा ग्रहण करती थीं।

(2) आधुनिक मनोवैज्ञानिक खोजों ने यह सिद्ध कर दिया है कि स्त्रियाँ मानसिक योग्यताओं में पुरुषों से पीछे नहीं हैं। वे सभी कार्य उतनी ही दक्षता से कर सकती हैं। जितना कि पुरुष इस प्रकार उनकी योग्यताओं का सदुपयोग न करना मानव शक्ति का अपव्यय है।

(3) स्त्रियाँ दिये हुये कार्य को अधिक गम्भीरता और लगन से करती हैं। उनके द्वारा किये गये कार्य में परिपक्वता अधिक होती है।

(4) किसी विभाग में स्त्रियों की उपस्थिति वहाँ अनुशासन उत्पन्न कर देती है। उनकी उपस्थिति में पुरुष अधिक मर्यादित और शालीन आचरण करते हैं।

(5) आज के जटिल युग में स्त्रियों द्वारा राजनीति में भाग लेने से उनके अन्दर सामाजिकता की भावना की वृद्धि होती है।

(6) राजनीति में भाग लेने से स्त्रियाँ अधिक आत्मनिर्भर होती हैं और उनका आत्मविश्वास बढ़ता है।

(7) आजकल के महँगाई के युग में उनका आर्थिक योगदान परिवार की सुख-सुविधाओं में वृद्धि करता है।

उपसंहार—स्त्रियों का राजनीति में भाग लेना वांछनीय ही नहीं श्रेयस्कर भी है यह स्वयं उनके, उनके परिवार के और राष्ट्र के हित में है।

●●

'भारतीय समाज में नारी का योगदान'

मनु महाराज ने कहा है—

यत्र नार्यस्तु पूज्यन्ते रमन्ते तत्र देवताः।
यत्रैतास्तु न पूज्यन्ते असफलास्तत्र सर्वाःक्रिया॥

प्राचीन भारतीय इतिहास के पृष्ठ भारतीय नारी की गौरवमयी कीर्ति एवं यश-गाथाओं से पूर्ण है। हमारे धर्म और पूर्वजों के विचार में जहाँ नारी की पूजा होती है, वहीं देवता निवास करते हैं। यहाँ पूजा से अर्थ सम्मान और मर्यादा से है। उन्हें अधिकार देकर उनकी रक्षा करने से है। वैदिक युग में उन्हें गृहलक्ष्मी, गृहदेवी के नाम से सम्बोधित किया जाता था। उस युग में उन्हें पुरुषों के समान ही अधिकार प्राप्त थे परिवार में उनका पद प्रतिष्ठा का था। गृहस्थी का प्रत्येक कार्य नारी के सहयोग से ही पूर्ण होता था। जीवन के कई क्षेत्रों में वह पति के आगे रहती है। कोई भी धार्मिक कार्य नारी के अभाव में अपूर्ण माना जाता था। धार्मिक और सामाजिक क्षेत्र में ही नहीं, राजनीति और रणक्षेत्र में भी वह पुरुष के साथ जाती थी। उन्हें स्वेच्छा से पति चुनने का अधिकार था। कैकेयी, शकुन्तला, सीता, अनुसुइया, सावित्री और दमयन्ती इसके उदाहरण हैं। सावित्री अपनी वाक्‌पटुता से यमराज को चकित और प्रभावित कर पति को वापस जीवन देने में सफल हुई। समय की परिवर्तनशीलता के साथ नारी की स्थिति में परिवर्तन हुआ। देश की स्वतन्त्रता के साथ नारी की स्थिति में भी परिवर्तन हुआ। मध्य युग में नारी की त्याग, बलिदान और समर्पण की भावना उनके गले का फन्दा बन कर रह गयी। पुरुष की अहं भावना ने उसे भोग्या बनाकर रख दिया। उन्हें पर्दे में बन्द कर दिया गया। उनकी शिक्षा पर प्रतिबन्ध लगा दिया गया। यहाँ तक कि तुलसी जैसे विद्वानों को नारी के विषय में कहना पड़ा—

ढोल, गँवार, शूद्र, पशु-नारी। सकल ताड़ना के अधिकारी।

अशिक्षा, अंध विश्वास, कुबुद्धि और दुर्बुद्धि आदि अवगुणों ने उसे हीन दशा में ही रहने दिया है।

धीरे-धीरे भारतीय विचारकों एवं नेताओं का ध्यान इस ओर आकर्षित हुआ। राजा राममोहनराय ने सती-प्रथा का अन्त कराने का सफल प्रयास किया। महर्षि दयानन्द सरस्वती ने पुरुषों की भाँति महिलाओं को भी समान अधिकार दिए जाने पर बल दिया। देश की स्वतन्त्रता के साथ-साथ नारी-वर्ग में भी चेतना का विकास हुआ। वह आज घर तक सीमित न होकर पुरुषों के समान कार्य-क्षेत्र में पर्दापण कर रही है। 'शारदा एक्ट' एवं 'उत्तराधिकार अधिनियम' द्वारा स्त्रियों की दशा को सुधारने का प्रयास किया गया। आज उन्हें पुरुषों के समान आर्थिक स्वतन्त्रता प्रदान की जा रही है। पिता की सम्पत्ति में पुत्रों की भाँति पुत्रियों के हिस्से की भी कानूनी व्यवस्था की गई है।

भारतीय नारी जीवन की कटुता और विषमताओं का विष पीकर भी कर्त्तव्य और त्याग का सन्देश देती रही है। रानी लक्ष्मीबाई के रूप में उसने अपना बलिदान देकर अपने देश की रक्षा के लिए अंग्रेजों से युद्ध किया। गाँधी जी को चरित्र-निर्माण की मूल प्रेरणा देने वाली उनकी माता पुतलीबाई ही थीं। श्रीमती सरोजिनी नायडू, विजयलक्ष्मी पण्डित, इन्दिरा गाँधी, राजकुमारी अमृत कौर, डॉक्टर सुशीला नय्यर आदि के रूप में हमें आज के प्रगतिशील नारी-समाज के दर्शन होते हैं। इन नारियों ने स्वयं राष्ट्र-निर्माण एवं जन-जागरण में भाग लेकर नारी-जाति का पथ-प्रदर्शन किया है।

आज की स्त्रियाँ घर के सीमित कार्य-क्षेत्र को छोड़कर समाज-सेवा की ओर बढ़ रही हैं, उनके हृदय में सामाजिक चेतना उत्पन्न हो रही है; किन्तु भारतीय नारी के सामूहिक जागरण के मार्ग में अनेक अवरोध उत्पन्न हो रहे हैं, अतः इन अवरोधों को नष्ट करके ही भारतीय नारी अपना उत्थान कर सकती है।

परन्तु पश्चिमी सभ्यता की नकल ने नारी का पथ भ्रष्ट कर दिया है वर्तमान समय में न तो वह गुप्त जी की अबला है और न सबला ही बन सकी है। आज भी देश व समाज के बहुत बड़े वर्ग में नारी की स्थिति दयनीय है। उसका जीवन आज भी अशिक्षा, आर्थिक निर्भरता की समस्या, पर्दा-प्रथा, आभूषणप्रियता व दोषपूर्ण विवाह पद्धति जैसी समस्याओं से ग्रस्त है।

हर्ष का विषय है कि वर्तमान संविधान ने नारी की स्थिति में सुधार के लिए नियम बनाये हैं। किन्तु नारी को स्वयं भी आगे बढ़कर अपने अधिकार और कर्त्तव्यों को समझना होगा।

●●

'असफलताएँ ही सफलता के स्तम्भ हैं।'

संसार कर्मप्रधान है। हर प्राणी बन्धन में बँधा है। जो व्यक्ति किसी भी कार्य को करता है और उसे कम या अधिक प्रयास के बाद पूरा कर लेता है वह सफल है और जो व्यक्ति कार्य को पूरा नहीं कर पाता वह असफल है। असफल होने का अर्थ यह नहीं कि वह जीवन में कभी भी सफल ही न हो सकेगा। यदि प्रयास एक बार विफल हो जाता है तो दुबारा प्रयत्न करने पर आशा से अधिक सफलता भी प्राप्त हो सकती है क्योंकि असफलताएँ ही सफलता के स्तम्भ है। इस प्रकार के उदाहरणों से भारतीय इतिहास भरा पड़ा है। बच्चा गिर-गिर कर ही चलना और दौड़ना सीखता है। किसी भी कार्य के सम्पादन के लिए अनेकानेक कष्टों या असफलताओं का सामना करना पड़ता है। कार्य जितना बड़ा होगा, मार्ग में उतनी ही बाधायें आयेंगी, किन्तु बाधाओं को देखकर मनुष्य को अपना मार्ग नहीं बदलना चाहिए। यदि मनुष्य तन, मन, धन से कार्य करता है और फिर भी असफल हो जाता है, तो वह असफलता कोई न कोई शिक्षा देकर प्रगति का नया मार्ग प्रशस्त करती है। अतः कहा जाता है कि 'असफलताएँ' मनुष्य की गुरु होती है। हमारी छोटी से छोटी भूल हमें कोई न कोई शिक्षा अवश्य देती है।

उदाहरण के लिए, रावण अपनी तपस्या में कई बार असफल हुआ किन्तु उसने हिम्मत नहीं हारी और अन्त में सफल होकर जो चाहा, सो पाया।

बालक ध्रुव पिता का प्यार पाने में असमर्थ रहे, किन्तु उन्होंने धैर्य से काम लिया। पिता का प्रेम पाने के लिए प्रयत्न करते रहे और अन्त में पिता के प्रेम के साथ ही परमपिता तक का प्रेम पाने में समर्थ रहे। यदि उन्हें आसानी से पिता का प्रेम मिल जाता, तो उनका प्रयास रुक जाता और उन्होंने सफलता की जो मंजिल पायी, वहाँ तक नहीं पहुँच पाते। मुहम्मद गजनवी ने 17 बार भारत पर आक्रमण किया। जिसमें 16 बार वह असफल रहा, किन्तु अन्त में सत्रहवीं बार सोमनाथ का मन्दिर लूटने में समर्थ हुआ।

महाकवि सूरदास और तुलसीदास लौकिक प्रेम पाने में असमर्थ रहे, किन्तु अन्त में ईश्वर का असीम प्रेम पाने में समर्थ रहे।

महात्मा गाँधी अँग्रेजों से अपमानित हुए। कई बार उनके बने हुए कार्य बिगड़े, किन्तु उन्होंने उन विपरीत परिस्थितियों से शिक्षा ग्रहण कर एक के बाद एक आन्दोलन किये और अन्त में देश को स्वतन्त्र कराने में समर्थ हुए।

महाकवि कालिदास उष्ट्र शब्द का भी शुद्ध उच्चारण न कर सके। फलतः पत्नी द्वारा घोर अपमानित हुए। गृहस्थ जीवन में असफल हुए किन्तु उन्होंने निराश न होकर कठिन परिश्रम किया और अन्त में सफल होकर संस्कृत साहित्य के विद्वान बने। उनकी बराबरी का साहित्य लिखने वाला आज तक उत्पन्न नहीं हुआ। अभिज्ञान शाकुन्तलम, मेघदूत आदि श्रेष्ठ काव्यों की उन्होंने रचना की।

भागीरथ की कई पीढ़ियाँ गंगा नदी को पृथ्वी पर लाने में असफल रहीं, किन्तु फिर भी उन्होंने हिम्मत न छोड़ी और अन्त में भागीरथ, भागीरथी को पृथ्वी पर लाने में समर्थ हुए, जो राजा सगर के 60 हजार पुत्रों के उद्धार का कारण बनीं। अगर एक पीढ़ी समाप्त होते ही, वे प्रयास छोड़ देते तो गंगा नदी का पृथ्वी पर आना सम्भव न हो पाता।

असफलता का मुख्य कारण कहीं-न-कहीं हमारे परिश्रम में कमी रह जाना ही होता है। असफल होने से मन में दृढ़ इच्छा शक्ति उत्पन्न होती है, फिर हम उसी कार्य को या उससे भी ऊँचे या श्रेष्ठ कार्य को और अधिक मनोयोग से करते हैं तथा पहले की असफलता के कारणों को ध्यान में रखते हुए परिश्रम करते है तो सफलता अवश्य मिलती है। हर कार्य अपने समय पर सम्पादित होता है, किन्तु कभी-कभी धैर्य के अभाव के कारण हम सफलता के पास पहुँचते-पहुँचते पीछे लौट आते हैं, तो बनता हुआ कार्य भी बिगड़ जाता है। जरूरत से अधिक शीघ्रता या आलस्य भी असफलता का या कार्य में रुकावट का एक कारण है। निष्ठापूर्वक धैर्य के साथ किया गया कोई भी कार्य असफल नहीं होता। यदि हो भी जाता है तो बहुत ऊँची सफलता देकर जाता है। ज्ञान के तन्तु खोलकर नई-नई दिशाओं का ज्ञान करा जाता है। अतः कहा जाता है कि "असफलताएँ ही सफलता की कुँजी है।"

●●

प्रौढ़ शिक्षा (चलो पढ़ायें कुछ कर दिखायें)

प्रस्तावना—संयुक्त राज्य अमेरिका के पूर्व राष्ट्रपति विल्सन का कथन था कि, "प्रजातन्त्र की सफलता के लिए हमें अपने स्वामियों (जनता) को पढ़ाना चाहिए।" कथन का अभिप्राय यह है कि प्रजातन्त्र की सफलता के लिए जनता का शिक्षित होना आवश्यक है। इसका कारण है कि प्रजातन्त्र में जनता ही स्वामी होती है। बड़े खेद का विषय है कि भारत में आज भी निरक्षरता का प्रतिशत काफी है। एक सूचना के अनुसार भारत में तीन में से दो व्यक्ति निरक्षर हैं। 15 से 35 वर्ष के अनपढ़ युवाओं की संख्या 10 करोड़ है। इस जटिल समस्या के समाधान के लिए सरकार की ओर से प्रौढ़ शिक्षा योजना के नाम से कार्यक्रम निश्चित किया गया है।

प्रौढ़ शिक्षा का अर्थ—प्रौढ़ शिक्षा का अर्थ है ऐसे निरक्षर व्यक्तियों को शिक्षा प्रदान की जाये, जो विषम परिस्थितियों में रहकर शिक्षा प्राप्त करने में असफल रहे और अपने व्यवसाय में लग गए। प्रौढ़ शिक्षा के माध्यम से ऐसे ही युवकों को शिक्षित करने का प्रयास किया जा रहा है। इसका उद्देश्य उन्हें शिक्षा प्रदान करने के साथ तकनीकी ज्ञान भी प्रदान करना है। इससे नागरिकता के कर्त्तव्यों के ज्ञान के साथ ही उन्हें राष्ट्र के सामने उपस्थित गम्भीर समस्याओं जैसे—बढ़ती जनसंख्या, अशिक्षा, बेकारी, मँहगाई आदि के विषय में जानकारी होगी और वे उन्हें हल करने के प्रयास में सक्रिय सहयोग देंगे।

भारत की स्वतन्त्रता को पचास वर्ष हो चुके हैं। इन वर्षों में राष्ट्र में शिक्षा के प्रचार-प्रसार की ओर विशेष ध्यान दिया गया है। विद्यालयों, महाविद्यालयों तथा विश्वविद्यालयों की स्थापना भी देश में तीव्र गति से हुई है इन सब प्रयासों के फलस्वरूप भी आज देश की 80% जनसंख्या अनपढ़ है जिसमें बच्चों के अलावा प्रौढ़ अधिक है। निरक्षरता का यह रूप नया नहीं अपितु सदियों पुराना है। प्राचीनकाल में मन्दिरों, मठों तथा मस्जिदों में छात्रों की शिक्षा की व्यवस्था थी। किन्तु जब अंग्रेजों ने भारत में अपना प्रभुत्व स्थापित किया तो प्राचीन शिक्षा व्यवस्था को समाप्त करके अंग्रेजी शिक्षा का प्रचार-प्रसार किया।

निरक्षरता एक ऐसा रोग व अभिशाप है जो किसी भी राष्ट्र की प्रगति में सबसे बड़ी बाधा है। गाँधी जी के अनुसार—

"सामूहिक निरक्षरता न केवल पाप है, प्रत्युत भारत के लिये लज्जाजनक बात भी है।"

नगरों तथा गाँव में रहने वाले 77 प्रतिशत प्रौढ़ आज भी निरक्षर है। उनका साक्षर होना उतना ही महत्वपूर्ण है जितना कि उनकी सन्तान का। शिक्षा केवल रोजगार की दिशा में ही आवश्यक नहीं है बल्कि यह व्यक्ति का सर्वांगीण विकास करती है। जब वयस्क व्यक्ति शिक्षित होंगे तो वह अपने देश की आर्थिक, सामाजिक तथा राजनीतिक स्थिति से अवगत होंगे तथा अपने परिवार को उन्नत बनाने के साथ-साथ देश के विकास में सहयोग देंगे।

इस क्षेत्र में योजनाएँ—इस योजना की कल्पना 1949 में की गयी। 1961 में एक कार्यक्रम की स्थापना की गयी। सितम्बर, 1969 को "प्रौढ़ शिक्षा मण्डल" की स्थापना की गयी। इस संस्था ने जहाँ इस कार्यक्रम को आगे बढ़ाया वहीं इसे पंचवर्षीय योजनाओं में स्थान दिया गया। इस उद्देश्य की पूर्ति के लिए प्रथम पंचवर्षीय योजना में 7·5 करोड़, तृतीय योजना में 12 करोड़ तथा छठी योजना में अरबों रुपयों की व्यवस्था की गयी।

इस कार्यक्रम में प्रौढ़ शिक्षा पाठ्यक्रम, शिक्षा प्रणाली, शिक्षण केन्द्र आदि बातों की ओर विशेष ध्यान दिया गया। कार्यक्रम 8 से 10 माह में समाप्त होना था। प्रौढ़ों को 35 घण्टे शिक्षा देने की व्यवस्था की गयी। इस कार्यक्रम में पुरुषों के साथ निरक्षर महिलाओं की शिक्षा की भी व्यवस्था की गयी है।

प्रौढ़ शिक्षा का पूर्ण लाभ तभी होगा जब यह सामाजिक विकास की प्रक्रिया पर आधारित हो। इस तथ्य को दृष्टि में रखते हुए भारत सरकार ने प्रौढ़ शिक्षा को विस्तार देकर सामाजिक शिक्षा का रूप प्रदान किया। शिक्षा के क्षेत्र में भारत के लिए प्रौढ़ शिक्षा की नितान्त आवश्यकता है। सरकार इस दिशा में जागरूक है तथा व्यक्तिगत स्तर पर भी प्रयास चल रहे हैं। सरकार द्वारा महाविद्यालयों में संचालित राष्ट्रीय सेवा-योजना के अन्तर्गत भी प्रौढ़ शिक्षा को विशेष महत्व दिया गया है।

प्रौढ़ शिक्षा को राष्ट्रीय कर्त्तव्य समझकर साक्षर युवक तथा युवतियों को निरक्षर लोगों को साक्षर बनाने का प्रयास करना चाहिए। सरकार द्वारा भी इस दिशा में महत्वपूर्ण प्रयास किये जा रहे हैं। हमें विश्वास है कि कुछ ही वर्षों में हमारे देश के अधिकांश प्रौढ़ साक्षर होंगे। साक्षर होने पर वे पत्र-पत्रिकाओं का अध्ययन कर सकेंगे। जिसके फलस्वरूप उनमें सामाजिक, सांस्कृतिक और राजनैतिक चेतना जाग्रत होगी तथा देश उन्नति के पथ पर अग्रसर होगा।

●●

अध्ययन का आनन्द

प्रस्तावना— मनुष्य एक सुखाभिलाषी प्राणी है। सुख या आनन्द की प्राप्ति के लिए ही उसकी सम्पूर्ण चेष्टाएँ और कर्म होते हैं। यद्यपि किसी भी कार्य में कुछ परिश्रम और कष्ट तो उठाना ही पड़ता है, उसकी परिणति आनन्द में तभी होती है। मनुष्य धन कमाता है, उससे ऐश्वर्य और विलास की अनेक वस्तुएँ खरीदता है। किसलिए ? आनन्द पाने के लिए ही न।

आनन्द के साधन—सुख या आनन्द प्राप्ति के अनेक साधन हैं। किसी को खेलों में रुचि होती है। किसी को अच्छे भोजन में ही सुख मिलता है। कोई सुरापान में, कोई मित्रों के साथ संलाप में ही आनन्द लेता है। किसी सात्विक विचारों के व्यक्ति को भगवद् भक्ति और सत्संग में आनन्द की प्राप्ति होती है तो किसी साधु संत को संसार से विरक्त हो ईश्वर के चिन्तन और योगाराधना में ही आनन्द की उपलब्धि होती है।

आनन्द प्राप्ति के अनेक साधन हैं, उन्हीं में एक प्रमुख साधन है सद्ग्रन्थों का अध्ययन करना। अध्ययन से भी असीम सुख मिलता है। एक नीति श्लोक में कहा गया है।

काव्य-शास्त्र विनोदेन कालो गच्छति धीमताय्।
व्यसेन न च मूर्खांणा निद्रयाकलेहन वा॥

विद्वानों और मनीषियों का कथन है कि सत्संगति से व्यक्ति को आनन्द मिलता है। भर्तहरि ने एक नीति-श्लोक में कहा है कि सत्संगति बुद्धि की जड़ता को दूर करती है, सत्य बोलना सिखाती है, सम्मान बढ़ाती है, पाप दूर करती है, मन को प्रसन्न करती है और चारों ओर यश को फैलाती है। सज्जनों, साधुपुरुषों और सन्त महात्माओं की संगति वो सत्संगति है पर यदि उनकी संगति प्राप्त न हो तो सद्ग्रन्थों का अध्ययन भी एक प्रकार की सत्संगति ही है।

अध्ययन से आनन्द व लाभ—वेद, शास्त्र, रामायण, महाभारत, साहित्य काव्य-ग्रन्थ आदि सद्ग्रन्थों के अध्ययन से आनन्द के साथ शिक्षा भी मिलती है। एक पाश्चात्य विद्वान् का कथन है कि "पुस्तकें अवकाश के समय मनोरंजन का अत्युत्तम साधन है। रोचक पुस्तकों के अध्ययन से मनुष्य जीवन की सारी चिन्ताओं से मुक्त हो जाता है।

रामचरित्मानस में डुबकी लगाइए। मन में अपार शान्ति छा जायेगी, समस्त अन्धकार दूर हो जायेगा और अलौकिक आनन्द से रोम-रोम पुलकित हो जायेगा। अध्ययन में रुचि के कारण वाल्मीकि, व्यास, कालिदास, सूरदास, तुलसीदास, रवीन्द्र नाथ टैगोर, प्रेमचन्द्र, जयशंकर प्रसाद और निराला जैसे साहित्यकारों से मित्रता हो जाती है। अध्ययनशील व्यक्ति ज्यों-ज्यों उनके साहित्य-सागर में गोते लगाता है त्यों-त्यों उसके हाथ में आनन्द के मोती आते जाते हैं। कबीर ने कहा है—

जिन ढूँढा तिन पाइया, गहरे पानी पैठ।

जब हम किसी पुस्तक को पढ़ते हैं तो व्यक्त भाव चित्त को आनन्द-मग्न कर देता है।

उपसंहार—मनुष्य को सच्चा और सात्विक आनन्द लेना है तो सत्-साहित्य का अध्ययन करना चाहिए। मनुष्य को अध्ययन के लिए सदैव उत्तम पुस्तकों का ही चुनाव करना चाहिए। अश्लील पुस्तकें भी आनन्द देती हैं पर वह आनन्द इन्द्रियों को उत्तेजित और मन को अस्वस्थ करने वाला ही होता है। जैसे चटपटी चाट खाने में अच्छी लगती है, पर खाने वाले को अस्वस्थ कर देती है, ऐसी ही अश्लील पुस्तकें मन को बीमार कर देती हैं। जीवन में साथी, मित्र, बन्धु नहीं हों तो सत्-साहित्य का स्वाद लो जीवन आनन्द से भर जायेगा और मनुष्य का श्रेष्ठ विकास भी होगा। अंग्रेजी में भी एक उक्ति है।

"Good books are the best friend"

अर्थात् उत्तम पुस्तकें सबसे उत्तम मित्र हैं। इन मित्रों की संगति (उनका अध्ययन) आनन्द देगी ही।

●●

अनुशासन का महत्व
अथवा
विद्यार्थी एवं अनुशासन

प्रस्तावना—प्रकृति के समस्त तत्व अनुशासन से प्रेरित हैं। संसार में सूर्य, चन्द्रमा, सन्ध्या, प्रातः, ऋतु आदि को नियमित रूप से आते-जाते देखकर स्पष्ट हो जाता है कि सृष्टि के मूल में एक सुनियोजित व्यवस्था कार्य कर रही है। 'अनुशासन' शब्द का अर्थ है—नियम के अनुसार चलना। अनुशासन का अर्थ पराधीनता नहीं है। समय, स्थान तथा परिस्थितियों के अनुरूप सामान्य नियमों का पालन करना ही अनुशासन कहलाता है।

अनुशासन का महत्व—अनुशासन का जीवन में विशेष महत्व है। समस्त प्रकृति नियमों के अनुसार चलती है, इसलिए उसके किसी भी क्रियाकलाप में बाधा नहीं आती है। दिन-रात नियमित रूप से आते रहते हैं। इससे स्पष्ट है कि अनुशासन के द्वारा ही जीवन को सार्थक बनाया जा सकता है। अनुशासन के मार्ग से भटक जाने पर व्यक्ति चरित्रहीन, दुराचारी, पतित तथा निन्दनीय हो जाता है। समाज में उसका कोई सम्मान नहीं रहता है। अनुशासन के अभाव में उसका तन तथा मन दोनों दूषित हो जाते हैं।

विद्यार्थी और अनुशासन—विद्यार्थी जीवन मनुष्य के भावी जीवन की आधारशिला है। आज के विद्यार्थी ही भावी नागरिक बनेंगें। विद्यार्थी अनुशासन में रहकर ही स्वास्थ्य, शिक्षा, व्यवहार तथा आचार ग्रहण कर सकता है। नियमित रूप से अध्ययन करना, विद्यालय जाना, व्यायाम करना, गुरुजनों से सद्व्यवहार करना ही विद्यार्थी-जीवन का अनुशासन है। इसके बिना विद्यार्थी आदर्श विद्यार्थी नहीं बन सकता है।

बच्चे का प्रथम सम्पर्क अपने माता-पिता तथा परिवार से होता है। अन्य प्रकार की शिक्षा के समान अनुशासन की शिक्षा भी बच्चे को सबसे पहले यहीं से प्राप्त होती है। इसके बाद विद्यालय तथा बाह्य समाज से अनुशासन की शिक्षा मिलती है। अनुशासन का पालन आत्म-नियन्त्रण तथा भय से होता है। आत्म-नियन्त्रण से होने वाला अनुशासन स्थिर माना गया है। इसकी शिक्षा संस्कारों से मिलती है। दूसरे प्रकार का अनुशासन बाहर के आतंक के कारण होता है। अनुशासन के द्वारा ही सफल जीवनयापन किया जा सकता है। इन्हीं के द्वारा तन तथा मन स्वस्थ रहते हैं, अनुशासन के कारण ही मनुष्य उच्च आदर्शों की ओर बढ़ता है। अनुशासन के द्वारा ही ज्ञान प्राप्ति सम्भव है। पवित्र मन तथा बुद्धि से ही ज्ञान का संचार होता है। चरित्र के निर्माण में अनुशासन का विशेष योग रहता है।

अनुशासनहीनता—अनुशासनहीनता एक कोढ़ है जो समाज को नष्ट कर रही है। दुर्भाग्यवश आज अनुशासनहीनता इतनी बढ़ गयी है कि विद्यालय, छात्रावास, बाजार, घर, समाज आदि सभी में अनुशासन का अभाव दिखायी पड़ता है। धर्म तथा समाज के नियन्त्रण समाप्त हो रहे हैं। प्रशासनिक अधिकारी, कर्मचारी आदि भी अनुशासनहीन हो गये हैं।

अनुशासन की आवश्यकता—अनुशासन में रहकर ही शक्ति का संचार होता है। जो राष्ट्र जितना अधिक अनुशासित होता है, वह उतना ही अधिक विकास करता है। अनुशासित कल-कारखाने, विद्यालय, कृषि, मजदूरी, नौकरी आदि के द्वारा ही देश तथा समाज को सुखी एवं सम्पन्न बनाया जा सकता है। दूसरे राष्ट्रों से सुरक्षित रहने के लिए भी अनुशासन आवश्यक है। सेना अनुशासन में रहकर ही युद्ध कर पाती है, विद्यार्थी अनुशासन में रहकर ही ज्ञान प्राप्त कर पाता है तथा व्यापारी एवं उद्योगपति भी अनुशासन का पालन करके ही अपना उत्तरदायित्व निभा पाता है।

उपसंहार—बिना अनुशासन के मानव-जीवन का कोई भी क्रिया-कलाप नहीं चल सकता है विद्यार्थी जीवन तो इसकी धुरी है। छात्रों के भविष्य को अनुशासन मंगलमय बनाता है। अनुशासनप्रिय छात्र सफलता को प्राप्त होता है। सफलता अथवा असफलता का मापदण्ड अनुशासन है। ये दैनिक जीवन को व्यवस्थित करता है। गुणों का बीजारोपण करने वाला है। सद्भावना का विस्तार करके विश्व जीवन को भव्यता प्रदान करता है। अनुशासनमय जीवन ही यथार्थ जीवन का परिचायक है। ●●

एक अविस्मरणीय चरित्र (महर्षि दयानंद)

भारतवर्ष के राजनैतिक तथा धार्मिक उत्थान में भारत के प्रदेश गुजरात ने भी सदैव अपना सहयोग दिया है। महात्मा गाँधी तथा सरदार पटेल ये दोनों ही महापुरुष गुजरात में उत्पन्न हुए थे पर ये दोनों ही राजनैतिक गुत्थियों को सुलझाने वाले थे। धार्मिक क्षेत्र में इनमें से किसी ने भी तथा यहाँ उत्पन्न होने वाले अन्य महापुरुषों ने भी कोई स्तुत्य कार्य नहीं किया। देश की राजनैतिक चेतना के साथ-साथ सांस्कृतिक या धार्मिक भावनाओं एवं हिन्दी के उत्थान में अपना बलिष्ठ कन्धा लगाने वालों में महर्षि दयानन्द का नाम विशेष रूप से स्मरणीय है। वह समाज सुधारक तथा आर्य संस्कृति के रक्षक थे। प्राचीनकाल में महापुरुषों ने अपने प्राणप्रण से आर्य-संस्कृति की रक्षा की और उसके स्थान पर उद्योग, परिश्रम और कर्मण्यता का पाठ पढ़ाया। धार्मिक कृत्यों में प्राचीन विचारधारा तथा आडम्बरपूर्ण रीतियों के स्थान पर नवीन आध्यात्मिक पूजा को महत्व दिया। रूढ़िवाद की पुरातन छिन्न-भिन्न शृंखलाओं को नष्ट करके जनता को धर्म के मूल तथ्यों को समझाया। जाति, वैषम्य, अस्पृश्यता और भेद-भाव को दूर किया। दुःखी हिन्दू जनता का ईसाई और मुस्लिम धर्म में धर्मान्तरण होता जा रहा था। हिन्दू जाति का एक बहुत बड़ा भाग धर्म परिवर्तन कर चुका था। महर्षि दयानन्द ने जातिवाद और वैषम्य की विषाक्त विचारधाराओं को समाज से जड़ सहित उखाड़ फेंक देने का सबल प्रयत्न किया। इन्होंने हिन्दू धर्म में पर्याप्त संशोधन उपस्थित किये। ईसाई मिशनरियों से टक्कर ली। इन सब बातों के अतिरिक्त देश की स्वतन्त्रता के महान् उद्घोषकों में भी दयानन्द जी का प्रमुख स्थान है।

महर्षि दयानन्द का प्रादुर्भाव सन् 1724, में गुजरात प्रान्त के मौरवी राज्य के टंकारा नामक गाँव में हुआ था। कुछ लोग इन्हें दयाल भी कह देते थे। इनके पिता का नाम कर्षन जी था। वे गाँव के बड़े जमींदार थे, परिवार सम्पन्न था। सनातन धर्म की पद्धति के अनुसार बालक मूलशंकर का पाँच वर्ष की अवस्था में यज्ञोपवीत संस्कार तथा विद्यारम्भ संस्कार कराया गया। संस्कृत की शिक्षा से आपके अध्ययन का श्रीगणेश हुआ। प्रारम्भ में अमरकोष और लघु कौमुदी आदि संस्कृत के ग्रन्थ याद कराये गये। यजुर्वेद की कुछ ऋचायें भी कण्ठस्थ करायी गयीं। प्रारम्भ से ही कुशाग्र बुद्धि होने के कारण थोड़े ही समय में इन्होंने संस्कृत का ज्ञान प्राप्त कर लिया।

महर्षि दयानन्द के पिता प्राचीन विचारों के पोषक थे, वे शैव थे। परिवार में शिवजी की उपासना होती थी। बालक मूलशंकर की आयु लगभग 13 वर्ष की होगी। शिवरात्रि का महापर्व आया। शैव सम्प्रदाय वालों के लिए यह दिन विशेष महत्व का होता है। पारिवारिक प्रथा के अनुसार इन्होंने भी सारे दिन व्रत रखा और रात्रि को रात्रि जागरण किया, शिवलिंग के निकट बैठे-बैठे जप करते रहे, जैसे परिवार के अन्य व्यक्ति कर रहे थे। अर्धरात्रि के समय इन्होंने देखा कि एक चूहा आया और शिवलिंग पर आकर बैठ गया। वह कभी चढ़ता और कभी उतरता, कभी रखे हुए भोग को खाता। वे विचित्र विस्मय में पड़ गये, सोचने लगे कि शिव तो अत्यन्त शक्तिशाली है, सारे विश्व का सृजन और संहार करते हैं, क्या वे इस चूहे से अपनी रक्षा नहीं कर सकते हैं ? उसी दिन से उन्हें मूर्ति पूजा के प्रति अनास्था हो गयी, हृदय में विचार विद्रोह होने लगा। बात तो साधारण थी, परन्तु तत्कालीन परिस्थितियों को दृष्टि में रखकर देखने से प्रतीत होता है कि इसका बड़ा महत्व था, क्योंकि जनता में अन्धविश्वास और अन्धभक्ति थी। उनको युगों-युगों की विचारधारा के विरुद्ध एक शब्द भी कहना बड़ा कठिन था, साधारण व्यक्ति के वश की बात नहीं थी।

इस घटना के दो वर्ष बाद इनकी बहन की मृत्यु हो गयी। बहन की मृत्यु ने इनके हृदय में संसार के प्रति अरुचि उत्पन्न कर दी। इनकी दृष्टि के सामने सदैव संसार की अस्थिरता, नश्वरता और क्षणभंगुरता नृत्य करने लगी। अपने तर्कों के आधार पर संसार को प्रिय लगने वाली माया विष प्रतीत होने लगी। अपने पुत्र में संसार के प्रति बढ़ती हुई घृणा को देखकर पिता चिन्तित हो उठे और इन्हें विवाह के बन्धन में बाँधने का निश्चय कर लिया। एक दिन, घर में मंगल गीत हो रहे थे, बाजे बज रहे थे, सभी लोग मूलशंकर के विवाह की खुशी मना रहे थे कि यह रात्रि को घर से निकल भागे। पैदल चलते-चलते आप अहमदाबाद पहुँचे, फिर कुछ दिन तक बड़ौदा रहे। नर्मदा के किनारे अनेक विद्वान, साधु-संन्यासियों की सत्संगति प्राप्त करते हुए आप ज्ञानार्जन में व्यस्त हो गये। उन्हें अधिकांश संन्यासी पाखण्डी और ढोंगी मिले। सन् 1760 में वह मथुरा पहुँचे। वहाँ स्वामी विरजानन्द जी से इनकी भेंट हुई। स्वामी जी नेत्रों से अन्धे थे, फिर भी इन्हें वेद, व्याकरण, ज्ञान और वैराग्य की शिक्षा देने लगे। स्वामी विरजानन्द जी को भी देश में फैले हुए पाखण्डों के कारण बड़ा कष्ट होता था। दयानन्द की शिक्षा-दीक्षा समाप्त होने के पश्चात् उन्होंने आज्ञा दी कि तुम देश में वैदिक धर्म का प्रचार करो, जनता के हृदय-पटल से अन्धकार को दूर करके वेदों की मर्यादा की रक्षा करो।

गुरु की आज्ञानुसार वे वैदिक धर्म के प्रचार में लग गये। उनके पास न धन-बल था, न संस्था थी, न सभा, केवल बुद्धि-बल था। उन दिनों हरिद्वार में कुम्भ का मेला हो रहा था। वहाँ जाकर उन्होंने 'पाखण्ड खण्डिनी पताका' लगाकर जनता को धर्म के गूढ़ रहस्यों को बताया। कुम्भ में यद्यपि उनको विशेष सफलता नहीं मिली, परन्तु फिर भी धीरे-धीरे उनके अनुयायियों की संख्या बढ़ती गयी। दयानन्द जी को शास्त्रों का अच्छा ज्ञान था, वे लोगों से शास्त्रार्थ करते थे। उन दिनों देश में शास्त्रार्थ का प्रचलन था। दो विभिन्न सिद्धान्तों के मानने वाले विद्वान् आपस में शास्त्रार्थ करते थे, जो विजयी हो जाता था, जनता उसकी बात मान लेती थी। दयानन्द अनेक शास्त्रार्थों में विजयी हुए। काशी, विद्वानों का गढ़ था। स्वामी दयानन्द जी के वहाँ पर भी कई शास्त्रार्थ हुए। दयानन्द जी की धूम सारे देश में मच गयी।

वह समय सामाजिक चेतना का समय था और राजा राममोहन राय सती प्रथा के विरुद्ध तथा विधवा विवाह के पक्ष में आन्दोलन कर रहे थे, दूसरी ओर भारतेन्दु हरिश्चन्द्र स्त्री शिक्षा के लिए प्रयत्नशील थे, स्वामी

दयानन्द समाज की सर्वांगीण उन्नति के लिए प्रयत्नशील थे, एक ओर उन्होंने अन्ध-विश्वास, पाखण्ड और मूर्ति-पूजा का विरोध किया, दूसरी ओर छूआ-छूत और बाल-विवाह को दूर करने तथा स्त्री शिक्षा एवं विधवा विवाह को प्रोत्साहन देने के लिए आन्दोलन किये।

सन् 1774 में, उन्होंने बम्बई (मुम्बई) आर्य समाज की स्थापना की, आर्य समाज के सिद्धान्तों का देश में तेजी से प्रचार और प्रसार होने लगा। देश के प्राय: सभी बड़े-बड़े नगरों में आर्य समाज मन्दिरों की स्थापना हो गयी। आर्य समाज ने सर्वप्रथम स्त्रियों की अशिक्षा दूर करने की आवाज उठाई। स्वामी दयानन्द जी ने स्वयं गुजराती होते हुए अपने सिद्धान्तों का प्रचार हिन्दी भाषा में किया, इससे हिन्दी की वृद्धि हुई, पंजाब जैसा उर्दू भाषी प्रान्त भी हिन्दी में रूचि लेने लगा। हिन्दी भाषा इसके लिए सदैव दयानन्द जी की ऋणी रहेगी।

भारतीय अपना स्वाभिमान खोते जा रहे थे। भारतीय विदेशी सभ्यता, संस्कृति और शिक्षा प्राप्त करने में अपने को गौरवशाली समझते थे तथा अपनी प्राचीन भारतीय संस्कृति को हीन। दयानन्द जी ने वेदों और संस्कृत साहित्य के अध्ययन पर बल दिया, अपने पूर्वजों के प्रति महान् श्रद्धा और निष्ठा जाग्रत की। ईसाई पादरी अपने मत का प्रचार करने में संलग्न थे। उन्हें शासन द्वारा सहयोग मिला हुआ था। दयानन्द जी ने उनके बढ़ते हुए प्रभावों को रोका, उन्हें मुँह तोड़ उत्तर दिए, शास्त्रार्थों में पराजित किया और वैदिक धर्म की महानता सिद्ध कर दी। इसी का विस्तृत विश्लेषण उनके ग्रन्थ "सत्यार्थ प्रकाश" में है। दयानन्द जी के अथक प्रयासों से जनता विधर्मियों के बहकावे में आने से बच गयी। दयानन्द जी के धर्म-प्रचार की यह विशेषता थी कि पढ़े-लिखे विद्वान लोग भी उनके धर्म से प्रभावित हुए। उन्होंने विद्वानों से टक्करें लीं, बुद्धि की कसौटी पर उनके विचार खरे उतरे। उनसे पूर्व भी अनेक धर्म-प्रचारक और समाज-सुधारक हुए। उन्होंने पहले अशिक्षित जनता के हृदय को स्पर्श किया। इसके पश्चात् वे आगे बढ़े। परन्तु दयानन्द जी के आर्य समाज को पहले शिक्षितों ने अपनाया फिर अशिक्षितों ने। कहने का तात्पर्य यह है कि स्वामी जी के आर्य समाज और उनके सिद्धान्तों का आधार बुद्धिवादी था, उन बातों को तर्क और व्यापार की कसौटी पर कसकर देख लिया गया था। शिक्षा प्रसार में भी स्वामी दयानन्द ने अमूल्य योगदान दिया। उन्होंने समस्त भारत में डी. ए. वी. हाईस्कूल स्थापित कराये।

स्वामी जी स्वतन्त्रता का मूल्य समझते थे। उन्होंने सत्यार्थ प्रकाश में लिखा है कि अपना बुरे से बुरा शासन भी अच्छा और पराया, अच्छे से अच्छा शासन भी बुरा है। सामाजिक, नैतिक और धार्मिक उत्थान के पश्चात् वे राजनीतिक क्षेत्र में सुधार करना चाहते थे। उनकी इच्छा थी कि पहले देशी रियासतों के सभी राजाओं को संगठित किया जाये तब कोई आगे ठोस कदम उठाया जाये। यह पवित्र कार्य उन्होंने प्रारम्भ कर दिया था, परन्तु विधाता की इच्छा कुछ और ही थी, इन्हें संसार छोड़कर जाना पड़ा।

एक बार स्वामी जी को जोधपुर नरेश महाराजा जसवन्तसिंह का निमन्त्रण प्राप्त हुआ। स्वामी जी गये और बड़ी श्रद्धा से उनका स्वागत किया गया। दूसरे दिन नगर की जनता के समक्ष आपका प्रवचन हुआ। महाराजा कई बार स्वामी जी के दर्शनों के लिए आये। एक दिन राजा ने स्वामी जी को राजमहल में आमन्त्रित किया। राजा के पास एक वैश्या बैठी हुई थी। स्वामी जी को यह देखकर अत्यन्त खेद हुआ। उन्होंने कहा "हे राजन! क्षत्रिय वीर कुमार को यह शोभा नहीं देता। वैश्या जगह-जगह पर भटकने वाली कुतिया के समान है।" इसी प्रकार के अन्य तिरस्कारपूर्ण शब्द वैश्या की उपस्थिति में ही राजा से कहे। वैश्या को बहुत बुरा लगा। उसके हृदय में प्रतिशोध की अग्नि भड़क उठी तथा अपना रास्ता साफ करने के लिए उसने रसोइये से मिल कर भोजन में विष मिलवा दिया। सारे शरीर में विष फैल गया बहुत उपचार किये गये परन्तु स्वामी जी स्वस्थ न हुए, कुछ रोगों ने स्थायी रूप से अपनी जड़ जमा ली। महाराजा जसवन्तसिंह उन्हें आबू पर्वत पर ले गये। बड़े-बड़े डॉक्टरों को दिखाया गया पर कोई लाभ नहीं हुआ। महाराजा बहुत खिन्न हुए परन्तु स्वामी जी ने उन्हें लौटा दिया। अन्त में दीपावली के दिन आपने अपने सभी शिष्यों को बुलाकर कहा कि "आज मेरा संसार से प्रस्थान का दिन है, तुम लोग अपने-अपने कर्तव्यों पर कायम रहना, संसार में संयोग और वियोग का होना स्वाभाविक है।" इतना कहकर वेद-मन्त्रों का पाठ करते हुए स्वामी जी ने अपना नाशवान शरीर छोड़ दिया।

हिन्दू जाति पर स्वामी जी के इतने उपकार हैं कि वह उनसे कभी उऋण नहीं हो सकती।

वीरतापूर्ण कार्य का वर्णन

प्रस्तावना–मानव-जीवन में घटनाओं का अम्बार है। यह सामान्य भी हो सकती हैं और विशेष भी। समय का मरहम सामान्य घटना के घावों को तो भर देता है, किन्तु कुछ घटनाओं के घाव इतने गहरे होते हैं कि समय का मरहम भी उन्हें भरने में असमर्थ रहता है। आज जिस घटना का वर्णन मैं करने जा रहा हूँ वह लगभग 20 वर्ष पूर्व की होने पर भी कल जैसी मालूम होती है।

घटना का वर्णन–वह घटना 14 नवम्बर की है। विद्यालय की ओर से कक्षा 11 तथा 12 के छात्र-छात्रायें बस द्वारा जयपुर के लिए चल दिये। सुबह के 5 बजे हम सब दो बसों में विद्यालय से चलकर 2 घण्टे में भरतपुर पहुँच गये। वहाँ आधा घण्टा रुककर चाय नाश्ता करने के बाद फिर आगे बढ़ गये। दोपहर को 1 बजे हम जयपुर के सवाई मानसिंह पैलेस होटल पहुँचे। बस से उतरकर अपने आरक्षित कमरों में गये। इसके बाद तरोताजा होकर 2 बजे भोजन के बाद कुछ समय विश्राम किया। शाम को 3 बजे हम सब आमेर के लिए रवाना हुए। वहाँ लगभग 2 घण्टे का समय व्यतीत करके हम जयपुर के लिए वापस चले। लगभग 6 बजे शाम को वापस होटल में आ गये। सभी निश्चिन्त हो गहरी नींद का आनन्द लेकर सुबह 3 बजे जागे और 4 बजे चल दिये।

वापसी की यात्रा में सभी में नया उत्साह था। सर्दी के दिन थे। भारी वाहनों की आवाज ही सुनाई दे रही थी। इस यात्रा के मध्य व्यवधान बनकर 8–10 नकाबपोश एक जीप में सवार होकर हमारी बस के आगे निकलकर सामने खड़े हो गए। अचानक व्यवधान से हतप्रभ चालक ने बस रोक दी। एक नकाबपोश ने फुर्ती से बस में सवार होकर चालक की कनपटी पर पिस्तौल लगा दी। दूसरा नकाबपोश बस के बीच में खड़ा यात्रियों को आतंकित कर रहा था। उसकी चेतावनी के बाद भी जब चालक ने दुस्साहस दिखाया तो उनमें से एक ने उसे गोली मार दी। उसके शव को एक किनारे फैंककर उन्हीं का साथी बस लेकर नये रास्ते पर चलने लगा। सुबह के 5 बजने के बाद भी अन्धेरा था। हम किसी सुनसान मार्ग पर थे। सभी पत्थर की बेजान मूर्ति बनकर रह गये थे। सारा जोश खत्म हो गया था। सभी छात्र-छात्राएँ किसी दैवीय-चमत्कार की आशा के लिए प्रार्थना कर रहे थे। अचानक डीजल खत्म होने के कारण बस किसी छोटे से उपमार्ग पर खड़ी हो गयी। उनकी जीप आगे निकलकर ओझल हो गयी थी। नकाबपोश स्वयं को विवश-सा अनुभव कर रहे थे। उन्होंने अपनी क्रोधपूर्ण दृष्टि पूरी बस में घुमाकर कहा, "बस का अपहरण हो चुका है। किसी भी चालाकी या दुस्साहस का परिणाम मौत होगा।" कुछ समय की शान्ति के पश्चात् नकाबपोश ने मुझे अपनी ओर आने का संकेत किया। साथियों के संकेत की चिन्ता न करके में रुक-रुककर कदम रखकर आगे बढ़ा और नकाबपोश तक जा पहुँचा। मेरे विषय में वह प्रश्न करने लगा। मैंने शान्ति से उत्तर दिये। इसके बाद छात्र-छात्राओं के विषय में जानकारी पाने की कोशिश करने लगा। अन्दर की घबराहट धीरे-धीरे कम हो रही थी। धीरे-धीरे मुझे वह व्यक्ति लापरवाह-सा दिखाई दिया। मैंने चक्कर खाने का अभिनय करके उसकी पिस्तौल उठाकर फायर ठोंक दिया। दूसरे नकाबपोश ने मुझे लक्ष्य बनाने का प्रयत्न किया, किन्तु दुर्भाग्यवश पहला साथी सामने आ गया। गोली उसके सिर में लगी और वह वहीं ढेर हो गया। यह घटना इतनी अचानक हो गयी कि कोई कुछ न समझा। मैं चिल्लाया "बस छोड़कर लुकते-छिपते पीछे भागो। मुख्य मार्ग पर अलग-अलग टोलियों में पहुँचो। हर समूह में लड़कियों को बीच में रखो। जहाँ जिसे जो साधन मिले आगरा पहुँचो।" इस प्रकार मानों मैं उनका नेतृत्व और मार्गदर्शन कर रहा था। मेरे कहने पर जितना जल्दी हो सके सब बस से उतर कर मुख्य मार्ग की ओर टोलियाँ बना कर भागे। सबसे अन्त में मैं 10 छात्राओं के साथ भागा। हल्का बैग सबके साथ था। लगभग 1 घण्टा भागने के बाद हम मुख्य मार्ग पर लगभग प्रात: 8 बजे पहुँचे। वहाँ P.C.O. से घर और विद्यालय में सूचना दी। धीरे-धीरे उपलब्ध साधनों से वापस घर पहुँचे।

उपसंहार–घर पहुँचकर भी यह विश्वास नहीं हो रहा था कि हम सुरक्षित हैं। मैं यह सोच रहा था कि अगर उनकी जीप वापस आ जाती। अगर मेरा प्रयास असफल रहता ....? हमने ईश्वर को धन्यवाद दिया।

●●

महिलाएँ पुरुषों से किसी प्रकार हीन नहीं

हर बात या वस्तु के दो पहलू होते हैं—पक्ष और विपक्ष। मैं सदा से पक्ष का समर्थक हूँ। अत: मैं यहाँ 'महिलाएँ पुरुषों से किसी प्रकार हीन नहीं' शीर्षक के पक्ष में विचार व्यक्त कर रहा हूँ।

इस संसार का निर्माण नर और नारी दो शक्तियों के योग से हुआ है। दोनों जीवन रथ के दो पहिए है। एक के अभाव में दूसरा सक्रिय नहीं हो सकता। नर को आकाश तो नारी को पृथ्वी की उपमा दी गयी है। दोनों में द्वन्द्व समास है। दोनों में से किसी को भी कम नहीं कहा जा सकता।

संसार एक रंगमंच है जहाँ स्त्री एवं पुरुष दोनों को ही अभिनय करना पड़ता है। देश की उन्नति में पुरुषों के समान स्त्रियों का भी महत्वपूर्ण योगदान है। भारतीय समाज में नारियों की पूजा विभिन्न रूपों में होती रही है। प्राचीन भारत के ऐतिहासिक पृष्ठ भारतीय महिलाओं की गौरव-गाथा से भरे हुए हैं। 'मनुस्मृति' में कहा गया है—

यत्र नार्यस्तु पूजयन्ते, रमन्ते तत्र देवता।

अर्थात् जहाँ नारियों की पूजा होती है, वहाँ देवता निवास करते हैं। नारी को श्रद्धा, शक्ति, देवी आदि सम्बोधनों से पुकारा जाता रहा है।

संसार का निर्माण करने वाली, अपनी कोख से राम, कृष्ण, बुद्ध, महावीर जैसे अवतारों को तथा गाँधी, चन्द्रशेखर आजाद जैसे देश भक्तों को जन्म देकर तथा पालन-पोषण करके योग्य बनाने का कार्य करने वाली नारी ही है। इसीलिए उसे प्रथम गुरु माना गया है। नारी ने प्रेम की वशीभूत होकर स्वयं को पुरुष के चरणों में समर्पित कर दिया, किन्तु पुरुष ने उसे बन्धनों में जकड़ लिया। समाज की घृणित विचारधारा ने उसका क्षेत्र केवल घर की चारदीवारी तक ही सीमित कर दिया। पर्दा-प्रथा आरम्भ होने के साथ ही स्त्रियों को शिक्षा प्राप्त करने के अधिकार से भी वंचित होना पड़ा। समाज में प्रचलित कुछ कुरीतियों ने नारियों को इतना दीन-हीन बना दिया कि वे अपने अस्तित्व को ही भूल गईं। राष्ट्रकवि मैथिलीशरण गुप्त ने नारी की इसी शोचनीय दशा का वर्णन निम्नलिखित पंक्तियों में किया है—

अबला जीवन हाय तुम्हारी यही कहानी,
आँचल में है दूध और आँखों में पानी।

मध्य युग में भोग की वस्तु समझी जाने वाली नारी की दशा स्वतन्त्रता प्राप्ति के लगभग 68 वर्षों के बाद भी दयनीय है। पुरुषों को अपनी संकुचित विचारधारा को त्याग कर नारी को समान स्थान देना होगा। समाज, देश और राष्ट्र का उद्धार बिना नारी के सहयोग के सम्भव नहीं है। संसार की उत्पत्ति एवं भरण-पोषण का मुख्य कार्य भी नारी करती है। पुरुष का साथ वह कभी मातृ शक्ति बनकर देती है तो कभी बहिन, कभी प्रेयसी के रूप में सहायता करती है, तो कभी पत्नी बनकर। हर परिस्थिति में वह पुरुष का साथ देती है। उसकी मानसिक शक्ति का अनुमान नहीं लगाया जा सकता। वह चाहे तो घर को स्वर्ग बना सकती है और चाहे तो नर्क से भी बदतर। गुप्त ने नारी शब्द कलेवर की शक्ति की व्याख्या करते हुए लिखा है—

एक नहीं दो-दो मात्राएँ
नर से बढ़कर नारी।

जब 'नारी' शब्द इतना भारी है तो साक्षात् नारी, नर से कितनी कुशल होगी, अनुमान लगा सकते हैं। इसी प्रकार मानसिक शक्ति की दृष्टि से, ज्ञान की दृष्टि से, धैर्य, विवेक और शारीरिक शक्ति किसी भी दृष्टि से देखा जाय तो आदिकाल से अब तक किसी भी युग में नारी नर से कमजोर नहीं रही है।

प्राचीनकाल में नारियों को पुरुषों के समान अधिकार प्राप्त थे। आवश्यकता होने पर स्त्रियाँ पुरुषों के साथ रणक्षेत्र में भी जाती थी। त्रेता-युग की वह घटना स्मरणीय है जिसमें कैकेयी ने अपने अद्वितीय कौशल से

महाराज दशरथ को भी विस्मित कर दिया था। अपनी योग्यता, विद्वता तथा विवेक-बुद्धि के बल पर द्रौपदी अपने पतियों को वनवासकाल और युद्धकाल में सत्परामर्श से प्रेरित करती थी।

अगणित ऐसी नारियाँ हुई है, जिन्होंने देश और समाज को परतन्त्रता की बेड़ियों से मुक्त कराने के लिए स्वतन्त्रता की चिंगारी हर मानव के हृदय में जगा दी। जिनमें मुख्य हैं—रानी लक्ष्मीबाई, अहिल्याबाई आदि।

ज्ञान के क्षेत्र में मन्दोदरी, सुलोचना, अनुसुइया, गार्गी, गौतमी, कात्यायनी, विद्योत्तमा आदि ऐसी नारियाँ हुई हैं जिन्होंने ज्ञान के क्षेत्र में अनेक बार पुरुषों को परास्त कर यह सिद्ध कर दिया है कि ज्ञान के क्षेत्र में नारी नर से पीछे नहीं है।

राजनीतिक क्षेत्र में क्वीन विक्टोरिया, प्रियदर्शनी इन्दिरा गाँधी आदि के नेतृत्व में हुई प्रगति ने संसार को विस्मित कर दिया।

नारी में धैर्य, साहस, सहनशीलता, विवेक, दृढ़ इच्छा शक्ति आदि ऐसे ईश्वर प्रदत्त स्वाभाविक गुण है जो हर क्षेत्र में उसकी सफलता में उसका पूर्ण सहयोग करते हैं। नारी जो ठान लेती है उसे बाधाओं के आने पर भी घबराकर छोड़ती नहीं। तन, मन तथा धन से उसे पूर्ण कर ही दम लेती है।

आचार्य रजनीश ने नारी शक्ति के विषय में विचार व्यक्त करते हुए लिखा है–

''जिस कार्य को नर तीन साल में करता है, उस कार्य को नारी तीन दिन में करने की क्षमता रखती है।''

आज नर भी नारी की शक्ति को पहचान रहा है। विज्ञान विधि, इतिहास, मनोविज्ञान, शिक्षा, घर-बाहर सभी क्षेत्रों में उसकी अद्‌भुत सफलता इस बात को सिद्ध करती है कि महिलाएँ किसी भी प्रकार पुरुषों से हीन नहीं है। इसी बात को व्यक्त करते हुए लोकनायक तुलसीदास जी ने कहा है–

कहा न पावक जल सके, कहा न समुद्र समाय।
कहा न करैं अबला प्रबल, केहि जग काल न खाय॥

●●

समाज में नारियों के साथ भेदभावपूर्ण व्यवहार

भारतीय समाज में नर और नारी दोनों को परिवार रूपी रथ के दो पहिए माना गया है। एक के अभाव में दूसरा ठीक प्रकार से गति नहीं कर सकता। प्राचीनकाल से आज तक हर युग में नारी का महत्व रहा है। वेदों में नारी को पूजनीय कहा गया है। उस समय की प्रथा थी–

यत्र नार्यस्तु पूज्यन्ते, रमन्ते तत्र देवताः।

अर्थात् जहाँ नारियों की पूजी होती है वहाँ सारी सुख-समृद्धियाँ तथा देवता निवास करते हैं और जहाँ इनका अपमान होता है, वहाँ सारे प्रयास निष्फल हो जाते हैं। भक्तिकाल में उनको शक्ति का दर्जा दिया गया था।

प्राचीनकाल में उसे भोग की वस्तु माना गया। वह पुरुष के हाथ की कठपुतली बन कर रह गयी। उस समय से आज तक नारी को भेद-भावपूर्ण दृष्टि से देखा जाता रहा है। इसके पक्ष में विचार करते हुए मैं स्पष्ट करना चाहता हूँ कि नारी को आज के समाज में भी भेद-भावपूर्ण दृष्टि से देखा जाता है। भारतीय समाज में भी पुत्र के जन्म पर खुशियाँ मनायी जाती हैं, बधाईयाँ गायी जाती हैं और खजाने लुटाने को तैयार रहते हैं लोग। पुत्र उत्पन्न होने की सूचना देने वाले को मुँह माँगा इनाम दिया जाता है, किन्तु पुत्री के उत्पन्न होने की सूचना सुनकर ऐसा व्यवहार करते हैं जैसे कोई गमी हो गयी है इसलिए मातम मना रहे हैं। पैदा होते ही उसे परायी धरोहर या पराये घर का धन समझकर ही उसके साथ व्यवहार किया जाता है। प्राचीनकाल में क्षत्रियों में बेटियों को पैदा होते ही मार दिया जाता था। यही नहीं, आज भी चम्बल पार के ग्रामीण क्षेत्रों में यही हाल है।

मेरे गाँव की एक लड़की की पहली लड़की पैदा हुई। उसकी सास ने उस नवजात बच्ची की गर्दन चारपाई के पाये के नीचे रखकर उससे कहा—बहू चढ़ जा पलंग पर। बेचारी जब पलंग पर चढ़ी तो उसे एक

हिचकी की आवाज सुनायी दी, नीचे झाँककर देखा तो एक औरत ने ही एक माँ के हाथ से उसकी ममता का गला घुटवा दिया। उसने रोते हुए सास से कारण जानना चाहा तो सास ने डाँटते हुए कहा—बेटी से कोई खानदान चलता है क्या ? चुप रह यहाँ की यही रीति है। नारी ही नारी के साथ जब ऐसा व्यवहार करती है, तो पुरुष पीछे क्यों रहेंगे ? यह एक ही ऐसी घटना नहीं है, ऐसी अगणित घटनाएँ रोजाना हो रही हैं। ममता बिलखती रह जाती है।

सती प्रथा भी भेद-भावपूर्ण व्यवहार का उदाहरण है। आज तक लाखों औरतों को पति के साथ जिन्दा जला दिया गया है, किन्तु आज तक आपने यह नहीं पढ़ा होगा कि किसी पति ने अपनी पत्नी की मृत्यु हो जाने पर स्वयं भी उसके साथ आत्महत्या कर ली हो।

यदि किसी की पत्नी की मृत्यु हो जाये तो पुरुष को दूसरा विवाह करने का अधिकार प्राप्त है, किन्तु भाग्यवश यदि कोई स्त्री विधवा हो जाती है तो लोग उसे डाइन, कुलक्षिणी आदि कहकर अपमानित करते हैं तथा मृत्यु समान जीवन व्यतीत करने को मजबूर कर देते हैं। यही नहीं कुछ गाँवों में तो बाल मुड़वाकर घर से बाहर निकाल देते हैं। बेचारी दिन-रात तीर्थ स्थानों पर जाकर अपना पूरा जीवन भीख माँगकर गुजारती है और समाज के कर्णधारों के कानों पर जूँ नहीं रेंगती।

पुत्री की शिक्षा-दीक्षा तथा खान-पान पर कोई ध्यान नहीं दिया जाता। जो माँ पुत्र के आने पर उसे खड़े होकर खाना-दूध आदि देती है, वही पुत्री के आने पर डाँटते हुए कहती है खाना-खाना है तो खा ले, नहीं तो काम कर। जन्म से ही उन्हें यह सिखाया जाता है कि तू स्त्री है तुझे दबकर रहना सीखना होगा।

आज संसार में उन्हें अबला बना दिया गया है। शक्ति की अवतार नारी की शक्ति के स्वाभाविक विकास को दबाकर रोक दिया जाता है। उसके काम को सराहा नहीं जाता। आज नारी अपना भी कार्य कर रही है और पुरुषों का भी। फिर भी पुरुष प्रधान समाज की नजरों में वह कुछ नहीं है। पुरुष जब चाहे उसका अपमान कर सकता है किन्तु धीरे-धीरे समय गुजरने के साथ स्थिति में बदलाव आता जा रहा है। अब नारियाँ इसके खिलाफ आवाज भी उठाती हैं तथा हर क्षेत्र में नारी ने अभूतपूर्व विकास किया है। पुरुष से दस गुना अधिक कार्य नारी प्रतिदिन करती है, किन्तु फिर भी यह समाज उसके साथ भेद-भावपूर्ण व्यवहार करता है। इस विचारधारा में बदलाव आना जरूरी है। आज शायद ही कोई ऐसा क्षेत्र हो जहाँ नारी ने कदम न रखा हो। वह पुरुष के समान सभी क्षेत्रों में समान रूप से कार्य कर रही है।

आज देश के विकास के लिए आवश्यक है कि नारी को समाज में उचित स्थान दिया जाय तथा उसके कार्य की उपलब्धियों को सराहा जाय। 'परलोक के लिए केवल पुत्र ही होना चाहिए', आदि मान्यताओं पर अधिक ध्यान न देकर 'कन्यादान सर्वश्रेष्ठ दान है' की मान्यता को बल देना चाहिए। जिसके कन्या नहीं होती उसका उद्धार नहीं होता। इस बात को ध्यान में रखते हुए नारी को समाज में उचित सम्मान मिलना चाहिए, क्योंकि नारी ही नर की शक्ति और जननी है।

●●

एक पर्वतीय यात्रा का वर्णन

सैर कर दुनियाँ की गाफिल, जिन्दगानी फिर कहाँ।
जिन्दगानी गर रही तो, यह जवानी फिर कहाँ।

किसी विद्वान का यह कथन अपने में बहुत ही महत्त्वपूर्ण तथा सत्य है। सभ्यता के आदिकाल से मानव घुमक्कड़ रहा है। इसीलिए अक्सर जीवन की तुलना नदी के बहते जल से की जाती है कहा जाता है 'रमता जोगी, बहता पानी'—भाव यह है कि बहता हुआ पानी भी साफ और स्वास्थ्यप्रद होता है। ठीक इसी प्रकार योगी वही सच्चा और पवित्र होता है जो बराबर घूमता रहता है। इसके विपरीत रुका हुआ पानी गन्दा तथा एक

ही स्थान पर अधिक समय तक रहने वाला योगी भी भ्रष्ट हो जाता है। अतः जीवन में घूमना आवश्यक है। इसी उद्देश्य को ध्यान में रखकर हम सब मित्रों ने भी जम्मू-कश्मीर तथा निकट के सभी पर्वतीय स्थानों की यात्रा का कार्यक्रम बनाया। गत वर्ष गर्मियों में 20 मई की शाम को हम सभी 'ताज-एक्सप्रेस' से दिल्ली के लिए रवाना हुए। सभी आवश्यक सामान हमारे साथ था। हम रात में लगभग 9.30 बजे हजरत निजामुद्दीन पहुँचे। वहीं से हमारा हिमसागर में स्थान आरक्षित था। यह गाड़ी 00.15 बजे जम्मू के लिए प्रस्थान करने वाली थी। कुछ समय इधर-उधर घूमकर व्यतीत करने के बाद हम अपने आरक्षित स्थान पर जम गए। गाड़ी समय पर रवाना हुई। कुछ समय तक अपने स्थान पर गप्पें मारने के बाद हम सभी नींद की गोद में समा गए। जब आँख खुली तो हम जालन्धर के निकट थे। एक-एक करके सभी दैनिक कार्यों से मुक्त हुए। तब सभी ने चाय पी। वहीं से समाचार पत्र लेकर देश-विदेश की स्थिति का ज्ञान किया। लगभग एक बजे हम जम्मू पहुँचे। वहाँ से हम अपने होटल के लिए बस से पहुँचे। दोपहर को खाने आदि के बाद दो-तीन घण्टे आराम किया। बाद में कटरा पहुँचे और रात में वैष्णों देवी की चढ़ाई आरम्भ की। वहाँ का वातावरण ही धर्ममय था। आने जाने वाले लोगों का जय घोष, भजन-कीर्तन के साथ स्थान-स्थान पर क्षणिक विश्राम लेकर सभी वैष्णों देवी पहुँचे। वहाँ दर्शन करके हम भैंरों जी के मन्दिर होते हुए वापस आए। दिन में आराम करके शाम को कटरा शहर घूमने निकले। रात में लौटने के बाद खाना खाकर सोये। दूसरे और तीसरे दिन कश्मीर घूमने निकल गए। वहाँ से लौट कर आस-पास के स्थानों की यात्रा के बाद हम 29 मई की शाम को वापस आए।

इस प्रकार हमारी लम्बी पर्वतीय यात्रा का अन्त हुआ। इस यात्रा में जहाँ अपने देश के प्रसिद्ध और महत्त्वपूर्ण स्थानों का ज्ञान हुआ। वहीं मानव स्वभाव के अनुरूप उन सभी प्राकृतिक स्थानों के विषय में जानकारी प्राप्त की।

●●

पर्यावरण प्रदूषण

प्रस्तावना—यह शब्द दो शब्दों (परि + आवरण) से मिलकर बना है। इसका अर्थ है—वायुमण्डल से सम्बन्धित चारों ओर का वातावरण। इसका क्षेत्र व्यापक है जिसमें जल, वायु एवं ध्वनि आदि सभी तत्व शामिल हैं, यह सभी तत्व सही मात्रा और अनुपात में होने पर ही वातावरण में सन्तुलन स्थापित करने में सहायता करते हैं। आज के वैज्ञानिक युग में बढ़ती हुई जनसंख्या तथा आवश्यकताओं की पूर्ति के लिए अधिकाधिक उत्पादन हो रहा है। इस क्रिया में हजारों कल-कारखानें रात-दिन कार्य कर रहे हैं, किन्तु इस औद्योगीकरण की अति ने वर्तमान में प्रदूषण की समस्या उत्पन्न कर दी है। इससे प्राकृतिक वातावरण दूषित हो गया है तथा विश्व का जैविक सन्तुलन बिगड़ गया है। सन्तुलन बिगड़ने से अनेक प्राणघातक रोगों का जन्म हुआ है। विषाक्त वातावरण में साँस लेना कठिन हो गया है। अनेक घातक बीमारियाँ मानव को काल का ग्रास बना रहीं हैं।

प्रदूषण के कारण तथा प्रकार—जल-प्रदूषण, वायु-प्रदूषण तथा ध्वनि-प्रदूषण प्रदूषण के मुख्य रूप हैं। अत्यधिक औद्योगीकरण पर्यावरण-प्रदूषण का मुख्य कारण है। इसके परिणामस्वरूप कारखानों के आस-पास अत्याधिक कचरा जमा होने लगता है। कचरे की दुर्गंध से प्राकृतिक-सुन्दरता भी नष्ट हो जाती हैं। नदियों में फेंके कारखानों के इस जल में अनेक रासायनिक तत्त्व घुले रहते हैं जो नदियों के जल को भी विषाक्त बना देते हैं। इससे जल चरों का जीवन नष्ट हो जाता है। उदाहरण के लिए—नदियों का जल दूषित और विषाक्त होने से सैकड़ों टन मछलियाँ मर गयीं। इस पानी की सिंचाई से मिट्टी भी विषैली हो जाती हैं। इस मिट्टी में उत्पन्न फसलें विषैली होकर मानव को पेट सम्बन्धी अनेक बीमारियों से ग्रस्त करती हैं।

आज वायु प्रदूषण मानव के सामने एक चुनौती उपस्थित कर रहा है। कारखाने, मोटर-वाहन, इंजनों का धुँआ तथा गैसें, घरों में जलाया जाने वाला कोयला, स्टोव में जलने वाला कैरोसिन आदि से कार्बन-

डाईऑक्साइड, कार्बन मोनोऑक्साइड, नाइट्रोजन एवं सल्फ्यूरिक ऐसिड आदि तत्त्व वायु प्रदूषण को विस्तृत कर देते हैं। यह प्रदूषित वायु मनुष्य के साँस लेने पर उसके शरीर में पहुँचकर अनेक रोग उत्पन्न करती है। इसका सर्वाधिक प्रभाव मनुष्य के फेफड़ों पर पड़ता है।

ध्वनि प्रदूषण भी हानिकारक हैं। महानगरों में वाहन, लाउडस्पीकर तथा मशीनों के शोर के कारण जन्म लेने वाले ध्वनि-प्रदूषण के कारण मानव की श्रवण शक्ति का ह्रास हुआ है। इसका मानव हृदय तथा मस्तिष्क पर घातक प्रभाव पड़ता है।

प्रदूषण से होने वाली हानियाँ—प्रदूषण से अनेक गम्भीर बीमारियाँ जन्म लेती हैं—चर्म रोग, श्वास रोग, खाँसी, दमा, जुकाम, क्षय तथा फेफड़ों का कैंसर आदि। ताप और दुर्गंध भी इसके कारण हैं। ताप तथा परमाणु बिजली घरों से निकलने वाली ऊष्मा जलवायु तथा ऋतु चक्र को बिगाड़ देती है। वायुमण्डल में कार्बन डाई ऑक्साइड की मात्रा बढ़ने से ताप अधिक हो जायेगा, जिससे हिम खण्ड पिघल जाऐंगे। इससे बाढ़ तथा प्रलय आ सकती है। अत: विश्व में प्राणी रक्षा के लिए पर्यावरण की रक्षा आवश्यक है।

उपसंहार—इस सम्बन्ध में सम्पूर्ण विश्व में पहली बार 5 मई 1977 को विचार हुआ। इसमें पर्यावरण की शुद्धि के उपायों पर विचार किया गया। कारखानों को बस्तियों से दूर करने का सुझाव दिया गया। धुँआ कम किया जाए। अधिक मात्रा में वृक्ष लगाए जाऐं।

●●

व्यायाम का महत्व

अंग्रेजी में कहावत है कि 'Health is Wealth' अर्थात् स्वास्थ्य ही धन है। अस्वस्थ मन अस्वस्थ विचारों का आश्रय स्थल है जो मनुष्य को अविवेकी, अकर्मण्य, क्रोधी और विचार शून्य कर देता है। तभी तो कहा गया है—"पहला सुख निरोगी काया" अर्थात् सबसे बड़ा सुख स्वस्थ शरीर है। स्वास्थ्य रक्षा के प्रमुख साधन है—व्यायाम, सन्तुलित और नियमित भोजन, स्वच्छता, संयमपूर्ण जीवन तथा ब्रह्मचर्य का पालन।

व्यायाम—डॉ. जॉन ने "बिना थकावट के परिश्रम को व्यायाम की संज्ञा दी है।" प्राण-शक्ति बढ़ाने का सर्वोत्तम साधन व्यायाम है। व्यायाम का अर्थ पहलवानी नहीं है। किसी भी ऐसे कार्य को व्यायाम कहा जा सकता है जिससे शरीर की शक्ति बढ़े, शरीर क्रियाशील होकर स्फूर्तिमान बने। व्यायाम नित्य करना चाहिए। भोजन के पहले तथा तुरन्त बाद व्यायाम वर्जित है। प्रात:काल शुद्ध तथा खुली हवा में व्यायाम करना अत्यन्त लाभकारी होता है। जिस प्रकार किसी मशीन से बहुत समय तक काम न लेने से उसमें जंग लग जाती है, ठीक उसी प्रकार शरीर रूपी यंत्र भी काम न लेने पर अनुपयोगी हो जाता है। व्यायाम द्वारा शरीर में रक्त संचार होता है तथा मांसपेशियों में बल आता है।

व्यायाम के लाभ—व्यायाम से शरीर पुष्ट तथा मुख कान्तिमय होता है। शरीर की माँसपेशियाँ मजबूत होती हैं। शरीर का आलस्य दूर होता है तथा मन में उत्साह का संचार होता है। व्यायाम के द्वारा शरीर के वर्ज्य पदार्थ शरीर से बाहर निकल जाते हैं। व्यायाम केवल शरीर को ही प्रभावित नहीं करता वरन् मस्तिष्क पर भी व्यापक प्रभाव डालता है। व्यायाम से मस्तिष्क की शक्ति बढ़ती है। मन में स्फूर्ति आती है और मन की यह शक्ति चेहरे पर स्पष्ट रूप से प्रकट होती है। नियमित व्यायाम करने वाले व्यक्ति पर बुढ़ापे का सहसा प्रभाव नहीं पड़ता। व्यायाम करने वाला व्यक्ति तो, "कुर्वन्नेह कर्माणि जिजीवितेषु: शतं समा:" अर्थात् कार्य करते हुए 100 वर्षों तक जीने की इच्छा करता है।

व्यायाम करने वाले व्यक्ति में धैर्य, क्षमा, संयम आदि गुण स्वत: ही आ जाते हैं। संयम और धैर्य मनुष्य को परम शक्तिशाली बना देते हैं। व्यायाम से मनुष्य में आत्म-विश्वास और आत्म-निर्भरता का भाव उत्पन्न होता है। आत्म-निर्भरता की भावना जीवन की सफलता का रहस्य है। आत्मविश्वास के सहारे मनुष्य स्वयं को

संसार के सब सुखों को भोगने के समर्थ बनाता है। जो मनुष्य मन तथा शरीर से पुष्ट एवं शक्तिशाली होगा वह समाज की रूढ़ियों और कुरीतियों को दूर करके समाज एवं देश को नयी राह दिखा सकता है।

मानव शरीर में अनेकानेक माँसपेशियाँ है। ये माँसपेशियाँ जितनी सुदृढ़ और लचीली होंगी शरीर के अंगों में उतनी ही क्रियाशीलता होगी। व्यायाम से रक्त का संचार सुचारु रूप से होता है जिससे शरीर में रोगों से लड़ने की क्षमता उत्पन्न होती है।

जो व्यक्ति नियमित रूप से व्यायाम करते हैं उनका शरीर सुगठित एवं निरोग हो जाता है। व्यायाम द्वारा शरीर के विकार दूर होते हैं। शरीर के विकारों के दूर होने से समाज के विकारों को दूर करने की शक्ति मिलती है। व्यायाम से मानसिक विकार भी दूर होते हैं। जिस व्यक्ति में दया, क्षमा, परोपकार आदि गुण होते हैं वही वीर और शक्तिशाली है। क्षमा वीरों का आभूषण है। वीर एवं दृढ़ निश्चयी व्यक्ति विधाता के लेख को भी बदल सकते हैं। आत्म-विश्वास, दृढ़-निश्चय की भावना तथा वीरता व्यायाम से ही उत्पन्न होती है। यजुर्वेद में व्यायाम के महत्व पर व्यापक रूप में प्रकाश डाला गया है।

उपसंहार— **नेम से व्यायाम को नित कीजिए।**
दीर्घ जीवन का सुधारस पीजिए।

उपरोक्त पंक्तियों में व्यायाम के महत्व पर प्रकाश डाला गया है। नित्यप्रति व्यायाम करने वाले व्यक्ति से रोग दूर रहते हैं। उसके शरीर तथा मन में कठिन से कठिन कार्य करने की शक्ति उत्पन्न होती है। नियमित व्यायाम से शरीर हल्का और फुर्तीला बना रहता है। हम सभी को व्यायाम के महत्व को समझते हुए इसे अपनी दैनिक दिनचर्या में सम्मिलित करना चाहिए।

●●

इस दिन की सुखद यादें मुझे कभी नहीं भूलेंगी।

समय को दिन-रात की संज्ञा में बाँध दिया है। इसे हम दिनों के माध्यम से व्यतीत करते हैं। जीवन में अनेकानेक ऐसी घटनाएँ होती है जिन्हें हम भूल जाते हैं किन्तु कभी-कभी कोई घटना मस्तिष्क को इतना प्रभावित कर जाती है कि हम भुला नहीं पाते। ऐसी घटनाओं में सुख और दु:ख दोनों प्रकार की घटनाएँ हो सकती है। सुख की घटनाएँ जीवन में आनन्द का संचार करती है अत: हम आनन्द से सम्बन्धित घटना को बार-बार याद करना चाहते हैं और दु:खदायी घटनाओं को भूल जाना चाहते हैं। किन्तु सत्य तो यह है कि दिल को प्रभावित करने वाली किसी भी घटना को भूला नहीं जा सकता। मेरे जीवन में अत्यन्त खुशी के क्षण थे जिन्होंने मुझे रोमांचित किया था, जिनकी स्मृति आज भी दिल को प्रसन्न कर देती है। ऐसी ही एक घटना मैं यहाँ बता रहा हूँ।

दिनांक 19 अगस्त, 2004 को हम अपने परिवार के साथ घूमने के लिए अमरनाथ गये। जब हम बर्फ की चढ़ाई पर चढ़ने लगे तो छोटे-छोटे बर्फ के कण हमारे ऊपर गिरते जा रहे थे। हमारे बरसाती वाले कपड़ों पर, जूतों पर, सिर पर लगे हुए टोप पर जब बर्फ के कण गिरकर जम गये तो ऐसे सुन्दर लग रहे थे मानो चाँदी की झीनी पर्त सबके ऊपर चढ़ा दी हो। तभी सुरक्षाकर्मियों ने हमसे आग्रह किया कि आगे खतरा है यहीं रुको, हम रुक गये तभी हमने देखा एक (बर्फ) का बहुत बड़ा टुकड़ा धड़ाम से कुछ दूरी पर गिरा। सब का हृदय भय और आनन्द से भर गया। भय इस बात का कि यदि हमारे ऊपर गिरता तो क्या होता ? आनन्द इस बात का कि ईश्वर ने हम सबको बचा लिया।

हम क्रमश: मन्दिर के पास पहुँचते हैं। मेरे सभी घरवाले पहले वहाँ कि प्राकृतिक छटा देखने चले जाते हैं, किन्तु मैं तो शीघ्र से शीघ्र अमरनाथ जी के दर्शन करना चाहता था। अत: मैंने उनसे कहा कि आप घूम आयें मैं यही मिलूँगा। सब चले गये। मैं मन्दिर की ओर चला। मेरा मन वहाँ के सौन्दर्य को देखकर अत्यन्त

प्रसन्न हो रहा था, तभी अचानक मैंने देखा एक पर्वत से दूध की धारा आकाश मार्ग से धनुष की आकृति बनाये हुए मन्दिर के बीच एक छोटे से छेद से होती हुई शिवलिंग के ऊपर गिर रही थी। उसे देखकर मेरा रोम-रोम प्रसन्न एवं पुलकित हो रहा था। मैं सोचता हूँ कि मन्दिर से इस दूध के निकलने का कोई-न-कोई रास्ता अवश्य होगा। उस रास्ते से थोड़ा-सा दूध प्रसाद के रूप में घरवालों को दे देता। इस विचार से मैं मन्दिर का चक्कर लगाता हुआ रास्ते की खोज करता हूँ। मेरा उद्देश्य सफल हो जाता है। मुझे दूध निकलने वाला रास्ता मिल जाता है, किन्तु तभी एक अड़चन पैदा होती है। दूध ले जाने के लिए मेरे पास कोई बर्तन नहीं, मैं सोचता हूँ रुमाल भिगोकर एक-एक बूँद सबको दे दूँगा। मैं अपना रुमाल निकालकर नीचे बिछा देता हूँ, किन्तु यह क्या रुमाल पर आते ही दूध खोये (थक्के) के रूप में जम जाता है। इस आश्चर्य को देखकर मैं आनन्द-विभोर हो गया। अपने मम्मी, पापा, भाई-बहिन आदि के पास आता हूँ और सारी घटना खुश होकर उन्हें सुनाता हूँ। सुनकर वे सोचते हैं कि हमने अपना सारा समय बेकार बिता दिया सच्चा आनन्द तो इसने प्राप्त किया। किन्तु आपको क्या पता कि मेरा कितना दुर्भाग्य था कि मेरी नींद टूट गई। सारा सुरम्य वातावरण मेरे स्मृति पटल पर अंकित होकर रह गया।

भले ही सोते में घूमा किन्तु मैं जानता हूँ कि अगर वास्तव में मैं अमरनाथ घूमने गया भी तो वैसा आनन्द शायद ही मुझे मिले। जो 19 अगस्त, 2000 को सोते-सोते मैंने पाया था। इस रोमांचकारी घटना को मैं जीवन में सदा स्मरण करता रहूँगा और कभी नहीं भुला पाऊँगा। यद्यपि यह घटना एक स्वप्न थी किन्तु मेरे लिए वह दिन अत्यन्त सुखद है, जिस दिन मैंने यह स्वप्न देखा। वह सुखद दिन, स्वप्न और उसकी यादें मैं कभी नहीं भुला पाऊँगा।

●●

यदि मैं प्रधानाचार्य बन जाऊँ

प्रस्तावना—विद्यालय एक परिवार है। जैसे परिवार में अनेक सदस्य होते हैं और उस का एक प्रमुख होता है, इसी प्रकार छात्र व शिक्षक विद्यालय परिवार के सदस्य तथा प्रधानाचार्य उस परिवार का प्रमुख होता है। यह उसका संचालक व नियता है। मेरे मन में भी अभिलाषा जाग्रत होती है कि शिक्षा समाप्त करने के पश्चात् क्यों न मैं भी विद्यालय का प्रधानाचार्य बन जाऊँ ? यदि संयोगवश मैं प्रधानाचार्य बन गया तो अपने विद्यालय के सर्वांगीण विकास के लिए प्रयत्नशील हो जाऊँगा।

अनुशासन की स्थापना—आज विद्यालयों में सबसे बड़ी समस्या अनुशासन की है। प्रधानाचार्य बनते ही मैं अनुशासन स्थापित करने पर पूरा ध्यान दूँगा। छात्र व शिक्षक समय पर विद्यालय पहुँचे इसके लिए मैं स्वयं निश्चित समय से पन्द्रह मिनट पूर्व विद्यालय में पहुँचूँगा। मेरे समय से पूर्व पहुँचने पर अन्य शिक्षक भी समय पर पहुँचेंगे, क्योंकि बड़े लोग जैसा आचरण करते हैं, छोटे भी वैसा ही करते हैं। ''यद् यदा चरित श्रेष्ठस्तत्तेवेतरे जना:।'' यदि वे ऐसा नहीं करेंगें तो मैं उन्हें प्रेम से समय पर आने का आग्रह करूँगा। जब मैं और मेरे अध्यापक समय पर विद्यालय आयेंगे तो छात्र भी निश्चित रूप से समय पर आयेंगे। जो छात्र उपस्थिति घण्टा पर कक्षा में न होगा, उसकी अनुपस्थिति लगा दी जायेगी। मैं समझता हूँ इस प्रकार विद्यालय में उपस्थिति नियमित हो जायेगी।

छात्र प्राय: कभी पानी के, कभी लघुशंका के और कभी किसी शिक्षक द्वारा बुलाये जाने के बहाने से कक्षा से बाहर निकलकर घूमते रहते हैं। मैं प्रधानाचार्य बनते ही इनकी निगरानी रखूँगा और व्यवस्था करूँगा कि घण्टा समाप्त न होने तक कोई भी छात्र कक्षा से बाहर न आये।

शिक्षकों की ढिलाई—छात्रों का ही नहीं कुछ शिक्षकों का भी स्वभाव बन गया है कि वे जमकर कक्षा में नहीं बैठते। वे मॉनीटर को कक्षा में पाठ पढ़ाने के लिए कहकर किसी अन्य शिक्षक के साथ बातचीत में मग्न

हो जाते हैं। अध्यापक की अनुपस्थिति में कक्षा में कोलाहल होता है, छात्र एक-दूसरे से लड़ते-झगड़ते हैं, गाली-गलौज करते हैं, मेज-कुर्सियाँ तोड़ते हैं, उन्हें बजाते हैं, या गन्दे फिल्मी गीत गाते रहते हैं। इससे पास वाली कक्षा के अध्ययन में बाधा पड़ती है। मैं अध्यापकों को आग्रहपूर्वक इस प्रवृत्ति को त्यागने को कहूँगा।

एक ही गण-वेश—हमारे विद्यालय में निर्धन व धनी सभी प्रकार के छात्र हैं। धनी तो अपनी अच्छी-सी वेश-भूषा में आते हैं और निर्धन सामान्य वेश-भूषा में। इससे धनी विद्यार्थियों में अहंभाव रहता है और निर्धनों में आत्महीनता की भावना जागती है। यदि मैं प्रधानाचार्य बन जाऊँगा तो सभी छात्रों को एक ही गणवेश में आना अनिवार्य कर दूँगा। एक जैसे गणवेश से अनुशासन सुदृढ़ होगा तथा छात्रों में मैत्री भाव विकसित होगा और किसी भी छात्र में हीनभावना अथवा उच्चता की भावना जाग्रत न होगी।

निर्धन छात्रों की सहायता—मैं प्रधानाचार्य बनने पर निर्धन छात्रों को विद्यालय की ओर से पुस्तकें और गणवेश दूँगा। इसके साथ ही शुल्क मुक्ति भी उन्हीं को दूँगा जो वास्तव में योग्य, उसके उचित अधिकारी तथा निर्धन होगे।

नैतिक और शारीरिक शिक्षा—मेरा प्रयास होगा कि छात्रों में उत्तम संस्कार जागें। संस्कार सम्पन्न छात्र ही अपने कुल और देश का गौरव होते हैं। अत: मैं प्रधानाचार्य बनने पर सप्ताह में एक दिन विद्यालय में नैतिक शिक्षा का पाठ अनिवार्य कर दूँगा। जिसमें शिक्षक बारी-बारी से छात्रों को धार्मिक व ऐतिहासिक कथा-कहानियों के द्वारा चारित्रिक शिक्षा देंगे। छात्रों के चरित्र की उन्नति के लिए मैं पूर्ण सचेष्ट रहूँगा। इसके साथ प्रत्येक शनिवार बाल-सभा का आयोजन भी करूँगा, जिससे छात्र कहानियाँ, कविताएँ व चुटकुले आदि सुनायें और विभिन्न विषयों पर भाषण देने का अभ्यास भी करें। इससे छात्रों में नैतिकता, सदाचार, विनम्रता तथा विवेक आदि सद्‌गुणों का विकास होगा।

मैं अपने छात्रों के लिए व्यायाम और खेलकूद भी अनिवार्य कर दूँगा। ताकि बौद्धिक विकास के साथ ही उनका शारीरिक विकास भी होता रहे। मेरा प्रयास यह भी रहेगा कि छात्र पुस्तकालय का उपयोग करें, जिससे उनके ज्ञान में अधिक वृद्धि हो।

उपसंहार—आज विद्यार्थी परीक्षा में नकल आदि के अनुचित ढंग अपनाते हैं। मैं छात्रों में ऐसी भावना भर दूँगा कि वे नकल करें ही नहीं। यदि किसी ने ऐसा दुस्साहस किया तो उसकी इस प्रवृत्ति को दृढ़तापूर्वक दबा दूँगा। प्रभु, मुझे सुअवसर दें कि मैं प्रधानाचार्य बनकर अपने विद्यालय और विद्यार्थियों की उन्नति कर सकूँ।

एक लम्बी यात्रा

भारत में हिमालय की किसी चोटी पर चढ़ना शायद उतना कठिन नहीं है जितना कि आमतौर पर किसी रेल में यात्रा करना। मेरा तो कुछ इसी प्रकार का ही अनुभव है। इस पहले अनुभव ने ही न केवल मुझे रेल यात्रा करने से इतना थका दिया, बल्कि भयभीत कर दिया है कि भविष्य में मैंने कभी भी रेल यात्रा न करने का पक्का मन बना लिया है। कोई मुझे किसी कुएँ या किसी खन्दक में कूद पड़ने को कहेगा तो एक बार इसलिए कूद भी लूँगा कि ऐसा करते समय अन्धाधुन्ध भीड़ व रेलवे अधिकारियों की अन्धेरगर्दी का सामना तो नहीं करना पड़ेगा। पर जैसा कि मैंने कहा रेल यात्रा से दूर ही रहने की कोशिश करता रहूँगा।

यदि आप मेरी पहली रेल यात्रा का पहला अनुभव सुनना चाहते हैं तो अवश्य सुनिए। बात तो अभी कुछ ही दिन पहले की है अपने एक रिश्तेदार के यहाँ किसी शुभ कार्य में भाग लेने हमें दिल्ली से इलाहाबाद तक जाना था। हमने रेल विभाग द्वारा द्वितीय श्रेणी में दिन की यात्रा के लिए स्लीपिंग कोच नामक एक नई श्रेणी में कोई बीस दिन पहले से ही अपने लिए तीन सीटें आरक्षित करवा ली थीं। इस नई श्रेणी में दिन भर की यात्रा का भाड़ा मात्र पचास रुपये एक सीट के हिसाब से अधिक देना पड़ा ! हमने यह सोचकर तीन सीटों के लिए

एक सौ पचास रुपया अधिक देना स्वीकार कर लिया कि चलो सारे दिन की यात्रा है आराम से कट जायेगी, लेकिन आराम से तो क्या कटनी थी यात्रा, हम पूरे के पूरे अपने गन्तव्य पर पहुँच सके बस इतना ही बहुत है।

यात्रा कैसी रहेगी, इसकी झलक दिल्ली से ट्रेन में सवार होते समय ही मिलने लगी थी। बाहर मुसाफिरखाने से गुजरकर गेट से प्लेटफार्म तक पहुँच पाना ही किसी पहाड़ की चोटी पर चढ़ने से कम कठिन नहीं था। जहाँ तक भी नजर जाती भीड़ ही भीड़ दिखाई दे रही थी। बस पूछो मत, अजीब सी बातें सुनते और अन्धे होने का खिताब पाते हुए किसी तरह लम्बी-चौड़ी सीढ़ियाँ पार कर प्लेटफार्म पर पहुँच ही गये। मैं बुरी तरह हाँफने लगा था। मेरी वृद्ध माता की क्या दशा होगी, सरलता से अनुमान किया जा सकता है क्योंकि गाड़ी प्लेटफार्म पर पहुँच ही रही थी, फिर कुली को भी किसी अन्य सवारी का सामान मजदूरी के लिए ढूँढ़ना था। इसलिए बिना साँस लेने का अवसर दिये वह हमारी आरक्षित सीट वाला कोच ढूँढ़ने के चक्कर में पहले से अधिक वेग से भागने लगा। उसके पीछे पहले से अधिक बुरी दशा में हमारा अपना भागना आवश्यक था, सो भागने लगे।

मैंने देखा ट्रेन अभी रुकने भी नहीं पायी थी और उतरने वाले यात्री उतर भी नहीं पाये थे कि साथ-साथ भाग रहे कुलियों ने खिड़कियों और दरवाजों से सामान भीतर फेंकना व कूदकर भीतर घुसना आरम्भ कर दिया। ट्रेन के जैसे प्रत्येक डिब्बे पर यात्री टूट पड़ रहे थे। यहाँ तक कि आरक्षित डिब्बों में आरक्षित स्थान वाले यात्रियों में भी सब्र नहीं था जबकि उन्हें पता था कि वही सीट बैठने को मिलेगी जिसका नम्बर उनके आरक्षित कराये गये टिकट पर लिखा हुआ था। कुली के उत्तेजना भरे आग्रह पर हम लोग भी ज्यों-त्यों ही धँस गये। भीतर हमारी आरक्षित सीटें दिखा उसने सामान ऊपर रखा, पैसे लिए और चलता बना। जैसे ही हम अपनी सीटों की तरफ बड़े हमें यह देखकर अचरज हुआ कि वहाँ तीन चार व्यक्ति पहले से पसीने से नहाये हुए बैठे थे। हम लोगों ने अपने टिकट दिखाते हुए जब उनसे कहा कि ये सीटें तो हमने रिजर्व करवा रखी हैं, तो वे लोग इधर-उधर सरकते हुए बोले आप लोग भी बैठिए। हमारे बार-बार कहने व टी. सी. को बुलाने जैसी धमकी भरी बातें सुनकर उनमें से एक उठकर सामने वाली सीट पर बैठकर अकड़ते हुए बोला ''आने दीजिए टी. सी. को भी, तब तक तो बैठिए।''

विवश होकर हमें खाली किए गये स्थान पर अड़ना पड़ा यानि तीन के लिए आरक्षित स्थान पर पाँच व्यक्ति बैठ गये। हम लोग इधर-उधर देखने लगे, देखा बाकी सीटों पर भी कुछ इसी तरह का चक्कर था। पचास रुपये अधिक देकर आरक्षण करवाने वाले हमारी तरह ही विवश और रोनी सूरत लिए हुए बँगले झाँक रहे थे। ट्रेन चलने के आधे पौने घण्टे बाद ही टी. सी. महोदय के दर्शन हुए। हमारी सीट पर बैठे व्यक्ति से टिकट पूछने पर उसने तीन टिकट दिखाये तो टी. सी. ने कहा—यह तो इस डिब्बे के टिकट नहीं है इसमें पचास रुपये और देने पडेंगे। एक टिकट के हिसाब से उस आदमी ने सौ और पचास का नोट निकाल कर दिया और टी. सी. उन्हें लेकर आगे बढ़ गया। हमने देखा ऐसा ही वह सब जगह कर रहा था। टी. सी. के आगे बढ़ते ही दो आदमी और आकर हमारे सामने वाली सीट पर एक-एक करके अड़ गये । इस प्रकार तीन-तीन के लिए आरक्षित उन सीटों पर छह यात्री हो गये।

इसके बाद टी. सी. के दर्शन इलाहाबाद आने के लगभग आधा घण्टे पहले हो पाए। मैंने देखा बिना आरक्षण करवाये जो दो-दो, तीन-तीन लोग प्रत्येक सीट पर बैठे हुए थे उनसे बीस रुपये प्रति सीट के हिसाब से लेते हुए टी. सी. महोदय अपनी जेबों में भरते जा रहे थे। हमारी न तो टिकट ही चैक की गई और न ही आँखें मिलाई गईं। मेरे विचार में उस एक डिब्बे से ही कम से कम तीन हजार रुपये टी. सी. की जेब में चले गये होंगे।

यदि कोई ईमानदार रेलवे कर्मचारी जुर्माना न भी लगाकर पचास-पचास रुपये की रसीद काटकर आरक्षित बैठे यात्रियों को देता तो रेलवे विभाग को सात-आठ हजार रुपये की शुद्ध आय हो जाती। जुर्माना करने पर यह आय कई गुना अधिक हो सकती थी, लेकिन आकण्ठ भ्रष्टाचार में डूबे और रिश्वतखोरी के आदी इन कर्मचारियों को परवाह नहीं, रेल विभाग घाटे में रहता है तो रहे, हर साल किराये में अन्धाधुन्ध बढोत्तरी होती

है तो हो इससे इन्हें क्या ? इन्हें एक तो मुफ्त यात्रा के पास मिलते हैं दूसरा किराया बढ़ने पर इनकी भ्रष्ट आमदनी में भी तो बढ़ोत्तरी हो जाती है।

तो ऐसा रहा मेरी पहली रेल यात्रा का वर्णन व अनुभव। समाचार पत्रों में आरक्षित डिब्बों में यात्रा करने वालों की दुर्दशा के जो समाचार आदि प्रकाशित होते रहते हैं, ऊपर तक भ्रष्टाचार फैले होने की चर्चा की जाती है, वह पूर्ण सत्य है।

●●

रेल दुर्घटना

मानव जीवन घटनाओं से पूर्ण है। घटनाएँ छोटी-बड़ी, महत्वहीन तथा महत्वपूर्ण होती है, कुछ घटनाओं के घाव को समय का मरहम ठीक कर देता है और वे विस्मृति के गर्भ में विलीन हो जाती हैं जबकि कुछ घाव ऐसे होते हैं जो समय के आँधी-तूफानों के बाद भी खत्म नहीं होते। ऐसी ही घटना मैं यहाँ वर्णित कर रहा हूँ।

बात लगभग दो या तीन वर्ष पुरानी है। अपने मित्र के भाई की शादी में भाग लेकर मैं परिवार के साथ आगरा लौट रहा था। हम हावड़ा मेल में यात्रा कर रहे थे। सर्दियों का मौसम था। हम इलाहाबाद से लगभग शाम 4·30 बजे गाड़ी में सवार हुए। स्टेशन पर मित्र से विदा ली। गाड़ी तेजी से आगे बढ़ रही थी। हम सभी पर मौसम और शादी में जागने का खुमार था। ऐसी दशा में रात को लगभग 1 बजे अन्य यात्रियों के साथ हमारा परिवार भी सो गया। आरक्षित बोगी, प्रथम-श्रेणी का डिब्बा तथा सभी दूर के यात्री होने के कारण सो गये। डिब्बे में ज्यादा भीड़ नहीं थी।

अर्द्ध-निद्रा की अवस्था कहें या तन्द्रा हमें ऐसा अनुभव हुआ जैसे हमारा डिब्बा तेजी से ऊँचा उठकर उड़ा और धूम-धड़ाम-धम्म की आवाज के साथ एक ओर लुढ़क गया। उसी अवस्था में चीख-पुकार और आर्तनाद सुनाई दिया। जब तक स्थिति समझते, अचानक बत्ती चली गयी और हम घुप्प अँधेरे में डूब गये।

सभी त्रस्त एवं आतंकित थे। बच्चे चीख रहे थे। एक-दूसरे का स्पर्श करके यह स्पष्ट हो गया कि हमारी गाड़ी दुर्घटना का शिकार हो गई थी। अब अन्दाज के सहारे किसी प्रकार टार्च निकाली। टार्च जलने पर स्थिति स्पष्ट हुई। डिब्बा एक ओर लुढ़का पड़ा था कई बार चीख-पुकार मचाई, डिब्बे को बुरी तरह खड़काया। छोटे बच्चे सहमे हुए से अपनी माँ की गोद में चिपके थे। बड़े लोग भी सहमे हुए थे। बार-बार चीख-पुकार तथा डिब्बे की ठोक-पीट का कोई प्रभाव नहीं पड़ रहा था। समय देखा सुबह के साढ़े तीन बजे थे। इस दुर्घटना को हुए दो घण्टे हो चुके थे। लगभग 5 बजे ठोक-पीट की आवाज सुनाई पड़ी। शोर बढ़ने लगा था। गाँव वाले तथा सरकारी कर्मचारी डिब्बा तोड़ने का शक्तिभर प्रयास कर रहे थे। अन्त में किसी प्रकार मैंने अन्दर से एक खिड़की खोलने में सफलता प्राप्त की क्योंकि बाहर की चोट से वह काफी कमजोर हो गयी थी। पहले मैंने एक-एक करके बच्चों और औरतों को बाहर निकाला। बाद में सभी पुरुष सदस्यों की सहायता से यथा-सम्भव सामान निकाला। भारी सामान बाद के लिए छोड़ दिया गया। किसी प्रकार बाहर निकले। तब मालूम हुआ कि दुर्घटना बहुत भयंकर थी। दो गाड़ियों के आमने-सामने की टक्कर थी। लगभग 4 बोगियाँ पूरी तरह नष्ट हो गयी थी। उन्हें काट कर यात्रियों को निकालना पड़ा। किसी-किसी का पूरा परिवार नष्ट हो गया था। सकुशल घर लौटने पर मैंने ईश्वर को धन्यवाद दिया। ●●

एक अविस्मरणीय घटना

"............और आज यह तीसरा अवसर था जबकि वैसा ही लिफाफा मेरा इन्तजार कर रहा था। पहले के समान टाइप किया हुआ था। वही सीमित शब्दों में दिया गया सन्देश था। आखिर तुम नहीं माने। तुमने हमारे आदेश को गम्भीरता से नहीं लिया। आज समय आ गया है, जब हम अपना कार्य करेंगे। रात के ठीक दस बजे..............हमारे सन्देश का इन्तजार करो (फोन पर) और बताये पते पर पहुँचो। बिलकुल अकेले।" इसके नीचे केवल कंकाल बना होता।

दो महीने पूर्व............जब मुझे पहली बार ऐसा लिफाफा मिला, उस समय शाम के चार बजे थे। मैं विद्यालय से वापस आकर चाय पीने की तैयारी कर रहा था। अचानक छोटी बहन ने एक हरा लिफाफा लाकर मेज पर रख दिया। उत्सुकतावश मैंने उसे उठाया और उलट-पलट कर देखा। उस पर केवल मेरा नाम तथा पता लिखा हुआ था। भेजने वाले के स्थान पर केवल कंकाल का चित्र बना था। मैंने उत्सुकतावश लिफाफा खोलकर ध्यान से देखा। एक सुन्दर से कागज पर मात्र कुछ वाक्य टाइप किये गये थे। उनका सार इस प्रकार का था। थोड़ा धन और सम्मान पाकर तुम्हारी आँखें शायद आकाश में टँग गयी हैं। तुम्हें धरती तथा यहाँ के मनुष्य नहीं दिखायी देते। सावधान। अपना व्यवहार सुधारो नहीं तो धरती का बोझ कम करना होगा। रात में वैसा ही फोन मिला। सार था समाचार मिल गया होगा। तुम्हारा अपराध अक्षम्य है। तुम्हारा नम्बर, हमारी सूची में नवाँ है। आज पहले अपराधी को दुनिया से उठाया जायेगा। तुम्हारा नम्बर तीन महीने में आयेगा।

इस पत्र को पढ़ते ही मेरा जीवन स्वयं मेरे लिए एक घुटन एवं बोझ बनकर रहा गया। किसी को बता भी नहीं सकता और न उस पर कोई चर्चा ही सम्भव थी। मेरे बदले चेहरे ने घर में सभी को चौंका दिया था। पूछने पर इधर-उधर के बहाने बना देता। लोगों को विश्वास नहीं हुआ है; यह मैं जानता था, किन्तु उन्हें सन्तुष्ट करने में असमर्थ था। खुद मैं इस मामले को समझ नहीं पा रहा था। जितना सोचता, उतनी ही परेशानी बढ़ती जा रही थी। मैं सोच रहा था कि मुझे न तो कोई पुरस्कार मिला है और न आकस्मिक रूप में कोई धन लाभ ही हुआ है। फिर मेरे द्वारा किसकी भावनाओं को इतनी चोट पहुँची कि उसने इस संगठन से मेरी शिकायत कर दी और वह संगठन मेरा जीवन लेने पर उतारू हो गया। इस सम्पूर्ण समय में मैं तनावग्रस्त ही रहा। किसी कार्य में मन नहीं लगता था। उसके बाद पूरे महीने कुछ नहीं हुआ। मैं भी इस पत्र तथा फोन को किसी बुरे स्वप्न के समान भूल गया।

अगले महीने भी, ठीक उसी दिन, उसी समय पर हरा लिफाफा, मुझे मिला। वही सन्देश और वैसा ही फोन कॉल। अब मुझे गम्भीर होना पड़ा। एक अन्तरंग ने सलाह दी कि पुलिस को सूचित करूँ। किन्तु क्या ? किसके विरुद्ध सूचना लिखाऊँ। वे भी मेरा मजाक उड़ायेंगे। उसके बाद पुनः एक महीने सब कुछ सामान्य रहा। आज भी वैसा ही रहा। फोन पर मैंने संवाद देने वाले को खूब बुरा-भला कहा, किन्तु दूसरी ओर से खिल-खिलाने का स्वर सुनाई दिया और सम्बन्ध विच्छेद हो गया।

अब मुझे यह स्पष्ट हो गया था कि चाहे कोई भी क्यों न हो, यह मेरी जान लेने पर तुला हुआ है। अतः अब तो इससे दो चार होना ही पड़ेगा। यह सोचकर रात के 12 बजे कब्रिस्तान के पास अन्तिम कोठी का दरवाजा खटखटाया। कुछ समय बाद सुनायी दिया, सीधे अन्दर आ जाओ और कमरे में रखी कुर्सी पर बैठ जाओ। रोशनी जलाने या और कोई चालाकी दिखाने की कोई भी कोशिश खतरनाक होगी। मैंने जान पर खेलने का निश्चय किया। बड़े जोर से दरवाजे पर प्रहार किया और अन्दाज से स्विच बोर्ड का बटन दबा दिया। मैं यह देखकर आश्चर्यचकित रह गया कि वहाँ मित्रों का समूह मौजूद था। वे सब हँस रहे थे। बाद में उन्होंने विस्तार से बताया कि वे मुझसे पार्टी लेना चाहते थे, जबकि मैं हाथ नहीं धरने दे रहा था। अन्त में मैंने उनकी शर्त स्वीकार कर ली तथा मेरे तनाव का अन्त हुआ।

●●

हास्य-विनोद पूर्ण घटना

मानव-जीवन सुख-दुःख, हानि-लाभ, यश-अपयश आदि से पूर्ण है। जन्म से मृत्यु तक संघर्षपूर्ण इस मानव-जीवन में अनेक घटनाएँ घटित होती रहती हैं। ये दुःखद और सुखद दोनों प्रकार की होती हैं। अधिकतर घटनाओं को मानव भूल जाता है, किन्तु कुछ घटनाएँ ऐसी होती हैं जिन्हें समय की आँधी और तूफान भी विस्मृत नहीं कर पाते। इस प्रकार दुःखद घटनाएँ यदि विषाद और निराशा की सृष्टि करती है, तो सुखद घटनाएँ मन को एक अद्भुत आह्लाद से भर देती हैं। ऐसी एक घटना का वर्णन में यहाँ कर रहा हूँ।

घटना आज से लगभग 20 वर्ष पुरानी है। मार्च का अन्तिम दिन था। विद्यालय का अवकाश था। मैं कुछ उदास स्थिति में घर में बैठा था। अचानक डाकिया मेरे नाम का एक पत्र द्वार पर लगी पत्र-पेटिका (Letter box) में डाल गया। उत्सुकतावश पत्र, पेटिका से बाहर निकालकर पढ़ा। दूसरे दिन जन्म-दिवस समारोह का

निमन्त्रण था। आग्रह कुछ अधिक ही था और दूसरे दिन शाम का समय फालतू था। अतः कार्यक्रम बनाकर शाम के समय एक बड़ा-सा उपहार लेकर हम उनके घर पहुँचे। यहाँ सब कुछ सामान्य-सा ही दिखायी दिया। अब पहुँच तो गये ही थे। विचार किया कि जो होगा सो देखा जायेगा। उत्सुकता दबाये इन्तजार करने लगे। परिवार के सभी सदस्य अचानक मेरे आगमन से कुछ आश्चर्यचकित थे, क्योंकि अनेक बार आग्रह किये जाने पर भी मैं वहाँ नहीं जाता था। औपचारिकता के बाद भी जब मुझे जन्म-दिवस मनाये जाने के कोई लक्षण न दिखाई दिये तो मैंने पूछा कि आज (उस दिन) किसी (नाम लेकर) के जन्म-दिवस मनाये जाने की सूचना मिली थी। जिसके कोई लक्षण अथवा तैयारी नहीं है। तब जाकर बात खुली। उसी समय सम्बन्धी की पुत्री चाय के साथ मिठाई और नमकीन आदि लेकर आयी। मेरे आग्रह पर उस बालिका के पिताजी भी शामिल हो गये। मैंने ध्यान दिया कि वे कुछ अधिक कृत्रिम गम्भीरता का आवरण लगाकर आचरण कर रहे थे। उनकी माँ के लिए कहा गया कि वे किसी सहेली से मिलने गयीं हैं। मुझे यह कुछ बनावटी तो मालूम हुआ किन्तु शान्त रहा।

चाय का पहला घूँट लेते ही मन कड़वाहट और कसैलेपन से भर गया। वे पिता-पुत्री मेरे चेहरे के भाव बड़े ध्यान से पढ़ रहे थे। कप रखकर मैंने बिस्कुट उठाया, किन्तु यह क्या ? वह पत्थर के समान कठोर। अब तक मैं भी सब कुछ समझकर नासमझ बनने का अभिनय कर रहा था। अन्त में मैंने विदा माँगी। मैने उपहार उस बालिका को भेंट किया और चलने वाला था कि बालिका की माताजी मुस्कराती हुईं सामने आयीं। जब उन्हें ज्ञात हुआ कि मुझे किस प्रकार मूर्ख बनाया गया है, तो वे बच्चों तथा उनके पापा पर बिगड़ीं। तभी उपहार का पैकिट खोलने पर उसमें असीमित तहों के बाद पुर्जा था।

ऐप्रिल फूल बनाया तो उनको गुस्सा आया।

अब पासा पलट गया। मुझे मूर्ख बनाने वाले स्वयं मूर्ख बन गये। बाद में अच्छे नाश्ते और गप्पों के बाद वापस लौटा। मैं यह घटना आज भी नहीं भुला पाता हूँ।

●●

जहाँ सुमति तहँ सम्पत्ति नाना

'जहाँ सुमति तहँ सम्पत्ति नाना, जहाँ कुमति तहँ विपत्ति निदाना।'

सुमति से सम्पन्नता और सम्मान प्राप्त होता है तथा कुमति से आपत्ति और विनाश का जन्म होता है। कलयुग में संघ में ही शक्ति मानी जाती है। अकेला चना भाड़ नहीं फोड़ सकता, जब तक उसके पीछे सामूहिक शक्ति न हो। जिस घर में सुमति और एकता होती है, वही बाहरी तथा आंतरिक रूप में प्रगति कर सकता है। यही बात राज्य और राष्ट्र के उदाहरण में भी चरितार्थ होती है।

परिवार एवं देश में सुमति से ही एकता आती है और एकता से शक्ति। शक्ति से सारे कार्य सुलभ हो जाते हैं। सच ही कहा है कि, अकेला मनुष्य यदि कुछ करना चाहे तो नहीं कर सकता। किन्तु यदि उसके पीछे सूत्रबद्ध सामूहिक शक्ति हो तो ऐसा कुछ भी नहीं जो असम्भव हो। देश की स्थिति भी परिवार जैसी है। जिस प्रकार यदि किसी घर में सदैव कलह और झगड़े बने रहते हैं वहाँ सदैव दरिद्रता का निवास होता है इसी प्रकार देश भी एक परिवार है यदि देश में विभिन्न स्तरों पर यहाँ के निवासियों में मतभेद होगा तो देश की उन्नति भी असम्भव है।

यह निर्विवाद सत्य है कि संगठित होकर ही समाज व राष्ट्र शक्ति एवं मजबूती प्राप्त करता है। सामाजिक और सामूहिक रूप से भी यह देश को शक्ति, सम्मान और सम्पन्नता के रूप में ईश्वरीय वरदान है।

वर्तमान में वही देश और समाज वंदनीय है जिनमें स्वाभिमान एवं परस्पर बन्धुत्व की भावना हो। ऐसा ही देश वास्तव में उन्नति के शिखर पर पहुँचेगा। ऐसा राष्ट्र आत्मरक्षा में सफल होता है। एकता के सूत्र में बँधा देश शक्तिशाली से शक्तिशाली शत्रु को भी परास्त कर सकता है। किसी में शक्ति नहीं कि ऐसे राष्ट्र की ओर आँख उठाकर भी देख सके। वह सामाजिक, राजनैतिक, आर्थिक, संक्षेप में हर क्षेत्र में सफलता प्राप्त करता है तथा सर्वांगीण विकास कर सकता है। जैसा कहा गया है कि एक धागे अथवा लकड़ी के एक टुकड़े को तोड़ना सरल है, जबकि अनेक धागों से मिलकर बने रस्से तथा लड़कियों के गट्ठर को तोड़ना कठिन होता है।

घर में यदि एक ही व्यक्ति कमाने वाला होता है तथा कई सदस्य खाने वाले होते हैं तो उस घर की आर्थिक स्थिति सुदृढ़ नहीं होती। जबकि जिस घर के बहुत से व्यक्ति मिलकर कमाते हैं तथा आवश्यकताओं की पूर्ति करते हैं। उस घर की आर्थिक स्थिति सदैव सुदृढ़ रहेगी। जिस घर के सभी सदस्य समर्थ हों, किन्तु व्यक्तिगत स्वार्थ में लीन रहते हों। वहाँ व्यापार की पूँजी ही डूब जाती है। सुमति होने पर सभी सदस्य पवित्र भावना से कार्य करते हैं और वहाँ सहयोग, स्नेह और भाईचारे का वातावरण बन जाता है, तब सम्पन्नता स्वतः ही मिल जाती है। प्राचीन काल में संगठन और सुमति होने के कारण हर क्षेत्र में भारत विश्व में सभी देशों का सिरमौर था। इसी प्रकार वर्तमान में अमेरिका, ब्रिटेन, फ्रांस जैसे देश अपनी सुमति, संगठन और एकता के कारण ही आज संसार के सिरमौर बन गए हैं। इन देशों के नागरिक देश के लिए व्यक्तिगत स्वार्थों का बलिदान कर देते हैं अतः आज विश्व में उन देशों की तूती बोल रही है।

विश्व में आज दो ही शक्ति प्रबल हैं—एक धन शक्ति और दूसरी मन शक्ति। जहाँ यह दोनों ही शक्तियाँ प्रबल होती हैं, वहाँ आस-पास के क्षेत्र में प्रभाव स्वतः ही बन जाता है। विश्व में अमेरिका, रूस और ब्रिटेन को यह कहने की आवश्यकता नहीं कि वे विकसित और प्रभावी राष्ट्र हैं।

दसवीं शताब्दी में संगठन शक्ति और एकता के अभाव में राजपूत संख्या में अधिक होने पर भी आक्रमणकारियों से पराजित हुए, क्योंकि राजपूतों में मिथ्या अहंकार था। उन्हें अपनी जाति, धर्म और देश के सम्मान का तनिक भी ध्यान नहीं था। यही कारण था कि देश पराधीन हो गया। जिस घर अर्थात् राष्ट्र में दिन-रात झगड़े होते हैं। लोग एक-दूसरे से घृणा करते है तथा प्राण लेने का प्रयत्न करते हैं, ऐसे स्थान पर कुमति और विनाश का गहरा अन्धकार व्याप्त रहता है।

यह दुर्भाग्य का विषय है कि अनेक धर्म, भाषा तथा संस्कृति होने के कारण भारत में कुमति और कलह का वातावरण व्याप्त है। व्यक्तिगत स्वार्थ ने देश को दयनीय अवस्था मैं ला पटका है। जनता भ्रमित है। वह अपने हित-अहित का निर्णय नहीं कर पा रही है। राष्ट्रीयता की भावना का अभाव है। ''विष्णु शर्मा'' रचित पंचतन्त्र में मनुष्य को आपस में मेल से रहने एवं सोच-विचार कर कार्य करने की प्रेरणा दी गयी है। जहाँ एक-दूसरे के सहयोग से कार्य किया जाता है वहाँ सम्पत्ति और सुख स्वयं निवास हेतु आते हैं किन्तु जहाँ आपस में भावनात्मक या क्रियात्मक टकराव होता है वहाँ बने हुए कार्य भी बिगड़ जाते हैं। सुख शान्ति का आधार सुमति ही।

उदाहरण के लिये, रावण बहुत शक्तिशाली था। उसको जीतना देवताओं के भी वश की बात नहीं थी। किन्तु जब उनमें फूट पड़ गई, एक-दूसरे के विचार आपस में टकराने लगे तो सर्वशक्तिमान व सर्वसाधनसम्पन्न रावण को केवल बन्दरों एवं अपने मनोबल के आधार पर भगवान श्रीराम विभीषण की सहायता से जीतने में समर्थ हुए। सुमति और कुमति का सर्वश्रेष्ठ उदाहरण रामायण है।

आज हमारे देश में ऐसे आदर्श महापुरुष और देशभक्त नेता की आवश्यकता है जो देश की जनता को सन्मार्ग पर ले जा सके। यदि हम जीवन में उच्च लक्ष्य प्राप्त करना चाहते हैं तो हमें एकता, सदाचार की भावना को हृदय में रखकर सुमति से चलना चाहिये।

●●

जैसे को तैसा

कर्मण्येवाधिकारस्ते, मा फलेषु कदाचन्।
मा कर्मफल हेतुर्भूमति सङ्गडस्त्वकर्मणि॥

अर्थात् मनुष्य को अपना कर्म करना चाहिये। फल देना तो ईश्वर का काम है। जो कर्म दूसरों की भलाई के लिए किये जाते हैं वे सत्कर्म कहलाते हैं। ऐसे कर्म करने वाला व्यक्ति सदैव सुखी रहता है। दूसरों को कष्ट पहुँचाने वाले कर्मों को असत् कर्म कहते हैं। हम जैसे भी कर्म करते हैं हमें वैसा ही फल मिलता है।

हम जैसा भी कार्य अर्थात् कर्म करते है हमें उसका वैसा ही फल मिलता है। प्रत्येक मनुष्य कर्म करने के लिये स्वतन्त्र है परन्तु उन कर्मों का फल तो ईश्वर देता है और प्रत्येक व्यक्ति को अपने कर्मों का जो भी फल हो भोगना ही पड़ता है।

प्राय: कर्म करते समय मनुष्य यह भूल जाता है कि अच्छे और बुरे जैसे भी कर्म कर रहा है। उन कर्मों का फल उसे अवश्य ही भोगना पड़ता है। प्रत्येक मनुष्य को उसके कर्म के अनुसार फल अवश्य मिलता है। इस सम्बन्ध में निम्न उदाहरण देखने को मिलते हैं। हम बीज बोकर अर्थात् कर्म करके भूल जाते हैं किन्तु बीज उगना नहीं भूलता।

भीष्म पितामह ने एक दुमही को तीर की नोंक से उठाकर बेरिया के पेड़ पर पटक दिया जहाँ उसे छ: महीने तड़पना पड़ा। वही फल शर-शय्या पर सोकर उन्हें भोगना पड़ा। राजा दशरथ ने श्रवण के तीर मारा। उनके माता-पिता ने पुत्र वियोग में प्राण त्याग दिये, उसी प्रकार पुत्र-वियोग में राजा दशरथ को प्राण त्यागने पड़े। दुर्योधन ने पाण्डवों को राज्य प्राप्ति की इच्छा से नाना प्रकार के कष्ट दिये तो अन्त में उसका फल उन्हें पराजय और नाश के रूप में भोगना पड़ा। आज भी लोग दुर्योधन से घृणा और युधिष्ठिर का सम्मान करते हैं। इन सभी उदाहरणों से स्पष्ट होता है कि जो जैसा कर्म करते हैं उन्हें उसका परिणाम अवश्य मिलता है।

विद्यार्थी जीवन में तो कर्म का विशेष महत्व है। क्योंकि विद्या रूपी धन को बिना परिश्रम के कोई भी प्राप्त नहीं कर सकता। जो विद्यार्थी परिश्रम एवं लगन से पढ़ाई करते हैं, वे हमेशा अच्छे अंकों से उत्तीर्ण होकर अपना, अपने माता-पिता का एवं विद्यालय का नाम रोशन करते हैं। इसके विपरीत जो विद्यार्थी अपना समय खेल में व्यर्थ बिताते हैं वे अक्सर परीक्षा में अनुत्तीर्ण होकर जीवन की दौड़ में पीछे रह जाते हैं तथा अपने माता-पिता और शिक्षकों के कोप का भाजन बनते हैं।

तुलसीदास, कबीरदास, गुरुनानक, चन्द्रशेखर आजाद, राजा हरिश्चन्द्र, राजा राममोहन राय, महात्मा गाँधी आदि महापुरुषों ने अपने कर्मों से यह सिद्ध कर दिया है कि जो जैसी करनी करता है उसका फल उसे वैसा ही मिलता है। दूसरों को सुख पहुँचाने वाला सुखी और दूसरों को दु:ख पहुँचाने वाला हमेशा दु:खी ही रहता है। कहा भी गया है जैसा बोओगे, वैसा काटना पड़ेगा—'As you sow, so you reap'. अपने द्वारा किये गये कर्म के फल से कोई भी बच नहीं सकता। तुलसीदास जी के अनुसार—

कर्म प्रधान विश्व करि राखा।
जो जस करइ सो तस फल चाखा॥

इतिहास ऐसे असंख्य उदाहरणों से भरा पड़ा है जिससे सिद्ध होता है कि जो व्यक्ति अपने जीवन का उद्देश्य ऊँचा बनाकर चलते हैं, वे ऊँचा प्रयास करते हैं और ऊँचाइयों पर पहुँच जाते हैं।

यदि हमारे कर्म ही अच्छे न हों तो हमें अच्छे फल की भी आशा नहीं करनी चाहिए। कहावत भी है—

बोया पेड़ बबूल का, आम कहाँ से होय।

अंगुलिमाल जब तक हिंसा के कर्मों में लगे रहे तब तक उन्हें शान्ति नहीं मिली। हिंसा छोड़कर ही उन्हें सुख शान्ति का अनुभव हुआ।

अत: कहने का तात्पर्य यह है कि हमें सदैव अच्छे कर्म करने चाहिए। यदि हमारे कर्म ही अच्छे न होंगे तो उनका फल कैसे अच्छा होगा। जो व्यक्ति दूसरों को कष्ट पहुँचाता है उसे स्वयं भी कष्ट उठाने पड़ते हैं। हमें सदैव दूसरों का उपकार करना चाहिये और उस कर्म के फल की आशा नहीं करनी चाहिये। क्योंकि फल तो एक न एक दिन अवश्य मिलेगा। केवल सत्कर्म करना ही मनुष्य का उद्देश्य होना चाहिये।

●●

अपठित गद्यांश

(UNSEEN PASSAGE)

Read the following passage and answer the questions that follow using your own words as far as possible.

निम्नलिखित अवतरण को पढ़कर नीचे दिये गये प्रश्नों के संक्षिप्त उत्तर दीजिए। प्रश्नों के उत्तर यथासम्भव आपके अपने शब्दों में होने चाहिए—

गद्यांश–1

ऐसा माना जाता रहा है कि मस्तिष्क की शक्ति जन्मजात होती है अर्थात् जन्म से ही कोई बुद्धिमान् होता है और कोई बुद्धिमान् नहीं होता। इस स्थिति में अन्तर नहीं आता। जैसे मारपीट कर गधे को घोड़ा नहीं बनाया जा सकता, किन्तु नवीनतम अन्वेषणों से पता चलता है कि सही प्रोत्साहन मिलने पर हमारे मस्तिष्क का रूप बदल सकता है अर्थात् हम पहले से कहीं अधिक बुद्धिमान् और क्रियाशील हो सकते हैं।

कहावत है—'स्वस्थ शरीर में स्वस्थ मस्तिष्क का वास।' अत: मस्तिष्क की दक्षता और कार्यकुशलता के लिए न केवल मानसिक अपितु शारीरिक व्यायाम भी अपेक्षित है। एक शोध के अनुसार जो लोग नियमित रूप से शारीरिक व्यायाम करते हैं वे मानसिक परीक्षाओं में बेहतर अंक लेते हैं। इसका कारण यह है कि मस्तिष्क में भी माँसपेशियाँ होती हैं। जब हम व्यायाम करते हैं, तो मस्तिष्क में रक्त संचार बढ़ जाता है और वह पहले से अधिक क्रियाशील हो जाता है।

शोध से पता चलता है कि आप भारतीय संगीत सुनें या पाश्चात्य आपका मस्तिष्क स्पन्दित होता है, क्रियाशील होता है। मस्तिष्क को अधिकाधिक क्रियाशील रखने के लिए आप अपने सामने चुनौतियाँ रखें। चुनौतियाँ शिक्षा सम्बन्धी भी हो सकती हैं और खेल-कूद सम्बन्धी भी। जैसे कक्षा में प्रथम आने की या स्वर्णपदक जीतने की, दोनों ही प्रोत्साहक हैं। कुछ नया करने की चेष्टा करें। चाहे नई-नई भाषाएँ सीखें या नृत्य, वाद्य, संगीत आदि कलाओं का प्रशिक्षण लें। सभी के पीछे एक ही उद्देश्य निहित है—मस्तिष्क को क्रियाशीलता प्रदान करना। इस दिशा में शतरंज, चौपड़, ताश, क्रासवर्ड, वीडियो गेम भी उपयोगी हैं। कोशिश करें अधिकाधिक व्यक्तियों के नाम स्मरण रखने की, जिनके सम्पर्क में आप आयें या जिनसे किसी भी रूप में आपका परिचय हुआ है। सहज स्मरण के लिए उनके व्यक्तित्व या उनके जीवन की घटना विशेष को उनके नाम के साथ जोड़ें। जैसे—'सत्याग्रह आन्दोलन' सुनते ही महात्मा गाँधी का नाम स्मरण हो आता है।

संक्षेप में, चुनौतियों का सामना करें, उनसे पलायन नहीं। कुछ नया सीखें तथा हमेशा कुछ नया करें, क्योंकि जीवन में अनुभव कुछ कर गुजरने से ही होता है। और हाँ, याद रहे—नया सीखने या नया करने के लिए कोई आयु सीमा निर्धारित नहीं।

प्रश्न : (i) मस्तिष्क की शक्ति (बुद्धि) के विषय में क्या प्राचीन मान्यता चली आ रही है ? आप इससे सहमत हैं या नहीं ? क्यों ?

(ii) उदाहरण देते हुए स्पष्ट कीजिए कि मस्तिष्क की कार्यकुशलता के लिए मानसिक ही नहीं, शारीरिक व्यायाम भी आवश्यक है।

(iii) चुनौतियों के नाम पर हम क्या-क्या कर सकते हैं ? क्या अधिकाधिक व्यक्तियों के नाम स्मरण रखना भी एक चुनौती है ? इसे कैसे सरल बनाया जा सकता है ?

(iv) प्रस्तुत गद्यांश से हमें क्या शिक्षा मिलती है ?

(v) 'नया सीखने में आयु कोई बाधा नहीं है।' इस कथन की समीक्षा कीजिए।

उत्तर : (i) प्राचीन मान्यता है कि मस्तिष्क की शक्ति जन्मजात होती है। दूसरे शब्दों में, जिस व्यक्ति में जन्म के समय जितनी बुद्धि होती है, उतनी ही रहती है। इसमें जीवन भर कोई परिवर्तन नहीं होता। भाव यह है कि मूर्ख को प्रयत्न करने पर भी बुद्धिमान नहीं बनाया जा सकता है। हम इस विचार से सहमत नहीं हैं। इसका कारण यह है कि मानव के मस्तिष्क एवं बुद्धि या विचार शक्ति का उसके शरीर के साथ विकास होता रहता है। इसका प्रमाण हमें जीवन की कई घटित घटनाओं में मिल जाता है।

(ii) मस्तिष्क की दक्षता तथा उसकी कार्यकुशलता का गहरा सम्बन्ध शारीरिक स्वास्थ्य से होता है। कहावत के अनुसार, स्वस्थ शरीर में ही स्वस्थ मस्तिष्क का निवास होता है। अत: मस्तिष्क की दक्षता और कार्यकुशलता के लिए शरीर के व्यायाम की बहुत अधिक आवश्यकता है। शरीर के अंग-प्रत्यंग के व्यायाम से मस्तिष्क का भी व्यायाम हो जाता है। यही कारण है कि शारीरिक परिश्रम करने वाले मानसिक परीक्षाओं में भी श्रेष्ठ अंक प्राप्त करते हैं।

(iii) चुनौतियों के नाम पर शिक्षा सम्बन्धी तथा खेल सम्बन्धी दोनों ही प्रकार की चुनौतियाँ आवश्यक हैं। शिक्षा सम्बन्धी चुनौतियों में कक्षा में प्रथम आना तथा अधिकाधिक व्यक्तियों का नाम स्मरण रखना और खेलकूद के क्षेत्र में अधिकाधिक पदक जीतना इसके उदाहरण हैं। नाम स्मरण के लिए हम व्यक्ति के नाम के साथ सम्बन्धित घटना को भी जोड़ सकते हैं।

(iv) इस गद्यांश से हमें चुनौतियों से पलायन करने के स्थान पर उनका सामना करने की शिक्षा मिलती है। हमें जीवन में हर समय कुछ नया सीखने तथा नया करने का प्रयास करना चाहिए।

(v) नया सीखने के लिए कुछ मनुष्य आयु को जिम्मेदार मानते हैं। उनके अनुसार प्रत्येक कार्य को करने की एक निश्चित आयु होती है तथा उस आयु के पश्चात् कार्य को सीखना असम्भव है। ऐसे मनुष्य एक कुंठित विचारधारा वाले होते हैं और कूप-मंडूक के समान होते हैं। इसके विपरीत हमें समाज में अनेक मनुष्य ऐसे मिलते हैं, जिन्होंने उम्र को नजरअंदाज करते हुए ऐसे कार्य किये जिन्हें कुछ लोग कठिन मानकर छोड़ देते हैं। परन्तु इसके लिए मस्तिष्क की क्रियाशीलता आवश्यक है तथा इसके लिए कुछ मानसिक क्रियाओं का सहारा लिया जा सकता है।

अत: हम कह सकते हैं कि नया सीखने में आयु कोई बाधा नहीं है। नया सीखने के लिए हमारे मन में उत्साह और परिश्रम करने का साहस होना चाहिए।

गद्यांश–2

वनों की रमणीय स्थली के बीच, वृक्षों की शीतल छाया के नीचे, भारतीय ऋषि और मुनियों के द्वारा विश्व श्रेष्ठ हमारी सभ्यता और संस्कृति समृद्धि को प्राप्त हुई थी। वनों में स्थित ऋषि आश्रम प्रात: और संध्याकाल के समय वेदों के मधुर निनाद से गूँजा करते थे। वनों के ही शान्त वातावरण में हमारे विद्यार्थी सरस्वती की आराधना किया करते थे। अशोक वृक्ष के नीचे महात्मा बुद्ध ने ज्ञान की अमर ज्योति प्राप्त की थी। भगवान राम ने वनवासी बनकर ही अपने जीवन के महान कार्य पूरे किये थे। कृष्ण ने वृन्दावन के हरे-भरे कुंजों में अपनी मनोहर क्रीड़ाएँ की थीं। ऋषिकन्या शकुन्तला तो बिना वृक्षों का जल सिंचन किए स्वयं जल भी ग्रहण नहीं करती थी। इसलिए तो हमारे प्राचीन ग्रन्थों और काव्यों में वनों की बड़ी महिमा पाई गई है। हमारे सभी उत्कृष्ट काव्य वनों की प्राकृतिक छटा और उसकी अतुल सुषमा से भरे पड़े हैं। वैदिक साहित्य में तो वनदेवियों की अर्चना की गई है। मनुस्मृति में वृक्ष विच्छेदक को बहुत बड़ा पापी माना गया है। किसी अच्छे गुण की उपमा जब दी जाती है, तो किसी न किसी वृक्ष से दी जाती है। सन्तों की उपमा देने के लिए सुन्दर फलदार वृक्षों के

अतिरिक्त कवियों को और कुछ नहीं सूझता। इस प्रकार हमारी सभ्यता, हमारी संस्कृति, हमारा साहित्य सभी कुछ वन प्रधान रहा है।

हमारे ये वन धार्मिक दृष्टिकोण से ही नहीं, भौतिक दृष्टि से भी अत्यन्त महत्वपूर्ण हैं। देश की आर्थिक समृद्धि में इन वनों का महत्वपूर्ण हाथ रहा है। सत्य तो यह है कि वनों से इतने अधिक लाभ हैं कि उनके बिना जीवनयापन भी असम्भव है। विभिन्न प्रकार की बहुमूल्य लकड़ी बाँस, चन्दन, कागज बनाने वाली घास, कपूर, राल, तारपीन, रेशम, रबड़ तथा अनेक जड़ी-बूटियाँ वनों से ही प्राप्त होती हैं साथ ही शहद, इलायची, दालचीनी, काली मिर्च, खजूर, साबूदाना भी वृक्षों की कृपा से प्राप्त होता है। परन्तु दुःख का विषय है कि वन जैसी अमूल्य धरोहर को हम सहेज कर नहीं रख सके। अपने छोटे-छोटे स्वार्थों के लिए हमने वृक्षों को काटना प्रारम्भ किया। वनोच्छेदन से हमारी कितनी हानि हुई है, इसका सबल प्रमाण तो सिन्ध प्रदेश के मोहनजोदड़ों और हड़प्पा के वे अवशेष खण्डहर हैं जो किसी दिन अत्यन्त समृद्धिशाली, धन-धान्य से भरे पूरे थे। परन्तु कालान्तर में वहाँ के वन नष्ट कर दिए गए, तभी वह शस्यश्यामला सिन्धु प्रदेश धीरे-धीरे मरुस्थल बनता गया।

प्रश्न : (i) प्राचीन भारतीय संस्कृति में वनों का क्या महत्व और उपयोग था ?

(ii) हमारे धर्मग्रन्थों में वनों के विषय में क्या लिखा है ?

(iii) वनों के आर्थिक महत्व के विषय में अपने विचार स्पष्ट कीजिए।

(iv) वनों के विनाश का देश की आर्थिक स्थिति पर क्या प्रभाव पड़ा है ?

(v) 'वनों के विनाश से मानव-जाति का भी विनाश होगा।' आप इस तर्क से कहाँ तक सहमत हैं ? सप्रमाण उत्तर दीजिए।

उत्तर : (i) प्राचीन भारतीय संस्कृति में वनों का विशेष महत्व था। वृक्षों की छाया में ही ऋषियों ने भारतीय संस्कृति और सभ्यता के विकास में योगदान किया। वेद और शास्त्रों का निर्माण वनों में ही हुआ। ऋषियों के आश्रम में सरस्वती की आराधना (ज्ञान-प्राप्ति) होती थी। सभी महापुरुषों ने वृक्षों की छाया में ज्ञान प्राप्त किया था। वैदिक साहित्य में वन के साथ वन देवी की कल्पना कर उसकी महिमा का गान किया गया है।

(ii) हमारे धर्म ग्रन्थों में वनों के महत्व का स्पष्ट उल्लेख है। वैदिक साहित्य में वनों की सेवा, वन देवी की कल्पना एवं अर्चना, शकुन्तला द्वारा वृक्षों के सिंचन के पश्चात् जल ग्रहण करने की प्रतिज्ञा तथा सज्जन व परोपकारी व्यक्तियों के गुण-गान में वृक्षों की उपमा देने की परम्परा प्राचीन धर्म-ग्रन्थों में भी दिखाई देती है।

(iii) देश की आर्थिक समृद्धि में वनों का महत्वपूर्ण स्थान है। वनों से हमें विभिन्न प्रकार की लकड़ी, बाँस, चन्दन, कागज बनाने वाली घास, कपूर, राल, तारपीन, शहद, इलायची, दालचीनी, कालीमिर्च, रेशम तथा रबड़ जैसी वस्तुएँ प्राप्त होती हैं। वनों से प्राप्त कच्चे माल पर हमारे उद्योग-धन्धों का विकास निर्भर है।

(iv) वनों के नष्ट होने से देश की आर्थिक स्थिति भी प्रभावित हुई है। वनों से प्राप्त होने वाले कच्चे माल के अभाव में उद्योग-धन्धों पर बुरा प्रभाव पड़ा है इसके अतिरिक्त पर्यावरण का सन्तुलन भी बिगड़ा है। वनों के अभाव में वर्षा की मात्रा कम हो जाती है और बाढ़, सूखा, रेगिस्तान का प्रसार आदि कुपरिणाम हमारे सामने आते हैं।

(v) मानव जाति अपने अस्तित्व के लिए वनों पर निर्भर है क्योंकि वनों से मनुष्य को आवश्यक वस्तुओं की प्राप्ति होती है। किसी भी देश की आर्थिक प्रगति में भी वनों का महत्व होता है। पर्यावरण की दृष्टि से भी वन मानव के लिए विशेष उपयोगी हैं, क्योंकि वन वर्षा कराने, भूमि अपरदन को रोकने आदि क्रियाओं में सहायक होते हैं। अतः वनों का विनाश करने से मानव जाति का भी विनाश होगा, तर्क सर्वथा उपयुक्त है। इसका प्रमाण सिन्ध प्रदेश के मोहनजोदड़ो और हड़प्पा के खण्डहर हैं, जो कभी अत्यन्त सम्पन्न और धन-धान्य से युक्त थे। परन्तु जब वहाँ वनों को नष्ट किया तो धीरे-धीरे सब कुछ नष्ट हो गया।

गद्यांश– 3

मानव अपने भाग्य का स्वयं निर्माता है। वर्तमान में यह विचार पूरी तरह न केवल सत्य सिद्ध हो चुका है बल्कि सैकड़ों वर्षों के मानव इतिहास ने भी इसे दर्पण के समान स्पष्ट कर दिया है। गत वर्ष विश्व के इतिहास में ऐसी अनेक घटनाएँ घटित हुई जिन्होंने न केवल सम्पूर्ण मानवता को खतरे में डाल दिया अपितु जिनके विषय में जानकर सभी स्तब्ध रह गए। दु:ख इस बात का है कि यह सब कुछ मानव के कर्मों का दुष्परिणाम है।

जी हाँ यह पूर्णत: सत्य है कि मानव ने अपने कर्मों से हमारी सभ्यता के अस्तित्व पर ही प्रश्न–चिन्ह लगा दिया था। आज विज्ञान और तकनीकी प्रगति के क्षेत्र में मानव ऊँचाइयों को छू चुका है। इस क्षेत्र की हर उपलब्धि विकास के क्षेत्र में महत्वपूर्ण स्थान रखती है। जहाँ एक ओर इस प्रगति ने हमारे जीवन को सुख और आराम से पूर्ण कर दिया है, वहीं इसने ऐसी अनेक दुर्घटनाओं को जन्म दिया जिसने सम्पत्ति तथा श्रम के साथ सैकड़ों मनुष्यों के जीवन को नष्ट कर दिया।

विज्ञान और तकनीकी ज्ञान आज अनेक देशों की रक्षा–योजनाओं का महत्वपूर्ण अंग बन गया है। आज अणु बम, आणविक युद्ध तथा अन्तरिक्ष–युद्ध इत्यादि वर्तमान जीवन में सामान्य बातें हो गयी हैं। प्रत्येक राष्ट्र इनसे होने वाले विनाश से अवगत है फिर भी इन क्षेत्रों में बराबर आगे बढ़ रहे हैं। आश्चर्य एवं दु:ख का विषय यह है कि हम इसके लिए एक दूसरे को दोषी मान रहे हैं। हिरोशिमा और नागासाकी पर बम वर्षा से केवल मानव जीवन का विनाश ही नहीं हुआ बल्कि इसके पड़ने वाले हानिकारक प्रभाव ने भविष्य के कुछ वर्षों में जैविक विकिरण ने मानव अस्तित्व को ही प्रदूषित कर दिया।

हम भोपाल में होने वाले गैस रिसाव तथा इसके कारण होने वाली सैकड़ों व्यक्तियों की जीवन हानि तथा बचे हुए लोगों के शरीर को इस गैस के विकिरण के कारण होने वाले घातक प्रभाव को कैसे भूल सकते हैं ? अध्ययन से यह बात पूर्णत: स्पष्ट हो गयी है कि अणु–शक्ति से प्रभावित क्षेत्रों में कार्यरत श्रमिकों में कैंसर के जीवाणुओं की संख्या अन्य क्षेत्रों की तुलना में अधिक मात्रा में होती है।

प्रश्न : (i) 'मानव अपने भाग्य का निर्माता स्वयं है' का अर्थ स्पष्ट कीजिए तथा यह भी स्पष्ट कीजिए कि यह विचार कहाँ तक सत्य है ?

(ii) मानव आपत्तियों को स्वयं कब और कैसे आमन्त्रित करता है ? स्पष्ट कीजिए।

(iii) हम किस प्रकार कह सकते हैं कि मानव अपने विनाश के लिए स्वयं उत्तरदायी है ?

(iv) यूनियन कार्बाइड फैक्ट्री भारत में कहाँ है ? यहाँ कब और क्या दुर्घटना घटित हुई तथा उसका क्या परिणाम हुआ ?

(v) उपर्युक्त गद्यांश के आधार पर बताइए कि विज्ञान और तकनीक मानव के लिए वरदान है या अभिशाप।

उत्तर : (i) इस वाक्य का अर्थ है कि मनुष्य का भाग्य उसके अपने हाथ में है। वह अपने प्रयत्न से चाहे तो उसे ऊँचा उठा सकता है और चाहे तो उसको पतन के गहरे गड्ढे में गिरा कर नष्ट कर सकता है।

यह विचार पूर्णत: सत्य है कि मानव ने अपने कर्मों से हमारी सभ्यता के अस्तित्व पर ही प्रश्न चिन्ह लगा दिया है। प्रगति के क्षेत्र में मानव ऊँचाइयों को छू चुका है। इसी प्रकार मानवता के विनाश के क्षेत्र में मानव ने घातक अस्त्र–शस्त्रों का निर्माण कर लिया है।

(ii) मानव को ईश्वर की सृष्टि का सबसे बुद्धिमान प्राणी माना जाता है। उससे यह आशा की जाती है कि वह अपनी बुद्धि का प्रयोग उचित तथा कल्याणकारी योजनाओं के लिए करे। किन्तु अक्सर जाने–अनजाने वह आपत्तियों को स्वयं आमन्त्रित करता है। यह दुर्घटनायें और आपत्तियाँ अक्सर मानव की असावधानी का परिणाम होती हैं तथा इन दुर्घटनाओं से धन–सम्पत्ति के साथ मानव जीवन की भी हानि होती है। जैसे—भोपाल गैस त्रासदी।

(iii) विज्ञान तथा तकनीक के क्षेत्र में इतनी प्रगति हो चुकी है कि जहाँ जीवन सुख और आराम से पूर्ण बन गया है, वहीं दूसरी ओर ऐसे विध्वंसक अस्त्र-शस्त्रों का निर्माण भी हो रहा है जिससे मानवता के अस्तित्व को ही खतरा उत्पन्न हो गया है। एक ओर यदि एक देश अपनी रक्षा की योजनाएँ बना रहा है वहीं दूसरी ओर वह दूसरों के विनाश की तैयारी भी कर रहा है।

(iv) यूनियन कार्बाइड फैक्ट्री भारत के भोपाल नामक शहर में है। इसमें सन् 1983 में गैस रिसाव की भयानक दुर्घटना हुई थी। इस दुर्घटना में सैकड़ों व्यक्ति मारे गए तथा हजारों हमेशा के लिए अपाहिज जैसा जीवन व्यतीत करने को बाध्य हुए।

(v) इसमें सन्देह नहीं है कि वर्तमान युग विज्ञान और तकनीक का युग है। आज विज्ञान और तकनीक ने अनेक उपलब्धियों को हासिल किया है। मानव को अनेक सुख-सुविधाएँ प्रदान करने का श्रेय इसी को है, साथ ही अनेक असाध्य रोगों के उपचार दिये हैं। परन्तु इसके दूसरे पहलू पर विचार करें तो इसने मनुष्य को बारूद के ढेर पर खड़ा कर दिया है। भोपाल गैस त्रासदी से अनेक लोग काल के गाल में समा गये तथा कुछ लोग अपाहिज हो गये। हिरोशिमा और नागासाकी पर बम वर्षा से जन-धन को भारी नुकसान पहुँचा। राष्ट्रों में अस्त्र-शस्त्रों की होड़ दिन-प्रतिदिन बढ़ती जा रही है। इस प्रकार हम कह सकते हैं कि यदि मनुष्य शान्तिपूर्ण ढंग से विज्ञान और तकनीक का उपयोग करे तो वह वरदान है अन्यथा अभिशाप।

गद्यांश-4

'नर' और 'नारी' दोनों परिवार और सामाजिक व्यवस्था के अभिन्न अंग हैं। पुरुष का समाज और परिवार दोनों में प्रमुख स्थान रहा है। 'नारी' को परिवार और समाज में उत्तम दर्जे का नागरिक माना गया है। आरम्भ में नारी को देवी का स्थान, परिवार और समाज में दिया गया था। उस युग में सहधर्मिणी के रूप में उसे सामाजिक, धार्मिक और यहाँ तक कि आर्थिक क्षेत्र में भी पुरुष के समान स्थान प्राप्त था। उसकी उपस्थिति हर कार्य में अनिवार्य थी। यही कारण है कि राजसूय यज्ञ के अवसर पर भगवान् श्रीराम को सीता-माता की स्वर्ण प्रतिमा रखनी पड़ी। महाराज दशरथ अपनी विदुषी महारानी कैकेयी से सलाह लिया करते थे। उस युग में नारी को गृह लक्ष्मी, सहधर्मिणी और काली का अवतार माना जाता था। बाद में उसका स्थान नीचे गिर गया। उसे 'अबला' कहकर पुकारा गया। किन्तु नारी का यह रूप भी चिर स्थायी न रह सका।

वर्तमान में नारी ने जीवन के हर क्षेत्र में पदार्पण कर लिया। आज राजनीति, विज्ञान, कृषि, चिकित्सा यहाँ तक कि अन्तरिक्ष में प्रगति के क्षेत्र में नारी का योगदान उल्लेखनीय रहा है। मारग्रेट थैचर, गोल्डा मायर, मावो भण्डारनायके, पी. टी. उषा तथा 'लौह-महिला' के नाम से विख्यात श्रीमती इन्दिरा गाँधी तथा वर्तमान में सोनिया गाँधी आदि महिलाएँ राजनीति में उल्लेखनीय योगदान कर रही हैं।

वर्तमान युग में तो स्थल, जल तथा वायु सेना की तीनों शाखाओं में नारी का प्रवेश हो गया है। इतना ही नहीं, वर्तमान युग में तो नारी का प्रयोग 'मानव बम' के रूप में भी किया जा रहा है। आज विश्व में चलने वाले सभी आतंकवादी संगठनों के प्रशिक्षण के केन्द्रों में नारी वर्ग का प्रयोग सामान्य रूप में किया जाने लगा। तमिल एलम के नेता प्रभाकरन के संगठन में भी नारी वर्ग का महत्वपूर्ण स्थान है। इस संगठन ने श्रीलंका के रक्षामन्त्री, राष्ट्रपति तथा हमारे पूर्व प्रधानमन्त्री राजीव गाँधी के चिथड़े उड़ा दिये थे। वे इतना अधिक मिल गए थे कि उन्हें श्री गाँधी के जूतों के कारण ही पहचाना जा सका था।

इस प्रकार नारी आज 'अबला' नहीं 'सबला' हो गयी है। वह ममता, त्याग, सेवा और आत्म-बलिदान की मूर्ति नहीं, काली के रूप में प्राण हरने वाली हो गयी है।

प्रश्न : (i) नारी का समाज और परिवार में क्या स्थान था ? इस रूप में परिवर्तन कब और कैसे हुआ ?

(ii) 'अबला' शब्द का अर्थ स्पष्ट करते हुए बताइए कि इस रूप में परिवर्तन कब और क्यों हुआ ?

(iii) 'सबला' शब्द का अर्थ स्पष्ट करते हुए बताइए कि वर्तमान सामाजिक प्रगति में नारी का क्या योगदान रहा है ?

(iv) आतंकवादी संगठन नारी का प्रयोग किस रूप में करते है ? किसी एक उदाहरण द्वारा स्पष्ट कीजिए।

(v) नारी के बारे में आपके क्या विचार हैं ? इंदिरा गाँधी 'लौह-महिला' के नाम से क्यों विख्यात हैं ?

उत्तर : (i) सभ्यता के आदि काल में नारी को 'गृहलक्ष्मी' का सम्मान प्राप्त था। परिवार में उसका स्थान महत्वपूर्ण था। उसे स्वामिनी, सहधर्मिणी, दुर्गा आदि रूप में सम्मान दिया जाता था। समाज और धर्म के प्रत्येक कार्य और अवसर पर वह पुरुष के समान ही भाग लेती थी।
पुरुष के मिथ्या-गर्व तथा क्षुद्र श्रेष्ठता की भावना के कारण नारी का महत्व कम होता चला गया। यह परिवर्तन उत्तर-वैदिक काल के अन्तिम समय से ही आरम्भ हो गया था।

(ii) 'बला' शब्द में 'अ' उपसर्ग जोड़कर इस शब्द की रचना की गयी। इसका अर्थ है शक्ति और बल से रहित। पुरुषों ने नारी के सारे अधिकारों को धीरे-धीरे छीनकर उसे मनोरंजन की सामग्री मात्र बनाकर रख दिया। ऐसा शायद गार्गी द्वारा महर्षि वशिष्ठ की पराजय जैसी घटनाओं के बाद तो अवश्य आरम्भ हो गया था।

(iii) 'सबला' शब्द का अर्थ है—शक्ति एवं साहस से पूर्ण व्यक्तित्व। नारी ने अथक तथा निरन्तर परिश्रम, सेवा, त्याग, साहस तथा सहनशीलता आदि गुणों की सहायता से अपनी स्थिति में सुधार कर लिया है।
वर्तमान सामाजिक प्रगति में नारी का महत्वपूर्ण योगदान है। आज एक बार फिर से नारी ने अपनी सामाजिक स्थिति में क्रान्तिकारी और उल्लेखनीय सुधार किया है। आज वह फिर से अपने उसी पुराने महत्व और सम्मान को प्राप्त करने के प्रयास में दिखाई देती है। आज विभिन्न कार्यालय, विज्ञान, व्यापार, सेना आदि सभी क्षेत्रों में नारी उल्लेखनीय कार्य करते हुए निरन्तर समाज तथा देश की प्रगति में योगदान दे रही है।

(iv) विश्व के सभी आतंकवादी संगठनों द्वारा नारी का प्रयोग 'मानव बम' के रूप में विश्व के महत्वपूर्ण व्यक्तियों की हत्या के कार्य के लिए किया जा रहा है।
उदाहरण के लिए—श्रीलंका के आतंकवादी संगठन 'लिट्टे' ने नारी (मानव बम) के प्रयोग द्वारा अपने राष्ट्रपति, रक्षा मन्त्री तथा हमारे युवा नेता तथा पूर्व प्रधानमन्त्री स्व. राजीव गाँधी की हत्या का घृणित कार्य किया था।

(v) नारी का समाज में महत्वपूर्ण स्थान होना चाहिए। वह नर की सहधर्मिणी है न कि उसकी दासी। उसे पुरुषों के समान अधिकार प्राप्त हों, देश की प्रगति में भागीदार हो, परिवार में आदरणीय स्थान प्राप्त हो। नारी को अबला नहीं समझा जाना चाहिए। उसे भी पुरुषों की तरह युद्ध का अवसर दिया जाये, जिससे वह अपने आपको सबला सिद्ध कर सके।
इंदिरा गाँधी ने महिला होते हुए भी मध्यावधि चुनाव कराना, आपातकाल के अन्तर्गत कड़ाई से शासन करना, बैंकों का राष्ट्रीयकरण जैसे अहम फैसले लिये। इन सब कारणों से इंदिरा गाँधी 'लौह महिला' के नाम से विख्यात हैं।

गद्यांश–5

आजकल देश में विघटनकारी तत्व बढ़ते जा रहे हैं। व्यक्ति, सम्प्रदाय, पार्टी और राज्य देश की महत्वपूर्ण इकाइयाँ हैं। एक तरफ सीमा के भीतर रहकर ये शासन को शक्ति प्रदान करती हैं, किन्तु सीमा के बाहर होने पर ये छोटी-छोटी इकाइयाँ स्वतन्त्रता के नाम पर विघटन को जन्म देती हैं, तोड़-फोड़ को बढ़ावा देती हैं। छोटी इकाइयों की स्वतन्त्रता वहीं तक स्वागत योग्य है जहाँ तक वह पारस्परिक योग में बाधक न हो और संघ की शक्ति को कम न करे। यदि आपसी झगड़ों में देश की शक्ति का ह्रास हो गया तो इन छोटी इकाइयों का

अस्तित्व भी खतरे में पड़ जाएगा। पार्टियों में भी अब गुट बनते जा रहे हैं जो प्राय: व्यक्ति केन्द्रित होते हैं। गुटों की पारस्परिक फूट पार्टी के लिए घातक है और पार्टी की शक्ति का कम होना देश की एकता और समृद्धि के लिए घातक है। देश व्यक्ति, पार्टी, सम्प्रदाय और राज्य सबसे बड़ा है। उसकी रक्षा और समृद्धि में सबकी रक्षा और समृद्धि है।

गणतन्त्र दिवस के इस पावन अवसर पर आज हम देश-हित को सर्वोपरि समझने का प्रयत्न करें। हम कोई ऐसा काम न करें जिससे देश के विघटनकारी तत्वों को पोषण मिले और देश की शक्ति का ह्रास हो। हम अपनी स्वतन्त्रता की रक्षा के लिए प्रयत्नशील रहते हुए देश की स्वतन्त्रता की जी-जान से रक्षा करें। हम विकेन्द्रीकरण की ओर जाएँ किन्तु इतना नहीं कि बेरस्सी के लकड़ी के गट्ठे की तरह बिखर जाएँ।

हम स्वतन्त्र देश के नागरिक होने का गर्व तभी सार्थक कर सकेंगे, जब हम आपस की फूट और वैमनस्य से बच कर देश की समृद्धि, सम्पन्नता एवं सुरक्षा में प्राण-प्रण से योग दें। देश की स्वतन्त्रता के लिए हमें अपनी अबाधित स्वतन्त्रता पर नियन्त्रण करना होगा। स्वतन्त्र देश के नागरिकों की भाँति हम अनुशासन में रहना सीखें, अपने चुने हुए नेता की बात का आदर करें, विपक्ष की बात सावधानी से सुनने को तैयार रहें और देश के हित को पार्टी, जाति, सम्प्रदाय और व्यक्तियों के हित की अपेक्षा अधिक महत्व दें।

प्रश्न : (i) विघटनकारी तत्व किन्हें कहते हैं ? व्यक्ति, पार्टी, सम्प्रदाय और राज्य कब विघटनकारी तत्व का रूप ले लेते हैं ?

(ii) छोटी इकाइयों से लेखक का क्या आशय है ? इनका अस्तित्व भी कब खतरे में पड़ जायेगा ?

(iii) पार्टी से लेखक का अभिप्राय धार्मिक दल है या राजनीतिक दल ? किसी पार्टी की शक्ति को कब धक्का लगता है ? देश और पार्टी में आप किसे बड़ा समझते हैं और क्यों ?

(iv) हमारा गणतन्त्र दिवस कब आता है ? उस दिन हमें क्या प्रण लेना चाहिए ?

(v) स्वतन्त्र देश के नागरिकों का क्या कर्त्तव्य है ? देश के हित में उन्हें क्या करना चाहिए ?

उत्तर : (i) ऐसे तत्व जो किसी न किसी रूप में विघटन और मतभेद फैलाकर देश की शान्ति व्यवस्था को बिगाड़ कर राष्ट्रीय एकता में बाधा डालते हैं। ऐसा ये तत्व तब करते हैं जब व्यक्तिगत स्वतन्त्रता की आड़ लेकर पार्टी में गुट या वर्ग का निर्माण करते हैं। इससे उनकी एकता और संगठन ध्वस्त हो जाता है तथा अनुशासनहीनता का प्रचार होता है।

(ii) व्यक्ति, परिवार, समूह गाँव, नगर आदि से ही लेखक का आशय छोटी इकाइयों से है।
जब इन इकाइयों में स्वार्थ तथा व्यक्तिगत स्वतन्त्रता की आड़ में छोटे-छोटे गुट या वर्गों का निर्माण कर दिया जाता है तो वे व्यक्तिगत स्वार्थों को पूर्ण करने के लिए अनुशासनहीनता तथा अव्यवस्था को जन्म देते हैं। अशान्ति और अस्थिरता की अवस्था में पार्टी का अनुशासन मिट्टी में मिल जाता है।

(iii) पार्टी से लेखक का अर्थ, सामान्य अवस्था में राजनैतिक दल से है। किसी भी पार्टी की शक्ति को तब धक्का लगता है जब उसमें दलगत अनुशासन के स्थान पर व्यक्तिगत स्वार्थ, व्यर्थ का गर्व और शक्ति प्रदर्शन की भावना जन्म लेती है।
हम इन सबमें देश को बड़ा मानते हैं क्योंकि इस पर देश का अस्तित्व एवं सम्मान निर्भर करता है।

(iv) यह दिन 26 जनवरी को मनाया जाता है। इस दिन हमें आपसी मतभेद भुलाकर देश की रक्षा का प्रण लेना चाहिए तथा आवश्यकता होने पर हमें अपने प्राणों का भी बलिदान देने के लिए तत्पर रहना चाहिए क्योंकि देश के सम्मान की रक्षा का दायित्व भी हमारा ही है। हमें इसके लिए ऐसे कार्य का संकल्प लेना चाहिए, जिससे कि हमारे देश का सिर गर्व से ऊँचा हो सके। इसके साथ ही देश की प्रगति के लिए कठोर परिश्रम करने का प्रण भी हमें लेना चाहिए।

(v) स्वतन्त्र देश के नागरिक के रूप में हमारा कर्त्तव्य है कि आपसी मतभेद, शत्रुता, ईर्ष्या, द्वेष तथा स्वार्थ भावना को त्यागकर देश के विकास के लिए कार्य करें।
स्वतन्त्र देश के नागरिकों का कर्त्तव्य है कि वे सभी विरोधी परिस्थितियों का दृढ़ता से सामना करते हुए अपने आत्म-सम्मान की रक्षा करें। देश के सम्मान की रक्षा के लिए उसे अपना सर्वस्व भेंट कर देना चाहिए।
देशहित में नागरिकों को पारस्परिक स्वार्थ तथा मतभेदों को शान्तिपूर्वक बातें करके सुलझाने की कोशिश करनी चाहिए। आवश्यकता पड़ने पर न्याय की रक्षा के लिए हमें अपने प्राणों का बलिदान कर देना चाहिए।

गद्यांश-6

इतिहास पढ़कर हमें यह सीखना चाहिए कि दुनिया ने कैसे आहिस्ता-आहिस्ता , लेकिन निश्चित रूप से तरक्की की है। दुनिया के आरम्भ के सरल जीवों की जगह पर अधिक उन्नत और पेंचीदा जीव कैसे आ गये और कैसे सबसे आखिर, जीवों का सिरताज आदमी पैदा हुआ और अपनी बुद्धि के जोर पर उसने कैसे दूसरों पर विजय पायी। बर्बरता से निकलकर सभ्यता की ओर मनुष्य की प्रगति का हाल इतिहास का विषय माना गया है, लेकिन कभी-कभी जब हम इतिहास के लम्बे जमानों पर नजर डालते हैं, तो यह विश्वास करना मुश्किल होता है कि हम लोग बहुत सभ्य या उन्नत हो गये हैं। सहयोग का अभाव आज भी बहुत ज्यादा पाया जाता है। एक मुल्क या कौम दूसरे मुल्क और दूसरी कौम पर खुदगर्जी से आक्रमण कर रहे हैं या सता रहे हैं; एक आदमी दूसरे आदमी से बेजा फायदा उठा रहा है। अगर करोड़ों बरस की तरक्की के बाद भी हम इतने पिछड़े और अपूर्ण हैं तो न जाने समझदार और वाजिब बात करने वाले आदमियों की तरह व्यवहार करना सीखने में हमें और कितने दिन लग जायेंगे। कभी-कभी हम इतिहास के उन बीते हुए जमानों के बारे में पढ़ते हैं, जो हमारे जमाने से बेहतर मालूम होते हैं और अधिक सुसंस्कृत और सभ्य जान पड़ते हैं। इससे हमें यह शक होने लगता है कि हमारी दुनिया आगे बढ़ रही है या पीछे हट रही है। गुजरे हुए जमाने में खुद हमारे देश में भी ऐसे उज्ज्वल युग जरूर बीते हैं जो हर हालत में वर्तमान से बहुत अच्छे थे।

आजकल बहुत से लोग हमारी महान सफलता और विज्ञान के चमत्कारों की डींग मारते रहते हैं। इसमें शक नहीं कि विज्ञान ने बहुत चमत्कार कर दिया है और बड़े-बड़े वैज्ञानिक हर तरह इज्जत के योग्य हैं, लेकिन जो डींग मारते हैं वे अक्सर बड़े नहीं हुआ करते। दूसरे, यह बात भी याद रखनी चाहिए कि बहुत-सी बातों में कुछ जीव आदमी से अब भी श्रेष्ठ हैं। यह बात बेवकूफी की-सी मालूम पड़ सकती है और जो लोग ज्यादा नहीं जानते, वे इसकी हँसी भी उड़ा सकते हैं, लेकिन अगर आपस के सहयोग को और समाज की भलाई के लिए त्याग को सभ्यता की कसौटी मान लें, तो हम कह सकते हैं कि इस लिहाज से मधुमक्खियाँ और चीटियां मनुष्य जाति से अच्छी हैं।

संस्कृत की हमारी एक पुरानी पुस्तक में एक श्लोक है, जिसका अर्थ है:'कुल के लिए व्यक्ति को, समाज के लिए कुल को, देश के लिए समाज को और आत्मा के लिए सारी दुनिया को छोड़ देना चाहिए।' आत्मा क्या चीज है, इसे हममें से न कोई समझता है और न बता सकता है और हर एक आदमी आत्मा का अर्थ अपने-अपने ख्याल के मुताबिक अलग-अलग किया करता है, लेकिन संस्कृत का यह श्लोक हमें उसी सहयोग की और सार्वजनिक हित के लिए त्याग करने की शिक्षा देता है।

प्रश्न : (i) इतिहास का विषय क्या है ? उससे हमें क्या सीखना चाहिए ?

(ii) क्या देखकर लेखक को शक होने लगता है कि हमारी दुनिया आगे बढ़ रही है या पीछे हट रही है ? इस विषय में आपका क्या मत है ?

(iii) लेखक ने किन जीवों को अब भी मनुष्य जाति से श्रेष्ठ माना है और क्यों ?

(iv) सभ्यता और बर्बरता में क्या अन्तर है ? संस्कृत के श्लोक में किसके लिए क्या त्याग की बात कही है ? उससे हमें क्या शिक्षा मिलती है ?

(v) लेखक के वर्तमान मानव-सभ्यता के बारे में क्या विचार हैं ?

उत्तर : (i) इतिहास का विषय मानव-जीवन के विकास की लम्बी कहानी है। इससे हमें ज्ञात होता है कि मानव ने धीरे-धीरे लेकिन निश्चित रूप से तरक्की की है। आरम्भ के सरल जीवों का स्थान वर्तमान के जटिल जीवों ने लिया है। मानव ने अपनी बुद्धि के बल पर दूसरों पर विजय प्राप्त की।

(ii) इतनी प्रगति तथा विकास के बाद भी मानव सभ्य होने का दावा तो करता है, किन्तु उसे पूर्ण नहीं कर पाता। आज स्वार्थप्रियता तथा पड़ोसी राष्ट्रों की दुर्बलता से लाभ उठाने की भावना के कारण वह सभ्य कहलाने का अधिकारी नहीं है। यह सब कुछ देखकर प्रतीत होता है कि मानव आगे बढ़ने के स्थान पर पीछे हट रहा है।
हमारे विचार में यह मत पूरी तरह सत्य और न्याय की भावना पर आधारित है।

(iii) मधुमक्खियाँ मधु-संग्रह दूसरों के लिए करती हैं तथा त्याग करने का सन्देश देती हैं। चींटियाँ भी एक पंक्ति में चलकर हमें एकता की शिक्षा देती हैं। जबकि मनुष्य अपने स्वार्थ के लिए जीवन-यापन करता है। वह अन्य किसी जीव की भलाई के बारे में नहीं सोचता है। इन कारणों से लेखक के विचार में मधुमक्खियाँ और चींटियों को मानव की तुलना में श्रेष्ठ माना है।

(iv) सभ्यता में मानव आत्म-सम्मान, नैतिकता, न्याय और समानता की भावना पर आधारित व्यवहार करता है। इससे मानवता का विकास होता है तथा मानव देवत्व को प्राप्त करने में सफल होता है। इसके विपरीत जब मानवता, भाईचारे, करुणा और सहानुभूति की भावना का त्याग करके, सभ्यता के विनाश की तैयारी कर ली जाती है, जब मानव के अस्तित्व पर भी प्रश्नचिह्न लग जाता है तब इसे बर्बरता कहा जाता है।

(v) लेखक के अनुसार वर्तमान मानव ने विज्ञान के क्षेत्र में आशातीत प्रगति की है तथा वैज्ञानिक सम्मान के योग्य भी हैं, परन्तु मानव सभ्य बनने में सफल नहीं हो सका है। वह सभ्यता के नाम पर विनाश की ओर बढ़ रहा है। वैज्ञानिक प्रगति के कारण राष्ट्रों में अस्त्र-शस्त्रों की प्रतिस्पर्धा बढ़ रही है। एक मनुष्य दूसरे मनुष्य का शोषण करता है जिससे आपसी सहयोग का अभाव होता जा रहा है।

गद्यांश–7

क्रोध विवेक का शत्रु है, इससे सम्मोह पैदा होता है और सम्मोह से बुद्धि भ्रष्ट होती है। क्रोध के आवेश में व्यक्ति कर्त्तव्याकर्त्तव्य का ज्ञान खो बैठता है, विवेक खो बैठता है।

क्रोध दूषित मनोविकार है। यह मनुष्य के रूप को विकृत कर देता है—शरीर को भयानक बना देता है, शब्दों को कुत्सित कर देता है, आँखों को विकराल बना देता है, चेहरे को आग के समान लाल कर देता है। यह मनुष्यता नहीं पशुता का चिह्न है, वीरता नहीं भीरुता का चिह्न है। यह दूसरों के साथ-साथ स्वयं के लिए भी दु:ख का कारण बनता है।

इतिहास साक्षी है कि क्रोध भीषण रक्तपात और विशाल साम्राज्यों के विनाश का कारण बना। क्रोध के ही वशीभूत होकर जयचन्द ने महाराज पृथ्वीराज को नीचा दिखाने के लिए मौहम्मद गौरी को इस देश पर आक्रमण करने के लिए आमन्त्रित किया। उसके कारण भारत को पराधीनता का मुँह देखना पड़ा। पृथ्वीराज तो मिटा ही, पर जयचन्द भी अपने को न बचा सका। गौरी ने यह कहते हुए कि जो अपनों का न हो सका, वह दूसरों का क्या होगा, उसके भी टुकड़े-टुकड़े कर दिये। कुछ हजार वर्ष और पीछे मुड़ें तो हम पायेंगे कि भारत को सदा-सदा के लिए जर्जरित कर देने वाले महाभारत के युद्ध का कारण भी क्रोध ही था। इन्द्रप्रस्थ में पाण्डवों के नवनिर्मित सभा-भवन के अद्भुत सौन्दर्य को देखकर विस्मित दुर्योधन का सिर द्वार समझकर जैसे ही स्फटिक की दीवार से टकराया तो द्रौपदी संयम खो बैठी और कह उठी—'अन्धे का अन्धा पुत्र।' इन अपमान भरे शब्दों से दुर्योधन का अभिमान आहत हो उठा और यही आगे चलकर महाभारत के युद्ध का कारण बना।

सचमुच क्रोध का भूत बड़ा ही भयंकर होता है। जो व्यक्ति इसके वश में हो जाता है, वह ऐसे-ऐसे अनर्थ कर बैठता है कि आजीवन पछताता है। अत: विवेक को अपनाकर क्रोध के भूत को सदा अपने से दूर रखना चाहिए। अभिमान क्रोध का जनक है। उसे पास न फटकने देना चाहिए। विनम्रता एक ऐसा मानवीय गुण है जिसे अपनाकर मनुष्य क्रोध रूपी दानव के दमन में समर्थ हो सकता है।

प्रश्न : (i) क्रोध का जनक कौन है और क्रोध के आवेश में व्यक्ति क्या खो बैठता है ?

(ii) क्रोध किसका चिह्न है ? क्रोध के आवेश में मनुष्य का क्या रूप हो जाता है ?

(iii) कोई एक उदाहरण देते हुए सिद्ध कीजिए कि क्रोध दूसरों के साथ-साथ अपने लिये भी दु:ख का कारण बनता है।

(iv) अभिमान और विनम्रता में से आप किसे अच्छा समझते हैं और क्यों ?

(v) 'महाभारत के युद्ध का कारण क्रोध था।' आप इस कथन से सहमत हैं या नहीं। समझाइयो।

उत्तर : (i) अविवेक ही क्रोध का जनक तथा विवेक का शत्रु है। क्रोध के प्रभाव से व्यक्ति का विवेक नष्ट हो जाता है। इससे सम्मोह पैदा होता है तथा सम्मोह से व्यक्ति की बुद्धि भ्रष्ट हो जाती है और वह अपना आपा खो बैठता है।

(ii) क्रोध, व्यक्ति के दूषित मनोविकारों का चिह्न तथा परिणाम है। यह मानव के रूप को विकृत कर देता है। शरीर की सुन्दरता को नष्ट करके इसे भयानक बना देता है। शब्द भी कुत्सित हो जाते हैं। आँखे लाल और विकराल हो जाती हैं। संक्षेप में क्रोध मानव को पशु और दानव बना देता है।

(iii) क्रोध एक हानिकारक मनोविकार है। यह दूसरे के साथ अपने आप के लिए भी हानिकारक होता है। हमारा इतिहास इसके प्रमाणों से भरा हुआ है। उदाहरण के लिए, पृथ्वीराज के प्रति क्रोध की भावना के कारण ही जयचन्द ने गजनी के सुल्तान मौहम्मद गौरी को आक्रमण के लिए बुलाया। उसके कारण ही देश को पराधीनता का सामना करना पड़ा। पृथ्वीराज के साथ ही जयचन्द भी नहीं बचा।

(iv) अभिमान और विनम्रता में हम विनम्रता को ही श्रेष्ठ मानते हैं, क्योंकि अभिमान और क्रोध की सहायता से हम दूसरों से दूर हटते जाते हैं, जबकि विनम्रता की सहायता से ही हम दूसरों के मन में अपने लिये सम्मान का भाव जाग्रत कर सकते हैं।

(v) पाण्डवों ने इन्द्रप्रस्थ में एक अद्‌भुत महल का निर्माण किया था। दुर्योधन इस महल के सौन्दर्य को देखकर आश्चर्यचकित हो जाता है। वह स्फटिक की एक दीवार को द्वार समझकर उससे टकरा जाता है। इस पर द्रोपदी उसका उपहास करते हुए कहती है—'अन्धे का पुत्र अन्धा।' इस कथन से दुर्योधन बहुत आहत होता है और इसे अपना अपमान समझकर क्रोधित हो उठता है। यही क्रोध आगे चलकर महाभारत के युद्ध का कारण बनता है। अत: उपर्युक्त कथन सत्य है।

गद्यांश–8

मानव को मानव के रूप में सम्मानित करके ही हम जातीयता, प्रान्तीयता, क्षुद्र राष्ट्रीयता और अन्तर्राष्ट्रीयता के भेद को तोड़ सकते हैं। आज मानव, मानव से दूर हटता जा रहा है। वह भूल चुका है कि देश, धर्म और जाति के भिन्न होते हुए भी हम सर्वप्रथम मानव हैं और समान हैं तथा सभी की भावनाएँ और लक्ष्य एक ही हैं। आज धर्म, सत्ता, धन आदि के भेद होने से एक मानव दूसरे मानव को मानव ही नहीं मानता। कभी-कभी स्वधर्मी विधर्मी को, स्वदेशी विदेशी को, अफसर चपरासी को, धनी निर्धन को तथा विद्वान निरक्षर को इंसान ही नहीं समझता है और भूल जाता है कि दूसरे को भी समान रूप से इच्छानुसार भूख और प्यास सताते हैं तथा उसे भी प्रेम और आदर चाहिए। वह भूल जाता है कि दूसरे में भी स्वाभिमान का पुट है, उसे भी विश्राम की आवश्यकता है और उसे भी अपने बच्चे प्रिय हैं अथवा वह भी अपनी सन्तान के लिए कुछ करना

चाहता है। सत्ताधारी मनुष्य दूसरों को कुचलकर सुख-सुविधाओं पर एकाधिकार कर लेना चाहता है, लेकिन एक आकाश के नीचे रहने वाले इंसान तो सब एक हैं, भले ही कोई कुदाल लेकर श्रमिक का कार्य करता हो, कोई कलम लेकर दफ्तर का, किन्तु लक्ष्य है; समाज का अभ्युदय। कार्यभेद होते हुए भी सब इंसानी बिरादरी के एक से हकदार हैं। सब भाई-भाई ही तो हैं, सब अपने-अपने स्थान पर विशेष हैं। मानव का नाता ही श्रेष्ठ नाता है। नौकर कहकर पुकारना मानो मानवता का अपमान है।

अपराधी को जेल में डालने और फाँसी देने के स्थान पर सुधारशालाओं में रखना चाहिए। उसमें लुप्त मानवता को पुनः जगाना मानवोचित है। जेल और फाँसी का विधान मानवता का कलंक है। दण्ड पशु के लिए है, मानव के लिए नहीं। एक सीमा तक दण्ड भी आवश्यक होता है, लेकिन दण्ड का आतंक समाज को पंगु बना देता है। हमें अपराध वृत्ति का शमन करके अपराधी को शिष्ट एवं सभ्य मानव बनाना चाहिए, किन्तु यह आदर्श स्थिति है और धीरे-धीरे ही इसकी उपलब्धि सम्भव है। दया मानवता का सार है। दया को छोड़कर सत्य भी सत्य नहीं। दया प्रेरित असत्य भी व्यवहारिक सत्य है। दया धर्म मानव धर्म है।

प्रश्न : (i) मानव-मानव समान हैं। फिर आज मानव-मानव से दूर क्यों हटता जा रहा है ? इस दूरी को कैसे मिटाया जा सकता है ?

(ii) धर्म, सत्ता और धन आदि के भेद ने आज मानव को कहाँ तक गिरा दिया है ? हम किस प्रकार कह सकते हैं कि कार्य-भेद होते हुए भी मानव-मानव समान हैं, भाई-भाई हैं ?

(iii) अपराधी के प्रति आज समाज का क्या दृष्टिकोण है ? मानवता की दृष्टि से उसके साथ कैसा व्यवहार होना चाहिए ? अपराधी को दण्ड देने के विषय में आपका अपना क्या मत है ?

(iv) आज का मानव क्या भूल चुका है ? इस भूल का परिणाम क्या हुआ है ?

(v) निम्न पंक्ति का भाव स्पष्ट कीजिए—
'दया प्रेरित असत्य भी व्यवहारिक सत्य है।'

उत्तर : (i) मानव-मानव समान होने पर भी मानव से दूर हटता जा रहा है क्योंकि आज मानव को मानव समझने में धर्म, धन तथा सत्ता और पद की प्रतिष्ठा सबसे बड़ी बाधा के रूप में सामने आ जाती है। इससे एक मनुष्य दूसरे मनुष्य को छोटा समझने लगता है।
इस दूरी को खत्म करने के लिए मानव को मानव से भिन्न तथा दूर करने वाले सभी भेदों को मिटाना होगा। स्थिति ऊँची या नीची होने के भेद को दूर करके उसे मानव का सम्मान देना होगा।

(ii) धर्म, सत्ता, धन के भेद ने मानव को ऊँचे और सम्मानित स्थान से नीचे गिरा दिया है। वह व्यक्तिगत स्वार्थ तथा धन कमाने में इतना नीचे गिर चुका है कि अच्छे बुरे के भेद को भूल चुका है। वह अपने जैसे मानव को मानव नहीं समझता, बल्कि पशु के समान मानता है।
मानव-मानव में कार्य-भेद के अलावा और किसी प्रकार का भेदभाव नहीं है। सभी के विचार समान है। सभी परिवार की शिक्षा तथा उन्नति के लिए कार्य करते हैं। सभी में समान रुप में आत्म-सम्मान की भावना है।

(iii) अपराधी के सम्बन्ध में समाज का दृष्टिकोण कठोर है। समाज छोटे से छोटे अपराध के लिए अपराधी को जेल यातना तथा गम्भीर अपराध की दशा में फाँसी का समर्थन करता है। मानवता की दृष्टि से अपराध की परिस्थितियों पर विचार करने के बाद अपराधी को जेल के स्थान पर सुधारशालाओं में रखा जाना चाहिए।

(iv) आज का मानव यह भूल चुका है कि हम सर्वप्रथम मानव हैं। हमारा देश, धर्म तथा जातिवाद में विश्वास करता है। जिसके कारण मानव अपने को श्रेष्ठ और दूसरे को हीन समझता है। अफसर चपरासी को, धनी निर्धन को तथा विद्वान अनपढ़ को निम्न दर्जे का इंसान समझते हैं। वह दूसरे की भावनाओं का कोई महत्व नहीं समझता है। ऐसे मनुष्य

समझते हैं कि न तो दूसरे को विश्राम की आवश्यकता है, न उसमें स्वाभिमान है और वह अपनी सन्तान के लिए भी कुछ करना नहीं चाहता है।

(v) दया का मानव जीवन में महत्वपूर्ण स्थान है। जिस मानव में दया नहीं है, वह सभ्य मानव कहलाने का अधिकारी नहीं है। यदि हम ऐसा असत्य भी बोलते हैं जो दया की भावना से पूर्ण हो तो वह भी मान्य है। दया की भवना को अपराधी में उत्पन्न करके, उसे शिष्ट एवं सभ्य बनाया जा सकता है। यदि हमारे मन में दूसरे के प्रति दया की भावना होगी तो हम कभी दूसरों का अहित नहीं करेंगे और इस प्रकार हम कह सकते हैं कि दया प्रेरित असत्य भी व्यवहारिक सत्य है।

गद्यांश–9

सम्राट अशोक के मन में कलिंग का पतन और अपनी विजय का परिणाम देखने की इच्छा का उत्पन्न होना स्वाभाविक था। अशोक अपनी सेना के अधिकारियों के साथ युद्धभूमि में गया। जहाँ तक दृष्टि जाती थी, मृतक सैनिकों के शव, कठिनाई से साँस लेते हुए, कराहते हुए हताहत सैनिकों का करुण चीत्कार, शवों पर मण्डराते हुए गिद्धों, श्वानों और शृंगालों का समूह, अपने प्रियजनों के वियोग में करुण विलाप करते हुए बालक-बालिकाएँ, महिलाएँ और अभिशप्त से वृद्धजन दृष्टिगत होते थे।

यह सब देखकर अशोक का कठोर हृदय भी करुणा से द्रवित हो गया और मन आत्म-ग्लानि से भर उठा। महान अनर्थकारी इस युद्ध का उसके जीवन पर गहरा प्रभाव पड़ा। उसने अनुभव किया कि इतने लोगों का सुख छीनकर उसने जो विजय प्राप्त की है, वह तो पराजय से भी बुरी है। इतनी हत्याएँ, जन-धन का इतना विनाश किसलिये ? क्या केवल इसलिये कि एक सम्राट की साम्राज्य लिप्सा पूरी हो सके ? इस चिन्तन से सम्राट अशोक का हृदय मानवता के प्रति करुणा से भर उठा और उसने अपने अब तक के नृशंस कार्यों के लिए प्रायश्चित करने का संकल्प किया।

बस, इतिहास उसी अशोक को आज भी श्रद्धा और सम्मान से याद करता है, जिसके मन में प्राणीमात्र के लिए करुणा का स्रोत प्रवाहित होता था, जो दूसरों को दु:ख देकर अपना सुख नहीं चाहता था अपितु स्वयं कष्ट सहकर दूसरों को सुखी देखने में सुख का अनुभव करता था। कलिंग का भयावह युद्ध उसके हृदय-परिवर्तन का कारण बना। उसने प्रण किया, "मैं साम्राज्य के विस्तार के लिए अब कभी शस्त्र न उठाऊँगा। भविष्य में मेरी विजय यात्रा 'शस्त्र विजय' के लिए न होकर 'धर्मविजय' के लिए होगी।" विचारों की इस क्रान्ति ने अशोक को हिंसा के छोर से उठाकर अहिंसा के छोर पर लाकर खड़ा कर दिया। उसने महात्मा बुद्ध के परम शिष्य उपगुप्त से बौद्धधर्म की दीक्षा ली और प्रजारंजन में लग गया। पथिकों की सुविधा के लिए उसने सड़कें और विश्राम गृह बनवाये, उद्यान लगवाये, कुएँ और बावड़ियाँ बनवायी, शिक्षार्थ तक्षशिला और नालन्दा जैसे विश्वविद्यालयों की स्थापना की और अपना शेष जीवन देश और विदेशों में बौद्ध धर्म के प्रचार और प्रसार में लगा दिया।

प्रश्न : (i) सम्राट अशोक कहाँ के शासक थे ? उन्होंने कलिंग पर आक्रमण किस उद्देश्य से किया ? कलिंग युद्ध से उनके मन में युद्ध के प्रति घृणा क्यों उत्पन्न हो गयी ?

(ii) कलिंग अब किस नाम से पुकारा जाता है ? कलिंग युद्ध के अनन्तर अशोक ने क्या अनुभव किया ?

(iii) कलिंग का युद्ध सम्राट अशोक के जीवन की महत्वपूर्ण घटना है। इसने उनका हृदय-परिवर्तन कर दिया, विचारों में क्रान्ति ला दी। कैसे ?

(iv) आचार्य उपगुप्त कौन थे ? उन्होंने सम्राट अशोक को किस धर्म की दीक्षा दी ? दीक्षा का उनके जीवन पर क्या प्रभाव पड़ा ?

(v) युद्ध के बारे में आपके क्या विचार हैं ?

उत्तर : (i) अशोक मगध सहित उत्तर भारत के एक बड़े भू-भाग के शासक थे। उन्होंने कलिंग पर अधिकार प्राप्ति तथा उसे अपने राज्य का एक भाग बनाने के उद्देश्य से आक्रमण किया था।

कलिंग युद्ध से अशोक के मन में युद्ध के प्रति घृणा उत्पन्न हो गयी, क्योंकि उस युद्ध में लाखों व्यक्ति शहीद हुए तथा इतने ही आहत और बन्दी हुए। अशोक ने सोचा कि इतने विनाश के बाद प्राप्त विजय से कोई लाभ या आत्म-शान्ति नहीं मिलती है।

(ii) यह प्रदेश अब उड़ीसा के नाम से पुकारा जाता है। कलिंग युद्ध के बाद अशोक ने अनुभव किया कि इतने लोगों की हत्या तथा सुख-चैन छीनकर उसने जो विजय प्राप्त की है, वह पराजय से भी बुरी है। इतनी हत्या और विनाश क्या केवल साम्राज्य बढ़ाने का लालच पूर्ण करने के लिए है।

(iii) कलिंग का युद्ध सम्राट अशोक के जीवन की महत्वपूर्ण घटना है। क्योंकि इसी युद्ध में हुए विनाश तथा हत्या को देखकर अशोक का हृदय परिवर्तित हो गया। उसे युद्ध से घृणा हो गयी। अशोक ने भविष्य में युद्ध न करने का निश्चय किया तथा साथ ही बौद्ध धर्म अपनाकर करुणा, प्रेम, सहानुभूति और प्राणीमात्र की सेवा का व्रत लिया।

(iv) आचार्य उपगुप्त महान विचारक, विद्वान एवं गौतम बुद्ध के प्रिय शिष्य थे। उन्होंने बुद्ध विचारों के प्रचार के लिए अपना जीवन अर्पित कर दिया।
उपगुप्त ने सम्राट अशोक को बौद्धधर्म की दीक्षा दी। शिक्षा के साथ ही सम्राट ने अपने आपको प्रजा के कल्याण कार्यों में लगा दिया। उसने पथिकों की सेवा के लिए विश्राम-गृह तथा उद्यान लगाने का कार्य किया। जल की सुविधा के लिए बावड़ियों को बनवाया तथा शिक्षा प्रचार के लिए तक्षशिला और नालन्दा जैसे विश्वविद्यालय बनवाये।

(v) किसी भी युद्ध का परिणाम दु:खद एवं विनाशकारी ही होता है। युद्ध से जन-धन की भयंकर क्षति होती है। निरीह, निर्दोष लोग मारे जाते हैं, बालक अनाथ हो जाते हैं, महिलाएँ विधवा हो जाती हैं, वृद्धजन असहाय हो जाते हैं। सैनिकों के परिवार में रोजी-रोटी का संकट उत्पन्न हो जाता है। अत: मात्र साम्राज्य विस्तार के लिए युद्ध उचित नहीं हैं। परन्तु कोई आक्रमणकारी अपने स्वार्थ के लिए किसी अन्य पर आक्रमण करता है, तब युद्ध करना आवश्यक हो जाता है, अन्यथा अधर्म और अत्याचार बढ़ते जायेंगे।

गद्यांश–10

आज का कार्यक्षेत्र कठिन है, विविध है, निश्चित नहीं है। हमारा वर्तमान समाज जाति-उपजाति, समता-विषमता में विभाजित है। हमारा धर्म अन्ध-विश्वास से ग्रसित है। हमारी राजनीति स्वार्थ में विभाजित है। हम केवल विभाजित ही विभाजित हैं। तब भी मैं यह विश्वास करती हूँ कि किसी युग का सबसे बड़ा निर्माण उसका विद्यार्थी है। किसी युग का सबसे बड़ा बसन्त उसका तारुण्य है, उसकी नई पीढ़ी है। जब वह पराजित होती है तो सब कुछ पराजित हो जाता है, सब कुछ व्यर्थ हो जाता है। यदि आप निराश हो, आप कहें कि समाज में हमारा स्थान नहीं है, कर्मक्षेत्र में हमारा स्थान नहीं है, राजनीति में हमारा कोई स्थान नहीं है, तो मैं आपको यही उत्तर दूँगी कि आप स्थान बनाइए। कोई नदी जो हिमालय के हृदय से निकलती है, चाहे बड़ी या छोटी धारा में निकले, शिलाओं से मार्ग नहीं माँगती। क्या उसने कभी कहा है कि घाट बनाइए, संगमरमर के, चाँदी या सोने के ? उसने यह कभी नहीं कहा है। वह शिलाओं को पार करती हुई अपने उच्छल वेग में सब कुछ पार करती हुई आगे बढ़ती है और उसका नियम है कि तट वह स्वयं बनाती है। इसी प्रकार प्रत्येक पीढ़ी अपना मार्ग आप बनाती है। लेकिन अपनी मर्यादा भी आप बताती है। जो नदी समुद्र से हिमालय को जोड़ती है वह नदी मर्यादा भी बनाती है, वह नदी तट भी बनाती है, तट उसे बने बनाए नहीं मिलते।

माना, आज का युग घोर वैज्ञानिक युग है। लेकिन मैं आपसे पूछती हूँ कि कोई आपसे कहे कि गौरी शंकर शिखर को हमें डायनामाइट से उड़ा देने दीजिए, हम आपको चन्द्रमा में स्थान दे देंगे। क्या आप स्वीकार करेंगे ? कोई आपसे कहे कि गंगा-यमुना दे दीजिए, हम आपको मंगल ग्रह तक पहुँचाते हैं, आप नहीं राजी होंगे, नहीं होंगे, नहीं होंगे। उसका कारण है आप इस धरती से बने हैं, इसके साथ आपकी आत्मा का सम्बन्ध

है। इसका एक कण भी आप नहीं दे सकते। न हिमालय दे सकेंगे, न गंगा-यमुना, न यह हरी-भरी धरती दे सकेंगे। संसार में इतना सुन्दर देश दूसरा नहीं है। जिन्होंने बाहर जाकर देखा है वे भी यहीं कहेंगे कि वास्तव में ऐसी हरी-भरी भूमि कहीं-नहीं जिसमें तुषार मण्डित हिमालय भी है, जिसमें सूर्य की किरणें केसर के फूलों की तरह शोभा बरसाती हैं, जिसके कण्ठ में गंगा-यमुना जैसी नदियों की माला पड़ी है, जिसके चरण सागर धोता है। कितनी हरी-भरी, कितनी सम-विषम, सुजला-सुफला है भारत की यह धरती!

प्रश्न : (i) क्या देखकर लेखिका खिन्न है ? वह किसकी ओर आशाभरी दृष्टि से देखती है तथा क्यों ?

(ii) नई पीढ़ी से लेखिका का क्या अभिप्राय है ? उसके लिए उसका क्या सन्देश है ? नदी से नई पीढ़ी को क्या प्रेरणा लेनी चाहिए।

(iii) भारत भूमि को लेखिका ने अनुपम क्यों कहा है ? उससे हमारा स्वाभाविक प्रेम क्यों है ?

(iv) निम्न पंक्ति का आशय स्पष्ट कीजिए—

'आज का कार्यक्षेत्र कठिन है, विविध है, निश्चित नहीं है।'

(v) उपर्युक्त गद्यांश के आधार पर भारत-भूमि के प्राकृतिक सौन्दर्य का वर्णन कीजिए।

उत्तर : (i) समाज के हर क्षेत्र में विभाजन तथा भेदभाव और मनुष्य द्वारा मनुष्य के शोषण को देखकर लेखिका खिन्न है।

वह देश के युवा वर्ग की ओर आशा भरी दृष्टि से देखती है, क्योंकि विद्यार्थी युवा है। उसमें असीमित वीरता, साहस, सहनशीलता और आत्म-विश्वास आदि गुण हैं जिनकी सहायता से वह समाज और राष्ट्र के सामने उपस्थित चुनौतियों का सामना करने में सफल होगा।

(ii) नयी पीढ़ी से लेखिका का अर्थ किसी राष्ट्र और समाज का युवा विद्यार्थी है। उनके लिए लेखिका का सन्देश है कि वे समाज से माँगने के स्थान पर शक्ति, साहस, परिश्रम और सहनशीलता आदि गुणों की सहायता से अपने स्थान तथा लक्ष्य को प्राप्त करें।

जिस प्रकार नदी अपने लिए मार्ग और सुन्दर घाट बनाने की किसी से प्रार्थना नहीं करती बल्कि खुद अपने मार्ग का निर्माण करती है, उसी प्रकार युवा पीढ़ी को भी समाज और राजनीति में अपना स्थान बनाना चाहिए।

(iii) भारत भूमि को लेखिका ने अनुपम कहा है क्योंकि यहाँ की भूमि, मिट्टी, नदी, झरने तथा तालाबों, प्रकृति के सुन्दर दृश्यों से हमें हृदय और आत्मा से प्रेम और लगाव है। यह स्वाभाविक लगाव इसलिए है क्योंकि यहाँ हमने जन्म लिया है। यहाँ कि मिट्टी, हवा और पानी से हमारा शरीर बना है।

(iv) आज हमारा समाज अनेक वर्गों में विभाजित हो गया है। राष्ट्रीयता के स्थान पर क्षेत्रीयता की भावना प्रबल होती जा रही है। जाति, धर्म, भाषा आदि के नाम पर लोगों ने समाज को बाँट दिया है। वे यह भूल गये हैं कि सर्वप्रथम एक मनुष्य है, जाति, धर्म, भाषा आदि बाद में हैं। हमारे नीति-नियन्ता अपना स्वार्थ सिद्ध करने में लिप्त हैं। आज का युवा निराशा एवं अवसाद से ग्रसित है। वह ऐसा जीवन चाहता है जिसमें वह दूसरों पर निर्भर हो, स्वयं कुछ करना नहीं चाहता।

(v) भारतभूमि का प्राकृतिक सौन्दर्य अद्‌भुत है। यहाँ प्राकृतिक विविधता है। कहीं अधिक वर्षा होती है तो कहीं बहुत कम वर्षा। कहीं बहुत गर्मी है तो कहीं बहुत ठण्ड। वन, नदी, झील, झरने, सागर, पर्वत, पठार सभी की शोभा मनोहारी है। इसमें पर्वतराज हिमालय है, जो सूर्य की किरणें पड़ने पर केसर के पुष्प की तरह शोभा बिखेरता है। गंगा-यमुना जैसी पवित्र नदियाँ भी हैं।

गद्यांश–11

प्रकृति के विभिन्न स्वरूपों और रूप चेष्टाओं का प्रभाव मनुष्य पर पड़ता है और वे ही उसके अभिव्यंजना के विषय बनते हैं तथा उसके मन में भाव उत्पन्न करते हैं। मनुष्य प्रकृति के नाना स्वरूपों को देखता है उसके रूप–लावण्य से मुग्ध हो जाता है और उसमें भावों का उद्रेक होता है। इन्हीं भावों को वह अभिव्यक्त करने का प्रयास करता है और कला का जन्म होता है। इस दृष्टि से कला और प्रकृति का घनिष्ठ सम्बन्ध प्रकट होता है। प्रकृति के कुछ चित्र अपनी विशेषताओं के कारण अथवा मनुष्य की अभिरुचि के कारण उसे अपनी ओर आकृष्ट करते हैं और उसके मन में अंकित हो जाते हैं। मनुष्य उन्हीं चित्रों को कलाओं के द्वारा अभिव्यक्त करता है। आदिकाल से मनुष्य प्रकृति की ओर आकृष्ट होता आया है। क्योंकि उससे उसकी वासनाओं की तृप्ति होती है। इस नैसर्गिक आकर्षण का परिणाम यह होता है कि मनुष्य प्रकृति के उन चित्रों को अपने हृदय के रस से सिक्त कर अभिव्यक्त करता है और वे ही भिन्न–भिन्न कलाओं के रूप में इसके हृदय को रसान्वित करते हैं। भारतीय साहित्य में इसे 'रस' कहते हैं। साहित्य के साथ ही साथ अन्य कलाओं से भी इसकी निष्पत्ति होती है। प्राकृतिक दृश्य को देखकर कलाकार के हृदय में भावना का उदय होता है। वह यदि उस भावना की तीव्रता अथवा स्थायित्व को वास्तविकता के साथ व्यक्त करने में समर्थ हो, तो उस अभिव्यक्ति से दर्शक, श्रोता अथवा पाठक समाज को भी उतनी तृप्ति हो सकती है, जितनी कलाकार की हुई थी जबकि उसका उस प्राकृतिक दृश्य के साथ साक्षात्कार हुआ था। कलाकार हृदय के माध्यम से साधारण जनता को प्रभावित करता है। वह जितना अधिक हृदय साम्य स्थापित कर सकेगा उतना ही सफल कलाकार माना जाएगा। कलाकार की अन्तरात्मा का सच्चा भाव उसकी कला वस्तु में निहित होता है। सहृदय पाठक को वही भाव रसान्वित करने में समर्थ होता है। यदि कलाकार का जीवन–सम्बन्धी अथवा जगत् सम्बन्धी अनुभव सच्चा न हो तो वह उन्हें रीति से व्यक्त करने में समर्थ नहीं हो सकता और उसकी अभिव्यक्ति दोषपूर्ण होती है—सशक्त नहीं होती और मानव समाज उसकी कृति से तृप्ति अनुभव नहीं करता। यही कलाकार की असफलता है।

प्रश्न : (i) मनुष्य प्रकृति के किन–किन चित्रों को अभिव्यक्त करता है ? कला और प्रकृति का घनिष्ठ सम्बन्ध कैसे है ?

(ii) मनुष्य प्रकृति की ओर आकृष्ट होता है ? उसका परिणाम क्या होता है ?

(iii) 'हृदय साम्य' क्या है ? वह कैसे स्थापित होता है ?

(iv) कलाकार की असफलता के क्या कारण हैं ? स्पष्ट कीजिए।

(v) आदर्श समाज के निर्माण में कलाकार का क्या योगदान है ?

उत्तर : (i) मनुष्य प्रकृति के विभिन्न स्वरूपों और रूप चेष्टाओं को अपनी रचनाओं में अभिव्यक्त करता है। मनुष्य प्रकृति के रूप लावण्य से मुग्ध हो जाता है और उसमें भावों का उद्रेक होता है इन्हीं भावों को अभिव्यक्त करने का प्रयास करता है, इस प्रकार कला का जन्म होता है। इस दृष्टि से कला और प्रकृति में घनिष्ठ सम्बन्ध है।

मनुष्य उन्हीं चित्रों को कलाओं द्वारा अभिव्यक्ति करता है जिससे उसकी वासनाओं की तृप्ति होती हैं। वे चित्र मानव हृदय को रसान्वित करते हैं।

(ii) प्रकृति की विशेषताओं तथा मनुष्य अपनी अभिरुचि के कारण प्रकृति की ओर आकृष्ट होता है। इससे उसकी वासनाओं की तृप्ति होती है। मनुष्य के स्मृति–पटल पर प्रकृति के चित्र अंकित हो जाते हैं और वह उन चित्रों को अपने हृदय के रस से सिक्त कर अभिव्यक्त करता है और वे ही भिन्न–भिन्न कलाओं के रूप में इसके हृदय को रसान्वित करते हैं।

(iii) "मन से समान होने का भाव।" प्राकृतिक दृश्य को देखकर कलाकार के हृदय में भावना का उदय होता है वह यदि उस भावना की तीव्रता अथवा स्थायित्व को वास्तविकता के साथ व्यक्त करने में समर्थ हो तो उस अभिव्यक्ति से दर्शक, श्रोता अथवा पाठक समाज को

भी उतनी ही तृप्ति हो सकती है जितनी कलाकार को हुई थी। कलाकार हृदय के माध्यम से साधारण जनता को प्रभावित करता है। वह जितना अधिक हृदय साम्य कर सकेगा उतना ही बड़ा कलाकार माना जायेगा।

(iv) यदि कलाकार का जीवन सम्बन्धी अनुभव सच्चा न हो तो वह अपने भावों को उचित रीति से व्यक्त करने में समर्थ नहीं होता। उसकी अभिव्यक्ति सशक्त नहीं होती। मानव समाज उसकी कृति से तृप्ति प्राप्त नहीं करता। यही कलाकार की असफलता है।

(v) कलाकार अपनी कला के माध्यम से समाज की कुरीतियों, बुराइयों, अन्धविश्वासों को सभी के समक्ष उजागर करता है और उनके समाधान का भी प्रयास करता है। वह अपनी रचना में उन अनुभवों को व्यक्त करता है, जिनका वह स्वयं साक्षात्कार करता है। इससे पाठक, श्रोता या दर्शक की भावनाओं की तृप्ति होती है, ज्ञान प्राप्त होता है, नैतिक शिक्षा मिलती है तथा साथ ही मनोरंजन होता है। इस प्रकार एक आदर्श समाज के निर्माण में कलाकार का महत्वपूर्ण योगदान है।

गद्यांश–12

ज्ञान-प्राप्ति के अनन्तर महात्मा बुद्ध ने अपना उपदेश सारनाथ में दिया। उसमें उन्होंने कहा—"जीवन के दो मार्ग हैं। एक मार्ग पर चलकर लोग सुख-साधनों को जुटाते हैं और भोगों से लिपटे रहते हैं। यह जीवन को सुखी नहीं बनाता। दूसरा मार्ग त्याग का है, तपस्या का है। इस पर चलकर लोग शरीर को कठोर यातनाएँ देकर भी अपने आपको सुखी नहीं बना पाते। अत: ज्ञान-प्राप्ति के लिए, मानसिक सुख-शान्ति के लिए बीच का मार्ग ही श्रेयस्कर है। बुद्ध का यही सिद्धान्त मध्यम-मार्ग के नाम से प्रसिद्ध है। कहते हैं कि महात्मा बुद्ध जहाँ बोधिवृक्ष के नीचे ध्यान-मग्न बैठे थे, उस मार्ग से एक भजन-मण्डली जा रही थी। गीत की स्वर-लहरी वातावरण को गुंजित कर रही थी। सहसा समाधिस्थ बुद्ध के कानों में गायिका के गीत के मधुर स्वर गूँज उठे—'वीणा के तारों को ढीला न छोड़ो, नहीं तो उससे मधुर स्वर नहीं निकलेगा और न उन्हें इतना कसो कि वे टूट ही जाएँ।' इन शब्दों से बुद्ध को मध्यम-मार्ग की प्रेरणा मिली। उन्होंने अनुभव किया कि न तो भोगों से पूर्णतया तृप्ति हो सकती है और न भोगों को पूर्णरूप से त्याग जा सकता है। अत: जीवन के लिए भोग और त्याग के बीच का मार्ग ही श्रेयस्कर है।

महात्मा बुद्ध का चिन्तन सरल और स्वाभाविक था। उनके मत में ऊँच-नीच का भेदभाव न था। राजा से लेकर रंक तक उनके लिए समान थे। उन्होंने धर्म के बाह्यडम्बरों की अपेक्षा आन्तरिक शुद्धि पर बल दिया। यज्ञ में दी जाने वाली पशुबलि का उन्होंने विरोध किया। जन-साधारण की भाषा में उन्होंने अहिंसा और प्रेम का जो उपदेश दिया उसने जादू का काम किया और देखते ही देखते लाखों नर-नारी उनके अनुयायी बन गये। पैंतालीस वर्षों तक उन्होंने घूम-घूमकर अपने अमृतमय उपदेशों से जन-कल्याण किया।

महात्मा बुद्ध जीवन के अस्सी वर्ष पार कर चुके थे। शरीर दिन पर दिन क्षीण होता जा रहा था। अन्त में उन्होंने कुशीनगर की ओर प्रस्थान किया। कुशीनगर पहुँचते-पहुँचते उनका शरीर निढाल हो गया। उनके प्रिय-शिष्य भिक्षु आनन्द ने उनके लिए शय्या तैयार की। वह उस पर लेट गये। शिथिलता बढ़ती जा रही थी। निर्वाण की घड़ियाँ आ पहुँची थीं। यह देख आनन्द की आँखों से आँसू फूट पड़े। बोले—"देव! अब हमारा मार्गदर्शन कौन करेगा ?" बुद्ध ने आँखें खोली। बोले—"आनन्द! तुम्हारे सामने विशाल कर्म-क्षेत्र है। जरा, रोग और मृत्यु से त्रस्त मानवता को अहिंसा और प्रेम का मार्ग दिखाओ। क्यों भूलते हो संसार नश्वर है। जन्म के बाद मृत्यु और मृत्यु के बाद जन्म प्रकृति का अटल नियम है। रही मार्ग-दर्शन की बात। कौन किसका मार्ग-दर्शन करता है ? कौन किसका मार्ग-दर्शन कर सकता है ? अप्प दीपो भव—अपना दीपक आप बनो।" यह कहते हुए तथागत सदा के लिए समाधिस्थ हो गये। वातावरण शोक से भर गया। तथागत के निष्पन्द पार्थिव शरीर के चारों ओर खड़े भिक्षु आँसू बहा रहे थे। रह-रहकर उनके कानों में तथागत के शब्द गूँज रहे थे—"भिक्षुओं! मुझ पर विश्वास मत करना। मैं जो कहता हूँ उस पर भी इसलिए विश्वास मत करना कि मैंने कहा है। सोचना, विचारना और अपने अनुभव की कसौटी पर जो खरा उतरे वही करना।"

प्रश्न : (i) मध्यम-मार्ग से आप क्या समझते हैं ? महात्मा बुद्ध को मध्यम-मार्ग की प्रेरणा कैसे मिली ?

(ii) महात्मा बुद्ध के मत की क्या विशेषताएँ थीं कि देखते ही देखते लाखों नर-नारी उनके अनुयायी बन गये ?

(iii) महात्मा बुद्ध ने शोकाकुल भिक्षु को क्या उपदेश दिया ? इससे हमें क्या शिक्षा मिलती है ?

(iv) महात्मा बुद्ध के निष्पन्द पार्थिव शरीर के चारों ओर खड़े शोकाकुल भिक्षुओं के कानों में क्या शब्द गूँज रहे थे ? इनसे क्या प्रेरणा मिलती है ?

(v) महात्मा बुद्ध के जीवन के अन्तिम समय का वर्णन कीजिए।

उत्तर : (i) जीवन में प्रथम मार्ग है, भोग का। इस मार्ग पर चलकर मानव स्वयं अधिक से अधिक भोगों का आनन्द लेकर जीवन सुख और आराम से व्यतीत कर सकता है। दूसरा मार्ग है—त्याग और आत्म-संयम का। इस मार्ग पर चलकर मानव त्याग और तपस्या से पूर्ण कठोर जीवन व्यतीत करता है। इन दोनों के मध्य का, आत्म-संयम और निष्ठा से पूर्ण जीवन ही मध्यम मार्ग है।

इस मार्ग की प्रेरणा महात्मा बुद्ध को बोधिवृक्ष के नीचे बैठे हुए, भजन-मण्डली की संगीत-स्वर लहरी को सुनकर प्राप्त हुई।

(ii) उनके मत की विशेषतायें निम्नलिखित थीं, जिनके कारण लाखों नर-नारी उनके अनुयायी बन गये—

(a) उनका चिन्तन सरल और स्वाभाविक था।

(b) समानता को अधिक महत्व दिया था।

(c) बाह्याडम्बरों की अपेक्षा आन्तरिक शुद्धि पर बल दिया।

(d) जनभाषा को अपनाया।

(e) अहिंसा और प्रेम पर जोर दिया।

(iii) गौतम बुद्ध ने शोकाकुल भिक्षु को उपदेश देते हुए कहा कि वह जन्म और मृत्यु से ग्रस्त मानवता को अहिंसा ओर प्रेम का मार्ग दिखाये। जन्म और मृत्यु प्रकृति के अटल नियम हैं। उसे अपना दीपक स्वयं बनना चाहिए। इससे हमें अपना मार्ग स्वयं दर्शन करने की शिक्षा मिलती है। इसके लिए प्राप्त ज्ञान एवं अनुभव का महत्वपूर्ण स्थान है।

(iv) पार्थिव शरीर के चारों ओर खड़े भिक्षुओं के कानों में तथागत के शब्द गूँज रहे थे कि भिक्षुओं को उन (तथागत) पर अन्धे के समान विश्वास न करके अपने ज्ञान और अनुभव के आधार पर निर्णय लेने पर विचार करना चाहिए।

इनसे हमें प्रेरणा मिलती है कि किसी का भी अन्धभक्त होने के स्थान पर आत्म-चिन्तन, आत्म-ज्ञान और अनुभव पर विश्वास करके ही कदम उठाना चाहिए।

(v) महात्मा बुद्ध पैंतालीस वर्ष तक घूम-घूमकर धर्म का उपदेश देते रहे। अब वे अस्सी वर्ष से ऊपर के हो गये थे। उनका शरीर दिन-प्रतिदिन क्षीण होता जा रहा था। वे अन्तिम समय में कुशीनगर पहुँच गये। यहाँ आकर उनका शरीर पूर्णरूप से निशक्त हो गया। भिक्षु आनन्द ने उनके लिए शय्या तैयार की और वह उस पर लेट गये। आनन्द ने दु:खी होकर उनसे पूछा कि हमारा मार्गदर्शन अब कौन करेगा, तो इस पर उन्होंने कहा कि स्वयं अपना मार्गदर्शन करो। ऐसा कहकर वे सदा के लिए समाधिस्थ हो गये।

गद्यांश–13

किसी राष्ट्र में क्रान्ति का सूत्रपात नवयुवक ही करते हैं। वह क्रान्ति सामाजिक और राजनैतिक किसी भी क्षेत्र में हो सकती है। भारतीय स्वतन्त्रता के इतिहास के अध्ययन से भी यह स्पष्ट हो चुका है कि स्वतन्त्रता प्राप्ति के पावन उद्देश्य की प्राप्ति के लिए आगे बढ़कर कष्ट सहने में भी युवकों का योगदान उल्लेखनीय था। गाँधी जी ने भी बिखरी हुई युवा शक्ति को संगठित कर उनमें राष्ट्रभक्ति एवं आत्म बलिदान की भावना को भर दिया था। गाँधी के इसी सफल उद्देश्य से प्रेरणा पाकर लगभग सभी राजनैतिक दलों ने युवा शाखा का गठन करके युवकों को स्थान दिया है। इसी भावना और युवा शक्ति को महत्व देकर उनके मन में आकर्षण की भावना को जन्म देने के उद्देश्य से पूर्व युवा प्रधानमन्त्री राजीव गाँधी ने मताधिकार की उम्र को 21 वर्ष से कम करके 18 वर्ष कर दिया। इसी वर्ग ने अवसर पाकर काँग्रेस को पराजित कराने में महत्वपूर्ण योगदान कर दिया।

युवा वर्ग की इस असीमित बिखरी शक्ति को संगठित उसे उचित मार्गदर्शन की जितनी आवश्यकता आज है उतनी कभी नहीं थी। तूफानी शक्ति एवं संसाधनों वाले इस युवा वर्ग की कोमल भावनाओं को भड़काकर अक्सर राजनैतिक दल और राजनीतिज्ञ अपनी स्वार्थसिद्धि के लिए प्रयोग करते दृष्टिगोचर होते हैं। यही कारण है कि वर्तमान में युवा वर्ग इन दलों की कठपुतली बनकर रह गया है। आज वह पूर्णत: लक्ष्य-भ्रष्ट हो चुका है। यही कारण है कि वह अपनी शक्ति का प्रयोग विध्वंसकारी कार्यों में कर रहा है। कक्षाओं से भागकर मुफ्त में सिनेमा देखना, परीक्षा में नकल करना तथा रोके जाने पर हड़ताल, तोड़-फोड़ आदि के द्वारा विनाश कर देने की सूचना प्राय: समाचार-पत्रों द्वारा अक्सर हमें प्राप्त होती है। आज तो वह नशे का शिकार बनकर रह गया है। भाँग, चरस, गाँजा तथा अफीम जैसे नशे का शिकार हो चुका है। अब समय आ गया है जब युवा वर्ग का सही मार्गदर्शन किया जाना चाहिए।

प्रश्न : (i) किसी भी राष्ट्र की मुख्य शक्ति से क्या आशय है ? उसे क्रान्ति उद्‌गम क्यों कहा गया है ? स्पष्ट कीजिए।

(ii) राष्ट्रीय स्वतन्त्रता के आन्दोलन में युवकों को किस महापुरुष ने क्या प्रेरणा दी तथा इसका क्या परिणाम हुआ ?

(iii) वर्तमान राजनीति में युवकों का क्या योगदान है ? राष्ट्र में क्रान्ति लाने में युवक कहाँ तक और क्या सहयोग दे सकते हैं ? स्पष्ट कीजिए।

(iv) वर्तमान युवा वर्ग में निराशा का क्या कारण है ? वे दिशाहीन क्यों हो रहे हैं ? इसका क्या परिणाम हुआ है ?

(v) आज का युवा वर्ग नशे का शिकार क्यों है ? वह किस प्रकार के पदार्थों से नशा करता है ? इस समस्या से मुक्त होने का क्या उपाय है ?

उत्तर : (i) किसी भी राष्ट्र की मुख्य शक्ति से अर्थ है—उसकी युवा शक्ति, उसका युवा वर्ग जो उस समाज, जाति और राष्ट्र के लिए रीढ़ के समान है। वह वर्ग उस धर्म, देश और समाज की व्यवस्था में क्रान्तिकारी परिवर्तन ला सकता है।

किसी भी समाज में तीव्रगामी परिवर्तन लाने के लिए युवा वर्ग ही क्रान्ति को जन्म दे सकता है। इसी वर्ग में यह योग्यता है कि देश और समाज के रूप में क्रान्ति के माध्यम से परिवर्तन ला सके। वही वर्ग इस कार्य को करने में सक्षम है।

(ii) राष्ट्रीय स्वतन्त्रता संग्राम में युग पुरुष महात्मा गाँधी ने युवकों का आह्वान करके उनकी बिखरी शक्ति को संगठित किया। उन्हें, उनके महत्व का ज्ञान कराया तथा राष्ट्र-प्रेम, राष्ट्र सेवा, सत्य, अहिंसा, सेवा, त्याग, आत्म-बलिदान तथा भाईचारे की भावना का प्रचार करके नि:स्वार्थ राष्ट्र-भक्ति की प्रेरणा दी। इसका यह परिणाम हुआ कि इसी वर्ग ने स्वयं

को एकता सूत्र में संगठित कर तथा गाँधीजी के दिखाए मार्ग पर चलकर राष्ट्र को स्वतन्त्र कराया।

(iii) वर्तमान राजनीति तथा राजनैतिक दल, दोनों ही युवकों के संगठन तथा उनकी शक्ति पर आधारित हैं। युवा नेता राजीव गाँधी ने युवा शक्ति को आकर्षित करने के लिए मताधिकार की आयु 21 वर्ष से कम करके 18 वर्ष कर दी जिसका परिणाम यह हुआ कि इस वर्ग के मत प्रतिशत ने कांग्रेस को पराजित कर दिया।

युवक अपनी संगठित शक्ति से असम्भव को सम्भव करके दिखाते हैं। समाज की कुरीतियों को नष्ट करने तथा उसे एक नया रूप देने में युवक महत्वपूर्ण योगदान कर सकते हैं। आज सभी राजनैतिक दलों में युवक है।

(iv) वर्तमान में युवा वर्ग अपने उद्देश्यों से पथ भ्रष्ट हो चुका है। आज राजनैतिक दल तथा राजनीतिज्ञ दोनों ही युवकों का प्रयोग अपनी स्वार्थ सिद्धि के लिए कर रहे हैं। वे युवकों को पथ भ्रष्ट करते हैं। उन्हें आकर्षक वादे और सपने दिखाते हैं। ये दल तथा राजनीतिज्ञ इन्हें इस ढंग से प्रयोग कर रहे हैं कि युवकों को अपना जीवन अनिश्चयपूर्ण एवं भविष्य अन्धकार तथा निराशापूर्ण दिखाई देता है। ये राजनैतिक दल छात्रों में वर्ष भर राजनीति में व्यस्त रहकर समय नष्ट करना, मुफ्त सिनेमा देखना, सालभर न पढ़ना तथा समय नष्ट करना, परीक्षा में नकल करना और रोके जाने पर तोड़-फोड़, हड़ताल, लूटमार आदि आदतों के विकास द्वारा समाज में अव्यवस्था फैलाते हैं। यही इनकी निराशा का कारण है।

(v) वर्तमान समय में युवा वर्ग राजनीतिज्ञों की कठपुतली बन गया है। वे युवाओं को दिशाहीन बना रहे हैं और इससे युवाओं में निराशा उत्पन्न होती है। इस निराशा को दूर करने के लिए युवा नशे का सहारा लेते हैं। भाँग, चरस, गाँजा तथा अफीम जैसे नशीले पदार्थों का सेवन करते हैं। युवा इस समस्या से तब मुक्त हो सकते हैं, जब कोई उनका उचित मार्गदर्शन करे।

गद्यांश–14

'पुलिस' को समाज एवं जनता का मित्र और समाज का रक्षक कहा जाता है। कहने के लिए तो यह विचार बहुत ही आकर्षक प्रतीत होता है, किन्तु व्यवहार में यह विचार केवल कल्पना मात्र ही मालूम होता है। किसी भी घटना पर ध्यान दें, पुलिस की हृदय-हीनता तथा अमानवीय व्यवहार स्पष्ट दृष्टिगोचर होता है। अक्सर यह देखा जाता है कि पुलिस शक्तिशाली असामाजिक तत्वों, कालाबाजारियों तथा गैर कानूनी धन्धों में लिप्त लोगों से दूर रहती है अथवा उन्हें सक्रिय सहयोग (प्रत्यक्ष या अप्रत्यक्ष) देते हुए दिखाई देती है, जबकि सज्जन और ईमानदार नागरिकों पर पुलिस अपनी शक्ति का प्रदर्शन करती हुई दिखाई देती है। पीड़ित, भुक्त-भोगी जब अपनी पीड़ा और अन्याय की शिकायत लेकर जाता है तो पहले उन्हें महत्व ही नहीं दिया जाता। अगर दिया जाता है तो बात को न तो ध्यान से सुना जाता है और न उनकी प्राथमिक सूचना को दर्ज किया जाता है। अक्सर तो सामान्य जनता को वैसे ही टहला दिया जाता है। अक्सर ऐसे उदाहरण भी मिलते हैं, जबकि शिकायत कर्त्ता के साहस के परिणामस्वरूप उसे ही थाने में बिठा दिया जाता है। अक्सर जाँच के नाम पर निर्दोष और निरीह लोगों को अनावश्यक रूप में थाने में लम्बे समय तक बिठाकर अमानवीय यातनाएँ दी जाती हैं। अक्सर बीमारी, दुर्बलता आदि की दशा में मृत्यु हो जाने पर पीड़ित पक्ष को ही आतंकित और प्रताड़ित किया जाता है। सामान्य रूप में पुलिस, शक्तिशाली गुण्डे और माफिया के लोगों से बचने का प्रयास करती हैं। अपनी कारगुजारी दिखाने के लिए पुलिस अक्सर निर्दोष लोगों को मुठभेड़ (encounter) में मारकर श्रेय प्राप्त कर लेती है।

प्रश्न : (i) 'पुलिस' का समाज में क्या स्थान और महत्व है ? समाज में पुलिस के सम्बन्ध में क्या धारणा है तथा इसकी वास्तविकता क्या है ?

(ii) पुलिस का समाज के शक्तिशाली वर्ग के प्रति क्या दृष्टिकोण होता है? पीड़ित-पक्ष के प्रति पुलिस कैसा व्यवहार करती है और क्यों ?

(iii) समाज के दुर्बल वर्ग के प्रति पुलिस का दृष्टिकोण अक्सर कैसा रहता है और क्यों ?

(iv) 'मुठभेड़' (encounter) का क्या अर्थ है ? अक्सर यह कार्य पुलिस किन लोगों के साथ करती है ?

(v) पुलिस किन लोगों पर शक्ति प्रदर्शन करती है ? पुलिस के बारे में लोगों के मन में क्या धारणा है ?

उत्तर : (i) सैद्धान्तिक रूप में पुलिस का समाज में महत्वपूर्ण स्थान है। उसे समाज का मित्र और रक्षक माना जाता है। वर्तमान युग में समाज में शान्ति और व्यवस्था स्थापित करना पुलिस का ही दायित्व माना जाता है। पुलिस के सम्बन्ध में समाज की धारणा है कि वह सताये गये लोगों को शरण देकर उनकी सुरक्षा करती है, जबकि आपराधियों को दण्ड देती है।

जबकि वास्तविकता यह है कि पुलिस अक्सर सत्ताधारी राजनीतिज्ञ, बड़े एवं शक्ति-सम्पन्न अधिकारी और अपराधियों से साँठ-गाँठ रखती है तथा सामान्य जनता को परेशान करती है।

(ii) समाज के शक्तिशाली वर्ग के प्रति पुलिस का दृष्टिकोण खुशामद से पूर्ण होता है। अक्सर पुलिस के छोटे-बड़े सभी अधिकारी ऐसे ही व्यक्तियों की सुख-सुविधा में समय व्यतीत करते हैं।

पीड़ित वर्ग के प्रति पुलिस का व्यवहार अधिकतर क्रूर और उपेक्षापूर्ण होता है। पुलिस उनके प्रति अन्याय एवं अमानवीयता पूर्ण व्यवहार करती है। चौकी या थाने में उन्हें उपेक्षा की दृष्टि से देखा जाता है। उनकी बात को न तो ध्यान से सुना जाता है और न ही प्राथमिक सूचना (F.I.R.) ही लिखने का प्रयास किया जाता है। उनकी सूचना पर कोई कार्यवाही करने के स्थान पर या तो डाँटकर भगा दिया जाता है अथवा उनको अनावश्यक रूप से थाने में ही बिठाए रखा जाता है। इसका कारण यह है कि उनके पास धन या सत्ता में से किसी की शक्ति नहीं होती।

(iii) समाज में दुर्बल वर्ग के प्रति पुलिस का व्यवहार बहुत ही अपमानजनक, अमानवीय एवं हृदयहीनता से पूर्ण होता है। अक्सर उन्हें पुलिस थाने और चौकी से धमकाकर भगा दिया जाता है। उनके द्वारा साहस किए जाने पर अनावश्यक रूप में पुलिस चौकी या थाने में कई-कई दिनों या घण्टों तक बिठाए रखा जाता है। इसका कारण है कि उनके पीछे धन या सिफारिश की शक्ति का अभाव।

(iv) 'मुठभेड़' (encounter) का अर्थ है आमना-सामना होना अथवा करना। इस स्थिति में अक्सर पुलिस अपने अधिकारियों की दृष्टि में श्रेष्ठता या सम्मान पाने के लिए निर्धन तथा अनजान लोगों को नुकसान पहुँचाती हैं। इसके लिए किसी शक्तिशाली और इनामी अपराधी के स्थान पर किसी निर्दोष व्यक्ति को जंगल में ले जाकर मुठभेड़ दिखाकर मार डालते हैं। ऐसा पुलिस इसलिए करती है कि शासन और समाज आदि में से किसी को इनकी चिन्ता नहीं होती।

(v) पुलिस सज्जन और ईमानदार लोगों पर शक्ति प्रदर्शन करती है। पुलिस के बारे में लोगों की विचारधारा अच्छी नहीं है। आम जनमानस पुलिस के पास जाने से डरता है क्योंकि पुलिस कार्यवाही के नाम पर उन्हें परेशान करती है, अमानवीय यातनाएँ देती है। पुलिस उन्हीं का सहयोग करती है जो शक्तिशाली और धनाढ्य हैं। सामान्य जनता की शिकायत को पुलिस दर्ज नहीं करती है।

गद्यांश–15

'निर्वाचन' और 'मताधिकार' प्रजातन्त्र की रीढ़ की हड्डी है। जब यहाँ जनता के शासन की बात की जाती है तब अभिप्राय यह होता है कि प्रजा द्वारा निर्वाचित प्रतिनिधि शासन चला रहे हैं। स्वराज्य के सम्बन्ध में वेदों में भी कहा गया है। मन्त्र का भाव है कि प्रजातन्त्र बहुमत की सम्मति से ही पालित होता है। हम सब विद्वान् विस्तृत और विद्वानों के लिए पालित स्वराज्य हेतु प्रयत्न करेंगे। जनता का मताधिकार ही उस शस्त्र के समान है जिसकी सहायता से वह संसद में अपने प्रतिनिधि तथा उनके आचरण पर नियन्त्रण रखती है। सभी निर्वाचित प्रतिनिधि अपने कार्यों के लिए जनता के सामने उत्तरदायी होते हैं। इस प्रकार जनता समवेत रूप में शासन के लिए अपने प्रतिनिधियों का निर्वाचन करती है। इस प्रकार 'निर्वाचन' 'प्रजातन्त्र की एक महत्वपूर्ण क्रिया है। यह जनता का अस्त्र और शस्त्र दोनों है। यह निर्वाचन एक निश्चित और सीमित समय के लिए किया जाता है। विशेष परिस्थिति या संकट की स्थिति में यह कार्यकाल बढ़ भी सकता है तथा सरकार समय से पूर्व स्वयं इस्तीफा भी दे सकती है अथवा राष्ट्रपति द्वारा भंग की जा सकती है।

इस सम्पूर्ण प्रक्रिया के लिए राजनीतिक दल बहुत आवश्यक और महत्वपूर्ण हैं। वे सभी राष्ट्रहित और जन–कल्याण को ध्यान में रखकर जनता को उसके अधिकार और कर्तव्यों की शिक्षा देकर प्रजातन्त्र को सुदृढ़ बना सकते हैं। यही कारण है कि राजनैतिक दल जनतन्त्र के स्तम्भ माने जाते हैं। इस सम्पूर्ण प्रक्रिया को सम्पन्न कराने के लिए सरकार निर्वाचन आयोग का गठन करती है।

प्रश्न : (i) 'प्रजातन्त्र' का क्या अर्थ है ? इसके विभिन्न अंग कौन–कौन से हैं ?

(ii) वेदों में प्रजातन्त्र के विषय में क्या कहा गया है ? वर्तमान में इस पद्धति के विषय में विद्वानों के क्या विचार हैं ?

(iii) 'निर्वाचन आयोग' क्या है ? इसके सदस्यों की नियुक्ति कौन और किसकी सलाह तथा कितने समय के लिए करता है ?

(iv) राजनैतिक दल का क्या अर्थ है ? इनका प्रजातन्त्र में क्या स्थान है ?

(v) प्रजातन्त्र की महत्वपूर्ण क्रिया कौन सी है तथा यह किस प्रकार सम्पन्न होती है ?

उत्तर : (i) प्रजातन्त्र का अर्थ है जनता की, जनता के लिए, जनता के द्वारा निर्वाचित सरकार ही प्रजातन्त्रीय सरकार कहलाती है। इसके अर्थ प्रजातन्त्र में जनता अपनी अच्छा से, निश्चित समय के लिए अपने प्रतिनिधियों का निर्वाचन करती है। इस प्रकार निर्वाचित सरकार एक निश्चित अवधि तक सरकार बनाकर देश का शासन कर सकती है। सरकार निश्चित समय से पूर्व भी त्यागपत्र दे सकती है। इसके तीन विभाग है—व्यवस्थापिका, कार्यपालिका तथा न्याय पालिका।

(ii) वेदों में इस सम्बन्ध में कहा गया है कि प्रजातन्त्र में बहुमत की सम्मति आवश्यक है। उसी से कार्य होता है। सभी विद्वान् विस्तृत और बहुतों के पालित स्वराज्य हेतु कार्य करेंगे।

इस पद्धति के विद्वानों के विचार हैं कि यह एक सफल पद्धति है। इसकी सहायता से जनता को एक ऐसा अस्त्र और शस्त्र मिल जाता है जिसकी सहायता से अपने प्रतिनिधियों के कार्यों पर नियन्त्रण रख सकते हैं। जनता की इच्छा के अनुसार कार्य न करने की स्थिति में जनता अपने प्रतिनिधियों को उनके पद से हटा भी सकती है, यह एक शक्ति है जिससे जनता के अधिकार बढ़ जाते हैं। यह एक सफल पद्धति है जिसमें जनता को अपने शासन में भाग लेने का अधिकार होता है।

(iii) 'निर्वाचन आयोग' स्वतन्त्र रूप में कार्य करने वाली संस्था है। इसका एक अध्यक्ष तथा शेष तीन सहायक सदस्य होते हैं। इनकी नियुक्ति प्रधानमन्त्री की सलाह पर देश का राष्ट्रपति करता है। यहाँ तक कि सरकार भी इस आयोग के अधिकारों में परिवर्तन नहीं कर सकती। निर्वाचन की प्रक्रिया आरम्भ होते ही सरकार की घोषणा बेकार हो जाती है। सरकार न तो कोई नियुक्ति कर सकती है, न स्थानान्तरण और न पदमुक्ति ही कर सकती है। इस प्रकार यह आयोग एक स्वतन्त्र एवं शक्तिशाली आयोग है। सामान्य रूप में यह नियुक्ति 60 वर्ष तक के लिए होती है।

(iv) राजनैतिक दल का अर्थ है राजनीतिक विचारों पर आधारित दल या समूह। इन दलों का गठन किसी-न-किसी राजनैतिक विचारधारा या उद्देश्य की पूर्ति के लिए किया जाता है। यह राजनैतिक दल स्वतन्त्र रूप से जनता को उसके अधिकार और कर्त्तव्यों का ज्ञान कराती है। जनता होने वाले अन्याय और अत्याचारों का विरोध करती है। इसके अतिरिक्त सरकार के अन्याय पूर्ण कार्य के विरुद्ध संघर्ष करती है।

(v) 'निर्वाचन' प्रजातन्त्र की एक महत्वपूर्ण क्रिया है। यह क्रिया जनता के द्वारा सम्पन्न होती है। वह अपने मताधिकार का प्रयोग करके जन प्रतिनिधियों का चुनाव करती है। यह निर्वाचन एक निश्चित समय के लिए होता है। पर सरकार विषम परिस्थितियों में समय से पूर्व त्याग पत्र दे सकती है अथवा राष्ट्रपति के द्वारा भंग की जा सकती है।

गद्यांश–16

वर्तमान में भ्रष्टाचार हमारे जीवन का पर्याय बन चुका है। जन्म हो या मृत्यु, शादी हो अथवा और कोई घटना, भ्रष्टाचार फल-फूल रहा है। बच्चे के विद्यालय में प्रवेश की बात हो, गृह अथवा सार्वजनिक परिचय हो, कोई साक्षात्कार हो अथवा नियुक्ति, हर क्षेत्र में भ्रष्टाचार नजर आता है। शिकायत अथवा प्रार्थना-पत्र की फाइल पर वजन हो तभी वह आगे खिसकती है। वजन के अभाव में आपकी शिकायत के पृष्ठ हवा में इधर से उधर उड़ते रहते हैं।

आज तो हालत यह है कि खेल जैसे सद्‌भावना से पूर्ण क्षेत्र में भी भ्रष्टाचार का प्रवेश हो चुका है। उदाहरण के लिए आज मैच फिक्सिंग एक ज्वलंत समस्या का रूप ग्रहण कर चुकी है। आज तो मैच खेलने से पूर्व ही सट्टेबाजों द्वारा खिलाड़ियों को ही खरीद लिया जाता है। पैसे के बल पर यह भी निश्चित हो जाता है कि मैच का फैसला कितने ओवर तथा कितनी रन संख्या पर हो जाएगा। इतना ही नहीं खेलने या न खेलने के लिए भी पैसे दिए जाते हैं। इस प्रकार भ्रष्टाचार की सहायता से खेल का भी व्यवसायीकरण हो गया है। अधिकतर खिलाड़ी देश के सम्मान के लिए नहीं व्यक्तिगत सम्मान तथा पैसे के लिए खेलते हैं। इस भ्रष्टाचार में बड़े-बड़े सटोरियों के अलावा चयन समिति के सदस्य, प्रबन्ध तन्त्र और अगर अन्यथा न लिया जाए तो कुछ अति महत्वपूर्ण व्यक्तित्व भी शामिल होते हैं। इस बुराई ने व्यक्तिगत जीवन में नैतिकता को पूर्णतः नष्ट कर दिया। इसके कुछ प्रमुख उदाहरण हैं आस्ट्रेलिया-पाकिस्तान, भारत-दक्षिण अफ्रीका आदि। आइए इस बुराई को खत्म करने की शपथ लें।

प्रश्न : (i) 'भ्रष्टाचार' का क्या अर्थ है ? इसने कब और किस रूप में जीवन को प्रभावित किया है ?

(ii) वर्तमान युग में भ्रष्टाचार के कितने रूप है तथा कहाँ देखने को मिलते हैं ?

(iii) 'सट्टेबाज' कौन होता है ? वह जीवन में कहाँ और किस रूप में पाया जाता है ?

(iv) मैच-फिक्सिंग का क्या अर्थ है ? इसने किस रूप में क्रिकेट के खेल को प्रभावित किया है ?

(v) खेल के व्यवसायीकरण का तात्पर्य स्पष्ट करते हुए इसके दुष्परिणामों का उल्लेख कीजिए।

उत्तर : (i) भ्रष्टाचार दो शब्दों से मिलकर बना है भ्रष्ट + आचार। इसका अर्थ है अनुचित या अनैतिक कार्य या आचरण। इस दशा में कोई भी नियम या नैतिक व्यवहार की सीमा नहीं होती।
आज यह बुराई हमारे व्यक्तिगत जीवन को, इसके प्रत्येक क्षेत्र में प्रभावित कर रही है। जीवन का कोई क्षेत्र ऐसा नहीं है जहाँ भ्रष्टाचार ने प्रवेश न किया हो। छोटा या बड़ा, महत्वहीन या महत्वपूर्ण, प्रत्येक कार्य भ्रष्टाचार से प्रभावित हो चुका है।

(ii) वर्तमान समय में व्यक्ति, व्यक्तिगत जीवन, समाज, सामाजिक जीवन, धर्म, धार्मिक भवन, राजनीति, नैतिकता, संक्षेप में जीवन के प्रत्येक क्षेत्र में इस बुराई ने पर्दापण कर लिया। यह भ्रष्टाचार निम्नलिखित प्रकार का है—सामाजिक, राजनैतिक, नैतिक, आर्थिक, व्यक्तिगत तथा सार्वजनिक और अब तो खेल जैसे कार्य में भी भ्रष्टाचार का प्रवेश हो चुका है। भ्रष्टाचार इस रूप में सामने आता है कि विद्यालय में प्रवेश, परीक्षा, पुलिस, कोर्ट, आवेदन, शिकायत, जन्म, विवाह, मृत्यु, हर क्षेत्र में बिना रिश्वत दिए कोई काम नहीं होता।

(iii) सट्टेबाज वह व्यक्ति होता है जो अपने अथवा दूसरे लोगों के पैसे की सहायता से किसी कार्य के निर्णय या परिणाम के विषय में पूर्व घोषणा करता है तथा सम्बन्धित पक्षों में पैसे देकर अपने निर्णय को प्रभावी बनाने का कार्य करता है। जैसे परीक्षा में नकल कराना (ठेके पर) परीक्षा की उत्तर-पुस्तिकाऐं स्वयं भरना, प्रवेश करना, और यहाँ तक कि बाजार-भाव, परीक्षा परिणाम, चुनाव परिणाम तथा देश की आर्थिक और राजनैतिक स्थिति पर नियन्त्रण स्थापित करना।

(iv) इस शब्द का अर्थ है धन के बल पर क्रिकेट के मैच में, आरम्भ से पूर्व मैच के परिणाम को निश्चित कर लेना। इस मैच में कौन-सा देश जीते या हारेगा। इसके लिए सट्टेबाजों द्वारा, बिचौलियों के माध्यम से धन उपलब्ध कराकर खिलाड़ियों को व्यक्तिगत आर्थिक लाभ के लिए, देश के विरुद्ध खेलने के लिए बाध्य करना।

(v) खेल के व्यवसायीकरण से तात्पर्य यह है कि खिलाड़ियों का देश के सम्मान के लिए न खेलकर आर्थिक लाभ के लिए खेलना। इसमें सट्टेबाजों के अतिरिक्त चयन समिति के सदस्य, प्रबन्ध तन्त्र और कुछ महत्वपूर्ण व्यक्ति भी शामिल होते हैं। इससे खिलाड़ियों में नैतिक भावना पूर्णरूप से समाप्त हो जाती हैं। उन्हें मात्र धन ही प्रिय लगता है और वे आत्म सम्मान की भावना से दूर हो जाते हैं।

गद्यांश-17

आज विश्व में उक्त विभिन्न प्रकार के विकलांग करोड़ों की संख्या में है। इसमें भारत में ही लगभग 50 लाख विकलांग हैं। यह विकलांग आज उपेक्षित जीवन व्यतीत कर रहे हैं। इन्हें पराश्रित तो रहना ही पड़ता है, समाज एवं परिवार भी भार समझकर इनकी उपेक्षा करता है। अतः इन अपाहिजों को अपना जीवन भार ही प्रतीत होता है, इनका जीवन भी निराशा से पूर्ण हो जाता है। विकलांगों की इसी अवस्था को लेकर उनकी ओर समाज और सरकार का ध्यान आकर्षित करने के लिए व उनके प्रति अपना दायित्व समझाने के लिए विकलांग वर्ष का रूप दिया गया है। उसी समय से समाज और सरकार ने ध्यान देना आरम्भ किया। यही कारण है कि सरकार ने इन अपंगों के विकास से सम्बन्धित योजनाएँ बनाना आरम्भ कर दिया है। इन सभी योजनाओं का उद्देश्य समाज के इस वर्ग को मुख्य धारा में शामिल करना है। मानसिक विकलांग (मन्दबुद्धि या पूर्ण विक्षिप्त) को छोड़कर केवल शारीरिक अपंग (लूले, लंगड़े और बहरे) अथवा किसी भी दुर्घटना में जिनका अंग-भंग हो गया हो, ऐसे सभी व्यक्ति समाज में भार बन कर नहीं जीना चाहते। वे समाज में आत्म-सम्मान का जीवन व्यतीत करना चाहते हैं। वे भी आत्म-निर्भर होकर रहना चाहते हैं। समाज का उपयोगी सदस्य बनने में उन्हें आत्म-गौरव का अनुभव होता है। इस दशा में उन्हें विकलांगता का बोध नहीं कराया जाना चाहिए। इसके साथ उनमें आत्म-सम्मान तथा आत्म-निर्भरता की भावना जाग्रत करनी चाहिए। तभी हम व्यक्ति और समाज के रूप में अपने कर्तव्य का पालन कर सकेंगे।

प्रश्न : (i) अपंगता का क्या अर्थ है ? यह कितने प्रकार की होती है ?

(ii) वर्तमान विश्व में इन विकलांगों की क्या स्थिति है ? इसका क्या कारण है ? इस व्यवहार का विकलांगों के हृदय पर क्या प्रभाव पड़ता है ?

(iii) समाज और परिवार के विकलांगों के प्रति क्या उत्तरदायित्व हैं ? वे उनका कहाँ तक पालन करने में सफल हैं ?

(iv) समाज और सरकार ने उनके विकास के लिए अब तक क्या-क्या प्रयत्न किए हैं ? अपने शब्दों में उल्लेख कीजिए।

(v) विकलांग व्यक्ति समाज के विकास में किस प्रकार सहयोगी हो सकते हैं ?

उत्तर : (i) अपंगता का अर्थ है शारीरिक और मानसिक अक्षमता या अभाव की स्थिति। दूसरे शब्दों में शरीर में किसी प्रकार की कमी तथा मानसिक रूप से अक्षम या दुर्बल व्यक्ति।
यह दो प्रकार की होती है—शारीरिक और मानसिक।

(ii) वर्तमान युग में वे समाज में उपेक्षित और अपमानित जीवन व्यतीत कर रहे हैं। समाज में उनका कदम-कदम पर अपमान होता है। कोई भी न तो उनकी बात सुनता है और न उन्हें महत्व देता है। इस प्रकार उपेक्षा और अपमान का जीवन व्यतीत करते-करते उनमें हीनता की भावना आ जाती है। इसका परिणाम यह होता है कि धीरे-धीरे उनके मन में समाज के प्रति विद्रोह की भावना जाग्रत हो जाती है।

(iii) समाज और परिवार का भी ऐसे शारीरिक रूप से अक्षम लोगों के प्रति कर्तव्य और उत्तरदायित्व बनता है। परिवार के लोगों को चाहिए कि वे उनके प्रति अपने कर्तव्य का पालन करें। ऐसे अक्षम या अपाहिज लोगों को उचित सम्मान दें। उनके परेशानियों को दूर करने के लिए सच्चाई, ईमानदारी, करुणा और सहानुभूति का व्यवहार करें। ऐसा कोई कार्य न करें जिससे उनके मन और विचारों को ठेस पहुँचे। सामाजिक व्यवहार भी उनके प्रति सहानुभूति और सम्मानपूर्ण होना चाहिए। समाज के सम्पन्न लोगों का कर्तव्य है कि वह अपने ऐसे दुर्बल सदस्यों की आर्थिक सहायता करें। उन्हें कार्य आरम्भ हेतु धन तथा साधनों से सहायता दें।

(iv) समाज और सरकार ने ऐसे शारीरिक अथवा मानसिक रूप से अक्षम व्यक्तियों (बच्चों, जवान) आदि की शिक्षा की व्यवस्था की है तथा कृत्रिम अंग प्रदान करके इन लोगों की सहायता करके उनके मन की हीनता की भावना को दूर किया है। सम्पन्न वर्ग की संस्थाएँ (क्लब अथवा मानवता पर आधारित संगठन) समय-समय पर इस वर्ग को जीवन आरम्भ करने में सहयोग देकर इस वर्ग के प्रति अपनी जिम्मेदारी को पूरा कर रहे है।

दूसरी ओर सरकार ने भी इस वर्ग के लिए चिकित्सा, शिक्षा, औद्योगिक-शिक्षा, आदि की व्यवस्था करके तथा इस वर्ग के लोगों को भी समाज का अंग स्वीकार करके उनमें आत्मविश्वास पैदा करने का प्रयास किया है।

(v) वर्तमान समय में सरकार अनेक ऐसी योजनाएँ क्रियान्वित कर रही है, जिससे विकलांग व्यक्ति लाभ उठा सकते हैं। विकलांगों को औद्योगिक शिक्षा देकर उन्हें आत्मनिर्भर बनाने में भी सरकार सहयोग कर रही है। समाजसेवी संगठन भी विकलांगों की योग्यता अनुसार उन्हें किसी एक कार्य में प्रवीण कर रहे हैं, जिससे विकलांग स्वयं कुछ कमा सकते हैं और देश के विकास में सहयोग दे सकते हैं।

गद्यांश–18

भारतीय संस्कृति का आधार केवल ज्ञान एवं नम्रता ही नहीं है अपितु वह तो असीमित शक्ति एवं अनन्त ऊर्जा के विस्फोट का प्रतीक है। भारत के मनीषियों ने वेद एवं उपनिषद् जैसे गहन ज्ञान की शिक्षा के साथ ही धर्नुविद्या की शिक्षा दी। प्रथम से यदि मानव का बौद्धिक विकास होता है तो द्वितीय से स्वाभिमान एवं आत्मसम्मान की भावना की रक्षा का आत्मविश्वास जाग्रत होता है। विनम्रता से पूर्ण शक्ति ही हमारी संस्कृति का आधार है। भारत में अशक्त संस्कृति का विकास केवल कल्पना की वस्तु है, कोई सिद्धान्त अथवा विचार नहीं। सत्यमेव का उद्घोष करने वाले हमारे पूर्वज गायक तथा स्वाभिमानी वीर थे। सत्य, धर्म एवं न्याय की रक्षा के लिए हमारे उन्हीं पूर्वजों ने अपने ही भाई-बन्धुओं से अनेक युद्ध किए।

आसुरी शक्ति के सामने हमारे पूर्वजों ने घुटने टेकने के स्थान पर उसका दृढ़ता से सामना करना पसन्द किया। इसके लिए उन्होंने विभीषण के समान अपने बन्धु के अन्याय को स्वीकार करने के स्थान पर उसका दृढ़ता से विरोध किया। इसके लिए घर छोड़कर सत्य और न्याय की स्थापना के लिए राघव का साथ दिया। उन्होंने कभी आसुरी शक्ति को न तो अमृत पान कराया न उसके प्रबल होने पर भयभीत हुए। 'सत्यमेव जयते'

के विचार में विश्वास प्रकट करते हुए असत्य और अन्य अन्याय का विरोध करके सत्य का साथ दिया। अन्याय न करना श्रेष्ठ मानव धर्म है। सत्य मानवता की रक्षा का अमोघ अस्त्र है। इस विचार का प्रचार व्यक्ति से सम्पूर्ण समाज तक किया। अन्याय करना और सहना कायरता की निशानी है। अतः अन्याय सहने वाला भी अन्याय का समर्थक माना जाता है।

स्वतन्त्रता के पश्चात् हमारे पतन एवं दुर्दशा का कारण अपनी संस्कृति की प्राचीन विशिष्टताओं को भुला देना था।

प्रश्न : (i) भारतीय संस्कृति की क्या विशेषता रही हैं ? इसका परिणाम हमारे सिद्धान्त एवं व्यवहार पर क्यों पड़ता है ?

(ii) 'अशक्त संस्कृति' का क्या अर्थ है ? इसके सम्बन्ध में हमारे पूर्वजों का विश्वास क्या था ? उसे कल्पना क्यों माना गया है ?

(iii) 'आसुरी शक्ति' का आशय स्पष्ट करते हुए बताइए कि हमारे पूर्वजों के इस नीति के सम्बन्ध में क्या विचार थे ? उसे व्यवहारिक जीवन में उन्होंने क्या स्थान दिया है ?

(iv) स्वतन्त्रता के पश्चात् हमारी दुर्दशा का क्या कारण है ? इसका क्या परिणाम हुआ है ? अपने खोए आत्म-सम्मान को हम कैसे प्राप्त कर सकते हैं ? स्पष्ट कीजिए।

(v) सत्यमेव जयते का क्या अर्थ है ? विभीषण कौन थे और उन्होंने राम का साथ क्यों दिया ?

उत्तर : (i) भारतीय संस्कृति की मुख्य और महत्वपूर्ण विशेषता है—ज्ञान-भक्ति एवं कर्म का समन्वय। हमारे पूर्वजों ने ज्ञान एवं नम्रता को महत्व देने के समय शारीरिक और मानसिक ऊर्जा को जीवन में स्थान दिया। हमने वैज्ञानिक ज्ञान के क्षेत्र में यदि वेद, उपनिषद् तथा पुराणों को महत्व दिया, वहीं शारीरिक तथा भौतिक शक्ति के रूप में धर्नुविद्या (अस्त्र-शस्त्र तथा युद्धकला) का व्यवहारिक अनुभव प्राप्त किया। इसका परिणाम यह हुआ कि हमने वैज्ञानिक शक्ति के साथ ही भौतिक शक्ति की ऊर्जा के ज्ञान से स्वाभिमान और आत्म-सम्मान की भावना की रक्षा की है।

इसका प्रभाव हमारे आचार और व्यवहार पर यह पड़ा कि हमने सत्य, न्याय, धर्म एवं कर्त्तव्य को जीवन का आधार बनाकर उसकी रक्षा के लिए सर्वस्व न्यौछावर करने, अन्याय का विरोध तथा सत्य और न्याय की रक्षा करने का प्रयास किया।

(ii) इसका अर्थ है कि कल्पना या दुर्बलता की नीति पर आधारित विचार है। इसे दूसरे शब्दों में इस प्रकार भी कह सकते हैं कि दुर्बलता की नीति पर आधारित संस्कृति या समझौतावादी संस्कृति। जिसमें व्यक्ति या राष्ट्र अपनी नम्रता या कायरता को छिपाने के लिए कदम-कदम पर हर किसी के सामने स्वाभिमान का बलिदान करे, अन्याय का सामना करके भी सत्य तथा न्याय की बात न करें, यह अनुचित है। यह व्यवहार से परे और केवल कल्पना की वस्तु है। भारतीय संस्कृति व्यवहारिक आदर्शवाद की मजबूत भूमि पर स्थित है।

(iii) इसका अर्थ है—शक्ति, असत्य-विचार, अन्याय एवं अत्याचार की भावना पर आधारित संस्कृति। इसमें अत्यधिक भौतिकता, बनावट, प्रदर्शन, अन्याय, अत्याचार तथा अतिवाद का प्रचार एवं समर्थन किया जाता है अथवा करना पड़ता है।

इस सम्बन्ध में हमारे पूर्वजों के विचार स्पष्ट एवं दृढ़ थे। उन्होंने कभी भी आसुरी शक्ति का समर्थन नहीं किया। हमने कभी किसी भी शक्तिशाली व्यक्ति अथवा समूह के अन्याय और अत्याचार का समर्थन करने के स्थान पर उसका दृढ़ता से सामना किया। सत्यमेव

जयते (सत्य की विजय हो) का समर्थन किया है। अन्याय के विरोध के लिए पूर्ण शक्ति से सामूहिक प्रयत्न किया।

(iv) स्वतन्त्रता के पश्चात् हमारे पतन और दुर्दशा का कारण अपनी संस्कृति की विशिष्टता को भुला देना था। हमने अपने आत्म-सम्मान स्वाभिमान, अन्याय का विरोध, न्याय की स्थापना, दृढ़ इच्छा-शक्ति एवं नम्रता को प्रोत्साहन तथा शक्ति को जीवन में महत्वपूर्ण स्थान देना था। किन्तु हम जाति व धर्म के व्यूह में फँसकर ऐसा नहीं कर सके। इसका परिणाम यह हुआ कि आज विश्व स्तर पर हमारा कहीं कोई स्थान नहीं है। हमारी कोई आवाज नहीं है। हमारी विदेश नीति सन्देह एवं कायरता का रूप ले चुकी है। विश्व के मंच पर हमारी बात गूँगे कानों से सुनी जाती है। हमारी अहिंसा नीति को कायरता समझकर उससे अनुचित लाभ उठाया जाता है। अपनी नीति में शक्ति, शस्त्र एवं दृढ़ता को अपना कर अपने आपको शक्तिशाली रूप में विश्व के सामने उपस्थित करना होगा।

(v) सत्यमेव जयते का अर्थ है सत्य की ही विजय हो। विभीषण लंका नरेश रावण के भाई थे। उन्होंने अपने भाई रावण को त्याग दिया और राम का साथ दिया। इसका कारण यह है कि उन्होंने अन्याय को स्वीकार नहीं किया और सत्य तथा धर्म की रक्षा के लिए राम का साथ दिया। विभीषण रावण की शक्ति से भयभीत नहीं हुए और रावण के पापों, अत्याचारों से लोगों को मुक्त कराने के लिए राम का साथ दिया।

गद्यांश–19

प्रकृति मानव की चिर-संगिनी रही है। दैनिक एवं नियमित कर्मों से जब भी उस का मन ऊबा तब-तब उसने प्रकृति का आश्रय लिया। उसने अनुभव किया कि प्रकृति उसके दुःख में दुःखी और सुख में सुखी है। आकाश, सूर्य, समुद्र, तारागण, मेघ बिजली, वृक्ष एवं लताऐं पशु-पक्षी, उषा की अरुणिमा, इन्द्रधनुष, हरियाली, ओस बिन्दु, लहराते खेत, नदी की उन्मत्त लहरों को देखकर उसे अपने संघर्षमय जीवन में कुछ विश्राम मिला। आगे बढ़ने की प्रेरणा एवं शक्ति प्राप्त हुई है। आज भी सितारों से जगमगाता आकाश एवं सरिता की उन्मादिनी तरंगों को देखकर मानव आत्म-विभोर हो जाता है। प्रातःकालीन उषा-मण्डित, हरियाली पर टहलते समय, वृक्ष की डाली पर बोलते पक्षियों को देखकर तथा आकाश में उड़ते पक्षियों को देखकर सहसा मन मयूर नाच उठता है।

मानव मन पर प्राकृतिक सौन्दर्य का स्थायी प्रभाव पड़ता है। सावन और भादो के काले बादल, बसंत की हरीतिमा, शरद पूर्णिमा की धवल ज्योति होली के अवसर पर पके-पकाए खेत तथा उनमें संलग्न विभिन्न पक्षियों की क्रीड़ा आदि सभी भावुक हृदयों को प्रसन्न करती है। कवि की वाणी मधुर एवं सुन्दर कविता के आधार पर मुखरित हो जाती है। कविता की सहायता से मानव प्रकृति से एक्य स्थापित करने का प्रयास करता है। इसमें उसे विशेष आनन्द का अनुभव होता है।

विश्व के अन्य साहित्यों के समान हिन्दी साहित्य में प्रकृति चित्रण का महत्वपूर्ण स्थान है। आदिकाल से लेकर आज तक, सभी युगों में तत्कालीन कवियों ने प्रकृति का किसी न किसी रूप में आश्रय ग्रहण किया है। चन्दवरदाई से लेकर वर्तमान कवियों ने किसी-न-किसी रूप में प्रकृति का उल्लेख अपने साहित्य में किया है।

आदिकाल की प्रकृति भी मानव को विलास की ओर प्रेरित करने के साथ देश, जाति और धर्म पर आत्म-बलिदान की प्रेरणा देती थी। इस युग में प्रकृति, उद्दीपन का साधन थी। यह भावनाओं को उत्तेजित करने का कार्य करती थी।

इस प्रकार प्रकृति ने कभी मन में प्रेम एवं श्रृंगार भावना को जागृत किया तो कभी आत्म-बलिदान, निस्वार्थ सेवा आदि की भावना को बढ़ाया। प्रकृति का चित्रण कुछ भक्त-कवियों द्वारा अपनी भक्ति भावना के प्रयोग के लिए किया गया।

प्रश्न : (i) मानव और प्रकृति में परस्पर क्या सम्बन्ध है ? इसका जीवन में क्या महत्व है ?

(ii) कवि प्रकृति से क्या-क्या प्रेरणा ग्रहण करता है ? उसके विचारों का रचनाओं पर क्या प्रभाव पड़ता है ?

(iii) हिन्दी साहित्य का पहला कवि कौन था ? वह किस युग में हुआ था ? उस युग में साहित्य और प्रकृति का स्वरूप कैसा था ?

(iv) हिन्दी साहित्य में प्रकृति का चित्रण किस-किस रूप में हुआ ? अपने पढ़े किसी एक कवि के प्रकृति-चित्रण का परिचय दीजिए।

(v) मानव मन पर किस सौन्दर्य का स्थायी प्रभाव पड़ता है ? कविता की मानव के लिए क्या उपयोगिता है ?

उत्तर : (i) अनादिकाल से प्रकृति मानव की सहचरी रही है। मनुष्य के प्रत्येक दु:ख तथा सुख में प्रकृति उसकी साथी है। प्रकृति मानव को प्रसन्नता एवं आनन्द प्रदान करती है।

प्राचीन काल से लेकर आज तक के सभी कवियों को प्रकृति के सौन्दर्य ने आकर्षित किया है। प्रात:काल का सूर्य, हरियाली, नदियों में उठती लहरें मनुष्य को आत्मविभोर कर देती हैं। प्रकृति मनुष्य की पूरक तथा जीवनाधार है।

(ii) कवि प्रकृति से प्रेम, शृंगार, बलिदान, परोपकार तथा भक्ति आदि की प्रेरणा ग्रहण करता है। प्रकृति द्वारा ग्रहण की गयी इन प्रेरणाओं का प्रभाव उसके काव्य पर पूर्ण रूप से दिखाई देता है। भक्त कवियों द्वारा भक्ति भावना एवं शृंगारी कवियों के द्वारा प्रेम और शृंगार के रूप में ये प्रेरणाएँ सामने आती हैं।

(iii) हिन्दी साहित्य का पहला कवि चन्द्रवरदाई था। वह आदिकाल में हुआ था। इस युग के कवि राज्याश्रित थे, अत: उन्होंने अपने आश्रयदाता को प्रसन्न करने के लिए साहित्य लिखा। इसमें वे या तो उनकी वीरता का वर्णन करते थे या किसी स्त्री के सौन्दर्य का वर्णन करते थे। प्रकृति का उपयोग इस काल में उद्दीपन रूप में हुआ। वह भावनाओं को उत्तेजित करने का साधन थी।

(iv) हिन्दी साहित्य के प्रतिभाशाली कवियों द्वारा प्रकृति का चित्रण आलम्बन और उद्दीपन दो प्रमुख रूपों में किया गया है। राष्ट्रकवि मैथिलीशरण गुप्त के शब्दों में प्रकृति-चित्रण का एक दृश्य—

चारु चन्द्र की चंचल किरणें, खेल रहीं है जल-थल में।
स्वच्छ चाँदनी बिछी हुई है, अवनि और अम्बर तल में।।

(v) मानव मन पर प्राकृतिक सौन्दर्य का स्थायी प्रभाव पड़ता है। वर्षा ऋतु के काले मेघ, बसंत की हरियाली, शरद पूर्णिमा की उज्ज्वल ज्योति, होली के अवसर पर लहलहाते खेत, पक्षियों की क्रीड़ा मानव मन को प्रसन्न कर देती हैं। कविता की मानव के लिए अत्यधिक उपयोगिता है। कविता के माध्यम से ही कवि प्रकृति के साथ तादात्म्य स्थापित करता है और फिर पाठक कवि की अनुभूति से तादात्म्य स्थापित करता है। इसमें कवि और पाठक दोनों विशेष आनन्द का अनुभव करते हैं।

गद्यांश–20

हमारे जीवन में धर्म का महत्वपूर्ण स्थान है, धर्म ही उसके जीवन को संयमित एवं आचरण को मर्यादित करता है। अपने धार्मिक संस्कारों से वह जीवन की कठिन परिस्थिति का सामना करने की प्रेरणा पाता है। यह बात अलग है कि प्रत्येक परिवार तथा समुदाय की पूजा पद्धति पृथक् है। भारत में अनेक सम्प्रदाय सैकड़ों वर्षों से साथ रहते आए है। विभिन्न धर्म या सम्प्रदायों की उत्पत्ति इसी भारत भूमि में हुई। इस भूमि ने सभी धर्म और सम्प्रदायों को फलने-फूलने का मौका दिया है। चाहे वे बौद्ध हो, जैन हो, सिक्ख हो, वे सभी हिन्दू धर्म

के अंग हैं तथा इसी से उत्पन्न होकर प्रथक् व्यक्तित्व के रूप में फल-फूल रहे हैं। वे सभी आरम्भ से भारत के वास्तविक निवासियों (सनातनियों) के साथ मिलकर रहते और फलते-फूलते रहे हैं। विदेशी धर्मों, इस्लाम और ईसाई मत को भी सम्मान और महत्व दिया गया है। उनके साथ भी प्रेम एवं सौहार्दपूर्ण व्यवहार किया गया है। दुर्भाग्य वश यह सौहार्द अब खत्म हो चुका है। विदेशी शासकों ने अपने स्वार्थ की पूर्ति के लिये विभाजन की नीति को अपनाया (फूट डालो, राज्य करो), उन्होंने हिन्दू और मुस्लिम को आपस में लड़वाया। उनमें अविश्वास एवं शत्रुता के बीज बोए।

स्वतन्त्रता प्राप्ति पर ऐसे हालात पैदा कर दिए कि हिन्दू एवं मुस्लिम धर्मावलम्बियों को आपस में लड़वाया। कोई एक, दूसरे को सहन करने को तैयार न था। इस परिस्थिति के लिए कट्टर मुस्लिम एवं संकुचित विचारों वाले मुस्लिम राजनीतिज्ञों का हाथ था। उन्हीं ने सत्य प्राप्ति के लिए देश में हिंसा, अराजकता को बढ़ावा दिया जिसकी परिणिति देश के विभाजन में हुई। मुसलमानों ने जिन्ना के नेतृत्व में अपने लिए एक स्वतन्त्र देश माँग लिया। इस प्रकार राष्ट्र का विभाजन भारत और पाकिस्तान के रूप में हो गया। उस समय के शिक्षित और राष्ट्रभक्त नेताओं को विश्वास था कि विभाजन के पश्चात् कट्टरवादी तो जा चुके हैं। अब राष्ट्र का भविष्य धार्मिक तटस्थता या धर्म निरपेक्षता में है। इसी आधार के कारण उन्होंने अपने लिए पृथक् राष्ट्र की माँग करने वाले मुस्लिम नेताओं को भी पाकिस्तान जाने से रोक दिया। तब हमें साम्प्रदायिक सौहार्द्र की आशा थी। दुर्भाग्यवश ऐसा कुछ न हुआ। स्थिति आज और विषम हो गयी है।

प्रश्न : (i) धर्म का मानव जीवन में क्या स्थान है ?

(ii) धर्म के विचार से भारत में विभिन्न धर्मावलम्बियों के बीच क्या सम्बन्ध रहा है ? यहाँ विभिन्न धर्मों की क्या स्थिति है ?

(iii) धार्मिक उदारता का क्या अर्थ है ? भारत में इसमें परिवर्तन कब और किस रूप में आया ?

(iv) अंग्रेजों की नीति आरम्भ से ही क्या रही ? उन्होंने ऐसा क्यों किया ? इसका क्या परिणाम हुआ ?

(v) मुसलमानों ने किसके नेतृत्व में स्वतन्त्र राष्ट्र की माँग की और इसका क्या परिणाम हुआ ?

उत्तर : (i) मानव जीवन में धर्म का महत्वपूर्ण स्थान है। धर्म, मनुष्य को परस्पर मिलजुल कर रहना सिखाते हैं। यह मानव के जीवन से कटुता, द्वेष, आदि की भावना निकालकर प्रेम और शान्ति की स्थापना करता है। मनुष्य के धार्मिक संस्कार उसे जीवन की कठिन से कठिन परिस्थिति का सामना करने की प्रेरणा देते हैं।

(ii) भारत में अनेक धर्मों के लोग सैकड़ों वर्षों से साथ रहते आए हैं। भारत के सभी निवासी चाहें वे किसी भी धर्म के मानने वाले हों एक दूसरे को अपना भाई समझते हैं तथा दूसरे धर्म और उनके मानने वालों का उतना ही सम्मान करते हैं जितना कि अपने धर्म का। सिक्ख, इस्लाम या ईसाई सभी धर्मों को भारत में समान महत्व तथा सम्मान दिया जाता है तथा उनके मानने वालों के साथ प्रेम और सौहार्द्र का व्यवहार किया जाता है।

(iii) धार्मिक उदारता से तात्पर्य है—सभी धर्मों का समान महत्व तथा सम्मान। जब भारत में विदेशी आक्रमण हुए तो विदेशी शासकों ने अपने स्वार्थ की पूर्ति हेतु विभाजन नीति को अपनाया तथा धर्म के नाम पर हिन्दू और मुसलमानों को आपस में लड़वाकर अराजकता को बढ़ावा दिया।

(iv) अंग्रेजों की प्रारम्भ से ही यह नीति रही कि फूट डालो और राज्य करो। उन्होंने ऐसा इसलिए किया ताकि भारत के लोग धर्म के नाम पर आपस में लड़ते रहें और एक दूसरे को अपना शत्रु समझें तथा अंग्रेजी शासन दिन प्रतिदिन सुदृढ़ होता जाये। इस आपसी फूट और धार्मिक विरोध का परिणाम यह हुआ कि देश का विभाजन हो गया तथा परिस्थितियाँ अत्यन्त विषम हो गयीं।

(v) मुसलमानों ने मोहम्मद अली जिन्ना के नेतृत्व में स्वतन्त्र राष्ट्र की माँग की। इसके बाद राष्ट्र का विभाजन हुआ और एक नये देश पाकिस्तान का उदय हुआ। इससे हिन्दू और मुसलमान के बीच सौहार्द्र की भावना समाप्त हो गयी और वे एक-दूसरे के शत्रु बन गये। राष्ट्र विभाजन से लाखों लोग मारे गये अनेक बेघर हुए तथा धन की भी बहुत हानि हुई।

गद्यांश-21

प्रत्येक राष्ट्र के जीवन-निर्वाह के लिए आवश्यक है कि देश की प्राकृतिक सम्पत्ति की रक्षा की जाय तथा उस सम्पत्ति को उन्नति देने के लिए पूरे-पूरे प्रयत्न किए जायें। देश की कृषि, देश की खानों की पैदावार तथा देश की दस्तकारी की बिना रक्षा किए, बिना उनकी उन्नति किए तथा देश के धन को बाहर जाने से रोके बिना किसी भी देश के बच्चों का पालन अथवा उन्हें दरिद्रता तथा दुष्काल के भयानक परिणामों से बचाना सर्वथा दुष्कर है। साथ ही हमें यह स्मरण रखना चाहिए कि राष्ट्रीय-जीवन तथा राष्ट्रीय उन्नति के लिए देश की प्राकृतिक सम्पत्ति को उन्नति देने की अपेक्षा देश की मानसिक और नैतिक सम्पत्ति को उन्नति देना आवश्यक है। जो राष्ट्र अपनी मानसिक सम्पत्ति की उचित रक्षा करता है तथा उसे उन्नत बनाने के पूरे-पूरे प्रयत्न करता है, केवल वह राष्ट्र ही मान, उत्साह तथा स्वतन्त्रता के साथ इस संसार में जीवित रह सकता है। राष्ट्र के बालक-बालिकाएँ राष्ट्र की मानसिक और नैतिक सम्पत्ति हैं, जो प्राकृतिक सम्पत्ति से अधिक मूल्यवान और महत्व की हैं। जो राष्ट्र इस धन की उचित रक्षा और उन्नति नहीं करता, वह राष्ट्र उन्नति के पथ से हटकर अवनति के गड्ढे की ओर फिसलने लगता है।

जिन सम्पत्तियों की ओर हम संकेत कर पाए हैं, उनकी रक्षा और वृद्धि उचित रक्षा के प्रभाव से ठीक-ठीक तभी हो सकती है, जब हम अपने-अपने कर्तव्यों और अधिकारों को समझें और अपने कर्तव्यों को पूरा करने और अधिकारों को प्राप्त करने के लिए कटिबद्ध हों। कर्तव्यविमूढ़ परतन्त्र देशों के लोग रत्नगर्भा भूमि पर रहते हुए भी निर्धन बने रहते हैं। अशिक्षित तथा अज्ञानान्धकार में डूबे दक्षिण अफ्रीका जैसे देशों के वाशिन्दे अपने पैरों के नीचे सोने की खान रखते हुए भी कंगाल हैं। वास्तव में किसी देश की प्राकृतिक सम्पत्ति की रक्षा तथा सम्वृद्धि उस देश की मानसिक सम्पत्ति की रक्षा तथा सम्वृद्धि पर निर्भर है।

प्रश्न : (i) 'शिक्षा किसी भी देश के विकास में महत्वपूर्ण भूमिका निभाती है।' आप इस तर्क से कहाँ तक सहमत हैं ?

(ii) राष्ट्र की प्राकृतिक सम्पत्ति क्या है ? उसकी रक्षा करना क्यों आवश्यक है ?

(iii) राष्ट्र की मानसिक सम्पत्ति क्या है ? राष्ट्र उसकी उपेक्षा करके क्या खोता है ?

(iv) दक्षिण अफ्रीका के मूल निवासी क्यों गरीब हैं, जबकि प्रकृति ने उन्हें सोने की खानों का उपहार दिया है ?

(v) राष्ट्र की प्राकृतिक सम्पत्ति एवं मानसिक सम्पत्ति में कौन और क्यों अधिक मूल्यवान और महत्त्वपूर्ण है ? उसकी रक्षा और वृद्धि कब हो सकती है ?

उत्तर : (i) किसी भी देश का विकास तभी सम्भव है जब वहाँ के नागरिक शिक्षित हों क्योंकि शिक्षित होने पर ही नागरिकों को अपने अधिकारों, कर्तव्यों, देश की वास्तविक जानकारी, प्राकृतिक सम्पदा आदि का ज्ञान होता है। जो राष्ट्र अपने बच्चों की शिक्षा का उचित प्रबन्ध नहीं करता है, वह विकास करने में पिछड़ जाता है और अवनति की ओर बढ़ता जाता है। ऐसे राष्ट्र प्राकृतिक सम्पदा होते हुए भी निर्धन बने रहते हैं। उदाहरणार्थ—दक्षिण अफ्रीका। अत: उपर्युक्त तर्क सही है।

(ii) देश की कृषि, देश की खानों की पैदावार, देश की दस्तकारी, देश के वन तथा उसकी खनिज सम्पदा ही उसकी प्राकृतिक सम्पत्ति है। इसकी रक्षा करना इसलिए आवश्यक है

क्योंकि प्राकृतिक सम्पदा की रक्षा और उसके विकास से ही राष्ट्र का विकास सम्भव है। उसकी उपेक्षा करने से राष्ट्र का भविष्य अवरुद्ध (रुक) हो जाता है। ऐसा राष्ट्र विकास यात्रा में पिछड़ जाता है।

(iii) किसी भी राष्ट्र का साहित्य, उसका ज्ञान तथा बालक-बालिकाएँ (विद्यार्थी) ही उस राष्ट्र की मानसिक सम्पत्ति कहलाती है। जो राष्ट्र अपनी मानसिक सम्पत्ति की रक्षा न करके उसकी उपेक्षा करता है, उस देश का सम्मान और अस्तित्व दोनों ही खतरे में पड़ जाते हैं। मानसिक सम्पदा की रक्षा के लिए बालकों का विकास बहुत आवश्यक है।

(iv) दक्षिण अफ्रीका प्राकृतिक दृष्टि से सम्पन्न है किन्तु शिक्षा (मानसिक सम्पदा) के अभाव के कारण वहाँ के अधिकतर देशों तथा उनकी जनता को इस विषय में कुछ भी जानकारी नहीं है। जिसका परिणाम यह है कि उनकी अशिक्षा और अज्ञान का लाभ यूरोप तथा अमेरिका आदि सभ्य, शक्तिशाली और सम्पन्न देश उठा रहे हैं।

(v) राष्ट्र के बालक और बालिका ही उसकी मानसिक और नैतिक सम्पत्ति हैं। मानसिक व प्राकृतिक सम्पत्ति में से मानसिक सम्पत्ति ही अधिक महत्वपूर्ण है क्योंकि मानसिक शक्ति के विकास और उसकी रक्षा से ही देश की प्राकृतिक सम्पदा का भी विकास सम्भव है।

गद्यांश–22

जल को मानव जीवन और अस्तित्व के लिए बहुमूल्य माना जाता है किन्तु मानव जीवन के लिए आवश्यक इस अमृत के लिए आज देश का 3/4 भाग तरस रहा है। वैष्णो देवी से लेकर कन्याकुमारी तथा द्वारिका से कामाख्या तक शायद ही ऐसा स्थान होगा जहाँ के लोग पानी के भारी संकट का सामना न कर रहे हों। समाजवाद से उदारवाद और साम्यवाद से प्रखर राष्ट्रवाद तक की कोई भी विचारधारा अभी तक लोगों की इस आवश्यक वस्तु को नहीं दिला सकी है। 21वीं सदी में प्रवेश करने की कल्पना तथा गत कुछ दिन पूर्व किए गए अणु विस्फोटों की सफलता का उत्साह भी नगर की डगर और गाँव की गैल से होकर वहाँ के लोगों की प्यास नहीं बुझा सके हैं।

प्राचीन युग में देश में हर गाँव और नगर में तालाब हुआ करते थे। राजा-महाराजा अपनी प्रजा के हित चिन्तन की कामना से प्रायः धर्मशाला तथा छायादार वृक्षों के साथ कुएँ और तालाबों का निर्माण कराते थे। साथ ही धनी-मानी और परोपकारी व्यक्ति भी इस पवित्र उद्देश्य के लिए कार्य करते थे। एक समय था जबकि देश के चप्पे-चप्पे पर तालाबों का जाल फैला हुआ था। इतना ही नहीं जल के अभाव वाले इलाके में भी शुद्ध और शीतल जल से युक्त बावड़ियों के पाए जाने का उल्लेख मिलता है। किन्तु बढ़ती हुई जनसंख्या के लिए आवास की व्यवस्था करने तथा शहरीकरण की प्रक्रिया तीव्र होने के साथ ही वनों को काटने के साथ ही तालाबों को पाटने का कार्य भी आरम्भ हो गया। आज स्थिति यह है कि शहरों और गाँवों में विभिन्न प्राधिकरणों के नाम पर वैध तथा अवैध हर प्रकार की इमारतें खड़ी कर दी गयी हैं। इससे जहां तालाबों के समाप्त होने पर जल-भण्डारण की व्यवस्था का अभाव हो गया। पचास के दशक में जहाँ 2000 टयूब-वैल पूरे देश में थे, अब यह संख्या लाखों में पहुँच गयी है। इससे भूमिगत जल का स्रोत तेजी से गिरता चला गया है। उदाहरण के लिए उत्तर प्रदेश और गुजरात में यह स्तर काफी नीचे पहुँच गया है।

प्रश्न : (i) जल का मानव जीवन में क्या स्थान है ? उसकी उपयोगिता के विषय में अपने विचार स्पष्ट कीजिए।

(ii) वर्तमान युग में मानव को पर्याप्त पेयजल न मिल पाने के लिए आप किसे उत्तरदायी मानते हैं और क्यों ? विचार स्पष्ट कीजिए।

(iii) प्राचीन युग में पर्याप्त जल की उपलब्धि के कारणों पर प्रकाश डालिए।

(iv) वर्तमान युग में जल के पर्याप्त मात्रा में उपलब्ध न होने के क्या कारण हैं ? स्पष्ट कीजिए।

(v) वर्तमान पेयजल संकट का वर्णन करते हुए इसके समाधान के बारे में अपने विचार स्पष्ट कीजिए।

उत्तर : (i) जल को मानव जीवन और अस्तित्व के लिए बहुमूल्य माना जाता है। यह मानव जीवन के लिए बहुत आवश्यक है। इसके बिना मानव जीवन की कल्पना भी असम्भव है। जल को जीवन कहा गया है।

जल सभी प्राणियों के लिए अमृत के समान है। जल पीने से लेकर जीवन के अन्य अनेक दैनिक उपयोगों के लिये महत्वपूर्ण है।

(ii) मानव को आवश्यकता के अनुसार पर्याप्त पेयजल न मिल पाने के लिए हम मुख्य रूप से सरकार की राष्ट्रीय जल नीति को ही उत्तरदायी मानते हैं। इसके अतिरिक्त बढ़ती हुई आबादी को जीवन के आवश्यक साधन प्रदान करने के लिए वनों को नष्ट करना तथा तालाबों को पाटना मुख्य कारण है। इसके अतिरिक्त जनता द्वारा जल की बर्बादी भी इसके लिए उत्तरदायी है।

(iii) प्राचीन युग में देश के कोने-कोने में तालाबों का जाल बना हुआ था। राजा-महाराजा अपनी प्रजा के लिए कुएँ और तालाबों का निर्माण कराते थे, छायादार वृक्ष लगाते थे। वनों का रक्षण प्रजा और राजा दोनों करते थे। जल की बर्बादी नहीं होती थी, लोग जल का मूल्य समझते थे। धनी और परोपकार मनुष्य भी प्राचीन युग में जलाशयों का निर्माण कराते थे। इन सब कारणों से प्राचीन समय में जल की उपलब्धता सुगम थी।

(iv) वर्तमान युग में बढ़ती जनसंख्या, जल की अपर्याप्त उपलब्धि का मुख्य कारण है। आवास की व्यवस्था, बढ़ता हुआ शहरीकरण, तालाबों को पाटने की प्रक्रिया तथा जल-संग्रह की पर्याप्त व्यवस्था का न होना भी इसका एक कारण है। इसके अतिरिक्त टयूब-वैल की बढ़ती संख्या के कारण जल का स्तर भी बड़ी तेजी से घटता जा रहा है।

(v) वर्तमान समय में पेयजल की समस्या अत्यन्त विकट है। आज देश का तीन-चौथाई भाग जल के लिए तरस रहा है। देश के अधिकांश भाग पानी के संकट का सामना कर रहे हैं। इस समस्या के समाधान के लिए निम्न उपाय हो सकते हैं—

(1) हमें जल को बर्बाद नहीं करना चाहिए।

(2) वर्षा के जल का उचित भण्डारण करना चाहिए।

(3) तालाबों की उचित देखभाल होनी चाहिए।

(4) वनों की अन्धाधुन्ध कटाई नहीं करनी चाहिए।

(5) जनसंख्या नियन्त्रण के उपाय किये जाने चाहिए।

गद्यांश–23

शान्ति में ही जीवन की समृद्धि निहित है। आज समस्त विश्व के सामने मानव ही नहीं, प्राणी मात्र के अस्तित्व पर प्रश्नचिन्ह लगता हुआ प्रतीत होता है। वैज्ञानिक प्रगति ने जहाँ मानव जीवन को सुख-सुविधाओं से पूर्ण कर दिया है, वहीं सृष्टि के विनाश की भी पूर्ण तैयारी कर ली है। विज्ञान की प्रगति के कारण चाँद पर पदार्पण के पश्चात् मानव मंगल जैसे ग्रहों पर पहुँचने के लिए तत्पर दिखाई देता है, वहीं हिरोशिमा और नागासाकी जैसे दो शहरों के अस्तित्व को मिट्टी में मिलाने वाले बमों से भी खतरनाक अस्त्र-शस्त्रों का निर्माण हो चुका है। आज का मानव बारुद्ध के विशाल ढेर पर बैठा हुआ अपने विनाश का स्वयं ही इन्तजार कर रहा है।

इस अन्धी शस्त्र दौड़ ने विश्व को दो स्पष्ट समूहों में विभक्त कर दिया है। एक परमाणु अस्त्र-शस्त्र से सम्पन्न राष्ट्र तथा दूसरे परमाणु शस्त्र-विहीन राष्ट्र। आज परमाणु शस्त्र सम्पन्न राष्ट्र स्वयं ही विश्व की राजनीति के केन्द्र में रहना चाहते हैं। वे नहीं चाहते कि अन्य राष्ट्र भी उनके समकक्ष बनें। उन्हें आशंका है कि ऐसा होने पर उनकी दादागिरी पर अंकुश लग जाएगा। अतः स्वयं को विकसित राष्ट्र घोषित कर वे अन्य राष्ट्रों को विकसित करने का उत्तरदायित्व वहन करके उन्हें हर तरह की सहायता का प्रलोभन दिखाकर अपने शिकंजे में फँसा लेते हैं। सबल राष्ट्र ऐसे राष्ट्रों को विभिन्न प्रकार की मानवीय, गैरमानवीय, आर्थिक, गैर-आर्थिक जैसी अनेक सहायता, अनुदान और ऋणों के द्वारा अपना पिछलग्गू बनने को बाध्य करते हैं। ऐसे राष्ट्र विश्व संगठन (संयुक्त राष्ट्र संघ) जैसी संस्था पर भी अपने-अपने धन और प्रभुत्व की शक्ति के आधार पर अपना वर्चस्व सिद्ध कर रहे हैं।

ऐसे राष्ट्र इस संगठन की सभी विभिन्न इकाइयों में अपने अधिक प्रतिनिधि नियुक्त कर लेते हैं। कभी-कभी अपने पिछलग्गू देशों को भी प्रवेश दिलाकर इस संगठन की उपयोगिता पर प्रश्नचिन्ह लगा दिया है। ऐसी दशा में यह विश्व संगठन भी एक खेल बनकर रह गया है।

प्रश्न : (i) शान्ति का मानव जीवन में क्या स्थान और क्या उपयोगिता है ?

(ii) वर्तमान युग में शान्ति के मार्ग में कौन-कौन सी बाधाएँ हैं ?

(iii) परिस्थितियों ने आज विश्व को किन-किन वर्गों में बाँट दिया है और क्यों ?

(iv) विश्व संगठन की उपयोगिता पर प्रश्नचिन्ह लगने का क्या कारण है ?

(v) विकसित और विकासशील राष्ट्र का अन्तर स्पष्ट कीजिए। विकसित देश किस प्रकार विकासशील देशों का शोषण करते हैं ?

उत्तर : (i) शान्ति का मानव जीवन में बहुत महत्वपूर्ण स्थान है। इसी में जीवन की सुख-समृद्धि छिपी हुई है। शान्त वातावरण में ही समाज तथा देश प्रगति के मार्ग पर अग्रसर हो सकता है। शान्ति काल में मानवता हर क्षेत्र में विकास कर सकती है।

इस प्रकार मानव को अपनी सभ्यता, संस्कृति तथा हर क्षेत्र में श्रेष्ठता सिद्ध करने का अवसर शान्तिकाल में ही प्राप्त होता है।

(ii) वैज्ञानिक प्रगति ने मानव और मानव सभ्यता के अस्तित्व पर प्रश्न-चिन्ह लगा दिया है। आज मानव अपने तथा देश के अस्तित्व को मिट्टी में मिलाने पर तुला हुआ है। विश्व राष्ट्रों में अन्धी शस्त्र-दौड़ आरम्भ हो चुकी है। आज शस्त्र-सम्पन्न तथा परमाणु शक्ति विहीन राष्ट्र एक दूसरे को शंका की दृष्टि से देखते हैं। आज शक्तिशाली राष्ट्र दूसरे राष्ट्रों को राजनीति के केन्द्र में नहीं आने देना चाहते हैं।

(iii) परिस्थितियों ने आज विश्व को शक्ति-सम्पन्न तथा शक्ति विहीन, विकसित तथा विकासशील राष्ट्रों में विभक्त कर दिया है। इस दशा में शक्तिशाली और सम्पन्न राष्ट्र विश्व राजनीति को अपने तक केन्द्रित करके रखते हैं।

(iv) विश्व संघ की उपयोगिता पर प्रश्न-चिन्ह लगने का कारण है शक्ति-सम्पन्न राष्ट्रों द्वारा इस संस्था पर पूरी तरह अपना आधिपत्य स्थापित करना। यह राष्ट्र दूसरे राष्ट्रों को अपना पिछलग्गू बनाने के लिए उन्हें विभिन्न प्रकार की सहायता देते रहते हैं तथा ऐसे राष्ट्रों को राष्ट्र संघ में प्रवेश दिला कर अपना उल्लू सीधा करते रहते हैं।

(v) ऐसे राष्ट्र जो पूर्ण विकास कर चुके हैं, विकसित राष्ट्र कहलाते हैं और जो राष्ट्र अभी विकास कर रहे हैं, वे विकासशील राष्ट्र कहलाते हैं। विकसित देश अपनी आर्थिक और सैन्य शक्ति के बल पर विकासशील राष्ट्रों पर नियन्त्रण करना चाहते हैं। विकासशील देशों को हर तरह की सहायता का प्रलोभन देकर अपने शिकंजे में फँसा लेते हैं। इस प्रकार विकसित देश विकासशील देशों से अपनी इच्छानुसार कार्य कराते हैं।

गद्यांश–24

पुस्तकों का मानव जीवन में महत्वपूर्ण स्थान है। कहते हैं कि पुस्तक एक गुरु, माता, पत्नी और मित्र आदि सभी रूपों और क्षेत्रों में मानव की सहायता करती हैं। यह अज्ञान के अन्धकार में भटकते हुए मानव के लिए ज्ञान का प्रकाश प्रदान कर उसकी आँखें खोलती हैं। कहते हैं कि जन्म के समय मानव और पशु में कोई खास भिन्नता नहीं होती। जब वह ज्ञान प्राप्त कर अपनी बुद्धि का विकास कर लेता है तो वह पशु से भिन्न होकर अपनी श्रेष्ठता सिद्ध करता है।

कहते हैं कि सभ्यता के आरम्भ में जब लिखने या छापने के साधन न थे तब यह ज्ञान कंठ से कंठ तक होता हुआ एक पीढ़ी से दूसरी पीढ़ी तक अबाध गति से चलता रहता था। इस प्रक्रिया में ब्रह्म बेला में शिष्य, गुरु के सामने अर्द्धचन्द्राकार वृत्त में आसन ग्रहण करते थे। वे अपनी आँखें ही नहीं शरीर और आत्मा तक गुरु चरणों में अर्पित कर देते थे। उस समय वे गुरु के अस्तित्व में स्वयं को विलीन कर देते थे। तब गुरु के श्रीमुख से निकला एक-एक शब्द, एक-एक वाक्य सीधे शिष्य के अन्तर्मन में प्रविष्ट हो जाता था। यह क्रिया कुछ दिन या वर्ष नहीं, सहस्त्रों वर्ष तक चलती रही। उसी अवस्था में कुछ विद्वान् गुरु अपने विचार ताड़-पत्र या भोज-पत्र पर लिखकर उसे धागे से गाँठ (ग्रन्थि) बाँध देते थे। इसी कारण प्रारम्भ में पुस्तक को ग्रन्थ भी कहा गया है। हमारे पुरातन पुराण, वेद आदि सभी ग्रन्थ कहलाये।

प्रकाशन की कला तथा कागज के आविष्कार ने इस विद्या के प्रचार और प्रसार में महान योगदान दिया है। पहले अधिकतम दो-चार पुस्तकें ही लिखी जाती थीं। राजा महाराजा अपने यहाँ आश्रित विद्वानों की सहायता से पुस्तकें लिखवाते थे। इसी प्रकार कुछ राजा भी अपने हाथों से प्रतियाँ लिखा करते थे। इस प्रकार ज्ञान कुछ व्यक्ति या परिवारों तक ही सीमित था। आज प्रकाशन की सुविधा होने के कारण ज्ञान सामान्य व्यक्ति के लिए भी सुलभ हो गया है।

प्रश्न : (i) पुस्तक की मानव जीवन में क्या उपयोगिता है ?

(ii) पुरातन युग में ज्ञान प्रदान करने के लिए कौन-सी प्रक्रिया अपनायी जाती थी ?

(iii) प्राचीन युग में ज्ञान प्राप्ति के लिए शिष्य में कौन-कौन से गुणों का होना आवश्यक था ? उस समय गुरु का समाज में क्या स्थान था ?

(iv) पुस्तक को ग्रन्थ क्यों कहा जाता था ? प्रकाशन की सुविधा में विकास का ज्ञान के प्रचार पर कहाँ तक प्रभाव पड़ा है ? स्पष्ट कीजिए।

(v) मानव पशु से किस प्रकार भिन्न है ? प्राचीन समय में ज्ञान कुछ लोगों तक ही सीमित क्यों था ?

उत्तर : (i) पुस्तकें मानव जीवन तथा विकास के लिये बहुत उपयोगी हैं। पुस्तक गुरु, माँ, मित्र और पत्नी आदि सभी रूपों में मानव का मार्गदर्शन करती हैं। पुस्तक मानव के अज्ञान को दूर कर उसके जीवन में ज्ञान का प्रकाश बिखेर देती हैं। इस प्रकार पुस्तकों की सहायता से मानव बुद्धि का विकास करता है तथा समाज में श्रेष्ठ स्थान को प्राप्त कर लेता है।

(ii) प्राचीन युग में ज्ञान प्राप्ति के लिए मौखिक विधि का सहारा लिया जाता था। शिष्य ब्रह्म-बेला में गुरु के सम्मुख अर्द्ध चन्द्राकर रूप में घेरा बनाकर बैठ जाते। वे अपना तन और आत्मा दोनों ही गुरु चरणों में अर्पित कर देते थे। शिष्यों का व्यक्तित्व गुरु के व्यक्तित्व में लीन हो जाता तब वे ज्ञान को आत्मसात कर लेते थे।

(iii) प्राचीन युग में ज्ञान प्राप्ति के लिए शिष्य में आत्म संयम, कठोर अनुशासन, सादगी, एकाग्रचित्तता और गुरु के प्रति श्रद्धा तथा विश्वास आदि गुण आवश्यक थे। उस समय गुरु को समाज में महत्वपूर्ण स्थान प्राप्त था। उसे भगवान से भी उच्च स्थान प्राप्त था क्योंकि गुरु के माध्यम से ही भगवान तक पहुँचा जा सकता था।

(iv) प्रकाशन कला के आविष्कार से पूर्व विद्वान् भोज-पत्र पर हाथ से लिखकर सभी भोज-पत्रों को एक स्थान पर एकत्रित करके उसमें ग्रन्थि (गाँठ) बाँध दिया करते थे। इसलिए पुस्तकों को ग्रन्थ कहा गया।

प्रकाशन की कला तथा कागज के आविष्कार ने ज्ञान के प्रचार में बहुत योगदान दिया है। पहले पुस्तकें सीमित मात्रा में लिखी जाती थीं लेकिन आज सैकड़ों और हजारों की संख्या में पुस्तकें लिखी जाती हैं।

(v) जन्म के समय मानव और पशु में कोई विशेष अन्तर नहीं होता है। परन्तु मानव ज्ञान प्राप्त करके अपनी बुद्धि का विकास करता है और पशु से श्रेष्ठ बन जाता है। प्राचीन समय में पुस्तकों के छापने के साधन नहीं थे इसलिए सामान्य जनता को ज्ञान प्राप्त नहीं हो पाता था। पहले राजा-महाराजा या तो स्वयं या राज्याश्रित विद्वानों से पुस्तकें लिखवाते थे, जो बहुत कम होती थीं। इस प्रकार प्राचीन समय में ज्ञान कुछ लोगों तक ही सीमित था।

गद्यांश–25

स्वतन्त्रता के तुरन्त बाद नवीन संविधान के निर्माण की आवश्यकता अनुभव हुई। इसका एक मात्र कारण है कि तत्कालीन संविधान अंग्रेजी सरकार द्वारा निर्मित तथा उनकी सुविधाओं को ध्यान में रखकर लिखा गया था। नयी परिस्थिति के अनुसार यह विधान सर्वथा अनुपयुक्त था। इसके लिए प्रारम्भिक तैयारी और विचार-विमर्श सन् 1948 में ही आरम्भ हो चुका था। सन् 1948 में संविधान सभा का निर्माण हुआ। उसमें से प्रमुख विद्वान, अनुभवी एवं योग्य कानूनविदों ने विश्व के प्रमुख देशों तथा विचारधाराओं का अध्ययन और मनन किया। इसके लिए डॉ. राजेन्द्र प्रसाद की अध्यक्षता वाली समिति के डॉ. बी. आर. अम्बेडकर के लगभग 30 महीने के कठोर परिश्रम और लगन के परिणामस्वरूप संविधान तैयार हुआ। यह विधान 26 जनवरी, सन् 1950 से लागू हुआ।

इस विधान के निर्माताओं ने इस बात का ध्यान रखा था कि कोई भी विधान सार्वकालिक और स्थायी नहीं होता अतः निर्माताओं ने इसमें संशोधन की व्यवस्था को भी स्थान दिया। इसके लिए फिर से सभी संविधानों में दी हुई प्रक्रिया का अध्ययन किया। समिति अन्त में इस निष्कर्ष पर पहुँची कि संशोधन की प्रक्रिया न तो इतनी सरल होनी चाहिए कि कोई सरकार अपने स्वार्थ के लिए इसमें चाहे जब परिवर्तन कर ले और न इतनी जटिल होनी चाहिए कि आवश्यक होने पर भी बदला न जा सके। अतः निर्माताओं ने संविधान संशोधन की ऐसी प्रक्रिया अपनायी जो सरल दिखाई देने पर भी किसी के लिए सम्भव नहीं। उदाहरण के लिए, वर्तमान में किसी भी संविधान संशोधन के प्रस्ताव के लिए संसद तथा सभी विधानमण्डलों के सदस्यों का दो तिहाई समर्थन होना आवश्यक है। इसी प्रकार संसद द्वारा उस संशोधन की स्वीकृति के लिए 3/4 सदस्यों का समर्थन अनिवार्य है। इस प्रकार किसी दल के लिए अपने स्वार्थ के लिए विधान में सरलता से संशोधन सम्भव नहीं है।

प्रश्न : (i) नवीन संविधान की आवश्यकता कब और क्यों अनुभव हुई ? स्पष्ट कीजिए।

(ii) प्राचीन और परम्परा पर आधारित संविधान में पूर्ण परिवर्तन के कारणों को स्पष्ट कीजिए।

(iii) परिवर्तन के सम्बन्ध में संविधान निर्माताओं का क्या विचार था ?

(iv) वर्तमान संविधान में परिवर्तन की क्या प्रक्रिया है ? स्पष्ट कीजिए।

(v) संविधान सभा का निर्माण कब हुआ ? इसके अध्यक्ष कौन थे ? संविधान किस प्रकार निर्मित हुआ और कब लागू हुआ है ?

उत्तर : (i) स्वतन्त्रता के तुरन्त बाद नवीन संविधान की आवश्यकता अनुभव हुई क्योंकि पुराना संविधान अंग्रेज शासकों द्वारा अपने स्वार्थ और आराम के लिए बनाया गया था। वह देश की वर्तमान आवश्यकताओं को पूर्ण करने में बाधक था।

(ii) प्राचीन संविधान तत्कालीन आवश्यकताओं और उस युग के शासकों की स्वार्थपूर्ति की भावना पर आधारित था। स्वतन्त्रता के बाद देश की राजनैतिक स्थिति में जो परिवर्तन हुआ, उसकी पूर्ति उस संविधान द्वारा सम्भव नहीं थी। इसलिए संविधान में परिवर्तन आवश्यक हो गया।

(iii) परिवर्तन के सम्बन्ध में संविधान निर्मात्री सभा का विचार था कि कोई भी विधान सार्वकालिक और स्थायी नहीं होता। अतः संविधान में परिवर्तन की बहुत आवश्यकता है। किन्तु उनके विचार में संविधान में परिवर्तन न तो इतना सरल होना चाहिए कि कोई भी सरकार अपने स्वार्थ की पूर्ति के लिए मनमाना परिवर्तन कर सके और न ऐसा कठिन हो कि परिवर्तन सम्भव ही न हो सके।

(iv) वर्तमान संविधान में प्रस्ताव के लिए संसद तथा विधान सभाओं के सदस्यों की कुल संख्या का 2/3 तथा अनुमोदन के लिए 3/4 सदस्य संख्या का समर्थन होना अनिवार्य है। इतना समर्थन पाना किसी भी सरकार के लिए सरल नहीं है। ऐसी स्थिति में कोई भी केवल अपनी स्वार्थपूर्ति हेतु संविधान में संशोधन नहीं कर सकता।

(v) सन् 1948 में संविधान सभा का निर्माण हुआ था। डॉ. राजेन्द्र प्रसाद इस सभा के अध्यक्ष थे। इनकी अध्यक्षता में प्रमुख विद्वान, अनुभवी एवं योग्य कानूनविदों ने विश्व के प्रमुख देशों के संविधानों का अध्ययन करके तथा डॉ. बी. आर. अम्बेडकर के लगभग तीस महीने के कठोर परिश्रम और लगन के परिणामस्वरूप संविधान तैयार हुआ। संविधान 26 जनवरी, सन् 1950 को लागू हुआ।

गद्यांश–26

ऐसा लगता है कि अब भ्रष्टाचार का दुष्ट ग्रह भारत की कुण्डली में स्थायी रूप से आसन जमाकर बैठ गया है। भ्रष्टाचार विरोधी हर आन्दोलन और हर प्रयास उसी पूर्वापेक्षा और प्रबल हर वक्तव्य बनाता जा रहा है। भ्रष्टाचार के इस प्रभाव से कोई भी दल अछूता नहीं है। देश के दलों के नेताओं को टटोला–परखा जाएगा, तो मरुस्थल की दूब की तरह कोई एकाध व्यक्ति ही ऐसा मिलेगा, जो भ्रष्टाचार में लिप्त न हो। किन्तु यदि उसकी भी गहराई से खोज की जाएगी, तो वह स्वयं न सही, उसकी पत्नी, पुत्र, भाई, भतीजे, भाँजे, दामाद, दल के विश्वासपात्र लोग और सलाहकार आदि में से कोई न कोई प्रधानमन्त्री, मुख्यमन्त्री आदि के पद का दुरुपयोग करके उसके नाम पर यह कार्य करता हुआ मिल जाएगा। यह कार्य लुक–छिपकर नहीं खुले आम कर रहे हैं उन्हें कोई रोकता–टोकता भी नहीं है। सरकारें बदलती हैं, सरकारी दल बदलते हैं, सांसद और विधायक बदलते हैं, सरकारी उपक्रम के अध्यक्ष भी बदलते हैं और प्रशासन के अधिकारी भी, किन्तु भ्रष्टाचार का रिवाज यथावत् चलता रहता है। भ्रष्टाचार की कार्यशाला इन सभी को साँचे में ढाल लेती है और देखते-देखते इनका भ्रष्टाचार सदाचार में रूपांतरित हो जाता है। इसकी सबसे बड़ी शोकांतिका यह है कि जिन भ्रष्टाचारियों पर सत्ता में आने के पहले कुछ दलों और नेताओं द्वारा प्रहार किया जा रहा होता है, सत्ता में आने की सम्भावना से ही वे इस भ्रष्टाचारी के गिरोह के समर्थक बन गये दिखाई देते हैं। वर्तमान शासन व्यवस्था के आगमन के साथ ही ऐसा अनुभव हुआ था कि इस बीमारी का अगर अन्त नहीं होगा तो कम से कम प्रभाव तो अवश्य ही कम होगा किन्तु यह विचार भी केवल कल्पना मात्र ही सिद्ध होकर रह गया।

इस शब्द का क्षेत्र और विस्तार तुलसीदास जी द्वारा वर्णित 'जस–तस सुरसा वदन बढ़ावा, तासु दून कपि रूप दिखावा।' यहाँ समय और परिस्थिति की नाजुकता को समझकर कपि 'हनुमान' ने तो अस्थायी रूप में ही सही अपने शरीर के आकार को संकुचित कर लिया था और सुरसा से क्षणिक ही सही, समझौता कर लिया था किन्तु वर्तमान में तो व्यवस्था ही हमें संकुचित होती दिखाई दे रही है। आज हमारे समाज, धर्म, राष्ट्र यहाँ तक कि नैतिकता तक को भ्रष्टाचार का महादैत्य ग्रसता जा रहा है। आज भ्रष्टाचार का यह महादैत्य, व्यवस्था को

पंगु करता जा रहा है। उसके सामने नियम और कानून सीमित हो रहे हैं। आज परिस्थिति विपरीत हो रही हैं। भ्रष्टाचार की सुरसा आज कपि हनुमान को ग्रस कर हजम करने के लिए तैयार है। आज कोई नया नियम बनता है तो भ्रष्टाचारी उसकी काट तैयार कर लेता है। आज तो रिश्वत लो और लेने दो का सिद्धान्त खूब फल-फूल रहा है।

प्रश्न : (i) भ्रष्टाचार का क्या अर्थ है ? समाज में उसका क्या स्थान है ?

(ii) वर्तमान में भ्रष्टाचार ने समाज तथा राजनीति के क्षेत्र को किस सीमा तक प्रभावित किया है ? स्पष्ट कीजिए।

(iii) राजनैतिक दल भ्रष्टाचार के प्रचार तथा प्रसार में कहाँ तक उत्तरदायी हैं ?

(iv) शासन और प्रशासन को भ्रष्टाचार ने कहाँ तक दूषित किया है और किस रूप में ? स्पष्ट कीजिए।

(v) भ्रष्टाचार की लेखक ने सुरसा से तुलना क्यों की है ?

उत्तर : (i) भ्रष्टाचार का अर्थ है अनुचित और अनैतिकता से पूर्ण आचरण। वर्तमान समाज में इसका बहुत ही प्रभावशाली, स्थायी और महत्वपूर्ण स्थान है। यह शासकों से आरम्भ होकर सम्पूर्ण समाज में गहरे रूप में व्याप्त हो चुका है। आज तो यह वायु, जल और भोजन के समान अनिवार्य हो गया है। हम इसके आदी हो चुके हैं।

(ii) वर्तमान में समाज और राजनीति दोनों भ्रष्टाचार के पर्याय बन गए हैं। राजनीति में भी भ्रष्टाचार की जड़ें बड़ी गहरी हैं। कोई भी राजनीतिज्ञ, अधिकारी यहाँ तक कि छोटे या बड़े सभी पदों पर आसीन प्रतिष्ठित व्यक्ति आकंठ भ्रष्टाचार में डूबे दिखाई देते हैं। रेगिस्तान की घास के समान सच्चरित्र व्यक्ति तो दुर्लभ हैं। जो भ्रष्टाचार में लिप्त नहीं उसे भी सफल होने के लिए भ्रष्टाचार में लिप्त होना पड़ता है अन्यथा उसे उखाड़कर फेंक दिया जाता है।

(iii) राजनैतिक दल, हर प्रकार से भ्रष्टाचार के पोषण में लीन हैं। सत्ता के बाहर नैतिकता का दावा करने वाले राजनीतिज्ञ भी सत्ता प्राप्ति के साथ ही भ्रष्टाचार में डूब जाते हैं। बड़े-बड़े प्रतिनिधि (M.L.A.), (M.P.), मुख्यमन्त्री तथा सांसद सभी बहती गंगा में हाथ धोने के अवसर को नहीं जाने देते। जो स्वयं इस कार्य को प्रत्यक्ष रूप में नहीं करते वे अपने पुत्र, पत्नी अथवा किसी अन्य सम्बन्धी के माध्यम से यह कार्य करते नजर आ रहे हैं।

(iv) शासन और प्रशासन में भ्रष्टाचार बहुत गहरे तक प्रवेश कर चुका है। प्रशासन के किसी भी विभाग में फाइल का आगे बढ़ना उस पर रखी हुई रिश्वत के वजन पर निर्भर होता है। बड़े-बड़े प्रशासनिक अधिकारी राजनीतिज्ञों को रिश्वत देकर इच्छित स्थान पर नियुक्ति कराते हैं तथा रिश्वत देकर ही स्थानान्तरण रुकवाते हैं।

(v) जिस प्रकार सुरसा हनुमान को ग्रसने के लिए अपना आकार बढ़ाती जा रही थी, उसी प्रकार आज भ्रष्टाचार भी बढ़ता जा रहा है। आज हमारे समाज, धर्म, राष्ट्र यहाँ तक कि नैतिकता को भ्रष्टाचार का महादैत्य ग्रस्ता जा रहा है। भ्रष्टाचार के समक्ष नियम और कानून छोटे सिद्ध हो रहे हैं। आज कोई नियम बनता है तो भ्रष्टाचारी उसकी काट तैयार कर लेता है। इसलिए लेखक ने भ्रष्टाचार की तुलना सुरसा से की है।

गद्यांश–27

'बजट' अंग्रेजी शब्द है जिसका छोटा अर्थ है आय-व्यय का विवरण। यह व्यक्तिगत भी हो सकता है और पारिवारिक भी। यह किसी स्थानीय संस्था का हो सकता है, तो राज्य और केन्द्रीय सरकार का भी। संक्षेप में यह विवरण व्यक्ति से लेकर सम्पूर्ण राष्ट्र तक को शामिल कर सकता है। समय के विचार से यह विवरण दैनिक, साप्ताहिक, पाक्षिक, मासिक, त्रैमासिक, अर्द्धवार्षिक और वार्षिक ही होता है। सामान्य रूप तथा अवस्था में इस विवरण की अवधि इससे अधिक नहीं होती है किन्तु विशेष परिस्थिति में यह घट-बढ़ भी सकती है।

बजट का मानव के व्यक्तिगत ही नहीं सामूहिक जीवन में भी बहुत महत्व होता है। यह व्यक्ति समूह तथा विस्तृत रूप में सम्पूर्ण राष्ट्र की आर्थिक स्थिति का प्रारूप स्पष्ट कर देता है। हर बुद्धिमान व्यक्ति अपनी आर्थिक स्थिति के अनुसार ही अपने भविष्य के जीवन की रूपरेखा निश्चित करता है। उसी रूपरेखा के आधार पर वह समाज के सामने स्वयं को प्रस्तुत करता है। घर में अगर व्यक्ति स्वयं अपना बजट बनाता है तो राष्ट्र का बजट सामान्य रूप में वित्तमन्त्री प्रस्तुत करता है। बजट सरकार की आर्थिक ही नहीं सामान्य नीति का परिचायक है। एक सफल वित्तमन्त्री समय, परिस्थिति तथा अपने अनुभव और सूझ-बूझ के आधार पर बजट प्रस्तावों को प्रस्तुत करता है। यहाँ ध्यान रखना चाहिए कि बजट सरकारी नीति और विचारों का परिचायक है।

इस प्रकार बजट का प्रस्ताव सरकार तथा उसकी नीति की स्थिरता तथा सफलता का परिचायक होता है। विरोधी दल जहाँ प्रयास करते हैं कि सरकारी प्रस्तावों में कटौती हो किन्तु वित्तमन्त्री तथा सरकारी पक्ष का यह प्रयास होता है कि बजट प्रस्ताव मूलरूप में ही स्वीकृत हो। इसी पर सरकार की प्रतिष्ठा और स्थिरता निर्भर करती है।

प्रश्न : (i) बजट शब्द का क्या अर्थ है ? तथा इसका मानव जीवन में क्या महत्व है ?

(ii) बजट की अवधि तथा समूह के आधार पर प्रकारों का वर्णन कीजिए।

(iii) किसी देश के बजट का उसकी आर्थिक स्थिति पर क्या प्रभाव पड़ता है ?

(iv) देश का बजट कौन प्रस्तुत करता है ? इसकी सफलता किस बात पर निर्भर करती है ?

(v) सरकारी नीतियों और विचारों का परिचय जनता को कैसे मिलता है ? विरोधी दल इसमें किस प्रकार बाधा पहुँचाते हैं ? सरकार इस स्थिति में क्या करती है ?

उत्तर : (i) 'बजट' शब्द का अर्थ है एक निश्चित समय के लिए व्यक्ति, परिवार, समाज, संस्था तथा किसी सरकार द्वारा बनाया गया आर्थिक स्थिति का विवरण। यह एक प्रारूप के रूप में होता है। इसमें व्यक्ति अथवा राष्ट्र की आय-व्यय का सम्पूर्ण उल्लेख होता है।

मानव जीवन में बजट का महत्वपूर्ण स्थान होता है। यह व्यक्तिगत, पारिवारिक, सामाजिक तथा राष्ट्र की आर्थिक स्थिति को विस्तृत रूप में स्पष्ट करता है।

(ii) अवधि के आधार पर बजट साप्ताहिक, पाक्षिक, मासिक, त्रैमासिक, अर्द्धवार्षिक, वार्षिक, पंचवर्षीय आदि होता है। सामान्य रूप में समय सीमा इससे अधिक नहीं होती। विशेष परिस्थिति में इसे कम या अधिक भी किया जा सकता है।

समूह के आधार पर यह विभाजन पारिवारिक, नगरीय, व्यावसायिक, सरकारी, व्यक्तिगत, विभागीय, राज्य एवं केन्द्रीय प्रकारों में किया जाता है।

(iii) बजट किसी व्यक्ति, समूह, समाज, राज्य एवं राष्ट्र की आर्थिक स्थिति को पूरी तरह समाज एवं विश्व के सामने प्रस्तुत कर देता है। बजट के अनुसार ही देश अपनी भावी योजनाओं का क्रियान्वन करता है। क्योंकि प्रत्येक बुद्धिमान व्यक्ति अपनी आर्थिक स्थिति के अनुसार ही भविष्य के जीवन की रूपरेखा निर्धारित करता है।

(iv) देश का बजट शासक दल का वित्तमन्त्री प्रस्तुत करता है। इसकी सफलता वित्तमन्त्री की व्यावहारिक सूझ-बूझ, अनुभव एवं योग्यता पर निर्भर करती है। उसे इस बात का ध्यान रखना होता है कि देश के प्रत्येक वर्ग को इसका लाभ मिले। सरकारी तथा निजी क्षेत्रों का भी ध्यान रखना पड़ता है।

(v) सरकारी नीतियों और विचारों का परिचय जनता को सरकार द्वारा प्रस्तुत बजट से प्राप्त होता है। विरोधी दल अनेक तर्क देकर यह प्रयास करते हैं कि बजट में कटौती किस प्रकार की जाये, जिससे जनता की सरकार के प्रति विचारधारा सही न रहे। पर सरकार भी यह प्रयास करती है कि बजट मूल रूप में ही प्रस्तुत हो।

गद्यांश–28

किसी भी देश की न्यायप्रियता तथा वहाँ की जनता का वहाँ की न्याय व्यवस्था में विश्वास इस बात की सफलता पर निर्भर करता है कि न्याय, वहाँ कितना शीघ्र, कितनी सरलता तथा कम से कम खर्चे के बाद सुलभ होता है। न्याय का जन–सामान्य के लिए सुलभ होना उसकी सरलता तथा सुलभता पर निर्भर है। न्याय व्यवस्था में जितनी अधिक पेचीदगी होगी, जितनी यह व्यवस्था लम्बी और खर्चीली होगी उतनी ही अधिक जनसामान्य के लिए दुष्कर होती जाएगी। प्राचीन युग से पंचायत व्यवस्था न्याय व्यवस्था का आधार है तो सर्वोच्च न्यायालय उसका मुकुट है। आज से सैकड़ों वर्ष पहले पंचायतें ही हमारी व्यवस्था का आधार थीं। उस समय पंचायतें आत्मनिर्भर तथा पूर्ण शक्ति सम्पन्न थीं। यही कारण है कि उस समय गाँव आत्मनिर्भर थे। एक के बाद दूसरी जाति तथा वंशों का शासन स्थापित हुआ और खत्म हो गया किन्तु किसी ने ग्राम पंचायतों के कार्य तथा उसकी व्यवस्था में हस्तक्षेप नहीं किया।

अंग्रेजी शासन के आगमन के साथ ही शासन का हस्तक्षेप बढ़ता गया। धीरे-धीरे अंग्रेजी सरकार ने ग्राम सभा तथा पंचायती व्यवस्था से भी अधिकारों को छीनकर उन्हें पंगु कर दिया। परिणाम यह हुआ कि न्याय व्यवस्था खर्चीली तथा लम्बी हो गयी। 40 से 50 वर्ष तक मुकदमें खिंचते जाते हैं। इस व्यवस्था में पेशकार और वकीलों का महत्व बढ़ता गया। जैसे-जैसे किसान न्याय पाने के लिए शहरों की ओर भागा, वह वकीलों पर निर्भर होता गया। न्याय दिलाने के लालच में दिन पर दिन वकील तथा इस व्यवस्था से जुड़े व्यक्ति सम्पन्न होते गए जबकि किसान अधिक से अधिक निर्धन होता गया। वह सामान्य से लेकर उच्च तथा उच्चतम न्यायालय के चक्कर लगाकर बूढ़ा होता गया। निर्धनता और तनावपूर्ण जीवन के साथ उसका सर्वस्व न्याय व्यवस्था की बलिवेदी पर बलिदान हो गया किन्तु उसे न्याय नहीं मिला। स्वतन्त्रता के पश्चात् पिछले 50 वर्षों में न्याय व्यवस्था में सुधार के दावे तो बहुत किए गए किन्तु कार्य नाममात्र का ही हुआ है।

प्रश्न : (i) न्याय व्यवस्था का किसी देश में क्या स्थान है ? इसका देश की शान्ति व्यवस्था पर क्या प्रभाव पड़ता है ?

(ii) न्याय व्यवस्था की सफलता का अर्थ स्पष्ट करते हुए बताइए कि इसका जनता पर क्या प्रभाव पड़ता है ?

(iii) प्राचीन भारत की न्याय व्यवस्था का क्या आधार था तथा वह सफल क्यों मानी जाती थी ?

(iv) वर्तमान न्याय व्यवस्था के दोषों का वर्णन करते हुए यह बताइए कि इसकी सफलता के लिए किन बातों की आवश्यकता है ?

(v) प्राचीन समय में हमारे ग्राम आत्म-निर्भर क्यों थे ? ग्रामों की आत्म-निर्भरता क्यों समाप्त हो गयी ?

उत्तर : (i) न्याय व्यवस्था का किसी भी देश में महत्वपूर्ण स्थान होता है। यदि न्याय व्यवस्था शीघ्र, सरल और सस्ती होगी तो उस देश की जनता को उसमें गहरा विश्वास होगा। इसके विपरीत यदि न्याय व्यवस्था जटिल, लम्बी और खर्चीली होगी तो जनता का उसमें विश्वास नहीं रहेगा। इस प्रकार न्याय-व्यवस्था पर देश की शान्ति-व्यवस्था भी निर्भर करती है।

(ii) किसी भी देश की न्याय व्यवस्था की सफलता का अर्थ है जनता को शीघ्रता व सरलता से न्याय मिलना है। जब जनता को न्याय शीघ्रता और सरलता से मिलता है तब जनता की दृष्टि में न्याय-व्यवस्था का सम्मान होता है। यदि इस व्यवस्था पर जनता का समय और धन अधिक खर्च होता है तो जनता का विश्वास खत्म हो जाता है।

(iii) प्राचीन भारत की न्याय-व्यवस्था का आधार पंचायत व्यवस्था थी। उस समय में गाँव आत्म-निर्भर थे। गाँव के ही निर्वाचित प्रतिनिधि न्याय-प्रक्रिया में भाग लेते थे। वे गाँव की

परिस्थितियों तथा घटना की वास्तविकता से भी सरलता से परिचित हो जाते थे। इसके साथ पंच में परमेश्वर का निवास मानने के कारण भी न्याय को धोखा नहीं दिया जा सकता था। इसी कारण यह व्यवस्था सफल मानी जाती थी।

(iv) वर्तमान न्याय व्यवस्था कोर्ट, वकील और गवाहों पर ही निर्भर करती है। न्यायालय में पेशकार, वकील, मुंशी का त्रिकोण न्याय प्रक्रिया को खर्चीला और लम्बा कर देता है। गवाह और सबूत पर पूरी तरह आधारित व्यवस्था में तो मुकदमे कभी-कभी 50 वर्ष से भी अधिक लम्बी अवधि तक खिंच जाते हैं। इसमें किसान का धन और सर्वस्व न्याय-व्यवस्था की भेंट चढ़ जाता है। इतने पर भी न्याय न पाने वाला या तो शान्त होकर बैठ जाता है अथवा कंगाल होकर वापस लौट आता है।

(v) प्राचीन समय में ग्राम-पंचायतें ही न्याय करती थीं और ये पूर्ण शक्ति सम्पन्न होती थीं। इसलिए प्राचीन समय में हमारे ग्राम आत्म-निर्भर थे। जब अंग्रेजी शासन का आगमन हुआ तो उसने धीरे-धीरे ग्रामीण न्याय व्यवस्था में हस्तक्षेप करना आरम्भ कर दिया। अंग्रेजों ने ग्राम-पंचायतों के अनेक अधिकारों को छीन लिया, जिससे वे शक्तिहीन हो गयीं। इससे ग्रामवासियों को भी न्याय के लिये शहरों की ओर आना पड़ा। इस प्रकार ग्रामों की आत्म-निर्भरता समाप्त हो गयी।

गद्यांश–29

वर्तमान वैज्ञानिक खोजों से यह स्पष्ट हो चुका है कि घास स्वास्थ्य के लिए बहुत लाभदायक है। यही कारण है कि घास खाने वाले जानवर मानव से अधिक स्वस्थ और मजबूत दिखाई देते हैं। वैज्ञानिक खोजों के आधार पर घास की उपयोगिता सिद्ध करते हुए कहा गया है कि घास खाने से आँखों की रोशनी बढ़ती है। इस प्रकार घास हमारे लिए बहुत उपयोगी बतायी गई है। आयुर्वेद तथा अरबी चिकित्सा पद्धति में घास पात के महत्व का वर्णन किया है। वहाँ कहा गया है कि घास और हरी सब्जियाँ भोजन का एक आवश्यक अंग होने पर मानव को बहुत सी बीमारियों से छुटकारा दिलाने में सहायक सिद्ध हुई हैं। उदाहरण के लिए, सोयाबीन एक प्रकार की घास ही तो है उसी प्रकार मेथी, पालक और बथुआ इन्हें हम हरे पत्तों वाली सब्जी के रूप में प्रयोग कर सकते हैं।

मूली, शलजम आदि हरे पत्तों वाली सब्जी का एक उदाहरण है। जिसका अन्दरूनी भाग खाने के उपयोग में आता है। इसी प्रकार सुबह शाम घास पर नंगे पैर घूमना आँखों को रोशनी देने के साथ-साथ दिल और दिमाग को शीतलता और शान्ति भी देता है। वर्तमान में जब भोजन में आवश्यक कैलोरी की बात की जाती है, उस समय भी बात घूम फिर कर हरी पत्तों वाली सब्जी अथवा घास पर आ जाती है। वर्तमान चिकित्सकों के विचार में कई विटामिन हरी सब्जी में पाये जाते हैं। अगर सभी मनुष्य सावधानी से और नियमित ढंग से हरी सब्जी का प्रयोग करें तो लोगों के चश्में खुद ही हट जायेंगे। यह बात गाय, भैंस, घोड़े, ऊँट और बकरी आदि पशुओं के जीवन के उदाहरण से स्वयं स्पष्ट हो जाती है। क्योंकि कोई भी पशु चश्में या लैन्स का प्रयोग नहीं करता। इसलिए हमें अपने भोजन और दिनचर्या में घास सहित हरी सब्जी के अधिक से अधिक प्रयोग पर ध्यान देना चाहिए।

प्रश्न : (i) वर्तमान वैज्ञानिक खोजों ने क्या स्पष्ट कर दिया है और क्यों ?

(ii) घास की उपयोगिता के सम्बन्ध में आयुर्वेद तथा अरबी चिकित्सा पद्धति में क्या कहा गया है ? आप इन विचारों से कहाँ तक सहमत हैं ?

(iii) 'हरी सब्जी' शब्द का क्या अर्थ है ? इसमें आप मुख्य रूप में किन-किन सब्जियों को शामिल करेंगे ? स्पष्ट कीजिए।

(iv) भोजन और स्वास्थ्य के सम्बन्ध को स्पष्ट करते हुए सन्तुलित भोजन में कैलोरी की उपयोगिता पर विचार प्रकट कीजिए।

(v) वर्तमान समय में चश्मे की समस्या क्यों बढ़ती जा रही है ? इससे छुटकारा कैसे मिल सकता है ? उदाहरण देते हुए बताइए।

उत्तर : (i) वर्तमान वैज्ञानिक खोजों ने यह स्पष्ट कर दिया है कि घास मानव स्वास्थ्य के लिए बहुत लाभदायक है यही कारण है कि घास खाने वाले जानवर मानव से अधिक स्वस्थ दिखाई देते हैं। वैज्ञानिक खोजों ने यह भी सिद्ध किया है कि घास खाने से आँखों की रोशनी बढ़ती है। इस प्रकार घास हमारे लिए बहुत महत्वपूर्ण एवं उपयोगी बताई गयी है।

(ii) घास की उपयोगिता के विषय में आयुर्वेद तथा अरबी पद्धति में कहा गया है कि घास खाने से आँखों की रोशनी बढ़ती है। भोजन का आवश्यक अंग होने के कारण घास और हरी सब्जी मानव को अनेक बीमारियों से छुटकारा दिला सकती है।

हम उपर्युक्त विचार से पूरी तरह सहमत हैं क्योंकि वर्तमान वैज्ञानिक खोजों ने भी इसकी सत्यता को स्पष्ट कर दिया है।

(iii) हरी सब्जी का अर्थ है ऐसी सब्जी जिसमें हरा रंग स्पष्ट दिखाई देता है तथा जो अपेक्षाकृत अधिक क्लोरोफिल के कारण विभिन्न प्रकार के विटामिनों से युक्त होती हैं। यह भोजन में कैलोरी की मात्रा की कमी को पूरा करती हैं।

इसमें सोयाबीन, मेथी, पालक, बथुआ, मूली तथा शलजम आदि शामिल हैं।

(iv) जब भोजन में कैलोरी की बात आती है तब भी हरी पत्तेदार सब्जी को ही महत्व दिया जाता है। क्योंकि चिकित्सकों के अनुसार हरी सब्जियों में कई प्रकार के विटामिन पाये जाते हैं तथा हरी घास पर प्रातःकाल नंगे पैर चलने से आँखों की रोशनी बढ़ती है। अतः चिकित्सकों के विचार से सभी मनुष्यों को नियमित रूप से हरी सब्जी का सेवन करना चाहिये तथा प्रातःकाल घास पर नंगे पैर घूमना चाहिये।

(v) वर्तमान समय में चश्मे की समस्या इसलिए बढ़ती जा रही है क्योंकि हम भोजन को आयुर्वेद के नियमानुसार नहीं करते हैं और असावधानीपूर्वक करते हैं। अगर सभी मनुष्य सावधानी से और नियमित ढंग से आयुर्वेदानुसार हरी सब्जियों का प्रयोग करें तो इस समस्या से निजात पाना सम्भव है। उदाहरण के लिए गाय, बकरी, भैंस आदि पशुओं को लिया जा सकता है क्योंकि ये चश्मे का प्रयोग नहीं करते हैं।

गद्यांश–30

भारतवर्ष में हर दस वर्ष पश्चात् होने वाली जनगणना में व्यक्ति की जाति पूछी और लिखी जाने की परम्परा रही है। सन् 2001 (21वीं सदी) के आगमन के अवसर पर यह एक प्रतिगामी फैसला होगा। इस निर्णय पर अब तक होने वाली सभी प्रतिक्रियाएँ उचित हैं। सभी तर्क उचित और वजनदार हैं। यह परम्परा अंग्रेजी शासन के आरम्भ में लागू की गयी किन्तु 30 तथा 40 के दशक में इस प्रथा को तिलांजलि भी दे दी गयी थी। इस परम्परा को एक बार त्यागने के बाद ऐसा कुछ भी नहीं हुआ कि इसे दुबारा आरम्भ किया जाए। यह सच है कि इससे जाति की दीवारें टूटने वाली नहीं है किन्तु प्रगति के माध्यम से एक ऐसा वर्ग पैदा हुआ है कि जो जाति के माध्यम से अपनी पहचान देने में अपमान का अनुभव करता है। प्रक्रिया धीमी होने पर भी निरन्तर चल रही है। इतने वर्ष बाद पुनः जनगणना में नाम के साथ जाति पूछना एक भयानक अपराध होगा।

यह आश्चर्य एवं दुःख का विषय है कि नये युग के द्वार पर खड़े राष्ट्र में एक बार पुनः जाति का उल्लेख दर्ज करने का विचार कैसे आ गया। आज राजनीति तथा राज्य व्यवस्था में जो कुछ हो रहा है यह आश्चर्य क्षणभंगुर होगा। मण्डल आयोग की रिपोर्ट आने से लेकर जिस राजनीति ने जोर पकड़ा है, वह लोगों की जातिगत पहचान से ही अपनी खुराक पाती है। जब 60 से 80% तक आरक्षण देने की बात की जाती है और

इसके लिए जनजातियाँ, पिछड़ी तथा अनुसूचित जातियों की सूचियाँ बनानी पड़ती हैं, तब इन्हीं आधारों पर उनकी जनगणना के लोभ को भी नहीं रोका जा सकेगा। इस विचार से जनगणना में पुनः जाति का उल्लेख करना जातिवादी राजनीति का ही अगला तार्किक और सफल कदम होगा। तब भी अलग जाति पूछने के स्थान पर पिछड़ा वर्ग शब्द जोड़कर काम चलाया जा सकता है। जिन जातियों का राज्य के क्रियाकलापों से कोई सम्बन्ध नहीं, उनकी जाति दर्ज करने का कोई लाभ नहीं है। अगर जातिगत राजनीति को उलट-पलट नहीं सकते तो इसे मजबूत और स्थायी बनाने का प्रयत्न तो कम से कम कर ही सकते हैं।

प्रश्न : (i) हमारे देश में जाति के सम्बन्ध में क्या परम्परा रही है ? इसका आरम्भ कब हुआ ?

(ii) जातिगत राजनीति का अर्थ स्पष्ट करते हुए बताइए कि इस परम्परा को जारी रखने को अपराध क्यों कहा गया है ?

(iii) जाति का उल्लेख राष्ट्रीय एकता में कहाँ तक बाधक हो सकता है ? स्पष्ट उल्लेख कीजिए।

(iv) वर्तमान में जातिगत राजनीति के दुष्परिणामों से किस प्रकार बचा जा सकता है ? स्पष्ट कीजिए।

(v) आरक्षण क्या है ? आरक्षण के लाभ और हानियों पर प्रकाश डालिए।

उत्तर : (i) हमारे देश में हर दस वर्ष बाद होने वाली जनगणना के समय व्यक्ति की जाति पूछ कर लिखने की परम्परा रही है। इस परम्परा का आरम्भ अंग्रेजी साम्राज्य की स्थापना के प्रारम्भिक वर्षों में हुआ था।

(ii) जातिगत राजनीति का अर्थ है जाति के आधार पर वर्गीकरण करके समाज को विभिन्न भागों तथा उपभागों में विभाजित करना तथा इसी आधार पर राजनीति को आगे बढ़ाकर सत्ता-प्राप्ति के अपने स्वार्थ को सिद्ध करना है। इस व्यवस्था में व्यक्ति की पहचान जाति के आधार पर ही होती है। इसी आधार पर यह प्रवृत्ति फल-फूल रही है।

इस परम्परा को आज अपराध माना जाता है क्योंकि वैज्ञानिक प्रगति के इस युग में जबकि मानव देश, जाति, धर्म, रंग आदि पर आधारित बन्धनों को तोड़कर विशुद्ध मानवता की भावना के विकास के लिए कार्य कर रहा है, जाति के आधार पर मानव-मानव के विभाजन की बात करना अनुचित होगा।

(iii) किसी राष्ट्र की एकता और मजबूती के लिये उसके नागरिकों के द्वारा एक जाति, एक धर्म तथा एक भाषा के आधार पर संगठित होना आवश्यक है। जब कोई राष्ट्र जाति, धर्म अथवा भाषा के आधार पर विभाजित हो जाता है, तब उसकी राष्ट्रीय एकता खतरे में पड़ जाती है। इससे व्यक्ति-व्यक्ति में व्यर्थ का भेद तथा ईर्ष्या-द्वेष का भाव जाग्रत हो जाता है।

(iv) वर्तमान जाति पर आधारित स्वार्थपूर्ण राजनति ने समाज और देश को इतने भाग और उपभागों में विभाजित कर दिया है कि कभी-कभी हमें अपने भारतीय होने पर सन्देह होता है। यह बुराई एक जहरीले फोड़े के समान बढ़ रही है। अतः जाति पर आधारित राजनीति को त्याग कर ही हम इस बुराई से मुक्ति पा सकते हैं।

(v) समाज की ऐसी जातियाँ जो सामाजिक और आर्थिक रूप से पिछड़ी हुई हैं, उनके लिए सरकारी सेवाओं, चुनाव आदि में एक नियत संख्या में स्थान सुरक्षित करना आरक्षण है। इससे इन जातियों को लाभ होता है। उनकी आर्थिक स्थिति में सुधार होता है, उन्हें भी समाज की मुख्य धारा में सम्मिलित होने का अवसर प्राप्त होता है, सम्मान प्राप्त होता है, परन्तु इससे समाज में भेदभाव बढ़ने लगता है। उच्च जातियाँ इससे प्रभावित होती हैं और उनके मन में ऐसी जातियों के प्रति घृणा उत्पन्न हो जाती है। राजनीतिज्ञ ऐसी जातियों के प्रति घृणा तथा आरक्षण का उपयोग अपने स्वार्थ के लिए करते हैं।

गद्यांश–31

बात करते समय किसी के मन को मोह लेने की शक्ति का नाम मधुर भाषण है। किसी की बढ़ाई करते हुए लोग कहते हैं कि अमुक व्यक्ति जब बात करता है तो मिसरी घोल देता है। दूसरा व्यक्ति, किसी अन्य व्यक्ति की प्रशंसा करते हुए कहता है कि उसकी वाणी में तो मानो फूल झड़ते हैं। यह मिसरी घोलना और फूल झाड़ना मीठी वाणी के लिए है। यह उसके संकेत हैं।

प्रभु की बनाई वाक् शक्ति में बहुत शक्ति है। मिठास इसका सर्वप्रिय गुण तथा कटुता सर्वप्रिय अवगुणहै। यदि मानव वाणी के मधुर गुण को ग्रहण करे तो वाणी उसे देव तुल्य पूज्य बना सकती है। दूसरी ओर इसकी अवहेलना करने पर मानव दानव से भी बढ़कर नीच और घृणास्पद हो जाता है। दूसरे शब्दों में, इस वाणी में लोकप्रियता के शिखर पर बिठाने की शक्ति है और निरन्तर अप्रिय होने की खाई में धकेल देने की शक्ति भी है।

मीठा बोलने वाले नर अथवा नारी बच्चे तथा बूढ़े सभी से प्रेम करते हैं। बच्चें भी उस बालक को जो कड़वा बोलता या गाली देता है, अपने साथ खिलाना पसन्द नहीं करते हैं। इसी प्रकार घर के जो वृद्ध व्यक्ति मधुर बोलते हैं, परिवार के लोग उन्हें बड़े सम्मान की दृष्टि से देखते हैं। उनकी सेवा करने में स्वयं को कृतकृत्य अनुभव करते हैं। उनकी बातें ध्यान से सुनते तथा उस पर अमल करते हैं। किन्तु यदि वे ही लोग कटुवादी हो जायें तो घर वाले उनसे तंग आ जाते हैं और भगवान से यही प्रार्थना करते हैं कि वह उन्हें शीघ्र से शीघ्र उठा ले। वे उस क्षण का इन्तजार करते हैं कि कब उनका अन्त हो और कब इससे हमारा पिण्ड छूटे।

यह सब वाणी की ही करामात है। जहाँ वाणी का संयम रहता है, उन घरों में पारिवारिक समस्याएँ नहीं होतीं। परस्पर प्रेमपूर्वक एक साथ रहते हुए वे लोग चौगुना ऐश्वर्य बढ़ा देते हैं किन्तु वाणी में कटुता आते ही घर की समृद्धि भी सिर पर पाँव रखकर भाग लेती है।

प्रश्न : (i) मधुर भाषण का क्या अर्थ है ? इसकी तुलना किससे की गयी है और क्यों ?

(ii) ईश्वर द्वारा प्रदत्त इस वाक् शक्ति का प्रमुख गुण तथा अवगुण क्या है ?

(iii) लोग किससे क्यों और किस दशा में पिण्ड छुड़ाना चाहते हैं ?

(iv) 'सिर पर पाँव रखकर भाग जाना' का क्या अर्थ है ? उपर्युक्त सन्दर्भ में इसका अर्थ स्पष्ट कीजिए।

(v) मधुर भाषण की उपयोगिता स्पष्ट कीजिए।

उत्तर : (i) इसका अर्थ है—मीठी बोली तथा मधुर ढंग से बातें और व्यवहार करना।

इस गुण की तुलना फूल झड़ने तथा मिसरी घोल देने की विशेषता से की गयी है। यह तुलना इसलिए की गई है क्योंकि मीठा बोलने से बोलने और सुनने वाले, दोनों पक्षों को शान्ति एवं प्रसन्नता का अनुभव होता है।

(ii) ईश्वर द्वारा दी गई वाक् शक्ति के विषय में कहा गया है कि इसका सबसे प्रिय गुण मिठास तथा अवगुण कटुता की भावना है। मानव मीठा बोलकर सबका प्रिय तथा कड़वा बोलकर सबका अप्रिय बन जाता है। इस प्रकार मीठी बोली के प्रयोग से मानव देवता बन सकता है तथा कड़वी बोली के प्रयोग से राक्षस।

(iii) लोग कड़वा बोलने तथा अप्रिय स्वभाव के व्यक्ति से इसलिए छुटकारा पाना चाहते हैं क्योंकि उनकी कड़वी और अप्रिय बातों से दुःखी और निराश होकर वे लोग उससे ऊब जाते हैं।

(iv) इसका अर्थ है जान छुड़ाकर भाग जाना या परेशान होकर भागना।

यहाँ इस शब्द का प्रयोग कटु बोली के परिणाम को प्रकट करने के लिए किया गया है वाणी की कटुता से घर की सुख, शान्ति और सद्भाव का वातावरण नष्ट हो जाता है। जो लोग मीठी वाणी का प्रयोग करते हैं उनकी समृद्धि दिन-प्रतिदिन बढ़ती ही जाती है।

(v) मधुर बोलने वाले से बच्चे, वृद्ध, नर, नारी सभी प्रेम करते हैं। बच्चे भी अपने साथ ऐसे बच्चों को खिलाना पसन्द करते हैं जो मीठा बोलते हैं। घर में जो वृद्ध मीठा बोलते हैं, परिवार में उन्हें सम्मान मिलता है। ऐसे लोगों की सेवा करना परिवार के सदस्यों के लिए सौभाग्य होता है। उनकी बातों को ध्यानपूर्वक सुना जाता है।

गद्यांश–32

रमणीयता और नित्य नूतनता आपस में घनिष्ठ सम्बन्ध रखती है। रमणीयता के अभाव में कोई भी चीज मान्य नहीं होती। नित्य नूतनता किसी भी सर्जन की मौलिक उपलब्धि की प्रामाणिकता सूचित करती है और उसकी अनुपस्थिति में कोई भी चीज वस्तुत: जनता जनार्दन द्वारा स्वीकृत नहीं होती। सड़ी-गली मान्यताओं से जकड़ा हुआ समाज जैसे आगे नहीं बढ़ पाता, वैसे ही पुरानी रीतियों और शैलियों की परम्परागत लीक पर चलने वाली भाषा भी जनचेतना को गति देने में प्राय: असमर्थ ही रह जाती है। भाषा समूची युग चेतना की अभिव्यक्ति का एक सशक्त माध्यम है और ऐसी शक्ति वह तभी अर्जित कर सकती है जब वह अपने युगानुकूल सही मुहावरों को ग्रहण कर सके। भाषा सामाजिक भावों को प्रकट करने के लिए है। इसके अतिरिक्त और कोई उपयोगिता कल्पना से परे है। इस उपयोगिता की सार्थकता सामयिक सामाजिक चेतना में प्राप्त अनेक प्रकार से मिश्रित विचारों की दुरुहता को दूर करने की शक्ति में छिपी है। कभी-कभी अन्य जातियों या संस्कृतियों के सम्पर्क से भाषा में नये शब्दों का प्रयोग होता है। इन शब्दों से सही पर्यायवाची शब्द अपनी भाषा में प्राप्त न हो, उन्हें वैसे ही अपनी भाषा स्वीकार करने में किसी भी भाषा-भाषी को आपत्ति नहीं होनी चाहिए। यही भाषा की आधुनिकता है। भाषा की सजीवता इस नवीनता को पूर्णरूप से स्वीकार करने पर ही निर्भर करती है। भाषा किसी म्यूजियम की वस्तु नहीं है, उसकी स्वत: सिद्ध एक सहज गति है जो सदैव नित्य नूतनता को ग्रहण कर चलने वाली है।

जब भाषा अपनी सामान्य विशेषताऐं एवं रूप को समय और परिस्थितियों के अनुसार नहीं बदलती तो वह भाषा रोगी होकर धीरे-धीरे अपना वास्तविक स्थान खोकर पतन के गहरे गर्त में लीन होकर सदा के लिए विश्व और समाज की दृष्टि से ओझल हो जाती है। इसलिए हर भाषा-भाषी का यह पुनीत कर्तव्य है कि अपनी भाषा और उसके स्वरूप को नष्ट होने से बचाए तो उसके वास्तविक रूप को, केवल अनिवार्य होने पर ही परिवर्तित होते रहने दें। उसमें किसी भी प्रकार की बाधा न डालें। इसी प्रकार हर साहित्यकार का यह कर्तव्य है कि अपनी भाषा में निरन्तर साहित्य का सृजन करता रहे। अगर ऐसा न हुआ तो वह भाषा और उसका साहित्य समाज, भाषा तथा मानवता के विकास में कोई सहयोग नहीं कर सकेगा।

प्रश्न : (i) 'रमणीयता' और 'नूतनता' का क्या अर्थ है ? इनका आपस में क्या सम्बन्ध है ?

(ii) 'जनता जनार्दन' का क्या आशय है ? वह किस वस्तु को कब और क्यों स्वीकार नहीं करती ? स्पष्ट उत्तर दीजिए।

(iii) 'जनचेतना' शब्द का आशय स्पष्ट करते हुए बताइए कि समाज कब आगे नहीं बढ़ पाता तथा भाषा कब समाज को गति देने में असमर्थ हो जाती है ?

(iv) भाषा की आधुनिकता का क्या अर्थ है ? यह कब उपयोगी बनकर जाति और समाज के उत्थान के लिए कार्य करती है ?

(v) भाषा क्या है ? भाषा की प्रमुख विशेषताएँ बताइए।

उत्तर : (i) 'रमणीयता' का अर्थ है सुन्दरता तथा आकर्षण की शक्ति। 'नवीनता' का अर्थ है कि किसी भी वस्तु में हर समय तथा हर दशा में एक प्रकार का नयापन आ जाना। इनका आपस में बहुत ही गहरा तथा भावात्मक सम्बन्ध है। जिस प्रकार एक जैसी वस्तु सुन्दर होने पर भी मन को आकर्षित नहीं कर पाती उसमें यदि नयापन न हो। इसी प्रकार नवीनता होने पर भी यदि वस्तु में आकर्षण नहीं तो वह व्यर्थ है।

(ii) 'जनता जनार्दन' का अर्थ है शक्तिशाली और प्रजातन्त्र में अधिकारों से सम्पन्न जनता।

जनता उस समय जबकि वस्तु में नवीनता और रमणीयता दोनों अथवा किसी एक का अभाव हो उसे अस्वीकार कर देती है क्योंकि वह नवीनता और रमणीयता दोनों को ही समझती है तथा उनके महत्व को स्वीकार करती है।

(iii) इसका अर्थ है साधारण जनता में अपने अधिकार के प्रति जागृति की भावना। इसी कारण देश और सार्वजनिक हित की प्रत्येक बात को ध्यान से सुनकर उस पर गम्भीरता से विचार करती तथा निर्णय करती है। वह सड़ी-गली परम्पराओं को स्वीकार नहीं करती है।
समाज तब आगे नहीं बढ़ने पाता जब उसमें सड़ी-गली परम्परा और रीति-रिवाजों का प्रचलन होता है।
भाषा उस समय समाज को गति देने में असमर्थ हो जाती है जब वह पुरानी रीतियों और शैलियों की परम्परागत लीक पर ही चलती रहती है। तथा स्वयं को नवीन वातावरण के अनुसार नहीं बदलती।

(iv) कभी-कभी अन्य जातियों या संस्कृतियों के सम्पर्क से भाषा में नये शब्दों का प्रयोग होता है। इन शब्दों के सही पर्यायवाची शब्द अपनी भाषा में प्राप्त न हो तो उन्हें भाषा द्वारा वैसे ही स्वीकार किया जाना ही भाषा की आधुनिकता है। भाषा की सजीवता इस नवीनता को स्वीकार करने पर ही निर्भर करती है।
जब भाषा समय और परिस्थितियों के अनुसार अपने स्वरूप को बदल कर समाज के अनुसार उपयोगी स्वरूप धारण करके समाज के उत्थान में सहायता करती है।

(v) भाषा वह साधन है जिसके द्वारा हम दूसरों के विचार आसानी से समझ सकते हैं तथा अपने विचार दूसरों पर भली-भाँति प्रकट कर सकते हैं।
भाषा की प्रमुख विशेषताएँ निम्नलिखित हैं—
(1) भाषा परिवर्तनशील है।
(2) भाषा सामाजिक वस्तु है।
(3) भाषा का कोई अन्तिम स्वरूप नहीं है।
(4) व्यक्ति भाषा को उत्पन्न नहीं कर सकता।
(5) प्रत्येक भाषा का एक मानक रूप होता है।

गद्यांश–33

भक्ति भारतीय संस्कृति के प्रधान अंगों में से एक है। सृष्टि के आदिकाल से ही सुख के अन्वेषण और दु:ख के निवारण के लिए मानव इसकी निर्मल और पावन धारा में आनन्द का अनुभव करता चला आ रहा है। वह किसी महान शक्ति की खोज करता है जो सुख में सहयोग तथा दु:ख में सहानुभूति प्रकट करे। यह महान शक्ति केवल ईश्वर है। सुख में नहीं तो दु:ख के लीलामय संग्राम में लड़ता हुआ मानव जब पराजित हो जाता है, उसकी शक्ति और आशा जब उसके सम्मुख प्रश्न चिन्ह लगा देती है, तभी उसका निराश हृदय ईश्वर की शरण में जा गिरता है और महान आदर्श शक्ति का स्मरण करके आत्म-सन्तोष का अनुभव करता है। इसी दशा में उसे आत्मज्ञान एवं जीवन के सत्य का ज्ञान प्राप्त होगा।

किसी भी देश और जाति पर तभी दु:ख के बादल छा जाते हैं, जब वह सुख और विलास के क्रीड़ास्थल में इन्द्रिय सुख का आनन्द लेने में निमग्न हो जाता है और भगवान के पवित्र नाम को विस्मृत कर देता है। इसी विस्मरण का दण्ड भोगने के लिए किसी न किसी रूप में मानव काल का ग्रास बनकर इन कष्टों से उद्धार हेतु फिर से भगवान की शरण में आता है। साहित्य और इतिहास इसी वास्तविकता को प्रमाणित करते आए हैं।

तुलसीदास मूलत: एक भक्त कवि हैं। उनकी भक्ति का आधार समन्वय की भावना पर आधारित है। मूल रूप में उसकी निम्नलिखित विशेषताएँ देखने को मिलती हैं—तुलसीदास की भक्ति भावना राम के प्रति है। उसमें दास्य भाव के दर्शन होते हैं। वह स्वयं को सेवक तथा राम को सेवा मान कर चले हैं। तुलसीदास की भक्ति में समन्वय की भावना है। वह विरोधी परिस्थिति में भी मेल और सहयोग करते हैं। उसमें राम और शिव, शिव और शक्ति तथा शिव और राम द्वारा एक दूसरे के प्रति भक्ति-भावना प्रदर्शित करते हैं। तुलसीदास की भक्ति और भक्ति-भावना सम्पूर्ण समाज के कल्याण की भावना पर आधारित है। शास्त्रों में जिस नवधा भक्ति का उल्लेख है, तुलसीदास के काव्य में वे सारी भावनाएँ एवं रूप सम्पूर्ण रूप में देखने को मिलते हैं।

प्रश्न : (i) भक्ति का मानव जीवन में क्या स्थान है ? इसे जीवन की पावन धारा क्यों कहा गया है ? मानव इसकी ओर आकर्षित क्यों रहा है ?

(ii) ईश्वर के सम्बन्ध में मानव के क्या विचार हैं ? वह उसकी आवश्यकता कब अनुभव करता है और क्यों ?

(iii) कोई जाति दुःख और निराशा के गहन अन्धकार में कब डूब जाती है और क्यों ?

(iv) 'काल का ग्रास बनना'— का क्या अर्थ है ? मानव काल का ग्रास कब बनता है और क्यों ?

(v) साहित्य और इतिहास कौन से विचार को प्रमाणित कर रहे हैं और किस रूप में ?

उत्तर : (i) भक्ति का मानव जीवन में बहुत महत्वपूर्ण स्थान है। सृष्टि के आरम्भ से ही सुख के अन्वेषण तथा दुःख और कष्टों को दूर करने के लिए मानव का मन इसकी पवित्र धारा में निमग्न रहा है। इसमें उसने परम आनन्द का अनुभव किया है।

भक्ति की धारा में निमग्न होकर मानव असीमित सुख और सन्तोष का अनुभव करता रहा है। इसीलिए इसे जीवन की पावन धारा कहा गया है।

किसी महान शक्ति की खोज के उद्देश्य से मानव सदैव से भक्ति की ओर आकर्षित होता रहा है।

(ii) ईश्वर के सम्बन्ध में मानव का विचार है कि वह सर्वशक्तिमान् है। वह मानव को दुःख के अन्धकार से मुक्ति दिलाकर सुख और शान्ति के मार्ग की ओर ले जाता है।

जब दुःख के महासंग्राम में संघर्ष करके मानव थकान और निराशा का अनुभव करता है, तब उसे ईश्वर की आवश्यकता अनुभव होती है क्योंकि ईश्वर ही उसे दुःख की निराशा से हटाकर सुख के प्रकाश की ओर ले जाता है।

(iii) कोई भी जाति तभी दुःख में डूब जाती है जब अत्यधिक सुख और विलास को पाने के लिए इन्द्रिय सुख की क्रीड़ा में डूब जाती है। इस अवस्था में भगवान की शक्ति को भूल कर स्वयं को ही भगवान समझ लेती है।

(iv) इसका अर्थ है—मृत्यु का शिकार या भोजन बनकर खत्म हो जाना। जब मानव ईश्वर का नाम और शक्ति भूल जाता है तब वह किसी न किसी घटना का शिकार बनकर नष्ट हो जाता है।

(v) साहित्य और इतिहास इसी भाव को प्रमाणित कर रहे हैं कि कष्टों से परेशान व्यक्ति जब सब कुछ भूलकर स्वयं को ईश्वर की शरण में डाल देता है तो ईश्वर उसकी रक्षा के लिए नया अवतार लेता है।

गद्यांश–34

वियोग भाव की साक्षात प्रतिमूर्तियाँ तो वे गोपियाँ बनी हुई हैं। जिनके नेत्र निस दिन बरसते रहते हैं और जिनके पठाँये सन्देशों से मधुवन के कूप तक भर गये। वहाँ गोपियों के बहाने से सूर ही अपने आराध्य प्रभु के विछोह में आँसू बहाते दिखाई पड़ते हैं। गोपियों के विरहदग्ध हृदय का चित्रण करते समय मानो सूर की विगलित भावुकता ही सहस्रधारा होकर फूट निकली है। सूरदास ने अपनी भावुकता को प्रत्येक पद में सशक्त अभिव्यक्ति प्रदान की है। तभी तो उनका काव्य सहृदयों के गले का हार बन पड़ा है। शब्दों का सार्थक और उपयुक्त रूप अलंकारों का भावोत्कर्ष हेतु प्रयोग तथा भाव की गेयात्मक अभिव्यक्ति—सभी ने मिलकर उनके काव्य को एक ऐसी उत्कृष्टता प्रदान की है कि उसकी टक्कर की कोई दूसरी कविता नहीं दिख पड़ती। सूर के गीतों में अनुभूति की गहराई इतनी अधिक है कि पाठक रस में डुबकियाँ लगाने लगता है। सूर का अन्तर्जगत राधा कृष्ण के माध्यम से व्यक्त हुआ है। विद्यापति के अन्तर्जगत का माध्यम भी राधा कृष्ण का युग्म ही है परन्तु विद्यापति ने केवल श्रृंगारपरक गीत ही लिखे हैं। सूर ने वात्सल्य, श्रृंगार और शान्त तीनों रस लिए हैं।

वात्सल्य में बाल-मनोविज्ञान का सूक्ष्म चित्रण है और शृंगार में प्रेम की वृत्ति का व्यापक दिग्दर्शन। भक्ति के पदों में सीधी अभिव्यक्ति है। इसलिए सूर का काव्य विद्यापति की भाँति वासनात्मकता विकलता से युक्त न होने के कारण अधिक प्रभावशाली बन पड़ा है।

सूर बाल मनोविज्ञान के अद्‌भुत पारखी थे। उनके काव्य में जीवन की जैसी मनोरम झाँकी मिलती है, किसी अन्य कवि के काव्य में नहीं। इस वर्णन में सहज स्वाभाविकता है, मनोवैज्ञानिकता है, सजीवता है, सरसता और समरसता है। उसमें मानव-मन के आकर्षण की शक्ति है। सूर मूल रूप में प्रेम और सौन्दर्य के कवि हैं। उनके आराध्य श्रीकृष्ण सर्वरूप में सुन्दर हैं तथा उनका अनन्त प्रेम ही सबसे बड़ी उपलब्धि है। श्रीकृष्ण की रूप माधुरी अनन्त है। मन उस पर निछावर हो जाता है।

प्रेम का पारिजात विरह के सरोवर में ही विकसित होता है। संसार के प्रायः सभी कवियों ने विरह के गीत गाए किन्तु सूर के शृंगार के चटक तथा वियोग के मार्मिक गीतों की समता कोई नहीं कर सकता।

प्रश्न : (i) सूर के काव्य में गोपियों का क्या स्थान है ? उनके द्वारा सूर किस रूप में अपना भाव प्रकट करना चाहते हैं ?

(ii) सूर के काव्य में कौन-सी विशेषताएँ मिलती हैं ?

(iii) विद्यापति और सूर के काव्य में क्या अन्तर है ?

(iv) वात्सल्य के क्षेत्र में सूर का क्या स्थान है ?

(v) 'प्रेम का पारिजात विरह के सरोवर में ही विकसित होता है।' इस तर्क से आप सहमत हैं या नहीं ?

उत्तर : (i) सूर के काव्य में गोपियों का महत्वपूर्ण स्थान है। उन्होंने जिस विरह भाव को प्रमुखता दी है, गोपियाँ उसकी साक्षात प्रतिमूर्तियाँ हैं। उनके नेत्र रात-दिन प्रियतम श्री कृष्ण के वियोग में बरसते रहते हैं। उनके संदेशों से मथुरा के कुएँ भी भर गए हैं। इस प्रकार मानो सूर ही अपने आराध्य के वियोग में आँसू बहाते हुए दिखाई देते हैं। गोपियों के विरह-पीड़ित हृदय के द्वारा मानो सूर की भावुकता ही सहस्त्रधारा के रूप में फूट पड़ी है।

(ii) सूर के काव्य में भावुकता को अभिव्यक्ति प्रदान की गयी है। शब्दों का सार्थक और उपयुक्त प्रयोग, अलंकारों का भावोत्कर्ष के रूप में प्रयोग, भाव की गीत द्वारा अभिव्यक्ति एवं संगीतात्मकता, सभी ने उनके काव्य को ऐसी उत्कृष्टता प्रदान की है कि उसकी टक्कर की कोई दूसरी कविता दिखाई नहीं पड़ती।

(iii) सूर में नम्रता और पवित्रता है तो विद्यापति में वासना की अधिकता दिखाई देती है। सूर के काव्य का आधार राधा-कृष्ण है। विद्यापति का माध्यम भी राधा-कृष्ण युग्म ही है किन्तु विद्यापति ने केवल शृंगारपूर्ण रचनाएँ ही की हैं। जबकि सूर ने वात्सल्य, शृंगार और शान्त, तीनों रस लिए हैं।

(iv) सूर के वात्सल्य वर्णन में बाल-मनोभावों का सूक्ष्म चित्रण है। सूर के वर्णन में सहजता, स्वाभाविकता, सजीवता और समरसता सर्वत्र दिखाई देती है। सूर ने भक्त के रूप में श्रीकृष्ण की बाल क्रीड़ाओं का अद्‌भुत वर्णन किया है। वह वात्सल्य के सम्राट कहे जाते हैं।

(v) गोपियाँ श्रीकृष्ण के विरह में व्याकुल रहती थीं और इस अवस्था में कृष्ण के प्रति उनका प्रेम बढ़ता था, उसमें तनिक भी कमी नहीं आती थी। इसी प्रकार सूरदास भी कृष्ण के दीवाने थे और उनसे अगाध प्रेम करते थे। उन्होंने अपनी भावनाओं को गोपियों के विरह-वर्णन के माध्यम से प्रकट किया है। गोपियाँ और सूरदास दोनों श्रीकृष्ण के विरह में व्याकुल रहते थे, पर प्रिय के प्रति प्रेम में कोई कमी नहीं आती थी। अतः उपर्युक्त तर्क सर्वथा उचित है।

गद्यांश–35

विद्या कला, कविता, साहित्य, धन और राजस्व से भी आचरण की सभ्यता अधिक ज्योतिष्मती है। आचरण की सभ्यता को प्राप्त करके एक कंगाल आदमी राजाओं के दिलों पर भी अपना प्रभुत्व जमा सकता है। इस सभ्यता के दर्शन से कला, साहित्य और संगीत को अद्भुत सिद्धि प्राप्त होती है। राग अधिक मृदु हो जाता है। विद्या का तीसरा शिवनेत्र खुल जाता है, चित्रकला मौन राग अलापने लग जाती है, वक्ता चुप हो जाता है। लेखक की लेखनी थम जाती है। मूर्ति बनाने वाले के सामने नये कपोल, नये नयन और नवीन छवि का दृश्य उपस्थित हो जाता है। आचरण की सभ्यतामय भाषा सदा मौन रहती है। इस भाषा का निघण्टु शुद्ध श्वेत पत्रों वाला है। इसमें नाममात्र के लिए भी शब्द नहीं। यह सत्याचरण नाद करता हुआ भी मौन है, व्याख्या देता हुआ भी व्याख्यान के पीछे छिपा है, राग गाता हुआ भी राग के सुर के भीतर पड़ा है। मृदु वचनों की मिठास में आचरण की सभ्यता मौन रूप से खुली हुई है। नम्रता, दया, प्रेम और उदारता सब के सब सत्याचरण की भाषा के मौन व्याख्यान हैं। मनुष्य के जीवन पर मौन व्याख्यान का प्रभाव चिरस्थायी होता है और उसकी आत्मा का एक अंग हो जाता है। न काला, न नीला, न पीला, न सफेद, न पूर्वी, न पश्चिमी, न उत्तरी, न दक्षिणी, वे नाम, वे निशान, वे मकान–विशाल आत्मा के आचरण से मौनरुपिणी सुगन्ध सदा प्रसारित हुआ करती है। इसके मौन से प्रसूत प्रेम और पवित्रता धर्म सारे जगत का कल्याण करके विस्तृत होते हैं। इसकी उपस्थिति से मन और हृदय की ऋतु बदल जाती है। तीक्ष्ण गर्मी से जले–भुने व्यक्ति आचरण के बादलों की बूँदा-बाँदी से शीतल हो जाते हैं।

आचरण की सभ्यता का क्षेत्र बहुत व्यापक है। यद्यपि देखने में तो इसका सम्बन्ध पूर्णतः व्यक्तिगत आचरण ही प्रतीत होता है तथापि सिद्धान्त तथा व्यवहार, व्यक्ति एवं समाज, भाव, वाणी और कर्म तथा घर और बाहर कोई भी क्षेत्र तो इस आचरण की सभ्यता से नहीं बचा। इस सभ्यता से आभूषित व्यक्ति अपनी दृष्टि में तो आत्मिक शान्ति का अनुभव करता है किन्तु समाज की दृष्टि में तो वह पूर्ण रूप में सम्मानित होता है। प्रकृति स्वयं उसकी प्रशंसा में प्रशस्ति गान करती है। बिजली की चमक, बादलों का गर्जन तथा मूसलाधार वर्षा आदि के द्वारा मानो ऐसे सभ्य एवं आचरण में सभ्य व्यक्ति के मस्तक पर तिलक लगाया जाता है।

प्रश्न : (i) आचरण की सभ्यता का क्या अर्थ है ? जीवन में इसका क्या स्थान है ?

(ii) आचरण की भाषा का क्या अर्थ है ? इसका मानव व्यवहार पर क्या प्रभाव पड़ता है ?

(iii) 'मौन रूपी व्याख्यान' का क्या अर्थ है ? जीवन में उसका क्या स्थान है ?

(iv) 'आचरण से ही व्यक्ति देवता बनता है और राक्षस भी'—कोई एक उदाहरण दीजिए।

(v) आचरण की सभ्यता का क्षेत्र बहुत व्यापक है, क्यों ? आचरण की सभ्यता से युक्त व्यक्ति कैसा अनुभव करता है ?

उत्तर : (i) इसका अर्थ दैनिक व्यवहार में एक दूसरे के साथ सभ्यता, पवित्रता तथा नैतिकता से पूर्ण व्यवहार से है। हमारे कर्म, विचार तथा व्यवहार सभी में नैतिकता, पवित्रता तथा धार्मिकता की भावना का पर्याप्त रूप में समावेश होना चाहिए।

जीवन में इसका बहुत ही महत्वपूर्ण स्थान होता है। इसकी सहायता से निर्धन, धनी हो जाता है, सामान्य व्यक्ति इसकी सहायता से राजाओं के दिलों पर राज्य करता है। इसकी सहायता से मानव को कला, संगीत, साहित्य में सफलता प्राप्त होती है।

(ii) अपने विचार और व्यवहार को प्रकट करने का ढंग। यह स्वयं मौन रह कर भी कार्य करती हुई नजर आती है। मीठे वचनों की मिठास में मौन रह कर भी आचरण की सभ्यता खुली रहती है।

जीवन में इसका प्रभाव गहरा और स्थायी होता है। यह उसके मन और आत्मा का अंग हो जाता है।

(iii) इसका अर्थ शान्त रहकर भी सब कुछ स्पष्ट कर देना है। बिना कुछ कहे तथा विचार प्रकट किए ही अपने व्यवहार से कार्य को पूर्ण रूप में स्पष्ट कर देना।

जीवन में इसका स्थान महत्वपूर्ण है। इसमें दिखावे के स्थान पर मानव अपने व्यवहार में पवित्रता, नैतिकता, उदारता तथा असीमित सहन-शक्ति आदि गुणों को प्राप्त कर लेता है। इससे वह सभी के मन को वश में कर लेता है।

(iv) यह विचार पूरी तरह स्पष्ट है कि अपने आचरण और व्यवहार से ही व्यक्ति देवता के समान महत्व और सम्मान प्राप्त कर लेता है और गलत, अनैतिक तथा अपवित्र स्वार्थपूर्ण आचरण उसे दानव बना देता है।

उदाहरण के लिए—रत्नाकर, जीवन के प्रारम्भ में डाकू के रूप में लोगों के धन और प्राण हर लेते थे। ऋषियों की सहायता से जब उन्हें ज्ञान हुआ तो उन्होंने आचरण सुधारा और वे रत्नाकर से महर्षि बन गए। उन्होंने 'रामायण' के रूप में संस्कृत में पहला महाकाव्य लिखा।

(v) यद्यपि देखने में आचरण की सभ्यता व्यक्तिगत प्रतीत होती है, परन्तु सिद्धान्त और व्यवहार, व्यक्ति एवं समाज, भाव, वाणी और कर्म तथा घर और बाहर कोई भी क्षेत्र इस आचरण की सभ्यता से नहीं बच सका है। इस प्रकार आचरण की सभ्यता का क्षेत्र बहुत व्यापक है। इस सभ्यता से युक्त व्यक्ति आत्म-सन्तोष का अनुभव करता है और समाज की दृष्टि में सम्मानित होता है।

गद्यांश–36

जगत के अनेक सम्प्रदाय अनदेखी और अनजानी वस्तुओं का वर्णन करते हैं। पर अपने नेत्र तो अभी माया पटल से बन्द हैं और धर्मानुभव के लिए मायाजाल में उनका बन्द होना आवश्यक भी है और धर्मानुभव के लिए इस कारण में उनके अर्थ कैसे जान सकता हूँ ? वे भाव, वे आचरण—जो उन आचार्यों के हृदय में थे और जो उनके शब्दों के अन्तर्गत मौनावस्था में पड़े हुए हैं। उनके साथ मेरा सम्बन्ध, जब तक मेरा भी आचरण उसी प्रकार का न हो जाये तब तक हो ही कैसे सकता है। ऋषि को तो मौन पदार्थ भी उपदेश दे सकते हैं। टूटे-फूटे शब्द भी अपना अर्थ भासित कर सकते हैं, तुच्छ से भी तुच्छ वस्तु उसकी आँखों में उसी महात्मा का चिह्न है जिसका उत्तम पदार्थ, राजा में फकीर छिपा है और फकीर में राजा, बड़े से बड़े मूर्ख में पण्डित। वीर में कायर और कायर में वीर सोता है। पापी में महात्मा और महात्मा में पापी डूबा हुआ है। वह आचरण जो धर्म सम्प्रदायों के अनुच्चारित शब्दों को सुनता है, हम में कहाँ ? जब वही नहीं तब फिर क्यों न ये सम्प्रदाय हमारे मानसिक महाभारतों के कुरूक्षेत्र बने ? क्यों न अप्रेम, अपवित्रता, हत्या और अत्याचार इन सम्प्रदायों के नाम से हमारा खून करें। कोई भी धर्म सम्प्रदाय आचरणरहित पुरुषों के लिए कल्याणकारक नहीं हो सकता है और आचरण वाले पुरुषों के लिए धर्म सम्प्रदाय अवश्य कल्याणपूरक है। सच्चा साधु धर्म को गौरव देता है। धर्म किसी को गौरवान्वित नहीं करता।

इस प्रकार सभी धर्म और सम्प्रदाय, जिनका हमारे व्यक्तिगत और सामाजिक दोनों ही क्षेत्रों में इतना महत्वपूर्ण स्थान है, जब तक मानव धर्म पर आधारित नहीं होते तथा जब तक उनमें प्राणिमात्र के प्रति करुणा और सहानुभूति की भावना का अभाव है, कम से कम व्यावहारिक अर्थ में तो धर्म का रूप और स्थान ग्रहण नहीं कर सकते। इस दशा में ऐसे सभी धर्म तब तक अधर्म ही कहलायेंगे जब तक वे मानव को मानव से, व्यक्ति को व्यक्ति से तथा समाज को समाज से लड़ा कर तथा उनमें धार्मिक आधार पर घृणा का प्रचार करके अपना स्वार्थ सिद्ध करने का कार्य ही करते रहेंगे। ऐसा धर्म और समाज, स्वार्थ का साधन तो बन सकते हैं किन्तु धर्म कहलाने के योग्य नहीं होते।

प्रश्न : (i) इस जगत के सम्प्रदायों की क्या विशेषता है ? वे अपने उद्देश्य में अक्सर असफल क्यों रहते हैं ?

(ii) लेखक विभिन्न धर्माचार्यों के विचारों को समझने में स्वयं को असमर्थ क्यों अनुभव करता है ? स्पष्ट कीजिए।

(iii) एक सच्चे महात्मा (ऋषि) की क्या विशेषताएँ बताई गयी हैं ? स्पष्ट कीजिए।

(iv) 'मानसिक महाभारत' का क्या अर्थ है ? लेखक के विचार में सभी सम्प्रदाय मानसिक महाभारत के कुरूक्षेत्र कैसे बन गए हैं ?

(v) धर्म और सम्प्रदायों के बारे में अपने विचार प्रकट कीजिए।

उत्तर : (i) इस जगत के सम्प्रदायों की यह विशेषता है कि वे काल्पनिक तथा अनजान वस्तुओं का उल्लेख करते हैं। धर्मानुभव के जाल में उनका बन्द होना अनिवार्य है। अत: इस ढंग से उसके अर्थ का ज्ञान कठिन है।

सम्प्रदाय अपने उद्देश्य में अधिकतर असफल रहते हैं क्योंकि हमारे उपदेशों और ज्ञान का सम्बन्ध मानव के व्यवहार और आचरण से होता है। दुर्भाग्यवश धर्म और समाज में इसका अभाव पाया जाता है।

(ii) वह विभिन्न धर्माचार्यों के विचारों को समझने में स्वयं को असमर्थ अनुभव करता है क्योंकि इन आचार्यों के धर्म सम्बन्धी विचार, केवल विचार तक ही सीमित होकर रह गए है। उनका सम्बन्ध आचरण या व्यवहार से तनिक भी नहीं होता। उनमें अक्सर विरोध की भावना होती है।

(iii) ऋषि में जिज्ञासा की भावना होती है। प्रकृति का जड़ और तुच्छ पदार्थ भी सच्चे ऋषि को शिक्षा दे सकता है। वह हर वस्तु में ईश्वर के दर्शन और उसका अनुभव कर लेता है। उसे बुरे से बुरे में अच्छा दिखाई दे जाता है। वह अपने मन की आँखें खुली रखता है।

(iv) इसका अर्थ मस्तिष्क या बुद्धि के क्षेत्र में हर समय जारी रहने वाला संघर्ष। यह संघर्ष अच्छे-बुरे, ऊँचे-नीचे, राजा-रंक, महात्मा-दुरात्मा, आदि में छिपे रहते हैं। ऐसी दशा में जैसे महाभारत का युद्ध कुरूक्षेत्र के मैदान में हुआ था ठीक वैसा ही युद्ध मानव के मन और मस्तिष्क में बराबर और हर युग में चलता रहता है।

इन सभी सम्प्रदायों के सिद्धान्त और व्यवहार में जो भिन्नता है उसके कारण यह सभी सम्प्रदाय मानसिक महाभारत के केन्द्र बन गए हैं।

(v) धर्म और सम्प्रदाय हमारे लिए तब कल्याणकारी हैं जब ये मानव धर्म पर आधारित हों, न कि देश, भाषा, वर्ग, क्षेत्र आदि कारकों पर। ऐसे सभी धर्म अधर्म ही कहलायेंगे जो मानव को मानव से, व्यक्ति को व्यक्ति से तथा समाज को समाज से लड़ाकर तथा उनमें धार्मिक उन्माद उत्पन्न करके अपना स्वार्थ सिद्ध करते हैं। ऐसे सभी धर्म समाज के लिए हानिकारक हैं।

गद्यांश–37

आये दिन विद्वानों, चिन्तकों और नेताओं से हम यह सुनते रहते हैं कि समाज बहुत कुरूप हो गया और इसके सुधार में अब विलम्ब नहीं होना चाहिए। इसके लिए आवश्यक है कि व्यक्ति अहिंसा, प्रेम, दया और सहानुभूति जैसे मानवीय मूल्यों को बढ़ावा दे और जहाँ भी ईर्ष्या-द्वेष की लपटें उठ रही हों, उन्हें नीचे लाये। व्यक्ति आगे बढ़ना चाहता है—यह न तो अस्वाभाविक है और न निन्दनीय। सिर्फ उसे यह देखकर चलना है कि खुद को आगे बढ़ाने की कोशिश में कहीं वह उन मूल्यों को तो नहीं कुचल रहा, जो एक व्यक्ति के वैयक्तिक विकास से कई गुना मूल्यवान हैं।

नेता बनने की कोशिश में लगे रहने से हर आदमी नेता नहीं बन सकता। बात कड़वी हो या मीठी, लेकिन आदमी वहीं तक जाता है, जहाँ तक जाने की उसमें मौलिक शक्ति होती है। ऐसा भी हुआ है कि इस नियम को तोड़कर लोग नेता के पद तक जा पहुँचे हैं, लेकिन ऐसे अपवादों के नतीजे अच्छे नहीं हुए, क्योंकि या तो वे जल्दी ही लुढ़ककर नीचे आ गये या उनका नेता बना रहना इन्सानियत के लिए हानिकारक साबित हुआ।

समाज का असली सुधार उसमें रहने वाले व्यक्तियों का सुधार है। व्यक्तियों के ही बुरे या भले होने से समाज को बुरा या भला कहते हैं। मुख्य बात यह नहीं है कि हम दूसरों को सुधारने का उपदेश दें, बल्कि यह है कि सुधार की जो बातें हमारे मन में उठती हों, पहले हम उन्हें अपने चरित्र और स्वभाव पर लागू करें। समाज की सुन्दरता दो चार नेताओं पर नहीं बल्कि लाखों व्यक्तियों के सुधार पर निर्भर करती है।

और नेता होता कौन है ? अक्सर वह मनुष्य जो जीवन मूल्यों को, अच्छाइयों को अपने चरित्र और व्यवहार में ढालता है और जो ऐसा नहीं करते, उन्हें समाज का हार्दिक सम्मान प्राप्त नहीं होता। अत: उचित यही है कि समाज की जिन कुरीतियों से हमारी नाराजी है, उन्हें सब से पहले हम छोड़ दें और जिन मूल्यों को हम समाज में लाना चाहते हैं, उन्हें भी अपने वैयक्तिक जीवन में सबसे पहले हम ही बरतना शुरू करें। समाज को योग्य नागरिकों की जरूरत है, नेताओं की नहीं।

प्रश्न : (i) समाज सुधार के लिए क्या आवश्यक है ? व्यक्ति का आगे बढ़ना, अपना विकास करना कब निन्दनीय बन जाता है ?

(ii) 'हर आदमी नेता नहीं बन सकता' इस कथन के पक्ष में लेखक ने क्या तर्क दिया है ? आप इससे कहाँ तक सहमत हैं ?

(iii) अपवाद किसको कहा गया है ? इसका क्या परिणाम दिखाया गया है ?

(iv) समाज को बुरा या भला किस आधार पर कहते हैं ? समाज-सुधार की दिशा में हमारे लिए मुख्य बात क्या है ?

(v) नेता में हम क्या विशेषता पाते हैं ? योग्य नागरिक बनने के लिए हमें क्या करना चाहिए ?

उत्तर : (i) समाज सुधार के लिए यह आवश्यक है कि व्यक्ति, अहिंसा, प्रेम, करुणा और सहानुभूति जैसे मानवीय मूल्यों को बढ़ावा दे। इतना ही नहीं ईर्ष्या और द्वेष की आग को शान्त करने का प्रयत्न भी करें।

जब व्यक्ति, खुद को आगे बढ़ाने के प्रयत्न में स्वार्थ भावना से प्रभावित होकर उन आधारभूत नैतिक मूल्यों को कुचलने को तैयार हो जाता है, जो व्यक्तिगत विकास के लिए आवश्यक है तो व्यक्ति का ऐसा विकास निन्दनीय बन जाता है।

(ii) इस सम्बन्ध में लेखक का तर्क है कि सभी सुविधाएँ मिलने के बाद भी व्यक्ति अधिकतम वहीं तक प्रगति करता है, जितनी उसमें शक्ति और योग्यता होती है। ऐसा न होने पर उन्नति करने वाला शीघ्र ही वापस अपने वास्तविक स्थान पर आ जाता है।

हम लेखक के विचार से पूरी तरह सहमत हैं। कुछ अपवादों को छोड़कर अधिकतर ऐसा ही देखने को मिलता है।

(iii) सर्वमान्य और सिद्ध नियम के विरुद्ध अगर कोई कार्य हो जाता है अथवा कोई घटना घटित हो जाती है तो उसे अपवाद कहते हैं।

ऐसे व्यक्ति जो अयोग्य होने पर भी किसी प्रकार प्रगति के ऊँचे शिखर तक पहुँच जाते हैं, वे योग्यता के अभाव में अधिक समय तक वहाँ नहीं रहते और शीघ्र अपनी वास्तविक स्थिति में पहुँच जाते हैं।

(iv) समाज का भला या बुरा होना उसमें रहने वाले व्यक्तियों के भले या बुरा होने पर निर्भर करता है। जिस समाज में बुरे व्यक्ति अधिक होते हैं, उसे बुरा कहा जाता है तथा जहाँ भले और परोपकारी व्यक्ति अधिक होते हैं, उसे भला समाज कहा जाता है।

अत: समाज सुधार के लिए समाज की अनैतिक, अव्यावहारिक तथा अन्धविश्वास से पूर्ण बुराइयों को दूर करना ही हमारे लिए आवश्यक कार्य है।

(v) नेता वह व्यक्ति होता है जो आवश्यक जीवन मूल्यों को, अच्छाइयों को अपने चरित्र और व्यवहार में ढालता है। योग्य नागरिक बनने के लिए यह आवश्यक है कि ऐसे जीवन मूल्यों को तथा अच्छाइयों को अपने चरित्र और व्यवहार में ढालें, जिन्हें हम समाज में लाना चाहते हैं।

गद्यांश–38

जिस दिन नेता सुधार के मार्ग पर पैर रक्खे, उसी दिन उसे अपने प्राणों का मोह छोड़ देना चाहिए क्योंकि सहयोगियों का विश्वासघात और विरोधियों की नंगी तलवार सदा उसके मस्तक पर नृत्य किया करती है। कभी–कभी ऐसा समय आ जाता है, जब अनुयायी सहारा छोड़कर सदा के लिए किनारा कर लेते हैं। कभी–कभी नेता के सहमत न होने पर वे उसके प्राणों के ग्राहक भी हो जाते हैं। प्रसिद्ध नाविक कोलम्बस पर ऐसी ही विपत्ति आयी थी, परन्तु ईश्वर ने उसकी सहायता की और दूसरे ही दिन अमरीका महाद्वीप के दर्शन पाकर उसके साथी नाविक बन्धुओं का क्रोध शान्त हो गया। महात्मा बुद्ध को भी उनके शिष्य छोड़ कर चले गये थे। इसी प्रकार यदि विरोधी प्रबल हो उठें तो समाज सुधारक को उनकी क्रूरता का शिकार होना पड़ता है। ऐसे अवसर पर सच्चे और दृढ़ संकल्प नेता कसौटी पर कसे जाते हैं। यह कह कर बच निकलना कि यदि मेरा अन्त हो गया तो सच्चाई का भी अन्त हो जाएगा—अतएव सत्य की रक्षा के लिए मुझे अपनी प्राण–रक्षा करनी चाहिए, मात्र पलायन है, कर्त्तव्य से दूर भागना है। सत्य और न्याय जैसे जीवन–मूल्य शाश्वत हैं। मनुष्य इनके संस्थापन या निर्मूलन में निमित्त मात्र है।

संसार के सभी नेताओं ने उक्त सिद्धान्त की सत्यता पर विश्वास करके आगे कदम बढ़ाया। अनुयायियों के विश्वासघात के भय से उन्होंने पलायन नहीं किया और न आततायियों के भय से उन्होंने उनके सामने अपना सिर झुकाया। 'मेरे जीवन की अपेक्षा मेरी मृत्यु से ही सत्य का अधिक कल्याण होगा।' यह कहते हुए महात्मा ईसा शूली पर चढ़ गए और महान् दार्शनिक सुकरात ने मुस्कराते हुए विष का प्याला पी लिया। इतिहास साक्षी है कि महात्मा ईसा के साथ उनका धर्म शूली पर नहीं चढ़ाया जा सका और न महामना सुकरात के साथ उनके शाश्वत सिद्धान्तों का अन्त हुआ।

प्रश्न : (i) नेता किसे कहते हैं ? उसे अपने प्राणों का मोह कब और क्यों त्याग देना चाहिए ?

(ii) 'सहयोगियों का विश्वासघात और विरोधियों की नंगी तलवार नेता के मस्तक पर नृत्य करती है।' इस कथन की सत्यता को उदाहरण देकर स्पष्ट कीजिए।

(iii) पलायन किसे कहते हैं ? प्राय: नेता पलायन के पीछे क्या तर्क देते हैं ?

(iv) संसार के महान् नेताओं ने किस सिद्धान्त की सत्यता पर विश्वास किया ? इससे उन्हें क्या प्रेरणा मिली ?

(v) महात्मा ईसा क्या कहते हुए सूली पर चढ़ गए ? उनके जीवन से हमें क्या प्रेरणा मिलती है ?

उत्तर : (i) जिसमें समाज, धर्म तथा राष्ट्र का उचित और सुचारू ढंग से नेतृत्व करने तथा मार्गदर्शन की योग्यता होती है, उसे ही नेता कह सकते हैं।

जब सिद्धान्त तथा आदर्शों की दृढ़ता के कारण उसके अनुयायी (विरोधी) स्वार्थ अथवा किसी अन्य कारण से कोई कट्टर विरोधी उसके प्राणों के शत्रु हो जाते हैं तब उस अवस्था में नेता को अपने स्थान से पलायन करने के स्थान पर प्राणों को खतरे में डाल कर ऐसे खतरनाक शत्रुओं का सामना करना चाहिए।

(ii) जितना ही नेता महान, आदर्श और सिद्धान्तवादी होगा तथा जितनी अधिक ऊँची जिम्मेदारी होगी उतना ही नेता का जीवन खतरे में होगा। इस दशा में उसे अपने सहयोगियों के विरोध अथवा विश्वासघात का खतरा वैसे ही परेशान करता रहता है, जैसे नंगी तलवार शासक के सामने रहती है।

(iii) इसका अर्थ है परेशानियों से डर कर भाग जाना। नेता प्राय: अपने प्राण, सम्मान अथवा पद के खतरे में पड़ने तथा कठिन परिस्थितियाँ आने पर अक्सर पलायन कर जाता है। उनका तर्क यह होता है कि इस कार्य में उनके प्राण चले जाने पर देश की बहुत बड़ी हानि हो जाती।

(iv) संसार के महान् नेता सत्य और न्याय के सिद्धान्त की सत्यता पर विश्वास करके जीवन के अमर मूल्यों की स्थापना के लिए अपना कदम आगे बढ़ाते हैं, और किसी भी अत्याचार के सामने सिर नहीं झुकाते हैं।
संसार के महान् नेता भविष्य अथवा किसी बड़े अवसर का इन्तजार नहीं करते बल्कि उपस्थित क्षण को ही महान् समझकर कार्य करते हैं। इससे उन्हें हर परिस्थिति में आगे बढ़ने की प्रेरणा मिली।

(v) 'मेरे जीवन की अपेक्षा मृत्यु से ही सत्य का अधिक कल्याण होगा', यह कहते हुए ईसामसीह सूली पर चढ़ गए। इससे हमें सत्य, न्याय तथा मानवता के विकास के लिए आत्म बलिदान की प्रेरणा मिलती है।

गद्यांश–39

'लपका'—हिन्दी भाषा का एक बहुत ही सामान्य किन्तु प्रचलित शब्द है। इस शब्द का प्रचार उत्तर भारत के कम से कम उत्तर प्रदेश, मध्य प्रदेश और राजस्थान आदि में पर्याप्त मात्रा में पाया जाता है। इस शब्द का अर्थ है—लपकने, झपटने या भागकर अपने शिकार तक पहुँचकर उसे अपने पंजे में जकड़ने वाला व्यक्ति। ऐसे व्यक्ति संसार में सबसे अलग होते हैं। वे स्वार्थ की प्रतिमूर्ति होते हैं। भावना का उनके जीवन में कोई स्थान नहीं है। वह तो शिकार को एक बार पकड़कर तब तक नहीं छोड़ता जब तक शिकार से कुछ भी मिलने की सम्भावना होती है।

'पर्यटन' भारत का एक प्रमुख उद्योग है। इस उद्योग में देशी और विदेशी दोनों ही स्थानों से पर्यटक आते हैं। उनका उद्देश्य देश-विदेश के प्राचीन इतिहास और संस्कृति के विचार से महत्वपूर्ण स्थान, धार्मिक तथा ऐसे ही स्थानों पर जाकर वहाँ के सामाजिक, धार्मिक, राजनैतिक महत्व के सम्बन्ध में जानकारी इकट्ठा करना होता है। इसके लिए पर्यटक पर्याप्त धन व्यय करने के बाद भी अनेक मुसीबतें उठाते हैं। इनमें धन और समय की बर्बादी प्रमुख है।

'लपका' प्रवृत्ति के व्यक्ति ऐतिहासिक महत्व के नगरों में बस-स्टैण्ड, रेलवे स्टेशन तथा प्राचीन ऐतिहासिक इमारतों के आस-पास घूमते रहते हैं। बस या रेल से उतरने वाले अपने शिकार को यह व्यक्ति लाखों में पहचानकर उसे अपनी बातों के जाल में इस ढंग से फुसलाते हैं कि वह स्वयं ही इन लपकों के जाल में फँस जाता है। अक्सर इन लोगों के पास न तो अपने कार्य के सम्बन्ध में कोई सैद्धान्तिक ज्ञान होता है और न व्यावहारिक अनुभव। यहाँ तक कि उनके पास कोई सरकारी अनुज्ञा (आज्ञा पत्र) भी नहीं होता। इतने पर भी पुलिस के सक्रिय सहयोग और सहमति से यह अपना गैर-कानूनी कार्य सफलता से करते हैं। इनके हाथों लुटने वाले व्यक्ति देश या विदेश में देश की बदनामी करते हैं। इससे व्यवसाय पर प्रभाव पड़ता है, इसकी चिन्ता न इस विभाग के उच्च अधिकारियों को है और न पुलिस को। यह लोग पर्यटन उद्योग के लिए अभिशाप बन गए हैं।

प्रश्न : (i) 'लपका' शब्द से क्या अभिप्राय है ? ऐसे व्यक्तियों की विशेषताएँ बताइए।

(ii) 'पर्यटन उद्योग' का देश में क्या स्थान है ? इसके सम्बन्ध में अपने विचार स्पष्ट कीजिए।

(iii) 'पर्यटक' का अपनी यात्रा के समय सामान्य रूप में क्या उद्देश्य होता है ? स्पष्ट कीजिए।

(iv) 'लपका' का इस उद्योग में क्या स्थान है ? वह किस प्रकार उद्योग के लिए हानिकारक है ? स्पष्ट कीजिए।

(v) किस प्रकार के व्यक्ति पर्यटन उद्योग के लिए अभिशाप बन गये हैं ? इस समस्या का समाधान क्या है ?

उत्तर : (i) 'लपका' शब्द का अर्थ है लपकने, झपटने या भाग कर अपने शिकार तक पहुँचने तथा पंजे में जकड़ कर सब कुछ छीन ले जाने वाला व्यक्ति। ऐसा व्यक्ति स्वार्थ की प्रतिमूर्ति होता है। वह संसार में सबसे अलग होता है। भावना अथवा मानवता का इनके जीवन में कोई स्थान नहीं होता। विदेशी या अनजान व्यक्ति को अकेला पाकर ये व्यक्ति उसका सब कुछ छीन लेते हैं।

(ii) पर्यटन देश का एक महत्वपूर्ण उद्योग है। यह देश को लाखों डालर विदेशी मुद्रा के रूप में दिलाता है। इस उद्योग में देशी और विदेशी दोनों ही प्रकार के पर्यटक भारत आते हैं। इनका उद्देश्य देश के प्राचीन इतिहास, संस्कृति, धर्म तथा ऐसे महत्व के स्थानों की यात्रा तथा उनका अध्ययन करके ज्ञान प्राप्त करना होता है। इस उद्देश्य के लिए पर्यटक काफी धन भी व्यय करते हैं।

(iii) सामान्य रूप में पर्यटक का उद्देश्य देश के सामाजिक, ऐतिहासिक, धार्मिक, सांस्कृतिक तथा आर्थिक दृष्टि से महत्वपूर्ण स्थानों की यात्रा करना तथा सम्बन्धित स्थान अथवा भवन के सम्बन्ध में अधिकतम जानकारी प्राप्त करना भी होता है।

(iv) 'लपका' का इस उद्योग में महत्वपूर्ण स्थान है। वह ऐतिहासिक, सामाजिक, आर्थिक तथा धार्मिक विचार से महत्वपूर्ण स्थान अथवा इमारतों के पास घूमते पाए जाते हैं। ऐसे लोग रेलवे स्टेशन एवं बस स्टैण्ड के आस-पास घूमते हुए नजर आते हैं। यह अवसर पाते ही भीड़ से भी अपने शिकार को पहचान कर उसे अपने जाल में फँसा लेते हैं तथा तभी उसे छोड़ते हैं जब सब कुछ छीन लेते हैं। उनके इस प्रकार के कार्य से देश-विदेश में हमारे देश की बदनामी होती है तथा पर्यटन उद्योग भी चौपट होने की स्थिति में पहुँच जाता है।

(v) लपका प्रवृत्ति के व्यक्ति पर्यटन उद्योग के लिए अभिशाप बन गये हैं। इस प्रकार के लोगों के पास न तो कोई सैद्धान्तिक ज्ञान होता है और न व्यावहारिक अनुभव। इनके पास कोई सरकारी आज्ञा पत्र भी नहीं होता है। इतने पर भी पुलिस के सहयोग से ये अपना गैर-कानूनी कार्य सफलता से करते हैं। इस पर उच्च अधिकारी भी ध्यान नहीं देते हैं। इस समस्या के समाधान के लिए सरकार को पुलिस तथा अधिकारियों को सख्त निर्देश देते हुए कार्यवाही करनी चाहिए।

गद्यांश-40

'धर्म' का मानव जीवन में बहुत महत्वपूर्ण स्थान है। मानव और धर्म दोनों एक-दूसरे के पूरक हैं। एक के अभाव में दूसरे के स्पष्ट व्यक्तित्व की कल्पना ही नहीं की जा सकती। 'धर्म' मानव के व्यक्तित्व को पूर्ण बनाता है। धर्म का उद्देश्य मानव के आचार और विचार में गुणात्मक सुधार करके उसे सु-संस्कृत बनाना तथा उसमें सामाजिकता की भावना जाग्रत करना है। धर्म मनुष्य को एक-दूसरे के निकट लाता है, उन्हें अलग नहीं करता है। धर्म का उद्देश्य समाज को जोड़ना है, उसे तोड़ना या विभाजित करना नहीं है। धर्म में सैद्धान्तिक अथवा वैचारिक मतभेद तो हो सकता है किन्तु सभी धर्मों का मूल उद्देश्य मानव जीवन में ईश्वर के अस्तित्व के प्रति आस्था तथा उसमें श्रद्धा की भावना को जाग्रत करना रहा है। समय-समय पर देश-विदेश तथा सभी युगों में विभिन्न संत, फकीर तथा अवतारों को जन्म दिया है। किन्तु अक्सर व्यावहारिक जीवन में कुछ अधकचरे ज्ञान तथा प्रवृत्ति वाले व्यक्ति समाज में सिद्धान्त की व्याख्या स्वार्थपूर्ण भावना तथा 'पूर्वाग्रह' के कारण गलत रूप में करते हैं। अक्सर इन गलत व्याख्याओं के कारण जनसामान्य एक-दूसरे को समझने के स्थान पर विरोध या आलोचना पर उतारू हो जाते हैं। ऐसे स्वार्थी प्रकृति के व्यक्ति वैमनस्य या मतभेद को जन्म देकर तथा समाज को तोड़कर उसे विभाजित करते हैं, जबकि उदार हृदय फकीर और संत अपने आचरण और व्यवहार से नि:स्वार्थ सेवा की भावना को जीवन का आधार बना लेते हैं। वे धर्म, जाति और देश के सीमित स्तर से ऊपर उठकर मानवता की सेवा के लिए कार्य करते हैं। ऐसे फकीर हर प्रकार के भौतिक आकर्षणों से दूर रहकर कार्य करते हैं। वे सभी के होते हैं और सब उनके हो जाते हैं।

ऐसे फकीर हर युग, परिस्थिति और समाज में जन्म लेते रहे हैं और लेते रहेंगे। ऐसे ही संत और फकीरों के उच्च और आदर्श चरित्र तथा पवित्र आचरण से व्यक्तिगत तथा सामाजिक दोनों ही जीवन प्रभावित होते हैं। एक निस्वार्थ प्रवृत्ति का महात्मा, प्राणि मात्र के प्रति करुणा और सहानुभूति की भावना से पूर्ण रहता है। उसका

जीवन मानव मात्र की सेवा और परोपकार का साकार रूप होता है। ऐसे महात्मा, संत और फकीर मानव को धर्म के पवित्र और वास्तविक रूप की शिक्षा देते हैं। वे ही वास्तविक रूप में मानव को मानव के तथा समाज को समाज के निकट लाने का प्रयास करते हैं। उनका अवतरण ही हर प्रकार की खाई को पाट कर ऐसे सेतु का निर्माण करते हैं जिसे कोई भी विस्फोट नहीं तोड़ पायेगा।

प्रश्न : (i) धर्म का मानव जीवन में क्या स्थान है ? स्पष्ट कीजिए।

(ii) धर्म का मूल उद्देश्य स्पष्ट करते हुए बताइए कि वह समाज की एकता के लिए क्या कार्य करता है ?

(iii) समाज में वैचारिक विरोध कब उत्पन्न होता है और क्यों ?

(iv) इस विरोध को दूर करने का कार्य कौन करता है और किस प्रकार ? स्पष्ट कीजिए।

(v) किस प्रकार के व्यक्ति समाज को विभाजित करते हैं और कैसे ?

उत्तर : (i) धर्म का मानव जीवन में महत्वपूर्ण स्थान है। मानव और धर्म एक-दूसरे के पूरक है। धर्म मानव के व्यक्तित्व को पूर्ण बनाता है। धर्म उसके जीवन में स्थिरता और शान्ति का प्रचार करता है। धर्म, मानव को एक-दूसरे के निकट लाता है। वह समाज में एकता एवं संगठन का प्रचार करता है।

(ii) धर्म का मूल उद्देश्य मानव के आचार और विचार में गुणात्मक सुधार करके उसे सुसंस्कृत बनाना तथा उसमें सामाजिकता की भावना जाग्रत करना है। धर्म का उद्देश्य समाज को जोड़ने का है। वह समाज में ईश्वर के अस्तित्व के प्रति विश्वास और श्रद्धा का विचार जाग्रत करता है।

(iii) समाज में वैचारिक मतभेद तभी उत्पन्न होता है जब अल्पज्ञान या वैचारिक मतभेद वाले स्वार्थी और अवसरवादी व्यक्ति धर्म के सिद्धान्तों की गलत व्याख्या करते हैं। इसका कारण पूर्वाग्रह भी हो सकता है। इससे जनसामान्य की आपसी समझ खत्म होकर उनमें मतभेद खत्म हो जाता है। इससे विरोध भावना जाग्रत हो जाती है।

(iv) इस विरोध को दूर करने का कार्य उदार हृदय फकीर, महान पुरुष और संत करते हैं। वे अपने आचरण में निस्वार्थ सेवा को आधार बना लेते हैं। वे धर्म, जाति और सम्प्रदाय के सामान्य भेदभाव से ऊपर उठकर कार्य करते हैं। उनके सामने सभी आकर्षण फीके पड़ जाते हैं।

(v) व्यावहारिक जीवन में कुछ अधकचरे ज्ञान तथा प्रवृत्ति वाले व्यक्ति समाज में सिद्धान्त की व्याख्या स्वार्थपूर्ण भावना तथा 'पूर्वाग्रह' के कारण गलत रूप में करते हैं। इन गलत व्याख्याओं के कारण जनसामान्य एक-दूसरे को समझने के स्थान पर विरोध या आलोचना करने लगते हैं। इस प्रकार व्यक्तियों में मतभेद होने लगते हैं और समाज विभाजित हो जाता है।

गद्यांश–41

मानव की प्रारम्भिक अवस्था को सच्चरित्रता और सदाचारिता आदि उपायों से सुरक्षित रखना प्रत्येक मनुष्य का परम कर्तव्य है। छात्रावस्था अबोधावस्था होती है। पहले माता-पिता तथा गुरुजनों के दबाव से वह कर्तव्य पालन करना सीखता है। माता-पिता तथा गुरुजनों की आज्ञाएँ ज्यों की त्यों स्वीकार करना ही अनुशासन कहा जाता है। अनुशासन विद्यार्थी जीवन का प्राण है। अनुशासनहीन विद्यार्थी न तो देश का सभ्य नागरिक बन सकता है और न अपने व्यक्तिगत जीवन में ही सफल हो सकता है, वैसे तो जीवन के प्रत्येक क्षेत्र में अनुशासन परमावश्यक है, परन्तु विद्यार्थी जीवन के लिए तो यह सफलता की एकमात्र कुँजी है।

आज विद्यार्थियों में अनुशासनहीनता बढ़ रही है। यही कारण है कि शिक्षा का स्तर दिन पर दिन गिर रहा है। अनुशासनहीन विद्यार्थी अपनी विद्या का विनाश तो करता ही है। साथ-साथ वह कुसंगति का भी शिकार हो

जाता है। सामूहिक मेलों और उत्सवों में विद्यार्थियों की चरित्रहीनता स्पष्ट दिखाई देती है। अनुशासनहीनता का मुख्य कारण है। माता-पिता की ढिलाई। बच्चे की प्राथमिक पाठशाला घर होती है। अत: माता-पिता प्यार या भय दिलाकर अनुशासन का पाठ बच्चे को पढ़ायें। तभी वह आगे चलकर विद्यालय में अनुशासन का पूर्ण पालन करेगा। अनुशासनहीनता का दूसरा कारण है आज की दोषपूर्ण शिक्षा प्रणाली। इसमें नैतिक या चारित्रिक शिक्षा का कोई स्थान नहीं है। पहले विद्यार्थी को दण्ड का भय रहता था, अत: वह अनुशासित रहता था। परन्तु आजकल शारीरिक दण्ड अवैध है। शिक्षा संस्थाओं का कुप्रबन्ध भी विद्यार्थी को अनुशासनहीन बनाता है।

प्रश्न : (i) अनुशासन क्या है ? विद्यार्थी जीवन में अनुशासन का महत्व बताइये।

(ii) वर्तमान समय में शिक्षा का स्तर गिरने का क्या कारण है ?

(iii) अनुशासनहीनता के दो प्रमुख कारणों को स्पष्ट करें।

(iv) विद्यार्थी जीवन की सफलता का क्या आधार है ?

(v) बच्चे की प्रथम पाठशाला क्या है ? अनुशासनहीन विद्यार्थी स्वयं का विनाश कैसे करता है ?

उत्तर : (i) बालक द्वारा माता-पिता तथा अध्यापक द्वारा बताये गये नियमों, कर्तव्यों तथा आज्ञाओं का सही-सही पालन करना ही अनुशासन है।

विद्यार्थी जीवन में अनुशासन का स्थान शरीर में प्राण की भाँति है। जो विद्यार्थी अनुशासन में रहकर अपने कर्तव्यों का पालन करते है वे ही आगे चलकर सभ्य नागरिक बनते हैं तथा समाज में उनका सम्मान होता है।

(ii) विद्यार्थियों में बढ़ती हुई अनुशासनहीनता शिक्षा के स्तर में गिरावट का मुख्य कारण है। अनुशासनहीन विद्यार्थी स्वयं अपना तो विनाश करते ही हैं साथ ही साथ विद्यालय के वातावरण को भी दूषित करके शिक्षा तथा अन्य अनुशासित विद्यार्थियों का भविष्य भी नष्ट करते हैं।

(iii) अनुशासनहीनता का सर्वप्रमुख कारण माता-पिता द्वारा बच्चों को प्रेम तथा भय दिखाकर अनुशासित न करना है। इसका दूसरा कारण हमारी वर्तमान शिक्षा प्रणाली है। जिसमें केवल पाठ्य-पुस्तकों का अध्ययन कराना ही आवश्यक है नैतिक या चारित्रिक शिक्षा का इसमें कोई स्थान नहीं है।

(iv) विद्यार्थी जीवन की सफलता का मुख्य आधार अनुशासन है। अनुशासित विद्यार्थी ही आगे चलकर उचचकोटि के नागरिक बनते हैं। उनके द्वारा किये गये कार्य माता-पिता तथा देश के सम्मान को बढ़ाते हैं।

(v) बच्चे की प्रथम पाठशाला घर है, जहाँ उसे माता-पिता तथा अन्य सदस्य शिक्षा देते हैं। अनुशासनहीन विद्यार्थी सर्वप्रथम अपनी पढ़ाई का विनाश करता है। साथ-साथ वह कुसंगति में पड़कर अपने सामाजिक स्तर को भी गिराता है। मेलों और उत्सवों में अपनी चरित्रहीनता दिखाते हैं, शिक्षण संस्थानों में तोड़-फोड़ करते हैं।

गद्यांश–42

शिक्षा का जीवन में महत्व है। उसे राष्ट्र निर्माण का आधार माना गया है। हमारे देश में शिक्षा जीवन की आवश्यकता मानी गयी है। अत: इस पर आरम्भ से ही अधिक व्यय होना चाहिए था किन्तु ऐसा सम्भव नहीं हुआ। गत 50 वर्षों में शिक्षा पर व्यय के आँकड़े इस तथ्य को स्वयं स्पष्ट करते हैं। दुर्भाग्यवश इस विषय पर न तो सरकार ने गम्भीरता से ध्यान दिया और न जनता की ओर से इस क्षेत्र में कोई प्रयत्न किया गया। सरकारी क्षेत्र में इस विषय पर उपेक्षा का दृष्टिकोण अपनाया गया। कारण कोई भी राजनैतिक दल इस विषय विवाद में

नहीं फँसना चाहता था। कारण स्पष्ट है कि शिक्षित जनता जागरूक होकर अपने हित–अनहित की बात समझ जाएगी। उस दशा में राजनीतिज्ञ उसे किसी भी लुभावने वादे अथवा किसी अन्य प्रकार से धर्म और जाति के आधार पर विभाजित कर उनकी भावनाओं को भड़का कर उन्हें अपने राजनैतिक अस्त्र के रूप में प्रयोग नहीं कर पाएंगे। निश्चय ही ऐसा ही विचार इन राजनीतिज्ञों का रहा होगा। अगर ऐसा न होता तो कम से कम तत्कालीन विरोधी दलों में से किसी ने भी इस महत्वपूर्ण विषय पर कोई सकारात्मक विरोध न तो प्रकट किया न सक्रिय कदम बढ़ाया। उधर जनता ने शिक्षा के महत्व को पूरी तरह नहीं समझा। इसका मुख्य कारण उसकी निर्धनता है। जिस देश की जनता का 40% से अधिक भाग गरीबी की रेखा से नीचे रहकर जीवन की आवश्यक सुविधाओं तक से वंचित हो। उसके लिए वर्तमान खर्चीली शिक्षा व्यवस्था को सहन करना आकाश कुसुम के समान है। उनके विचार में बढ़ती जनसंख्या में हर नया पेट दो हाथ भी लेकर आता है। अत: शिक्षा प्राप्ति की उम्र से ही वे चाय के होटलों, मिल–फैक्ट्रियों और दुकानों पर परिश्रम करके 2 से 5 रु. प्रतिदिन तक कमाकर परिवार की गरीबी दूर करते हुए दिखाई देते हैं। सरकार द्वारा अनिवार्य शिक्षा की घोषणा केवल फाइलों में ही कैद होकर रह गयी है। देखना है, वर्तमान सरकार इस विषय में क्या कदम उठाती है।

प्रश्न : (i) शिक्षा के विषय में लेखक ने क्या विचार व्यक्त किए हैं और क्यों ? स्पष्ट कीजिए।

(ii) हमारे देश में शिक्षा के सम्बन्ध में सरकार का अब तक क्या दृष्टिकोण रहा है और क्यों ? तर्कसंगत उत्तर दीजिए।

(iii) शिक्षा के महत्व में भारतीय जनता की उदासीनता का उल्लेख करते हुए इसके कारण भी दीजिए।

(iv) अनिवार्य शिक्षा का क्या अर्थ है ? सरकार द्वारा अब तक क्या कदम उठाए गए हैं ? इनमें असफलता के लिए आप किसे उत्तरदायी मानते हैं ? सकारण उत्तर दीजिए।

(v) 'शिक्षा का हमारे जीवन में महत्वपूर्ण स्थान है।' आप इस तर्क से कहाँ तक सहमत हैं और क्यों ?

उत्तर : (i) शिक्षा, मानव जीवन की आवश्यक प्रक्रिया है। यह मानव को मानव बना देती है। यह किसी भी राष्ट्र की दृढ़ता और उन्नति का आधार है। हमारी जनसंख्या का एक बड़ा भाग आज भी अशिक्षित और निर्धन है। यह मानव के चरित्र और व्यक्तित्व को पूर्ण बना कर उसे अपनी मूलभूत आवश्यकताओं और अधिकारों के प्रति जागरूक करती है।

(ii) गत 50 वर्षों में सरकार का दृष्टिकोण शिक्षा के प्रति सकारात्मक नहीं रहा है। सरकार ने शिक्षा पर आवश्यकता से कम खर्च किया है।

इसके पीछे शायद राजनेताओं का यही दृष्टिकोण रहा है कि जनता को पूरी तरह से शिक्षित न होने दिया जाए क्योंकि शिक्षित जनता अपने अधिकार एवं कर्त्तव्यों को पहचान कर जागरूक हो जाएगी। उसमें स्वतन्त्र चिन्तन शक्ति का विकास होगा। इससे राजनेताओं की चालों का शिकार न हो पाएगी।

(iii) भारतीय जनता की शिक्षा के सम्बन्ध में दृष्टिकोण उदासीनता से पूर्ण रहा है। इसका कारण उसकी निर्धनता और भाग्यवादिता है। परिस्थितियों ने भाग्य और भगवान् पर इतना अधिक निर्भर कर दिया है कि बच्चों को भगवान् की देन समझता है। वह शिक्षा प्राप्त करने की उम्र में बच्चों को नौकरी पर भेजते हैं। छोटे–छोटे बालक शिक्षा पाने के स्थान पर चाय के होटल, दुकान तथा ऐसे ही कार्यों में लगकर पेट भरते दिखाई देते हैं।

(iv) इसका अर्थ 5 वर्ष से 14 वर्ष तक के प्रत्येक बच्चे को अनिवार्य रूप से विद्यालय में शिक्षा प्राप्त करनी चाहिए। इस उम्र के सभी बच्चे विद्यालय नियमित रूप से जाने चाहिए। जो

माँ-बाप अपने बच्चों को विद्यालय नहीं भेजते उन्हें इस सम्बन्ध में जानकारी दी जानी चाहिए।

सरकार द्वारा अब तक कागजी प्रचार ही अधिक किया गया है। जनता को शिक्षा के महत्व से पूरी तरह परिचित नहीं कराया गया है। राजनेताओं एवं अधिकारियों पर ऐसा करने का दबाव नहीं डाला गया है। इसके लिए सरकारी नीति और उदासीनता ही अधिक उत्तरदायी है।

(v) शिक्षा ही राष्ट्र निर्माण और व्यक्ति निर्माण का आधार है। शिक्षित होकर ही हम अपने और राष्ट्र के विषय में सही ढंग से जान सकते हैं और राष्ट्र निर्माण में अपना योगदान दे सकते हैं। शिक्षा के अभाव में राजनीतिज्ञ, अधिकारी आदि हमारा शोषण करते रहते हैं। राजनीतिज्ञ हमारी भावनाओं को भड़का कर अपने स्वार्थ पूर्ति करते हैं। अतः शिक्षा का हमारे जीवन में महत्वपूर्ण स्थान है।

गद्यांश–43

प्रकृति का अनिवार्य नियम है कि जिसको आप जैसा समझते हैं वह आपको भी वैसा ही समझता है। नागरिक के कर्तव्यों और अधिकारों का ज्ञान अस्पृश्यता रूपी कलंक को हम में से निकाल देगा और सच्चा भ्रातृ-भाव हमारे बीच फैलायेगा। वह हमको बतायेगा कि जो बात अपने को बुरी लगती है वह दूसरों को भी बुरी लगती है। वह विवश करेगा कि जैसा व्यवहार हम दूसरों से चाहते हैं, वैसा ही व्यवहार हम दूसरों के साथ करें। सब चीजें चाहती हैं कि हमारे साथ सद्व्यवहार किया जाय, चाहे ये जड़ हो, चाहे चेतन। दुर्व्यवहार करने पर सभी वस्तुयें अपना बदला लेंगी। यदि भाई, नौकर, पड़ोसी आदि चेतन जीवों से आप दुर्व्यवहार करते हैं, तो वे अपना बदला लेते ही है। अचेतन वस्तुएँ भी ऐसा करती हैं। जूते के साथ दुर्व्यवहार कीजियेगा, उसे साफ नहीं रखियेगा, तो वह काट लेगा। छाते की फिक्र न कीजियेगा उससे लापरवाही से पेश आइयेगा तो समय आने पर आप उसकी कमानी टूटी और कपड़ा कटा, अर्थात् उसे बेकार पाइयेगा। यदि सुई की फिक्र न रखियेगा तो बेवक्त वह आपके शरीर में चुभकर अपने अस्तित्व का प्रमाण आपको देगी। कार्य-कुशल पुरुष सबके साथ सदा अच्छा और उचित व्यवहार करता है। इस कारण वह अपनी सब वस्तुएँ हर समय ठीक प्रकार से ठीक स्थान पर पाता है और सब चीजें उसकी सेवा करती हैं। उसका घर गन्दा नहीं रहता। उसके कपड़े मैले नहीं रहते। वह सदा चिढ़चिढ़ाया हुआ, घबराया, दूसरों पर अपना दोष मढ़ता हुआ परेशान नहीं पाया जाता। उसका शरीर, उसका मस्तिष्क, सब स्वस्थ, स्थिर और प्रसन्न रहते हैं।

प्रश्न : (i) कर्तव्य और अधिकार हमें क्या बताते हैं?

(ii) लेखक ने दुर्व्यवहार और सद्व्यवहार का कैसा विश्लेषण किया है ?

(iii) जड़ या चेतन वस्तुयें हमसे किस प्रकार के व्यवहार की इच्छा करती हैं ?

(iv) अगर हम जड़ वस्तुओं के प्रति लापरवाह रहेंगे तो उनका हमारे प्रति कैसा रवैया रहेगा ?

(v) कार्य-कुशल व्यक्ति किस प्रकार अपना काम करता है ?

उत्तर : (i) कर्तव्य और अधिकारों का ज्ञान हमें बतलाता है कि समाज में हमारा अस्तित्व या स्थान क्या है तथा दूसरों से हम क्या आशा रखते हैं। इसी प्रकार कर्तव्यों का ज्ञान हमें यह सिखाता है कि हमारा समाज के प्रति तथा उसके प्रत्येक व्यक्ति के प्रति क्या कर्तव्य है।

(ii) लेखक के विचार में मानव का व्यवहार समाज में उसके स्थान को निश्चित करता है। हमारे सद्व्यवहार के परिणामस्वरूप समाज के सदस्यों में हमारे प्रति अपनत्व और प्रेम की जागृति होगी। इसके विपरीत दुर्व्यवहार की दशा में उस व्यक्ति, वर्ग विशेष अथवा समाज में ही हमारे प्रति विरोध की भावना जाग्रत हो जाएगी।

(iii) जड़ ही नहीं चेतन वस्तु भी हमसे सद्व्यवहार की आशा रखती है। सभी जीवित व्यक्ति, पशु और पक्षियों में स्वाभिमान एवं आत्म सम्मान का भाव होता है। वे सम्मानपूर्ण व्यवहार

की आशा करते हैं। इसी प्रकार जड़ या निर्जीव पदार्थ दुर्व्यवहार की दशा में मानव को अपनी प्रतिक्रिया से परिचित करा देते हैं, जैसे उपेक्षा या लापरवाही की दशा में सुई जैसा तुच्छ पदार्थ अपनी उपस्थिति से परिचित करा देता है।

(iv) जड़ वस्तुएँ हमारे सद्व्यवहार की दशा में हमारी लम्बे समय तक सेवा करती रहती हैं किन्तु उपेक्षा और लापरवाही की दशा में वे वस्तुएँ हमारी सेवा करने से इन्कार कर देती हैं।

(v) कार्यकुशल व्यक्ति सबके साथ सद्व्यवहार करता है। वह हर वस्तु को उसके उचित स्थान पर सावधानी से रखता, उचित ढंग से उसका प्रयोग करता है। इससे सभी वस्तुएँ लम्बे समय तक उसकी सेवा करती हैं।

गद्यांश–44

देश के पिछड़े भाग तथा निर्धन और कमजोर वर्गों में आत्महत्याओं के समाचार प्रायः मिलते रहते हैं। पिछले दिनों देश भर में किसानों ने भारी संख्या में आत्महत्याएँ कीं और यह सिलसिला अभी भी बराबर जारी है। बेरोजगारी से तंग आकर अथवा कैरियर की आकाशवाणी से आहत होकर बहुत से नौजवान आत्महत्या कर रहे हैं। यहाँ तक कि जवानी की दहलीज पर कदम रखने वाले किशोर तक आत्महत्या का रास्ता अख्तियार कर रहे हैं। दहेज के विकराल दानव से भयभीत होकर बड़ी संख्या में युवतियाँ भी आत्महत्या पर विवश हैं। लालची ससुराल वालों के जुल्मों-सितम और तानों से तंग आकर बहुएँ भी जान दे रही हैं। समस्त मध्यवर्ग एवं उच्चमध्य वर्ग, जैसे आत्महत्या की महामारी का शिकार हो रहा है। फिर भी आत्महत्या को धर्म और नैतिकता ने महामारी की संज्ञा दी है और कानून ने अपराध भी करार दिया है। फिर भी आत्महत्या करने वालों की तादाद दिन व दिन बढ़ती ही चली जा रही है। आत्महत्या करने वालों को कानून का खौफ भला कैसे रोक सकता है ? कानून के पास इससे बड़ी और बड़ी सजा क्या है जो आत्महत्या करने वाला स्वयं को दे देता है।

आत्महत्या के इस उभरते वातावरण के लिए कौन जिम्मेदार है ? क्या हिन्दुस्तान की आर्थिक, सामाजिक और राजनीतिक व्यवस्था इतनी जर्जर हो चुकी है कि इसमें बहुत से लोगों के लिए जीना सम्भव नहीं रह गया है और जीने की अपेक्षा मरना उन्हें आसान लगता है अथवा महत्वाकांक्षियों की नाकामियों ने उन्हें इतना पीड़ित, दुःखी और परेशान कर दिया है कि मौत की शरण में जाना ही श्रेयस्कार समझा है। वैसे भारतीयों को बहुत आत्म सन्तोषी माना जाता रहा है क्योंकि न तो कोई इतनी गरीबी झेल सकता है और न कोई इतनी बीमारी झेल सकता है और न कोई इतना जुल्मों सितम और बेईमानी झेल सकता है जितनी कि हम भारतवासी झेलने के सदियों से अभ्यस्त हो चुके हैं। हमारा मुल्क हजारों वर्षों से यह सब झेल रहा है। फिर भी अपने उल्लास और आनन्द में मगन रहा है। किन्तु अब जिन्दगी रोज व रोज बदल रही है। पश्चिम के गहन सम्पर्क में आकर भारत की मनोदशा बदली है। पश्चिम ने वैज्ञानिक प्रगति और सुख साधनों के रूप में हमें बहुत कुछ दिया है किन्तु हमारी शान्ति और सहनशीलता को छीन लिया है।

प्रश्न : (i) आत्महत्या शब्द का क्या अर्थ है ? बताइए कि आत्महत्या के पीछे कौन-सी मनोवृत्ति काम करती है ?

(ii) आत्महत्या के कारणों को स्पष्ट कीजिए।

(iii) भारतवासियों की कौन-सी विशेषताएँ बताई गई हैं ? उनको चारित्रिक विशेषताओं के आधार पर स्पष्ट कीजिए।

(iv) पश्चिमी संस्कृति के सम्पर्क ने इस भावना को बढ़ाने में योगदान दिया है। इस सम्बन्ध में अपने विचार स्पष्ट कीजिए।

(v) भारतीयों को आत्म-सन्तोषी क्यों माना गया है ?

उत्तर : (i) इसका अर्थ है स्वेच्छा तथा बिना किसी बाहरी दबाव के अपने जीवन का अन्त करना या स्वयं को मौत के हवाले कर देना।

इसके पीछे भविष्य की अनिश्चितता, बेरोजगारी, लम्बी बीमारी, जीवन की असफलता और निराशा की भावना प्रमुख कारण है। इसके अतिरिक्त दहेज प्रथा के कारण परिवार द्वारा उपेक्षा एवं अन्याय के व्यवहार की मनोवृत्ति काम करती है।

(ii) आत्महत्या के मुख्य कारण हैं भविष्य की अनिश्चितता, बेरोजगारी, लम्बी बीमारी, निर्धनता, उद्देश्य में असफलता, उपेक्षा, अभाव, अपमान तथा दहेज प्रथा के कारण जीवन में आने वाला तनाव।

(iii) भारतवासियों में सन्तोष की भावना असीमित होती है। वे गरीबी, बीमारी, उपेक्षा, अन्याय, अपमान, तनाव किसी भी प्रकार के अत्याचार को सह सकते हैं। वे सन्तोषी, सहनशील, आत्म-विश्वासी, और स्वाभिमानी हैं।

(iv) पश्चिमी सभ्यता और संस्कृति के सम्पर्क और प्रभाव ने भारतवासियों में सुख भोग, दिखावे, आत्म-सम्मान, स्वार्थप्रियता और अवसरवादिता आदि का लालच बढ़ा कर हमारी सहनशीलता को छीन लिया है।

(v) भारतीयों को आत्म-सन्तोषी माना गया है क्योंकि न तो कोई इतनी गरीबी झेल सकता है और न कोई इतनी बीमारी झेल सकता है और न कोई इतना जुल्मों-सितम और बेईमानी झेल सकता है जितनी कि हम भारतवासी सदियों से झेलते आ रहे हैं, हमारा देश हजारों वर्षों से यह सब झेल रहा है, फिर भी अपने आनन्द और उल्लास में मगन रहता है।

गद्यांश–45

आजकल समता का सिद्धान्त जो प्रचलित हो रहा है, उसका आधार प्रेम नहीं, यही सम्पत्ति और प्रभुत्व है। वैज्ञानिकों के ज्ञान और नीतिज्ञों की नीति दोनों का लक्ष्य इसी सम्पत्ति और प्रभुत्व की बुद्धि है। उसी के कारण जीवन में संघर्ष है और देश-देश में युद्ध है। यन्त्रों की वृद्धि हो रही है, उद्योगों की उन्नति हो रही है, व्यवसायों का विस्तार हो रहा है, पर उन्हीं के साथ राष्ट्रों में संघर्ष बढ़ रहा है, देश के भीतर अशान्ति भी फैल रही है। यदि सचमुच में हम में समता और बन्धुत्व का भाव आ जाये, तो यही संसार स्वर्ग हो जाये। पर एक मात्र सम्पत्ति को ही प्रधानता देकर हम लोगों में जो एक असन्तोष और अशान्ति की प्रबलता हो रही है, पर क्या हमें सचमुच सुख और शान्ति के पथ पर ले जा रही है ?

इन्हीं चिन्ताओं में व्यस्त रहकर जब मैं सन्ध्या समय नदी तट पर पहुँचा, तब देखा कि वहाँ कैसी शान्ति है, कैसी शोभा है, कैसा माधुर्य है। रात्रि की भयानकता न जाने कहाँ विलीन हो गयी थी। नदी कलकल करती बहती जा रही थी। वृक्षों पर पक्षी कलरव कर रहे थे और कुछ नदी में ही विहार कर रहे थे। पवन भी मन्द-मन्द गति से बह रही थी। सूर्यास्त के कारण आकाश बहुवर्ण-रंजित हो गया था। सर्वत्र सौन्दर्य का एक अप्रतिम राज्य था। यहीं तो हम सच्ची शान्ति का अनुभव करते हैं। पर क्या मूक प्रकृति में ही यह सौन्दर्यमय जीवन है ? क्या मनुष्यों के जीवन में अभावों के कष्ट और चिन्ताओं की ही वेदनाएँ हैं ? उससें क्या कहीं विशुद्ध सौन्दर्य, विशुद्ध आनन्द या विशुद्ध मुक्ति और चिन्ताओं की ही वेदनाएँ हैं ? उससें क्या कहीं विशुद्ध सौन्दर्य, विशुद्ध आनन्द या विशुद्ध मुक्ति की अवस्था नहीं है ? बाह्य जगत में जिस अलक्षित शक्ति द्वारा अलौकिक सौन्दर्य की सृष्टि होती है, उसने क्या हमारे अन्तर्जगत में किसी भी सौन्दर्य की रचना नहीं की ? वहाँ क्या हिंसा और वासनाओं की ही आँधी रहती है ? वहाँ क्या प्रेम की मृदु तरंगें नहीं उठती हैं ? क्रमशः अन्धकार फैल गया और मैं घर लौट आया। पर इस एक ही दिन में जीवन में कला का अनुभव किया और कला में जीवन का।

प्रश्न : (i) लेखक समता और बन्धुत्व का भाव क्यों लाना चाहता हैं ?

(ii) जीवन में संघर्ष और देश-देश में युद्ध का क्या कारण है ?

(iii) एकमात्र सम्पत्ति को ही प्रधानता देने से क्या हमें सच्चा सुख और सच्ची शान्ति मिल सकती है ? अगर नहीं, तो क्यों ?

(iv) 'क्या मूक प्रकृति में ही यह सौन्दर्यमय जीवन है' का क्या तात्पर्य है ?

(v) लेखक ने कला पर अधिक जोर क्यों दिया है ?

उत्तर : (i) लेखक मानव जीवन में समता और बन्धुत्व का सिद्धान्त इसलिए लागू करना चाहता है क्योंकि केवल इसी भावना मात्र के प्रचार से ही मानव के सभी मतभेद नष्ट हो जायेंगे तथा यह संसार स्वर्ग के समान सुन्दर और सुख शान्ति का स्थान बन जाएगा।

(ii) जीवन में संघर्ष, तनाव और मतभेद तथा राष्ट्रों में पारस्परिक कटुता तथा युद्ध का प्रमुख कारण भौतिक सम्पत्ति तथा सत्ता या अधिकार प्रदर्शन की भावना ही है।

(iii) एकमात्र सम्पत्ति को ही जीवन में प्रमुखता देने से ही मानव को सच्चा सुख और सच्ची शान्ति नहीं मिल सकती है क्योंकि सम्पत्ति के द्वारा मानव वैभव और शक्ति का प्रदर्शन करके अपनी श्रेष्ठता प्रदर्शित करना चाहता है जिससे इनसे रहित व्यक्ति स्वयं को हीन और अपमानित अनुभव करता है। ऐसे में ईर्ष्या, द्वेष तथा वैमनस्य की भावना का उदय होता है जो व्यक्ति तथा राष्ट्र के विनाश का कारण बनता है।

(iv) जी हाँ, मूक प्रकृति में ही यह सौन्दर्य जीवन व्याप्त है। इसका अर्थ है कि प्रकृति हर समय अपने पवित्र और सुन्दर रूप का प्रचार करती है। प्रकृति अपने सम्पर्क में आने वाले प्रत्येक मानव के मन को अपने ही समान पवित्र बना देती है।

(v) लेखक ने जीवन में कला पर अधिक जोर दिया है। सौन्दर्य का अनुभव तथा उसकी कल्पना को साकार रूप कला की सहायता से ही दिया जा सकता है। इस प्रकार यदि हम यह कहें कि कला ही सौन्दर्य की अभिव्यक्ति है, तो कोई अनुचित बात न होगी।

गद्यांश–46

परमाणु शक्ति होने के उत्साह में क्या भारत की जनता महँगाई का बोझ खुशी-खुशी वहन कर लेगी। वित्त मन्त्री की धारणा तो यही जान पड़ती है। उनके द्वारा पेश 1998–99 के बजट की जिस एक बात से इन्कार नहीं किया जा सकता वह यह कि यह बजट महँगाई बढ़ाने वाला होगा। पेट्रोल की कीमतें एक झटके में तीन-चार रुपये से ज्यादा बढ़ गईं। जब पेट्रोल की कीमतें बढ़ती हैं तो उन सारी चीजों की कीमतें बढ़ जाती हैं जो एक से दूसरी जगह ले जाने के लिए पेट्रोल पर निर्भर हैं। यानी पेट्रोल की कीमत बढ़ने से झटका सिर्फ उन्हीं लोगों को नहीं लगता जो पेट्रोल से चलने वाले वाहनों का प्रयोग करते हैं। उसका झटका क्या अमीर, क्या गरीब प्रत्यक्ष या अप्रत्यक्ष रूप से सभी को लगता है। जाहिर है व्यावहारिक अर्थ में गरीब पर उसकी मार ज्यादा पड़ती है। इसलिए जब कुछ लोगों को कीमत वृद्धि के सिलसिले में यह दलील देते सुना जाता है कि परमाणु गौरव प्राप्त करना है तो कीमत तो चुकानी होगी। तब बरबस कुछ सवाल पैदा होते हैं। एक तो यही कि क्या करों की प्रणाली हमारे देश में उपभोग की विसंगतियों और असमानताओं को और पुख्ता और मजबूत नहीं कर रही है। मसलन पेट्रोल के ही मामले में एक-एक विसंगतियाँ यह हैं कि जो लोग अत्यन्त जरूरी कामों से दोपहिया वाहनों का प्रयोग करते हैं और जो महँगी कारों, लम्बे और अनावश्यक सफर करते हैं, दोनों एक ही कीमतों पर पेट्रोल खरीदते हैं। इसका सबसे बड़ा विदूष यह है कि जिन चीजों के दाम अब भी बाजार की शर्तों से निर्धारित नहीं हैं और सरकारी अनुदान प्राप्त वस्तुएँ हैं, उनके अनावश्यक और असंगत इस्तेमाल की कीमतें, देश के सभी आय वर्गों के करदाता अदा करते हैं यानी सामान्य करदाता का अपने द्वारा इस्तेमाल पेट्रोल की कीमत का कुछ हिस्सा भी उसकी जेब से ही जाएगा। जो महज सुविधा का या शानशौकत के लिए उसका दुरुपयोग करते

हैं। यह स्थिति बिजली के मामले में है। जो लोग वातानुकूलन की सुविधा वहन कर सकते हैं और उसके लिए बिजली की ज्यादा खपत करते हैं। उनकी खपत पर भी भारत के करदाताओं की जेब से उतना ही अनुदान दिया जाता है, जितना उन लोगों के द्वारा प्रयुक्त बिजली पर जो मुश्किल से एक बल्ब और पंखे पर गुजर करते हैं। इस प्रकार अनुदान वाली वस्तुओं का अधिक प्रयोग, अमीर वर्ग द्वारा अधिक मात्रा में किया जा रहा है।

प्रश्न : (i) वित्तमन्त्री की धारणा क्या है ? क्या जनता उनके विचार से सहमत है ? यदि नहीं तो क्यों ?

(ii) बजट को महँगाई बढ़ाने वाला किन कारणों से बताया गया है ?

(iii) बजट की मार का क्या अर्थ है ? यह किस वर्ग को अधिक प्रभावित करती है और कैसे ?

(iv) 'सुविधा भोगी' शब्द का क्या अर्थ है ? वह वर्ग किस प्रकार अनुचित रूप में सुविधाओं का उपयोग करता है ? स्पष्ट कीजिए।

(v) उदाहरण सहित स्पष्ट कीजिए कि भारतीय कर प्रणाली में विसंगतियाँ हैं ?

उत्तर : (i) वित्तमन्त्री का विचार है कि परमाणु-शक्ति सम्पन्न राष्ट्र होने के गर्व और सम्मान की रक्षा के लिए जनता पेट्रोल तथा ऐसी ही अन्य वस्तुओं की मूल्य वृद्धि को स्वीकार कर लेगी। ऐसा करने में उसे सम्मान या स्वाभिमान की भावना का अनुभव होगा।

देश की जनता वित्तमन्त्री के विचार से पूरी तरह असहमत है क्योंकि मूल्य वृद्धि की स्थिति में उस वस्तु का उपभोग करने वाले लोगों पर तो प्रभाव पड़ता ही है साथ ही उस वस्तु से प्रत्यक्ष या अप्रत्यक्ष सम्बन्ध रखने वाली वस्तुओं का मूल्य भी बढ़ जाता है। इस प्रकार इस वृद्धि का व्यापक प्रभाव उस जन सामान्य पर अधिक पड़ता है जो उस वस्तु का उपयोग ही नहीं करता।

(ii) इसका कारण है कि देश की जनता के सीमित वर्ग के ऐश-आराम की वस्तुओं की आपूर्ति तथा सुरक्षा और देश के स्वाभिमान की रक्षा के लिए देश को अधिक व्यय करना पड़ता है। जनता का सम्पन्न और उच्च वर्ग अक्सर हर वस्तु का अत्यधिक दुरुपयोग करता है किन्तु बढ़ी हुई कीमत सम्पूर्ण जनता को चुकानी पड़ती है।

(iii) इसका अर्थ बजट के द्वारा लगाए गए कर अथवा अधिभार। यह कर लगते ही सम्बन्धित वस्तु की कीमत ही नहीं बढ़ती बल्कि उस वस्तु से सम्बन्धित सभी वस्तुओं की कीमत भी बढ़ जाती है।

इसका प्रभाव जन साधारण पर अधिक पड़ता है। उसके द्वारा प्रयोग की जाने वाली अनिवार्य एवं जीवन-पोषक तथा रक्षक वस्तुओं के बढ़े मूल्य का प्रभाव उसकी आर्थिक स्थिति पर पड़ता है।

(iv) इसका अर्थ है सभी प्रकार के सुख और आराम उठाने वाला सम्पन्न वर्ग। किसी भी वस्तु के मूल्य की वृद्धि का इसके स्तर पर कोई प्रभाव नहीं पड़ता। ऐश-आराम के साधनों का प्रयोग यह वर्ग अधिक करता है, जबकि इसका मूल्य नाममात्र को बिजली और पेट्रोल जैसे इन साधनों को प्रयोग करने वालों पर इसका प्रभाव अधिक होता है।

(v) भारतीय कर प्रणाली में विसंगतियाँ हैं क्योंकि सरकारी अनुदान प्राप्त वस्तुओं के लिए प्रत्येक वर्ग को समान कर देना पड़ता है। उदाहरणार्थ पेट्रोल को ले सकते हैं। इसमें यह विसंगति है कि जो लोग अत्यन्त जरूरी कामों से दोपहिया वाहनों का प्रयोग करते हैं और जो महँगी कारों, लम्बे और अनावश्यक सफर करते हैं, दोनों एक ही कीमत पर पेट्रोल खरीदते हैं। यही स्थिति बिजली के मामले में भी है। जो लोग वातानुकूलित का उपयोग करते हैं तथा जो मुश्किल से एक पंखा और बल्ब का प्रयोग करते हैं, दोनों को एक ही कीमत देनी पड़ती है।

●●

व्याकरण

(GRAMMAR)

मुहावरे तथा लोकोक्तियाँ

(IDIOMS AND PROVERBS)

लोकोक्ति और मुहावरे देते भाषा में है ज्ञान।
अतः इनके प्रयोग पर दीजिए पूरा-पूरा ध्यान॥

मुहावरे (IDIOMS)

भाषा में प्रवाह, सजीवता एवं विशेषता लाने के लिए मुहावरों का प्रयोग किया जाता है। वाक्य का ऐसा अंश जो साधारण अर्थ का बोध न करा कर उसमें विलक्षणता उत्पन्न करे, उसे 'मुहावरा' कहते हैं।

वाक्यों में मुहावरों का प्रयोग माधुर्य, चमत्कार तथा प्रभाव उत्पन्न करने के लिए किया जाता है। मुहावरों तथा लोकोक्तियों में अन्तर होता है। मुहावरा वाक्य का एक अंश होता है जबकि लोकोक्ति एक पूर्ण वाक्य। लोकोक्ति का प्रयोग पूरे वाक्य के रूप में किया जाता है तथा इसे बदला नहीं जा सकता जबकि मुहावरे लिंग, वचन और क्रिया के अनुरूप परिवर्तित हो जाते हैं।

1. अपने मुँह मियाँ मिट्ठू बनना—(अपनी प्रशंसा स्वयं करना) सज्जन पुरुषों को अपने मुँह मियाँ मिट्ठू बनना शोभा नहीं देता।
2. अपना सा मुँह लेकर रह जाना—(लज्जित होना, खिसियाकर रह जाना) मैंने दुष्यन्त से ऐसी कड़वी बात कही कि वह अपना सा मुँह लेकर रह गया।
3. अन्धे की लकड़ी—(एकमात्र सहारा) श्रवण कुमार अपने माँ-बाप के लिए अन्धे की लकड़ी था।
4. अगर-मगर करना—(टालना) जब अफसर ने चपरासी से ताला खुला रह जाने के विषय में पूछा तो वह अगर-मगर करने लगा।
5. अपने पैरों पर खड़ा होना—(स्वावलम्बी बनना) मनीष को अब किसी की परवाह नहीं क्योंकि वह अपने पैरों पर खड़ा हो गया है।
6. अक्ल के पीछे लाठी लिए फिरना—(अक्ल से काम न लेना) स्टेशन पर अपना सामान छोड़कर पानी पीने जाना अक्ल के पीछे लाठी लिये फिरने के समान है।
7. अक्ल के घोड़े दौड़ाना—(दूर की सोचना) श्याम किसी काम को करने से पहले अक्ल के घोड़े दौड़ाता है।
8. अक्ल के दुश्मन—(मूर्ख) तुम्हें जरा सा प्रश्न नहीं आता तुम तो अक्ल के दुश्मन मालूम पड़ते हो।
9. अपना राग अलापना—(अपनी ही बात करते रहना) सुरेश तो किसी की सुनता ही नहीं, वह अपना राग अलापता रहता है।
10. अपना उल्लू सीधा करना—(स्वार्थ सिद्ध करना) हरीश तो भोले-भाले आदमियों को दबाकर अपना उल्लू सीधा करता है।
11. आस्तीन का साँप—(कपटी मित्र) मित्र बनाने में सावधान रहना चाहिये क्योंकि अधिकतर लोग आस्तीन के साँप होते हैं।

12. आड़े हाथों लेना—(फटकारना) जब अध्यापक ने उसे आड़े हाथों लिया तब उसने सच्चाई बतायी।
13. आकाश-पाताल का अन्तर—(अत्यधिक भेद) प्राचीन काल व वर्तमान समय के राजनेताओं में आकाश-पाताल का अन्तर है।
14. आपे से बाहर होना—(अत्यधिक क्रोध करना) प्राचीन काल में ऋषि-मुनि जरा सी बात पर आपे से बाहर होकर श्राप दे दिया करते थे।
15. आनन-फानन में—(तुरन्त) शिक्षा निदेशक के यकायक आ जाने से आनन-फानन में उनके स्वागत की तैयारी करनी पड़ी।
16. आग बबूला होना—(क्रोधित होना) दुर्वासा ऋषि जरा-सी बात पर आग बबूला हो जाते थे।
17. आग लगाना—(भड़काना) जयचन्द ने अपनी बातों से पृथ्वीराज चौहान और आल्हा-उदल के बीच आग लगा दी।
18. आसमान में उड़ना—(कल्पना लोक में रहना) घर में कुछ भी चल रहा हो पर संजय को तो आसमान में उड़ने से मतलब है।
19. आग पर पानी डालना—(क्रोध शान्त करना) राम ने महर्षि परशुराम से आदरपूर्वक बात करके आग पर पानी डाल दिया।
20. आकाश चूमना—(बहुत ऊँचा होना) हिमालय की कई चोटियाँ आकाश चूमती दिखाई देती हैं।
21. आकाश के तारे तोड़ना—(असम्भव काम करना) आधुनिक युग के वैज्ञानिक आकाश के तारे तोड़ने का दम रखते हैं।
22. आकाश-पाताल एक करना—(भरसक प्रयत्न करना) गाँधीजी ने भारत की स्वाधीनता के लिए आकाश-पाताल एक कर दिया था।
23. आसमान से बातें करना—(इतराना) चार पैसे हो जाने पर आदमी आसमान से बातें करने लगता है।
24. आँख का तिनका—(दु:ख देने वाला) सीता तो सदैव से अपनी सौतेली माँ की आँख का तिनका थी।
25. आँच न आना—(कोई हानि न होना) जो लोग ईश्वर की उपासना करते हैं उन पर कभी कोई आँच नहीं आती।
26. आँखें पथरा जाना—(मरणासन्न होना) कृष्ण की राह देखते-देखते गोपियों की आँखें पथरा गयीं।
27. आँखें भर आना—(दु:खी होना) गोपियों की दयनीय दशा देखकर सूर की आँखें भर आयीं।
28. आँखें नीली-पीली करना—(क्रोधित होना) अरे भाई, मुझ पर आँखें नीली-पीली क्यों करते हो, मैंने तुम्हारा क्या बिगाड़ा है ?
29. आँखों में खून उतरना—(क्रोधित होना) तुम्हारी बदमाशी देखकर मेरी आँखों में खून उतरने लगता है।
30. आँख उठाकर देखना—(सामना करना) रणजीत सिंह जी की वीरता के कारण उनकी तरफ आँख उठाकर देखने का साहस किसी में न था।
31. आँख का अन्धा—(मूर्ख) आशीष जैसा आँख का अन्धा कभी संसार में सफल नहीं हो सकता।
32. आँख खुलना—(सचेत होना) धोखा खाने के बाद निधि की आँखें खुल गईं।
33. आँख का पानी उतरना—(बेशर्म हो जाना) पंकज से चाहे कितना ही भला-बुरा कहो उस पर कोई असर नहीं होता, उसकी तो आँखों का पानी ही उतर गया है।
34. आँखों से गिर जाना—(आदर कम हो जाना) ट्यूशनखोरी के चलते आजकल के शिक्षक अभिभावकों की आँखों से गिर गये हैं।

35. आँखों में धूल झोंकना—(धोखा देना) राजेश महाजन ऐसा चालबाज है कि स्कूल के सभी अध्यापकों की आँखों में धूल झोंककर भाग जाता है।
36. आँखें दिखाना—(धमकाना) बच्चे आँखें दिखाने से ही ठीक काम करते हैं।
37. आँखें चुराना—(सामने न आना) काम पूरा न होने के कारण शरद भूगोल के घण्टे में अध्यापक से आँखें चुराता है।
38. आँसू पीना—(बहुत दुःख सहना) बेचारे गरीब अत्याचार सहते हैं और आँसू पीकर रह जाते हैं।
39. आँसू पोंछना—(नुकसान करके सन्तोष या सांत्वना देना) पहले धोखे से उसकी जमीन अपने नाम लिखवा ली अब दो हजार रुपया देकर उसके आँसू पोंछते हो।
40. आँखें फेरना—(सम्बन्ध समाप्त कर लेना) सुरेश की दुकान और घर नीलाम होते ही उसके सब रिश्तेदारों ने उससे आँखें फेर लीं।
41. आँखों पर पर्दा पड़ना—(समझ न आना) रमेश की आँखों पर तो अपने मित्र राघव की मित्रता का पर्दा पड़ गया है।
42. आँखों में खटकना—(बुरा लगना) पाण्डव सदैव दुर्योधन की आँख में खटकते रहे।
43. अँधेर खाता—(अन्याय) आजकल अपराधियों को सजा नहीं मिलती अँधेर खाता जो खुला हुआ है।
44. आँखें चार होना—(निगाह मिलना) उससे आँखे चार होते ही वह सबको मोह लेता है।
45. आँख की पुतली होना—(अति प्रिय) कृष्ण यशोदा की आँख की पुतली थे।
46. आँखों का काँटा—(अप्रिय) सीमा की बहन उसकी आँखों का काँटा बन गई है।
47. आँखों का तारा—(अति प्रिय) तानसेन अपने माता-पिता की आँखों का तारा थे।
48. आसमान सिर पर उठाना—(बहुत शोर करना) महेश के थोड़ी देर से घर पहुँचने पर उसके पिता ने आसमान सिर पर उठा लिया।
49. अंकुश रखना—(दबाव में रखना) सन्तान को चरित्रवान बनाने के लिए उन पर अंकुश रखना आवश्यक है।
50. अंकित होना—(कभी न भूल पाना) कुम्भ के मेले की दुर्घटना का दृश्य मेरे हृदय पटल पर अंकित हो गया।
51. आँखें बिछाना—(बहुत आदर करना) राम के वन में पधारने पर वनवासियों ने आँखें बिछा दीं।
52. अँगूठा दिखाना—(इन्कार करना) धीरज ने दिनेश से पुस्तक माँगी लेकिन उसने अँगूठा दिखा दिया।
53. अपने पाँव आप कुल्हाड़ी मारना—(अपनी ही हानि करना) पढ़ने का समय खेल में गँवा कर ललित ने अपने पाँव आप कुल्हाड़ी मार ली।
54. अंक भरना—(प्यार करना) माँ ने बेटे को देखते ही अंक में भर लिया।
55. अँगारे उगलना—(जली-कटी कहना) गन्दी मानसिकता के रोगी जरा सी बात पर अँगारे उगलने लगते हैं।
56. इधर की उधर लगाना—(चुगली करना) रमेश की बड़ी बुरी आदत है वह सदैव इधर की उधर लगाया करता है।
57. ईंट से ईंट बजाना—(मुँहतोड़ जबाव देना) उसके द्वारा लगाये आक्षेपों का जबाव हमने उसकी ईंट से ईंट बजा कर दिया।
58. ईद का चाँद होना—(बहुत दिनों बाद दिखाई देना) अरे भाई रोहित, तुम तो ईद के चाँद हो गये हो।

59. ईंट का जबाव पत्थर से देना—(करारा जबाव देना) जब भारत पर पाकिस्तान का आक्रमण हुआ तब भारत ने ईंट का जबाव पत्थर से दिया।
60. इधर-उधर की हाँकना—(गप्पें मारना) तुम काम-काज करने की अपेक्षा इधर-उधर की हाँकने में ही समय नष्ट कर देते हो।
61. उँगली पर नचाना—(वश में रखना) चतुर स्त्रियाँ अपने भोंदू पतियों को उँगली पर नचाती हैं।
62. उँगली उठाना—(कमी निकालना) किसी के ऊपर उँगली उठाना अच्छा नहीं होता।
63. उल्टी गंगा बहाना—(नियम के विरुद्ध चलना) अपने पिता पर रौब दिखाकर तुम तो उल्टी गंगा बहाते हो।
64. उल्टी माला फेरना—(अहित चाहना) कल तक तुम गिरधारी के अभिन्न मित्र थे, अब उसके लिए उल्टी माला फेरने लगे।
65. उगल देना—(सच-सच बोलना) पुलिस की मार के आगे बड़े-बड़े अपराधी सारी बात उगल देते हैं।
66. ऐड़ी-चोटी का जोर लगाना—(अत्यधिक प्रयास करना) श्यामबाबू ऐड़ी-चोटी का जोर लगाने पर भी उस मकान को नहीं खरीद पाये।
67. ओखली में सिर देना—(जान-बूझकर परेशानी में फँसना) मूर्खों की लड़ाई के बीच में बोलना ओखली में सिर देना है।
68. कलम तोड़ना—(बहुत अच्छा लिखना) रामचन्द्र शुक्ल ने हिन्दी साहित्य का इतिहास क्या लिखा है, बस कलम तोड़ दी है।
69. कान पर जूँ न रेंगना—(ध्यान न देना) कितनी बार पढ़ने के लिए कहा, लेकिन तुम्हारे कान पर जूँ भी नहीं रेंगती है।
70. कलेजा ठण्डा होना—(असीम शान्ति मिलना) डाकू के मरने पर क्षेत्रीय जनता का कलेजा ठण्डा हो गया।
71. कलेजे पर साँप लोटना—(जलन होना) उसकी पदोन्नति सुनकर तुम्हारे कलेजे पर साँप क्यों लोट गया ?
72. कलई खुलना—(असलियत का पता लग जाना) सुरेश अपनी प्रतिभा की बड़ी प्रशंसा किया करता था, किन्तु नकल में पकड़े जाने पर उसकी सारी कलई खुल गयी।
73. किस्मत ठोंकना—(भाग्य को दोष देना) आलसी हमेशा किस्मत ठोंकते रहते हैं।
74. कुत्ते की मौत मरना—(बुरी तरह मरना) अपराधी सदैव कुत्ते की मौत मारे जाते हैं।
75. कोल्हू का बैल—(रात-दिन काम में लगे रहना) जगन्नाथ ने अपने नौकर को कोल्हू का बैल बना रखा है।
76. काई सी फटना—(तितर-बितर होना) पुलिस के फायर करते ही भीड़ में काई सी फट गई।
77. कागजी घोड़े दौड़ाना—(केवल लिखा-पढ़ी करना) सरकार रचनात्मक काम तो करती नहीं है केवल कागजी घोड़े दौड़ा रही है।
78. कदमों पर चलना—(अनुसरण करना) हमें गाँधी जी के कदमों पर चलना चाहिए।
79. कान पकना—(परेशान होना) रोज वही बातें सुन-सुनकर रीता के कान पक गये हैं।
80. कन्धे से कन्धा मिलाना—(पूरी सहायता करना) गाँधी जी के साथ स्वतन्त्रता आन्दोलन में प्रत्येक देशवासी ने कन्धे से कन्धा मिलाया।

81. कसौटी पर कसना—(जाँच करना) सोने की जाँच कसौटी पर कस कर ही (घिस कर) होती है।
82. कठपुतली बनना—(अधीन रहना) राम प्रकाश तो अपनी पत्नी के हाथ की कठपुतली बन गया है।
83. कानों में तेल डालना—(बात न सुनना) इतनी देर से आवाज दे रहा हूँ लेकिन अवधेश तो जैसे कानों में तेल डालकर बैठा है।
84. कोढ़ में खाज—(कष्ट में अधिक कष्ट) मोती पैर के फोड़े से पहले ही परेशान था, अब उसे मलेरिया भी हो गया। यह कोढ़ में खाज होने के समान था।
85. कहर मचाना—(मुसीबत पैदा करना) थोड़ा सा अनाज किसान द्वारा रख लेने पर जमींदार ने कहर मचा दिया।
86. काफूर हो जाना—(गायब हो जाना) इंजैक्शन की बात सुनकर राजू का सारा पेट दर्द काफूर हो गया।
87. जले पर नमक छिड़कना—(नाराज व्यक्ति को और परेशान करना) रमेश के मित्र उससे बार-बार यात्रा के विषय में पूछकर उसके जले पर नमक छिड़क रहे थे।
88. कान कतरना—(धोखा देना) मुझे तुमसे ऐसी उम्मीद न थी, तुम्हारी यह हरकत कान कतरने के समान है।
89. काली करतूत—(बुरा काम) दुर्योधन द्वारा द्रोपदी के चीर-हरण की काली करतूत ने धृतराष्ट्र और गान्धारी का सिर झुका दिया।
90. कान खड़े होना—(सावधान होना) रुपये की बात आते ही लोभी व्यक्तियों के कान खड़े हो जाते हैं।
91. किंकर्त्तव्यविमूढ़ होना—(कुछ न सूझना) रमेश के माथे का बहता हुआ खून देखकर उसकी माँ किंकर्त्तव्यविमूढ़ सी हो गयीं।
92. कलेजा मुँह को आना—(अत्यन्त व्याकुल होना) गुजरात में आये भूकम्प की तबाही देखकर कलेजा मुँह को आने लगता था।
93. काम तमाम कर देना—(मार देना) आतंकवादियों के लिये किसी का भी काम तमाम कर देना बड़ा आसान काम है।
94. काया पलट होना—(बहुत परिवर्तन होना) एक दुर्घटना ने तो रमेश की काया ही पलट दी।
95. कान का कच्चा होना—(बिना विचार किये विश्वास कर लेना) महिलाएँ कान की बहुत कच्ची होती हैं।
96. कही खेत की सुनी खलिहान की—(कुछ का कुछ सुनना) राम ने दवा के बारे में कहा और तुमने हवा सुना यह तो वही बात हुई कि कही गई खेत की सुनी खलिहान की।
97. कान भरना—(चुगली करना) रमेश की माँ हमेशा उसकी पत्नी के खिलाफ उसके कान भरती रहती है।
98. कोई चारा न होना—(उपाय न होना) अपनी दुकान बेचने के सिवा राधेलाल के पास कोई चारा न था।
99. खाक चाटना—(हार जाना) राणा प्रताप के सामने मुगल सैनिक खाक चाटते फिरते थे।
100. खाक में मिलना—(बरबाद होना) रामनाथ ने अपने गलत व्यसनों की वजह से अपने घर को खाक में मिला दिया।
101. खाक छानना—(मारे-मारे फिरना) अशोक अच्छी-भली नौकरी को लात मारकर आज खाक छान रहा है।
102. खून सूखना—(चिन्ता में कमजोर होना) घर की चिन्ताओं के कारण मेरा तो खून सूखा जा रहा है।

103. खून खौलना—(अत्यधिक क्रोधित होना) बलवीर की उल्टी बात सुनकर उसके पिता का खून खौल उठा।
104. खेत रहना—(मारे जाना) युद्ध में हजारों सैनिक खेत रहे।
105. खून का प्यासा—(जान का दुश्मन) राजवीर अपने भाई के खून का प्यासा है।
106. खून का घूँट पीना—(अपमान सहना) जब रमेश ने अपने पिता को उल्टा जबाव दिया तो वे खून का घूँट पीकर रह गये।
107. खटाई में पड़ना—(बाधा आना) परीक्षा कार्यक्रम स्थगित होने से उसका विवाह में लखनऊ जाना खटाई में पड़ गया।
108. कपोल-कल्पित (केवल कल्पना मात्र) प्राचीन काल में हवा में उड़ना कपोल कल्पित था।
109. खटपट होना—(झगड़ा होना) सुनीता की कुछ समय से अपनी सहेली से खटपट चल रही है।
110. गढ़े मुर्दे उखाड़ना—(बीती-बातों को कहना) गढ़े मुर्दे उखाड़ कर रामू को क्यों दु:खी करते हो ?
111. गज भर की छाती होना—(गर्व होना) रमेश द्वारा आई. ए. एस. की परीक्षा उत्तीर्ण कर लेने से उसके पिता की छाती गज भर हो गयी।
112. गागर में सागर भरना—(थोड़े में बहुत कहना) बिहारी ने अपने दोहों में गागर में सागर भर दिया।
113. गुड़-गोबर करना—(बना काम बिगाड़ देना) तुमने यहाँ आकर सारा गुड़-गोबर कर दिया।
114. गाल बजाना—(व्यर्थ की बातें करना, शेखी मारना) कुछ लोग व्यर्थ में गाल बजाते रहते हैं।
115. गुलछर्रे उड़ाना—(मौज उड़ाना) जयदीप अपने पिताजी के धन से गुलछर्रे उड़ा रहा है।
116. गुदड़ी का लाल—(छिपा गुणवान) शास्त्री जी सचमुच भारत के गुदड़ी के लाल थे।
117. गूलर का फूल होना—(कल्पना की वस्तु) प्राचीनकाल में धरतीवासियों के लिए चाँद पर पहुँचना गूलर के फूल के समान था।
118. गले का हार होना—(अत्यधिक प्रिय होना) गोकुल में कृष्ण सभी गोपियों के गले का हार बने हुए थे।
119. गला काटना—(अहित करना) आज के युग में लोग एक दूसरे का गला काटने में लगे रहते हैं।
120. गले न उतरना—(समझ में न आना) बहुत कोशिश करने पर भी राजेश की बात मेरे गले नहीं उतरी।
121. गंगा नहाना—(काम पूरा होना) बेटी की शादी करके माता-पिता गंगा नहा लेते हैं।
122. गीत गाना—(एक ही बात बार-बार दुहराना) माना तुमने बहुत अच्छा कार्य किया है पर कब तक इसका गीत गाते रहोगे।
123. गले पड़ना—(पीछे पड़ना) कुछ लोगों में बेकार ही गले पड़ने की आदत होती है।
124. गीदड़ भभकी—(सिर्फ डराने के लिये) रमेश जानता है कि यह बातें केवल गीदड़ भभकी है और कुछ नहीं।
125. गुरु घंटाल—(बहुत चालाक) अपनी हरकतों से तुम बड़े गुरु घंटाल मालूम होते हो।
126. गर्दन पर छुरी फेरना—(अत्याचार करना) आजकल के अधिकारी अपने से निम्न पद पर कार्यरत कर्मचारियों के गले पर छुरी फेरते हैं।
127. घाव पर नमक छिड़कना—(कष्ट में और कष्ट देना) दु:खी व्यक्ति से भला बुरा कहना उसके घाव पर नमक छिड़कने के समान है।
128. घर फूँक तमाशा देखना—(सब कुछ नष्ट करना) मनोहर की बीबी घर फूँककर तमाशा देखने वालों मे से है।

129. घी के दिये जलाना—(खुशी मनाना) अवधेश बोला रमा का रिश्ता किसी अच्छे परिवार में तय होने पर मैं घी के दिये जलाऊँगा।
130. घुटने टेकना—(हार मानना) पत्नी की हठधर्मिता के आगे पति को घुटने टेकने ही पड़े।
131. घड़ों पानी पड़ना—(लज्जित होना) बेईमानी का भेद खुलने पर रोहित पर घड़ों पानी पड़ गया।
132. घुटकर रह जाना—(इच्छा दबाना) परिवार की आर्थिक परिस्थितियों के वशीभूत नैना की उच्च शिक्षा की इच्छा मन में घुटकर रह गई।
133. घोड़े बेचकर सोना—(बेफ़्रिक होना) तुम्हारी माँ तो घोड़े बेचकर सोती है।
134. घर करना—(समझ में आना) अध्यापक की बात ने विद्यार्थी के मन-मस्तिष्क में घर कर लिया।
135. घाट-घाट का पानी पीना—(बहुत अनुभवी होना) राजेश के भईया तो घाट-घाट का पानी पिये हुए हैं।
136. चार चाँद लगाना—(शोभा बढ़ाना) राकेश के आ जाने से बारात में चार चाँद लग गये।
137. चेहरे का रंग उड़ना—(घबरा जाना) अरे श्याम, तुम्हारे चेहरे का रंग क्यों उड़ रहा है ?
138. चैन की बंसी बजाना—(मौज उड़ाना) प्रधानाचार्य की कृपा से लिपिक चैन की बंसी बजाते हैं।
139. चादर से बाहर पैर पसारना—(आय से अधिक व्यय करना) महँगाई के इस युग में मध्यम वर्ग के लोगों को चादर से बाहर पैर नहीं पसारने चाहिए।
140. चूर-चूर होना—(पूरी तरह नष्ट हो जाना) नौकरी के लिये देखे गये सारे सपने पढ़ाई समाप्त करके नौकरी ढूँढ़ने पर पूरी तरह चूर-चूर हो जाते हैं।
141. चाँदी काटना—(खूब धन कमाना) अनुचित तरीकों से चाँदी काटने वालों को समाज में सम्मान नहीं मिलता है।
142. चुल्लू भर पानी में डूब मरना—(बहुत लज्जित होना) हाईस्कूल की परीक्षा देने में भी तुम्हारी जान निकल रही है, तो चुल्लू भर पानी में डूब मरो।
143. चोली-दामन का साथ होना—(परस्पर घनिष्ठ प्रेम होना) श्रीकृष्ण और अर्जुन का चोली-दामन का साथ था।
144. चींटी के पर निकलना—(मृत्युकाल निकट आना) जब बुरा समय आता है तो चींटी के पर निकल आते हैं।
145. चिराग तले अँधेरा—(सम्मानित पुरुष का बुराई में लिप्त होना) नेताओं द्वारा धन के लिये देश को धोखा देना चिराग तले अँधेरे जैसा है।
146. चोर की दाढ़ी में तिनका—(शक होना) चोर अपनी करतूत कितनी भी छिपाये लेकिन चोर की दाढ़ी में तिनका होता है।
147. छाती पीटना—(विलाप करना) बेटे के न रहने पर माँ का छाती पीटना स्वाभाविक था।
148. छाती पर मूँग दलना—(कष्ट देना, दिल दुखाना) मैंने तुम्हारा क्या बिगाड़ा है जो मेरी ही छाती पर मूँग दल रहे हो।
149. छक्के छूटना—(हिम्मत हारना) शिवाजी के सामने दुश्मनों के छक्के छूट जाते थे।
150. जान के लाले पड़ना—(जान बचाना मुश्किल होना) सन् 1965 के युद्ध में पाकिस्तानियों को अपनी जान के लाले पड़ गये थे।
151. जहर का घूँट पीना—(कठोर बातों को सुनकर भी चुप रहना) अपने पुत्र के विषय में पड़ोसियों की तरह-तरह की बातें सुनकर दिवाकर के पिता जहर का घूँट पी लेते हैं।

152. जड़ खोदना—(अहित करना) आज के समय में सभी क्षेत्रों में लोग एक दूसरे की जड़ खोदने में लगे हैं।

153. टूट पड़ना—(आक्रमण करना) हमारे वीर सिपाही सीमा पर मौका मिलते ही दुश्मनों पर टूट पड़ने के लिये तैयार थे।

154. टका सा मुँह लेकर रह जाना—(लज्जित होना) अपने पुत्र के जबाव देने पर सीताराम जी टका सा मुँह लेकर रह गये।

155. टोपी उछालना—(अपमान करना) आजकल जरा सा भी दहेज कम मिलने पर लड़के वाले लड़की के पिता की टोपी उछालने से भी नहीं चूकते।

156. टस से मस न होना—(विचलित न होना) चाहे कोई विपत्ति आये साहसी व्यक्ति अपने मार्ग से टस से मस नहीं होते।

157. टेढ़ी खीर—(कठिन काम) मेहनत के बिना उन्नति करना बड़ी टेढ़ी खीर है।

158. टाँग अड़ाना—(बाधा डालना) मेरे हर काम में दुश्मन टाँग अड़ा देते हैं।

159. डींग मारना—(शेखी बघारना) किसी काम में सफलता पाने के लिए परिश्रम की आवश्यकता होती है केवल डीगें मारने से काम नहीं चलता।

160. डकार जाना—(हड़प जाना) अशोक बेईमानी से अपनी मौसी का मकान डकार गया।

161. डंके की चोट पर—(घोषणापूर्वक) वह जो भी काम करता है डंके की चोट पर करता है।

162. तारे गिनना—(दु:ख में समय काटना) बेचारी ममता पति वियोग में तारे गिन-गिन कर रात काट रही है।

163. तिल का ताड़ बनाना—(छोटी-सी बात को बहुत बढ़ा देना) ब्रजेश ने छोटी सी बात पर तिल का ताड़ बना दिया।

164. तूती बोलना—(दबदबा होना) काँग्रेस सरकार में इन्दिरा गाँधी की तूती बोलती थी।

165. तीन तेरह होना—(तितर-बितर होना) पिता की मृत्यु के बाद उसका परिवार तीन तेरह हो गया।

166. तीन-पाँच करना—(बेईमानी करना) आज के समय में वही व्यक्ति आगे बढ़ सकता है जो तीन-पाँच करना जानता हो।

167. थूककर चाटना—(बात को कह कर बदल जाना) उसकी बात का कोई भरोसा नहीं वह तो थूककर चाटने वालों में से है।

168. थाली का बैंगन—(अस्थिर विचार वाला) आज के नेताओं को थाली का बैंगन कहा जाना उचित ही लगता है।

169. दाँत खट्टे करना—(पराजित करना) युद्ध में चन्द्रगुप्त ने सिकन्दर के दाँत खट्टे कर दिये।

170. दाँतों तले उँगली दबाना—(आश्चर्य करना) युद्ध में भारतीय सैनिकों की वीरता देखकर संसार के लोग दाँतों तले उँगली दबाने लगे।

171. दाल में काला—(शक, सन्देह होना) सन्तोष की बातों से मुझे ऐसा लगता है कि अवश्य ही दाल में कुछ काला है।

172. दो टूक बात करना—(कम शब्दों में साफ बात कहना) मैंने सीमा से दो टूक बात करना उचित समझा।

173. दुम दबाकर भाग जाना—(भयभीत होकर चले जाना) उसकी बात खुलने वाली थी इसलिए वह दुम दबाकर भाग गया है।

174. दिन दूनी रात चौगुनी होना—(अत्यधिक उन्नति होना) जब से श्री अटल बिहारी बाजपेयी देश के प्रधानमन्त्री बने हैं। देश दिन दुनी रात चौगुनी उन्नति कर रहा है।
175. दिल पसीज जाना—(दया आना) रहीम के दुःख से मेरा दिल पसीज गया।
176. दोनों हाथों में लड्डू होना—(बहुत लाभ होना) जब से निमेष ने नौकरी के साथ व्यापार प्रारम्भ किया है तब से उसके दोनों हाथों में लड्डू हैं।
177. धूल में मिलना—(बरबाद होना) जरा-सी गलती से नीना की सारी मेहनत धूल में मिल गई।
178. धज्जियाँ उड़ाना—(स्थिति खराब कर देना) राजा ने अपने बुद्धि चातुर्य से दरबारियों की धज्जियाँ उड़ा दीं।
179. धरती पर पाँव न पड़ना—(खुशी से फूला ना समाना) विद्यालय में अपना परिणाम जानकर घर लौटते में राजू के पाँव धरती पर नहीं पड़ रहे थे।
180. नाक रगड़ना—(मजबूर होना) रघुवीर बड़ा खलीफा बनता था अब देखों कैसी नाक रगड़ने लगा है।
181. नाकों चने चबाना—(बहुत तंग करना) युद्ध में राणा प्रताप ने मुगलों को नाकों चने चबवा दिये थे।
182. नौ दो ग्यारह होना—(भाग जाना) पुलिस को देखकर चोर नौ दो ग्यारह हो गये।
183. नाक-भौं सिकोड़ना—(अरुचि दिखाना) सिलाई-कढ़ाई का नाम सुनते ही लड़कियाँ नाक-भौं सिकोड़ने लगती हैं।
184. नाक रखना—(सम्मान बढ़ाना या बचा लेना) रामचन्द्र ने माता कैकेयी के कहने पर वन जाकर अपने पिता की नाक रख ली।
185. नाक ऊँची होना—(सम्मान बढ़ना) प्रत्येक क्षेत्र में भारतीय वैज्ञानिकों द्वारा किये गये आविष्कारों ने विश्व में हमारे देश की नाक ऊँची कर दी है।
186. नाक कटना—(बदनामी होना) बच्चों के गलत कर्मों से माता-पिता की नाक कट जाती है।
187. पत्थर की लकीर—(अमिट) महाराजा हरिश्चन्द्र का निर्णय पत्थर की लकीर होता था।
188. साँप लोटना—(ईर्ष्या होना) आज के समय में अपने ही परिचितों को आगे बढ़ते देखकर लोगों की छाती पर साँप लोटने लगते हैं।
189. छठी का दूध याद दिलाना—(सबक सिखाना, बुरी तरह परास्त करना) भीम ने दुर्योधन को महाभारत के युद्ध में छठी का दूध याद दिला दिया।
190. पापड़ बेलना—(कष्ट में जीवन बिताना) स्वतन्त्रता सेनानियों ने स्वतन्त्रता के लिये अपने जीवन में बहुत से पापड़ बेले।
191. पानी में आग लगाना—(असम्भव कार्य करना) वर्तमान वैज्ञानिक पानी में आग लगाने की ताकत रखते हैं।
192. पीठ दिखाना—(हार कर भाग जाना) जीतने की कोई आशा न रहने पर राहुल पीठ दिखाकर कर भाग गया।
193. पगड़ी उछालना—(अपमानित करना) जरा-सी बात पर दिनेश ने अपने पिता की सबके सामने पगड़ी उछाल दी।
194. पानी की तरह रुपया बहाना—(अंधाधुंध खर्च करना) मेरे पिताजी ने मेरे इलाज के लिये रुपया पानी की तरह बहा दिया।
195. फूँक-फूँक कर पैर रखना—(सावधानी से काम करना) अजहरुद्दीन हर कार्य करते समय फूँक-फूँक कर पाँव रखता है।

196. बाल बाँका न होना—(तनिक भी अहित न होना) जिस पर भगवान की कृपा है उसका कोई भी बाल बाँका नहीं कर सकता।
197. बाल-बाल बचना—(वक्त पर रक्षा होना) दुर्घटना तो बहुत भयंकर थी लेकिन राकेश बाल-बाल बच गया।
198. बाग-बाग होना—(बहुत प्रसन्न होना) परीक्षा में उत्तीर्ण होने की सूचना पाकर मेरा दिल बाग-बाग हो गया।
199. बायें हाथ का खेल—(मामूली काम) ग्रामीण ने रितेश से कहा कि नदी पार करना उसके बायें हाथ का खेल है।
200. बाल की खाल निकालना—(नुक्ताचीनी करना) मेरी माँ को हर बात में बाल की खाल निकालने की आदत है।
201. बगलें झाँकना—(निरुत्तर हो जाना) अध्यापक द्वारा गृह कार्य के अपूर्ण होने के विषय में पूछने पर रवि बगलें झाँकने लगा।
202. बट्टा लगना—(कलंक लगना) राधा द्वारा भाग कर शादी कर लेने से उसके पिता की इज्जत पर बट्टा लग गया।
203. बहती गंगा में हाथ धोना—(अवसर का लाभ उठाना) अभियंता महोदय के साथ-साथ घोटाले में सहायकों ने भी बहती गंगा में हाथ धोने का अवसर पाया।
204. बखिया उधेड़ना—(पोल खोलना) अन्त में तंग आकर सीता ने अपने भाई की बखिया उधेड़ दी।
205. बात बढ़ाना—(बहस करना) अमित को तो जरा सी बात को बहुत बढ़ाने की आदत है।
206. बिल्ली के भाग्य से छींका टूटना—(संयोग से लाभ मिलना) दिनेश के व्यापार में बिल्ली के भाग्य से छींका टूट ही गया।
207. बेपेंदी का लोटा—(मौकापरस्त) राजू तो बिल्कुल बेपेंदी का लोटा है वह कभी किसी का साथ नहीं देता।
208. मिट्टी पलीद करना—(दुर्दशा करना) नेताओं ने देश की आर्थिक व्यवस्था की मिट्टी पलीद कर दी है।
209. मूँछों पर ताव देना—(अहंकार दिखाना) अमीर होने के कारण ही राजेश मूँछों पर ताव देता रहता है।
210. मुँह देखते रह जाना—(अचम्भित होना) शीला के बेटे की बातें सुनकर मैं उसका मुँह देखती रह गयी।
211. मुँह में खून लगना—(बुरी आदत पड़ जाना) कर्मचारियों के मुँह में रिश्वत का खून लग चुका है।
212. मक्खियाँ मारना—(बेकार बैठे रहना) हजारों युवक एम. ए. पास करके मक्खियाँ मार रहे हैं।
213. मुँह में पानी भरना—(लालच में आना) रसगुल्ला देखते ही अनिल के मुँह में पानी भर आता है।
214. मुँह ताकना—(दूसरे के सहारे रहना) मोहन हर समय दूसरों का मुँह ताकता रहता है।
215. मुट्ठी गरम करना—(रिश्वत देना) किसी भी सरकारी विभाग में अपना काम कराने के लिये अधिकारी की मुट्ठी गरम करनी पड़ती है।
216. मिट्टी का माधो—(मूर्ख, बेकार) कुछ लोग काम के नाम पर केवल मिट्टी के माधो होते हैं।
217. रंगा सियार—(कपटी) आजकल के जमाने में अधिकतर लोग रंगे सियार निकलते हैं।
218. रंग में भंग पड़ना—(आनन्द में विघ्न पड़ना) प्रधानाचार्य के आ जाने से विद्यार्थियों के रंग में भंग पड़ गया।
219. रफू-चक्कर होना—(भाग जाना) पुलिस के आते ही चोर रफू-चक्कर हो गये।

220. रंग लाना—(प्रभाव दिखाई देना) चाहे कुछ भी हो जाये यदि मेहनत की है तो वह एक न एक दिन अवश्य रंग लायेगी।
221. रंगे हाथों पकड़ा जाना—(मौके पर पकड़े जाना) सुरेश को उसके पिताजी ने अपनी जेब से रुपये निकालते हुए रंगे हाथों पकड़ लिया।
222. राई का पहाड़ बनाना—(जरा-सी बात को व्यर्थ में बढ़ाना) दरवाजा खुला रह जाने की जरा-सी बात को निमिष ने राई का पहाड़ बना दिया।
223. पेट में चूहे कूदना—(बहुत तेज भूख लगना) पेट में चूहे कूद रहे हैं इसलिये मुझसे कोई काम न हो सकेगा।
224. पाँवों तले जमीन खिसकना—(भयभीत हो जाना) शिकार करने गये पर शेर को सामने देखकर ही पाँवों तले की जमीन खिसक गई।
225. पहाड़ टूटना—(एक साथ कई विपत्तियाँ आना) नीरज की नौकरी क्या गई, उस पर तो विपत्तियों का पहाड़ टूट पड़ा।
226. पानी-पानी हो जाना—(लज्जित होना) सुरेश से उसकी गलती के विषय में पिताजी द्वारा पूछे जाने पर वह पानी-पानी हो गया।
227. लोहा लेना—(युद्ध करना) आज के समय में भारत के पास अस्त्र-शस्त्रों का खजाना होने से अब हम विश्व के किसी भी देश से लोहा ले सकते हैं।
228. लेने के देने पड़ना—(कुछ का कुछ हो जाना) कभी-कभी ज्यादा चालाकी दिखाने से लेने के देने भी पड़ जाते हैं।
229. लुटिया डुबोना—(काम बिगाड़ देना) रहीम ने अच्छे-भले चलते हुए व्यापार की लुटिया डुबो दी।
230. लकीर के फकीर—(अन्ध विश्वासी) वैज्ञानिक युग में भी लकीर के फकीर लोगों की कमी नहीं है।
231. लोहे के चने चबाना—(कठिन काम करना) रिश्वतखोरी मिटाना सरकार के लिए लोहे के चना चबाना है।
232. लोहा मानना—(शक्ति को स्वीकार करना) सिकन्दर ने पोरस की वीरता का लोहा मान लिया।
233. विष उगलना—(बुराई करना) लोकेश हमेशा अपने भाई के बारे में विष उगलता रहता है।
234. शेर के दाँत गिनना—(दुस्साहस करना) प्रधानाचार्य के कार्यालय में जाकर बात करना शेर के दाँत गिनने जैसा है।
235. शैतान के कान काटना—(अति चतुर होना) आजकल के बच्चे शैतान के कान काटते नजर आते हैं।
236. सिर खपाना—(दिमागी कार्य करना) किसी-किसी प्रश्न को हल करने के लिए बहुत सिर खपाना पड़ता है।
237. सिर ओखली में देना—(आफत में फँसना) नीता को हिन्दी पढ़ाने की जिम्मेदारी देकर मैंने अपना सिर ओखली में दे दिया।
238. सिर नीचा होना—(अपमानित होना) नेताओं द्वारा किये जाने वाले घपलों ने देश का सिर नीचा कर दिया है।
239. सिर मुँड़ाते ही ओले पड़ना—(आरम्भ में ही हानि होना) नयी दुकान खरीदते ही उसमें आग लग जाने से सुरेश को सिर मुँड़ाते ही ओले पड़ गये।
240. सिर थाम कर बैठ जाना—(बहुत दुःख करना) व्यापार में बहुत बड़ा घाटा होने पर सेठ धनीराम अपना सिर थाम कर बैठ गये।

241. सिर पर भूत सवार होना—(धुन सवार होना) राहुल के सिर पर क्रिकेट मैच देखने का भूत सवार हो गया है।

242. सिर आँखों पर बैठाना—(सम्मान करना) शबरी ने राम के उसकी कुटिया में आने पर उन्हें सिर आँखों पर बैठाया।

243. सब्ज बाग दिखाना—(व्यर्थ की आशाएँ बँधाना) ढोंगी ज्योतिषी लोगों को सब्ज बाग दिखाकर उनसे धन लूटते हैं।

244. साँप सूँघ जाना—(निश्चेष्ट हो जाना) रुपयों की बात आते ही सेठ जी को साँप सूँघ गया।

245. साँप के बिल में हाथ डालना—(खतरनाक काम करना) मैंने राजेश से कहा कि मुझे साँप के बिल में हाथ डालने का कोई शौक नहीं है।

246. हँसों के बीच कौआ होना—(शोभा न देना) साक्षर लोगों के बीच अनपढ़ हँसों के बीच कौआ प्रतीत होते हैं।

247. हाथ-पाँव फूलना—(घबरा जाना) अचानक मेहमानों के आ जाने से कपीश के हाथ-पाँव फूल गये।

248. हत्थे चढ़ना—(कब्जे में आना) आज श्रुति बाहर खेलती हुई अपने पिताजी के हत्थे चढ़ गई।

249. हवा के घोड़े पर सवार होना—(बहुत जल्दी में होना) रमेश से तो कुछ काम कहना बेकार है वो तो हमेशा हवा के घोड़े पर सवार रहता है।

250. हाथ तंग होना—(धन का अभाव) पति की नौकरी जाने से आजकल रीना का हाथ बहुत तंग है।

251. हुलिया बिगाड़ना—(बुरी हालत कर देना) जेबकतरे के रंगें हाथों पकड़े जाने पर राह चलते राहगीरों ने मार-मार कर उसका हुलिया बिगाड़ दिया।

252. हिरन हो जाना—(लुप्त हो जाना) पुलिस के आते-आते चोर हिरन हो गये।

253. हवा से बातें करना—(तेज चलना) हिम सागर एक्सप्रेस चलते में मानो हवा से बातें करती है।

254. हँसी में उड़ाना—(ध्यान न देना) रमेश अपनी माँ की हर बात हँसी में उड़ा देता है।

255. हाथ मलना—(पछताना) जो व्यक्ति समय रहते काम नहीं करते उन्हें बाद में हाथ मलना पड़ता है।

256. हाथ धोकर पीछे पड़ना—(बुरी तरह से पीछे पड़ना) श्याम की माँ अपनी बहू के पीछे हाथ धोकर पड़ गयी है।

257. हाथ साफ करना—(चोरी करना) कुछ लोगों को घर की वस्तुओं पर भी हाथ साफ करने की आदत पड़ जाती है।

लोकोक्तियाँ (PROVERBS)

लोकोक्ति को कहावत भी कहते हैं। वह पूरे वाक्य के समान होती है और साधारण अर्थ के स्थान पर विशेष अर्थ को प्रकट करती है।

मुहावरों की भाँति लोकोक्तियों का प्रयोग भाषा को सुन्दर, सरल एवं प्रभावपूर्ण बनाने के लिये होता है। लोकोक्तियाँ कहानी या चिर सत्य पर आधारित होती हैं। लोकोक्तियाँ भाषा को अलंकृत करती हैं।

1. अन्धों में काना राजा—(मूर्खों में अल्पज्ञ) अनपढ़ समाज में हाईस्कूल पास दिनेश अन्धों में काना राजा है।

2. अकेला चना भाड़ नहीं फोड़ता—(संगठन के बिना सफलता नहीं मिलती) सबको मिल-जुल कर ही काम करना चाहिए, क्योंकि अकेला चना भाड़ नहीं फोड़ता।

3. अधजल गगरी छलकत जाय—(नीच अधिक इतराता है) थोड़ा सा धन आ जाने पर मनुष्य कितना बदल जाता है ठीक ही कहा है अधजल गगरी छलकत जाय।

4. आँख के अन्धे नाम नयनसुख—(गुणहीन को यश मिलना) मोहन राजनीति में तो कुछ भी जानता नहीं, बातें बहुत करता है। वह तो आँख का अन्धा नाम नयनसुख है।

5. आगे नाथ न पीछे पगहा—(सम्बन्धी रहित) रामनाथ खूब धन खर्च करता है क्योंकि उसके आगे नाथ न पीछे पगहा है।

6. अन्धे के हाथ बटेर लगना—(अनायास इच्छित वस्तु मिल जाना) नितान्त खिलाड़ी होते हुए भी सुरेश अपनी परीक्षा में प्रथम श्रेणी में उत्तीर्ण हुआ सच है अन्धे के हाथ बटेर लग गई।

7. अपनी-अपनी ढपली अपना-अपना राग—(समूह में रहकर स्वतन्त्र आचरण) भाई हमारे यहाँ की तो विचित्र दशा है, सभी अपनी-अपनी ढपली, अपना-अपना राग अलाप रहे हैं।

8. आम के आम गुठलियों के दाम—(दोहरा लाभ प्राप्त करना) छात्र अपनी पुस्तकों से साल भर पढ़ने के बाद उन्हें बेचकर आम के आम गुठलियों के दाम प्राप्त कर लेते हैं।

9. अपनी करनी पार उतरनी—(कर्मों का फल अवश्य मिलता है) अब पश्चाताप करने से कोई लाभ नहीं क्योंकि अपनी करनी पार उतरनी।

10. अरहर की टट्टी गुजराती ताला—(छोटी बात के लिए बड़ा प्रबन्ध) रमेश ने बच्चे के जन्म दिन को अरहर की टट्टी गुजराती ताला बना दिया।

11. आँख के अन्धे गाँठ के पूरे—(मूर्ख धनवान) यदि तुम पुरानी साइकिल को 300 रुपये में बेचना चाहते हो तो किसी आंख के अन्धे गाँठ के पूरे को जाकर पकड़ो।

12. अक्ल बड़ी की भैंस—(बुद्धि में ही बल है) राम से अध्यापक ने प्रश्न पूछा किन्तु उसके गलत जवाब से यह स्पष्ट हो गया कि अक्ल बड़ी या भैंस।

13. उल्टे बाँस बरेली को—(विपरीत कार्य) आगरा में पेठा लाकर बेचना उल्टे बाँस बरेली के समान है।

14. उल्टा चोर कोतवाल को डाँटे—(दोषी होते हुए भी आँख दिखाना) एक तो सारे दिन विद्यालय से गायब रहे पूछने पर आँख दिखाने लगे, कैसी अजीब बात है। उल्टा चोर कोतवाल को डाँटे।

15. ऊँची दुकान फीका पकवान—(बाहरी आडम्बर मात्र) प्रजातन्त्र शासन व्यवस्था तो बिल्कुल ऊँची दुकान फीका पकवान सिद्ध हो रही है।

16. ऊँट के मुँह में जीरा—(आवश्यकता का न्यूनतम निदान) 50 पूड़ियाँ खाने वाले रामसिंह के लिए 10 पूड़ियाँ ऊँट के मुँह में जीरा हो गयीं।

17. एक म्यान में दो तलवारें—(दो समान पदों का एक साथ रहना) एक कालेज में दो प्रधानाचार्य नहीं हो सकते कहीं क्योंकि एक म्यान में दो तलवारें रह नहीं सकती हैं।

18. एक पन्थ दो काज—(दोहरा लाभ) इलाहाबाद उच्च न्यायालय में तारीख पर उपस्थित हो जाऊँगा और संगम पर स्नान भी। अपने तो एक पंथ दो काज हो जायेंगें।

19. एक अनार सौ बीमार—(एक वस्तु के अनेक चाहने वाले) विद्यालय में एक अध्यापक की नियुक्ति के लिए पचास प्रार्थना पत्र आने पर प्रबन्धक ने कहा कि मैं क्या करूँ एक अनार सौ बीमार हैं।

20. एक और एक ग्यारह होते हैं—(संगठन में शक्ति होती है) सभी को मिलकर राष्ट्रोत्थान में सहयोग देना चाहिए क्योंकि एक और एक ग्यारह हो जाते हैं।

21. कहाँ राजा भोज कहाँ गंगू तेली—(दो व्यक्तियों की स्थिति में बहुत अन्तर होता है) मुन्शी प्रेमचन्द प्रसिद्ध कहानी लेखक थे, उमेश जैसे कल के लड़के से उनकी क्या समानता, कहाँ राजा भोज कहाँ गंगू तेली।

22. काटो तो खून नहीं—(अत्यन्त भयभीत हो जाना) घर में आग लग जाने के कारण मेरी ऐसी दशा हो गई कि काटो तो खून नहीं।

23. काला अक्षर भैंस बराबर—(अशिक्षित) आज भी कुछ ऐसे गाँव हैं जहाँ के लोग के लिए काला अक्षर भैंस बराबर हैं।

24. कंगाली में आटा गीला—(दु:ख में और दु:खी होना) नरेश का बैल भी मर गया और चोरी भी हो गई। उस बेचारे का कंगाली में आटा गीला हो गया।

25. खग जाने खग ही की माया—(जैसे की बात तैसा ही समझता है) उस बनिये के पास तुम्हारे जाने से ही काम बनेगा क्योंकि खग जाने खग ही की भाषा।

26. खिसियानी बिल्ली खम्भा नोंचे—(शक्तिशाली पर वश न चलने पर कमजोर व्यक्ति पर क्रोध प्रदर्शित करना) खिसियानी बिल्ली खम्भा नोंचे की तरह पिताजी पर वश न चलने पर सतीश ने छोटे भाई को ही पीट दिया।

27. खुदा गंजे को नाखून न दे—(बुरे व्यक्ति को अधिकार या सुविधा से वंचित रखना ही ठीक है) रमेश के पिताजी ने उसे अपना कारोबार न सौंपकर ही अच्छा किया क्योंकि खुदा गंजे को नाखून न दे वही अच्छा है।

28. खोदा पहाड़ निकली चुहिया—(कठिन परिश्रम करने पर अल्प परिणाम निकलना) बहुत ढूँढ़ने पर चार में से एक पुस्तक मिली यह तो खोदा पहाड़ निकली चुहिया वाली बात हुई।

29. खाने के दाँत और दिखाने के दाँत और—(कहना कुछ करना कुछ) वर्तमान समय के राजनीतिज्ञों के खाने के दाँत और दिखाने के कुछ और होते हैं।

30. घर का भेदी लंका ढाये—(घर का दुश्मन बहुत हानि पहुँचाता है) अपने भाई से होशियार रहना क्योंकि घर का भेदी लंका ढाये।

31. घर की मुर्गी दाल बराबर—(सहज प्राप्त मूल्यवान वस्तु का महत्व न होना) रमेश चाहे कितना भी काम क्यों न कर ले लेकिन अपने पिताजी की आँखों में सदैव घर की मुर्गी दाल बराबर ही रहेगा।

32. चमड़ी जाये, पर दमड़ी न जाये—(बहुत अधिक कंजूस) सेठ धनीराम जी किसी को एक रुपया भी नहीं देंगे उनका उसूल है चमड़ी जाये पर दमड़ी न जाये।

33. चार दिन की चाँदनी फिर अन्धेरी रात—(थोड़े दिन का सुख) पिता के एकत्रित किए हुए धन को थोड़े दिन और व्यय कर लो बाद में चार दिन की चाँदनी फिर अन्धेरी रात ही होगी।

34. चोर पर मोर—(बेईमान के साथ बेईमानी करना) सतीश ने सेठ रामलाल को धोखा देकर चोर पर मोर का काम कर दिखाया है।

35. छोटे मुँह बड़ी बात—(अपनी मर्यादा से बढ़कर बात कहना) छोटे मुँह बड़ी बात कभी अच्छी नहीं होती है।

36. जल में रह कर मगरमच्छ से बैर—(अधीनता में रहकर शत्रुता नहीं की जा सकती) नौकरी करने पर अपने अधिकारी की बात न मानकर जल में रहकर मगरमच्छ से बैर नहीं करना चाहिए।

37. जैसा देश वैसा भेष—(समयानुसार व्यवहार) मेरे एक मित्र के अनुसार पुरानी मान्यताओं पर चलने का कोई लाभ नहीं होता। आज के समय में तो जैसा देश हो वैसा ही भेष बना लेना चाहिए।

38. जिसकी लाठी उसकी भैंस—(बलवान की जीत) सन्तोष ने अपने भाई को उसका हिस्सा नहीं दिया ऊपर से धमकी और दे दी। ठीक ही है जिसकी लाठी उसकी भैंस।

39. जंगल में मंगल होना—(सुनसान (वीरान) स्थान में भी चहल-पहल हो जाना) भिलाई में रूसी इस्पात का कारखाना खुलने से जंगल में मंगल हो गया।

40. जितने मुँह उतनी बातें—(भिन्न-भिन्न तरह की अफवाहें) कश्मीर समस्या के प्रश्न पर जितने मुँह उतनी बातें सुनने को मिलती हैं।

41. जो गरजते हैं वो बरसते नहीं—(डींग हाँकने वाले कुछ नहीं कर पाते) अब और अधिक वीरता के गुण मत बखानिये मैं भली प्रकार जानता हूँ जो गरजते हैं सो बरसते नहीं।

42. झूठे का मुँह काला, सच्चे का बोलबाला—(अन्त में सत्य की विजय होना) झूठ बोलने वाला व्यक्ति कुछ भी कर ले, किन्तु अन्त में झूठे का मुँह काला और सच्चे का बोलबाला होता ही है।

43. डूबते को तिनके का सहारा—(संकटकाल में थोड़ी सहायता भी बहुत होती है) नौकरी हाथ से जाने के बाद विक्रांत को अल्प पूँजी से छोटा सा व्यापार खुलवाकर राजू ने डूबते को तिनके का सहारा देने जैसा कार्य किया।

44. ढोल के भीतर पोल—(थोथी शान) आजकल लोगों की आमदनी कम है ऊपरी आडम्बर अधिक। अधिकांश लोगों में ढोल के भीतर पोल है।

45. तीनों लोक से मथुरा न्यारी—(सबसे अलग रहना) सुनील का व्यवहार परिवार से अलग है आपकी तो तीनों लोक से मथुरा न्यारी है।

46. तुम्हारे मुँह में घी शक्कर—(ईश्वर करे तुम्हारा कथन सत्य हो) रमेश ने अपनी बहन द्वारा नौकरी मिल जाने की बात पर कहा कि यदि मुझे नौकरी मिल जाये तो तुम्हारे मुँह में घी शक्कर।

47. थोथा चना बाजे घना—(बाहरी दिखावा) अशोक अनपढ़ होते हुए भी बड़े ठाट-बाट से रहता है सच है थोथा चना बाजे घना।

48. दूर के ढोल सुहावने—(दूर की प्रशंसा) आजकल कॉलेज तो बस नाम मात्र का रह गया है, पढ़ाई-लिखाई कुछ नहीं होती। सच ही तो है दूर के ढोल सुहावने लगते हैं।

49. दीवारों के भी कान होते हैं—(गुप्त बात छिपी नहीं रहती) मैं यह बात तुमसे एकान्त में कहूँगा जानते नहीं हो दीवारों के भी कान होते हैं।

50. दूध का दूध पानी का पानी—(ठीक-ठीक निर्णय करना) राष्ट्र संघ परिषद की स्थापना दूध का दूध पानी का पानी करने के लिए हुई है।

51. धोबी का कुत्ता घर का न घाट का—(बिल्कुल बेकार) नये व्यापार में ज्यादा फायदा सोच रविश ने पुरानी दुकान बन्द कर अपनी स्थिति धोबी का कुत्ता घर का न घाट का वाली बना ली।

52. न रहैगा बाँस न बजेगी बाँसुरी—(झगड़े की जड़ नष्ट कर देना) मैं दोनों को यहाँ से स्थानान्तरित कर रहा हूँ फिर न रहेगा बाँस न बजेगी बाँसुरी।

53. नौ नगद न तेरह उधार—(उधार से लाभ होने की आशा हो तो वह बुरी है) जो मनुष्य नौ नगद न तेरह उधार का उद्देश्य लेकर व्यापार करते हैं वह मूर्ख होते हैं।

54. नौ दिन चले अढ़ाई कोस—(अधिक परिश्रम का थोड़ा फल) प्रतिदिन 10 घण्टे पढ़ने पर भी उसका द्वितीय श्रेणी में उत्तीर्ण होना नौ दिन चले अढ़ाई कोस की बात को सिद्ध करता है।

55. नाँच न आवै आँगन टेढ़ा—(अपना दोष दूसरे के सिर पर मढ़ना) स्वयं तो लिखना आता नहीं दोष स्याही और कलम को देते हो—नाच न आवै आँगन टेढ़ा।

56. नया नौ दिन पुराना सौ दिन—(नया अस्थाई व पुराना स्थाई होता है) ताजमहल की भव्य सुन्दरता एवं मजबूती और नवीन इमारतों के खोखलेपन को देखकर यही कहना पड़ता है कि नया नौ दिन पुराना सौ दिन।

57. पाँचों अँगुली घी में—(सब प्रकार से लाभ होना) खुदरा व्यापारियों की प्राय: पाँचों अँगुली घी में रहती हैं।

58. बन्दर क्या जाने अदरक का स्वाद—(मूर्ख व्यक्ति गुणों को नहीं पहचानता) तुम जब संगीत को सुनते ही नहीं हो तो उसके बारे में क्या समझ सकते हो। ठीक भी है—बन्दर क्या जाने अदरक का स्वाद।

59. भैंस के आगे बीन बजाना—(मूर्ख के सामने ज्ञान की बात करना व्यर्थ है) छोटे बच्चों के आगे गीता का उपदेश देना भैंस के आगे बीन बजाना है।

60. मन चंगा तो कठौती में गंगा—(चित्त प्रसन्न हो तो घर में आनन्द है) मोहन ने कहा धार्मिक मेले में क्या रखा है मन चंगा तो कठौती में गंगा।

61. मुल्ला की दौड़ मस्जिद तक—(व्यक्ति की शक्ति बहुत सीमित होती है) आप हमारी शिकायत डिप्टी इन्सपेक्टर से करने गये बस मुल्ला की दौड़ मस्जिद तक ही होती है।

62. यथा राजा तथा प्रजा—(जैसा स्वामी होता है वैसे ही सेवक होते हैं) भारतीय सेनाओं ने कोरिया में जाकर शान्ति स्थापना की क्योंकि अपने यहाँ के प्रधानमन्त्री नेहरूजी भी शान्ति के पुजारी थे। सच ही है यथा राजा तथा प्रजा।

63. रस्सी जल गई पर बल न गया—(बरबाद हो जाने पर भी अभिमान करना) जमींदारी की जमींदारी चली गयी फिर भी व्यर्थ अकड़ किसानों पर दिखाते हैं यह कैसी बात है कि रस्सी जल गई पर बल न गया।

64. लाल गुदड़ी में नहीं छिपते—(गुणवान का गुण छिपाये नहीं छिपता) कर्मठ की कर्मठता ज्ञानी का ज्ञान एक न एक दिन उजागर जरूर होगी। क्योंकि लाल गुदड़ी में नहीं छिपते।

65. लेना एक न देना दो—(किसी से कोई मतलब न होना) श्याम के झगड़े में राम को व्यर्थ में ही तंग किया गया जबकि उस बेचारे का न किसी से लेना एक न देना दो।

66. सीधी उँगली से घी नहीं निकलता है—(सीधेपन से काम नहीं चलता) अध्यापक के बराबर कहने पर भी विद्यार्थी पाठ याद करके नहीं लाये। अध्यापक ने सभी को पीटते समय कहा। अब मैंने समझ लिया सीधी ऊँगली से घी नहीं निकलता।

67. साँप मरे पर लाठी न टूटे—(हानि भी न हो काम भी बन जाये) आप शौक से मेरी कार ले जा सकते हैं परन्तु साँप मरे पर लाठी न टूटे वाली बात ध्यान रखियेगा।

68. न सावन सूखे न भादों हरे—(सदैव समान हालत में रहना) आप मेरे वस्त्रों की चिन्ता मत करिये मेरा तो यही कुर्ता पाजामा ठीक है। यहाँ तो न सावन सूखे न भादों हरे।

69. सौ सुनार की, एक लुहार की—(बलवान की एक चोट निर्बल की सौ चोट के बराबर होती है) वह मुझे खूब दुःख पहुँचा ले परन्तु यह समझ लीजिए सौ सुनार की एक लुहार की।

70. सिर मुड़ाते ही ओले पड़ना—(कार्य प्रारम्भ होते ही हानि होना) नया व्यापार आरम्भ करते ही कच्चे माल की आमद न हो पाने के कारण मोहन को सिर मुड़ाते ही ओले पड़ गए।

71. हाथ कंगन को आरसी क्या—(प्रत्यक्ष के लिए प्रमाण की क्या आवश्यकता) कार्य करने वाले व्यक्ति को हाथ कंगन को आरसी क्या के समान अपने कार्य का प्रमाण देने की कोई आवश्यकता नहीं होती।

उपरोक्त के अतिरिक्त अन्य कुछ लोकोक्तियाँ व उनके अर्थ इस प्रकार हैं—

1. अंधा बाँटे रेवड़ी फिर-फिर अपनों को दे—पक्षपातपूर्ण व्यवहार करना।

2. आप काज महाकाज—अपना काम स्वयं करने से ठीक होता है।

3. कोयले की दलाली में हाथ काले—बुरे काम में बुराई मिलती है।

4. का वर्षा जब कृषि सुखानी—आवश्यकता पूरी हो जाने पर वस्तु मिलना बेकार है।

5. जाको राखे साइयाँ मार सके न कोय—ईश्वर जिसकी रक्षा करता है उसे कोई हानि नहीं पहुँचा सकता।

6. मन के हारे हार है मन के जीते जीत—मन की भावना के अनुसार कार्य में सफलता या असफलता मिलती है।

7. साँच को आँच नहीं—जो मनुष्य सच्चा है उसे डर नहीं।

8. दीवारों के भी कान होते हैं—गुप्त बात एकान्त में भी कही जाये तो भी कोई न कोई सुन ही लेता है।

9. हथेली पर सरसों जमाना—कोई बड़ा काम जल्दी नहीं होता।

10. टेड़ जानि शंका सब काहू—कुटिल व्यक्ति से सब डरते हैं।

वाक्य शुद्धिकरण

(RECTIFICATION OF SENTENCES)

अशुद्ध वाक्य	शुद्ध वाक्य
1. लोकसभा के बीच कल विचार होगा।	कल लोक सभा में विचार होगा।
2. मैंने आज जाना है।	मुझे आज जाना है।
3. मशीनों के धुँए से वायु मण्डल में हवा दूषित हो रहा है।	मशीनों के धुँए से पर्यावरण दूषित हो रहा है।
4. हमको तुमको और श्याम को अवश्य जाना है।	श्याम, तुम्हें तथा मुझे अवश्य जाना है।
5. इस समस्या की औषधि उसके पास है।	इस समस्या का समाधान उसके पास है।
6. विज्ञानिकों ने धरती को स्वर्ग बना दिया है।	वैज्ञानिकों ने धरती को स्वर्ग बना दिया है।
7. प्रातः भ्रमण में कैसी आनन्द आती है।	प्रातः भ्रमण में कैसा आनन्द आता है।
8. माताजी मंसूरी से कब आ रहे हैं ?	माताजी मंसूरी से कब आ रही हैं ?
9. हमारे कक्षा में 40 छात्र-छात्रा हैं।	हमारी कक्षा में 40 छात्र-छात्राएँ हैं।
10. ईश्वर उनका सहायता करता है जो अपनी सहायता आप करता है।	ईश्वर उनकी सहायता करता है जो अपनी सहायता आप करते हैं।
11. हम वह दुःखद घटना नहीं देख सका।	हम वह दुःखद घटना नहीं देख सके।
12. मैं सभी वस्तुओं को क्रम से सजाई।	मैंने सभी वस्तुओं को क्रम से सजाया।
13. पैसा देना उस के लिए बड़ा बात नहीं।	पैसा देना उसके लिए बड़ी बात नहीं।
14. जरा सी बात को लेकर तिल का पहाड़ न बनाओ।	जरा-सी बात को लेकर तिल का ताड़ न बनाओ।
15. इतिहासिक पुरुष अपनी अमिट छाप छोड़ जाते हैं।	ऐतिहासिक पुरुष अपनी अमिट छाप छोड़ जाते हैं।
16. मात्रभूमि की रक्षा हमारा पुनीत कर्त्तव्य है।	मातृभूमि की रक्षा हमारा पुनीत कर्त्तव्य है।
17. शिवाजी औरंगजेब की आँखों का तारा था।	शिवाजी, औरंगजेब की आँखों का काँटा थे।
18. यह दुःखद घटना मुझे आजन्म नहीं भूलेगी।	मैं यह दुःखद घटना आजन्म नहीं भूलूँगा।
19. आर्थिक संकट में ऋण के लिए भारत विश्वबैंक का कृतघ्न है।	आर्थिक संकट में ऋण के लिए भारत विश्व बैंक का कृतज्ञ है।
20. स्वतन्त्रता के विगत वर्षों में भारत ने भारी उद्योगिक उन्नति की है।	स्वतन्त्रता के विगत वर्षों में भारत ने भारी औद्योगिक उन्नति की है।
21. दादीजी अभी-अभी आए हैं।	दादीजी अभी-अभी आयीं हैं।
22. स्वार्थी मित्र काम निकलते ही आँखें नीची कर लेते हैं।	स्वार्थी मित्र काम निकलते ही आँखें फेर लेते हैं।
23. देश का भविष्य उसके नागरिकों पर अवलम्बन है।	देश का भविष्य उसके नागरिकों पर अवलम्बित है।

24. तुम्हारा सब काम ऐसा ही होता है।	तुम्हारे सब काम ऐसे ही होते हैं।
25. शेर की चिंघाड़ सुनकर मैं डर गई।	शेर की दहाड़ सुनकर मैं डर गयी।
26. यहाँ कितना हरा-भरा घास है!	यहाँ कितनी हरी-भरी घास है।
27. पूज्यनीय देशभक्तों को शत-शत प्रणाम।	पूजनीय देशभक्तों को शत-शत प्रणाम।
28. याद रहे:'धोबी का कुत्ता घर का न बाहर का।'	याद रहे, ''धोबी का कुत्ता घर का ना घाट का।''
29. मेरे को वह दृश्य नहीं देखा गया।	मुझसे वह दृश्य न देखा गया।
30. शीला ने जाते हुए कहा:''मैं फिर आयेंगी।''	शीला ने जाते हुए कहा, ''मैं फिर आऊँगी।''
31. विज्ञानिक आविष्कारों ने आज संसार की काया पलट दी है।	वैज्ञानिक आविष्कारों ने आज संसार की काया पलट दी है।
32. निर्दयी चंगेजखां की क्रूरता आज भी कृपा देती है।	चंगेज खाँ की क्रूरता आज भी कंपा देती है।
33. मेरे माताजी आज ही मद्रास से आये हैं।	मेरी माताजी आज ही चेन्नई से आयीं हैं।
34. हिमालय की उच्च शिखरें किसका मन नहीं मोहतीं।	हिमालय के उच्च शिखर किसका मन नहीं मोहते।
35. शिवाजी ओरंगजेब की आँखों में धूल फेंककर बन्दीगृह से निकल भागे।	शिवाजी औरंगजेब की आँखों में धूल झोंककर बन्दीगृह से निकल भागे।
36. मेरी रुचि अच्छा-अच्छी पुस्तकें पढ़ने में है।	मेरी रुचि अच्छी-अच्छी पुस्तकें पढ़ने में है।
37. महात्मा गाँधी का देश सदा आभारी रहेगा।	देश महात्मा गाँधी का सदा आभारी रहेगा।
38. हम यह घटना कभी नहीं भूलेगा।	हम यह घटना कभी नहीं भूलेंगे।
39. हमारा लक्ष्य देश की चहुँमुखी प्रगति होनी चाहिए।	हमारा लक्ष्य देश की चहुँमुखी प्रगति होना चाहिए।
40. यह सारा कार्य मैंने करा है।	यह सारा कार्य मैंने किया है।
41. तुम्हें झूठ मत न बोलना चाहिए।	तुम्हें झूठ नहीं बोलना चाहिए।
42. लोक सभा के बीच कल विवाद होगा।	लोक सभा में कल बहस होगी।
43. अनेक कामों की भीड़ में मैं परेशान हूँ।	कार्य की अधिकता से मैं परेशान हूँ।
44. यह सुनकर मैं अति विस्मय हुआ।	यह सुनकर मुझे अत्यन्त विस्मय हुआ।
45. उसने केवल कुछ रुपये मात्र में अपना ईमान बेच दिया।	उसने केवल कुछ रुपयों में अपना ईमान बेच दिया।
46. रात होते रात के तिमिर का अंधकार फैल गया।	रात होते ही तिमिर/अँधेरा चारों ओर फैल गया।
47. आपत्ति में सहयोग के लिए देश विश्व बैंक का कृतघ्न रहेगा।	आपत्ति में सहयोग के लिए देश विश्व बैंक का कृतज्ञ रहेगा।
48. रामू और राजा का विरोध छत्तीस के अंक के समान है।	रामू और राजा में इन दिनों छत्तीस का आँकड़ा है।

49. दृढ़ निश्चय का भावना सफलता के मूलमन्त्र हैं।	दृढ़ निश्चय की भावना सफलता का मूल-मन्त्र है।
50. मैंने आज वहाँ जाना है।	मुझे आज वहाँ जाना है।
51. यहाँ न लिखो।	यहाँ न लिखें।
52. दुष्ट हत्यारे को मृत्युदण्ड की सजा मिलेगी।	दुष्ट हत्यारे को मृत्युदण्ड मिलेगा।
53. वह लोग आ गए हैं।	वे लोग आ गए हैं।
54. वह नपा-तुला शब्द बोलता है।	वह नपे-तुले शब्दों में अपनी बात कहता है।
55. तुम्हें तुम्हारी पुस्तकें सुरक्षित ढंग से रखनी चाहिए।	तुम्हें अपनी पुस्तकें सुरक्षित ढंग से रखनी चाहिए।
56. वह लोग आ गए हैं।	वे लोग आ गए हैं।
57. तू झूठ मत बोलिओ।	तुम झूठ मत बोलना।
58. मैं आपका दर्सन करने आया हूँ।	मैं आपके दर्शन करने आया हूँ।
59. वे भगवान् की श्रद्धा करते हैं।	वे भगवान् में श्रद्धा रखते हैं।
60. दादाजी रेलगाड़ी पर आया है।	दादाजी रेलगाड़ी से आए हैं।
61. यह पुस्तक मैं पढ़ा हूँ।	मैंने यह पुस्तक पढ़ी है।
62. अनेक परिक्षार्थी प्रश्न भी नहीं समझ सके।	अनेक परीक्षार्थी प्रश्न भी नहीं समझ सके।
63. यहाँ फालतू न बैठो।	यहाँ फालतू न बैठें।
64. आज हमारा सूखा ग्रस्त देश है।	आज हमारा देश सूखा ग्रस्त है।
65. आपको मेरे नमस्कार पहुँचे।	आपको मेरा नमस्कार पहुँचे।
66. उसने अनेकों ग्रन्थ लिख डाले हैं।	उसने अनेक ग्रन्थ लिखे हैं।
67. उसका प्राण तुरन्त निकल गया।	उसके प्राण तुरन्त निकल गए।
68. हिन्दी हमारा राष्ट्र भाषा है।	हिन्दी हमारी राष्ट्रभाषा है।
69. उसके बहन दिल्ली में रहते हैं।	उसकी बहन दिल्ली में है।
70. इन लड़के तो रात में ही आ गए।	ये लड़के तो रात में ही आ गए।
71. प्रधान अध्यापक ने स्वतन्त्रता दिवस पर छात्रों की शिक्षा दी।	प्रधानाध्यापक ने स्वतन्त्रता दिवस पर छात्रों का उद्‌बोधन किया।
72. चिड़ियाँ बाग में मीठा बोलती हैं।	चिड़ियाँ बाग में मधुर स्वर में बोलती हैं।
73. राधा, सीता और सुवामा बाजार गए।	सुवामा, सीता और राधा बाजार गयीं।
74. शहीदों का देश हार्दिक कृतज्ञ है।	देश, शहीदों के प्रति हार्दिक कृतज्ञता प्रकट करता है।
75. उसके आगमन ने उत्सव में शोभा बढ़ा दिया।	उसके आगमन ने उत्सव की शोभा बढ़ा दी या उसके आगमन से उत्सव की शोभा बढ़ गयी।
76. पुलिस को देखकर चोर आठ तीन ग्यारह हो गए।	पुलिस को देखकर चोर नौ दो ग्यारह हो गए।
77. करुणा के सभी सहेली कल ही आ गईं।	करुणा की सभी सहेलियाँ कल ही आ गईं।
78. आयो यहाँ बैठो और काम करो।	आएँ, यहाँ बैठें और काम करें।

79. उसे बड़ों में भक्ति है।	उसे बड़ों में श्रद्धा है।
80. मेरे को मेरे सभी शिक्षक पसन्द करते हैं।	मुझे सभी शिक्षक पसन्द करते हैं।
81. आज वहाँ उसने आना है।	उसे आज यहाँ आना है।
82. एक विरोध-प्रदर्शन मन्त्री जब आए, किया गया।	जब मन्त्री आये, विरोध-प्रदर्शन किया गया।
83. उसके पिताजी एक-एक दाँ को पैसे से पकड़ते हैं।	उसके पिताजी एक-एक पैसे को दाँत से पकड़ते हैं।
84. उसके भईया जी बहुत उदार हैं।	उसके भाई बहुत उदार हैं।
85. सूर्यास्त के छिपते ही वातावरण में अँधेरा छा गया।	सूर्यास्त होते ही वातावरण में अँधेरा छा गया।
86. शहीदों का यह देश सदा आभारी रहेगा।	यह देश शहीदों का सदा आभारी रहेगा।
87. देखते ही काले-काले बादलों ने आकाश ढक दिया।	देखते ही देखते काले-काले बादलों ने आकाश ढँक लिया।
88. एकमात्र राज ऐसा व्यक्ति था जो समय पर शादी में आया।	राज ही एकमात्र व्यक्ति था जो समय पर शादी में आया।
89. उसके भाभीजी इन दिनों बीमार हैं।	उसकी भाभीजी इन दिनों बीमार हैं।
90. क्या इसका अनूकरण हो सकता है ?	क्या इसका अनुसरण हो सकता है ?
91. आज हमारा तबीयत ठीक नहीं है।	आज मेरी तबियत ठीक नहीं है।
92. जो किसी का पक्ष न ले उसे निस्पक्ष कहते हैं।	जो किसी का पक्ष न ले उसे निष्पक्ष कहते हैं।
93. पिताजी अभी विदेश से नहीं आई हैं।	पिताजी अभी विदेश से नहीं आए हैं।
94. यह मेरा व्यक्तीगत निर्णय है।	यह मेरा व्यक्तिगत निर्णय है।
95. पिछला साल तुम कहाँ गया था ?	पिछले साल तुम कहाँ गये थे ?
96. महात्मा बुद्ध की चिन्तन सरल व स्वाभाविक थे।	महात्मा बुद्ध का चिन्तन सरल व स्वाभाविक था।
97. मनुष्य के सामान के रक्षा के लिए मदर टेरेसा ने नि:स्वार्थ सेवा किया।	मनुष्य के सम्मान की रक्षा के लिए मदर टेरेसा ने नि: स्वार्थ सेवा की।
98. शिकारी ने अपनी गोली से शेर को धाराशायी कर दिया।	शिकारी ने अपनी गोली से शेर को धराशायी कर दिया।
99. यह एक विद्वान नारी है।	यह एक विदुषी है।
100. मुझे घमण्डी लोग अच्छा नहीं लगता।	मुझे घमण्डी लोग अच्छे नहीं लगते।
101. मेरा काला घोड़ा हरा घास खाता है।	मेरा काला घोड़ा हरी घास खाता है।
102. राम अब भी आया है।	राम अभी आया है।
103. चोर में बल से दरवाजा तोड़ लिया।	चोर ने बल से दरवाजा तोड़ दिया।
104. मेरा ऐनक गुभ हो गया।	मेरी ऐनक गुम हो गयी।
105. उसे साँप ने खा लिया।	उसे साँप ने डस लिया।
106. केवल मात्र कहने से कुछ नहीं होगा।	केवल कहने मात्र से कुछ नहीं होगा।
107. नीती सास्त्र में नैतिकता की बातें होती है।	नीतिशास्त्र में नैतिकता की बातें होती हैं।
108. मेरे माता आज घर पर नहीं है।	मेरी माता आज घर पर नहीं हैं।
109. हम यह काम नहीं कर सकता।	मैं यह काम नहीं कर सकता।
110. वह घर जा रहे हैं।	वह घर जा रहा है।

111.	तुम अपना काम कर लिया।	तुमने अपना काम कर लिया।
112.	रोगी को पथ देना चाहिए।	रोगी को पथ्य देना चाहिये।
113.	आप क्या करोगे ?	आप क्या करेंगें ?
114.	सात दिन में सप्ताह होता है।	सप्ताह सात दिन का होता है।
115.	जाओ, देखो, ठहरो।	ठहरो, देखो और जाओ।
116.	यह कार्य तत्काल अभी पूर्ण करना है।	यह कार्य तत्काल पूर्ण करना है।
117.	हमें लोगों में दु:ख बाँटने चाहिए।	हमें लोगों के दु:ख बाँटने चाहिए।
118.	आज भी कुछ लोग काला अक्षर भैंस बराबर है।	शिक्षा आज भी कुछ लोगों के लिए काला अक्षर भैंस बराबर है।
119.	गीता में श्रीकृष्ण ने अर्जुन को उपदेश दिया।	श्रीकृष्ण ने, अर्जुन को गीता का उपदेश दिया।
120.	संगति का व्यक्ति के व्यवहार पर प्रभाव होता है।	संगति का प्रभाव व्यक्ति के व्यवहार पर पड़ता है।
121.	उसका उधार का पैसा मारा गया।	उसका उधारी का पैसा मारा गया।
122.	एक किलोग्राम के एक हजार ग्राम होते हैं।	एक किलोग्राम में एक हजार ग्राम होते हैं।
123.	इस फाइल पर उचित टिप्पणी करो।	इस फाइल पर उचित टिप्पणी लिखो।
124.	ऊँट के गले कुत्ता की कहावत उन दोनों पर लागू होती है।	ऊँट के गले बिल्ली वाली कहावत उन दोनों पर लागू होती है।
125.	महाभारत व्याजजी ने लिखा।	महाभारत ग्रन्थ व्यासजी ने लिखा या महाभारत की कथा व्यास जी ने लिखी।
126.	चोर-चोर चचेर भाई।	चोर-चोर मौसरे भाई।
127.	अपने बुरे दुष्कर्मों के कारण वह आज कंगाल है।	अपने दुष्कर्मों के कारण आज वह कंगाल हो गया है।
128.	ताजमहल शाहजहाँ ने बनाया था।	ताजमहल शाहजहाँ ने बनवाया था।
129.	होली रंग का पर्व कहलाता है।	होली रंगों का पर्व कहलाता है।
130.	ह्रास और रुदन जीवन कंग होता है।	ह्रास और रुदन जीवन के अंग होते हैं।
131.	बीज से ही फल होता है।	बीज से ही फल पैदा होता है।
132.	आजकल ब्याज की दर सौ रुपये पर छ: प्रतिशत है।	आजकल ब्याज की दर छ: प्रतिशत है।
133.	भारत, पाकिस्तान का पड़ोसी है।	भारत और पाकिस्तान पड़ोसी हैं।
134.	प्राकृतिक सौन्दर्यता किसका मन नहीं मोहती।	प्राकृतिक सौन्दर्य किसका मन नहीं मोहता या प्राकृतिक सुन्दरता किसका मन नहीं मोहती।
135.	समुद्र की उत्ताल तरंगों को देखकर कैसा आनन्द आता है।	समुद्र की उत्ताल तरंगें देखकर कितना आनन्द आता है।
136.	जो व्यक्ति स्वार्थी होते हैं, वे देश हित की बातें नहीं सोचते।	स्वार्थी व्यक्ति देशहित की बात नहीं सोचते।
137.	सज्जन किसी का अहित नहीं चाहते।	सज्जन किसी का अहित नहीं चाहते या सज्जन सभी का हित चाहते हैं।
138.	अभी तो दस बजा है।	अभी तो दस बजे हैं।
139.	वह लोग कब आ रहे हैं ?	वे लोग कब आ रहे हैं ?
140.	मात्रभूमि की रक्षा हमारा पुनीत कर्तव्य है।	मातृभूमि की रक्षा करना हमारा पुनीत कर्तव्य है।
141.	राणा प्रताप अकबर की आँख का तारा थे।	राणा प्रताप अकबर की आँख का काँटा थे।

142.	अपराधी को दण्ड न देना केवल मात्र उसके अपराध को बढ़ावा देना है।	अपराधी को दण्ड न देना केवल उसके अपराध को बढ़ावा देना है।
143.	रोगी की दिशा ठीक नहीं है।	रोगी की दशा ठीक नहीं है।
144.	धनमान व्यक्तियों का उदार होना चाहिए।	धनवान व्यक्तियों को उदार होना चाहिए।
145.	हम यह काम नहीं कर सकता।	हम यह काम नहीं कर सकते।
146.	विद्वान पत्नी ने कालीदास को मूर्ख से विद्वान बना दिया।	विदुषी पत्नी ने कालिदास को मूर्ख से विद्वान बना दिया।
147.	रत्नावली ने गो. तुलसीदास की जीवन धारा बदल दी।	रत्नावली ने गो. तुलसीदास के जीवन की धारा को ही बदल दिया।
148.	बुरा से बुरा आदमी भी अच्छे व्यवहार की आशा करता है।	बुरे से बुरा आदमी भी अच्छे व्यवहार की आशा रखता है।
149.	मेरे को अपनी पुस्तक देकर जाना।	मुझे अपनी पुस्तक दे जाना।
150.	यह सुनकर मैं अतिविस्मय हुआ।	यह सुनकर मुझे अति विस्मय हुआ।
151.	क्या यह सारा काम तुमने करा है ?	क्या यह सारा काम तुमने किया है ?
152.	अनेकों बार समझाने पर भी वह नहीं समझता।	अनेक बार समझाने पर भी वह नहीं समझा।
153.	आज वहाँ राम ने जाना है।	आज राम को वहाँ जाना है।
154.	वह लोग आ गये हैं।	वे लोग आ गये हैं।
155.	यहाँ देवतों की पूजा होती है।	यहाँ देवताओं की पूजा होती है।
156.	यह बात राम को पूछो।	यह बात राम से पूछिये।
157.	उसका भाई सैक्रेटरी लगा हुआ है।	उसका भाई सैक्रेटरी है।
158.	सुरेश को रमेश को और मोहन को कल मैंने साथ-साथ देखा।	सुरेश, रमेश और मोहन को कल मैंने साथ-साथ देखा।
159.	देखते-देखते यह सब कुछ हो गया। उनकी आँखों के सामने।	उनकी आँखों के सामने देखते-देखते वह सब कुछ हो गया।
160.	हमको और तुमको और राम को अवश्य जाना है।	मुझे, तुम्हें और राम को अवश्य जाना है।
161.	कमीज तो सिल गया है, लेकिन बटन नहीं टँका है।	कमीज तो सिल गई है, लेकिन बटन नहीं टँके हैं।
162.	यहाँ नहीं लिखो!	यहाँ मत लिखो।
163.	इन सबों ने काम नहीं करा है।	इन सब ने काम नहीं किया है।
164.	उसने बम्बई जाना है।	उसे मुंबई जाना है।
165.	भयानक दृश्य देखकर हमारा तो प्राण निकल गया।	भयानक दृश्य देखकर हमारे तो प्राण ही निकल गये।
166.	उसकी ख्याति सारे देश भर में फैली है।	उसकी ख्याति सारे देश में फैली है।
167.	रोकर बालक की आँखों से आँसू निकलने लगे।	बालक रोने लगा और उसकी आँखों से आँसू निकलने लगे।

सारा आकाश

[SAARA AKASH]

—राजेन्द्र यादव

उपन्यास की परिभाषा— हिन्दी गद्य साहित्य की अनेक विधाएँ होती हैं, जैसे—निबन्ध, उपन्यास, कहानी, नाटक, जीवनी, आत्मकथा, संस्मरण, रेखाचित्र, गद्यकाव्य, यात्रावृत्त, एकांकी, आलोचना, रिपोर्ताज, भेंटवार्ता और डायरी।

उपन्यास कहानी का ही वृहद् और रोचक स्वरूप है। उपन्यास में ऐसी कथावस्तु होती है जिसमें पात्रों के चरित्र-चित्रण, कथोपकथन, घटनाओं को उद्देश्यपूर्ण, भावना प्रधान तथा कला से रंजित करके प्रस्तुत किया जाता है। साहित्यकारों ने उपन्यास के छः तत्व स्वीकार किये हैं—

(1) कथावस्तु, (2) पात्रयोजना, (3) संवाद, (4) देशकाल एवं वातावरण, (5) भाषा शैली तथा (6) उद्देश्य।

हिन्दी के सुप्रसिद्ध उपन्यासकार हुए हैं—

प्रेमचन्द, भगवती चरण वर्मा, जैनेन्द्र कुमार, यशपाल, शिवानी आदि।

हिन्दी के प्रथम उपन्यासकार श्रीनिवास दास हैं। उनके उपन्यास का नाम 'परीक्षा गुरू' है।

उपन्यास के प्रकार— सामाजिक (सारा आकाश, गोदान, गबन) ऐतिहासिक (ध्रुवस्वामिनी, चन्द्रगुप्त, ज्वालामुखी के फूल, झाँसी की रानी), आंचलिक (रेणु, मैला आंचल), जासूसी (अनेक उपन्यास हैं), मनोवैज्ञानिक, राजनीतिक, पौराणिक, क्रान्तिकारी।

उपन्यासकार का परिचय— राजेन्द्र यादव का जन्म आगरा (उ. प्र.) में 28 अगस्त, 1929 को हुआ था। इनकी प्रारम्भिक शिक्षा आगरा में हुई। इन्होंने 1949 में बी. ए. पास किया फिर 1951 में आगरा यूनिवर्सिटी में हिन्दी में एम. ए. किया।

इनका पहला उपन्यास 'प्रेत बोलते हैं' 1951 में प्रकाशित हुआ फिर 1960 में 'सारा आकाश' लिखा। 1969 में वसू चटर्जी, फिल्म निर्माता एवं निदेशक ने इस उपन्यास पर इसी नाम से फिल्म बनाई। इनका अगला उपन्यास 'उखड़े हुए लोग' आया। इसके बाद दो उपन्यास 'कुल्टा' और 'शह और मात' लिखे गये।

इनके अलावा इन्होंने कई कहानियाँ भी लिखीं। लेखक होने के साथ-साथ इनको 1999 में प्रसार भारती के बोर्ड का सदस्य नामित किया गया। 2013 में उत्तर प्रदेश सरकार ने इनको 'यश भारती सम्मान' से सम्मानित किया।

राजेन्द्र यादव का देहान्त दिल्ली में 28 अक्टूबर, 2013 को हुआ। इन्होंने लिखने के सिवाय कोई अन्य काम नहीं किया। इन्होंने शुरू में कलकत्ता में लेखक बनने के लिए संघर्ष किया फिर अपनी पत्नी मन्नू भण्डारी के साथ दिल्ली में बस गये और लेखक के तौर पर नाम कमाया।

अपने लेखन के साथ-साथ इन्होंने कुछ अनुवाद भी किये जैसे चेखव के तीन नाटक, उपन्यास : टक्कर, हमारे युग का एक नायक आदि। इन्होंने कविता संग्रह 'आवाज तेरी है' 1967 में लिखा। इसके साथ-साथ सम्पादन का कार्य भी किया।

पूर्वार्द्ध : साँझ

एक

शब्दार्थ—प्राण पखेरू उड़ जाना = मृत्यु होना, **अनिष्ट** = बुरा, **फुरसत** = खाली समय, **गोधूलि** = शाम का समय, **नमामि भक्त वत्सलम** = भक्तों पर कृपा करने वाले को नमस्कार, **नाक-नक्शा** = चेहरे की बनावट, **दया निधि** = दया के सागर, **उदासीनता** = ध्यान न देना, **सदैव** = हमेशा।

सारांश

बिना किसी ताल और लय के ढमाढम पिटती ढोलक और औरतों के गीतों के स्वर आचानक रुक गये। 'क्या हुआ ?' पूछते हुए सारी औरतें, बच्चे गली वाले जंगले और छज्जों पर से झाँककर देखने लगे। नीचे फाटक पर नाचते और ताली बजाते हिजड़े 'अये-जियो-जियो रे लला' का अलाप भूलकर ऊपर की ओर ताकने लगे।

गली के पार ठीक हमारे घर के सामने वाले साँवल की बहू मिट्‌टी का तेल डालकर कोठरी में जलकर मर गयी थी। किवाड़ तोड़ते-तोड़ते लोग अन्दर गये; लेकिन तब तक उसके प्राण पखेरू उड़ चुके थे। बड़ी चीख-पुकार और भाग-दौड़ मच गई थी। लाख समर अपने को विश्वास दिलाता था कि आज उसकी सुहागरात है, लेकिन उसे विश्वास नहीं होता था।

'देश को साहसी और कर्मठ युवकों की जरूरत है' का नारा देने वाला यह युवक भी अब चौपाया हो गया है। समर एक कर्मठ कार्यकर्ता है वह दो हफ्तों से शाखा नहीं गया है और अपने साथियों से आँख चुराता फिर रहा है। वह मन्दिर की ओर जा रहा है। वहाँ बैठकर शान्ति का अनुभव करेगा। वह अपनी शादी के दृश्य को याद करता है। वह एक निम्न मध्यम वर्गीय परिवार का दूसरा लड़का है। उसके संयुक्त परिवार में माता-पिता, विवाहित बड़ा भाई, दो छोटे भाई और एक विवाहित बहन जो ससुराल के अत्याचारों से पीड़ित होकर अपने मायके में रह रही है।

वह एक लड़के से बचते हुए आगे बढ़ा। वह सोचता है कि कैसा बोझीला प्रारम्भ है जिन्दगी का ! वह अभी इण्टर में पढ़ रहा है। उसके मन के खिलाफ उसकी शादी कर दी गयी थी। वह मन में सोचता है कि कहीं भाग जाऊँ। न जाने किसको मेरे गले बाँध दिया है ? बड़े भाई के विवाह को आठ साल हो गये। अम्मा और बाबूजी रोज यही मनौती मनाते कि कब मेरी शादी हो जाये।" उसने अपनी डायरी में लिखा कि वह इतनी जल्दी अपनी हिम्मत क्यों हार जाता है ? सभी के जीवन में परीक्षा के क्षण आते हैं। यह उसकी परीक्षा का क्षण है। राणा प्रताप और शिवाजी का रक्त उसकी धमनियों में है, उसे लजाना नहीं है। वह भगवान से प्रार्थना करता है कि "मैं झुक न जाऊँ-कहीं मैं हार न जाऊँ।" कोई कहता, "प्रभा (पत्नी) दसवीं पास है। मैंने तो उसके हाथ के सिवा कुछ देखा नहीं है। जो भी है, मुझे तो उससे कोई सम्बन्ध नहीं रखना है।" भाभी कहती है कि चेहरे पर हल्के-हल्के चेचक की झाँई है। खैर जो भी हो मुझे इन सबसे क्या लेना-देना ?

समर सोचता है कि वह अपनी नवविवाहिता पत्नी से एकदम बात करना शुरू नहीं करेगा और उसे समझायेगा कि वह पहले अपनी शिक्षा पूरी करना चाहता है। फिर अचानक वह सोचता है कि उसे इन सब बातों के मोहजाल में नहीं फँसना है।

दो

शब्दार्थ—तड़फड़ाया = परेशान होना, **झनझनाहट** = आवाज, **खुसर-पुसर** = धीरे-धीरे बात करना, **भकभकाकर** = जोर से, **स्पष्ट** = साफ, **वज्रमूर्ख** = सबसे बड़ा मूर्ख, **अपलक** = बिना पलक झपके, **अज्ञात** = जो मालूम न हो।

हलके से धक्का देकर भाभी ने पीछे से किवाड़ बन्द कर दिये तो समर कमरे में आ गया। उस समय प्रभा जंगले में सिर रखे खड़ी थी, जैसे खड़ी-खड़ी सो गई हो। थोड़ी देर खड़े रहकर वह पलंग पर बैठ गया। इस समय उसका दिल धड़क रहा था। वह दूसरे लड़कों की तरह नहीं है जो कि लड़कियों को न जाने क्या समझते हैं। मन ही मन दुहराता रहा।. . . .नारी अंधकार है, नारी मोह है, नारी माया है। इस समय स्टूल पर रखा पंखा अपनी झनझनाहट से अपनी उपस्थिति दर्ज करा रहा था। विवाह के अवसर पर बिजली पड़ोसी से उधार ले ली गई थी। समर के पलंग पर बैठते ही प्रभा ने सिर उठाकर देखा, इस तरह फिर सिर खिड़की पर टिका दिया। वह बुद्धू की तरह पंखे को देखता रहा। धीरे से पलंग पर आड़ा ही लेट गया। उसे आशंका हो रही

थी कि वह उसकी कठोरता पर फूट-फूट कर रो उठेगी और उसके पैरों पर गिर कर अपना अपराध पूछेगी। पर ऐसा कुछ नहीं हुआ और आधी रात बीत गई। उसे लगा कि वह यहाँ आया ही क्यों ? समर के घर वाले तो बिना पढ़े-लिखे हैं और वह है मैट्रिक पास। वह सोचने लगा कि वह झुकेगा नहीं। प्रभा शायद यह सोच रही होगी कि वह आयेगा और उसे मनाकर पलंग पर बिठायेगा। तभी पहली बार समर का ध्यान उसकी अशिष्टता पर गया कि उसके आने पर नमस्कार-प्रणाम कुछ नहीं। समर को अपना अपमान लगा। तब भी उसके मन में भाव आया कि जब वह चलेगा तो वह उसका हाथ या कुरते का छोर पकड़ लेगी। लेकिन उसने ऐसा कोई भाव नहीं दिखाया। समर ने किवाड़ खोले तो उसने सिर उठाकर उसे देखा; लेकिन रुका नहीं। वह सीढ़ियाँ चढ़कर खुली छत पर आ गया। चाँदनी छिटक रही थी। अब देखना है कि वह इस अपमान का बदला किस प्रकार चुकाता है। इसी दिमागी उठक-पटक में उसकी आँखें बुरी तरह डबडबा आईं। पता नहीं किस तरह की लड़की को उसके गले मढ़ दिया है ? कैसे चलेगी जिन्दगी. . . ?

अपने मन की गहराई में वह सोचता रहा कि अभी उठे और बिना किसी से कहे-सुने बाहर निकल पड़े तो कैसा रहेगा ? कहीं चला जायेगा, कलकत्ता, बम्बई या हरिद्वार. . .।

तीन

शब्दार्थ—तथाकथित = कही जाने वाली, **गूढ़** = गहरा, **कतराना** = बच के रहना, **निरुद्देश्य** = बिना उद्देश्य के, **जाहिलो** = गवारों, **परीजादी** = परी जैसी सुन्दर, **अमरित** = अमृत, **बोझीला** = न सहने योग्य, **उत्कंठा** = तीव्र इच्छा, **नौकाकार** = नौका की आकृति जैसी, **उत्सुकता** = जानने की इच्छा, **रिस्टवाच** = कलाई में पहनने वाली घड़ी।

वन में लगी भयंकर आग की तरह समाचार सारे घर में फैल गया कि समर प्रभा से नहीं बोला। वह अपने कमरे में बैठा-बैठा जाने क्या-क्या सोचता रहा। उदासी थी कि अँधेरे के साथ-साथ बढ़ती चली आ रही थी। सुबह से कई लोग पूछ चुके थे। शायद प्रभा से भी पूछा हो। लेकिन दोनों (समर और प्रभा) ने ऐसी अनिच्छा दिखाई कि फिर किसी के पूछने की हिम्मत ही नहीं पड़ी वह अपनी तथाकथित पत्नी से नाराज जरूर था, लेकिन यह भी जानना चाहता था कि उसने उसके खिलाफ क्या-क्या कहा है ? अभी तक उसके सुनने में कुछ नहीं आया था। अगर वह सबसे कुछ न कुछ कहती फिरती, तब भी शायद क्या नया नहीं लगता।

बाबूजी ने अत्यन्त गूढ़ रहस्य जानने की मुद्रा में पूछा, "कुछ खास बात हुई क्या ?" वह चुप रहा। फिर उन्होंने पूछा, "लड़ाई-वड़ाई तो नहीं हो गई।" वह चुपचाप निकल गया। वह पिताजी से डरता है। बचपन की मार वह भूला नहीं है। उस समय तो उसका साहस डगमगा गया जब मुन्नी (बहन) ने कहा कि बाबूजी ने बुलाया है। वह उनके पास गया। वह फर्शी पीते हुए धुआँ निकाल रहे थे। आस-पास की खाली कुर्सी और मूढ़े को देखकर लगा कि कुछ लोग उठकर गये हैं। बैठने के संकेत को देखकर वह एक तरफ बैठ गया। बाबूजी बोले—"क्या बात है ? बहू तुझे पसन्द नहीं आई ? साफ बता न इसमें झिझक की क्या बात है ? सुनते हैं तू उससे बोला भी नहीं।" वह चुपचाप सुनता रहा। वे बोलते रहे—"यह भी तो सोचो कि वह बेचारी पराई लड़की किसके बूते आई है ?. . . . माना कि शादी करने की तुम्हारी इच्छा नहीं थी; लेकिन बेटा, यह लोक व्यवहार है. . . ।" उसके फूट-फूटकर रोने से उनकी बात बीच में ही रह गई।

अपने पढ़ने की कोठरी के दरवाजे पर बैठा वह निरुद्देश्य न जाने क्या-क्या सोचता रहा। वह सोचने लगा कि आखिर ये बात बाबूजी को किसने बताई ? उसी ने कहा होगा। अम्मा से न कहा हो, पर मुन्नी या भाभी से जरूर कहा होगा। तभी जाने किधर से भाभी ने आकर कहा, "लालाजी, क्या सोच रहे हो ऐसे डूबे हुए ? तुम्हारी तो शादी न हुई, लगता है दुनिया भर की चिन्ताओं का बोझ तुम्हारे ऊपर ही आ गया।" वह चौंक गया जैसे चोरी करते हुए पकड़ा गया हो। उसने इन्कार किया कि कुछ नहीं। भाभी के इस प्रश्न पर कि "बनी नहीं क्या ?" उसने जवाब दिया कि बन भी नहीं सकती। भाभी ने कहा कि प्रभा को अपनी खूबसूरती और पढ़ाई का गुमान तो है। भाभी उसके बारे में उल्टी-सीधी बातें करती रहीं। फिर खाने के लिए कहा।

सुबह से ही घर का वातावरण उबाने वाला लग रहा था। रात को फिर अम्मा, बाबूजी, मुन्नी और भाभी ने उसे समझाया। प्रभा उसके पास दूध लेकर आई। वह सोच रहा था कि वह उससे माफी माँगेगी और दूध पीने के लिए कहेगी। उसने कुछ नहीं कहा। यह देखकर वह गुस्से से बाहर निकल गया। उस रात उसने दो निर्णय लिये। एक तो यह कि अब चाहे वह अपनी ओर से बोले या न बोले, वह नहीं बोलेगा। दूसरा खूब ध्यान से पढ़ेगा।

सुबह प्रभा ने पहली बार खाना बनाया। उसके हाथ की रसोई से समर को ही खाना था। जब वह रसोई में आया तो मुन्नी, अम्मा, भाभी और अमर (छोटा भाई) बगैरह बैठे थे। उसने रसोई में उसके गोरे हाथ को देखा जिसमें वह अँगूठी, सोने की चूड़ी और हाथ की घड़ी पहने थी। उसने रोटी का टुकड़ा दाल में डुबोकर खाया तो 'ओ-ओ' करते हुए वह कौर उगल दिया और बाहर आ गया। दाल में बहुत नमक था। घर में बवाल मचा। दूसरे दिन प्रभा के भाई आये और वह मायके चली गई।

चार

शब्दार्थ—स्वाभाविक = स्वभाव के अनुसार, **निहाल** = खुश, **यथार्थ** = जैसा होना चाहिए, **करुणापूर्ण** = दुःख भरे, **तटस्थ** = अलग, किसी का पक्ष न लेने वाला, **अनिच्छा** = बिना इच्छा के, **लाक्षागृह** = लाख (एक प्रकार का गोंद) का घर, **शरणार्थी** = शरण लेने वाले, **रोचक** = मन को भाने वाली, **भगवा ध्वज** = पीला झण्डा, **हताश** = निराश, **षड्यन्त्र** = किसी के विरुद्ध योजना बनाना।

समर को अमर ने नीचे बुलाया। दो स्वयंसेवक खड़े थे। उन्होंने कहा कि शाखा नहीं आते हो। उसने कोई बहाना बना दिया। लगता था अम्मा भी प्रभा से खुश नहीं थी। तभी तो उसने कहा, "हमारे लड़कों को लड़कियों की क्या कमी है ? हम तो समर की दूसरी शादी कर देंगे।" समर ने अम्मा को डाँटते हुए कहा कि एक शादी ने ही निहाल कर दिया अब तो उसे पढ़ लेने दें। विवाह के दिनों का सारा दिखावा समाप्त हो चुका था और लेन-देन वालों से रोज महाभारत होता था। बाबूजी अम्मा और भाई साहब से कहते रहते, "अब आगे कैसा होगा, इस पर भी सोचा ?" हकीकत यह थी कि बाबूजी को पच्चीस रुपये पेंशन मिलती थी और भाई साहब को निन्यानवे रुपये सिर्फ। शादी में साइकिल मिली थी उसे ही घसीट रहे थे। अम्मा बैठी-बैठी माला जपती हुई बुदबुदाया करती हैं। दो-तीन बच्चे पढ़ने को हैं। अमर मैट्रिक देगा। छोटा कुँवर अभी छठे में है और समर को इण्टर करना है।

घर में मुन्नी सबसे अभागिन है। सोलह-सत्रह की उम्र में उसकी शादी कर दी थी। ससुराल से मुन्नी के करुणापूर्ण खत आते। यहाँ आती तो बिलख-बिलख कर रोती। पति और सास मिलकर उस पर अत्याचार करते। पति का चाल-चलन भी ठीक नहीं था। उसने किसी औरत को लाकर घर में रख लिया। समर को उसके पति पर गुस्सा आता। वह सब कुछ सहती रही, लेकिन जब नहीं सहा गया तो हमारे पास आ गई।

अब बहू के बारे में कोई बात नहीं करता। भाभी प्रभा के बारे में समर के कान भरती रहती कि औरत को तो दबाकर ही रखना चाहिए। घर में रुपये-पैसों की तंगी के बखान से उसका मन भारी-भारी सा रहने लगा। पहले जो पढ़ने का चाव था वह मरता जा रहा है। घर में रहने का मन नहीं करता। दो वक्त खाना और सोना मजबूरी है। दिन का समय वह यों ही घूमने या किसी दोस्त के यहाँ जाने में काट देता। कभी पार्क में पड़ा रहता। कॉलेज के लड़के कितने मस्त और लापरवाह रहते हैं। वह सोचता है कि इन लड़कों को फिल्म की मधुबाला और अशोक कुमार से क्या लेना देना। मन्दिर के एकान्त में बैठकर सोचने में सुख मिलता है। जब देखा कि पुजारी ने एक भिखारी को मार-मारकर भगाया तो फिर उसने मन्दिर जाना भी छोड़ दिया। वह सोचता कि उसके विवाह ने घरवालों की आशाओं को पूरा नहीं किया तो यह क्या उसका अपराध है। बाबूजी से उसे भय लगता। भाई साहब को उसकी ओर देखने की फुर्सत नहीं मिलती।

उसे अपनी पत्नी से न बोलने का कहीं न कहीं मन में दुःख भी है, लेकिन इसका कारण वह प्रभा के व्यवहार में अहंकार को मानता है।

पाँच

शब्दार्थ—**सहसा** = अचानक, **खुशामद** = तारीफ करना, **घुटन** = कष्ट, **अन्यमनस्क** = अनमने भाव से, **अरमान** = इच्छाएँ, **घमण्डिन** = अभिमानी, **निहायत** = बिल्कुल, **दृष्टिकोण** = सोच, **अदवायन** = मूँज की बनी खाट को कसने वाली रस्सी।

एक दिन खाना देते समय मुन्नी ने उससे पूछा कि भैया तुम भाभी से नहीं बोले ? दूसरी शादी करोगे क्या ? उसके मुँह से निकला कि "हाँ-हाँ, एक शादी कराके जो उसे रूला रही हो, दूसरी किसके नाम को रोयेगी।" वह यह कह तो गया पर दूसरे ही क्षण ख्याल आया कि घर वालों के व्यवहार से प्रभा जाने कितनी दु:खी हुई होगी। उसकी ओर से कभी किसी ने सोचा ही नहीं। उसने मुन्नी से पूछा कि तुमसे क्या यह अम्मा ने कहा ? मुन्नी इस बात को टाल गई। भाभी कपड़े धोकर आई थी और बोली कि आज तो मुन्नी लालाजी को खाना दे रही है। थकान से भाभी हाँफ रही थीं, पेट से थीं। भाभी ने धुले कपड़ों को सुखाने के लिए मुन्नी से विनती की। वह छोटे-छोटे टुकड़े खाता रहा। खाने की इच्छा नहीं थी। वह प्रभा के बारे में जानना चाहता था पर कुछ पता नहीं चला। लेकिन भाभी ने यह कहा, "तुम्हारा ब्याह भी क्या हुआ, लालाजी ! क्या-क्या अरमान थे, सब पर पानी फिर गया। लेन-देन की तो खैर कोई बात नहीं, एकाध साल में आई-गई बात हो जाती है।"

समर ने अपनी भाभी से ताना मारा कि उसे (भाभी) ही बड़ा शौक था कि बहू ऐसी ही, वैसी ही। भाभी ने बताया कि वह (प्रभा) बड़ी घमण्डी है। समर खाना खाने बैठा और थोड़ा खाकर उठ गया कि उसे कॉलेज के लिए देर हो रही है। भाभी ने समर से बहू को दबाकर रखने की बात कही। वह सोचने लगा कि प्रभा को मायके गये हुए छः महीने हो गये, जाने उसका क्या हुआ। एक चिट्‌ठी भी उसने नहीं लिखी। कभी-कभी तो वह सिहर उठता कि इस घमण्डी लड़की के साथ उसकी जिन्दगी कैसे कटेगी ? उसको बोर्ड की फीस भरने के लिए पच्चीस रुपये की आवश्यकता थी। उसने सोचा कि भाभी से माँग लूँ, पर फिर सोचा कि उनके पास होंगे तो भी नहीं देंगी । हार कर बाबूजी के पास गया। साँझ के समय बाबूजी एक खाट की अदवायन को कस रह थे। समर ने निहायत ही मुलायम स्वर में उनसे अपनी बात कही। सुनकर बाबूजी तमतमा गये और बोले, "ये मेरी पेंशन के पच्चीस रुपये आये हैं, सो इन्हें तुम ले लो। हमारा क्या है, हमें तो हड्डे पेलने हैं जिन्दगी भर, सो तुम्हारे लिए करेंगे। करम में लिखा के लाये थे कि लड़के धींगरे-ऊँट हो जायें तब तक खिलाना, सो खिलायेंगे।. . ."

समर की हिम्मत नहीं हो रही थी नोट उठाने की, पर मजबूरी थी इसलिए उठा लिए और सोचा कि परेशानियों ने बाबूजी को चिड़चिड़ा बना दिया है। बाबूजी ने उससे प्रभा को मायके से लाने की बात कही, तो उसने जवाब दिया कि अमर को भेज दें, वह नहीं जायेगा। इस पर बाबूजी नाराज भी हुए।

भाभी ने एक दिन मजाक के स्वर में कहा कि लालाजी, बाबूजी अम्माजी से कह रहे थे कि समर से कहो कि वह किसी डॉक्टर-वैद्य को दिखा दे, फीस जो होगी सो देंगे। वह कहने लगा कि उसे क्या हुआ है ? भाभी हँसती रही और समर क्रोध में भर गया। उसे यह बात बुरी लग रही थी कि जब भी पढ़ने के लिए पैसे माँगो तभी तकरार होती है। बहू को बुलाना है तो बुलाओ, न बुलाना हो तो मत बुलाओ, पर उसे प्रभा से बोलने को मजबूर नहीं कर सकते।

छः

शब्दार्थ—**तारीफ** = प्रशंसा, **विरुद्ध** = खिलाफ, **आश्चर्य** = अचम्भा, **अध्यवसाय** = पढ़ना व कठिन परिश्रम करना, **जल्दबाज** = जल्दी करने वाला, **उपेक्षापूर्ण** = न ध्यान देना, **आहिस्ता** = धीरे से, **सरसराहट** = कपड़े निकालने की आवाज, **अनुमान** = अन्दाज, **दाम्पत्य जीवन** = नव विवाहित जीवन, **उल्लास** = प्रसन्नता, **दुर्निवार** = न रोके जाने वाली, **दंभ** = घमण्ड, **अक्लमन्द** = होशियार, **तीसमारखाँ** = बहुत होशियार, **लयपूर्ण** =

स्वर में, **निष्क्रिय** = बिना उछल कूद के, **'नेवर द फील्ड वाज लॉस्ट नॉर द फ्री सेण्ड'** = न कभी मैदान छोड़ा न कोई बच निकला, **सन्तुलन** = एक सा रहना।

कॉलेज से लौटते समय अमर ने बताया कि वह भाभी को मायके से ले आया है। उनके घरवालों ने उन्हें बड़ी मुश्किल से भेजा है। लेकिन समर की सब तारीफ करते हैं। उसे आश्चर्य हुआ। इसका मतलब प्रभा ने उसके बारे में कुछ नहीं कहा है, उन लोगों ने उसकी पढ़ाई के बारे में पूछा। उसे अपने अनुचित व्यवहार पर क्षोभ हुआ। अमर ने बताया कि भाभी कुछ कमजोर हो गई हैं। बाबूजी कह रहे थे कि बहू आ गई है उसी से सारा काम कराना है। वह घर की तरफ जा रहा था। घर पहुँचते ही मुन्नी ने कहा कि भैया, भाभी आ गई है। अपनी कोठरी में उसका सन्दूक देखा। उसने सोचा कि अब तो उसे बोलना ही पड़ेगा।

दिन ढल चुका था। वह कोठरी से बाहर आ गया। सड़क पर चलते हुए फेरीवालों को दुकान लगाते हुए देखा। उसे प्रभा की अच्छाई नजर आने लगी कि उसने अपने मायके में कुछ नहीं कहा। काफी देर बाद जब आया तो भाभी ने खाना खाने के लिए कहा क्योंकि प्रभा भूखी बैठी थी। उसने जल्दी खाना देने को कहा क्योंकि उसे पढ़ना है, बोर्ड के इम्तिहान हैं। उसके पास पढ़ने के लिए एक लालटेन थी, जबकि उसके दोनों छोटे भाई एक ही लालटेन से पढ़ते थे। वह बाहर निकल कर आया यह देखने कि घर में क्या हो रहा है। वह अन्दर आ गया तो प्रभा भी अपना सब काम करके कोठरी में आई। फिर वह सन्दूक खोलकर कपड़े निकालने लगी। उसने क्रम-क्रम से उठते हुए उसके पगों को बाहर जाते देखा। भाभी ने उससे कहा कि उसे ऊपर ही सोना है। चारपाई न हो तो वह डाले जाती है। उसे तो सारी जिन्दगी बितानी है यह तो सब होता ही रहता है। समर को उसके अंहकार पर गुस्सा आ रहा था। सोच रहा था कि प्रभा से अब उसे कोई सम्बन्ध नहीं रखना है।

रात और गहरी होती चली गई। वह सोने का प्रयत्न करने लगा। कभी सामने सिकुड़ी पड़ी प्रभा को घृणा से देख लेता फिर अपने आप में खो जाता।

सात

शब्दार्थ—भावावेश = भावों के आवेश में, **संयोगवश** = भाग्यवश, **विस्मय** = आश्चर्य, **लाड़ली** = प्यारी, **कुठड़ियाँ** = कोठरी, **आफत** = मुसीबत, **सहानुभूति** = दया की भावना, **कटने लगी** = बचने लगी, **आशंका** = शंका, **अभ्यस्त** = अभ्यास डालना, **तत्कालिक** = उस समय का, **पहली डिग्री** = बड़ा खर्चा, **नामकरण** = बच्चे के नाम रखने का उत्सव, **अनिच्छा** = बिना इच्छा के, **कायदा** = नियम, **बेहयाई** = बेशरमी, **सैद्धान्तिक रूप से** = सिद्धान्त के अनुसार, **शिष्टाचार** = अच्छे गुण, **कसूर** = गलती, **सगुन-साइत** = सगुन के साथ, **बिफरकर** = रोकर, **ग्लानि** = दु:ख, **प्रचंड** = बहुत बड़ा, **निस्पन्द** = बिना हिले डुले।

जब-जब प्रभा की बात को याद करता, अपने आप दाँत भिच जाते और हर बार विस्मय से दुहराता जैसे मानो पहली बार यह सत्य उसके सामने प्रकट हो रहा है। वह बोला—"कितना दर्प ? खाना देते समय भाभी से बोर्ड के इम्तिहान का नाम क्या ले दिया, उसी पर ताना ?" खाना खाते समय भाभी से बोला—"भाभी तुम मुझे पास होना देना चाहती हो या नहीं।" समर का कहना ये था कि एक अलग कोठरी उसने अपनी पढ़ाई के लिए साफ की उसमें भी कोई न कोई आ जाता है तो वहाँ कोई कैसे पढ़ेगा ?

भाभी ने समर से प्रभा के बारे में शिकायत करना शुरू किया कि उस महारानी से तो किसी काम की उम्मीद नहीं है। अम्माजी भी कोई ज्यादा खुश नहीं हैं। प्रभा ने अपने मायके में कहा होगा कि रुपये के भूखे हैं, ऐसे हैं, वैसे हैं। इससे बदनामी तो अपनी ही होगी। भाभी की बातें सुनकर समर झुँझला गया और कहने लगा कि उसे इन सब बातों से कोई मतलब नहीं है, बस उसे पढ़ने दिया जाये। भाभी ने समझाया कि वह ऐसी बात न करे। समर ने कहा कि मुझे तो शादी अभी करनी नहीं थी।

किताबें लेकर कॉलेज जाते हुए एक बात समर के मन में उठी। सब लोग प्रभा को सुन्दर बताते हैं, एक बार सूरत को अच्छी तरह देख ही लेनी चाहिए। लेकिन फिर मन में आया कि नहीं। मेरा रास्ता कुछ बनने का है। वह दिन भर खुश रहा। रात को प्रभा समर की कोठरी में नहीं सोई।

अगले दिन समर ने भाभी से कहा कि भाभी अब तुम क्यों व्यर्थ में पिसती रहती हो ? यह समय तो आराम का है। घर में और लोग भी तो हैं काम करने को। इसके बाद सारे घर का दोनों वक्त का खाना प्रभा को बनाने को दे दिया गया। समर ने मुन्नी से कहा कि वह क्यों नहीं काम करवा लेती।

अजब वातावरण था घर का। सभी भाभी के लड़का होने की बात करते। लड़के की बात पर अम्मा बाबूजी खुश थे, लेकिन खर्चे के बारे में सोचकर सहम जाते। आखिर भाभी के लड़की हो गई। बाबूजी ने चैन की साँस ली क्योंकि उनका खर्च बच गया।

प्रभा न जाने कब सुबह उठकर भाभी के लिए हरीरा बनाना शुरू कर देती। खाना बनाती और चौका बर्तन का काम करती। वह खूब काम करती, लेकिन अनिच्छा या थकान नहीं दिखाई देती। बाबूजी ने उसे एक दिन पर्दा न करे हुए देख लिया तो सुना दिया कि बहू पर्दा नहीं करती है। समर को भी उन्होंने डाँटा।

समर पर्दे के खिलाफ है, लेकिन अपने घर में कुछ न कर सका। आखिर घर में समझौते का भाव आ गया। नये प्राणी के आने से घर पर खर्चा बढ़ गया था। घरवालों की इच्छा थी कि समर इण्टर करके कहीं नौकरी पर लग जाये।

घर की चिल्ल-पौं के बाद भी समर के काम निर्बाध रूप से चलते रहे। उसकी कोठरी साफ मिलती। समर ने सोचा कि उसे अपनी पढ़ाई पर ध्यान देना चाहिए। वह प्रभा के बारे में ही ज्यादा सोचता। भाई साहब भी उससे कहते कि कभी-कभार बहू के पास जाकर बैठ लिया करे। बच्ची का नामकरण संस्कार हुआ। एक दिन प्रभा ने पूजा के लिए मिट्टी के ढेले से बने गणेशजी ले लिए और उससे बर्तन माँज लिए। इससे सारे घर में बवाल खड़ा हो गया। प्रभा चुपचाप अपराधी बनी खड़ी थी। उसके माँ-बाप तक को खरी-खोटी सुनाई गई। अम्माजी की सिसकियाँ सुनाई दे रही थीं। समर ने जाकर एक चाँटा प्रभा के गाल पर दे मारा। सब एकदम स्तब्ध रह गये। उसे इस पर दुःख भी हुआ। सात-आठ महीने में पहली बार बोला वह भी तमाचे से। उसे बहुत दुःख हुआ और वह रोने लगा।

आठ

शब्दार्थ—सत्यार्थ प्रकाश = आर्य समाज की एक पुस्तक जिसमें हिन्दू धर्म के आडम्बरों का खण्डन किया गया है, **निर्लक्ष्य** = बिना लक्ष्य के, **निरुद्देश्य** = बिना उद्देश्य के, **नियन्त्रण** = अधिकार, **संकल्प** = निश्चय, **श्रद्धा** = भक्ति, **मानसिक** = मन से सम्बन्धित, **अनोखा** = अजब ही, **अधिकांश** = अधिकतर, **दिक्कत** = परेशानी, **फूहड़** = साफ सफाई न रखने वाली, **अपरिवर्तनीय** = न बदलने वाला, **एहसान** = किया गया अच्छा काम, **अन्तर्बाह्य** = अन्दर-बाहर का।

मुन्नी ने समर से पूछा कि तुम्हारे इम्तिहान कब से हैं। उसको याद ही नहीं आया कि इम्तिहान कब से हैं। मुन्नी की उपस्थिति और उसके द्वारा पूछी गई बात को एकदम भूल ही गया। लगा जैसे वह पागल तो नहीं होता जा रहा, हर समय ग्लानि भरी रहती। और सोचता कि प्रभा पर हाथ उठा ही कैसे ? फिर सोचता कि उसे भी तो ऐसा करना नहीं चाहिए। मिट्टी और गणेश जी में अन्तर नहीं समझ में आया। अच्छा हुआ एक सबक मिल गया।

उस घटना के दूसरे दिन उसकी बाहर निकले की हिम्मत ही नहीं हुई। वह अपने आप से पूछता कि बात-बात पर चिड़चिड़ाना, दूसरे को कष्ट पहुँचाकर आनन्द लेना अच्छी बात नहीं है। बहुत दिनों बाद मन्दिर के बाहर ही बैठा सोचता रहा कि उससे बड़ा अपराध हो गया। क्लास में गया तो गुमसुम बैठा रहा। ईश्वर से अपनी गलतियों की क्षमा माँगी। उस दिन के बाद उसमें परिवर्तन आया। पहले घर और बाहर की बातें परेशान करतीं, पर अब केवल अपने इम्तिहान के बारे में ही सोचता। दिन का अधिकांश भाग दिवाकर के साथ कटता। वह गिरीष भाई साहब से मिलने की बात करता। उस दिन की घटना पर किसी ने कोई बात न की। केवल भाभी प्रसन्न थीं। भाभी अपनी बच्ची की देखभाल में लगी रहतीं। घर का सारा काम प्रभा के ऊपर ही आ गया

था। प्रभा के मायके से कोई खत आता तो कोई न कोई उसे खोलकर पढ़ लेता तब उसे दिया जाता। उसके पत्र को भी पढ़ा जाता। अम्मा ने कहा कि वह अपने पीहर चिट्ठी डाल दिया करे। जाने कितने दिन बाद उसने अम्मा का नरम स्वर सुना। समर तटस्थ-सा रहने लगा। प्रभा चाय रख जाती तो उसे चुपचाप पी लेता। खाना उसे खुद परोसती थी। बिना बोले-चाले खाना खाकर चला जाता। वह यह तो भूल ही गया ता कि प्रभा का उससे कोई सम्बन्ध भी है। कभी-कभी यह महसूस होता कि वह सिर्फ संसार और अपने आस-पास को ही नहीं, अपने आपको भी भूले चला जा रहा है।

दस बजने को आये पर अभी खाना तैयार नहीं था। मुन्नी ने प्रभा से कहा कि वह भाभी को दूध पहुँचा दे। प्रभा ने मुन्नी से खुद दूध पहुँचाने को कहा। लेकिन कटोरी से ढका दूध फैल गया। उधर अमर ने अम्मा से शिकायत कि दस बज गये हैं अभी तक खाना नहीं बना, कब पढ़ने जाऊँगा। तभी अम्मा की रामायण शुरू हो गई। प्रभा बेचारी अकेला क्या-क्या काम करे पर इस घर में उसकी सुनने वाला कोई नहीं था। समर तो किताब उठाकर पढ़ने चला गया। समर को लगने लगा कि न तो प्रभा से ही उसका कोई सम्बन्ध है न घरवालों से ही।

बीच में एक दो पीरियड खाली देखकर घर आया तो उसने देखा कि कोठरी में थाली ढकी रखी है।

फरवरी में जाड़ा शुरू हो गया था। मार्च के शुरू में इम्तिहान थे। इसलिए छुट्टियाँ हो गई थीं। समर दिवाकर के यहाँ पढ़ने चला जाता। घर में तो कोई न कोई विघ्न-बाधा आती ही रहती। कभी अम्मा रो रही है, कभी भाभी बड़बड़ा रही है।

सुबह दिवाकर के यहाँ से लौटा तो अम्मा प्रभा को डाँट रही थीं कि कभी-कभी सिर तो धो लिया करे। उसने बताया कि घर में इतना काम है कि समय ही नहीं मिलता। पर अम्मा जी में संवेदना ही नहीं थी। इधर भैयाजी गरजे—''क्या दिन रात चख-चख होती रहती है ? दिन निकला और शुरू हो गया। कोई और काम नहीं है क्या ? नौ बज रहे हैं।'' उनकी बात को किसी ने नहीं सुना। अम्माजी बड़बड़ाईं—''चख-चख होती रहती है तब तो यह हाल है, न हो तो एक दिन सारे घर का पटरा ही बैठ जाये। एक दिन प्रभा ने ऊपर छत पर बाल धोये तो बाबूजी नाराज हुए। मुन्नी ने प्रभा का बचाव किया। समर के अन्दर कोई बोलता, महसूस करता है या नहीं, यह भी वह नहीं जान पाया। परीक्षा में पाँच-सात दिन रह गये थे।

नौ

शब्दार्थ—दार्शनिक = दर्शनशास्त्र को जानने वाला, **भरसक** = बहुत, **प्रतीक्षा** = इन्तजार, **संजीदगी** = दुःख से, **अकल-दाढ़** = समझ आ गई, **चंपत** = गायब, **पीहर** = मायका, **चीत्कार** = रोने की जोर की आवाज, **थर्राकर** = काँपकर, **दुर्व्यवहार** = बुरा व्यवहार, **भावातिरेक** = भावों की अधिकता, **हिस्टीरिया** = एक बीमारी जिसमें दौरे पड़ते हैं, **डकराकर** = बहुत जोर से रोना, **समाधिस्थ** = समाधि लगे हुए जैसे, **मुर्दनी** = खामोशी जो दु:ख में हो।

आखिरी पेपर करके अमर हॉल से निकला तो उसकी तबियत हल्की और खुश थी। पेपर अच्छे हो गये थे। दिवाकर ने सिनेमा देखने की सलाह दी और कहा—''आज हम दिखायेंगे और अगर माताजी राजी हो गईं तो किरन (पत्नी) को भी ले चलेंगे। बेचारी को कब से सिनेमा देखने को नहीं मिला। सोचती होगी अच्छी कुए में आ फँसी।'' दिवाकर ने शाम को आने को कहा।

समर घर आया तो उसे पता चला कि मुन्नी के पति उसे लेने आये हैं और बाबूजी की उनसे बातें हो रही हैं। दो ढाई साल से सुध नहीं ली और अब लेने आये हैं। इतना मारा-पीटा कि उसके शरीर पर अभी तक निशान बने हुए हैं। आज उनको आते देखकर सभी हक्के-बक्के रह गये। बैठक में बाबूजी और उनके दमाद की गम्भीरतापूर्वक बातें चल रही थीं। आखिर मामला क्या है, जानने के लिए घर के सभी लोग पास घिर आये। बाबूजी दामाद की खुशामद और माफी माँगने पर सन्तुष्ट हो गये और रात को खाना इत्यादि खिला चुकने के बाद बाबूजी ने अम्मा को बताया कि ''कल मुन्नी जायेगी, सुबह दस बजे की गाड़ी से।'' सारे घर में

सन्नाटा छा गया। अम्मा झुँझलाकर बोलीं—"बैठो तो सही, कुछ बताओगे भी कि चले आये, कल मुन्नी जायेगी। ऐसी क्या आफत आ गई अब निपूते पर ? दो साल से कौन-सी मक्खी छींक गई थी ?" मुन्नी एक ओर दीवार से लगी पहले ही बैठी थी। भाभी भी बच्ची को सुलाकर वहाँ आ गई। प्रभा नहीं दिखाई दी। बाबूजी ने बताया कि वह (दामाद) बहुत माफी माँग रहा है। अब कभी कोई शिकायत नहीं आयेगी। बिरादरी का दण्ड भुगतने को भी तैयार है। जो औरत उसने अपने घर में रखी थी वह सब कपड़े-जेबर समेटकर चंपत हो गई। कुँवर ने मुन्नी को न भेजने की राय दी। अम्मा की भी यही राय थी। बाबूजी ने विश्वास दिलाते हुए कहा, "भाई वह कसम खा रहा है, विश्वास दिलाता है। बातों से भी लगता है कि अब समझ आ गई है। धीरज की माँ, हो गई गलती एक बार। अब क्या कोई जिन्दगी भर यही करता रहेगा। इस उम्र में आदमी को होश नहीं रहता। हमने उससे सारी बातें साफ-साफ कर ली हैं।" अम्मा नहीं मानीं। उसी तरह लापरवाही से बोलीं, "तुम्हारी बातों का क्या है ? जिसने जैसा समझा दिया वैसा ही मान गये।"

इस बात पर बाबूजी को गुस्सा आ गया। उन्होंने यह स्पष्ट कर दिया कि वे मुन्नी को जिन्दगीभर तो नहीं रख सकते। इससे अच्छा मौका फिर नहीं मिलेगा। यह सुनकर मुन्नी फूट-फूटकर रोने लगी। भाई साहब ने हमदर्दी से उससे पूछा कि वह बताये अपने रोने का कारण। समर को मुन्नी के प्रति घरवालों का उपेक्षित व्यवहार अच्छा नहीं लग रहा था। वह सोच रहा था कि मुन्नी को वह अपने पास रखेगा। मुन्नी ने बाबूजी से रोते हुए कहा, "बाबूजी, मैं किसी का चौका-बरतन कर लूँगी, पीस-कूट लूँगी, मुझे वहाँ मत भेजो उनके साथ।" बाबूजी ने उसे समझाते हुए कहा, "पगली हुई है, बेटी ! हम लोग क्या कोई गैर हैं ? तू आधी रात को यहाँ आ जाइयो, कोई ऐसी-वैसी बात देखे तो। यह तेरा घर पहले है, हमारा बाद में। पर तू इस बार तो मान जा, अब कोई बात न होगी।" मुन्नी फफक-फफककर रोते होते हुए बोली, "नहीं बाबूजी नहीं ! मुझे उस कुएँ में मत धकेलो बाबूजी।" बाबूजी ने फिर उसे सान्त्वना दी, लेकिन मुन्नी को किसी तरह धीरज नहीं बँध रहा था। वह निरन्तर रोये जा रही थी। बाबूजी के सामने किसी की भी नहीं चली।

अगले दिन सुबह मुन्नी को विदा कर दिया गया। सभी की आँखें सजल थीं। प्रभा से लिपटकर मुन्नी इस तरह रोई जैसे दोनों जन्म-जन्मातरों को विदा ले रही हैं। सभी को उसके (मुन्नी) जाने से दु:ख हो रहा था, पर समर को अत्यन्त दु:ख हो रहा था। वह अपनी कोठरी में किवाड़ बन्द करके बैठ गया। पूरे घर में मुन्नी के जाने से उदासी छाई हुई थी।

दस

शब्दार्थ—कसक = दु:ख, **धिक्कारना** = भला-बुरा करना, **अनमना** = उदास, **प्रण-प्रतिज्ञाएँ** = पत्नी की सुरक्षा के लिए किये गये प्रण या प्रतिज्ञा, **लक्खनों** = लक्षणों, **सिर खपाना** = बहुत सोचना, **कोलाहल** = शोरगुल, **मस्तिष्क** = दिमाग, **नि:शक्त** = बिना शक्ति वाला, **बेकसूर** = निर्दोष, **पश्चाताप** = पछताना, **मर्मान्तक पीड़ा** = अन्दर का दु:ख, **आधार** = सहारे।

समर खाना खाकर दिवाकर के यहाँ से निकला तो ग्यारह बज चुके थे। यह तो निश्चित था कि घर पर डाँट पड़ेगी। कुहरा गलियों में छाया हुआ था। रात के दस बजे सिनेमा समाप्त हुआ। दिवाकर की पत्नी भी हमारे साथ गई थी। समर के कपड़े उनके कपड़ों के सामने नीचे दर्जे के थे। अपनी उठी हुई चोटी खोलकर उसने बालों में ही मिला ली थी। दिवाकर ने उससे पूछा कि अब क्या करना है। समर के भाई साहब चाहते थे कि रिजल्ट आने के बाद वह नौकरी करे। ये तीनों चले जा रहे थे।

उनको लग रहा था कि दिवाकर की माताजी तो खूब नाराज हो रही होंगी। किरण ने उपेक्षा से कहा—"कहाँ तक दिन रात मरें। छह महीने में एक बार सिनेमा आये हैं, अगर अब भी वह गालियाँ दें तो कोई क्या करे ?" दिवाकर ने समर से अपनी पत्नी को उनके घर लाने को कहा। समर ने कहा कि इस समय तो वह अपने मायके गई है। अगली बार आयेगी तो मिलवाऊँगा।

समर और भाई साहब भीतर गये तो देखा बाबूजी दुर्वासा का रूप धारण किये हैं और प्रभा अपराधिनी की मुद्रा में खड़ी थी। वह छत पर बैठकर दाल बीन रही थी। बाबू जी को ये बातें बिल्कुल पसन्द नहीं है। बाबूजी ने बताया कि मुहल्ले में ही पाण्डेजी की लड़की भाग गई। धीरज (भाई साहब) ने बताया कि मास्टर के साथ भागी होगी। भाभी ने अपनी बच्ची अम्मा की गोद में दे दी। अम्मा ने फिर भी न कहने लायक बात भी कह दी।

एक दिन समर फिर सिनेमा चला गया। घर पहुँचा तो अमर ने किवाड़ खोले और कहा कि सब लोग परेशान हो रहे थे कि कहाँ चले गये थे। कोठरी में देखा तो खाना रखा नहीं था।

रिजल्ट आने में अभी दो-ढाई महीने हैं। भाई साहब का कहना है कि अपने दोस्त से कहकर कहीं नौकरी लगा लो अभी अमर और कुँवर को तो पढ़ाना ही है। घर का खर्च नहीं चलता है। समर ने दिवाकर से नौकरी के लिए कहा।

मार्च का महीना था ठण्ड कम हो गई थी। रात में पानी पीने के लिए वह उठा तो देखा कि बाहर ओस में सफेद-सफेद सा कोई बैठा है। वह प्रभा थी। वह रो रही थी। वह पानी पीकर लौट आया और बिस्तर पर लेटे-लेटे करवटें बदलता रहा और सोचता रहा कि वह बाहर बैठकर रो क्यों रही है। कुछ देर बाद वह फिर बाहर गया और पानी पीकर प्रभा के सामने जाकर खड़ा हो गया और बड़ी हिम्मत करके पूछा—"आधी रात को यहाँ बैठकर क्या कर रही हो ?" उसने एक बार समर की तरफ देखा और फिर सिर झुका लिया। समर को अपनी उपस्थिति अनावश्यक और अपमानजनक लगी फिर भी उसने कह ही दिया, "सुबह रो लीजिए न, ओस में तबियत खराब हो जायेगी। अब रात काफी हो गई है।" उसने रुआँसे स्वर में कहा—"आपको क्या है ? आप जाकर सोइए न।" इस बार पल्ला हटाकर उसने सिर उठाया और जैसे तड़पकर कहा—"एक साल से कभी आपको चिन्ता हुई कि मरती है या जीती है ? ऐसा क्या खास जरूरत आ पड़ी अब ! आप जाकर सोइए न।"

निःशक्त और टूटा हुआ समर वहीं उसके सामने बैठ गया। समर ने सकपकाते हुए कहा, "प्रभा, तुम मुझसे नाराज हो ?" उसने उसके कन्धे पकड़कर कहा—"तुम मुझे बताओ, मैंने तुम्हारा क्या बिगाड़ा है ? क्या कसूर किया है मैंने तुम्हारा ? मैं तुम्हारे लायक नहीं हूँ, मैं तुम्हें पसन्द नहीं हूँ, तो अपने हाथों से मेरा गला घोंट दो, मैं चू नहीं करूँगी, तुम शौक से दूसरी शादी कर लो, लेकिन मुझे बताओ तो सही. . ." यह कहकर वह उसके कंधे पर लिपट गई। समर को खुद भी होश नहीं था कि कब वह रोने लगा।

अब उसे अपने हृदय में दुःख होता कि उसने उसके प्रति कितने अत्याचार किये हैं। कभी यह जानने की कोशिश नहीं की कि उसके भी तो जान है। अपने किये का पश्चाताप क्या किसी रूप में नहीं हो सकता। समर उसे वहाँ से उठाकर अपनी कोठरी में लाया। सारी रात वे दोनों बिल्कुल नहीं सोये।

सुबह किसी के जागने से पहले ही वह उठकर बाहर चली गई। जाते हुए दूसरी ओर मुँह करके इतना कहा, "मुझे एक पोस्टकार्ड दे दीजिए, मैं बहुत दिनों से माँ को खत लिखना चाह रही थी—पैसे नहीं थे।"

उत्तरार्द्ध : सुबह

प्रश्न—पीड़ित दस दिशाएँ

एक

शब्दार्थ—आह्लादकारी = खुशी देने वाला, **ज्योतिर्मय** = चमकता हुआ, **उलाहना भरे** = शिकायत करते हुए, **प्राण सुखाना** = चिन्ता करना, **प्रतिध्वनि** = आवाज की गूँज, **संस्कृति** = सभ्यता, **उपयोगिता** = लाभ, **भोग-विलास** = आराम, **अमानुषिक** = मनुष्य के स्वभाव के विपरीत, **थिगलियाँ** = फटे कपड़े पर ऊपर से छोटा टुकड़ा लगाकर सिलना, **विभीषिका** = संकट, **मटरगस्ती** = बेकार घूमना, **संयत गांभीर्य** = सधी हुई गंभीरता, **विश्लेषण** = समझाना, **नासपीटे** = नाश करने वाले, **बखत** = समय, **आटे-दाल का भाव** = महँगाई की जानकारी होना।

सुबह का सुहावना मौसम देखकर समर को अति प्रसन्नता हुई। वह सूरज आज नई खुशियाँ लेकर आया है। उसे लगा जैसे वह जिन्दगी में पहली बार सूर्योदय देख रहा है। उसे लगा कि अब बाबूजी उससे खुश हो जायेंगे। पहले प्रभा की याद करके उसके हृदय में आग लग जाती थी, पर आज उसकी याद करके खुद-ब-खुद मुस्करा उठता। उसे पोस्टकार्ड वाली बात याद आई। बाजार की गलियों में समर लोगों को देखता हुआ जा रहा है। दिवाकर के यहाँ पहुँचा तो वह बोला कि सुबह सात बजे ही आ गया। समर आकर बैठक में बैठ गया। दिवाकर ने बताया कि अभी तक माताजी का मुँह फूला है कल सिनेमा जाने की बात पर।

समर अब सिर्फ प्रभा के बारे में ही सोचता रहता है, दिवाकर ने बताया कि उसके चचेरे भाई आने वाले हैं। समर से कहा कि अपनी चोटी कटवा लेना उन्हें ढोंग बिल्कुल पसन्द नहीं है। समर ने दिवाकर को समझाया कि देश के रहन-सहन, वस्त्रों या विचारों की एक संस्कृति होती है। हम लोग अपनी संस्कृति का अध्ययन नहीं करते। फिर उसे प्रभा के द्वारा मिट्टी के गणेश जी को उठा लेने की बात याद आई तो अपने अशिष्ट व्यवहार पर दुःख हुआ। दिवाकर ने उसके कपड़े पहनने की ढंग और मोटी चोटी पर कसकर ताना मारा। पर उसे नहीं मालूम के समर के पास ऐसे ही कपड़े हैं।

समर ने उससे दो चार पोस्टकार्ड माँग लिए। दिवाकर बोला लड़के अपने नम्बर बढ़वाने को निकल पड़ते हैं और अपना काम करवा भी लेते हैं। दोनों फिर अपने पास होने की बात करने लगे। समर ने बात ही बात में कह दिया कि अब तो सौ-पचास रुपये की नौकरी मिल जाये तो अच्छा है। इण्टर पास को कौन नौकरी देता है। दिवाकर ने उसे पोस्टकार्ड लाकर दिये। समर ने उसे बताया कि प्रभा आ गई है।

जब घर पहुँचा तो बाबूजी ने टोका—"नवाब साहब, कहाँ मटरगश्ती कर आये ? न खाने की चिन्ता न पीने की।" समर ने बताया कि वह दिवाकर के यहाँ गया था नौकरी की बात करने। बाबूजी कुछ नरम हुए। वह रसोई में गया, प्रभा ने खाना लगा दिया। उसका चेहरा सूखा जरूर था, लेकिन आज एक अजब सन्तोष की आभा दिख रही थी। खाना रखकर जाने लगी तो समर ने देखा कि उसकी धोती जगह-जगह से फटी है। किसी ने भी उसके बारे में नहीं सोचा कि उसे (प्रभा) भी किसी चीज की जरूरत है। भाभी के पास चार-छह धोतियाँ रखी होंगी, लेकिन उन्होंने भी नहीं सोचा प्रभा के बारे में। चौका-बरतन और घर के काम-धन्धे में लगे रहने के कारण उसकी गोरी खाल काली पड़ गई थी। थाली सरका कर वह उठ खड़ा हुआ तो प्रभा ने पूछा 'क्यों' तो उसने उत्तर दिया कि दिवाकर के यहाँ से खाकर आया हूँ। ऊपर जंगले में से देखा तो भाभी कह रही थी—"दोनों अब तो आपस में बोलने लगे।" उनकी आवाज में हलका व्यंग्य था।

शाम को फिर अपराधी की तरह निकल गया। चारों तरफ के वातावरण के प्रति उपेक्षा का भाव देखते हुए समर इस तरह का व्यवहार करने की कोशिश करने लगा जैसे उसके जीवन में कुछ भी नया नहीं हुआ है। अम्मा ने समर को बाबूजी को बुलाने भेजा। वे नवलकिशोर पण्डित जी के यहाँ भारतीय लोगों और संस्कृति के बारे में बात कर रहे थे। समर ने कहा कि आपको घर पर बुलाया है। समर को अन्दर से बच्ची को लाने की कहकर वे चल दिये। पण्डिताइन ने अपने बेटे के बारे में समर से कहा कि उनका बेटा मन्दिर का पूरा चढ़ावा अपनी बीवी को दे देता है। उसके बेटे (विशन) की बहू ने सास की तरफ ठेंगा दिखाया और बच्ची लाकर समर को दे दी।

दो

शब्दार्थ—कमबख्त = अभागी, **अविचलित** = बिना डिगे हुए, **उष्णता** = गर्मी, **साकार** = स्वरूप में, **दुर्गुण** = बुरा गुण, **परिस्थिति** = रहने का वातावरण, **एक्सपर्ट** = किसी काम में विशेष योग्यता, **नगण्य** = तुच्छ, **लायक** = बराबर, **उन्मुक्त** = स्वतन्त्र, **आज्ञाकारिणी** = आज्ञा मानने वाली, **परिहास** = हँसी, **खातिर** = स्वागत, **जमुहाइयाँ** = सोने का प्रयास।

प्रभा ने बताया कि उस दिन जब मैंने खाना बनाया था तो भाभी ने सब्जी में मुट्ठी भर नमक डाल दिया था। समर को सुनकर आश्चर्य हुआ। उसने पूछा कि तभी बताना चाहिए था। प्रभा ने कहा कि अब पुरानी बातें करने से क्या फायदा।

कोठरी के अंधेरे में दोनों बात कर रहे थे। दोनों में प्रेम उमड़ रहा था। समर ने पूछ ही लिया कि अम्मा और भाभी उससे नाराज क्यों रहती हैं ? प्रभा ने कहा कि मेरी किस्मत में ऐसा लिखा होगा। फिर उसने साफ कहा कि दहेज न लाने के कारण अम्मा और बाबूजी नाराज हैं। भाभी अम्मा के दिन-भर कान भरती रहती हैं। फिर समर ने पूछा कि कल तुम छत पर क्यों रो रही थीं। उसने बताया कि घर वाले मेरे चरित्र पर सन्देह करने लगे तब रोना आया। समर ने अपने पहले किये गये कार्यों की क्षमा माँगी। अब वह प्रभा के बारे में अच्छा ही सोचता है कि यह पढ़ी-लिखी तो है ही, साथ साथ ही बोल-चाल में अच्छे शहरी परिवार की लगती है। प्रभा ने बताया कि वह बहुत बोलने लगी है, यदि कोई बात बुरी लग जाये तो बुरा मत मानना। फिर उसने रमा नाम की एक क्लासफैलो के बारे में बताया कि किस तरह वह अपने जीवन के लिए योजनाएँ बनाती रहती थी।

समर ने बात काट कर प्रभा से पूछा—"अच्छा प्रभा, तुम्हें शादी करने का बहुत अफसोस है ?" उसने कहा, "नहीं तो, क्या मैंने तुमसे ऐसा कहा ?" समर चुप हो गया। फिर उसने पूछा कि क्या उसे थर्ड ईयर ज्वॉइन करना चाहिए या नहीं ? उसने सहमति या असहमति नहीं दिखाई और समर के ऊपर ही छोड़ दिया। फिर समर ने खुद ही बताया कि घर वाले तो चाहते हैं कि मैं कुछ काम करूँ, पर नौकरी क्या इतनी आसान है इण्टर, बी. ए. बेकार घूम रहे हैं। उसने प्रभा की हालत पर अफसोस जताया। उसके मन में तो यह है कि खूब पढ़े फिर अच्छी सी नौकरी करे।

सुबह का उजाला आकाश में उभरता चला आ रहा था। प्रभा अब उठकर जाने को थी। वह बोली, "लेकिन अच्छी नौकरी के बाद फर्ज ज्यादा अच्छी तरह अदा नहीं किया जा सकता।" समर उसके कहने का मतलब नहीं समझ पाया।

तीन

शब्दार्थ—निर्णय = फैसला, **बेमन** = बिना मन के, **नोच खायेंगी** = परेशान करेंगी, **गिन्नियाँ** = सोने के बने हुए सिक्के, **दुभाँति** = दो तरह का व्यवहार, **निरुद्विग्न भाव से** = शान्त भाव से, **वनमानुषों** = वन में रहने वाले मनुष्य, **हुलस पड़ी** = खुश हो गई, **आत्मकथा** = जीवन की सच्ची कहानी, **किलबिल** = छोटे-छोटे बच्चों की आवाज, **विष** = जहर, **प्रोत्साहन** = आगे बढ़ाने के लिए प्रोत्साहित करना, **तलाश** = खोज।

समर एम्प्लायमेंट एक्सचेंज गया था। वहाँ की भीड़ देखकर निराश हुआ और घर लौटा। घर पहुँचकर उसने भाभी से पूछा कि यदि उनके पास एक धोती हो तो प्रभा को दे दें। भाभी ने मना कर दिया। अब वह अम्मा के पास गया तो उन्होंने उल्टे ताने मारने शुरू कर दिये और कहा कि प्रभा ने ही तुझे पढ़ा-लिखाकर भेजा होगा। बाबूजी ने आकर अम्मा को डाँटा तो वह उल्टा बोल उठीं—"तुम्हारा लड़का बहू की तरफदारी लेकर आया है।" बाबूजी ने क्रोध से उसे देखा और कह दिया, "कमाने-धमाने को कौड़ी नहीं और बहू की तरफदारी को शेर।"

तभी वहाँ प्रभा आ गई और बोली—"यहाँ आकर यह सब काण्ड करने को तुमसे किसने कहा था ?" तभी नीचे से आवाज आई कि दाल उफन-उफन कर चूल्हे में जा रही है।

अपना मैट्रिक का सर्टीफिकेट लेकर समर बाहर निकल गया। घर में तो हर समय चक-चक होती रहती है। सड़क पर आकर याद करता रहा कि कहाँ जाना है। एम्प्लायमेंट एक्सचेंज गया तो वहाँ हजारों की भीड़ थी। लगा कि कोई नेता भाषण दे रहा होगा। किसी ने पीठ पर हाथ रखकर कहा, "कहिए, स्वयंसेवक जी !" जब समर ने मुड़कर देखा तो उस व्यक्ति ने गलत समझने की क्षमा माँगी। उस व्यक्ति का चेहरा आकर्षक लगा। उसने बताया कि आज यहाँ क्लर्कों और मजदूरों की भरती हो रही है। थोड़ी देर बाद वह सिर लटकाये घर लौट आया। दिवाकर ठीक कहता था कि जब तक डिग्री न हो तब तक अच्छी नौकरी नहीं मिल सकती। उसके (समर) सपने सभी चूर-चूर हो गये। समर सोचने लगा कि उस व्यक्ति को शायद कहीं देखा है पर याद नहीं आ रहा।

दोपहर बाद जब घर पहुँचा तो अमर के हाथ में एक चिट्ठी देखी। रमा की चिट्ठी थी जो जोधपुर से प्रभा के लिए आई थी। पत्र प्रभा को दिया। उसने समर से पूछा कि आज खाना क्यों नहीं खाया मैं अभी तक भूखी बैठी हूँ। समर ने उस समय खाना माँगा और प्रभा ने ताजा बनाकर दिया। प्रभा ने रमा के पत्र का जवाब दिया कि घर में काम है अतः कम समय मिल पाता है। स्कूल कॉलेज और घर की बातें लिखीं। पत्र समाप्त हुआ। उस रात उसने प्रभा से अपनी पढ़ाई करने या नौकरी करने की बात पूछी। प्रभा ने अपने मन की बात यह बताई कि वह खूब पढ़े एम.ए. तो कर ले। समर ने घर की तंगी की हालत बताई। उसने प्रभा से कहा कि वह उसकी हिम्मत बढ़ाती रहे। समर ने कहा कि वह नौकरी की तलाश करेगा।

चार

शब्दार्थ—**आत्म विश्वास** = अपने पर विश्वास, **लज्जा** = शरम, **क्षोभ** = दुःख, **इत्मीनान** = विश्वास, **कृतज्ञता** = एहसान मानना, **मुखातिब** = मुख की तरफ देखकर, **बर्राने** = कुछ न कुछ कहने जिसका कोई मतलब नहीं है, **बोखला** = गुस्सा, **संग्रहालय** = जहाँ पुरानी ऐतिहासिक चीजें रखी जाती हैं, **गोबर-संस्कृति** = बेकार की संस्कृति, **अर्पित** = देना, **अवैज्ञानिक** = विज्ञान से अलग, **आध्यात्मिक** = आत्मा से सम्बन्धित, **संकुचित** = सिकुड़ना, **आत्मीयता** = अपने पन से।

एम्प्लायमेंट एक्सचेंज पर मिले सज्जन की बात प्रभा को बताई। वह दिवाकर के पास गया। दिवाकर ने उसके घर में सोफे पर बैठे हुए व्यक्ति से परिचय कराया। वह शिरीष भाई साहब हैं। वह अपनी बहिन का इलाज कराने लाये हैं, उसे हिस्टीरिया के दौरे पड़ते हैं अतः उसे मेंटल हॉस्पीटल में भरती कराना है। छोटी उम्र में उसकी शादी कर दी। पतिदेव उस समय पढ़ रहे थे। पति को पता चला कि उसकी पत्नी अशिक्षित है, तो उसने उसे छोड़ ही दिया। ज्यादा सोच विचार और टेंशन के कारण यह हालत हुई है। भाई साहब ने निष्कर्ष निकाला कि समर भावनाओं के आवेश में घुटने वाले व्यक्ति हैं। अखबार बुरी खबरों से भरे पड़े हैं। मजबूरी में घुल-घुलकर और घुट-घुटकर मरने को भारतीय नारी की सहनशीलता का नाम देकर नहीं पूजना चाहिए। समर ने पूछा, ''हमारे ऋषि-मुनियों के बनाये सारे धर्म-नियम आपकी निगाह में बेकार हैं ?'' शिरीष भाई साहब की राय में तो सब बेकार हैं। उन्होंने सिगरेट जलाई। जब समर ने हिन्दू-धर्म की श्रेष्ठता के बारे में पूछा। उनका यही विचार था कि अन्य धर्म जैसे ईसाई धर्म भी लोगों के हित के लिए स्कूल, अस्पताल खोलता है। यहाँ तो बस तपस्या कर लेते हैं। समर को बात पसन्द नहीं आईं। शिरीष भाई साहब ने कहा, ''तब तो आप कच्चे हिन्दू हैं। सच्चा हिन्दू सोचता और जाँचता कुछ नहीं, वह तो चाहे आध्यात्मिक ज्ञान हो या रिश्वत और ब्लैक का रुपया, सबको ग्रहण करना जानता है। खैर, मेरी कोई बात आपको अगर बुरी लगी हो तो माफ कीजिए।'' फिर उन्होंने राय दी कि आगे खूब पढ़िये। शिरीष भाई साहब ने अपने बारे में बताया कि वह सरकारे-हिन्द में डेढ़ सौ रुपये में क्लर्क हैं। समर ने दिवाकर को बाहर बुलाकर कहा कि उसे कहीं नौकरी दिलवा दे। दिवाकर ने उसे आश्वासन दिया।

पाँच

शब्दार्थ—**ख्याल** = ध्यान, **निर्निमेष** = लगातार, **उद्धत** = तेज स्वभाव से, **भन्नाया** = क्रोधित, **हिमायत** = तरफदारी, **धड़धड़ाता** = तेजी से, **उद्दण्डता** = गँवारपन, **हेकड़ी** = अकड़, **उपद्रव** = ऊधम, **तमीज-सलीका** = संस्कार की अच्छी बातें, **हक्का-बक्का** = होश-हवाश खोये हुए, **तिरस्कार** = उपेक्षापूर्ण, **नामोनिशान** = बिल्कुल न होना, **सन्नाटा** = खामोशी, **आशंकित** = शंका से भरा।

साँझ हो रही थी और गाय-भैंसों का झुण्ड सारी सड़क के रिक्शा-ताँगों को एक ओर समेट, धूल उड़ाता, गोबर फैलाता लौट रहा था। मन्दिर या संघ जाने का तो समर को ख्याल ही नहीं आता जैसे इन चीजों से काफी दूर चला गया हो। पार्क में जाकर चुपचाप बैठ गया और वहाँ आये लोगों, औरतों और बच्चों को देखता रहा।

घर पर अमर ने रोटियों में कम घी लगने की बात प्रभा से कही। प्रभा ने बताया कि घी खत्म हो गया है। अमर को अपनी उपेक्षा लगी। उसने समर को घी खिलाने का ताना दिया। समर के आने पर वह चुप हो गया। समर ने पीछे से उसे लात मारी और अमर भनभनाता हुआ थाली फैंककर बाहर चला गया और जोर-जोर से रोने लगा। अम्मा ने अमर की तरफदारी की। समर और अमर की तनातनी हो गई। अम्मा रोने लगी। समर ने कहा, "तुम तो कुछ सोचो मत और अगर दूसरा कहे तो बहू की आड़ हो गई। अब महीनों हो गये, ख्याल है किसी को कि कब खाती है ? कब सोती है ? एक कपड़ा माँगा तो दुनियाभर का महाभारत ? भाभी क्या कुछ भी करने लायक नहीं हैं. . .।" यह सुनकर भाभी भी मोरचे पर आ गईं। उन्होंने प्रभा को एक तरफ कर दिया और रोटियाँ बनाने लगीं। प्रभा ने बच्ची को गोद में लिया तो उठकर उसके हाथ से बच्ची को छीन लिया।

प्रभा को लगा कि इस सारे काण्ड की जिम्मेदारी उस पर डाल दी गई है। समर हक्का-बक्का खड़ा इस सारी स्थिति को देखता रहा।

पार्क वाली घटना याद आई कि दरोगाजी ने अपने बीमार घोड़े को गोली से मार दिया था। समर को यह बहुत बुरा लगा।

रात को दस बजे समर जब घर लौटा तो उसकी समझ में कुछ भी नहीं आ रहा था। माथे में दर्द था। घर में सब सो चुके थे। अपनी कोठरी में जाकर बिना कपड़े उतारे ही जा पड़ा। अप्रैल बीत चुका था। सब लोग ऊपर छतों पर ही सो रहे थे। प्रभा आकर उसके पास बैठ गई और बोली—"खाना नहीं खाओगे ?" समर ने उससे पूछा कि उसने खा लिया क्या ! प्रभा ने नहीं में उत्तर दिया। समर का हृदय दुःख से भरा हुआ था और रोते हुए बोला, "प्रभा. . . प्रभा बताओ, हम क्या करें, कहाँ चलें।"

छः

शब्दार्थ—**शिष्टता** = अच्छा व्यवहार, **उतावली** = जल्दी करने वाली, **कृतज्ञता** = अहसान मानना, **अड़ियल** = बात न मानने वाला, **हतप्रभ** = भौचक्का, **अहसान फरामोशी** = अहसान न मानना, **आध्यात्मिक** = धर्म से सम्बन्धित, **मनःस्थिति** = मन की स्थिति, **घुप्प** = गायब, **उलझाये** = फँसाये हुए, **झुँझलाहट** = गुस्सा, **फिलहाल** = इस समय, **प्रूफ रीडिंग** = प्रेस में छपने वाले कागजों के शब्दों में गलती को शुद्ध करना, **विह्वलता** = भावुकता, **जहन्नुम** = नरक, **ओवर टाइम** = अधिक देर तक काम करना, **कूढ़मगज** = नाकारा, काम न करने वाला, **मनःस्थिति** = मन के विचार, **स्थित-प्रज्ञता** = अपनी स्थिति का ज्ञान, **ब्रह्मज्ञान** = ईश्वर का ज्ञान, **कुम्भीपाक** = एक नरक का नाम, **कृतघ्नता** = अहसान को न मानना, **आत्मज्ञान** = अपनी आत्मा का ज्ञान, **मानव कल्याण** = मनुष्य मात्र की भलाई, **अभिप्राय** = मतलब, **अर्थान्तरित** = अर्थ बताना, **व्याख्या** = अर्थ समझाना, **परसाद** = प्रसाद, **बदतमीजी** = अपमान करना, **पलभर** = थोड़ी देर में, **काफूर** = गायब, **आत्मप्रवाह** = लगातार, **सामर्थ्य** = ताकत, **निराधार** = बिना आधार के, **आश्वासन** = भरोसा, **एम्प्लायमेंट एक्सचेंज** = नौकरी दिलाने वाला दफ्तर, **खण्डन** = विरोध, **भीगी बिल्ली बनी** = डरी हुई, **अनैतिक** = नीति के विरुद्ध, **अनुचित** = गलत।

दिवाकर ने समर को बताया कि एक नौकरी है, पर है बहुत दूर शहर के दूसरे छोर पर। पर शर्त यह है कि कॉलेज में थर्ड ईयर में दाखिला लोगे। एक प्रेस में प्रूफ रीडिंग का काम है। सुबह पाँच बजे से ग्यारह बजे का टाइम है और पचहत्तर रुपये महीने का है और बाद में बढ़ भी सकता है। समर तो खुशी के मारे उछल पड़ा और दिवाकर के प्रति कृतज्ञता जाहिर की। उसे विश्वास नहीं हो रहा था कि पचहत्तर रुपये की नौकरी उसे मिल गई है। सुबह वह जल्दी उठेगा और खाना प्रभा बना दिया करेगी। समर ने दिवाकर से बीस रुपये उधार माँग लिए। चलते हुए समर ने पूछा कि इतवार की तो छुट्टी रहा करेगी। दिवाकर ने हाँ में जवाब दिया। शिरीष भाई साहब से मुलाकात हुई।

समर ने अपनी चुटिया कटवाकर बालों में ही मिला ली थी। शिरीष भाई ने संसार को मायाजाल बताया। शिरीष भाई ने बताया कि एक बार नदी पार करने के लिए विवेकानन्द नौका का इन्तजार कर रहे थे। तभी एक बाबा आया और बोला कि तुम कैसे योगी हो एक छोटी सी नदी पार नहीं कर सकते ? उसने गर्व से नदी के ऊपर चलते हुए नदी पार की और वापस आ गया। उसने बताया कि हिमालय की गुफाओं में तीस साल तपस्या करने के बाद यह सिद्धि प्राप्त की है, स्वामी जी हँसे कि नदी पार करने के लिए जीवन के तीस साल बर्वाद कर दिये। नदी तो दो पैसे नाव में देकर आसानी से पार हो जाती है। ये तीस साल आप मानव-कल्याण में लगा सकते थे।

उनकी बात सुनकर समर प्रभा की बात सोचने लगा कि उसने उस पर बहुत अत्याचार किये हैं। यह बात तो किसी से छिपी नहीं है। शिरीष भाई साहब ने उपर्युक्त बात के साथ-साथ यह भी कहा कि कविता में तो यों भी सारे इतिहास को रूपक, प्रतीक, उत्प्रेक्षा और व्यंजना से लाद दिया जाता है। समर ने यह कहते हुए विदा ली कि उसे जल्दी है।

दिवाकर ने उसे बताया कि सुबह साढ़े चार या पौने पाँच बजे यहाँ से एक गाड़ी जाती है उससे तुम प्रेस चले जाया करो। समर ने अपनी पत्नी के लिए एक धोती खरीदी। वह सोचने लगा कि प्रभा को सीधा दूँगा तो भाभी और अम्मा बुरा मान जायेगी। समर ने धोती का बण्डल अम्मा की गोद में डाल दिया। अम्मा ने धोती को देखकर उसे देते हुए कहा कि उसी को दे दे जिसके लिए लाया है।

उसी दिन खाना खाते-खाते समर ने भाई साहब से कहा कि वह सोच रहा है कि इस साल थर्ड ईयर में प्रवेश ले ही ले। भाई साहब ने कहा कि बाबूजी से पूछ लो। फिर उन्होंने खर्चे का दुखड़ा रोया। धोती पर प्रभा नाराज भी हुई और खुश भी। नौकरी की बात सुनकर प्रभा उछल पड़ी। पहले तो वह कॉलेज नाम लिखवायेगा फिर फीस माफ करायेगा। दोनों सपनों की सुहानी दुनिया की सैर करने लगे। निश्चय कल रविवार को जाकर काम देख लेगा फिर घरवालों को बतायेगा कि दिवाकर ने नौकरी इस शर्त पर दिलाई है कि वह पढ़ेगा। प्रभा किरण (दिवाकर की पत्नी) के सामने होने की कल्पना से सकुचा उठी, समर ने प्रभा को शिरीष भाई साहब की बातें बताईं। यकायक उनकी कोठरी की किवाड़ों को जोर से किसी ने धक्का मारा। समर ने बाहर जाकर देखा तो बाबूजी चिल्ला रहे हैं—"जवानी हमें भी आई थी, पर ऐसी नहीं कि न दिन देखें न रात ! जब देखो बहू को लिए पड़े हैं। अरे, घर में बच्चे हैं, बड़े-बूढ़े हैं—किसी का तो लिहाज करो। दस बजने को आ रहे हैं और बाबूजी का अभी सबेरा ही नहीं हुआ. . .।" बाबूजी अपना आलाप समाप्त करके चले गये तब प्रभा धीरे से निकलकर नीचे आई।

सात

शब्दार्थ—वात्सल्य = माता-पिता का बच्चे के प्रति प्रेम, **दिलचस्प** = मन को पसन्द, **अजीबो गरीब** = बेतुके, **व्यभिचार** = गलत काम करना, **सेक्सन** = कक्षा, **मिलिट्री ट्रेनिंग** = फौजी ट्रेनिंग, **विभीषिकाएँ** = परेशानियाँ, **विचलित** = डिगाना, **तेजोज्जल** = तेज प्रकाश, **अरुणाभा** = लाल प्रकाश, **ज्योतिर्मण्डल** = प्रकाश समूह, **रोमांचित** = अधिक प्रसन्न।

नौकरी की बात पता लगते ही घर वालों का व्यवहार समर और प्रभा के प्रति नरम हो गया था। अम्मा कहतीं कि यदि समर सहारा देगा तो घर की मुसीबतें कम हो जायेंगी। समर सोच रहा था कि पढ़ाई का भी खर्च है घर वालों की मदद कैसे हो पायेगी। पच्चीस-तीस रुपये तो पढ़ाई में निकल जायेंगे और प्रभा के लिए धोती ब्लाउज भी लाना है, बीस रुपये दिवाकर के देने है। फिर दोनों बातें करने लगे घरवालों की

समर ने अपनी नौकरी पर जाना शुरू कर दिया। प्रभा पूरे दिन बैल की तरह जुटी रहती है। समर ने पहले तो बिना टिकिट ही जाना शुरू किया। शुरू में तो काम ठीक लगा बाद में अरुचि होने लगी। शुरू में गलितयाँ भी हुईं। प्रेस में शोरगुल इतना रहता कि सिर में दर्द होने लगे। काम करने वाले लोग इतने दिलचस्प

थे कि बाद में मन लगने लगा। जब बारह बजे कड़कती धूप में पसीने से तर-बतर होकर घर आता तो दो गिलास पानी पी लेता फिर भूख ही नहीं रहती। प्रभा ने बताया कि घर के काम-काज के बाद इसी समय छुट्टी मिलती है। दोनों ने साथ-साथ खाना खाया।

रिजल्ट आया कि समर तो सैकण्ड डिवीजन में पास हो गया, पर अमर फेल हो गया। अमर रो रहा था, सभी दुःखी थे। भाभी अपना खर्च का दुःख रोती रहीं। समर अपना नाम कॉलेज में लिखवा आया। पुराना विद्यार्थी होने के कारण एडमीशन तो हो गया। प्रेस से छूटते ही उसे कॉलेज भागना पड़ता और वहाँ से तीन बजे छुट्टी मिलती। दोनों बात करते रहे। प्रभा ने कहा कि वह सुबह जल्दी उठकर खाना बना दिया करेगी। समर कहने लगा कि वह कहीं क्लर्की देखेगा जिससे कि दस बजे जाकर पाँच बजे आ सकता है। प्रभा ने बताया कि उसमें बहुत ज्यादा जीवनी-शक्ति है। इससे भी ज्यादा मुसीबतों में वह विचलित नहीं हो सकती। समर ने बताया कि वह हारा नहीं है उसके लिए जरूर कुछ करेगा।

आठ

शब्दार्थ—खुलासा = साफ-साफ बताना, **खानदान** = परिवार, **अनिच्छा** = इच्छा के बिना, **कहन-सुनन** = कहना-सुनना, **अशिष्टता** = असभ्यता, **अदब-कायदा** = परिवार में बड़ों के सम्मान के लिए बनाये गये नियम, **पुनर्कथन** = दुबारा कहना, **ईजाद** = खोज करना, **अप्रत्याशित** = जो सोचा नहीं गया हो, **हतप्रभ** = अचम्भित, **सकपका गया** = घबरा गया, **संयुक्त** = मिला हुआ, **भावुकता** = भावना से सम्बन्धित, **आर्दता** = गीलापन।

घर में मामाजी को आया हुआ देखकर समर को आश्चर्य हुआ। वह अमर के लिए कोई लड़की बताने आये थे। कह रहे थे कि आप स्वयं लड़की देख लेते तो अच्छा होता। अमर को और दो-चार मुहल्ले वालों को भी दिखा दो और बाकी बातें खुद ही कर लें। समर ने टोका कि अभी जल्दी क्या है ? बाबूजी अभी तो अमर फेल होकर चुका है। मामाजी ने कहा कि फेल-पास तो लगा ही रहता है। लेन-देन की बात साफ कर लेना। समर उठने लगा तो मामाजी ने हाथ पकड़कर उसे बैठा लिया। बाबूजी ने उसके ऊपर ताना मारा कि नौ बजे से पहले तो इनका सबेरा ही नहीं होता। मामाजी ने उसे समझाया कि कुछ घर की तरफ भी ध्यान दो। समझदार आदमी को तो औरतों की बातों में आना ही नहीं चाहिए। उसने मामाजी से कहा कि वह आगे पढ़ना चाहता है। मामाजी ने कहा कि पढ़ने की कौन मना करता है ? पर सब घर की हालत देखकर किया जाता है। तुम धरम-करम को छोड़ते चले जा रहे हो ? धरम-करम के बिना दुनिया कैसे रहेगी ? बाबूजी जोर से बोले—"तुम किस पत्थर को समझा रहे हो, चन्दन ? कहा है, 'सीख दीजिए ताहि को जाको सीख सुहाय. . .।" समर वहाँ से चला आया। प्रभा को मामाजी की बातें बताईं-बहू को दबाकर रखा करो आदि। अमर की शादी का प्रस्ताव लेकर आये हैं। कुछ देर बाद समर घर से बाहर चला गया और सड़कों पर भटकता रहा। दिवाकर मिल गया। समर ने दिवाकर को बताया कि उसके घर में कितने झंझट हैं, शिरीष भाई भी साथ में थे। शिरीष भाई बोले—"भाई समर जी, आपकी अपनी या दिवाकर की वास्तविक स्थिति जानकर एक बात मेरी समझ में आती जा रही है—इस संयुक्त परिवार की परम्परा को तोड़ना ही होगा।" गिरीष भाई साहब और भी बातें करते रहे। आखिर में यही कहा—"भैया मेरे, सीधा-सादा हल यही है कि आप अलग रहिये और घर के लिए जो जिम्मेदारी महसूस करते हैं, वह पूरी कीजिए।"

समर उसकी विश्लेषण प्रतिभा पर चकित था। रास्तेभर समर सोचता आया कि सारी बातें प्रभा को बतायेगा।

नौ

शब्दार्थ—अवचेतन = चेतना रहित, **याचना भरे** = प्रार्थना करते हुए, **ढर्रा** = चलना, **असाध्य** = जिस बीमारी का इलाज न हो सके, **फर्ज** = कर्त्तव्य, **अतीत-जीवी** = भूतकाल पर जीने वाला, **गरिमा** = महिमा, **अक्षत** = चावल, **खयाल** = ध्यान, **भाव-भंगिमाओं** = चहरे पर आते-जाते भाव, **निष्फल** = असफल।

समर थोड़ा लेटा था तो प्रभा आकर बोली कि वह उसके पैर दबा देती है क्योंकि समर ने आज बहुत काम किया है। समर को उस पर दया आई कि खुद कितना काम करती है। प्रभा समर का बहुत खयाल रखती है। समर ने नीचे से बाल्टी भर-भरकर ऊपर छत पर छिड़काव कर दिया था ताकि गर्मी कुछ शान्त हो। खाटों पर भी पानी डाल दिया था। सभी अपनी अलग-अलग जगहों पर छत पर ही सोते थे। समर की आँख लग गई, प्रभा ने उसे जगाया और पैर दबाने लगी और दोनों बात करने लगे। समर पैर दबाने की मना करता रहा। प्रभा ने बताया कि आज उसने और भाभी ने व्रत रखा था इसलिए खीर-पूरी और हलुआ बना था। समर ने उससे अपने स्वास्थ्य का ध्यान रखने को कहा।

समर को व्रत वगैरा में विश्वास नहीं है। प्रभा ने उसकी हाँ में हाँ मिलाई कि विश्वास तो उसे भी नहीं है पर घर में रहकर यह सब करना पड़ता है। समर ने इसी बात पर डाँटा तो वह रोने लगी। समर को उस पर दया आई और उसने उसे रोने से मना किया।

भाभी की बेटी रात को जाकर रोती रही। भाई साहब भाभी को ही डाँट रहे थे। रात को डेढ़ बजा था। समर पुरानी बात सोचने लगा जब वह लालटेन की रोशनी में 'रुस्तम और सोहराब' की किताब पढ़ रहा था और प्रभा नाराज होकर एक कोने में पड़ी थी। प्रभा को भी नींद नहीं आ रही थी। समर ने बताया कि दिवाकर की पत्नी ने उसे (प्रभा) कई बार बुलाया है। एक दिन वह चले। आजकल शिरीष भाई साहब भी वहीं हैं। उनकी बातों के बारे में समर ने प्रभा को बताया। प्रभा उनकी (शिरीष) बातों का समर्थन करती है। समर ने सोचा कि समय-समय पर वह उसे ये बातें बताता रहे तो वह बहुत कुछ सीख जायेगी। प्रभा ने पूछा कि आखिर वे मानते किसको हैं ? समर ने भी यही बात उनसे पूछी थी। उनका जवाब था—"ईश्वर, धर्म, अन्तरात्मा और संस्कार के बाद जो कुछ भी बाकी बच जाता है, मैं उस सबको मानता हूँ। अगर मानने लायक सारी बात इन्हीं चार-पाँच शब्दों की बपौती है, तो यह समझ लीजिए कि मैं किसी को नहीं मानता।" अपने पुरखों के बारे में शिरीष भाई की अपमानजनक बातें समर को अच्छी नहीं लगीं। लेकिन उनका गुस्सा देखकर उसे (समर) को भी जोश आ जाता है। सुनते-सुनते लगा कि प्रभा सो गई। उसने प्रभा को जगाया। उसे प्रभा की कमर में कोई गोली जैसी चीज बँधी हुई देखी तो उसने सख्ती से पूछा कि यह क्या है ? आखिर प्रभा ने बताया कि अवस्थीजी की बीवी के कहने पर अम्माजी और भाभी ने सैयद बाबा की धूनी बाँधी है। इससे बच्चा हो जायेगा। समर ने क्रोध में आकर उस गाँठ को तोड़ दिया। प्रभा ने कहा कि माताजी और भाभी दिन भर मेरी जान खाती हैं कि वह बाँझ है। समर खाट की पाटी से सिर टिकाये अपना माथा कूट रहा था और प्रभा घुटनों में सिर दबाये रो रही थी।

दस

शब्दार्थ—अनुरोध = आग्रह, **क्षमा याचना** = क्षमा माँगना, **स्निग्ध** = भीगे, **सख्त** = कठोर, **उम्मीद** = आशा, **कृतार्थ** = धन्य, **उत्सुकता** = जानने की इच्छा, **मनहारिन** = चूड़ी पहनाने वाली, **झलमलाना** = चमकना, **निश्चिन्तता** = बिना चिन्ता के प्रसन्न होकर, **कटखने** = काटने वाले, **उत्तेजना** = क्रोध के साथ, **साज-सिंगार** = सजावट का सामान, **विचित्र** = अजीब, **सन्नाटा** = खामोशी, **आतंकोत्पादिनी** = डर उत्पन्न करने वाली, **अविभाज्य** = बिना बँटा हुआ, **तन्द्रा** = नींद।

"यहाँ क्यों बैठे हो सुबह से ? कुछ काम नहीं है ? कॉलेज नहीं जाना है आज ?" प्रभा ने आकर समर से पूछा। समर प्रेस से आने के बाद सुस्त और उदास सा ऊपर छज्जे पर ही बैठ गया था। प्रभा ने उसकी कलाई छूकर देखा कि कहीं बुखार तो नहीं है। नीचे आँगन में चूड़ी वाली भाभी को चूड़ी पहना रही थी। समर की चुप्पी देखकर प्रभा ने कारण पूछा कि अभी तक नाराज हो उस बात पर ? अम्मा ने प्रभा को नीचे बुलाया। समर इस बात से दु:खी था कि उसकी नौकरी चली गयी है तथा पचहत्तर रुपये कहकर साठ रुपये दिये और पार्टटाइम कहकर पूरा टाइम काम लिया। प्रभा ने कहा कि दिवाकर से इस बारे में बात करो। समर ने कहा कि कल आखिरी बार जाऊँगा—पन्द्रह दिन ही सही इतने तो मिल ही जायें कि उधार चुक जाये। प्रभा ने नीचे जाते

हुए कहा कि वह (समर) चिन्ता न करे, उसके (प्रभा) पास थोड़ा-बहुत जेवर है, वह किस काम आयेगा। प्रभा के मना करने पर भी अम्मा जी ने उसे चूड़ी पहनवा दीं। समर नीचे आया और गुस्से में प्रभा के दोनों हाथों को एक-दूसरे से टकराकर चूड़ियों को तोड़ दिया। चूड़ियों के टुकड़े समर की हथेली और उँगलियों में चुभ गये थे, खून निकल आया था। उसके बाद वह ऊपर लौट गया।

नीचे बाबूजी के साथ समर बैठा था तो बाबूजी ने उसकी तनख्वाह के बारे में पूछा कि दस तारीख से काम शुरू किया था। समर ने लापरवाही से कहा कि नौकरी तो छूट भी गई। बाबूजी गुस्सा हुए कि समर ने पहली तनख्वाह अपने बाप को नहीं दी थी। अन्य अनकही बात भी कहीं। गुस्से में वह कुछ भी कह देते हैं। अमर और भाई साहब के रोकते हुए भी उन्होंने समर पर लात, घूँसों और थप्पड़ों की बौछार कर ही दी। घर के लोग और बाहर की स्त्रियाँ इकट्ठी होकर पूछने लगीं कि क्या बात हो गयी ? समर ने कहा कि अब वह यहाँ से चला ही जायेगा। बाबूजी ने तुरन्त ही कह दिया कि दोनों निकल जाओ इस घर से। अम्मा ने उससे चुप होने को कहा। समर ने कहा कि अब वह यहाँ नहीं रहेगा।

अचानक प्रभा ने समर को जगा दिया—"चार बज गये. . . जागोगे नहीं आज।" समर उठ बैठा। प्रभा ने खाना बनाकर उसे दे दिया। वह दरवाजे के पास आया तो द्वार पर एक तारवाला खड़ा था। समर ने तार लिया और खोलकर देखा तो उसमें लिखा था—"मुन्नी मर गई," वह बाहर चला गया यह जानकर कि घर में रोना-पीटना होगा। वह बार-बार यहीं सोचता रहा कि मुन्नी मरी नहीं, उसे मार दिया गया। गाड़ी में बैठा और अगले स्टेशन पर उतरा। सोचने लगा कि सामने आती हुई गाड़ी के सामने आ जाये तो सारी मुसीबतें समाप्त हो जायेंगी। इस सवाल के साथ ही बन्दूक पकड़े हुए दरोगाजी की तस्वीर कौंध गई। सारी तस्वीर ऐसी सजीव होकर सामने आ गई कि उसे लगा, कहीं यह सब कर ही न डालूँ। काफी देर तक विभिन्न प्रकार के विचार उसके दिमाग को परेशान करते रहे। और फिर एक साथ ही सारी तस्वीरें एक बड़ी तस्वीर में बदल जाती हैं। अखबार में उसकी तस्वीर छपी है—"प्रिय बेटा समर, तुम्हारी माँ की तबीयत बहुत खराब है, एक बार वे तुम्हें देखना चाहती है ?"

सामने वाली रेल की सीटी से चौंककर वह तन्द्रा से जागा—सामने वाली ट्रेन का उसके आगे वाला पहिया धीरे-धीरे घूमा-अगर दो डिब्बों के बीच की खाली जगह में अचानक कूद पड़े तो ? या लपककर हैण्डिल पकड़कर डिब्बे में चढ़ जाये तो ?

अब पीछे वाली ट्रेन भी खिसकने लगी थी—दोनों गाड़ियाँ दो विरोधी दिशाओं की तरफ सरक रही थीं। समर को लगा जैसे वह तेजी से चक्कर खाते चाक पर खड़ा है—भीतर कोई दुहराये चला जा रहा है. . . कूद पड़. . . चढ़ जा ! . . . कूद पड़ ! . . . चढ़ जा . . . ! घबराकर उसने ऊपर देखा. . . सारा आकाश डग-डग घूमने लगा था।

अभ्यास-प्रश्न

प्रश्न 1. आज किसकी सुहागरात है ? वह बाहर निकलकर दोस्तों से आँख चुराते हुए मन्दिर की ओर गया। वहाँ का दृश्य कैसा था ?

उत्तर—आज समर की सुहागरात है। वह पढ़ रहा था, घरवालों ने जबरदस्ती उसकी शादी कर दी। 'देश को साहसी और कर्मठ युवकों की जरूरत है' का नारा देने वाला यह युवक भी अब चौपाया हो गया है। जो समर आँधी-पानी में नहीं रुका, वही आज दो दिन से शाखा नहीं गया है। अपने ही साथियों से आँख चुराता फिर रहा है। इस समय वह मेहमानों, मित्रों, परिचितों की आँखों से बचता हुआ मन्दिर की ओर चल दिया। मन्दिर वह जगह है जहाँ वह शान्ति से बैठकर इस परिवर्तन के बारे में सोचेगा, रात को देर से लौटेगा, तब तक हल्ला-गुल्ला भी शान्त हो चुकेगा। चूँकि उसका मन नहीं था अभी शादी करने का इसलिए उसका मन शादी के बाद के किसी कार्यक्रम में नहीं लग रहा था। यदि वह कहीं भाग जाये तो कल के अखबार में ही

निकलेगा—'बेटा तुम्हारी माँ की तबीयत बहुत खराब है। हमें अब कोई शिकायत नहीं है।' इसलिए वह भाग भी नहीं सकता।

गोधूलि के बाद का कोहरा चारों ओर छाया हुआ है। समर ने मन्दिर पहुँचकर उसके खम्भे से अपना माथा टेक दिया। उसका सिर कुछ भारी-सा हो रहा था। संगमरमर के सुन्दर काले-सफेद टुकड़ों से बनी शतरंजी-ठाकुर जी के सामने वाले द्वार तक चली गई खम्भों की दो कतारें उन पर टिका बड़ा भारी हॉल—बीचों-बीत मूर्ति के सामने मँजीरा, मृदंग, हारमोनियम, सितार इत्यादि लेकर गाते हुए कुछ भक्त लोग—"मेरे तो गिरधर गोपाल, दूसरा न कोई. . . . अरे हाँ मेरे तो गिरधर गोपाल. . . अत्यन्त मनभावन और सुन्दर लग रहे थे। आसपास गूँजते भक्ति के उद्‌गार—'जय वंशीवाले की. . . नन्द के लाले की. . . नमामि भक्तवत्सलम्. . .।' गूँजती झाँझ, लोबान और अगरबत्ती की सुहावनी गंध, धुँधली-धुँधली रोशनियाँ मन्दिर की सुन्दरता में चार-चाँद लगा रही थीं। खम्भे से टेक लगाये समर बाहर की सीढ़ियों पर बैठ गया और सोचने लगा कि वह किस विपदा में फँस गया है। उसने अपनी शादी के लिए बहुत मना किया और गिड़गिड़ाता रहा—'मेरे पाँव में चक्की मत बाँधो।' पर किसी ने उसकी बात नहीं सुनी। वह सोच रहा है कि समर्थ गुरु रामदास माँडा छोड़कर उठ भागे थे। सभी लोगों का यही विचार था कि अब तो बहू आनी ही चाहिए। बड़े की शादी हुए आठ साल से ऊपर हो गये। सगे सम्बन्धी भी उसके घरवालों पर दवाब डालने लगे। आखिर समर को अनिच्छा होते हुए भी विवाह करना पड़ा।

फिर उसे ख्याल आया कि उसे निराशावादी नहीं होना चाहिए। अपनी हिम्मत वह क्यों जल्दी हार जाता है ? कभी वह सोचता कि जैसे उसकी महत्वाकांक्षाएँ मर गई हैं। लेकिन यह उसकी अग्निपरीक्षा का समय है। सोना आग में तपकर ही कुन्दन बनता है। अब उसके सामने आज परीक्षाफल है—हमेशा तो रहेगा नहीं। बीच में आये इस माया जाल और मोहिनी में अपने को फँस जाने दे या इस झाड़ी से कतराकर निकल जाये। यह प्रश्न उसके मस्तिष्क को मथने लगा, लेकिन कोई सटीक उत्तर वह खोज नहीं पा रहा है।

प्रश्न 2. प्रभा के बारे में समर को क्या विचार थे ? वह उसे क्या समझाना चाहता है ?

उत्तर—जैसे भी कहो प्रभा समर की पत्नी है। अभी तक उसने न तो प्रभा को देखा है और न ही उससे बात की है। स्वाभाविकता से तो पति अपनी नवविवाहिता को देखने की और उसे बात करने की उत्कंठा रखता है, लेकिन यहाँ समर के साथ उलटा ही हो रहा है। वह पहले से ही सोच रहा है कि वह अपनी पत्नी की रंगीनियों और झंझट में नहीं फसेगा। उसने सोच रखा है कि यह उसके बनने का समय है, उसका निर्माण काल है।

लोग कहते हैं कि प्रभा दसवीं पास है। समर ने उसके हाथ के सिवाय कुछ नहीं देखा है। भाँवरों पर जब वह आगे चल रही थी तो महावर लगे हुए पाँव देखे थे। उसे लग रहा है कि उसे कम-से-कम उसका चेहरा तो देख ही लेना चाहिए था। भाभी कहती हैं कि चेहरे पर चेचक की हल्की-हल्की झाँई हैं। आज उसकी सुहागरात है और वह घर से बाहर है। उसने सोच रखा है कि उसे प्रभा से कोई सम्बन्ध ही नहीं रखना है। यदि बात करनी ही पड़ी तो मतलब की ही एक-दो बातें करेगा, बस। अब तक तो दवाब और कहने में आकर शादी कर ली, यही बहुत है। उसका काम तो बस पढ़ना है। उसका मन चाहता है कि खूब परिश्रम करके अपनी शिक्षा-दीक्षा पूरी कर ले, फिर वह घर-गृहस्थी देखेगा। तब तक प्रभा कहाँ रहेगी, क्या करेगी उसे नहीं मालूम। यह सब घर वाले देखेंगे जिन्होंने कि उसे शादी के बन्धन में बाँध दिया है। किसी ने समर से कहा कि बहू बहुत समझदार है। समझदार है तो अच्छी बात है। वह अपना काम करे और उसको अपना काम करने दे।

समर सोचने लगा कि वह प्रभा को समझायेगा कि वे दोनों ही समझदार हैं। माँ-बाप जैसे भी हैं या जो भी कर सकते हैं उन्होंने कर दिया; लेकिन उनका (समर और प्रभा) जीवन तो उन्हें ही देखना है। सबसे पहले उन्हें अपनी शिक्षा पूरी करनी होगी। यदि यह सब सुनकर वह रोने लगी, तो भी वह अपनी बात पर अडिग

रहेगा जैसे भगवान बुद्ध को उनकी पत्नी यशोधरा का सौन्दर्य बाँधकर नहीं रख पाया, गोपियों के प्यार ने भगवान कृष्ण को योगीराज बनने से नहीं रोका। पत्नी पति के कार्यों में बाधा नहीं बनतीं। पर कुछ-कुछ अशिक्षित या संस्कारहीन पत्नियाँ कभी-कभी अपनी अल्पबुद्धि या स्वार्थ के कारण पति के मार्ग में बाधा बन जाती हैं, लेकिन सर्वथा ऐसा नहीं होता। वह प्रभा को भी यही बतायेगा कि वह उसे पढ़ने दे। समर सोचता है कि वह हृदय से बहुत कमजोर है। तब तक उपेक्षा उसका अस्त्र है और उदासीनता उसकी ढाल. . . आँसुओं और वासना के दलदल में पाँव जमा-जमाकर उसे चलना है।

प्रश्न 3. अपनी सुहागरात का समय समर का कैसे बीता ?

उत्तर—सुहागरात एक ऐसा समय होता है जब दो अनजान या जाने पहचाने युवक और युवती शादी के पवित्र गठबन्धन में बँधकर पहली बार मिलते हैं और रातभर अपने प्यार का इजहार करके अपने साथी की भावना को तोलते हैं। सभी के लिए यह एक प्रसन्नता का अवसर होता है। लेकिन यहाँ पर सब कुछ उलटा ही हुआ। न तो समर प्रभा से बोला और न प्रभा ने ही हिम्मत दिखाई। दोनों में कोई बोलचाल नहीं हुई। प्रभा पर इसका क्या प्रभाव पड़ा यह तो उसने प्रकट नहीं किया केवल उसके आँसू ही उसके हृदय की तकलीफ को बयां करने वाले थे। पहल युवक की तरफ से होती है क्योंकि लड़की तो नये वातावरण में आकर संकोच व शर्म के मारे चुपचाप सिमटी सी बैठी रहती है। यहाँ बातचीत न होने का कारण समर ही रहा।

हल्के से धक्का देकर भाभी ने पीछे से किबाड़ बन्द कर दिये तो समर कमरे में आ गया। उस समय प्रभा जंगले में सिर रखके खड़ी थी, जैसे खड़ी-खड़ी सो गई हो। थोड़ी देर समर यों ही खड़ा रहा और फिर धीरे से आकर पलंग के सिरे पर इस तरह बैठ गया जैसे डर लग रहा हो। सोचा था कि पलंग पर जाकर सो जायेगा और सुबह से पहले जागना उसने नहीं जाना। मन ही मन वह दुहराता रहा. . . नारी अंधकार है, नारी मोह, नारी माया है, नारी देवत्व की ओर उठते हुए मनुष्य को बाँधकर राक्षसत्व के गहरे अंधे कुएं में डाल देती है। नारी पुरुष की सबसे बड़ी कमजोरी है। इस कमरे में आने से पहले वह सोच रहा था कि जैसा सभी विवाहों में होता है, प्रभा सजीली नव-वधू की तरह गठरी बनी होगी, उसी साज-सज्जा से उसका स्वागत करने को तैयार होगी। यही तो वह क्षण है जब उसे अपने को सावधान रखना होगा। लेकिन उसने ऐसा कुछ नहीं किया और वह चुपचाप सामने के जंगले पर खड़ी रही। इस समय तो बस कमरे के सन्नाटे में स्टूल पर रखे पंखे की खड़खड़ाहट की आवाज ही आ रही थी। विवाह के समय पर पड़ोसी से बिजली उधार ले ली थी। समर भरसक उपेक्षा और लापरवाही दिखाना चाहता था। वह बुद्धू की तरह पंखे को देखता रहा फिर धीरे से पलंग पर आड़ा ही लेट गया। वह सोच रहा था कि वह आकर उसे क्षमा माँगेगी, लेकिन ऐसा नहीं हुआ। कभी-कभी चूड़ियों की खनक सुनाई पड़ती थी। वह सोचने लगा कि यहाँ आया ही क्यों ? कहीं और चला जाता तो ऐसा अपमान तो न होता। वह मैट्रिक तक पढ़ी है और उसके (समर के) घरवाले बेपढ़े हैं। वह समझती है कि दूसरे लड़कों की तरह वह भी उसे मनायेगा और खुशामद करेगा। पहले उसने सोचा था कि वे दोनों शिक्षित हैं, समझदार हैं। आपस में बातें करके अपने को अधिक से अधिक योग्य बनाने की ओर ध्यान देंगे। लेकिन नहीं। इसकी मर्जी यही है तो यही सही।

जब कुछ क्षण यों ही बैठे-बैठे बीत गये तो वह एक झटके से उठकर खड़ा हो गया और भड़ाक से दरवाजा खोला तो लगा चौंककर उसने सिर उठाकर देखा। एक क्षण वह बाहर रुका और सीढ़ियाँ चढ़कर खुली छत पर आ गया। सभी लोग चारपाइयों या जमीन पर सो चुके थे। उसने कुछ नहीं देखा और एक कोने में धरती पर सो गया। लेकिन रातभर नींद न आई और सोचता रहा कि मान लो, अभी उठे और बिना किसी से कुछ कहे-बाहर निकल पड़े—कलकत्ता, बम्बई या हरिद्वार।

प्रश्न 4. अगले दिन बाबूजी ने समर से क्या पूछा ? और बहू का समर्थन किन शब्दों में किया ? समर बाबूजी से इतना क्यों डरता था ?

उत्तर—सुबह से कई लोग समर और प्रभा से पूछ चुके थे। लेकिन दोनों ने ऐसी अनिच्छा का भाव दिखाया कि फिर पूछने की किसी की हिम्मत ही नहीं पड़ी। भाभी ने पहले व्यंग्य में प्रश्न किया फिर गम्भीरता से जानना चाहा। अम्मा ने भी पूछा। लेकिन सबको टाल दिया। सारा दिन वह मुँह छुपाते हुए इधर-उधर घूमता रहा। वह अपनी पत्नी से नाराज जरूर था, लेकिन यह भी जानना चाहता था कि उसने उसके (समर) खिलाफ क्या-क्या कहा है ? उसे आश्चर्य हो रहा था कि अभी तक उसके सुनने में कुछ नहीं आया। लगा, उससे घर वाले कुछ भी नहीं निकाल पाये। कभी लगा कि यह कहीं उसे प्रभावित करने का ढंग तो नहीं, थोड़ी देर बाद मुन्नी ने सूचना दी कि उसे बाबूजी ने बुलाया है। बाबूजी ने अत्यन्त गूढ़ रहस्य जानने की मुद्रा में पूछा "कुछ खास बात हुई क्या ?" समर चुप रहा। फिर उन्होंने पूछा—"लड़ाई-वड़ाई तो नहीं हो गई ?" समर चुपचाप बैठा रहा तो उन्होंने फिर कहा—"क्या बात है ? बहू तुझे पसन्द नहीं आई ?" समर को चुपचाप देखकर फिर पूछा, "साफ बता न, इसमें झिझक की क्या बात है ? सुनते हैं तू उससे बोला भी नहीं।"

बाबूजी ने बहू का समर्थन किया, "यह भी तो सोचो कि वह बेचारी पराई लड़की किसके बूते पर आई है ? कोई घर में आता है तो इस व्यवहार के लिए ? क्या कहेगी वह घर जाकर ? माना कि शादी करने की तुम्हारा इच्छा नहीं; लेकिन बेटा यह लोक व्यवहार है। और जो हो जाता है उसे निभाना तो पड़ता ही है। मान लो कि. . .।"

बाबूजी के सामने आने से समर हमेशा ही डरता रहा है; यों तीन-चार साल से उन्होंने हाथ नहीं उठाया, लेकिन शरीर पर पड़ी हुई पुरानी नीलें अभी भी उनके आतंक को ताजा कर देती हैं। किस विषय में वे क्या कर बैठे, इस बात का कोई ठिकाना नहीं। जिन दिनों वे उसे मारते, एक अल्हड़ और जिद्दी निश्चिन्तता रहती कि ज्यादा से ज्यादा पीट ही तो देंगे। हॉकी-फुटबॉल में भी तो चोट लग जाती है और सब उसे सह ही लेते हैं। लेकिन इधर तो एक अजब रहस्यमय खौफ उसे उनके हर व्यवहार में लगता था। अपनी किसी गलती पर जब वह पीटे जाने या डाँटे जाने की आशंका करता और वे टाल देते तो लगता जैसे उसके खाते में जाने कितनी सजा इकट्ठी हो गई है। नतीजे में उनसे कतराना और डरना उसका स्वभाव बन गया था। बाबूजी का आतंक समर की नस-नस में इस तरह समा गया था कि उनके सामने उसकी जुबान नहीं खुलती थी।

प्रश्न 5. बहू के खाना बनाने वाले दिन घर में क्या उत्सव जैसा वातावरण बना ? खाने के समय कैसा दृश्य उपस्थित हुआ ?

उत्तर—सुबह का खाना बन रहा था। समर का न बोलने का निश्चय अभी भी यों ही था। लेकिन यह कुछ ज्यादती लगने लगी। यह तो तय था कि आज प्रभा के हाथ का खाना समर को ही पहले खाना है। यों घर में विवाह के जितने रीति रिवाज हो रहे थे उनसे उसे कोई सरोकार नहीं था। रोज पास-पड़ोस की औरतों की फौजें आतीं और तीन बजे से रात के ग्यारह बजे तक ढोलक पीटी जाती। गीतों के बाद अँजलियाँ भर-भरकर बूँदी के लड्डू और बताशे बाँटे जाते। मुन्नी का तो गाते-गाते गला खराब हो गया था। भाभी बड़ी-बूढ़ियों के पैर लगते-लगते और उनके लिए पान लगाते-लगाते बड़बड़ाने लगी थी। ऐसे समय में अकेली कमरे में चुपचाप कोई किताब पढ़ती या अपनी सहेलियों से, जो उसे देखने या मिलने आई होती, बातें करती प्रभा के पास वे पानों की डलिया और पानदान रख जातीं। और जब कभी सुन आतीं कि छोटी बहू बड़ी से ज्यादा सुन्दर, सलीकेदार और शिष्ट है तो आकर प्रभा से कहतीं—"तुमने अभी तक पान नहीं लगाये बहू, वहाँ मौसीजी और अम्माजी मेरी जान खाये जा रही हैं कि ला, पान ला। लाओ मैं लगा डालूँ जल्दी-जल्दी। तुम नई बहू हो न, सो शरमा रही हो ?" और फिर दो-चार लगे हुए पानों को ले जाकर बाहरवालियों की बातों में शामिल हो जातीं कि इस शादी में उन लोगों को कितना कम मिला है।

समर खाना खाने की मना कर रहा था, लेकिन अम्माजी ने कहा कि यह तो शगुन है कि बहू के हाथ का बना हुआ खाना उसका पति ही पहले खाता है। इस सारे काण्ड में अम्मा ने पहली बार मुझे समझाया था

कि यह तो घर की रीति है, अन्न देवता का अपमान नहीं किया जाता। समर को आश्चर्य हो रहा था कि बात-बात पर डाँटने वाली अम्मा आज चुप क्यों है ?

जब समर को खाना खाने के लिए बुलाया तो रसोई में मुन्नी, अम्मा, भाभी और अमर बगैरह सभी बैठे थे। समर प्रभा को खाना बनाते हुए नहीं देख पा रहा था, लेकिन खाना लगाते हुए उसके हाथ दिखाई पड़ रहे थे। दो उँगलियों में सोने की अँगूठियाँ, एक हाथ में सोने की चूड़ियाँ, काँच की चूड़ियों के बीच में, दूसरे हाथ में काले रेशमी फीते से बँधी छोटी सी रिस्ट वाच स्पष्ट दिखाई दे रही थी। उसने काँपते हुए हाथों से खाने की थाली बढ़ाई तो भाभी ने संभलकर समर की ओर सरका दी। थाली में दो पतली-पतली रोटियाँ, तीन साग, एक दाल, रायता, दो चटनियाँ, पापड़ और अचार। मुस्कराते हुए समर ने पानी पिया और पहला टुकड़ा रोटी में से तोड़कर दाल में डुबोकर कर मुँह में डाला तो 'ओ-ओ' करता हुआ बाहर भागा और बाहर वह कौर उलट दिया। सभी पूछने लगे कि क्या हुआ। समर ने झल्लाकर कहा कि दाल कड़वी जहर कर रखी है। उसने एक टुकड़ा तोड़कर माथे से लगाया और थाली में ठोकर मारी कि कटोरियाँ उछलकर नीचे गिरीं। समर जल्दी से बाहर चला गया।

पूरा दोष प्रभा के सिर पर लगा जबकि वह बार-बार कहती रही कि दाल चख ली थी ऐसा कुछ भी नहीं था। भाभी ने खूब ताना मारा। मुन्नी ने बाद में समर को बताया कि भैया भाभी ने दाल में एक मुट्ठी नमक डाल दिया था। समर को प्रभा पर दया आई और अपने किये पर शर्मिन्दगी।

प्रश्न 6. समर के विवाह के बाद कौन-सा कठोर यथार्थ सामने आ गया था ? मुन्नी सबसे अभागिन क्यों है ?

उत्तर—विवाह में समर की जिद्द के कारण पहले से कोई सौदा न किया जा सका और जितनी उम्मीद थी उतना मिला नहीं। इसलिए अम्मा अक्सर ही कहतीं, "कहें क्या चन्दन (समर का मामा) शादी के तो सारे होंसले ही मर गये।" मामाजी ने ही शादी कराई थी।

विवाह के दिनों का सारा दिखावा समाप्त हो चुका था और अब वही कठोर यथार्थ आ गया था। चीनी वाले, गेहूँ वाले सभी को पैसे देने में घर में रोज महाभारत होता। अक्सर ही बिना किसी कारण, बाबूजी अम्मा और भाई साहब से कहते रहते, "अब आगे क्या होगा, इस पर भी सोचा ?" उन्हें पच्चीस रुपये पेंशन मिलती थी और महँगाई भत्ता सब मिलाकर निन्यानवें रुपये भाई साहब को गिलते थे। अम्मा चारपाई पर बैठी-बैठी माला जपती हुई घर के खर्चे और पढ़ाई के खर्चे का रोना रोती रहती थीं।

इस घर में मुन्नी ही सबसे अभागिन है। समर से वह दो साल छोटी है। दो तीन साल पहले सोलह-सत्रह की उम्र में पढ़ाई छुड़वाकर उसकी शादी कर दी। कुछ चीजें बेचकर और भाई साहब को मिले सामान को मिलाकर दहेज दे दिया। लेकिन ससुराल में उसे कोई सुख नहीं मिला। ससुराल से उसके बड़े ही करुणामय खत आते। यहाँ आती तो बिलख-बिलख कर रोती। सास और पति मिलकर जो-जो अत्याचार करते, उन्हें किसी से कह भी नहीं सकती थी। एक डेढ़ साल तो किसी तरह उसने काट लिया, लेकिन सास के मरते ही उसके पति ने दूसरी औरत लाकर घर में रख ली। सुनते हैं कोई ब्राह्मण जाति की थी। नौकरानी की तरह मुन्नी घर में टहला करती रहती थी। दो-दो, तीन-तीन दिन तक उसे खाना नहीं देता था।

एक दिन शरीर पर बेंतों के निशान लिए हुए मुन्नी अपने मायके आ गई। तब से वह यहीं है। समर को मुन्नी के पति पर बहुत क्रोध आता। मुन्नी पता नहीं कुछ सोचती है या नहीं। अधिक-से-अधिक चुप और तटस्थ रहना उसका स्वभाव बन गया है। न जाने क्या-क्या उलटा सीधा सोचती रहती है। वह दिन पर दिन कमजोर होती जा रही है। शायद जिंदगी भर उसे यहीं रहना है। बाबूजी ने उस आदमी को न जाने कितना लिखा है, शहर और बाहर बिरादरी के प्रमुख लोगों द्वारा उस पर बहुत दबाव डलवाने की कोशिश की है, लेकिन कुछ नहीं हुआ। इतनी पढ़ी-लिखी भी नहीं है कि कुछ कर सके। सिलाई-कढ़ाई सीखने में भी दो-एक

साल लग जायेंगे फिर इतना पैसा भी नहीं है। मुन्नी जब आई-आई थी तो सभी उसके प्रति हमदर्दी दिखाते, उसकी हिम्मत बढ़ाते थे। अब तो प्राय: सभी भूल चुके हैं। हाँ ! अगर नहीं भूली है तो वह स्वयं घर के ऊपर बोझ है।

प्रश्न 7. बोर्ड की फीस भरने के लिए समर ने किससे रुपये माँगे ? उसे इस बारे में क्या-क्या सुनना पड़ा ?

उत्तर—समर को अपने इम्तिहान की बोर्ड की फीस भरनी थी। वह बोर्ड की फीस माँगने अम्मा के पास गया तो पच्चीस रुपये का नाम सुनकर अम्मा का मुँह खुला रह गया। "हाय इतने रुपये मेरे पास कहाँ हैं भैया ! अपने बाबूजी से ही माँगना।" वह बाबूजी से नहीं माँगना चाहता था। एक बार भाभी से माँगने की बात मन में आई कि उनके पास पच्चीस-तीस रुपये तो रखे ही होंगे। जरूरत के लिए पर वे उन्हें देंगी नहीं।

आखिर बाबूजी के पास ही जाना पड़ा। साँझ घिरे बाबूजी एक खाट की अदवायन को कस रहे थे। समर ने कहा कि बोर्ड की फीस जानी है। बाबूजी ने पूछा कि कितनी फीस भरनी है। समर ने जवाब दिया—पच्चीस रुपये। उन्होंने हुंकार भरी और फिर एक रस्सी को खींचा। उसे कुहनी से दबाकर बोले—"ये मेरी पेंशन के पच्चीस रुपये आये हैं, सो इन्हें तुम ले लो। हमारा क्या है, हमें तो हड्डे पेलने हैं जिन्दीग भर सो तुम्हारे लिए करेंगे। करम में लिखा के लाये थे कि लड़के धींगरे-ऊँट हो जायें तब तक खिलाना, सो खिलायेंगे। कल-परसों अमर रो रहा था कि उसकी फीस जानी है, अभी दिवाली गई है खर्चे के मारे ढेर हुआ जा रहा है। कमाने वाला वही एक धीरज है, सो उसे तुम. . .।" उन्होंने कमीज के भीतर हाथ डालकर बनियान की जेब से नोट निकाले, और बिना गिने ही उसके सामने खाट पर डाल दिये और बोले—"अब उठा लो इन्हें, यों खड़े-खड़े मेरा मुँह क्यों ताक रहे हो ?" समर की हिम्मत नहीं थी कि इतना सुनने के बाद सामने पड़े नोटों को उठा ले। उसके मन में आया कि यों ही उल्टे पैर चला जाऊँ और इस सारी पढ़ाई लिखाई में लात मारकर कहीं से लाकर रुपयों का इतना बड़ा ढेर लगा दूँ कि इन लोगों का भी मन भर जाये।

एक बार उसे यों ही खड़ा देखकर बाबूजी ने सिर झुका लिया फिर एकदम बदले स्वर में बोले, "कितनी परेशानियाँ हैं समर। तुम्हीं सोचो। हमारा ही दिल जानता है। बताओ मैं क्या करूँ ? कहीं दुबारा नौकरी करने की हाथ पैरों में दम नहीं है। इधर उस धीरज की बहू के दिन भी पूरे हो रहे हैं. . .जान को एक नई आफत। बड़ी बहू का पहला बच्चा है, तुम जानो कम खर्च होगा ? सारे बच्चे स्कूल कॉलेज जाने वाले हैं। ठीक समय पर उन्हें भी खाना-पहनना होना चाहिए। तुम्हारी अम्मा चूल्हे में सिर झोंकते-झोंकते इस हालत को आ गई है। बुढ़ापे का शरीर। बहुत किया उस बेचारी ने भी। तीसियों साल से बिना साँस लिए वही तो करती रही है। न हो तो जरा जाकर अपनी बहू को ही लिवा लाओ। कुछ तो मदद मिलेगी। अब मुन्नी को भी यहीं रहना है। सारी बिरादरी के लोग थूकते हैं, लेकिन करें क्या, एक मुसीबत है।"

बाबूजी की स्थिति देखकर उन पर दया आई। अगर वे चिड़चिड़े हो गये हैं तो इसमें उन बेचारों का कसूर नहीं है। समर ने रुपये उठा लिए और चला गया।

प्रश्न 8. दूसरी बार छोटी बहू आई है और सारा काम उसी से कराने की योजनाएँ बन गई हैं। ऐसा क्यों है ?

उत्तर—अमर छोटी भाभी को मायके से ले आया है। समर ने यह पूर्ण विश्वास था कि प्रभा ने अपने मायके में उसकी शिकायत जरूर की होगी क्योंकि उसने (समर) उसके (प्रभा) साथ अनुचित व्यवहार किया था। समर ने अमर से इस बारे में पूछा तो अमर ने बताया कि वहाँ तो सब उसकी तारीफ करते हैं। वे बस यही कह रहे थे कि कितनी पढ़ाई और रह गई है। प्रभा के जाने से उनकी पढ़ाई का नुकसान तो नहीं होगा। उन्हें तो उसकी पढ़ाई से खुशी होगी। आत्म-प्रशंसा सुनकर समर खुश तो हुआ, लेकिन उसकी समझ में नहीं आ रहा था कि यह सब कैसे हुआ ? अमर ने बताया कि वे कह रहे थे कि प्रभा कमजोर हो गई है, कुछ तबियत यदि खराब हो तो दवा दिलवा दें और ध्यान रखने को कहलवाया है।

यहाँ बाबूजी कह रहे थे कि ठीक समय पर खाना-पीना मिल जायेगा। दूसरी बार बहू आई है और सारा काम-काज उसी से कराने की योजनाएँ बन गई हैं। कम-से-कम दो-एक बार तो आ जाने देते। ऐसा समर सोच रहा है कि उसके घर का रवैया अजब है।

समर को यह विश्वास नहीं हो पा रहा था कि प्रभा ने उसके बारे में कुछ नहीं कहा होगा। अगर उसने कुछ भी कहा होता तो अमर से ताने में ढालकर किसी न किसी तरह कह जरूर दी जाती और लोगों के बारे में भी तो कहा ही गया। समर को इस बात पर अपनी मूर्खता समझकर क्रोध आ रहा था कि जी भरकर उसका चेहरा भी नहीं देखा। घर पहुँचते ही मुन्नी ने बताया कि भाभी आ गई है। घर के सब लोग खुश थे कि घर में काम करने के लिए एक व्यक्ति आ गया है। घर का ज्यादातर काम प्रभा से ही कराया जाने लगा। मुन्नी तो काम के मारे घबराती थी और भाभी अपने को बड़ी मानकर सास के स्थान पर रखकर काम नहीं करना चाहती थी। घर में ऐसा कोई नहीं था जो सोचता कि प्रभा भी तो इंसान है, उसे भी तो कुछ आराम की जरूरत है। प्रभा भी चुपचाप अपने काम में लगी रहती। उसे यह सब अखरता था कि किसी के अन्दर संवेदना नहीं है। उसका पति भी उसकी उपेक्षा करता है। उससे बोलता भी नहीं है। बोलता भी है तो बस एक-दो शब्द जितने की जरूरत होती। जिसके सहारे उसके माता-पिता ने उसे इस घर में भेजा है, वहीं उससे अलग-अलग सा रहता है। उसे इस घर में वह सम्मान और प्यार नहीं मिला जिसकी कि वह हकदार है।

समर बाहर से आकर सीधा अपनी कोठरी में गया। मन में उत्सुकता हुई कि क्या-क्या नई चीजें आ गई हैं। अब तो वह इसी कोठरी में आयेगी क्योंकि उन दोनों के लिए यही कोठरी नियुक्त थी। उसने मन में सोचा कि अब तो बोलना ही पड़ेगा देर से या जल्दी।

प्रश्न 9. ''जबरदस्ती वहीं कहीं जाकर सो जाऊँ ? मुझसे तो नहीं होता जिठानी जी, कि कोई दुत्काराता रहे और पूँछ हिलाते रहो, ठोकर मारता रहे और तलुए चाटते रहो। उनके बोर्ड के इम्तिहान हैं, मैं क्यों तंग करूँ ?'' ऐसा प्रभा ने क्यों कहा ? क्या उसे अपने तिरस्कार का दुःख है या उसके हृदय की वेदना बाहर निकल रही है ?

उत्तर—प्रभा के ऐसा कहने से पता चलता है कि उसके हृदय में अपने तिरस्कार, अपमान की वेदना है जो शब्दों के रूप में बाहर निकल रही है। जिसके भरोसे वह इस घर में आई है, वही उससे नहीं बोलता है इससे बड़ा दुःख और क्या होगा ? अपने दुःख-दर्द को वह कहना चाहे तो किससे कहे। यह कैसी विडम्बना है कि पति अपनी नव विवाहिता पत्नी से बोल नहीं रहा है। जबकि नई बहू की कोई गलती नहीं है। यदि समर को शादी से कोई परेशानी थी तो वह शादी करने से ही मना कर देता। लेकिन शादी करने के बाद बहू का अपमान करे यह बात सही नहीं, कोई भी व्यक्ति इस बात की प्रशंसा नहीं करेगा। यह तो अपनी पत्नी का जीवन अन्धकार में डालने वाली बात हुई।

छत के दूसरे सिरे से भाभी का स्वर सुनाई पड़ा—''नहीं, प्रभा, वहीं जाकर सोओ। चारपाई न हो तो मैं डाले आती हूँ। यहाँ अभी तुम्हारे जेठजी आते होंगे।'' जब भाभी ने उससे पूछा कि आखिर वह समर की कोठरी में सोना क्यों नहीं चाहती ? तब प्रभा ने यह जवाब दिया कि जबरदस्ती वहाँ जाकर क्यों सोये ? वहाँ उसका कोई सम्मान नहीं होता, बल्कि अपमान होता है।

प्रभा के प्रत्येक शब्द के जहर-बुझे तीर जैसा दम्भ और अहंकार घनघनाता था ऐसा समर को लगा। वह उसके दिल के जख्म को समझ नहीं पाया। इन शब्दों का मतलब ही उसने उलटा निकाला। प्रभा ने तो अपनी हकीकत बयान की थी कुछ इस लहजे में कि उसके पति का उसके प्रति व्यवहार उसे कतई पसन्द नहीं है। यह उसके आत्मसम्मान को ठेस पहुँचाने वाला है। कोई भी स्वाभिमानी स्त्री ऐसा अपमान क्यों बर्दाश्त करेगी ? अब तक तो प्रभा ने बड़े धीरज से काम लिया है कोई प्रतिवाद नहीं किया। आज पहली बार जिठानी के पूछने पर ही उसने अपने हृदय की पीड़ा को बताया है।

इन शब्दों का मान लो समर पर प्रतिकूल प्रभाव पड़ा हो, लेकिन समर तो पहले से ही उसके समर्थन में नहीं था। वह तो यहाँ तक निश्चय कर चुका था कि उसे इस स्त्री से कोई सम्बन्ध ही नहीं रखना है।

प्रश्न 10. घर में बच्चा होने के समय से ही लोग क्या-क्या आशाएँ लगाये थे। बाबूजी का क्या विचार था ? बच्ची के होने पर उन्हें किस बात पर सन्तोष हुआ ?

उत्तर—समर ने नहा-धोकर भाभी से कहा कि वही क्यों सब काम करती है, घर में और भी तो लोग हैं। अगर सबको खाने का हक है तो काम के लिए बाहर से आदमी तो नहीं बुलाये जायेंगे। मुन्नी भी मदद कर सकती है। उसने देखा कि प्रभा रात के जूठे बर्तनों के ढेर के पास बैठी बर्तन साफ कर रही है। समर को सन्तोष हुआ कि अब इसकी अकड़ ठिकाने आ जायेगी। उसके बाद सारे घर का दोनों वक्त का खाना उसे ही बनाने को दे दिया गया। भाभी तो यही चाह रही थी। मुन्नी ने एक-दो दिन काम करवाया फिर बहाने बनाकर काम से दूर होने लगी। वैसे जुबानी हमदर्दी उसकी प्रभा के साथ रहती।

मुन्नी भाभी से कह रही थी—''भाभी, लल्ला होगा तो सारे कपड़े ले लूँगी। फिर तुम इधर-उधर टालो, हाँ। पहले से बात तय है।'' घर का वातावरण अजब था। महतरानी ने धोती-ब्लाउज पहले ही अपनी तरफ से लेने की घोषणा कर दी थी। जो भी आता, इसी बारे में बात करता। यों सभी चाहते थे कि लड़का ही हो, और इसीलिए सारे समय लड़के की ही बातें करते। वैसे सबको विश्वास यही था कि लड़का ही होगा। घर में पहला पोता होगा, इसलिए खुश तो अम्मा बाबूजी सभी थे; लेकिन उसके खर्चे की कल्पना करते तो यही कहते, ''भगवान जाने क्या होगा।'' क्योंकि उस हालत में दुनिया भर के खर्चे होंगे, एक बड़ी-सी दावत देनी पड़ेगी। इस प्रकार लड़का-लड़की के विश्वास-अविश्वास में दिन गुजर रहे थे।

एक रात को बारह बजे खूब भाग-दौड़ के बाद भाभी ने पुत्री को जन्म दिया। अम्मा ने माथे पर हाथ मारकर कहा, ''लो, घर में पहली भवानी ही आई।'' ऊपर से सभी खुश होने का नाटक कर रहे थे। पता नहीं भाभी को कैसा लगा ? लेकिन बाबूजी ने तो निश्चय ही प्रसन्नता की दबी साँस छोड़ी, तत्कालिक खर्चा बचा। अब कोई कहेगा तो कह देंगे, लड़की होने पर कोई मिठाई-दावत माँगता होगा। उनके विचार से घर में पहली डिग्री आ गई थी। समर को तो इस बात से खुशी हुई कि प्रभा के ऊपर काम बढ़ गया है। प्रभा के ज्यादा काम करने पर उसे खुशी होती—ऐसी कुछ प्रवृत्ति उसने बना ली थी। उसने ठीक से प्रभा को समझाने की कोशिश ही नहीं की। भाभी को सेवा-सुश्रूषा के लिए एक आदमी चाहिए। अम्मा तो अपनी आयु और बीमारी की बात बता कर हाथ में माला फेरती रहतीं, लेकिन घर की पूरी खोज-खबर रखती थीं।

प्रभा सुबह न जाने कब उठकर भाभी के लिए हरीरा बनाना शुरू कर देती। सुबह छः बजे तक प्रायः उनके सारे काम पूरे हो जाते। फिर रात के बर्तन आदि साफ होते, चौका धुलता और नहा-धोकर जल्दी ही रसोई में घुस जाती कि कॉलेज जाने वालों को खाने के लिए देर न हो जाये। बारह बजे तक खाना बन जाता और फिर चौका-बर्तन का काम निपटा देती। घर के पूरे काम में रात के साढ़े ग्यारह-बारह बज जाते। इस बात पर समर को आश्चर्य होता कि सब काम प्रभा चुपचाप मशीन की तरह करती थी। हर नये काम को ऐसी स्वाभाविकता से ग्रहण करती चली जाती कि लगता ही नहीं था कि उसे वह काम करने में कहीं भी अनिच्छा या थकान है।

प्रश्न 11. घर में किस बात का बवाल मचा ? समर पर क्या प्रभाव पड़ा और उसने फिर क्या किया ? क्या उसे बाद में अपने किये पर पश्चाताप हुआ ?

उत्तर—नामकरण का दिन बहुत व्यस्त दिन होता है। दुनिया भर के काम होते हैं घर में। सब लोग इधर-उधर भागते रहते हैं। शाम को समर घर आया तो देखा कि घर में खूब हल्ला-गुल्ला मचा हुआ है। अम्मा बुरी तरह चिल्ला-चिल्लाकर कह रही है, ''जब तक कुछ कहें नहीं तो सिर पर चढ़ी चली आती है, दुनिया का सारा काम तुम्हारे ही मन से तो होगा ? हम तो कुछ हैं ही नहीं। हम तो सब इतने बड़े मूर्ख हैं। बस ज्ञान

तो एक तू ही घुट्टी में पीकर आई है। सगुन-साइत के दिन क्या करके धरा है ? बोलो, हमें पता भी नहीं और वहाँ इतना सब हो भी लिया।''

सब सहमे से एक ओर खड़े थे। कोठरी में अपनी चारपाई पर पड़ी भाभी खूब फूट-फूटकर रो रही थी, ''आग लगे ऐसी पढ़ाई में। पढ़ाई अपने लिए होगी कि दूसरे की जान लेने की होगी। हाय राम, पता नहीं अब क्या होने वाला है ?'' मुन्नी एक ओर खड़ी चुपचाप देख रही थी। समर इतना तो समझ ही गया कि कोई गम्भीर बात हुई है ? अपराधी की तरह खड़ी प्रभा ने धीरे से कहा, ''अम्माजी मुझे पता होता तो मैं कभी भी ऐसा नहीं करती। मैंने समझा कि कोई सादा मिट्टी का ढेला है।'' अम्माजी और गरम हो गई कि तुझे दिखाई थोड़े ही दिया था कि उस ढेले पर कलावा बँधा हुआ था। जवाब देने को तो सबसे ऊपर है। मुन्नी ने समर को बताया कि पण्डित जी ने मिट्टी के ढेले में कलावा बाँधकर गणेशजी बनाये थे तो भाभी ने उसे मिट्टी का ढेला समझकर जूठे बर्तन माँज लिए। इस बात पर सभी परेशान थे कि कोई अशुभ घटना घट सकती है।

समर क्रोध में भर गया और दाहिने हाथ से पूरी शक्ति से प्रभा के गाल पर तमाचा ऐसा मारा कि उसके गाल पर पाँचों उँगलियाँ उभर आईं। वह एक ओर झोंका खाकर गिरते-गिरते सँभली और यों ही धम से नीचे बैठ गई। समर ने कहा, ''हरामजादी, यहाँ रहना है तो ठीक से रहो। नहीं तो जहाँ जगह दीखे अभी चली जाओ। बड़ी नास्तिक की बच्ची बनी है।'' ये शब्द प्रभा के हृदय में चुभ गये, लेकिन वह कुछ बोली नहीं। सब लोग यह देखकर स्तब्ध रह गये।

लेकिन चाँटा मारने के बाद ऐसी आत्मग्लानि का झटका समर को लगा कि वहाँ वह ठहर नहीं सका। कोठरी के भीतर आकर वह पश्चाताप के समुद्र में डूबने-उतराने लगा। यह कार्य बड़ा अमानुषिक और निंदनीय था जोश में आकर उसने सबके सामने चाँटा मार तो दिया, लेकिन अब अपनी करनी पर पश्चाताप की आग में जलने लगा। न जाने किस आवेश में वह ऐसा कर गया। सात-आठ महीने में पहली बार उससे बोला और वह भी गाली से। बार-बार उसकी आत्मा उसे धिक्कार रही थी।

प्रश्न 12. काम के बारे में अम्मा ने क्या-क्या ताने प्रभा को मारे और धोती के बारे में क्या प्रवचन दिया ?

उत्तर—बाहर का एक-आध काम समर को भी करना पड़ता। वह दिवाकर के यहाँ अक्सर चला जाता पढ़ने क्योंकि उसके पास अलग कमरा था। अतः दोनों साथ-साथ बैठकर पढ़ते। समर के घर में तो बिल्कुल भी शान्ति नहीं थी। जब भी घर जाता तो या तो कोई तकरार हो रही होती या हो चुकी होती। प्रभा का चेहरा उसने सदैव अपरिवर्तनीय और भावहीन देखा। हमेशा गम्भीर चेहरा लोगों को पसन्द भी नहीं आता।

जब वह दिवाकर के घर से लौटा तो अम्मा उसे समझा रही थी कि कभी-कभी तो सिर को धो लिया करे। उसने हिम्मत करके कह ही दिया—''अम्माजी, अब तुम्हीं बताओ किस वक्त धोऊँ ?'' इतने कहने पर ही अम्मा भड़क उठीं और उल्टा-सीधा सुनाने लगीं। जैसे—''ओहो, अब तो ये जताने लगी कि मैं इतना काम करूँ, क्यों ? वाह री ! अच्छी बहू है, तू तो काम के ताने देने लगी। अरे, तुझे अपना काम करने की फुर्सत नहीं मिलती ? खाने की तो मिल ही जाती है ना ? जरा गिना तो दे मुझे, ऐसा कौन-सा काम करै तू ? दोनों बखत की रोटी ही का काम, एक काम कह लो। सो इसमें चाहो तो सारा दिन लगा दो। मुझे तो बता, कौन सा घर है, जहाँ बहुएँ काम नहीं करतीं ? भैना, तेरे बाप के यहाँ दस नौकर लगे होंगे, हमारे यहाँ तो सब बहुएँ ही करेंगी काम।'' समर नल के पास कोयले से दाँत साफ कर रहा था। भाभी जो हमेशा कुछ-न-कुछ भिड़ाती रहती थी, ने उसकी तरफ इशारा करके कहा, ''देख लो जरा-सा काम क्या करना पड़ा, रोज हल्ले करवा रही है। बोलो हम नहीं करते थे ? कहा किसी भी दिन अम्माजी ने कुछ ? जरा-सी करने क्या लगी, एहसान जता रहा है, एहसान। मेरे काम काम का तो एहसान जताइयो मती बहू, जितना तूने किया है मैं तो सब ब्याज समेत चुका दूँगी। हाँ, कहीं कल को कहे. . .''

यह सब इसलिए सुनाया जा रहा था कि प्रभा तो कुछ काम करती ही नहीं, जबकि बेचारी सुबह से लेकर रात तक घर के काम में खटती रहती। उधर भाई साहब बोले कि इस घर में चख-चख होती रहती है। दिन निकला और शुरू हो गई। उनकी बात को किसी ने नहीं सुना पर अम्माजी ने यह स्पष्ट कर दिया कि चख-चख होती रहती है, तब तो यह हाल है, न हो तो घर का पटरा ही बैठ जाये। उनका कहने का मतलब था कि यहाँ तो सभी लातों के देवता हैं। जब तक कुछ कहो नहीं क्या मजाल कि पत्ता भी हिल जाये।

अब धोती को ले बैठीं कि धोती फट रही है पर सिली नहीं जायेगी। मैल के मारे चीखट हो रही है, पर धुलेगी नहीं। उलटा प्रभा से ही पूछने लगीं कि उसे फटी और मैली धोती दिखाई नहीं देती क्या ? या यों कहो कि धोने के नाम पर दम निकलता है। कौन मेहनत करे। वहाँ तो पलंग पर बिठा दो और हाथ में पकड़ा दो किताब. . .। यह सब अम्माजी ताने भरे स्वर में कह गईं कि जैसे सच ही कह रही हैं। इतना सब सुनने के बाद भी प्रभा का चुप रहना उसके संस्कार का ही द्योतक है। अम्मा और भाभी का उसके प्रति व्यवहार कतई उचित और शिष्ट नहीं है। सब काम करते हुए भी इस तरह के ताने कसे जायें तो बेचारी कहाँ तक सहे। सब कुछ सहना उसकी मजबूरी है कि उसका पति भी उसकी बात नहीं सुनता है। वह उसके दु:ख दर्द में सहायक नहीं है। उसने निरपराध प्रभा को गँवार और अशिक्षित घरवालों के रहम-करम पर छोड़ दिया है। फिर भी प्रभा धैर्यवान है जो बात-बात पर बिफर नहीं जाती और न ही किसी से अपने प्रति किये गये कटाक्षों और अधिक काम की शिकायत करती। जो बुरा व्यवहार उसके पति, भाभी, बाबूजी और अम्माजी ने किया है वह अपेक्षित नहीं था। दहेज न मिलने के ताने भी उसे सुनने पड़ते, पर बेचारी सब कुछ बर्दाश्त करती और अपना काम करती रहती।

प्रश्न 13. मुन्नी के पति के आने से घर में क्या हलचल मच गई ? बाबूजी की घर वालों से क्या बातें हुई और क्या निर्णय लिया गया ?

उत्तर—भाग्यहीन मुन्नी की कहानी बड़ी दु:खभरी है। उसकी पढ़ाई छुड़वाकर उसकी शादी कर दी गई थी। उसकी ससुराल अच्छी नहीं थी। उसका पति उसे मारता-पीटता था। एक दिन जब दूसरी औरत को वह घर में ले आया तो मुन्नी को बर्दाश्त नहीं हुआ और वह अपने मायके चली आई। सबने उसके शरीर पर मार पड़ने के नील देखे और दु:खी होकर रहने लगे।

एक दिन अचानक मुन्नी के पति उसे लेने के लिए आ गये। उनके यहाँ आने से पूरे घर में हलचल मच गई। सब हक्के-बक्के रह गये। बाबूजी और मुन्नी के पति में बात-चीत शुरू हुईं। हर कोई यह जानने को उत्सुक था कि क्या बातें हो रही हैं। भाभीजी और अम्मा धीरे-धीरे बातें कर रही थीं और बार-बार कुँवर को बाहर भेजतीं कि जा चुपके से सुनके आ कि बाबूजी और उनमें क्या-क्या बात हो रही हैं ? सभी इस अप्रत्याशित हृदय परिवर्तन का कारण जानना चाहते थे। बैठक में काफी गम्भीरतापूर्वक बातें चल रही थीं।

रात का खाना इत्यादि खिला चुकने के बाद बाबूजी ने आकर अम्मा को सूचना दी, "कल मुन्नी जायेगी, सुबह दस बजे की गाड़ी से।" यह सुनकर सारे घर में सन्नाटा छा गया। अम्मा ने इतनी देर मामला जानने की प्रतीक्षा में जो कष्ट सहा था, इससे वे झल्ला रही थीं। झुँझलाकर बोलीं—"बैठो तो सही, कुछ बतलाओगे भी कि चले आये, कल मुन्नी जायेगी। ऐसी क्या आफत आ गई अब निपूते पर ? दो साल कौन सी मक्खी छींक गई थी ?" यह उन्होंने जोर से नहीं कहा क्योंकि बैठक तक उनकी आवाज न पहुँचे। बाबूजी खाट पर बैठ गये। जमीन पर छोटी-सी लालटेन रखी थी। मुन्नी एक ओर दीवार से लगी पहले ही बैठी थी। जबरदस्ती बच्ची को सुलाकर घूँघट निकाले भाभी भी आ गई थी। समर, भाई साहब, अमर और कुँवर वहीं पास में बैठ गये। बाबूजी ने कहना शुरू किया, "भई वह मुन्नी को लेने आया है। बहुत माफी-वाफी माँग रहा है, अफसोस जाहिर कर रहा है कि गलती हो गई, अब कभी ऐसा नहीं होगा। अगर ऐसी बात सुनी तो कान पकड़ लेना। जो बिरादरी का दण्ड होगा, भरूँगा। जब रुआँसा हो आया तो मैं क्या करता।" अम्मा ने अपने जमाई के लिए जिन शब्दों का इस्तेमाल किया उसके लिए वह सर्वथा योग्य था। अम्मा का कहना था, "तो

आखिर कुछ बात भी कि यों ही रुआँसा-सा हो आया ? अब आचनक कौन-सी अकल-दाढ़ फूट आई उस कम्बख्त के ? उस चुड़ैल को क्या हुआ ?''

बाबूजी ने बताया कि उस चुड़ैल के कारण ही तो अकल आई है। सब कपड़े-जेबर समेट कर भाग गई। इसलिए उसका दिमाग ठिकाने लगा है। कुँवर ने झल्लाकर मुन्नी को न भेजने की बात कही। लेकिन उसकी बात को गम्भीरता से नहीं लिया गया। पूरी पंचायत में कोई भी मुन्नी को भेजने को राजी नहीं था सिवाय बाबूजी के। अम्मा ने क्रोध में कहा, ''अब ऐसे आदमी का ठीक क्या है ? कल किसी दूसरे के बहकावे में आ जायेगा। मैं तो अपनी बेटी को नहीं भेजती। पहले अधमरी कर दिया था, अब तो मार ही डालेगा।''

बाबूजी ने फिर समझाया कि अब लगता है उसे समझ आ गई है। उससे सारी बातें साफ-साफ करली हैं। अम्मा को राजी न होने पर बाबूजी ने उन्हें डाँट दिया। उन्हें विश्वास हो गया था कि अब वह मुन्नी को ठीक से रखेगा। और फिर यहाँ भी इतना नहीं है कि मुन्नी को पढ़ा-लिखा सकें या कोई हुनर सिखा दें कि कुछ काम करने लगे। आखिर कब तक रखेंगे। बिरादरी वाले भी इधर-उधर की बातें करते हैं। या फिर हम लोग मुन्नी की दूसरी शादी कर दें। इस पर अम्मा क्रोधित हुईं कि बच्चों के सामने ऐसी बातें करते हैं। इतने में ही मुन्नी के फूट-फूट कर रोने की आवाज आने लगी। सबके पूछने पर बड़ी मुश्किल से उसने रोते-रोते कहा, ''बाबूजी, तुम मुझे अपने हाथ से जहर देकर मार डालो, मेरा गला घोंट दो. . . मुझे वहाँ मत भेजो—मुझे वहाँ मत भेजो बाबूजी मैं वहाँ मर जाऊँगी. . . मैं तुम्हारे हाथ जोड़ती हूँ। पाँव पड़ती हूँ . . . मुझे कहीं मत जाने दो। '' और फिर वह बाबूजी के पैरों से लिपट गई और बिलख-बिलख कर रोने लगी। सब लोगों की आँखों में आँसू भर गये। सभी को यह सोचकर कष्ट हो रहा था कि इतनी दु:खी लड़की के प्रति उनकी कितनी उपेक्षाएँ रहीं फिर बाबूजी ने उसे समझाया कि यह घर भी उसी का है, कोई ऐसी-वैसी बात देखे तो तुरन्त यहाँ चली आये।

इस तरह समझा बुझाकर मुन्नी को उसके पति के साथ भेज दिया गया।

प्रश्न 14. समर और भाई साहब घर के भीतर गये तो क्या देखा ? इस पर अम्मा की क्या प्रतिक्रिया थी ?

उत्तर—समर और भाई साहब घर के भीतर गये तो देखा कि सिर झुकाये ही सामने प्रभा अपराधिनी की मुद्रा में खड़ी है और बाबूजी दुर्वासा का रूप धारण किये हाथ ऊँचे उठा-उठाकर गरज रहे हैं। अम्मा भी इसमें कभी-कभी सहयोग दे देती है। भाभी भी घूँघट निकाले किवाड़ के पीछे छिपी खड़ी हैं। बाबूजी ने इन दोनों को देखकर फिर से किस्से को दुहरा दिया, ''और कोई जगह दाल बीनने की रह ही नहीं गई, दाल छत पर ही बिनेगी। ऐसे ही उस दिन छत पर बाल्टी ले जाकर सिर धोया गया। उस दिन तो मैं चुप हो गया, मुन्नी ने सिफारिश कर दी। बस, अब तो खाना-सोना सभी छत पर होने लगा। हमेशा गूँगी की तरह मनहूस-सी घूमती रहेगी, आँखें चुराती रहेगी।'' उनका तात्पर्य था कि वह बार-बार छत पर क्यों जाती है। उनके विचार से प्रभा के क्या दिमाग हैं समझ में नहीं आता। उन्हें औरतों का छत पर जाना पसन्द नहीं है। जाड़े के दिन हैं। बीस आदमी छत पर धूप खाने के बहाने से ताक-झाँक करते हैं। बहू कायदे से रहे। जैसा वह चाहते हैं वैसा ही कार्य करे। बाबूजी भी शक्की दिमाग के आदमी हैं और पुराने ख्यालों को आधुनिक लोगों पर लादना चाहते हैं। इतने बड़े होकर अपनी बहू को गूँगी और मनहूस कहना उन्हें शोभा नहीं देता। यह उनके गँवारपने को ही जाहिर करता है।

इसी प्रकार अम्मा का व्यवहार भी बहू प्रभा के प्रति अच्छा नहीं है। उनकी बोली भी अशिष्ट, अनचाही और असभ्य है। बुजुर्गी के हिसाब से उनकी बोली उचित नहीं है। अपनी ही बहू से यह कह देना कि वह छत पर बैठी रहती है इसलिए पड़ोसियों के नैना लड़ते रहते हैं। आखिर वह क्यों भाग-भाग कर छत पर जाती है। प्रभा पर तमाम पाबन्दियाँ लगा दी हैं जैसे यह कर, यह मत कर। प्रभा के हृदय में उनके ताने तीर की तरह चुभ

रहे थे। लेकिन चुपचाप खड़ी सभी प्रहार सह रही थी। फिर जिक्र हुआ कि मुहल्ले के पण्डित जी की लड़की किसी के साथ भाग गई है। अम्माजी इस बात पर जमाने को कोसने लगीं। भाई साहब का विचार तो यह था कि पढ़ी-लिखी लड़कियाँ ही ऐसा काम करती हैं। अम्मा ने असहज होकर कहा, ''हमारी तरफ से दुनिया भाड़ में जाये, लेकिन ये भाग-भाग कर ऊपर क्यों जाती है ? इसका वहाँ कौन बैठा है ? खबरदार जो आज से उधर पैर रखा, मुझसे बुरा कोई न होगा।'' इसके बाद भी अम्मा के कटु शब्द निकलते रहे। जो नहीं कहना चाहिए था, वह भी कह गईं। यहाँ तक कह दिया कि वह मरे तो लड़के की दूसरी शादी कर दूँ।

क्या ऐसा कहना उचित था ? एक बुजुर्ग व्यक्ति को ऐसा बोलना निहायत ही गैर जिम्मेदाराना और असभ्य था। ऐसा लगता है कि किसी पुरानी खुंदस का बदला वह प्रभा से अपनी तीखे और कटु वचनों से ले रही हैं।

समर को अम्माजी का व्यवहार बुरा तो लग रहा था, लेकिन वह तटस्थ ही रहा और यह सोच लिया कि यहाँ तो रोज ऐसे ही झगड़े होते रहते हैं। कहाँ तक कोई उनकी तरफ ध्यान दे।

प्रश्न 15. निम्न पात्रों का चरित्र चित्रण कीजिए—

(1) समर, (2) प्रभा, (3) दिवाकर, (4) बाबूजी, (5) अम्माजी।

उत्तर—(1) समर का चरित्र—समर उपन्यास 'सारा आकाश' का नायक है और प्रभा का पति है। उसका अभी विद्यार्थी जीवन चल रहा है। उसकी इच्छा के खिलाफ शादी कर दी गई है, इसलिए अपनी नव-विवाहिता पत्नी से सामीप्य नहीं बना पाता।

(i) पढ़ने वाला—प्रारम्भ में वह एक पढ़ने वाले विद्यार्थी के रूप में सामने आता है। उसकी लगन पढ़ने में है इसीलिए वह नहीं चाहता था कि उसका विवाह कर दिया जाये। उसकी इच्छा के प्रतिकूल विवाह होने से उसकी पढ़ाई में बाधा पड़ती है। घर में रोज किसी न किसी बात पर चख-चख होती रहती है इसलिए वह अक्सर अपने मित्र दिवाकर के घर पर पढ़ने के लिए चला जाता है। पढ़ने में व्यवधान न पड़े इसलिए वह अपनी पत्नी से भी बोलचाल नहीं करता। वह इण्टर में पढ़ रहा है और कॉलेज जाता है। वार्षिक परीक्षा में वह द्वितीय श्रेणी में पास हुआ। इससे प्रकट होता है कि वह पढ़ने में होशियार है।

(ii) शुरू में निराशावादी—विवाह के बाद जो उत्साह और उमंग युवकों में होता है, उसका समर में अभाव है। वह अपने साथियों से कतराता, परिचित-अपरिचितों से आँख चुराता है कि वे उससे सुहागरात के सम्बन्ध में मजाक करेंगे। वह प्रारम्भ को बोझीला मानता है और कहता है कि उसमें भागने का साहस नहीं है। उसने अपनी डायरी में लिखा था, ''मैं इतनी जल्दी अपनी हिम्मत क्यों हार जाता हूँ ? अभी से क्यों सोचता हूँ कि मेरी सारी महत्वाकांक्षाएँ मर गईं ?. . . . मुसीबतों से इतनी जल्दी घबरा जाना अच्छी आदत नहीं है।'' भाभी के कथानुसार कि लालाजी क्या सोच रहे हो ? तुम्हारी तो शादी न हुई, दुनियाभर की चिन्ताओं का बोझ तुम्हारे ऊपर आ गया हो। इस कथन से उसकी निराशा मालूम पड़ती है और लड़कों की तरह वह हँस बोल नहीं पाता जैसे उसका मन ही मर गया है। एक गहरी निराशा, सूक्ष्म किन्तु व्यापक थकान उसकी रग-रग में बैठ गई है।

(iii) शान्त स्वभाव वाला—वह घर में शान्ती चाहता है, लेकिन वह उसे घर में नहीं मिल पाती। घर में रोजाना किसी न किसी बात पर चख-चख होती रहती इसलिए वह पढ़ नहीं पाता। अक्सर पढ़ने के लिए वह दिवाकर के घर पर चला जाता है। अम्माजी और बाबूजी को तो रोज ही प्रभा के काम-काज के बारे में जली-कटी सुनानी होतीं और इस माहौल में वह अशान्त हो जाता। पढ़ाई के लिए शान्त वातावरण आवश्यक है जो समर को नहीं मिल पाता। वह सुहागरात वाले दिन से ही प्रभा से बोला नहीं। बहुत दिनों बाद उससे बोलचाल प्रारम्भ हुई। एक दिन घर के कलेश ने उसे अशान्त और क्रोधित कर दिया जिसके कारण उसने प्रभा को जोर का चाँटा मार दिया। लेकिन बाद में उसे अपने किये पर पश्चाताप हुआ।

(iv) सच्चा मित्र—वह दिवाकर का सच्चा मित्र है। उन दोनों में प्रगाढ़ता है। समर उसके घर में पढ़ने चला जाता है और कभी-कभी वहाँ खाना भी खा लेता है। वह उसका आदर करता है। जब कभी रुपयों की

आवश्यकता होती है तो दिवाकर उसे उधार रुपये भी दे देता है। दिवाकर ने उसकी नौकरी की व्यवस्था भी की। उन दोनों में खूब गहरा प्रेम है। उसने कभी भी दिवाकर की आलोचना नहीं की। कभी-कभी मजाक में दिवाकर उसके पहनावे के जरूर टोक देता। कभी सिनेमा जाते तो साथ-साथ जाते। उसे दिवाकर के पास आकर सच्चा सुख मिलता है।

(v) पुराने विचारों और पहनावे वाला—समर पुराने विचारों वाला व्यक्ति है और साधारण कपड़े पहनने वाला है। उसे चटक-मटक और फैशन वाले कपड़े पसन्द नहीं हैं और न ही वह इतना खर्च कर सकता है। दिवाकर ने एक दिन उससे कहा, "देशी और विदेशी की बात नहीं जानता, लेकिन देशीपने का नाम लेकर कार्टून जैसी सूरत बनाये रखना भी मुझे पसन्द नहीं है। मेरी बात का बुरा मत मानना, लेकिन अगर मैं पूछूँ कि ऊँची-ऊँची बिना क्रीज-इश्तरी की पतलून और गंदी सिकुड़ी कमीज या अंग्रेजी ढंग से कटे लटकती लट्ठ जैसी गाँठ वाली चोटी ही अगर देशीपना है तो हम इसे दूर से प्रणाम करते हैं।" समर ने उसे व्यक्तिगत पसन्द और विश्वास कहकर टाल दिया। उसे क्या पता कि उसके (समर) के पास बस यही कपड़े हैं।

(vi) शुरू में पत्नी के खिलाफ, बाद में प्यार करने वाला—प्रारम्भ में तो समर अपनी नव विवाहिता पत्नी के खिलाफ ही रहा क्योंकि उसकी मर्जी के खिलाफ घरवालों ने उसकी शादी कर दी थी। इसलिए वह बहुत दिनों तक उससे बोला भी नहीं। हमेशा उससे गुस्सा ही रहा। कभी उसने यह जानने की कोशिश भी नहीं कि की वह कैसे रह रही है। लेकिन उत्तरार्द्ध में वह उससे बोलने भी लगा और प्यार भी करने लगा। वह उसकी स्थिति और अधिक काम का भी ध्यान रखता और घरवालों से उसकी खातिर उलझ भी जाता।

(vii) शिरीष भाई की बातों पर विश्वास करने वाला—पहले तो शिरीष भाई की बातें समर की समझ में ही नहीं आईं। पर धीरे-धीरे वह उन पर विश्वास करने लगा। उसने हिन्दू समाज के ढाँचे के बारे में बताया कि शादी-विवाह एक पवित्र बन्धन है। शिरीष भाई ने बताया कि ऋषि मुनियों के बनाये सारे धर्म-नियम संग्राहलय में रखने लायक हैं, किसी काम में आने लायक नहीं हैं। धर्म के नाम पर पैसा कमाना, लोगों को धोखा देना ठीक नहीं है, उनके विचार से सच्चा हिन्दू सोचता या जाँचता कुछ नहीं, वह तो चाहे आध्यात्मिक ज्ञान हो या रिश्वत और ब्लैक का रुपया, सबको ग्रहण करना जानता है। शिरीष भाई के अनुसार तो मनुष्य का धर्म 'मानवता' है बाकी सब ढकोसला है। धीरे-धीरे समर भी उनकी बात मानने लगा था।

सब मिलाकर समर का चरित्र मेधावी, निराशावादी, स्वाभिमानी और अपने फैसले पर अडिग रहने वाला है। वह घर में परेशान रहता है, और बाहर जाकर खुश रहता है। उसका सम्पूर्ण जीवन निराशा और कष्टों में बीतता है। अन्त में तो वह आत्महत्या तक करने को तैयार हो जाता है लेकिन अपनी सूझ-बूझ से आत्महत्या करने से अपने को बचा लेता है।

(2) प्रभा का चरित्र—प्रभा एक आदर्श गृहणी है। उसकी उम्र अधिक नहीं है। वह सूझ-बूझ से काम लेने वाली है। दूरदर्शिता और कुशलता के गुण उसमें दिखाई देते हैं। वह धैर्यवान है और मुसीबतों में घबराती नहीं है तथा अपना अपमान सहकर भी काम करती रहती है।

(i) कुशल गृहणी—प्रभा एक कुशल गृहणी है। समर से उसका विवाह होता है। वह निम्न मध्यम-परिवार से आई है और ससुराल भी उसी हालत में मिली है, जहाँ आमदनी का अभाव है और खर्च पूरे परिवार का है। शादी के बाद स्त्री का सबसे बड़ा उत्तरदायित्व घर के प्रति ही होता है। प्रभा अपने धर्म का पूरी तरह पालन करती है। घर के हर काम को उसने सम्भाल लिया है। यहाँ तक कि आठ व्यक्तियों के बड़े परिवार के सब कामों को अकेले ही सम्भालने की हिम्मत दिखाई है। वह अपने परिवार का भला ही चाहती है।

(ii) सुन्दर शरीर और अच्छे स्वभाव वाली स्त्री—वह अपने स्वरूप से सुन्दर है और उसका स्वभाव भी अच्छा है। उसने कभी भी कोई अपशब्द अपने ससुराल के किसी व्यक्ति के लिए नहीं बोला। अपने पति से उसकी बहुत दिनों तक बिल्कुल भी बोलचाल नहीं रही। इसका कारण उसके पति का नाराज होना था। इसकी भी शिकायत उसने कभी किसी से नहीं की। समर ने अपनी सुहागरात के दिन या और किसी दिन उसका चेहरा देखने की कोशिश भी नहीं की। भाँवरों के समय उसने उसके सुन्दर पैर और खाना बनाते समय उसके गोरे

हाथ देखे। उसकी भाभी ने समर से कहा था कि उसके चेहरे पर चेचक के दागों की झाँई-सी है। लेकिन बाद में एक स्थान पर यह जिक्र आया है कि वह बड़ी बहू से सुन्दर है। मुँह दिखावनी वाले दिन भी मोहल्ले की औरतों का कहना था कि बहू तो सुन्दर है।

(iii) स्वाभिमानी—वह एक स्वाभिमानी स्त्री है। वह चाहती है कि घर के सभी लोग उसके स्वाभिमान का खयाल रखें, लेकिन ऐसा हो नहीं पाता। कई बार बाबूजी, अम्माजी और भाभी ने उसके स्वाभिमान की परवाह न कर उसकी उपेक्षा की है। वह अपमान का घूँट पीकर चुप रह जाती है पर उन लोगों का अपमान नहीं करती। वह हाथ में घड़ी पहनकर काम करती है और घरवालों के बार-बार टोकने पर भी घड़ी नहीं उतारती। न ही वह किसी से पर्दा करती है। इसमें उसकी कोई जिद्द या गलत मंशा नहीं है।

(iv) चरित्रवान स्त्री—उसका चरित्र उज्ज्वल है। पति के न बोलने पर भी वह प्रतिकार नहीं करती और घर के कामों में लगी रहती है। एक दो बार उसके ससुर ने छत पर बाल धोने और दाल बीनने के बारे में ऐतराज किया तो फिर दुबारा उसने ऐसा नहीं किया सिर्फ रोकर रह गई। मुन्नी (ननद) ने उसका पक्ष लिया। उसने अपने पति से जरूर इस बात की शिकायत की कि सभी उसके चरित्र पर उँगली उठाते हैं। उसके पति ने उसको समझाकर शान्त किया। उसने अपने सास, ससुर और जेठानी का आदर ही किया। उनके विरुद्ध कभी अपशब्दों का इस्तेमाल नहीं किया।

(v) आभूषण प्रियता का अभाव— अधिकतर यह देखने में आता है कि स्त्रियाँ और विशेषकर नव विवाहित स्त्रियाँ आभूषण प्रिय होती हैं, पर प्रभा इसके विपरीत है। उसके माता-पिता ने न तो दहेज ही दिया था और न ही उसे ससुराल से गहने मिले। उसके पास कुल मिलकार दो-चार सोने की चीजें थीं जैसे— अँगूठी, जंजीर, सोने की चूड़ियाँ बस। वे चीजें भी उसकी सन्दूक में रखी थीं। जब उसके पति ने एक बार धनहीनता का जिक्रकिया कि वह कैसे पढ़ पायेगा तो उसने कह दिया कि मेरे पास जो थोड़ा-सा जेवर है उसे बेच दो। वह सिर्फ अपने हाथ में घड़ी पहने रहती है।

(vi) पतिव्रता स्त्री—वह अपने पति से बहुत प्रेम करती है। पहले चार-छह महीने तक समर ने उससे अधिक बात नहीं की तब भी उसने न तो घर में उसकी बुराई की और न ही अपने मायके में उसकी बुराई की। सिर्फ इतना ही कहा कि वे पढ़ाई कर रहे हैं, कोई बाधा नहीं चाहते। वह अपने पति को खाना खिलाकर ही स्वयं खाना खाती है। उसके ससुर ने समर के देर से आने पर कहा था—"बड़ी देर लगा देते हो समर, आखिर बहू खाने को भी तो बैठी रहती है। खाना-वाना खाकर ही घूमने निकल जाया करो न। फिर ठण्डा खाना शरीर को लगता भी तो नहीं है।" इस कथन से यह बात स्पष्ट हो जाती है कि वह अपने पति का कितना सम्मान करती है।

(vii) धैर्यवान और विवेकशील—धैर्य और विवेक उसके अनुपम गुण हैं। इनके सहारे ही वह अपने दुःख-भरे दिन काट देती है। उसका पति उससे बोलता नहीं था, सास-ससुर के ताने सुनकर उसका हृदय फट जाता था। भाभी का व्यवहार भी कोई अच्छा नहीं था। केवल मुन्नी उससे जुबानी हमदर्दी जरूर रखती थी, लेकिन घर के काम तो प्रभा को ही करने पड़ते थे। ऐसे वातावरण में उसने धीरज से काम लिया और विवेक का सहारा लिया। तमाम विरोधों के बाद भी वह यहीं ससुराल में ही बनी रही, गुस्सा होकर अपने मायके नहीं गई। वह जानती थी कि मायके जाकर भी उसकी समस्या हल नहीं होगी, बल्कि और बढ़ जायेगी।

प्रभा के चरित्र की उपर्युक्त वर्णित विशेषताओं के आधार पर हम कह सकते हैं कि प्रभा एक आदर्श भारतीय नारी है जो त्याग, कर्मठता, ममता, स्नेह, विवेकशीलता, सच्ची मित्र, सेवाभाव, स्वाभिमानी आदि गुणों से सुशोभित है। अपनी चारित्रिक विशेषताओं के कारण ही वह 'सारा आकाश' उपन्यास की केन्द्र बिन्दु बन गई है।

(3) बाबूजी का चरित्र—बाबूजी, धीरज, समर, अमर, कुँवर और मुन्नी के पिता हैं। वरिष्ठ नागरिक हैं, जिन्हें पच्चीस रुपये महीने पेंशन मिलती है। वह गरीब परिवार के मुखिया हैं। वह क्रोधी, अशिष्ट भाषा बोलने वाले तथा शकी दिमाग वाले व्यक्ति हैं। उनमें दूरदर्शिता की कमी है। जल्दी ही किसी पर विश्वास कर लेते हैं।

(i) घर के मुखिया की जिम्मेदारी सम्भालने वाले—नई बहू को मिलाकर आठ लोग इनके परिवार में हैं। वह गरीब जरूर हैं, लेकिन स्वयं को परिवार का मुखिया मानते हैं। तम्बाकू की इनको आदत है इसलिए बैठक में बैठकर हुक्का गुड़गुड़ाते रहते हैं। इनकी पच्चीस रुपये पेंशन और बड़े बेटे धीरज की नौकरी के निन्यानवें रुपयों से ही पूरे घर का खर्चा चलता है। बात-बात पर ये घरवालों को निर्देश देते रहते हैं।

(ii) क्रोध स्वभाव वाले—इनका स्वभाव क्रोधी है, क्रोध में आकर उलटा-सीधा तो बोल ही जाते हैं और एक दिन समर को लात-घूँसों से पीट भी दिया। जरा सी बात पर गुस्सा आना इस बात का संकेत देता है कि वह व्यक्ति अवसाद से घिरा है और अपना प्रभुत्व स्थापित करना चाहता है। प्रभा के छत पर बाल धोने पर उनका गुस्सा इस तरह निकला—"अरे, तुम से पर्दा नहीं होता तो मत करो। छाती पर पत्थर रखकर उसे भी सह लेंगे; लेकिन बेशर्मी की ऐसी हद तो मत करो। ऊपर जाकर सिर धोते समय तुम्हें दीखा नहीं कि चारों तरफ लोग क्या कहेंगे. . .।" एक दिन वह भड़क उठे और बोले—"ऐसा पता होता कि तू ऐसा निकलेगा तो हम तो तुझे पैदा होते ही खोदकर गाड़ देते। क्या निहाल कर दिया आपने ! अब पढ़ा-लिखाकर हाथी बना दिया है न, तो हमारी ही छाती रोंदोगे।" उसके बाद उन्होंने समर जो विवाहित लड़का है उसे लात-घूसों और थप्पड़ों से मारा।

(iii) अशिष्ट व्यवहार—उनका व्यवहार अशिष्ट और अशिक्षित व्यक्ति जैसा लगता है। क्रोध में वह भूल जाते हैं कि किससे क्या बोलना है ? बात-बात पर अपनी पत्नी को डाँटना और प्रभा को भी अशिष्टता से डाँटना वह ठीक समझते हैं। गरीबी के कारण उनका दिमाग शान्त नहीं रहता। सभी उनसे डरते हैं, लेकिन उनकी पत्नी उनसे ज्यादा नहीं डरती और सटीक भाषा में उनको जवाब दे देती है।

(iv) अदूरदर्शी और दूसरे पर विश्वास करने वाले—अपनी लड़की मुन्नी की पढ़ाई छुड़वाकर कम उम्र में ही उसकी शादी कर देना उनकी अदूरदर्शिता को बताता है। उसके बाद मुन्नी के दुबारा लेने आये उसके पति की भी बातों पर विश्वास कर लिया कि वह अब सुधर गया है और अब वह मुन्नी को अच्छी प्रकार से रखेगा। सभी घरवालों के विरोध और मुन्नी के लगातार रोने के बावजूद उन्होंने मुन्नी को उसके पति के साथ भेज दिया। उनकी अदूरदर्शिता के परिणामस्वरूप मुन्नी मर गयी। दूसरे अपने छोटे बेटे अमर की शादी करने को तैयार हो जाते हैं जबकि वह हाईस्कूल में फेल हो गया है। बाबूजी मानवीय दुर्बलताओं से पूर्ण, अदूरदर्शी, क्रोधी और शंकालु व्यक्ति हैं।

(4) अम्माजी का चरित्र—अम्माजी चार पुत्रों, एक पुत्री की माँ और बाबूजी की पत्नी हैं। वह गँवार, अपशब्द बोलने वाली, बहुओं पर रौब गाँठने वाली, बीमार और खाट पर माला जपते हुए पूरे घर की निगरानी रखने वाली महिला हैं।

(i) साधारण महिला—अम्मा एक गरीब निम्न मध्यम-परिवार की महिला है। उसे घर का कोई काम करते हुए नहीं बताया गया है, लेकिन घर की पूरी खोज खबर रखती है। दो बहुएँ घर में हैं और वे ही पूरे घर का काम करती हैं। इनका काम तो खाट पर माला जपते रहना या माला जपने का ढोंग करना और बहुओं को विशेषकर छोटी बहू को डाँटना है।

(ii) क्रोधी और शंकालु—वह अपने पति की तरह क्रोधी और शंका करने वाली है। उनका क्रोध समर पर तथा उसकी पत्नी प्रभा पर उतरता है। जब बाबूजी प्रभा को छत पर जाने के लिए डाँट लगाते हैं तो वे भी चुप नहीं रहतीं। प्रभा ने जब गणेशजी बने हुए मिट्टी के ढेले से बर्तन माँज लिए तो अम्माजी फुँकार उठीं—"सादा मिट्टी का ढेला तो है ही, और हमारी पुरखा हमें जवाब दिये चली जा रही है। तूने समझा काहे को। तेरे तो हिथे-माथे की फूट गई थी न ? अन्धी थी दिखाई थोड़े ही दिया होगा कि इसमें कलावा बँधा था या नहीं ? बात पर बात कहे चली जा रही है, जो एक भी बात बिना जवाब दिये छोड़ी हो। अच्छी सीख सिखाई है तेरे माँ-बाप ने, बड़ों से जुबान लड़ाने की।"

जब बाबूजी ने छोटी बहू के छत पर जाने की बात उठाई तो अम्मा ने भी उसके चरित्र पर शंका की और अनकहे शब्द कहे।

(iii) अदूरदर्शी— अम्मा में भी दूरदर्शिता का अभाव है। वह अपनी बेटी को यद्यपि प्यार करती है, लेकिन ससुराल जाने से उसे रोक नहीं सकी। उनमें अगर दूरदर्शिता होती तो मुन्नी को हरगिज नहीं जाने देतीं। उन्होंने विरोध तो किया, लेकिन सादा रूप में कहकर। यदि वह अड़ जातीं तो मुन्नी वहाँ नहीं जा पाती और उसकी जान भी बच जाती।

(iv) समर और छोटी बहू प्रभा पर क्रोधित रहने वाली— एक दिन समर ने अपने छोटे भाई अमर की उद्दण्डता पर उस पर हाथ उठा दिया तो अम्मा उसका पक्ष लेते हुए बोली— "खबरदार जो लड़के पर हाथ उठाया, अभी तो मैं जिन्दा हूँ। देखती हूँ, मेरे रहते कैसे तू उसकी तरफ टेढ़ी नजर से देखता है। अब तो तुझे हम दुश्मन लगते ही होंगे। हम तो तेरे इन लक्षणों को पहले ही जानते थे। देखो कोई, उस काले सिर वाली के लिए भाई पर हाथ उठा रहा है।"

अम्माजी ने अपनी कुछ मानवीय दुर्बलताओं जैसे कठोर वाणी, बिना सोचे समझे कुछ भी कह देना, बहुओं पर रौब जमाना, अपने को बीमार बताकर खाट पर बैठे रहना और अपने ऊँचे औहदे का पूरा फायदा उठाना आदि के होते हुए भी प्रधान भूमिका निभाई है। उनके चरित्र के अनुसार उनके काम में या बोलने में कोई कमी दिखाई नहीं देती।

(5) दिवाकर का चरित्र— दिवाकर का एक आदर्श पात्र है। वह समर का सहपाठी और सच्चा मित्र है। वह एक शादीशुदा युवक है, जिसकी पत्नी का नाम किरण है। वह एक सहायक, निर्भीक, प्रसन्न, बाधाओं से न घबराने वाला एक सम्पन्न परिवार का होनहार बेटा है।

(i) एक आदर्श पात्र— दिवाकर राजेन्द्र यादव द्वारा लिखित उपन्यास 'सारा आकाश' का एक मुख्य व आदर्श पात्र है। वह एक सम्पन्न परिवार का आदर्श व्यक्तित्व वाला युवक है। उसकी सच्चरित्रता, परमार्थ, सच्ची मित्रता और सभ्य बोलचाल उसके आदर्श होने के गुण हैं।

(ii) सच्चा मित्र— दिवाकर एक सच्चा मित्र है। वह अपने मित्र समर की हर सम्भव सहायता करता है। वह उसके सुख-दु:ख में सहायक है। जब भी समर को पैसों की जरूरत होती है वह उसे पैसे उधार देता है। जब समर को नौकरी की आवश्यकता हुई तो उसने अपने पिताजी से कहकर एक प्रेस में प्रूफ रीडर की नौकरी लगवा दी। तनख्वाह भी पचहत्तर रुपये जो समर के लिए बड़ी रकम थी। समर इस नौकरी के प्राप्त होने पर बहुत प्रसन्न हुआ। इसके अलावा उसकी और भी कोई समस्या हो तो उसे भी सुलझाने को तैयार रहता। उसने उसको ढंग से कपड़े पहनने और बड़ी और लम्बी चुटिया को छोटी करने की सलाह दी। समर उसकी किसी बात का बुरा नहीं मानता। वह उसके पास आकर ही पढ़ता था और कभी-कभी खाना खाकर भी जाता था।

(iii) मेधावी— वह बुद्धिमान और पढ़ाई में रुचि रखने वाला व्यक्ति है। उसके घर में पढ़ने का अलग कमरा है जिसमें वह और समर पढ़ते हैं। इण्टर के बाद उसकी आगे पढ़ने की इच्छा है। वह समर से भी कहता है कि वह भी आगे पढ़े। पढ़ने के लिए उसके सामने कोई आर्थिक परेशानी नहीं है।

(iv) एक जिम्मेदार पति— वह एक जिम्मेदार पति है। अपनी पत्नी का ख्याल रखता है। वह उसे सिनेमा दिखाने भी ले जाता है ताकि घर के काम-काज से थकी हुई किरण का कभी-कभी मनोरंजन हो जाया करे। एक दिन जब दिवाकर, किरण और समर सिनेमा गये और रात को लौटकर आये तो दिवाकर की माँ नाराज हुईं। तो किरण ने उपेक्षा दिखाते हुए कहा, "कहाँ तक दिन-रात मरें। छह महीने में एक बार सिनेमा आये हैं, अगर अब भी वह गालियाँ दें तो कोई क्या करे ?" यह सुनकर भी दिवाकर ने कोई प्रतिक्रिया या नाराजगी नहीं दिखाई।

(v) एक सच्चा मददगार— दिवाकर एक सच्चे मददगार के रूप में हमारे सामने आता है। उसके एक चचेरे भाई हैं, शिरीष। वह अपनी बहन के इलाज के लिए यहाँ आये हैं। शिरीष और दिवाकर ने बहन को

मानसिक अस्पताल में भरती करवा दिया। उसे हिस्टीरिया की बीमारी है। हफ्ते-दो हफ्ते बाद शिरीष भाई आते हैं और दिवाकर के यहाँ ही ठहरते हैं। वह शिरीष भाई के सिद्धान्तों से प्रभावित है। वह धार्मिक आडम्बर और ढकोसलों के खिलाफ है। उसका स्वभाव शान्त है और उसके जीवन में कोई उलझन नहीं है।

दिवाकर के माध्यम से उपन्यासकार ने एक आदर्शवादी, स्वाभिमानी, सच्चरित्र, बुद्धिमान, सच्चे मित्र और दृढ़ निश्चयी युवक का चित्रण किया है।

प्रश्न 16. संवाद योजना की दृष्टि से 'सारा आकाश' उपन्यास की समीक्षा कीजिए।

उत्तर—मानव एक सामाजिक प्राणी है। समाज में रहने वाले प्रत्येक व्यक्ति को एक-दूसरे से सम्पर्क स्थापित करने के लिए संवादों का सहारा लेना पड़ता है। वह अपने भावों की अभिव्यक्ति कथोपकथनों या संवादों के माध्यम से करता है। राजेन्द्र यादव लिखित उपन्यास 'सारा आकाश' के कथानक में संवादों का विशेष महत्व है। संवाद कथानक की गतिशीलता का आधार हैं। कथोपकथन की दृष्टि से 'सारा आकाश' की समीक्षा इस प्रकार की जा सकती है—

(1) कथानक के विकास में सहायक—पात्रों के पारस्परिक वार्तालाप से ही कथा आगे बढ़ती है। संवाद ही वर्तमान और भविष्य की घटनाओं की जानकारी देते हैं। समर, बाबूजी, अम्माजी, प्रभा, दिवाकर और शिरीष भाई के संवाद इसी प्रकार के हैं। पात्रों की भाषा उनके चरित्र के अनुरूप ही है। कथानक के संवाद कहानी को गतिशील बनाने के साथ ही साथ पात्रों की मन:स्थिति तथा परिस्थितियों का पूर्ण ज्ञान करा देते हैं। यथा—"उठो-उठो फेरों का वक्त हो गया। सोना ही है तो जाकर जनमासे में सोना।. . . यहाँ पड़े हो, न शरीर का होश, न कपड़ों का ख्याल. . . क्या कहेंगे लोग कि अच्छे बराती लेकर आये हैं. . . उठो. . . उठो।"

(2) पात्रों की चारित्रिक विशेषताओं को उद्‌घाटित करने वाले—संवादों के माध्यम से उपन्यासकार अपने पात्रों की चारित्रिक विशेषताओं को अभिव्यक्त करता है। समर, बाबूजी, अम्माजी और शिरीष भाई के संवाद इसी प्रकार के हैं। प्रारम्भ में समर के संवादों से उसके निराशावादी और कमजोर व्यक्तित्व का पता चलता है। जैसे—"मुन्नी मैं सच कहता हूँ, मैं घर छोड़कर भाग जाऊँगा। भले ढंग से पढ़ना चाहता हूँ सो पढ़ाया तक तो जाता नहीं, अब चार-चार शादियाँ करके रख दो।"

(3) पात्रानुकूलता—इस उपन्यास के संवाद निम्न मध्यम वर्ग के पात्रों की भावनाओं को अभिव्यक्त करने के कारण पात्रों के अनुकूल हैं। चिन्ता, पीड़ा और धन का अभाव संवादों के माध्यम से व्यक्त हुआ है। उपन्यास के कुछ पात्र ही शिक्षित हैं। ऐसी स्थिति में उनके संवाद भी उन्हीं के अनुसार हैं। पात्रों के संवादों की अनुकूलता इस प्रकार है—

समर—शिक्षित है, लेकिन घर की परिस्थिति में पढ़ नहीं पा रहा है। ऊपर से उसकी इच्छा के विरुद्ध उसकी शादी भी कर दी है। भाभी ने समर से कहा—"तुम्हारा ब्याह भी क्या हुआ, लालाजी ! क्या-क्या अरमान थे, सब पर पानी फिर गया। लेन-देन की तो खैर कोई बात नहीं, एक आध साल में आई-गई बात हो जाती है। लेकिन वह महारानी जी तो जिन्दगीभर को बँध गई। उन लोगों ने शायद भेजने को लिखा है।"

बाबूजी—इनके संवादों में कठोरता और असभ्यता दिखाई देती है। "और कोई जगह दाल बीनने की रह ही नहीं गई ? दाल छत पर ही बिनेगी ! ऐसे ही उस दिन छत पर बाल्टी ले जाकर सिर धोया गया।. . . . कुछ दिमाग ही समझ में नहीं आते साहबजादी के।"

अम्मा जी—बुर्जुग महिला है और प्रभा और भाभी की सास हैं इनकी भाषा में कठोरता और रौब दिखाई देता है—"ओहो, अब तो ये जताने लगी कि मैं इतना काम करूँ, क्यों ? वाह री ! अच्छी बहू है, तू तो काम के ताने देने लगी। अरे ! तुझे अपना काम करने की फुर्सत नहीं मिलती ? खाने की तो मिल जाती है न ?"

(4) भावानुकूलता और संक्षिप्तता—'सारा आकाश' के संवाद पात्रों की भावनाओं को प्रकट करने वाले तथा पाठकों के अन्तःस्थल को छू लेते हैं। इसके संवाद पाठकों को पात्रों की भावनाओं से जोड़ देते हैं।

उपर्युक्त विवरण के आधार पर कहा जा सकता है कि संवादों की दृष्टि से 'सारा आकाश' उपन्यास एक सफल रचना है। उपन्यास के संवाद सरल, संक्षिप्त लेकिन कहीं-कहीं बड़े भी, मनोभावों के अनुकूल हैं। किसी-किसी पात्र के एक संवाद से उसका चरित्र हमारे सम्मुख स्पष्ट हो जाता है।

प्रश्न 17. 'सारा आकाश' उपन्यास में उपन्यासकार राजेन्द्र यादव ने पाठकों के सामने क्या उद्देश्य रखा है ?

उत्तर—उपन्यासकार ने 'सारा आकाश' उपन्यास साधारण बोलचाल की भाषा में लिखा है। सरल पात्रों के द्वारा समाज में फैली बुराइयों जैसे दहेज न मिलने के कटु अनुभव, गरीब परिवार की मुश्किल, कम उम्र में विवाह कर देने पर पुत्री के कष्ट, बेरोजगार और विद्यार्थी का विवाह कर देने से उनके सामने समस्याएँ, सच्चे-मित्र के गुण और एक परिवार में निरन्तर चलते हुए विवाद मानसिक अशान्ति उत्पन्न करते हैं, इन उद्देश्यों को प्रदर्शित करने में वह सफल हुआ है।

उपन्यासगकार ने समाज में फैली कुण्ठा और सास-बहू के रोज-रोज के झगड़ों को यथार्थ रूप में प्रस्तुत किया है। समाज में जैसा होता है वैसा ही दिखाया गया है। कोई भी कथन या पात्र बनावटी या असम्भव सा नहीं लगता।

समर प्रमुख पात्र है। उसके सामने यह समस्या है कि वह पढ़ना चाहता है। जब वह इण्टर की पढ़ाई कर रहा है तभी उसकी शादी कर दी जाती है। यह शादी उसकी इच्छा के विरुद्ध हुई है इसलिए कई महीनों तक वह उससे बात नहीं करता। घर के झगड़ों से वह न तो पढ़ पा रहा है और न ही उसका मन शान्त रहता है।

आज की बहुएँ किस प्रकार से सासुओं की प्रताड़नाएँ सुनती हैं और चुप रहकर इस दुःख को झेलती हैं। धनाभाव में तो अन्य समस्याएँ भी खड़ी हो जाती हैं। उपन्यासकार ने स्पष्ट किया है कि धनाभाव को अधिक परिश्रम करके और कम खर्च करके कम किया जा सकता है। लेकिन जो अशान्ति आपसी झगड़ों और नासमझदारी के आधार पर उत्पन्न होती है, वह शिक्षा, दूरदर्शिता और सूझ-बूझ से दूर हो सकती है। उपन्यास में उपन्यासकार ने पात्रों के द्वारा आडम्बरों, अन्धविश्वासों और समाज में प्रचलित बुराइयों का विरोध मुखरित किया है।

इस उपन्यास में यथार्थ और आदर्श का भी समावेश हुआ है। दिवाकर एक आदर्श मित्र के रूप में हमारे सामने आता है और समर के सामने गरीबी का यथार्थ प्रस्तुत होता है। वह अपने मन की अशान्ति से घिरा रहता है, परन्तु न चाहते हुए भी वह अन्त तक अशान्त ही रहता है। पाठकों को यह बताने का उद्देश्य भी उपन्यासकार का रहा है कि घर की अशान्ति और हर समय होने वाले झगड़े अध्ययन में बाधा तो डालते ही हैं और उसे ऐसी स्थिति में ले जाकर खड़ा कर देते हैं कि जहाँ वह अपना जीवन ही समाप्त करने को उद्यत हो जाता है।

प्रश्न 18. प्रभा को अपने चरित्र वाली बात पर बहुत दुःख हुआ। किसने क्या कहा था ?

उत्तर—कोई भी स्वाभिमानी और चरित्रवान महिला को अपने चरित्र पर लांछन सुनकर अवश्य ही दुःख होता है। प्रभा अत्यन्त ही कुशल, कार्य करने वाली, सहनशील और सुन्दर चरित्र वाली महिला है। बहुत दिनों तक पति के न बोलने पर भी वह अपना काम सुचारू रूप से करती रही।

समर और भाई साहब घर के भीतर गये तो देखा कि सिर झुकाये प्रभा अपराधिनी की मुद्रा में खड़ी है और बाबूजी दुर्वासा का रूप धारण कर गरज रहे हैं—"और कोई जगह दाल बीनने की रह ही नहीं गई ? दाल छत पर ही बिनेगी ! ऐसे ही उस दिन छत पर बाल्टी ले जाकर सिर धोया गया। उस दिन तो चुप हो गया,

मुन्नी ने सिफारिश कर दी। . . . हमेशा गूँगी की तरह मनहूस सी धूमती रहेगी, आँखें चुराती रहेगी। कुछ दिमाग ही समझ में नहीं आते साहबजादी के। वहाँ छत पर तेरा क्या रखा है ? हमें भी तो बता ! मैं आज साफ-साफ कह देता हूँ, मुझे ये बातें जरा भी पसन्द नहीं हैं, कान खोलकर सुन लो। जाड़े के दिन हैं, बीस आदमी छत पर धूप खाने का बहाना करके ताक-झाँक करते हैं। बहू के कायदे से रहो।'' इसके बाद अम्मा भी अपशब्द कहने से नहीं चूकीं—''सबसे बचकर अकेली छत पर नहीं बैठी रहे, तो पड़ोसियों से नैना कैसे लड़ें ? और भाग-भागकर छत पर जाती क्यों है ?''

प्रभा जब से सिर झुकाये बिना कुछ बोले सुन रही थी, इस बात से एकदम झटक कर उसका सिर उठ गया। उसने एक बार तीखी निगाहों से अम्मा की ओर देखा और धीरे से सिर झुका लिया। उसकी आँखों से आँसू भी गिरे। यह तो उसके चरित्र पर सीधा आघात था। इसे कैसे सह रही थी यह तो वही जाने। फिर बताया गया कि मुहल्ले के पाण्डेजी की लड़की उसे पढ़ाने वाले मास्टर के साथ भाग गई।

अम्माजी से न रहा गया और फिर बोली—''अरे हमारी तरफ से दुनिया भाड़ में जाये, लेकिन ये भाग-भागकर ऊपर क्यों जाती है ? इसका वहाँ कौन बैठा है ? खबरदार जो आज से उधर पैर रखा, मुझसे बुरा कोई न होगा।''

समर तो यह सब सुनकर ऊपर अपनी कोठरी में चला गया। लेकिन प्रभा रोती रही। इस तरह बिना किसी कारण के उस पर लांछन लगाया जा रहा है। वह नहीं समझती कि एक दो बार काम से छत पर जाने से ऐसा क्या अनर्थ हो गया जो इन लोगों को नहीं पच रहा है। वह तो बिल्कुल साफ-हृदय वाली है, उसके अन्दर कोई पाप नहीं है। सास-ससुर के तानों ने उसके हृदय को बड़ी तकलीफ दी है। वह रोती रही पर कुछ कह न सकी।

प्रश्न 19. समर की मुलाकात शिरीष भाई साहब से कहाँ हुई ? वे यहाँ क्यों आये थे ? उनकी बहन को क्या हुआ था ? उसका कारण क्या था ?

उत्तर—समर की मुलाकात शिरीष भाई साहब से दिवाकर के घर पर हुई। वैसे शिरीष से समर की मुलाकात एम्प्लायमेंट एक्सचेंज के पास हुई थी, लेकिन दोनों का परिचय नहीं हुआ था। यहाँ पर दिवाकर ने उनका परिचय कराया कि वह उसके चचेरे भाई हैं और अपनी बहन को यहाँ मानसिक अस्पताल में भर्ती कराने के लिए आये हैं।

उसने बताया कि उसकी बहन को हिस्टीरिया के दौरे पड़ते थे। फिर अचानक वह पागलों जैसी हरकत करने लगी है ? उन दौरों (Fits) का समय बढ़ता गया। डॉक्टर ने बताया कि जल्दी से जल्दी इसे किसी मेंटल हॉस्पीटल में दाखिल न किया गया तो केस काफी खराब हो जायेगा। इसलिए उसे परसों भर्ती करके आये हैं। समर के पूछने पर कि इसे, ''हिस्टीरिया के दौरे क्यों आने लगे हैं, डॉक्टरों ने इसके बारे में कुछ नहीं बताया ?''

शिरीष ने कहा कि इसके बारे में डॉक्टर क्या बतायेंगे। यह तो मानसिक परेशानियों, बहुत अधिक चिन्ताओं और नर्वस दवाब से आने लगते हैं। गलती शिरीष के परिवार वालों की ही रही थी। शिरीष की बहन की शादी छोटी उम्र में कर दी थी। मुश्किल से तब वह ग्यारह-बारह साल की रही होगी। उसके पति उस समय पढ़ रहे थे। जब उन्होंने पढ़ाई पूरी की तो उन्हें मालूम हुआ कि उसकी पत्नी अशिक्षित है। जिसके कारण तब से एक तरह उसे छोड़ ही रखा है। शिरीष ने अपने साथ रखकर उसे मैट्रिक तो करा दिया। अगर यह रोग न लगा होता तो इस साल इण्टर कर लेती। बहुत समझाया पर उसने किसी की भी न सुनी। रात को सोते-सोते बर्राने लगती है। कुछ देर बाद वह बोले, ''मैं तो राह देख रहा हूँ कि हिन्दू कोड-बिल पास करके या वैसे ही नेता लोग एकाध कानून बना दें तो तलाक दिलाकर कहीं और शादी कर-करा दूँ।

प्रश्न 20. अमर की छोटी भाभी से क्या तकरार हुई जिसके कारण समर को गुस्सा आया ? उसने फिर क्या किया ? अम्माजी ने किसकी तरफदारी की ?

उत्तर– प्रभा खाना बना रही थी और अमर खाना खाने बैठा था। प्रभा ने थाली लगा कर दी। अमर बोला, "रोटियों में आज घी क्यों नहीं लगा रहीं, भाभी ?" प्रभा ने नम्रता से कहा, "घी खत्म हो गया, लालाजी !" वह एकदम तेज हो गया और बोला, "अभी कल-परसों ही तो सेर-भर लाया था, खत्म भी हो गया ? प्रभा ने बताया–"था ही कितना ? अब तुम देख ही रहे हो। घर में ही काम आ रहा है।" अमर को इस बात पर अपनी उपेक्षा लगी और बोला, "यों, क्यों नहीं कहतीं कि सारा अपने खसम को चटा दिया ? घर का नाम क्यों लेती हो ? हमें दीखता नहीं है, घर में किसी को मिले या न मिले, लेकिन समर भैया की दाल में खूब घी डाला जायेगा, रोटियाँ खूब चुपड़ी जायेंगी। बस हमारे लिए. . .।"

समर वहीं खड़ा यह सब सुन रहा था। अमर बैठा था। समर ने एक जोर की लात उसकी पीठ पर मारी और कहा, "बेशर्म बात करने की तमीज नहीं है। लगाम मुँह में है ही नहीं ? जो जी में आया सो बक दिया ? मैट्रिक में पढ़ते हैं ये !"

तभी सारा दम लगाकर अम्मा वहीं चारपाई से बोलीं–"क्यों रे समर के बच्चे, इधर तो आ जरा ! बस तेरी ही वह बहू लगती है, किसी और की कुछ नहीं लगती।" समर ने फिर अमर को फटकारा तो अम्माजी को क्रोध आ गया और बोली, "खबरदार जो लड़के पर हाथ उठाया ? अभी तो मैं जिन्दा हूँ। देखती हूँ, मेरे रहते कैसे उसकी तरफ टेढ़ी नजर से देखता है ? अब तो तुझे हम सब दुश्मन लगते होंगे। हम तो तेरे इन लक्षणों को पहले ही जानते थे। देखो कोई, उस काली सिरवाली के लिए भाई पर हाथ उठा रहा है। अरे मैं पूछती हूँ, तुझे शर्म नहीं आ रही जो तू उसे शर्म की सीख दे रहा है। किस मुँह से यह सब कह रहा है ? अच्छा तू बोलने लगा अपनी फूलंदे रानी से, तूने तो सारा आसमान सिर पर उठा लिया। रोज एक न एक उपद्रव, रोज एक न एक ऊधम ! इससे अच्छा तो जब बोलता नहीं था तभी था।"

इस प्रकार समर और अमर में और कहासुनी हुई और यह दृश्य समाप्त हुआ।

प्रश्न 21. शिरीष भाई साहब के विचारों के बारे में समर ने प्रभा को क्या बताया ? समर की कोठरी की किबाड़ों को जोर से धक्का किसी ने मारा तो बाबूजी दहाड़कर क्या-क्या कर रहे थे ?

उत्तर–अपनी कोठरी में बैठे हुए समर और प्रभा दिवाकर के यहाँ जाने की बात कर रहे थे। तभी समर ने बताया कि वहाँ शिरीष भाई से भी मिल लेना। प्रभा के यह पूछने पर कि शिरीष भाई कौन हैं, समर ने उनका परिचय दिया और उनके विचारों के बारे में बताया कि पहले उनसे एम्प्लॉयमेंट एक्सचेंज पर मुलाकात हुई, लेकिन परिचय नहीं हुआ, परिचय दिवाकर के घर पर हुआ। फिर वह बोला, "सच प्रभा, कभी-कभी तो मैं उस आदमी की इस बात पर आश्चर्य करता हूँ। हर चीज को देखने का उसका अपना अलग ही तरीका है। वह तो जैसे किसी चीज को मानता ही नहीं। जिसे देखो, उसी का खण्डन ! कहता है, हमारे पास अपना इतिहास है ही नहीं। जो कुछ है, वह पुराण हैं, जिनमें धर्म, अंधविश्वास और कविताओं का घपला है और वहाँ सच्चाई का पता ही नहीं चलता। या फिर किराये के भाटों द्वारा लिखे हुए कुछ राजाओं के प्रशस्ति-काव्य हैं जिनमें पाँच गाँवों के राजा को धरती का सिरमौर बताया जाता है। कहता था कि शास्त्रों और स्मृतियों के नाम पर हमारे पास वे चीजें हैं जिनमें कहा गया है कि नियम-कायदे पहले बने कैसे, और किसके लिए ? इस समय हिन्दू, मुसलमान, क्रिश्चियन किसी धर्म की आदमी को जरूरत नहीं है। इस समय तो एक ही धर्म चाहिए। वह है, 'मानवता'।

लेकिन समर की बात बीच में ही टूट गई। किसी ने किबाड़ों को ऐसे जोर से धक्का दिया मानो पूरी ताकत से लात मारी हो। उन लोगों पर जैसे बिजली टूट पड़ी। घबराहट में सम्भल कर देखा तो बाहर चीख-पुकार शुरू हो गई। पहले तो समझ में नहीं आया कि यह अचानक क्या हुआ ? फिर बाबूजी के चीखने का स्वर सुनाई देने लगा। वे मुहल्ले-पड़ोस के सुनने की चिन्ता किये बिना जोर-जोर से दहाड़ रहे थे। प्रभा अपने कपड़े ठीक करने लगी थी और समर किबाड़ की दरारों से झाँककर देख रहा था। बाबूजी एक तरफ खड़े

जोर-जोर से कह रहे थे, ''जवानी हमें भी आई थी, पर ऐसी नहीं कि न दिन देखें न रात ! जब देखो, तब बहू को लिए पड़े हैं। अरे, घर में बच्चे हैं, बड़े-बूढ़े हैं—किसी का तो लिहाज करो ? दस बजने आ रहे हैं और बाबूजी का अभी सबेरा ही नहीं हुआ है। ऐसी भी बेशर्मी किस काम की साली! रातभर ही-ही, हो-हो ! मस्त हो रहे हैं ! चूर हैं जवानी में ! न दुनिया का ध्यान है, न आँखों की शर्म। आग लगे ऐसे अंधेपन में। नहीं बोलते थे तो ऐसे डरते थे कि औरत नहीं हो गई कोई शेरनी हो गई, और अब बोलने लगे तो जब देखो तब उसी के पास मँडरा रहे हैं। सारा घर नहा-धो लिया, काम-काज सारा खत्म हो गया और यहाँ अभी गुलछर्रे ही उड़ रहे हैं।'' उनका भाषण निर्बाध जारी था, ''हालत तो यह है कि हिम्मत उल्लू के पट्ठों की देखो—ये आगे पढ़ेंगे लाड़साहब ने खत्ती गाड़ दी है न ? साले नवाबजादे कहीं के।''

डरते-डरते वे दोनों नीचे आये। प्रभा तो भीगी बिल्ली बनी-चुपचाप निकलकर नीचे चली गई। ससुर का ऐसे अपशब्दों का अपनी बहू और बेटे से बोलना उनकी असभ्यता और गँवारपन का ही प्रतीक है।

प्रश्न 22. प्रूफ रीडिंग का काम क्या वास्तव में थकाऊ और कष्टदायक था ? प्रेस के वातावरण का वर्णन करते हुए बताइए कि वहाँ काम करने वाले लोग कैसे थे ?

उत्तर—समर ने प्रूफ रीडिंग के काम पर जाना शुरू किया। वह रेल से जाता था इसलिए उसे आने में थकान नहीं होती थी। लेकिन काम शुरू में जितना रोचक लगा, बाद में तबियत उतनी ही ऊबने लगी। पाँच से ग्यारह तक प्रूफ के गीले खुरदरे कागजों पर फैलती स्याही से छह घण्टे लगातार उलटे-सीधे निशान बनाते-बनाते सिर भन्नाने लगता था। उस समय समर और भी डर जाता कि अगर यह काम सचमुच इतना ही थका देने वाला और कष्टदायक है तो कॉलेज के दिनों में यहाँ से जाने के बाद पढ़-लिख क्या पाऊँगा ? कुछ समझ में ही नहीं आयेगा। पहले कुछ दिन तो जोश-जोश में उसने इतने सारे पन्नों के प्रूफ एक-साथ देख डाले कि सारे प्रेस वाले चकित रह गये। लगता था कि इस जरा-से काम में दिक्कत ही क्या है ? केवल पढ़ना ही तो है, जहाँ गलत लगे वहाँ निशान लगा दो। लेकिन मैनेजर ने बाद में सारे पन्ने लौटा दिये क्योंकि उनमें ढेरों गलतियाँ भरी पड़ी थीं। एक-एक अक्षर कॉपी से मिला-मिलाकर जाँचने के बाद उसका दिमाग थककर चूर हो जाता। प्रेस की मशीनों की खस्स और खटर-खटर चलती रहती है और इन आवाजों के ऊपर सारे गले से चीखकर दिये गये हुक्म गूँजते रहते, 'नोट, टाइप उभर क्यों नहीं रहा है ?' अब स्याही ज्यादा आने लगी। 'अब देख क्या रहा है मुँह फाड़कर, कागज लगा।'

मैनेजर अपनी स्याही लगी पतलून में दोनों हाथों को ठूँसे पास आकर खड़ा हो जाता और उसे प्रूफ देखते हुए देखता तो उसके मन में अजीब सी घबराहट होने लगती। फिर चलते-चलते कह जाता—''बड़े सुस्त प्रूफ देख रहे हैं मिस्टर, मशीन खाली पड़ी है। अभी तो करैक्शन भी टाइम लेगा। जरा ध्यान से देखिए और कई बार देखिए।' एक तरफ सुमेरा बैठा-बैठा पानी में भिगो-भिगोकर कुछ कूटता रहता और दूसरी तरफ मशीन मैन चूल्हे पर स्याही औटाया करते। सरेस की बदबू से उबकाई आती। ऐसा था यह प्रूफ रीडिंग का काम।

लेकिन वहाँ काम करने वाले लोग इतने दिलचस्प थे कि मन ऊबता नहीं था। पहले तो बड़ा अजनबी-अजनबी सा लगता था, लेकिन जल्दी ही वे समर को अच्छे लगने लगे। टाइपों को केसों में डिस्ट्रीब्यूट करते या कम्पोज करते हुए बड़े रस ले-लेकर किसी लड़की की प्रेम कहानी, अपने पड़ोसी की व्यभिचार-कथा, काल्पनिक या कई सिनेमाओं के ताल-मेल से तैयार किये गये अजीबोगरीब किस्सों का बखान हुआ करता। चाहे बात सिनेमा की हो या अपने जीवन की, सबके पास विस्मय एक ही था अपने-अपने अनुभवों का वर्णन। इस प्रकार वे अपने इस उबाऊ जीवन को दिलचस्प बना लेते थे। रोज समर इन किस्सों को प्रभा को सुनाता था।

प्रश्न 23. मामाजी ने समर को क्या-क्या कहकर समझाया ?

उत्तर—बैठक में मामाजी (चन्दन) और बाबूजी बैठे हुए बात कर रहे थे। समर अपनी कोठरी में था। उसे बैठक में बुलाया गया। मामाजी उससे गले मिले और खुश हुए। दरअसल मामाजी छोटे भाई अमर का रिश्ता लेकर आये थे। समर की शादी भी इन्होंने ही कराई थी। समर ने इसका विरोध किया कि अभी वह पढ़

रहा है, मैट्रिक तक तो अभी की नहीं है। अभी से उसके पैरों में बेड़ी क्यों डालते हो ? बाबूजी ने और मामाजी ने उसकी बात पर ज्यादा ध्यान नहीं दिया। मामाजी ने समर को प्यार से समझाना शुरू किया। कारण यह रहा होगा कि बाबूजी ने घर की सारी रामकहानी (विशेष रूप से प्रभा और समर की) नमक-मिर्च मिलाकर कही होगी तभी तो मामाजी को पता चला और उन्होंने कहा होगा कि मैं समझाऊँगा समर को।

मामाजी ने कहना शुरू किया—"शादी-ब्याह तो सभी के होते हैं भाई, लेकिन इसके लिए कोई अपने भाई-बहन, माँ-बाप को थोड़े ही छोड़ देता है ? जहाँ चार बरतन होते हैं, खटकते ही हैं। औरतों का क्या है, पल में इधर, पल में उधर, समझदार आदमी को तो उनकी बातों में आना ही नहीं चाहिए। तुम खुद हमसे ज्यादा पढ़े-लिखे हो, अच्छी तरह समझते हो। वे तो अलग घर, अलग खानदान से आई है, उन्हें किसी के आपसी रिश्ते से क्या लेना-देना ! खून का रिश्ता तो तुम्हारा आपस में है। वह अलग थोड़े ही हो जायेगा। सो बेटा, ये सब तो घर-गिरस्ती के मामले हैं। खूब फूँक-फूँककर कदम रखना चाहिए।" समर ने मन ही मन सोचा कि इस घर की हालत अगर मामाजी जानते तो अमर की शादी का रिश्ता लेकर नहीं आते। समर चुपचाप उनकी बातें सुनता रहा।

"तुम कहो, सास-बहू की कहन-सुनन ? तो भैया किस घर में यह नहीं होता ? बड़े-बड़े लखपतियों के घर की हालत तो मैं जानता हूँ। घर-घर मिट्टी के चूल्हे हैं समझे।" मामाजी ने उसके कन्धे पर हाथ रखते हुए कहा। समर ने उनके सामने यह कहा कि वह पढ़ना चाहता है। तब उन्होंने कहा—"पढ़ने को कौन नहीं पढ़ाना चाहता, बेटे! लेकिन भैया, सब कुछ अपने घर की हालत देखकर होता है। तुम्हारा भैया भी है। वह भी तो अपना फर्ज पूरा कर रहा है या नहीं ? घर में रहकर सब सोचना पड़ता है, मेरे मुन्ना ! अब तुम गिरस्ती में आये हो, समझने की कोशिश करो कि दुनिया चलती कैसे है ? बहू को जरा दबा के रखो, उसे अदब-कायदा सिखाओ। और तुम्हारे बाबूजी कह रहे थे कि तुम पूजा-पाठ, धरम-करम सब छोड़ते चले जा रहे हो ? ऐं ? कहीं पढ़ना-लिखना इसलिए होता है बेटा ? सारे लोग धरम-करम को छोड़ दें तो दुनिया रहेगी कैसे ? हकीकतराय, बन्दा बहादुर पर क्या-क्या जुल्म नहीं ढाये गये। भैया, अपने धरम-करम का ही तो प्रताप है कि हम-तुम यहाँ बैठे हैं।"

बाबूजी यह सब सुन रहे थे और महसूस कर रहे थे कि इस पर कोई प्रभाव नहीं पड़ रहा है। बोले—"तुम किस पत्थर को समझा रहे हो चन्दन ! कहा है, 'सीख दीजिए ताहि को जाको सीख सुहाय. . . सीख न दीजे बाँदरा घर बया कौ जाय।" उनको बीच में ही टोकते हुए मामाजी ने आखिरी बाण चलाया जो शहद में लिपटा हुआ था। नहीं जी कोई बच्चा थोड़े ही है हमारा समर बेटा। समझता तो सब है, जरा-सा लड़कपन है। क्यों, है न बेटा ? बाबूजी से माफी माँग लेना बेटा ! यह बड़े हैं। यह सब सुनकर समर बिना कुछ कहे ऊपर अपने कमरे चला गया।

प्रश्न 24. संयुक्त परिवार के बारे में शिरीष भाई साहब के क्या विचार थे ?

उत्तर—शिरीष भाई साहब दिवाकर के चचेरे भाई हैं और अपनी बहन का इलाज कराने उसके यहाँ आये थे। अपनी बहन को मेंटल हॉस्पीटल में भरती करा दिया है और उससे मिलने आते रहते हैं। उनसे समर और दिवाकर की बात हुई और उन्होंने उन दोनों के परिवार की स्थिति जानी और जानकर इस निष्कर्ष पर पहुँचे कि लगातार चलने वाली तकरार या आपस के झगड़े संयुक्त परिवार के कारण ही होते हैं। या तो परिवार इतना समर्थ हो कि एक घर में रहते हुए भी सबको अलग-अलग सुविधाएँ मिलें और स्वाभिमान की भी रक्षा हो सके तो ही संयुक्त परिवार चल सकता है अन्यथा अर्थभाव और अशिक्षा में रहकर तो अशान्ति ही बनी रहेगी।

इस प्रकार स्थिति को जानकर शिरीष भाई बोले, "भाई समरजी ! आपकी अपनी या दिवाकर की, सबकी वास्तविक स्थिति जानकर एक बात मेरी समझ में आती जा रही है—इस संयुक्त परिवार की परम्परा को

तोड़ना ही होगा। अब आपके लिए ही कहूँ कि अगर आप खुद जिन्दा रहना चाहते हैं या चाहते हैं कि आपकी पत्नी भी जिन्दा रहे तो इसके सिवाय कोई रास्ता नहीं है कि अलग रहिए। जैसा भी हो अलग रहिए. . .।'' उनकी सलाह अप्रत्याशित थी इसलिए समर स्तब्ध रह गया। उन्होंने फिर समझाया—''आप बुरा न मानिये, लेकिन समर भाई, सच्चाई यह है कि आपकी पत्नी की सारी आकांक्षाएँ और आपके सारे प्रयत्न इस वातावरण में बिल्कुल बेबस होकर घुट-घुटकर मर जायेंगे। एक के बाद एक मुसीबतें निकलती आयेंगी और आप लोग शायद सुख की नींद के सपने में ही जिन्दगी बिता देंगे।''

फिर उन्होंने कहा, आज की आर्थिक स्थिति में संयुक्त परिवार चल नहीं सकता। अगर चलेगा भी तो ऊपर से देखने में चाहे जो भी हो, लेकिन अन्दर से उसमें छोटे-छोटे परिवारों की कई इकाइयाँ बन जायेंगी।

फिर उन्होंने अपनी बात आगे बढ़ाई—''संयुक्त परिवार का शाब्दिक अर्थ चाहे कितना महान हो, उसका सबसे बड़ा नुकसान यह होता है कि परिवार का कोई भी सदस्य अपने व्यक्तित्व का विकास नहीं कर पाता। सारा समय तो समस्याएँ बनाने में या बनी-बनाई समस्याओं को सुलझाने में चला जाता है। लड़ाई-झगड़ा, खींचतान, बदला, ग्लानि, सब मिलाकर वातावरण ऐसा विषैला और दमघोंटू बना रहता है कि आप भी जानते हैं। नतीजे में हम दो हिस्सों में बँटे रहते हैं। बाहर अपनी आर्थिक लड़ाई लड़ो और भीतर अपनी पारिवारिक उलझनें सुलझाओ ! सीधे-सरल दिल-दिमाग का आदमी इन्हीं झंझटों में पिस जाता है।''

दिवाकर ने पूछ लिया, ''लेकिन यह तो स्थिति हुई, परिणाम कहाँ हुआ ?''

शिरीष बोले—''मैंने बताया न, परिणाम यही होता है कि आप अपने व्यक्तित्व का विकास नहीं कर पाते। अपनी शक्तियों और प्रतिभा को सही दिशा में बढ़ाने का आपको अवसर ही नहीं मिलता। या कहें कि आप अपने-आपको ऐसी बातों में उलझाकर थका डालते हैं कि आपका दिल-दिमाग अपने सपने पूरे करने लायक नहीं रह जाता। पढ़ाई-लिखाई या किसी भी बौद्धिक और मानसिक विकास के लिए आपके पास शक्ति बच ही कहाँ पाती है।'' आखिर में उन्होंने कहा, ''भैया मेरे, सीधा-सादा हल यही है कि आप अलग रहिए और घर के लिए जो जिम्मेदारी महसूस करते हैं, वह पूरी कीजिए।

अब उनकी बातें सुनकर समर भी यह महसूस करने लगा कि बात तो वे सही कह रहे हैं। उन्हें संयुक्त परिवार में रहकर कितने ताने सुनने पड़ते हैं और प्रभा को दिन-रात काम में जुटे रहना पड़ता है। संयुक्त परिवार का एक नुकसान यह भी है कि प्रत्येक व्यक्ति काम करने से बचना चाहता है और दूसरे से काम करवाना चाहता है।

प्रश्न 25. बाबूजी ने पूछा, ''क्यों रे समर, तूने तो शायद दस तारीख से काम करना शुरू किया था ?'' समर ने लापरवाही से जवाब दिया, ''बाबूजी नौकरी छूट भी गई।'' इसके बाद बाबूजी के कटु भाषण और प्रतिक्रिया का वर्णन करिए।

उत्तर—बड़ी देर तक बाबूजी बैठे रहे और प्रतीक्षा करते रहे कि समर ही कुछ कहे। लेकिन हारकर उन्होंने यह बात पूछ ही ली कि क्या उसने दस तारीख से काम शुरू किया था ? समर का रूखा जवाब सुनकर उनको थोड़ा असहज लगा और स्पष्ट कर दिया कि उन्होंने इसलिए नहीं पूछा है कि वह उन्हें कुछ दे। उद्धत स्वर में समर ने कहा कि वे साफ-साफ माँग तो नहीं रहे हैं तो फिर कहने का क्या मतलब है। इस पर बाबूजी भड़क गये और हवा में हाथ फेंककर कहा—''जानता है तो क्या फाँसी पर चढ़ा देगा ? बड़े जानते हैं ये ! हमने तो एक बात पूछी सो सीधा जवाब तो दिया नहीं, काटने दौड़े। आ, बैल मुझे मार ! बेटा, हम तो तुम्हारी नस-नस जानते हैं। हमारे सामने ही तो बड़े हुये हो। अब साफ-साफ माँगने की धमकी देने लगे ? हिम्मत तो देखो पूत की ! अरे, हमने अपनी पहली तनख्वाह लाकर बाप को दी थी, सो अदब-कायदा गया चूल्हे-भाड़ में, साफ-साफ माँगने की धमकी देने लगे। हरामी ! तुझे पाला-पोसा, पढ़ाया-लिखाया, सब इसलिए कि तू यों

हमारी इज्जत उतारकर रख दे ? छाती पर चढ़-चढ़कर आये। सीधी-सीधी बात करो तो कटखने पागल कुत्ते की तरह भौंके ?''

समर ने बड़ी नम्रता से कहा कि उसने तो ऐसा कुछ कहा नहीं है। इस पर भी उन्होंने सुना दिया कि और वह क्या कहेगा। वे अंधे नहीं हैं। अब क्या है उसे पढ़ा दिया, ब्याह कर दिया। अब माँ-बाप का क्या है ? वे जायें चूल्हे-भाड़ में और वह अपनी मस्ती में जीवन गुजारे।

उनसे नहीं रहा गया तो और भी न कहने वाली बात भी कही। ऐसा पता होता तो वे उसे पैदा होते ही मार देते। अब तो वह अपनी मर्जी का मालिक बन गया है और घर में कोई बड़ा जैसे है ही नहीं। चूड़ियों का ताना उन्होंने दिया कि बहू को चूड़ियाँ पहनाई थी तो सहाबजादे ने जाकर तोड़ दी। उनका कहना जारी रहा—''हम तो सोचें कि कौन मुँह लगे, कौन मुँह लगे ! समझदार लड़का है, खुद ही सारी बातें समझता है, पर उन्हें तो अच्छे से अच्छा खाने को मिलता है न, तो उसकी सोचे, बताये ! अपने लिए पढ़ लें, अपने लिए कपड़े आ जायें, अपनी बहू का साज-सिंगार हो जाये। बस, सब अपना ही अपना हो जाये। जब तक कोई कुछ बोले-कहे नहीं, तब तक सिर पर ही चढ़े चले आते हैं।'' समर ने, 'साज-सिंगार वह कब लाया है ? ऐसा पूछा तो और भड़क गये और उन्होंने समर को लात, घूँसे और थप्पड़ों से मारना शुरू कर दिया। भाई साहब ने उन्हें रोका और दूसरी तरफ ले गये। फिर भी बड़बड़ाते रहे कि वह लाख बूढ़े और मरे गिरे हैं, लेकिन अभी भी वह समर की अकल ठिकाने लगा के रहेंगे।

उनका कटु कथन चलता रहा और घर की औरतें पूछती रहीं कि क्या हुआ ? एक-दो औरतें पड़ोस से भी आ गई थीं।

समर ने यह सब अपमान सहकर कहा—''हाँ, बाबूजी, अब चला ही जाऊँगा।''

प्रश्न 26. इच्छा होती है, उसके पति को पकड़कर भरे बाजार में ठोकरों और कोड़ों से खूब पीटूँ—'राक्षस अपनी फूल-सी बहन हमने इसलिए तुझे दी थी ? देख, शरीर पर चोट यों लगती है।'

(i) वक्ता का नाम लिखते हुए उसका परिचय दीजिए।

(ii) मुन्नी का पति मुन्नी पर क्या-क्या अत्याचार करता था ?

(iii) मुन्नी के पति के प्रति समर के क्या विचार हैं ?

(iv) पति को त्यागने के बाद मुन्नी की स्थिति का वर्णन करें।

उत्तर—(i) वक्ता समर है। वह 'सारा आकाश' उपन्यास का नायक है। वह मेधावी, शान्त स्वभाव वाला, पुराने विचारों वाला स्वाभिमानी युवक है। उसकी इच्छा के विरुद्ध उसका विवाह प्रभा के साथ कर दिया जाता है। विवाहोपरान्त उसका जीवन निराशामय हो जाता है और वह अन्तर्द्वन्द्व से ग्रस्त हो जाता है।

(ii) मुन्नी का पति उस पर नाना प्रकार के अत्याचार करता था। वह चरित्रहीन था और एक ब्राह्मण स्त्री उसकी रखैल थी। वह मुन्नी से नौकरानी की तरह अपनी सेवा करवाता था। मुन्नी को दो-दो, तीन-तीन दिन तक खाना नहीं देता था। रात-रातभर मुन्नी की दोनों हथेलियों पर चारपाई के पैर रखकर उसे कुढ़ाने और जलाने को अपनी आनन्द-क्रीड़ा समझता था। वह बेतों से उसे मारता था, जिससे उसके शरीर पर नीले निशान पड़ गये। एक-डेढ़ वर्ष तो गाड़ी रोते-झींकते खिंचती रही, लेकिन सास के मरते ही मुसीबतों का पहाड़ अर्राकर टूट पड़ा। अब मुन्नी के पति को रोकने वाला कोई नहीं था अब वह मुन्नी पर और अत्याचार करने लगा।

(iii) समर की दृष्टि में मुन्नी का पति बहुत बुरा इंसान है। वह जब मुन्नी को देखता है तो उसे मुन्नी के पति पर अत्यन्त क्रोध आता है। वह उन अत्याचारों का प्रतिकार करना चाहता है जो मुन्नी के पति ने मुन्नी पर किये थे। वह कहता है कि वह उसके पति को समाज के समक्ष ले जाकर कोड़ों और ठोकरों से पीटे

जिससे उसके पति को यह अनुभव हो जाये कि चोट का दर्द क्या होता है। समर के मन में उसके पति के प्रति बहुत घृणा है और वह उसके पति को राक्षस भी कहता है।

(iv) अपने पति को त्यागने के बाद मुन्नी अपने मायके में रह रही है। वह बहुत कम बोलती है और तटस्थ रहती है। उसका स्वास्थ्य दिन-प्रतिदिन गिरता जा रहा है। उसे देखकर ऐसा लगता है कि वह दु:ख के पाले में मुरझा गयी है। वह इतनी पढ़ी लिखी नहीं है कि कहीं नौकरी कर सके और सिलाई-कढ़ाई सीखने के लिए भी एक-दो वर्ष चाहिए। इसके अतिरिक्त आर्थिक तंगी भी इन कार्यों में एक बाधा है। जहाँ लड़कों को पढ़ाने की आफत मची रहती है, वहाँ लड़कियाँ कैसे पढ़ सकती हैं ? मुन्नी जब आई-आई थी तो सभी उसके प्रति हमदर्दी दिखाते, उसे हिम्मत बँधाते थे। अब परिवार के प्राय: सभी सदस्य उसे भूल चुके हैं। परिवार में मुन्नी ही अभागिन है। वह किसी से कुछ कहती नहीं, परन्तु मन ही मन सोचती रहती है, भीतर जैसे कोई चीज उसे पीसे डाल रही हो। जब सभी नीचे होते हैं तो वह ऊपर चली जाती है। वह सभी की नजरों से बचने का प्रयास करती है।

इस प्रकार हम कह सकते हैं कि पति को त्यागने के बाद भी मुन्नी की स्थिति शोचनीय और दयनीय है।

प्रश्न 27. देखो कोई, उस काले सिरवाली के लिए भाई पर हाथ उठा रहा है। अरे मैं पूछती हूँ, तुझे शरम नहीं आ रही जो तू उसे शरम की सीख दे रहा है।

(i) यहाँ कौन किसको काले सिरवाली कह रहा है ?

(ii) उक्त कथन में 'तुझे शरम नहीं आ रही·········' पंक्ति का आशय स्पष्ट करें।

(iii) यहाँ किस भाई की बात हो रही है, क्यों ?

(iv) अम्माजी का समर और प्रभा के प्रति कैसा व्यवहार है ?

उत्तर—(i) यहाँ अम्माजी समर की पत्नी प्रभा को काले सिरवाली कह रही है।

(ii) उक्त कथन में 'तुझे शरम नहीं आ रही·········' पंक्ति समर से कही गयी है। अम्माजी को जब यह ज्ञात होता है कि समर ने अमर को मारा है तो वह क्रोधित हो जाती है। वह अमर का समर्थन करती है और समर को फटकारती हैं। समर से कहती है तू छोटे-बड़े किसी को नहीं समझता है। जो भी तेरे मन में आता है, करता रहता है। वह कहती है कि अभी तो मैं जिन्दा हूँ और मेरे होते हुए तुम अमर पर हाथ कैसे उठा सकते हो, समर तू ही बेशरम है और अमर को शरम की सीख दे रहा है।

(iii) यहाँ समर के छोटे भाई अमर की बात हो रही है। इसका कारण समर का अमर के ऊपर हाथ उठाना है। यह घटना इस प्रकार है कि अमर एक बार बाजार से घी लाया था। अमर को एक दिन बिना घी की रोटी मिलती हैं तो वह प्रभा से कहता है कि तुमने सारा घी अपने पति को खिला दिया। समर इस बात को सुनकर आग बबूला हो जाता है और अमर को मारता है। इस कारण यहाँ अमर के बारे में बात हो रही है।

(iv) अम्माजी समर और प्रभा के प्रति बहुत बुरा व्यवहार करती है। वह समर से घृणा करती हैं, इसलिए जब समर अमर को उसकी गलती के लिए मारता है तो भी वे अमर का ही पक्ष लेती हैं और समर को फटकारती हैं। वह समर के इस व्यवहार का कारण उसकी पत्नी प्रभा को मानती हैं। वह प्रभा से अनेक अपशब्द कहती हैं, अशिष्ट व्यवहार करती हैं। वे प्रभा को कलमुँही कहती हैं और प्रभा को समर की गुरू बताती हैं। बेटा कल तक तू पैदल चलना नहीं जानता था, अब आसमान पर उड़ने लगा है। धरती पर चल बेटा, धरती पर। बेटा (समर) तू बहुत बेशर्म है, तुझे माँ-बाप का बिल्कुल ख्याल नहीं है। जब देखो तब बहू (प्रभा) का पक्ष लेता रहता है। अब प्रभा ही तेरे लिए सब कुछ है और हमको तू अपना दुश्मन समझता है। अम्माजी के मन में जो कुछ आता है वही समर से कहती रहती है।

इस प्रकार हम कह सकते हैं कि अम्माजी का समर और प्रभा के प्रति जो व्यवहार है, वह संयुक्त परिवार में रहने के कारण स्वाभाविक है।

प्रश्न 28. **"लेकिन रमा, कल्पनाएँ ही सच हो जाया करती तो फिर कहना ही क्या है। हमारी हर हँसी पर भाग्य दाँत पीसता है। हम रोते हैं तो वह खिलखिलाता है।"**

(i) रमा का संक्षिप्त परिचय दीजिए।

(ii) 'हमारी हर हँसी पर भाग्य दाँत पीसता है।' प्रभा ने ऐसा क्यों कहा ?

(iii) रमा और प्रभा की मित्रता का वर्णन करें।

(iv) यहाँ किन कल्पनाओं की बात हो रही है ?

उत्तर—(i) रमा, प्रभा की सहेली है। वे दोनों एक ही स्कूल में पढ़ती थीं। रमा जोधपुर में रहती है। दोनों में बहुत प्रेम था।

(ii) 'हमारी हर हँसी पर भाग्य दाँत पीसता है।' प्रभा ने ऐसा इसलिए कहा क्योंकि मनुष्य को वह मिलता है जो उसके भाग्य में होता है, वह नहीं मिलता है जो वह सोचता है। उसके अनुसार सभी भाग्य के समक्ष विवश हैं। वह कहती है कि हम कितने भी प्रयत्न करें परन्तु भाग्य के लिखे को बदल नहीं सकते। प्रभा ने ऐसा स्वयं अनुभव किया था, उसने विवाह से पहले अनेक सपने देखे थे, परन्तु विवाह के बाद उसे यह अनुभव हुआ कि भाग्य ही प्रधान है।

(iii) रमा और प्रभा घनिष्ठ मित्र हैं। स्कूल के दिनों में रमा जब प्रभा से नाराज हो जाती थी तो स्कूल के पीछे वाले अनार के पेड़ के पास मुँह फुलाकर बैठ जाती थी और प्रभा उसे मनाने जाती थी। रमा प्रभा से कहती थी कि तुम्हें सर्कस में नौकरी करनी चाहिए। प्रभा शादी के बाद भी रमा के पास जाना चाहती है, परन्तु परिस्थितिवश नहीं जा पाती और रमा भी उसको पत्र लिखती रहती है। दोनों में इतना प्रेम है कि वे एक-दूसरे से दूर होना नहीं चाहती हैं। कुल मिलाकर दोनों एक-दूसरे की सच्ची मित्र हैं।

(iv) यहाँ प्रभा, रमा से उन कल्पनाओं के बारे में कह रही है जो विवाह से पूर्व एक लड़की की होती हैं। प्रभा कहती है, मुझे अब यह अनुभव हुआ कि हमारी कल्पनाएँ कितनी झूठी होती हैं। हम लोग न जाने क्या-क्या चाहते हैं। हमारे चाहने की कोई सीमा नहीं होती है। संसार की हर अच्छी वस्तु को चाहने की कल्पना स्कूल के दिनों में होती है। रमा, हमें उस समय कोई क्यों नहीं बताता कि यह सब झूठ है।

प्रभा कहती है कि किसी भी लड़की की शादी होती तो मैं उसके पति को जाकर देखती और कहती थी कि मेरा पति ऐसा नहीं होगा, वह तो प्रोफेसर होगा, कहीं अफसर होगा, किसी बड़ी कम्पनी का मैनेजर होगा। परिवार में बस हम दोनों ही होंगे तथा हमारी एक सुन्दर कोठी होगी। उसमें तरह-तरह के सामान होंगे। घर में तीन-चार नौकर होंगे। कहीं बैडमिण्टन या टैनिस कोर्ट होगा। मेरा पति सुबह मुझे उठायेगा और मैं चाय पीते-पीते समाचार पत्र पढ़ूँगी। पति के दफ्तर जाने के बाद मैं अकेली रह जाऊँगी तो समय व्यतीत करने के लिए किसी पड़ोसिन के यहाँ चली जाया करूँगी या उसे बुला लिया करूँगी। शाम को हम दोनों सिनेमा देखने या किसी परिचित के घर जाया करेंगे।

इस प्रकार शादी से पहले एक लड़की की अनेक कल्पनाएँ होती हैं।

प्रश्न 29. हाँ, इस बात का बुरा मान रहे थे कि पहली बार तुम्हें ही लेने जाना चाहिए था, यह कायदा है। मैंने समझा तो दिया था कि गौना तो शादी के साथ ही हो गया था।

(i) वक्ता का नाम लिखते हुए उसका परिचय दीजिए।

(ii) प्रभा के मायके वालों ने समर के बारे में क्या कहा और अमर ने उन्हें कैसे समझाया ?

(iii) गौना किसे कहते हैं ? यहाँ किसके गौने की बात हो रही है ?

(iv) समर का चरित्र-चित्रण कीजिए।

उत्तर—(i) वक्ता अमर है। वह परिवार में समर से छोटा है और कुँवर से बड़ा है। उसका अभी विद्यार्थी जीवन चल रहा है। हाईस्कूल में फेल होने के बाद भी बाबूजी उसका विवाह करना चाहते हैं।

(ii) अमर जब अपनी भाभी के घर जाता है तो वे अमर से कहते हैं कि पहली बार प्रभा को लेने के लिए समर को आना चाहिए था, यही नियम होता है। अमर उन्हें समझाते हुए कहता है कि गौना तो शादी के साथ ही हो गया था। समर भैया इस समय पढ़ाई में व्यस्त हैं, इसलिए नहीं आ सके।

(iii) गौना विवाह के उपरान्त की रीति है। विवाह के कुछ समय पश्चात् वधू पिता के घर से पहली बार ससुराल आती है तो उसे गौना कहते हैं। यहाँ समर की पत्नी प्रभा के गौने के बारे में बात हो रही है।

(iv) समर 'सारा आकाश' उपन्यास का नायक है। उसके चरित्र में निम्न विशेषताएँ हैं—

(1) मेधावी छात्र—समर एक मेधावी छात्र है वह पढ़ना चाहता है, परन्तु घरवाले उसकी शादी कर देते हैं। घर का वातावरण भी पढ़ने योग्य नहीं है, फिर भी समर इण्टर में द्वितीय श्रेणी में उत्तीर्ण होता है।

(2) पुराने विचारों और पहनावे वाला—वह पुराने विचारों वाला युवक है। वह अपने मित्रों की तरह चटक-मटक के कपड़े नहीं पहनता है। उसका मित्र दिवाकर उसकी वेशभूषा पर कटाक्ष भी करता है, फिर भी वह साधारण कपड़े ही पहनता है।

(3) स्वाभिमानी—समर एक स्वाभिमानी युवक है। प्रभा समर से नहीं बोलती है तो वह भी प्रभा से नहीं बोलता है। वह हिन्दू धर्म को सर्वश्रेष्ठ मानता है और स्वयं पर गर्व करता है कि वह एक हिन्दू है।

(4) परिवर्तनशील स्वभाव—समर प्रारम्भ में प्रभा से नाराज रहता है और उस पर कोई ध्यान नहीं देता है। एक घटना के बाद प्रभा के प्रति समर का व्यवहार परिवर्तित हो जाता है और प्रभा से प्रेम करने लगता है।

(5) सच्चा मित्र—वह दिवाकर का सच्चा मित्र है। वह कभी-कभी दिवाकर के घर भोजन भी कर लेता है। वह कभी भी दिवाकर की बुराई नहीं करता है।

प्रश्न 30. मिट्टी के ढेले और गणेशजी में उसे अन्तर नहीं दिखाई दिया ? अगर किसी के घर इस तरह के विश्वास है भी तो उनका अपमान करने का अधिकार उसे किसने दिया ?

(i) उक्त कथन कौन किसके बारे में तथा क्यों कह रहा है ?

(ii) प्रभा ने क्या कर दिया था ?

(iii) यहाँ किन विश्वासों की बात हो रही है ?

(iv) प्रभा ने जो गलती की थी, उस पर घरवालों की क्या प्रतिक्रिया हुई ?

उत्तर—(i) उक्त कथन समर अपनी पत्नी प्रभा के बारे में कह रहा है। इसका कारण यह है कि प्रभा ने गलती की थी।

(ii) प्रभा से नामकरण वाले दिन एक गलती हो जाती है। जब भाभी की पुत्री का नामकरण हुआ तो पण्डित जी ने गणेशजी की पूजा की तथा उससे कलावा बाँध दिया। प्रभा गणशजी को साधारण मिट्टी का ढेला समझकर उससे बर्तन साफ कर लेती है।

(iii) यहाँ अपनी संस्कृति के प्रति विश्वासों की बात हुई है। समर कहता है कि कोई कितना भी पढ़ ले, परन्तु उसे अपने पूज्य देवों का अपमान नहीं करना चाहिए। गणेशजी का हिन्दू पूजा-पद्धति में प्रथम और पूज्यनीय स्थान है। इसी विश्वास की उक्त कथन में चर्चा हुई है।

(iv) प्रभा ने जो गलती की थी उस पर घर में खूब हंगामा हुआ। सभी लोग प्रभा की बुराई कर रहे थे। अम्मा चिल्ला-चिल्लाकर कह रही थीं कि सगुन-सादूत के दिन इसने बहुत बुरा किया है। कोठरी में अपनी चारपाई पर पड़ी भाभी खूब फूट-फूटकर रो रही थीं और प्रभा के लिए अपशब्द कह रही थीं। वह इसके लिए प्रभा की पढ़ाई को दोष देते हुए कह रहीं थीं कि अगर कुछ हो गया तो इसका क्या बिगड़ेगा जो कुछ होगा सो हमें भुगतना पड़ेगा।

अम्माजी भी प्रभा से कहती हैं कि क्या अंधी हो गई थी ? दिखाई नहीं दिया कि उसमें कलावा बँधा है या नहीं ? समर जब बाहर से आता है तो वह भी प्रभा पर अपना क्रोध प्रकट करता है। पूरी शक्ति के साथ प्रभा के गाल पर थप्पड़ मारता है, प्रभा से कहता है कि यहाँ रहना है तो ढंग से रहो अन्यथा जहाँ जाना चाहो चली जाओ। इसके बाद सब चुप हो जाते हैं।

प्रश्न 31. दाल छत पर बिनेगी। ऐसी ही उस दिन छत पर बाल्टी ले जाकर सिर धोया गया ? उस दिन तो चुप हो गया, मुन्नी ने सिफारिश कर दी।

(i) छत पर सिर धोने कौन तथा क्यों गया था ?

(ii) बाबूजी प्रभा से छत पर जाने के लिए क्यों मना करते हैं ?

(iii) मुन्नी ने किसकी तथा क्या सिफारिश की थी ?

(iv) इस घटना के बाद घरवालों ने प्रभा के बारे में क्या कहा और प्रभा पर उसका क्या प्रभाव पड़ा ?

उत्तर—(i) छत पर सिर धोने समर की पत्नी प्रभा गयी थी क्योंकि नीचे बहुत सर्दी थी।

(ii) बाबूजी इस बात से बहुत नाराज होते हैं कि प्रभा दाल बीनने, सिर धोने छत पर जाती है। वे कहते हैं कि सर्दियों का समय है और हर आदमी धूप में बैठने के लिए ऊपर जाता है। जब तुम छत पर जाती हो तो लोग ताक-झाँक करते हैं। यह अच्छी बात नहीं है। एक सभ्य परिवार की बहू को ऐसा नहीं करना चाहिए।

(iii) मुन्नी ने बाबूजी से प्रभा की सिफारिश की थी। एक बार प्रभा ने छत पर सिर धोया था। बाबूजी इससे बहुत नाराज हुए और प्रभा को डाँटते हैं। उस समय मुन्नी प्रभा के पक्ष में बोलती है कि बाबूजी सर्दियों का समय है और हमें सिर धोने में बहुत समय लगता है। प्रभा इस कारण छत पर सिर धोने गयी थी कि नीचे बहुत सर्दी है। इसके बाद बाबूजी चुप हो जाते हैं।

(iv) इस घटना के बाद प्रभा को बहुत ताने सुनने पड़ते हैं। बाबूजी कहते हैं कि अब तो खाना-सोना सभी छत पर होने लगा है। हमेशा गूँगी की तरह मनहूस-सी घूमती रहती है। छत पर तू क्यों जाती है ? वहाँ तेरा क्या है ? किसके लिए छत पर जाती है ? ऐसी अनेक बातें बाबूजी प्रभा से कहते हैं और कहते हैं कि बहू हो कायदे से रहो। और अम्माजी तो उनके चरित्र पर आरोप लगाती हैं और कहती हैं कि अगर छत पर नहीं जायेगी तो पड़ोसियों से नैना कैसे लड़ायेगी ? बाबूजी भी कहते हैं कि कहीं पाण्डे की लड़की की तरह भाग न जाये। इस प्रकार प्रभा को चरित्रहीन बताया जाता है।

इन बातों का प्रभा पर गहरा प्रभाव होता है। इससे पहले उसे इतना दु:ख कभी नहीं हुआ था जितना अब हो रहा है। वह रात भर बाहर बैठी रोती रही।

प्रश्न 32. बाबूजी, तुम मुझे अपने हाथ से जहर देकर मार डालो, मेरा गला घोंट दो……मुझे वहाँ मत भेजो……मुझे वहाँ मत भेजो……बाबूजी।

(i) उक्त कथन कौन, किससे तथा कब कह रहा है ?

(ii) उक्त कथन के आधार पर बाबूजी के वक्ता के प्रति दृष्टिकोण को स्पष्ट करें।

(iii) वक्ता अपनी ससुराल क्यों नहीं जाना चाहती है ?

(iv) बाबूजी मुन्नी को ससुराल भेजने को कब तैयार हुए और मुन्नी की क्या प्रतिक्रिया थी ? स्पष्ट करें।

उत्तर—(i) उक्त कथन मुन्नी ने बाबूजी से उस समय कहा जब वह मुन्नी को ससुराल भेजने को तैयार हो जाते हैं।

(ii) बाबूजी का मुन्नी के प्रति दृष्टिकोण अदूरदर्शी और अव्यावहारिक है। वे मुन्नी को अपने ऊपर बोझ समझते हैं, इसलिए मुन्नी के मना करने के बाद भी उसे ससुराल भेजने को तैयार हो जाते हैं। वे परम्परावादी विचारों के व्यक्ति हैं, इसलिए सोचते हैं कि एक लड़की जिसकी शादी हो चुकी है, उसे ससुराल में ही रहना चाहिए। उनके हठ के कारण ही मुन्नी का निधन हो जाता है।

(iii) मुन्नी अपनी ससुराल इसलिए नहीं जाना चाहती है क्योंकि उसका पति चरित्रहीन था और उस पर अनेक अत्याचार करता था। उसे दो-दो, तीन-तीन दिन तक भूखा रखता और बेतों से उसकी पिटाई करता था। पिटाई से उसके शरीर पर नीले निशान पड़ गये थे। उसका पति रात-भर इधर-उधर घूमता रहता था। एक स्त्री को भी अपने घर लाया था और मुन्नी से नौकरानी की तरह काम कराता था।

(iv) बाबूजी मुन्नी को उसकी ससुराल भेजने को उस समय तैयार हो जाते हैं जब उसका पति उसे लेने आया है। उसका पति बाबूजी से क्षमा माँगता है। वह अफसोस जाहिर करता है कि गलती हो गयी, अभी कभी ऐसा नहीं होगा। अगर ऐसी बात सुनी तो कान पकड़ लेना। जो बिरादरी वाले दण्ड देंगे उसे स्वीकार होगा। वह बात कहते-कहते बहुत उदास हो जाता है। बाबूजी पर इन बातों का गहरा प्रभाव पड़ता है और मुन्नी को उसके साथ भेजने के लिए हाँ कर देते हैं।

मुन्नी को जब यह पता चलता है तो वह बहुत दु:खी होती है। वह रोने लगती है और बाबूजी से लिपट जाती है। वह कहती है कि उसे ससुराल मत भेजो, वह दूसरों के घर काम करके अपना पेट भर लेगी। ससुराल भेजने से तो अच्छा है कि आप मुझे जहर लाकर दे दो, परन्तु मुझे ससुराल मत भेजो।

प्रश्न 33. कोई और लड़की होती तो घर जाकर मेरी बुराई करती कि मुँह दिखाने की हिम्मत न पड़ती। बताया होगा कि पढ़ने में व्यस्त हैं, परीक्षा पास आ रही है।

(i) यहाँ किस लड़की की बात हो रही है ?

(ii) उक्त कथन के आधार पर बताइये कि समर प्रभा के बारे में क्या सोचता है ?

(iii) प्रभा ने अपने मायके में समर के बारे में क्या कहा ? उसके मायके वाले किस बात का बुरा मान रहे थे ?

(iv) समर ने ऐसा क्यों कहा कि 'और कोई लड़की होती.........हिम्मत न पड़ती।' कारण सहित स्पष्ट करें।

उत्तर—(i) यहाँ समर की पत्नी प्रभा की बात हो रही है। वह पढ़ी-लिखी, स्वाभिमानी, त्याग भावना से युक्त एक आदर्श गृहणी है।

(ii) समर प्रभा से नाराज रहता था, इसलिए उसने सोचा कि प्रभा ने अपने मायके जाकर मेरी बुराई की होगी। उसे जब यह ज्ञात होता है कि प्रभा ने उसकी बुराई नहीं की तो वह कहता है कि एक पढ़ी-लिखी और अनपढ़ स्त्री में यही अन्तर होता है। प्रभा के स्थान पर कोई और लड़की होती तो मेरी बुराई अवश्य करती।

(iii) प्रभा समर के प्रति समर्पण भावना से युक्त है। वह अपने मायके में जाकर समर के बारे में कहती है कि उनके बोर्ड के इम्तिहान हैं, वे खूब मन लगाकर पढ़ाई कर रहे हैं, व्यस्त हैं। वह उनकी पढ़ाई में बाधा नहीं चाहती है। प्रभा के मायके वाले इस बात का बुरा मान रहे थे कि पहली बार समर को आना चाहिए था, यही नियम होता है।

(iv) समर ने ऐसा इसलिए कहा क्योंकि उसने प्रभा पर अनेक अत्याचार किये थे। वह सुहागरात वाले दिन भी प्रभा से नहीं बोलता है। प्रभा की उपेक्षा करता रहता है। प्रभा जब कष्ट में होती है तो उसे देखकर समर को आनन्द की प्राप्ति होती है। नामकरण वाले दिन प्रभा गणेशजी को भूलवश मिट्टी का ढेला समझ

लेती है और उससे बर्तन साफ कर लेती है। इसके लिए समर उसे मारता है। प्रभा से कहता है कि तुम्हें यहाँ रहना है तो कायदे से रहो अन्यथा जहाँ स्थान मिले, वहाँ चली जाओ। घर के अन्य सदस्य जब प्रभा के साथ दुर्व्यहार करते हैं, तब भी समर तटस्थ रहता है। प्रभा को चरित्रहीन बताया जाता है, इस बात पर भी समर किसी से कुछ नहीं कहता है। उसे प्रभा से कोई मतलब नहीं है, चाहे वह जिये या मरे।

प्रश्न 34. और तो कुछ उम्मीद महारानीजी से है नहीं यह ठीक से कर दें तो प्रसाद बाँटूँगी। मुझे तो दीखे, उसमें भी बीस बातें उठेंगी।

(i) यहाँ प्रसाद बाँटने की बात कौन कह रहा है तथा क्यों ?

(ii) यहाँ महारानीजी किसे कहा गया है, क्यों ?

(iii) भाभी का प्रभा के प्रति कैसा व्यवहार है ?

(iv) प्रभा से किस कार्य की उम्मीद की जा रही है और वह उसमें कितनी सफल होती है ?

उत्तर—(i) यहाँ प्रसाद बाँटने की बात समर की भाभी कह रही हैं क्योंकि उन्हें प्रभा पर विश्वास नहीं है कि वह घर को सम्भाल पायेगी।

(ii) यहाँ महारानीजी प्रभा को कहा गया है। भाभी प्रभा को घमण्डी समझती है। उनके अनुसार प्रभा पढ़ी-लिखी तो है परन्तु उसे कुछ आता नहीं है। उसे अपनी सुन्दरता और पढ़ाई का घमण्ड है। इस कारण भाभी प्रभा पर व्यंग्य करते हुए उसे महारानीजी कहती हैं।

(iii) भाभी का व्यवहार प्रभा के प्रति अच्छा नहीं है। वह प्रभा की पढ़ाई-लिखाई से ईर्ष्या करती हैं और कहती हैं कि प्रभा कोई इन्द्र की परी नहीं है जो इतने नखरे दिखाती है। कुछ गुण हों तो नखरे सहे भी जायें। जब प्रभा गणेश जी की मूर्ति से बर्तन साफ कर लेती है तो वे प्रभा से रुष्ट हो जाती हैं।

(iv) समर की भाभी के पुत्री होने वाली थी, इसलिए घर के सभी उत्तरदायित्व प्रभा के ऊपर थे। सभी के लिए खाना बनाना, बर्तन साफ करना, कपड़े धोना आदि। प्रभा से इन्हीं कार्यों की उम्मीद की जा रही है। प्रभा ने अपनी तरफ से इन उत्तरदायित्वों का निर्वाह करने का पूरा प्रयास किया था। वह हर काम को ऐसी आसानी से और चुपचाप करती चली जाती थी मानो मशीन हो और उसे यह सब करने में कोई तकलीफ नहीं होती थी। हर नये काम को आसानी से कर लेती थी। वह दिन भर कार्य में लगी रहती है। कभी भाभी के कार्यों को करती तो कभी घर के कार्यों को करती। उसे तनिक भी फुर्सत नहीं मिलती थी। उससे जल्दबाजी में कुछ गलतियाँ भी हो जाती थीं।

कुल मिलाकर प्रभा ने काफी हद तक अपने उत्तरदायित्वों को सम्भाल लिया था।

प्रश्न 35. अपने काँपते और बेजान हाथों को निहायत डरते-डरते उसके कन्धे पर रखकर भर्राये और खण्डित स्वर में कहा, "प्रभा, तुम मुझसे नाराज हो.......?"

(i) समर के हाथ क्यों काँप रहे थे ?

(ii) "प्रभा, तुम मुझसे नाराज हो.......?" समर ने उक्त कथन प्रभा से कब कहा ?

(iii) प्रभा समर से क्यों नाराज थी ?

(iv) "प्रभा, तुम मुझसे नाराज हो.......?" समर के ऐसा कहने की प्रभा पर क्या प्रतिक्रिया हुई और समर पर उसका क्या प्रभाव पड़ा ?

उत्तर—(i) समर के हाथ इसलिए काँप रहे थे कि वह पहली बार प्रभा से बोल रहा था।

(ii) प्रभा के चरित्र पर आरोप लगाये जाते हैं तो वह इसे सहन नहीं कर पाती है और छत पर बैठी रो रही थी। समर जब रात को पानी पीने जाता है तो प्रभा को देखता है कि वह रो रही है। समर कहता है कि प्रभा तुम सुबह रो लेना। इस पर प्रभा कहती है कि आपको मुझसे क्या मतलब ? आप जाकर सोइये। इन बातों से समर प्रभावित होकर प्रभा से पूछता है कि प्रभा तुम मुझसे नाराज हो ?

(iii) समर का व्यवहार प्रभा के प्रति अच्छा नहीं था। वह उससे बोलता नहीं था। प्रभा की बुराई करता था। अगर घरवाले प्रभा को डाँटते थे तो भी किसी से कुछ नहीं कहता था। प्रभा को कष्ट देने में उसे आनन्द आता था। प्रभा को पहली बार लेने भी नहीं गया था और प्रभा के लिए उसके मन में सदैव घृणा रहती थी। इन सब कारणों से प्रभा समर से नाराज रहती थी।

(iv) "प्रभा, तुम मुझसे नाराज हो…… ?" समर के ऐसा कहने के बाद प्रभा ने अपने दोनों हाथ बढ़ाकर समर के कन्धे पकड़ लिए और समर से आवेश में पूछा—'मुझे बताओ, मैंने तुम्हारा क्या बिगाड़ा ? अगर मैं तुम्हारे योग्य नहीं हूँ तो अपने हाथों से मेरी हत्या कर दो, मैं कुछ भी नहीं कहूँगी। तुम मुझे किस अपराध का दण्ड दे रहे हो ? ये बातें कहते-कहते प्रभा रोने लगती है और समर से लिपट जाती है।

समर की इन बातों से बहुत प्रभावित होता है। वह भी रोने लगता है और दोनों बहुत देर तक रोते रहते हैं। इस घटना के बाद समर का व्यवहार प्रभा के प्रति परिवर्तित हो जाता है और वह प्रभा से प्यार करने लगता है।

प्रश्न 36. यार इस इम्तिहान की ही याद मत दिलाया कर। मेरी जान निकल जाती है। पता नहीं, पास भी होंगे या नहीं। फेल ही हो गये तो सचमुच, हमें मरने की भी जगह नहीं है।"

(i) उक्त कथन कौन किससे कब कह रहा है ?

(ii) यहाँ किस इम्तिहान की क्या बात हो रही है ?

(iii) वक्ता का संक्षिप्त परिचय दीजिए।

(iv) दिवाकर का चरित्र-चित्रण कीजिए।

उत्तर—(i) उक्त कथन समर दिवाकर से उस समय कहता है जब वह उसके घर गया था।

(ii) यहाँ समर दिवाकर से बोर्ड के इम्तिहानों के बारे में बात कर रहा है। उन दोनों ने इम्तिहान के समय बहुत मेहनत की थी। वे दोनों साथ-साथ पढ़ते थे। समर तो उन दिनों की याद करके ही परेशान हो जाता है। उसे इम्तिहान के परिणाम से बहुत भय लगता है। वह दिवाकर से कहता है कि पता नहीं फेल होंगे या पास। यदि फेल हो गये तो बहुत बदनामी होगी। हम किसी को मुँह दिखाने लायक भी नहीं रहेंगे।

(iii) उक्त कथन का वक्ता समर है। वह 'सारा आकाश' उपन्यास का नायक है। वह पढ़ने वाला, शान्त स्वभाव और पुराने विचारों वाला स्वाभिमानी युवक है। उसका विवाह उसकी इच्छा के विरुद्ध प्रभा के साथ कर दिया गया है। विवाहोपरान्त उसका जीवन निराशामय हो जाता है।

(iv) दिवाकर समर का सहपाठी है और उसका सच्चा मित्र भी है। दिवाकर के चरित्र की विशेषताएँ निम्न हैं—

(i) सच्चा मित्र—वह समर का सच्चा मित्र है। वह समर की हर प्रकार से सहायता करता है। समर आवश्यकता होने पर दिवाकर से रुपये भी लेता है। दिवाकर ने समर को नौकरी भी दिलाई है।

(ii) पढ़ने वाला युवक—दिवाकर भी समर की तरह मेधावी है और इण्टर के बाद भी पढ़ना चाहता है। वह समर से भी इण्टर के बाद पढ़ने के लिए कहता है।

(iii) आदर्श पति—दिवाकर एक आदर्श पति है। वह अपनी पत्नी किरण का पूरा ध्यान रखता है। वह उसे कभी-कभी सिनेमा दिखाने भी ले जाता है।

(iv) आधुनिक विचारों वाला—दिवाकर आधुनिक विचारों वाला युवक है। वह समर की तरह पुराने ढंग के कपड़े नहीं पहनता है और समर की इसी कारण आलोचना भी करता है।

(v) आदर्शवादी—दिवाकर एक आदर्शवादी युवक है। वह अपने आदर्शों की कभी भी उपेक्षा नहीं करता है। वह अपने उच्च आदर्शों के कारण समर की सहायता भी करता है और बदले में कुछ भी नहीं चाहता है।

कुल मिलाकर दिवाकर का चरित्र एक आदर्श युवक का है।

प्रश्न 37. ''दासी वह काहे को, दासी तो हम हैं, जिन्दगी भर ठेक-ठेककर खिलाया, अब और खिलायेंगे। पहले एक को खिलाया, अब दो-दो को खिलायेंगे।

(i) स्वयं को दासी कौन कह रहा है तथा क्यों ?

(ii) उक्त कथन के आधार पर बताइये कि कौन किससे तथा क्यों रुष्ट है ?

(iii) अम्माजी ने अपने क्रोध को किन शब्दों में व्यक्त किया ?

(iv) अम्माजी और प्रभा का सम्बन्ध कैसा था ? उक्त कथन के आधार पर विवेचना कीजिए।

उत्तर—(i) स्वयं को दासी अम्माजी कह रही हैं। इसका कारण समर का प्रभा के पक्ष में बोलना है।

(ii) अम्माजी समर से रुष्ट हैं। समर अम्माजी से प्रभा के बारे में कहता है कि उस पर कोई ध्यान नहीं देता है। उसकी किसी को कोई परवाह ही नहीं है कि वह कब खाती, कब सोती है। मैंने प्रभा के लिए एक कपड़ा माँगा था, उसे भी नहीं दे सकतीं। सब जिम्मेदारियाँ प्रभा पर ही है। क्या भाभी कुछ भी करने लायक नहीं है ? इन बातों से अम्माजी समर से रुष्ट हो जाती हैं।

(iii) अम्माजी ने समर से क्रोधित होकर कहा कि तू बहू के कहने से ऐसा कर रहा है। तू तो कल तक पैदल चलना भी नहीं जानता था, उसी ने तुझे यह शिक्षा दी है। अब तू हमें तमीज़ सिखाने वाला है। तेरी पत्नी तो महारानी है। वह क्यों कार्य करेगी ? हम दासी हैं सो उसे कर-करके खिलायेंगे। पहले तुम्हें खिलाते थे, अब दोनों को खिलायेंगे।

(iv) अम्माजी और प्रभा के मध्य सम्बन्ध अच्छे नहीं थे। अम्माजी प्रभा से पर्दा करने के लिए कहती थीं, पर प्रभा पर्दा नहीं करती थी, क्योंकि वह एक पढ़ी-लिखी स्त्री है। अम्माजी अक्सर समर की शादी को लेकर प्रभा को ताने देती रहती थीं क्योंकि समर की शादी में दहेज कम मिला था। वे समर की दूसरी शादी करना चाहती थीं। वे समर के कारण भी प्रभा से नाराज रहती थीं क्योंकि वह समर की अपेक्षा अमर से अधिक स्नेह करती थीं। प्रभा के चरित्र पर भी अम्माजी शंका करती हैं और उसे फटकारती रहती हैं। नामकरण वाले दिन प्रभा से गलती हो गयी थी। उसने मिट्टी के गणेशजी से बर्तन साफ कर लिए थे। इसके बाद अम्माजी प्रभा से कहती हैं कि क्या तू अंधी है ? प्रभा भी अम्माजी की कोई बात नहीं मानती है और वही करती है जो उसे अच्छा लगता है।

इस प्रकार हम कह सकते हैं कि प्रभा और अम्माजी के मध्य सम्बन्ध बहुत चिन्ताजनक हैं।

प्रश्न 38. फिर जाने क्या मेरे चेहरे की ओर देखकर बोली, ''रात को खाना-वाना खाकर जब भाभी अम्मा के पैर दबाती है न, तभी अक्सर इस तरह की बातें होती रहती हैं।''

(i) उक्त कथन कौन किससे कब कह रहा है ?

(ii) वक्ता का संक्षिप्त परिचय दीजिए।

(iii) मुन्नी समर को क्या बताना चाहती है ?

(iv) घरवाले किसकी दूसरी शादी करना चाहते हैं और क्यों ? समर के इस बारे में क्या विचार हैं ?

उत्तर—(i) उक्त कथन मुन्नी ने समर से उस समय कहा जब वह भोजन कर रहा था।

(ii) वक्ता मुन्नी है। वह समर की बहन है। सत्रह-अठारह वर्ष की आयु में घर की कुछ वस्तुएँ बेचकर उसकी शादी हो जाती है। ससुराल में पति उस पर बहुत अत्याचार करता था, इसलिए वह अपने पिता के घर लौट आयी है। अब वह अधिक-से-अधिक चुप रहती है और मन ही मन कुढ़ती रहती है। मुन्नी का पति मुन्नी को लेने आता है और अपनी गलती की माफी माँगता है और बाबूजी मुन्नी को भेज देते हैं। कुछ दिनों बाद मुन्नी का स्वर्गवास हो जाता है।

(iii) मुन्नी समर को बताना चाहती है कि घरवाले उसकी दूसरी शादी करना चाहते हैं। समर मुन्नी से पूछता है कि इस तरह की बातें तुझे कैसे मालूम हुईं। मुन्नी उसे बताती है कि रात को भाभी जब अम्मा के पैर दबाती हैं, उस समय तुम्हारी दूसरी शादी के बारे में बातें होती हैं।

(iv) घरवाले समर की दूसरी शादी कराना चाहते हैं क्योंकि समर की जिद के कारण उन्हें शादी में कुछ नहीं मिला, अपितु जो उम्मीद थी उससे भी कम मिला। इसके अतिरिक्त प्रभा भी एक कारण है। घरवाले प्रभा से नाराज रहते हैं क्योंकि वह घरवालों की बात नहीं मानती है। घरवाले उससे पर्दा करने के लिए कहते हैं, परन्तु वह ऐसा नहीं करती है। वे प्रभा को चरित्रहीन भी समझते हैं और छत पर जाने से मना करते हैं, क्योंकि छत पर धूप का बहाना करके आस-पड़ोस के लोग ताँक-छाँक करते हैं। प्रभा उनकी बात पर ध्यान नहीं देती है। भाभी भी प्रभा को घमण्डी औरत समझती है। उनके अनुसार प्रभा को अपनी पढ़ाई-लिखाई और सुन्दरता का घमण्ड है, परन्तु उसे आता कुछ नहीं है। वह प्रभा से घृणा करती हैं। अम्माजी भी प्रभा को डाँटती रहती है।

प्रश्न 39. किस समय वे क्या कर बैठेंगे, कोई ठिकाना नहीं। जिन दिनों वे मुझे मारते थे, उन दिनों तो एक अल्हड़ और जिद्दी निश्चिन्तता रहती थी कि ज्यादा से ज्यादा पीट ही तो देंगे।

(i) यहाँ किसकी तथा क्या बात हो रही है ?

(ii) उक्त कथन के आधार पर बाबूजी के स्वभाव का परिचय दीजिए।

(iii) यहाँ समर किन दिनों की क्या बात कर रहा है ?

(iv) 'बाबूजी' का चरित्र परिस्थितियों से निर्मित हुआ है।' इस कथन की समीक्षा कीजिए।

उत्तर—(i) यहाँ बाबूजी की बात हो रही है। समर उनके बारे में बता रहा है कि वे कभी भी कुछ भी कर देते हैं उनका कोई विश्वास नहीं है।

(ii) बाबूजी परिवार के मुखिया हैं। वह सभी पर अपना अधिकार समझते हैं। उनके मन में जो होता है वे वह बिना सोचे समझे कह देते हैं। समर कहता है कि उसे बाबूजी पर तनिक भी विश्वास नहीं है। वे कब क्या काम करेंगे, कुछ कहा नहीं जा सकता। वे कब क्या काम करेंगे कुछ कहा नहीं जा सकता। वे अचानक मुझे मारने लेगेंगे या किसी को डाँटने लगेंगे। इस प्रकार बाबूजी का स्वभाव बड़ा कठोर है।

(iii) यहाँ समर विवाह से पूर्व के दिनों की बात कर रहा है। उन दिनों वह खुश रहता था और किसी बात का कोई फर्क नहीं पड़ता था। वह बाबूजी से डरता था लेकिन कहता था कि बाबूजी ज्यादा से ज्यादा पीट ही तो देंगे और क्या करेंगे। खेलने में भी तो चोट लग जाती है और हम उसे सहन कर लेते हैं।

(iv) बाबूजी के परिवार में कई सदस्य हैं—अम्माजी, धीरज, समर, अमर, कुँवर, मुन्नी, बड़ी बहू और प्रभा तथा धीरज की पुत्री। घर में खर्चे बहुत हैं और कमाने वाला अकेला धीरज है। समर, अमर और कुँवर का पढ़ाई का खर्चा है। मुन्नी को उसके पति ने छोड़ दिया है। उसका बोझ भी बाबूजी पर है। बाबूजी को पच्चीस रुपये पेंशन के मिलते हैं। समर की शादी करने के बाद घर पर पैसे माँगने वाले आते रहते हैं। कभी गेहूँ वाला, कभी घी वाला, कभी राशन वाला और घर पर प्रतिदिन इनके कारण लड़ाई होती रहती है।

बाबूजी अम्माजी से प्राय: कहते रहते हैं कि अब आगे क्या होगा ? वह धीरे-धीरे चिड़चिड़े होने लगते हैं। बात-बात पर समर को फटकारते रहते हैं। प्रभा के छत पर जाने वाली बात से इतने क्रोधित हो जाते हैं कि प्रभा को चरित्रहीन कहते हैं। समर जब बोर्ड की फीस माँगने जाता है तो उसे डाँटते हैं। वे मुन्नी को भी अपनी जिद के कारण ससुराल भेज देते हैं। उनकी अदूरदर्शिता के कारण मुन्नी का देहान्त हो जाता है।

उपर्युक्त विवेचन के आधार पर हम कह सकते हैं कि बाबूजी का चरित्र परिस्थितियों से निर्मित हुआ है।

प्रश्न 40. स्नेह और आत्मीयता से भाभी बोलीं, "चलो, खाना खा लो। सब धीरे-धीरे ठीक हो जायेगा। तुम्हारा भी खून गरम है और वह भी अभी बच्ची ही है। मैं समझा दूँगी उसे।"

(i) भाभी ने समर से ये कथन कब और क्यों कहे ?

(ii) भाभी किसे समझाने की बात कह रही है तथा क्यों ?

(iii) भाभी ने समर से ऐसा क्यों कहा कि सब धीरे-धीरे ठीक हो जायेगा

(iv) भाभी का चरित्र-चित्रण कीजिए।

उत्तर—(i) भाभी ने समर से ये कथन भोजन करने के समय कहे क्योंकि समर उनसे शिकायत कर रहा था कि प्रभा बहुत घमण्डी है।

(ii) भाभी समर की पत्नी प्रभा को समझाने की बात कर रही हैं। इसका कारण प्रभा और समर के मध्य सामंजस्य का अभाव है। वे दोनों एक-दूसरे से नहीं बोलते हैं। समर चाहता है कि प्रभा पहले बोलना शुरू करे जबकि प्रभा का कहना है कि वह किसी की खुशामद नहीं कर सकती। अतः भाभी कहती हैं कि तुम्हारा भी खून नया है और वह भी अभी छोटी है, इसलिए मैं उसे समझा दूँगी।

(iii) समर और प्रभा की शादी हुए अभी कुछ ही दिन हुए हैं। यह शादी समर की इच्छा के विरुद्ध हुई थी। इसलिए वह प्रभा के ऊपर कोई ध्यान नहीं देता है। प्रभा सुहागरात को भी समर से नहीं बोली और बाद में भी नहीं बोलती है। इस बात के लिए समर भाभी को दोष देता है कि तुमने ही कहा था कि लड़की पढ़ी-लिखी, अच्छी है। तुम्हें ही शादी की पड़ी थी। तब भाभी ने समर से कहा कि सब धीरे-धीरे ठीक हो जायेगा।

(iv) भाभी समर के बड़े भाई धीरज की पत्नी हैं। उनके एक पुत्री भी है। उनके चरित्र की विशेषताएँ निम्नलिखित हैं—

(1) ईर्ष्यालु प्रवृत्ति—भाभी ईर्ष्यालु प्रवृत्ति से युक्त हैं। वे समर की पत्नी से ईर्ष्या करती हैं क्योंकि वह पढ़ी-लिखी है। इसके अतिरिक्त प्रभा का सुन्दर होना भी एक कारण है।

(2) परिवार की बड़ी बहू—भाभी परिवार की सबसे बड़ी बहू हैं। जब प्रभा की शादी हो जाती है तो वे चाहती हैं कि प्रभा उनके अनुसार कार्य करे। वे प्रभा से घड़ी उतारने के लिए कहती हैं और प्रभा को समर के कमरे में ही सोने के लिए कहती हैं। यह सब कहना वह बड़ी बहू होने के कारण अपना अधिकार समझती है।

(3) अंधविश्वासी—भाभी पढ़ी-लिखी नहीं है तथा अंधविश्वासी हैं। प्रभा गणेशजी को गलती से मिट्टी का ढेला समझ लेती है और उससे बर्तन साफ कर लेती है तो भाभी बहुत रोती हैं। वे कहती हैं कि यह हमारे लिए एक अनहोनी है।

(4) परिश्रमी—वह एक परिश्रमी महिला हैं। वह सारे दिन घर के काम में लगी रहती थी। कपड़े धोना, खाना बनाना, बर्तन साफ करना और रात को अम्माजी के पैर दबाना उनका कार्य था।

(5) छिद्रान्वेषी—वे छिद्रान्वेषी स्वभाव की हैं। वे अवसर मिलने पर दूसरों की बुराई करती हैं। प्रभा में बुराई ढूँढ़ती रहती हैं और उसे घमण्डी बताती है। प्रभा के बारे में समर से उन्होंने ही कहा था कि उसके चेहरे पर चेचक के निशान हैं।

इस प्रकार भाभी का चरित्र एक साधारण महिला का है।

प्रश्न 41. ''धीरज की माँ, बड़ा खर्च होने लगा है। बेचारा धीरज भी क्या करे ? करते-करते तो मरा जाता है। उसका कसूर भी क्या ? कुनबा छोटा है।

(i) बाबूजी ने ऐसा क्यों कहा कि बड़ा खर्च होने लगा है ?

(ii) धीरज का संक्षिप्त परिचय दीजिए।

(iii) परिवार की आर्थिक स्थिति का वर्णन करें।

(iv) परिवार में कितने सदस्य हैं ? उनका परिचय दीजिए।

उत्तर—(i) बाबूजी ने ऐसा इसलिए कहा क्योंकि परिवार में एक सदस्य और आ गया था—धीरज की पुत्री। इस कारण परिवार का आर्थिक ढाँचा चरमराने लगा था।

(ii) धीरज परिवार में सबसे बड़ा पुत्र है। उसकी पत्नी को परिवार में भाभी कहते हैं। उसकी एक पुत्री है। उसे निन्यानबे रुपये वेतन मिलता है। परिवार के खर्चों का अधिकांश उत्तरदायित्व उसी का है। वह बहुत

मेहनत करता है। वह बीमार रहने लगा है और शादी में जो साइकिल मिली थी उसी से काम चला रहा है, इसलिए उसका शरीर कमजोर हो गया है।

(iii) परिवार की आर्थिक स्थिति बहुत चिन्ताजनक है। कमाने वाला अकेला धीरज है। समर, अमर, कुँवर पढ़ाई कर रहे हैं। घर में प्रायः पैसों के लिए लड़ाई होती रहती है। बाबूजी को मात्र पच्चीस रुपये पेंशन के मिलते हैं। मुन्नी का बोझ भी है। समर की शादी में भी जितनी उम्मीद थी, उतना नहीं मिला। धीरज के पुत्री होने के बाद घर की आर्थिक स्थिति और खराब हो जाती है।

(iv) परिवार में कुल दस सदस्य हैं। बाबूजी, अम्माजी, धीरज, समर, अमर, कुँवर, बड़ी बहू, प्रभा, मुन्नी तथा धीरज की पुत्री।

(1) बाबूजी—बाबूजी परिवार के मुखिया हैं। उनकी पत्नी को सभी अम्माजी कहते हैं। उन्हें पेंशन मिलती है। वे परिवार के सदस्यों को निर्देश देते रहते हैं।

(2) अम्माजी—वे परिवार में वृद्ध महिला हैं। वे चारपाई पर बैठे-बैठे माला जपती रहती हैं और कोई घटना होने पर चिल्लाती रहती हैं।

(3) धीरज—धीरज परिवार में सबसे बड़ा पुत्र है। वह नौकरी करता है और एक पुत्री का पिता है। घर के खर्चे की जिम्मेदारी उसी के कंधों पर है।

(4) समर—समर परिवार में धीरज से छोटा और अमर, कुँवर से बड़ा है। वह अभी पढ़ाई कर रहा है। उसकी शादी प्रभा के साथ हुई है।

(5) अमर और कुंवर—अमर और कुँवर समर से छोटे हैं तथा दोनों पढ़ाई कर रहे हैं। अमर प्रभा से घृणा करता है।

(6) बड़ी बहू—धीरज की पत्नी परिवार में बड़ी बहू है। वह प्रभा से ईर्ष्या करती है और समर से उसकी बुराई भी करती है।

(7) प्रभा—प्रभा समर की पत्नी है। परिवार में सभी उससे घृणा करते हैं। समर भी प्रारम्भ में उससे नहीं बोलता है। वह पढ़ी-लिखी, स्वाभिमानी व आदर्श गृहणी है।

(8) मुन्नी और धीरज की पुत्री—मुन्नी परिवार में सबसे ज्यादा अभागिन है। वह पति के अत्याचारों के कारण मायके में रह रही है। वह गुमशुम रहती है और सबसे अलग रहने का प्रयास करती है, धीरज को कुछ ही दिन पहले पुत्री हुयी है, जिससे घर की आर्थिक स्थिति प्रभावित होती है।

●●

आषाढ़ का एक दिन

[ASHADH KA EK DIN]

—मोहन राकेश

नाटककार का परिचय

मोहन राकेश का जन्म 8 जनवरी, 1925 को हुआ था। वे नई कहानी आन्दोलन के सशक्त हस्ताक्षर थे। उन्होने पंजाब विश्वविद्यालय से हिन्दी और अंग्रेजी में एम. ए. किया। जीविकोपार्जन के लिए अध्यापन का कार्य किया। कुछ वर्षों तक 'सारिका' के सम्पादक भी रहे। इन्हें 'संगीत नाटक अकादमी' से सम्मानित किया गया था। 3 जनवरी, 1972 को नयी दिल्ली में इनका आकस्मिक निधन हो गया। मोहन राकेश हिन्दी के बहुमुखी प्रतिभा सम्पन्न नाट्य लेखक और उपन्यासकार हैं। समाज के संवेदनशील व्यक्ति और समय के प्रवाह से एक अनुभूति क्षण चुनकर उन दोनों के सार्थक सम्बन्ध को खोज निकालना, राकेश की कहानियों एवं नाटकों की विषय-वस्तु है।

नाटक का परिचय

'आषाढ़ का एक दिन' सन् 1948 में प्रकाशित और नाटककार मोहन राकेश द्वारा रचित एक हिन्दी नाटक है। इसे कभी-कभी हिन्दी नाटक के आधुनिक युग का प्रथम नाटक भी कहा जाता है। 1949 में इसे वर्ष का सर्वश्रेष्ठ नाटक होने के लिए 'संगीत नाटक अकादमी' पुरस्कार से सम्मानित किया गया और कई प्रसिद्ध निर्देशक इसे मंच पर ला चुके हैं। 1971 में निर्देशक 'मणि कौल' ने इस पर आधारित एक फिल्म बनाई, जिसने आगे जा कर साल की सर्वश्रेष्ठ फिल्म का 'फिल्मफेयर' पुरस्कार जीत लिया। आषाढ़ का एक दिन महाकवि कालिदास के निजी जीवन पर केन्द्रित है, जो 100 ई. पू. से 500 ईसवीं के अनुमानित काल में व्यतीत हुआ।

यह नाटक दर्शाता है कि कालिदास के महानता पाने के प्रयास की मल्लिका और कालिदास को कितनी बड़ी कीमत चुकानी पड़ती है। जब कालिदास मल्लिका को छोड़कर उज्जयिनी में बस जाता है तो उसकी ख्याति और उसका रुतबा तो बढ़ता है लेकिन उसकी सृजनशक्ति चली जाती है। लाखों प्रयत्न करने और अनुकूल वातावरण बनाने का प्रयास करने के उपरान्त भी कालिदास सन्तुष्ट नहीं हो पाता है।

'आषाढ़ का एक दिन' नाट्य लेखन के क्षेत्र में एक महत्वपूर्ण उपलब्धि है। वस्तुत: हिन्दी के जिन एक-दो लेखकों ने नाटकों में यथार्थपरकता और काव्यात्मकता का श्रीगणेश किया था, 'आषाढ़ का एक दिन' उसकी महत्वपूर्ण परिणिति है। इस नाटक की प्रत्यक्ष विषय-वस्तु कालिदास के जीवन से सम्बन्धित है। सारी घटनाएँ आषाढ़ के एक दिन पर ही घटित होती हैं। प्रेयसी मल्लिका के आग्रह पर कालिदास उसे छोड़कर चला जाता है। उसे सारी सुख-सुविधाएँ मिल जाती हैं, परन्तु अपने मानसिक द्वन्द्व की वजह से उसे कहीं शान्ति नहीं मिलती है।

सुप्रसिद्ध नाट्य समालोचक नेमिचन्द्र जैन के अनुसार, ''नाट्य रूप की दृष्टि से 'आषाढ़ का एक दिन' एक सुगठित यथार्थवादी नाटक है। इसमें बाह्य ब्यौरे की अपेक्षा परिस्थिति के काव्य को अभिव्यक्त करने का प्रयास किया है।'' हिन्दी में यह पहला यथार्थवादी नाटक है जो बाह्य और आन्तरिक यथार्थ के अन्तर्द्वन्द्व को संवेदनशीलता के साथ देखता है। इस उपन्यास में अतीत का न तो तथाकथित विवरण है, न पुरूत्थानवादी गौरव गान। इस प्रकार 'आषाढ़ का एक दिन' नाटक सही अर्थ में आधुनिक हिन्दी नाटक की शुरूआत का सूचक है।

हिन्दी नाटक के परिप्रेक्ष्य में, भाव-वस्तु और रूपबन्ध दोनों के स्तर पर 'आषाढ़ का एक दिन' ऐसा पर्याप्त, सघन, तीव्र और भावोद्दीप्त लेखन प्रस्तुत करता है जैसा हिन्दी नाटकों में कम ही हुआ है।

नाटक का सारांश

अंक एक

(कालिदास के आगमन तक की घटना का सारांश)

शब्दार्थ—अनन्तर = बाद, **विलीन** = धीरे से गायब होना, **प्रकोष्ठ** = कमरा, **तल्प** = पलंग, **कुम्भ** = घड़ा, **उपत्यकाएँ** = पहाड़ की तलहटी, **अंशुक** = ओढ़नी, **उष्णता** = ताप अथवा गर्मी, **अस्पृश्य** = अछूता, **भर्त्सना** = निन्दा, **अनिष्ट** = बुरा, **निरर्थक** = बेवजह, **प्रलाप** = बक-बक, **वितृष्णा** = घृणा,**आत्म-प्रवंचना** = खुद को छलना।

नाटक के आरम्भ में पर्दा उठने पर साधारण-सा कमरा दिखाई देता है। आषाढ़ का पहला दिन है वर्षा हो रही है, रह-रहकर बिजली चमक उठती है। ऐसे समय में उस कमरे में पूरी तरह से भीग चुकी मल्लिका का प्रवेश होता है। वह अपनी माँ से मूसलाधार वर्षा का वर्णन करती है। मल्लिका अपनी माँ से सूखे वस्त्र के सन्दर्भ में पूछते हुए यह कहती है कि इन गीले कपड़ों में उसे सर्दी लग जायेगी। अम्बिका ने उसके वस्त्र पलंग पर रखे हैं, क्योंकि उसे पता था कि मल्लिका भीगकर आयेगी। मल्लिका वस्त्र बदलने चली जाती है। वापस आने के पश्चात् मल्लिका वर्षा ऋतु के सौन्दर्य का चित्रमय वर्णन करती है। माँ अम्बिका अपने कार्य में प्रवृत्त है तथा मल्लिका के वार्तालाप पर ध्यान नहीं देती है। उसे शर्करा मिश्रित दूध पीकर तख्त पर आराम करने के लिए कहती है। लेकिन मल्लिका यह कहकर कि वह थकी नहीं है, आराम करने के लिए नहीं जाती है। वह अपनी माँ अम्बिका से उसकी उदासी का कारण पूछती है। उसी समय उन्हें पता चलता है कि राज्य के कुछ कर्मचारी आये हैं। अम्बिका यह कहती है कि राज्य के कर्मचारियों का आना अशुभ है। ये लोग तभी आते हैं जब किसी महामारी या युद्ध की सूचना देनी होती है। यह भी बताती है कि तुम्हारे पिता की मृत्यु के समय भी ये आकृतियाँ देखी गई थीं।

अम्बिका अग्निमित्र को मल्लिका के विवाह के सन्दर्भ में कहीं भेजती है जिस बात को सुनकर मल्लिका नाराज हो जाती है। नाराजगी के साथ मल्लिका अपने विवाह न करने का निर्णय सुनाती है। यह कहती है कि जीवन उसका है, किसी अन्य को उसके जीवन पर निर्णय सुनाने का अधिकार नहीं है। उसी समय कालिदास के आने के स्वर सुनाई देते है और अम्बिका भीतर चली जाती है।

(मातुल के प्रवेश तक की कथा)

शब्दार्थ—स्पर्श = छूना, **आहत** = घायल, **भाजन** = बर्तन, **रुष्ट** = नाराज, **सामुद्रिक** = ज्योतिष, **लाँछन** = आरोप, **आस्तरण** = बिस्तर, **संवेदना** = दया, **हरिणशावक** = हिरण का बच्चा, **प्रताड़ना** = दु:ख, **पूर्वाग्रह** = झुकाव, **उपादान** = सहारा।

कालिदास एक घायल हिरण के बच्चे को लिए हुए आता है। वह उससे बात करते हुए यह कहता है कि उँगलियों का कोमल स्पर्श उसके प्राण बचा सकता है। कालिदास मल्लिका को एक पात्र में दूध लाने के लिए कहता है। मल्लिका अम्बिका की कही बात कालिदास से भी कहती है कि जब भी राज्य के कर्मचारी गाँव में आते हैं कुछ न कुछ अनिष्ट अवश्य होता है। कालिदास उस हिरण के बच्चे से बात करते हुए दूध पिलाने का प्रयास करता रहता है। उसी समय राजपुरुष दंतुल का प्रवेश होता है। दंतुल कालिदास से यह प्रश्न पूछता है कि मेरे बाण से घायल हिरण को क्यों यहाँ लाये हैं ? तब कालिदास और दंतुल का परिचय होता है। मल्लिका दंतुल के द्वारा कालिदास के ऊपर लगाये गये चोरी के आरोप का विरोध करती है। उस समय कालिदास यह कहकर उस हिरण के बच्चे को देने से इन्कार कर देता है कि यह प्रकृति की सम्पत्ति है। कालिदास मल्लिका से हरिणशावक को बिस्तर पर सुलाने के लिए कहता है, तब अम्बिका यह कहकर इन्कार कर देती है कि बिस्तर मनुष्यों के सोने के लिए है पशुओं के सोने हेतु नहीं। तब कालिदास उस शावक को लेकर जाने लगता है। तभी दंतुल भी तलवार लेकर उसके पीछे जाने को उद्यत होता है, तभी मल्लिका द्वारा उसे यह पता लगता है कि शावक की रक्षा करने वाला व्यक्ति कोई और नहीं महान कवि कालिदास हैं। यह सुनकर वह आश्चर्यचकित हो जाता है।

दंतुल मल्लिका को यह बताता है कि उज्जयिनी के महाराज कालिदास की रचना 'ऋतुसंहार' से प्रभावित होकर उनका सम्मान करना चाहते हैं। इसी उद्देश्य से आचार्य वररुचि यहाँ आये हैं। यह कहकर दंतुल वहाँ से चला जाता है। दंतुल की बात सुनकर मल्लिका प्रसन्न हो जाती है और यह बात अपनी माँ अम्बिका को बताती है। यह सुनकर अम्बिका कालिदास के दोषों का विवेचन करने लगती है। तब कालिदास के दोष के सन्दर्भ में अम्बिका कहती है कि वह तुमसे विवाह क्यों नहीं कर रहा है ? इसके प्रत्युत्तर में मल्लिका यह कहती है कि अभावग्रस्त जीवन में विवाह की कल्पना करना भी असम्भव है। माँ मल्लिका से कहती है कि मेरी अनुपस्थिति में जब भोजन की व्यवस्था भी मुश्किल हो जायेगी ऐसी परिस्थिति में तुम्हें मेरे कथन के औचित्य का आभास होगा। मल्लिका यह कहना चाहती है कि आज कालिदास का जीवन एक नई दिशा का ग्रहण कर रहा है ऐसी परिस्थिति में वह अपने स्वार्थ अथवा अपने लाभ की बात नहीं कर सकती। माता व पुत्री की इस बात-चीत के दौरान ही मातुल के शब्द सुनाई देते हैं।

(मातुल के प्रवेश की कथा)

शब्दार्थ—भागिनेय = भाँजा, **निष्णात** = निपुण, **अभ्यागत** = मेहमान, **विचक्षणता** = अनोखापन, **आग्रह** = अनुरोध, **वंचित** = रहित, **अग्रिकाष्ठ** = जलाऊ लकड़ी, **वृत्ति** = आदत, **अप्रत्याशित** = अनपेक्षित, **अनर्गलता** = असंयमिता, **बाध्य** = विवश, **रिक्तता** = खालीपन, **पथ** = रास्ता, **प्रशस्त** = उत्कृष्ट।

अम्बिका को पुकारते हुए मातुल प्रवेश करता है। मातुल कहता है कि वह पूरे गाँव में घोषणा करने वाला है कि कालिदास से अब मेरा कोई सम्बन्ध नहीं है, क्योंकि उज्जयिनी से आचार्य वररुचि आये हैं और वे कालिदास को सम्मानित करने के लिए अपने साथ उज्जयिनी ले जाना चाहते हैं, परन्तु कालिदास इन्कार कर रहे हैं। अम्बिका कहती है कि कालिदास उज्जयिनी अवश्य जायेगा। इस वार्तालाप के दौरान एक ग्रीमाण आता है। वह मातुल से कहता है कि उज्जयिनी से आये आचार्य आपकी प्रतीक्षा कर रहे हैं। इस दौरान मातुल और ग्रामीण में वाद-विवाद होता है। ग्रामीण यह बताता है कि आचार्य, कालिदास को जन्म देने वाले इस ग्राम-प्रदेश का दर्शन करना चाहते हैं। मातुल निक्षेप को कालिदास को खोजकर लाने के लिए कहता है और यह कहते हुए चला जाता है। मातुल यह भी कहता है कि मेरा मन करता है कि जैसे भी हो मैं कालिदास को आचार्य के सामने अवश्य पेश करूँ।

मातुल के जाने के पश्चात् निक्षेप मल्लिका को यह बताता है कि कालिदास जगदम्बा के मन्दिर में हैं। वह मल्लिका को यह भी बताता है कि कालिदास तब तक घर नहीं जायेंगे जब तक कि उज्जयिनी से आये अतिथि चले नहीं जाते। वह यह बताता है कि कालिदास को राजकीय सम्मान का मोह नहीं है। निक्षेप यह प्रकट करता है कि कालिदास अवसर का तिरस्कार कर रहे हैं। वह उनके न जाने का कारण कटुता समझता है। मल्लिका अम्बिका के विरोध के बावजूद कालिदास को समझाने के लिए निक्षेप के साथ चली जाती है।

मल्लिका के जाने के बाद विलोम का आगमन होता है। अम्बिका उसे यह कहकर वापस भेजना चाहती है कि उसका यहाँ आना मल्लिका को अच्छा नहीं लगता है। विलोम यह बताता है कि मल्लिका को यह अच्छा इसलिए नहीं लगता क्योंकि कालिदास को मेरा यहाँ आना पसन्द नहीं है। विलोम अम्बिका से यह कहता है कि कालिदास के उज्जयिनी जाने से पूर्व मल्लिका व कालिदास का विवाह हो जाना चाहिए, क्योंकि सारे प्रान्त में उनके सम्बन्ध को लेकर बातें की जा रही हैं। विलोम और अम्बिका की बातचीत के दौरान ही मल्लिका और कालिदास का प्रवेश होता है। कालिदास और विलोम के बीच बहस होती है। विलोम को अपने घर देखकर मल्लिका को तनिक भी अच्छा नहीं लगता है। विलोम कालिदास के सामने यह प्रश्न रखता है कि क्या तुम राजधानी के वैभव में जाकर अपने प्रान्त के लोगों को भूल तो नहीं जाओगे ?

विलोम और कालिदास एक-दूसरे के विपरीत स्वभाव के सन्दर्भ में चर्चा करते हैं। विलोम कालिदास से यह प्रश्न करते हैं कि क्या आप मल्लिका को अपने साथ लेकर उज्जयिनी जायेंगे ? मल्लिका इस प्रश्न से कालिदास का बचाव करते हुए यह कहती है कि कालिदास आपके प्रश्नों का उत्तर देने के लिए बाध्य नहीं हैं।

कालिदास, विलोम की उपस्थिति को अनाधिकार मानते हैं। मल्लिका विलोम को अनचाहा अतिथि कहती है। अन्ततः विलोम कालिदास को शुभकामनाएँ देते हुए प्रस्थान करता है।

अब मल्लिका और कालिदास के बीच यह वार्तालाप होती है कि कालिदास को उज्जयिनी जाना चाहिए। मल्लिका के अनुसार ग्रामीण प्रान्त में रहने से कालिदास की प्रतिभा का विकास नहीं हो सकता। वह यह भी कहती है कि वह उसे घेरना नहीं चाहती। कालिदास भी मल्लिका को यह बताने का प्रयास करता है कि वह मातृ-भूमि से जुड़ा रहना चाहता है। वह यह भी बताता है कि उसके मन में कोई उत्साह नहीं है। फिर भी मल्लिका के बार-बार समझाने पर कालिदास उज्जयिनी जाने के लिए तैयार हो जाता है। कालिदास के जाने के बाद मल्लिका रोती है और अम्बिका उसे सांत्वना प्रदान करती है। इस प्रकार नाटक के पहले अंक का समापन होता है।

अंक दो

(अनुनासिक और अनुस्वार के प्रस्थान तक)

शब्दार्थ—**अनन्तर** = बाद, **प्रतियाँ** = अनुकृति, **रंगशाला** = नाट्यशाला, **अपवाद** = बदनामी, **राजदुहिता** = राजकन्या, **आग्रह** = अनुरोध, **ग्लानि** = पछतावा, **क्षति** = नुकसान, **झरोखे** = खिड़की, **सहसा** = अचानक, **वेशभूषा** = पहनावा, **अभिप्राय** = अर्थ, **स्थानीय** = देशीय, **आँचलिक** = क्षेत्रीय, **राजकीय-नियोजन** = सरकारी उद्देश्य, **पृष्ठभूमि** = परवर्ती जीवन, **निःश्वास** = गहरी साँस, **असमंजस** = दुविधा, **अनुचर** = सेवक, **साक्षात्कार** = भेंट, **प्रणेता** = लेखक अथवा रचयिता, **उपवेश** = गृह-बैठक, **गवाक्ष** = खिड़की, **विवादास्पद** = विवादित, **संदिग्ध** = अनिश्चित।

कालिदास के जाने के कुछ वर्षों के बाद फिर वही कमरा है। इस अंक का प्रारम्भ उसी कमरे से होता है, परन्तु कमरे की स्थिति अब पहले से अधिक खराब हो चुकी है। घर में जगह-जगह से मिट्टी उखड़ रही है। कमरे में एक चौकी पर मल्लिका बैठकर खरल में दवा पीस रही है। तभी निक्षेप का आगमन होता है। निक्षेप आते ही अम्बिका के ज्वर के सन्दर्भ में पूछता है, क्योंकि अम्बिका को दो वर्षों से निरन्तर एक-सा ज्वर है। मल्लिका के अनुसार अम्बिका औषधि का सेवन भी नियमित रूप से नहीं करती है। निक्षेप कहता है कि मल्लिका दुबली हो गई है। निक्षेप मल्लिका को यह बताता है कि कालिदास उज्जयिनी जाकर पूरी तरह से यहाँ के लोगों को भूल गये हैं। उन्हें यह पता है कि कालिदास उज्जयिनी में नये काव्यों की रचना कर रहे हैं। निक्षेप के अनुसार कालिदास ने गुप्तवंश की राजकुमारी से विवाह भी कर लिया है। जबकि जब वे यहाँ थे तो उन्होंने आजीवन विवाह न करने का निर्णय लिया था। मल्लिका यह कहती है कि कालिदास असाधारण हैं इसलिए उस विदुषी राजकन्या से उनका विवाह होना उचित ही है। निक्षेप इन सबका दोषी अपने-आपको मानता है क्योंकि उसी के कहने पर मल्लिका ने कालिदास को उज्जयिनी जाने पर विवश किया था। आज उसी निर्णय की वजह से मल्लिका की यह स्थिति हो गई है।

निक्षेप झरोखे से देखकर यह बताता है कि राज्य के कुछ वही कर्मचारी आज फिर से आये हैं जो कालिदास को लेने के लिए आये थे। झरोखे के पास से ही निक्षेप एक घोड़े पर सवार कालिदास को जाते हुए देखता है। वह बताता है कि कालिदास पर्वत-शिखर की ओर गये हैं। वह उनका पता लगाने के लिए चला जाता है।

मल्लिका विचार-मग्न रहती है कि वह कलिदास के साथ किन-किन विषयों पर वार्तालाप करेगी। उसी समय रंगिनी और संगिनी का आगमन होता है जो उज्जयिनी की नाट्यशाला में काम करती हैं। रंगिनी नृत्य व नाटक का अभ्यास करती है वहीं दूसरी ओर संगिनी वीणा वादन का अभ्यास करती है। वे यहाँ ग्रामीणों का घर देखने आई हैं। वे जब मल्लिका से उसका परिचय पूछती हैं तो वह कोई जवाब नहीं देती है। रंगिनी और

संगिनी यहाँ स्थानीय शब्दों को जानने के लिए आई हैं। 'प्रकोष्ठ' और 'कुम्भ' जैसे शब्दों को सुनकर यह कहती हैं कि यहाँ के स्थानीय शब्द कुछ भी नहीं हैं। संगिनी के अनुसार इस प्रदेश में असाधारण प्रतिभा वाले कालिदास ने जन्म लिया है तो यहाँ की प्रत्येक वस्तु असाधारण होनी चाहिए। रंगिनी बताती है कि वे कालिदास की पृष्ठभूमि का अध्ययन करने के लिए आई हैं। अन्तत: वे दोनों चली जाती हैं।

रंगिनी और संगिनी के जाने के बाद मल्लिका अपने विचारों में खो जाती है। वह यह सोचती है कि आज भी वैसा ही वातावरण है। मैं एक बार फिर प्रेम की वर्षा में भीगूँगी। फिर बताऊँगी कि मैंने तुम्हारी सारी रचनाएँ पढ़ी हैं। तुम्हारी नई रचनाओं के लिए पृष्ठ तैयार किया है। मल्लिका इन्हीं विचारों में खोई रहती है। तभी दरवाजे पर दस्तक होती है। मल्लिका दरवाजा खोलती है तो अनुनासिक और अनुस्वार नामक दो अधिकारियों का प्रवेश होता है।

अनुस्वार बताता है कि ऋतुसंहार, कुमारसम्भव, मेघदूत एवं रघुवंश के प्रणेता कश्मीर के भावी शासक मातृगुप्त की पत्नी प्रियंगुमंजरी आपसे मिलने के लिए उत्सुक हैं। हम इसकी सूचना देने के लिए आपके समक्ष उपस्थित हैं। मल्लिका समझ नहीं पा रही थी कि इन ग्रन्थों की रचना तो कालिदास ने की थी ये किसका नाम ले रहे हैं ? अनुस्वार द्वारा उसे पता चलता है कि मातृगुप्त उन्हीं का नया नाम है।

अनुस्वार और अनुनासिक प्रियंगुमंजरी के आगमन के पूर्व उनके स्वागत के लिए घर के उस कमरे में साज-सज्जा को ध्यान में रखकर कुछ परिवर्तन करना चाहते हैं। वे दोनों अधिकारी प्रकोष्ठ में आकर वस्तुओं का बारीकी से निरीक्षण करते हैं। वे सर्वप्रथम आसन को लेकर आपस में बहस करते हैं और दोनों के दृष्टिकोण बिल्कुल अलग हैं। अत: विवादित विषय होने के कारण उसे यथावत रखने का निर्णय लेते हैं। इसी प्रकार कुम्भ, वस्त्र सुखाने की रस्सी, बर्तन, चौकी और चूल्हे आदि के सन्दर्भ में भी यही होता है। अन्त में वे चारों ओर एक बार फिर से दृष्टि डालने का विचार करते हैं। तभी मातुल का उत्तेजित स्वर सुनाई देता है। मातुल अधिकारियों को बताता है कि देवी प्रियंगुमंजरी बाहर पहुँच चुकी हैं और वह अब अन्दर आना चाहती हैं। यह सुनकर वे दोनों मातुल के साथ ही बाहर चले जाते हैं।

(प्रियंगु के प्रस्थान तक के दृश्य का सारांश)

शब्दार्थ—विनीत = शिष्ट, **चाटुकारिता** = खुशामद, **अभिवादन** = नमस्कार करना, **कुलीनता** = रईसी, **आत्म-श्लाघा** = आत्म-प्रशंसा, **योजन** = दूरी की एक इकाई, **अनुचर** = सेवक, **आतिथ्य** = मेहमाननवाजी, **विदग्धतापूर्ण** = चतुराई पूर्ण, **निर्व्याज** = छल रहित, **स्पर्धा** = होड़, **हेय** = उपेक्षित, **उपभोग** = आनन्द अथवा सुख, **आत्मविस्मृत** = अपने आपको भूल जाना, **जागरूक** = चौकस, **जर्जर** = पुरानी, **परिसंस्कार** = नवीनीकरण, **स्थपति** = वास्तुकार या भवन निर्माण करने वाला, **श्लक्ष्ण** = सुन्दर, **विमूढ़** = हक्का-बक्का, **रूँधे** = अवरोधित, **शिथिल** = ढीला।

मातुल, मल्लिका की प्रशंसा करते हुए प्रियंगुमंजरी के साथ प्रवेश करता है। मातुल प्रियंगुमंजरी की चाटुकारिता करता रहता है। प्रियंगुमंजरी बार-बार मातुल को जाने के लिए कहती हैं, लेकिन मातुल तरह-तरह की बातें बनाता रहता है। अन्तत: जब प्रियंगुमंजरी मल्लिका से बात करना प्रारम्भ करती है तब मातुल प्रकोष्ठ से प्रस्थान करता है। प्रियंगुमंजरी यह कहती है कि मल्लिका उसे अपरिचित नहीं लग रही है। मल्लिका आतिथ्य करना चाहती है तब प्रियंगुमंजरी यह कहती है कि वह यहाँ उसका घर देखने आई हैं। प्रियंगु के अनुसार मेघदूत लिखते समय कालिदास प्राय: इस घर की चर्चा किया करते थे। प्रियंगु यह कहती हैं कि उनके विशेष आग्रह करने के कारण ही कालिदास यहाँ आये हैं। प्रियंगु यहाँ आने का एक कारण और भी बताती है कि वह इस स्थान को सिर्फ देखना ही नहीं चाहती थी बल्कि यहाँ के कुछ वातावरण को भी अपने साथ ले जाना चाहती है।

मल्लिका प्रियंगु को रुकने का प्रस्ताव देती है, परन्तु प्रियंगु यह कहते हुए अस्वीकार कर देती हैं कि उन्हें रुकने का अवकाश नहीं है। उनके अनुसार कश्मीर की स्थिति बड़ी ही संकटपूर्ण है। जब प्रियंगु मल्लिका के घर में कालिदास की कुछ रचनाओं को देखती है तब वह मल्लिका को बताती है कि कालिदास अब

मातृगुप्त के नाम से जाने जाते हैं। वह बताती है कि कालिदास यहाँ के जीवन की चर्चा करते हुए आत्मविस्मृत हो जाते हैं, वह यह भी बताती है कि उनका अधिकतर समय केवल इसी प्रयास में लग जाता है कि कालिदास का राजनीति की तरफ बढ़ा कदम पीछे न हट जाये। इन्हीं कारणों से यहाँ का वातावरण अपने साथ ले जाना चाहती है। कुछ हरिण शावक, वनस्पतियाँ आदि। वे यहाँ से कुछ अनाथ बच्चों को भी अपने साथ ले जाकर उनकी शिक्षा का प्रबन्ध करेंगे।

इन बातों के बीच प्रियंगु मल्लिका के घर के परिसंस्कार के सन्दर्भ में कहती है तो उसके जवाब में मल्लिका यह कहती है कि हमें ऐसे ही घर में रहने का अभ्यास है। वह यह कहती है कि मल्लिका तुम मेरे साथ चलो, अपनी माँ को भी साथ ले चलो। तब तक स्थपति इस घर का परिसंस्कार करते रहेंगे। परन्तु मल्लिका प्रियंगु के इस प्रस्ताव को बड़ी उदारता से अस्वीकार कर देती है। प्रियंगु यह भी प्रस्ताव करती है कि जो दो अधिकारी घर का निरीक्षण करने के लिए आये थे तुम उनमें से किसी एक के साथ विवाह कर लो। मल्लिका यह निवेदन करती है कि आप विवाह की चर्चा छोड़ दीजिए।

इसी समय अम्बिका उनकी तरफ आती है। यह कहती है कि मल्लिका तो भावनाओं के आधार पर जीती है। मल्लिका, अम्बिका को मना करती है कि उसका स्वास्थ्य ठीक नहीं है इसलिए वह लेटी रहें। लेकिन अम्बिका राजवधू से बातें करते हुए उन्हें यह बताती है कि मैं जब ठीक थी तब अच्छी तरह से घर को सम्भाला करती थी। तब प्रियंगु यह कहती है कि घर की स्थिति ठीक नहीं है इसलिए वे इस घर को गिराकर इसके स्थान पर एक नया घर बनाने का आदेश देकर जायेंगी। जिसे सुन मल्लिका चौंक जाती है और उन्हें घर गिराने के आदेश को वापस लेने का निवेदन करती है। इस बीच अम्बिका बार-बार कुछ कहना चाहती है लेकिन वह कह नहीं पाती है क्योंकि बीच-बीच में उसे खाँसी आ जाती है। अन्ततः प्रियंगु उनकी सहायता का आश्वासन देकर चली जाती हैं।

शब्दार्थ—भित्तियाँ = दीवारों, **परिचारिका** = सेविका, **क्षुब्ध** = नाराज, **क्षुद्र** = तुच्छ अथवा छोटा, **अनुकृति** = प्रति, **अनुरोध** = निवेदन, **विक्षुब्ध** = परेशान, **अयाचित** = अवांछित, **स्तब्ध** = अविचल, **व्यंगात्मक** = व्यंगपूर्ण, **हताशा** = निराशा।

प्रियंगुमंजरी के जाने के बाद अम्बिका व्यंग्यपूर्ण शब्दों में मल्लिका से मेघदूत की पंक्तियाँ पढ़ने के लिए कहती है। वह मल्लिका से कहती हैं कि कालिदास की जिस कोमलता की बातें वह करती थी वह कोमलता अब साकार हो उठी है। अम्बिका कहती है आज कालिदास शासक है, उसने अपनी शक्ति और सम्पत्ति का परिचय देने के लिए ही घर की दीवारों का परिसंस्कार करने की बात की है। मल्लिका माँ से इसी विषय में बात करती रहती है तभी विलोम बाहर से आता है।

विलोम आते ही अम्बिका से यह कहता है कि तुम क्यों नाराज हो ? जिस घर में राजपरिवार के किसी व्यक्ति का आगमन होता है वह धन्य हो जाता है। अम्बिका कहती है हमारे वर्षों के दुःख व अभाव झेलने का कितना अच्छा परिणाम मिला है कि हमारे घर की दीवारों की अब मरम्मत की जायेगी। विलोम कहता है कि आज तुम्हारी बातों को सुनने का वक्त किसी के पास नहीं है। आज ग्राम का प्रत्येक व्यक्ति अतिथियों के लिए सामग्री जुटाना चाहता है। आज यहाँ पत्थर भी मूल्यवान हो गये हैं। ग्राम में आज बहुत उत्साह है। राजकन्या अपने साथ हरिणशावकों को ले जा रही हैं। यहाँ का कोई पेड़-पत्ता भी बाकी न रहेगा, जिसकी अनुकृति न बने।

विलोम की इन सब बातों को सुनकर मल्लिका कहती है कि इनके पीछे कुछ दूसरा प्रयोजन भी तो हो सकता है। विलोम कहता है कि यहाँ की हर चीज उनके लिए विचित्र उदाहरण की भाँति है। एक कलाकार यहाँ की धूप में अपनी छाया को रेखांकित कर रहा है। इस बीच अम्बिका कुछ कहती है और उसे खाँसी आ

जाती है। विलोम बताता है कि कालिदास ने यहाँ आना उचित नहीं समझा। इसे सुन अम्बिका यह कहती है कि कालिदास को पता है कि अम्बिका अभी जीवित है इसीलिए वह यहाँ नहीं आया। विलोम कहता है कि कालिदास तो कवि हृदय है फिर वह ऐसे सम्बन्ध कैसे तोड़ सकता है ? विलोम की बातें सुन मल्लिका विलोम को जाने के लिए कहती है।

विलोम यह कहता है कि कालिदास के जाने के समय वह उससे यहीं मिला था। शायद आज भी वह यहीं मिलना चाहता है। मल्लिका विलोम का हाथ पकड़ उसे जाने के लिए कहती है। वह यहाँ तक कहती है कि यह मेरा घर है और मैं यह चाहती हूँ कि आप यहाँ से चले जाये। उसी समय घोड़ों के टापों के स्वर नजदीक आते हैं और धीरे-धीरे दूर चले जाते हैं। जिससे यह स्पष्ट हो जाता है कि कालिदास यहाँ आने वाला नहीं है। अम्बिका को कालिदास का न आना सामान्य लगता है। परन्तु विलोम ऐसे समय में मल्लिका की मित्रता पर व्यंग्य करता है। मल्लिका हताश होकर कठोरता से विलोम से जाने के लिए कहती है। विलोम जाते समय दोनों की ओर देखता है और चला जाता है।

अम्बिका का भाव हताशा से करुणा में बदल जाता है। मल्लिका दोनों हाथों से मुँह ढककर रोने लगती है। अम्बिका, मल्लिका को सटाये उसे सांत्वना देते हुए यह कहती है कि तुम अब भी उस व्यक्ति के लिए रो रही हो जिसने तुम्हारी इतनी उपेक्षा की। इसके जवाब में मल्लिका अम्बिका से कालिदास के बारे में कुछ भी न बोलने के लिए कहती है। इस प्रकार दूसरे अंक की भी समाप्ति हो जाती है।

अंक तीन
(कालिदास के आगमन तक)

शब्दार्थ—बैसाखी = आधार, **जीर्णता** = अवस्था, **राज-प्रसाद** = राजमहल, **प्रतिहारी** = द्वारपाल, **अप्रतिभ** = उत्तर रहित अथवा मूक, **आहत** = घायल, **अभियोगपूर्ण** = आरोप, **उद्विग्न** = व्याकुल, **तटस्थ** = उदासीन, **उपार्जित** = अर्जित, **वारांगणाओं** = वेश्या, **अन्तर्मुख** = आत्मविश्लेषी।

कुछ वर्षों के, इसी प्रकोष्ठ से तीसरे अंक का भी प्रारम्भ होता है। आज यह प्रकोष्ठ पूरी तरह जीर्ण-शीर्ण हो चुका है। वर्षा हो रही है बीच-बीच में मेघों की गर्जना हो रही है। प्रकोष्ठ पूरी तरह से अस्त-व्यस्त है। दीवारों पर बने स्वास्तिक और शुभ-लाभ के निशान लगभग विलीन हो चुके हैं। प्रकोष्ठ में कोई नहीं है। ऐसे समय में मातुल भीगे वस्त्रों में बैसाखी के सहारे प्रकोष्ठ में प्रवेश करता है। बीच में आकर मल्लिका को पुकारता है। मल्लिका को बताता है कि वर्षा में उसकी क्या हालत हो गई है। आज मातुल का व्यक्तित्व भी काफी कमजोर दिखाई दे रहा है।

मल्लिका के पूछने पर आर्य मातुल, यहाँ आने का कारण इस वर्षा को बताता है। वह बताता है कि इस वर्षा में तुम्हारे घर के सिवाय दूसरा कोई आसरा नहीं था। आज बैसाखी के सहारे चलना पड़ता है। वर्षा के कारण कभी पाँव फिसलता है तो कभी बैसाखी। राजमहल में पाँव टूटा है और घर में कितने पत्थर लगे हैं जो बहुत फिसलते हैं। इन कारणों से घर में रहना भी मुश्किल हो गया है। इस बातचीत के दौरान मल्लिका मातुल को आसन ग्रहण करने के लिए कहती है।

आसन ग्रहण करने के बाद भी मातुल राजमहल में रहने वाले दु:खों के बारे में बताता है। वह कहता है कि राजमहल में रहने से बड़ा दु:ख इस संसार में नहीं है। लोग यूँ ही अभिवादन और वंदना करते रहते हैं। इसलिए यहाँ आकर रहना मुझे अच्छा लगता है, परन्तु वर्षा से ही मुझे अधिक कष्ट मिलता है। मल्लिका मातुल के वस्त्र सुखाने के लिए आग जलाने के लिए कहती है। मातुल मना कर देता है। तब मातुल यह कहता है कि अम्बिका की मृत्यु के पश्चात् ऐसा लग रहा है कि इस घर में कोई व्यवस्था रह ही नहीं गई है। मल्लिका तुमने प्रियंगुमंजरी द्वारा दी गई सुविधाओं को अस्वीकार कर दिया। तुमने ही उनके द्वारा भेजी गई स्वर्ण मुद्राओं, वस्त्र और घर के परिसंस्कार के प्रस्ताव को भी यह कहकर ठुकरा दिया कि तुम्हें इन चीजों की आवश्यकता नहीं है।

मातुल झरोखे से देखकर कहता है कि वर्षा अब थम रही है घर जाकर वस्त्रों को सुखाऊँगा। मातुल कश्मीर के सम्बन्ध में बात करते हुए कहता है कि राजनीति में कुछ भी असम्भव नहीं है। मल्लिका आश्चर्य से समाचार पूछती है। मातुल के अनुसार सम्राट् की मृत्यु हो चुकी है और विद्रोह बढ़ता जा रहा है। कालिदास ने कश्मीर छोड़ दिया है और उज्जयिनी भी नहीं गये हैं। कुछ लोग तो यह कहते हैं कि उन्होंने संन्यास ले लिया और काशी चले गये हैं। मातुल यह कहता है कि वह जो कुछ भी समझने की कोशिश करता है उसका विपरीत ही होता है। मल्लिका पास रखे ग्रन्थ को उठाकर उसे हृदय से लगाकर यह कहती है कि यह सच नहीं हो सकता। मातुल प्रस्थान करता है।

मातुल के प्रस्थान के बाद मल्लिका ग्रन्थ को हाथ में लिए हुए स्वयं से बात करते हुए कहती है, कि तुमने मेरी शुभकामनाओं को नहीं स्वीकार किया। मैं तुम्हारे जीवन का अंग भले न बन पाई, लेकिन तुम हमेशा मेरे जीवन में बने रहे। तुम्हारी सार्थकता ही मेरी जीवन की सार्थकता थी। मल्लिका अन्दर का दरवाजा खोलकर पालने की तरफ देखकर यह कहती है कि यह जीव मेरे अभाव की संतान है। जो भाव तुम थे आज तक वह स्थान कोई नहीं ले पाया लेकिन अभाव की अनेक आकृतियाँ हैं। मैंने बहुत सुना कि तुम्हारे अनेक वारांगणाओं के साथ सम्बन्ध रहे हैं, क्या आज तुम मुझे देखकर पहचान सकते हो ? आज भी मैं उसी तरह तुम्हारी रचनाओं को पढ़ती हूँ। मेरे भाव वहीं हैं, पर अभावों की पीड़ा का अनुमान शायद तुम नहीं लगा सकते हो। आज तक मैंने यह सब सहा कि तुम्हारा विकास हो रहा है क्योंकि मैं तुम्हीं में स्वयं को देखती थी। आज वही आषाढ़ का दिन है। आज सब कुछ वैसा ही है। बादलों की गर्जना के साथ ही बिजली चमकती है और दरवाजा खुलता है।

(कालिदास का प्रवेश)

शब्दार्थ—**क्षत** = जख्मी, **जड़** = अविचल, **यथार्थ** = वास्तविकता, **यथास्थान** = उचित स्थान, **कलेवर** = शरीर, **आत्मीयता** = घनिष्ठता,, **स्मृति** = याद, **आगन्तुक** = आने वाला, **निराधार** = आधारहीन, **प्रतिक्रिय** = प्रतिकार, **उपहास** = मजाक, **अनुभूति** = अनुभव, **सालती** = दुःख देती है, **खण्डित** = टूटना, **सर्वथा** = बिल्कुल, **मूक प्रश्न** = मौन प्रश्न, **संवरण** = अन्त, **द्वन्द्व** = अस्तव्यस्तता, **संचय** = संग्रह, **विरह-विमर्दिता** = वियोग से दुःखी, **विलाप** = क्रंदन तथा रोना, **वेदना** = कष्ट, **अभिव्यक्ति** = अभिव्यंजना, **प्रतीत** = महसूस, **कोरे पृष्ठ** = सादा पन्ना, **स्वेद कण** = पसीने की बूँदें, **सीलन** = नमी, **अथ** = शुरू, **स्तंभित-सा** = शक्तिहीन सा।

कालिदास दरवाजा खुलने के पश्चात् भी द्वार पर ही खड़ा रहता है। उसकी हालत पीड़ित और चोटिल-सी है। मल्लिका कालिदास के प्रवेश करने पर उसे अविचल रूप से देखती रह जाती है। कालिदास कहते हैं कि शायद तुमने मुझे पहचाना ही नहीं और पहचानोगी भी तो कैसे ? मैं वह व्यक्ति हूँ ही नहीं जिसे तुम पहचानती रही हो। कालिदास प्रकोष्ठ में इधर-उधर देखता है और आसन पर जाकर बैठ जाता है। मल्लिका दरवाजा बन्द कर उसकी तरफ आगे बढ़ती है।

मल्लिका को भी यह विश्वास नहीं हो रहा है। कालिदास के अनुसार यह स्वप्न नहीं यथार्थ है। यह सच है कि मैं थका-हारा यहाँ यथार्थ को देखने आया हूँ। मल्लिका कालिदास के भीगे वस्त्रों को देखकर चिन्तित है। जिसे जान कालिदास यह कहता है कि मैं सूखना ही नहीं चाहता। मैं बहुत थक गया था, ज्वर आ गया था लेकिन इस वर्षा से मेरी थकान कम हो गई है। मल्लिका कहती है कि तुम सचमुच पहचाने नहीं जाते। कालिदास यह कहते हैं कि सब कुछ कितना बदल गया है भले तुमने न बदला हो पर ये सब कुछ बदल गया है। कालिदास ने कभी नहीं सोचा था कि यहाँ प्रत्येक वस्तु अपरिचित लगेगी। कहीं ऐसा तो नहीं कि मेरी दृष्टि ही बदल गई है। कालिदास ने कहा कि कश्मीर जाते समय जिस कारण से नहीं आया था, आज उसी कारण से आया हूँ।

मल्लिका ने मातुल की कही बात कालिदास से कही कि तुमने कश्मीर छोड़ दिया है। कालिदास ने इसके जवाब में कहा कि आज में सत्ता और प्रभुता सबसे मुक्त हूँ। सब यह सोचते हैं कि मैंने संन्यास ले लिया

है लेकिन मैं सिर्फ मातृगुप्त के चरित्र से मुक्त हुआ हूँ। मैं कालिदास बनकर जीना चाहता हूँ क्योंकि यहाँ की सी आत्मीयता मुझे कहीं नहीं मिली। जाने के दिन मैंने तुम्हारा जो रूप देखा था वह आज तक मुझे याद है। तभी द्वार पर दस्तक होती है। कालिदास दरवाजा खोलना चाहता है लेकिन मल्लिका उसे द्वार खोलने से रोक देती है। बाहर से आने वाले का नशीला स्वर सुनाई देता है कि हर समय दरवाजा बन्द ही रहता है। मल्लिका कहती है बस बैठकर बातें करते रहो।

कालिदास अम्बिका की बात को याद कर कहते हैं कि मैं इसलिए नहीं जा रहा था क्योंकि मुझे अपने आप पर विश्वास नहीं था। मेरा जीवन इस प्रकार परिवर्तित होगा कि मेरे जीवन की दिशा ही बदल जायेगी। ये आशंकाएँ निराधार नहीं थीं। कश्मीर का शासक बनने में मानो एक प्रतिशोध की भावना थी कि जिन्होंने मेरा उपहास उड़ाया, उनसे प्रतिशोध लिया जाये। परन्तु न तो मैं बदला और न ही सुखी हो सका। मैं प्रभुता और सुविधा के मोह में कवि से राज्याधिकारी बनने लगा। अनन्तः मैं खण्डित होता गया।

मैंने सोचा था कि कभी मिलने पर तुम्हें बताऊँगा कि मैंने वहाँ के वातावरण से कुछ भी नहीं लिखा। जो भी लिखा उसमें तुम ही थीं, कुमारसम्भव की तपस्विनी उमा तुम हो। मेघदूत में यक्ष की पीड़ा मेरी पीड़ा है और विरह में डूबी यक्षिणी तुम हो। मेरी शकुन्तला भी तुम थी। मैंने जो भी लिखा है वह मेरे जीवन का इतिहास था। मैं यह चाहता था कि मेरी सारी रचनाओं को तुम पढ़ पातीं। मल्लिका ने बताया कि उसने सारी रचनाएँ व्यापारियों से मँगाकर पढ़ ली हैं।

कालिदास यह बताते हैं कि यहाँ मुझे बहुत पहले ही आ जाना चाहिए था जिससे मैं यहाँ की वर्षा में बैठकर वह सब लिखता जो वर्षों से मेरे अन्दर बादलों की तरह घुमड़ रहा है। आज तक मैं उन्हें लिख न पाया क्योंकि उन्हें प्रतिकूल वातावरण ही नहीं मिला। कालिदास पास में पड़े एक ग्रन्थ को उठाकर देखता है तो उसमें केवल कोरे पृष्ठ हैं। मल्लिका ने बताया कि ये पन्ने अपने हाथों से तुम्हें भेंट करने के लिए बनाये गये थे लेकिन तुम यहाँ आकर भी नहीं आये। कालिदास पन्नों को पलटता है और कहता है कि तुम चाहती थी कि मैं इस पर एक महाकाव्य की रचना करूँ, परन्तु सच तो यह है कि तुमने अपनी आँखों से गिरने वाले आँसुओं से बहुत कुछ लिखा है। इन पर अनन्त सर्गों के महाकाव्य की रचना हो चुकी है। हम फिर से जीवन की शुरुआत कर सकते हैं। तभी अन्दर से बच्ची के रोने का स्वर सुनाई देता है। मल्लिका कालिदास को यह बताती है कि यह मेरा वर्तमान है और घर के अन्दर चली जाती है।

(विलोम का प्रवेश)

शब्दार्थ—कोसना = फटकारना, **लालसा** = इच्छा, **आकस्मिक** = संयोग, **उपक्रम** = शुरुआत, **सामर्थ्य** = शक्ति, **शाश्वत** = सदैव के लिए, **निर्दय** = कठोर, **चेतना** = आपा, **कम्पन** = सिहरन, **आवेश** = जोश।

किसी के पैर की चोट से दरवाजा अपने-आप खुल जाता है। विलोम वस्त्र और कीचड़ से लथपथ है। वह नशे में लड़खड़ाता हुआ अन्दर आता है। बड़बड़ाता रहता है लेकिन कालिदास को देखकर रुक जाता है। बड़े सन्देह से कहता है कि मेरी आँखों को जाने क्या हो गया है कि अपरिचित आकृतियाँ भी परिचित दिखाई देती हैं ? मल्लिका बाहर आने लगती है लेकिन विलोम को देखकर ठिठक जाती है।

कालिदास कहता है कि आकृति भले बदल गई हो पर तुम्हारे सामने खड़ा व्यक्ति वही है। विलोम कहता है कि स्वर और शब्द दोनों ही परिचित से लगते हैं। फिर अचानक हँसते हुए कहता है कि तुम्हें बहुत देखने की लालसा थी। वह मल्लिका से यह भी कहता है कि वह आज तो इस घर में अवांछित-सा नहीं है। विलोम आज इस घर में अधिकार से आता है। आज फिर से यह कैसा संयोग आया है कि हमारी मुलाकात यहीं हुई। तुम जब भी आते हो हमारी मुलाकात यहीं होती। कालिदास को हरिणशावकों से बहुत मोह है। एक हरिणशावक इस घर में भी है। मल्लिका की बच्ची की आँखें भी हरिणशावकों के नेत्रों से कम नहीं है। मल्लिका विलोम को रोकना चाहती है, परन्तु विलोम कहता है कि अष्टावक्र की बात सच है या असत्य कि बच्ची की आकृति विलोम से मिलती है। मल्लिका हाथों में अपना मुँह छिपाये रहती है और कालिदास विलोम

को जाने के लिए कहता है। विलोम कहता है कि जानता हूँ तुम्हारा अधिकार तो शाश्वत है। मैं आज चला जाता हूँ इसलिए नहीं कि तुम्हारा आदेश है बल्कि इसलिए कि अतिथि के शब्दों को मान दे रहा हूँ। कालिदास का भली-भाँति सत्कार करना वह फिर आये या न आये, ऐसा मल्लिका से कहते हुए विलोम चला जाता है।

विलोम के जाने के बाद मल्लिका के पूछने पर कालिदास कहता है कि मैं वही सोच रहा हूँ कि आषाढ़ का ऐसा ही दिन था वातावरण भी वैसा ही है लेकिन इन कोरे पृष्ठों का महाकाव्य तब नहीं लिखा गया था। मैं फिर से शुरुआत करना चाहता था लेकिन समय और इच्छा के बीच समय ज्यादा प्रभावी है क्योंकि वह प्रतीक्षा नहीं करता। इस वार्तालाप के दौरान ही बच्ची के रोने की आवाज आती है और मल्लिका अन्दर चली जाती है।

मल्लिका के जाने के बाद कालिदास थोड़ी देर कुछ सोचता है फिर बाहर चला जाता है। बादलों का गर्जन होता रहता है, मल्लिका बच्ची को हृदय से चिपकाये बाहर आती है लेकिन कालिदास को न पाकर दरवाजा खोल देती है। वह बाहर जाना चाहती है, परन्तु बच्ची को बाहों में देख वहीं रुक जाती है। बिजली चमकती रहती है, मेघ गरजते रहते हैं और यह अंक समाप्त हो जाता है।

अभ्यास-प्रश्न

प्रश्न 1. नाटककार के रूप में मोहन राकेश जी की विशेषताओं का उल्लेख कीजिए।

अथवा

'मोहन राकेश एक युगान्तकारी नाटककार हैं।' इस कथन के आलोक में मोहन राकेश की नाटक कला की विशेषताएँ बताइए।

अथवा

हिन्दी नाट्य-साहित्य में मोहन राकेश का क्या योगदान है ?

उत्तर—मोहन राकेश आधुनिक काल के सशक्त नाटककार माने जाते हैं। मोहन राकेश के नाटकों का शिल्प बेजोड़ है। रंगमंच की दृष्टि से मोहन राकेश ने कई सफल नाटकों की रचना की है, जिनमें 'आषाढ़ का एक दिन', 'लहरों के राजहंस' और 'आधे-अधूरे' प्रमुख हैं। राकेश जी के नाटकों की विशेषता यह है कि पाठक उन्हें पढ़कर आनन्दित तो होता ही है, परन्तु रंगमंच पर इनका प्रदर्शन देखकर नाटककार की रचनाधर्मिता से भी प्रभावित हुए बिना नहीं रहता।

राकेश जी के नाटक भारत के अनेक महत्वपूर्ण नगरों में तो मंचित हुए ही हैं, उनका मंचन अंग्रेजी माध्यम से विदेशों में भी हुआ है। मोहन राकेश के लिखे नाटकों को पढ़कर और उनका मंचन देखकर यह स्पष्ट हो जाता है कि वे कथात्मक और नाट्य-विधा दोनों पर समान अधिकार रखते हैं दोनों विधाओं पर उनकी गहरी पकड़ है। वे कहीं भी कथात्मकता के चक्कर में नाट्य-विधा को पीछे नहीं छोड़ते। उन्होंने दोनों का समान निर्वाह किया है।

मोहन राकेश को कहानी के बाद सफलता नाट्य-लेखन के क्षेत्र में मिली। हिन्दी नाटकों में भारतेन्दु और प्रसाद के बाद का दौर मोहन राकेश का दौर है जिसने हिन्दी नाटकों को फिर से रंगमंच से जोड़ा। हिन्दी नाट्य साहित्य में भारतेन्दु और प्रसाद के बाद यदि लीक से हटकर कोई नाम उभरता है तो मोहन राकेश का। हालांकि बीच में और भी कई नाम आते हैं जिन्होंने आधुनिक हिन्दी नाटक की विकास-यात्रा में कई महत्वपूर्ण पड़ाव तय किये हैं; किन्तु मोहन राकेश का लेखन एक-दूसरे ध्रुवान्त पर नजर आता है। इसलिए ही नहीं कि उन्होंने अच्छे नाटक लिखे, बल्कि इसलिए भी कि उन्होंने हिन्दी नाटक को अन्धेरे बन्द कमरों से बाहर निकाला और उसे युगों के रोमानी ऐन्द्रजालिक सम्मोहक से उबारकर एक नये दौर के साथ जोड़कर दिखाया। वस्तुतः मोहन राकेश के नाटक केवल हिन्दी के नाटक नहीं हैं। वे हिन्दी में लिखे अवश्य गये हैं, किन्तु समकालीन भारतीय नाट्य प्रवृत्तियों के द्योतक हैं। उन्होंने हिन्दी नाटक को पहली बार अखिल भारतीय स्तर ही नहीं प्रदान किया वरन् उसके सदियों के अलग-थलग प्रवाह को विश्व नाटक की एक सामान्य धारा की ओर

भी अग्रसर किया। प्रमुख भारतीय निर्देशकों में इब्राहम, ओम शिवपुरी, अरविन्द गौड़, श्यामानन्द जालान, राम गोपाल बजाज और दिनेश ठाकुर ने मोहन राकेश के नाटकों का निर्देशन किया।

मोहन राकेश के दो नाटकों 'आषाढ़ का एक दिन' तथा 'लहरों के राजहंस' में ऐतिहासिक पृष्ठभूमि को लेने पर भी आधुनिक मनुष्य के अन्तर्द्वन्द्व और संशयों की ही गाथा कही गयी है। एक नाटक की पृष्ठभूमि जहाँ गुप्तकाल है तो दूसरा बौद्धकाल के समय के ऊपर लिखा गया है। 'आषाढ़ का एक दिन' में जहाँ सफलता और प्रेम में एक को चुनने के द्वन्द्व से जूझते कालिदास एक रचनाकार और एक आधुनिक मनुष्य के मन की पहेलियों को सामने रखते हैं, वहीं प्रेम में टूटकर भी प्रेम को नहीं टूटने देने वाली इस नाटक की नायिका के रूप में हिन्दी साहित्य को एक अविस्मरणीय पात्र मिला है। 'लहरों के राजहंस' में और भी जटिल प्रश्नों को उठाते हुए जीवन की सार्थकता, भौतिक जीवन और अध्यात्मिक जीवन के द्वन्द्व, दूसरों के द्वारा अपने मत को दुनिया पर थोपने का आग्रह जैसे विषय उठाये गये हैं। राकेश के नाटकों को रंगमंच पर मिली शानदार सफलता इस बात की गवाह बनी कि नाटक और रंगमंच के बीच कोई खाई नहीं है।

प्रश्न 2. 'आषाढ़ का एक दिन' नाटक की कथानक के आधार पर समीक्षा कीजिए।

अथवा

'आषाढ़ का एक दिन' नाटक के कथावस्तु की विवेचना कीजिए।

उत्तर—हिन्दी नाटक के परिप्रेक्ष्य में, भाव वस्तु और रूपबन्ध दोनों के स्तर पर 'आषाढ़ का एक दिन' ऐसा पर्याप्त, सघन, तीव्र और भावोद्दीप्त लेखन प्रस्तुत करता है जैसा हिन्दी नाटकों में कम ही हुआ है। यह सुगठित यथार्थवादी नाटक है। हिन्दी में यह पहला यथार्थवादी नाटक है जिसमें बाह्य और आन्तरिक यथार्थ के अन्तर्द्वन्द्व को संवेदनशीलता के साथ दर्शाया गया है। किसी नाटक की सफलता और असफलता उस नाटक निर्माण में प्रयुक्त तत्वों के सफल संयोजन से ही होती है।

कथानक नाटक का मेरुदण्ड होता है। कथानक द्वारा ही नाटक का ताना-बाना बुना जाता है। इस लक्ष्य को ध्यान में रखकर ही कथानक का चयन किया जाना चाहिए। कथानक न तो इतना जटिल हो जो नाटक को शिथिल बना दे और न अधिक या कम अव्यवस्थित हो जिसमें कथा-सूत्रों का पारस्परिक सगुंफन न हो सके और उसकी गति अवरुद्ध हो जाये। कथानक के विकास के आधार पर इनकी तीन अवस्थाएँ होती हैं—प्रारम्भ, विकास और चरम सीमा।

इन तीनों अवस्थाओं के आधार पर 'आषाढ़ का एक दिन' नाटक के कथानक का विवेचन भी किया जा सकता है।

कथानक का प्रारम्भ—नाटक का प्रारम्भ मल्लिका के भीगकर घर आने से होता है जो कालिदास के उज्जयिनी जाने के निर्णय के सन्दर्भ में पाठकों में जिज्ञासा जाग्रत करता है जिससे जिज्ञासा और कौतुहल की सृष्टि होती है। मल्लिका के समझाने पर कालिदास उज्जयिनी जाने के लिए तैयार हो जाता है। उसी समय अनेक पात्रों के संयोजन द्वारा स्वाभाविक रूप से अन्य चरित्रों का परिचय दिया जाता है। मातुल, विलोम, अम्बिका तथा निक्षेप आदि पात्र नाटक के कथानक को कौतुहलपूर्ण और जिज्ञासावर्धक बनाने में सहायक होते हैं। इस प्रकार यदि कथानक के प्रारम्भ की समीक्षा की जाये तो यह स्पष्ट हो जाता है कि 'आषाढ़ का एक दिन' नाटक के कथानक में कौतुहल और जिज्ञासा की सृष्टि की है जो इस नाटक के कथानक के प्रारम्भ को सफल बनाता है।

कथानक का विकास—नाटक के कथानक के विकास के दौरान कथानक में गतिशीलता, रोचकता व घटनाओं का संयोजन इस प्रकार से होना चाहिए कि दर्शकों और पाठकों में कथानक के प्रति रोचकता बनी रहे। 'आषाढ़ का एक दिन' नाटक के कथानक के विकास में रोचकता को बनाये रखने के लिए मध्य में रंगिनी-संगिनी, अनुनासिक व अनुस्वार की घटनाओं का संयोजन किया गया है जिसमें नाटककार को पूरी सफलता मिली है। इन घटनाओं ने नाटक की प्रवाहमयता को और भी रोचक बना दिया है। इस प्रकार

कथानक का विकास संगठित एवं हास-परिहास की घटनाओं से गुंफित है जो नाटक को एकरस होने से बचाता है।

नाटक के कथानक की चरम सीमा— चरम सीमा से अभिप्राय कथानक के विकास की उस स्थिति से है, जहाँ नाटकीय स्थितियों का संघर्ष और दर्शक की जिज्ञासा अपने तीव्रतम रूप में प्रकट होती है। 'आषाढ़ का एक दिन' नाटक के कथानक में भी इस बात का विशेष ध्यान रखा गया है। नाटक के अन्त में स्थितियों का संघर्ष इस प्रकार बढ़ जाता है कि दर्शक की जिज्ञासा स्वत: बढ़ती जाती है। दर्शक अन्तिम समय तक यह निर्णय नहीं कर पाते कि कथानक किस ओर करवट लेगा। यह जिज्ञासा व संघर्ष की चरम सीमा पर पहुँचा देता है।

इस प्रकार कथानक के आधार पर जब 'आषाढ़ का एक दिन' नाटक की विवेचना की जाती है तो यह पाया जाता है कि नाटक का कथानक सुगठित, रोचक, जिज्ञासापूर्ण तथा प्रवाहमय है जो नाटक की सफलता में महत्वपूर्ण योगदान देता है।

प्रश्न 3. पात्र एवं चरित्र-चित्रण की दृष्टि से 'आषाढ़ का एक दिन' नाटक की समीक्षा कीजिए।

अथवा

'आषाढ़ का एक दिन' नाटक की पात्र-योजना के सम्बन्ध में अपने विचार लिखिए।

अथवा

पात्र योजना की दृष्टि से 'आषाढ़ का एक दिन' नाटक को कितनी सफलता मिली है ?

उत्तर—हिन्दी नाटक की विकास यात्रा में 'आषाढ़ का एक दिन' कई प्रकार से एक महत्वपूर्ण पड़ाव तो है ही, साथ ही इस दौर के नाटक लेखन की श्रेष्ठतम उपलब्धियों में गिनने योग्य भी है। यदि कथानक नाटक का मेरुदण्ड है तो पात्र नाटक के प्राण हैं, जो कथानक के निर्जीव शब्दों में प्राण फूँक देते हैं। पात्र नियोजन इसलिए भी महत्वपूर्ण है क्योंकि नाटक की मूल घटनाएँ और अनुभूति इसी के द्वारा प्रकट की जाती है। पात्रों के चरित्र-चित्रण, इन्हीं के मानसिक संघर्ष और इन्हीं की गतिशीलता द्वारा ही नाटक में स्वाभाविक रूप से नाटकीय आरोह-अवरोह उपस्थित होता है। पात्रों की कल्पना दो कोटियों में होती है—**मूल पात्र, गौण पात्र। 'मूल पात्र'** नाटक के चरम लक्ष्य का नायक होता है, यही वह शक्ति होती है जिसके सहारे नाटक की मूल संवेदना चरम सीमा पर पहुँचती है। **'गौण पात्र'** नाटक की मूल संवेदना को उत्तेजित करने में सहायक होते हैं तथा मूल पात्र की आत्माभिव्यक्ति में माध्यम का कार्य करते हैं। नाटक में पात्रों की संख्या सीमित होनी चाहिए साथ ही साथ उनके चरित्र-चित्रण में विश्वसनीयता का बोध होना चाहिए।

'आषाढ़ का एक दिन' नाटक में मल्लिका और कालिदास मुख्य पात्र हैं। मातुल, विलोम, निक्षेप, अम्बिका, रंगिनी-संगिनी, अनुस्वार, अनुनासिक और प्रियंगुमंजरी इस नाटक के गौण पात्र हैं।

कालिदास और मल्लिका को इस नाटक का मुख्य पात्र माना गया है क्योंकि पूरा कथानक इन्हीं दो पात्रों पर आधारित है। मल्लिका कालिदास की सृजनात्मकता को एक नया आयाम देने के उद्देश्य से अपने से दूर कर देती है। वहीं कालिदास को सारी सुख-सुविधाएँ तो मिल जातीं हैं परन्तु उसकी रचनात्मकता समाप्त हो जाती है। यहाँ कालिदास के चरित्र के माध्यम से बाह्य और आन्तरिक यथार्थ के अंतर्द्वन्द्व को प्रस्तुत करने का प्रयास किया है।

'आषाढ़ का एक दिन' नाटक में कालिदास और मल्लिका के अतिरिक्त विलोम एक ऐसा पात्र है कि उसे खलनायक कहकर टाला नहीं जा सकता है। वह कालिदास से भी अधिक विकसित पात्र है। उसके बिना यह नाटक भावुकतापूर्ण और शिथिल रह जाता। उसके तर्कों में ही नहीं, उसकी पूरी जीवन दृष्टि में एक ऐसी आवश्यकता और अनिवार्यता है कि उसकी गिनती हिन्दी नाटक के कुछ अविस्मरणीय पात्रों में होगी।

इस नाटक में मल्लिका की माँ और कालिदास का मामा मातुल दोनों बुजुर्ग हैं, नाटक के दो प्रमुख तरुण पात्रों के अभिभावक। फिर भी दोनों के स्वभाव एक-दूसरे से एकदम भिन्न हैं। दोनों के बीच यह भिन्नता अनेक स्तरों पर दिखाई देती है। इस कारण से मल्लिका और कालिदास दोनों के चरित्र अधिक सूक्ष्मता

और रोचकता के साथ रूपायित हो सके हैं। ऐसी ही विसदृशता निक्षेप और कालिदास तथा मल्लिका और प्रियंगुमंजरी के बीच भी दिखाई देती है।

इसी तरह रंगिनी-संगिनी और अनुस्वार-अनुनासिक की दो जोड़ियों के द्वारा बहुत संयत और प्रभावी ढंग से, व्यंग्य और हास्य के साथ समकालीन स्थितियों की अनुगूँज पैदा की गई है। ये पात्र थोड़ी देर के लिए ही आते हैं पर बड़ी कुशलता से कई बातें व्यंजित कर जाते हैं। इस प्रकार सभी पात्रों ने अपनी-अपनी भूमिकाओं का बड़ी सफलता से निर्वाह किया गया है।

इस प्रकार से 'आषाढ़ का एक दिन' में लेखन और प्रदर्शन दोनों ही स्तरों पर व्यापक सफलता का आधार उसकी बेहद सधी हुई, संयमित और सुचिन्तित पात्र योजना है।

प्रश्न 4. इस नाटक में मल्लिका की भूमिका पर प्रकाश डालिए।

अथवा

नाटक के आधार पर मल्लिका का चरित्र-चित्रण कीजिए।

अथवा

मल्लिका 'आषाढ़ का एक दिन' नाटक की एक महत्वपूर्ण पात्र है जिसके चरित्र ने सर्वाधिक प्रभावित किया है। अतः मल्लिका की चारित्रिक विशेषताओं का वर्णन कीजिए।

उत्तर—'आषाढ़ का एक दिन' नाटक पात्रों की दृष्टि से भी एक सफल नाटक है क्योंकि पात्रों की योजना कथानक के अनुसार है। मोहन राकेश के इस नाटक में दो प्रमुख पात्र हैं, कालिदास और मल्लिका। जिनमें मल्लिका का चरित्र नाटक के सन्देश को अपने में समेटे हुए है। नाटक का यह चरित्र नाटक का प्राण है जिसने कालिदास व अन्य पात्रों के सहयोग से नाटककार के उद्देश्य को पूरा करने में महत्वपूर्ण भूमिका निभाई है। मल्लिका के चरित्र की अनेक विशेषताएँ हैं जो नाटक को प्रभावशाली बनाने में सहायक हैं। मल्लिका ने अपने चरित्र का बड़ी सफलता से निर्वाह किया है।

मल्लिका के चरित्र की प्रमुख विशेषताएँ निम्नवत हैं—

प्रकृति प्रेमी—'आषाढ़ का एक दिन' नाटक के प्रारम्भ में जब मल्लिका वर्षा में भीगकर आती है और अम्बिका से प्रकृति के सौन्दर्य का वर्णन करती है तब प्रकृति से उसके प्रेम का आभास हो जाता है। मल्लिका प्रकृति के बहुत करीब है। मल्लिका का यह कथन उसके प्रकृति प्रेम को प्रदर्शित करता है।

"माँ, आज के वे क्षण मैं कभी नहीं भूल सकती। सौन्दर्य का ऐसा साक्षात्कार मैंने कभी नहीं किया। जैसे वह सौन्दर्य अस्पृश्य होते हुए भी माँसल हो।"

इस तरह मल्लिका को मेघ-मालाओं से आच्छादित पर्वत शिखरों को देखने के बाद अपने तन-मन की भी सुध नहीं रहती है जो उसके प्रकृति प्रेम को प्रमाणित करता है।

त्याग की प्रतिमूर्ति—मल्लिका ने पूरे नाटक में जहाँ आवश्यकता पड़ी है, अपने स्वार्थ को दरकिनार रखकर निर्णय किया है जो उसके अन्तर्निहित त्याग की भावना को दर्शाती है। मल्लिका नाटक के प्रारम्भ में भी अपने विवाह की बात कालिदास से न करके कालिदास की प्रतिभा को पल्लवित होने का पूरा अवसर देती है। इतना ही नहीं कालिदास के जाते समय मल्लिका एक बार भी अपने प्रेम के पाश में उसे बाँधने का प्रयास नहीं करती और अपने बारे में बिना कुछ सोचे उसे जाने के लिए प्रेरित करती है। मल्लिका का यह कथन उसकी त्याग की भावना को स्पष्ट करता है। वह कालिदास से कहती है कि "जानती हूँ कि कोई भी रेखा तुम्हें घेर न ले, तो तुम घिर जाओगे। मैं तुम्हें घेरना नहीं चाहती। इसलिए कहती हूँ, जाओ।"

इस प्रकार मल्लिका कालिदास के जाने के समय अपने स्वार्थ का पूरी तरह से त्याग कर उसे जाने के लिए प्रेरित करती है वहीं दूसरी ओर जब अन्तिम दृश्य में बच्ची को लेकर कालिदास को रोकने जाती है और बच्ची का ध्यान आते ही रुक जाती है, वहाँ भी उसका त्याग ही प्रदर्शित होता है।

भावुक—मल्लिका एक भावुक पात्र है जो हमेशा लोगों की भावनाओं को समझती है। मल्लिका भावनाओं को विशेष स्थान देती है। उसने पूरे नाटक के दौरान सभी की भावनाओं का पूरा ध्यान रखा है तथा अपने किसी भी कार्य व्यापार से किसी अन्य पात्र की भावनाओं को आहत नहीं होने दिया। अम्बिका ने कई बार यह कहा है कि मल्लिका, भावनाओं से बढ़कर भी दुनिया में बहुत कुछ है लेकिन हर बार मल्लिका ने भावनाओं को ही वरीयता दी है।

स्वाभिमानी—मल्लिका जिसका व्यक्तित्व एक तरफ भावुक और कोमल भावनाओं वाला है वहीं दूसरी ओर उसने कभी भी अपने आत्म-सम्मान को आहत नहीं होने दिया। मुश्किल से मुश्किल परिस्थिति में होते हुए कभी भी किसी से दया की अपेक्षा नहीं की बल्कि प्रियंगुमंजरी की तरफ से कई बार सहायता देने के बाद भी उसे स्वीकार नहीं करती और अपने स्वाभिमान से समझौता नहीं करती है। मातुल का यह कथन उसके चरित्र के इस गुण को इस प्रकार उद्घाटित करता है—

"प्रियंगुमंजरी ने तुम्हारे लिए कुछ वस्त्र और स्वर्ण मुद्राएँ भिजवायी थीं जो तुमने लौटा दीं ?"

सच्ची प्रेयसी—मल्लिका ने एक सच्ची प्रेयसी के धर्म का निर्वाह करते हुए बिना किसी अपेक्षा के कालिदास की प्रतिभा को विकसित होने के लिए कहीं भी अपने प्रेम को बाधा नहीं बनने देती है। अम्बिका के कहने पर कि 'विवाह के लिए तुम क्यों नहीं कहती ?' इस प्रश्न के जवाब में मल्लिका का कथन उसके सच्चे प्रेम को प्रदर्शित करता है। "तुम उनके प्रति सदा अनुदार रही हो, माँ! . . . . . . , मातुल के घर में उनकी क्या दशा रही है। उस साधनहीन और अभावग्रस्त जीवन में विवाह की कल्पना ही कैसे की जा सकती थी ?"

संघर्षशील—मल्लिका का जीवन कालिदास के जाने के बाद पूर्णतया संघर्षपूर्ण रहा है। प्रारम्भ में माँ के साथ विचारों का संघर्ष कालिदास के जाने के बाद दैनिक जीवन में संघर्ष के रूप में परिणित हो जाता है। मल्लिका ने पूरे नाटक में जीवन से संघर्ष किया और कभी अपनी इस अवस्था का जिम्मेदार किसी को नहीं ठहराया। अन्ततः वह एक वारांगना का जीवन व्यतीत करने पर विवश है, परन्तु वह कभी परिस्थितियों के समक्ष समर्पण नहीं करती।

इस प्रकार मल्लिका नाटक की प्रमुख भूमिका का निर्वाह करती है जिनमें इनके अतिरिक्त अनेक गुण विद्यमान हैं जो उसके चरित्र की सफलता में सहायक हैं।

प्रश्न 5. 'आषाढ़ का एक दिन' नाटक के शीर्षक की सार्थकता पर अपने विचार प्रकट कीजिए।

उत्तर—नाटकों में युगीन समस्याओं का चित्रण करते हुए उनका समाधान करने का भी प्रयास किया जाता है। मानव जीवन की सजीव, मूर्त एवं प्रत्यक्ष झाँकी जैसी नाटक में दिखाई जाती है वह दूसरी विधाओं में कठिन है। जनता में जागृति का संचार करने में नाटकों की प्रमुख भूमिका रहती है। नाटक में दृश्यों और अभिनय के आधार पर रंगमंच पर ऐसे वातावरण का निर्माण किया जाता है जिसे देखकर दर्शक आत्मविस्मृत हो जाता है। यही आत्मविस्मृति ही नाटक की सफलता कहलाती है। किसी नाटक की सफलता और असफलता उस नाटक के निर्माण में प्रयुक्त तत्वों के सफल संयोजन से ही होती है।

'आषाढ़ का एक दिन' नाटक का शीर्षक सार्थक है क्योंकि इसमें शीर्षक के सभी गुणों का समावेश है। शीर्षक जिज्ञासावर्धक है, जिसे सुनकर यह जानने की इच्छा होती है कि आखिर आषाढ़ के एक दिन क्या होता ? इस नाटक की सारी घटनाएँ शीर्षक के इर्द-गिर्द घूमती हैं। प्रत्येक अंक का प्रारम्भ इसी दिन से होता है। नाटक में तीन अंक हैं और तीनों अंकों की समाप्ति पर कालिदास हर बार मल्लिका को छोड़कर चला जाता है।

आषाढ़ के पहले दिन जब वर्षा होती है तब उज्जयिनी के राजा आचार्य वररुचि को कालिदास को लाने के लिए भेजते हैं और आषाढ़ के ही दिन कालिदास मल्लिका के समझाने के उपरान्त उज्जयिनी जाने के लिए तैयार होते हैं और आषाढ़ के दिन ही कालिदास मल्लिका को छोड़कर चले जाते हैं।

नाटक के दूसरे अंक का प्रारम्भ निक्षेप और मल्लिका की बातचीत के दौरान होता है। उसी समय निक्षेप कालिदास को जाते हुए देखता है। रंगिनी-संगिनी, अनुस्वार और अनुनासिक का आगमन होता है, वे

कुछ समय के लिए नाटक पर व्यंगात्मक प्रभाव छोड़ते हैं। प्रियंगुमंजरी का आगमन होता है जो मल्लिका के विवाह और घर के परिसंस्कार के सन्दर्भ में बातें करती हैं। इतना होने के बावजूद कालिदास मल्लिका से मिलने के लिए नहीं आता है और एक बार फिर कालिदास मल्लिका को छोड़कर चला जाता है।

नाटक के तीसरे अंक में एक बार फिर वही आषाढ़ का एक दिन है, वर्षा हो रही है और एक बार फिर कालिदास का आगमन होता है। कालिदास और मल्लिका तरह-तरह की बातें करते हैं। अथ से प्रारम्भ करने की भी बात होती है, लेकिन तभी मल्लिका की बेटी रोती है जिसे मल्लिका अपना वर्तमान कहकर सम्बोधित करती है। यह सब जानकर कालिदास एक बार फिर उसी वर्षा और मेघ-गर्जन के बीच में मल्लिका को छोड़कर चला जाता है।

इस प्रकार नाटक का प्रारम्भ और अन्त दोनों ही आषाढ़ की वर्षा के समय होता है। यह शीर्षक जिज्ञासावर्धक व नाटक को केन्द्र में रखकर रखा गया है। नाटक की घटनाएँ शीर्षक के आस-पास ही रहती हैं, अत: नाटक का यह शीर्षक सर्वथा सार्थक प्रतीत होता है।

प्रश्न 6. इस नाटक के आधार पर कालिदास का चरित्र-चित्रण कीजिए।

अथवा

नाटक के आधार पर कालिदास की चारित्रिक विशेषताओं का वर्णन कीजिए।

अथवा

कालिदास के चरित्र में सबलताओं और दुर्बलताओं का समन्वय है। इस कथन के आधार पर कालिदास की चारित्रिक विशेषताओं का वर्णन कीजिए।

उत्तर—'आषाढ़ का एक दिन' नाट्य लेखन के क्षेत्र में एक महत्वपूर्ण उपलब्धि है। वस्तुत: हिन्दी के जिन एक-दो लेखकों ने नाटकों में यथार्थपरकता और व्याख्यात्मकता का श्रीगणेश किया था, 'आषाढ़ का एक दिन' उसकी महत्वपूर्ण परिणिति है। इस नाटक की प्रत्यक्ष विषय-वस्तु कालिदास के जीवन से सम्बधित है। सारी घटनाएँ आषाढ़ के एक दिन पर ही घटित होती हैं। प्रेयसी मल्लिका के आग्रह पर कालिदास उसे छोड़कर चला जाता है। उसे सारी सुख-सुविधाएँ मिल जाती हैं, परन्तु अपने मानसिक द्वन्द्व की वजह से उसे कहीं भी शान्ति नहीं मिलती है। इस प्रकार कालिदास का चरित्र ही नाटक के कथानक का आधार है, अत: कालिदास की चारित्रिक विशेषताएँ अग्रवत है—

दयालु—नाटक के प्रथम अंक में कालिदास का प्रवेश ही हरिणशावक के साथ होता है जो किसी शर (तीर) से आहत हुआ है। जिसे लेकर कालिदास मल्लिका के घर आता है और उससे कहता है कि अँगुलियों का कोमल स्पर्श तुम्हें प्राण दे सकता है। इस प्रकार कालिदास का मंच पर आगमन ही जीवों पर दया करने वाले एक कोमल हृदय वाले व्यक्तित्व से होता है। जो उसके चरित्र की एक महत्वपूर्ण विशेषता को उद्घाटित करता है।

निर्भीक—कालिदास में निर्भीकता भी है, जो उनके चरित्र के महत्वपूर्ण पक्ष को उजागर करता है। नाटक के प्रथम अंक में ही दंतुल जब कालिदास को प्राणों और शक्ति का भय दिखाते हुए यह कहता है कि उसे हरिणशावक को देना ही पड़ेगा अन्यथा परिणाम बुरा होगा। तब यह सुनने के बाद भी कालिदास किसी भी परिणाम की चिन्ता किये बिना हरिणशावक को लेकर चले जाते हैं। इस प्रकार यह प्रकट हो जाता है कि कालिदास के चरित्र में निर्भीकता और शरणागत-वत्सलता है जो उनके चरित्र के निर्माण में एक महत्वपूर्ण योगदान करता है।

सन्तोषी—कालिदास का वर्तमान बड़े संघर्ष से बीत रहा है, वह मातुल की गाय चराने के लिए जाता है। जीविकोपार्जन भी कालिदास के समक्ष एक बड़ी समस्या बन जाती है। ऐसे समय में आचार्य वररुचि उज्जयिनी के राजा की तरफ से कालिदास को सम्मानित करने के लिए अपने साथ ले जाने के लिए आये हैं। कालिदास

को यह पता है कि उन्हें राजकवि का सम्मान दिया जायेगा। उनकी जीविकोपार्जन की समस्या का अन्त हो जायेगा। यह सब जानकर भी कालिदास उज्जयिनी जाने से इंकार कर देते हैं। मातुल के द्वारा कालिदास के सन्दर्भ में कहा गया यह कथन उनकी सन्तोषवृत्ति को दर्शाता है।

"....... और वे वंशावतंस कहते हैं कि, मुझे यह सम्मान नहीं चाहिए. .। मैं राजकीय मुद्राओं से क्रीत होने के लिए नहीं हूँ।"

प्रतिभाशाली—कालिदास का व्यक्तित्व एक असाधारण प्रतिभा से सम्पन्न है। उनकी कृतियाँ और उन कृतियों की प्रसिद्धि कालिदास की असाधारण प्रतिभा को व्यक्त करतीं है। अनेक स्थलों पर भिन्न-भिन्न पात्रों द्वारा नाटककार ने यह बात बताई है। जब संगिनी के पूछने पर मल्लिका उसे यह बताती है कि हमारा जीवन हर दृष्टि से बहुत साधारण है तो इस कथन के जवाब में कहा गया संगिनी का यह कथन कालिदास की प्रतिभा का परिचायक है—

"यह मैं नहीं मान सकती। इस प्रदेश ने कालिदास जैसी असाधारण प्रतिभा को जन्म दिया है। यहाँ की तो प्रत्येक वस्तु असाधारण होनी चाहिए।"

मानसिक अंतर्द्वन्द्व का शिकार—कालिदास ही नाटककार का वह पात्र है जिसे नाटककार ने बाह्य और आन्तरिक द्वन्द्व को प्रदर्शित करने के लिए चुना। कालिदास के माध्यम से राकेश जी ने एक ऐसे पात्र की सृष्टि की है जिसका जीवन यथार्थ और आदर्शवाद के बीच झूलता रहता है। अंक तीन में मल्लिका से बातचीत के दौरान कालिदास ने अपने कथन द्वारा अपने चरित्र के इस द्वन्द्व के सन्दर्भ में खुद ही कहा है—

"...... मैं यह आशा लिए हुए चला गया कि कल एक ऐसा समय आयेगा जब मैं तुमसे यह सब कह सकूँगा और तुम्हें अपने मन के द्वन्द्व का विश्वास दिला सकूँगा।"

निर्णय लेने में अक्षम—कालिदास को जब भी किसी प्रकार का निर्णय लेना होता है तो पूरी तरह से एक निर्णय पर पहुँच नहीं पाता जिससे उसका सम्पूर्ण जीवन द्वन्द्व में बीतता है। पहली बार उज्जयिनी जाने के सन्दर्भ में निर्णय लेने में मल्लिका उसकी सहायता करती है, दूसरी बार वह आकर भी मल्लिका से नहीं मिलता, तीसरे अंक में कालिदास अथ से प्रारम्भ करने की बात तो करता है परन्तु दूसरे ही क्षण वह मल्लिका को पुनः छोड़कर चला जाता है।

निष्कर्ष—अन्त में निष्कर्ष के रूप में यह कहा जा सकता है कि कालिदास का प्रभाव पूरे नाटक पर पड़ता है। जहाँ कालिदास अप्रतिम प्रतिभा का स्वामी है वहीं दूसरी ओर उसके चरित्र में अनेक ऐसे गुण भी हैं जो उसके चरित्र की दुर्बलता को भी उद्घाटित करते हैं। कहीं-कहीं तो ऐसा प्रतीत होता है कि मल्लिका के इस कष्टपूर्ण जीवन का एकमेव उत्तरदायी कालिदास ही है। कालिदास के चाहे बिना मल्लिका का औदात्य आत्मदान अकेला छूट जाता है। कुछ भी हो कालिदास ने नाटक में अपने चरित्र का बड़ी ही सफलता से निर्वाह किया है।

प्रश्न 7. 'संवाद योजना' की दृष्टि से 'आषाढ़ का एक दिन' नाटक की समीक्षा कीजिए।

उत्तर—संवाद का अर्थ है—बातचीत। नाटक के तत्वों में संवाद का अत्यन्त महत्वपूर्ण स्थान है। वास्तव में संवाद के बिना नाटकरूपी भवन का निर्माण असम्भव है। इसी कारण कुछ विद्वानों ने संवाद को 'नाटक का सर्वस्व' तो कुछ ने इसे 'नाटक की आत्मा' शब्दों से भी अभिहित किया है। नाटक में संवाद योजना कथासूत्र को आगे बढ़ाने, पात्रों के व्यक्तित्व का उद्घाटन करने तथा प्रतिपाद्य के अनुरूप वातावरण की सृष्टि करने के लिए किया जाता है। संवाद संक्षिप्त और पात्रानुकूल होने चाहिए। वस्तुतः संक्षिप्त और चुस्त संवाद नाटक को शक्ति एवं गति प्रदान करते हैं। संवाद ही वातावरण के निर्माण में सहायक होते हैं। पात्र लेखक के विचारों का वाहक होते हैं इसलिए उनके संवादों के द्वारा ही लेखक का उद्देश्य और अधिक स्पष्ट हो जाता है। आवश्यकतानुसार संवाद में हास्य-व्यंग्य का पुट संवादों को और भी चुस्त और आकर्षक बना देता है। जिससे

संवाद बोझिल व उबाऊ नहीं रहते। संवादों में स्वाभाविकता, रोचकता, उपयुक्तता, अनुकूलता, संबद्धता, संक्षिप्तता, सोद्देश्यता तथा नाटकीयता आदि गुणों का होना आवश्यक है। इन्हीं गुणों के द्वारा ही संवाद को प्रभावशाली बनाया जा सकता है। नाटकों में स्वगत कथन का प्रयोग कम से कम होना चाहिए।

कथानक के विकास में सहायक— पात्रों में पारस्परिक संवाद के द्वारा ही कथानक का विकास होता है। संवाद ही वर्तमान और भविष्य की घटनाओं की जानकारी देते हैं। पात्र अपने संवादों द्वारा ही अपने चरित्र की विचारधारा को प्रकट करते हैं। 'आषाढ़ की एक दिन' नाटक के कथानक पूरी तरह से नाटक के कथानक विकास में सहायक हैं। संवाद कथानक की प्रवाहमयता एवं गतिशीलता को बनाये रखते हैं।

पात्रानुकूलता— यह कथानक उस समय का है जब कालिदास का रचनाकाल था। उस समय की स्वाभाविकता को बनाये रखने के लिए नाटककार ने हिन्दी के तत्सम और तद्भव का प्रयोग बड़ी ही सफलता से किया है जिससे संवादों में स्वाभाविकता परिलक्षित होती है। कालिदास का यह संवाद नाटक में संवादों की पात्रानुकूलता को सिद्ध कर देता है।

''कालिदास—यह हरिणशावक इस पार्वत्य-भूमि की सम्पत्ति है, राजपुरुष ! और इसी पार्वत्य-भूमि के निवासी हम इसके सजातीय हैं।''

नाटकीयता— संवादों की नाटकीयता कथानक को नयी दिशा प्रदान करती है। नाटकीयता के कारण ही पात्रों में सजीवता का आभास होता है। उदाहरणार्थ, मल्लिका के सम्बन्ध में रंगिनी का यह संवाद है—''रहने दे संगिनी ! यह यहाँ के सम्बन्ध में विशेष कुछ नहीं जानती।''

इस प्रकार 'आषाढ़ का एक दिन' नाटक के संवाद पूरी तरह से नाटकीय हैं जो नाटक की प्रवाहमयता एवं स्वाभाविकता को बनाये रखते हैं।

संक्षिप्तता एवं रोचकता—'आषाढ़ का एक दिन' नाटक पूरी तरह से मंचन के अनुकूल है क्योंकि नाटक की सफलता पात्रों के कथन पर आधारित होती है। यदि संवाद संक्षिप्त न हों तो बोझिल बन जाते हैं और संवाद का आनन्द, अभिनेता और दर्शक दोनों को ही नहीं मिल पाता। इसलिए संवादों का संक्षिप्त और रुचिकर होना बहुत आवश्यक है। 'आषाढ़ का एक दिन' नाटक में प्रयुक्त संवाद बहुत ही संक्षिप्त और रोचक हैं। प्रस्तुत है नाटक के संवादों के संक्षिप्तता की एक बानगी—

''मातुल—अधिकारी-वर्ग, आपका कार्य यहाँ पूरा हो गया।

अनुनासिक—क्यों अनुस्वार ?

अनुस्वार—हाँ, पूरा हो गया। हो गया न ? क्यों अनुनासिक ?''

भावानुकूलता—'आषाढ़ का एक दिन' नाटक में भावों के अनुरूप ही संवादों की सर्जना की गई है जो नाटक की सफलता का एक महत्वपूर्ण कारक है। नाटक में प्रयुक्त सभी संवाद भावों के अनुरूप ही हैं जो दर्शकों व पाठकों के हृदय को छू जाते हैं। ये संवाद पूरी तरह से पाठकों व दर्शकों को पात्रों से जोड़ देते हैं। नाटक के तीसरे अंक में मल्लिका का यह कथन पूरी तरह से मल्लिका के जीवन में कालिदास के स्थान को व्यक्त करता है।

मल्लिका—. . . . . ''मैं यद्यपि तुम्हारे जीवन में नहीं रही, परन्तु तुम मेरे जीवन में सदा बने रहे हो। मैंने कभी तुम्हें अपने से दूर नहीं होने दिया। तुम रचना करते रहे और मैं समझती रही कि मैं सार्थक हूँ, मेरे जीवन की भी कुछ उपलब्धि है।''

इस प्रकार संवाद-योजना की दृष्टि से 'आषाढ़ का एक दिन' नाटक पूरी तरह से सफल नाटक है क्योंकि नाटक के संवाद में वे सभी गुण विद्यमान हैं जो नाटक की सफलता में सहायक होते हैं।

प्रश्न 8. 'आषाढ़ का एक दिन' नाटक के आधार पर मोहन राकेश के भाषा एवं शैली की विशेषताओं का वर्णन कीजिए।

अथवा

भाषा और शैली की दृष्टि से 'आषाढ़ का एक दिन' नाटक की समीक्षा कीजिए।

उत्तर— भाषा के प्रयोग में नाटककार को देश, काल, वातावरण, पात्रों की पात्रता अर्थात् चरित्र की अनुकूलता का ध्यान रखना आवश्यक है। भाषा में सरलता, प्रवाहमयता और बोधगम्यता होनी चाहिए। कहीं-

कहीं भाषा में काव्यात्मकता का प्रदर्शन भाषा को प्रभावशाली बनाने में सहायक होता है। शब्द भण्डार सटीक व समृद्ध होना चाहिए। शब्दों का चयन भावों के अनुकूल होना ही नाटककार की सफलता का रहस्य होता है।

नाटक, उपन्यास अथवा कहानी को प्रस्तुत करने के ढंग को शैली कहते हैं। इसमें कृतिकार का व्यक्तित्व विशेष रूप से झलकता है। नाटक की शैली के अन्तर्गत पात्रों की भाषा, रंगमंच की व्यवस्था, नाटककार का व्यक्तित्व आदि बातें आती हैं। इसे हम नाटक का कलापक्ष भी कह सकते हैं।

भाषा—इस नाटक में भाव स्थिति की गहराई में जाने का प्रयास है और पूरा नाटक एक साथ कई स्तरों पर प्रभावकारी है। ऐसे प्रभावकारी विषय-वस्तु को प्रस्तुत करने के लिए भाषा का प्रभावशाली होना आवश्यक है। आषाढ़ का एक दिन नाटक में भाषा पात्रानुकूल है। भाषा में प्रवाहमयता तथा बोधगम्यता है। भाषा की काव्यात्मकता नाटक को प्रभावशाली बनाने में सहायक है। नाटक में कालिदास के रचनाकाल के अनुसार ही भाषा का प्रयोग किया गया है जिससे नाटक के संवादों में भाषा की स्वाभाविकता आ सके। शब्दों का चयन भावों के अनुकूल किया गया है। जैसे—

''मल्लिका—ठहरो, राजपुरुष ! हरिणशावक के लिए हठ मत करो। तुम्हारे लिए प्रश्न अधिकार का है, उनके लिए संवेदना का, कालिदास निःशस्त्र होते हुए भी तुम्हारे शस्त्र की चिन्ता नहीं करेंगे।''

इस प्रकार यदि इस कथन में देखें तो राजपुरुष, हरिणशावक, निःशस्त्र और संवेदना आदि ऐसे शब्द हैं जो पात्रों के भावानुकूल है तथा भाषा की प्रवाहमयता को बनाये रखने में सहायक हैं।

नाटक में नाटककार ने टूटा-हारा, अपरवाद, निरर्थक प्रलाप, सौन्दर्य का साक्षात्कार, प्रकोष्ठ, आतिथ्य, निष्ठुर, आत्मसीमित, स्थपति, तल्प, अभ्यर्थना आदि ऐसे शब्दों का प्रयोग किया जो नाटक की भाषिक समृद्धता को प्रदर्शित करते हैं।

शैली—शैली की दृष्टि से आधुनिक चाक्षुष बिम्बों के साथ भाषा के शब्दों में जो व्यंजक बिम्ब है, वे ही सोना है। नाटक में कुछ ऐसे बिम्ब हैं जो दर्शकों को काफी समय तक बाँधे रखने में सहायक हैं। इनमें आरम्भ में बिजली की चमक के साथ अम्बिका का चिन्तित रूप में प्रवेश, कालिदास के पैरों की दूर होती आहट, मल्लिका का काले वस्त्र पहने हुए, अकेलापन और एक बार फिर अलग होते दो प्रेमी, कालिदास की धीमी चहलकदमी, मल्लिका का आँसुओं में डूबा हुआ चेहरा और तूफान के दृश्य अत्यन्त प्रभावकारी हैं।

'आषाढ़ का एक दिन' सुगठित यथार्थवादी नाटक है इसमें बाह्य ब्योरे की अपेक्षा परिस्थिति के काव्य को अभिव्यक्त करने का प्रयास किया गया है। नाटक में कार्य व्यापार के संयोजन में गति पर्याप्त तीव्र ही नहीं है, उस तीव्रता के भीतर लय की विविधता है। विभिन्न भावों और स्थितियों एवं पात्रों को इस प्रकार सामने रखा गया है कि वे अपने आप में नाटकीय प्रभाव उत्पन्न करते हैं।

इस प्रकार भाषा और शैली दोनों को आधार बनाकर जब 'आषाढ़ का एक दिन' नाटक की समीक्षा की जाती है तो यह पता चलता है कि नाटककार ने नाटक में इनका बड़ी सफलता व अनुकूलता के साथ प्रयोग किया है जो नाटक के कलेवर में चार चाँद लगाते हैं।

प्रश्न 9. प्रियंगुमंजरी का चरित्र-चित्रण करते हुए यह बतायें कि उसके द्वारा नाटककार ने कौन-सा सन्देश दिया है ?

उत्तर—मल्लिका के बार-बार कहने पर जब कालिदास उज्जयिनी चला जाता है तो वह वहाँ जाकर वहाँ की विदुषी राजदुहिता से विवाह कर लेता है। वही राजदुहिता प्रियंगुमंजरी है, जो नाटक में एक गौण पात्र है। प्रियंगुमंजरी एक गौण पात्र होते हुए भी मल्लिका और कालिदास जैसे प्रमुख पात्रों के चरित्र को विकसित करने में महत्वपूर्ण योगदान करती है। इस प्रकार प्रियंगुमंजरी के चरित्र में अनेक विशेषताएँ हैं।

विनम्रता—प्रियंगुमंजरी बड़े ही विनम्र स्वभाव की है। विनम्रता उसके चरित्र की एक महत्वपूर्ण विशेषता है। उसकी कुलीनता उसके स्वभाव से प्रदर्शित होती है। प्रियंगुमंजरी जब मल्लिका के घर में आती है

तो मल्लिका आतिथ्य करने का प्रयास करती है तो उसके जवाब में राजदुहिता द्वारा दिया गया जवाब उनकी विनम्रता की मिसाल है।

''प्रियंगु—आतिथ्य की बात मच सोचो। मैं तुम्हारे यहाँ अतिथि के रूप में नहीं आयी हूँ। . . . सम्भव था ये न भी आते, परन्तु मैं ही विशेष आग्रह के साथ इन्हें लायी हूँ। मैं स्वयं एक बार इस प्रदेश को देखना चाहती थी। इसके अतिरिक्त. . . .।''

समझदार—प्रियंगुमंजरी के चरित्र में समझदारी कूट-कूटकर भरी है। वह मल्लिका से मिलने के दौरान उसके घर की हालत को देखकर उसकी सहायता का प्रस्ताव देती है जो उसकी समझदारी का परिचायक है। इतना ही नहीं वह उसे अपने साथ ले जाना चाहती है। वह उसके घर का परिसंस्कार कराना चाहती है। मल्लिका के घर में जब कालिदास की रचनाएँ देखती है तो उसका यह कथन उसकी समझदारी को प्रमाणित करता है।

''प्रियंगु—मैं समझ सकती हूँ। उनसे जान चुकी हूँ कि तुम बचपन से उनकी संगिनी रही हो। उनकी रचनाओं के प्रति तुम्हारा मोह स्वाभाविक है।''

पतिपरायणा—प्रियंगुमंजरी बड़ी ही पतिपरायणा है। प्रियंगुमंजरी कालिदास के अनुरूप वातावरण का निर्माण करने हेतु वह यहाँ से कई चीजें अपने साथ ले जाना चाहती है जिससे कालिदास के अनुकूल वातावरण बनाया जा सके। ''कुछ हरिणशावक जायेंगे, जिनका हम अपने उद्यान में पालन करेंगे। यहाँ की औषधियाँ उद्यान के क्रीड़ा-शैल पर तथा आस-पास के प्रदेश में लगवा दी जायेंगी।'' इस प्रकार प्रियंगुमंजरी अपने पति की रचनात्मकता का विकास करना चाहती है।

संवेदनशील—प्रियंगुमंजरी में बड़ी संवेदनाशीलता है। वह दूसरों के दु:ख को समझ सकती है और उनके लिए ही चिन्तित नहीं है बल्कि मल्लिका और मातुल के लिए भी उसकी उतनी ही संवेदना है। मल्लिका के विवाह के साथ ही वह विलोम का भी घर बनवाना चाहती है। वह मल्लिका के घर को गिराकर उसके स्थान पर एक नया घर बनवा देना चाहती थी, परन्तु जैसे ही उसने यह सुना कि इस घर को गिराने से उन्हें दु:ख होगा वह अपना निर्णय तुरन्त बदल देती है।

''प्रियंगु—मैं तुम्हारी सुविधा के लिए ही कह रही थी। तुम्हें इसमें असुविधा है, तो. . . . . ठीक है। मैं ऐसा आदेश नहीं दूँगी। फिर भी चाहती हूँ कि तुम्हारे लिए कुछ न कुछ कर सकूँ।''

इस प्रकार प्रियंगुमंजरी के चरित्र की इन विशेषताओं के साथ अन्य विशेषताएँ भी हैं जो उसके चरित्र को प्रभावपूर्ण बना देती हैं।

प्रश्न 10. नाटक के आधार पर विलोम का चरित्र-चित्रण कीजिए ?

उत्तर—'आषाढ़ का एक दिन' नाटक में कालिदास और मल्लिका के अतिरिक्त विलोम भी एक पात्र है। उसे खलनायक कहकर टाला नहीं जा सकता। वह कालिदास से भी अधिक विकसित पात्र है। उसके बिना यह नाटक भावुकतापूर्ण और शिथिल रह जाता। उसके तर्कों में ही नहीं, उसकी पूरी जीवन दृष्टि में एक ऐसी आवश्यकता और अनिवार्यता है कि उसकी गिनती हिन्दी नाटक के कुछ ऐसे ही अविस्मरणीय पात्रों में होगी। इस प्रकार से विलोम का चरित्र मोहन राकेश की एक अनुपम नाटकीय चरित्र-सृष्टि है।

विलोम के चरित्र में अनेक चारित्रिक विशेषताएँ हैं जो उनके चरित्र की प्रबलता को प्रदर्शित करती हैं।

समझदारी—विलोम एक ऐसा पात्र है, जो नाटक पर कालिदास से अधिक प्रभाव छोड़ता है। वह बहुत ही समझदार है। जब अम्बिका विलोम से यह कहती है, कि तुम्हारा यहाँ आना मल्लिका को सह्य नहीं है तो उस प्रश्न के जवाब में विलोम द्वारा कहा गया कथन उसकी समझदारी को प्रदर्शित करता है।

''विलोम-मल्लिका को सह्य नहीं है, जानता हूँ अम्बिका ! मल्लिका बहुत भोली है। वह लोक जीवन के सम्बन्ध में कुछ नहीं जानती।

वह नहीं चाहती कि मैं इस घर में आऊँ, क्योंकि कालिदास नहीं चाहता।''

स्पष्टवादी—विलोम के चरित्र की यह महत्वपूर्ण विशेषता है कि उसे प्रमुख पात्रों की भाँति गौरव प्राप्त नहीं है फिर भी वह गौण पात्र होते हुए स्पष्टता से बातों को कहता है, जो किसी भी दृष्टिकोण से अप्रासांगिक प्रतीत नहीं होती हैं। कालिदास के उज्जयिनी जाने के सन्दर्भ में तथा कालिदास और मल्लिका के सन्दर्भ में सारे ग्राम प्रान्त में फैल रहे अपवाद को ध्यान में रखते हुए यह स्पष्ट करना चाहता है कि कालिदास मल्लिका को अपने साथ ले जायेगा अथवा नहीं। उसके द्वारा कालिदास से पूछा गया यह प्रश्न उसकी स्पष्टवादिता का प्रतीक है—

"विलोम—. . . . . क्या यह उचित नहीं कि कालिदास यह स्पष्ट बता दें कि उसे उज्जयिनी अकेले जाना है या. . . . .।"

दूरदर्शी—विलोम एक दूरदर्शी पात्र है। उसके अन्दर दूर तक सोचने और समझने की शक्ति है। विलोम की दूरदर्शिता का सबसे बड़ा उदाहरण यह है कि वह अंक एक में कालिदास के सन्दर्भ में जो बातें कहता है वही बातें अंक दो तक पूर्णत: सत्य प्रतीत होती है।

"विलोम—. . . सुना है, वहाँ जाकर व्यक्ति बहुत व्यस्त हो जाता है। वहाँ के जीवन में कई तरह के आकर्षण हैं—रंगशालाएँ, मदिरालय और तरह-तरह की विलास भूमियाँ !"

वाक्पटु—विलोम बड़ी ही वाकपटु है उसके वाक्‌चातुर्य के अनेक उदाहरण नाटक में भरे पड़े हैं। जब प्रथम अंक में मल्लिका के यह कहने पर कि उसकी उपस्थिति अनचाहे के रूप में है। तब विलोम का कथन उसकी वाकपटुता को प्रदर्शित करता है।

"विलोम—यह अनुभव करने की मैंने आवश्यकता नहीं समझी। तुम मुझसे घृणा करती हो, मैं जानता हूँ, परन्तु मैं तुमसे घृणा नहीं करता। मेरे यहाँ होने के लिए इतना ही पर्याप्त है।"

व्यंग्यात्मक वक्ता—विलोम के द्वारा कही गई बातें सत्य के करीब होते हुए भी यथार्थ पर इस प्रकार व्यंग्य करती हैं कि उसके व्यंग्य बाणों की चुभन से आहत हुए बिना कोई नहीं रह सकता।

"विलोम—. . . . . . मैं कब कहता हूँ कि दूसरा अर्थ नहीं है ? अर्थ बहुत स्पष्ट है। वे यहाँ से जाकर दूसरों को दिखाना चाहते हैं। तुम, मैं, यह घर, ये पर्वत सब उनके लिए विचित्र उदाहरण हैं।"

इस प्रकार विलोम का व्यक्तित्व पूरे नाटक पर छाया हुआ है। विलोम इस नाटक में खलनायक ही नहीं बल्कि एक खलनायक से बढ़कर है। यह ऐसा चरित्र है जिसकी अधिकांश बातें सत्य प्रतीत होती हैं। इस प्रकार एक गौण पात्र होते हुए भी नाटक के सफल होने में महत्वपूर्ण योगदान देता है।

प्रश्न 11. नाटक के आधार पर मातुल का चरित्र-चित्रण कीजिए।

अथवा

मातुल ने नाटक में किस प्रकार अपनी भूमिका का निर्वाह किया है। उसमें उसे कितनी सफलता मिली है ?

उत्तर—अनजान मातुल बाह्य सामाजिक संक्रान्ति के मूल्यों की पंगुता का प्रतीक बने ऐसी नाटककार की कोशिश है। इसलिए कहानी के अन्त में उसे बैसाखी के साथ दिखाया गया है। यह दिखाने का प्रयास किया गया है कि किस प्रकार सामाजिक संक्रान्ति के मूल्यों के कारण उसे अन्तत: पंगु बनाना पड़ता है। मातुल का चरित्र का एक प्रतीक भले हो लेकिन उसका चरित्र प्रमुख पात्रों के चरित्र निर्माण में सहायक है। उसके चरित्र की कुछ महत्वपूर्ण विशेषताएँ हैं।

दूरदर्शी—जब उज्जयिनी से आचार्य वररुचि आते हैं और कालिदास को ले जाकर उनका राजकीय सम्मान करना चाहते हैं तो ऐसी परिस्थिति में मातुल जो कालिदास के मामा हैं, वह यह भी सोचते हैं कि कालिदास के राजकीय सम्मान के अस्वीकार करने पर कहीं अहित न हो जाये। उसके सन्दर्भ में उनके विचार पूर्ण रूप से उनकी दूरदर्शिता को प्रकट करते हैं।

''मातुल–. . . . . तुम सोचो कि सम्राट रुष्ट भी तो हो सकते हैं कि एक साधारण कवि ने उनका सममान नहीं किया।''

चाटुकार—मातुल बड़ा ही चाटुकार है, वह अनावश्यक ही लोगों की खुशामद करता है। नाटक के दूसरे अंक में जब प्रियंगुमंजरी मल्लिका के घर पर आती है तो मातुल द्वारा प्रियंगुमंजरी की की गई खुशामद की एक बानगी इस प्रकार है—

''मातुल—मुझे थकाया है ? आपने ? आपके कारण मैं थकूँगा ? मुझे आप दिन-भर पर्वत-शिखर से खाई में और खाई से पर्वत-शिखर पर जाने को कहती रहें, तो भी मैं नहीं थकूँगा। मातुल का शरीर लोहे का बना है, लोहे का।''

'**ईर्ष्यालु**—मातुल जब निक्षेप द्वारा यह सुनता है कि आचार्य कालिदास के जन्म प्रवेश का अवलोकन करना चाहते तब मातुल जो कथन कहता है, यह कथन उसके मन के ईर्ष्या के भाव को प्रकट करता है—

''मातुल—कलिदास की कविता ! न जाने इतने बड़े आचार्य को इसकी कविता में क्या विशेषता दिखाई देती है।''

भ्रमित—नाटक के तीसरे अंक में मातुल जब आषाढ़ की वर्षा में भीगकर मल्लिका के घर में प्रवेश करता है, तब वहाँ आकर कश्मीर के सन्दर्भ में जब अपने विचार व्यक्त करता है। उस दौरान उसके द्वारा कहा गया कथन उसके भ्रम को प्रकट करता है।

''मातुल—. . . . मैं समझता हूँ कि जो कुछ मैं समझ पाता हूँ, सत्य सदा उसके विपरीत होता है। और मैं जब उस विपरीत तक पहुँचने लगता हूँ तो सत्य उस विपरीत से विपरीत हो जाता है।''

आत्म-प्रवंचक—मातुल जब मल्लिका से तीसरे अंक में मिलता है तो वह राज-प्रासाद की तमाम बातें करता है। उसी दौरान यह भी कहता है कि राज-प्रासाद में रहने से अधिक कष्टकर स्थिति संसार में हो ही नहीं सकती। कथन तो यह है लेकिन उसकी आड़ में मातुल अपने वैभव का बखान भी करता है जो उसकी आत्मप्रवंचना का द्योतक है।

''मातुल—. . . . . बताओ मातुल में ऐसा क्या है जिसके आगे कोई सिर झुकाएगा ? मातुल न देवी है न देवता, न पण्डित है न राजा है। तो बताओ फिर क्यों कोई सिर झुकाकर मातुल की वंदना करे परन्तु नहीं। लोग मातुल तो क्या मातुल के शरीर से उतरे वस्त्रों तक की वंदना करने को प्रस्तुत थे।''

इस प्रकार मातुल की भूमिका नाटक में छोटी भले हो लेकिन वह बड़ा सशक्त चरित्र है, जिसके बिना नाटक की सफलता की कल्पना की ही नहीं जा सकती।

प्रश्न 12. 'माँ का जीवन भावना नहीं कर्म है।' कथन के आलोक में अम्बिका की चारित्रिक विशेषताएँ लिखिए।

अथवा

नाटक के आधार पर अम्बिका का चरित्र-चित्रण कीजिए ?

उत्तर—'आषाढ़ का एक दिन' नाटक में कालिदास की प्रेयसी मल्लिका की माँ की भूमिका अम्बिका ने निभाई है। अम्बिका के चरित्र में एक माँ के सभी गुण विद्यमान हैं। अम्बिका एक माँ की तरह हमेशा मल्लिका के भविष्य को लेकर चिन्तित रहती है। एक कुशल माँ की तरह बार-बार अपनी पुत्री से बात कर उसे समझाने का प्रयास करती रहती है। इस प्रकार उसके चरित्र की विशेषताओं का अध्ययन इस प्रकार से किया जा सकता है।

कुशल माँ—नाटक के प्रारम्भ में जब मल्लिका भीगकर आती है तब वह अपनी माँ से कहती है कि वह उसे डाँटे कि वह भीगकर क्यों आई है ? तो इस कथन के प्रत्युत्तर में अम्बिका द्वारा यह कथन कहा गया है—''अम्बिका—मुझे सब अच्छा लगता है। तुम्हारे यहाँ रहते मैं अकेली नहीं होती।''

पुत्री के भविष्य को लेकर सशंकित—अम्बिका हमेशा मल्लिका के भविष्य को लेकर चिन्तित रहती है। उसे यह चिन्ता सताती रहती है कि कालिदास को लेकर तरह-तरह का अपवाद है जो मल्लिका के भविष्य को लेकर बाधक है। अम्बिका, मल्लिका का विवाह करना चाहती है, उसकी दृष्टि में कालिदास एक आत्मसीमित व्यक्ति है। वह मल्लिका से कहती है—

"अम्बिका—मैं जानती हूँ कि तुम पर आज अपना अधिकार भी नहीं है। किन्तु. . . . इतना बड़ा अपवाद मुझसे सहा नहीं जाता है।"

समझाने वाली—अम्बिका बार-बार अपनी पुत्री को समझाने का प्रयास करती है कि भावनाओं और कल्पनाओं से जीवन के यथार्थ का सामना नहीं किया जा सकता। वह यह समझाने का प्रयास करती है कि भावना और कल्पना से जीवनयापन नहीं किया जा सकता है।

"अम्बिका—तुम जिसे भावना कहती हो वह केवल छलना है और आत्म-प्रवंचना है।. . . . . भावना ने भावना का वरण किया है।. . . . मैं पूछती हूँ कि भावना का वरण क्या होता है ? उससे जीवन की आवश्यकताएँ किस प्रकार पूरी होती हैं ?

कर्म में विश्वास रखने वाली—अम्बिका नाटक के प्रथम अंक के प्रारम्भ से ही हमेशा अपने कर्म में प्रवृत्त रहती है। बीच-बीच में मल्लिका से बात करती रहती है। वह अपने कार्य पर विशेष ध्यान देती है। उसके चरित्र के इस गुण को देखकर यह लगता है कि वह कर्म में विश्वास रखने वाली है—

"अम्बिका—माँ का जीवन भावना नहीं कमई है। उसे घर में बहुत कुछ करना है।"

इस तरह अम्बिका बार-बार मल्लिका को यह समझाना चाहती है कि जीवन में कर्म का स्थान भावना से बढ़कर है।

दूरदर्शी—अम्बिका, मल्लिका और कालिदास के बीच के सम्बन्ध को क्षणिक मानती है। वह कालिदास के व्यक्तित्व को सामान्य नहीं मानती है उसके अनुसार कालिदास के जीवन में मल्लिका का स्थान स्पष्ट नहीं है जिसे लेकर अम्बिका सशंकित रहती है—

"अम्बिका—मैं ऐसे व्यक्ति को अच्छी तरह समझती हूँ, तुम्हारे साथ उसका इतना ही सम्बन्ध है कि तुम एक उपादान हो जिसके आश्रय से वह अपने से प्रेम कर सकता है।"

इस प्रकार अन्त में यह कहा जा सकता है कि अम्बिका का चरित्र पूर्णतया एक ऐसी माँ का चरित्र है जो अपनी पुत्री के भविष्य को लेकर चिन्तित रहती है। अम्बिका को नाटक के विकास में जो भी जिम्मेदारी दी गई है उसने उसे बड़ी सफलता से निभाया है।

प्रश्न 13. "मेरे भीगे होने की चिन्ता मत करो।. . . . . . जानती हो, इस तरह भीगना भी जीवन की एक महत्वाकांक्षा हो सकती है ? वर्षों के बाद भीगा हूँ। अभी सूखना नहीं चाहता।" उक्त वाक्य किसने, किससे और किस सन्दर्भ में कहा है ? क्या इसका कोई अन्तर्निहित अर्थ भी हो सकता है ? यदि है तो स्पष्ट करें।

उत्तर—'आषाढ़ का एक दिन' नाटक तीन अंकों का नाटक है। इस नाटक के तीसरे अंक में मातुल द्वारा मल्लिका जब कालिदास के सन्दर्भ में तरह-तरह की बातें सुनती है कि कालिदास अब सन्यासी हो गया, उनका कुछ भी अता-पता नहीं है तो यह सब जानकार मल्लिका दु:खी हो जाती है।

इस कथन का सन्दर्भ उस समय का है जब आषाढ़ का दिन है और मेघ गरज रहे हैं। आज का वातावरण भी ठीक उसी दिन के वातावरण की तरह है जब कालिदास उज्जयिनी गया था। ऐसे समय में कालिदास क्षत-विक्षत सा मल्लिका के प्रकोष्ठ में प्रवेश करता है। वे एक-दूसरे को देखकर आश्चर्य में पड़

जाते हैं। मल्लिका जब यह कहती है कि तुम बहुत भीग गये हो, सूखे वस्त्र भी मेरे पास नहीं है। तब यह सुनने के बाद कालिदास उक्त कथन कहता है।

इस कथन में अन्तर्निहित अर्थ यह हो सकता है कि कालिदास राजनीतिक जीवन में प्रवेश करने के बाद जब मातृगुप्त का कलेवर धारण करता है तब वह महत्वाकांक्षी हो जाता है। कालिदास के अनुसार उसका वह जीवन अभावपूर्ण जीवन की एक स्वाभाविक प्रतिक्रिया थी। उसके मन में प्रतिशोध लेने की भावना थी। वह स्वयं को उस वातावरण में ढालने का प्रयास करता है और असफल रहता है। कालिदास की सृजनात्मकता अपने जन्म प्रदेश के वातावरण में पल्लवित हुई थी। कालिदास आज इसलिए सूखना नहीं चाहता क्योंकि वह इनसे वर्षों तक दूर रहा। आज इस वातावरण में भीगे वस्त्रों ने उसके कविरूप को पुनर्जीवित कर दिया है। मातृगुप्त के कलेवर में उसमें प्रतिशोध लेने की महत्वाकांक्षा थी, आज वर्षा में भीगना भी एक महत्वाकांक्षा हो सकती है।

इस प्रकार 'आषाढ़ का एक दिन' इस प्रकार का नाटक है जिसमें कालिदास के बाह्य एवं आन्तरिक अन्तर्द्वन्द्व को प्रकट करने का प्रयास किया गया है। कालिदास इस प्रकार महत्वाकांक्षा के प्रवाह में बह जाता है कि अपने वास्तविक यथार्थ से दूर होता जाता है। आज जब वह वापस उस वातावरण में आता है तो उसे ऐसा लगता है जैसे चलते-चलते बहुत थक गया है। आज इस वर्षा से उसकी सारी थकान मिट गई है।

कालिदास के अनुसार यहाँ की एक-एक वस्तु में जो आत्मीयता थी, वह यहाँ से जाकर उसे कहीं नहीं मिली। उसे यहाँ की एक-एक वस्तु के रूप और आकार का स्मरण है। आज भी कालिदास को जाने का दिन जैसे का तैसा अंकित है। आज उसका भीगा शरीर उसके उस अतीत से जुड़ा है। उसे अतीत से प्रेम है अत: वह भीगा रहकर अपने अतीत से जुड़ा रहना चाहता है। उक्त कथन में यही अर्थ अन्तर्निहित है।

प्रश्न 14. ''आश्चर्य ? मुझे विश्वास ही नहीं हो रहा कि तुम, तुम हो और मैं जो तुम्हें देख रही हूँ, वास्तव में मैं, मैं ही हूँ।'' यह किस पात्र का कथन है और किस सन्दर्भ में कहा गया है ? इस तरह की बात व्यक्ति कब करता है और उसका अर्थ क्या होता है ?

उत्तर—'आषाढ़ का एक दिन' नाटक के तीसरे अंक में यह कथन कहा गया है। इस कथन का सन्दर्भ उस समय का है जब आषाढ़ का दिन है और मेघ गरज रहे हैं। आज का वातावरण भी ठीक उसी दिन के वातावरण की तरह है जब कालिदास उज्जयिनी गया था। ऐसे समय में कालिदास क्षत-विक्षत सा मल्लिका के प्रकोष्ठ में प्रवेश करता है। वे एक-दूसरे को देखकर आश्चर्य में पड़ जाते हैं। उसी दौरान मल्लिका कालिदास से यह कथन कहती है।

जब कालिदास प्रकोष्ठ में प्रवेश करने के बाद यह कहता है कि सम्भवत: तुमने मुझे पहचाना नहीं। मैं तो ऐसा व्यक्ति हूँ जो स्वयं को नहीं पहचानता। कालिदास के इस कथन के जवाब में मल्लिका यह कथन कहती है। मैं इस समय तुम्हें देखकर आश्चर्यचकित हो गई हूँ। समझ नहीं पा रही हूँ कि यह सत्य है अथवा असत्य। यह मैं ही हूँ जो तुम्हें अपने सामने खड़ा देख पा रही हूँ।

इस तरह की बात व्यक्ति तब करता है जब उसके साथ कुछ अप्रत्याशित होता है। कुछ इस प्रकार की घटना होती है जिसकी उसे आशा तक नहीं होती है। ऐसे समय जब वह उस अप्रत्याशित घटना को देखता है तो यह तय नहीं कर पाता कि यह यथार्थ है अथवा स्वप्न। यह विचार सोचकर व्यक्ति इस प्रकार की बातें करता है। उसके आन्तरिक यथार्थ और बाह्य यथार्थ के बीच में द्वन्द्व की स्थिति है। व्यक्ति का अन्तर्मन उसके बाह्य यथार्थ को स्वीकार करने में असमर्थ है।

इस प्रसंग में मल्लिका कालिदास को अचानक अपने समक्ष पाकर हतप्रभ हो जाती है। उसे स्वयं पर विश्वास ही नहीं हो रहा है कि वह सच में खुद ही है, जो कुछ देख रही है देखने वाली स्वयं ही है अथवा यह

कोई भ्रम है। मल्लिका का यह कथन कि "आश्चर्य ? मुझे विश्वास ही नहीं हो रहा कि तुम, तुम हो और मैं जो तुम्हें देख रही हूँ, वास्तव में मैं, मैं ही हूँ ?" मल्लिका की मन:स्थिति को व्यक्त करता है। यह कथन यह व्यक्त करता है कि कालिदास का आगमन उसके लिए किसी स्वप्न से कम नहीं है। कालिदास के इस समय यहाँ उपस्थित होने की कल्पना भी नहीं की जा सकती थी। इस प्रकार जब कुछ ऐसा होता है जो कल्पना के भी परे हो तब व्यक्ति इस तरह की बातें करता है। इससे यह स्पष्ट हो जाता कि मल्लिका की मन:स्थिति अस्थिर है।

जब व्यक्ति इस तरह की बातें करता है तब उसका यह अर्थ होता है कि घटना का असर इतना प्रभावी है जिसने व्यक्ति की मन:स्थिति को पूरी तरह से झकझोर कर रख दिया है।

प्रश्न 15. "वर्षों का व्यवधान भी विपरीत को विपरीत से दूर नहीं कर सकता।" यह बात किसने, किससे और किस सन्दर्भ में कही है ? इस कथन की प्रासांगिकता के सन्दर्भ में अपने विचार व्यक्त कीजिए।

उत्तर— उक्त कथन कालिदास ने विलोम से नाटक के प्रथम अंक में कही है। यह कथन उस समय का है जब कालिदास के उज्जयिनी जाने के सन्दर्भ में वार्तालाप होता रहता है। इस वार्तालाप में विलोम यह स्पष्ट करना चाहता है कि क्या कालिदास मल्लिका को अपने साथ उज्जयिनी लेकर जायेगा ? तब मल्लिका और कालिदास, विलोम के इस हस्तक्षेप का विरोध करते हैं।

इस विवाद के दौरान इस कथन का सन्दर्भ आता है जब विलोम कहता है कि हम एक-दूसरे के विपरीत हैं। विलोम एक असफल कालिदास है और कालिदास एक सफल विलोम है। तब विलोम के इस कथन को सुनकर उसका प्रत्युत्तर देते हुए कालिदास यह कथन कहता है।

कालिदास यह कहता है कि वर्षों का व्यवधान आये तब भी विपरीत को विपरीत से दूर नहीं किया जा सकता। मैं तुम्हारे निकट हूँ जो भी प्रश्न पूछना चाहो पूछ सकते हो। ये बातें सुनकर विलोम यह प्रश्न पूछता है कि क्या आज भी तुम वही कालिदास हो अथवा राजकीय सम्मान की घोषणा होने के बाद तुम्हारे अन्दर कुछ परिवर्तन भी आया है ? जब कालिदास और विलोम की बातचीत होती रहती है। उस दौरान बीच-बीच में मल्लिका विलोम को मना करती रहती है। विलोम के चरित्र की यह महत्वपूर्ण विशेषता है कि उसे प्रमुख पात्रों की भाँति गौरव प्राप्त नहीं है फिर भी वह गौण पात्र होते हुए स्पष्टता से बातों को कहता है, जो किसी भी दृष्टिकोण से अप्रासांगिक प्रतीत नहीं होती हैं।

'आषाढ़ का एक दिन' नाटक में कालिदास और मल्लिका के अतिरिक्त विलोम एक ऐसा पात्र है कि उसे खलनायक कहकर टाला नहीं जा सकता है। वह कालिदास से भी अधिक विकसित पात्र है। उसके बिना यह नाटक भावुकतापूर्ण और शिथिल रह जाता। उसके तर्कों में ही नहीं, उसकी पूरी जीवन दृष्टि में एक ऐसी आवश्यकता और अनिवार्यता है कि उसकी गिनती हिन्दी नाटक के कुछ अविस्मरणीय पात्रों में होगी।

यहाँ विपरीत स्वभावों के व्यक्ति एक दूसरे की आलोचना करने के कारण एक-दूसरे के निकट हो जाते हैं। यह निकटता हर परिस्थिति में विद्यमान रहती है। उसी प्रकार कालिदास और विलोम विपरीत स्वभाव के होने के कारण भी एक-दूसरे के स्वभाव से भली-भाँति परिचित हैं। कालिदास के सन्दर्भ में विलोम जो बातें अंक एक में करता है वही बातें जाकर दूसरे अंक में अक्षरश: सत्य हो जाती हैं। कालिदास में परिवर्तन अवश्य आ जाता है। इसी परिवर्तन का अनुमान विलोम ने पहले से लगा रखा था।

प्रश्न 16. "यह लोकनीति है मैं तो कहूँगा कि लोकनीति और मूर्ख नीति दोनों का एक ही अर्थ है।" उक्त वाक्य किसने किस सन्दर्भ में किससे और क्यों कहा ?

उत्तर— यह कथन मातुल ने अम्बिका से कहा है। इस कथन का सन्दर्भ उस समय का है जब मातुल कालिदास को खोजते हुए मल्लिका के घर आता है। वह वहाँ आकर यह कहता है कि कालिदास मेरा भागिनेय होकर भी वंशद्रोही हो गया है। आचार्य वररुचि उसे उज्जयिनी ले जाने के लिए आये हैं। लेकिन कालिदास यह

कहकर अस्वीकार कर देता है कि वह क्रीत दास नहीं है। कालिदास ही नाटककार का वह पात्र है जिसे नाटककार ने बाह्य और आन्तरिक द्वन्द्व को प्रदर्शित करने के लिए चुना है। कालिदास के माध्यम से राकेश जी ने एक ऐसे पात्र की सृष्टि की है जिसका जीवन यथार्थ और आदर्शवाद के बीच झूलता रहता है।

यह सब सुनने के बाद अम्बिका यह कहती है कि वह उज्जयिनी अवश्य जायेगा क्योंकि सम्मान प्राप्त होने पर सम्मान के प्रति प्रकट की गई उदासीनता व्यक्ति के महत्व को बढ़ा देती है। अम्बिका मातुल से यह कहती है कि तुम्हें प्रसन्न होना चाहिए कि तुम्हारा भाँजा लोकनीति में निपुण है।

मातुल अम्बिका का यह कथन सुनने के पश्चात् यह कहता है कि सम्मान के प्रति कालिदास द्वारा व्यक्त की जाने वाली उदासीनता मूर्ख नीति कहलायेगी। क्योंकि जो व्यक्ति सम्मान दे रहा है, वह भी रुष्ट हो सकता है। सम्मान करने का निर्णय बदल सकता है। यदि ऐसा हुआ तो भाँजे की यह नीति मूर्ख नीति कही जायेगी। अनजान मातुल बाह्य सामाजिक संक्रान्ति के मूल्यों की पंगुता का प्रतीक बने ऐसी कोशिश है। इसलिए कहानी के अन्त में उसे बैसाखी के साथ दिखाया गया है। यह दिखाने का प्रयास किया गया है कि किस प्रकार सामाजिक संक्रान्ति के मूल्यों के कारण से उसे अन्ततः पंगु बनना पड़ता है। मातुल का चरित्र एक प्रतीक भले हो लेकिन उसका चरित्र प्रमुख पात्रों के चरित्र निर्माण में सहायक है।

इस प्रकार यह वाक्य यह प्रदर्शित करता है कि मातुल अवसर का लाभ उठाना चाहता है, वह यह नहीं चाहता है कि कालिदास उस सम्मान के निमन्त्रण को अस्वीकार करे।

प्रश्न 17. 'अथ से प्रारम्भ' करने का क्या अभिप्राय है ? यहाँ अथ से आरम्भ करने की बात क्यों की जा रही है ?

उत्तर—'अथ से प्रारम्भ करने का अभिप्राय है एक नई शुरुआत करना। यह कथन नाटक के तीसरे अंक में कालिदास द्वारा कहा गया है। जब कालिदास कश्मीर छोड़कर चला जाता है तथा गायब हो जाता है। कोई यह नहीं जानता कि वह कहाँ है ? ऐसे समय में कालिदास क्षत-विक्षत स्थिति में मल्लिका के घर में प्रवेश करता है।

कालिदास जबसे मल्लिका को छोड़कर गया है उसे कहीं भी स्थिरता नहीं मिली। उसकी सृजनात्मकता राजनीतिक वातावरण में नष्ट हो गई। प्रियंगुमंजरी कालिदास के लिए अनेक उपादानों द्वारा अनुकूल वातावरण की सृष्टि करने का प्रयास करती है, परन्तु कालिदास के लिए मल्लिका नहीं बन पाती है।

कालिदास का मन अस्थिर हो जाता है और वह शान्ति के प्रयास में बिना कुछ कहे चल देता है। कालिदास का जीवन पूर्णतया बिखर जाता है। वह न तो योग्य राजनीतिज्ञ बन पाता है और न ही नवीन सर्जना कर पाता है। जब वह मल्लिका से मिलता है, तो उसे समझ में नहीं आता कि वास्तव में क्या बदल गया है ?

मल्लिका के प्रेम को देखकर कालिदास अतीत की स्मृतियों के सागर में डूबकर बीते कल के स्थान पर नवीन दृष्टि करना चाहता है। उसके नैराश्यपूर्ण जीवन में मल्लिका के रूप में आशा की एक धुँधली आकृति दिखाई दे जाती है। उसी आशा के आलोक में कालिदास के मुख से यह शब्द निकल जाते हैं।

कालिदास का एक जीवन जिसमें वह मातृगुप्त के कलेवर में रहता है। वह उसका अन्त कर चुका है। वह मल्लिका के द्वारा बनाये गये कोरे पृष्ठों के अनन्त सर्गों वाले महाकाव्य को देखकर भाव-विभोर हो जाता है और यह विचार करता है कि जीवन अभी समाप्त नहीं हुआ है, अब भी अथ से प्रारम्भ किया जा सकता है।

इस प्रकार अथ से प्रारम्भ करने की यह बात कहने वाला कालिदास जब मल्लिका की पुत्री के रोने की आवाज सुनता है तो फिर अपना निर्णय बदलकर मल्लिका को बिना कुछ बताये चला जाता है। यहीं कालिदास के चरित्र की दुर्बलता दिखाई दे जाती है। जहाँ कालिदास अप्रतिम प्रतिभा का स्वामी है वहीं दूसरी ओर उसके चरित्र में अनेक ऐसे गुण भी हैं जो उसके चरित्र की दुर्बलता को भी उद्घाटित करते हैं। कहीं-कहीं तो ऐसा प्रतीत होता है कि मल्लिका के इस कष्टपूर्ण जीवन का एकमेव उत्तरदायी कालिदास ही है। कालिदास के चाहे बिना मल्लिका का औदात्य आत्मदान अकेला छूट जाता है और कालिदास अथ से प्रारम्भ नहीं कर पाता है।

प्रश्न 18. 'आषाढ़ का एक दिन' नाटक की उद्देश्य की दृष्टि से समीक्षा कीजिए।

अथवा

'आषाढ़ का एक दिन' नाटक का उद्देश्य स्पष्ट कीजिए।

अथवा

'आषाढ़ का एक दिन' नाटक में नाटककार का कौन-सा उद्देश्य निहित है ? समझाकर लिखें।

उत्तर—आषाढ़ का एक दिन एक सुगठित यथार्थवादी नाटक है। इसमें बाह्य ब्यौरे की अपेक्षा परिस्थिति के काव्य को अभिव्यक्त करने का प्रयास किया है। हिन्दी में यह पहला यथार्थवादी नाटक है जिसमें बाह्य और आन्तरिक यथार्थ के अन्तर्द्वन्द्व को संवेदनशीलता के साथ दर्शाया गया है। इस उपन्यास में अतीत का न तो तथाकथित विवरण है, न पुरुत्थानवादी गौरव गान। इस प्रकार 'आषाढ़ का एक दिन' नाटक सही अर्थ में आधुनिक हिन्दी नाटक की शुरूआत का सूचक है।

आषाढ़ का एक दिन मोहन राकेश की एक ऐसी कृति है जिसमें बाह्य यथार्थ तथा आन्तरिक यथार्थ के अन्द्वन्द्व को दिखाया गया है। यही इस नाटक का उद्देश्य है। अपने इसी उद्देश्य के कारण ही 'आषाढ़ का एक दिन' नाटक नाट्य लेखन के क्षेत्र में एक महत्वपूर्ण उपलब्धि है। वस्तुत: हिन्दी के जिन एक-दो लेखकों ने नाटकों में यथार्थपरकता और काव्यात्मकता का श्रीगणेश किया था 'आषाढ़ का एक दिन' उसकी महत्वपूर्ण परिणिति है। इस नाटक की प्रत्यक्ष विषय-वस्तु कालिदास के जीवन से सम्बन्धित है। सारी घटनाएँ आषाढ़ के एक दिन पर ही घटित होती हैं।

हिन्दी नाटक के परिप्रेक्ष्य में, भाव-वस्तु और रूपबन्ध दोनों के स्तर पर 'आषाढ़ का एक' दिन ऐसा पर्याप्त, सघन, तीव्र और भावोद्दीप्त लेखन प्रस्तुत करता है जैसा हिन्दी नाटकों में कम ही हुआ है। यह सुगठित यथार्थवादी नाटक है। किसी नाटक की सफलता और असफलता उस नाटक निर्माण में प्रयुक्त तत्वों के सफल संयोजन से ही होती है जिसमें उद्देश्य का एक महत्वपूर्ण योगदान होता है।

अन्त में निष्कर्षत: यह कहा जा सकता है कि जीवन के अन्तर्द्वन्द्व को संवेदनशीलता के साथ दिखाकर दर्शकों को उसकी अनुभूति कराना ही इस नाटक के नाटककार का उद्देश्य है। उद्देश्य की सफलता समाज और मानवता के मार्मिक पक्षों का जीवन्त प्रस्तुतीकरण करने में होती है। इस प्रकार इस नाटक की विषय-वस्तु द्वारा मानव जीवन के अन्तर्द्वन्द्वों का सजीव चित्र प्रस्तुत किया है जिसके कारण यह नाटक उद्देश्य की दृष्टि से भी एक सफल नाटक बन जाता है।

प्रश्न 19. ''माँ आज के वे क्षण मैं कभी नहीं भूल सकती। सौन्दर्य का ऐसा साक्षात्कार मैंने कभी नहीं किया। जैसे वह सौन्दर्य अस्पृश्य होते हुए भी मांसल हो। मैं उसे छू सकती थी, देख सकती थी, पी सकती थी। तभी मुझे अनुभव हुआ कि वह क्या है जो भावना को कविता का रूप देता है। मैं जीवन में पहली बार समझ पायी कि क्यों कोई पर्वत-शिखरों को सहलाती मेघ-मालाओं में खो जाता है, क्यों किसी को अपने तन-मन की अपेक्षा आकाश में बनते-मिटते चित्रों का इतना मोह हो रहा है।''

(i) उपरोक्त संवाद में नायिका ने किन क्षणों को कभी न भूल सकने की बात कही है ?

(ii) नायिका ने अपने किस अनुभव का वर्णन उपरोक्त पंक्तियों में किया है ?

(iii) 'जैसे वह सौन्दर्य अस्पृश्य होते हुए भी मांसल हो।' उक्त कथन का आशय अपने शब्दों में स्पष्ट कीजिए।

(iv) प्रस्तुत संवाद में कवियों के जीवन-चरित्र से जुड़ी किन विशेषताओं का उल्लेख किया गया है ?

उत्तर—(i) नायिका आषाढ़ के प्रथम दिवस की वर्षा में भीग कर घर में प्रवेश करती है। उपत्यकाओं पर मूसलाधार गिरते हुए मेघों के चित्रमयी दृश्य ने उसे नैसर्गिक सौन्दर्य के जिस रूप का साक्षात्कार करवाया

है, वह उसके लिए अप्रतिम है। सौन्दर्य के साथ हुए इस अद्‌भुत साक्षात्कार के क्षणों को ही नायिका कभी नहीं भूल सकती।

(ii) आषाढ़ की प्रथम वर्षा से नायिका के समक्ष सौन्दर्य का जो अप्रतिम दृश्य प्रस्तुत हुआ है, वह नायिका के लिए किसी अविस्मरणीय अनुभव के समान है। इस दृश्य ने उसे यह बोध कराया है कि ऐसे सौन्दर्य के उद्‌वेग से मन में जिन कोमल भावों का जन्म होता है, वही भाव शायद काव्य का रूप धारण कर लेते हैं। इसी अनुभव का वर्णन नायिका द्वारा उपरोक्त पंक्तियों में किया गया है।

(iii) उक्त कथन का आशय यह है कि नायिका ने नैसर्गिक सौन्दर्य के जिस स्वरूप को जाना है उसे केवल अनुभूत किया जा सकता है। उसे स्पर्श कर सकने का कोई साधन नायिका के पास नहीं है, किन्तु अस्पृश्य होने के बावजूद भी नायिका को उसकी अनुभूति किसी देह के स्पर्श के समान ही प्रतीत हो रही है। सौन्दर्य की इस दैहिक अनुभूति के कारण ही नायिका ने उसे छू सकने, देख सकने और पी सकने योग्य कहा है।

(iv) कवियों की कल्पनाशीलता एवं संवेदनाएँ सदैव ही उनके व्यक्तित्व का असाधारण गुण मानी जाती रही है। अपनी कल्पनाशीलता के चलते ही एक कवि किसी सामान्य से सामान्य दृश्य अथवा घटना को अत्यन्त असाधारणता के साथ प्रस्तुत कर पाने में पूर्णतया सक्षम होता है। नायिका को जिस नैसर्गिक सौन्दर्य की अनुभूति हुयी है, उससे ही उसे यह एहसास हुआ है कि कोई कवि किस प्रकार पर्वत-शिखरों को सहलाती मेघ-मालाओं में खो जाता है, तथा किस प्रकार वह अपने तन-मन की सुध-बुध खोकर आकाश में बनते-मिटते चित्रों के प्रति इतना मोह व संवेदनशीलता प्रदर्शित कर सकने में सक्षम है। कवियों के जीवन-चरित्र से जुड़ी इसी कल्पनाशीलता व संवेदनशीलता जैसी विशेषताओं का उल्लेख प्रस्तुत संवाद में किया गया है।

प्रश्न 20. ''हम जियेंगे हरिणशावक ! जियेंगे न ? एक बाण से आहत होकर हम प्राण नहीं देंगे। हमारा शरीर कोमल है, तो क्या हुआ ? हम पीड़ा सह सकते हैं। एक बाण प्राण ले सकता है, तो उँगलियों का कोमल स्पर्श प्राण दे भी सकता है। हमें नये प्राण मिल जायेंगे। हम कोमल आस्तरण पर विश्राम करेंगे। हमारे अंगों पर घृत का लेप होगा। कल हम फिर वनस्थली में घूमेंगे। कोमल दूर्वा खायेंगे। खायेंगे न ?''

(i) प्रस्तुत पंक्तियों में नायक किससे संवाद कर रहा है, सन्दर्भ सहित लिखिए।

(ii) 'हमारा शरीर कोमल है, तो क्या हुआ ? हम पीड़ा सह सकते हैं।' नायक ने ऐसा क्यों कहा है ?

(iii) हरिण-शावक को कालिदास क्या सांत्वना दे रहे हैं ?

(iv) 'एक बाण प्राण ले सकता है, तो उँगलियों का कोमल स्पर्श प्राण दे भी सकता है।' पंक्ति का आशय स्पष्ट कीजिए।

उत्तर—(i) प्रस्तुत पंक्तियों में नायक ने लहूलुहान हरिणशावक को, जो किसी आखेटक के बाण से आहत है, अपनी गोद में उठा रखा है। इसी हिरण के शावक से नायक संवाद कर रहा है।

(ii) नायक सुकोमल एवं भावुक कवि-हृदयीं व्यक्तित्व का धनी है। अपनी इसी भावुकता के कारण उसे आखेटक के बाण से आहत हरिणशावक के प्रति विशिष्ट अनुराग है। वह उसकी पीड़ा के प्रति न केवल सहानुभूति प्रदर्शित करता है अपितु तन के साथ-साथ उसके मन की सुकोमलता हरिणशावक के प्रति उसे समानुभूति के भाव से भर देती है। हरिणशावक जिस पीड़ा का अनुभव कर रहा है स्वयं नायक भी उसी पीड़ा का अनुभव कर रहा है। उसकी पीड़ा की अनुभूति के चलते ही वह हरिणशावक को पीड़ा सह सकने का ढाढस बँधाने का प्रयत्न कर रहा है। इसीलिए नायक ने उक्त कथन कहा है।

(iii) हरिणशावक से कालिदास कह रहे हैं कि वह अपनी पीड़ा को सहन करे। यदि बाण में प्राण लेने की क्षमता है तो कोमल हाथों का स्पर्श प्राणों को बचा भी सकता है। वह घबराये नहीं, उसे प्रेम के स्पर्श से

नये प्राण मिल जायेंगे। हम कोमल आस्तरण पर विश्राम करेंगे। अंगों पर घृत का लेप लगायेंगे, वनस्थली घूमेंगे, दूर्वा खायेंगे।

(iv) नायक हरिणशावक के बाण लगने से अत्यन्त आहत व द्रवित है। समानुभूति की उत्पत्ति उसे पीड़ा के उसी धरातल पर ला खड़ा करती है जिस पीड़ा को यह शावक अनुभूत कर रहा है। अपने कवि-हृदयी व्यक्तित्व के कारण वह प्रेम को सदैव घृणा और हिंसा से ऊपर पाता है। वह अपनी सुकोमल उँगलियों के स्पर्श से हरिणशावक को पीड़ा से राहत प्रदान करने का प्रयास करता है। उसे पूर्ण विश्वास है कि यदि एक बाण प्राण हर लेने की क्षमता रखता है, तो संवेदनाओं के सम्मिश्रण से ओत-प्रोत प्रेम सहित किया गया उसकी उँगलियों का वह कोमल स्पर्श भी उसके प्राण बचा सकने की क्षमता से परिपूर्ण है।

प्रश्न 21. ''जाने क्या कर रहे हैं !............कभी वर्षों में ये आकृतियाँ यहाँ दिखायी देती हैं। और जब भी दिखायी देती हैं, कोई न कोई अनिष्ट होता है। कभी युद्ध की सूचना आती है, कभी महामारी की। पिछली महामारी में जब तुम्हारे पिता की मृत्यु हुई, तब भी मैंने ये आकृतियाँ यहाँ देखी थीं।''

(i) 'जाने क्या कर रहे हैं !' किसने किससे, किसके बारे में तथा क्यों कहा है ?

(ii) उपरोक्त संवाद में वर्णित आकृतियाँ वास्तव में कौन हैं, और वे कब दिखायी देती हैं ?

(iii) वक्ता ने जब पहले इन आकृतियों को देखा था, तब क्या घटना घटी थी ?

(iv) आकृतियों के दिखने पर वक्ता चिंतित क्यों है ?

उत्तर—(i) प्रस्तुत वाक्य नाटक की प्रमुख नायिका मल्लिका की माता अम्बिका ने, मल्लिका से कहा है। उक्त वाक्य अम्बिका ने नगर में यदा-कदा दिखने वाली संदिग्ध आकृतियों के बारे में कहा है। अम्बिका ने यह वाक्य मल्लिका द्वारा अपनी माँ से इन आकृतियों के बारे में पूछे जाने पर कहा है।

(ii) उपरोक्त संवाद में वर्णित आकृतियाँ वास्तव में राजा के दरबार में कर्मरत् राज्य के कर्मचारी है। वे यहाँ लम्बे अंतराल के पश्चात् कभी वर्षों में यदा-कदा ही दिखायी देते हैं।

(iii) वक्ता ने जब पहले इन आकृतियों को देखा था, तब महामारी फैल गयी थी। इस महामारी की चपेट में वक्ता के पति भी आ गये थे, और इसके चलते ही उनकी मृत्यु हो गयी थी।

(iv) आकृतियों के दिखने पर वक्ता इसलिए चिंतित है, क्योंकि उसे जब-जब यह आकृतियाँ दिखायी देती हैं तब-तब कोई न कोई अप्रिय घटना घट जाती है। उसे किसी न किसी अनिष्ट की चिंता सताने लगती है। उनके दिखने पर कभी युद्ध की सूचना सुनाई पड़ती है, कभी किसी महामारी के फैलने का अशुभ सन्देश सुनने को मिलता है। पहले भी जब यह आकृतियाँ दिखी थीं तब महामारी के चलते उसे अपने पति को खोना पड़ा था।

प्रश्न 22. ''मैं जानती हूँ माँ, अपवाद होता है। तुम्हारे दुःख की बात भी जानती हूँ। फिर भी मुझे अपराध का अनुभव नहीं होता। मैंने भावना में एक भावना का वरण किया है। मेरे लिए वह सम्बन्ध और सब सम्बन्धों से बड़ा है। मैं वास्तव में अपनी भावना से प्रेम करती हूँ जो पवित्र है, कोमल है, अनश्वर है....।''

(i) माँ ने किस अपवाद की ओर संकेत किया है ?

(ii) उपरोक्त संवाद में नायिका को अपनी किस बात पर अपराध का अनुभव नहीं होता ?

(iii) नायिका ने किस सम्बन्ध को सभी सम्बन्धों से बड़ा क्यों बताया है ?

(iv) नायिका ने प्रेम की जिस अनुभूति का वर्णन किया है, उसे अपने शब्दों में लिखिए।

उत्तर—(i) माँ नायिका का विवाह करवाना चाहती है, किन्तु नायिका अपने विवाह के पक्ष में नहीं है। एक माँ होते हुए भी अपनी पुत्री पर सहज प्राप्त होने वाले अधिकार से भी वह वंचित है। यह अपवाद उसके लिए असहनीय है, तथा इसी अपवाद की ओर उसने संकेत किया है।

(ii) नायिका अपने विवाह की बात अस्वीकार कर देती है। पुत्री के विवाह की इच्छापूर्ति न होते देख माँ अवसादग्रस्त हो जाती है। विवाह-योग्य पुत्री का विवाह करना हर माँ का दायित्व भी है और अधिकार भी। किन्तु वह इस अधिकार से वंचित है। यह स्थिति उसे असहनीय अपवाद से भर देती है। नायिका माँ के इस दु:ख को महसूस भी करती है, किन्तु इसे महसूस करने के बावजूद वह इसके लिए स्वयं को अपराधी नहीं मानती।

(iii) नायिका ने अपने मन की भावना में भी एक भावना का वरण कर लिया है। मन की भावना में भी एक भावना के वरण को वह परिणय-सूत्र के वरण से भी ऊपर मानती है। मन का यह वरण स्पष्ट तौर पर उसकी अपनी भावनाओं के साथ एक सम्बन्ध स्थापित कर रहा है। और इस सम्बन्ध को ही नायिका सभी सम्बन्धों से बड़ा बता रही है।

(iv) नायिका भावनावश अपनी भावना का ही वरण कर लेती है। उसे अपनी भावना से प्रेम है। भावनावश अपनी भावना का ही किया गया यह वरण उसके प्रेम को एक विशिष्टता प्रदान कर रहा है। अपने इस प्रेम में उसे पवित्रता की अनुभूति होती है। यह पवित्रता उसके सम्बन्धों की कोमलता का प्रतिबिम्ब भी है। भावना की यह पवित्रता और कोमलता उसके प्रेम को कभी न नष्ट होने वाले अनश्वर, अजर-अमर प्रेम में परिवर्तित कर रही है। प्रेम की इसी अनुभूति को नायिका ने संवाद के माध्यम से प्रस्तुत किया है।

प्रश्न 23. ''तुम जिसे भावना कहती हो वह केवल छलना और आत्म-प्रवंचना है।....भावना में भावना का वरण किया है ! मैं पूछती हूँ भावना में भावना का वरण क्या होता है ? उससे जीवन की आवश्यकताएँ किस तरह पूरी होती हैं ? .... भावना में भावना का वरण ! हाँ !''

(i) उपरोक्त संवाद किसके द्वारा किस सन्दर्भ में कहा गया है ?

(ii) 'मैं पूछती हूँ भावना में भावना का वरण क्या होता है ?' मल्लिका की माँ अम्बिका ने ऐसा क्यों कहा है ?

(iii) 'भावना में भावना का वरण ! हाँ।' वक्ता उक्त वाक्य में अपना आश्चर्य क्यों प्रकट कर रहा है ?

(iv) 'तुम जिसे भावना कहती हो वह केवल छलना और आत्म प्रवंचना है।' आशय स्पष्ट कीजिए।

उत्तर—(i) उपरोक्त संवाद नायिका की माता अम्बिका द्वारा कहा गया है। यह संवाद अम्बिका ने अपनी पुत्री मल्लिका की उस बात पर कहा है जहाँ उसने भावना में भी एक भावना का वरण करने की बात कही है।

(ii) मल्लिका की माँ अम्बिका ने ऐसा इसलिए कहा है क्योंकि वह अपनी पुत्री मल्लिका के उस वक्तव्य से पूर्णत: असहमत है जिसमें उसने भावना में एक भावना का वरण करने की बात कही है। माता अम्बिका को अपनी पुत्री का यह वक्तव्य यथार्थ की अस्वीकृति जैसा प्रतीत हो रहा है।

(iii) वक्ता द्वारा उक्त वाक्य में आश्चर्य इसलिए प्रकट किया गया है क्योंकि वह अपनी पुत्री के इस वक्तव्य से सहमति प्रकट नहीं करती। उसके मुताबिक यह वक्तव्य यथार्थ की परिधि से कोसों दूर है। उसका मानना है कि भावना के वरण से जीवन का यथार्थ नहीं बदल जाता। जीवन जीने की अपनी आवश्यकताएँ होती हैं और भावना का वरण उन आवश्यकताओं की पूर्ति की कसौटी पर खरा नहीं उतरता।

(iv) उक्त पंक्ति का आशय यह है कि केवल भावना के संबल से जीवन नहीं जिया जा सकता। भावना जीवन के कटु सत्य का पर्याय नहीं हो सकती। जीवन की अपनी आवश्यकताएँ हैं। इन आवश्यकताओं की पूर्ति जीवन के यथार्थ की स्वीकारोक्ति के द्वारा ही सम्भव हो सकती है। जब तक हम इस यथार्थ को स्वीकार नहीं करते तब तक केवल भावना के आधार पर जीवन की नैया को पार लगाना मुमकिन नहीं है। यदि हम भावना के प्रवाह में बहकर जीवन के यथार्थ की अनदेखी करते हैं तो यह स्वयं के साथ किये गये छल अथवा आत्म प्रवंचना के अतिरिक्त और कुछ नहीं है।

प्रश्न 24. **''ठहरो, राजपुरुष ! हरिणशावक के लिए हठ मत करो। तुम्हारे लिए प्रश्न अधिकार का है, उनके लिए संवेदना का। कालिदास निःशस्त्र होते हुए भी तुम्हारे शस्त्र की चिन्ता नहीं करेंगे।''**

(i) उपरोक्त संवाद में राजपुरुष हरिणशावक के लिए क्या हठ कर रहा है ?

(ii) 'कालिदास निःशस्त्र होते हुए भी तुम्हारे शस्त्र की चिन्ता नहीं करेंगे।' कथन का आशय स्पष्ट कीजिए।

(iii) 'तुम्हारे लिए प्रश्न अधिकार का है, उनके लिए संवेदना का।' आशय स्पष्ट कीजिए।

(iv) आपके विवेक से हरिणशावक पर किसका अधिकार होना चाहिए, राजपुरुष का अथवा कालिदास का ? संक्षिप्त विवेचना कीजिए।

उत्तर—(i) राजपुरुष ने हरिणशावक का शिकार किया है। शावक घायल है और वह भाग कर कालिदास की गोद में आ गया है। राजपुरुष कालिदास से हरिणशावक को पुनः प्राप्त करने का हठ कर रहा है।

(ii) उक्त कथन का आशय है कि राजपुरुष हरिणशावक पर अपने अधिकार का दावा प्रस्तुत कर रहा है, जबकि कालिदास शावक की घायल स्थिति को देखते हुए उसे राजपुरुष को सौंपने को तैयार नहीं है। राजपुरुष विवाद बढ़ता देख तलवार से उस पर वार करना चाहता है। तब नायिका उसे सचेत करते हुए कहती है कि तुम भले ही शस्त्र से उन पर हमला करो किन्तु हरिणशावक के प्राणों की रक्षा करने के लिए कालिदास निःशस्त्र रह कर भी उसके प्राणों को बचायेंगे। कथन के माध्यम से नायिका ने कालिदास के निर्भीक व्यक्तित्व पर भी प्रकाश डाला है।

(iii) उक्त कथन नाटक की प्रमुख नायिका मल्लिका द्वारा कहा गया है। राजपुरुष और कालिदास दोनों हरिणशावक को अपने साथ ले जाना चाहते हैं। इस कारण दोनों में वाद-विवाद होने लगता है। राजपुरुष शिकारी के अधिकार के तहत शावक को प्राप्त करना चाहता है और कालिदास के लिए शावक के प्राण बचाना प्रीतिकर है। उनके लिए शावक के प्राण बचाना उनकी संवेदनशीलता को प्रदर्शित कर रहा है।

(iv) हरिणशावक पर राजपुरुष शिकारी होने के कारण अपना अधिकार जता रहा है, जबकि कालिदास उसके प्राणों को बचाना चाहते हैं। इस कारण वह भी हरिणशावक को राजपुरुष के हवाले नहीं करना चाहते। ऐसी परिस्थिति में हमारे विवेक से हरिणशावक पर कालिदास का अधिकार सर्वोपरि है, क्योंकि वह प्राणरक्षक हैं। व्यवहृत विश्व में यह सत्य सिद्ध है कि प्राण हरने वाले से बड़ा अधिकार प्राण बचाने वाले का है। अतः कहा जा सकता है कि हरिणशावक पर प्रथम एवं अन्तिम अधिकार कालिदास का होना चाहिए।

प्रश्न 25. **''नहीं उठो नहीं। इसी तरह बैठी रहो ...... राज्य उन्हें सम्मान दे रहा है, माँ ! राजकवि का आसन प्राप्त होगा .... उस व्यक्ति को, जिसे उसके निकट के लोगों ने आज तक समझने का प्रयत्न नहीं किया। जिसे घर में और घर से बाहर केवल लांछना और प्रताड़ना ही मिली है। ..... अब तो तुम विश्वास करती हो माँ, कि मेरी भावना निराधार नहीं है ?''**

(i) राज्य किसे और कौन-सा सम्मान दे रहा है ?

(ii) 'उस व्यक्ति को, जिसे उसके निकट के लोगों ने आज तक समझने का प्रयत्न नहीं किया।' नायिका ने ऐसा क्यों कहा है ?'

(iii) 'जिसे घर में और घर से बाहर केवल लांचना और प्रताड़ना ही मिली है।' आशय स्पष्ट कीजिए।

(iv) नायिका ने क्यों कहा कि उसकी भावना निराधार नहीं है ?

उत्तर—(i) राज्य महाकवि कालिदास को सम्मानित कर रहा है। वह कालिदास को राजकवि के पद पर आसीन करना चाहता है।

(ii) नायिका को कवि कालिदास के राजकवि के पद पर आसीन करने का समाचार जब ज्ञात होता है तब वह गौरवान्वित महसूस करती है। लेकिन उसे यह अवसाद भी होता है कि जिस कवि को आज राज्य इतने

महत्वपूर्ण पद पर सुशोभित करना चाहता है, उसके व्यक्तित्व को उसके अपने नगर, उसके अपने समीपस्थ लोग ही उपेक्षा की दृष्टि से देखते आये हैं। इसीलिए नायिका ने ऐसा कहा है।

(iii) उक्त कथन में नायिका अपनी माँ को यह समझाने का प्रयास कर रही है कि हम जिसे साधारण व्यक्तित्व का व्यक्ति समझते रहे, उसी कालिदास को आज राज्य राजकवि के पद पर आसीन करने का इच्छुक है। वह साधारण व्यक्ति नहीं है, असाधारण है। किन्तु ऐसे असाधारण व्यक्ति को भी अपने ही घर में और अपने ही लोगों से उपेक्षा का शिकार होना पड़ा है। किस प्रकार उसे अपने ही लोग लांछित करते हैं और किस प्रकार वह लोगों की अवांछित प्रताड़ना का शिकार होता रहा है।

(iv) नायिका महाकवि कालिदास से प्रेम करती है। उसका यह प्रेम दैहिक आकर्षण मात्र न होकर उसकी अप्रतिम भावना का द्योतक है। आज जब कालिदास को राज्य गौरवान्वित करना चाहता है, तब नायिका स्वयं भी गौरव का अनुभव करती है। राज्य के इस निर्णय से वह प्रफुल्लित हो उठी है। उसका हृदय कालिदास के महान व्यक्तित्व के प्रति असीम श्रद्धा से भर जाता है, वह भाव-विभोर हो उठती है। मन में उठी तरंगों के वशीभूत वह अपनी माँ से कहती है कि महाकवि के प्रति उसके मन में जो भाव हैं, वह निराधार नहीं है और राज्य द्वारा उन्हें जो सम्मान का अवसर प्राप्त हुआ है उससे इसका आधार और प्रबल हुआ है।

प्रश्न 26. "तुम उनके प्रति सदा अनुदार रही हो, माँ ! तुम जानती हो उनका जीवन परिस्थितियों की कैसी विडम्बना में बीता है। मातुल के घर में उनकी क्या दशा रही है। उस साधन-हीन और अभाव-ग्रस्त जीवन में विवाह की कल्पना ही कैसे की जा सकती थी ?"

(i) नायिका ने कालिदास के जीवन की किस विडम्बना की ओर संकेत किया है ?

(ii) उपरोक्त कथन से कालिदास के जीवन का जो चित्र आप कल्पित कर रहे हैं, उसका संक्षिप्त वर्णन कीजिए।

(iii) नायिका ने अपनी माँ को कालिदास के प्रति अनुदार क्यों कहा है ?

(iv) साधन-हीन और अभाव-ग्रस्त जीवन में विवाह की कल्पना क्यों नहीं की जा सकती ?

उत्तर—(i) नायिका ने कालिदास के जीवन में जो आर्थिक विषमता है तथा इस विषमता के कारण उनके जीवन में जो दरिद्रता का भाव है, उसकी ओर संकेत किया है।

(ii) कथनानुसार कालिदास के जीवन की प्रथमदृष्ट्या जो तस्वीर उभर कर आती है वह उनके जीवन में व्याप्त दरिद्रता को प्रदर्शित करती है। ऐसा प्रतीत होता है कि कालिदास का जीवन अभावों का पिटारा है। उनके माता-पिता की मृत्यु के पश्चात् उनके मामा ने उनका लालन-पालन किया। मामा के घर पर भी अभाव-ग्रस्त परिवेश में ही उनका लालन-पालन हुआ। यहाँ तक कि अपनी युवावस्था में भी दरिद्रता का यह जीवन परछाईं की भाँति उनके साथ-साथ चलता हुआ प्रतीत होता है।

(iii) नायिका की माँ अपनी युवा पुत्री का विवाह करना चाहती है। नायिका और कालिदास एक-दूसरे से प्रेम-बन्धन में बँधे होने के बावजूद वैवाहिक बन्धन से दूर हैं। कालिदास का स्वाभिमानी चरित्र व अभाव-ग्रस्त जीवन इसमें बड़ी बाधा है। नायिका भी अपने इस सम्बन्ध को भावना का सम्बन्ध मानती है। यह सारी बातें नायिका की माँ को कुंठित करती रहती हैं। यही कुंठा उनमें कालिदास के प्रति एक रोष का भाव उत्पन्न कर देती है जिसके प्रभाव से वह उनके प्रति अनुदारता का वरण कर लेती है।

(iv) वैवाहिक जीवन जहाँ एक ओर भावनात्मक अनुभूति एवं दम्पत्ति के परस्पर समर्पण व त्याग का प्रतीक है वहीं व्यवहार व यथार्थ के धरातल पर जा कर सोचें तो दाम्पत्य जीवन में भावनात्मकता के साथ-साथ उचित भौतिक संसाधनों का होना भी नितान्त आवश्यक होता है। इन संसाधनों को जुटाने हेतु आवश्यक साधनों का अभाव किसी के भी सुखद दाम्पत्य पर प्रश्नचिह्न लगा सकता है। केवल भावों के संबल पर वैवाहिक जीवन की कल्पना नहीं की जा सकती। अभाव सदैव कुंठाओं का जन्मदाता रहा है। अतः सुखद

दाम्पत्य के लिए अभावों से मुक्त होना इसकी महत्वपूर्ण कड़ी माना जा सकता है। इसीलिए साधन-हीन व अभाव-ग्रस्त जीवन में विवाह की कल्पना नहीं की जा सकती।

प्रश्न 27. ''मैं ऐसे व्यक्ति को अच्छी तरह समझती हूँ। तुम्हारे साथ उसका इतना ही सम्बन्ध है कि तुम एक उपादान हो, जिसके आश्रय से वह अपने से प्रेम कर सकता है। परन्तु तुम क्या सजीव व्यक्ति नहीं हो ? तुम्हारे प्रति उसका या तुम्हारा कोई कर्तव्य नहीं है ? कल तुम्हारी माँ का शरीर नहीं रहेगा, और घर में एक समय के भोजन की व्यवस्था भी नहीं होगी, तो जो प्रश्न तुम्हारे सामने उपस्थित होगा, उसका तुम क्या उत्तर दोगी ? तुम्हारी भावना उस प्रश्न का समाधान कर देगी ? फिर कह दो कि यह मेरी नहीं, विलोम की भाषा है।''

(i) मैं ऐसे व्यक्ति को अच्छी तरह समझती हूँ।' उक्त वाक्य किसने, किससे तथा किसके लिए कहा है ?

(ii) माँ अम्बिका ने नायिका मल्लिका को उपादान क्यों कहा है ?

(iii) 'परन्तु तुम क्या सजीव व्यक्ति नहीं हो ?' आशय स्पष्ट कीजिए।

(iv) माँ अपना शरीर न रहने पर किस प्रकार की आशंका से ग्रस्त है ?

उत्तर—(i) उपर लिखित वाक्य माता अम्बिका ने अपनी पुत्री मल्लिका से महाकवि कालिदास के विषय में कहा है।

(ii) माँ अम्बिका ने नायिका से ऐसा इसलिए कहा है क्योंकि कालिदास और मल्लिका के मध्य जो प्रेम-प्रसंग स्थापित है उसके विषय में उनकी यही धारणा है कि कालिदास मल्लिका को किसी प्राप्य वस्तु के समान मानता है, जिसके सहारे वह बस खुद से प्रेम कर सके।

(iii) प्रस्तुत वाक्य में नायिका मल्लिका की माता अपनी पुत्री से यह प्रश्न पूछ रही है कि उसका अस्तित्व क्या केवल किसी उपभोक्ता वस्तु के समान है, जिसे मात्र अपनी किसी आवश्यकतापूर्ति के लिए उपयोग में लाया जा सके। क्या उसका व्यक्तित्व किसी अन्य जीते-जागते व्यक्ति जैसा नहीं है, जिसकी अपनी आकांक्षाएँ और कर्तव्य हों।

(iv) माँ अपना शरीर न रहने पर इस आशंका से ग्रस्त है, कि यदि वह नहीं रही तो उसकी अविवाहित पुत्री का क्या होगा। उसे चिन्ता है कि उसके न रहने की स्थिति में उसके भोजन-पानी की व्यवस्था किस प्रकार होगी। जीवन के यथार्थ से जुड़े अनेक प्रश्न जब सम्मुख खड़े होंगे तब वह क्या करेगी। आज वह जिस भावना में बह रही है क्या तब यही भावना उसे जीवन जीने में सहायक सिद्ध हो सकेगी ?

प्रश्न 28. ''माँ आज तक का जीवन किसी तरह बीता ही है। आगे का भी बीत जायेगा। आज जब उनका जीवन नयी दिशा ग्रहण कर रहा है, मैं उनके सामने अपने स्वार्थ की घोषणा नहीं करना चाहती।''

(i) उपरोक्त कथन किसने, किससे कहा है ? सप्रसंग उल्लेख कीजिए।

(ii) किसका जीवन नयी दिशा ग्रहण करने जा रहा है, और कैसे ?

(iii) नायिका अपने किस स्वार्थ की घोषणा नहीं करना चाहती और क्यों?

(iv) 'माँ आज तक का जीवन किसी तरह बीता ही है। आगे का भी बीत जायेगा।' नायिका के इस कथन को आप किस तरह देखते हैं ?

उत्तर—(i) उपरोक्त कथन मल्लिका ने अपनी माता अम्बिका से उस समय कहा जब वह उसके भविष्य के प्रति अपनी आशंका जाहिर करती है।

(ii) महाकवि कालिदास का जीवन नयी दिशा ग्रहण करने जा रहा है। महाकवि को उनका राज्य राजकवि के पद पर आसीन करना चाहता है। इस पद पर आसीन होने पर उनके जीवन की दशा और दिशा

दोनों परिवर्तित हो जायेंगे। कालिदास का अब तक का जीवन संघर्ष और चुनौतियों से भरा रहा है। राजकवि हो जाने पर उनके जीवन का संघर्ष विराम लेगा और वह एक प्रतिष्ठित कवि के रूप में स्वयं को स्थापित कर सकेंगे।

(iii) नायिका कालिदास से अगाध प्रेम करती है। और आज जब यह अवसर आया है कि कालिदास राजकवि के रूप में प्रतिष्ठा पाने जा रहे हों तब ऐसे में वह अपने प्रेम के चलते उनके सम्मुख विवाह का प्रस्ताव रखे, ऐसा वह कदापि नहीं करना चाहती। वह अपने विवाह की घोषणा को अपने स्वार्थ की घोषणा के रूप में देखती है।

(iv) नायिका अपनी माँ की आशंकाओं को लेकर दु:खित भी है किन्तु अपने प्रेमी कालिदास के महिमामंडन से प्रसन्न भी है। ऐसे में जब कालिदास को राजकवि का गौरव प्रदान होने वाला हो, वह किसी भी प्रकार से उनके मार्ग में बाधा उत्पन्न नहीं करना चाहती। वह अपनी माँ की आशंकाओं को यह कह कर दिलासा देने का भरसक प्रयत्न कर रही है कि संघर्षों और कठिनाइयों के साथ जिस प्रकार अब तक का जीवन येन-केन प्रकारेण व्यतीत हो चुका है, उन्हीं चुनौतियों के साथ भविष्य में भी इसी प्रकार बचा-खुचा जीवन भी व्यतीत हो ही जायेगा।

प्रश्न 29. ''मैंने कहा, 'कविवर्य आपको साथ उज्जयिनी ले जाने के लिए आये हैं। राज्य की ओर से आपका सम्मान होगा।' सुनकर रुके। रुककर जलते, अंगारे की सी दृष्टि से मुझे देखा।— 'मैं राजकीय मुद्राओं से क्रीत होने के लिए नहीं हूँ।'—ऐसे कहा जैसे राजकीय मुद्राएँ आपके विरह में घुली जा रही हों, और चल दिये। ...... मेरे लिए धर्मसंकट खड़ा हो गया कि अनुनय करता हुआ आपके पीछे-पीछे जाऊँ, या अभ्यागतों को देखूँ।''

(i) कविवर्य, आचार्य किसको साथ उज्जयिनी ले जाना चाहते हैं और क्यों ?

(ii) कालिदास ने अपने मातुल को जलते अंगारे की दृष्टि से क्यों देखा ?

(iii) 'मैं राजकीय मुद्राओं से क्रीत होने के लिए नहीं हूँ।' आशय स्पष्ट कीजिए।

(iv) 'जैसे राजकीय मुद्राएँ आपके विरह में घुली जा रही हों।' मातुल ने ऐसा क्यों कहा ?

उत्तर—(i) कविवर्य, आचार्य महाकवि कालिदास को उज्जयिनी ले जाना चाहते हैं। वे उन्हें इसलिए साथ ले जाना चाहते हैं क्योंकि राज्य उन्हें राजकवि के पद पर सुशोभित कर सम्मानित करना चाहता है।

(ii) कालिदास स्वाभिमानी प्रकृति के व्यक्ति हैं। वे उज्जयिनी जाकर सम्मानित होने के प्रति अनिच्छुक दिखाई पड़ते हैं। अपनी इसी अनिच्छा के कारण उन्होंने अपने मातुल को जलते अंगारे की दृष्टि से देखा।

(iii) उक्त कथन के माध्यम से कालिदास अपनी स्वाभिमानी प्रकृति का उद्घोष कर रहे हैं। राज्य का उन्हें राजकवि के रूप में सम्मान देने का निर्णय उचित नहीं लग रहा। उन्हें लगता है कि सम्मान के तहत राजकीय मुद्राओं का दिया जाना उनकी कला को खरीदने जैसा है। कला अनमोल होती है, उसका क्रय-विक्रय नहीं किया जा सकता। यही बात उन्हें कचोट रही है और वे इस तरह स्वयं को क्रय किये जाने का विरोध करते प्रतीत होते हैं।

(iv) मातुल कालिदास के उज्जयिनी न जाने का निर्णय सुन हतप्रभ हैं। उन्हें लगता है कि कालिदास अपने अहंकार के कारण हाथ में आये इस अवसर को गँवा रहे हैं। वह कालिदास के इस आचरण से क्रोध में भर उठते हैं। कालिदास पर उन्हें खीझ उत्पन्न होने लगती है। वे कालिदास को यह बताना चाहते हैं कि जिस अवसर को वह मुद्राओं से क्रीत होना कहकर गँवा देना चाहते हैं वह हर किसी को उपलब्ध नहीं होता और जिन राजकीय मुद्राओं का वह अपमान कर रहे हैं उन्हें प्राप्त कर पाना सर्वसाधारण को सरल सुलभ नहीं है।

प्रश्न 30. ''कालिदास अपनी भावुकता में भूल रहे हैं कि इस अवसर का तिरस्कार करके वे बहुत कुछ खो बैठेंगे। योग्यता एक चौथाई व्यक्तित्व का निर्माण करती है। शेष पूर्ति प्रतिष्ठा द्वारा होती है। कालिदास को राजधानी अवश्य जाना चाहिए।''

(i) प्रस्तुत कथन का वक्ता कौन है और वह यह कथन किससे व क्यों कह रहे हैं ?

(ii) कालिदास भावुकता में क्या भूल कर रहे हैं ? इससे उन्हें क्या नुकसान उठाना पड़ सकता है ?

(iii) 'कालिदास को राजधानी अवश्य जाना चाहिए।' क्या आप निक्षेप के इस कथन से सहमत हैं ?

(iv) 'योग्यता एक चौथाई व्यक्तित्व का निर्माण करती है। शेष पूर्ति प्रतिष्ठा द्वारा होती है।' सूक्ति की व्याख्या कीजिए।

उत्तर—(i) प्रस्तुत कथन का वक्ता निक्षेप है। वह नाटक की प्रमुख नायिका मल्लिका की माता अम्बिका से यह बात इसलिए कह रहे हैं क्योंकि वे चाहते हैं कि कालिदास उज्जयिनी जा कर सम्मान ग्रहण करें।

(ii) कालिदास भावुकतावश उज्जयिनी न जाकर सम्मान न ग्रहण करने की भूल कर रहे हैं। यह उनके जीवन में आया एक बड़ा अवसर है। यदि वे इस अवसर को हाथ से निकल जाने देते हैं तो उन्हें आजीवन आर्थिक कठिनाइयों से जूझना पड़ेगा जो उनके लिए कतई हितकर सिद्ध नहीं रहेगा।

(iii) हाँ, हम निक्षेप के इस कथन से सहमत हैं। कालिदास के जीवन में यह अवसर एक नया मोड़ लेकर उपस्थित हुआ है। इस अवसर का उचित लाभ उठाकर वे अपने जीवन की चुनौतियों एवं कठिनाइयों से उबर सकते हैं। यह अवसर उनके जीवन में केवल सम्मान के रूप में नहीं आया है, बल्कि उन्होंने अब तक जो कुछ अर्जित किया है उसके सापेक्ष प्रस्तुत हुआ है। अतः अब तक अर्जित पूँजी के उपलक्ष्य में वे इस सम्मान को पाने के पूर्ण हकदार हैं।

(iv) प्रस्तुत सूक्ति के माध्यम से यह बताने का प्रयास किया गया है कि किसी भी व्यक्ति के जीवन में योग्यता और प्रतिष्ठा दोनों का महत्वपूर्ण स्थान है। जहाँ एक ओर योग्यता को अर्जित कर कोई व्यक्ति अपने एक चौथाई व्यक्तित्व का ही निर्माण कर पाता है। किन्तु जीवन का शेष तीन चौथाई व्यक्तित्व तभी निर्मित हो सकता है जब व्यक्ति की योग्यता प्रतिष्ठित हो जाती है। बिना प्रतिष्ठा प्राप्त किये योग्यता आधी-अधूरी है। योग्यता अर्जन का सुखद परिणाम तभी फलीभूत होता है जब आप अपनी योग्यता के बलबूते समाज में स्वयं को प्रतिष्ठित कर पाने में भी सफलता प्राप्त कर लेते हैं।

प्रश्न 31. "उस कटुता को केवल तुम्हीं दूर कर सकती हो, मल्लिका ! अवसर किसी की प्रतीक्षा नहीं करता। कालिदास यहाँ से नहीं जाते है, तो राज्य की कोई हानि नहीं होगी। राजकवि का आसन रिक्त नहीं रहेगा। परन्तु कालिदास जो आज हैं, जीवन भर वही रहेंगे—एक स्थानीय कवि। जो लोग आज 'ऋतु-संहार' की प्रशंसा कर रहे हैं, वे भी कुछ दिनों में उन्हें भूल जायेंगे।"

(i) किस कटुता का वर्णन उपरोक्त पंक्तियों में किया गया है ?

(ii) राजकवि का आसन रिक्त क्यों नहीं रहेगा ?

(iii) कालिदास के राजधानी न जाने की स्थिति में वक्ता ने क्या सन्देह व्यक्त किया है ?

(iv) 'अवसर किसी की प्रतीक्षा नहीं करता।' सूक्ति की व्याख्या कीजिए।

उत्तर—(i) राजपुरुष द्वारा कालिदास से हरिणशावक को हठपूर्वक प्राप्त करने का दुराग्रह कालिदास के मन में गहरी टीस पैदा कर देता है। यह टीस ही राजपुरुष व राज्य की व्यवस्थाओं के प्रति कालिदास के मन में कटुता का स्थान ले लेती है।

(ii) कालिदास राजधानी जा कर राजकवि के पद पर आसीन होने के प्रति अपनी उदासीनता प्रदर्शित कर रहे हैं। निश्चय ही यह एक बड़ा अवसर है, किन्तु यदि कालिदास इस पद को ग्रहण नहीं करते तब भी राज्य की व्यवस्था को सुचारु रूप से चलाने हेतु यह पद किसी अन्य को प्रदान कर दिया जायेगा। यही कारण है कि राजकवि का आसन रिक्त न रहने की बात कही गयी है।

(iii) कालिदास के राजधानी न जाने की स्थिति में राज्य को कोई हानि नहीं होगी। देर-सवेर राजकवि के पद पर किसी और को सुशोभित कर दिया जायेगा। किन्तु ऐसा होने पर कालिदास मात्र एक स्थानीय कवि हो कर रह जायेंगे और उनका काव्य 'ऋतु-संहार' जो आज चहुँओर प्रशंसा प्राप्त कर रहा है, कुछ दिनों बाद लोग उसे भूल जायेंगे।

(iv) प्रस्तुत सूक्ति में स्पष्ट किया गया है कि प्रत्येक व्यक्ति को जीवन में कभी न कभी एक बार किसी सुअवसर की प्राप्ति अवश्य होती है, किन्तु यदि व्यक्ति उस समय उस अवसर का लाभ प्राप्त करने से चूक जाता है तो वह अवसर उसे पुनः प्राप्त नहीं होता। इस प्रकार अवसर से चूक जाने पर व्यक्ति अपनी हानि स्वयं कर लेता है। महाकवि तुलसीदास ने रामचरित् मानस में भी अपनी चौपाई से इस तथ्य की पुष्टि की है—'का बरखा जब कृषि सुखाने, समय चूकि पुनि का पछताने।'

प्रश्न 32. ''तुम समझते हो कि तुम इस अवसर को ठुकराकर यहाँ रह जाओगे, तो मुझे सुख होगा ? मैं जानती हूँ कि तुम्हारे चले जाने से मेरे अन्तर को एक रिक्तता छा लेगी। बाहर भी सम्भवतः बहुत सूना प्रतीत होगा। फिर भी मैं अपने साथ छल नहीं कर रही। मैं हृदय से कहती हूँ तुम्हें जाना चाहिए।''

(i) नायिका कालिदास के अवसर को ठुकराने पर सुखी क्यों नहीं होगी ?

(ii) 'फिर भी मैं अपने साथ छल नहीं कर रही।' नायिका ने ऐसा क्यों कहा ?

(iii) 'मैं जानती हूँ कि तुम्हारे चले जाने से मेरे अन्तर को एक रिक्तता छा लेगी।' आशय स्पष्ट कीजिए।

(iv) उपरोक्त कथन के आलोक में नायिका के चरित्र का विश्लेषण कीजिए।

उत्तर—(i) नायिका कालिदास से अगाध प्रेम करती है। वह उनके संघर्षपूर्ण जीवन को भी भली-भाँति जानती है। उसे ज्ञात है कि आज जो अवसर कालिदास को प्राप्त हुआ है वह उनके जीवन को एक नई दिशा प्रदान कर सकता है। अतः वह कालिदास के अवसर ठुकराने की स्थिति में स्वयं को सुखी नहीं पाती।

(ii) नायिका कालिदास के साथ अटूट प्रेम के बन्धन में बँधी हुई है। उनके राजधानी चले जाने पर उसे विरह की असहनीय पीड़ा का सामना करना पड़ेगा। किसी भी प्रेयसी के लिए अपने प्रिय का बिछोह अत्यधिक कष्टकारी होता है। वह इसे भली-भाँति समझती है, किन्तु कालिदास के भविष्य की सुखमय कल्पना को अनुभूत कर वह इस विरहाग्नि को सहने को सहर्ष तैयार है। वह कालिदास को इसके प्रति आश्वस्त कर देना चाहती है और इसीलिए उसने ऐसा कहा है कि वह अपने साथ किसी भी प्रकार का छल नहीं कर रही।

(iii) उक्त पंक्ति का आशय यह है कि कालिदास के राजधानी चले जाने पर नायिका को प्रियबिछोह का जो संताप सहना पड़ेगा, वह अत्यधिक कष्टप्रद एवं असहनीय होगा। कालिदास की उपस्थिति उसके जीवन का संबल है। कालिदास के चले जाने पर उसका जीवन शून्य हो कर रह जायेगा ठीक उसी प्रकार जिस प्रकार किसी रंग-बिरंगे चित्र को रंगविहीन कर दिया जाये।

(iv) उपरोक्त कथन नायिका के बलिदानी एवं त्यागी चरित्र की पराकाष्ठा को इंगित कर रहा है। नायिका इससे भली-भाँति परिचित है कि कालिदास के चले जाने से उसका जीवन शून्यता से भर जायेगा। किन्तु कालिदास के सुखद भविष्य की कामना के समक्ष उसे अपने जीवन की शून्यता का कोई मूल्य नहीं लगता। सच्चे प्रेम की सबसे बड़ी कसौटी त्याग ही होती है। नायिका त्याग का ऐसा उदाहरण प्रस्तुत कर अमर प्रेम की नवीन परिभाषा को गढ़ने का दायित्व निर्वाह कर रही है।

प्रश्न 33. ''तुम यहाँ से जाकर भी मुझसे दूर हो सकते हो.... ? यहाँ ग्राम-प्रान्तर में रहकर तुम्हारी प्रतिभा को विकसित होने का अवसर कहाँ मिलेगा ? यहाँ लोग तुम्हें समझ नहीं पाते। वे सामान्य की कसौटी पर तुम्हारी परीक्षा करना चाहते हैं। विश्वास करते हो न कि मैं तुम्हें जानती हूँ ? जानती हूँ कि कोई भी रेखा तुम्हें घेर ले, तो तुम घिर जाओगे। मैं तुम्हें घेरना नहीं चाहती। इसीलिए कहती हूँ जाओ।''

(i) 'तुम यहाँ से जाकर भी मुझसे दूर हो सकते हो.... ?' अपने कथन में नायिका क्या कहना चाहती है ?

(ii) ग्राम-प्रान्तर में रहकर कालिदास की प्रतिभा के विकसित न हो सकने के क्या कारण नायिका ने बताये हैं ?

(iii) 'विश्वास करते हो न कि मैं तुम्हें जानती हूँ ?' नायिका ने ऐसा क्यों कहा ?

(iv) 'जानती हूँ कि कोई भी रेखा तुम्हें घेर ले, तो तुम घिर जाओगे।' नायिका का कथन स्पष्ट कीजिए।

उत्तर—(i) नायिका इस कथन में कालिदास को यह जताना चाहती है कि उनका परस्पर प्रेम इतना अगाध व दृढ़ है कि स्थान की निकटता व दूरी उसे कमजोर नहीं कर सकते।

(ii) नायिका ने ग्राम-प्रान्तर में रहकर कालिदास की प्रतिभा के विकसित न हो सकने के जो कारण बताये हैं, वे निम्नलिखित हैं—

(1) ग्राम-प्रान्तर में लोग कालिदास की काव्य-प्रतिभा को सही से समझ नहीं सकेंगे।

(2) वे कालिदास के कर्म की परीक्षा किसी सामान्य मानव की तरह ही कर सकेंगे।

(iii) नायिका ऐसा इसलिए कह रही है क्योंकि वह कालिदास को यह जताना चाहती है कि वह उसके व्यक्तित्व के सभी पहलुओं से भली-भाँति परिचित है। कालिदास का मन उज्जयिनी जाने के विचार से विचलित हो रहा है। नायिका इस विचलन को भाँप चुकी है। वह कालिदास को यह एहसास कराना चाहती है कि उसके मन में जिस ऊहापोह ने घमासान मचा रखा है वह उसे सीधे-सीधे देख व अनुभूत कर पा रही है।

(iv) इस कथन के जरिये नायिका कालिदास की मनोदशा को चित्रित कर रही है। वह उसे यह ज्ञात करा रही है कि वह जिस असमंजस की स्थिति से गुजर रहा है, ऐसे में यदि कोई विचार उसके सम्मुख विघ्न-रेखा के रूप में उपस्थित हो जायेगा तो वह उस विघ्न-रेखा में स्वयं को घिरा हुआ पायेगा और यह विघ्न-रेखा उसके सुखमयी भविष्य को प्रभावित कर उसे उज्जयिनी जाने से रोक देगी।

प्रश्न 34. ''मैं अनुभव करता हूँ कि यह ग्राम-प्रान्तर मेरी वास्तविक भूमि है। मैं कई सूत्रों से इस भूमि से जुड़ा हूँ। उन सूत्रों में तुम हो, यह आकाश और ये मेघ हैं, यहाँ की हरियाली है, हरिणों के बच्चे हैं, पशुपाल हैं। यहाँ से जाकर मैं अपनी भूमि से उखड़ जाऊँगा।''

(i) प्रस्तुत कथन किसने, किससे कहा है ?

(ii) कालिदास ने भूमि से जुड़े होने के जो तर्क प्रस्तुत किये हैं, उनका उल्लेख अपने शब्दों में कीजिए।

(iii) 'यहाँ से जाकर मैं अपनी भूमि से उखड़ जाऊँगा।' इस वाक्य में कालिदास अपनी किस वेदना का परिचय दे रहे हैं ?

(iv) प्रस्तुत कथन से कालिदास के चरित्र की किन विशेषताओं का पता चलता है ?

उत्तर—(i) प्रस्तुत कथन नाटक के नायक महाकवि कालिदास ने अपनी प्रेयसि व नाटक की नायिका मल्लिका से कहा है।

(ii) कालिदास ने भूमि से जुड़े होने के सम्बन्ध में कहा है कि यह ग्राम-प्रान्तर ही उनकी वास्तविक कर्मभूमि है। इस भूमि में वह स्वयं से जुड़े लोगों व परिवेश को महत्ता प्रदान करते हैं। वह अपनी प्रेयसि मल्लिका से कहते हैं कि यह भूमि उन्हें इसलिए प्रिय है क्योंकि इस भूमि से वह भी जुड़ी हुई है। इस भूमि से जुड़ा आकाश व उस पर छाये हुये मेघ, सुदूर पर्वतों पर फैली हरियाली, यत्र-तत्र विचरण करते हिरन-शावक और गाँव के पशुपालक, ये सभी उन्हें अपनी भूमि से जोड़े रखने के महत्वपूर्ण सूत्र हैं।

(iii) इस वाक्य में कालिदास अपनी मातृभूमि से बिछुड़ जाने के प्रति अपनी वेदना का परिचय दे रहे हैं। उन्हें अपनी मातृभूमि व उसके परिवेश से बेहद लगाव है। इस लगाव के कारण वह यहाँ से अन्यत्र नहीं जाना चाहते। वह अपने परिवेश की प्रत्येक वस्तु से अपना जुड़ाव पाते हैं अतः यहाँ से दूर जाने का विचार भी उन्हें उदास कर देता है।

(iv) प्रस्तुत कथन से कालिदास की स्वयं से जुड़े लोगों व आस-पास की वस्तुओं के प्रति प्रदर्शित भावुकता का पता चलता है। इस कथन में वे अपनी प्रेयसि, आकाश, मेघ, हरियाली, हरिण-शावकों एवं अपने ग्राम के पशुपालकों सभी के साथ अपना जुड़ाव स्थापित करते हैं। वे स्वभाव से कवि हैं तथा कवि का अपने परिवेश से जुड़ाव सर्वविदित है। साथ ही उक्त कथन में कालिदास का अपनी मातृभूमि के प्रति विशिष्ट प्रेम भी देखने को मिल रहा है।

प्रश्न 35. ''यह क्यों नहीं सोचते कि नयी भूमि तुम्हें यहाँ से अधिक सम्पन्न और उर्वरा मिलेगी। इस भूमि से तुम जो कुछ ग्रहण कर सकते थे, कर चुके हो। तुम्हें आज नयी भूमि की आवश्यकता है, जो तुम्हारे व्यक्तित्व को अधिक पूर्ण बना दे।''

(i) नायिका कालिदास से यह कथन क्यों कह रही है ?

(ii) 'यह क्यों नहीं सोचते कि नयी भूमि तुम्हें यहाँ से अधिक सम्पन्न और उर्वरा मिलेगी।' नायिका का आशय स्पष्ट कीजिए।

(iii) 'इस भूमि से तुम जो कुछ ग्रहण कर सकते थे, कर चुके हो।' आशय स्पष्ट कीजिए।

(iv) नायिका कालिदास से यह क्यों कह रही है कि उसे नयी भूमि की आवश्यकता है ?

उत्तर—(i) कालिदास का मन अपनी मातृभूमि को छोड़कर जाने के लिए सहमत नहीं है। वह स्वयं को अपनी धरा के परिवेश से जुड़ा हुआ पाते हैं। किन्तु नायिका उन्हें ऐसा कहकर नयी सम्भावनाओं की ओर उन्मुख करना चाहती है जहाँ उनके काम को और अधिक पहचान मिल सके व उनका व्यक्तित्व पहले की तुलना में और अधिक निखर सके। इसीलिए कालिदास को वह अपने कथन के माध्यम से प्रेरित करना चाहती है।

(ii) उक्त कथन में नायिका कालिदास को यह समझाने का प्रयास कर रही है कि निःसन्देह उनकी मातृभूमि उनके सृजन की पृष्ठभूमि रही है, और उन्हें अपनी मातृभूमि से लगाव भी है, किन्तु उन्हें यहाँ से आगे जाकर अपनी सर्जकता को और अधिक निखारने की आवश्यकता है। इस हेतु यदि वे मातृभूमि को छोड़कर नये स्थान पर जाते हैं तो उनकी कल्पना की उड़ानों को नये पंख मिलेंगे जो काव्य के नूतन प्रतिमानों को प्रतिस्थापित करने में उनके लिए सहायक सिद्ध होंगे।

(iii) नायिका ने अपने इस कथन में कालिदास को यह समझाने का प्रयास किया है कि अपने परिवेश व अपनी भूमि से वह अपनी काव्य-प्रतिभा को जितना निखार सकते थे, निखार चुके। अब इससे अधिक की क्षमता यहाँ सम्भव नहीं है। अपने काव्य को निखारने के लिए जिन बिम्बों, प्रतीकों व प्रतिमानों को यहाँ रहकर वे तलाशते फिरते हैं सब पुराने हो चुके हैं।

(iv) चूँकि कालिदास स्वभावगत कवि हैं, अतः कल्पनाओं के धनी हैं। एक कवि के तौर पर कल्पना की उड़ान को किसी भी परिस्थिति में नये पंख मिल सकते हैं। स्थान-विशेष उसमें कोई बड़ी बाधा नहीं है। किन्तु फिर भी नये स्थानों का अवलोकन कल्पनाओं को नई धार प्रदान कर सकता है व प्रतिभा को नई ऊँचाइयाँ प्रदान करने में सहायक हो सकता है। अतः इसमें कोई सन्देह नहीं कि यदि कालिदास उज्जयिनी जाकर राजकवि के रूप में कर्मरत् हों तो उनकी काव्य-प्रतिभा को नई व विशिष्ट पहचान प्राप्त हो सकती है।

प्रश्न 36. ''अब भी उत्साह का अनुभव नहीं होता..... ? विश्वास करो तुम यहाँ से जाकर भी यहाँ से अलग नहीं होओगे। यहाँ की वायु, यहाँ के मेघ और यहाँ के हरिण, इन सबको तुम साथ ले जाओगे.....। और मैं भी तुमसे दूर नहीं होऊँगी। जब भी तुम्हारे निकट होना चाहूँगी, पर्वत-शिखर पर चली जाऊँगी और उड़कर आते मेघों में घिर जाया करूँगी।''

(i) नायिका कालिदास को उत्साह का अनुभव कैसे कराती है ?

(ii) नायिका कालिदास को यह विश्वास कैसे दिलाती है कि वह यहाँ से जाकर भी यहाँ से अलग नहीं होंगे ?

(iii) नायिका ने कालिदास के अलग होने पर भी अपनी निकटता होने के क्या तर्क प्रस्तुत किये हैं ?

(iv) प्रस्तुत संवाद में नायिका के व्यक्तित्व का कौन-सा पहलू उजागर हो रहा है ?

उत्तर—(i) कालिदास के मन में उज्जयिनी जाने को लेकर अनेक आशंकाएँ हैं जो उन्हें हतोत्साहित कर देती हैं। नायिका कालिदास को अपनी आँखों में देखने को कहती है। इस प्रकार वह उन्हें उत्साह का अनुभव कराती है।

(ii) नायिका कालिदास को यह विश्वास दिलाती है कि यहाँ से दूर चले जाने पर भी वह यहाँ से अलग नहीं होंगे। नायिका कहती है वे जहाँ भी जायेंगे यहाँ की वायु, यहाँ के मेघ तथा यहाँ के हरिण भी उनकी कल्पनाओं व कविताओं के माध्यम से उनके साथ ही जायेंगे। वे हमेशा अपने होने का एहसास दिलाते हैं।

(iii) नायिका कालिदास से कहती है कि वह भी उनसे दूर नहीं है। वह उन्हें विश्वास दिलाती है कि वह जब भी उनके निकट आना चाहेगी तो वह उन पर्वत-शिखरों पर चली जायेगी जो उनके प्रेम के साक्षी रहे हैं। वह यह भी कहती है कि वह स्वयं उड़कर आते हुए मेघों से लिपट जायेगी और उन मेघों के माध्यम से वह अपना सन्देश उन तक पहुँचा देगी।

(iv) प्रस्तुत संवाद में नायिका के प्रेम की उत्कृष्टता का प्रमाण मिल रहा है। यह संवाद नायिका के निश्छल प्रेम की पराकाष्ठा को परिलक्षित करता प्रतीत होता है। नायिका अपने प्रेमी को श्रेष्ठता की मनोरम मीनार पर स्थापित होते हुए देखना चाहती है। इसके लिए वह बड़े से बड़ा त्याग करने से भी पीछे नहीं हटना चाहती। हतोत्साहित हो चुके कालिदास को वह निरन्तर सांत्वना व संबल प्रदान करती है। जिस समय असमंजस व अपने मातृभूमि के प्रति प्रेम के कारण वह राजधानी जाने के विचार से डिगते हुए प्रतीत होते हैं तब नायिका मेरुदंड के समान उन्हें संबल प्रदान कर उनका उत्साहवर्द्धन करती है। वह उन्हें स्पष्ट करती है कि अलग होने की स्थिति में भी प्रेम की एक अटूट डोर है जो उन्हें हमेशा एक-दूसरे से बाँधे रहेगी।

प्रश्न 37. ''यह क्यों नहीं सोचते कि नयी भूमि तुम्हें यहाँ से अधिक सम्पन्न और उर्वरा मिलेगी। इस भूमि से तुम जो कुछ ग्रहण कर सकते थे, कर चुके हो। तुम्हें आज नयी भूमि की आवश्यकता है, जो तुम्हारे व्यक्तित्व को अधिक पूर्ण बना दे।''

(i) नायिका कालिदास से यह कथन क्यों कह रही है ?

(ii) 'यह क्यों नहीं सोचते कि नयी भूमि तुम्हें यहाँ से अधिक सम्पन्न और उर्वरा मिलेगा।' नायिका का आशय स्पष्ट कीजिए।

(iii) 'इस भूमि से तुम जो कुछ ग्रहण कर सकते थे, कर चुके हो।' आशय स्पष्ट कीजिए।

(iv) नायिका कालिदास से यह क्यों कह रही है कि उसे नयी भूमि की आवश्यकता है ?

उत्तर—(i) कालिदास का मन अपनी मातृभूमि को छोड़कर जाने के लिए सहमत नहीं है। वह स्वयं को अपनी धरा के परिवेश से जुड़ा हुआ पाते हैं। किन्तु नायिका उन्हें ऐसा कह कर नयी सम्भावनाओं की ओर उन्मुख करना चाहती है जहाँ उनके काम को और अधिक पहचान मिल सके व उनका व्यक्तित्व पहले की तुलना में और अधिक निखर सके। इसीलिए कालिदास को वह अपने कथन के माध्यम से प्रेरित करना चाहती है।

(ii) उक्त कथन में नायिका कालिदास को यह समझाने का प्रयास कर रही है कि निःसन्देह उनकी मातृभूमि उनके सृजन की पृष्ठभूमि रही है, और उन्हें अपनी मातृभूमि से लगाव भी है, किन्तु उन्हें यहाँ से

आगे जा कर अपनी सर्जकता को और अधिक निखारने की आवश्यकता है। इस हेतु यदि वे मातृभूमि को छोड़कर नये स्थान पर जाते हैं तो उनकी कल्पना की उड़ानों को नये पंख मिलेंगे जो काव्य के नूतन प्रतिमानों को प्रतिस्थापित करने में उनके लिए सहायक सिद्ध होंगे।

(iii) नायिका ने अपने इस कथन में कालिदास को यह समझाने का प्रयास किया है कि अपने परिवेश व अपनी भूमि से वह अपनी काव्य-प्रतिभा को जितना निखार सकते थे, निखार चुके। अब इससे अधिक की क्षमता यहाँ सम्भव नहीं है। अपने काव्य को निखारने के लिए जिन बिम्बों, प्रतीकों व प्रतिमानों को यहाँ रहकर वे तलाशते फिरते हैं वे सब पुराने हो चुके हैं।

(iv) चूँकि कालिदास स्वभावगत कवि हैं, अतः कल्पनाओं के धनी हैं। एक कवि के तौर पर कल्पना की उड़ान को किसी भी परिस्थिति में नये पंख मिल सकते हैं। स्थान-विशेष उसमें कोई बड़ी बाधा नहीं है। किन्तु फिर भी नये स्थानों का अवलोकन कल्पनाओं को नई धार प्रदान कर सकता है व प्रतिभा को नई ऊँचाइयाँ प्रदान करने में सहायक हो सकता है। अतः इसमें कोई सन्देह नहीं कि यदि कालिदास उज्जयिनी जा कर राजकवि के रूप में कर्मरत् हों तो उनकी काव्य-प्रतिभा को नई व विशिष्ट पहचान प्राप्त हो सकती है।

प्रश्न 38. ''उनके प्रसंग में मेरी बात कहीं नहीं आती। मैं अनेकानेक साधारण व्यक्तियों में से हूँ। वे असाधारण हैं। उन्हें जीवन में असाधारण का ही साथ चाहिए था। ...... सुना है राजदुहिता बहुत विदुषी हैं।''

(i) प्रस्तुत संवाद से नायिका के मन के किस भाव का बोध हो रहा है ?

(ii) नायिका ने स्वयं को साधारण व कालिदास को असाधारण व्यक्तित्व क्यों कहा है ?

(iii) नायिका के मुताबिक कालिदास को असाधारण का ही साथ क्यों चाहिए ?

(iv) 'उनके प्रसंग में मेरी बात कहीं नहीं आती।' क्या आपको नायिका का यह तर्क उचित प्रतीत होता है ?

उत्तर—(i) प्रस्तुत संवाद में नायिका कालिदास की प्रतिभा-सम्पन्नता की भूरि-भूरि प्रशंसा कर रही है तथा वह उनके लिए मंगल-कामना भी कर रही है।

(ii) नायिका यह भली-भाँति जानती व समझती है कि कालिदास की काव्य-प्रतिभा अप्रतिम है। वह निश्चय ही युग के श्रेष्ठ कवि हैं। भले ही उनकी प्रतिभा को उनके नगर के लोग न समझ पाये हों किन्तु उनकी प्रशस्ति राज्य में चहुँओर फैल चुकी है। जबकि नायिका उनकी तुलना में गाँव की अनपढ़ यौवना है। कालिदास के समक्ष उनका ज्ञान तुच्छ है। यही कारण है कि वह कालिदास को असाधारण व स्वयं को साधारण व्यक्तित्व का धनी मानती है।

(iii) कालिदास कवि-श्रेष्ठ हैं। उनकी प्रतिभा का गुणगान समस्त राज्य में हो रहा है। उनकी कीर्ति चहुँओर फैली है। इसीलिए नायिका उन्हें असाधारण व्यक्तित्व का धनी मानती है। नायिका का ऐसा मानना है कि जब कालिदास असाधारण व्यक्ति हैं, तब उनकी जीवन-संगिनी भी असाधारण ही होनी चाहिए। यही कारण है कि नायिका ने कहा है कि कालिदास को असाधारण का ही साथ चाहिए।

(iv) नायिका कालिदास के बाल्यकाल की संगिनी है। वह उनके सृजन की साक्षी भी है, और उनका केन्द्र भी। कालिदास के साधारण से असाधारण व्यक्तित्व में परिवर्तित होने में नायिका की भूमिका ही मुख्य है। कालिदास यदि आज राजकवि के पद पर आसीन हैं तो नायिका ही इसकी सूत्रधार है। इन तथ्यों से ज्ञात होता है कि नायिका कालिदास के जीवन के हर प्रसंग में अपनी महत्वपूर्ण भूमिका का निर्वाह कर रही है। ऐसे में नायिका का यह तर्क कि 'उनके प्रसंग में मेरी बात कहीं नहीं आती' सर्वथा अनुचित प्रतीत होता है।

काव्य मंजरी

[KAVYA MANJARI]

1. साखी

—कबीरदास

जीवन परिचय—कबीरदास निर्गुण काव्यधारा के ज्ञानमार्गी शाखा के प्रमुख कवि हैं। उनका जन्म 1398 में हुआ था। जनश्रुति के आधार पर कहा जाता है कि वे एक विधवा ब्राह्मणी के परिव्यक्त सन्तान थे। इनका पालन-पोषण एक जुलाहा दम्पत्ति ने किया था जिनका नाम नीरू और नीमा था। इन्होंने इनका नाम कबीर रखा।

इनकी शिक्षा विधिवत नहीं हुई। स्वयं कबीर कहते हैं—''मसि कागद छुओ नहीं,कलम गही नहिं हाथ।'' इनके गुरु का नाम रामानन्द था। इनकी पत्नी का नाम लोई, पुत्र का नाम कमाल और पुत्री का नाम कमाली था। कबीर पाखण्ड और अन्धविश्वास के विरोधी थे। कबीर जीवन के अन्तिम दिनों में मगहर चले गये। सन् 1518 में इनका देहान्त हो गया।

कबीर ने पदों और साखियों की रचना की है जो मुख्यत: कबीर ग्रन्थावली में संगृहीत है, कबीर पंथियों के अनुसार 'बीजक' ही कबीर की रचनाओं का प्रामाणिक संग्रह है। कबीर की कुछ रचनाएँ 'गुरु ग्रन्थ साहब' में भी संकलित हैं।

कबीर की रचनाओं को तीन रूपों में संकलित किया है—(1) साखी, (2) सबद, (3) रमैनी। कबीर निर्गुण ब्रह्म के उपासक थे। कबीर के 'राम' निर्गुण, निराकार परब्रह्म हैं।

सामाजिक जीवन में व्याप्त जाति-भेद, साम्प्रदायिकता, अन्धविश्वास पाखण्ड एवं आडम्बर और मूर्तिपूजा आदि के मिटाने के लिए कबीर की वाणी थोड़ी कर्कश हो उठी थी। इन्होंने समाजगत बुराइयों का खण्डन तो किया ही, लेकिन इसके साथ आदर्श जीवन के लिए नीतिपूर्ण उपदेश भी दिया। कबीर समाज सुधारक एवं युग निर्माता के रूप में जाने जाते हैं।

(1)

पीछे लागा जाई था लोक वेद के साथि।
आगैं थैं सतगुरु मिल्या, दीपक दिया हाथि।। 1।।
कबीर बादल प्रेम का, हर पर बरष्या आइ।
अंतरि भीगी आत्मां हरी भई बनराइ।। 2।।
बासुरि सुख, नाँ रैजि सुख, ना सुख सुपिनै माहिं।
कबीर बिछुट्या राम सूँ, ना सुख धूप न छाँह।। 3।।

शब्दार्थ—**लोक** = संसार, **वेद** = धार्मिक पुस्तक, **दीपक** = ज्ञानरूपी दीपक, **अंतरि** = अन्दर से, **बासुरि** = दिन, **रैणि** = रात, **सुपिनै** = सपने में।

प्रसंग—कबीर इन साखियों में ज्ञान, प्रेम और राम से बिछड़ने के दु:ख का वर्णन करते हैं।

भावार्थ—कबीर कहते हैं कि मैं तो लोक (संसार) और वेद को मानकर उनकी बातों पर विश्वास कर आगे बढ़ रहा था, पर मार्ग में मेरी सतगुरु से भेंट हुई। उन्होंने ज्ञानरूपी दीपक मेरे हाथ में दे दिया जिससे मेरे अज्ञान का अँधेरा मिट गया।

कबीर कहते हैं कि प्रेमरूपी बादल हम पर ऐसे बरसा कि हमारे अन्दर आत्मा तक उससे भीग गई और बाहर की प्रकृति (हमारा शरीर भी) हरी भरी हो गई। ईश्वरीय प्रेम की वर्षा जब होती है तो बाहर-भीतर सब कुछ प्रेममय हो जाता है।

कबीर कहते हैं कि राम (निर्गुण ब्रह्म) से बिछड़ने के बाद न तो दिन में चैन (सुख) पड़ता है, न रात में और न ही सपने में। ईश्वर से अलग होने पर न धूप में चैन पड़ता है, न छाँव में।

(2)

मूवां पीछे जिनि मिलै, कहै कबीरा राम।
पाथर घाटा लौह सब, (तब) पारस कोणें काम।। 4 ।।
अंखड़ियाँ झाईं पड़ी, पंथ निहारि-निहारि।
जीभड़ियाँ छाला पड़्या, राम पुकारि-पुकारि।। 5 ।।
जो रोऊँ तो बल घटै, हँसौं तो राम रिसाइ।
मनहि मांहि बिसूरणां ज्यूँ घुंण काठहि खाइ।। 6।।

शब्दार्थ—मूवां = मरने पर, **पाथर** = पत्थर, **पारस** = एक ऐसा पत्थर जो लोहे को स्पर्श करके सोना बना देता है, **निहारि** = देखकर, **बिसूरणां** = शोक।

प्रसंग—यहाँ पर कबीर ने राम (ईश्वर) के विरह में दुःख का वर्णन किया है।

भावार्थ—कबीर कहते हैं कि मरने के बाद भी राम (ईश्वर) नहीं मिले तो क्या लाभ ? जैसे लोहे के बदले पत्थर ले लिया तब पारस मिलने से भी कोई लाभ नहीं।

ईश्वर की राह देखते-देखते आँखों में झाईं पड़ गई और राम पुकारते-पुकारते जीभ में छाला पड़ गया पर राम (ईश्वर) की प्राप्ति नहीं हुई।

संसार को देखकर रोऊँ तो बल घटता है अर्थात् संसार के लिए रोने से कोई लाभ नहीं। यदि उस पर हँसू तो ईश्वर को बुरा लगता है क्योंकि संसार तो उन्हीं की बनाई हुई कृति है। मेरे मन में तो दुःख ऐसे बैठ गया है जैसे अन्दर लगा हुआ घुन लकड़ी को खाता रहता है।

(3)

परवति-परवति मैं फिर्‌या, नैन गँवाये रोइ।
सो बूटी पाँऊ नहीं, जातैं जीवन होई।। 7 ।।
आया था संसार में, देषण कौं बहु रूप।
कहै कबीरा संत हौ, पड़ि गयां नजरि अनूप।। 8 ।।
जब मैं था तब हरि नहिं, अब हरि है मैं नाहिं।
सब अँधियारा मिटि गया, जब दीपक देख्या माहिं।। 9।।
तन कौं जोगी सब करैं, मन कौं विरला कोइ।
सब विधि सहजै पाइए, जे मन जोगी होइ।। 10।।

शब्दार्थ—परवति = पर्वत, **बूटी** = दवा, **जीवन** = सुखी जीवन जो राम को पास के, **देषण** = देखने को, **मैं** = अभिमान (घमंड), **दीपक** = ज्ञान का दीपक, **जोगी** = योगी, साधु, **बिरला** = कोई-कोई ही, **सहजै** = आसानी से।

प्रसंग—राम की प्रप्ति के उपाय बताये हैं।

भावार्थ—कबीर कहते हैं कि मैं राम (निर्गुण ब्रह्म) की प्राप्ति की लिए पर्वत-पर्वत पर घूमा और नैनों से रोता रहा, लेकिन मुझे कहीं भी दवा न मिली जिससे ईश्वर की प्राप्ति हो और जीवन सफल हो जाये।

कबीर कहते हैं कि मैं संसार में मनुष्यों के अनेक रूप देखने को आया। लेकिन जब सन्त के रूप में मैंने दर्शन किये तो उस ईश्वर के भी दर्शन हो गये। अर्थात् किसी सच्चे संत ने मुझे ईश्वर का दर्शन करा दिया।

जब मेरे हृदय के अन्कर अभिमान (घमण्ड) था तब हरि (भगवान) उसके अन्दर नहीं थे और जब हरि हृदय के अन्दर आ गये हैं तो अभिमान वहाँ से चला गया।

कबीर कहते हैं कि शरीर से जोगी (योगी, साधु) तो सब हो जाते हैं, लेकिन मन से कोई बिरला ही जोगी हो पाता है. यदि मन से कोई जोगी (योगी, साधु) हो गया तो आसानी से ईश्वर को प्राप्त कर सकता है।

अभ्यास-प्रश्न

प्रश्न 1. प्रस्तुत कविता में कबीसदास जी ने क्या सन्देश दिया है ? साहित्य में उनका क्या स्थान था ?

उत्तर— कबीरदास द्वारा रचित साखी में उन्होंने उपदेशात्मक भाषा में भगवान को प्राप्त करने के मार्ग बतायें हैं। कबीर निर्गुण ब्रह्म के उपासक थे। इनके राम निर्गुण ब्रह्म हैं। उनके राम सर्वव्यापक और सर्वकालिक हैं। उनका ब्रह्म, अरूप, अनाम, अजन्मा, अनुपम और सूक्ष्म है।

ईश्वर को पाने के लिए वह संसार और वेदमार्ग पर चलता रहे, लेकिन कोई काम नहीं आया। जब सतगुरु ने ज्ञान का दीपक हाथ में दे दिया तो अज्ञान रूपी अँधेरा मिट गया। जब प्रेम रूपी बादल बरसता है तो बाहर-भीतर सब भीग जाता है अर्थात् आत्मा तक उससे प्रसन्न हो जाती है।

कबीर का यह कहना है कि जब वह राम से बिछुड़ गये तो उन्हें न दिन में चैन पड़ा न रात में और न सपने में ही चैन पड़ा। वह कहते हैं कि कहीं भी उन्हें सुख प्राप्त नहीं हुआ चाहे वे धूप में रहे या छाँव में। कहने का तात्पर्य है कि सच्चा सुख तो ईश्वर की प्राप्ति में ही है।

मरने के बाद भी यदि राम से भेंट नहीं हुई तो पूरा जीवन व्यर्थ चला गया, जैसे लोहे को कोई काठ से बदल ले फिर उसे पारस (पत्थर जो लोहे को सोने में बदल देता है) मिले तो उसके लिए पारस की प्राप्ति बेकार है। उसी प्रकार जीवन में ही ईश्वर की प्राप्ति ही सुखदायक और कल्याणकारी है।

राम की राह देख-देखकर आँखें दुखने लगीं और राम पुकार-पुकारकर जीभ में छाला पड़ गया, लेकिन राम नहीं मिले। कहने का तात्पर्य यह है कि आडम्बर छोड़कर मन से राम का भजन करना चाहिए।

कबीर का यह मानना है कि अगर वे संसार को देखकर रोते हैं तो उनका बल कम होता है और यदि हँसते हैं तो ईश्वर नाराज होगा क्योंकि उसकी कृति पर वह हँस रहे हैं। ईश्वर से न मिलने का शोक उनके हृदय के अन्दर बैठ गया है और अन्दर ही अन्दर उन्हें खाये जा रहा है जैसे लकड़ी में लगा हुआ घुन उसे अन्दर ही अन्दर खाता रहता है।

ईश्वर की प्राप्ति के लिए वह पर्वत-पर्वत पर घूमे और रो-रोकर अपने नेत्र खराब कर लिए, लेकिन उन्हें ऐसी कोई दवा न मिली जिससे कि ईश्वर की प्राप्ति हो जाती और उनका जीवन सफल हो जाता।

कबीर कहते हैं कि मैं संसार में ईश्वर के बनाये हुए बहुत से रूपों को देखने आया था। जब मैं सन्त हुआ या मुझे सन्तों का साथ मिला तभी उस अनूप (ईश्वर) के दर्शन हो गये। अत: कबीर का मत है कि ईश्वर का दर्शन सन्तों के सत्संग से ही सम्भव है।

जब तक हृदय में अभिमान रहता है, तब तक उस हृदय में ईश्वर प्रवेश नहीं करते, लेकिन जैसे ही हृदय में ईश्वर का निवास हुआ, हृदय से अभिमान (घमण्ड) चला गया। अभिमान मनुष्य को नष्ट कर देता है इसलिए उसे ईश्वर का समर्थन नहीं मिलता।

संसार में शरीर से तो जोगी (योगी, साधु) सब बन जाते हैं। लेकिन मन से जोगी कोई बिरला ही बन पाता है। यदि मन से कोई जोगी बन गया तो वह सहज में ही ईश्वर को प्राप्त कर लेता है।

कबीर सच्चे अर्थों में युगदृष्टा थे, जिन्होंने जीवन भर अपनी सधुक्कड़ी भाषा में तत्कालीन समाज में व्याप्त रूढ़ियों और आडम्बरों का डटकर विरोध किया। इसलिए वे युग निर्माता और क्रान्तिकारी महात्मा के रूप में पूजित हैं। कबीरदास अशिक्षित थे लेकिन अद्भुत प्रतिभा के धनी थे। खुले आकाश के नीचे आसपास

बैठे लोगों के बीच में अपनी अनुभूति को अभिव्यक्त करना ही उनकी साहित्य सेवा थी। उन्होंने राम (ईश्वर) को जानने की प्रेरणा दी है, जैसे—

"कबीर एक न जाँणियाँ, तौ बहु जाँण्यौ क्या होइ।
एक तैं सब होत है, सब तैं एक न होई।।

प्रश्न 2. कबीर द्वारा रचित 'साखी' कविता का केन्द्रीय भाव लिखिए।

उत्तर—कविता में अपने समाज का यथातथ्य चित्रण और उसका दिशा निर्देशन होता है। कबीरदास ने समाज के अन्तर्विरोधों को यथार्थ के स्तर पर अनुभव किया और सामाजिक परिवर्तन के लिए अपनी कविताओं में क्रान्तिकारी कदम उठाया। इस कविता में उन्होंने कहा है कि जब तक वह संसार और वेदों (धार्मिक पुस्तकें) के मार्ग पर चलते रहे तब तक उन्हें कुछ भी प्राप्त नहीं हुआ, लेकिन जैसे ही सन्तों का संग मिला तो ईश्वर के दर्शन हो गये।

प्रेम का बादल बरसने से अन्दर और बाहर सब जगह शान्ति मिल गई। प्रेम के आने से आत्मा तक प्रसन्न हो उठी। यहाँ प्रेम का तात्पर्य ईश्वर के प्रेम से है।

जब भी कबीर का राम से बिछोह हुआ तो उन्हें न दिन में चैन (सुख) मिला न रात में, न सपने में, न धूप में और न ही छाया में चैन मिला। कहने का तात्पर्य है कि ईश्वर के सामीप्य में ही सुख है, संसार के साधनों में नहीं। मरने के बाद भी यदि राम नहीं मिले तो संसार में आना ही बेकार हो गया। जैसे लोहे के बदले कोई काठ (लकड़ी) ले ले तो उसके लिए तो पारस पत्थर किसी काम का नहीं होता। उसी प्रकार यदि मरने के बाद भी ईश्वर की प्राप्ति नहीं हुई तो संसार में आना बेकार है।

ईश्वर की राह देखते-देखते आँखें दुखने लगीं और राम (ईश्वर) पुकारते-पुकारते जीभ में छाला पड़ गया लेकिन ईश्वर की प्राप्ति नहीं हुई। कहने का तात्पर्य है कि दिखावा छोड़कर सच्चे मन से ईश्वर का ध्यान या भजन करना चाहिए तभी ईश्वर की प्राप्ति होगी।

संसार के लिए रोने से तो बल का ह्रास होता है और हँसने से ईश्वर नाराज होता है कि हम उसके द्वारा रचित संसार पर हँस रहे हैं। यह तो मन में बैठा वह दु:ख है जो घुन की तरह लकड़ी को खाता रहता है। पर्वत-पर्वत पर घूमने से और राम के लिए रोने से कोई लाभ नहीं हुआ। उसे कोई ऐसी दवा न मिली जिससे उसका जीवन सफल हो जाये। मैं संसार के लोगों के अनेक रूपों को देखने आया था। जब मैं सन्तों के साथ रहा तो उनकी कृपा से ईश्वर के दर्शन भी हो गये।

यहाँ पर कहा गया है कि अभिमान और ईश्वर एक साथ नहीं रहते। अगर हमारे हृदय में अभिमान है तो ईश्वर नहीं रहेंगे और यदि ईश्वर है तो अभिमान नहीं रहेगा, जैसे ज्ञान के दीपक से अज्ञानरूपी अँधेरा मिट जाता है, उसी प्रकार ईश्वर के आने से घमण्ड रूपी अंधेरा मिट जाता है।

संसार में शरीर से सभी जोगी (योगी, साधु) बन जाते हैं पर मन से तो कोई बिरला ही जोगी बन पाता है। एक बार मन से जोगी कोई हो गया तो उसे ईश्वर की प्राप्ति सहज ही हो जाती है।

कबीर ने समाज की बुराइयों का खण्डन तो किया ही इसके साथ आदर्श जीवन के लिए नीतिपूर्ण उपदेश भी दिया।

प्रश्न 3. पीछे लागा जाई था लोक वेद के साथि।
आगैं थैं सतगुरु मिल्या, दीपक दीया हाथि।।
कबीर बादल प्रेम का, हम पर बरष्या आइ।
अंतरि भीगी आत्मा हरी भई बनराय।।

(i) कबीर क्या कर रहे थे और बाद में उन्हें क्या मिला ?

(ii) सतगुरु ने उन्हें क्या दिया ? उससे उन्हें क्या लाभ हुआ।

(iii) प्रेम के बादल के बरसने से क्या हुआ ?

(iv) प्रस्तुत पंक्तियों का अर्थ लिखिए ?

उत्तर—(i) कबीर लोक वेद के अनुसार चल रहे थे संसार में। कुछ समय बाद उन्हें सतगुरु की प्राप्ति हुई।

(ii) सतगुरु ने उन्हें ज्ञान का दीपक प्रदान किया जिससे कि उनके जीवन में अज्ञान का अंधेरा मिट गया और ज्ञान का प्रकाश जगमगाने लगा।

(iii) भगवान के प्रेमरूपी बादल के बरसने से उनके अन्दर आत्मा तक और उससे बाहर की प्रकृति (हमारा शरीर भी) हरी भरी हो गयी। ईश्वर की प्रेमरूपी वर्षा जब होती है तो बाहर-भीतर सब कुछ प्रेममय हो जाता है।

(iv) कबीर कहते हैं कि मैं तो लोक (संसार) और वेद को मानकर उनकी बातों पर विश्वास करके आगे बढ़ रहा था, तभी मार्ग में मेरी सतगुरु से भेंट हुई। उन्होंने ज्ञानरूपी दीपक मेरे हाथ में दे दिया जिससे मेरे अज्ञान का अँधेरा मिट गया।

कबीर कहते हैं कि प्रेमरूपी बादल इस पर ऐसे बरसा कि हमारे अन्दर आत्मा तक उससे भीग गयी और बाहर की प्रकृति (हमारा शरीर भी) हरी भरी हो गई। ईश्वर के प्रेम की वर्षा जब होती है तो बाहर-भीतर सब कुछ प्रेममय हो जाता है।

प्रश्न 4. बासुरि सुख, नां रेणि सुख, ना सुख सुपिनैं माहिं।
कबीर बिछुट्या राम सूं, ना सुख धूप न छाँह।।
मूवां पीछे जिनि मिलै, कहे कबीरा राम।
पाथर घाटा लौह सब, (तब) पास कोणें काम।।

(i) किसको दिन या रात में सुख नहीं है ?

(ii) मरने के बाद कौन मिलता है तथा उससे क्या लाभ या हानि है ?

(iii) कबीर किसके उपासक थे ?

(iv) प्रस्तुत पद्यांश का अर्थ लिखिए।

उत्तर—(i) कबीरदास को न तो दिन में सुख मिलता है न रात में। इसका कारण यह है कि उनका राम (ब्रह्म) से बिछोह हो गया है।

(ii) कबीर के अनुसार अगर मरने के बाद भी राम (ईश्वर) नहीं मिले तो क्या लाभ ? जैसे लोहे के बदले पत्थर ले लिया तब पारस मिलने से भी कोई लाभ नहीं। यदि हमारे पास लोहा होता तो वह पारस पत्थर के छूने से सोना बन जाता, लेकिन पत्थर को पारस सोने में परिवर्तित नहीं कर सकता।

(iii) कबीर राम (निर्गुण ब्रह्म) के उपासक थे। उनके राम एक निर्गुण ब्रह्म हैं और उन्हीं में उनकी अनन्य भक्ति है। उन्होंने समाज की बुराइयों का खण्डन तो किया ही इसके साथ आदर्श जीवन के लिए नीतिपूर्ण उपदेश भी दिया। वे एक सच्च युगदृष्टा थे जिन्होंने जीवनभर अपनी सधुक्कड़ी भाषा में तत्कालीन समाज में व्याप्त रूढ़ियों और आडम्बरों का डटकर विरोध किया। उन्होंने राम (ईश्वर) को जानने की प्रेरणा दी है। जो उन्हें मन को अनन्य भाव से प्राप्त करना चाहता है वह प्राप्त कर सकता है।

(iv) कबीर कहते हैं कि राम (निर्गुण ब्रह्म)के बिछड़ने के बाद न तो दिन मैं चैन (सुख) पड़ता है और न ही रात में चैन पड़ता है। ईश्वर से बिछड़ने पर न तो धूप में चैन (सुख) पड़ता है और न छाँव में।

उनके अनुसार यदि मरने के बाद राम मिले तो क्या लाभ। जीवन में ही उनके मिलने से लाभ है। जैसे हमने लोहे के बदले पत्थर ले लिया तब पारस मिलने से कोई लाभ नहीं क्योंकि पारस धातु लोहे को ही सोने में बदल सकती है, पत्थर को नहीं।

प्रश्न 5. जब मैं था तब हरि नहिं, अब हरि हैं मैं नाहिं।
सब अँधियारा मिट गया, जब दीपक देख्या माहिं।।
तन कौं जोगी सब करैं, मन कौं बिरला कोइ।
सब विधि सहमे पाइए, जे मन जोगी होइ।।

(i) जोगी होने से क्या होता है ?

(ii) ईश्वर को सहज में कैसे प्राप्त किया जा सकता है ?

(iii) हरि कहाँ पर कब नहीं थे और उनके आने से क्या हुआ ?

(iv) उपर्युक्त पंक्तियों का अर्थ लिखिए।

उत्तर—(i) कबीर कहते हैं कि मनुष्य शरीर से नहीं, बल्कि मन से जोगी होगा तभी ईश्वर की प्राप्ति होगी।

(ii) कबीर कहते हैं कि जो व्यक्ति शरीर से नहीं बल्कि मन से जोगी हो जायेगा वह सहज ही ईश्वर को प्राप्त कर लेगा। मन का जोगी ही अपनी अनन्य भक्ति से ईश्वर को प्राप्त कर सकता है।

(iii) हरि (ईश्वर) कबीर के हृदय में तब नहीं थे जब उनके हृदय में अहंकार भरा हुआ था। जैसे ही उनके हृदय का अहंकार हटा, वैसे ही ईश्वर का उनके हृदय में बास हो गया। ईश्वर के आते ही उनके हृदय का अँधेरा मिट गया जैसे दीपक के आने पर अँधेरा मिट जाता है। ईश्वर के आने से उनके हृदय का अज्ञान रूपी अँधेरा मिट गया।

(iv) कबीर कहते हैं कि जब मेरे हृदय में अभिमान था तब हरि (ईश्वर) उसके अन्दर नहीं थे और जब भगवान हृदय के अन्दर आ गये तो अभिमान वहाँ से चला गया। शरीर से साधु (जोगी) तो सब हो जाते हैं, परन्तु मन से कोई बिरला ही जोगी हो पाता है। यदि मन से कोई जोगी (योगी) हो जाये तो सहज में ही ईश्वर को प्राप्त कर सकता है।

2. बाल-लीला

—सूरदास

कवि परिचय—हिन्दी साहित्य आकाश को सूर्य के समान दैदीप्यमान करने वाले कवि शिरोमणि सूरदास भक्तिकाल के सर्वश्रेष्ठ कवि हैं। इनका जन्म सन् 1478 ई. में आगरा के समीप 'रुनकता' गाँव में हुआ था। कुछ विद्वान् दिल्ली के समीप 'सीही' नामक गाँव में इनका जन्म स्वीकार करते हैं। सूर जन्म से अँधे थे। इस विषय में भी विद्वानों में मतभेद हैं।

सूरदास बल्लभाचार्य जी के शिष्य थे। वे मथुरा के गऊघाट स्थित श्रीनाथ जी के मन्दिर में रहते थे तथा कृष्ण लीला का गान करते थे। कहते हैं कि इन्होंने कृष्ण भक्ति में लीन होकर सवा लाख पदों की रचना की। परन्तु अभी तक दस हजार पद ही उपलब्ध हो सके हैं। गोबरधन पर्वत के समीप पारसौली नामक गाँव में सन् 1563 ई. में इनकी मृत्यु हो गई।

बल्लभाचार्य जी के पुत्र बिट्ठलनाथ ने 'अष्टछाप' नाम से आठ कवियों का संगठन किया, जिसमें सूरदास सर्वश्रेष्ठ कवि थे। सूर ने अपनी रचनाओं में कृष्ण की बाल लीलाओं का ऐसा सजीव वर्णन किया कि हर किसी को आश्चर्य होता है कि क्या कोई अंधा व्यक्ति भी ऐसा वर्णन कर सकता है ? कृष्ण की बाल-लीलाओं के अतिरिक्त सूर ने कृष्ण के प्रति उनके माता-पिता तथा गोपिकाओं के प्रेम का अत्यन्त सजीव वर्णन किया है। इसलिए सूर वात्सल्य रस के सम्राट् कहे जाते हैं। इनके पदों में बाल-हट, चपलता, नटखटपन आदि का वर्णन अति उत्तम है।

सूरदास के प्रमुख ग्रन्थ सूरसागर, सूरसारावली, साहित्यलहरी हैं।

हिन्दी में ही नहीं, अपितु विश्व की किसी भी भाषा में बाल सुलभ चेष्टाओं का ऐसा अनूठा वर्णन कोई नहीं कर सका है। श्रीकृष्ण का बालहठ, माखनचोरी, शिशु सुलभ चपलता, खीझ, स्पर्धा, नटखटपन आदि का वर्णन बड़ा मनोहारी है।

भाषा शैली—सूर की भाषा ब्रजभाषा है। यद्यपि इन्होंने संस्कृत, अरबी, फारसी, गुजराती, पंजाबी आदि भाषाओं के शब्दों का प्रयोग किया किन्तु उनका स्वभाव ब्रजभाषा में ही अधिक रहा। सूर ने मुक्तक शैली को अपनाया है। इनके सभी पद गेय हैं। अलंकारों का प्रयोग भी इनके काव्य में चार चाँद लगा देता है।

सूरदास ने वात्सल्य के साथ श्रृंगार रस के संयोग और वियोग दोनों पक्षों का मार्मिक एवं हृदयग्राही चित्रण किया है। सूर के काव्य में भाव पक्ष के साथ ही साथ कला पक्ष का भी उत्कृष्ट रूप देखने को मिलता है।

निष्कर्ष रूप से हम कह सकते हैं कि सूर का काव्य हिन्दी साहित्य की अनूठी धरोहर है, जिसमें वात्सल्य की मधुरता, भक्ति की तन्मयता और आनन्द की विभोरता है। सूर ने शृंगार के सतरंगी रंगों से अपने काव्य को इन्द्रधनुष जैसा बना दिया है जो हर पाठक को लुभाता है।

सूरदास के सम्बन्ध में निम्न दोहा प्रचलित है—

सूर सूर तुलसी शशी उडगन केशवदास।
अब के कवि खद्योत सम, जहँ तहँ करत प्रकाश।।

(1)

शोभित कर नवनीत लिए।
घुटुरुन चलत रेनु-तन-मंडित, मुख दधि लेप किये।
चारु कपोल लोल लोचन, गोरोचन तिलक दिये।
तट लटकनि मनु मत्त मधुप-गन, मादक मधुहिं पिये।

कठुला कंठ वज्र केहरि नख, राजत रुचिर हिये।
धन्य सूर एको पल इहि सुख, का सत कल्प जिये॥

शब्दार्थ—**शोभित** = सुन्दर, **नवनीत** = मक्खन, **कर** = हाथ, **घुटुरुन** = घुटनों के बल चलना, **रेनु** = धूल, **मंडित** = लगी हुई है, **दधि लेप** = दही लिपटा है, **चारु** = सुन्दर, **कपोल** = गाल, **लोल** = सुन्दर, **लोचन** = नेत्र, **गोरोचन** = तिलक लगाने की खड़िया, **लटकनि** = लटकते हुए, **मनु** = मानो, **मत्त** = मस्त, **मधुप गन** = भोंरों के झुंड, **मादक** = मस्त करने वाला, **मधुहिं** = रस, **कठुला** = कठला गले में पहनने का, **केहरि** = शेर का, **राजत** = सुन्दर लगता है, **रुचिर हिए** = सुन्दर गले में, **एको पल** = एक पल भी, **इहि** = ऐसा, **का** = क्या, **सत** = सौ, **कल्प** = बहुत बड़ा समय, **जिए** = जिन्दा रहे।

प्रसंग—प्रस्तुत पंक्तियाँ सूरदास द्वारा रचित 'बाल-लीला' से ली गई है। सूरदास जी ने इस पद में बाल कृष्ण की सुन्दरता का वर्णन किया है।

भावार्थ—सूरदास कहते हैं कि बाल कृष्ण अपने हाथ में मक्खन लिए हुए शोभित हो रहे हैं। वे घुटनों के बल चल रहें हैं और उनका शरीर धूल से लिपटा हुआ भी शोभित लग रहा है। उनके मुख पर दही लिपटा हुआ है। उनके गाल अत्यन्त सुन्दर हैं और नेत्र भी सुन्दर लग रहे हैं। उनके माथे पर गोरोचन का तिलक लगा हुआ है। उनकी लटकती हुई लटें ऐसी लगती है कि मानो मस्त भंवरों के झुंड मस्त होकर मधु (रस) पान कर रहे हैं। उन्होंने गले में वज्र और शेर के नाखून का कठुला पहना हुआ है जो उनके सुन्दर गले पर अत्यन्त मोहक लग रहा है। सूरदास कहते हैं कि एक पल भी अगर उनके दर्शन का सुख मिल जाये तो उसके सामने सौ कल्प तक जीने में भी कोई लाभ नहीं है।

(2)

कहन लागे मोहन मैया-मैया।
नंद महर सौं बाबा-बाबा, अरु हलधर सौं भैया।
ऊँचे चढ़ि-चढ़ि कहति जसोदा, लै-लै नाम कन्हैया।
दुरि खेलन जनि जाहु लला रे, मारैगी काहु की गैया।
गोपी ग्वाल करत कौतूहल, घर-घर बजति बधैया।
सूरदास प्रभु तुम्हरे दरस कौं, चरननि की बलि जैया।।

शब्दार्थ—**नंद-महर** = नंद बाबा, **अरु** = और, **हलधर** = बलदाऊ, **ऊँचे** = ऊँची जगह पर, **दुरि** = दूर, **जनि** = नहीं, **जाहु** = जाओ, **काहु की** = किसी की, **कौतूहल** = शोरगुल, **बजति** = बजती है, **बधैया** = बधाई, **चरननि** = चरणों की, **बलि जैया** = बलिहारी जाती हूँ।

प्रसंग—इस पद में कवि ने बताया है कि बाल कृष्ण बोलने लगे हैं।

भावार्थ—अब बाल कृष्ण बोलने लगे हैं। यशोदा माँ से 'मैया-मैया' कहकर पुकारते हैं और नन्द से 'बाबा-बाबा' कहने लगे हैं। इनके अलावा बलदाऊ से 'भैया' कहकर बुलाते हैं। ऊँचे स्थान पर चढ़कर यशोदा कन्हैया कहकर कृष्ण को बुलाती हैं और कहती हैं कि हे कन्हैया, दूर खेलने मत जाना किसी की गाय तुझे मारेगी। गोपी-ग्वाल सब मिलकर खेलते हैं और कौतूहल करते हैं। घर-घर में बधाई के गीत गाये जा रहे हैं। सूरदास कहते हैं कि हे प्रभु ! तुम्हारे दर्शन के लिए मैं तुम्हारे चरणों की बलिहारी जाता हूँ या तुम्हारे चरणों में प्रणाम कर तुम्हारे दर्शन की अभिलाषा रखता हूँ।

(3)

मैया मोहि दाऊ बहुत खिझायौ।
मौं सो कहत मोल को लीन्हो, तू जसुमति कब जायो।

कहा करौं इहि रिस के मारे, खेलन हौं नहिं जात।
पुनि-पुनि कहत कौन है माता, को है तेरौ तात।
गोरे नंद जसोदा गोरी, तू कत स्याम शरीर।
चुटकी दै दै हँसत ग्वाल सब, सिखै देत बलवीर।
तू मोहि को मारन सीखी, दाउहि कबहुँ न खीझै।
मोहन मुख रिस की ये बातें, जसुमति सुनि-सुनि रीझै।
सुनहु कान्ह बालभद्र चबाई, जनमत ही को धूत।
सूर स्याम मोहि गोधन की सौं, हौं माता तू पूत।

शब्दार्थ—**खिजायौ** = चिढ़ाना, **इहि** = इस, **रिस** = गुस्से में, **पुनि-पुनि** = बार-बार, **तात** = पिता, **कत** = कैसे, **स्याम** = साँवला, **सरीर** = शरीर, **चुटकी दै दै** = चुटकी मार कर, **सिखै** = सिखाना, **खीझै** = डाँटना, **रीझै** = प्रसन्न होती है, **जनमत** = जन्म से ही, **धूत** = दुष्ट, **सौं** = सौगन्ध, **हौं** = मैं।

प्रसंग—यहाँ बाल कृष्ण अपनी माता से बलदाऊ भैया की शिकायत करते हैं कि वह मुझे चिढ़ाते हैं।

भावार्थ—बाल कृष्ण अपनी माँ यशोदा से अपने बड़े भैया बलदाऊ की शिकायत करते हैं कि वह मुझे चिढ़ाते हैं। मुझसे कहते हैं कि मुझे तो मोल लिया था, यशोदा माता ने तुझे जन्म नहीं दिया है। क्या करूँ ? इसके कारण गुस्सा होकर मैं खेलने भी नहीं जाता हूँ। बार-बार मुझसे पूछते हैं कि तेरी माता और तेरे पिता कौन हैं ? फिर यह भी कहते हैं कि नन्द बाबा गोरे हैं, यशोदा माता गोरी हैं, फिर तू साँवला कैसे हो गया ? उनके कहने का तात्पर्य है कि मैं उनका पुत्र होता तो गोरा होता। फिर वे ग्वाल-बालों को सिखा देते हैं और सभी ग्वाल-बाल ताली दे-देकर हँसते हैं। कृष्ण यशोदा माता से कहते हैं कि तू तो मुझे ही मारना जानती है, दाऊ से कुछ नहीं कहती। यशोदा मोहन के गुस्से से भरे मुख की सुन्दरता देखकर और उसकी बातें सुनकर मन ही मन प्रसन्न होती हैं। वह कहने लगी, हे कृष्ण सुनो ! बलदाऊ तो जन्म से ही दुष्ट (धूर्त) है। सूरदासजी कहते हैं कि यशोदा कृष्ण को विश्वास दिलाती है कि हे कृष्ण ! मैं गायों की सौगन्ध खाकर कहती हूँ कि मैं तेरी माता हूँ और तू मेरा पुत्र है।

अभ्यास-प्रश्न

प्रश्न 1. सूरदास की भक्ति का परिचय और 'बाल-लीला' को उदाहरण सहित वर्णन कीजिए।

उत्तर—सूरदास सगुण ब्रह्म के उपासक थे। उन्होंने भगवान की अनन्य उपासना की है और वही उनकी सगुण भक्ति कहलाई। सगुण ईश्वर गान करने में उन्हें अधिक रुचि लगी क्योंकि निर्गुण ब्रह्म का ज्ञान ऐसा ही है जैसे गूँगे व्यक्ति को मीठा फल दिया जाये तो वह उसका अनुभव तो कर सकता है पर उसका वर्णन नहीं कर सकता। इसलिए उन्होंने सगुण ब्रह्म की उपासना की और उनका वर्णन किया।

सूर के अनुसार भक्त परमात्मा की कृपा को सबसे बड़ा आशीर्वाद मानता है। बड़े प्रेम भाव से वह भगवान की लीलाओं का गुणगान करता है और इन्हीं लीलाओं के माध्यम से और इसी भाव से अपने प्रभु का दर्शन भी कर लेता है। कवि हमें हरि के विमुख व्यक्ति से सदा दूर रहने का सन्देश देता है क्योंकि नास्तिक व्यक्ति सदा ही आस्तिक को भी अपनी तरह बनाना चाहता है। सूरदास ने आस्तिक बनकर सत्संगति पर बड़ा बल दिया है। सत्संगति में रहकर वह माया, मोह, क्रोध का त्याग कर सकता है। जब तक मनुष्य इन बुराइयों का साथ नहीं छोड़ता तब तक उसे ज्ञान, भक्ति और ईश्वर-दर्शन नहीं हो सकता। ईश्वर-दर्शन में मोह-माया बड़ा व्यवधान पैदा कर देती हैं। मोह माया के चक्कर में पड़कर बन्धनों में बँधकर उसे न ज्ञान की प्राप्ति होती है न ईश्वर की प्राप्ति। अतः इन मोह माया के झंझटों का त्याग करना अति आवश्यक है। माया मनुष्य को नचाती रहती है और ईश्वर की तरफ नहीं जाने देती। क्या अच्छा है तथा क्या बुरा है ? यह समझाने में कठिनाई

भी मोह-माया के कारण ही होती है। सूरदास श्रीकृष्ण के प्रति अपनी अनन्य भक्ति प्रकट करते हैं तथा उनका मन श्रीकृष्ण के चरणों में ही आश्रय तथा सुख पा सकता है।

सूरदास का मन श्रीकृष्ण की बाल-लीलाओं के वर्णन में अधिक लगा है। उन्होंने बाल-लीलाओं का ऐसा सजीव चित्रण किया है जैसे सूर स्वयं ही उन लीलाओं को देख रहे हों। जैसे—

'शोभि कर नवनीत लिए
घुटुरुन चलत रेनु-तन-मंडित, मुख दधि-लेप किए
चारू कपोल लोल लोचन, गोरोचन तिलक किए।'

दूसरे स्थान पर उन्होंने कृष्ण के बोलना शुरू करने पर अति हर्ष प्रकट किया है, जैसे माता-पिता अपने पुत्र या पुत्री को पहले बोलते हुए सुनते हैं तो अति हर्षित होते हैं। देखिए—

'कहन लागे मोहन मैया-मैया।
नंद-महर सौं बाबा-बाबा, अरु हलधर सौं भैया।
ऊँचे चढ़ि-चिढ़ कहति जसोदा, लै-लै नाम कन्हैया।
दुरि खेलन जनि जाहु लला रे, मारैगी काहु की गैया।'

इस प्रकार हम देखते हैं कि सूर सगुण भक्ति के उपासक थे और 'अष्ट छाप' कवियों में श्रेष्ठ थे। कृष्ण भक्ति की तन्मयता और बाल-चेष्टाओं से प्रेम उनके रचित पदों में मिलता है।

अन्त में सूरदास का कहना है कि निर्गुण ब्रह्म की उपासना से सगुण ब्रह्म की उपासना सरल, प्रेमोत्पादक और मोहक है। सगुण भक्ति सरल होने के साथ-साथ व्यावहारिक भी है। इसीलिए सूरदास ने भगवान कृष्ण की बाल-लीलाओं से लेकर उनकी रास लीला तथा जीवन के प्रत्येक पहलू के गीत गाये हैं। सूर वात्सल्य रस के सर्वोत्कृष्ट कवि हैं।

प्रश्न 2. बाल कृष्ण अपनी माता यशोदा से बलराम की क्या शिकायत करते हैं ?

उत्तर—बलदाऊ और कृष्ण अन्य ग्वाल-बालों के साथ बाहर खेलने जाते हैं तो बलदाऊ भिन्न-भिन्न प्रकार से उन्हें चिढ़ाते हैं। श्रीकृष्ण अपने बड़े भाई बलदाऊ की शिकायत करते हुए अपनी माता से कहते हैं कि मैया बलदाऊ भाई मुझे बहुत चिढ़ाते हैं। मुझसे कहते हैं कि मुझे यशोदा माँ ने जन्म नहीं दिया है बल्कि किसी से मोल लिया है। मैं क्या बताऊँ ? इस गुस्से के कारण मैं खेलने भी नहीं जाता हूँ। मुझसे बार-बार पूछते हैं कि तेरे माता-पिता कौन हैं ? तू नन्द-यशोदा का बेटा तो हो ही नहीं सकता क्योंकि तू साँवले रंग का है जबकि वे दोनों गोरे हैं। यह तर्क बलदाऊ ने इसलिए दिया क्योंकि कृष्ण इसे काट न सकें। ऐसी मान्यता है कि गोरे माता-पिता की सन्तान भी गोरी ही होती है। फिर उन्होंने कहा कि इस बात पर सभी ग्वाल-बाल ताली दे-देकर हँसते हैं। सभी ग्वाल-बालों को बलदाऊ भैया सिखा देते हैं और सभी हँसते हैं, तब मैं खीझकर रह जाता हूँ। तू सिर्फ मुझे ही मारना सीखी है दाऊ से कभी कुछ भी नहीं कहती। कृष्ण के गुस्से से भरे मुख को बार-बार देखकर और उनकी रिस भरी बातें सुनकर यशोदा अत्यन्त प्रसन्न होती हैं। प्रसन्नता से भरे मुख से यशोदा जी कहती हैं हे कृष्ण ! बलदाऊ तो चुगलखोर है और जन्म से ही धूर्त है। सूरदास जी कहते हैं यशोदा जी कहने लगीं—मुझे गोधन (सभी गायों) की सौगन्ध है, मैं तेरी माता हूँ और तूरा मेरा पुत्र है। इस कथन से माँ ने कृष्ण के गुस्से को दूर कर दिया। सूर के वात्सल्य प्रेम में प्रेम का निश्छल, उदार और शिशु सुलभ स्वभाव के दर्शन होते हैं। शिशु के सुन्दर स्वरूप, आकर्षक मुद्राओं और उनके अबोध व्यवहारों के प्रदर्शन से अनुपम वात्सल्य भाव पाठक के हृदय में संचरित होता है।

प्रश्न 3. सूर ने बाल कृष्ण की सुन्दरता का किस प्रकार वर्णन किया है ?

उत्तर—सूरदास ने कृष्ण की बाल-सुलभ चेष्टाओं का बड़ा सटीक, सुन्दर और रोचक वर्णन किया है। इनके पदों को पढ़कर पाठकों के सामने श्रीकृष्ण की लीलाओं का चित्र-सा उपस्थित हो जाता है जिससे उनके

हृदय में श्रीकृष्ण के प्रति प्रेम और भक्ति का समावेश होता है। सूरदास बाल कृष्ण की लीलाओं का वर्णन करते हुए कहते हैं कि कृष्ण अपने छोटे हाथ में मक्खन लिए हुए अति शोभायमान लग रहे हैं। अभी वे चलना नहीं जानते इसलिए घुटनों के बल चल रहे हैं, उनके शरीर में धूल लिपटी हुई है और सुन्दर मुख पर दही लिपटा हुआ है। बाहर खेलने के कारण धूल शरीर पर लग गई है और उन्होंने पहले दही खाया होगा तो वह मुख पर लगा रह गया है। कहने का तात्पर्य है कि यह दृश्य अत्यन्त सुन्दर लग रहा है। उनके गाल सुन्दर हैं और आँखें भी अति सुन्दर हैं। उनके माथे पर गोरोचन का तिलक भी शोभा को प्राप्त हो रहा है। उनकी लटकटी हुई लटें उनके चेहरे पर ऐसे शोभायमान हैं जैसे काले भंवरों के झुंड मधुर रस का पान किसी सुन्दर फूल पर बैठकर कर रहे हों। वह गले में वज्र तथा शेर का नाखून लगा हुआ कठुला पहने हैं। अन्त में सूरदास कहते हैं कि श्रीकृष्ण के दर्शन का ऐसा सुख जो यशोदा जी को मिल रहा है, वह यदि मिल जाये तो सैंकड़ों कल्प जीने से कोई लाभ नहीं। अर्थात् श्रीकृष्ण दर्शन का सुख संसार के सभी सुखों से श्रेष्ठ है। यशोदा जी कितनी भाग्यशाली हैं कि भगवान कृष्ण की बाल-लीलाओं का आनन्द प्रत्यक्ष रूप से उठा रही हैं। जो सुख ऋषि-मुनि और देवताओं को भी दुर्लभ है वह सुख यशोदा जी सहज में ही प्राप्त कर रही हैं।

प्रश्न 4. शोभित कर नवनीत लिए।
घुटुरन चलत रेनु-तन मंडित, मुख दधि-लेप किए।
चारू कपोल लोल लोचन, गोरोचन तिलक दिए।
लट लटकनि मनु मत्त मधुप-गन मादक मधुहिं पिए।
कठुला कंठ वज्र केहरि नख, राजत रुचिर हिए।
धन्य सूर एको पल इहि सुख, का सत कल्प जिए।।

(i) प्रस्तुत पद्यांश में कौन और कैसे शोभा पा रहे हैं ?

(ii) प्रस्तुत पद्यांश में सूर कैसे धन्य हो जाते हैं ?

(iii) कृष्ण के बाल किस प्रकार शोभा पाते हैं ?

(iv) सूर ने कृष्ण की बाल लीलाओं का कैसा वर्णन किया है, उदाहरण सहित लिखिए।

उत्तर—(i) प्रस्तुत पद्यांश में बाल कृष्ण अपने हाथ में मक्खन लिए, मुख पर दही का लेप किये हुए और माथे पर गोरोचन का तिलक किये हुए शोभा पा रहे हैं।

(ii) प्रस्तुत पद्यांश में सूर एक पल भी बाल कृष्ण की सुन्दर छवि का दर्शन करके अपने को धन्य मानते हैं।

(iii) बाल कृष्ण की लटकती हुई लटें ऐसी लगती हैं कि मानो मस्त भँवरों के झुण्ड मस्त होकर मधु (रस) का पान कर रहे हैं।

(iv) सूरदास बड़े प्रेम भाव से बाल कृष्ण की लीलाओं का गुणगान करते हैं। उन्होंने भगवान कृष्ण की अनन्य उपासना की है। वे इन्हीं लीलाओं के माध्यम से अपने प्रभु का दर्शन भी कर लेते हैं। वे सगुण ब्रह्म के उपासक थे। संसार में मोह-माया के बन्धन को त्यागकर ही ईश्वर की प्राप्ति सम्भव है। वे श्रीकृष्ण के प्रति अपनी अनन्य भक्ति प्रकट करते हैं उनका मन श्रीकृष्ण के चरणों में ही आनन्द तथा सुख पा सकता है। माया-मोह मनुष्य को ईश्वर की तरफ जाने से रोकते हैं।

प्रश्न 5. कहन लागे मोहन मैया-मैया।
नंद महर सौं बाबा-बाबा, अरु हलधर सौं भैया।
ऊँचे चढ़ि-चढ़ि कहति जसोदा, लै लै नाम कन्हेया।
दुरि खेलन जनि जाहु लला रे, मारेगी काहु की मैया।
गोपी ग्वाल करत कौतूहल, घर-घर बजति बधैया।
सूरदास प्रभु तुम्हारे दरस कौं, चरननि की बलि जैया।।

(i) कौन क्या कहने लगे ?

(ii) जसोदा कृष्ण से क्या कह रही है ?

(iii) सूर की भक्ति का संक्षिप्त परिचय दीजिए।

(iv) प्रस्तुत पद्यांश का अर्थ लिखिए।

उत्तर—(i) बाल कृष्ण जसोदा से मैया, नंद से बाबा और हलधर से भैया कहने लगे।

(ii) ऊँचे स्थान पर चढ़कर यशोदा कृष्ण से कह रही हैं कि दूर खेलने मत जाना क्योंकि किसी की गाय तुझे मारेगी।

(iii) सूरदास सगुण ब्रह्म के उपासक थे। सगुण ईश्वर भी लीलाओं का गान करने में उन्हें अधिक रुचि लगी क्योंकि निर्गुण ब्रह्म का ज्ञान ऐसा है जैसे गूंगा व्यक्ति मीठे फल के रस का अनुभव तो कर सकता है पर उसका वर्णन नहीं कर सकता। इसलिए उन्होंने सगुण ब्रह्म की उपासना की। उन्होंने बड़े प्रेमभाव से भगवान की लीलाओं का वर्णन किया है। वह हरि के विमुख लोगों से दूर रहने का सन्देश देता है। सत्संगति में रहकर वह माया, मोह, क्रोध का त्यागकर सकता है। माया मनुष्य को ईश्वर की तरफ नहीं जाने देती।

(iv) अब बाल कृष्ण बोलने लगे हैं। यशोदा से 'मैया', नन्द बाबा से 'बाबा' और हलधर से 'भैया-भैया' कहने लगे हैं। ऊँचे स्थान पर चढ़कर यशोदा कन्हैया कहकर कृष्ण को बुलाती है और दूर खेलने जाने की मना करती है क्योंकि किसी की गाय मारेगा। गोपी ग्वाल सब मिलकर खेलते हैं और कौतूहल करते हैं। घर-घर में बधाई के गीत गाये जा रहे हैं सूरदास कहते हैं कि हे प्रभु ! तुम्हारे दर्शन के लिए मैं तुम्हारे चरणों की बलिहारी जाता हूँ।

प्रश्न 6. मैया मोहि दाऊ बहुत खिजायौ।
मो सौं कहत मोल को लीन्हो, तू जसुमति कब जायो।
कहा करौं इहि रिस के मारे, खेलत हौं नहि जात।
पुनि-पुनि कहत कौन है माता,को है तेरौ तात।
गोरे नंद जसोदा गोरी, तू कत स्याम शरीर।
चुटकी दै दै हँसत ग्वाल सब, सिखै देत बलवीर।

(i) प्रस्तुत पद्यांश में कृष्ण अपनी माँ से किसकी शिकायत कर रहे हैं ?

(ii) सूर किसके उपासक थे ? उनका ब्रह्म निर्गुण था या सगुण ?

(iii) किसके कारण वे खेलने नहीं जाते हैं ?

(iv) प्रस्तुत पंक्तियों का अर्थ लिखिए।

उत्तर—(i) प्रस्तुत पद्यांश में कृष्ण अपनी माँ से अपने भाई बलदाऊ की शिकायत कर रहे हैं।

(ii) सूरदास भगवान कृष्ण के अनन्य उपासक थे। वे सगुण ब्रह्म की उपासना करते थे। उनके भगवान श्रीकृष्ण थे। वह भगवान कृष्ण की लीलाओं का गायन करते करते उनका दर्शन भी कर लेते थे। उन्होंने आस्तिक बनकर सत्संगति पर बड़ा बल दिया है।

(iii) माँ के मना करने पर बाल कृष्ण दूर खेलने नहीं जाते हैं क्योंकि उन्हें कोई गाय मारेगी। माँ ने गाय के माध्यम से उन्हें डरा दिया है ताकि वे कहीं दूर खेलने न जायें।

(iv) बालकृष्ण अपनी माँ यशोदा से बलदाऊ भैया की शिकायत करते हैं कि वह उन्हें चिढ़ाते हैं। उनसे कहते हैं कि उसे तो मोल लिया था, यशोदा माता ने उन्हें जन्म नहीं दिया है। इसके कारण गुस्से से मैं खेलने भी नहीं जाता हूँ। बार-बार मुझसे पूछते हैं कि तेरे माता-पिता कौन हैं। नन्द बाबा और यशोदा माता गोरी है तो फिर तू साँवला कैसे हो गया। उनके सिखाने पर ही ग्वाल बाल ताली दे-देकर हँसते हैं।

●●

3. एक फूल की चाह

—सियारामशरण गुप्त

जीवन परिचय—आधुनिक हिन्दी साहित्य में गाँधीवादी विचारधारा के पोषक कवि सियारामशरण गुप्त का जन्म सन् 1885 में झाँसी जिले के चिरगाँव में एक वैश्य परिवार में हुआ था। ये राष्ट्रकवि मैथिलीशरण गुप्त के छोटे भाई थे। घर पर ही इन्होंने संस्कृत, अंग्रेजी और बंगला आदि भाषाओं का ज्ञान प्राप्त किया। इन्होंने अपनी कविताओं में सामाजिक बुराइयों पर करारी चोट की है। इनकी रचनाओं में सत्य, अहिंसा, करुणा, विश्वबन्धुत्व की छाप स्पष्ट दिखाई देती है। इन्होंने कथात्मक, भावनात्मक और विचारात्मक सभी प्रकार की कविताओं का प्रणयन किया है। सन् 1963 में इनका देहावसान हो गया।

इनकी कृतियों में इनका सरल और विनयशील व्यक्तित्व स्पष्ट प्रतिबिम्बित हुआ है। उत्कृष्ट कवि होने के साथ-साथ ही ये एक सफल उपन्यासकार, नाटककार, कहानीकार तथा निबन्धकार भी थे। 'आर्द्रा', 'मौर्य विजय', 'नकुल', 'दूर्वादल', 'पाथेय', 'मृण्मयी', 'बापू', 'दैनिकी', 'विषाद', 'उन्मुक्त', 'आलोत्सर्ग' आदि इनकी प्रसिद्ध काव्य कृतियाँ हैं।

(1)

बहुत रोकता था सुखिया को,
"न जा खेलने को बाहर"
नहीं खेलना रुकता उसका,
नहीं ठहरती वह पल-भर।
मेरा हृदय काँप उठता था,
बाहर गई निहार उसे,
यही मानता कि बचा लूँ,
किसी भाँति इस बार उसे।
भीतर जो डर रहा छिपाए,
हाय ! वही बाहर आया।
एक दिवस सुखिया के तन को
ताप-तप्त मैंने पाया।
ज्वर में विह्वल हो बोली वह,
क्या जानूँ किस डर-से-डर,
मुझको देवी के प्रसाद का,
एक फूल ही दो लाकर।

शब्दार्थ—निहार = देखकर, **ताप-तप्त** = बुखार से पीड़ित, **विह्वल** = भाव में भरकर।

प्रसंग—प्रस्तुत कविता में बुखार से तप्त बेटी का वर्णन है जो अपने पिता से 'देवी माँ' का प्रसाद लाने को कहती है।

भावार्थ—सुखिया को उसका पिता बाहर खेलने जाने से बहुत रोकता था, पर उसका खेलना नहीं रुकता और वह पल भर भी घर में नहीं ठहरती थी। उसे बाहर जाते हुए देखकर पिता का हृदय काँप उठता और सोचता कि किसी प्रकार उसे मैं बचा लूँ अर्थात् वह बीमार न पड़ जाये।

जो डर उसके अन्दर था, वही बाहर दिखाई दिया। एक दिन सुखिया बेटी को तेज बुखार ने घेर लिया। वह न जाने किस डर से डरकर अपने पिता से बोली—'मुझको देवी के प्रसाद का एक फूल ही लाकर दे दो।'

(2)

क्रमश: कंठ क्षीण हो आया,
शिथिल हुए अवयव सारे,
बैठा था, नव-नव उपाय का,
चिंता में मैं मन मारे।
जान सका न, प्रभात सजग से,
हुई अलस कब दोपहरी,
स्वर्ण घनों में कब रवि डूबा,
कब लौटी संध्या गहरी।

सभी ओर दिखलाई दी बस,
अंधकार की ही छाया,
छोटी सी बच्ची को ग्रसने,
कितना बड़ा तिमिर आया।
ऊपर विस्तृत महाकाश में
जलते-से अंगारों से,
झुलसी-सी जाती थीं आँखें,
जगमग जगते तारों से।

प्रसंग—पिता अपनी बेटी की बीमारी से दु:खी है।

भावार्थ— कवि कहता है कि उस बेटी का कंठ सूख-सा गया और सभी अंग शिथिल हो गये थे। उसका पिता अपने मन में नये-नये उपायों के बारे में सोचकर दु:खी बैठा था। उसे यह भी पता नहीं चला कि कब प्रभात से आलस लाने वाली दोहपर हो गई और कब सूर्य बादलों में डूब गया और न जाने कब संध्या हो गई।

सभी ओर पिता को अंधकार ही अंधकार दिखाई दे रहा है। उस छोटी-सी बच्ची के प्राण लेने के लिए कितना बड़ा अँधेरा आया है। ऊपर विस्तृत आकाश में मानो अंगारे जल रहे हों जिनसे उसकी आँखें झुलस रही थीं। जगमग करते हुए तारे भी उसे तपती हुई आग के समान लग रहे थे।

(3)

देख रहा था जैसे सुस्थिर हो,
नहीं बैठती थी क्षण-भर,
हाय वही चुपचाप पड़ी थी,
अटल शान्ति सी धारण कर।
सुनना यही चाहता था मैं,
उसे स्वयं ही उकसाकर,
मुझको देवी के प्रसाद का,
एक फूल दो लाकर।

ऊँचे शैल शिखर के ऊपर,
मन्दिर था विस्तीर्ण विशाल,

स्वर्ण-कलश-सरसिज विहँसित थे,
पाकर समुदित रवि-कर-जाल।
दीप धूल से अच्छादित था,
मन्दिर का आँगन सारा,
गूँज रही थी भीतर-बाहर,
मुखरित उत्सव की धारा।

शब्दार्थ—**सुस्थिर** = दृढ़, **अटल** = न टलने वाली, **विस्तीर्ण** = फैला हुआ, **विहँसित** = खिल रहे थे, **सरसिज** = कमल, **समुदित** = प्रसन्न होकर, **रवि-कर-जाल** = सूर्य की किरणों से, **आच्छादित** = ढका हुआ, **मुखरित** = शोर करते हुए।

प्रसंग—एक पिता अपनी बीमार बेटी के बारे में सोच रहा है इसका वर्णन कवि ने इन पंक्तियों में किया है।

भावार्थ—मैं यह देख रहा था कि मेरी बेटी जो एक क्षण भी बैठती नहीं थी, वही आज अटल शान्ति को ओढ़े हुए चुपचाप पड़ी है। मैं उससे यही सुनना चाहता था कि मुझे देवी के प्रसाद का एक फूल ही लाकर दे दो।

ऊँचे पर्वत की चोटी पर एक विशाल मन्दिर था। उसके ऊपर स्वर्ण कलश चमक रहे थे और सूर्य की किरणों का स्पर्श प्राप्त कर कमल खिल रहे थे। दीप-धूप के धुएँ से मन्दिर जैसे ढका हुआ लगता था। मन्दिर के भीतर और बाहर उत्सव का शोरगुल सुनाई दे रहा था।

(4)

भक्त-वृंद सब मधुर कंठ से
गाते थे सभक्ति मुद-मय
''पतित तारिणी, पाप-हारिणी
माता तेरी जय-जय-जय !''
''पतित तारिणी, तेरी जय-जय-जय''
मेरे मुख से भी निकला;
बिना बढ़े ही मैं आगे को
जाने किस बल से ढिकला।

मेरे दीप-फूल लेकर वे
अंबा को अर्पित करके,
दिया पुजारी ने प्रसाद जब
आगे को अंजलि भर के।
भूल गया उसका लेना झट
परम लाभ-सा पाकर मैं।
सोचा बेटी को माँ के ये
पुण्य पुष्प दूँ जाकर मैं।

शब्दार्थ—**भक्त-वृंद** = भक्त लोग, **सभक्ति** = भक्ति के साथ, **मुद-मय** = प्रसन्न होकर, **पतित तारिणी** = पापियों का उद्धार करने वाली, **ढिकला** = आगे को बढ़ गया, **पुण्य पुष्प** = पुण्य फूल।

प्रसंग—कवि कहता है कि पिता बेटी के लिए प्रसाद लेने मन्दिर में गया।

भावार्थ—कवि कहता है कि मन्दिर में मधुर कंठ से भक्त लोग प्रसन्न होकर भजन गा रहे थे और 'पापियों को तारने वाली और पापों को नष्ट करने वाली देवी की जय हो' ऐसे बोल रहे थे। पिता के मुख से भी यही शब्द निकले और पीछे से ऐसा धक्का आया कि वह आगे तक पहुँच गया।

पुजारी ने उसका दीप-फूल देवी माँ को अर्पित करके उसके हाथ में प्रसाद दिया और उसने अपनी अंजलि में लिया और सोचने लगा कि बेटी को माता का प्रसाद जाकर दूँगा।

(5)

सिंह पौर तक भी आँगन से
नहीं पहुँचने मैं पाया
सहसा यह सुन पड़ा कि—"कैसे
यह अछूत भीतर आया ?
पकड़ो, देखो भाग न जाए,
बना धूर्त है यह कैसा,
साफ-स्वच्छ परिधान किये है
भले मनुष्यों के जैसा।

पापी ने मन्दिर में घुसकर
किया अनर्थ बड़ा भारी,
कलुषित कर दी है मन्दिर की,
चिरकालिक शुचिता सारी।"
ऐं ! क्या मेरा कलुष बड़ा है
देवी की गरिमा से भी ?
किसी बात में हूँ मैं आगे,
माता की महिमा के भी ?

शब्दार्थ—**सिंह पौर** = दालान, **अछूत** = नीच जाति का, **कलुषित** = अपवित्र, **कलुष** = पाप, दोष, **चिरकालिक** = बहुत समय से, **शुचिता** = पवित्रता, **कलुष** = पाप, दोष, **गरिमा** = स्वाभिमान, पवित्रता, **महिमा** = ऐश्वर्य।

प्रसंग—बीमार बच्ची का पिता मन्दिर में जाता है।

भावार्थ—बच्ची का पिता आँगन से दालान तक पहुँच भी नहीं पाया कि उसने सुना कि यह अछूत कैसे मन्दिर में घुस आया ? पकड़ो यह दुष्ट कहीं भाग न जाये। वह भले आदमियों जैसे साफ कपड़े पहनकर आया है। इस पापी ने मन्दिर में घुसकर बड़ा अनर्थ कर दिया। मन्दिर की पुराने समय से चली आ रही पवित्रता समाप्त कर दी है। वह सोचने लगा कि क्या उसका यह पाप देवी माँ की गरिमा से भी बड़ा है ?

(6)

माँ के भक्त हुए तुम कैसे,
करके यह विचार खोटा ?
माँ के सम्मुख ही माँ का तुम
गौरव करते हो छोटा ?

कुछ न सुना भक्तों ने, झट से
मुझे घेरकर पकड़ लिया,
मार-मारकर मुक्के घूँसे
धम-से नीचे गिरा दिया।

मेरा हाथों से प्रसाद भी
बिखर गया हा ! सब-का-सब,
हाय अभागी बेटी, तुझ तक
कैसे पहुँच सके वह अब !
अन्तिम बार गोद में बेटी;
तुझको लेन सका मैं हा
एक फूल माँ के प्रसाद का
तुझको दे न सका मैं हा !

शब्दार्थ—खोटा = बुरा, **सम्मुख** = सामने, **गौरव** = गरिमा, **झट से** = तुरन्त, **बिखर गया** = नीचे गिर गया, **अभागी** = बुरे भाग्यवाली।

प्रसंग—मन्दिर में उस व्यक्ति के साथ मार-पीट की गई। वह पूछता है कि क्या उसका पाप माँ के गौरव से भी बड़ा है ?

भावार्थ—मन्दिर में गये हुए उस व्यक्ति ने माँ के भक्तों से पूछा कि तुम इतना बुरा विचार करके माँ के सामने उनके गौरव को छोटा करते हो। यह सब भक्तों ने नहीं सुना और उस व्यक्ति को घेरकर पकड़ लिया। उसे नीचे गिरा कर मुक्के, घूँसों से पीटा जिससे उसके हाथ का प्रसाद नीचे गिर कर बिखर गया। वह सोचने लगा कि अब यह प्रसाद कैसे मेरी बेटी तक पहुँच पायेगा ? दुःख के साथ वह कहता है कि हे बेटी ! अन्तिम बार मैं तुम्हें गोद में ले न सका और माँ के प्रसाद का एक फूल भी तुम्हें न दे सका। यह उसकी करुण पुकार है।

अभ्यास-प्रश्न

प्रश्न 1. यहाँ कवि ने कौन से प्रसाद की बात कही हैं ? पुराने समय में अछूतों के साथ कैसा व्यवहार होता था ?

उत्तर—यहाँ पर कवि कहता है कि एक व्यक्ति की बेटी बीमार है। उसकी श्रद्धा है कि उसे देवी माँ के प्रसाद का एक फूल भी मिल जाये तो अच्छा रहेगा। उसका पिता सोचता है कि उसे अपनी बेटी की यह इच्छा पूरी करनी ही चाहिए।

वह उसे बाहर जाकर खेलने की मना करता था क्योंकि उसे भय था कि वह कहीं बीमार न पड़ जाये। जो डर उसको था बेटी के बीमार पड़ने का वह सच हो गया। एक दिन उसका शरीर ताप से जलने लगा, उसे बुखार ने बुरी तरह से घेर लिया। वह ज्वर से ग्रस्त बोली कि उसको देवी माँ के प्रसाद का एक फूल ही लाकर दे दो शायद उसके प्रसाद से वह ठीक हो जाये। धीरे-धीरे उसका गला बैठ गया और शरीर भी शिथिल हो गया था। पिता को उसके प्राणों की चिन्ता होने लगी। उसका पिता मन में नये-नये उपाय सोचने लगा। उसको उस चिन्ता में यह भी नहीं पता चला कि कब सुबह से दोपहर हो गयी और दोपहर से कब शाम हो गई।

सभी ओर उसे अंधकार ही अंधकार दिखाई देता था जैसे बच्ची को निगलने ही महाअंधकार आया है। वह चुपचाप अपने बिस्तर पर पड़ी थी। वह उसके मुँह से एक बार यही शब्द सुनना चाहता था कि देवी माँ के

प्रसाद का एक फूल ही लाकर मुझे दे दो। देवी माँ का मन्दिर बहुत बड़ा था। उसके ऊपर स्वर्ण कलश शोभित थे। रवि किरणों से कमल के फूल खिल रहे थे। मन्दिर दीपों और धूपों के सुगन्धित धुएँ से घिरा हुआ था और मन्दिर के भीतर-बाहर भक्तों की मधुर ध्वनि गूँज रही थी। भक्तजन मधुर कण्ठों से भक्ति के गीत गा रहे थे और पाप-हारिणी और पतित-पावनी माता की जय-जयकार कर रहे थे।

उस बच्ची के पिता ने माँ के लिए प्रसाद लेकर पुजारी को माता पर अर्पित करने को दिया और वह व्यक्ति अपने हाथों में उस प्रसाद को लेकर सोचने लगा कि वह यह प्रसाद उसकी बीमार बेटी को जाकर देगा। वह मन्दिर के दालान तक भी नहीं पहुँच पाया था कि उसे सुनाई पड़ा—कैसे यह अछूत मन्दिर में प्रवेश कर गया ? बोलने वाला व्यक्ति उससे परिचित होगा, इसीलिए उसने ऐसा कहा। और जोर के शब्द सुनाई पड़े कि पकड़ो, यह धूर्त कहीं भाग न जाये। अतः उसे लोगों ने घेर लिया और मुक्कों-घूँसों से उसकी खूब पिटाई की। इस पिटाई के समय उसके हाथ से माँ का प्रसाद नीचे गिरकर बिखर गया। वह सोचने लगा क्या उसका यह छोटा सा पाप कि वह अछूत होकर मन्दिर में घुस आया है, माँ के गौरव से भी बड़ा है ? इस दीन अवस्था में वह सोच रहा है कि हे बेटी ! मैं तुझे माँ के प्रसाद का फूल भी लाकर न दे सका।

प्राचीन काल में हिन्दू धर्म में अछूतों की दशा बड़ी दयनीय थी। उनको समाज में बराबर का दर्जा हासिल नहीं था। मन्दिर में प्रवेश की आज्ञा उनको नहीं थी। वैसे तो कोई अछूत मन्दिर में जाता नहीं था, यदि कोई इस प्रकार मन्दिर में पकड़ा जाये तो उसकी पिटाई की जाती थी ताकि वह दुबारा ऐसी हिम्मत न करे। हमारे देश में छूआछूत जैसी कुप्रथाओं पर बहुत काम हुआ। इस सम्बन्ध में कानून भी बनाया गया कि अछूत भी साफ-स्वच्छ होकर मन्दिर में प्रवेश कर सकता है। समाज की उन्नति तभी होगी जब सब मिलकर आगे बढ़ें और गिरे हुओं को उठायें। हम सभी ईश्वर की सन्तान हैं, कोई छोटा बड़ा नहीं हैं।

प्रश्न 2. 'एक फूल की चाह' कविता का केन्द्रीय भाव लिखिए।

उत्तर—कवि सियारामशरणगुप्त ने बड़े ही मार्मिक ढंग से यह कविता लिखी है। इस कविता में एक बीमार बेटी ने अपने पिता से देवी माँ के प्रसाद का एक फूल उसको लाकर देने की माँग की है क्योंकि उसे लगता है कि देवी माँ की कृपा से वह ठीक हो जायेगी। उसका पिता उसे खेलने जाने की मना करता था इसलिए कि वह कहीं बीमार न पड़ जाये। हुआ भी यही कि एक दिन वह बुखार से पीड़ित हो गई। बुखार इतना अधिक था कि उसका गला क्षीण हो गया और हाथ-पैर शिथिल हो गये। उसका पिता नये-नये उपाय सोचकर दु:खी बैठा था तो बेटी ने भावना में भरकर कहा, हे पिता ! मुझको देवी माँ के मन्दिर से उसके प्रसाद का फूल लाकर दे दो। चिन्तामग्न पिता का सवेरा और दोपहर शाम में कब बदल गया उसे पता ही नहीं चला। उसे लगा जैसे यह भयंकर अंधकार उसकी बेटी को छीनने आया है। वह एक क्षण भी शान्त नहीं बैठती थी लेकिन आज वह स्थिर और शान्त पड़ी हुई है। पिता उससे फिर यही सुनना चाहता था कि देवी माँ के मन्दिर जाकर उनके प्रसाद का एक फूल ही उसको लाकर दे दे।

मन्दिर ऊँचे शैल पर बना हुआ था। मन्दिर बड़ा विशाल और सुन्दर था। स्वर्ण कलश शोभायमान थे और सूरज की किरणों से कमल खिल रहे थे। मन्दिर का आँगन धूप-दीप से आच्छादित था। मन्दिर में एक उत्सव जैसा वातावरण बना हुआ था। भक्त-जन मधुर कण्ठों से माता के गीत गा रहे थे और पतित तारिणी, पाप-हारिणी माता तेरी जय-जय-जय के नारे लगा रहे थे। बच्ची के पिता ने भी यही नारा लगाया। फिर धक्के से वह आगे बढ़ा और अपने हाथ का प्रसाद पुजारी के हाथ में दे दिया कि माता को अर्पण कर दे। पुजारी जी ने माता का भोग लगाकर उसके हाथ में वह प्रसाद दे दिया। तभी उसने सुना कि यह अछूत मन्दिर में कैसे प्रविष्ट हुआ ? पकड़ो, कहीं यह दुष्ट भाग न जाये। इस धूर्त ने भले आदमी जैसे स्वच्छ कपड़े पहन रखे हैं। इस पापी ने मन्दिर में आकर इसकी प्राचीन काल से चली आ रही पवित्रता नष्ट कर दी। वह व्यक्ति यह सोचने लगा कि मेरा यह छोटा सा पाप क्या देवी माँ के गौरव से भी बड़ा है ? माता के भक्त होकर तुम कैसा छोटा विचार लिए हुए हो।

उन्होंने उसे घेरकर पकड़ लिया और मारना शुरू कर दिया। इस कारण उसके हाथ से प्रसाद नीचे गिरकर बिखर गया। उसे यह महान दु:ख है कि वह अपनी बेटी की अन्तिम इच्छा भी पूरी न कर सका। माँ के प्रसाद का एक फूल भी उसे लाकर न दे सका।

प्रश्न 3. भीतर जो डर रहा छिपाये,
हाय ! वही बाहर आया।
एक दिवस सुखिया के तन को
ताप-ताप्त मैंने पाया।
ज्वर में विह्वल हो बोली वह,
क्या जानूँ किस डर-से-डर,
मुझको देवी के प्रसाद का,
एक फूल ही दो लाकर।

(i) उसके पिता के हृदय में कौन सा डर बैठा था ?

(ii) एक फूल की चाह किसने और क्यों की थी ?

(iii) ज्वर आने पर उसने क्या कहा ? उसका क्या विश्वास था ?

(iv) प्रस्तुत पद्यांश का अर्थ लिखिए।

उत्तर—(i) बेटी के पिता के हृदय में यह डर बैठा रहता कि यह बाहर खेलने गयी तो इसको बुखार आ सकता है।

(ii) एक फूल की चाह एक अछूत व्यक्ति की बुखार से तप्त बेटी ने की है। उसे यह विश्वास था कि देवी के प्रसाद का एक फूल उसको ठीक कर देगा।

(iii) ज्वर से तप्त उस बेटी ने देवी माँ के प्रसाद का एक फूल लाकर देने को कहा है। उसे अपने मन में कुछ भरोसा हो रहा था कि यदि मन्दिर से देवी माँ के प्रसाद का एक फूल उसको मिल जायेगा तो वह ठीक हो जायेगी।

(iv) सुखिया को उसके पिता बाहर खेलने जाने से मना करता था क्योंकि उसे डर था कि बाहर खेलने से वह कहीं बीमार न हो जाये। जो डर उसके अन्दर हृदय में बैठा था, वही निकलकर बाहर आया। उसकी बेटी सुखिया को ताप ने घेर लिया। ज्वर से तप्त वह अपने पिता से बोली न जाने किस डर से डरकर कि उसको मन्दिर जाकर देवी माँ के प्रसाद का एक फूल लाकर दे दो।

प्रश्न 4. देख रहा था—जैसे सुस्थिर हो,
नहीं बैठती थी क्षण-भर
हाय वही चुपचाप पड़ी थी,
अटल शान्ति-सी धारण कर।
सुनना यही चाहता था मैं,
उसे स्वयं ही उकसाकर,
मुझको देवी के प्रसाद का,
एक फूल ही दो लाकर।

(i) प्रस्तुत पंक्तियों में किसके बारे में क्या कहा गया है ?

(ii) 'देख रहा था—जैसे सुस्थिर हो, नहीं बैठती थी क्षण-भर' पंक्ति का अर्थ स्पष्ट कीजिए।

(iii) 'सुनना यही चाहता था मैं, उसे स्वयं ही उकसाकर', पंक्तियों का भावार्थ लिखिए।

(iv) प्रस्तुत पंक्तियों का अर्थ लिखिए।

उत्तर—(i) प्रस्तुत पंक्तियों में सुखिया के बारे में बताया गया है कि जो पहले क्षण भर भी नहीं बैठती थी वह आज चुपचाप बुखार में पड़ी है।

(ii) प्रस्तुत पंक्तियों में सुखिया की बीमार दशा को बताते हुए उसके पिता कहते हैं कि जो कभी स्थिर होकर एक क्षण के लिए भी नहीं बैठती थी आज वही अटल शान्ति धारण किये हुये चुपचाप बिस्तर पर पड़ी हुयी है। अपनी पुत्री को पीड़ा में देखकर पिता अत्यन्त दुःखी है।

(iii) प्रस्तुत पंक्तियों में सुखिया के पिता की पीड़ा का मार्मिक वर्णन किया गया है। वह अपनी पुत्री को स्थिर रूप से शान्त बैठा देखकर सोचता है कि जो कभी एक क्षण-भर के लिए शान्त नहीं बैठती थी आज वह अटल शान्ति धारण किये हुए है। उसके पिता चाहते हैं कि सुखिया शान्ति को त्यागकर बस इतना ही कह दे कि 'मुझको देवी के प्रसाद का एक फूल ही दो लाकर।'

(iv) सुखिया का पिता देख रहा था कि उसकी बेटी एक क्षण भी बैठती नहीं थी, वही आज अटल शान्ति को ओढ़े हुए चुपचाप पड़ी है। वह उससे यही सुनना चाहता था कि वह उसे देवी माँ के प्रसाद का एक फूल लाकर दे दे। न जाने किस डर से डरकर उसने देवी माँ के प्रसाद का एक फूल लाकर उसे देने को अपने पिता से कहा।

प्रश्न 5. मेरे दीप फूल लेकर वे
अंबा को अर्पित करके,
दिया पुजारी ने प्रसाद जब
आगे को अंजलि भर के।
भूल गया उसका लेना झट
परम लाभ सा पाकर मैं।
सोचा बेटी को माँ के ये
पुण्य पुष्प दूँ जाकर मैं।

(i) प्रस्तुत पंक्तियों में किसके बारे में कहा गया है ?

(ii) वह मन्दिर में क्यों गया था ? उसे क्या विश्वास था ?

(iii) मन्दिर से क्या लाने को किसने किससे कहा और क्या सोचकर कहा ?

(iv) प्रस्तुत पंक्तियों का अर्थ लिखिए।

उत्तर—(i) प्रस्तुत पंक्तियों में बुखार से पीड़ित बच्ची सुखिया के पिता के बारे में कहा गया है।

(ii) सुखिया ने अपने पिता से माँ के प्रसाद का एक फूल मन्दिर से लाने को इसलिए कहा क्योंकि उसे यह विश्वास था कि माँ के प्रसाद का एक फूल उसके बुखार को ठीक कर उसे पहले जैसा हृष्ट-पुष्ट बना सकता है।

(iii) मन्दिर में जाने के लिए सुखिया ने अपनी पिता से देवी माँ के प्रसाद का एक फूल लाकर देने को कहा। उसने यह सोचकर कहा था कि देवी माँ के प्रसाद के फूल से उसका बुखार ठीक हो जायेगा।

(iv) मन्दिर के पुजारी ने उसका दीप-फूल देवी माँ को अर्पित करके उसके हाथ में प्रसाद दिया और उसने वह प्रसाद अपनी अंजलि में लिया और सोचने लगा कि बेटी को माता का प्रसाद जाकर दूँगा क्योंकि उसे यह विश्वास था कि देवी माँ के प्रसाद से उसकी बेटी जो भयंकर ज्वर से पीड़ित है, ठीक हो जायेगी।

4. आ : धरती कितना देती है

—सुमित्रानन्दन पंत

जीवन परिचय—प्रकृति के सुकुमार कवि सुमित्रानन्दन पंत का जन्म सन् 1900 में अल्मोड़ा के निकट कौसानी ग्राम में हुआ था। इनके बचपन का नाम गोसाईं दत्त था। इनके जन्म के समय ही इनकी माता का देहान्त हो गया था। इनकी दादी और पिताजी ने इनका लालन-पालन किया। इन्होंने मात्र 7 वर्ष की उम्र में ही कविता की रचना प्रारम्भ कर दी थी।

आपने अल्मोड़ा में फिर उसके बाद काशी के क्वींस कॉलेज में विद्याध्ययन किया और साथ-साथ काव्य-रचना भी चलती रही। इन पर सरोजिनी नायडू, कवीन्द्र रवीन्द्र, महात्मा गाँधी और श्री अरविन्द का भी गहरा प्रभाव पड़ा। 28 दिसम्बर, 1977 को इनका देहावसान हो गया।

'वीणा', 'पल्लव', 'ग्रन्थि', 'गुंजन', 'युगान्त', 'युगवाणी', 'उत्तरा', 'चिदंबरा', 'लोकायतन', 'ग्राम्या', 'स्वर्ण धूलि', 'कला और बूढ़ा चाँद', 'युगपथ' इनकी प्रमुख रचनाएँ हैं।

पंत जी प्रकृति के कवि हैं। इनकी काव्य-रचनाओं में प्रकृति का सुन्दर चित्रण हुआ है। प्रसाद और निराला की भाँति ये भी छायावादी कवि हैं। तथा रूस की सरकार ने भी इन्हें पुरस्कृत किया।

हिन्दी काव्यधारा में पंत जी का स्थान एक उत्कृष्ट कवि तथा मानवता के प्रति आस्थावान शिल्पी के रूप में वर्णित है। वे छायावाद तथा प्रगतिवाद के उन्नायक कवि हैं। आधुनिक काव्य को प्राचीन रूढ़ियों की धारा से मुक्त कर नवीन दिशा की ओर मोड़ने तथा खड़ी बोली को रमणीय रूप में प्रदान करने में पन्त जी का विशेष योगदान है।

(1)

मैंने छुटपन में छिपकर पैसे बोये थे,
सोचा था पैसों के प्यारे पेड़ उगेंगे।
रुपयों की कलदार मधुर फसलें खनकेंगी।
और फूल-फलकर मैं मोटा सेठ बनूँगा।
पर बंजर धरती में एक न अंकुर फूटा,
बंध्या मिट्टी ने न एक भी पैसा उगला।
सपने जाने कहाँ मिटे, सब धूल हो गये।
मैं हताश हो बाट जोहता रहा दिनों तक,
बाल कल्पना के अपलक पाँवड़े बिछाकर,
मैं अबोध था, मैंने गलत बीज बोये थे,
ममता को रोपा था, तृष्णा को सींचा था।

शब्दार्थ—**छुटपन** = बचपन, **कलदार** = खूब अच्छी, **बंजर** = जिस जमीन में कुछ न उगे, **बंध्या** = न पैदा करने वाली, **हताश** = निराश, **जोहता** = देखता रहा, **अबोध** = अनजान, **ममता** = प्रेम, **तृष्णा** = तीव्र इच्छा।

प्रसंग—इस कविता में कवि ने अपने बचपन की एक घटना धरती में पैसे बोकर रुपयों की खेती करना का वास्तविक चित्र प्रस्तुत किया है।

भावार्थ—कवि ने अपने बचपन में छिपकर (किसी की जानकारी में न होना) कुछ पैसे जमीन में बोये थे। कवि का विचार था कि इन पैसों के अच्छे-अच्छे पौधे उगने लगेंगे। इस तरह उन पैसों से उगे हुए पौधों पर रुपयों की सुन्दर फसलें उगने लगेंगी। रुपयों की खनक भी सुनाई देगी। इसका परिणाम यह होगा कि कवि फूल-फलकर बड़ा धनवान सेठ बन जायेगा।

लेकिन बोये हुए पैसों का एक भी पौधा नहीं उगा। कवि ने सोचा कि धरती बंजर होगी। उस बाँझ बनी मिट्टी ने एक भी पैसे को रुपये के रूप में अंकुरित नहीं होने दिया। कवि की सभी कल्पनाएँ (सपने और इच्छाएँ) इसी धूल में मिल गईं। वह हताशा से उद्विग्न था। फिर भी बहुत दिनों तक उसने प्रतीक्षा की। ये उसके सपने उसके बचपन के थे। कवि पलक पाँवड़े बिछाये उन पैसों के बीजों से रुपयों के पेड़ उगने का इन्तजार करता रहा। वह अज्ञानी और अबोध था। उसने अपनी अज्ञानतावश गलत बीजों को बोया था। अनुचित बीजों की बुवाई से कवि ने लालच का रोपण किया था और तृष्णा (तीव्र इच्छा) का पानी लगाकर ममता का सिंचन किया था।

(2)

अर्धशती हहराती निकल गई है तब से
कितने ही मधु पतझर बीत गये अनजाने,
ग्रीष्म तपे, वर्षा झूलीं, शरदें मुसकाईं,
सी-सीकर हेमन्त कँपे, तरु झरे, खिले वन,
और जब फिर से गाढ़ी ऊदी लालसा लिए,
गहरे कजरारे बादल बरसे धरती पर;
मैंने कौतूहलवश आँगन के कोने की
गीली तह को यों ही उँगली से सहलाकर;
बीज सेम के दबा दिये मिट्टी के नीचे,
भू के अंचल में मणि-माणिक बाँध दिये हों,
मैं फिर भूल गया इस छोटी सी घटना को,

शब्दार्थ—**अर्धशती** = पचास वर्ष, **हहराती** = झूमती, **मधु** = बसन्त, **पतझर** = पतझड़ की ऋतु, **शरदें** = शरद ऋतु, **हेमंत** = हेमंत ऋतु, **ऊदी** = सुगन्ध लिए हुए, **लालसा** = इच्छा, **कजरारे** = काले, **कौतूहलवश** = जिज्ञासा, **अंचल** = आँचल, **मणि-माणिक** = मणियाँ।

प्रसंग—यहाँ पर कवि ने बदलते हुए समय और ऋतुओं का वर्णन किया है। उसने अनजाने ही धरती में सेम के बीज बो दिये।

भावार्थ—कवि कहता है कि बचपन की घटना के बाद समय बदला और जीवन के पचास साल यूँ ही जल्दी से निकल गये। कितने ही बसंत, पतझड़, ग्रीष्म, वर्षा, शरद और हेमन्त ऋतु निकल गईं। पेड़ों के पत्ते गिरे और वन खिल गये। जब फिर से सुगन्ध (सुन्दर) लालसा लिए काले धरती पर बादल बरसे तो कवि ने जिज्ञासावश आँगन के एक कोने की गीली मिट्टी को उँगली से खोदकर कुछ सेम के बीज मिट्टी के नीचे दबा दिये जैसे कि पृथ्वी के अन्दर मणियाँ बो दी हों। कवि इस छोटी सी घटना को भूल गया।

(3)

और बात भी क्या थी, याद जिसे रखता मन,
किन्तु, एक दिन, जब मैं संध्या को आँगन में
टहल रहा था, तब सहसा मैंने जो देखा,
उससे हर्ष विमूढ़ हो उठा मैं विस्मय से।
देखा आँगन के कोने में कई नवागत
छोटी-छोटी छाता ताने खड़े हुए हैं।

छाता कहूँ या विजय पताकाएँ जीवन की
या हथेलियाँ खोले थे वे नन्हीं, प्यारी-
जो भी हो, वे हरे-भरे उल्लास से भरे
पंख मारकर उड़ने को उत्सुक लगते थे,
डिंब तोड़कर निकले चिड़ियों के बच्चों से।
निर्निमेष, क्षण भर, मैं उनको रहा देखता
सहसा मुझे स्मरण हो आया, कुछ दिन पहले,
बीज सेम के रोपे थे मैंने आँगन में।

शब्दार्थ—**हर्ष विमूढ़** = खुशी से पागल-सा, **विस्मय** = आश्चर्य, **नवागत** = नई अंकुरित, **विजय पताकाएँ** = विजय की पताका लिए हुए, **उत्सुक** = गहरी लालसा या इच्छा रखने वाला, **डिंब** = अण्डा, **निनिर्मेष** = लगातार, **रोपे** = बोये थे।

प्रसंग—यहाँ कवि अपने आँगन में बोये हुए सेम की बीजों को अंकुरित होते देखकर आश्चर्यचकित होता है, इसी का सुन्दर चित्रण किया है।

भावार्थ—यह छोटी-सी बात (सेम के बीज मिट्टी में दबा देने की) ऐसी नहीं थी जिसे याद रखा जाता। वह उस बात को भूल गया। किन्तु एक दिन शाम के समय वह अपने आँगन में टहल रहा था, तो अचानक कुछ देखा जिसे देखकर वह आश्चर्य और हर्ष से जैसे पागल-सा हो गया। उसने देखा कि उसके आँगन के कोने में कई अंकुर एक बेल (लता) के फूट पड़े हैं। ऐसा लगता है कि वे छोटे-छोटे छाते ताने हुए खड़े हैं। कवि सोचता है कि उनकी पंक्तियों को विजय पताका कहे या उनकी खुली हथेलियाँ कहे। जो भी हो वे भी प्रसन्नता से भरे हुए लग रहे थे। ऐसा लगता था मानो वे अण्डे तोड़कर निकले चिड़ियों के बच्चे जैसे पंख फैलाकर उड़ना चाहते हैं। वह क्षणभर बिना पलक झपके उन्हें देखता रहा। फिर उसे याद आया कि कुछ दिन पहले उसने अपने आँगन के एक कोने में कुछ सेम के बीज रोपे थे।

(4)

और उन्हीं से बौने पौधों की यह पलटन
मेरी आँखों के सम्मुख अब खड़ी गर्व से,
नन्हें नाटे पैर पटक, बढ़ती जाती है।
तबसे उनको रहा देखता, धीरे-धीरे,
अनगिनती पत्तों से लद, भर गईं झाड़ियाँ,
हरे-भरे टँग गये कई मखमली चँदोवे ।
बेलें फैल गईं बल खा, आँगन में लहरा,
और सहारा लेकर बाड़े की टट्टी का,
हरे-हरे सौ झरने फूट पड़े ऊपर को,
मैं अवाक् रह गया वंश कैसे बढ़ता है।

शब्दार्थ—**बोने** = छोटे कदम के, **सम्मुख** = सामने, **नन्हें** = छोटे, **पैर पटक** = मार्च करते हुए, **अनगिनती** = बहुत संख्या में, **लद** = भरकर, **मखमली** = रेशमी या मुलायम, **चँदोवे** = शामियाने, **बल खा** = लिपटकर, **बाड़े की टट्टी** = घेर के लिए बनाई गई बाँस की छपट्टी की टटिया, **अवाक्** = अचम्भित।

प्रसंग—कवि अपने आँगन में सेम की बेल के अंकुरों को देखकर प्रसन्न है। वह इसी का वर्णन करता है।

भावार्थ— कवि कहता है कि उन्हीं छोटे पौधों की जैसे कोई पलटन खड़ी हो ऐसा लगता है। वह पलटन उसकी आँखों के सामने खड़ी है और कवि को लग रहा है कि वह बौने पौधों की फौज अपने छोटे-छोटे पैरों से मार्च करती हुई आगे बढ़ रही है। कवि उनको धीरे-धीरे देखता रहा। वह बेल अनगिनत पत्तों से भर गई और एक झाड़ी का सा रूप ले लिया। ऐसा लगता है मानो हरे भरे कई मुलायम शामियाने तान दिये गये हों। कवि ने आँगन में घेर के लिए बाँसों की टटिया बनाई थी, उसका सहारा लेकर हरे-हरे अनेक अंकुर ऊपर की ओर बढ़ रहे हैं। कवि यहाँ पर वंश के बढ़ने को देखकर दंग रह गया है।

(5)

छोटे तारों से छितरे, फूलों के छींटे,
झागों-से लिपटे लहरी श्यामल लतरों पर,
सुन्दर लगते थे, मावस के हँसमुख नभ-से,
चोटी के मोती से, आँचल के बूटों-से।
ओह समय पर उनमें कितनी फलियाँ टूटीं,
कितनी सारी फलियाँ, कितनी सारी फलियाँ,
यह धरती कितना देती है, धरती माता
कितना देती है अपने प्यारे पुत्रों को,
नहीं समझ पाया था मैं उसके महत्व को,
बचपन में छिः स्वार्थ लोभवंश पैसे बोकर।

शब्दार्थ—**श्यामल** = साँवली, **लतरों** = लताओं, **मावस** = अमावस्या, **लोभवश** = लालच में।

प्रसंग—यहाँ पर कवि आँगन में उगी हुई सेम की बेलों पर लगी फलियों के सम्बन्ध में बता रहा है।

भावार्थ— कवि कहता है कि सेम की बेलें तारों के समान और फूलों के समान सुन्दर लग रही हैं। साँवले रंग की लताओं पर अमावस के सुन्दर आकाश के समान लिपटे हुए अंकुर अत्यन्त सुन्दर लग रहे हैं। उनमें कितनी सारी फलियाँ लग आई हैं। कवि प्रसन्न होता है कि यह धरती माता अपने पुत्रों के लिए कितना देती है। वह कहता है कि बचपन में वह मिट्टी के महत्व को नहीं समझ पाया था और स्वार्थ और लोभवश उसने पैसे बोये थे। उस समय वह इस बात से अनजान था कि धरती माता में कौन से बीज डाले जाते हैं।

(6)

रत्न प्रसविनी है वसुधा, अब समझ सका हूँ।
इसमें सच्ची समता के दाने बोने हैं,
इसमें जन की क्षमता के दाने बोने हैं,
इसमें मानव ममता के दाने बोने हैं,
जिसमें उगल सके फिर धूल सुनहली फसलें,
मानवता की जीवन श्रम से हँसे दिशाएँ,
हम जैसा बोयेंगे वैसा ही पायेंगे।

शब्दार्थ—**प्रसविनी** = पैदा करने वाली, **वसुधा** = पृथ्वी, **ममता** = प्रेम, **उगल सके** = पैदा कर सके, **मानवता** = मनुष्यता, **श्रम** = परिश्रम।

प्रसंग—कवि ने इन पंक्तियों में परिश्रम के महत्व को समझाया है।

भावार्थ— कवि कहता है कि अब जैसे-जैसे समय बीता है वैसे-वैसे ही उसने भली-भाँति समझ लिया है कि यह धरती माता रत्नों को जन्म देने वाली है। इसमें पैसों के बीज बोकर धन उत्पन्न नहीं किया जा सकता। इसमें तो ममता के बीज बोये जाते हैं। इसमें मानवता की सुनहरी फसलें उगाई जायेंगी। मनुष्य के परिश्रम का परिणाम ही चारों ओर प्रसन्नता भर देगा। यह प्रकृति का नियम है कि हम जैसा बीज बोयेंगे वैसा

ही फल प्राप्त करेंगे। यदि हम अपनी सद्भावना से प्रेम, सहयोग, समता, ममता और एक-दूसरे के प्रति सहानुभूति के बीज बोयेंगे तो पृथ्वी पर सर्वत्र ही सुख और शान्ति की आनन्ददायी फसल उत्पन्न होगी। इस प्रकार मनुष्य के परिश्रम से पृथ्वी पर धन-धान्य भरपूर रहेगा। इसके लिए मनुष्य-मनुष्य में आपसी प्रेम, सद्भाव, समता और सहानुभूति उत्पन्न करना आवश्यक है।

अभ्यास-प्रश्न

प्रश्न 1. बचपन में कवि ने पृथ्वी में क्या बोया था और वर्षों के बाद बड़े होकर क्या बोया था ? दोनों स्थितियों का क्या परिणाम हुआ ?

उत्तर— बचपन में कवि अनजान और अबोध था। उसने सोचा कि पृथ्वी में जो बोते हैं वह कुछ दिन बाद बहुलता में उग आता है। अत: उसने चुपचाप बिना किसी को बताये जमीन खोदकर पैसे गाढ़ दिये और सोचने लगा कि कुछ समय बाद पैसों के पेड़ उगेंगे और उन पर ढेर सारे पैसे लगेंगे, तब मैं धनी सेठ बन जाऊँगा। सभी सुख मुझे प्राप्त हो जायेंगे। लेकिन जब अधिक दिनों तक प्रतीक्षा करने के बाद भी कुछ नहीं उगा तो उसे बड़ी निराशा हुई। लेकिन उसे यह नहीं मालूम था कि उसने गलत बीज बोये थे। यह सब उसने लोभ, लालच और स्वार्थवश किया था इसलिए निष्फल हुआ।

उसके बाद पचास वर्ष ऐसे ही जल्दी से बीत गये। उनमें कई बसंत, पतझड़, वर्षा, ग्रीष्म, शरद और हेमन्त ऋतुएँ निकल गईं। फिर एक दिन काले बादल आये और बरसने लगे। कवि ने कौतूहलवश अपने आँगन के एक कोने में जमीन में खोदकर सेम के कुछ बीज दबा दिये। बिना कुछ सोचे हुए उसने ऐसा किया और इस बात को भूल गया क्योंकि यह कोई ऐसी महत्वपूर्ण बात नहीं थी जिसे याद रखा जाये।

एक दिन जब वह अपने आँगन में टहल रहा था। तो उसने अपने आँगन में सेम के अंकुरों को उगते हुए देखा तो आश्चर्य और हर्ष से वह उछल पड़ा। उसने देखा कि हरे-भरे कई अंकुर एक बेल के फूट निकले हैं। कवि सोचता है कि उनकी पत्तियों को उनकी विजय पताका कहे या उनके हाथ की खुली हथेलियाँ। कवि को वह छोटी-छोटी पत्तियाँ ऐसी लग रहीं थी जैसे कोई चिड़िया का बच्चा अण्डा तोड़कर बाहर निकला हो और पंख फैलाकर उड़ना चाहता हो। वह निर्निमेष उनको देखता रहा। फिर उसके दिमाग में आया कि कुछ समय पूर्व उसने अपने आँगन में सेम के कुछ बीज बोये थे। यह उन्हीं बीजों की फसल है। तभी कवि ने सोचा कि पृथ्वी हमको कितना कुछ देती है। जो हम बोते हैं उसको हजारों गुना करके हमें लौटा देती है। वह हमें धन-धान्य से परिपूर्ण करती है। हम धरती का उचित उपयोग करें तो हम बहुत कुछ प्राप्त कर सकते हैं। उन्नत भारत की लालसा में धरती माता अपना भरपूर सहयोग करती है। मनुष्य अपने परिश्रम से इस धरती को रत्नगर्भा बना देता है। परिश्रम न करने की अवस्था में उसे कुछ भी प्राप्त नहीं होता।

प्रश्न 2. कवि ने परिश्रम के महत्व को कब समझा ?

उत्तर— अपने जीवन के पचास वर्ष निकल जाने के बाद जिसमें कई बसंत, पतझर, ग्रीष्म, वर्षा, शरद और हेमन्त ऋतुएँ बीत गईं, तब कवि ने परिश्रम के महत्व को समझा। बचपन में जब उसने लोभ, लालच और स्वार्थ के वश में होकर पैसे जमीन में बोये थे, तब उसे यह ज्ञान नहीं था कि धरती में कौन से बीज बोये जाते हैं और कौन से नहीं। अब जब उसने अपने आँगन में सेम के बीज बोये तो वे नई फसल के रूप में उत्पन्न हुए। उनके अंकुर अत्यन्त सुन्दर और आह्लादकारी प्रतीत हो रहे थे। कवि उन्हें देखकर प्रसन्नता से नाच उठा। उसका कुछ समय पूर्व किया गया थोड़ा सा परिश्रम आज पौधे के रूप में उसके सामने उपस्थित हुआ। समय के साथ कवि यह समझ गया है कि पृथ्वी रत्नों को जन्म देने वाली है। इसमें पैसों के बीज बोकर धन उत्पन्न नहीं किया जा सकता। इसमें तो ममता के बीज बोने चाहिए तभी इसमें मानवता की सुनहरी फसलें उगेंगी। यहाँ कवि ने मनुष्य के कल्याण की बात कही है। जब वह परस्पर मिलकर भाईचारा, सद्भावना, प्रेम, सहयोग, ममता और सहानुभूति अपनायेगा तभी उसका और उसके देश का कल्याण होगा। इन सभी मानवीय गुणों के

अपनाने से पृथ्वी पर सर्वत्र सुख और शान्ति स्थापित होगी। कवि की कामना है कि हम सब परस्पर मिलकर रहें और देश के विकास के लिए भूमि का सदुपयोग करें। 'जैसा बोयेंगे वैसा ही काटेंगे' का सिद्धान्त शत प्रतिशत सही है। यदि हम गलत बीज का रोपण करते हैं तो गलत (नुकसानदायक) पौधा उत्पन्न होगा इसलिए अच्छे पौधे के लिए तो अच्छा बीज ही बोना होगा। गलत बीज के लिए ही कहा गया है, ''बोया पेड़ बबूल का आम कहाँ से होइ।'' इसीलिए कवि चाहता है कि हम परस्पर सद्व्यवहार करें तो हमें भी सद्व्यवहार ही मिलेगा। अच्छा कर अच्छा पा के सिद्धान्त से सर्वत्र सुख-संपन्नता दिखाई देगी।

प्रश्न 3. मैंने छुटपन में छिपकर पैसे बोये थे,
सोचा था पैसों के प्यारे पेड़ उगेंगे।
रुपयों की कलदार मधुर फसलें खनकेंगी।
और फूल-फलकर मैं मोटा सेठ बनूँगा।
पर बंजर धरती में एक न अंकुर फूटा।
बंध्या मिट्टी ने न एक ही पैसा उगला।
सपने जाने कहाँ मिटे, सब धूल हो गये।

(i) यदि धरती से पैसे उग आते तो कवि क्या बन जाता ?

(ii) बचपन में कवि ने क्या सोचा था और क्या किया ?

(iii) कवि ने मिट्टी में जो कुछ बोया क्या उसका फल उसे मिला ?

(iv) प्रस्तुत पंक्तियों का अर्थ लिखिए।

उत्तर—(i) यदि उसकी सोच के अनुसार धरती से पैसे उग आते तो कवि मोटा (बड़ा) सेठ बन जाता।

(ii) बचपन में सेम के बीज बोने से उसका पौधा उगने पर कवि ने सोचा कि यदि पृथ्वी में पैसे बो दिये जायें तो उनके भी पौधे उगेंगे जिन पर कलदार रुपयों की फसल उगेगी। इसलिए उसने पृथ्वी में पैसे बो दिये।

(iii) सेम के बीज मिट्टी में बोने पर मिट्टी में से उसके अंकुर फूट निकले, लेकिन कवि द्वारा मिट्टी में पैसे बोने से उसमें से कोई अंकुर नहीं फूटा। अर्थात् कवि की अपेक्षा के विपरीत पैसों के अंकुर नहीं फूटे।

(iv) कवि ने अपने बचपन में छिपकर कुछ पैसे जमीन में बोए थे। कवि का विचार था कि इन पैसों के अच्छे-अच्छे पौधे उगने लगेंगे। इस तरह रुपयों की कलदार फसलें खनकेंगी और फूल-फल कर उन रुपयों से वह मोटा सेठ बन जायेगा परन्तु बंजर धरती में एक अंकुर भी नहीं फूटा। कवि के सपने जाने कहाँ धूल बनकर मिट गये क्योंकि मिट्टी में से कोई अंकुर नहीं निकला।

प्रश्न 4. तब से उनको रहा देखता, धीरे-धीरे,
अनगिनती पत्तों से लद, भर गई झाड़ियाँ
हरे-भरे रंग गये कई मखमली चँदोवे।
बेलें फैल गई बल खा, आँगन में लहरा,
और सहारा लेकर बाड़े की टट्टी का,
हरे-हरे सौ झरने फूट पड़े ऊपर को,
मैं अवाक् रह गया वंश कैसे बढ़ता है।

(i) कवि अपने आँगन में क्या देखता रहा ?

(ii) कवि के आँगन में क्या लहरा उठा ?

(iii) कवि क्या देखकर अवाक् रह गया ?

(iv) प्रस्तुत पद्यांश का अर्थ लिखिए।

उत्तर—(i) कवि आँगन में यह देखता रहा कि सैम की बेलें चारों तरफ धीरे-धीरे फैलने लगी हैं।

(ii) कवि ने कुछ दिन पहले मिट्टी में सेम के कुछ बीज बो दिये थे। उन बीजों के अंकुर फूटे और अनगिनत पत्तों से वह बेलभर गयी और उन्होंने झाड़ी का सा रूप ले लिया है जिसे देखकर ऐसा लगता है कि मानो हरे-भरे कई मुलायम शामियाने तान दिये गये हों।

(iii) कवि ने आँगन में घेर के लिए बाँसों की टटिया बनाई थी, जिसका सहारा लेकर हरे-भरे अनेक अंकुर ऊपर की ओर बढ़ रहे हैं। कवि यहाँ पर वंश के बढ़ने को देखकर अवाक् रह गया।

(iv) कवि ने जो सेम के बीज रोपे थे उनमें से बौने पौधों की पलटन उगने लगी थी जिसे कवि धीरे-धीरे बढ़ता हुआ देख रहा था। धीरे-धीरे वह बेल अगिनत पत्तों से भर गयी और उन्होंने झाड़ी का रूप ले लिया। झाड़ियों को देखकर ऐसा लग रहा है जैसे हरे-भरे कई मुलायम शामियाने तान दिये गये हों। कवि ने आँगन में घेर के लिए बाँसों की टटिया बनायी थी जिसका सहारा लेकर हरे-हरे अनेक अंकुर झरने की भाँति फूट पड़े थे ऊपर की ओर। कवि कहता है कि इस प्रकार वंश के बढ़ने अर्थात् सेम की बेल के बढ़ने को देखकर वह दंग रह गया।

प्रश्न 5. रत्न प्रसविनी है वसुधा, अब समझ सका हूँ।
इसमें सच्ची समता के दाने बोने हैं,
इसमें जन की क्षमता के दाने बोने हैं,
इसमें मानव सभ्यता के दाने बोने हैं,
जिससे उगल सके फिर धूल सुनहली फसलें,
मानवता की जीवन श्रम से हँसें दिशाएँ,
हम जैसा बोयेंगे वैसा ही पायेंगे।

(i) यह वसुधा हमें क्या देती है ?

(ii) 'हम जैसा बोयेंगे वैसा ही पायेंगे' से क्या सन्देश मिलता है ?

(iii) धरती माता को कैसा बताया गया है ?

(iv) प्रस्तुत पंक्तियों का अर्थ लिखिए।

उत्तर—(i) यह वसुधा रत्न प्रसविनी है। जो कुछ हम इसमें बोते हैं वह अनेक गुना करके लौटा देती है।

(ii) धरती में जैसा बोते हैं वैसा ही फल पाते हैं। यदि आम का बीज बोते हैं तो उससे आम ही प्राप्त होंगे। कहावत भी है कि बोये पेड़ बबूल का आम कहाँ ते होइ। जो भी अन्न हम पृथ्वी में बोते हैं उसका कई गुना करके पृथ्वी हमें लौटा देती है।

(iii) धरती माता को रत्न प्रसविनी बताया गया है। धरती में हम जो भी बोते हैं उसको वह अनेक गुना करके लौटा देती है। इसीलिए इसे रत्न प्रसविनी बताया गया है। यह प्रकृति का नियम है कि हम जैसा बीज बोयेंगे वैसा ही फल प्राप्त करेंगे। यदि हम अपनी सद्भावना से प्रेम, सहयोग, समता, एक दूसरे के प्रति सहानुभूति के बीज बोयेंगे तो हमें वही प्राप्त होगा।

(iv) धरती माता रत्नों को जन्म देने वाली है। इसमें पैसों के बीज न बोकर ममता के बीज बोने चाहिए। इसमें मानवता की सुनहरी फसलें उगाई जायेंगी। मनुष्य का परिश्रम चारों ओर प्रसन्नता भर देगा। यदि हम सदभावना का बीज बोयेंगे तो पृथ्वी पर सुख-शान्ति की आनन्ददायी फसल उत्पन्न होगी। इस प्रकार मनुष्य के परिश्रम से पृथ्वी पर धन-धान्य भरपूर रहेगा। इसके लिए मनुष्य-मनुष्य में आपसी प्रेम, सद्भाव, समता और सहानुभूति उत्पन्न करना होगा।

●●

5. नदी के द्वीप

—सच्चिदानंद हीरानंद वात्सायन 'अज्ञेय'

जीवन परिचय— सच्चिदानंद हीरानंद वात्सायन 'अज्ञेय' का जन्म 7 मार्च, 1911 को उत्तर प्रदेश के देवरिया जनपद के 'कसिया' नामक गाँव में हुआ था। इनके पिता का नाम हीरानंद शास्त्री था। क्रान्तिकारी आन्दोलन में भाग लेने के कारण इन्हें कई बार जेल-यात्रा भी करनी पड़ी। पिता की सेवानिवृत्ति के बाद कुछ समय तक ये 'सैनिक' और 'विशाल भारत' के सम्पादकीय विभाग में कार्यरत रहे।

1943 से 1946 तक ये सेना में रहे। यहाँ से मुक्त होने पर इलाहाबाद में प्रकाशित 'प्रतीक' से जुड़ गये। इन्होंने अनेक पत्र-पत्रिकाओं का सम्पादन भी किया। कुछ दिन ये आकाशवाणी से भी सम्बद्ध रहे। कैलीफोर्निया विश्वविद्यालय में इन्होंने कुछ समय तक अध्यापन कार्य भी किया। 4 अप्रैल, 1987 को इनका निधन हो गया।

अज्ञेय जी की प्रतिभा बहुमुखी है। 'जीवन के पार द्वार', 'इत्यलम्' 'हरी घास पर क्षण भर', 'इन्द्रधनुष रौंदे हुए', 'अरी ओ करुणा प्रभामय', 'सुनहले शैवाल', 'कितनी नावों में कितनी बार' तथा 'पूर्वा' इनकी प्रसिद्ध रचनाएँ हैं। सन् 1978 में 'कितनी नावों में कितनी बार' नामक काव्य रचना पर इन्हें ज्ञानपीठ पुरस्कार भी प्राप्त हुआ। इनकी कविता में जीवन की गहरी अनुभूति तथा कल्पना की ऊँची उड़ान का सुन्दर समन्वय हुआ है।

(1)

हम नदी के द्वीप हैं
हम नहीं कहते कि हमको छोड़कर स्रोतस्विनी बह जाए।
वह हमें आकार देती है।
हमारे कोण, गलियाँ, अन्तरीप, उभार, सैकत-कूल,
सब गोलाइयाँ उसकी गढ़ी हैं।

शब्दार्थ—स्त्रोतस्विनी = नदी, **अन्तरीप** = द्वीपों के बीच में उठान, **आकार** = रूप, **कोण** = कोने, **उभार** = उठाव, **सैकत-कूल** = बालू के किनारे, **गढ़ी** = निर्मित।

प्रसंग—प्रस्तुत पद्यांश हमारी पाठ्य पुस्तक के 'नदी के द्वीप' नामक पाठ से लिया गया है।

भावार्थ— कवि कहता है नदी ही द्वीप का निर्माण करती है। वही द्वीप को आकार में ढालती है। द्वीप नहीं चाहता कि नदी उसकी उपेक्षा करती हुई आगे निकल जाये। द्वीप के कोण, उसके मध्य का उठान, उसके मार्ग, बालू के किनारे सभी गोलाकार आकृति नदी की ही देन हैं। द्वीप को नदी से अलग नहीं किया जा सकता।

(2)

माँ है वह ! इसी से हम बने हैं,
किन्तु हम हैं द्वीप ! हम धारा नहीं हैं,
स्थिर समर्पण है हमारा, हम सदा से द्वीप हैं स्रोतस्विनी के।
किन्तु हम बहते नहीं हैं।
क्योंकि बहना रेत होना है।
हम बहेंगे, तो रहेंगे ही नहीं।
पैर उखड़ेंगे, प्लवन होगा, ढहेंगे, सहेंगे बढ़ जायेंगे,
और फिर हम पूर्ण होकर भी कभी क्या धार बन सकते ?

रेत बनकर हम सलिल को तनिक गँदला ही करेंगे।
अनुपयोगी ही बनायेंगे।

शब्दार्थ—**समर्पण** = त्याग, **प्लवन** = धरती का जल से पूर्ण होना, **ढहेंगे** = टूट गकर गिर जायेंगे, **सलिल** = जल, **गँदला** = गंदा, **अनुपयोगी** = जो उपयोग के लायक न हो।

प्रसंग—कवि कहता है कि द्वीप का अस्तित्व स्थिर रहने पर ही है। यदि नदी इनका कटाव कर देगी तो इनका अस्तित्व नहीं रहेगा।

भावार्थ—कवि कहता है कि द्वीप को नदी से अलग नहीं किया जा सकता। नदी से ही इसका जन्म होता है। द्वीप कभी भी नदी की प्रवाहित होने वाली धारा नहीं बन सकते। द्वीप का अस्तित्व स्थिर रहते हुए त्याग की भावना में है। वे हमेशा ही नदी के द्वीप कहलाते हैं। वे नदी की गति के साथ नहीं चलते। यदि वे नदी के साथ प्रवाहित हो जायेंगे तो स्वयं रेत बन जायेंगे और उनका अस्तित्व समाप्त हो जायेगा। यदि ये अपने स्थान से डिग जायेंगे, तो सभी स्थान जल से पूर्ण हो जायेंगे, इनके किनारे कट-छँटकर गिरेंगे जिसे उन्हें सहन करना पड़ेगा। यदि ये चूर्ण हो जायें तो भी धारा नहीं बन सकते। रेत बनने के बाद ये द्वीप जल को गंदा ही करेंगे। वह जल पीने के उपयोग में नहीं रहेगा।

व्यक्ति का अस्तित्व समाज के अनुरूप चलने में है। समाज के विपरीत चलने में उसका कोई अस्तित्व नहीं है। समाज के हित में कार्य करने से व्यक्ति के व्यक्तित्व का विकास होगा। व्यक्ति अपनी विकृतियों को समाज में मिश्रित न होने दे तभी समाज का परिवेश दूषित नहीं होगा।

(3)

द्वीप हैं हम ! यह नहीं है शाप, यह अपनी नियति है।
हम नदी के पुत्र हैं, बैठे नहीं की क्रोड में,
वह वृहत भूखंड से हमको मिलाती है,
और वह भूखंड अपना पितर है।

शब्दार्थ—**शाप** = अभिशाप, **नियति** = भाग्य, **क्रोड** = गोद, **वृहद** = विशाल, **भूखंड** = भू भाग, **पितर** = पिता।

प्रसंग—द्वीप का यही भाग्य है कि वह नदी के बीच में है। नदी ने उसे सजाया और सँवारा है।

भावार्थ—कवि कहता है कि द्वीप बनना कोई अभिशाप नहीं है। यह तो उनका भाग्य है कि वे नदी के पुत्र हैं तथा उसकी बीच धारा में बैठे हैं। वे नदी की गोद में बैठे हैं। नदी उनका अस्तित्व शेष भू-भाग से जोड़ती है। इस विशाल भू-भाग से ही उनका जन्म हुआ है। अतः यह भू-भाग ही उनके पिता के समान है। कहने का तात्पर्य है कि व्यक्ति को समाज ने ही मानवीय गुणों को दिया है। समाज ही उसके व्यक्तित्व का निर्माण करता है। समाज के बीच में ही मनुष्य रहता है इसलिए समाज ही उसका निर्माता है।

अभ्यास-प्रश्न

प्रश्न 1. 'नदी के द्वीप' नामक कविता कवि ने प्रतीकात्मक रूप में लिखी है। नदी के द्वीप किसके प्रतीक हैं और कैसे ?

उत्तर—कवि द्वीप के प्रतीकात्मक अर्थ के माध्यम से कहते हैं कि जिस प्रकार नदी द्वीप का निर्माण करती है, उसी प्रकार समाज के द्वारा व्यक्ति के व्यक्तित्व का निर्माण होता है। नदी ही द्वीप का निर्माण करती है। वही द्वीप को आकार में ढालती है। द्वीप नहीं चाहता कि नदी उसकी उपेक्षा करती हुई आगे बह जाये। जैसे द्वीप को नदी से अलग नहीं किया जा सकता उसी प्रकार मनुष्य का निर्माण समाज के द्वारा होता है। उसका अस्तित्व समाज के कारण ही है। इसलिए मनुष्य को समाज से अलग नहीं किया जा सकता है।

द्वीप कभी धारा में नहीं बह सकते। द्वीप का अस्तित्व स्थिर रहते हुए त्याग की भावना में है। यदि द्वीप अपने स्थान से डिग जायेंगे, तो सभी स्थान जल से परिपूर्ण हो जायेंगे। व्यक्ति का अस्तित्व समाज के साथ चलने में है। समाज के विपरीत चलने में उसका अस्तित्व ही नष्ट हो जाता है। समाज के हित में काम करने से व्यक्ति के व्यक्तित्व का विकास होगा। व्यक्ति को चाहिए कि वह अपनी विकृतियों को समाज में मिश्रित न होने दे। इससे समाज का परिवेश दूषित होगा जो सभी व्यक्तियों को हानि पहुँचायेगा। द्वीप का बनना कोई अभिशाप नहीं है। यह तो उसका भाग्य है कि वह नदी की गोद में बैठा है। नदी द्वीपों के अस्तित्व को शेष भू-भागों से जोड़ती है। ये भू-भाग द्वीप के पिता के समान हैं। कहने का तात्पर्य है कि व्यक्ति को समाज ने ही मानवीय गुणों को दिया है। समाज ही उसके व्यक्तित्व का निर्माण करता है। समाज के बीच में ही मनुष्य रहता है। अर्थात् समाज ही मनुष्य का जन्मदाता है।

प्रश्न 2. हम नदी के द्वीप हैं,
हम नहीं कहते कि हमको छोड़कर स्रोतस्विनी बह जाये।
वह हमें आकार देती है।
हमारे कोण; गलियाँ, अन्तरीय, उभार, सैकत-कूल, सब गोलाइयाँ, उसकी गढ़ी हैं।

(i) द्वीप आखिर क्या है ?

(ii) द्वीपों की अभिलाषा क्या है ?

(iii) द्वीपों की शकल कौन बनाता है ?

(iv) प्रस्तुत पंक्तियों का अर्थ लिखिए।

उत्तर—(i) द्वीप नदी के बीच में छोड़ी हुई जगह है जो नदी के साथ बह नहीं जाती। वह अपने स्थान पर स्थिर रहती है।

(ii) द्वीप यह नहीं चाहते कि नदी उन्हें छोड़कर आगे बढ़ जाये। नदी ने ही उन्हें बनाया है, इसलिए नदी उनकी उपेक्षा नहीं कर सकती।

(iii) द्वीपों को शक्ल नदी ही देती है। वह उन्हें आकार देती है। उनके कोण, गलियाँ, अन्तरीय, उभार, सैकत-कूल और गोलाइयाँ नदी के द्वारा ही निर्मित है।

(iv) द्वीप कहते हैं कि हम नदी के ही द्वीप हैं। हम नदी की ही देन हैं। हम यह नहीं कहते कि नदी हमारी उपेक्षा करके आगे बढ़ी चली जाये। वह हमें आकार देती है। हमारे कोण, गलियाँ, अन्तरीय, उभार, सैकत-कूल और सब गोलाइयाँ नदी की ही देन है।

प्रश्न 3. माँ है वह ! इसी से हम बने हैं,
किन्तु हम हैं द्वीप ! हम धारा नहीं हैं,
स्थिर समर्पण है हमारा, हम सदा से द्वीप हैं स्रोतस्विनी के।
किन्तु हम बहते नहीं हैं।
क्योंकि बहना रेत होना है।
हम बहेंगे तो रहेंगे ही नहीं।
पैर उखड़ेंगे, प्लवन होगा, ढहेंगे, सहेंगे बढ़ जायेंगे,
और फिर हम पूर्ण होकर भी कभी क्या धार बन सकते ?
रेत बनकर हम सलिल को तनिक गँदला ही करेंगे।
अनुपयोगी ही बनायेंगे।

(i) द्वीप चूर्ण होकर क्या बन सकते हैं ?

(ii) यहाँ किसके बारे में क्या कहा गया है

(iii) द्वीप क्यों नहीं बहना चाहते ?

(iv) प्रस्तुत पंक्तियों का अर्थ लिखिए।

उत्तर—(i) द्वीप यदि चूर्ण भी हो जायें तो भी नदी की धारा नहीं बन सकते। वे रेत बनकर पानी को कुछ गंदा ही करेंगे।

(ii) यहाँ नदी के द्वीपों के बारे में कहा गया है कि वे बहती नदी में भी स्थिर हैं, उसके साथ बहते नहीं हैं। वे रेत नहीं बनना चाहते क्योंकि रेत बनने से पानी थोड़ा गन्दा ही होगा।

(iii) द्वीप रेत बनकर बहना नहीं चाहते क्योंकि इससे उनका अस्तित्व ही समाप्त हो जायेगा और नदी का पानी भी गन्दा हो जायेगा। वे तो स्थिर हैं और स्थिर ही रहना चाहते हैं।

(iv) कवि कहता है कि द्वीप को नदी से अलग नहीं किया जा सकता। नदी से ही उसका जन्म होता है। द्वीप कभी भी नदी की प्रवाहित होने वाली धारा नहीं बन सकते। द्वीप का अस्तित्व स्थिर रहते हुए त्याग की भावना में है। वे हमेशा ही नदी के द्वीप कहलाते हैं। वे नदी की गति के साथ नहीं चलते। यदि वे नदी के साथ प्रवाहित हो जायेंगे तो स्वयं रेत बन जायेंगे और उनका अस्तित्व समाप्त हो जायेगा। यदि वे अपने स्थान से डिग जायेंगे, तो सभी स्थान जल से पूर्ण हो जायेंगे, इनके किनारे कट-छँटकर गिरेंगे जिसे उन्हें सहन करना पड़ेगा। यदि वे चूर्ण हो जायें तो भी धारा नहीं बन सकते। रेत बनने के बाद वे द्वीप जल को गन्दा ही करेंगे। वह जल पीने के उपयोग में भी नहीं रहेगा।

प्रश्न 4. द्वीप हैं हम ! यह नहीं है शाप, यह अपनी नियति है।
हम नदी के पुत्र हैं, बैठे नदी की क्रोड में,
वह वृहत भूखण्ड से हमको मिलती है,
और वह भूखण्ड अपना पिता है।

(i) द्वीप की नियति क्या है ?

(ii) द्वीप अपने को कैसा मानते हैं ?

(iii) द्वीप के माता और पिता कौन हैं ?

(iv) इन पंक्तियों का अर्थ लिखिए।

उत्तर—(i) द्वीप अपने को शाप नहीं मानते बल्कि अपने को भाग्यवश द्वीप बनना मानते हैं।

(ii) द्वीप अपने को शाप नहीं बल्कि अपना भाग्य मानते हैं। द्वीप होना उनके भाग्य में लिखा था इसलिए वे द्वीप हैं।

(iii) द्वीप की माता नदी है और पिता भूखण्ड है। वे अपनी माता नदी की गोद में बैठे हैं।

(iv) कवि के अनुसार द्वीप कहते हैं कि वे शाप नहीं हैं बल्कि उनका द्वीप होना उनका भाग्य है। वे नदी के पुत्र हैं और नदी की गोद में बैठे हैं। नदी उनको एक बड़े भूखण्ड से उनको मिलाती है। वह भूखण्ड उनका पिता है।

6. तुलसीदास के पद

—तुलसीदास

जीवन परिचय—महाकवि तुलसीदास के जन्म और मृत्यु के विषय में विद्वानों में अलग-अलग मत हैं। अधिकांश विद्वान मानते हैं कि इनका जन्म उत्तर प्रदेश के बाँदा जिले के राजापुर नामक गाँव में सन् 1532 में हुआ था। कुछ विद्वान इनका जन्म स्थान सोरों मानते हैं। इनके पिता का नाम आत्माराम दुबे और माता का नाम हुलसी था। कहते हैं कि बचपन में ही इनके माता-पिता की मृत्यु हो गई थी इसलिए इनको दासी की माँ ने पाला था। कुछ विद्वानों का मत है कि इनके जन्म को अनिष्ट मानकर इनके माता-पिता ने अपनी दासी को दे दिया था और दासी इनको अपनी माँ के यहाँ छोड़ आई। सत्य जो भी हो इनका बचपन तो बड़ी कठिनाई में बीता। इनके गुरु नरहरिदास थे जिन्होंने इनको अध्ययन करवाया और काशी में इन्होंने पुराण तथा अन्य शास्त्रों का अध्ययन किया। इनका विवाह रत्नावली के साथ हुआ जो सुशिक्षित थी। इनकी मृत्यु सन् 1623 में हुई थी।

तुलसी राम के अनन्य भक्त थे। संवत् 1631 में इन्होंने 'रामचरित मानस' की रचना प्रारम्भ की। इसके अतिरिक्त 'दोहावली', 'गीतावली', 'कवितावली', 'विनय पत्रिका', 'जनकी मंगल', 'हनुमान बाहुक', आदि इनके प्रमुख ग्रन्थ हैं।

तुलसी की भाषा ब्रज और अवधी दोनों रही हैं। 'रामचरित मानस' इनका सर्वाधिक लोकप्रिय ग्रन्थ है। इसकी गणना विश्व के प्रमुख ग्रन्थों में की जाती है। इस ग्रन्थ में भारतीय संस्कृति, धर्म, दर्शन तथा भक्ति का अद्‌भुत समन्वय देखने को मिलता है। इसमें मर्यादा पुरुषोत्तम राम के जीवन का मार्मिक रूप से वर्णन किया गया है। यह ग्रन्थ आज भी जनमानस को आदर्श जीवन के निर्माण की प्रेरणा देता है। तुलसी ने राम के शक्ति, शील तथा सौन्दर्य समन्वित रूप की अवतारणा की है। 'कवितावली' और 'विनय पत्रिका' भी जनमानस में प्रमुख रूप से देखे और पढ़े जाते हैं।

(कवितावली : बालकांड)

(1)

दूलह श्री रघुनाथ बने दुलही सिय सुन्दर मन्दिर माहीं।
गावति गीत सबै मिलि सुन्दर बेद जुवा जुरि विप्र पढ़ाहीं॥
राम को रूप निहारति जानकी, कंकन के नग की परछाहीं।
यातें सबै सुधि भूलि गई कर टेकि रही पल टारत नाहीं।।

शब्दार्थ—**जुवा** = युवा, **जुरि** = इकट्ठे, **विप्र** = ब्राह्मण, **निहारति** = देखतीं, **नग** = गहनों में लगाया जाने वाला कीमती पत्थर, **परछाहीं** = परछाईं, **यातै** = इससे, **सबै** = सब, **सुधि** = याद, **टारत** = जाने देना।

प्रसंग—प्रस्तुत पद तुलसीदास द्वारा रचित 'कवितावली' से लिया गया है। इसमें श्रीराम और सीताजी के विवाह का वर्णन किया गया है।

भावार्थ—तुलसीदास कहते हैं कि दूल्हा बने श्रीराम और दुल्हन बनी सीताजी सुन्दर भवन में बैठे हैं, सुन्दर स्त्रियाँ मिल कर गीत गा रही हैं और युवा विप्र (ब्राह्मण) मिलकर वेद मन्त्रों का मधुर उच्चारण कर रहे हैं। सीताजी संकोचवश श्रीराम का रूप प्रत्यक्ष नहीं देख पाई हैं इसलिए अब अपने हाथ में पहने हुए कंगन के नग में उनके सुन्दर रूप की परछाईं देखकर प्रसन्न हो रही हैं। उनके रूप की सुन्दरता देखकर सभी सुधि भूल गईं और अपने हाथ को वहीं रखे रहीं और एक पल को भी उस नग से अपनी नजर नहीं उठाई। श्रीराम की अनुपम सुन्दरता का वर्णन बड़ा ही सजीव है और जानकी जी की लज्जा का भी समावेश इसमें प्रदर्शित होता है।

(2)

(कवितावली : अयोध्या काण्ड)

कागर कीर ज्यों भूषण-चीर सरीरु लस्यो तजि नीरू ज्यों काई।
मातु-पिता प्रिय लोग सबै सनमानी सुभायै सनेह सगाई।।
संग सुभामिनि, भाइ भलो, दिन, द्वै जनु औध हुते पहुनाई।
राजिव लोचन रामु चले तजि बाप को राज बटाऊ की नाईं॥

शब्दार्थ—**कागर** = मुलायम पर, **कीर** = तोता, **भूषण** = गहने, **चीर** = वस्त्र, **लसे** = सुन्दर लगता है, **सनमानी** = सम्मान किया, **सुभायै** = अच्छे लगे, **सुभामिन** = सुन्दर स्त्री (सीताजी), **दन द्वै** = दो दिन, थोड़ी अवधि तक, **जनु** = मानो, **औध** = अयोध्या, **हुते** = हुए, **पहुनाई** = मेहमान, **राजिव लोचन** = कमल के समान सुन्दर नेत्रों वाले, **बटाऊ** = पथिक, यात्री, **नाई** = के समान।

प्रसंग—इन पंक्तियों में तुलसीदास जी ने यह वर्णन किया है राम अपनी पत्नी सीता और भाई लक्ष्मण के साथ पिता के राज्य को छोड़कर वन को चल दिये।

भावार्थ—तुलसीदास कहते हैं कि तोता अपने मुलायम पर छोड़ देता है, शरीर अपने राजसी वस्त्र और आभूषण तज कर भी सुन्दर लगता है जैसे काई के हट जाने से जल निर्मल लगता है। कहने का तात्पर्य यह है कि सीता रामजी और लक्ष्मण जी ने राजसी वस्त्र और आभूषण त्यागकर गेरुए वस्त्र धारण किये थे फिर भी उनके शरीर ऐसे ही सुन्दर लग रहे थे जैसे काई के हट जाने से नीर निर्मल और सुन्दर लगता है। तोते के अपने मुलायम पर को त्यागने से उसकी सुन्दरता पर कोई प्रभाव नहीं पड़ता है उसी प्रकार इन तीनों के राजसी वस्त्र और आभूषण त्याग देने से कोई प्रभाव नहीं पड़ा। जब तक ये अयोध्या में रहे तब माता-पिता, प्रिय लोग सभी ने इनसे प्रेम किया और इनका सम्मान किया। दो दिन (वह अवधि जब तक राम, सीता और लक्ष्मण अयोध्या में रहे) तक ये अयोध्या में रहे तो इनका मेहमान की भाँति आदर सत्कार किया गया। कवि ने इनको मेहमान इसलिए कहा कि अब ये अयोध्या से वन के लिए प्रस्थान कर रहे हैं। कमल के समान सुन्दर नेत्रों वाले राम अपने पिता के राज्य को ऐसे ही छोड़कर चल दिये जैसे कोई पथिक विश्राम करने के बाद निर्लेप भाव से उस स्थान को छोड़कर चल देता है। श्रीराम को भी पिता के राज्य का कोई लोभ-लालच नहीं है।

(3)

(विनय पत्रिका)

जाऊँ कहाँ तजि चरन तुम्हारे।
काको नाम पतित पावन जग केहि अति दीन पियारे।
कौने देव बराइ बिरद हठ, हठि-हठि अधम उधारे।
खग, मृग, व्याघ, पषान, विटप जड़, जवन-कवन सुर तारे।
देव, दनुज, मुनि, नाग, मनुज सब, माया-बिबस बिचारे।
तिनके हाथ दास तुलसी प्रभु, कहा अपनुपौ हारे।।

शब्दार्थ—**तजि** = छोड़कर, **काको** = किसका, **पावन** = पवित्र, **जग** = संसार में, **केहि** = किसको, **कौने** = कौन, **देव** = देवता, **विरद हठ** = अपने प्रण की रक्षा के लिए, **हठि-हठि** = हठ करके, **मृग** = हिरन (मारीच), **व्याध** = बहेलिया (बाल्मीकि), **विटर** = पेड़ (यमलार्जुन), **माया-बिबस** = माया के वश में, **अपनयौ हारे** = अपने को हार कर।

प्रसंग—यहाँ कवि कलियुग के दु:खों से दु:खी होकर भगवान राम से विनय कर रहा है कि उसका उद्धार करें।

भावार्थ—यहाँ कविवर तुलसीदास कहते हैं कि हे नाथ (श्रीराम) आपके चरणों को छोड़कर और कहाँ जाऊँ ? संसार में 'पतित पावन' नाम और किसका है ? और आपकी तरह दीन-दुखियारे लोग किसे बहुत प्यारे हैं ? अर्थात् न तो कोई देवता पापियों का उद्धार करने वाला है और न ही किसी को दीन-हीन प्यारे हैं।

आज तक किस देवता ने अपने बाने को रखने के लिए हठपूर्वक चुन-चुनकर पापियों का उद्धार किया है ? किस देवता ने पक्षी (जटायु), मृग (मारीच), व्याध (बाल्मीकि), पषान (अहिल्या), जड़ वृक्ष (यमलार्जुन) और यवनों का उद्धार किया है ?

देवता, दैत्य, मुनि, नाग, मनुष्य आदि सभी बेचारे माया के वश में हैं अर्थात् ये स्वयं बँधे हुए हैं तो दूसरों के मायारूपी बन्धन को कैसे खोल सकते हैं ? अर्थात् नहीं खोल सकते। इसीलिए हे प्रभो ! यह तुलसीदास अपने को उन लोगों के हाथ में सौंप कर क्या करे ? मैं तो आपकी शरण में ही आया हूँ।

अभ्यास-प्रश्न

प्रश्न 1. 'तुलसीदास अपने युग के लोक नायक थे।' इस कथन की समीक्षा कीजिए।

उत्तर— जब कोई समाज अपनी उन्नति का मार्ग नहीं ढूँढ़ पाता तब उसे जो व्यक्ति वास्तविक मार्ग दिखाता है वह समाज का लोकनायक माना जाता है जिस युग में तुलसीदास ने 'रामचरित् मानस' की रचना की थी उस युग में भारतीय समाज अपने प्राचीन गौरव, भारतीय प्राचीन आदर्श परम्परा और उस दर्शन को भूल चुका था, जिसका प्रकाश भारत के प्राचीन ऋषियों ने फैलाया था। आपसी द्वेषभाव एवं विदेशी आक्रमण के कारण यहाँ की परम्परागत शिक्षा-व्यवस्था नष्ट हो चुकी थी। देश की राज्य व्यवस्था तथा सामाजिक व्यवस्था भी आदर्श रूप में नहीं थी। भारत विदेशी शासकों का गुलाम हो चुका था। समाज में कोई दिशा नहीं दिख रही थी। सामान्य कविताओं में भक्ति की जो धारा बह रही थी, वह भारतीयों को आध्यात्मिक मार्ग पर तो ले जा रही थी, लेकिन एक आदर्श व्यवस्था से परिचय कराने में वह सक्षम नहीं थी।

ऐसे समय में तुलसीदास ने 'रामचरित् मानस' नामक एक ऐसे ग्रन्थ की रचना की जो राज्य-व्यवस्था, सामाजिक व्यवस्था, नीति व्यवस्था और मानव चरित्र की उत्कृष्ट छवि प्रस्तुत करने में समर्थ था। आध्यात्मिक ग्रन्थ होने के साथ-साथ इसमें दर्शन, सामाजिक व्यवस्था, शिष्टता, राजा-प्रजा, भाई-भाई, पिता-पुत्र एवं पति-पत्नी के आदर्श रूप की अभिव्यक्ति भी थी। इन्होंने अंधकार में भटकते भारतीय समाज को जीवन के उस आदर्श से परिचित कराया, जो वास्तव में भारतीय समाज का मौलिक जीवन दर्शन था और उसे भारतीय समाज भूल चुका था। जब मुगल-संस्कृति राज्य एवं सम्पत्ति के लिए छल-प्रपंच, हिंसा एवं अत्याचार का मार्ग अपनाने हेतु जनमानस को प्रेरित कर रही थी, उस समय तुलसीदास ने राम और भरत के रूप में एक आदर्श प्रस्तुत किया। इसमें भाई-भाई का प्रेम, पिता-पुत्र का प्रेम, राजा का आदर्श और प्रजा का कर्तव्य श्रेष्ठ रूप में प्रस्तुत किया गया है। राम एक आदर्श राजा हुए जिनके राज्य में पूरी प्रजा सुखी थी। राम के चरित्र में तुलसीदास ने मानव-व्यक्तित्व के सभी आदर्श गुणों को समाविष्ट कर दिया। उन्होंने गुरु-शिष्य, पिता-पुत्र, माता-पुत्र के सम्बन्ध और सामाजिक शिष्टता के आदर्श का चित्रण किया। इसके साथ ही तुलसी ने विश्व-मानवता के लिए आध्यात्मिक आदर्श प्रस्तुत किया।

तुलसीदास ने अपने ग्रन्थ में दिशाहीन भारतीय समाज को प्रत्येक क्षेत्र में मार्ग दिखाया और उसके सामने मानव जीवन के एक ऐसे आदर्श को रखा, जो वास्तव में संसार के प्रत्येक मनुष्य और प्रत्येक समाज के लिए आदर्श हो सकता है। तुलसी का यह ग्रन्थ भारतीय समाज के घर-घर में पूजा की वस्तु बन गया। इस ग्रन्थ के साथ उन्होंने कवितावली, गीतावली, हनुमान बाहुक, विनय पत्रिका आदि पुस्तकें लिखकर मनुष्य को धर्म के मार्ग पर चलने को प्रेरित किया। विनय पत्रिका में तो उन्होंने कलियुग के पापों और मोहमाया से बचते हुए भगवान राम की शरणागति के लिए मनुष्य को प्रेरित किया है। इन्होंने भारतीय समाज के बिखरते आदर्शों को फिर से संगठित कर दिया और सम्पूर्ण मानव-समाज के लिए आदर्श भावात्मक समाज की रूपरेखा प्रस्तुत की। इसी कारण तुलसीदास को अपने युग का लोकनायक कहा जाता है।

प्रश्न 2. प्रस्तुत पुस्तक में तुलसीदास ने अपने पहले और दूसरे पद में क्या बात कही है ?

उत्तर—पहले पद में तुलसीदास ने रामजी और सीताजी के विवाह का वर्णन किया है कि जनकपुर के सुन्दर भवन में रघुनाथ जी दूल्हा बने हैं और जानकीजी दुल्हन बनी हैं और स्त्रियाँ मंगल गीत गा रही हैं और युवा विप्र वेद मन्त्रों का उच्चारण कर रहे हैं। जानकी जी श्रीराम के सुन्दर रूप की परछाईं अपने हाथ के कंगन के नग में एकटक देख रही हैं। वे इस परछाईं की सुन्दरता को देखती रहीं और सब बातें भूल गईं।

दूसरे पद में तुलसी ने कहा है कि राम अपनी भार्या और भाई लक्ष्मण के साथ अपने पिता के राज्य को ऐसे छोड़कर वन को चले गये जैसे कोई राहगीर विश्राम करके उस जगह को छोड़कर आगे बढ़ जाता है। उसे उस स्थान से कोई लगाव नहीं रहता क्योंकि उसे तो आगे बढ़ना है इसलिए उस स्थान से मोह-ममता नहीं रखता। इसी प्रकार राम ने भी अपने माता-पिता, भाई और अयोध्यावासियों को छोड़कर वन जाने के लिए प्रस्थान किया। अयोध्या में जितने दिन भी रहे एक पाहुने (मेहमान) की तरह रहे और कुछ दिन बाद अयोध्या को छोड़ अपने मार्ग पर चल दिये। उनके साथ सीताजी और भाई लक्ष्मण स्वेच्छा से बन को गये।

प्रश्न 3. तुलसीदास जी ने विनय पत्रिका में बताया है कि भगवान राम ने पतित-पापियों का उद्धार किया है जैसे खग, मृग, व्याध, पषान, विटप-जड़। इनके बारे में संक्षिप्त रूप में बताइए।

उत्तर—तुलसीदास जी ने अपनी पुस्तक 'विनय पत्रिका' में बताया है कि कलियुग के पापों से भगवान राम ही रक्षा कर सकते हैं। उनका नाम पापियों का उद्धार करने वाला और दीन-दु:खियों के कष्ट को दूर करने वाला है। ऐसा कोई देवता नहीं है जो पापियों का उद्धार कर सके। देव, दनुज, मुनि, नाग और मनुष्य सभी भगवान की माया के वश में भ्रमित हैं। ये लोग किसी का कल्याण नहीं कर सकते। जिन-जिन का प्रभु ने उद्धार किया उनका संक्षिप्त वर्णन निम्नलिखित है—

(1) खग—खग जटायु के लिए आया है। जब रावण सीताजी का हरण कर आकाश मार्ग से जा रहा था, तब जटायु ने उड़कर उस पर आक्रमण कर सीताजी को बचाने का प्रयास किया। रावण ने अपनी तलवार से उसके पंख काट दिये जिससे कि वह नीचे गिर पड़ा। जब रामजी लक्ष्मण के साथ आये तो जटायु से उनका वार्तालाप हुआ और उन्होंने अपने हाथों से जटायु का दाह संस्कार किया। इस प्रकार वह उनके धाम को चला गया।

(2) मृग—मृग मारीच राक्षस बना था। वह लंका के राजा रावण का मामा था। उसने मारीच को कपट मृग बनकर राम को भ्रमित करने के लिए कहा। मारीच ने राम के हाथ से मरने में ही अपना कल्याण सोचा। इस प्रकार वह राम के बाण से मारा गया और उनके धाम को चला गया।

(3) व्याध—यहाँ व्याध वाल्मीकि को कहा गया है जो यात्रियों को लूटते थे और बहेलिए का काम भी करते थे। उन्हें नारद जी ने उपदेश दिया और उन्हें 'राम नाम' का मन्त्र दिया। वे राम न कहकर मरा-मरा जपने लगे जो राम हो गया और वही महर्षि वाल्मीकि बने। इनके बारे में एक चौपाई भी है—"उलटा नाम जपत जग जाना। वाल्मीकि भये ब्रह्म समाना।"

दूसरा व्याध वह था जिसने श्रीकृष्ण के पैर पर तीर मारा था और श्रीकृष्ण अपनी लीला समाप्त कर अपने धाम को चले गये थे और बहेलिए का भी कृष्ण के द्वारा उद्धार किया गया।

तीसरी कथा ऐसे है कि एक बहेलिए को एकादशी के दिन कोई पक्षी नहीं मिला और वह भूखा-प्यासा रहा और अगल दिन उसकी मृत्यु हो गई। एकादशी के प्रभाव से उसका भी उद्धार हुआ।

(4) पषान—पाषाण 'अहिल्या' के लिए प्रयोग हुआ है। ये गौतम ऋषि की पत्नी थी। गौतम ऋषि के श्राप से वह पत्थर बन गई थी। श्रीराम लक्ष्मण और विश्वामित्र के साथ यहाँ पर आये तो उन्होंने इस शिला के बारे में पूछा। विश्वामित्र के कहने पर श्रीराम ने अपनी चरण-रज उससे लगा दी जिससे वह स्त्री रूप में परिवर्तित हो गई और राम की स्तुति करक अपने पति के पास चली गई।

(5) विटप-जड़—ये दो वृक्ष थे और श्रापवश यमलार्जुन से वृक्ष बन गये और यशोदा के आँगन में खड़े थे। श्रीकृष्ण को जब यशोदा ने ऊखल से बाँध दिया था तो वे इन दोनों वृक्षों के बीच से होकर निकले। इनके बीच में ऊखड़ फँस गया। जब कृष्ण ने जोर लगाया तो ये दोनों वृक्ष उखड़कर गिर गये और दो दिव्य पुरुष बनकर भगवान की स्तुति करने लगे फिर स्वर्ग को चले गये।

इस प्रकार तुलसीदास जी ने विनय पत्रिका में इनका जिकर इसलिए किया है कि ऐसे अधम जीवों का भी भगवान ने उद्धार किया। मनुष्य को अपनी मोहमाया को छोड़कर भगवान का ही भजन करना चाहिए ?

प्रश्न 4. दूलह श्री रघुनाथ बने दुलही सिय सुन्दर मंदिर माहीं।
गावति गीत सबै मिलि सुन्दर बेद जुवा जुरि विप्र पढ़ाहीं।।
राम को रूप निहारहि जानकी, कंगन के नग की परछाहीं।
यातें सबै सुधि भूलि गई कर टेकि रही पल टारत नाहीं।।

(i) राम का रूप कौन और कैसे निहार रही है ?

(ii) दूल्हा और दुल्हन कौन बने ? बेद कौन पढ़ रहे हैं ?

(iii) सीताजी सब सुधि क्यों भूल गई ?

(iv) प्रस्तुत पंक्तियों का अर्थ लिखिए।

उत्तर—(i) श्रीराम के सुन्दर रूप को सीताजी अपने कंगन के नग में निहार रही हैं।

(ii) दुल्हा अयोध्या के राजा दशरथ के पुत्र श्री रघुनाथ जी बने और दुल्हन जनकपुर के राजा जनक की पुत्री सीताजी बनीं। युवा विप्र इकट्ठे होकर वेदपाठ कर रहे थे।

(iii) श्रीराम के सुन्दर रूप की परछाईं सीतजी के हाथ के कंगन के नग में पड़ रही थी। सीताजी उनकी इस सुन्दर छवि को अपने कंगन के नग में देखकर सब सुधि भूल गईं।

(iv) तुलसीदास कहते हैं कि श्री रघुनाथ जी दूल्हा बने और दुल्हन बनी हुई श्री सीताजी सुन्दर भवन में बैठे हैं। सुन्दर स्त्रियाँ मिलकर गीत गा रही हैं और युवा ब्राह्मण मिलकर वेद मन्त्रों का मधुर उच्चारण कर रहे हैं। सीताजी संकोचवश श्रीराम का रूप प्रत्यक्ष नहीं देख पा रही है इसलिए अपने हाथ के कंगन के नग में उनके सुन्दर रूप की परछाईं देखकर प्रसन्न हो रही है। उनके सुन्दर रूप को देखकर सभी सुधि भूल गईं अपने हाथ को कहीं रखे रहीं और एक पल को भी उस नग से अपनी नजर नहीं उठाई। राम की अनुपम सुन्दरता का वर्णन बड़ा ही सजीव है।

प्रश्न 5. कागर कीर ज्यों भूषण-चीर सरीस लस्यौ तजि नीरू ज्यों काई।
मातु-पिता प्रिय लोग सबै सनकानी सुभायै सनेह सगाई।।
संग सुभामिनि, भाइ चलो, दिन, द्वै जनु औध हुते पहुनाई।
राजिव लोचन रामु चले तजि बाद को राज बटाऊ की नाईं।।

(i) काई के बिना नीर कैसा लगता है ? यह किसके लिए कहा गया है ?

(ii) राम के पिता का राज कैसे छोड़ दिया और क्यों ?

(iii) राम के साथ कौन-कौन और कहाँ गये ?

(iv) प्रस्तुत पंक्तियों का अर्थ लिखिए।

उत्तर—(i) जिस प्रकार काई के हट जाने से पानी की शोभा बढ़ जाती है उसी प्रकार राजसी वस्त्र त्यागकर भी रामजी की शोभा अत्यन्त निराली लग रही है।

(ii) राम ने अपने पिता दशरथ (अयोध्या के राजा) का राज्य ऐसे छोड़ दिया जैसे कोई राहगीर विश्राम के लिए किसी स्थान पर बैठता है और थोड़े विश्राम के बाद उस स्थान को छोड़कर चल देता है। राजा

दशरथ की रानी कैकेयी ने अपने दो वरदानों में से एक में भरत को राज्य और दूसरे वरदान में राम को चौदह वर्ष का वनवास माँगा था।

(iii) राम के साथ उनकी भार्या सीताजी और भाई लक्ष्मण चौदह वर्ष के लिए वन को गये।

(iv) तुलसीदास कहते हैं कि तोता अपने मुलायम पर छोड़कर सुन्दर लगता है उसी प्रकार शरीर भी राजसी वस्त्र और आभूषण तजकर भी सुन्दर लगता है, जैसे काई के हट जाने पर जल निर्मल हो जाता है। तोते के अपने मुलायम पर त्यागने पर उसकी सुन्दरता पर कोई प्रभाव नहीं पड़ता। उसी प्रकार राम, सीता और लक्ष्मण के अपने राजसी वस्त्र त्यागकर गेरुए वस्त्र धारण करने से उनकी सुन्दरता पर कोई प्रभाव नहीं पड़ा। जब तक वे अयोध्या में रहे तब माता-पिता, प्रिय लोग सभी ने इनसे प्रेम किया और इनका सम्मान किया। दो दिन (वह अवध जब वे अयोध्या में रहे) तक वे अयोध्या में रहे तो इनका मेहमान की तरह आदर सत्कार किया। कमल के समान सुन्दर नेत्रों वाले राम अपने पिता के राज्य को पथिक की भाँति छोड़कर चल दिये। राम को पिता के राज्य का कोई मोह नहीं है।

प्रश्न 6. जाऊँ कहाँ तजि चरन तुम्हारे।
काको नाम पतित पावन जग केहि अति दीन पियारे।
कौने देव बराइ बिरद हिव, हठि हठि अधम उधारे।
खग, मृग, व्याध, पषान, विटपजड़, जवन कवन सुर तारे।
देव, दनुज, मुनि, नाग, मनुज सब, माथा बिबस बिचारे।
तिनके हाथ दास तुलसी प्रभु, कहा अपुनयौ हारे।।

(i) किसका नाम पतित पावन है और किसे दीन अत्यन्त प्यारे हैं ?

(ii) माया के वशीभूत कौन-कौन हैं ?

(iii) किसने अपनी प्रतिज्ञा (प्रण) की रक्षा के लिए पापियों का उद्धार किया ?

(iv) प्रस्तुत पंक्तियों का अर्थ लिखिए।

उत्तर—(i) तुलसीदास जी के अनुसार श्रीरामजी का नाम पतित पावन है और उन्हें ही दीन-दु:खी अत्यन्त प्रिय हैं।

(ii) ईश्वर की माया के वशीभूत देव, दनुज, मुनि, नाग और मनुष्य सब हैं। माया का प्रभाव उनके जीवन पर पड़ता है और वे माया के अधीन ही रहते हैं।

(iii) तुलसीदास कहते हैं कि कौन प्रभु श्रीराम की तरह उदार तथा दयालु है जिन्होंने अपने प्रण को रखने के लिए हठपूर्वक चुन-चुनकर पापियों का उद्धार किया। किस देवता ने उदार होकर पक्षी (जटायु), मृग (मारीच), व्याध (बाल्मीकि), पषान (अहिल्या), जड़ वृक्ष (यमलार्जुन) और यवनों का उद्धार किया है।

(iv) देवता, दैत्य, मुनि, नाग, मनुष्य आदि सभी बेचारे माया के वश में हैं अर्थात् ये स्वयं बँधे हुए हैं तो दूसरों के मायारूपी बन्धनों को कैसे खोल सकते हैं ? इसीलिए हे प्रभु ! तुलसीदास अपने को उन लोगों के हाथ में सौंपकर क्या करे ? मैं तो अपनी शरण में ही आया हूँ।

7. जाग तुझको दूर जाना है

—महादेवी वर्मा

जीवन परिचय—महादेवी वर्मा का जन्म 26 मार्च सन् 1907 को फर्रुखाबाद में एक सभ्रान्त कायस्थ परिवार में हुआ। इनके पिता गोविन्द प्रसाद भागलपुर विद्यालय में प्रधानाचार्य थे। इनकी माता हेमरानी देवी विदुषी और भक्त महिला थीं इनको अपनी माँ से काविता, साहित्य तथा भक्ति की प्रेरणा प्राप्त हुई।

इनकी प्राथमिक शिक्षा इन्दौर में हुई। बाल्यकाल से ही इनका झुकाव काव्य की ओर था। इनका विवाह ग्यारह वर्ष की अवस्था में डॉ. स्वरूपनारायण वर्मा के साथ हुआ। इनके ससुराल के विरोध के कारण शिक्षा में विघ्न पड़ा। उन्होंने देहावसान के बाद पुनः शिक्षा प्रारम्भ हुई और संस्कृत में एम. ए. किया।

11 सितम्बर, 1987 को इनका देहान्त हो गया। इनकी प्रसिद्ध रचनाएँ 'नीहार', 'रश्मि', 'नीरजा', 'सांध्य गीत', 'यामा', 'दीपशिखा', 'साधिनी' (काव्य रचनाएँ), 'अतीत के चलचित्र', स्मृति की रेखाएँ', 'श्रृंखला की कड़ियाँ' (निबन्ध संग्रह) तथा आलोचनात्मक निबन्ध संग्रह हैं।

इनके काव्य संग्रह 'नीरजा' पर 'सेक्सरिया पुरस्कार' तथा 'यामा' पर 'मंगला प्रसाद पारितोषिक' प्राप्त हुआ। भारत सरकार ने इन्हें 'पद्म भूषण' की उपाधि से सम्मानित किया। इन्हें ज्ञानपीठ पुरस्कार से भी सम्मानित किया गया। हिन्दी साहित्य सम्मेलन में इन्हें भारतेन्दु पुरस्कार मिला।

(1)

चिर सजग आँखें उनींदी, आज कैसा व्यस्त बाना।
जाग तुझको दूर जाना।।
अचल हिमगिरि के हृदय में आज चाहे कंप हो ले,
या प्रलय के आँसुओं में मौन अलसित व्योम रो ले;
आज पी आलोक को डोले तिमिर की घोर छाया,
आज या विद्युत-शिखाओं में निठुर तूफान बोले !
पर तुझे है नाश-पथ पर चिह्न अपने छोड़ जाना।
जाग तुझको दूर जाना।।

शब्दार्थ—**सजग** = जागरूक, **उनींदी** = नींद से भरी, **बाना** = वेशभूषा, **अलसित** = अलसाया हुआ, **व्योम** = आकाश, **निष्ठुर** = कठोर, **नाश पथ** = विनाश का मार्ग।

प्रसंग—ये पंक्तियाँ महादेवी वर्मा द्वारा कृत 'गीत' से ली गई हैं। इनमें जीवन मंजिल के लिए तय करने वाले अपने मन को विकास की ओर बढ़ने के लिए प्रेरित किया है।

भावार्थ—कवयित्री कहती हैं कि सदैव जागरूक रहने वाले हे मन ! आज तेरी आँखों में नींद कैसे भरी हुई है और तेरी वेशभूषा अस्त-व्यस्त क्यों है ? तू जाग ! क्योंकि तुझे अभी दूर जाना है। तुझे किसी प्रकार की बाधाओं के कारण रुकना नहीं है। चाहे अचल हिमालय के हृदय में कम्पन हो उठे अथवा मौन रहने वाला अलसाया हुआ सा आकाश प्रलय के आँसू बहाकर रो उठे। अर्थात् आकाश में छाये बादल भयंकर वर्षा करने लगें, चाहे अंधकार प्रकाश को पी जाये अथवा बिजली की तरंगों में कठोर तूफान जागकर गर्जन करने लगे, फिर भी तुझे इस विनाश के मार्ग पर अपने निर्माण के चिन्ह छोड़कर आना है। अर्थात् तुझे इन सभी बाधाओं को हटाकर प्रगति पथ पर आगे बढ़ना है। अतः हे राहगीर ! तू सावधान हो जा, तुझे अभी दूर तक जाना है।

(2)

बाँध लेंगे क्या तुझे, यह मोम के बंधन सजीले ?
पंथ की बाधा बनेंगे तितलियों के पर रंगीले ?

विश्व का क्रन्दन भुला देगी मधुप की मधुर गुनगुन,
क्या डुबा देंगे तुझे यह फूल के दल ओस-गीले ?
तू न अपनी छाँह को अपने लिए कारा बनाना।
जाग तुझको दूर जाना।।

शब्दार्थ—**मोम के बंधन** = सांसारिक बन्धन, **सजीले** = आकर्षक, **क्रन्दन** = करुण पुकार, **कारा** = जेल।

प्रसंग—यहाँ कवयित्री ने मन को सजग किया है कि वह सांसारिक आकर्षणों की ओर ध्यान न दे।

भावार्थ—कवयित्री कहती हैं कि हे मन ! क्या सांसारिक आकर्षण तुझे विचलित कर देंगे और तुम अपने लक्ष्य तक नहीं पहुँच पाओगे ? इस क्षण भंगुर संसार के आकर्षण बड़े मोहक हैं, इनसे तुम्हें सावधान रहना है। तितलियों के पंख जैसे सुन्दर और रंगीले आकर्षण क्या तुम्हारे मार्ग में बाधक बनेंगे ? क्या भंवरों की मधुर गुंजार तुझे संसार के करुण-क्रन्दन को भुला देगी ? तुम्हें यह समझ लेना चाहिए कि सांसारिक आकर्षण छाया के समान हैं, स्थिर नहीं है। इसलिए तुम इनके बन्धन में मत पड़ना क्योंकि तुमको अभी दूर तक जाना है और अपना लक्ष्य प्राप्त करना है।

(3)

वज्र का उर एक छोटे अश्रुकण में धो गलाया ?
दे किसे जीवन-सुधा दो घूँट मदिरा माँग लाया ?
सो गई आँधी मलय की बात का उपधान ले क्या ?
विश्व का अभिशाप क्या चिर नींद बनकर पास आया ?
अमरता-सुत चाहता क्यों मृत्यु को उर में बसाना ?
जाग तुझको दूर जाना।।

शब्दार्थ—**मलय** = एक पर्वत का नाम जहाँ चन्दन होता है, **बात** = वायु, **उपधान** = तकिया, **अमरता सुत** = देव पुत्र।

प्रसंग—कवयित्री यहाँ पर मन को दूर लक्ष्य तक पहुँचने की प्रेरणा देती है।

भावार्थ—कवयित्री कहती है कि हे मेरे मन ! तेरा हृदय वज्र के समान था, क्या तूने उसे आँसुओं से धोकर गला दिया है ? क्या तूने अपने असीम साहस को दु:खों से घबराकर खो दिया है ? क्या तूने जीवन रूपी अमृत देकर उसके बदले में केवल दो घूँट मदिरा माँग ली है। संसार के झूठे सुखों के लिए अपने अमूल्य जीवन को नष्ट कर दिया है।

हे मेरे मन ! क्या तुझमें उठने वाली उत्साह रूपी आँधी, मोह एवं आलस्य रूपी मलय का तकिया लगाकर सो गई ? क्या विश्व का अभिशाप आलस्य रूपी नींद के रूप में तुम्हारे पास आ गया है ? तात्पर्य है कि मन में आलस्य आ गया है जिसने उत्साह को समाप्त कर दिया है। हे देव पुत्र ! तू अपने हृदय में मृत्यु को क्यों बसाना चाहता है ? तू सजग बन, आलस्य को त्यागकर अपने पथ पर आगे बढ़ क्योंकि अभी तुझे बहुत दूर तक जाना है।

(4)

कह न ठंडी साँस में अब भूल वह जलती कहानी,
आग हो उर में तभी दृग में सजेगा आज पानी;
हार भी तेरी बनेगी मानिनी जय की पताका,
राख क्षणिक पतंग की है अमर दीपक की निशानी,

है तुझे अंगार शैय्या पर मृदुल कलियाँ बिछाना।
जाग तुझको दूर जाना।।

शब्दार्थ—**ठण्डी साँस** = आह भरना, **जलती कहानी** = कष्टपूर्ण बात, **उर** = हृदय, **दृग** = नेत्र, **अंगार शैया** = तकलीफ भरी परिस्थिति।

प्रसंग— कवयित्री कहती है कि साधना का मार्ग कष्टों और कठिनाइयों से भरा हुआ है। तुमको आहें भरकर इन कष्टों का वर्णन कर हताश नहीं होना चाहिए, बल्कि इन कठिनाइयों पर विजय प्राप्त करते हुए आगे बढ़ना है। आँखों से बहने वाले आँसुओं की महिमा तभी है जब मन में कुछ करने की तीव्र इच्छा की आग हो। साधना पर चलते हुए मिली पराजय भी अन्त में जय की पताका बनती है। अर्थात् साधना के मार्ग के कष्टों को सहने से मन में दृढ़ता, साहस प्राप्त होता है। जैसे पतंगा जलकर भी दीपक की अमर कहानी बन जाता है। तुझको अंगारों की शैया के समान कष्टकारक साधना पथ पर भी मधुर भावना रूपी कलियाँ बिछानी हैं तभी तुझे लक्ष्य की प्राप्ति होगी। अतः तू आलस्य त्यागकर जाग जा क्योंकि तुझे अभी बहुत दूर जाना है।

अभ्यास-प्रश्न

प्रश्न 1. इस कविता में कवयित्री ने अपने मन और मानव को क्या शिक्षा दी है ?

उत्तर—कवयित्री ने इस कविता में अपने मन को सम्बोधित करते हुए मनुष्य को यह सन्देश दिया है कि आज तेरी आँखों में नींद क्यों भरी हुई है और तेरी वेशभूषा अस्त-व्यस्त क्यों है ? तू जाग कि तुझे अभी दूर जाना है। तुझे किसी भी प्रकार की बाधाओं के कारण बीच में रुकना नहीं है। चाहे कितनी ही बड़ी मुसीबत क्यों न आये ? चाहे हिमालय में कम्पन होने लगे या आकाश से प्रलय के बादल बरसें, चाहे अंधकार प्रकाश को लील ले, हमें विनाश के मार्ग पर निर्माण के चिन्ह छोड़कर हमेशा आगे बढ़ना है। ऐसी प्रेरणा कवयित्री ने अपने मन के माध्यम से मनुष्य को दी है।

सांसारिक आकर्षणों में न फसने की राय कवयित्री ने दी है क्योंकि संसार के रंगीन आकर्षणों में फँसकर लोग अपना लक्ष्य भूल जाते हैं और अपने जीवन को नष्ट कर बैठते हैं। संसार के आकर्षण बड़े मोहक होते हैं और राहगीर को अपना रास्ता भुलाकर भटका देते हैं। उनसे सावधान रहना है। भौंरों की मधुर गुंजन में तू संसार में उठते करुण क्रन्दन को भूल मत जाना। तू संसार के किसी बन्धन में न पड़ कर अपनी राह की तरफ अपने कदम बढ़ाता चल।

तूने क्या अपने वज्र जैसे हृदय को आँसुओं में धोकर गला तो नहीं दिया है ? क्या तेरा असीम साहस दुःखों से घबराकर खो गया है ? ऐसा तो नहीं है कि अपने जीवन रूपी अमृत के बदले दो घूँट मदिरा माँग ली है ? अर्थात् संसार के झूठे सुखों के लिए अपने जीवन को नष्ट कर दिया है, तेरे मन में आया आलस्य तेरे उत्साह को समाप्त कर देगा फिर कैसे तू अपने पथ पर आगे बढ़ेगा ? तू जाग और बाधाओं से लड़ता हुआ आगे बढ़।

आगे कवयित्री ने कहा है कि साधना का मार्ग कष्टों से भरा हुआ है। तुझे दुःखी होकर इन कठिनाइयों का वर्णन करके हताश नहीं होना चाहिए। मन में कुछ करने की तीव्र इच्छा हो। अपने मार्ग पर चलते हुए यदि पराजय भी मिलती है तो वह भी अन्त में में जय की पताका बन जाती है। अपने जीवन में आगे बढ़ते हुए कठिनाइयों को सहने पर मन में दृढ़ता और साहस प्राप्त होता है, जैसे पतंगा जलकर भी दीपक की अमर कहानी बन जाता है। तुझको अंगारों की शैया के समान कष्टदायक साधना पथ पर भी मधुर भावना रूपी कलियाँ बिछानी हैं तभी तुम्हें लक्ष्य की प्राप्ति होगी।

कवयित्री ने कहा है कि मन को (मानव) आलस्य त्यागकर निरन्तर अपने निर्माण पथ पर आगे बढ़ना है। कोई संसार का आकर्षण तुम्हारे गति में बाधा न डाल पाये ऐसा प्रयास करना चाहिए।

प्रश्न 2. 'जाग तुझको दूर जाना' कविता का केन्द्रीय भाव लिखिए।

उत्तर—'जाग तुझको दूर जाना' कविता महादेवी वर्मा द्वारा रचित है। इसमें कवयित्री ने अपने मन से कहा है कि तू आलस्य में क्यों है, तुझे इस समय नींद क्यों आ रही है ? तुझे तो अभी बहुत दूर जाना है। रास्ता कठिन है, संसार की बाधाएँ रास्ता रोके खड़ी हैं। तुझे तो उन बाधाओं पर विजय प्राप्त करनी है। चाहे रास्ता कितना ही कठिन हो तेरी गति में रुकावट नहीं आनी चाहिए। हो सकता है कि तेरे सामने प्रकृति की विनाशलीला ही आ जाये पर तुझे किसी हालत में रुकना नहीं है। चाहे हिमालय काँप उठे या आकाश से भीषण वर्षा होने लगे, चाहे अंधकार प्रकाश को निगल जाये तो भी तेरे पग रुकने नहीं चाहिए। तुझे सावधान रहकर आगे बढ़ना है।

हे मेरे मन ! तुझे संसार के आकर्षण अपनी ओर आकर्षित न करने पावें। तू सजग रह क्योंकि ये आकर्षण किसी को भी अपनी ओर खींचकर उसकी राह भुला सकते हैं। भौंरों की मधुर गुंजार मनुष्य को संसार का करुण-क्रन्दन नहीं सुनने देती। अतः उसे सजग रहना चाहिए। संसार के आकर्षण छाया के समान हैं, स्थिर नहीं हैं। इसलिए मन को इनके बंधन में न पड़कर अपने लक्ष्य पर ध्यान केन्द्रित करना है।

अन्य स्थान पर कवयित्री कहती है कि हे मन, तूने अपना वज्र के समान कठोर हृदय आँसुओं में धोकर गला तो नहीं दिया है ? लगता है तूने अपना असीम साहस दुःखों से घबराकर खो दिया है। अपना जीवनरूपी अमृत देकर दो घूँट मदिरा माँग ली है अर्थात् संसार के थोड़े से सुख की खातिर अपना जीवन नष्ट कर दिया है। हे मेरे मन ! क्या तुझमें उठने वाली उत्साहरूपी आँधी मोह एवं आलस्यरूपी मलय का तकिया लगाकर सो गई है ? क्या विश्व का अभिशाप आलस्यरूपी नींद के रूप में तुम्हारे पास आ गया है ?

जीवन में साधना का मार्ग कठिनाइयों से भरा हुआ है तुम्हें इन कष्टों का वर्णन कर हताश नहीं होना चाहिए। आँखों में बहने वाले आँसुओं की महिमा तभी है जब मन में कुछ करने की तीव्र इच्छा की आग हो। साधना पर चलते हुए मिली पराजय भी अन्त में जय की पताका बनकर फहराती है। कष्टों को सहने से मन में दृढ़ता और साहस प्राप्त होता है। अंगारों की शैया (कष्ट) पर तुम्हें भावना रूपी कलियाँ बिछानी हैं तभी तुझे अपने मार्ग में सफलता मिलेगी। हे राही ! जाग तुझको अभी दूर जाना है।

प्रश्न 3. चिर सजग आँखें उनींदीं, आज कैसा व्यस्त बाना।
जाग तुझको दूर जाना।
अचल हिमगिरि के हृदय में आज चाहे कंप होते,
या प्रलय के आँसुओं में मौन अलसित व्योम रो ले;
आज पी आलोक को डोले तिमिर की घोर छाया,
आज या विद्युत-शिखाओं में निठुर तूफान बोले !
पर तुझे है नाश-पथ पर चिन्ह अपने छोड़ आना।
जाग तुझको दूर जाना।

(i) जाग तुझको दूर जाना से क्या तात्पर्य है ?

(ii) कवयित्री ने मनुष्य को इस कविता के माध्यम से क्या प्रेरणा दी है ?

(iii) प्रतिकूल परिस्थितियों में भी मनुष्य साहस और वीरता के साथ आगे बढ़ता है तो क्या सम्भव है ?

(iv) प्रस्तुत पंक्तियों का अर्थ लिखिए।

उत्तर—(i) इस कथन का तात्पर्य यह है कि समय बीतता जा रहा है ऐसे में तुझे जाग जाना चाहिए क्योंकि तुझे जीवन में अभी बहुत से काम करने हैं। जागरुक होकर निरन्तर आगे बढ़ना है।

(ii) कवयित्री ने इस कविता के माध्यम से मनुष्य को यह प्रेरणा दी है कि आज सोने का नहीं बल्कि जागने का समय है। ऐसे समय में तू ऐसे आलस्य में क्यों है ? चाहे कितनी ही बाधाएँ तेरे मार्ग में आयें तू उन सबको परास्त करता हुआ अपने कर्मपथ पर आगे बढ़ा। कितना ही कठिन मार्ग हो पर तू कर्मवीर की तरह उस पथ पर अपने पैरों के निशान छोड़ता चला जा।

(iii) प्रतिकूल परिस्थितियों में भी जब मनुष्य वीरता के साथ आगे बढ़ता है तो सफलता उसका स्वागत करती है। वह अन्य मनुष्यों के लिए जो आगे बढ़ने वाले हैं, मार्ग पर अपने पद चिन्ह छोड़ जाता है। यह संकेत है कि इस पथ पर उससे पहले और भी लोग गये हैं।

(iv) कवयित्री कहती है कि सदैव जागरूक रहने वाले हे मन ! आज तेरी आँखों में नींद कैसे भरी हुई है और तेरी वेशभूषा अस्त-व्यस्त क्यों है ? तू जाग ! क्योंकि तुझे अभी दूर जाना है। तुझे किसी प्रकार की बाधाओं के कारण रुकना नहीं है चाहे अचल हिमालय के हृदय में कम्पन हो उठे अथवा मौन रहने वाला अलसाया हुआ सा आकाश प्रलय के आँसू बहाकर रो उठे अर्थात् आकाश में छाये बादल भयंकर वर्षा करने लगे, चाहे अंधकार प्रकाश को पी जाये अथवा बिजली की तरंगों में कठोर तूफान जमकर गर्जन करने लगे, फिर भी तुझे इस विनाश के मार्ग पर अपने निर्माण के चिन्ह छोड़कर जाता है अर्थात् तुझे इन सभी बाधाओं को हटाकर प्रगति पथ पर आगे बढ़ना है। अत: हे राहगीर ! तू सावधान हो जा क्योंकि तुझे अभी दूर जाना है।

प्रश्न 4. बाँध लेंगे क्या तुझे, यह मोम के बंधन सजीले ?
पंथ की बाधा बनेंगे तितलियों के पर रँगीले ?
विश्व का क्रंदन भुला देगी मधुय की मधुर गुनगुन ?
क्या डुबा देंगे तुझे यह फूल के दल ओस-गीले ?
तू न अपनी छाँह को अपने लिए कारा बनाना ?
जाग तुझको दूर जाना।

(i) पथ की बाधा कौन बनेंगे ?

(ii) कवयित्री ने इन पंक्तियों में क्या अपेक्षा की है ?

(iii) जाग तुझको दूर जाना से कवयित्री का क्या आशय है ?

(iv) प्रस्तुत पंक्तियों का अर्थ लिखिए।

उत्तर—(i) मनुष्य के पथ की बाधा संसार के आकर्षण बनते हैं।

(ii) इन पंक्तियों में कवयित्री ने अपने मन को सजग किया है कि वह सांसारिक आकर्षणों की ओर ध्यान न दे। वह पूछती हैं कि क्या सांसारिक आकर्षण तुझे विचलित कर देंगे और तुम अपने लक्ष्य तक नहीं पहुँच पाओगे ? तुम आकर्षणों को अपने मार्ग में बाधा न बनने देना।

(iii) यहाँ कवयित्री ने अपने मन को सजग किया है कि वह सांसारिक आकर्षणों की ओर ध्यान न दे। इस क्षण भंगुर संसार के आकर्षण बड़े मोहक हैं, इनसे तुम्हें सावधान रहना है। तितलियों के पंख जैसे सुन्दर और रंगीले आकर्षण क्या तुम्हारे मार्ग में बाधक बनेंगे ? तुम्हें समझ लेना चाहिए कि सांसारिक आकर्षण छाया के समान हैं, स्थिर नहीं हैं।

(iv) कवयित्री कहती है कि हे मन ! क्या सांसारिक आकर्षण तुझे विचलित कर देंगे और तुम अपने लक्ष्य तक नहीं पहुँच पाओगे ? इस क्षण भंगुर संसार के आकर्षण बड़े मोहक हैं, इनसे तुम्हें सावधान रहना है। तितलियों के पंख जैसे सुन्दर और रंगीले आकर्षण क्या तुम्हारे मार्ग में बाधा बनेंगे ? क्या भँवरों की मधुर गुंजार तुझे संसार के करुण-क्रन्दन को भुला देगी ? तुम्हें यह समझ लेना चाहिए कि सांसारिक आकर्षण छाया के समान हैं, स्थिर नहीं हैं। इसलिए तुम इनके बन्धन में मत पड़ना क्योंकि तुमको अभी दूर तक जाना है और अपना लक्ष्य प्राप्त करना है।

प्रश्न 5. कह न ठंडी साँस में अब भूल वह जलती कहानी,
आग हो उर में तभी दृग में सजेगा आज पानी;
हार भी तेरी बनेगी मानिनी जय की पताका,
राख क्षणिक पतंग की है अमर दीपक की निशानी,
है तुझे अंगार शैया पर मृदुल कलियाँ बिछाना।
जाग तुझको दूर जाना।

(i) हार भी जय की पताका कब बन जाती है ?

(ii) कवयित्री ने हमसे क्या अपेक्षा की है ?

(iii) पतंगें की कहानी क्या है ? वह दीपक की लौ पर अपने को क्यों बलिदान कर देता है ?

(iv) प्रस्तुत पंक्तियों का अर्थ लिखिए ?

उत्तर—(i) मनुष्य जब अपने प्रबल मन में साहस और उत्साह भरकर अपने पथ पर आगे बढ़ता है तो उसकी हार भी जय में बदल जाती है।

(ii) कवयित्री को हमसे यह अपेक्षा है कि हमें अपने मार्ग की बाधाओं से दु:खी होकर हताश नहीं होना चाहिए। मन में कुछ करने की तीव्र इच्छा हो। अपने मार्ग पर चलते हुए यदि पराजय भी मिलती है तो वह भी अन्त में जय की पताका बन जाती है। अपने जीवन में आगे बढ़ते हुए कठिनाइयों को सहने पर मन में दृढ़ता और साहस प्राप्त होता है।

(iii) पतंगा दीपक की लौ पर जलकर दीपक की अमर कहानी बन जाता है। दीपक की लौ अपना सर्वस्व बलिदान करने के लिए आकर्षित करती है। अत: वह मोहित होकर दीपक की लौ पर न्योछावर हो जाता है।

(iv) कवयित्री कहती है कि साधना का मार्ग कष्टों और कठिनाइयों से भरा हुआ है। तुम्हें इन कष्टों से हताश नहीं होना चाहिए, बल्कि इन कठिनाइयों पर विजय प्राप्त करते हुए आगे बढ़ाना है। आँखों से बहते हुए आँसुओं की महिमा तभी है जब मन में कुछ करने की तीव्र इच्छा हो। साधना पर चलते हुए मिली पराजय भी अन्त में जय की पताका बन जाती है। अर्थात् साधना के मार्ग के कष्टों को सहने से मन में दृढ़ता व साहस प्राप्त होता है। जैसे पतंगा जलकर भी दीपक की अमर कहानी बन जाता है। तुझको अंगारों की शैया के समान कष्टदायक साधना पथ पर भी मधुर भावनारूपी कलियाँ बिछानी हैं तभी तुझे लक्ष्य की प्राप्ति होगी। अत: तू आलस्य त्यागकर जाग जा क्योंकि तुझे अभी बहुत दूर जाना है।

8. उद्यमी नर

—रामधारी सिंह 'दिनकर'

जीवन परिचय—रामधारी सिंह 'दिनकर' का जन्म 30 सितम्बर, 1906 को बिहार राज्य के मुंगेर जिले के सिमरिया गाँव में हुआ। भारत सरकार ने इन्हें 'पद्म भूषण' से सम्मानित किया। 24 अप्रैल, 1974 को इनका निधन हो गया।

दिनकर जी की कविता का मूल स्वर सौन्दर्य, प्रेम, राष्ट्रवाद, प्रगतिशीलता, प्रकृति चित्रण, भारत के अतीत का गुणगान तथा क्रान्तिकारी भावना है। इन्होंने गद्य और पद्य दोनों क्षेत्रों में अपनी प्रतिभा को निखारा है। इन्होंने यात्रा, संस्मरण, आलोचना, संस्कृति, इतिहास, धर्म और दर्शन के क्षेत्र में भी रचनाएँ की हैं। इनके काव्य 'उर्वशी' पर इन्हें भारतीय ज्ञानपीठ की ओर से एक लाख रुपये का पुरस्कार प्राप्त हुआ।

दिनकर जी ने भारत सरकार की हिन्दी समिति के सलाहकार और आकाशवाणी में निर्देशक के पद पर रहकर हिन्दी के उत्थान के लिए कार्य किये। दिनकर प्रारम्भ से ही लोक के प्रति निष्ठावान, सामाजिक उत्तरदायित्व के प्रति सजग और जनसाधारण के प्रति समर्पित कवि थे।

इनकी प्रमुख रचनाएँ हैं—'रेणुका', 'हुंकार', 'रसवन्ती', 'द्वन्द्वगीत', 'सामधेनी', 'कुरुक्षेत्र', 'रश्मिरथी', 'उर्वशी' एवं 'परशुराम की प्रतिज्ञा'। इन्होंने हिन्दी काव्य को नई धारा प्रदान की। इन्होंने देश तथा समाज को अपने काव्य का विषय बनाया।

इनकी भाषा शुद्ध खड़ी बोली है। ये अपनी भाषा में तत्सम शब्दों का प्रयोग करते हैं। इनका शब्द-चयन अत्यन्त पुष्ट और भावानुकूल होता है। इनकी शैली ओजप्रधान है। इनकी प्रतिभा बहुमुखी है। ये अत्यन्त लोकप्रिय कवि हैं। ये अपने युग के प्रतिनिधि कवि हैं।

(1)

इतना कुछ है भरा विभव का, कोष प्रकृति के भीतर,
निज इच्छित सुख-भोग, सहज ही पा सकते नारी-नर।
सब हो सकते तुष्ट, एक-सा सब सुख पा सकते हैं,
चाहें तो, पल में धरती को स्वर्ग बना सकते हैं।

छिपा दिए सब तत्व आवरण के नीचे ईश्वर ने,
संघर्षों से खोज निकाला उन्हें उद्यमी नर ने।
ब्रह्मा से कुछ लिखा भाग्य में मनुज नहीं लाया है,
अपना सुख उसने अपने भुजबल से ही पाया है।

शब्दार्थ—**विभव** = वैभव, **तुष्ट** = सन्तुष्ट, **आवरण** = पर्दा, **संघर्षों** = कड़ी मेहनत, **उद्यमी** = परिश्रम करने वाले, **भुजबल** = अपने भुजाओं की शक्ति से।

प्रसंग—कवि कहता है कि ईश्वर ने मनुष्य के लिए सभी वैभव पृथ्वी पर दिये हैं, वह उन्हें अपने परिश्रम से प्राप्त कर सकता है।

भावार्थ—कवि कहता है कि ईश्वर ने मनुष्य के सभी सुख-साधन पृथ्वी के अन्दर सहेज कर रख दिये हैं। उस प्रकृति के द्वारा प्रदत्त संसाधनों से सभी मनुष्य सन्तुष्ट हो सकते हैं और एक समान सभी सुख प्राप्त कर सकते हैं। यदि सभी मनुष्य चाहें तो एक पल में पृथ्वी को स्वर्ग के समान सुन्दर और सुखद बना सकते हैं।

ईश्वर ने अनेक मुख्य तत्व पृथ्वी के अन्दर छिपाकर रख दिये हैं। और उनको उद्यमी नर ने अपने परिश्रम से खोज निकाला है। मनुष्य ऊपर से ब्रह्मा के हाथ से कुछ लिखवा कर नहीं लाया है। अर्थात् भाग्य

जैसी कोई चीज लिखकर ब्रह्मा ने नहीं दी है। जो कुछ सुख-साधन मनुष्य ने इकट्ठे किये हैं वे सब अपनी भुजाओं की शक्ति से इकट्ठे किये हैं। अर्थात् परिश्रम करके अपने लिए धन-धान्य प्राप्त किया है।

(2)

प्रकृति नहीं डर कर झुकती है, कभी भाग्य के बल से,
सदा हारती वह मनुष्य के उद्यम से, श्रमजल से।
ब्रह्मा का अभिलेख पढ़ा करते निरुद्यमी प्राणी,
धोते वीर कुअंक भाल का बहा भ्रुवों से पानी।

भाग्यवाद आवरण पाप का और शस्त्र शोषण का,
जिससे रखता दबा एक जन से भाग दूसरे जन का।
पूछो किसी भाग्यवादी से, यदि विधि-अंक प्रबल है,
पद पर क्यों देती न स्वयं वसुधा निज रतन उगल है ?

शब्दार्थ—**उद्यम** = परिश्रम, **श्रमजल** = पसीना, **अभिलेख** = लिखा हुआ, **निरुद्यमी** = परिश्रम न करने वाला, **कुअंक भाल** = बुरा लिखा हुआ, **भ्रुवों से पानी** = अधिक परिश्रम करके, **आवरण** = पर्दा, **शस्त्र** = हथियार, **शोषण** = अधिक काम लेना, **भाग्यवादी** = भाग्य को मानने वाला, **विधि अंक** = ब्रह्मा का लिखा हुआ, **प्रबल** = ताकतवर, **वसुधा** = पृथ्वी, **निज** = अपने, **रत्न** = धन, **उगल** = दे देती।

प्रसंग—यहाँ पर कवि मनुष्य के परिश्रम पर ही जोर देता है कि बिना परिश्रम के कोई भी वस्तु प्राप्त नहीं होती।

भावार्थ—कवि कहता है कि किसी का भाग्य देखकर पृथ्वी झुकती नहीं है। वह तो केवल मनुष्य के कठिन परिश्रम और पसीने से ही हार मानती है। अर्थात् परिश्रमी मनुष्य ही धरती से अपनी इच्छित वस्तु ले सकता है। जो परिश्रम नहीं करते हैं वे भाग्य का रोना रोते रहते हैं। लेकिन परिश्रमी मनुष्य अपने बुरे भाग्य को भी अपने श्रम के बल से बदल देते हैं अर्थात् अच्छा कर देते हैं।

भाग्यवाद तो पाप का आवरण है और शस्त्र मनुष्य से दूसरे मनुष्य का शोषण करवाते हैं। कवि कहता है कि हम किसी भाग्यवादी गनुष्य से पूछें कि यदि भाग्य में लिखा है तो यह पृथ्वी अफने आप अपने अन्दर दबे हुए रत्नों को उगलकर बाहर क्यों नहीं कर देती ? उन्हें प्राप्त करने के लिए परिश्रम क्यों करना पड़ता है ?

(3)

उपजाता क्यों विभव प्रकृति को सींच-सींच वह जल से ?
क्यों न उठा लेता निज संचित कोष भाग्य के बल से ?
एक मनुज संचित करता है अर्थ पाप के बल से,
और भोगता उसे दूसरा भाग्यवाद के छल से।

नर-समाज का भाग्य एक है, वह श्रम, वह भुजबल है,
जिसके सम्मुख झुकी हुई पृथिवी, विनीत नभ-तल है।
जिसने श्रम-जल दिया, उसे पीछे मत रह जाने दो,
विजित प्रकृति से सबसे पहले उसको सुख पाने दो।

शब्दार्थ—**संचित** = इकट्ठा किया हुआ, **मनुज** = मनुष्य, **सम्मुख** = सामने, **विनीत** = विनम्र, **श्रमजल** = परिश्रम से बहाया पसीना, **विजित** = जीती हुई, **विभव** = धन।

प्रसंग—कवि कहता है कि अपने परिश्रम से ही मनुष्य पृथ्वी से अन्न और रत्न खोजकर निकालता है।

भावार्थ—कवि कहता है कि भाग्य प्रबल नहीं है, बल्कि मनुष्य का परिश्रम प्रबल है। धरती को जल से सींचकर मनुष्य उससे धान्य उत्पन्न करता है। यदि भाग्य की प्रबलता होती तो वह बिना परिश्रम किये ही पृथ्वी से धन-सम्पदा प्राप्त कर लेता। जब मनुष्य पाप करके धन इकट्ठा करता है तो दूसरा मनुष्य अपने भाग्य के छल से उसे भोगता है। अर्थात् दूसरे का कमाया हुआ धन अपरिश्रमी मनुष्य यह कहकर भोगता है कि उसके भाग्य में लिखा है। ऐसा कहना मात्र धोखा है। भाग्य से उसे कोई धन नहीं मिल सकता।

मनुष्य के समाज का एक भाग्य सिर्फ उसका परिश्रम और भुजाओं की शक्ति है। परिश्रम के बल से ही पृथ्वी और आकाश-पाताल झुकते रहते हैं। जिस मनुष्य ने अपने परिश्रम से पृथ्वी को जीता है अर्थात् अपने परिश्रम से सभी सुख-साधन एकत्र किये हैं उन पर सर्वप्रथम उसी का अधिकार है उसे उन्हें प्राप्त करने दो। ऐसा न हो कि कोई अपरिश्रमी मनुष्य उसे छीन कर ले जाये।

अभ्यास-प्रश्न

प्रश्न 1. उद्यमी नर का संसार में महत्व क्यों है ? क्या भाग्य उसका साथ देता है ?

उत्तर—उद्यमी नर ही संसार में इच्छित सुख-साधनों को भोगने में समर्थ हो पाता है। ईश्वर ने इस पृथ्वी के अन्दर सभी धन-धान्य छिपाकर रख दिये हैं। उद्यमी मनुष्य ही उन्हें प्राप्त करता है। उद्यमी नर कभी भी भाग्य के भरोसे रहकर पछताता नहीं, वह तो कार्य को पूरा करके दिखा देता है। संत कबीर ने कहा है—

"कर बहियाँ बल आपणी, छाँड़ परायी आस।
जिनके आँगन है नदी, सो कत मरत पियास।"

इससे यह साबित होता है कि मनुष्य को अपनी भुजाओं के बल पर विश्वास रखना चाहिए। ईश्वर ने पूरा कोष प्रकृति के भीतर छिपाकर रख दिया है। इसे उद्यमी नर ही भोग सकता है। यदि अब भी कोई मनुष्य उन्हें परिश्रम करके प्राप्त नहीं करता है तो इसमें ईश्वर का दोष कहाँ है। तुलसीदास जी ने कहा है—

"सकल पदारथ हैं जग माहीं। करमहीन नर पावत नाहीं।"

संसार के सभी पदार्थ कर्मशील मनुष्य के लिए हैं, कर्महीन के लिए नहीं। इतिहास इस बात का साक्षी है कि परिश्रमशील और उद्यमी व्यक्ति को हमेशा सफलता मिलती है। गीता में श्रीकृष्ण ने अर्जुन को कर्मयोग का ही उपदेश दिया। संस्कृत का यह श्लोक कि—

"उद्यमेन हि सिध्यन्ति कार्याणि न मनोरथैः।
न हि सुप्तस्य सिंहस्य प्रविशत्ति मुखे मृगाः।।

ये इस बात को प्रमाणित करता है कि बिना परिश्रम के मनुष्य को कुछ प्राप्त नहीं होता। ईश्वर ने जो-जो भी बहुमूल्य वस्तुएँ या जीवन के लिए महत्वपूर्ण साधन पृथ्वी के अन्दर छिपाकर रख दिये हैं, वे सब मनुष्य के हितार्थ ही हैं, ईश्वर या प्रकृति के काम तो आने नहीं हैं। मनुष्य उन्हें अपने परिश्रम के बल से ही प्राप्त कर सकता है। आकाश पृथ्वी पर जल वर्षा कर अन्न उत्पन्न करने का साधन बना देता है, लेकिन मनुष्य को हल चलाकर बीज बोना पड़ेगा और उगती फसल की रक्षा करनी होगी तभी उसे खाने के लिए अन्न प्राप्त होगा। कवि के अनुसार परिश्रम के सम्मुख पृथ्वी, नभ-तल सभी झुके रहते हैं। वे परिश्रम करने वाले का विरोध नहीं करते, बल्कि सहयोग करते हैं।

भाग्य के भरोसे रहकर मनुष्य कुछ प्राप्त नहीं कर सकता। ब्रह्मा ने भी मनुष्य के भाग्य में ऐसा कुछ लिखा हो कि उसे बिना कुछ किये सब कुछ मिल जायेगा, ऐसा कोई प्रमाण नहीं मिलता। कर्मवीर न तो भाग्य-भरोसे रहता है और न ही भाग्य के भरोसे रहकर पश्चाताप करता है। प्रकृति कभी भाग्य के सामने झुकती नहीं हैं। भाग्य के भरोसे रहना मनुष्य की सबसे बड़ी भूल है। कोई भी मनुष्य ब्रह्मा से अपने भाग्य में सुख लिखाकर लाया हो, ऐसा नहीं है। भाग्य के भरोसे तो आलसी ही रहते हैं। यदि भाग्य ही प्रबल हो तो मनुष्य को पृथ्वी में संचित कोष अपने आप प्राप्त हो जायें, पर ऐसा नहीं होता।

इस सम्बन्ध में भाग्य उसकी कोई सहायता नहीं करता। कवि भाग्यवादी नहीं है, वह तो उद्यमी नर की ही प्रशंसा करने वाला व्यक्ति है। यहाँ एक प्रश्न अवश्य उठता है कि किसी का कमाया हुआ धन कोई भोग रहा है। कवि का कहना है कि पाप से जो संचित धन है उसे भाग्य के छल से कोई और भोगता है, यह एक धोखा है जो भाग्य का नाम लेकर धनी व्यक्ति के धन का उपभोग करता है। ऐसा भोग बहुत कम समय तक ही चलता है। कवि ने नर-समाज का भाग्य मनुष्य का परिश्रम और परिश्रम से बहाया हुआ पसीना बताया है।

इस कविता में कवि ने यही प्रेरणा दी है कि भाग्य के भरोसे न रह कर कर्मशील और परिश्रमी बनो। अपने कार्य से कभी विरक्त मत हो।

प्रश्न 2. प्रस्तुत कविता का केन्द्रीय भाव लिखिए।

उत्तर—'उद्यमी नर' नामक कविता में रामधारी सिंह दिनकर ने बताया है कि उद्यम करने वाला मनुष्य ही संसार में सब कुछ प्राप्त करता है, भाग्यवादी नहीं। ईश्वर ने प्रकृति में इतना सारा धन-धान्य छिपाकर रखा है कि मनुष्य परिश्रम करके उसे प्राप्त करे और सुख से रहे। कवि की इच्छा है कि परिश्रम के बल पर सभी मनुष्य सुख प्राप्त करें और इस पृथ्वी को स्वर्ग जैसा सुन्दर और सुखद बना दें। पृथ्वी के आवरण में ईश्वर ने जो भी तत्व छिपा दिये हैं, उन्हें उद्यमी नर ने परिश्रम करके खोज निकाला है। ब्रह्मा ने उसके भाग्य में कुछ लिखा नहीं है। अपना सुख उसने अपने भुजबल से ही प्राप्त किया है।

प्रकृति कभी भाग्य के बल से झुकती नहीं है वह केवल मनुष्य के उद्यम और परिश्रम के द्वारा बहाये हुए पसीने के सम्मुख हार मान लेती है। यदि उद्यमी नर नई-नई खोज नहीं करते तो इतने सुख-साधन हमें प्राप्त नहीं होते। भाग्यवाद का रोना निरुद्यमी नर ही रोते हैं। जिन्हें काम नहीं करना होता है वे कह देते हैं कि हमारे भाग्य में नहीं लिखा है।

भाग्यवाद पाप का आवरण है। यानी अपने पाप को हम भाग्य का नाम देकर छुपा देते हैं। शस्त्र दुनिया में शोषण कराते हैं। जो बलवान है वह अपनी शक्ति के बल पर गरीब लोगों का शोषण करता है। यदि हम किसी भाग्यवादी से पूछें कि यदि भाग्य प्रबल है तो पृथ्वी अपने आप अपने धन-धान्य को बाहर क्यों नहीं उगल देती। वह इसका उत्तर नहीं दे पायेगा क्योंकि ऐसा होता नहीं है। यदि कोई मनुष्य पाप करके धन कमा लेता है और दूसरा कोई उस धन को अपने भाग्य का भरोसा देकर भोगता है तो यह धोखा है। यह धन अल्प समय तक ही उपभोग में रहता है फिर नष्ट हो जाता है।

नर समाज का एक ही भाग्य है और वह है परिश्रम और उनकी भुजाओं का बल। परिश्रम के सम्मुख यह पृथ्वी और नभ-तल झुके हुए हैं। झुकने से तात्पर्य है कि वे उद्यमी नर की सहायता करने को तत्पर रहते हैं। जिसने भी परिश्रम से काम किया है उसे उसका हक मिलना चाहिए। ऐसा न हो कि वह सुख प्राप्त करने में सबसे पीछे रह जाये। उसे पीछे मत रहने दो। उसे तो पहले लाकर सुख, शान्ति और धन प्रदान करो।

कवि ने यहाँ भाग्यवाद की भर्त्सना कर उद्यम की प्रशंसा की है और हमें प्रेरणा दी है कि हम परिश्रमी बनें और अपने परिश्रम के बल पर सुख-सम्पत्ति भोगें। सबकी सहायता करते हुए सबको समान अवसर दें और पीछे रहने वाले परिश्रमी व्यक्ति को आगे लायें।

प्रश्न 3. प्रकृति नहीं डर कर झुकती है, कभी भाग्य के बल से,
सदा हारती वह मनुष्य के उद्यम से, श्रमजल से,
ब्रह्मा का अभिलेख पढ़ा करते निरुद्यमी प्राणी,
धोते वीर कुअंक भाल का बहा ध्रुवों से पानी।

(i) जो व्यक्ति आलसी हैं, परिश्रम नहीं करना चाहते ? क्या कहते सुने जाते हैं ?

(ii) भाग्य के भरोसे कौन व्यक्ति रहते हैं और क्यों ?

(iii) प्रकृति किस से हार मानती है ?

(iv) प्रस्तुत पंक्तियों का अर्थ लिखिए ?

उत्तर—(i) निरुद्यमी प्राणी हमेशा यह कहते सुने जाते हैं कि यदि भाग्य में होगा तो अवश्य ही हमें मिलेगा और भाग्य में नहीं होगा तो नहीं मिलेगा। वैसे ये धारणा गलत है।

(ii) भाग्यवादी लोग ही भाग्य के भरोसे रहते हैं, वे निरुद्यमी होते हैं और आलस्य के कारण शरीर से श्रम नहीं करते। समाज में वे अपनी भाग्यवादी सोच के कारण नुकसान भी उठाते हैं। उनके काम नहीं बन पाते। पुरुषार्थी लोग अपने पुरुषार्थ से अच्छे काम बना लेते हैं जबकि भाग्यवादी लोग अपने भाग्य के भरोसे रहकर अपने काम बिगाड़ लेते हैं।

(iii) प्रकृति कर्मवीर के उद्यम एवं श्रमजल से हार मान लेती है अर्थात् उसके परिश्रम के आगे वह अपनी कठोरता को भी मुलायम बना देती है और उसके सब काम निरन्तर बनते चले जाते हैं। कर्मवीर कभी भी बहाना बनाकर काम को टालते नहीं हैं। वे तो दुगुने उत्साह के साथ उसे पूर्ण करने में लग जाते हैं। ऐसा कोई काम नहीं जो कर्मवीर के करने से न हो।

(iv) कवि कहता है कि किसी का भाग्य देखकर प्रकृति (पृथ्वी) झुकती नहीं है। वह तो केवल मनुष्य के कठिन परिश्रम के पसीने से ही हार मानती है। अर्थात् परिश्रमी व्यक्ति ही धरती से अपनी इच्छित वस्तु प्राप्त कर सकता है। जो परिश्रमी नहीं हैं वे अपने भाग्य का रोना रोते रहते हैं। लेकिन परिश्रमी व्यक्ति अपने बुरे भाग्य को भी अपने परिश्रम के बल से बदल देते हैं अर्थात् अच्छा कर देते हैं।

प्रश्न 4. भाग्यवाद आवरण पाप का और शस्त्र शोषण का,
जिससे रखता दबा एक जन से भाग दूसरे जन का।
पूछो किसी भाग्यवादी से यदि विधि अंक प्रबल है,
पद पर क्यों देती न स्वयं वसुधा निज रतन उगल है।

(i) एक मनुष्य दूसरे मनुष्य को कैसे दबा लेता है ?

(ii) प्रथम पंक्ति को स्पष्ट कीजिए।

(iii) कवि ने भाग्यवादी से क्या प्रश्न पूछा है ?

(iv) प्रस्तुत पद्यांश का अर्थ लिखिए।

उत्तर—(i) पैसे वाला व्यक्ति गरीब मजदूर के भाग्य में ऐसा ही लिखा था कहकर इससे अपने काम कराता रहता है।

(ii) कवि ने भाग्यवाद को पाप का आवरण बताया है। अर्थात् धनी व्यक्ति गरीब व्यक्ति को उसके भाग्य का वास्ता देकर हतोत्साहित करते हैं और अपने काम उससे कराते रहते हैं। भाग्यवाद की परिभाषा अपने मन से बनाकर गरीबों का शोषण करते हैं और उन्हें भाग्य के नाम से अपने काम कराते रहते हैं।

(iii) कवि भाग्य के भरोसे रहने वाले व्यक्ति से पूछता है कि यदि भाग्य का अंक प्रबल है तो पृथ्वी अपने अन्दर छिपे हुए रत्नों को उगलकर बाहर क्यों नहीं दे देती ? उसे तो भाग्यवादी को बैठे-बैठे ही हर सुविधा प्रदान करनी चाहिए। पर ऐसा होता नहीं है, जो परिश्रम के बल पर भरोसा करते हैं उन्हीं को कार्य में सफलता मिलती है, भाग्यवादी को नहीं।

(iv) कवि कहता है कि भाग्यवाद तो पाप का आवरण है और शस्त्र मनुष्य से दूसरे मनुष्य का शोषण करवाते हैं। हम किसी भाग्यवादी व्यक्ति से पूछें कि यदि भाग्य में लिखा है तो यह पृथ्वी अपने आप अपने अन्दर दबे हुए रत्नों को उगलकर बाहर क्यों नहीं कर देती ? उन्हें प्राप्त करने के लिए परिश्रम क्यों करना पड़ता है ? यहाँ पर कवि का मानना है कि भाग्य नहीं मनुष्य द्वारा किया गया परिश्रम अधिक प्रबल है।

प्रश्न 5. नर-समाज का भाग्य एक है, वह श्रम, वह भुजबल है,
जिसके सम्मुख झुकी हुई पृथिवी, विनीत तभ-तल है।
जिसने श्रमजल दिया, उसे पीछे मत रह जाने दो,
विजित प्रकृति से सबसे पहले उसको सुख पाने दो।

(i) जिसने परिश्रम किया है उसके लिए कवि क्या कहता है ?

(ii) किसके सामने पृथ्वी और नभ तल झुके हुए हैं ?

(iii) नर-समाज का भाग्य क्या है ?

(iv) प्रस्तुत पंक्तियों का अर्थ लिखिए।

उत्तर—(i) जिसने परिश्रम किया है, यदि वह किसी कारणवश पीछे रह जाता है तो उसे पीछे मत रहने दो अपने साथ लेकर चलो।

(ii) परिश्रमी व्यक्ति के सामने पृथ्वी और नभ-तल झुके हुये हैं अर्थात् कर्मवीर व्यक्ति ने ही पृथ्वी और नभ-तल का भेद जान लिया है और उससे अपने कार्य बहुत समय पूर्व से ही बनाने आरम्भ कर दिये हैं। उसके सामने ऐसा कोई कार्य नहीं जिसे वह न कर सके।

(iii) नर-समाज का भाग्य उसका श्रम और भुजबल है। मनुष्य की भुजाओं में बल है और कार्य करने का उत्साह मन में है तो वह हर काम पूरा कर लेता है। परिश्रम के अलावा कोई और भाग्य नहीं है जो कर्महीन व्यक्ति के काम को पूरा कर सके। अत: मनुष्य को भाग्यवादी न होकर कर्मवीर होना चाहिए।

(iv) कवि कहता है कि मनुष्य का भाग्य उसका परिश्रम और भुजाओं का बल है। मनुष्य के परिश्रम के सामने पृथ्वी, नभ और तल सभी झुके हुए हैं अर्थात् उन्होंने मनुष्य के परिश्रम से हार मान ली है। जिस व्यक्ति ने भी अपने परिश्रम के बल से प्रकृति को जीता है, उसे साथ लेकर चलो, पीछे मत रह जाने दो। उसके परिश्रम का मूल्य उसको मिलना चाहिए।

●●

9. बादल को घिरते देखा है

—नागार्जुन

जीवन परिचय—नागार्जुन के जन्म का नाम वैद्‌यनाथ मिश्र था। इनका जन्म सन् 1911 में बिहार राज्य में दरभंगा जिले के तरौनी नामक गाँव में हुआ था।

इन्होंने कविता, कहानी, उपन्यास जैसी सभी विधाओं पर अपनी लेखनी चलाई है। 'युगधारा', 'प्यासी पथराई आँखें', 'खून और शोले', 'सतरंगे पंखों वाली', 'तालाब की मछलियाँ', 'हजार-हजार बाहों वाली', 'रत्नगर्भा', 'तुमने कहा था', 'प्रेत का बयान' आदि इनके प्रमुख काव्य ग्रन्थ हैं। 'नई पौध', 'बाबा बटेसरनाथ', 'जनमिया का बाबा', 'रतिनाथ की चाची', इनके प्रसिद्ध उपन्यास हैं।

सन् 1968 में इन्हें मैथिली में साहित्य अकादमी पुरस्कार तथा 1988 में 'मैथिलीशरण गुप्त सम्मान' और 'भारत भारती' पुरस्कार से सम्मानित किया गया। इन्हें मध्य प्रदेश का 'कबीर' तथा बिहार का 'राजेन्द्र प्रसाद' सम्मान भी प्राप्त हुआ। सन् 1998 में इनका देहावसान हो गया। इनके काव्य में प्रकृति प्रेम, जीवन के उतार-चढ़ाव, सुख-दुःख तथा मानवतावादी दृष्टिकोण की प्रधानता है।

(1)

अमल धवल गिरि के शिखरों पर,
बादल को घिरते देखा है।
छोटे-छोटे मोती जैसे
उनके शीतल तुहिन कणों को
मानसरोवर के उन स्वर्णिम
कमलों पर गिरते देखा है।
बादल को घिरते देखा है।

शब्दार्थ—**अमल** = स्वच्छ, **धवल** = सफेद, **तुहिन कणों** = ओस की बूँदों, **स्वर्णिम** = सुनहरे।

प्रसंग—प्रस्तुत पंक्तियों में कवि ने अपने प्रकृति प्रेम का परिचय देकर बादल को सजीव रूप देकर उसका मानवीकरण किया है।

भावार्थ—कवि कहता है कि स्वच्छ एवं श्वेत पर्वत शिखरों पर उसने अचानक बादल को घिरते हुए कई बार देखा है। बादलों से गिरने वाली बर्फ जैसे सफेद मोती के समान तथा तरल बूँदों को ओस कणों के समान मानसरोवर झील में खिले हुए कमलों पर गिरकर दृश्य को और अधिक मनमोहक बनते हुए भी देखा है।

(2)

तुंग हिमालय के कंधों पर
छोटे-बड़ी कई झीलें हैं
उनके श्यामल नील सलिल में
समतल देशों से आ-आकर
पावस की ऊमस से आकुल
तिक्त मधुर बिसतंतु खोजते,
हंसों को तिरते देखा है।
बादल को घिरते देखा है।

शब्दार्थ—**तुंग** = ऊँचे, **श्यामल नील सलिल** = काला नीला जल, **तिक्त** = मधुर, **बिसतन्तु** = तीखे मधुर रेशे जैसे, **उमस** = घुटन।

प्रसंग—इन पंक्तियों में कवि ने हिमालय की चोटियों पर स्थित झीलों में हंस जैसे अनेक पक्षियों की व्याकुलता का सजीव चित्रण किया है।

भावार्थ—कवि कहता है कि हिमालय की ऊँची-ऊँची चोटियों पर स्थित झीलों के स्वच्छ नीले और चमकदार जल में अनेक कमल खिले हैं। उन कमलों तथा वहाँ के वातावरण में आस-पास के मैदानों से अनेक पक्षी आते हैं। वे पक्षी तालाबों में खिले कमलों में बिसतन्तु (कोमल धागे जैसे श्वेत) खोजकर उसके तीखे मधुर स्वाद का आनन्द लेते हुए दृष्टिगोचर होते हैं।

(3)

ऋतु वसंत का सुप्रभात था
मंद-मंद था अनिल बह रहा
बालरुण की मृदु किरणें थीं
अगल-बगल स्वर्णिम शिखर थे
एक-दूसरे से विरहित हो,
अलग-अलग रहकर ही जिनको
सारी रात बितानी होती,
निशाकाल से चिर-अभिशापित
बेबस उस चकवा-चकई का,
बंद हुआ क्रंदन, फिर उनमें
उस महान सरवर के तीरे,
शैवालों की हरी दरी पर,
प्रणय-कलह छिड़ते देखा है।
बादल को घिरते देखा है।

शब्दार्थ—**बालरुण** = लाल रंग का सूर्य, **मृदु** = कोमल, **विरहित** = अलग, **चिर-अभिशापित** = हमेशा शापग्रस्त, **क्रंदन** = शोर, **शैवालों** = पानी पर पड़ी काई, **प्रणय-कलह** = प्रेमपूर्ण झगड़ा।

प्रसंग—इन पंक्तियों में कवि ने हिमालय के प्राकृतिक सौन्दर्य, पक्षियों के कलरव, चकवा-चकवी के सम्बन्ध में विचार व्यक्त किये हैं।

भावार्थ—कवि कहता है कि उसने बसंत के मौसम में एक प्रातःकाल शीतल, मंद और सुगन्धित वातावरण तथा रक्तिम किरणों वाले बाल सूर्य के प्रकाश में चमकते हुए शिखरों वाले पक्षियों को विभिन्न क्रीड़ाओं में मग्न देखा है, इस मौसम में आस-पास के प्रदेश तथा उमस भरे मैदानों की गरमी से व्याकुल अनेक प्रकार के पक्षी आकर अपना समय व्यतीत करते हैं। चकवा पक्षी के समान रात में एक-दूसरे से अलग रहकर विरहपूर्ण जीवन व्यतीत करते हैं। भाव यह है कि चकवा और चाँद का प्रेम होने के कारण वह वृक्षों की अगली डाली पर बैठकर रात व्यतीत करने को बाध्य होता है। कुछ समय तक शान्त रहने के बाद इसी तालाब के किनारे उनमें अक्सर प्रणय-कलह आरम्भ हो जाता है। यह स्थान हरी घास (शैवाल) से घिरे क्षेत्र के रूप में बड़ा ही सुन्दर दिखाई देता है।

(4)

दुर्गम बर्फानी घाटी में
शत सहस्त्र फुट ऊँचाई पर
अलख नाभि से उठने वाले
निज के ही उन्मादक परिमल
के पीछे धावित हो-होकर
तरल तरुण कस्तूरी मृग को
अपने पर चिढ़ते देखा है।
बादल को घिरते देखा है।

शब्दार्थ—**बर्फ से पूर्ण, शत सहस्त्र** = सैकड़ों हजारों, **अलख नाभि** = अलखनन्दा, **उन्मादक** = उन्माद से पूर्ण, **परिमल** = सुगन्ध, **धावित** = दौड़ना।

प्रसंग—इन पंक्तियों में कवि ने सैकड़ों फीट ऊँचे पर्वतीय प्रदेश की सुन्दरता और अलखनन्दा के प्रदेश में व्याप्त कस्तूरी मृग की चिढ़न का वर्णन किया है।

भावार्थ— कवि कहता है कि हिमालय के दुर्गम और बर्फीले प्रदेश में सैकड़ों फीट की ऊँचाई पर अलकनन्दा के किनारे के प्रदेश में घूमते हुए कस्तूरी मृग अपनी ही नाभि से उठती हुई सुगन्ध की तीव्र गन्ध से पागल होकर इधर से उधर, अपने आप से ही चिढ़ते हुए दिखाई देते हैं।

(5)

कहाँ गया धनपति कुबेर वह
कहाँ गई उसकी वह अलका
नहीं ठिकाना कालिदास के
व्योम-प्रवाही गंगाजल का,
ढूँढा बहुत परन्तु लगा क्या,
मेघदूत का पता कहीं पर।
कौन बताये वह छायामय
बरस पड़ा होगा न यहीं पर,
जाने दो, वह कवि-कल्पित था,
मैंने तो भीषण जाड़ों में
नभ-चुंबी कैलाश शीर्ष पर,
महामेघ को झंझानिल से,
गरज-गरज भिड़ते देखा है।
बादल को घिरते देखा है।

शब्दार्थ—**व्योम प्रवाही** = आकाश में प्रवाहित, **छायामय** = काल्पनिक, **कवि कल्पित** = कवि की कल्पना, **कैलाश शीर्ष** = कैलास पर्वत की चोटी, **झंझानिल** = आँधी तूफान।

प्रसंग—कवि ने पर्वतीय प्रदेश के सौन्दर्य का वर्णन किया है।

भावार्थ— कवि कहता है कि हिमालय पर आज कुबेर और उसकी अल्कापुरी का कोई अस्तित्व नहीं है। इसी प्रकार कालिदास द्वारा वर्णित मेघदूत और गंगा-जल का उल्लेख तो है, किन्तु वर्तमान में उनका कोई अस्तित्व नहीं है। कवि को अभी तक पता नहीं कि 'मेघदूत' का मेघ कहाँ गया। वह अनुमान लगाता है कि निश्चय ही वह कालिदास की कल्पना होगा। वह कहीं न कहीं बरस गया होगा। कवि कहता है कि उसने सर्दी में कैलाश पर्वत के उच्च शिखरों पर तूफानी बादलों को आपस में संघर्ष करने के बाद बरसते देखा है।

(6)

शत-शत निर्झर-निर्झरणी-कल
मुखरित देवदारु कानन में,
शोणित धवल भोज पत्रों से
छाई हुई कुटी के भीतर,
रंग-बिरंगे और सुगन्धित,
फूलों से कुंतल को साजे,
इंद्रनील की माला डाले
शंख-सरीखे सुघढ़ गलों में,
कानों में कुवलय लटकाये,
शतदल लाल कमल वेणी में,
रजत-रचित मणि-खचित कलामय
पान पात्र द्राक्षासव पूरित
रखे सामने अपने-अपने
लोहित चन्दन की त्रिपदी पर,
नरम निदाघ बाल-कस्तूरी
मृगछालों पर पलथी मारे
मदिरारुण आँखों वाले उन
उन्मद किन्नर-किन्नरियों की
मृदुल मनोरम अँगुलियों को
वंशी पर फिरते देखा है।
बादल को घिरते देखा है।

शब्दार्थ—**निर्झर-निर्झरिणी** = झरने और नदियाँ, **कल मुखरित** = मधुर स्वर में आवाज करना, **शोणित धवल** = लाल और सफेद (स्वच्छ), **कुंतल** = बाल, **कुवलय** = कलियाँ, **रजत-रचित** = चाँदी से बने हुए, **द्राक्षासव** = अंगूर का रस, **पूरित** = पूर्ण, **लोहित चंदन** = लाल चंदन, **त्रिपदी** = तिपाही, **निदाग** = बिना दाग के, **मदिरारुण** = शराब के नशे में लाल, **उन्मद** = उन्मत्त, **मृदुल** = कोमल, **मनोरम** = सुन्दर।

प्रसंग—कवि ने पर्वतीय प्रदेश के सौन्दर्य तथा किन्नर जाति के काल्पनिक सौन्दर्य तथा उनके प्रेममय जीवन का वर्णन किया है।

भावार्थ—कवि कहता है कि सैकड़ों झरने तथा नदियों के स्वर से पूर्ण देवदारू वृक्षों के वनों में लाल भोजपत्रों से बनी कुटियों में रंग बिरंगे तथा सुगन्धित फूलों से अपने बालों को सजाये हुए किन्नर और किन्नरियाँ बैठे दिखाई देते हैं। इनके शंख जैसे गले में इन्द्रनील मणियों की माला डाले हुए, कानों में कलियाँ तथा चोटी में लाल कमल धारण किये तथा कलापूर्ण ढंग से चाँदी से बने तथा मणियों से जड़े पान-पात्र शोभित हैं। ये पात्र द्राक्षासव (अंगूर की शराब) से पूर्ण हैं और अपने सामने लाल चंदन की तिपाई पर रखे हुए दिखाई देते हैं। ये सब कस्तूरी वाले मृग के चर्म से बने आसन पर बैठकर आसव के नशे में लाल नेत्रों से स्वयं को देखते हुए मस्त किन्नर युगलों को वंशी की मधुर ध्वनि प्रवाहित करते हुए देखते हैं।

अभ्यास-प्रश्न

प्रश्न 1. 'एक दूसरे से विरहित हो, अलग-अलग रहकर ही जिनको सारी रात बितानी होती, निशाकाल के चिर अभिशापित' पंक्तियों में कवि ने क्या कहना चाहा है। विरहित का अर्थ बताते हुए लिखिए कि कौन विरहित हैं और क्यों ?

उत्तर—विरहित शब्द का अर्थ है वियोग सहते हुए अलग रहना। यहाँ पर कवि ने चकवा-चकवी के अलग रहने का उल्लेख किया है। उन्हीं को एक-दूसरे का वियोग सहते हुए जीवन व्यतीत करना पड़ता है। इसका कारण है कि चकवा पक्षी अपने अगाध प्रेम के कारण चाँद की ओर ही देखता रहता है। इससे उसे रातभर अपनी पत्नी (चकवी) से अलग रहना पड़ता है। ऐसा विश्वास किया जाता है कि सृष्टि के आरम्भ से चकवे को अपनी चकवी से रात में अलग रहने का शाप मिला। चकवा चाँद के प्रति अपने अगाध प्रेम के कारण अपने परिवार से अलग रहकर चाँद को रातभर देखता रहता है। आगे कवि ने बताया है कि इस कारण चकवा-चकवी के मध्य कलह-क्रंदन होता है पर चकवा नहीं मानता। यह क्रंदन किसी भी सहृदय पाठक को करुणा से पूर्ण कर देता है। यह कलह प्रेमपूर्ण कलह है, ऐसा भाव है। सुबह होते ही वे दोनों दुबारा मिल जाते हैं। यह क्रंदन हिमालय के शिखरों पर स्थित झीलों वाले प्रदेश में होकर बन्द हो जाता है।

प्रश्न 2. 'रंग बिरंगे और सुगन्धित फूलों से कुंतल को साजे, इन्द्रनील की माला डाले शंख सरीखे सुघढ़ गलों में'—इन पंक्तियों में कवि ने किन लोगों का वर्णन किया है ? समझाकर लिखिए।

उत्तर—इन पंक्तियों में कवि ने किन्नर (गाने बजाने के कार्य द्वारा जीवनयापन करने वाली) जाति के सौन्दर्य एवं श्रृंगार का वर्णन किया है। यह जाति विभिन्न रंगों एवं गंध के सुन्दर पुष्पों का प्रयोग अपने श्रृंगार के लिए करते हैं। ये लोग अपने बाल, चोटी और गजरे तथा करधनी के लिए पुष्पों का प्रयोग करते हैं। गले में ये लोग इन्द्रनील मणि की माला धारण करते हैं।

स्वभाव से ही प्राकृतिक जीवन और वातावरण के प्रेम करने वाले ये प्राणी कला प्रेमी भी होते हैं। इनकी कुटिया सादा और भोजपत्रों से निर्मित होती है। इसका निर्माण बहुत ही कलापूर्ण ढंग से होता है। यह जाति प्राकृतिक जीवन को प्रेम कर वैसे ही व्यतीत करना पसन्द करती है। इनकी कुटिया के पान-पात्र चाँदी के बने होते हैं और चन्दन की बनी हुई तिपाही पर शराब से भरे हुए रखे रहते हैं। ये लोग नृत्य, संगीत तथा ललित कलाओं को अगाध प्रेम करते हैं। जीवन में कला, संगीत और नृत्य का महत्वपूर्ण स्थान होता है। किन्नर जाति के लोग मुख्यत: वंशी बजाना अधिक पसन्द करते हैं। द्राक्षासव (अंगूर की बनी शराब) पीने के आदी होते हैं।

प्रश्न 3. ऋतु बसंत का सुप्रभात था
मंद-मंद था अनिल बह रहा
बाल रूण की मृदु किरणें थीं
अगल-बगल स्वर्णिम शिखर थे
एक-दूसरे से बिरहित हो,
अलग-अलग रहकर ही जिनको
सारी रात बितानी होती,
निशा काल से चिर-अभिशापित
बेबस उस चकवा-चकई का,
बंद हुआ क्रंदन, फिर उनमें
उस महान सरवर के तीरे,
शैवालों की हरी दरी पर

प्रणय-कलह छिड़ते देखा है।
बादल को घिरते देखा है।

(i) कौन-कौन क्रंदन कर रहे थे ? उनका क्रंदन कब बन्द हुआ ?

(ii) किस ऋतु का कौन-सा प्रभात था ?

(iii) रात में क्रंदन किनका था ?

(iv) प्रस्तुत पद्यांश का अर्थ लिखिए।

उत्तर—(i) चकवा चकवी रात में क्रंदन कर रहे थे। जब सुबह हुई तो वे दोनों आपस में मिल गये और उनका क्रंदन समाप्त हो गया।

(ii) यहाँ बसन्त ऋतु का सुप्रभात है। मन्द-मन्द हवा चल रही थी। मौसम बड़ा सुहावना था। इस प्रभात में चकवा-चकवी अपनी रात की विरह को भुलाकर अपनी प्रसन्नता प्रकट कर रहे हैं। वे दोनों सरोवर के किनारे अपनी खुशी मना रहे हैं।

(iii) रात में क्रन्दन चकवा-चकवी करते हैं क्योंकि वे दोनों रात में अलग-अलग हो जाते हैं। आने वाला प्रभात उनके लिए प्रसन्नता लेकर आता है। रात के दु:ख को भुलाकर प्रभात के अवसर पर प्रसन्न हो रहे हैं। प्रभात ने ही उन दोनों को मिलाया है।

(iv) कवि कहता है कि उसने बसंत के मौसम में एक प्रात:काल शीतल, मन्द और सुगन्धित वातावरण तथा रक्तिम किरणों वाले बाल सूर्य के प्रकाश में चमकते हुए शिखरों पर पक्षियों को विभिन्न क्रीड़ाओं में मग्न देखा है, इस मौसम में आस-पास के प्रदेश तथा उमस भरे मैदानों की गर्मी से व्याकुल अनेक प्रकार के पक्षी आकर अपना समय व्यतीत करते हैं। चकवा पक्षी के समान रात में एक-दूसरे से अलग रहकर विरहपूर्ण जीवन व्यतीत करते हैं। भाव यह है कि चकवा और चाँद का प्रेम होने के कारण वह वृक्षों की अगली डली पर बैठकर रात व्यतीत करने को बाध्य होता है। कुछ समय तक शान्त रहने के बाद इसी तालाब के किनारे उनमें अक्सर प्रणय-कलह आरम्भ हो जाता है। यह स्थान हरी घास (शैवाल) से घिरे क्षेत्र के रूप में बड़ा ही सुन्दर दिखाई देता है।

प्रश्न 4. दुर्गम बर्फानी घाटी में
शत-सहस फुट ऊँचाई पर
अलख नाभि से उठने वाले
निज के ही उन्मादक परिमल
के पीछे धावित हो-होकर
तरल तरुण कस्तूरी मृग को
अपने पर चिढ़ते देखा है।
बादल को घिरते देखा है।

(i) उन्मादक परिमल किसको कहा गया है ?

(ii) हिमालय में कवि ने क्या देखा ?

(iii) कस्तूरी मृग कौन होता है और वह क्यों चिढ़ रहा है ?

(iv) प्रस्तुत पंक्तियों का अर्थ लिखिए।

उत्तर—(i) कस्तूरी मृग की नाभि में कस्तूरी होती है। उस कस्तूरी की मस्त करने वाली खुशबू को उन्मादक परिमल कहा गया है।

(ii) हिमालय की दुर्गम बर्फानी घाटी में सहस्त्र फुट की ऊँचाई पर युवा कस्तूरी मृग को अपनी सुगन्ध से मोहित होकर इसलिए चिढ़ते हुए देखा है क्योंकि वह सुगन्ध की खोज में भागता रहता है पर यह जान नहीं पाता कि यह सुगन्ध कहाँ से आ रही है।

(iii) कस्तूरी एक बड़ी ही मोहक सुगन्ध को धारण करने वाला पदार्थ है जो कस्तूरी मृग की नाभि में स्थित रहती है। इसकी जानकारी उस मृग को नहीं हो पाती। वह सुगन्ध को चारों ओर खोजने के लिए दौड़ता है पर उसे प्राप्त नहीं कर पाता। उस सुगन्ध को वह खोज नहीं पाता है इसलिए वह चिढ़ रहा होता है।

(iv) कवि कहता है कि हिमालय के दुर्गम और बर्फीले प्रदेश में सैकड़ों फीट की ऊँचाई पर अलकनन्दा के किनारे के प्रदेश में घूमते हुए कस्तूरी मृग अपनी ही नाभि से उठती हुई सुगन्ध तीव्र गन्ध से मोहित होकर इधर से उधर भागते हुए अपने आप से ही चिढ़ते हुए देखा है।

प्रश्न 5. कहाँ गया धनपति कुबेर वह
कहाँ गई उसकी वह अलका
नहीं ठिकाना कालिदास के
व्योम-प्रवाही गंगाजल का,
ढूँढ़ा बहुत परन्तु लगा क्या,
मेघदूत का पता कहीं पर।
कौन बताये वह छायामय
बरस पड़ा होगा न यहीं पर,
जाने दो, वह कवि कल्पित था,
मैंने तो भीषण जाड़ों में
नभ चुंबी कैलाश शीर्ष पर,
महामेघ को झंझानिल से,
गरज-गरज भिढ़ते देखा है।
बादल को घिरते देखा है।

(i) कुबेर के बारे में संक्षेप में बताइए।

(ii) कवि ने मेघदूत के बारे में क्या कहा है ? मेघदूत कौन था ?

(iii) कुबेर की नगरी कौन सी थी ? क्या उसका अभी भी अस्तित्व है ?

(iv) प्रस्तुत पंक्तियों का अर्थ लिखिए।

उत्तर—(i) देवताओं में कुबेर का प्रमुख स्थान है। वह धन का देवता था। उसके पास 'पुष्पक' विमान था जो आकाश में उड़ता था और यथायोग्य स्थान बना सकता था।

(ii) कवि ने बताया है कि 'मेघदूत' कवि कालिदास द्वारा लिखित रचना है। 'मेघदूत' उनकी प्रमुख रचना है जो हिमालय पर घटित हुई दिखाई गयी है। यहाँ मेघदूत बादल को कहा गया है।

(iii) धन के स्वामी कुबेर की नगरी अल्कापुरी थी जो हिमालय पर्वत पर बसी थी। एक स्थान पर कवि संकेत देता है कि वह नगरी कवि की कल्पना थी।

(iv) कवि कहता है कि हिमालय पर आज कुबेर और उसकी अल्कापुरी नगरी का कोई अस्तित्व नहीं है। इसी प्रकार कालिदास द्वारा वर्णित मेघदूत और गंगाजल का उल्लेख ही है, किन्तु वर्तमान में उनका कोई अस्तित्व नहीं है। कवि को अभी तक पता नहीं है कि मेघदूत का मेघ कहाँ गया। यह अनुमान लगता है कि निश्चय ही वह कविवर कालिदास की कल्पना होगा। वह कहीं न कहीं बरस गया होगा। कवि ने यहाँ कैलाश पर्वत के उच्च शिखरों पर तूफानी बादलों को आपस में संघर्ष करने के बाद बरसते देखा है।

●●

10. अँधेरे का दीपक

—हरिवंशराय 'बच्चन'

जीवन परिचय—हरिवंशराय 'बच्चन' छायावादी युग के आस्थावादी कवि थे। इनका जन्म इलाहाबाद में सन् 1907 में एक सम्पन्न कायस्थ परिवार में हुआ था। इनके पिता का नाम प्रतापनारायण था। माता-पिता की धार्मिक रुचियों व संस्कारों का इनके ऊपर गहरा प्रभाव पड़ा। इलाहाबाद विश्वविद्यालय से उच्च शिक्षा प्राप्त कर वहीं अंग्रेजी के प्राध्यापक नियुक्त हुए। इन्होंने कैम्ब्रिज विश्वविद्यालय से पी.एच.डी. की उपाधि प्राप्त की। कुछ महीने आकाशवाणी में कार्य करने के अनन्तर सन् 1955 में इनकी नियुक्ति भारत सरकार के विदेश मन्त्रालय में हिन्दी विशेषज्ञ के पद पर हुई। सन् 1966 में ये राज्य सभा के सदस्य मनोनीत हुए।

'बच्चन' व्यक्ति-प्रधान गीतों के कवि हैं। इनके गीतों की भाषा सरस और स्वाभाविक है। उसमें उर्दू-कविता जैसा प्रवाह है। 'मधुशाला', 'एकान्त संगीत', 'आकुल अन्तर', 'निशा निमन्त्रण', 'सतरंगिनी', 'सूत की माला', 'मिलन-यामिनी', 'हलाहल', 'आरती और अंगारे', 'धार के इधर-उधर', 'बहुत दिन बीते', आदि इनकी प्रसिद्ध काव्य-रचनाएँ हैं। सन् 1976 में इन्हें 'पद्मभूषण' की उपाधि से अलंकृत किया गया। सन् 2003 में इनका देहावसान हो गया।

'बच्चन' जी की कविताओं में जीवन की अनुभूतियों की सहज अभिव्यक्ति हुई है। भाव-भावनाओं के सहज चितेरे 'बच्चन' का साहित्य में श्रेष्ठ स्थान है। व्यक्तिवादी कवि होते हुए भी इन्होंने सामाजिक जन-जीवन पर अपनी मनोभावनाओं को व्यक्त किया है।

(1)

है अँधेरी रात, पर दीवा जलाना कब मना है ?
कल्पना के हाथ से कमनीय जो मन्दिर बना था,
भावना के हाथ ने जिसमें वितानों को तना था।
स्वप्न ने अपने करों से, था जिसे रुचि से सँवारा,
स्वर्ग के दुष्प्राप्य रंगों से, रसों से जो सना था।
ढह गया वह तो जुटाकर ईंट, पत्थर, कंकड़ों को,
एक अपनी शान्ति की कुटिया बनाना कब मना है ?
है अँधेरी रात पर दीवा जलाना कब मना है ?

शब्दार्थ—**दीवा** = दीपक, **कमनीय** = सुन्दर, **भावना** = सोच, कल्पना, **वितानों** = तम्बुओं, **रुचि** = इच्छा, **दुष्प्राप्य** = जो प्राप्त न हो सके, **कुटिया** = कुटी।

प्रसंग—यहाँ कवि अपनी भावना के आधार पर कहता है कि यदि अँधेरी रात है तो प्रकाश के लिए दीपक जलाओ। यदि आपका सुन्दर भवन टूट गया है तो उसे फिर से बनाओ।

भावार्थ—कवि हरिवंश राय 'बच्चन' कहते हैं कि अँधेरी रात है तो उसे बुरा न कहकर अपने लिए एक दीपक जला लो तो प्रकाश हो जायेगा और अंधकार दूर हो जायेगा। कल्पना से जो सुन्दर भवन बनाया था और भावना के आधार पर सुन्दर तम्बुओं को ताना था। अपनी कल्पना के हाथों से उसे सुन्दरता प्रदान की थी और स्वर्ग के से दुष्प्राप्य रंगों से उसको सजाया था। यदि वह टूट गया है तो उसके बिखरे सामान को इकट्ठा करके पुनः अपने लिए एक कुटिया बना लो जिसमें शान्ति से तुम रह सको। अर्थात् विनाश के बाद निर्माण की प्रक्रिया चलती रहनी चाहिए।

(2)

बादलों के अश्रु से धोया गया नभ-नील, नीलम
का बनाया था गया मधु-पात्र मनमोहक, मनोरम,

प्रथम ऊषा की किरण की लालिमा–सी लाल मदिरा,
थी उसी में चमचमाती, नव घनों में चंचला सम।
वह अगर टूटा, मिलाकर हाथ दोनों की हथेली,
एक निर्मल, स्त्रोत से, तृष्णा बुझाना कब मना है ?
है अँधेरी रात पर दीवा जलाना कब मना है ?

शब्दार्थ—नभनील = नीला आकाश, **नीलम** = नीलम मणि, **मधु-पात्र** = शराब पीने का पात्र, **मनमोहक** = मन को अच्छा लगने वाला, **मनोरम** = सुन्दर, **लालिमा** = लाली, **लाल मदिरा** = लाल रंग की शराब, **नवघनों** = नये बादलों, **चंचला सम** = बिजली के समान, **निर्मल** = साफ, **स्त्रोत** = पानी का झरना, **तृष्णा** = प्यास।

प्रसंग—यहाँ कवि कहता है कि मनुष्य को यदि मदिरा न मिल पाये तो निर्मल जल से प्यास बुझाना ही एक मात्र उपाय है। किसी नुकसान पर उदास न होकर फिर से प्रफुल्लित होने का प्रोत्साहन दिया है।

भावार्थ—कवि कहता है कि बादलों के अश्रुओं (पानी की बूँदों)से नीला आकाश साफ दिखाई दे रहा है। नीलम मणि का बनाया हुआ सुन्दर सुरा–पात्र है और उसमें उषा (प्रभात) की लाल किरण के समान लाल शराब भरी हुई है। वह उसमें ऐसे ही चमक रही है जैसे नये बादलों में बिजली चमक रही हो। यदि वह मदिरा से भरा हुआ पात्र टूट गया है तो अपने हाथ की दोनों हथेलियाँ मिलाकर निर्मल स्त्रोत के जल से प्यास बुझाना कब मना है। अर्थात् सुख रूपी मदिरा का पात्र टूट गया है तो दुःख न मना कर सन्तोष रूपी प्यास सादा जल (अन्य सुखभरे साधन) से बुझानी चाहिए। किसी से बिछड़ जाने पर अधिक दुःखी न होकर धीरज रखना चाहिए।

(3)

क्या घड़ी थी, एक भी चिन्ता नहीं थी पास आई,
कालिमा तो दूर, छाया भी पलक पर थी न छाई
आँख से मस्ती झलकती, बात से मस्ती टपकती,
वो हँसी ऐसी जिसे सुन, बादलों ने शर्म खाई।
वह गई तो ले गई, उल्लास के आधार माना,
पर अथिरता पर समय की, मुसकराना कब मना है ?
है अँधेरी रात पर दीवा जलाना कब मना है ?

शब्दार्थ—घड़ी = समय, **कालिमा** = काला, **शर्म** = लज्जा, **अथिरता** = कसौटी।

प्रसंग—यहाँ पर कवि ने मनुष्य के सुखमय समय का वर्णन किया है जब उसे किसी प्रकार की चिन्ता या दुःख नहीं था।

भावार्थ—कवि कहता है कि एक वह समय था जब एक भी चिन्ता का नामोनिशान नहीं था उसके चेहरे पर। अँधेरा तो दूर की बात है एक छाया तक उसके सामने नहीं थी। आँखों में मस्ती थी, बातों में बेपरवाही थी। हँसी ऐसी थी कि बादल भी अपनी गरज पर शरमाते थे। लेकिन जब वह (साथी, पत्नी) उसके जीवन से दूर चली गई जिसे कवि ने अपनी प्रसन्नता का आधार माना था। यह तो समय की अस्थिरता है अर्थात् समय एक जैसा नहीं रहता—सुख के बाद दुःख आता है। अतः हमें समय की अस्थिरता को देखकर दुःखी न होकर मुस्कुराना चाहिए क्योंकि यह सबके साथ ही होता आया है और होता रहेगा। अतः इस वजह से दुःखी न होकर धीरज रखना चहिए।

अँधेरे में दीपक जलाना ही बुद्धिमानी है।

(4)

हाय वे उन्माद के झोंके कि जिनमें राग जागा,
वैभवों से फेर आँखें, गान का वरदान माँगा।
एक अन्तर से ध्वनित हों, दूसरे में जो निरन्तर,
भर दिया अंबर-अवनि को मत्तता के गीत गा-गा।
अंत उनका हो गया तो, मन बहलाने के लिए ही,
ले अधूरी पंक्ति कोई, गुनगुनाना कब मना है ?
है अँधेरी रात पर दीवा जलाना कब मना है ?

शब्दार्थ—**उन्माद** = मस्ती, **राग** = गीत, प्रेम, **वैवभों** = सुख-सम्पत्ति, **गान** = गीत, **वरदान** = आशीर्वाद, **ध्वनित** = ध्वनि पूर्ण, **निरन्तर** = लगातार, **अम्बर-अवनि** = आकाश और धरती, **मत्तता** = मस्ती।

प्रसंग—कवि ने संकेत किया है कि सुख के बाद यदि दु:ख आये तो निराश न होकर धीरज का परिचय देकर प्रसन्न रहना चाहिए।

भावार्थ—कवि कहता है कि एक वह समय था जब हम मस्त होकर प्रेम प्रसंग में मग्न रहते थे और सुख-वैभव को छोड़कर गीत गाते थे। एक-दूसरे से मिलकर मधुर संगीत से आकाश और पृथ्वी को गुंजा दिया था। यदि उन गीतों का अन्त हो गया (या वह प्रिय साथी बिछड़ गया जिसके साथ प्रेम गीत गाये थे) तो उनकी (गीतों की) अधूरी पंक्ति को गुनगुनाना मना नहीं है। अर्थात् पूर्व के सुख को अनुभव करके इस समय को भी उसी प्रकार मधुर बनाने का प्रयास करना चाहिए। अँधेरे में दीपक जलाना मना नहीं है।

(5)

हाय वे साथी कि चुम्बक-लौहा से जो पास आए,
पास क्या आये, हृदय के बीच ही गोया समाए,
दिन कटे ऐसे कि कोई तार वीणा से मिलकर
एक मीण और प्यारा, जिन्दगी का गीत गाए।
वे गये तो सोचकर यह, लौटने वाले नहीं वे,
खोज मन का मीत, कोई लौ लगाना कब मना है ?
है अँधेरी रात पर दीवा जलाना कब मना है ?

शब्दार्थ—**चुम्बक** = वह धातु जो लोहे को अपनी ओर खींचती है, **लौहा** = लोहा, **वीणा** = वाद्य यन्त्र, **मीण** = मनुष्यों की एक जाति, **मीत** = प्रिय, मित्र।

प्रसंग—यहाँ कवि अपने साथी के बिछड़ जाने का जिक्र करते हुए दु:खी न होने की प्रेरणा दे रहा है।

भावार्थ—कवि कहता है कि उसको ऐसा साथी मिला कि वे एक-दूसरे के सम्पर्क में इस प्रकार आये जैसे चुम्बक लोहे की तरह अपनी ओर आकर्षित कर लेता है। दोनों के हृदय एक-दूसरे से मिल गये। उन दोनों के दिन सुख से कटने लगे जैसे वीणा के तार प्यारा संगीत निकाल रहे हों। एक ऐसा प्रिय मित्र मिला जिसने जिन्दगी के गीत गाये। वह मीत मृत्यु की गोद में चला गया कि वह अब कभी वापस नहीं आयेगा। तो धीरज रखकर उस दु:ख के समय को निकाल दो और फिर दूसरा कोई अपने मन का मीत खोजकर अपने मन को लगाना शुरू कर दो। अर्थात् यह जीवन हमेशा दु:ख मनाते रहने के लिए नहीं है। जीवन के यथार्थ को समझकर प्रसन्न रहने का प्रयत्न करना चाहिए।

अँधेरे में दीपक जलाना मना नहीं है।

(6)

क्या हवाएँ थीं कि उजड़ा प्यार का वह आशियाना,
कुछ न आया काम तेरा, शोर करना गुल मचाना,
माना कि उन शक्तियों के साथ चलता जोर किसका
किन्तु ऐ निर्माण के प्रतिनिधि, तुझे होगा बताना
जो बसे हैं, जो उजड़ते हैं, प्रकृति के जड़ नियम से,
पर किसी उजड़े हुए को, फिर बसाना कब मना है ?
है अँधेरी रात पर दीवा जलाना कब मना है ?

शब्दार्थ—आशियाना = घर, **शोरगुल** = रोना पीटना, **उन शक्तियों** = ईश्वर की शक्तियाँ, **निर्माण के प्रतिनिधि** = फिर से निर्माण करने वाले मनुष्य, **जड़ नियम** = कठोर नियम।

प्रसंग—यहाँ कवि संसार के जीवन और मृत्यु के नियम को बताते हुए कहता है कि विनाश के बाद मनुष्य को निर्माण करना चाहिए।

भावार्थ—कवि कहता है कि कुछ ऐसी प्रकृति की हवाएँ चलीं कि कवि के प्रेम का आशियाना उजड़ गया और परिवार के लोगों का रोना-धोना कुछ काम नहीं आया। तभी हम मान लेते हैं कि ईश्वर (प्रकृति) के कठोर नियमों के सामने मनुष्य का कोई जोर (शक्ति) नहीं चलता। अर्थात् जिसको संसार से जाना है, उसे कोई रोक नहीं सकता। अन्त में कवि यही सन्देश देता है कि जो विनाश का कार्य हो गया वह तो हो ही गया, लेकिन किसी उजड़े हुए मनुष्य को फिर बसाना होगा। निर्माण का प्रतिनिधि मनुष्य है वही पुनः निर्माण करता है। बसे हुए मनुष्य को फिर उजड़ना पड़ सकता है। इसलिए मनुष्य को चाहिए कि उजड़े हुओं को फिर से बसाये। यही कवि का सन्देश है।

अभ्यास-प्रश्न

प्रश्न 1. कवि ने इस कविता में क्या सन्देश दिया है ?

उत्तर—'अँधेरे का दीपक' नामक कविता में 'हरिवंशराय बच्चन' ने पाठकों को यह सन्देश दिया है कि यदि अँधेरी रात है तो दिया जलाकर उस अंधकार से मुक्ति पाओ। अँधेरे को कोसने के स्थान पर उसका निवारण करना चाहिए। जिस प्रकार अँधेरे का निवारण दिये जलाने से होता है उसी प्रकार हर दुःख से उबरने का उपाय भी मनुष्य को खोजना पड़ता है। कवि के अनुसार तो दुःख में न रोकर उसे भूलने का प्रयत्न करना चाहिए और अपने आप को प्रसन्न रखने का प्रयत्न करना चाहिए।

अनेक उदाहरणों द्वारा कवि ने स्पष्ट किया है कि यदि आपका सुन्दर घर किसी कारण से टूट गया है तो कंकड़, पत्थर इकट्ठे करके अपनी शान्ति की कुटिया फिर बना लो। कभी आपकी सुन्दर चमचमाती शराब की प्याली टूट जाती है तो निराश न हों और अपनी दोनों हथेलियाँ जोड़कर किसी निर्मल झरने के स्वच्छ पानी से अपनी प्यास बझाओ।

अन्य स्थान पर कवि ने कहा है कि यदि कोई अति प्रिय साथी बिछड़ गया है तो इसको समय की अस्थिरता मानकर दुःख छोड़कर प्रसन्नता की ओर अग्रसर होना चाहिए। जो जन चले गये हैं वे कभी वापस नहीं आते यह प्रकृति का कठोर नियम है, जिसको न तो बदला जा सकता है और न ही इसमें कुछ संशोधन हो सकता है। ऐसे में अपने को निःसहाय मानकर ज्यादा सोच-विचार मत करो, बल्कि अपने को उस वातावरण में ढालने का प्रयत्न करो और अपने हृदय को प्रसन्न रखो। प्यार का आशियाना टूट जाने पर भी निराश होकर रोने से भी कोई लाभ नहीं होगा। मनुष्य को धैर्य रखकर पुनः वैसा ही आशियाना बनाने का प्रयत्न करना चाहिए। मनुष्य निर्माण का प्रतिनिधि है, वह पुनः निर्माण कर सकता है, उसने कभी प्रकृति के विनाश से हार नहीं मानी है। कवि को विश्वास है कि वह फिर से अपना आशियाना स्थापित कर लेगा।

प्रश्न 2. 'अँधेरे का दीपक' नामक कविता का केन्द्रीय भाव लिखिए।

उत्तर—कवि कहता है कि अँधेरा तो अपने स्वभावगत गुण के कारण पृथ्वी पर फैले प्रकाश को दूर कर देता है। ऐसे में मनुष्य का कर्तव्य है कि वह दीपक जलाकर प्रकाश को जगमगा दे। यदि किसी कारण से हमारा सुन्दर भवन टूट गया है तो पुन: शान्ति की कुटीर बनाना मना नहीं है।

ऐसे ही मनोरम, सुन्दर मधु-पात्र जिसमें लाल रंग की शराब भरी है और वह किसी कारण से टूट गया है तो कवि कहता है कि अपनी तृष्णा को निर्मल जल से बुझाओ।

कवि ने निराशा का विरोध किया है और अपनी कविता में आशा का संचार किया है। ऐसा भी हो सकता है कि तुम्हारा खुशनुमा समय दु:ख में बदल जाता है, तो भी निराश न होकर समय की अस्थिरता को समझकर धैर्य धारण करना ही एक उपाय है और कुछ नहीं। पुन: प्रफुल्लित होने के लिए मना नहीं है।

उन्माद भरे गीत जो उसे प्रसन्नता दे रहे थे वे कभी टूट जाये तो दु:ख तो अवश्य होता है, लेकिन उन्हीं गीतों की अधूरी पंक्ति गुनगुनाने से थोड़ी राहत तो मिल ही जाती है। अत: प्रसन्नता के साथ उस गीत की कोई पंक्ति गुनगुनानी चाहिए।

यदि कभी तुम्हारे अत्यन्त प्रिय व्यक्ति का विरह हो जाता है यानी उसकी मृत्यु हो जाती है तो वह कभी वापस नहीं आयेगा। यह निश्चित है, क्योंकि प्रकृति का नियम अटल है, जो गया है वह कभी वापस नहीं आयेगा। कवि कहता है कि दूसरा मन का मीत खोजकर फिर से सुख का जीवन बिताने का प्रयास करना चाहिए। यहाँ पर कवि शायद अपनी पहली पत्नी की मृत्यु की ओर इशारा कर रहा है। अन्त में कवि कहता है कि एक समय ऐसी आँधियाँ चलीं कि मनुष्य का प्रेम से बनाया हुआ आशियाना उजड़ गया तो उसे रोना-चिल्लाना नहीं चाहिए क्योंकि इससे कुछ होगा भी नहीं और न ही प्रकृति की शक्तियों को चुनौती दी जा सकती है। मनुष्य निर्माण का प्रतिनिधि है, उसे तो पुन: अपना आशियाना बनाना होगा।

कवि की यह आस्थावादी और आशावादी कविता है। कवि पाठकों से यही अपेक्षा करता है कि आशा को अपने पास रखो और प्रकृति के नियमों में विश्वास रखो। संसार में दु:ख से दु:खी होकर निराशावादी मत बनो, बल्कि आशावादी बनो।

प्रश्न 3. है अँधेरी रात, पर दीवा जलाना कब मना है ?
कल्पना के हाथ से कमनीय जो मन्दिर बना था,
भावना के हाथ ने जिसमें वितानों को तना था।
स्वप्न ने अपने करों से, था जिसे रुचि से सँवारा,
स्वर्ग के दुष्प्राय रंगों से, रसों से जो सना था।
ढह गया वह तो जुटाकर ईंट, पत्थर, कंकड़ों को,
एक अपनी शान्ति की कुटिया बनावा कब मना है ?
है अँधेरी रात पर दीवा जलाना कब मना है ?

(i) प्रस्तुत पद्यांश में क्या सन्देश कवि ने दिया है ?

(ii) कवि किस युग के कैसे कवि थे ?

(iii) 'भावना के हाथ से जिसमें वितानों को तना था' का तात्पर्य बताइए।

(iv) प्रस्तुत पद्यांश का अर्थ लिखिए।

उत्तर—(i) कवि ने यहाँ यह सन्देश दिया है कि यदि रात अँधेरी है तो अँधेरी रात को न कोस कर अँधेरे को दूर करने के लिए दीपक जलाना चाहिए।

(ii) कवि 'हरिवंशराय बच्चन' छायावादी युग के आस्थावादी कवि थे। छायावाद प्रकृति से अधिक सम्बन्ध रखता है। वह प्रकृति के साथ-साथ ईश्वर में विश्वास करने वाले कवि थे। उनकी ईश्वर में और उनकी बनाई हुई रचना में अटूट विश्वास था। यदि मनुष्य की सुविधा के अनुसार प्रकृति में कोई कमी है तो मनुष्य को उस कमी को स्वयं दूर करना चाहिए।

(iii) मनुष्य ने अपनी कल्पना से जो सुन्दर भवन बनाया था, भावना के आधार पर उसे सुन्दरता प्रदान की थी और स्वर्ग के दुष्प्राप्य रंगों से उसे सजाया था। यदि वह टूट गया है तो पुन: बिखरे सामान को इकट्ठा करके अपने लिए एक कुटिया का निर्माण कर लो।

(iv) कवि 'हरिवंशराय बच्चन' कहते हैं कि अँधेरी रात है तो उसे बुरा न कहकर अपने लिए एक दीपक जला लो जिससे प्रकाश हो जायेगा और अँधेरा दूर हो जायेगा। कल्पना से जो सुन्दर भवन बनाया था और भावना के आधार पर सुन्दर तम्बुओं को ताना था। अपनी कल्पना के हाथों से उसे सुन्दरता प्रदान की थी और स्वर्ग के दुष्प्राप्य रंगों से उसे सजाया था। यदि वह टूट गया है तो उसके बिखरे सामान को इकट्ठा करके अपने लिए एक कुटिया बना लो जिसमें शान्ति से तुम रह सको। अर्थात् विनाश के बाद निर्माण की प्रक्रिया चलती रहनी चाहिए।

प्रश्न 4. क्या घड़ी थी, एक भी चिन्ता नहीं थी पास आई,
कालिमा तो दूर, छाया भी पलक पर भी न छाई
आँख से मस्ती झलकती, बात से मस्ती टपकती,
थी हँसी ऐसी जिसे सुन, बादलों ने शर्म खाई।
वह गई तो ले गई, उल्लास के आधार माना,
पर अस्थिरता पर समय की, मुसकराना कब मना है ?
है अँधेरी रात पर दीवा जलाना कब मना है ?

(i) किसको सुनकर किसने शर्म खाई ?

(ii) कवि को किस-किस में मस्ती झलकती थी ?

(iii) कवि ने समय को अस्थिर क्यों कहा है ?

(iv) प्रस्तुत पंक्तियों का अर्थ लिखिए ?

उत्तर—(i) कवि की हँसी इतनी मस्त थी कि जिसे सुनकर बादलों को भी शर्म आती थी।

(ii) कवि और उसकी पत्नी का साथ था तब उसकी आँख से मस्ती झलकती थी और बात करने में भी मस्ती झलकती थी। यानी उसका जीवन खुशियों से भरा हुआ था।

(iii) कवि ने समय को अस्थिर इसलिए कहा है क्योंकि यह कभी भी स्थिर अर्थात् ठहरने वाला नहीं रहता। यह हमेशा बदलता हुआ आगे बढ़ता है। आज जो चीजें हैं वे कल वैसी ही नहीं रहेंगी। अर्थात् उनमें कुछ-न-कुछ बदलाव जरूर हो जायेगा।

(iv) कवि कहता है कि एक वह समय था जबकि एक भी चिन्ता का नामोनिशान नहीं था उनके चेहरे पर। अँधेरा तो दूर की बात है एक छाया तक उसके सामने नहीं थी। आँखों में मस्ती थी। बातों में भी मस्ती थी। हँसी ऐसी थी कि बादल भी अपनी गरज पर शर्माते थे। लेकिन जब वह (साथी, पत्नी) उसके जीवन से दूर चली गई जिसे कवि ने अपनी प्रसन्नता का आधार माना था, तो सब चला गया। यही तो समय की अस्थिरता है अर्थात् समय एक जैसा नहीं रहता सुख के बाद दु:ख आता है। अत: हमें समय की अस्थिरता को देखकर दु:खी न होकर मुस्कुराना चाहिए क्योंकि यह सबके साथ ही होता चला आ रहा है और होता रहेगा। अत: इस कारण दु:खी न होकर धीरज रखना चाहिए। अँधेरे में दीपक जलाना ही बुद्धिमानी है।

प्रश्न 5. क्या हवाएँ थीं कि उजड़ा प्यार का वह अशियाना,
कुछ न आया काम तेरा, शोर करना गुल मचाना,
माना कि उन शक्तियों के साथ चलता जोर किसका
किन्तु ऐ निर्माण के प्रतिनिधि, तुझे होगा बताना
जो बसे हैं, जो उजड़ते हैं, प्रकृति के जड़ नियम से,
पर किसी उजड़े हुए को, फिर बसाना कब मना है ?
है अँधेरी रात पर दीवा जलाना कब मना है ?

(i) प्रस्तुत पंक्तियों की प्रथम दो पंक्तियों में क्या कहा है ?

(ii) निर्माण के प्रतिनिधि से कवि ने क्या पूछा है ?

(iii) अँधेरा रात है तो हमें क्या करना चाहिए ?

(iv) प्रस्तुत पंक्तियों का अर्थ लिखिए ?

उत्तर—(i) प्रस्तुत पद्यांश की प्रथम दो पंक्तियों में यह कहा गया है कि कुछ ऐसी प्रकृति की हवाएँ चलीं कि कवि के प्रेम का आशियाना उजड़ गया और परिवार के लोगों का रोना-धोना कुछ काम नहीं आया।

(ii) निर्माण के प्रतिनिधि (मनुष्य) से कवि ने यह पूछा है कि प्रकृति के जड़ नियम से जो लोग बसे हैं वे उजड़ जाते हैं, लेकिन उन उजड़े हुओं को फिर से बसाना चाहिए।

(iii) अँधेरी रात में हमें अँधेरे को न कोस कर प्रकाश के लिए एक दीपक जलाना चाहिए। अँधेरी रात में हमें दीपक जलाकर प्रकाश करना चाहिए और अपने काम को पूरा करना चाहिए।

(iv) कवि कहता है कि कुछ ऐसी प्रकृति की हवाएँ चलीं कि कवि के प्रेम का आशियाना उजड़ गया और परिवार के लोगों का रोना-धोना कुछ काम नहीं आया। तभी हम मान लेते हैं कि ईश्वर (प्रकृति) के कठोर नियमों के सामने मनुष्य का कोई जोर नहीं चलता। अर्थात् जिसको संसार से जाना है, उसे कोई रोक नहीं सकता। अन्त में कवि यही सन्देश देता है कि जो विनाश का कार्य हो गया वह तो हो ही गया, किन्तु किसी उजड़े मनुष्य को फिर बसाना होगा। निर्माण का प्रतिनिधि मनुष्य है वही पुनः निर्माण करता है। बसे हुए मनुष्य को उजड़ना पड़ सकता है। इसलिए मनुष्य को चाहिए कि उजड़े हुओं को फिर से बसायें। यही कवि का सन्देश है।

गद्य संकलन

[GADYA SANKALAN]

1. पुत्र-प्रेम

—मुंशी प्रेमचन्द

प्रेमचन्द जी ने कथा साहित्य को मनोरंजन के स्तर से ऊपर उठकर जीवन के साथ जोड़ने का कार्य किया। प्रेमचन्द जी के साहित्य पर सर्वत्र शिव का शासन है, सत्य और सुन्दर शिव के अनुचर होकर आते हैं। उनकी कला स्वीकृत रूप में जीवन के लिए थी और जीवन का अर्थ उनका वर्तमान सामाजिक जीवन ही था।

लेखक परिचय—हिन्दी के कथा एवं उपन्यास सम्राट प्रेमचन्द का जन्म उत्तर प्रदेश में वाराणसी के निकट लमही गाँव में 31 जुलाई, सन् 1880 में हुआ। बचपन में इनका नाम धनपतराय था। इनके पिता अजायबराय डाकखाने में काम करते थे। बचपन में पिता का देहावसान होने के बाद इनका पूरा बचपन संघर्ष में ही बीता। ये पहले उर्दू में 'नवाबराय' के नाम से कहानियाँ लिखा करते थे। हिन्दी में लेखन के लिए इन्होंने 'प्रेमचन्द' नाम का प्रयोग किया। इनका निधन 8 अक्टूबर, 1936 को बनारस में हुआ।

साहित्य में योगदान—प्रेमचन्द जी के लेखन पर गाँधीवादी विचारधारा का प्रभाव है। प्रेमचन्द जी की कहानियाँ 'मानसरोवर' (आठ भागों) में प्रकाशित हैं। निर्मला, गोदान, गबन, कर्मभूमि, रंगभूमि आदि प्रेमचन्द के उल्लेखनीय उपन्यास हैं।

प्रेमचन्द के साहित्य की महत्वपूर्ण विशेषता है उनका आदर्शोन्मुखी यथार्थवाद जिसके कारण वे पाठकों में अत्यधिक लोकप्रिय हुए। प्रेमचन्द जी का साहित्यिक जीवन विविध पहलुओं से जुड़ा हुआ है। विषयवस्तु एवं शिल्प दोनों ही दृष्टियों से यदि प्रेमचन्द जी के साहित्य की समीक्षा की जाये तो यह पता चलता है कि प्रेमचन्द जी का साहित्य अप्रतिम है।

पुत्र-प्रेम प्रेमचन्द जी की ऐसी अनूठी कहानी है जिसमें उन्होंने जीवन के यथार्थ को चित्रित करने का प्रयास किया है।

शब्दार्थ—अर्थशास्त्र = धन का शास्त्र, **व्यर्थ** = बेकार, **श्रेणी** = कक्षा, **ज्वर** = बुखार, **क्षीण** = कमजोर, **शुभ-संवाद** = अच्छा समाचार, **विस्मयकारी** = आश्चर्यजनक, **गुप्तरीति** = छुपकर, **पूर्णरीति** = पूरी तरह, **अस्थिरचित्त** = अशान्त मन, **अपव्यय** = खर्च, **संदिग्ध फल** = संदेहास्पद परिणाम, **सद्भाव** = अच्छे भाव, **शर** = बाण, **प्रारब्ध** = संभावित, **अवाक** = स्तब्ध, **परिमित** = पर्याप्त, **गालिब** = प्रभावी, **विरक्तावस्था** = विछोह की अवस्था, **दग्धकारिणी** = जलाने वाली, **देहात** = गाँव, **संतप्त** = दुःखी।

सारांश

बाबू चैतन्यदास अर्थशास्त्र के ज्ञानी थे। वे अपने अर्थशास्त्र के ज्ञान का उपयोग अपने लोकव्यवहार में भी बड़ी सफलता से किया करते थे। पेशे से वकील थे, उनकी जमींदारी थी और बैंक में भी पैसे जमा कर रखे थे। वे बहुत सोच समझकर खर्च किया करते थे। जिस खर्च में किसी किस्म का लाभ न हो वे ऐसे खर्चों से भागते थे।

चैतन्यदास के दो पुत्र थे। एक प्रभुदास तो दूसरा शिवदास। दोनों पुत्र होनहार और चतुर युवक थे। लेकिन पिता चैतन्यदास को अपने बड़े पुत्र प्रभुदास से कुछ विशेष अपेक्षाएँ थीं। वे प्रभुदास को इंग्लैण्ड भेजकर बैरिस्टर बनाना चाहते थे। किन्तु बी. ए. की परीक्षा देने के बाद प्रभुदास को ज्वर होने लगा। काफी दवा कराने के बावजूद ज्वर कम नहीं हुआ। दिनों-दिन प्रभुदास कमजोर होने लगा। धीरे-धीरे वह इतना कमजोर हो गया कि उसके उठने-बैठने की शक्ति भी समाप्त हो गई।

प्रभुदास ने बी. ए. की परीक्षा प्रथम श्रेणी में उत्तीर्ण की, पर यह समाचार भी उसके मन को उल्लासित न कर सका। वह हमेशा चिन्तित रहने लगा तथा उसे जीवन बोझ की भाँति प्रतीत होने लगा। डॉक्टर से पूछने पर चैतन्यदास को यह सुनकर आश्चर्य हो जाता है कि प्रभुदास को तपेदिक हो गया है। डॉक्टर के अनुसार यह बीमारी अभी फेफड़ों तक नहीं पहुँची है। तीन-चार महीनों में स्वस्थ हो सकते हैं। परन्तु मानसिक परिश्रम से बचना आवश्यक है।

जब मानसिक परिश्रम न कर पाने की बात चैतन्यदास सुनते हैं तो यह मान लेते हैं कि प्रभुदास का जीवन तो अब नष्ट हो गया। प्रभुदास की दशा भी दिनों-दिन खराब होती जा रही है। वह हमेशा इस रोग के बारे में ही सोचता रहता है। कभी जब ज्वर कम होता तो किताबें पढ़ने लगता लेकिन जब ज्वर का प्रकोप बढ़ जाता तब वह फिर से निराश हो जाता।

अन्ततः उसे विश्वास हो गया कि इस रोग से मुक्ति असम्भव है। यह सोच उसने दवाओं का सेवन भी बन्द कर दिया। खान-पान के उचित और अनुचित का विचार त्याग दिया। उसमें उदासीनता आ गई थी। वह दार्शनिकों की तरह बातें करता था। बीच-बीच में चैतन्यदास के मन में यह शंका उठा करती थी कि जब इस रोग के परिणाम को जान रहा हूँ फिर भी व्यर्थ धन क्यों खर्च कर रहा हूँ ? इस प्रकार से धन खर्च करने का क्या लाभ ? परन्तु पुत्र-प्रेम और लोकलाज के भय से उन्होंने इलाज जारी रखा।

एक बार जाड़े के समय में चैतन्यदास ने डॉक्टर से पूछा कि कुछ अन्तर आया कि नहीं ? तो डॉक्टर के यह कहने पर कि रोग और असाध्य होता जा रहा है, चैतन्यदास नाराज हो जाते हैं। वह डॉक्टर से यह कहते हैं कि आप लोग तो सिर्फ अपना मतलब साधते हैं। उनकी बात सुनकर डॉक्टर उन्हें यह बताता है कि रोग का सिर्फ अनुमान किया जा सकता है जो पूर्णतया सत्य हो यह निश्चित नहीं है। उसी समय शिवदास कमरे में प्रवेश करता है। जिसे देखते ही चैतन्यदास नाराज हो जाते हैं। वह डॉक्टर से पूछता है कि भाई साहब के लिए क्या किया जा सकता है ?

शिवदास के पूछने पर डॉक्टर साहब यह बताते हैं कि अब केवल एक ही रास्ता बचा है। इन्हें इटली के सेनेटोरियम में भेज दिया जाये। जिसमें करीब तीन हजार का खर्चा होगा, परन्तु यह रोग भयंकर है, यह निश्चित रूप से नहीं कहा जा सकता कि वे अच्छे होकर ही आयेंगे। इससे मन को यह महसूस होगा कि हम जो कर सकते थे वो सब कुछ किया। डॉक्टर के इस प्रस्ताव पर आधी रात तक शिवदास, चैतन्यदास और माँ तपेश्वरी के बीच बहस होती रही। एक ऐसे कार्य के लिए जिसमें परिणाम तय नहीं है, तीन हजार रुपये खर्च करना चतुराई नहीं है। शिवदास और चैतन्य दोनों का एक ही मत था, लेकिन माँ के समझाने के बाद शिवदास माँ के पक्ष में हो गया। तपेश्वरी ने अनेक तर्कों द्वारा पति को समझाने का प्रयास किया, लेकिन सफलता न मिली। अन्ततः अश्रु-वर्षा का सहारा लिया जिससे प्रभावी होकर चैतन्यदास ने यह कहा कि तुम जो कहती हो वही होगा।

तपेश्वरी ने पूछा कि मेरा कहना कब होगा तब चैतन्यदास ने रुपयों का बहाना किया। रुपयों के सन्दर्भ में तपेश्वरी कहती है कि जायदाद हैं और बैंक में भी रुपये हैं। यह सुनकर चैतन्यदास यह कहते हैं कि पूर्व पुरुषों की संचित जायदाद और रखे हुए रुपये मैं अनिश्चित हित की आशा पर बलिदान नहीं कर सकता। इसका प्रत्युत्तर देते हुए तपेश्वरी कहती है कि आधी जायदाद तो प्रभुदास की ही है। यह सुनकर चैतन्यदास यह कहते हैं कि मैं भावुकता के फेर में पड़कर धन का नाश नहीं कर सकता। अन्त में कुछ नहीं हो सका।

इस प्रस्ताव के छः महीने बाद शिवदास ने बी. ए. की परीक्षा उत्तीर्ण की जिसके लिए चैतन्यदास ने अपनी जमींदारी का कुछ हिस्सा बंधक रखकर उसे इंग्लैण्ड भेजा। मन में यही इच्छा थी कि इसमें उसे परिमित लाभ होगा। लेकिन दूसरी ओर प्रभुदास अपनी उच्च अभिलाषाओं के लिए परलोक सिधार गया।

प्रभुदास की मृत्यु के पश्चात चैतन्यदास अपने मित्रों के साथ चिता की ज्वाला को आँसुओं से भीगे नेत्रों के साथ देख रहे थे। इस अवस्था में बार-बार वह मन में यही कल्पना कर रहे थे कि यदि मैं प्रभुदास को इटली ले जाता तो शायद वह स्वस्थ हो जाता। मैंने तीन हजार के लिए अपने बेटे को खो दिया। यह सोचकर उन्हें बहुत ग्लानि हो रही थी। उनके मन के पश्चाताप की आग चिता की ज्वाला से कम ज्वलनशील नहीं थी।

चैतन्यदास इसी सोच में थे कि तभी उन्होंने एक समूह को गाजे-बाजे के साथ अर्थी लाते हुए देखा। लोग आये चिता सजने लगी तभी एक युवक उनके पास आकर खड़ा हो जाता है। जिससे पूछने पर यह पता चला कि वे इस देहात में अपने दादा को लेकर आये हैं। चैतन्यदास के पूछने पर युवक ने बताया कि बीमारी का पता नहीं चला लेकिन जिसने जहाँ बताया वहाँ लेकर गये, कोई कसर नहीं छोड़ी।

इतने में युवक का साथी बताता है कि नारायण लड़का दें तो ऐसा दें। घर की सारी पूँजी और कुछ जमीन तक पिता के इलाज के लिए बेच दी। लेकिन काल के आगे किसी का वश नहीं चलता। युवक खुशी से कहता है कि पैसा तो आज है कल नहीं पर मनुष्य दोबारा नहीं मिलता। आज भी यदि कोई मेरे पिता को एक बार बुलवा दे तो मैं सारा घर द्वार दे दूँ। क्योंकि धन से प्यारी जान, जान से प्यारा ईमान। आज अगर उनके इलाज में कोई कसर रखता तो रोते भी न बनता। जब उनकी आत्मा सुख से रहेगी तो मेरा सब तरह कल्याण ही होगा।

बाबू चैतन्यदास इन बातों को सुन रहे थे पर ये बातें उनको बाणों के समान चुभ रही थी। आज उन्हें अपनी हृदयहीनता और निरन्तरता पर ग्लानि हो रही थी। इस घटना का उनके मन पर इतना गहरा प्रभाव पड़ा कि उन्होंने प्रभुदास के अन्तिम संस्कार में खुले हाथों से खर्च किया। उनके मन की शान्ति के लिए अन्त में सिर्फ यही उपाय बाकी रह गया था।

अभ्यास-प्रश्न

प्रश्न 1. ''व्यक्ति लोभ में किस प्रकार हृदयहीन और निष्ठुर हो जाता है।'' पुत्र-प्रेम कहानी इसका जीवन्त उदाहरण हैं। स्पष्ट कीजिए।

अथवा

''पुत्र-प्रेम कहानी एक मनुष्य की हृदयहीनता की कहानी है।'' यह स्पष्ट कीजिए।

उत्तर—हिन्दी साहित्य के क्षेत्र में प्रेमचन्द का आगमन एक ऐतिहासिक घटना थी। उनकी कहानियों में ऐसी घोर यन्त्रणा, दुःखद गरीबी, असह्य दुःख, महान स्वार्थ और मिथ्या आडम्बर आदि से तड़पते हुए व्यक्तियों की अकुलाहट मिलती है, जो मन को कचोट जाती है और हमारे हृदय में टीस पैदा करती है।

व्यक्ति और लोभ दोनों का वर्षों का साथ है। यह एक ऐसा भाव है जो व्यक्ति के जीवन मूल्यों पर बड़ी सफलता से अपना प्रभाव छोड़ देता है। प्रस्तुत कहानी में प्रेमचन्द ने नैतिक मूल्यों का निर्वाह करने की कोशिश की है, लेकिन कभी-कभी स्वार्थ और लोभ अहम नैतिक मूल्यों पर हावी होकर मनुष्य को हृदयहीन और निष्ठुर बना देता है।

प्रस्तुत कहानी में चैतन्यदास का स्वार्थ उनके नैतिक मूल्यों पर इस प्रकार से हावी हो जाता है कि वे कब हृदयहीन और निष्ठुर बन जाते हैं इसका पता ही नहीं चलता है। कहानी के प्रारम्भ में प्रभुदास पर पिता का अधिक स्नेह था। पिता को उससे बड़ी-बड़ी आशाएँ थीं। लेकिन जैसे ही उनके मन में इस शंका ने जन्म लिया कि इस रोग का परिणाम विदित है तो फिर उन्हें धन का अपव्यय करने से क्या लाभ ? लेकिन डॉक्टर के यह बताने पर कि इटली के किसी सेनेटोरियम में भेजने से लाभ हो सकता है। एक आशा की किरण जगती है।

बाबू चैतन्यदास का यह प्रश्न कि यह निश्चय है कि वह वहाँ से अच्छे होकर आयेंगे। इस प्रश्न में स्वार्थ ने स्थान ले लिया। जब धन और अनिश्चित परिणाम की बात आई तो पिता ने धन का चुनाव किया।

चैतन्यदास का कथन था कि एक संदिग्ध फल के लिए तीन हजार का खर्च उठाना बुद्धिमानी नहीं है। इन तर्कों के दौरान पिता हृदयहीन हो गया था और उस हृदयहीनता का पता उसे भी नहीं चल पाया।

चैतन्यदास अपने सगे-सम्बन्धियों के साथ बैठकर चिता की ओर देख रहे थे। एक क्षण के लिए पुत्र-प्रेम जागृत हो गया। उस अवस्था में उन्होंने यही सोचा कि मुझे प्रभुदास को इटली भेजना चाहिए था, शायद वहाँ जाकर प्रभुदास स्वस्थ हो जाता। यह सोचकर उसका मन ग्लानि से भर आया। इस कहानी में युवक एक आदर्श को प्रस्तुत करता है। उस युवक के माध्यम से कहानीकार ने आदर्शोन्मुखी यथार्थवाद का सन्देश दिया है। इस प्रकार पुत्र-प्रेम कहानी में लोभ, लोभ का दुष्परिणाम और पश्चाताप को दिखाया गया है।

इस प्रकार इस कहानी में लोभ में व्यक्ति के हृदयहीन और निष्ठुर होने का प्रमाण प्रस्तुत किया गया है।

प्रश्न 2. तपेश्वरी प्रभुदास को इटली भेजने के लिए किन-किन तर्कों द्वारा समझाने का प्रयास करती है ?

अथवा

इस कहानी में माँ की भूमिका किस प्रकार की है ? तपेश्वरी ने अपने पुत्र के इलाज के लिए क्या प्रयास किया ?

उत्तर—हिन्दी के महान उपन्यासकार एवं कथा सम्राट मुंशी प्रेमचन्द ने अपनी कृतियों में मानव जीवन के अनेक पहलुओं का विवेचन किया है। मनुष्य किस प्रकार लाभ-हानि को जीवन में महत्वपूर्ण स्थान देकर अपने सम्बन्धों को छोटा बना देता है। पुत्र-प्रेम कहानी द्वारा प्रेमचन्द जी ने इसी उहा-पोह को प्रदर्शित करने का प्रयास किया है।

कहानी पुत्र-प्रेम में पिता और भाई लाभ-हानि अथवा संदिग्ध लाभ के फेर में पड़कर प्रभुदास को इटली भेजने के पक्ष में नहीं हैं। मनुष्य जीवन हेतु अर्थ को महत्वपूर्ण समझता है, परन्तु यही अर्थ कब जीवन से अधिक महत्वपूर्ण हो जाता है, मनुष्य को इस बात का पता भी नहीं चल पाता। ऐसी विषम परिस्थिति में जबकि पिता और प्रभुदास का भाई शिवदास दोनों ही संदिग्ध परिणाम को मुख्य आधार बनाकर यह निर्णय सुना देते हैं कि प्रभुदास को इटली भेजना बुद्धिमानी नहीं है।

ऐसे समय में माँ तपेश्वरी अकेली शिवदास और बाबू चैतन्यदास द्वारा लिए गये निर्णय का विरोध करती हैं। सबसे पहले पिता और भाई दोनों को धिक्कारती हैं। उनकी धिक्कार भरी बातें सुनकर शिवदास लज्जित हो जाता है और माँ के समर्थन में आ जाता है।

जब शिवदास माँ के विचारों से सहमत हो जाता है तब माँ तपेश्वरी देवी ने तर्क से काम लिया। पति के स्वभावों को प्रज्वलित करने की चेष्टा की। यह बताने का प्रयास किया कि धन नश्वर है। मनुष्य धन से अधिक महत्वपूर्ण है। इतना ही नहीं तपेश्वरी देवी ने अपने कथन के समर्थन में अनेक लोकोक्तियाँ कहीं, पर चैतन्यदास पर इनका कोई प्रभाव नहीं पड़ा।

जब तपेश्वरी देवी को अपने सारे प्रयास विफल होते दिखाई पड़े तब उन्होंने जल-बिन्दुओं के शर का प्रहार किया। जिससे बाबू चैतन्यदास नहीं बच पाये। तपेश्वरी की अश्रुवर्षा ने उन्हें स्वीकार करने पर विवश कर दिया। उन्होंने यह कहा कि रुपयों का उचित प्रबन्ध हो जाने पर वे प्रभुदास को इटली भेजेंगे। इसके प्रत्युत्तर में तपेश्वरी कहती हैं कि बैंक में रुपये हैं, जायदाद है और तीन हजार रुपयों का प्रबन्ध करना तुम्हारे लिए कोई बड़ी बात नहीं है। जिसके जवाब में चैतन्यदास यह कहते हैं कि अनिश्चित हित की आशा पर मैं पूर्वजों की सम्पत्ति का बलिदान नहीं कर सकता।

तब तपेश्वरी अन्त में यह तर्क देती है कि इस जायदाद में प्रभुदास का भी तो आधा हिस्सा है। उसके हिस्से की जायदाद का उपयोग उसके ही इलाज में किया जाये तो ठीक है। यहाँ भी चैतन्यदास यह कहते हैं कि मैं भावुकता के फेर में पड़कर धन का नाश नहीं कर सकता।

इस प्रकार तपेश्वरी, तर्क देने के बावजूद चैतन्यदास के कथन को सुनकर आश्चर्यचकित हो जाती हैं। अन्त में इतना तर्क देने के बाद भी माँ जीतकर भी हार जाती है।

प्रश्न 3. प्रभुदास को लेकर चैतन्यदास के मन में कौन-कौन-सी सदिच्छाएँ थीं और अन्त में उनका क्या परिणाम हुआ ?

उत्तर—मनुष्य की इच्छाएँ अनन्त हैं। इच्छाओं का प्रभाव जन्म से ही हो जाता है। जब शिशु माँ के गर्भ में रहता है तभी से उसको लेकर अनेक इच्छाओं का और स्वप्नों का सृजन किया जाता है। बाबू चैतन्यदास भी इससे अछूते नहीं रहे। चैतन्यदास के दो पुत्र थे, प्रभुदास और शिवदास। उनका अनुराग प्रभुदास की तरफ अधिक था।

प्रभुदास को लेकर चैतन्यदास के मन में अनेक सदिच्छाएँ भी थी। बाबू चैतन्यदास पुत्र प्रभुदास को अधिक से अधिक पढ़ाना चाहते थे। वे चाहते थे कि उनका बड़ा बेटा प्रभुदास इंग्लैण्ड में जाकर वहाँ से शिक्षा प्राप्त करे। बाबू चैतन्यदास प्रभुदास को बैरिस्टर बनाना चाहते थे। चैतन्यदास इन सारी अभिलाषाओं को पूरा करना चाहते थे। परन्तु यहाँ विधि के हाथों से अलग प्रकार की लीला रची जा रही थी।

जहाँ एक ओर बाबू चैतन्यदास अपने पुत्र को लेकर सपने सजाने में लगे हुए थे वहीं दूसरी ओर विधाता को मानों कुछ और ही मंजूर था। वह बाबू चैतन्यदास से कुछ और ही करवाना चाहता था। संयोग ऐसा हुआ कि प्रभुदास को बी. ए. की परीक्षा के बाद ज्वर आने लगा। डॉक्टरों की दवा होने लगी पर ज्वर में किसी भी प्रकार की कमी नहीं आई। प्रभुदास दिनों-दिन क्षीण होता चला जा रहा था। अपने बी. ए. की परीक्षा में उसने प्रथम श्रेणी प्राप्त की। यह समाचार भी प्रभुदास के ऊपर प्रभाव न डाल सका। वह सदैव गहरी चिन्ता में डूबा रहता। उसे अपना जीवन बोझ-सा लगने लगा। दो महीने हो गये मगर ज्वर जस का तस, हिलने का नाम ही नहीं लेता है।

चैतन्यदास को डॉक्टरों द्वारा यह पता चलता है कि उनके पुत्र में तपेदिक के लक्षण दिखाई दे रहे हैं। इस जवाब से बाबू चैतन्यदास विस्मित रह जाते हैं। उन्हें यह पता चला कि गुप्तरीति से इस रोग ने प्रभुदास के शरीर में प्रवेश किया है। यह सब सुनकर बाबू चैतन्यदास डॉक्टर से यह प्रश्न पूछते हैं कि क्या ठीक होने के बाद प्रभुदास अध्ययन में उसी प्रकार का परिश्रम कर सकेगा ?

अन्ततः डॉक्टर के द्वारा दिया गया यह जवाब सुनकर कि इसका मानसिक परिश्रम से बचना आवश्यक है, यह कथन ही बाबू चैतन्यदास कि इच्छाओं पर तुषारापात करता है। इस प्रकार उनकी सदिच्छाएँ और उनके स्वप्न डॉक्टर के इस कथन के साथ ही समाप्त हो जाते हैं।

प्रश्न 4. बाबू चैतन्यदास के साथ मणिकर्णिका घाट पर कौन-सी ऐसी घटना हुई जिसने उन्हें उनकी हृदयहीनता और आत्मशून्यता का आभास कराया ?

उत्तर—पुत्र-प्रेम कहानी में जिस महत्वपूर्ण बिन्दु को उद्‌घाटित करने का प्रयास किया गया है वह यह है कि मनुष्य की लोलुपता किस प्रकार उसकी हृदयहीनता बनकर उसके अपनों के नाश का कारण बन जाती है। बाबू चैतन्यदास का यह विचार कि पूर्व पुरुषों की संचित जायदाद और रुके हुए रुपये किसी अनिश्चित हित की आशा पर बलिदान नहीं कर सकता। इसी के परिणामस्वरूप प्रभुदास की मृत्यु हो जाती है।

चैतन्यदास अपने पुत्र की मृत्यु के पश्चात जब मणिकर्णिका घाट पर बैठे अपने पुत्र की चिता—ज्वाला की ओर देख रहे थे तो उस समय एक क्षण के लिए उनके मन में पुत्र-प्रेम जाग्रत होता है। वह मन में सोचने लगते हैं कि मैंने प्रभुदास को इटली न भेजकर गलती की। यदि मैं उसे इटली भेजता तो शायद वह स्वस्थ हो जाता। मैंने तीन हजार का मोह करके अपने पुत्र को खो दिया। बाबू चैतन्यदास का हृदय आज ग्लानि, शोक और पश्चाताप के बाणों से बिंध रहा था।

दु:खी चैतन्यदास यह सोचते रहते हैं कि तभी धूम-धाम से ढोल और शहनाइयों के साथ होती पुष्प वर्षा के बीच घाट पर एक अर्थी उतारी गई। बाबू विस्मित होकर पास खड़े युवक से पूछते हैं तो उन्हें पता चलता है कि ये एक पिता (दादा) की अर्थी है, जिसके बीमार होने पर उनके पुत्र ने बहुत इलाज करवाया। जिसने जहाँ बताया वहाँ लेकर गये। वैद्यों ने जो कुछ भी कहा उसमें कोई कसर नहीं की। उसी समय उसके साथी के मुँह से यह सुनकर कि इसने रुपयों को ठीकरे समझा। घर की सारी पूँजी पिता की दवा-दारू में स्वाहा कर दी। थोड़ी-सी जमीन भी बेच दी, फिर भी इसके पिता ठीक न हो सके।

इन सब बातों को सुन युवक कहता है कि भैया रुपया-पैसा हाथ का मैल है। कम से कम मन में यह लालसा तो न रह गई कि कुछ और करता तो अपने पिता के प्राण बचा लेता 'धन से प्यारी जान और जान से प्यारा ईमान।'

युवक के द्वारा कही गई इन बातों और इस घटना के प्रकाश में बाबू चैतन्यदास को अपनी आत्मशून्यता और अपनी हृदयहीनता दिखाई दे रही थी जो बड़ी भयावह थी। उनके अन्दर की ज्वाला उस चिता की ज्वाला से कम दग्धकारिणी नहीं थी। इस घटना का प्रभाव चैतन्यदास पर इतना गहरा पड़ा कि उन्होंने प्रभुदास की अन्त्येष्टि में हजारों रुपये खर्च कर डाले।

प्रश्न 5. कहानी के आधार पर बाबू चैतन्यदास का चरित्र-चित्रण कीजिए।

अथवा

पुत्र-प्रेम कहानी के प्रमुख पात्र का चरित्र-चित्रण कीजिए।

उत्तर—प्रेमचन्द जी ने अपनी कहानी की विषय-वस्तु के प्रभाव को व्यक्त करने के लिए ऐसे चरित्रों की सृष्टि की जो उनके विचारों के वाहक बन सकें। इस कहानी के प्रमुख पात्र बाबू चैतन्यदास हैं जिनके चरित्र के माध्यम से मुंशी जी ने यह जताने का प्रयास किया है कि शिक्षित, समृद्ध और बुद्धिमान व्यक्ति भी किस प्रकार हानि-लाभ के प्रभाव में पड़ जाता है और अपने प्रिय व्यक्ति को खो देता है। पुत्र-प्रेम कहानी का सर्वाधिक प्रभावित करने वाला प्रमुख पात्र है—बाबू चैतन्यदास। मुंशी प्रेमचन्द जी के इस चरित्र में अनेक विशेषताएँ और दुर्बलताएँ हैं जो मिलकर कहानी के प्रवाह और विषय-वस्तु को प्रभावी बनाती हैं।

शिक्षित और समृद्ध—बाबू चैतन्यदास पढ़े-लिखे व्यक्ति व पेशे से वकील थे। वे शिक्षा के महत्व को जानते थे। वे बहुत समृद्ध भी थे। दो-तीन गाँवों में उनकी जमींदारी भी थी जो कि उनकी आर्थिक सुदृढ़ता का प्रमाण थी। इस प्रकार मुंशी जी का यह पात्र इस लायक था कि अपने पुत्र के प्रति धन खर्च कर सके।

अर्थ-प्रेमी—मुंशी जी के चरित्र की यह सबसे महत्वपूर्ण विशेषता है कि उनका चरित्र अर्थ (धन) को सर्वाधिक महत्व देता है। बाबू चैतन्यदास की समृद्धता उनके अर्थशास्त्र के ज्ञान का परिणाम थी। वे व्यर्थ को विषय के समान समझते थे। उनके जीवन में अर्थ के महत्व को व्यंजित करने के लिए मुंशी जी ने लिखा—

"अर्थशास्त्र के सिद्धान्त उनके जीवन के स्तम्भ हो गये थे।"

महत्वाकांक्षी पिता—बाबू चैतन्यदास एक महत्वाकांक्षी पिता थे इसीलिए वे अपने पुत्रों को अधिक से अधिक पढ़ाना चाहते थे। वे प्रभुदास को इंग्लैण्ड भेजकर बैरिस्टर बनाना चाहते थे। अन्त में उन्होंने अपने बेटे शिवदास को शिक्षा हेतु इंग्लैण्ड भेजा। उनके मन में सदिच्छाओं से परिमित लाभ होने की आशा थी।

हृदयहीन और भौतिकवादी—बाबू चैतन्यदास के चरित्र में हृदयहीनता और भौतिकता विद्यमान थी। तपेश्वरी के बार-बार समझाने पर भी प्रभुदास को इटली न भेजने का निर्णय बाबू चैतन्यदास की हृदयहीनता का द्योतक है। वे अनिश्चित हित की आशा पर अपने धन का बलिदान नहीं करना चाहते थे। उनके द्वारा कहा

गया यह कथन उनके चरित्र की इस विशेषता को उद्घाटित करता है—"मैं भावुकता के फेर में पड़कर धन का ह्रास नहीं कर सकता।"

इस प्रकार बाबू चैतन्यदास के चरित्र के अनेक ऐसे गुण हैं जो कहानी में रसोद्रेक करने के साथ ही साथ कहानी के सन्देश को पाठकों के समक्ष प्रस्तुत करने में सहायक हैं।

प्रश्न 6. "युवक ने गदगद् स्वर में कहा—भैया, रुपया-पैसा हाथ का मैल है। कहाँ आता है, कहाँ चला जाता है, मनुष्य नहीं मिलता।" उक्त कथन का सन्दर्भ स्पष्ट करते हुए कथन के सम्बन्ध में अपने विचार लिखें।

उत्तर—प्रेमचन्द जी की रचनाएँ आदर्शोन्मुखी यथार्थवाद पर आधारित होती हैं। यहाँ बाबू चैतन्यदास का चरित्र एक यथार्थ को प्रस्तुत करता है तो दूसरी ओर उस युवक का चरित्र यथार्थ से दूर अपेक्षित आदर्श को प्रस्तुत करता है।

उक्त कथन का सन्दर्भ उस समय का है जब चैतन्यदास मणिकर्णिका घाट पर चिन्तामग्न बैठा है। उसी समय धूम-धूम से जो अर्थी लाई जाती है। उसके सम्बन्ध में जब वे उस युवक से बातचीत करते हैं तो उसी दौरान वह युवक, जो कि अपने पिता का अन्तिम संस्कार करने आया था यह कथन कहता है।

इस कथन से यह सन्देश स्पष्ट हो जाता है कि मनुष्य के जीवन से बढ़कर धन नहीं है। मैं उस युवक के कथन से पूरी तरह से सहमत हूँ। मेरी दृष्टि में रुपया-पैसा आता जाता रहता है। ये धन-सम्पत्ति और भौतिक संसाधन मनुष्य के लिए हैं। मनुष्य इन चीजों के लिए नहीं है।

मनुष्य के जीवन के लिए ये वस्तुएँ सहायक हैं, प्रधान अथवा मूलभूत नहीं है क्योंकि मनुष्य स्वयं प्रधान है। हमें यह कभी नहीं भूलना चाहिए कि जीवन एक बार ही मिलता है। मनुष्य धन का उपयोग करने के लिए बना है इसलिए धन मनुष्य से बढ़कर कभी नहीं हो सकता।

इस प्रकार मैं उस युवक के द्वारा कहे गये विचारों से पूरी तरह से सहमत हूँ। कहानी के द्वारा यही सन्देश देने का प्रयास किया गया कि मनुष्य को पूरी तरह से भौतिकवादी बनकर निर्णय नहीं लेना चाहिए जिससे बाद में पश्चाताप न करना पड़े। इस कहानी में बाबू चैतन्यदास का पश्चाताप इसी सन्देश का पर्याय है।

प्रश्न 7. "वे वकील थे, दो तीन गाँवों में उनकी जमींदारी भी थी, बैंक में भी कुछ रुपये थे ?"

(i) वकील कौन हैं ? उनके स्वभाव के विषय में दो पंक्तियाँ लिखें।

(ii) वकील साहब की आर्थिक स्थिति के विषय में बताइये।

(iii) धन खर्च करने का उनका दृष्टिकोण किस प्रकार का था ? समझाकर लिखिए।

(iv) वकील साहब के परिवार का परिचय दीजिये।

उत्तर—(i) लेखक प्रेमचन्द के द्वारा रचित कहानी 'पुत्र-प्रेम' के प्रधान पात्र चैतन्यदास ही वकील थे। वह अर्थशास्त्र के अच्छे ज्ञाता थे। साथ ही जीवन में वह उसका यथायोग्य व्यवहार करते थे।

(ii) चैतन्यदास पेशे से वकील थे। दो तीन गाँवों में उनकी जमींदारी थी। इसके अतिरिक्त बैंक में भी उनका कुछ पैसा जमा था। यह सब उनके अर्थशास्त्र के ज्ञान के कारण था।

(iii) धन खर्च करने के विषय में वह बड़े व्यावहारिक थे। उनके सामने जब कोई खर्च आता तब वह यह सोचते थे कि यहाँ धन खर्च करने में स्वयं मेरा लाभ होगा अथवा किसी अन्य पुरुष का ? यदि इन दोनों में से किसी का भी लाभ नहीं हो तो वह बड़ी कठोरता से अपना हाथ खींच लिया करते थे।

(iv) वकील चैतन्यदास के परिवार में उन्हें सम्मिलित करके कुल चार सदस्य, जिनमें वह, उनकी पत्नी तपेश्वरी एवं उनके दो पुत्र प्रभुदास एवं शिवदास थे। दोनों पुत्र कॉलेज में पढ़ते थे तथा उनमें एक श्रेणी

का अन्तर था। दोनों पुत्र चतुर व होनहार थे तथापि चैतन्यदास अपने ज्येष्ठ पुत्र प्रभुदास से बहुत स्नेह करते थे, क्योंकि उसमें सदुत्साह अधिक था। इसीलिए वह उसे विद्योन्नति के लिए इंग्लैण्ड भेजकर बैरिस्टर बनाना चाहते थे।

प्रश्न 8. ''युवक ने गद्‌गद् स्वर में कहा—भैया, रुपया पैसा हाथ का मैल है, कहाँ आता है, कहाँ जाता है, मनुष्य नहीं मिलता। जिन्दगानी है तो कमा खाऊँगा, पर मन में यह लालसा तो नहीं रह गई कि हाय ! यह नहीं किया उस वैद्य के पास नहीं गया नहीं तो शायद बच जाते।''

(i) युवक कौन है ? वह वहाँ किसके साथ व क्यों आया ?

(ii) ''रुपया पैसा हाथ का मैल है।'' युवक ने ये शब्द किस घटना के सन्दर्भ में कहे हैं ? समझाकर लिखिए।

(iii) उसने पैसा किसके लिये खर्च किया ? उस व्यक्ति से उसका क्या सम्बन्ध था ? युवक की उस व्यक्ति के प्रति संवेदनाओं का वर्णन कीजिए।

(iv) पुत्र-प्रेम कहानी में अभिव्यक्त सन्देश पर प्रकाश डालिये।

उत्तर—(i) चैतन्यदास मणिकर्णिका घाट पर बैठे अपने प्रिय पुत्र प्रभुदास की जलती चिता को देख रहे थे उसी समय मनुष्यों का एक समूह वहाँ एक अर्थी को लेकर आया। वे ढ़ोल बजाते, गाते और पुष्प बरसाते आये थे। यह युवक उसी समूह में था। दरअसल वह मनुष्यों का समूह इस युवक के पिता की अर्थी के साथ आया था। युवक के पिता का देहान्त हो गया था वह उनकी अन्तिम क्रिया हेतु वहाँ पर अपने मित्रों व सम्बन्धियों आदि के साथ आया था।

(ii) उसने प्रसन्न होकर कहा ''भैया रुपया पैसा हाथ का मैल है'' क्योंकि उसने अपने पिता की बीमारी में अपनी सारी धन-दौलत लुटा दी थी साथ ही उनकी इच्छानुसार वह मृत्युपरान्त उस घाट पर लाया था, जहाँ पर उसके पिता अपनी अन्तिम क्रिया चाहते थे। वह बहुत खुश था कि उसने अपने पिता की सब इच्छाएँ पूरी कीं।

(iii) उसने पैसा अपने पिता के लिए खर्च किया। जिसने जहाँ बताया लेकर गया। चित्रकूट, हरिद्वार, प्रयाग सभी स्थानों में लेकर घूमा। वैद्यों ने जो कहा वही सब किया। उसका कारण था कि वह उसके पिता थे तथा वह उन्हें बचाना चाहता था।

वह युवक संवेदनाओं में खोकर कहता है—''रुपया पैसा हाथ का मैल है। कहाँ आता है कहाँ जाता है पैसा तो मिलता है परन्तु मनुष्य नहीं मिलता। कोई हमारा सारा घर द्वार लिखा ले पर दादा को एक बोल बुला दे।''

(iv) 'पुत्र-प्रेम' प्रेमचन्द की बहुचर्चित तथा मार्मिक कहानी है। यह एक कृपण, धन के लोभी तथा प्रत्येक सन्दर्भ में धन के खर्च से होने वाले लाभ तथा हानि के विषय में सोचने वाले व्यक्ति चैतन्यदास की कहानी है। चैतन्यदास के लिए प्रत्येक विषय में धन के खर्च से लाभ होना आवश्यक था क्योंकि वह किसी भी अलाभकारी विषय पर धन व्यय करना व्यर्थ समझते थे। इस कहानी के माध्यम से लेखक ने मनुष्य के जीवन में धन से अधिक मनुष्य के महत्व को दर्शाया है। कहानी के अन्तिम पृष्ठों में लेखक ने स्पष्ट किया है कि धन मनुष्य से अधिक महत्वपूर्ण नहीं होता, धन तो जाकर आ जाता है परन्तु मनुष्य जाकर कभी वापस नहीं आता है। धन की सार्थकता उसके सदुपयोग में है अपितु उसे संचित करके रखने में नहीं।

2. गौरी

—सुभद्राकुमारी चौहान

लेखिका परिचय—सुभद्राकुमारी चौहान हिन्दी की सुप्रसिद्ध कवयित्री और लेखिका थीं। उनके दो कविता संग्रह तथा तीन कथा संग्रह प्रकाशित हुए पर उनकी प्रसिद्धि 'झाँसी की रानी' कविता के कारण है। ये राष्ट्रीय चेतना की एक सजग कवयित्री रही हैं। इन्होंने स्वाधीनता संग्राम में अनेक बार जेल यातनाएँ सहने के पश्चात अपनी अनुभूतियों को कहानी में भी व्यक्त किया। वातावरण चित्रण-प्रधान शैली की भाषा सरल तथा काव्यात्मक है, इस कारण इनकी रचना की सादगी हृदयग्राही है।

उनका जन्म नागपंचमी के दिन इलाहाबाद के निकट निहालपुर नामक गाँव में रामनाथ सिंह के जमींदार परिवार में हुआ था। बाल्यकाल से ही वे कविताएँ रचने लगी थीं। उनकी रचनाएँ राष्ट्रीयता की भावना से परिपूर्ण हैं। सुभद्राकुमारी चौहान, चार बहनें और दो भाई थे। उनके पिता ठाकुर रामनाथ सिंह शिक्षा के प्रेमी थे और उन्हीं की देख-रेख में उनकी प्रारम्भिक शिक्षा भी हुई। 1919 में खण्डवा के ठाकुर लक्ष्मण सिंह के साथ विवाह के बाद वे जबलपुर आ गई थीं। 1929 में गाँधीजी के असहयोग आन्दोलन में भाग लेने वाली वह प्रथम महिला थीं। वे दो बार जेल भी गई थीं। सुभद्राकुमारी चौहान की जीवनी, इनकी पुत्री, सुधा चौहान ने 'मिला तेज से तेज' नामक पुस्तक में लिखी है। इसे हंस प्रकाशन, इलाहाबाद ने प्रकाशित किया है। वे एक रचनाकार होने के साथ-साथ स्वाधीनता संग्राम की सेनानी भी थीं। डॉ. मंगला अनुजा की पुस्तक सुभद्राकुमारी चौहान उनके साहित्यिक व स्वाधीनता संघर्ष के जीवन पर प्रकाश डालती है। साथ ही स्वाधीनता आन्दोलन में उनके कविता के जरिये नेतृत्व को भी रेखांकित करती है। 15 फरवरी, 1948 को एक कार दुर्घटना में उनका आकस्मिक निधन हो गया था।

भारतीय तटरक्षक सेना ने 28 अप्रैल, 2006 को सुभद्राकुमारी चौहान की राष्ट्रप्रेम की भावना को सम्मानित करने के लिए नये नियुक्त एक तटरक्षक जहाज को सुभद्राकुमारी चौहान का नाम दिया है। भारतीय डाकतार विभाग ने 6 अगस्त, 1976 को सुभद्राकुमारी चौहान के सम्मान में 25 पैसे का एक डाक-टिकट जारी किया है।

शब्दार्थ—आग्रहपूर्वक = निवेदनपूर्वक, **आत्मग्लानि** = पछतावा, **व्यथित** = दु:खी, **यथेष्ट** = आवश्यक, **सरीके** = जैसे, **परिपूर्ण** = भरा, **तन्मय** = तल्लीन, **नालिशें** = शिकायतें, **प्रलोभन** = लालच, **निरीह** = मासूम, **निंद्य कर्म** = बुरे कर्म, **विकल** = व्याकुल।

सारांश

बाबू राधाकृष्ण अपनी बेटी गौरी के विवाह के सन्दर्भ में कहीं बाहर गये थे जब वह वापस आते हैं तब उनसे पत्नी कुंती चाय पीने का आग्रह करती है। इस दौरान गौरी अपराधिनी की तरह माता-पिता की दृष्टि से बचती हुई चाय बना रही है। वह यह सोचती है कि यदि उसका जन्म न हुआ होता तो उसके पिता को स्थान-स्थान पर वर की तलाश में न घूमना पड़ता। वह अपने माता-पिता से यह कहना चाहती है कि चाहे जिसके साथ उसकी शादी कर दी जाये अथवा शादी न भी करें तब भी वह सुखी है। वह यही सोच रही थी कि मेरे विवाह हेतु मेरे माता-पिता को कितना कष्ट उठाना पड़ रहा है। इस प्रकार आत्मग्लानि और क्षोभ से उसका रोम-रोम व्यथित हो उठा।

राधाकृष्ण जी गौरी का विवाह योग्य वर के साथ करना चाहते थे, परन्तु उनके पास उतनी सम्पत्ति नहीं थी। गौरी 19 साल की हो गई थी। माता-पिता की अकेली संतान थी। गौरी का स्वभाव निर्भीक और दृढ़-निश्चयी था। वह हजार बार यह निश्चय कर चुकी थी कि अपने पिता से यह कह दूँगी कि विवाह मेरे लिए आवश्यक नहीं पर वह लज्जा से कुछ भी कह न पाई।

राधाकृष्ण जी चाय पी रहे थे तब कुन्ती उनसे यह प्रश्न पूछना चाहती है कि वह जहाँ गये थे वहाँ बात बनी या नहीं। उसने डरते-डरते यह प्रश्न पूछा, जिसके जवाब में राधाकृष्ण जी यह कहते हैं कि वह लड़का नहीं आदमी है। मेरी बेटी के साथ वह चपरासी दिखेगा।

लड़के के दो बच्चे हैं, उसकी उम्र 35 से 36 साल है। वो अपने बच्चों के लिए एक धाय चाहते हैं। वो साफ-साफ कहते हैं कि मैं बच्चों के लिए ही दूसरा विवाह करना चाहता हूँ। कुन्ती के यह कहने पर कि दूसरे विवाह के लिए सभी बच्चों का ही बहाना बनाते हैं, इस कथन के जवाब में राधाकृष्ण जी कहते हैं कि उनका हृदय तो दर्पण की तरह साफ है। खादी कुर्ता, गाँधी टोपी, फटी चप्पल देखकर यही लगता है कि कि वे नेता बनने के योग्य हैं किसी का दूल्हा बनने के योग्य नहीं। कांग्रेस के दफ्तर में 30 रुपये की तनख्वाह पर काम करते हैं। तीन बार जेल जा चुके हैं। आदमी तो बुरे नहीं लेकिन गौरी का पति बनने के लायक नहीं हैं फिर भी मैंने उन्हें इतवार को बुलाया है जिससे तुम लोग भी उन्हें देख सको। गौरी ने दरवाजे की आड़ में ये बातें सुन ली और उसके हृदय में उनके प्रति श्रद्धा के भाव जागृत हो उठे।

अगले इतवार के दिन सीताराम जी देखने आने वाले हैं इस बात को बाहर वालों से गुप्त रखा गया है। भीतर आँगन में ही उनके बैठने का प्रबन्ध किया गया है। निर्धारित समय पर सीताराम जी अपने दोनों बच्चों के साथ आये। बच्चे भी वही खादी के कुर्ते और हाफ पैण्ट पहने थे। दोनों ही बड़े प्रसन्न और हँसमुख थे। आते ही वे घर में खेलने लगे। उन्हें देख कुंती को यह घर नन्दन कानन-सा जान पड़ा। वह बच्चों के खेल में इतनी तन्मय हो गई कि उन्हें सीताराम जी से बात करनी है यह भी भूल गईं। तभी छोटा बच्चा पिता के पास जाकर यह प्रश्न पूछता है कि माँ को दिखाने लाये हो तो बताओ माँ कहाँ है ? इसी दौरान बिल्ली के पीछे दौड़ते बच्चे घर के अन्दर पहुँच गये। छोटे बच्चे ने गौरी का आँचल खींचते हुए यह पूछा कि तुम हमारी माँ हो ? गौरी ने हाँ कहा। कुछ क्षण बाद कुन्ती ने देखा कि बच्चे गौरी के साथ खुश हैं।

माता-पिता के बुलाने पर गौरी सीताराम जी से मिलने आई। बच्चे गौरी को माँ समझकर उसके पिता की बहुत-सी शिकायतें करते रहे। जाते समय सीताराम जी ने राधाकृष्ण जी की तरफ देखकर कहा कि मुझे पत्नी की उतनी जरूरत नहीं जितनी मेरे बच्चों को माँ की जरूरत है जो मेरे जेल जाने पर इनकी देखभाल कर सके। सीताराम जी के जाने के बाद राधाकृष्ण जी ने सोचा कि मेरी लड़की उनके बच्चों की धाय बनेगी। कुन्ती ने सोचा कि उन दोनों बच्चों का पालन करके कोई भी अपना जीवन सार्थक बना सकता है। गौरी ने भी यह सोचा कि किसी विलासी युवक की पत्नी बनने से तो अच्छा है कि इन बच्चों की माँ बन जाऊँ। सीतारामजी को पक्का विश्वास था कि विवाह यहीं होगा।

काफी प्रतीक्षा करने के बाद भी सीताराम जी को किसी किस्म का आश्वासन नहीं मिला तो उन्होंने राधाकृष्णजी को पत्र लिखा जिसके जवाब में जन्मपत्री मँगाई गई और अन्त में राधाकृष्ण जी ने यह कहते हुए इन्कार कर दिया कि जन्मपत्री नहीं मिल रही।

वहीं दूसरी ओर राधाकृष्णजी ने गौरी के लिए एक दूसरा वर खोज लिया था जो नायब तहसीलदार था। देखने में तनिक भी सुन्दर भी नहीं था, फिर भी आगामी आषाढ़ में विवाह होना सुनिश्चित हुआ। कुन्ती और राधाकृष्ण जी दोनों बहुत ही खुश थे। दूसरी ओर गौरी के हृदय में बच्चों का भोला-भाला चेहरा और सीताराम जी की प्रतिमा उभर आती है। वह यह सोचती थी कि सीताराम जी बी. ए. पास करके नायब तहसीलदार बन सकते थे लेकिन उन्होंने देशभक्ति का मार्ग चुना। जहाँ नायब तहसीलदार अंग्रेजों की गुलामी करने वाला है। यह सब सोचकर गौरी की चिन्ता विवाह की तिथि के नजदीक आने के साथ-साथ बढ़ती जाती थी।

विवाह की तय की गई तारीख से 15 दिन पहले नायब तहसीलदार के पिता का देहान्त हो जाता है। जिसके कारण विवाह सालभर के लिए टल जाता है और गौरी की चिन्ता दूर हो जाती है। इसी बीच स्वतन्त्रता के आन्दोलन की लहर बड़ी तेजी से फैलती है। लोग गिरफ्तार होते और उन्हें सजा भी मिलती है। यह सब

देख गौरी को बच्चों की बड़ी चिन्ता होती। इसी दौरान एक दिन गौरी ने अखबार में पढ़ा कि सीताराम जी गिरफ्तार हो गये और उन्हें एक साल की सजा भी हो गई। गौरी कुछ समय तक विचार करती रही फिर अपनी माँ से कानपुर जाने की बात करती है। थोड़ी-सी बहस के बाद कुन्ती गौरी का विरोध न कर सकी। अन्त में गौरी उसी शाम एक नौकर के साथ कानपुर चली गई।

अब एक साल बाद जब सीताराम जी घर के लिए चलते हैं तो यह सोचते रहते हैं कि कहारिन ने मेरे बच्चों को किस प्रकार रखा होगा ? रास्ते में उन्होंने बच्चों के लिए गरम-गरम जलेबियाँ खरीदी और घर में यह सोचते हुए घुसे कि बच्चों की हालत क्या होगी ? लेकिन आँगन में वह गौरी को देखकर आश्चर्यचकित हो गये और गौरी ने भी उनकी पद-धूलि माथे से लगाई। इस प्रकार कहानी समाप्त हो जाती है।

अभ्यास-प्रश्न

प्रश्न 1. कहानी के आधार पर गौरी का चरित्र-चित्रण कीजिए।

अथवा

कहानी के प्रमुख पात्र का चरित्र चित्रण कीजिए।

उत्तर—'गौरी' कहानी की मुख्य पात्र और नायिका गौरी है। उसके चरित्र का ताना-बाना सहज, मानवीयता और उच्च आदर्श के द्वन्द्व से बुना गया है। उसके अन्तर्द्वन्द्व का सजीव चित्र प्रस्तुत कर कहानीकार सुभद्राकुमारी चौहान जी ने सांस्कृतिक वैभव, कर्तव्यनिष्ठा, देशप्रेम और उत्सर्ग की उदात्त भावनाओं को उजागर किया है। गौरी के चरित्र में अनेक विशेषताएँ हैं—

लज्जाशाली—गौरी भारतीय कन्याओं की प्रतिमूर्ति है और लज्जा उसका आभूषण। निर्भीक, दृढ़-निश्चयी होने के बावजूद उसकी जबान पर लज्जा का ताला लगा रहता है। लेखिका की ये पंक्तियाँ गौरी के इसी गुण को प्रमाणित करती हैं।

"उनकी यह परेशानी इतनी चिन्ता अब उससे सही नहीं जाती। किन्तु संकोच और लज्जा जबान पर ताला सा डाल देते हैं।"

संवेदनशील—गौरी बड़ी ही भावुक और संवेदनशील थी। जब उसने सीताराम जी के बच्चों को देखा और उनके छोटे बच्चे ने उसका आँचल पकड़कर खींचते हुए यह पूछा—"क्या तुम अमारी माँ हो ?" इस प्रश्न को सुनकर गौरी ने उस बालक को गोद में उठाकर कहा "हाँ।" इस प्रकार यह प्रसंग गौरी की बच्चों की प्रति संवेदनशीलता को प्रकट करता है। इससे यह स्पष्ट हो जाता है कि गौरी बच्चों से कितना प्रेम करती है।

देशप्रेमी—गौरी की भावनाएँ देशप्रेम से ओत-प्रोत हैं। वह सीताराम जी की देशभक्ति से बहुत प्रभावित थी। उसके हृदय में देशभक्त और त्यागी वीरों के लिए बड़ा सम्मान था। उसे तनिक भी इच्छा न थी कि वह माता-पिता द्वारा खोजे गये वर नायब तहसीलदार से विवाह करे, कहानीकार ने उसके द्वन्द्व को इस प्रकार व्यक्त किया है। 'ज्यों-ज्यों विवाह कि तिथि नजदीक आती, गौरी की चिन्ता बढ़ती ही जाती थी।"

दृढ़ निश्चयी—सीताराम जी के गिरफ्तार हो जाने की खबर अखबार में पढ़ते ही गौरी स्तब्ध हो गई। थोड़े ही समय में उसने अपना कर्तव्य निश्चित कर लिया कि वह सीताराम जी के बच्चों की देखभाल करने के लिए कानपुर अवश्य जायेगी। माँ के बार-बार समझाने पर भी उसका निर्णय नहीं बदलता, जो उसके निर्णय की दृढ़ता का उदाहरण हैं—

"गौरी-नहीं माँ, मैं पागल नहीं हूँ। बच्चों को तुम भी जानती हो उनके पिता को राजद्रोह के मामले में सालभर की सजा हो गई है। बच्चे छोटे हैं। मैं जाऊँगी माँ, मुझे जाना ही पड़ेगा।"

इस प्रकार गौरी का चरित्र पूरी कहानी में सजीव एवं जीवन्त रूप में मुखरित हुआ है जो उसे कहानी के मुख्य पात्र के रूप में प्रतिस्थापित करता है।

प्रश्न 2. विवाह तय होने के बाद भी किन कारणों से गौरी की चिन्ता बढ़ती जा रही थी ? अन्त में ये चिन्ता किस प्रकार दूर हुईं ?

उत्तर—'गौरी' कहानी में जहाँ दहेज की समस्या के कारण यथेष्ट वर का न मिलना एक समस्या के रूप में दिखाया गया है वहीं दूसरी ओर गौरी के माध्यम से किसी स्त्री के भावों को प्रकट करने की विवशता का भी प्रदर्शन किया गया है। गौरी जो कि प्रारम्भ से ही विवाह के सन्दर्भ में अपने विचार चाह कर भी अपने माता-पिता के समक्ष प्रस्तुत न कर सकी। अब जबकि उसका विवाह एक नायब तहसीलदार से हो रहा है, उसके मन में उथल-पुथल मची हुई है। जिसकी तरफ किसी का ध्यान ही नहीं जाता।

गौरी से कौन पूछता कि उसके हृदय में कैसी हलचल मच रही है ? रह-रहकर उसे उन बच्चों का भोला-भाला चेहरा और मीठी-मीठी बातें याद आ जाती हैं और साथ ही याद आ जाते विनयी, नम्र और सादगी की प्रतिमा सीताराम जी। उनकी याद आते ही श्रद्धा से गौरी का माथा अपने-आप ही झुक जाता है। देशभक्त और त्यागी वीरों के लिए उसके हृदय में बड़ा सम्मान था।

सीताराम जी ने भी तो वीर बनकर देश के लिए अपने जीवन का उत्सर्ग कर लिया है। नहीं तो बी. ए. पास करने के बाद क्या प्रयत्न करने पर उन्हें भी नायब तहसीलदारी न मिल जाती ? मिलती क्यों नहीं ? पर सीताराम जी सरकार की गुलामी पसन्द करते तब न ! दूसरी ओर थे उनके होने वाले वर नायब तहसीलदार साहब, जिन्हें अपने आराम, अपनी ऐश के लिए ब्रिटिश गवर्नमेण्ट के जरा से इशारे मात्र पर निरीह देशवासियों के गले पर छुरी फेरने में जरा भी संकोच या हिचक न होती; जिनके सामने चाँदी के कुछ टुकड़े फेंक दिये जाते हैं और वे दुम हिलाते हुए निंद्य कर्म करने में किंचित भी लज्जित नहीं होते। घृणा से गौरी का जी भर जाता। किन्तु उसके मनोभावों को जानने वाला यहाँ कोई भी न था। वह रात-दिन एक प्रकार की अव्यक्त पीड़ा से विकल-सी रहती थी। बहुत चाहती थी कि अपनी माँ से कह दे कि वह नायब तहसीलदार से शादी नहीं करना चाहती वह इसी से चिन्तित है।

अन्त में चिन्ता इस प्रकार दूर हुई कि विवाह की निश्चित तारीख से पन्द्रह दिन पहले एक दिन एकाएक तार आया कि नायब तहसीलदार के पिताजी का देहान्त हो गया है। इस मृत्यु के कारण विवाह साल-भर को टल गया। गौरी के माता-पिता बड़े दुःखी हुए, किन्तु गौरी के सिर से जैसे चिन्ता का पहाड़-सा हट गया।

प्रश्न 3. 'गौरी' कहानी में कहानीकार का क्या उद्देश्य है ? स्पष्ट कीजिए।

उत्तर—साहित्य वही सार्थक होता है जिसमें समाज का हित सन्निहित होता है। सुभद्राकुमारी चौहान जी ने 'गौरी' कहानी के माध्यम से जीवन के यथार्थ को प्रदर्शित करने का प्रयास किया है। प्रस्तुत कहानी में कहानीकार ने समस्या को कलात्मक ढंग से प्रस्तुत किया है तथा पाठकों को उनके समाधान के प्रयास की ओर उन्मुख किया है। कहानी के माध्यम से कहानीकार जीवन के महत्तर मूल्यों को विवेचित-विश्लेषित कर पाठकों को नया प्रकाश दे सकता है। इस विधा में सूक्ष्मता से आन्तरिक व बाह्य कृत्यों का पूरी स्वतन्त्रता से आकलन व विवेचन हो सकता है। इस प्रकार से कहानी का उद्देश्य आनन्द प्रदान करने के साथ-साथ मंगलकारी व सन्देशयुक्त होना चाहिए।

'गौरी' कहानी में कहानीकार का उद्देश्य स्पष्ट है। 'गौरी' कहानी में जहाँ दहेज की समस्या के कारण यथेष्ट वर का न मिलना एक समस्या के रूप में दिखाया गया है वहीं दूसरी ओर गौरी के माध्यम से किसी स्त्री के भावों को प्रकट करने की विवशता का भी प्रदर्शन किया गया है। गौरी जो कि प्रारम्भ से ही विवाह के सन्दर्भ में अपने विचार चाहकर भी अपने माता-पिता के समक्ष प्रस्तुत न कर सकी। अब जबकि उसका विवाह एक नायब तहसीलदार से हो रहा है, उसके मन में उथल-पुथल मची हुई है। जिसकी तरफ किसी का ध्यान ही नहीं जाता। इस प्रकार अन्त में गौरी द्वारा लिए निर्णय की घटना के माध्यम से भी एक अव्यक्त सन्देश देने का प्रयास किया है।

इस प्रकार कहानी का उद्देश्य जीवन के नैतिक मूल्यों को विवेचित करता है। 'गौरी' कहानी में कहानीकार का उद्देश्य सिर्फ आनन्द प्रदान करना नहीं बल्कि मंगलकारी सन्देश भी देना है।

प्रश्न 4. 'गौरी' कहानी के शीर्षक के औचित्य पर प्रकाश डालिए।

उत्तर—सुभद्राकुमारी चौहान जी ने हिन्दी कथा साहित्य में अपनी रचनाओं से विशिष्ट स्थान बनाया है। इनकी रचनाएँ सोद्देश्य तथा समाज का दर्पण होती है। अपनी रचनाओं के माध्यम से चौहान जी ने इस कथन को "साहित्य समाज का दर्पण होता है।" चरितार्थ करते हुए अपनी रचनाओं में दर्पण की भाँति सामाजिक विसंगतियों का प्रतिबिम्ब समाज के समक्ष प्रस्तुत किया है। कहानी का शीर्षक जिज्ञासावर्धक, संक्षिप्त और सारभाव अन्तर्निहित होना चाहिए। यदि इन तत्वों को आधार बनाकर गौरी कहानी के शीर्षक की समीक्षा की जाये तो यह पता चलता है कि कहानी का शीर्षक सार्थक है।

प्रस्तुत कहानी का शीर्षक कथानक के अनुरूप है। इस कहानी का कथानक गौरी और उसके साथ होने वाली घटनाओं पर आधारित है। कहानी के सभी भाव गौरी के चरित्र पर आधारित हैं अतः कहानी का शीर्षक कथानक के उद्देश्य एवं भाव को पूर्णतया स्पष्ट करता है।

कहानी का शीर्षक जिज्ञासावर्धक होना आवश्यक है, क्योंकि कहानी शीर्षक पढ़ने की उत्कंठा को जागृत करता है। जब यह उत्कंठा प्रबल हो जाती है तभी कहानी पढ़ी जाती है। कहानी के शीर्षक का संक्षिप्त होना भी आवश्यक है। 'गौरी' कहानी का शीर्षक इस दृष्टि से भी महत्वपूर्ण है। इतना ही नहीं कहानी के शीर्षक में कहानी का सारभाव अन्तर्निहित है जो पूरी कहानी के सारभाव को समेटे हुए है। इस प्रकार शीर्षक के गुणों की दृष्टि से गौरी कहानी एक सफल कहानी है। यह शीर्षक पूरी तरह से सटीक और सार्थक है जो सफल शीर्षक के समस्त गुणों को अपने भीतर समेटे हुए।

प्रश्न 5. सीतारामजी के घर आने के बाद एक ही व्यक्ति और रिश्ते के प्रति राधाकृष्ण जी, कुन्ती और गौरी के मन में क्या विचार उठते हैं ?

उत्तर—'गौरी' कहानी में सुभद्राकुमारी चौहान जी ने एक ही घटना के प्रति अलग-अलग पात्रों में किस प्रकार अलग-अलग विचार उठते हैं, उसे दिखाने का बड़ा ही सफल प्रयास किया है। निर्धारित समय पर जब सीताराम जी अपने दोनों बच्चों के साथ आते हैं तब उन्हें और उनके बच्चों को देखकर कुन्ती, राधाकृष्ण जी व गौरी के मन में अलग-अलग विचार उठते हैं।

कुन्ती सीताराम जी के हँसमुख और प्रसन्न बच्चों को देखकर भावातिरेक से भर जाती है। बच्चों के कोलाहल से परिपूर्ण घर क्षणभर के लिए नन्दन कानन-सा जान पड़ता है। उसने मन ही मन सोचा कितने अच्छे बच्चे हैं। कोई भी स्त्री ऐसे बच्चों का लालन-पालन कर अपना जीवन सार्थक बना सकती है। वह यह तक सोच लेती है कि बिना किसी प्रकार का सम्बन्ध हुए भी यदि सीताराम जी इन बच्चों को सम्भालने का कार्य सौंप दें तो वह सहर्ष स्वीकार कर लेगी।

वहीं राधाकृष्ण जी के मन में सीताराम जी और उनके बच्चों को देखकर एक अलग ही विचार आया। उनके अनुसार सीतारामजी की उमंगे और उत्साह सब ठण्डा पड़ गया है, वे अपने बच्चों के लिए एक धाय चाहते हैं। वह यह सोचते हैं कि सीताराम जी तो बच्चों के लिए विवाह करना चाहते हैं। उनके इस उद्देश्य से गौरी की संवेदनाओं और उसके सपनों की पूर्ति नहीं की जा सकेगी। इस प्रकार मेरी बेटी तो सीताराम जी के बच्चों की धाय बन जायेगी। सीताराम जी और उनके बच्चों को देखकर राधाकृष्ण जी के मन में यही विचार उत्पन्न हुए।

वहीं सीताराम जी को देखकर गौरी बहुत प्रभावित हुई। सीताराम जी के प्रति गौरी के हृदय में अनजाने ही कुछ श्रद्धा के भाव जागृत हो गये। उसके अनुसार सीताराम जी ने वीर बनकर देश के लिए अपने जीवन का उत्सर्ग कर लिया है। इस प्रकार गौरी के मन में सीताराम जी के प्रति भी स्नेह और संवेदना के भावों का उद्रेक हुआ।

इस तरह से सीताराम जी के आगमन और उनके बच्चों के प्रति कुंती, राधाकृष्ण जी और गौरी के मन में जो भाव जागृत हुए वे पूरी तरह से एक-दूसरे से भिन्न थे, जो कहानीकार के भाव संयोजन का अनूठा उदाहरण है।

प्रश्न 6. कहानी के तत्वों के आधार पर 'गौरी' कहानी की समीक्षा कीजिए।

उत्तर—सुभद्राकुमारी चौहान द्वारा लिखित 'गौरी' कहानी में सामाजिक विसंगतियों प्रमुखतया दहेज की समस्या को आधार बनाया गया है। इस कहानी में लेखिका ने गौरी के चरित्र के माध्यम से स्त्रियों के अन्तर्द्वन्द्व की भावना को प्रकट करने का प्रयास किया है। सुभद्राकुमारी चौहान की इस कहानी की सफलता का मुख्य रहस्य उनकी कहानी कला है। कहानी के तत्वों का सफलतापूर्वक संयोजन ही उनके कहानी लेखन की विशेषता है।

कहानी के संगठनात्मक तत्वों की दृष्टि से प्रस्तुत कहानी का स्वरूप कुछ इस प्रकार है—

कथानक—प्रस्तुत कहानी का कथानक एक निश्चित उद्देश्य की दिशा में यथार्थ घटनाओं एवं पात्रों के माध्यम से विकसित होता है। यह कथानक सामाजिक, व्यवहारिक एवं पारिवारिक व्यवस्था का सजीव चित्र प्रस्तुत करता है।

'गौरी' कहानी एक ऐसी नायिका की कहानी है, जिसके माता-पिता उसके विवाह के लिए बहुत चिन्तित हैं परन्तु आर्थिक परिस्थितियाँ अनुकूल न होने के कारण योग्य वर की प्राप्ति करना बड़ा ही मुश्किल है। यहाँ एक देशभक्त, अधिक आयु वाले तथा दो बच्चों के पिता सीताराम जी का विकल्प आता है, जिसे गौरी के पिता द्वारा अस्वीकार कर दिया जाता है। परन्तु गौरी बच्चों की स्थिति तथा सीताराम जी की सादगी से प्रभावित हो जाती है। अन्त में अच्छा नायब तहसीलदार वर मिलने के बाद भी गौरी परिस्थिति की आवश्यकता के अनुरूप सीताराम जी का ही चुनाव करती है।

पात्र तथा चरित्र-चित्रण—प्रस्तुत कहानी में पात्रों का संयोजन बड़ी ही कुशलता से किया गया है। कहानी के सभी पात्र यथार्थ जगत से ही सम्बन्धित हैं। इस कहानी में गौरी प्रमुख पात्र है तथा राधाकृष्ण जी, कुन्ती तथा सीताराम जी गौण पात्र हैं।

राधाकृष्ण जी व कुन्ती माता-पिता की ऐसी भूमिका में हैं जो अपनी पुत्री के सुखद भविष्य को आधार बनाकर निर्णय लेना चाहते हैं। ये दोनों पात्र माता-पिता के वास्तविक यथार्थ को प्रस्तुत करते हैं।

सीताराम जी गौण पात्र होते हुए भी इतने प्रभावशाली हैं कि पूरी कहानी उनके चरित्र की सादगी, देशभक्ति एवं पितृकतर्व्य के गुणों पर आधारित हैं।

इस प्रकार गौरी में भी प्रमुख पात्र के सभी गुण हैं जो कहानीकार के उद्देश्य की पूर्ति में सहायक हैं।

संवाद अथवा कथोपकथन—प्रस्तुत कहानी में समस्या को उभारने वाले, वस्तुस्थिति की व्याख्या करने वाले और पात्रों के मनोभावों को चित्रित करने वाले संवादों को प्रस्तुत किया है। कहानी के संवाद मौलिक, रोचक तथा पात्रानुकूल हैं। संवादों की पात्रानुकूलता का यह उदाहरण दर्शनीय है।

जब सीताराम जी का छोटा बेटा गौरी के पास जाता है तो वह गौरी से इस प्रकार पूछता है—

''क्या तुम अमारी माँ हो ?''

भाषा-शैली—कहानीकार सुभद्रा कुमारी चौहान पात्रानुकूल, भावानुकूल और परिस्थिति के अनुकूल भाषा का प्रयोग करने में सिद्धहस्त हैं। प्रस्तुत कहानी में भी भाषा-शैली का प्रयोग पात्र, विषय और परिस्थिति के अनुकूल हुआ है। इस कहानी में सरीखे, इंगित, व्यथित आदि भावप्रवीण शब्दों के समन्वित प्रयोग से अभिव्यक्त सहज स्पष्ट और सशक्त हो उठी है।

कहानी में वर्णनात्मक शैली की प्रधानता है तथा कहीं-कहीं चित्रात्मक वर्णन भी उपलब्ध है। संवादों की योजना से कहानी में नाटकीयता भी आई है। इस प्रकार भाषा और शैली की दृष्टि से यह कहानी एक सशक्त कहानी है।

देशकाल अथवा वातावरण— कहानीकार घटना और पात्रों के माध्यम से परिस्थितियों का चित्रण करने में कुशल है। इस कहानी में परिस्थितियों की योजना विशेष उद्देश्य से कराई गई है। तत्कालीन समाज व स्वतन्त्रता के संघर्ष का समय है। उस समय में व्याप्त समाज की विसंगतियों का चित्रण किया गया है।

प्रश्न 7. ''चलो हाथ पैर धोलो, चाय तैयार है।''

(i) यह कथन किसने, किससे व कब कहा है ?

(ii) श्रोता कहाँ से आया है ? उसकी मनः स्थिति का वर्णन कीजिए। क्या वह उदास है ? यदि हाँ तो क्यों ?

(iii) चाय की बात सुनकर श्रोता क्यों चौंक गये वक्ता से उनका क्या सम्बन्ध है ? वक्ता व श्रोता दोनों किस बात से चिन्तित हैं ?

(iv) यह कहानी हमारे समाज की किस बुराई की ओर संकेत करती है ? समझाकर लिखिए।

उत्तर—(i) उपर्युक्त कथन कुन्ती ने अपने पति राधाकृष्ण जी से कहा है। जब वह अपनी पुत्री गौरी के विवाह हेतु एक वर की तलाश में गये थे तथा वहाँ से लौटकर थके-हारे से घर पर आये हैं।

(ii) श्रोता राधाकृष्ण जी कानपुर अपनी पुत्री गौरी के लिए वर की तलाश में गये थे। वहाँ से अभी गोधूलि के समय ही वापस घर पर आये हैं। उनका मन उदास है क्योंकि जिस वर को वह देखने गये थे, वह वर नहीं बल्कि दो बच्चों का बाप है। उसकी पत्नी की मृत्यु हो चुकी है। राधाकृष्ण जी की पुत्री से वह उम्र में बहुत बड़ा है। गौरी अभी उन्नीसवें वर्ष में है। परन्तु वर अर्थात् सीताराम 35-36 साल का आदमी है अतः अपनी पुत्री के लिए उचित वर न होने के कारण राधाकृष्ण दुःखी थे।

(iii) चाय की बात सुनकर श्रोता राधाकृष्ण इसलिए चौंक गये क्योंकि वह पुत्री के लिए वर देखकर आये थे। उसमें उन्हें निराशा हाथ लगी वह उन्हीं विचारों में खोये हुए थे। वक्ता कुन्ती व श्रोता राधाकृष्ण जी दोनों अपनी पुत्री के विवाह को लेकर चिन्तित थे। उन्हें उनकी पुत्री के लिए योग्य वर नहीं मिल रहा था और पुत्री की दिनों-दिन उम्र बढ़ती जा रही थी। इधर योग्य वर का मूल्य चुकाने के लिए उनके पास यथेष्ठ सम्पत्ति भी नहीं थी।

(iv) 'गौरी' कहानी हमारे समाज की 'दहेज प्रथा' नामक बुराई की ओर संकेत करती है। यही कारण है कि भारत देश में कन्याओं को अभिशाप समझा जाता है। 'भ्रूण हत्या' इसी बुराई की देन है। लड़के वाले अपने गुणहीन पुत्रों के लिए सुशील संस्कारी पुत्रियों की बोली लगाते हैं। उसके बाद भी उन्हें प्रताड़ित करके उनका जीवन नारकीय बना देते हैं। अतः इस बुराई का अन्त होना चाहिये।

प्रश्न 8. ''दूसरी ओर थे उनके होने वाले वर-नायब तहसीलदार साहब, जिन्हें अपने आराम, अपनी ऐश के लिए ब्रिटिश गवर्नमेंट के जरा से इंगित मात्र पर निरीह देशवासियों के गले पर छुरी फेरने में जरा भी संकोच या हिचक नहीं।''

(i) यह नायब तहसीलदार कौन हैं ? इनका परिचय दीजिए। साथ ही बताइये कि ये क्या काम करते हैं ?

(ii) ''देशवासियों के गले पर छुरी फेरना'' इन शब्दों का प्रयोग यहाँ किस सन्दर्भ में किया गया है ? समझाकर लिखिए।

(iii) इस कहानी के लिखे जाने के समय देश में कैसा वातावरण था ?

(iv) कहानी की प्रधान पात्र गौरी के हृदय में सीताराम जी एवं नायब तहसीलदार के प्रति कैसे भाव थे ? क्या वह नायब तहसीलदार से विवाह करने में प्रसन्न थी ? यदि नहीं तो क्यों ? समझाइये।

उत्तर—(i) राधाकृष्ण जी ने गौरी के लिए दूसरा वर ढूँढ़ लिया था जो नायब तहसीलदार के पद पर नियुक्त था। बी. ए. पास था देखने में सुन्दर न था। आगे उन्नति की आशा थी। उम्र यही 24-25 वर्ष थी। माँ, बाप, भाई तथा बहिन से भरा पूरा परिवार था।

(ii) "देशवासियों के गले पर छुरी फेरना" इस कथन से अभिप्राय है कि नायब तहसीलदार अंग्रेजों की गुलामी में काम करता था। उसे अपने ऐश व आराम के लिए अंग्रेजों के इशारे पर यदि देशवासियों के गले पर छुरा भी चलाना पड़ता तो वह पीछे न रहता। वह देश के प्रति गद्दार एवं अँग्रेजों का गुलाम था।

(iii) इस कहानी के लिखे जाने के समय भारत देश पर अँग्रेजों का अधिकार था। भारत एक गुलाम देश तथा प्रत्येक भारतीय अँग्रेजों का गुलाम था। उस समय पूरे देश में स्वतन्त्रता आन्दोलन चल रहे थे। अँग्रेजों के अत्याचार दिन-प्रतिदिन बढ़ते जा रहे थे जिनके विरुद्ध पूरे देश में आन्दोलन चल रहे थे। परन्तु कुछ भारतीय ऐसे भी थे जिन्हें अपने ऐश-आराम के लिए अँग्रेजों की गुलामी करने में किंचित मात्र भी आपत्ति नहीं थी।

(iv) 'गौरी' कहानी की प्रधान नायिका गौरी देशभक्त, सेवा भावी, कर्तव्यपरायण एवं त्याग प्रवृत्ति की आदर्श नारी है। उसके हृदय में सीता रामजी के प्रति आदर के भाव थे वह उनके त्याग, सेवा, देशभक्ति एवं सादगी से बहुत प्रभावित थी और मन ही मन वह उन्हें स्वीकार कर चुकी थी। इसके विपरीत वह नायब तहसीलदार से घृणा करती थी। वह उसे देशद्रोही, अँग्रेजों का चाटुकार व अपने देशवासियों के साथ गद्दारी करने वाला मानती थी।

वह नायब तहसीलदार से विवाह करने में बिल्कुल रुचि नहीं रखती थी क्योंकि उसका मानना था कि नायब तहसीलदार धन के लिए कुछ भी कर सकता है वह उनमें से है जिनके सामने कुछ चाँदी के टुकड़े फेंक दिये जाते हैं और वे दुम हिलाते हुए निन्द्य से निन्द्य कर्म करने में भी किंचित लज्जित नहीं होता। इसलिए वह उससे घृणा करती थी।

●●

3. शरणागत

—वृन्दावनलाल वर्मा

लेखक परिचय—वृन्दावनलाल वर्मा का जन्म 9 जनवरी, 1889 तथा मृत्यु 23 फरवरी, 1969 में हुई। वृन्दावनलाल वर्मा एक ऐतिहासिक उपन्यासकार एवं निबन्धकार थे। इनका जन्म मऊरानीपुर, झाँसी, उत्तर-प्रदेश में हुआ था। इनके पिता का नाम अयोध्या प्रसाद था। वृन्दावनलाल वर्मा जी के विद्या-गुरु स्वर्गीय पण्डित विद्याधर दीक्षित थे। 1909 ई. में वृन्दावनलाल वर्मा जी का 'सेनापति ऊदल' नामक नाटक छपा, जिसे सरकार ने जब्त कर लिया। 1920 ई. तक यह छोटी-छोटी कहानियाँ लिखते रहे। इन्होंने 1921 से निबन्ध लिखना प्रारम्भ किया। स्कॉट के उपन्यासों का इन्होंने स्वेच्छापूर्वक अध्ययन किया और उससे ये प्रभावित हुए। ऐतिहासिक उपन्यास लिखने की प्रेरणा इन्हें स्कॉट से ही मिली। देशी-विदेशी व अन्य उपन्यास-साहित्य का भी इन्होंने यथेष्ट अध्ययन किया।

वृन्दावनलाल वर्मा जी ने सन् 1927 ई. में 'गढ़ कुण्डार' दो महीने में लिखा। उसी वर्ष 'लगन', 'संगम', 'प्रत्यागत', 'कुण्डली चक्र', 'प्रेम की भेंट' तथा 'हृदय की हिलोर' भी लिखा। 1930 ई. में 'विराट की पद्मिनी' लिखने के पश्चात कई वर्षों तक इनका लेखन स्थापित रहा। इन्होंने 1939 ई. में धीरे-धीरे व्यंग्य तथा 1942-1944 ई. में 'कभी न कभी', 'मुसाहिब जू' उपन्यास लिखा। 1946 ई. में इनका प्रसिद्ध उपन्यास 'झाँसी की रानी लक्ष्मीबाई' प्रकाशित हुआ। तब से इनकी कलम अबाध रूप से चलती रही। 'झाँसी की रानी', के बाद इन्होंने 'कचनार', 'मृगनयनी', 'टूटे काँटें', 'अहिल्याबाई', 'भुवन विक्रम', 'अचल मेरा कोई' आदि उपन्यासों और 'हंसमयूर', 'पूर्व की ओर', 'ललित विक्रम', 'राखी की लाज' आदि नाटकों का प्रणयन किया। 'दबे पाँव', 'शरणागत', 'कलाकार दण्ड' आदि कहानीसंग्रह भी इस बीच प्रकाशित हो चुके हैं।

वृन्दावनलाल वर्मा जी को भारत सरकार, राज्य सरकार, उत्तर प्रदेश, मध्य प्रदेश राज्य के साहित्य पुरस्कार तथा डालमिया साहित्यकार संसद, हिन्दुस्तानी अकादमी, प्रयाग (उत्तर प्रदेश) और नागरी-प्रचारिणी सभा, काशी के सर्वोत्तम पुरस्कारों से सम्मानित किये गये हैं। अपनी साहित्यिक सेवाओं के लिए वृन्दावनलाल वर्मा जी आगरा विश्वविद्यालय द्वारा डी.लिट. की उपाधि से सम्मानित किये गये। इनकी अनेक रचनाओं को केन्द्रीय एवं प्रान्तीय राज्यों ने पुरस्कृत किया है।

शब्दार्थ—**कर्मण्य** = काम करने वाले, **बसेरे** = रहने का स्थान, **शामत का मारा** = परेशानी का मारा, **आगंतुक** = आने वाले, **सरोकार** = मतलब, **तीव्र** = तेज, **क्षुब्ध** = दुःखी।

सारांश

रज्जब जो कि कसाई है अपना रोजगार करके ललितपुर लौट रहा था। साथ में उसके द्वारा कमाई करीब दो-तीन सौ की बड़ी रकम और उसकी बीवी भी थी। रास्ता काफी सुनसान था और बीच में ही उसकी पत्नी की तबियत खराब हो गई जिसके कारण उसने यह तय किया कि मड़पुरा गाँव में रातभर के लिए रुक जाये क्योंकि बैलगाड़ी किराये पर करने में ज्यादा खर्च आता। लेकिन उसकी समस्या यह थी कि गाँव के लोग उसे जानते हैं कि वह कसाई है इसलिए कोई भी आश्रय न देगा। उसने अपने व्यवहारियों से यहाँ रात-भर के लिए स्थान देने के लिए याचना की लेकिन सभी ने उसको आश्रय देने से इन्कार कर दिया।

अन्त में उसने गाँव के एक ठाकुर के घर जाने का निर्णय किया। ठाकुर का छोटा सा मकान था। गाँव के लोग ठाकुर को डर के मारे राजा कहा करते थे। परेशानी का मारा रज्जब उसी ठाकुर के घर अपनी बीमार पत्नी को लेकर जाता है। ठाकुर के पूछने पर रज्जब उसे अपनी परेशानी बताता है और रात-भर के लिए दो हाथ जगह देने के लिए प्रार्थना करता है। ठाकुर के पूछने पर वह यह बताता है कि वह कसाई है। जिसे सुनते ही ठाकुर नाराज हो जाता है। तब रज्जब कहता है कि जब किसी ने जगह नहीं दी जो राजा की शरण में आया हूँ। अन्त में ठाकुर यह कहता है कि अपनी चिलम ले आओ और अपनी पत्नी को लेकर हमारी पौर के एक कोने में पड़े रहना। ठाकुर ने यह पूछा कि कुछ नफा हुआ है तो रज्जब ने कहा बस पेट के लायक कुछ मिल गया है। और रज्जब अपनी पत्नी के साथ वहाँ सो जाता है।

काफी रात बीते कुछ लोग ठाकुर के घर के बाहर आकर कहते कि आज कुछ भी हाथ नहीं लगा है। ठाकुर पूछता है कि कोशिश की थी ? इस प्रश्न के जवाब पर उन्होंने कहा कि एक कसाई रुपये बाँधे इसी ओर

आया है। यह सुनते ही ठाकुर ने कहा कि कसाई का पैसा नहीं छुयेंगे। लोगों ने उसे शुद्ध करने की बात की और चले जाते हैं।

ठाकुर सुबह उठकर देखता है कि सवेरा होने के बाद भी कसाई नहीं गया तो वह उसे तुरन्त बाहर निकल जाने का हुक्म देता है। उस समय रज्जब की पत्नी एक कदम भी चलने के योग्य न थी। वह जाकर एक पेड़ के नीचे बैठ जाता हैं और यह सोचता है कि उसकी पत्नी शायद कुछ समय में ठीक हो जाये। परन्तु ऐसा न हुआ अन्त में उसने एक गाड़ी किराये पर लेकर आगे जाने का निर्णय लिया। बड़ी मुश्किल के बाद उसे एक छोटी जाति का व्यक्ति अधिक किराया लेकर ले जाने के लिए राजी हुआ। परन्तु पत्नी की अधिक तबियत खराब होने के वजह से रज्जब को दिनभर इंतजार करना पड़ा। वह गाड़ीवान को जल्दी से चलने के लिए कहता है तो गाड़ीवान अधिक किराये की माँग करता है। तब कसाई दया की बात करता है जिसे सुनकर गाड़ीवान को हँसी आ गई। वह गाड़ीवान को पैसे देता है तब गाड़ीवान आगे चलता है।

कुछ दूर चलने के बाद संध्या हो गई रास्ता काटने के उद्देश्य से रज्जब ने बातचीत की पहल की और गाड़ीवान से पूछा कि गाँव यहाँ से कितनी दूर मिलेगा ? इसी बीच रज्जब के मुँह से बातचीत के दौरान ही यह निकल जाता है कि अगर गड़बड़ करेगा तो छुरी से काटकर फेंक दूँगा। यह सब सुनकर गाड़ीवान पूरी तरह से डर गया था।

इस बातचीत के दौरान गाड़ी थोड़ी दूर चली होगी कि बैल रुक गये। रास्ते में एक टुकड़ी खड़ी हुई थी जिसमें से एक आदमी ने कहा कि खबरदार जो आगे बढ़ा। रज्जब ने देखा कि चार-पाँच लठैत रास्ता रोके खड़े हैं। वे रज्जब से उसका नाम पूछते हैं और यह जानने पर कि वह कसाई है। उसमें से एक ने कहा इसका नाम रज्जब है इसे छोड़ दो। लेकिन उसकी बात को अनसुना कर एक लठैत गाड़ी पर चढ़ जाता है और रज्जब को सारा माल निकालने के लिए कहता है। तभी नीचे खड़े व्यक्ति ने कहा उतर आओ उसे छोड़ दो, उसकी औरत बीमार है।

गाड़ी पर खड़े लठैत ने कहा मैं आपकी बात न मानूँगा। जिस पर नीचे खड़े लठैत ने कहा कि उसे छूना मत नहीं तो मैं तुम्हारी खोपड़ी चूर कर दूँगा क्योंकि यह मेरी शरण में आया था। इतना कहने के बाद गाड़ीवान से कहा कि इसे ठिकाने तक पहुँचाना और इस बात का जिक्र किसी से मत करना नहीं तो जलाकर खाक कर दूँगा।

जिस लठैत ने रज्जब के सिर पर वार करने की कोशिश की थी वह दुःखी होकर यह कहता है कि दाऊजी मैं आगे से आपके साथ कभी नहीं जाऊँगा। दाऊजी ने यह बात सुनकर कहा कि मत आना मेरे साथ, मैं अकेला ही काफी हूँ लेकिन बुंदेला शरणागत के साथ कभी धोखा नहीं करता है।

अभ्यास-प्रश्न

प्रश्न 1. 'शरणागत' कहानी का उद्देश्य स्पष्ट कीजिए।

उत्तर— भारत का साहित्य देश के गौरवमयी इतिहास की झाँकी है। यहाँ शिबि जैसे राजा हुए जिन्होंने अपने शरण में आये पक्षी की रक्षा के लिए अपने प्राणों की परवाह तक न की। 'शरणागत' कहानी में भी वृन्दावनलाल वर्मा ने पुनः एक ऐसा ही उदाहरण समाज के समक्ष प्रस्तुत किया है। इस कहानी में लेखक ने आधुनिक काल में भी उस प्राचीन मूल्य को प्रासांगिक बताया है। कहानीकार ने अपने पाठकों की आन्तरिक प्रवृत्तियों के विकास के साथ कुछ ठोस तथा गम्भीर अनुभूति भी प्रदान की है। इस प्रकार से कहानी का उद्देश्य आनन्द प्रदान करने के साथ-साथ सन्देशयुक्त भी है।

'शरणागत' कहानी में कहानीकार का उद्देश्य स्पष्ट है। कहानीकार ने इस कहानी के माध्यम से यह बताने का प्रयास किया है कि प्रतिकूल परिस्थिति के होने के बावजूद भी किस प्रकार उस ठाकुर ने रज्जब की और उसकी पत्नी की रक्षा की। जबकि पूरा गाँव किसी कसाई को शरण देने के लिए तैयार भी नहीं था। जो

समाज की अस्पृश्यता की समस्या को प्रकट करता है। ऐसी परिस्थिति में ठाकुर ने उसे शरण दी। वहीं दूसरी ओर कहानीकार ने शरणागत की रक्षा की घटना के माध्यम से भी एक अव्यक्त सन्देश देने का प्रयास किया है।

वृन्दावनलाल वर्मा की विचारधारा उनकी कहानी से स्पष्ट हो जाती है। इनकी दृष्टि सर्वदा राष्ट्र के पुनः निर्माण की ओर रही है। भारत के पतन के मूल कारण रूढ़ि-जर्जर समाज को इन्होंने अपनी सभी प्रकार की रचनाओं में प्रयोगशाला बनाया है तथा सामाजिक कुरीतियों की ओर इंगित किया है। ये श्रम के महत्व के प्रबल पोषक हैं। वर्मा जी मानव जीवन के लिए प्रेम को एक आवश्यक तत्व मानते हैं। यही नहीं, उनके विचार से प्रेम एक साधना है, जो साधक को सामान्य भूमि से उठाकर उच्चता की ओर ले जाती है। जीवन के प्रति इनका दृष्टिकोण प्रायः वही है, जिसका प्रतिपादन प्राचीन भारतीय संस्कृति करती है। इनके विचार से मनुष्य को केवल कर्म करने का अधिकार है, फल का नहीं।

प्रश्न 2. शरणागत कहानी के शीर्षक के औचित्य पर प्रकाश डालिए।

उत्तर—वृन्दावनलाल वर्मा जी श्रम के महत्व के प्रबल पोषक हैं। वर्मा जी मानव जीवन के लिए प्रेम को एक आवश्यक तत्व मानते हैं। यही नहीं, उनके विचार से प्रेम एक साधना है, जो साधक को सामान्य भूमि से उठाकर उच्चता की ओर ले जाती है। इसलिए वर्मा जी ने अपनी कहानी में इसी उद्देश्य को प्रमुख माना है। उनकी कहानी का शीर्षक ही उनके उद्देश्य पर प्रकाश डालता है। शीर्षक में कुछ महत्वपूर्ण गुणों का होना आवश्यक है। शीर्षक जिज्ञासावर्धक, संक्षिप्त और सारभाव अन्तर्निहित होना चाहिए। यदि इन तत्वों को आधार बनाकर शरणागत कहानी के शीर्षक की समीक्षा की जाये तो यह पता चलता है कि कहानी का शीर्षक सार्थक है।

कहानी का शीर्षक 'शरणागत' है जो कि यह जिज्ञासा बढ़ाता है कि यहाँ किस शरणागत की बात की जा रही है ? कहानी के शीर्षक का संक्षिप्त होना भी आवश्यक है। इस प्रकार शीर्षक के गुणों की दृष्टि से शरणागत कहानी एक सफल कहानी है। यह शीर्षक पूरी तरह से सटीक और सार्थक है जो सफल शीर्षक के समस्त गुणों को अपने भीतर समेटे हुए है।

प्रश्न 3. शरणागत कहानी के पात्रों का चरित्र-चित्रण कीजिए।

उत्तर—यदि कथानक कहानी का मेरूदण्ड होता है तो पात्र कहानी के प्राण हैं, जो कथानक के निर्जीव शब्दों में प्राण फूंक देते हैं। पात्र नियोजन इसलिए भी महत्वपूर्ण है क्योंकि कहानी की मूल घटनाएँ और अनुभूति इसी के द्वारा प्रकट की जाती हैं। पात्रों के चरित्र-चित्रण, मानसिक संघर्ष और गतिशीलता द्वारा ही कहानी में स्वाभाविक रूप से आरोह-अवरोह उपस्थित होता है। पात्रों की कल्पना दो कोटियों में होती है। **मूल पात्र, गौण पात्र**। मूल पात्र कहानी के चरम लक्ष्य का नायक होता है, यही वह शक्ति होती है जिसके सहारे कहानी की मूल संवेदना चरम सीमा पर पहुँचती है। गौण पात्र कहानी की मूल संवेदना को उत्तेजित करने में सहायक होते हैं तथा मूल पात्र की आत्मभिव्यक्ति में माध्यम का कार्य करते हैं। कहानी में पात्रों की संख्या सीमित होनी चाहिए साथ ही साथ उनके चरित्र-चित्रण में विश्वसनीयता का बोध होना चाहिए।

कहानी का मुख्य पात्र ठाकुर है। ठाकुर गरीब है तथा उसके पास थोड़ी-सी ही जमीन है। वह दबंग किस्म का व्यक्ति है। जिसके प्रभाव को व्यक्त करने के लिए कहानीकार ने लिखा है कि गाँव के लोग डर के मारे उसे 'राजा' कहा करते हैं। वर्मा जी ने कहानी के इस पात्र के द्वारा यह सन्देश देने का प्रयास किया है कि जब कोई रज्जब की सहायता नहीं करता ऐसी परिस्थिति में वह यह जानते हुए भी कि गाँव के लोगों को पता चलने पर उन्हें बुरा लगेगा, रज्जब को अपने यहाँ शरण देता है। रज्जब के अन्दर निर्भीक, स्वाभिमानी, दयालु जैसे अनेक गुण हैं, जो कहानीकार के उद्देश्य की पूर्ति में सहायक हैं।

अन्य पात्रों में रज्जब की पत्नी, ठाकुर के साथी और बैलगाड़ी वाला है। इन सभी पात्रों ने रज्जब और ठाकुर के चरित्र को मुखरित होने के लिए उपयुक्त वातावरण तैयार किया है। ये सभी पात्र कहानी के कथानक की प्रवाहमयता को बनाने के साथ ही साथ कहानी के उद्देश्य की पूर्ति में भी सहायक हैं।

प्रश्न 4. ''रज्जब ने उत्तर दिया।'' बहुत कोशिश की, परन्तु मेरे खोटे पेशे के कारण कोई सीधा नहीं हुआ। इस कथन का सन्दर्भ स्पष्ट करते हुए बताइए कि किसके सीधा न होने और किस प्रकार सीधा न होने की बात की जा रही है ?

उत्तर—प्रस्तुत कथन का सन्दर्भ उस समय का है जब रज्जब कसाई की पत्नी बीमारी की वजह से जा नहीं सकती थी इसलिए रज्जब को मजबूरीवश उस गाँव में रुकना पड़ा। उसने गाँव के लोगों से रातभर रहने के लिए जगह माँगी लेकिन उसे किसी ने भी शरण नहीं दी सिर्फ इसलिए कि वह पेशे से कसाई है। उसका पेशा खोटा है। उसका पेशा जानवरों का वध करना है, जो कि तत्कालीन समाज में निन्दनीय है। इसी कारण कोई उसे शरण नहीं देता है। यहाँ गाँव वालों के शरण न देने को ही सीधा न होने की बात की जा रही है।

यहाँ जब गाँव के किसी भी व्यक्ति ने उसे रात गुजारने के लिए जगह नहीं दी तब वह वहाँ के ठाकुर जिसे लोग राजा कहते थे उसके यहाँ जाकर उससे यही कथन कहता है कि गाँव वालों ने मेरे खोटे पशे के कारण जगह नहीं दी, इसी को रज्जब ने कहा कि गाँव में कोई सीधा नहीं हुआ। रज्जब यह कहता है कि यह राजा का घर है इसीलिए शरण में आया हूँ। रज्जब की इस बात को सुनकर ठाकुर को तरस आ जाता है और वह अंधेरे में जाने की बात सुनकर रज्जब को रातभर के लिए रुकने की जगह दे देता है।

प्रश्न 5. ''परन्तु बुंदेला शरणागत के साथ घात नहीं करता, इस बात को गाँठ में बाँध लेना।'' यहाँ कौन शरणागत है ? यहाँ किस घात की बात की जा रही है ?

उत्तर—'शरणागत' कहानी इसी के इर्द-गिर्द घूमती है। रज्जब को किसी के द्वारा सहायता नहीं मिली तब वह ठाकुर की शरण में जाता है। ठाकुर उसे रातभर रहने की शरण देता है। वहीं से शरणागत के सन्दर्भ का प्रारम्भ होता है। यह कथन उस समय का है जब ठाकुर के मित्र कसाई को लूटने की बात करते हैं, तब ठाकुर अपने मित्रों को यह कहता है कि मैं अकेले ही बहुत कुछ कर सकता हूँ। यहाँ उस घात की बात की जा रही है कि मैं अपने शरणागत रज्जब के साथ धोखा नहीं कर सकता क्योंकि रज्जब को मैंने शरण दी थी। रज्जब को जब किसी ने शरण नहीं दी तब मैंने उसे अपने घर में रखा इसलिए इसकी सुरक्षा की जिम्मेदारी भी मेरी है।

यहाँ ठाकुर ही बुंदेला है वह अपने वंश को बताते हुए यह कहता है कि रज्जब बुंदेला का शरणागत है। बुन्देला हमेशा शरणागत की रक्षा करता है। रज्जब मेरी शरण में आया था इसलिए तुम लोग उसे लूट नहीं सकते हैं। यहाँ उसी घात की बात की जा रही है। जब रज्जब बैलगाड़ी से अपने गाँव ललितपुर जा रहा होता है तभी उसे कुछ लोग घेर लेते हैं और उसे लूटने का प्रयास करते हैं। तभी उसी समूह का एक सदस्य यह कथन कहता है कि बुन्देला शरणागत के साथ घात नहीं करता। यह कथन ही इस कहानी का प्राण है और कहानी के सभी भावों को अपने भीतर समेटे हुए है।

प्रश्न 6. ''परन्तु ठहरता कहाँ ? जात छिपाने से काम नहीं चलता था।''

(i) यहाँ पर किसने ठहरने की बात कही है ? जात छिपाने से क्या अभिप्राय है ? कौन किसकी जात छिपाने की कोशिश कर रहा है ?

(ii) कहानी के मुख्य पात्र रज्जब का परिचय देते हुए बताइये वह कहाँ से आ रहा है ? वहाँ वह क्यों गया था ? उसके साथ कौन है ? उसे कहाँ जाना है ?

(iii) उसने रात व्यतीत करने के लिए किससे प्रार्थना की ? क्या उसकी प्रार्थना स्वीकार की गयी ? यदि नहीं तो अन्त में उसे किसने रात व्यतीत करने के लिए स्थान दिया ?

(iv) स्थान देने वाले व्यक्ति ठाकुर के चरित्र की विशेषताएँ लिखिये। इस कहानी में समाज में व्याप्त किस बुराई का उल्लेख किया गया है ?

उत्तर—(i) यहाँ पर श्री वृन्दावन लाल वर्मा के द्वारा रचित कहानी 'शरणागत' के मुख्य पात्र रज्जब ने रात को ठहरने की बात कही थी। वह जाति से कसाई था। वह अपनी जाति की बात इसलिए छिपाना चाहता था क्योंकि जाति बताकर उसे कोई अपने घर रात बिताने नहीं देगा।

(ii) रज्जब एक गरीब इँसान है। वह जाति से कसाई तथा ललितपुर का रहने वाला था। इस समय रोजगार के लिए वह बाहर गया था जहाँ से लगभग तीन सौ रुपये की कमाई करके वह लाया था। उसके साथ

उसकी पत्नी थी जो बुखार से तप रही थी। लौटते में देर हो गयी थी इसलिए उसे रात बिताने के लिए दो हाथ जगह चाहिए थी। उसे वापस ललितपुर जाना है।

(iii) उसने अपने व्यवहारियों से रातभर बसेरे के लिये दो हाथ जगह की याचना की, किन्तु किसी ने भी मंजूर नहीं किया। तत्पश्चात् उसी गाँव के ठाकुर के दरवाजे पर अपनी ज्वरग्रस्त पत्नी को ले जाकर रात बिताने के लिए गिड़गिड़ाने लगा। ठाकुर को दया आ गयी उसने अँधेरे में निकल जाने की हिदायत देकर अपनी पौर में रात बिताने के लिए दो हाथ जगह दे दी।

(iv) रज्जब को रात व्यतीत करने के लिए दो हाथ जगह देने वाला ठाकुर जाति से बुन्देला परन्तु सिद्धान्त का धनी था। उसके पास थोड़ी सी जमीन थी जिसको किसान जोतते थे। उसके पास अपना हल-बैल नहीं था लेकिन अपने किसानों से दो-तीन साल का पेशगी लगान वसूल करने में ठाकुर को किसी विशेष बाधा का सामना नहीं करना पड़ता था। छोटा-सा मकान था परन्तु उसे गाँव वाले गढ़ी के आदर व्यंजक शब्द से पुकारा करते थे और ठाकुर को डर के मारे 'राजा' शब्द से सम्बोधित करते थे। 'शरणागत' कहानी में जातीय भेदभाव को दर्शाया गया है। प्रस्तुत कहानी में रज्जब को कोई भी गाँववासी सिर्फ इसलिए रुकने की जगह नहीं देना चाहते थे क्योंकि वह एक कसाई है।

प्रश्न 7. ''जारे हाँक ले जा गाड़ी। ठिकाने तक पहुँचा आना, तब लौटना, नहीं तो अपनी खैर मत समझियो और तुम दोनों में से किसी ने भी कभी इस बात की चर्चा कहीं की तो भूसी की आग में जलाकर खाक कर दूँगा।''

(i) यह कथन किसने, किससे, कब व क्यों कहा ? समझाकर लिखिए।

(ii) गाड़ीवान गाड़ी लेकर कहाँ बढ़ गया ? वह कौन था जिसने गाड़ी पर चढ़कर रज्जब पर लाठी तानी थी ? उसने ऐसा क्यों किया ?

(iii) उस व्यक्ति ने क्षुब्ध होकर दाऊजी से क्या कहा ? दाऊजी ने उसकी बात का क्या उत्तर दिया ?

(iv) 'शरणागत' कहानी के आधार पर बताइये कि यहाँ पर शरणागत की रक्षा हेतु ठाकुर साहब ने क्या किया ? उनके विचारों पर प्रकाश डालिए।

उत्तर—(i) यह कथन गाड़ी से नीचे खड़े व्यक्ति ठाकुर बुन्देला ने उस गाड़ीवान से कहा। जब एक लठैत लाठी लेकर गाड़ी में बैठे रज्जब पर आक्रमण करने चढ़ा था। उसने स्पष्ट शब्दों में लठैत से कहा कि यदि वह रज्जब पर आक्रमण करेगा तो वह उसका सिर चूर कर देगा क्योंकि रज्जब ठाकुर का शरणागत था।

(ii) गाड़ीवान गाड़ी लेकर ललितपुर की ओर बढ़ गया। एक लठैत ने गाड़ी पर चढ़कर रज्जब की छाती में लाठी अड़ा दी और उससे रुपया पैसा निकालने को कहा तथा वह व्यक्ति चार-पाँच लठैतों में से एक व्यक्ति था। वह रज्जब से रुपया पैसा निकलवाना चाहता था।

(iii) चार-पाँच लठैतों में से एक ने ठाकुर बुन्देला की सहमति के विरुद्ध रज्जब पर आक्रमण करके जब उससे रुपये पैसे छीनने का प्रयास किया तब ठाकुर ने उसका विरोध किया। तब व्यक्ति ने क्षुब्ध स्वर में कहा ''दाऊजी ! आगे से कभी आपके साथ न आऊँगा।''

(iv) श्री वृन्दावन लाल वर्मा द्वारा रचित कहानी 'शरणागत' के माध्यम से लेखक ने ठाकुर बुन्देला की 'शरणागत रक्षा' की गरिमा का सुन्दर वर्णन किया है। रज्जब जाति का कसाई था। वह समाज में नीच जाति का हेय प्राणी समझा जाता था किन्तु ठाकुर में जाति-पाँति, ऊँच-नीच के साथ-साथ मानव हृदय एवं दयालुता के गुण भी थे। रज्जब जब पत्नी के ज्वरग्रस्त होने पर गिड़गिड़ाया तथा उसने ठाकुर को 'राजा' कहकर सम्मान दिया तो 'ठाकुर' गद्‌गद् हो गया। जिसके बाद उसने उसे रात व्यतीत करने के लिए अपनी पौर में दो हाथ जगह दी।

वह शरणागत की रक्षा करने वाला बुन्देला है। उसने मर्यादा के विरुद्ध आचरण करने वाले एक लठैत को रज्जब पर आक्रमण करने से रोका। साथ ही उसे उसके गाँव भेजने में सहायता की तथा अपनी शरणागति की गरिमा को बनाये रखा।

●●

4. सती

—शिवानी

लेखिका परिचय—हिन्दी साहित्य में शिवानी एक जाना पहचाना नाम है। इन्होंने काफी सारे उपन्यास, कहानियाँ, आलेख और निबन्ध लिखकर हिन्दी साहित्य को अपना योगदान दिया है। इनके लेखन में भावों का सुन्दर चित्रण, भाषा की सादगी तो होती ही है साथ ही साथ पहाड़, वहाँ रहने वाले भोले-भाले लोग और वहाँ की संस्कृति का जीता जागता वर्णन होता है। अगर आपने उनका लिखा साहित्य पढ़ा है तो समझ लीजिए कि कुमाऊँनी तो आप आसानी से समझ लेंगे क्योंकि उनके लेखन में कुमाऊँनी शब्दों और मुहावरों की भरमार रहती है। उन्हीं के शब्दों में, "मेरा लेखन कोई कल्पना की उड़ान नहीं, यह सच्चाई से जुड़ा है।"

हिन्दी कथा साहित्य में शिवानी जी की कथाएँ व उपन्यास एक अनमोल धरोहर हैं। शिवानी जी की कहानियाँ आधुनिक जीवन के यथार्थ पर आधारित है। इनकी कहानियों में बड़े ही कटीलेपन से आधुनिक जीवन की विसंगतियों को उजागर किया है। शिवानी का जन्म सन् 1923 में सौराष्ट्र में हुआ, उनके पिता अश्विनी कुमार पांडे रामपुर स्टेट में दिवान थे, वह वायसराय के बार काउंसिल के सदस्य भी थे। उनकी माता संस्कृत की विदुषी ही नहीं वरन् लखनऊ महिला विद्यालय की प्रथम छात्रा भी थीं। 1935 से 1943 के मध्य उन्होंने रविन्द्रनाथ टैगोर के शान्ति निकेतन में विद्या अध्ययन किया और 1943 में कलकत्ता से स्नातक की उपाधि प्राप्त की। उन्हें गुजराती, बंगाली, संस्कृत, अंग्रेजी और उर्दू का भी अच्छा ज्ञान था। मार्च 2003 को नई दिल्ली में अपने बच्चों में दीदी के नाम से विख्यात इस ईजा (माँ) का देहान्त हुआ।

शिवानी जी ने अपनी कृतियों से सामाजिक रूढ़ियों तथा आडम्बरों पर करारा व्यंग्य किया है। इनकी प्रमुख रचनाएँ विषकन्या, करिये छिमा, लाल हवेली, अपराधिनी आदि हैं। चौदह फेरे, कैजा, कृष्णकली, मायापुरी इनके प्रमुख उपन्यास हैं।

शब्दार्थ—**ठसाठस** = ठूँसकर भरी, **तसल्ली** = तसकीन या आश्वासन, **नासिका गर्जन** = खर्राटे भरना, **उपालम्भ** = ताने, **लावण्य** = सुन्दरता, **रीतापन** = खालीपन, **मलिन** = गंदा, **विस्थापित** = विधवा व तलाकशुदा, **संचालिका** = चलाने वाली, **गोष्ठी** = सभा, **स्वल्पभाषिणी** = कम बोलने वाली, **प्रोत्साहित** = प्रेरित, **परिपाटी** = रीति अथवा शैली, **केशराशि** = बालों की मात्रा, **वर्तुलाकार** = घुमावदार, **आबद्ध** = टिक गई, **त्रुटिहीन** = बिना गलती के, **धारा-प्रवाह** = प्रवाहमय, **सद्य वैधव्य** = नवीन विधवा, **खादीधारी** = खादी धारण करने वाली, **उदधि** = सागर, **भुवनमोहिनी** = संसार को मोहित करने वाली, **अर्धविक्षिप्त** = आधा पागल।

सारांश

प्रस्तुत कहानी का प्रारम्भ प्रयाग स्टेशन से होता है। जहाँ अर्धकुम्भ के मेले की वजह से बड़ी भीड़ है। लेखिका आरक्षण सूची देखकर आश्वस्त हो जाती है कि उसकी सहयात्री महिलाएँ हैं। लेखिका के अनुमान के अनुसार एक महाराष्ट्री तो दूसरी पंजाबी थी। उन दोनों के साथ भारी-भरकम सूटकेस के साथ बड़े-बड़े और ठँसे-ठँसे होल्डाल थे। लेखिका के पास एक छोटा बटुआ था, क्योंकि वे सिर्फ एक दिन के लिए बाहर जा रही हैं। उन दोनों के समान देखकर लेखिका यह सोचती है कि बिना सामान के यात्रा करना बेहद सुखद है।

मराठी महिला प्रत्येक वस्तु को उचित स्थान पर रखती है और एक मराठी पत्रिका पढ़ने लगती है। दूसरी पंजाबी महिला का सामान बेतरतीबी से बिखरा पड़ा है। पंजाबी महिला एक अंग्रेजी भाषा में जासूसी उपन्यास पढ़ रही है, लेकिन उनका सुराहीदान बार-बार उनके पढ़ने में व्यवधान उत्पन्न कर रहा है।

लेखिका के अनुमान से पंजाबी महिला शायद किसी सभा में भाग लेने के लिए जा रही हैं, क्योंकि वे अपने साथ एक फाइल लिए हुए है, जिसे वे बीच-बीच में खोलकर देखती हैं और फिर उपन्यास पढ़ने लगती हैं। पंजाबी महिला का पहनावा पूरी तरह से खद्दर का ही था। उनके चेहरे पर रोब था, परन्तु किसी प्रकार की सुन्दरता नहीं थी। उन्हें देख ऐसा प्रतीत होता है कि वे प्रौढ़ा कुमारी हैं अथवा विधवा। उस पंजाबी महिला ने

खुद ही अपना परिचय दिया और यह बताया कि वह विस्थापित स्त्रियों के लिए बनाये गये आश्रम की संचालिका है। वे एक समाज सेविका थीं, जो किसी गोष्ठी में भाग लेने के लिए लखनऊ जा रही थी।

वहीं दूसरी ओर मराठी महिला अपनी पत्रिका को पढ़ने में पूरी तरह से व्यस्त थी। वह पत्रिका पढ़ते हुए कभी मुस्कराती तो कभी उदास हो जाती थी। वह डिब्बे में होकर भी नहीं थी। वे शोलापुरी साड़ी पहने हुए थी। कानों में कर्णफूल था और एक मंगलसूत्र भी पहने थी जिस पर उनके पति का नाम लिखा हुआ था, मेजर वनोलकर।

इस बीच जब गाड़ी ने सीटी दी तभी चौथी महिला ने प्रवेश किया और गाड़ी चल दी। उनके हाथ में बेंत की एक टोकरी थी और एक बटुआ था। ये तीनों उन्हें देखने लगती हैं। जिसे समझकर उन्होंने कहा कि मैं छह फुट साढ़े दस इंच लम्बी हूँ। अच्छा ही है कि इस डिब्बे में चारों महिलाएँ ही हैं नहीं तो पुरुष भी मुझे घूरते। उसने सभी से प्रश्न पूछा लेखिका के साथ ही पंजाबी महिला ने बेरुखी से जवाब दिया लेकिन मराठी महिला ने यह कहकर टाल दिया कि वे हिन्दी नहीं जानती।

तब उस चौथी महिला ने अपना परिचय दिया कि उसका नाम मदालसा सिंघाड़िया है जो प्रिटोरिया से अपने पति की मृत देह लेने आई हैं। यह सुनकर तीनों चौंक जाती हैं। वह ताजी विधवा सी नहीं लग रही थी। उसने बताया कि उसके पति पर्वतारोहण के लिए भारत आये थे और एक तूफान में दबकर उनकी मृत्यु हो गई। भारत सरकार की सूचना पर वह भारत आई है। वे अपने मर्दाने रूमाल से कभी आँख पोंछती तो कभी नाक। इस प्रकार उसके इस वर्णन से तीनों एकदम प्रभावित हो जाती हैं।

मदालसा की ये बातें सुनकर मराठी महिला यह पूछती है कि क्या आप अपने पति का शव लेकर प्रिटोरिया जायेंगी ? इस प्रश्न के उत्तर को सुनकर सभी चकित हो जाते हैं। वह यह बताती हैं कि वह सती होने के लिए भारत आई है। यह सुनते ही समाज सेविका भाषण की गोलीबारी झाड़ने लगी। उन्होंने यह तक कह दिया कि मैं आपके पति के अन्तिम संस्कार में आपकी सहायता कर आपको अपने आश्रम में ले चलूँगी।

इन सब बातों को सुन मदालसा ने कहा कि मेरा निश्चय दृढ़ है। यह सती होने का रोग खानदानी है। परनानी, नानी और माँ सब सती हुई थीं और अब मैं। मेरे निर्णय को ब्रह्मा भी नहीं बदल सकते।

इन सब बातों के बाद मदालसा यह कहती है कि क्यों न हाथ मुँह धोकर कुछ खा लिया जाये। यह कहकर मदालसा गुसलखाने चली गई तो हम आपस में बातें करने लगे। मराठी महिला के अनुसार इस जमाने में ऐसे कोई सती-फती नहीं होती। समाज सेविका ने कहा कि यह कितनी निष्पाप, पवित्र और उदार है। वह जरूर ऐसी मूर्खता कर सकती है। लगता है कि पुलिस को खबर देनी पड़ेगी।

जब मदालसा हाथ-मुँह धोकर आती है तो आते ही उसने नाश्तादान निकाल लिया। कटोरियाँ सजाने लगी। जिसे देखकर सभी को भूख लग गई। उसने एक साथ ही खाने की बात की जिसे सब मान गये। उसने बहुत से घृत मिश्रित मसालेदार पकवान परोस रखे थे। वहीं हमारे पास कुछ पूरियाँ और अचार ही था। मदालसा के स्वादिष्ट भोजन को चटखारे लेकर तीनों ने साफ कर दिया और मदालसा ने भी अकेले ही हम तीनों के नाश्तादान को साफ कर दिया।

अन्त में मदालसा एक पानदान निकालती है और यह कहते हुए कि यह मेरा अन्तिम सफर है कल सुबह क्या होगा कोई नहीं जानता। उसका दिया पान खाने के बाद हम तीनों को ऐसी नींद आई जैसे पहले कभी नहीं आई थी।

आँख खुलते ही हमारे होश उड़ गये। मिसेज वनोलकर के स्टील का बक्सा, समाज सेविका का सूटकेस और मेरा पर्स गायब था। चेन खींचकर गाड़ी रोकी गई। सचमुच समाज सेविका को पुलिस को खबर देनी पड़ी, पर सती को बचाने के लिए नहीं अपितु पकड़वाने के लिए।

अभ्यास-प्रश्न

प्रश्न 1. सती कहानी में कहानीकार का क्या उद्देश्य है ?

अथवा

सती कहानी के माध्यम से कहानीकार कौन-सा सन्देश देना चाहता है ?

उत्तर—हिन्दी कहानीकार शिवानी जी की कहानी 'सती' की जब उद्देश्य के आधार पर समीक्षा की जाती है, तो यह पाया जाता है कि आजकल ट्रेनों में होने वाली जहरखुरानी की घटनाएँ दिन-प्रतिदिन बढ़ती चली जा रही हैं। समाचार पत्रों पर नजर डालें तो यह पता चलता है कि ट्रेन का सफर कितना खतरनाक बन चुका है। यात्री की इस समस्या को अपनी कहानी द्वारा प्रस्तुत करना ही कहानीकार का उद्देश्य है।

लेखिका अपनी इस कहानी में यह दिखाने का प्रयास करती हैं कि किस प्रकार ठगने वाले लोग मनुष्य की संवेदनशीलता का लाभ उठाते हैं। मनुष्य का संवेदनशील होना भी उसके लिए प्राणघातक अथवा उसके नुकसान का कारण हो सकता है। इस कहानी में जिस तथ्य की ओर संकेत किया गया है वह है मदालसा का स्त्री होना। इसके माध्यम से कहानी में यह भी स्पष्ट किया गया है कि महिलाएँ जिन्हें बहुत सुकोमल और संवेदनशील माना जाता है उनमें भी कुछ ऐसी महिलाएँ होती हैं जो इस प्रकार के कार्यों में संलिप्त रहती हैं और मानवता को शर्मसार करती हैं।

समाज की इस बड़ी समस्या को दिखाना एक लोकमंगल का कार्य है जो समाज के हित से जुड़ा हुआ है। इसके द्वारा समाज को यह सन्देश जाता है कि हमें अपनी संवेदनाओं एवं सहानुभूति पर काबू रखना चाहिए। जिससे हम जहरखुरानी का शिकार न बन सकें। कहानीकार ने कहानी के द्वारा यही सन्देश देने का प्रयास किया है।

प्रश्न 2. सती कहानी के शीर्षक के औचित्य पर प्रकाश डालिए।

उत्तर—शिवानी द्वारा लिखित 'सती' कहानी के शीर्षक की विवेचना करने पर यह पता चलता है कि कहानी का शीर्षक पूरी तरह से उचित है। शीर्षक में जिन गुणों का होना आवश्यक है, वे सारे गुण इस कहानी के शीर्षक में उपलब्ध हैं।

कहानी का शीर्षक 'सती' जिज्ञासावर्द्धक है। मदालसा के यह कहने के बाद कि वह सती होने के लिए भारत आई है, कहानी एक नया मोड़ लेती है जिसमें सहानुभूति और संवेदनाओं का एक मिश्रण तैयार होता है। यह पता ही नहीं चल पाता है कि आगे क्या होगा ? इस प्रकार पाठक की जिज्ञासा बढ़ती जाती है जो कहानी को पढ़ने के लिए प्रेरित करती है।

प्रस्तुत कहानी में सती प्रमुख है। कहानी का सम्पूर्ण घटनाएँ उस होने वाली सती पर आधारित हैं। यह सती कहानी का केन्द्र बिन्दु है। कहानी में मदालसा का आगमन और उसके सती होने की बात कथानक को एक प्रवाह देती है। कहानी का शीर्षक जिज्ञासावर्धक है, क्योंकि कहानी शीर्षक पढ़ने की उत्कंठा को जागृत करता है। जब यह उत्कंठा प्रबल हो जाती है तभी कहानी पढ़ी जाती है। कहानी के शीर्षक का संक्षिप्त होना भी आवश्यक है, सती कहानी का शीर्षक इस दृष्टि से भी महत्वपूर्ण है। इतना ही नहीं कहानी के शीर्षक में कहानी का सारभाव अन्तर्निहित है जो पूरी कहानी के सारभाव को समेटे हुए है। इस प्रकार शीर्षक के गुणों की दृष्टि से सती कहानी एक सफल कहानी है।

प्रश्न 3. ''नहीं, आपको ऐसी मूर्खता करने का कोई अधिकार नहीं है। यह एक अपराध है, क्या आप यह नहीं जानती ?'' इस कथन में कैसी मूर्खता करने की बात की जा रही है ? यह मूर्खता कौन करने वाला है ?

उत्तर—'सती' कहानी में शिवानी जी ने सती प्रथा के आधार पर अपनी कहानी का व्यंग्य तैयार किया है। प्रस्तुत कथन उस समय का है जब मराठी महिला के पूछने पर मदालसा यह कहती है कि मैं असल में सती होने के लिए भारत आई हूँ। यह सुनकर खादीधारी समाज सेविका यह कथन कहती है।

इस कथन में मदालसा के सती होने की बात को मूर्खतापूर्ण कार्य कहा गया है, जिसे खादीधारी समाज सेविका ने मदालसा से कहा। उसके अनुसार सती होना मूर्खता है। उन्होंने इसे अपराध भी बताया जिससे मदालसा यह सब जानकर अपना निर्णय बदल दे। वहीं पंजाबी महिला, मदालसा को इस प्रकार समझाने लगी कि मानों चिता प्रज्वलित हो चुकी है और सती लपटों में कूदने को तत्पर है।

समाज सेविका ने मदालसा को भिन्न-भिन्न तरीकों से समझाने का प्रयास किया। उन्होंने कहा कि नारी भावावेश के दुर्बल क्षणों में कभी-कभी बचपना कर बैठती है, मुझे इसका व्यापक अनुभव है। वह मदालसा को यह बताती है कि भारत विभाजन के समय ही मेरे पति की हत्या कर दी गई थी पर मैंने तब सती होने का निर्णय नहीं लिया। अगर मैं उस समय सती हो जाती तो दीन-दु:खियों के काम न आ पाती।

यह मूर्खता मदालसा करने वाली है। वह यह कहती है कि ब्रह्मा भी अब उसको सती होने के निर्णय से नहीं डिगा सकते। वह यह बताती है कि उसकी परनानी, नानी और माँ भी सती हुई थीं।

यह सब मदालसा का अभिनय था, क्योंकि अन्त में वह सभी को मूर्ख बनाकर नशे की दवा पान में खिलाकर उनका सारा सामान लेकर चंपत हो जाती है।

प्रश्न 4. सती कहानी के आधार पर शिवानी जी की भाषागत विशेषताओं का उल्लेख कीजिए।

उत्तर—हिन्दी साहित्य में शिवानी एक जाना पहचाना नाम है। इन्होंने काफी सारे उपन्यास, कहानियाँ, आलेख और निबन्ध लिखकर हिन्दी साहित्य को अपना योगदान दिया है। इनके लेखन में भावों का सुन्दर चित्रण, भाषा की सादगी तो होती ही थी साथ ही साथ पहाड़, वहाँ रहने वाले भोले भाले लोग और वहाँ की संस्कृति का जीता जागता वर्णन होता था।

भाषा के प्रयोग में लेखक को देश, काल, वातावरण, पात्रों की पात्रता अर्थात चरित्र की अनुकूलता का ध्यान रखना आवश्यक है। कहानीकार को विषयवस्तु, पाठक और पात्र के अनुरूप भाषा का प्रयोग करने से पाठक को उसी अनुभूति का आभास होगा जिसकी लेखक ने अभिव्यक्ति करनी चाही है। भाषा में सरलता, प्रवाहमयता और बोधगम्यता होनी चाहिए। कहीं-कहीं भाषा में काव्यात्मकता का प्रदर्शन भाषा को प्रभावशाली बनाने में सहायक होता है। शब्द भण्डार सटीक व समृद्ध होना चाहिए। कहीं-कहीं भाषा में काव्यात्मकता का प्रदर्शन भाषा को प्रभावशाली बनाने में सहायक होता है। शब्द भंडार सटीक व समृद्ध होना चाहिए। सूक्तियों और मुहावरों का प्रयोग भाषा को प्रवाहपूर्ण, प्रभावशाली व आकर्षक बनाने में सहायक होता है। शब्दों का चयन भावों के अनुकूल होना ही लेखक की सफलता का रहस्य होता है।

प्रस्तुत कहानी भाषा की दृष्टि से एक समृद्ध कहानी है। कहानी में भाषा के प्रयोग में शिवानी जी ने पात्रों के चरित्र के अनुकूल ही भाषा का प्रयोग किया है। इस कहानी में शिवानी जी की भाषा सरल, प्रवाहमय तथा बोधगम्य है। शिवानी जी के शब्दों का चयन भावों के अनुकूल है। शिवानी जी के भाषा की एक बानगी देखिए—

सती कहानी में मराठी महिला जो कि प्रारम्भ में यह कहती है कि उसे हिन्दी बोलना नहीं आता उसका यह संवाद उसके कथन को प्रमाणित करता है जिसमें हिन्दी की अपेक्षा अंग्रेजी के शब्द अधिक है।

"तो क्या आप अपने 'हसबैंड' का 'डैड बॉडी' लेकर प्रिटोरिया फ्लाई करेगा ?"

प्रश्न 5. 'सती' कहानी के किस पात्र ने आपको सर्वाधिक प्रभावित किया है और क्यों ?

अथवा

'सती' कहानी में मदालसा के चरित्र की कौन-कौन सी विशेषताएँ हैं ?

उत्तर—सती कहानी एक समस्या को उजागर करने वाली कहानी है। कहानी की पात्र योजना कहानी के उद्देश्य के अनुरूप है। इस कहानी में कुल चार पात्र हैं, जिनमें मदालसा का चरित्र प्रमुख है। इसी पात्र ने कहानी

के उद्देश्य की पूर्ति में सर्वाधिक योगदान दिया है। यही एक ऐसा पात्र है जिसने पाठकों को सर्वाधिक प्रभावित किया है।

मदालसा के चरित्र की अनेक विशेषताएँ हैं—

शारीरिक बनावट—मदालसा के चरित्र का कहानी में परिचय उसके शारीरिक बनावट के साथ हुआ है। मदालसा की लम्बाई-चौड़ाई उसके नकारात्मक व्यक्तित्व को और पुष्टता प्रदान करती है।

''वह हँसी, छह फीट साढ़े दस इंच टु बी एक्जैक्ट,''

संवाद में निपुण—मराठी महिला ने जब यह कहा कि मैं हिन्दी नहीं जानती। तब मदालसा ने त्रुटिहीन अंग्रेजी में धाराप्रवाह भाषण झाड़ दिया। जो उसकी संवाद में निपुणता को व्यक्त करता है। इतना ही नहीं, मदालसा ने ही सर्वप्रथम बातचीत का सिलसिला शुरू किया। लेखिका के अनुसार—

''फिर वे दनादन हमारा इंटरव्यू लेने लगीं।''

व्यवहार कुशल—मदालसा बड़ी ही व्यवहार कुशल थी। उसने बड़ी शीघ्रता से अपने बात व्यवहार से अपने सहयात्रियों के साथ निकटता स्थापित कर ली। उसकी बातों और उसके व्यवहार से ही तीनों सहयात्री प्रभावित हो जाती हैं। अन्ततः वे तीनों भी उसके साथ खाना खाने के लिए तैयार हो जाती हैं।

''उसकी भुवनमोहिनी हँसी ने हमें पराजित कर दिया।''

कुशल अभिनेत्री—मदालसा की अभिनय कला भी विशिष्ट थी। उसके अभिनय का प्रभाव इतना प्रबल था कि तीनों सहयात्रियों ने उसके द्वारा सुनाई गई घटना को सच मान लिया। उसने अभिनय में इस प्रकार की सहजता रखी कि उसके सहयात्रियों को पता ही नहीं चला कि ये झूठ भी हो सकता है।

अन्त में यह कहा जा सकता है कि सती कहानी में मदालसा एक ऐसी पात्र है जिसने कहानी की सफलता में सबसे अधिक योगदान दिया है। मदालसा का चरित्र एक ऐसा चरित्र है जिससे पाठक प्रभावित हुए बिना नहीं रह सकता।

प्रश्न 6.''रिजर्वेशन-स्लिप में अपना नाम ढूँढ़ा और बड़ी तसल्ली से अन्य तीन नामों की सूची देखी।''

(i) रिजर्वेशन-स्लिप में अपना नाम किसने ढूँढ़ा ? वह कहाँ से कहाँ जा रही थी ? उसके पास क्या सामान था ?

(ii) उन्होंने रिजर्वेशन-स्लिप में अन्य तीन नामों की सूची क्यों देखी ? वे तीन कौन थीं ? उनका वर्णन कीजिए।

(iii) गाड़ी ने जैसे ही सीटी दी गाड़ी में किसका प्रवेश हुआ ? उसका वर्णन कीजिए।

(iv) लेखिका ने यह क्यों कहा कि ''हम तीनों की ही दृष्टि उस चौथी पर आबद्ध हो गयी।'' इस भाव को स्पष्ट कीजिए।

उत्तर—(i) 'सती' कहानी की लेखिका शिवानी ने रिजर्वेशन-स्लिप में अपना नाम ढूँढ़ा फिर उन्होंने बड़े धैर्य से अन्य तीन लोगों का नाम देखा। तीनों महिला हैं यह जानकर उन्हें तसल्ली हुयी। वह प्रयाग से कहीं आस-पास ही एक दिन के लिए जा रही थी। इसलिए उनके पास कोई भारी भरकम सामान न था मात्र एक बटुआ ही था।

(ii) उन्होंने रिजर्वेशन-स्लिप में अन्य तीन नामों की सूची इसलिए देखी क्योंकि वह जानना चाहती थीं कि उनके कोच में अन्य तीन कौन हैं ? देखने पर उन्हें यह जानकर तसल्ली हुयी कि वे तीनों भी महिलाएँ ही थीं। उनमें से एक महाराष्ट्री, एक गुजराती और एक गाड़ी चलने पर उस कोच में चढ़ी जो छः फीट साढ़े दस इंच की लम्बी व आकर्षक व्यक्तित्व की नारी थी।

(iii) गाड़ी ने ज्यों ही सीटी दी ठीक उसी समय चौथी महिला ने डिब्बे में प्रवेश किया। उसके हाथ में बेंत से बनी एक छोटी सी टोकरी थी और काँख में चौकोर बटुआ दबा था। गाड़ी के धक्के के साथ ही महिला सीट पर लुढ़क पड़ी। वह बोली—"ओफ़, लगता था गाड़ी छूट ही जायेगी, बाप रे बाप कैसी दौड़ लगानी पड़ी।"

(iv) लेखिका ने "हम तीनों की ही दृष्टि उस पर आबद्ध हो गयी।" यह कथन इसलिए कहा क्योंकि वह चीज ही देखने लायक थी। उसकी हर अदा में कुछ न कुछ विशेषता थी। स्वयं उसने भी तीनों महिलाओं के द्वारा घूरा जाना स्वीकार किया और कहा, "केम, बेन, बहुत लम्बी हूँ न मैं, छह फीट, साढ़े दस इंच टु बी इग्जैक्ट, शायद भारत की सबसे लम्बी नारी।" उसने अपना परिचय देते हुए कहा, "मुझे मदालसा कहते हैं, मदालसा सिंघाड़िया। कल ही प्रिटोरिया से आयी हूँ, अपने पति की मृत देह लेने।" इसी प्रकार की उसकी अजीब-अजीब हरकतों ने लेखिका व अन्य दोनों महिलाओं को अपनी ओर आकृष्ट कर लिया था।

प्रश्न 7. "हाय मेरे स्टील का बक्स" मिसेज बनोलकर बर्थ से उतरते ही लड़खड़ा गयी।

(i) यह कथन किसने व कब कहा ? इस दुर्घटना का क्या कारण था ?

(ii) स्टील का बक्स चोरी होने पर उनकी दशा का वर्णन कीजिये।

(iii) समाज-सेविका दोनों हाथों से सिर थामे क्यों बैठ गयी ? ऐसी कौन सी वस्तु थी जिसके कारण महिलाओं को गहरी नींद आ गयी वर्णन कीजिए।

(iv) सती लेखिका शिवानी का क्या ले गयी ? विस्तार से वर्णन कीजिए।

उत्तर—(i) यह कथन लेखिका शिवानी के साथ गाड़ी के डिब्बे में यात्रा कर रही एक महाराष्ट्रियन महिला ने तब कहा जब उसके सामान में से एक स्टील का बक्स रहस्यमय ढंग से गायब हो गया।

इस दुर्घटना का कारण उनके डिब्बे में छह फीट साढ़े दस इंच वाली महिला मदालसा थी जिसने स्वादिष्ट पकवान खिलाने के बाद लेखिका सहित अन्य दो महिलाओं को पान खिलाकर सुला दिया व उनका सामान गायब कर दिया।

(ii) महाराष्ट्री व समाज सेविका के सामान की चोरी के बाद लेखिका का ध्यान अपने बटुए की ओर गया। उस समय उनका दिमाग भी गोल-गोल घूमते डिब्बे में गोल-गोल घूम रहा था। उनके दिमाग ने उन्हें सूचित किया कि "तुम्हारा बटुआ भी वह ले गयी है।" लेखिका के बटुए में पचपन रुपये और एक फर्स्ट क्लास का टिकिट था।

सती की चिता में लेखिका यही घृताहुति दे पायी थी।

(iii) समाज-सेविका दोनों हाथों से सिर थामे बिलख रही थी। "हाय, मैं तो लुट गयी। मेरे सूटकेस में आश्रम का दस हजार रुपया था।" लेखिका का मानना था कि यह कोई कुकुरमुत्तों को पीसकर बनाया गया विष भी हो सकता था जो ऐसे ही मीठे स्वप्न दिखाता है। इसका असर कई दिनों तक नहीं उतरता। सती ने ऐसे ही किसी विष का प्रयोग करके अपने प्रति सहानुभूति का लाभ प्राप्त कर सभी महिलाओं को लूटा है।

(iv) मिसेज़ बनोलकर अपने सामान में स्टील का बक्सा गायब देखकर बर्थ से उतरते ही लड़खड़ा गयी और बोली, "उसमें मेरे विवाह का जड़ाऊ सेट था।" उन्होंने कहा लगता है वह सती की बच्ची हमें कुछ विष खिला गई। सिर फटा जा रहा है। उनका गला भर्रा गया।

महाराष्ट्रीयन महिला अनुभव कर रही थी कि स्वादिष्ट भोजन व पान खिलाने के बाद मदालसा ने तीनों महिला साथियों से कहा था कि अब नींद में प्यारे-प्यारे सपने देखिए। वह बात सही ही थी। उसे पंखें के चारों ओर बल्ब, बल्ब के चारों ओर छत और छत के इर्द-गिर्द रेशमी साड़ियाँ और भारी-भारी आभूषण पहने वह स्वयं लट्टू सी घूम रही थी।

●●

5. आउट साइडर

—मालती जोशी

लेखिका परिचय—हिन्दी कहानी लेखिका मालती जोशी का जन्म 4 जून, सन् 1934 को औरंगाबाद में हुआ था। इन्होंने आगरा विश्वविद्यालय से सन् 1956 में हिन्दी विषय में एम. ए. की डिग्री प्राप्त की। आपने अनगिनत कहानियाँ, बाल कथाएँ तथा उपन्यासों की रचना की है। इनमें से अनेक रचनाओं का विभिन्न भारतीय तथा विदेशी भाषाओं में अनुवाद भी किया जा चुका है। संप्रति भोपाल में रहकर ये साहित्य सृजन में संलग्न हैं।

साहित्य में योगदान—'अपने आँगन की छाँव', 'परख', 'जीने की राह', 'दर्द का रिश्ता', 'आनन्दी'—आदि इनके प्रसिद्ध कहानी संग्रह हैं। इनकी कई कहानियों का रंगमंचन रेडियो तथा दूरदर्शन पर प्रस्तुत किया जा चुका है।

मालती जी की भाषा-शैली अत्यन्त रोचक, व्यवहारिक तथा सरस है। इनकी भाषा में बोलचाल के शब्दों की प्रचुरता है।

मालती जी को हिन्दी और मराठी की विभिन्न साहित्यिक संस्थाओं द्वारा सम्मानित व पुरस्कृत किया जा चुका है। इन्हें मध्य प्रदेश हिन्दी-साहित्य सम्मेलन द्वारा वर्ष 1998 के भवभूति अलंकरण सम्मान से विभूषित किया जा चुका है।

मालती जी की भाषा आडम्बरों से मुक्त सहजता एवं संवेदनशीलता से परिपूर्ण है। आपकी भाषा में मुख्यत: तत्सम शब्दों का प्रयोग हुआ है, किन्तु आवश्यकता के अनुसार तद्भव, देशज और विदेशी शब्दों को भी आपने यथासम्भव स्थान दिया है। यत्र-तत्र लक्षणा और व्यंजना का पुट पाठक के मास का स्पर्श करता है। मुहावरे, अलंकार आदि का प्रयोग भाषा को अधिक सम्प्रेषणीय बनाने में सहयोगी रहा है। वाक्य रचना सरल एवं सुस्पष्ट है। अनुभूति और अभिव्यक्ति के विशिष्ट कौशल के कारण मालती जोशी की पहचान हिन्दी कहानीकारों में अलग ही है। आधुनिक युग के संवेदनशील कहानीकारों में उन्हें बड़े सम्मान की दृष्टि से देखा जाता है। वर्तमान कथाकारों में उनका विशिष्ट स्थान है।

शब्दार्थ

संपन्न = परिपूर्ण, **निपट जाने** = फुरसत हो जाना, **दुबक जाना** = छिप जाना, **इरादा** = इच्छा, **कुशलक्षेम** = हालचाल, **अतिरिक्त** = अलावा, **आपाधापी** = भागदौड़, **मुल्तवी** = टालना, **भावविभोर** = भावना में बहना, **जुमला** = वाक्य, **जनरेशन** = पीढ़ियाँ, **बचकानी** = बच्चों जैसी, **इत्मिनान** = आराम से, **दायरे** = सीमाएँ, **अभियान** = कार्यक्रम, **ब्योरा** = पूर्ण जानकारी, **परफेक्ट कंवेनियन** = सही साथी, **दिलेर** = दिलवाला, **तनाव** = दिमागी उलझन, **सुस्ताने** = आराम करने, **मोहलत** = वक्त, **कद्र** = परवाह, **हुजूरी** = चापलूसी, **अनब्याही** = कुँआरी, **अरमानों** = इच्छाओं, **अहसास** = महसूस करना, **त्रस्त** = पीड़ित, **ममता** = प्रेम, **बेवक्त** = बिना वक्त के, **गुड़ गोबर** = काम बिगाड़ना, **मशरूफ** = व्यस्त, **काठ** = लकड़ी, **निजात** = मुक्ति, **हैसियत** = औकात।

सारांश

स्टेशन से लौटते हुए रात के ग्यारह बज गये थे। नये जोड़े के हनीमून पर रवाना होते ही शादी का कार्यक्रम एक तरह से सम्पन्न हो गया था। नीलम थकान से निढाल हो रही थी। पर सब कुछ ठीक से निपट जाने से, मन एकदम हल्का हो गया था। अब वह निश्चिन्त होकर बिस्तर में दुबक जाना चाहती थी।

पर जनता का इरादा कुछ और ही था। बच्चों को जबरदस्ती सोने के लिए भेजकर, सबके सब ड्राइंगरूम में ही जम गये थे। पम्मी ठीक ही कर रही थी। घर की इस आखिरी शादी में, पूरा परिवार इकट्ठा हो गया था। सुदीप तो इतनी दूर कनाडा से आया था। उससे कुशलक्षेम पूछने के अतिरिक्त ज्यादा बात करने का वक्त नहीं मिल पाया था। पूरे वक्त आपाधापी ही मची रही। अब आकर थोड़ी फुरसत मिली है। अब इन लोगों के जाने

की घड़ी पास आ गई है। पूनम चार दिन बाद अपने ससुराल चली जायेगी। सुदीप भी अपने ससुराल वालों से मिलना चाहेगा।

सोने का प्रोग्राम मुल्तवी कर नीलम अपनी प्रिय कुर्सी पर बैठ गई। एक सुमीत को छोड़कर उसका पूरा परिवार उसके सामने था। सुदीप-सुजीत दोनों भाई, उनकी बहुएँ—सुषमा और अलका-बहन पूनम और उसके पति नरेश। अपने इसी परिवार के लिए, वह पिछले पच्चीस वर्षों से खटती आ रही थी। आज छोटे भाई की शादी के साथ उसकी सारी जिम्मेदारियाँ पूरी हो गईं थीं। वह अपने आप को बहुत हल्का और कृतार्थ अनुभव कर रही थी।

सुजीत कुछ कहते-कहते रुक गया और उसने संकोच से आँखें झुका लीं, किन्तु पूनम तो हमेशा से बोल्ड रही है। वह तुरन्त बोली, ''दीदी, बड़े भैया का मतलब है कि अब आपकी सारी जिम्मेदारियाँ समाप्त हो गईं हैं। अब आपको भी शादी कर सैटल हो जाना चाहिए। यह सुनकर नीलम ने क्रोधित होकर बहन को बुरी तरह डाँट दिया। तभी नरेश बोल उठे, ''दीदी पम्मी ठीक कह रही है। यह सिर्फ इनकी नहीं हम सबकी इच्छा है। इस घर के लिए आपने अपनी पूरी जिन्दगी ही होम कर दी है।''

नीलम ने इसे महज मजाक समझकर उनकी बातों का कोई जवाब नहीं दिया। वे लोग नीलम के लिए दर्जन भर प्रस्ताव बटोर लाये थे। ऐसा लग रहा था कि छोटे भाई की शादी तो बहाना है, वे लोग शायद इसी अभियान के लिए इकट्‌ठा हुआ थे। फिर भी उसने इसे गम्भीरता से नहीं लिया।

तभी सुदीप ने एकाएक पूछ लिया कि उन्हें (नीलम दीदी) को लखनऊ वाला प्रपोजल कैसा लगा ? नीलम के मना करने पर सुषमा ने बरेली वालों को देखने की बात कही। नीलम का कहना था कि वह इस उम्र में इतना तनाव नहीं झेल पायेगी। परिस्थितियों से लड़ते-लड़ते वह तंग आ गई है। अब वह सुस्ताना चाहती है तथा जिन्दगी को आनन्द के साथ जीना-चाहती है। तीनों वहाँ से उठकर कमरे से बाहर दो-चार कदम गये होंगे कि सुषमा के ये शब्द नीलम के कानों में पड़े—''मुझे मालूम था वे मना कर देंगी। इतने दिनों तक इस घर में बॉसिंग करती रही हैं। ससुराल में धौंस-डपट सहना उनके बस का थोड़े ही है।'' उसे लगा शायद सुषमा ठीक ही कह रही है। पम्मी ने नीलम से कहा कि सुजीत और अलका उसे (नीलम) बोझ समझते हैं। अलका तो कहती है कि वह नीलम के कारण जिन्दगी को ठीक से एनजॉय नहीं कर पाई। पम्मी की बात सुनकर नीलम ने कहा कि वह उम्र में भले ही ज्यादा हो गई है, किन्तु उसके सपने अभी भी किशोर हैं। उसके भाई के द्वारा लाये गये प्रस्तावों का उसके साथ कोई मेल नहीं है। उनके प्रस्तावों को वह मजाक ही समझती रही। दरअसल, अब शादी की बात उसके मन में उतर गई थी।

नीलम की बात सुनकर पम्मी ने कहा—''तुमने इस घर को लाख अपने खून से सींचा हो, पर यह घर कभी तुम्हारा अपना नहीं हो सकता। तुम यहाँ हमेशा आउट साइडर ही रहोगी।'' अभी तो तुम्हारे पास नौकरी है, परन्तु रिटायर होने के बाद इस घर में तुम्हारी हैसियत एक फालतू सामान की सी रह जायेगी। तब तुम्हें मेरी बात याद आयेगी। नीलम को अपने भाई-बहनों से बहुत प्रेम था, किन्तु अपनी माँ से शिकायत थी कि उन्होंने नीलम के साथ पक्षपात किया तथा कमाने का भार अपनी बेटी के कंधों पर डालकर बाकि बच्चों का लालन-पालन करती रहीं। यहाँ तक कि नीलम की बढ़ती उम्र से भी वह अनजान बनी रही।

पिता की आकस्मिक मृत्यु के बाद, घर की बागडोर नीलम ने यह सोचकर सम्भाली थी कि कल जब भाई किसी लायक हो जायेंगे तब वह अपनी जिन्दगी जी पायेगी, किन्तु ऐसा हो न सका। सुजीत बी. कॉम करके बैंक में लग गया था, पर उसका सामर्थ्य इतना नहीं था कि वह पूनम की शादी भी करता और सुमीत की मैडिकल की पढ़ाई का खर्च भी उठाता। इसलिए नीलम को मोर्चे पर डटे रहना पड़ा। नीलम दीपू के साथ समय बिताना चाहती थी अतः वह शादी के लिए ली गई पन्द्रह दिन की छुट्टियों को बढ़ाने के लिए एक एप्लीकेशन लेकर कॉलेज गई। प्रिंसीपल मैडम ने उससे कहा कि उसे ट्रांसफर प्रमोशन के साथ मिल रहा और

वह प्रिंसीपल बनकर बस्तर जा रही है। मैडम ने उन्हें यह भी समझाया कि बार-बार प्रमोशन रिफ्यूज करना ठीक नहीं है।

घर आते हुए रास्ते में उसने ढेर सारी खरीददारी की। घर पहुँचकर नीलम अपने कमरे में जाने के बजाय सीधे दीपू के कमरे की ओर ही चली गई। दरवाजे पर ही उसने देवरानी-जिठानी का वार्तालाप सुन लिया। अलका कहा रही थी, ''आप तो लकी हैं जिज्जी ! फुर्र से उड़ जायेंगी। ये नेहा भी चार दिन बाद छोटू के साथ बंगलौर चली जायेगी। उम्रकैद तो हम लिखवाकर लाये हैं, सो भुगतेंगे।''

नीलम को अपने कानों पर विश्वास नहीं हुआ। उसके सामने इतना मीठा बोलने वाली अलका उसके पीठ पीछे उसके साथ को उम्रकैद बोल रही थी। अब नीलम की समझ में आ गया था कि कि शायद इस उम्रकैद से रिहाई पाने के लिए ही उसकी शादी का प्रपंच रचा जा रहा है।

रात को खाने की मेज पर रसगुल्लों का डोंगा सजाकर उसने (नीसम) ऐलान किया कि, ''यह मेरे प्रमोशन की मिठाई है। प्रिंसीपल बनकर जा रही हूँ।'' फिर वह बोली कि, ''इस आपाधापी से तंग आ गई हूँ। फिर बार-बार प्रमोशन ठुकराना अच्छा भी नहीं लगता। पहले तो खैर मजबूरी थी। अब तो कोई बहाना भी नहीं रहा।''

इस बात पर सभी एकमत थे। रात बिस्तर पर लेटी हुई वह दिनभर की घटनाओं का मन ही मन जायजा ले रही थी। किसी ने भी तो प्रतिवाद नहीं किया। पम्मी ठीक ही कह रही थी। बल्कि उसने तो रिटायरमेंट के बाद की बातकही थी। पर नीलम को लग रहा था कि घर में उसकी हैसियत तो अभी से किसी फालतू सामान की तरह हो गई है।

अभ्यास-प्रश्न

प्रश्न 1. प्रस्तुत कहानी में 'आउट साइडर' किसको कहा गया है और क्यों ?

उत्तर—'आउट साइडर' का तात्पर्य है घर से बाहर का व्यक्ति। यहाँ पर 'आउट साइडर' नीलम को कहा गया है जोकि अपने सभी भाई बहनों से बड़ी है और वही घर का पूरा खर्च भी चला रही है। जब सभी भाई-बहनों की शादी उसने कर दी तो उसे कुछ फुर्सत का आभास हुआ। वह एक स्कूल में अध्यापिका थी और अपने वेतन से ही पूरे परिवार का खर्च चला रही थी। छोटे भाई की शादी हो गई तो उन्हें हनीमून पर भेज दिया। शादी का कार्यक्रम एक तरह से सम्पन्न हो गया था। नीलम थकान से निढाल हो रही थी। लेकिन बच्चों को जबरदस्ती सोने के लिए भेजकर सभी भाई-बहन ड्राइंगरूम में ही जम गये। आपस में एक-दूसरे की बात होने लगी। नीलम अपने सोने के प्रोग्राम को मुल्तवी कर एक कुर्सी पर बैठ गई। एक सुमीत को छोड़कर पूरा परिवार उसके सामने था सुदीप-सुजीत दोनों भाई, उनकी बहुएँ सुषमा और अलका, बहन पूनम और उसके पति नरेश। अपने इसी परिवार के लिए वह पिछले पच्चीस वर्षों से खटती आ रही थी। आज छोटे की शादी के बाद उसकी (नीलम) सारी जिम्मेदारियाँ पूरी हो गई थीं। वह अपने आपको बहुत हल्का और कृतार्थ अनुभव कर रही थी।

फिर वार्ता का दौर शुरू हुआ। पूनम ने कहा, ''दीदी, बड़े भैया का मतलब है कि अब आपकी सारी जिम्मेदारियाँ समाप्त हो गई हैं। अब आपको भी सैटिल हो जाना चाहिए। नीलम नहीं समझ पाई कि सैटिल होने का क्या मतलब है। तब उन्होंने स्पष्ट कर दिया कि उसको भी अब शादी कर लेनी चाहिए। नीलम को यह बात कुछ अच्छी नहीं लगी क्योंकि उसकी उम्र अब पैंतालीस वर्ष की हो गई थी। वे सभी एक राय थे और उन्होंने शादी के अजीब से प्रस्ताव नीलम के समक्ष प्रस्तुत किये जिन्हें नीलम ने ठुकरा दिया। उसने कहा कि इतनी उम्र में अब कोई तनाव वह झेल नहीं पायेगी। वह सोचने लगी कि उसकी माँ ने उसके बारे में कुछ नहीं सोचा बस घर का खर्च चलाने वाली बना दिया। पिता की आकस्मिक मृत्यु के बाद जब उसने घर की बागडोर सम्भाली थी, तब यह नहीं सोचा कि यह उसकी नियति होगी। मन में एक क्षीण आशा थी कि कल को भाई जब किसी लायक हो जायेंगे तो वह अपनी जिन्दगी जी सकेगी। पर वह आशा दुराशा ही साबित हुई।

एक दिन नीलम अपने कमरे में जाने के बजाय, सीधे दीपू के कमरे की ओर चली गई। भीतर देवरानी और जिठानी बात कर रही थीं। अलका कह रही थी, ''आप तो लकी हैं जिज्जी ! फुर्र से उड़ जायेंगी। ये नेहा भी चार दिन के बाद छोटू के साथ बंगलौर चली जायेगी। उम्र कैद तो हम लिखवाकर लाये हैं, सो भुगतेंगे।'' यह सुनकर नीलम उलटे पाँव लौट गई। उसे विश्वास ही नहीं हुआ कि उसके बारे में लोगों की कितनी घटिया सोच है। इसीलिए उसकी शादी का प्रपंच रचा जा रहा है। वह अपना ट्रान्सफर 'बस्तर' के लिए लेकर आई है कि यहाँ से दूर चली जायेगी। नीलम को लग रहा था कि घर में उसकी स्थिति किसी फालतू सामान जैसी हो गई है।

प्रश्न 2. नीलम की अपनी माँ से क्या शिकायत रही ? क्या माँ को उसके बारे में सोचना नहीं चाहिए था ?

उत्तर—घर में छोटे की शादी के बाद सब लोग जैसे फुर्सत में आ गये थे। नीलम थकान से निढाल हो रही थी। पर सब कुछ ठीक से निपट जाने से मन एकदम हल्का हो गया था। सब लोगों का इरादा और ही था। वे नीलम से बात करना चाहते थे कि अब उनको भी अपनी शादी के बारे में सोचना चाहिए। नीलम उम्र में सबसे बड़ी थी तथा उसके परिवार में सुदीप और सुजीत दो भाई, उनकी बहुएँ—सुषमा और अलका, बहन पूनम और उसका पति नरेश थे। अपने इसी परिवार के लिए वह पिछले पच्चीस वर्षों से खटती आ रही थी। आज छोटे की शादी के बाद उसकी सारी जिम्मेदारियाँ पूरी हो गई थीं। वह अपने आपको बहुत हल्का अनुभव कर रही थी। वे लोग जो कहना चाह रहे थे उसकी शुरुआत पूनम ने की। उसने कहा कि अब आपकी सारी जिम्मेदारियाँ समाप्त हो गई हैं। अब आपको भी सैटल हो जाना चाहिए। इस बात से नीलम असहज हो गई। या यों कहें कि पैंतालीस वर्ष की उम्र में कोई शादी की बात क्यों सोचेगा। पर सब लोग किसी न किसी तरह एक ही बात पर जोर डालते रहे। नरेश ने कहा, ''दीदी, पम्मी ठीक कह रही है। यह सिर्फ उसकी और बड़े भैया की बात नहीं है, हम सबकी यही इच्छा है। इस घर के लिए आपने इतना कुछ किया है। एक तरह से अपनी पूरी जिन्दगी ही होम कर दी है। इसलिए सब चाहते हैं कि अब आप भी इत्मीनान की, आराम की जिन्दगी बसर करें। आप नहीं जानती कि अपनी गृहस्थी में रच-बस जाने के बाद भी इन सबके मन में अपराध-बोध पलता रहता है।'' नीलम ने कोई जवाब नहीं दिया।

अपने भाई-बहनों पर नीलम की अपार ममता है। शिकायत कभी अगर थी तो अम्मा से थी। माँ होकर भी उन्होंने बहुत पक्षपात किया। कमाने का भार बड़ी बेटी के कन्धों पर डालकर वे बाकी बच्चों का लालन-पालन करती रहीं। नीलम की मुट्ठी में से उम्र रेत की तरह फिसलती रही और अम्मा जानकर भी अनजान बनी रही। पिता की आकस्मिक मृत्यु के बाद जब उसने घर की बागडोर सम्भाली थी, तब यह नहीं सोचा था कि अब यही उसकी नियति होगी, मन में क्षीण आशा थी कि कल को भाई जब किसी लायक हो जायेंगे तो वह अपनी जिन्दगी जी सकेगी परन्तु ऐसा हुआ नहीं।

माँ को नीलम के भविष्य के बारे में सोचना चाहिए था। यदि माँ उसके बारे में सोचती तो आज नीलम की हालत ऐसी नहीं होती।

प्रश्न 3. नीलम ने किनको ऐंटीक पीस कहा ? उसने ऐसा क्यों कहा ?

उत्तर—घर में सब लोग इस फिराक में थे कि नीलम दीदी को किसी तरह शादी के लिए राजी किया जाये। लेकिन नीलम को ये बातें बचकानी लगीं क्योंकि उसकी उम्र अब शादी की नहीं रही थी। लेकिन इधर सब लोगों ने एक लम्बी चौड़ी लिस्ट थमा दी थी। उसे फुर्सत से विचार करने के लिए कहा गया था। पर सुदीप और सुषमा दूसरे ही दिन उसके कमरे में आ गये। उन्हें शायद सबसे ज्यादा जल्दी थी। कनाडा जाने से पहले वे सब कुछ तय करके जाना चाहते थे। उनके पीछे-पीछे सुजीत भी आ गया। लगा कि दोनों भाई दल बाँधकर उस पर हमला करना चाहते हैं थोड़ी देर इधर-उधर की बातें होती रहीं, फिर सुदीप ने एकाएक पूछ लिया, ''दीदी, तुम्हें लखनऊ वाला प्रपोजल कैसा लगा ?''

नीलम बोली, ''न बाबा शादी के तुरन्त बाद नानी बनने का अपना कोई इरादा नहीं है।'' सुषमा ने सुझाव दिया, ''तो बरेली वालों को देख लेते हैं उनके दो बेटे ही हैं शायद वे भी अभी छोटे हैं और उन बेटों को वे हॉस्टल में रखने को तैयार हैं।

नीलम ने कहा, "इसी को कहते हैं हिप्पोक्रैसी। इधर तो वे प्रचारित करेंगे कि हम सिर्फ बच्चों की खातिर शादी कर रहे हैं और फिर उन्हीं बच्चों को हॉस्टल में ठूँसने को भी तैयार हो जायेंगे। ऐसे दो मुँहे लोगों से मुझे सख्त नफरत है।" यह सुनकर सुजीत बोला, "मुझे तो नरेश के जीजाजी वाला प्रस्ताव बहुत अच्छा लगा है। एक तो महाशय डिप्टी कलेक्टर हैं। दूसरे, थोड़ा-बहुत लिखने का शौक भी रखते हैं। ही बिल बी ए परफेक्ट कंपेनियन।" नीलम ने कहा, "उन्हीं की बात कर रहे हो न जिनकी लड़की ने आत्महत्या की धमकी दी है ? अरे, क्यों मेरे सिर हत्या थोपना चाहते हो।"

यह सब देखकर ही नीलम ने इनको 'ऐंटीक पीस' कहा है।

प्रश्न 4. कहानी के आधार पर मुख्य पात्र नीलम का चरित्र-चित्रण कीजिए।

उत्तर— कहानी की नायिका नीलम निस्वार्थ भावना वाली, आत्मनिर्भर, दयालुता की भावना लिए हुए, अपने परिवार को प्रेम करने वाली, दूरदर्शी, बुद्धिमान और परिश्रमी थी।

(1) निस्वार्थ भावना वाली— नीलम निस्वार्थ भावना से अपने परिवार (भाई-बहन) का पालन-पोषण करती रही। उसने-अपनी पूरी जिन्दगी परिवार के पालन में ही खत्म कर दी। अपने बारे में कुछ नहीं सोचा। उसने परिवार का पालन ही अपनी नियति मान लिया और अपने जीवन को उसी में खपाती रही।

(2) आत्मनिर्भर— नीलम अपनी पैंतालीस वर्ष की अवस्था तक काम करती रही है और उसकी आमदनी से घर का पालन करती रही है। उसने अपने बारे में न सोचकर भाई-बहनों के पालन-पोषण पर ध्यान दिया। वह एक कॉलेज में अध्यापिका थी और अपनी तनख्वाह से घर का खर्च चलाती थी।

(3) दयालु— उसके स्वभाव में दयालुता थी। भाई-बहनों की अनकहीं बातें सुनकर भी क्रोध नहीं करती थी। उनके प्रति उसकी ममता अधिक थी।

(4) अपने परिवार से प्रेम करने वाली— नीलम एक आदर्श व अविवाहित महिला है। उसने अपनी पूरी जिन्दगी परिवार के पालन-पोषण में ही लगा दी।

(5) दूरदर्शी— वह दूरदर्शी थी। उसे ज्ञात था कि अपनी शादी करने के बाद भी उसे सुख नहीं मिलेगा। सुख सिर्फ कल्पना की बात है। काफी जोर-जबरदस्ती के बाद भी वह अपनी शादी के लिए तैयार नहीं हुई।

(6) बुद्धिमान और परिश्रमी— वह बुद्धिमान थी। भाई-बहनों की बातों को तो वह बचकानी बताती है। परिश्रम का गुण तो उसके जीवन के साथ जुड़ा हुआ था तथा परिश्रम करने से वह थकती नहीं थीं।

प्रश्न 5. कहानी के तत्वों के आधार पर 'आउट-साइडर' कहानी की समीक्षा कीजिए।

उत्तर— मालती जोशी द्वारा लिखित कहानी 'आउट-साइडर' एक स्त्री के मनोभावों को प्रकट करती है। नीलम के चरित्र के माध्यम से स्त्रियों के अन्तर्द्वन्द्व की भावना को प्रकट करने का प्रयास किया है। मालती जोशी की इस कहानी की सफलता का मुख्य रहस्य उनकी कहानी कला है। कहानी के तत्वों का सफलतापूर्वक संयोजन ही उनकी कहानी लेखन की विशेषता है।

कथानक— प्रस्तुत कहानी का कथानक एक निश्चित उद्देश्य की दिशा में यथार्थ घटनाओं और पात्रों के माध्यम से विकसित होता है। यह कथानक सामाजिक, व्यवहारिक एवं परिवारिक व्यवस्था का सजीव चित्र प्रस्तुत करता है।

पात्र एवं चरित्र-चित्रण— प्रस्तुत कहानी में पात्रों का संयोजन बड़ी ही कुशलता से किया गया है। इस प्रकार नीलम में प्रमुख पात्र के सभी गुण हैं जो कहानीकार के उद्देश्य की पूर्ति में सहायक है।

संवाद एवं कथोपकथन— प्रस्तुत कहानी में समस्या को उभारने वाले, वस्तुस्थिति की व्याख्या करने वाले और पात्रों के मनोभावों को चित्रित करने वाले संवादों को प्रस्तुत किया है। कहानी के संवाद मौलिक, रोचक तथा पात्रानुकूल हैं। संवादों की पात्रानुकूलता का यह उदाहरण दर्शनीय है।

''दीपू, मेरा मतलब इस जनरेशन की शादियों से था। तुम्हारी प्रिया तो अभी बहुत छोटी है।''

''बट आय एम क्वाइट वेल सैटल्ड।''

भाषा-शैली—कहानीकार पात्रानुकूल, भावानुकूल और परिस्थिति के अनुकूल-भाषा का प्रयोग करने में सिद्धहस्त हैं। प्रस्तुत कहानी में भाषा शैली का प्रयोग पात्र, विषय और परिस्थिति के अनुकूल हुआ है। इनकी भाषा-शैली अत्यन्त रोचक, व्यवहारिक तथा सरस है। इनकी भाषा में बोलचाल के शब्दों की प्रचुरता है; जैसे—दरअसल, जनरेशन, भागमभाग, रौनक, बौसिंग आदि।

प्रश्न 6. ''वट आइ एम क्वाइट वेल सेटल्ड।''

(i) उक्त कथन किसने कहा है ? उनका परिचय दें।

(ii) नीलम के भाई-बहन उसका विवाह क्यों करवाना चाहते थे ?

(iii) सेटल्ड होने को लेकर नीलम और उसके भाई-बहनों के नजरिये के अन्तर को स्पष्ट कीजिए।

(iv) 'नीलम एक आधुनिक नारी है।' विवेचना कीजिए।

उत्तर—(i) उक्त कथन की वक्ता नीलम है। नीलम, मालती जोशी द्वारा लिखित कहानी 'आउट साइडर' की नायिका है। वह अपने सभी भाई-बहनों में सबसे बड़ी है। पिता की आकस्मिक मृत्यु के बाद उसने ही परिवार की जिम्मेदारियाँ संभालते हुए परिवार के सदस्यों का भरण-पोषण किया है।

(ii) पिता की असामयिक मृत्यु के बाद नीलम ने घर की बागडोर अपने हाथों में ले ली थी। बड़ी बहन होने के नाते उसने स्वयं अविवाहित रहकर अपने सभी भाई-बहनों का भविष्य सँवारा तथा सबके विवाह सम्पन्न कराये। अब जब सब अपनी-अपनी गृहस्थी में सुख से रह रहे थे तो ऐसे में नीलम उन्हें 'जिम्मेदारी' प्रतीत होने लगी थी। इसलिए वे उसकी शादी करवाकर इस जिम्मेदारी रूपी बोझ से मुक्ति पाना चाहते थे।

(iii) नीलम के भाई-बहन उसे 'सेटल' करना चाहते थे। उनकी नजर में 'सेटल' का अर्थ था कि नीलम विवाह कर अपनी नयी गृहस्थी बसा ले और नये सिरे से जीवन शुरू करे। परन्तु उनके 'सेटल' होने के अभिप्राय को न समझते हुए नीलम का मानना था कि वह 'सेटल्ड' ही है। क्योंकि नीलम के अनुसार 'सैटल्ड' का अर्थ था कि उसके पास जीविकोपार्जन का साधन भी था तथा वह अपनी सारी जिम्मेदारियों का निर्वाहन भी अच्छी तरह कर चुकी थी। अत: दोनों के नजरिये से 'सैटल्ड' होने के मानक भिन्न थे।

(iv) आधुनिक नारी 'मल्टीटास्कर' होती है। आधुनिक नारी की ज्यादातर विशेषताएँ जैसे स्वाभिमान, कर्त्तव्यपरायणता, आत्मनिर्भरता, कार्यकुशलता, पारिवारिक तथा पेशेवर जिन्दगी में सन्तुलन, नेतृत्व क्षमता, निर्णय लेने की क्षमता आदि नीलम के चरित्र में परिलक्षित होती है।

नीलम अपने परिवार की मुखिया है और इस जिम्मेदारी का वह पूरे कौशल के साथ निर्वाहन भी करती है। वह अविवाहित है परन्तु अपने जीवन के इस खालीपन को परिवार के प्रति अपनी जिम्मेदारियों के बीच नहीं आने देती।

भाई-बहनों द्वारा लाये गये विवाह के प्रस्तावों को वह ठुकरा देती है क्योंकि वह स्वाभिमानी है अत: अपनी शर्तों पर विवाह करने की अभिलाषी है, न कि सिर्फ विवाह के नाम पर खानापूर्ति करने की।

जब वह स्वयं को अलका से तिरस्कृत होते हुए देखती है तो अचानक अपने तबादले को स्वीकर करने का निर्णय लेती है क्योंकि उसके लिए स्वाभिमान से बढ़कर कुछ नहीं है। इस आधार पर हम कह सकते हैं कि नीलम एक आदर्श आधुनिक नारी के रूप को प्रदर्शित करती है।

प्रश्न 7. ''तुम यहाँ हमेशा आउट साइडर ही रहोगी।''

(i) उक्त कथन किसने कहा है ? इस कथन के पीछे वक्ता का क्या उद्देश्य है ?

(ii) नीलम अपनी इस दशा के लिए किसे जिम्मेदार मानती है और क्यों ?

(iii) क्या नीलम पूनम के उक्त विचार से सहमत है ? अंत में उसके विचारों में क्या बदलाव आता है ?

(iv) इस कहानी के माध्यम से लेखिका मालती जोशी क्या सन्देश देना चाहती है ?

उत्तर—(i) उक्त कथन पम्मी का है। वह नीलम की छोटी बहन है। आयु में छोटी होने पर भी वह व्यावहारिक ज्ञान में नीलम से आगे है। इस कथन के द्वारा वह नीलम की आँखों पर बँधी परिवार के प्रति प्रेम व त्याग की पट्टी को खोलना चाहती है। उसे यह अहसास दिलाना चाहती है कि न तो वह घर ही उसका अपना है और न ही उस घर के लोग। वह सबके लिए एक बोझ से बढ़कर कुछ नहीं है।

(ii) नीलम इस बात को अच्छी तरह समझती है कि उसके अकेलेपन का कारण सुदीप द्वारा अपनी जिम्मेदारियों को नजरअन्दाज करना है परन्तु वह उसे दोष नहीं देना चाहती। उसकी नजर में उसकी इस बदहाल दशा की दोषी उसकी अपनी ही माँ है। पिता की मृत्यु के बाद जब नीलम घर की जिम्मेदारी उठाने का बीड़ा उठाती है तो उसकी माँ बड़ी निश्चित होकर सारी जिम्मेदारियाँ उस पर छोड़कर बाकी बच्चों के लालन-पालन में व्यस्त हो जाती है। सुदीप की नौकरी लगते ही वे उसका विवाह करा उसे सपत्नीक कनाडा भेज देती है। यदि वे नीलम के सपनों एवं आकांक्षाओं का मान रखना चाहती, उसके भविष्य की चिन्ता करती तो परिवार की जिम्मेदारी सुदीप और सुजीत को सौंपकर, नीलम के विवाह के विषय में सोचतीं।

माँ के गैर जिम्मेदाराना रवैये के कारण ही नीलम परिवार की जिम्मेदारियों में उलझी रह गयी और अन्त में एकांकी जीवन जीने के लिए विवश हो गयी।

(iii) "तुम यहाँ हमेशा आउटसाइडर ही रहोगी।" पूनम के कथन की इस गम्भीरता को पहले तो नीलम ने गहराई से नहीं लिया। बहन-भाइयों के प्रति प्रेम का उसकी आँखों पर पर्दा पड़ा था। उसे लगता था कि जितना वह अपने भाई-भाभियों से प्यार करती है, बदले में वे भी उसे उतना ही स्नेह और मान देते हैं। उसका यही विश्वास तब भी झलकता है जब वह अपनी प्रिंसिपल से कहती है कि उसके भाई उसे इतनी दूर अकेले नहीं जाने देंगे पर उसका यह विश्वास तब टूटकर बिखर जाता है जब वह अलका के मुँह से अपनी मौजूदगी को 'उम्रकैद' के समान समझते हुए सुनती है। ऐसा सुनते ही उसका विश्वास और स्वाभिमान 'चोटिल' हो जाता है। इस बात से उसे अहसास हो जाता है कि पम्मी अपनी जगह पर सही थी। इस प्रकार उसके विचारों में बदलाव आ जाता है और वह अपने प्रमोशन और ट्रांसफर के आर्डर स्वीकार कर लेती है।

(iv) मालती जोशी द्वारा लिखित कहानी 'आउट साइडर' आधुनिक समाज के स्वार्थी और खोखले रिश्तों पर प्रहार करती है। यह कहानी समाज के नजरिये में बदलाव लाने का सन्देश देती है।

मनुष्य कितना भी आधुनिक होने का ढिंढोरा पीटे परन्तु वास्तविकता यह है कि इस पुरुष प्रधान समाज में नारी का स्थान आज भी दोयम दर्जे का ही है। सक्षम होने के बावजूद भी आज की नारी अपना अस्तित्व बचाने के लिए अनवरत प्रयास में लगी रहती है। इसके लिए उसे घर से लेकर बाहर तक संघर्षों से जूझना पड़ता है।

कहानी 'आउट साइडर' ऐसा ही सन्देश देकर नारी-शक्ति को सतर्क करना चाहती है। पारिवारिक जिम्मेदारियाँ सम्भालना गलत नहीं है परन्तु इन जिम्मेदारियों के चक्रवाती तूफान में फँसकर अपनी जिन्दगी, अपनी खुशियों की पूर्णरूप से कुर्वानी दे देना गलत है। यह नारी के मौलिक अधिकारों का हनन है। अपने परिवार के प्रति समर्पण आवश्यक है परन्तु उसकी भी सीमा निश्चित होनी चाहिए।

इस कहानी की नायिका नीलम ऐसे ही समर्पण की शिकार है। उसके परिवारीजन उसके त्याग और प्रेम को एक बोझ तथा बन्धन समझते हैं जो कि सर्वथा अनुचित है। यदि नीलम भी ऐसी स्वार्थी होती तथा उस कठिन वक्त में अपने भविष्य की आहुति देकर परिवार की बागडोर न सँभालती तो सबका जीवन गरीबी और लाचारी की गर्त में तथा भविष्य की अनिश्चितताओं के अन्धकार में डूब जाता।

6. दासी

—जयशंकर प्रसाद

लेखक परिचय— जयशंकर प्रसाद जी हिन्दी के छायावादी युग के चार प्रमुख स्तम्भों में से एक हैं। प्रसाद जी का जन्म माघ शुक्ल 10, संवत् 1946 वि. में काशी के सरायगोवर्धन में हुआ। इनके पितामह बाबू शिवरतन साहू दान देने में प्रसिद्ध थे और वह कलाकारों का आदर करते थे। इनका काशी में बड़ा सम्मान था और काशी की जनता काशी नरेश के बाद 'हर हर महादेव' से बाबू देवीप्रसाद का ही स्वागत करती थी। किशोरावस्था के पूर्व ही माता और बड़े भाई का देहावसान हो जाने के कारण 17 वर्ष की उम्र में ही प्रसाद जी पर आपदाओं का पहाड़ टूट पड़ा। घर के वातावरण के कारण साहित्य और कला के प्रति उनमें प्रारम्भ से ही रुचि थी और कहा जाता है कि नौ वष्र की उम्र में ही उन्होंने 'कलाधर' के नाम से ब्रजभाषा में एक सवैया लिखकर अपने गुरु 'रसमय सिद्ध' को दिखाया था। उन्होंने वेद, इतिहास, पुराण तथा साहित्यशास्त्र का अत्यंत गंभीर अध्ययन किया था। अंततः क्षय रोग से जनवरी 14, 1937 (उम्र 47) को उनका देहांत काशी में हुआ।

जयशंकर प्रसाद जी की प्रमुख रचनाएँ निम्नवत हैं—

काव्य—कामायनी, आँसू, प्रेमपथि, झरना आदि।

नाटक—स्कंदगुप्त, चंद्रगुप्त, ध्रुवस्वामिनी, जनमेजय का नागयज्ञ आदि।

उपन्यास—कंकाल, तितली, इरावती (अधूरा)

कहानी संग्रह—छाया, प्रतिध्वनि, आकाशदीप, आँधी, इन्द्रजाल।

कथा के क्षेत्र में प्रसाद जी आधुनिक ढंग की कहानियों के आरम्भकर्ता माने जाते हैं। सन् 1912 ई. में 'इन्दु' में उनकी पहली कहानी 'ग्राम' प्रकाशित हुई। प्रायः तभी से गतिपूर्वक आधुनिक कहानियों की रचना हिन्दी में आरम्भ हुई। प्रसाद जी ने कुल 72 कहानियाँ लिखी हैं। उनकी अधिकतर कहानियों में भावना की प्रधानता है किन्तु उन्होंने यथार्थ की दृष्टि से भी कुछ श्रेष्ठ कहानियाँ लिखी हैं। 'दासी' कहानी एक ऐतिहासिक कहानी है जो भावनाओं की मिठास तथा कवित्व से पूर्ण हैं।

शब्दार्थ—**शिल्पकला** = मूर्तिकला, **कटार** = खंजर, **दम्भ** = अक्खड़पन, **कलह** = विवाद, **विचलित** = चलायमान, **आकांक्षा** = लालसा, **आनन्दातिरेक** = आनन्द की अधिकता, **कृतज्ञता** = आभार, **उज्जवलता** = दीप्तिमय, **आरक्त** = रक्तिम, **चतुष्पद** = चौराहा, **कुत्सित** = घृणित, **पाखण्ड** = कपट, **प्राचीर** = बाहरी दीवार, **हताश** = निराश, **विकल** = व्याकुल, **अनाहार** = बिना आहार के, **प्रधान भाग** = मुख्य हिस्सा, **काफिर** = धर्म निन्दक, **प्रत्यावर्तन** = एकान्तरण, **प्रवाह** = धारा, **वेदना विमंडित** = पीड़ित मुख, **मूर्छित** = बेहोश, **विस्मित** = हक्का-बक्का, **समाधि** = मकबरा।

सारांश

कहानी के प्रारम्भ में बलराज अपने ही हाथों अपने जीवन का अन्त कर लेने के उद्देश्य से छुरा कलेजे में भोंककर मर जाना चाहता है। उसी समय फिरोजा नामक एक युवती उसे ऐसा करने से रोक देती है। वह उसे समझाती है कि यदि वह तुर्कों से युद्ध करते हुए शहीद हो जाता तो वह कब्र बनवाती उसका सम्मान करती, परन्तु ऐसी बात नहीं है आज तुम आत्महत्या करना चाहते जो कि एक बचपना है। बलराज के अनुसार तुर्क ही सुल्तान के अपने, बाकी सब बेगाने हैं, यह कहते हुए बलराज छुरा फेंक देता है।

बलराज के छुरा फेंकने के बाद फिरोजा बलराज से यह पूछती है कि वह क्यों और किसके लिए मर जाना चाहता है ? तब बलराज यह कहता है कि वह भी मेरी तरह कंगाल है। मैंने यह सोचा था कि जब अमीर बन जाऊँगा तब उससे ब्याह करूँगा। यह सुनते ही फिरोजा कहती है कि यह सब होने के बाद भी तुम उससे मिलने की बजाय मर जाना चाहते हो ? और यह कहकर वह उससे रूठ जाती है।

फिरोजा की ये बातें सुनकर बलराज उसके भोलेपन पर विचार करने लगता है। वह फिरोजा से यह कहता है कि युद्ध में पकड़े जाने के बाद मिली गुलामी के बाद भी तुम्हारे जीवन में इतनी खुशी कैसे है ? इस प्रश्न के उत्तर में फिरोजा कहती है कि अहमद ने एक हजार सिक्के भेजकर मुझे छुड़ाने का वादा किया है, मैं छुटकारा पा जाऊँगी और गुलामी में भी रोने की कोई बात नहीं है। आज जो गुलाम है कल सुल्तान हो सकता है तो जितना समय हँस सकती हूँ उसे रोने में क्यों बिताऊँ ?

बलराज कहता है कि फिरोजा तुमने मुझे मरने से रोककर ठीक नहीं किया। हमारी धार्मिक और सामाजिक भावनाएँ अलग हैं। लेकिन फिरोजा यह सब सुनकर भी बलराज से कहती है कि हिन्दुस्तान जाने पर किसी झोंपड़ी में ही जीवन बिता लेना। कुछ भी हो लेकिन मैं तुम्हें मरने नहीं देना चाहती। मेरे पास राजा के दिये पाँच दिरम हैं जिन्हें लेते जाओ और उससे जाकर भेंट कर लेना। बलराज को मुद्राएँ देकर फिरोजा झाड़ियों में चली जाती है।

फिरोजा, के जाने के बाद राजा साहब आकर यह कहते हैं कि मैंने तुम्हारी सारी बातें सुन लीं हैं, जिससे मेरा मन विचलित हो उठा है। मैं भी तुमको हिन्दुस्तान जाने की सलाह देता हूँ।

राजा साहब कहते हैं कि मैं प्रतिकूल परिस्थितियों में चुप रहना ठीक समझता हूँ। हिन्दुस्तान का एक कंगाल था, जो साधारण स्थिति से सुल्तान का सलाहकार बन गया। मैंने सुल्तान के दरबार से बनावटी गम्भीरता, छलपूर्ण विनय आदि बहुत-सी चीजें सीखी हैं जिनसे मेरी छाती में हृदय है, यह भी सन्देहास्पद हो गया है। लेकिन आज मेरे स्वभाव की धारा का प्रवाह प्रबल हो गया है।

राजा साहब बलराज को दूसरे विद्रोही गुलाम के साथ जाने के लिए कहते हुए बलराज के हाथों में एक थैली रख देते हैं और बलराज चुपचाप वहाँ से चला जाता है।

राजा तिलक सुल्तान महमूद का अत्यन्त विश्वासपात्र हिन्दू कर्मचारी था जो प्रतिष्ठा दृढ़ रखने के कारण सुल्तान मसऊद के शासन काल में भी उपेक्षित नहीं था। लेकिन आज बलराज की बातों को सुनकर वह विचलित हो गया था। उन्होंने फिरोजा को बुलाकर पूछा कि तुम बिना डरे बताओ कि क्या तुम अहमद के पास हिन्दुस्तान जाना चाहती हो ? मैं तुम्हें बिना किसी शर्त के भेजना चाहता हूँ। जिसे सुनकर फिरोजा आश्चर्यचकित हो जाती है। राजा तिलक फिरोजा से कहता है कि तुम्हें जाकर अहमद को समझाना है कि वह लूट-मार न करे, मैं मालगुजारी का अधिकार उसे भी दिला दूँगा।

फिरोजा, शायद इन कामों के लिए सुल्तान मुझे हिन्दुस्तान भेजना चाहे लेकिन मैं हिन्दुस्तान नहीं जाना चाहता। मेरी एक बहन इरावती थी जो पता नहीं किस हाल में होगी। मैं अपनी जन्मभूमि और उसके दुःख-दर्द को भूल गया हूँ। मैं वहाँ जाकर पागल हो जाऊँगा। अपनी बहन को क्या मुँह दिखलाऊँगा ?

राजा तिलक की इन बातों को सुनकर फिरोजा कहती है कि मैं इरावती को ढूँढ़ निकालूँगी। आपके इस दुःख को मैं कभी समझ न सकी। राजा तिलक फिरोजा से गीत गाने को कहा। फिरोजा उसे गीत सुनाती है।

बलराज मन्दिर के खम्भों से धक्के खाते हुए धूम रहा है, वह यह सोच रहा है कि यदि उसे (इरावती) को एक बार देख लेता। वह सोच रहा है कि उसकी क्या स्थिति होगी ? तभी गर्भ-गृह के द्वारपाल उसे देखते हैं। अचानक ही उसका मन देव के सम्मान में झुक जाता है। वह यह कहता है कि मैंने अपने जीवन में कोई पाप नहीं किया है। एक बार मुझ पर कृपा करो, मुझे अपनी प्रेम प्रतिमा का दर्शन करा दो।

प्रार्थना करने के बाद जब बलराज ने सिर उठाया तो उसे किसी के अपने पास से खिसकने का एहसास होता है। बलराज उसके पीछे जाता है। संदिग्ध स्वर में उसे बुलाया और आलिंगन करने के लिए दौड़ा लेकिन इरावती उसे रोक देती है। कहती है कि बलराज तुम मेरी रक्षा नहीं कर सके। मैं अब कलंकित हो गई हूँ, अब मैं तुम्हारे स्नेह के योग्य नहीं रही। जिसे सुन बलराज कहता है कि मेरे प्रेम के पवित्रता की अग्नि तुम्हारी पवित्रता को और उज्ज्वल कर देगी।

इरावती यह कहती है कि मैं अब तुम्हारे साथ नहीं जा सकती। आज मैं खरीदी हुई दासी हूँ जिसे म्लेच्छों ने काशी के एक महाजन को पाँच सौ रुपये में बेच दिया। नियम भी ऐसे कि मैं घर का कुत्सित से कुत्सित कार्य करूँगी। मेरे शरीर पर आजीवन उसका अधिकार रहेगा। इन सभी शर्तों में मेरी स्वीकृति है। मेरी स्वामिनी का रथ दूर चला गया होगा, अब मुझे जाना ही होगा।

बलराज निराश होकर कहता है कि फिरोजा ने व्यर्थ ही आशा दी। इस प्रकार बलराज इरावती की बातें सुनकर दुःखी हो गया। इरावती जिस ओर गई वह भी उसी ओर चला गया। इरावती को देखने के लिए बलराज रात-दिन धनदत्त के उपवन से नगर तक का चक्कर लगाता रहता। अन्त में हताश होकर यह निश्चय करता है कि वह काशी छोड़कर चला जायेगा। असुरों के समान बलवाला उसका शरीर आज निर्जीव सा प्रतीत

हो रहा है। तभी वह कुछ घुड़सवारों से टकराता है, वे बलराज से रास्ता पूछते हैं तो बलराज यह कहता है कि मैं तुम्हारा नौकर नहीं। तब नियाल्तगीन उसे पकड़ने का हुक्म देता है तो वह बलराज को पहचान जाता है।

नियाल्तगीन बलराज को बनारस जाने का कारण बताता है कि वह नगर देखने और फिरोजा के लिए बनारसी जरी के कपड़े लेने आया है। वह यह कहता है कि बलराज तुम नहीं बदले। बातचीत के दौरान नियाल्तगीन के मुँह से फिरोजा के बारे में सुनकर बलराज उनके साथ पड़ाव पर चलने के लिए राजी हो जाता है।

वे अब बनारस की गलियों में थे। फिरोजा कमख्वाब देख रही थी और नियाल्तगीन अपने लिए नग चुन रहा था। फिरोजा ने कपड़े के थान छाँट लिए। जिसे देख दुकानदार ने कहा कि सिर्फ तंग करने आए कुछ लिया ही नहीं। उनकी बातों को सुनकर बलराज ने डाँटा। जिससे दुकानदार क्रोधित होकर यह कहता है कि तू तुर्की गुलाम का दास है, जिसे सुनते ही नियाल्तगीन की तलवार उसके गले तक पहुँच गई। तभी युद्ध आरम्भ हो जाता है, नियाल्तगीन के साथी बहुमूल्य पदार्थों को लूटने लगते है। उसी समय बलराज ने इरावती की आवाज सुनी। वह लोगों को रोकता है। फिरोजा के पूछने पर बलराज बताता है कि यही इरावती है। यह सुनकर फिरोजा, बलराज, नियाल्तगीन और इरावती को लेकर चले जाते हैं।

चन्द्रभागा के तट पर फिरोजा, इरावती से पूछती है कि क्या तुम बलराज से प्रेम करती हो ? जिसके जवाब में इरावती कहती है कि मैं तो दासी हूँ। तुमने मेरे प्राण तो बचाये हैं लेकिन हृदय नहीं बचा सकी। बलराज ने इन बातों को सुना और वह वहाँ से चला जाता है।

रावी के किनारे अहमद नियाल्तगीन के महल में आज शयन कक्ष की सज्जा भार फिरोजा का था जो अन्ततः थककर इरावती को सहेजकर सो जाती है। थकान के कारण इरा भी वहीं सो जाती है। जब अहमद ने इरावती के वेदना विमंडित सौंदर्य को देखा। तो अहमद की आँखों में पशुता नाच उठी। लेकिन ठीक समय पर फिरोजा आ जाती है और अहमद के इस कृत्य की निंदा करती है। वह जाने लगती है तो इरा भी उसी के साथ चली जाती है।

बहुत दिनों के बाद चन्द्रभागा के तट पर आकर बलराज जाटों के बीच एक नई जान फूँक देता है। जाट विद्रोह करना प्रारम्भ कर देते हैं। फिरोजा के जाने के बाद अहमद अपनी कोमल वृत्तियों को खो बैठा। यह पता चलने पर कि गजनी की सेना लेकर तिलक भी आ रहा है। वह यह विचार करता है कि जाटों के मिल जाने से गजनी के हाथों से पंजाब लिया जा सकता है।

फिरोजा और इरावती घने जंगल में एक वृक्ष के नीचे हैं, तभी जाटों का एक दल आता है जिसका नेतृत्व बलराज करता है। बलराज फिरोजा को उसकी सुरक्षा का वादा करता है। उसी समय अहमद आ जाता है और फिरोजा और इरावती को देखकर उन्हें पकड़ने की बात करता है। तब बलराज और अहमद के बीच युद्ध शुरू हो जाता है। उसी समय तुर्कों की सेना राजा तिलक के साथ आ जाती है। उनके आने से युद्ध तो रुक जाता है लेकिन तब तक बलराज का भाला अहमद का सीना चीर देता है। बलराज भी घायल हो जाता है। फिरोजा अहमद का सिर गोद में लिए हुए है और इरा बलराज का सिर गोद में लिए हुए है। तिलक यह दृश्य देखकर विस्मित हो जाता है। बलराज और इरा के संवाद से तिलक को यह पता चलता है कि यह इरा ही उसकी बहन है। इस प्रकार अंत में तिलक वर्षों बाद अपनी बहन इरा से मिलता है। बलराज चनाब प्रांत के जाटों का सरदार बन जाता है और इरा वहाँ की रानी। वहीं फिरोजा के प्रेमी रूपी प्रसन्नता (अहमद) की समाधि बन गई है और फिरोजा उस समाधि की दासी बनकर आजीवन उसकी देखभाल करती रही।

अभ्यास-प्रश्न

प्रश्न 1. 'दासी' कहानी में कहानीकार का क्या उद्देश्य है ?

अथवा

'दासी' कहानी के माध्यम से कहानीकार कौन-सा सन्देश देना चाहता है ?

अथवा

'दासी' कहानी के माध्यम से कहानीकार ने तत्कालीन समाज की किस समस्या को उद्घाटित करने का प्रयास किया है ?

उत्तर—'दासी' कहानी में कहानीकार ने अपने चरित्रों के द्वारा तत्कालीन समाज में व्याप्त दासप्रथा अथवा गुलामी की समस्या को दिखाया है। इसके साथ ही कहानीकार ने कहानी की घटनाओं से पाठकों को दासप्रथा के वातावरण की अनुभूति कराने का प्रयास भी किया है। जिसमें कहानीकार को आशातीत सफलता भी प्राप्त हुई है।

इस कहानी में पात्रों के मनोवैज्ञानिक चित्रों के माध्यम से उनकी मनोस्थिति को पाठकों के समक्ष रखा है। बलराज की मानसिक स्थिति निराश और हताश प्रेमी की है जिसके जीवन में जीवन का कोई मोल नहीं है और वह आत्महत्या करना चाहता है।

वहीं दूसरी ओर फिरोजा एक ऐसी गुलाम है जो गुलाम होते हुए भी जीवन के प्रति आशान्वित है। उसका यह विचार है कि जितनी देर हँसा जा सकता है उस समय को रोने में बिताना मूर्खता है।

राजा तिलक की मनोस्थिति को ही देख लें। उनकी मनोवृत्तियों में भयानक हलचल है। वह यह भी सोचने लगता है कि जीवन कितना बनावटी और छल-कपट से भरा है। छाती में यह हृदय है भी या नहीं इसमें उन्हें संदेह सा लगने लगता है।

इस प्रकार कहानीकार ने अपने पात्रों के माध्यम से केवल इतिहास व सामाजिक विसंगतियों को ही अपनी कहानी का उद्देश्य नहीं बनाया बल्कि उसके साथ-साथ मानव मन की संवेदनाओं को भी पाठकों के समक्ष रखा है।

प्रसाद जी की 'दासी' कहानी भी एक भावना प्रधान कहानी है। इस कहानी के माध्यम से कहानीकार ने एक ऐतिहासिक आदर्शवाद को प्रस्तुत करने का प्रयास किया है। इस कहानी में प्रसाद जी का उद्देश्य भारतीय इतिहास की गौरवमयी झाँकी प्रस्तुत कर यह दिखाना है कि इतिहास में भी प्रेम के लिए कौन-कौन से बलिदान किए गए हैं ? अंत में फिरोजा का अहमद की समाधि की सेवा करना उसके अद्वितीय प्रेम का उदाहरण है।

कहानी के द्वारा प्रसाद जी यह सन्देश भी देना चाहते हैं कि जहाँ दास-प्रथा व गुलामी जैसी समस्याएँ थीं, वही बलराज का फिरोजा के सम्मान की रक्षा करने की प्रतिज्ञा, उस समाज में आशा की किरण थी जो नारी के सम्मान से बढ़कर कुछ भी नहीं थी। इस सन्देश से यह स्पष्ट हो जाता है कि भारत अस्थिर भले रहा हो पर महान तब भी था।

अंत में यह कहा जा सकता है कि 'दासी' कहानी में प्रसाद जी का उद्देश्य बड़ा ही व्यापक है। जो सामाजिक विसंगतियों, ऐतिहासिक आदर्शों, मानव जीवन के संघर्ष की प्रतिभूति कराकर समाज को एक नया संदेश देता है।

प्रश्न 2. 'दासी' कहानी के शीर्षक के औचित्य पर प्रकाश डालिए।

उत्तर—प्रस्तुत कहानी 'दासी' का शीर्षक एक ओर जिज्ञासा को प्रबल करता है तो वहीं दूसरी ओर यह शीर्षक संक्षिप्त भी है। कहानी के कथानक की केन्द्रीय संवेदना दासियाँ ही है। इस कहानी के माध्यम से दासियों की तत्कालीन परिस्थिति को भी कहानी के अन्य भावों के साथ व्यक्त करने का प्रयास किया गया है। इस शीर्षक में कहानी का सारभाव भी अंतर्निहित है जो शीर्षक की उपयुक्तता को सिद्ध करता है।

इस कहानी में कहानी की दो नायिकाएँ प्रमुख हैं और दोनों नायिकाएँ फिरोजा और इरावती दासी हैं, जो गुलामों की भाँति जीवन व्यतीत करती हैं। ये कहानी उन्हीं दासियों के प्रेम और जीवन पर आधारित है तथा उनका जीवन ही कथानक की घटनाओं का केन्द्रबिन्दु है।

कहानी के प्रारम्भ में ही दासी फिरोजा के माध्यम से कहानीकार ने एक निराश और हताश प्रेमी के जीवन में आशा का संचार करवाया। फिरोजा की बातों से बलराज में एक बार आशा जाग्रत होती है वहीं राजा तिलक के मन में बसे उद्‌गार भी पाठकों के समक्ष आ जाते हैं। फिरोजा की बातों ने उसकी मनोवृत्तियों में भयानक हलचल मचा दी थी। अंत में तिलक फिरोजा को भी वापस हिन्दुस्तान भेज देते हैं।

कहानी के दूसरे अंश में भी यदि देखें तो दूसरी दासी इरावती जिसका भाई तिलक प्रतिकूल परिस्थितियों के कारण अपनी बहन को छोड़कर चला जाता है। जो बलराज की प्रेमिका बन जाती है, लेकिन बलराज भी

धन कमाने की हसरत में इरा से दूर चला जाता है। इसके बाद इरा को दासी की भाँति जीवन व्यतीत करना पड़ता है। जिसके संदर्भ में बलराज से मिलन होने पर इरावती द्वारा कही गई बातों से लेखक ने उस समय के मानव व्यापार को प्रदर्शित करने का प्रयास किया। अहमद द्वारा इरा के साथ दुर्व्यवहार किए जाने पर दासी और प्रेमिका फिरोजा द्वारा एक महत्वपूर्ण निर्णय लिया जाता है। इसी निर्णय ने अंत में बलराज और अहमद को आमने-सामने कर दिया।

कहानी के अंत में बलराज और अहमद के बीच होने वाले युद्ध के समय ही तिलक भी अपनी सेना के साथ आता है। लेकिन तब तक घायल बलराज का भाला अहमद का सीना चीर चुका होता है। उसी समय घायल बलराज और इरा के संवाद से तिलक को इरा के बारे में पता चल जाता है। इस प्रकार दासी का जीवन व्यतीत करने वाली इरा को उसका प्रेमी और भाई मिल जाता है वहीं दूसरी ओर फिरोजा एक समर्पित प्रेमिका की भाँति अहमद की समाधि के रख-रखाव में अपना जीवन बिता देती है।

इस प्रकार अंत में निष्कर्ष के रूप में देखा जाए तो सारी कहानी दासी फिरोजा और इरा के आस-पास ही मंडराती है। कहानी के प्रारम्भ से लेकर अंत तक उसका ही चरित्र पाठकों को सर्वाधिक प्रभावित करता है। अत: प्रस्तुत कहानी का शीर्षक दासी सर्वथा उपयुक्त है।

प्रश्न 3. दासी कहानी के आधार पर जयशंकर प्रसाद जी की भाषागत विशेषताओं का उल्लेख कीजिए।

उत्तर—प्रस्तुत कहानी भाषा की दृष्टि से एक समृद्ध कहानी है। प्रसाद जी ने अपनी इस कहानी में सरल और क्लिष्ट दोनों प्रकार की भाषाओं का प्रयोग किया है। इस कहानी में प्रसाद जी की भाषा सरल, प्रवाहमय तथा बोधगम्य है। प्रसाद जी के शब्दों का चयन भावों के अनुकूल है। दासी कहानी के आधार पर प्रसाद जी की प्रमुख भाषागत विशेषताएँ निम्नवत् हैं—

पात्रानुकूल भाषा—प्रसाद जी ने दासी कहानी में पात्रों के चरित्र को ध्यान में रखकर भाषा का प्रयोग किया है, जो चरित्र का एक चित्र-सा उपस्थित कर देते हैं। फिरोजा का परिचय प्रसाद जी ने इस प्रकार से दिया है, ''अल्हड़पन, चंचलता और हँसी से बनी हुई वह तुर्क बाला सब हृदयों के समीप थी।''

संस्कृतनिष्ठ हिन्दी—कहानी में प्रसाद जी ने अधिकतर संस्कृतनिष्ठ शब्दों का प्रयोग किया है लेकिन उनकी भाषा में संस्कृत के शब्दों का यह प्रयोग प्रवाहमयता के अनुकूल है। उदाहरणार्थ—''राजा तिलक हिन्दुस्तान ने जाने की विवशता को इस प्रकार प्रकट करता है, चिरनिर्वासित, विस्तृत अपराधी !''

काव्यात्मकता—प्रसाद जी की भाषा की यह एक महत्वपूर्ण विशेषता है, जो कहानियों में उनके काव्यात्मक भाषिक संयोजन को प्रकट करता है। जिसकी एक बानगी दृष्टव्य है,"''अहमद ने वारूणीविलसित नेत्रों से देखा, उस रूपमाधुरी को, जिसमें स्वाभाविकताा थी, बनावट नहीं।''

नाटकीयता—प्रसाद जी एक नाटककार थे जिसकी झलक दासी कहानी में उनके भाषिक विश्लेषण के दौरान परिलक्षित होती है। 'दासी' कहानी में इरावती और फिरोजा के द्वारा सरल और संक्षिप्त संवादों का प्रयोग कहानीकार के भाषा की नाटकीयता को प्रकट करता है—

''बलराज को तुम प्यार करती हो ?
–मैं नहीं जानती-आकस्मिक उत्तर मिला ?''

अन्य भाषाओं के शब्दों का प्रयोग—जयशंकर प्रसाद जी ने इस कहानी में भाषा को पात्रानुकूल और स्वाभाविक बनाने हेतु यत्र-तत्र अन्य भाषाओं के शब्दों का प्रयोग भी बड़ी कुशलता से किया है जैसे—जिहून, गुलामी, सलाह, दीनारें, मालगुजारी, कमख्वाब, फौजी आदि ऐसे अनेक शब्द हैं जो कहानी की भाषिक समृद्धता को प्रकट करते हैं।

मुहावरे और लोकोक्तियों का प्रयोग—दासी कहानी में भाषा को भावानुरूप बनाने में प्रसाद जी ने मुहावरों और लोकोक्तियों का भी सुन्दर संयोजन किया है। जैसे—''जिस दुख से मनुष्य छाती फाड़कर चिल्लाने लगता हो, सिर पीटने लगता हो, वैसी प्रतिकूल परिस्थितियों में भी केवल सिर नीचा कर चुप रहना अच्छा समझता हूँ।''इस प्रकार प्रसाद जी की भाषा में यही नहीं अनेक विशेषताएँ परिलक्षित होती हैं जो कहानीकार की भाषिक दक्षता को प्रकट करती हैं।

प्रश्न 4. कहानी के अंत में बलराज, इरावती और फिरोजा के साथ कौन-सी घटना होती है ?

अथवा

कहानी के अन्त में कौन-सी ऐसी घटना होती है जिसके द्वारा राजा तिलक अपनी बहन से मिल पाता है ?

अथवा

कहानी की किस घटना ने आपको सर्वाधिक प्रभावित किया है ?

उत्तर—प्रस्तुत कहानी प्रसाद जी की ऐसी कहानी है जिसके माध्यम से प्रसाद जी ने एक विशेष संदेश देने का प्रयास किया है। यह प्रदर्शित करने का प्रयास किया है कि किस प्रकार मानसिक अस्थिरता मनुष्य के व्यवहार को विकृत कर देती है। कहानी में अहमद द्वारा इरावती के साथ किया गया दुर्व्यवहार उसकी मानसिक विकृति को प्रकट करता है। कहानी की ये घटना जहाँ मन पर गहरा प्रभाव डालती है वहीं कहानी की दिशा को भी परिवर्तित कर देती है। जिसके कारण कहानी का अंत रोचक बन जाता है।

कहानी के अंत में जब अहमद इरावती के साथ दुर्व्यवहार करता है तब फिरोजा इरावती को साथ लेकर निकल पड़ती है। जब वे दोनों जंगल में एक वृक्ष के नीचे आराम करती रहती है। तभी कुछ जाट घुड़सवार आते हैं जिनका नेतृत्व बलराज करता रहता है। वह फिरोजा को उसकी रक्षा का आश्वासन देता है तभी अहमद आ जाता है और फिरोजा और इरा को देखते ही वह ललकारता है कि पकड़ लो इन औरतों को ! इसी के साथ युद्ध प्रारम्भ हो जाता है।

बलराज का भाला अहमद की छाती से पार हो जाता है। उसी समय तिलक भी सेना लेकर आ जाता है। सबके अस्त्र तो रूक जाते हैं लेकिन अहमद के प्राणों को न रोका जा सका। फिरोजा अहमद का सिर गोद में रखकर रोती है, वहीं दूसरी ओर घायल बलराज इरावती की गोद में है तथा इरावती उसे पानी पिलाती है, जिसके बाद बलराज ने कहा कि मैं अब न मरूँगा। इरा का नाम सुनते ही तिलक विस्मित हो जाता है। इस प्रकार से अंत में भाई-बहन का मेल होता है।

कहानी के अंत में बलराज जाटों का सरदार बन जाता है और इरावती उसकी रानी। किन्तु फिरोजा की प्रसन्नता अर्थात अहमद की समाधि वहीं बना दी जाती है। अपने सच्चे प्रेम का निर्वाह करती हुई फिरोजा आजीवन दासी की तरह उस समाधि की देखभाल करती है।

कहानी की अन्तिम घटना मुझे सर्वाधिक प्रभावित करती है जिसमें एक ही क्षण में दृश्य परिवर्तन हो जाता है। अहमद की मृत्यु, तिलक का अपनी बहन से मिलना ये सभी घटनाएँ अंत में एक साथ होती हैं जो कहानी को एक पूर्ण अन्तिम पड़ाव की ओर ले जाती हैं।

प्रश्न 5. 'दासी' कहानी के आधार पर फिरोजा का चरित्र-चित्रण कीजिए।

अथवा

'दासी' कहानी के प्रमुख पात्र फिरोजा का चरित्र-चित्रण कीजिए।

अथवा

कहानी के किस पात्र ने आपको सर्वाधिक प्रभावित किया है ? उस पात्र का चरित्र-चित्रण कीजिए।

उत्तर—'दासी' कहानी एक ऐतिहासिक कहानी है। जिसमें तत्कालीन दास-प्रथा को व्यक्त करने का प्रयास किया गया है। इस कहानी में फिरोजा एक प्रमुख पात्र है। सम्पूर्ण कहानी उसी के आस-पास घटित होती है। फिरोजा के चरित्र की कुछ प्रमुख विशेषताएँ निम्नवत् हैं—

चंचल बाला—कहानी के प्रारम्भ में ही जब फिरोजा, बलराज जो कि आत्महत्या करने जा रहा था, उसका हाथ रोक लेती है और उस गम्भीर परिस्थिति में भी खिल-खिलाकर हँस देती है। कहानीकार फिरोजा का स्वभाव कुछ इस प्रकार से व्यक्त करता है—"अल्हड़पन, चंचलता और हँसी से बनी हुई वह तुर्क बाला सब हृदयों के स्नेह के समीप थी।"

संवेदनशील—फिरोजा बड़ी संवेदनशील थी। वह दूसरों की भावनाओं को अच्छी तरह से समझने के साथ ही साथ उनका आदर भी करती थी। फिरोजा जब बलराज को आत्महत्या करने से रोकती है और उसे पाँच दिरम देकर हिन्दुस्तान जाने के लिए कहती है। उस समय वह भावोद्वेलित हो जाती है—"फिरोजा की आँखों में आँसू भरे थे, तब भी वह जैसे हँस रही थी।"

आशावादी—ऐसी परिस्थिति में जबकि बलराज निराश होकर अपनी इहलीला समाप्त करना चाहता है। फिरोजा पूरी तरह से आशावान है कि उसकी गुलामी के दिन अवश्य समाप्त होंगे। उसका यह कथन इस तथ्य को प्रमाणित करता है—"जो आज गुलाम है; कल वही सुल्तान हो सकता है।"

स्वाभिमानी—फिरोजा बड़ी स्वाभिमानी है। वह अहमद से सच्चा प्रेम करती है परन्तु जब वह इरावती के साथ अभद्रता करता है तो वह उसे छोड़कर चली जाती है। उसका स्वाभिमान उसके इस कथन में प्रकट होता है—"मैं बिकी हूँ अहमद ! भला तुम मेरे हाथ क्यों बिकने लगे ? लेकिन तुमको मालूम है कि तुमने अभी राजा तिलक को मेरा दाम नहीं चुकाया; इसलिए जाती हूँ।"

सच्ची प्रेयसी—फिरोजा के चरित्र की यह एक महत्वपूर्ण विशेषता है। कहानी के अंत में अहमद की मृत्यु के बाद उसकी समाधि की सेवा करना उसके अद्वितीय प्रेम को प्रदर्शित करता है। जिसे लेखक ने इन शब्दों में व्यक्त किया है—"उस समाधि की वह आजीवन दासी बनी रही।"

इस प्रकार फिरोजा का चरित्र दासी कहानी में कहानीकार के उद्देश्य की पूर्ति में एक महत्वपूर्ण योगदान देता है जो कहानी की सफलता का एक महत्वपूर्ण कारण है।

प्रश्न 6. "तो जाओ फिरोजा ! मुझे बचाने के लिए, उस भयानक आग से, जिससे मेरा हृदय जल उठता है, मेरी रक्षा करो !" इस कथन में राजा तिलक किस आग की बात कर रहे हैं और इस समय उनकी मनोस्थिति कैसी है ?

अथवा

प्रस्तुत कहानी में राजा तिलक कौन है और उसे किस बात का पछतावा है ?

अथवा

राजा तिलक की मनोदशा कब अस्थिर हो जाती है, वह किससे और किस प्रकार बचने का उपाय बताता है ?

उत्तर—तिलक सुल्तान महमूद का अत्यन्त विश्वासपात्र हिन्दू कर्मचारी था। बलराज की बातें सुनने के बाद आज उसकी मनोवृत्तियों में भयानक हलचल मच गई थी। अपनी इस बातचीत के दौरान राजा तिलक अपने मन का उद्‌गार व्यक्त करता है। राजा तिलक के अनुसार उन्होंने आकांक्षा का नशा पी लिया है जिसके कारण वह बेबस हो गया है राजा तिलक यह बताता है कि वह भी हिन्दुस्तान का एक कंगाल था जो सुल्तान के सलाहकार के पद तक तो पहुँच गया, पर इस दौरान वह इतना निर्मम हो गया कि लोगों को यह संदेश भी होने लगा कि इसकी छाती में दिल है भी या नहीं।

प्रस्तुत कहानी में यह कथन राजा तिलक ने फिरोजा से कहा है। फिरोजा जो राजा तिलक के यहाँ गुलाम का जीवन जी रही है। बलराज जो कि सुल्तान की सरकार में काम करता है उसे आत्महत्या करने से रोकती है। बलराज के हृदय में जीवन के प्रति प्रेम समाप्त हो गया है, वह बिना किसी आधार के जीवन नहीं जीना चाहता है इसलिए वह आत्महत्या करना चाहता है। बलराज और फिरोजा जब आपस में बात करते रहते हैं तभी उनकी बातें तिलक सुन लेता है। तब तिलक बलराज को हिन्दुस्तान जाने की सलाह देता है।

वह प्रस्तुत कथन तब कहता है जब फिरोजा उससे यह कहती है कि वह उसे अन्य तुर्क सरदारों की तरह ही समझती थी, लेकिन आज उसे पता चला कि तिलक के अन्दर भी एक ज्वालामुखी है, जिसकी आग से उसका हृदय भी जलता रहता है। वह जो इतना कठोर दिखाई देता है उसकी भी भावनाओं का एक सागर है जो किल्लोल करता रहता है। तिलक यह स्वीकार करता है कि आज उसके स्वभाव की धारा का बाँध टूट गया है।

तिलक के मन में एक टीस-सी है, जिसके कारण वह हिन्दुस्तान नहीं जाना चाहता है। जिसका कारण उसकी ग्लानि है। उसकी एक छोटी बहन थी, जिसे वह वहीं छोड़ आया और बरसों से उसके बारे में जानने की कोई कोशिश भी नहीं की। इन्हीं कारणों से वह शर्मिंदा हो रहा है। वह यह सोचता है कि यदि वह हिन्दुस्तान जाएगा तो अपनी बहन इरावती से क्या कहेगा। वह हिन्दुस्तान जाकर अपनी बहन के सामने कौन-सा मुँह लेकर खड़ा होगा। जो उसके लिए किसी सजा से कम नहीं है।

अपनी बहन के साथ किए गए इस व्यवहार के कारण ही उसका मन क्षोभ से भरा है और उसके मन में एक आग-सी जल रही है। इस समय तिलक की मनोस्थिति बड़ी ही संघर्षपूर्ण है। जिस पश्चाताप की अग्नि में

वह जल रहा है, वह अतीत उसके वर्तमान पर हावी हो गया है। उसने उस अतीत के समक्ष अपनी हार मान ली है इसीलिए वह फिरोजा से अपनी रक्षा की बात कर रहा है। यदि फिरोजा उसकी बहन का पता लगा ले और उसे हिन्दुस्तान न जाना पड़े तो इस आत्मग्लानि का साक्षात्कार करने से वह बच जाएगा। इसी संदर्भ में वह फिरोजा से अपनी रक्षा की गुहार करता है।

प्रश्न 7. ''यदि एक बार उसे फिर देख पाता; पर यह होने का नहीं। निष्ठुर नियति ! उसकी पवित्रता पंकिल हो गई होगी।'' इस कथन में किसे देखने की अभिलाषा व्यक्त की जा रही है और नियति ने वक्ता के साथ किस प्रकार की निष्ठुरता दिखाई है ?

उत्तर—इस कथन का वक्ता बलराज है। बलराज ने अपनी प्रेमिका इरावती से यह कहा था कि वह लड़ाई पर जाएगा और लूट में जब सोने-चाँदी की ढ़ेरी पाकर अमीर हो जाएगा, तब उससे विवाह करेगा। लेकिन वह अपना वचन पूरा नहीं कर पाता है और आज गजनी में अपने ही छुरे से अपनी इहलीला समाप्त करना चाहता है तभी उसे वहीं की एक गुलाम फिरोजा रोक देती है और अपनी बातों से उसमें निराशा की जगह आशा का संचार कर देती है।

वह फिरोजा और राजा तिलक के कहने पर हिन्दुस्तान आ तो जाता है, लेकिन अब भी उसे अपनी प्रेयसी का कोई पता नहीं मिल पाता है। वह फिर निराश होकर यह कथन कहता है कि नियति बड़ी निर्मम है। पता नहीं उसका हाल कैसा होगा ? वह बार-बार यह सोचता है कि मेरी पवित्र प्रेमिका पर संसार ने पता नहीं कितना जुल्म किया होगा ? वह यह विचार करने लगता है कि उसकी कल्पनाएँ तो एकदम सोने के मन्दिर की भाँति थी पर आज वे कल्पनाएँ एक खण्डहर बन चुकी होंगी।

इस कथन में बलराज अपनी प्रेयसी के दर्शन की अभिलाषा की बात कर रहा है। नियति ने उसके साथ बड़ी निष्ठुरता की है। उसने अपने भविष्य के जो भी सपने संजोये थे वे काँच के टुकड़ों की तरह टूटकर बिखर जाते हैं। उसका यह विचार है कि जीवन में उसने किसी प्रकार का कोई पाप नहीं किया जिसके लिए वह क्षमा माँगे। वह ईश्वर से यह प्रार्थना करता है कि एक बार उसे उसकी प्रेम की प्रतिमा का दर्शन करा दें।

अंत में जब उसका अपनी प्रेयसी से मिलन होता है तब वह उसकी दशा देखकर दु:खी हो जाता है। वह अपने प्रेम की पवित्रता की दुहाई देता है लेकिन प्रेयसी इरावती स्वयं को क्रीत दासी बताती है। वह यह बताती है कि उसके जाने के बाद उसके साथ बहुत अत्याचार हुआ। उसे रोज चौराहे पर लटकाया जाता था और अंत में काशी के एक महाजन ने उसे खरीदकर अपनी दासी बना लिया। उसके स्वामी उसके साथ किसी भी किस्म का व्यवहार कर सकते हैं। उसने अपने बिक्री में स्वीकृति भी दी है, इसलिए वह उस सत्य को तोड़ भी नहीं सकती।

इस प्रकार लाख प्रयास करने व अनेक प्रकार के तर्क देने पर भी बलराज उसे रोक नहीं पाता और वह चली जाती है। यह नियति की बलराज के प्रति निष्ठुरता ही तो है जिसके लिए वह आज लौटकर आया था, वही उसे छोड़कर चली जाती है।

प्रश्न 8. 'दासी' कहानी में इरावती की भूमिका पर प्रकाश डालिए।

उत्तर—'दासी' कहानी के महत्वपूर्ण पात्रों में से एक इरावती है जो कहानी की अधिकांश घटनाओं का केन्द्र बिन्दु है। इरावती तिलक की बहन है जिसे तिलक बरसों पहले हिन्दुस्तान में ही छोड़कर चला जाता है। वही इरावती बलराज की प्रेयसी है जिससे बलराज प्रेम करता है। वह बलराज की वाग्दत्ता है। कहानी के अंत में इसी इरावती को उसका भाई और प्रेमी दोनों ही मिल जाते हैं।

कहानी के प्रारम्भ में बलराज निराश होकर आत्महत्या करना चाहता है, लेकिन फिरोजा उसे समझाती है और इरा का वास्ता देकर उसे आत्महत्या करने से रोकती है। जब बलराज उससे मिलने आता है, तो उसके द्वारा कहा गया हर कथन उस समय की दास प्रथा की व्यथा को प्रकट करता है।

इरावती बताती है कि म्लेच्छों ने से मुल्तान की लूट में पकड़ लिया था। वे रोज उसे कोड़े मारते और उसे बाँधकर लटकाया जाता था। जिसे बाद में उन आततायियों ने पाँच सौ दिरम में काशी के एक महाजन को बेच दिया। मेरी बिक्री के साथ जो शर्तें थीं कि मैं कुत्सित कर्म करूँगी। मेरे शरीर पर आजीवन उनका ही अधिकार रहेगा। इस प्रकार इरावती का जीवन गुलामों की भाँति बीता था।

दूसरे चरण में वह जब नियाल्तगीन और उसके साथ फिरोजा के साथ अभद्रता करने के कारण काशी के व्यापारियों को लूटने लगते हैं तब इरावती अपने स्वामी की सुरक्षा में नियाल्तगीन के तलवार के समक्ष प्रस्तुत हो जाती है। जिसे बाद में बलराज द्वारा बचाया जाता है। तब फिरोजा उसे अपने साथ अहमद के महल ले जाती है। एक बार जब फिरोजा की अनुपस्थिति में जब अहमद इरावती के साथ अभद्रता करता है। तब इरावती और फिरोजा दोनों ही अहमद का महल छोड़कर चले जाते हैं।

कहानी के अन्तिम चरण में बलराज के पास पहुँच जाती हैं जहाँ बलराज इनकी सुरक्षा का आश्वासन देता है। तभी वहाँ अहमद का आगमन होता है और वह इन्हें पकड़ना चाहता है। जिसकी वजह से बलराज से युद्ध हो जाता है। उसी समय तिलक आ जाता है। लेकिन तब तक अहमद की मृत्यु हो जाती है। बलराज का सिर अपने गोद में रखी इरावती जब उससे बात करती है तभी तिलक उनकी बातों से यह जान जाता है कि यही उसकी बहन इरावती है।

इस प्रकार कहानी के अन्त में इरावती ही एक ऐसी पात्र हैं जिसे उसका प्रेमी और भाई दोनों ही मिल जाते हैं और उसकी दुखभरी कहानी का अन्त सुखमय हो जाता है।

प्रश्न 9. पात्रों के संयोजन की दृष्टि से दासी कहानी की समीक्षा कीजिए।

उत्तर—यदि कथानक कहानी का मेरूदण्ड होता है तो पात्र कहानी के प्राण हैं, जो कथानक के निर्जीव शब्दों में प्राण फूँक देते हैं। पात्र नियोजन इसलिए भी महत्वपूर्ण है क्योंकि कहानी की मूल घटनाएँ और अनुभूति इसी के द्वारा प्रकट की जाती है। कहानी के पात्रों की रचना सोद्देश्य की जाती है क्योंकि पात्र ही कहानीकार के उद्देश्य की पूर्ति में योगदान देते हैं और कहानीकार के निर्जीव शब्दों में प्राण डाल देते हैं। पात्र मुख्य रूप से दो प्रकार के होते हैं, मुख्य पात्र तथा सहायक पात्र।

दासी कहानी में प्रमुख पात्र फिरोजा और बलराज हैं तथा अन्य पात्र अपनी भूमिकाओं द्वारा प्रमुख पात्र के चरित्र-निर्माण में सहायक बनते हैं। अपने पात्रों के माध्यम से प्रसाद जी ने भारत की ऐतिहासिकता तथा तत्कालीन सामाजिक विसंगतियों को प्रदर्शित किया है। फिरोजा के चरित्र में स्वाभिमानी नारी दिखाई देती है जो अपने स्वाभिमान की रक्षा के लिए अपने उस प्रेम को ठुकरा देती है जिसके लिए वह हिन्दुस्तान आयी है। वहीं कहानी के अन्त में वह अहमद की समाधि की सेवा कर अपने पुष्ट प्रेम का उदाहरण प्रस्तुत करती है।

बलराज जो कहानी के प्रारम्भ में ही आत्महत्या करना चाहता है, फिरोजा के समझाने पर मान जाता है। अन्त में वही फिरोजा को अपनी बहन बनाता है और फिरोजा और इरावती की रक्षा के लिए अहमद से युद्ध करता है। बलराज का चरित्र एक भावुक और सशक्त पात्र का चरित्र है। इसी प्रकार अन्य पात्र भी कहानी की मूल संवेदना को उत्तेजित करने में सहायता प्रदान करते हैं। प्रस्तुत कहानी के सभी पात्रों में विश्वसनीयता परिलक्षित होती है। इस प्रकार पात्रों के संयोजन की दृष्टि से भी दासी कहानी एक सफल कहानी है।

प्रश्न 10. उसने कहा—'वही तो, न जाने क्यों मैं उसी दिन नहीं मरा, जिस दिन मेरे इतने वीर साथी कटार से लिपटकर इसी गजनी की गोद में सोने चले गये।'

(i) उक्त कथन किसके लिए कहा गया है ?

(ii) सुल्तान ने क्या किया था ?

(iii) कौन मरना चाहता था ? उसे किसने रोका ?

(iv) फीरोजा की गुलामी कैसे दूर होगी ?

उत्तर—(i) यह कथन बलराज ने फीरोजा के सामने कहा है।

(ii) सुल्तान ने सिल्जूको से हारे हुए तुर्क और हिन्दू दोनों को ही नौकरी से अलग कर दिया था।

(iii) बलराज कटार लेकर अपने आपको मारना चाहता था। फीरोजा ने आकर उसको रोका तो बलराज ने कटार फेंक दी।

(iv) फीरोजा को यह ज्ञात है कि वह अब गुलाम नहीं रहेगी। अहमद ने हिन्दुस्तान जाते समय राजा साहब से कहा था कि वह एक हजार सोने के सिक्के भेजेगा। तिलक वह लेकर फीरोजा को छोड़ देगा। यदि वह हिन्दुस्तान जाना चाहे तो उसे हिन्दुस्तान भेज देगा।

प्रश्न 11. आज तक अपनी आकांक्षा में भूला हुआ, अपने आराम में मस्त, अपनी उन्नति में विस्मृत, गजनी में बैठा हुआ हिन्दुस्तान को अपनी जन्मभूमि को और उसके दुःख-दर्द को भूल गया हूँ।

(i) यहाँ कौन किससे यह कथन कह रहा है ?

(ii) गजनी में बैठा हुआ कौन क्या काम करता था ?

(iii) वह हिन्दुस्तान क्यों नहीं जाना चाहता था ?

(iv) किसने किससे गीत गाने को कहा ? उसने क्या गीत गाया ?

उत्तर—(i) यहाँ तिलक फीरोजा से यह बात कहा रहा है।

(ii) गजनी में बैठा हुआ तिलक सुल्तान के लूटों की गिनती करता, उस रक्त रंजित धन की तालिका बनाना, हिन्दुस्तान के ही शोषण के लिए सुल्तान को नई-नई तरीकीबें बताना यही उसका काम था।

(iii) तिलक हिन्दुस्तान जाना नहीं चाहता था। वह चिरनिर्वासित और विस्मृत अपराधी है। इरावती उसकी बहन है जिसने हिन्दुस्तान में रहकर कष्ट पाये, लेकिन वह उसके लिए कुछ नहीं कर सका इसका उसको दुःख है।

(iv) राजा तिलक ने फीरोजा से वह गीत गाने को कहा जो वह अक्सर गाती थी। उसने यह गीत गाया—

'मैं जलती हुई दीपशिखा हूँ और तुम हृदय-रंजन प्रभात हो। जब तक देखती नहीं, जला करती हूँ और जब तुम्हें देख लेती हूँ, तभी मेरे अस्तित्व का अन्त हो जाता है—मेरे प्रियतम !'

प्रश्न 12. शयन-कक्ष की सेवा का भार आज उसी पर था। वह अहमद के आगमन की प्रतीक्षा करते-करते सो गयी थी। अहमद इन दिनों गजनी से मिले समाचार के कारण अधिक व्यस्त था।

(i) किसके शयन कक्ष की सेवा का भार आज किस पर था ?

(ii) अहमद किस बात में व्यस्त था ?

(iii) अहमद की अभिलाषा क्या थी ?

(iv) दालान में आकर अहमद ने क्या देखा ?

उत्तर—(i) पंजाब के सेनानी अहमद नियाल्तगीन के शयन-कक्ष की सेवा का भार आज इरावती पर था।

(ii) अहमद इन दिनों गजनी से मिले समाचार के कारण अधिक व्यस्त था। सुल्तान के रोष का समाचार उसे मिला था जिसने उसे विचलित कर दिया था।

(iii) पंजाब का स्वतन्त्र शासक बनने की अभिलाषा उसके मन में जग गई थी। फिरोजा ने कई बार उसे इस अभिलाषा को त्याग देने के लिए कहा परन्तु अहमद ने राजकीय कामों में साधारण तुर्क दासी के विचारों का कोई मूल्य न समझकर अपनी महत्वकांक्षा को अधिक तरजीह दी।

(iv) दालान में आकर अहमद ने इरावती की स्वाभाविक रूप माधुरी को अपनी वारुणीविलसित निगाह से देखा। एक बार सशंक दृष्टि से उसने चारों ओर देखा फिर इरावती का हाथ पकड़कर हिलाया। इरावती चौंककर खड़ी हो गई।

7. क्या निराश हुआ जाए ?

— हजारी प्रसाद द्विवेदी

लेखक परिचय—आचार्य हजारी प्रसाद द्विवेदी का जन्म 9 अगस्त, 1907 में बलिया जिले के 'दुबे-का-छपरा' नामक ग्राम में हुआ था। उनका परिवार ज्योतिष विद्या के लिए प्रसिद्ध था। उनके पिता पं. अनमोल द्विवेदी संस्कृत के प्रकांड पण्डित थे। द्विवेदी जी के बचपन का नाम बैजनाथ द्विवेदी था। इनकी प्रारम्भिक शिक्षा गाँव के स्कूल में ही हुई और वहीं से उन्होंने मिडिल की परीक्षा पास की। इसके पश्चात् उन्होंने इण्टर की परीक्षा और ज्योतिष विषय लेकर आचार्य की परीक्षा उत्तीर्ण की। शिक्षा प्राप्ति के पश्चात द्विवेदी जी शान्ति निकेतन चले गये और कई वर्षों तक वहाँ हिन्दी विभाग में कार्य करते रहे। शान्ति-निकेतन में रवीन्द्रनाथ टैगोर तथा आचार्य क्षितिमोहन सेन के प्रभाव से साहित्य का गहन अध्ययन और उसकी रचना प्रारम्भ की। अन्ततः 19 मई, 1979 में आचार्य हजारी प्रसाद द्विवेदी का देहावसान हो गया।

द्विवेदी जी का व्यक्तित्व बड़ा प्रभावशाली और उनका स्वभाव बड़ा सरल और उदार था। वे हिन्दी, अंग्रेजी, संस्कृत और बांग्ला भाषाओं के विद्वान थे। भक्तिकालीन साहित्य का उन्हें अच्छा ज्ञान था। लखनऊ विश्वविद्यालय ने उन्हें डी. लिट्. की उपाधि देकर उनका विशेष सम्मान किया था।

द्विवेदी जी के निबन्धों के विषय भारतीय संस्कृति, इतिहास, ज्योतिष, साहित्य विविध धर्मों और सम्प्रदायों का विवेचन आदि हैं। द्विवेदी जी के निबन्धों में विचारों की गहनता, निरीक्षण की नवीनता और विश्लेषण की सूक्ष्मता रहती है।

द्विवेदी जी की भाषा परिमार्जित खड़ी बोली है। उन्होंने भाव और विषय के अनुसार भाषा का चयनित प्रयोग किया है। उनकी भाषा के दो रूप दिखलाई पड़ते हैं—(1) प्राँजल व्यवहारिक भाषा, (2) संस्कृतनिष्ठ शास्त्रीय भाषा।

द्विवेदी जी का हिन्दी निबन्ध और आलोचनात्मक क्षेत्र में महत्वपूर्ण स्थान है। वे उच्च कोटि के निबन्धकार और सफल आलोचक हैं। उन्होंने सूर, कबीर, तुलसी आदि पर जो विद्वत्तापूर्ण आलोचनाएँ लिखी हैं, वे हिन्दी में पहले नहीं लिखी गईं। उनका निबन्ध-साहित्य हिन्दी की स्थाई निधि है। उनकी समस्त कृतियों पर उनके गहन विचारों और मौलिक चिन्तन की छाप है। विश्व-भारती आदि के द्वारा द्विवेदी जी ने सम्पादन के क्षेत्र में पर्याप्त सफलता प्राप्त की है।

शब्दार्थ—भष्टाचार = कदाचार, **आरोप** = इल्जाम, **आध्यात्मिक** = आत्मविषयक, **गह्वर** = गड्ढा, **सतह** = तल, **अनुकरणीय** = निदर्शनात्मक, **माहौल** = वातावरण, **जीविका** = रोजी-रोटी, **निरीह** = निर्दोष, **पर्याय** = समानार्थी, **बेबस** = मजबूर, **विकराल** = भयानक, **आस्था** = धारणा, **समकालीन** = सामयिक, **निर्मित** = बनाई गई, **त्रुटियाँ** = गलतियाँ, **संशोधन** = सुधार, **दुर्व्यवस्था** = अव्यवस्था, **जटिल** = पेंचीदा, **आलोढ़ित** = विचलित, **हताश** = निराश, **आन्तरिक** = अन्दरूनी, **संग्रह** = संचय, **दरिद्रजन** = मुहताज, **विश्वासघात** = धोखा।

सारांश

'क्या निराश हुआ जाये ?' आचार्य हजारी प्रसाद द्विवेदी जी द्वारा लिखा विचारात्मक निबन्ध है जिसमें सामाजिक सम्बन्धों के सन्दर्भ में विचार व्यक्त किये गये हैं।

आधुनिक समय में आरोप-प्रत्यारोप का दौर बहुत बढ़ गया है। ऐसा लगता है कि देश में अब कोई ईमानदार व्यक्ति रह ही नहीं गया। आज कोई भी कार्य किया जाये लोग उसमें दोष खोजने लगते हैं तथा उस कार्य के गुणों को भुला दिया जाता है। आज प्रत्येक व्यक्ति दोषी अधिक दिखाई दे रहा है। लेखक यही सोचता है कि गाँधी, तिलक, विवेकानन्द और रामतीर्थ का भारतवर्ष मानों कहीं खो गया है। लगता है कि यह कोलाहल और उथल-पुथल सिर्फ सतह पर है, परन्तु केन्द्र में अब भी गाम्भीर्य अचंचल महान भारत है।

माहौल में परिवर्तन हो गया है जिसमें श्रमजीवी व्यक्ति पिस रहा है और झूठ का व्यापार करने वाले लोग फल-फूल रहे हैं। ऐसी स्थिति में जीवन में महान मूल्यों के सन्दर्भ में लोगों का विश्वास अब डगमगाने लगा है।

लेखक के अनुसार यह परिस्थिति नई नहीं है, ऐसा माहौल पहले भी था। तुलसीदास जी ने भी अपने ग्रन्थ रामचरित्मानस में इस समस्या को व्यक्त किया है। तब और अब की परिस्थिति में सिर्फ यही अन्तर है कि आज आधुनिक सुख-सुविधाओं के बीच इस संकट को कुछ अधिक बढ़ावा मिला है। इतना होने पर भी जीवन मूल्यों के प्रति आस्था तब भी लोगों ने नहीं त्यागी और आज भी उसे त्यागने की आवश्यकता नहीं प्रतीत होती है।

आज ऊपरी सतह पर जो कोलाहल अथवा उथल-पुथल है, वह मनुष्य द्वारा बनाई गई नीतियों की त्रुटियों की वजह से है। ये नीतियाँ परिस्थितियों का सामना करने के लिए बनाई जाती है, जो समय-समय पर बदलती रहती हैं। मनुष्य की बुद्धि से निर्मित व्यवस्था हमेशा त्रुटियुक्त होती है।

भारत में भौतिक वस्तुओं के संग्रह को प्रधानता नहीं दी गई। जब बुद्धि काम, क्रोध आदि इशारे पर चलने लगती है तो आचरण निकृष्ट हो जाता है। इसे संयम में बाँधकर रखने के लिए ही उपाय किये गये हैं। देश के दरिद्र और हीन व्यक्तियों की दशा सुधारने के लिए अनेक कानून बनाये गये। यह लक्ष्य तो उत्तम है लेकिन जिन्हें इस कार्य में लगना है उनका मन कभी-कभी अपवित्र हो जाता है। और लक्ष्य का स्थान विकारों ने ले लिया। जो भी हो इससे पुराने आदर्श और उपयोगी दिखाई देने लगे हैं।

भारतवर्ष में कानून को धर्म माना जाता है आज कानून और धर्म में अन्तर आ गया है, जिसके कारण धर्म का पालन करने वाले लोग भी अब कानून की कमजोरियों का लाभ उठाने से नहीं हिचकिचाते। भारतवर्ष में अब भी धर्म, कानून से बड़ी चीज है। सेवा, ईमानदारी, सच्चाई और आध्यात्मिकता के मूल्य दब अवश्य गये हैं परन्तु अब भी बने हुए हैं। आज भी मनुष्यों के बीच प्रेम तथा महिलाओं का सम्मान है। गलत सही की समझ है। समाचार पत्रों में भ्रष्टाचार के प्रति लोगों का आक्रोश यह साबित करता है कि लोग इन चीजों को गलत समझते हैं।

दोषों का दर्शन कराना उचित है लेकिन बुराई में रस लेना ठीक नहीं है, ठीक उसी प्रकार अच्छाई में रस लेने के बाद भी अच्छाई उजागर न करना भी ठीक नहीं है। अच्छाई तो उजागर करने से लोगों में अच्छाई के प्रति भावना जाग्रत होती है। लेखक यह बताता है कि एक बार गलती से दस रुपये की जगह सौ का नोट देने के बाद वह आकर ट्रेन में बैठ गया जबकि टिकट दस रुपये का था जबकि टिकट दस रुपये का था, थोड़ी ही देर में टिकट बाबू विनम्रता के साथ उसे नब्बे रुपये लौटा देता है। यह कहना कि अब ईमानदारी लुप्त हो गई है, यह अनेक बेईमानी की घटनाओं से अधिक शक्तिशाली है।

लेखक वहीं दूसरे प्रसंग में यह कहता है कि मैं अपनी पत्नी और तीन बच्चों के साथ जा रहा था, निर्धारित स्थान से पहले एक निर्जन स्थान पर बस ने जवाब दे दिया। रात के दस बजे का समय था। तब कंडक्टर साइकिल लेकर चलता बना। लोगों ने सोचा कहीं वही डकैतों को न भेज दे। बच्चे पानी माँग रहे थे। कुछ नौजवान ड्राइवर को मारने की योजना बना रहे थे। मैंने बड़ी मुश्किल से ड्राइवर को बचाया। उसी समय हम यह देखते हैं कि बस अड्डे से खाली बस लेकर कण्डक्टर आ रहा है। आते ही उसने कहा कि यह बस चलने लायक नहीं है इसलिए वह नई बस लाया है। साथ ही वह लेखक के बच्चों के लिए पानी और दूध भी लाया था। अन्त में लोगों ने अपने व्यवहार के लिए ड्राइवर से माफी माँगी।

इन उदाहरणों को देखकर यह नहीं कहा जा सकता कि मनुष्यता एकदम समाप्त हो गई है। लेखक के अनुसार मैंने कितनी बार धोखा खाया है। लेकिन मुझे सिर्फ उसका हिसाब रखना हो तो मुश्किल हो जायेगा। लेकिन अच्छी बातों ने निराश मन को हिम्मत भी बंधाई है। लेखक ईश्वर से यह प्रार्थना करता है कि नुकसान के अवसरों पर भी मैं ईश्वर पर सन्देह न करूँ।

इस प्रकार आशा अब भी है जिसमें भारत के महान बनने की सम्भावना बनी हुई है। इसलिए मन को निराश होने की आवश्यकता नहीं है।

अभ्यास-प्रश्न

प्रश्न 1. क्या निराश हुआ जाये ? निबन्ध में निबन्धकार का क्या उद्देश्य है ?

अथवा

क्या निराश हुआ जाये ? निबन्ध के माध्यम से निबन्धकार कौन-सा सन्देश देना चाहता है ?

उत्तर—आचार्य हजारी प्रसाद द्विवेदी जी ने अपने निबन्ध 'क्या निराश हुआ जाये ?' की रचना एक विशेष उद्देश्य से की है। इस निबन्ध की रचना के दौरान निबन्धकार का उद्देश्य स्पष्ट रूप से परिलक्षित होता है। निबन्ध के प्रारम्भ में ही लेखक ने देश की वर्तमान स्थिति की विवचना की है। लेखक यह बताना चाहता है कि आज देश में एक ऐसे वातावरण का निर्माण हो गया है कि जिसे देख ऐसा प्रतीत होता है कि देश में कोई ईमानदार आदमी रह ही नहीं गया है। आज हर जगह दोष और भ्रष्टाचार ही दिखाई देता है। यदि इस पृष्ठभूमि पर विचार करें तो हर व्यक्ति दोषी दिखाई देता है। इसलिए यह चिन्तन का विषय है।

इस आधार पर यह कहना कि अब देश के लोगों में गुणों का अभाव है, यह अवश्य ही असंगत होगा। दोषों को बढ़ा-चढ़ाकर दिखाया जाता है तो गुण उसमें छिप जाते हैं और हमारा ध्यान उस ओर नहीं जा पाता है। ऐसी परिस्थिति में हमें चिन्तन करने की आवश्यकता है या निराश होने की ?

लेखक ने अपने बस चालक और टिकट बाबू की ईमानदारी की घटना के उदाहरणों द्वारा यह स्पष्ट रूप से प्रमाणित किया है कि समाज में अभी सच्चाई और ईमानदारी बाकी है। द्विवेदी जी ने यह समझाया कि सिर्फ कपटपूर्ण घटनाओं का हिसाब रखने से हमें कष्ट की अनुभूति होती है, वहीं दूसरी ओर जब हम ऐसी घटनाओं पर ध्यान देते हैं जिसमें लोगों ने अकारण की सहायता की है, तो ऐसी घटनाएँ मन को आशा और हिम्मत देती हैं।

इस प्रकार लेखक यह सन्देश देना चाहता है कि जब हम दोषों को दूर करने की दृष्टि से देश को देखते हैं तो हमें तमाम दोष जैसे—भ्रष्टाचार, बेरोजगारी, बालश्रम तथा स्त्रियों की दशा आदि दिखाई देते हैं और हम इन दोषों को देखकर निराश होने लगते हैं। इस प्रकार जब हम दोषों पर अधिक ध्यान देते हैं तो गुणों की अनदेखी हो जाती है। यह गुणों की अनदेखी ही हमारी निराशा का कारण बन जाती है। क्या वास्तव में हमें निराश होना चाहिए ? इसी समस्या पर पाठकों का ध्यान आकृष्ट करना ही निबन्धकार का उद्देश्य है।

प्रस्तुत निबन्ध के माध्यम से द्विवेदी जी ने आजकल की स्वाभाविक प्रवृत्ति को दोषोद्घाटन से हटाकर अन्तर्निहित सकारात्मक पहलुओं की ओर ले जाने की बात की है। जहाँ अनेक त्रुटियों से भ्रष्टाचार आदि अनेक समस्याओं का जन्म हुआ है ऐसे समय में आशा की ज्योति अब भी बुझी नहीं है, यही बताना ही निबन्धकार का उद्देश्य है। निबन्धकार का यह उद्देश्य मंगलकारी और सन्देशयुक्त है।

प्रश्न 2. 'क्या निराश हुआ जाये ?' निबन्ध के शीर्षक के औचित्य पर प्रकाश डालिए।

उत्तर—प्रस्तुत निबन्ध का शीर्षक पूर्णतया निबन्ध के उद्देश्य पर आधारित है। आज भारतवर्ष ठगी, डकैती, चोरी, तस्करी और भ्रष्टाचार से जूझ रहा है। इन परिस्थितियों को देखकर अब ऐसा लगने लगा है, कि शायद इस देश में कोई ईमानदार आदमी नहीं रह गया है। जीवन के महान मूल्यों के सन्दर्भ में लोगों की आस्था डगमगाने लगी है। द्विवेदी जी का यह निबन्ध भी जहाँ एक ओर संस्कृति व समाज में व्याप्त बुराइयों के बारे में बताता है, वहीं दूसरी अच्छाइयों को बताते हुए यह भी समझाने का प्रयत्न करता है कि हमें निराश होने की आवश्यकता नहीं है।

निबन्ध के प्रारम्भ में ही देश की वर्तमान स्थिति का वर्णन किया गया है जिसके सत्य को लेखक स्वीकार करता है साथ ही यह भी बताने का प्रयास किया गया है कि "ऊपर की सतह पर जितना भी कोलाहल और उथल-पुथल क्यों न दिखाई दे रही हो, नीचे शान्त अचंचल गाम्भीर्य में अब भी भारत महान है,

अनुकरणीय है।'' आज की इस अस्थिरता के सन्दर्भ में विचार करें तो आज की स्थिति मनुष्य के द्वारा बनाई गई नीतियों की त्रुटियों के कारण है।

अब भी समाज में सेवा, ईमानदारी, सच्चाई और आध्यात्मिकता के मूल्य बने हुए हैं लेकिन भ्रष्टाचार के स्वर में उनका स्वर दब अवश्य गया है परन्तु नष्ट नहीं हुआ है। एक बार की घटना में लेखक ने जब जल्दीबाजी में टिकट बाबू को ज्यादा पैसे दे लिए वह लेखक को खोजकर उन अधिक पैसों को लौटाता है। लेखक टिकट बाबू की घटना का विवरण देते हुए यह कहते हैं कि यह नहीं कहा जा सकता कि लोगों में दया-माया रह ही नहीं गई। लेखक के द्वारा बताई गई घटनाएँ अब भी आशा की ज्योति की तरह हैं। इसलिए में निराश होने की आवश्यकता है अथवा नहीं है, यह प्रश्न स्वाभाविक हो जाता है जिसे निबन्धकार ने एक शीर्षक के रूप में पाठकों के समक्ष प्रस्तुत किया है।

इस प्रकार निबन्ध की केन्द्रीय संवेदना में यही प्रश्न बार-बार आता है कि दोषों और गुणों पर विचार करने के बाद भी 'क्या निराश हुआ जाये ?' इस निबन्ध का शीर्षक पूरी तरह से सार्थक है, निबन्ध के विचारों की शृंखला भी निबन्धकार के इसी प्रश्न के इर्द-गिर्द ही घूमती है। अत: यह शीर्षक सर्वथा उचित है।

प्रश्न 3. 'जीवन के महान मूल्यों के बारे में लोगों की आस्था हिलने लगी है।' निबन्ध के आलोक में इस कथन की व्याख्या कीजिए।

उत्तर—इस कथन के माध्यम से लेखक ने यह बताने का प्रयास किया है कि हमारे मनीषियों के सपनों का भारत है और रहेगा। भ्रष्टाचार और अस्थिरता के रूप में जो हलचल है, वह हलचल केवल ऊपरी सतह पर है। भारत के आन्तरिक सतह पर अब भी शान्ति हैं। भारत अब भी महान है। इन दिनों इस प्रकार का माहौल बना है कि नादान और भोले-भाले मेहनती लोग ही पिस रहे हैं वहीं दूसरी ओर झूठ और फरेब का सहारा लेकर जीवन-यापन करने वाले लोग फल-फूल रहे हैं। ईमानदारी को अब मूर्खता समझा जा रहा है।

आधुनिक परिदृश्य को देखकर यह प्रश्न उठता है कि क्या यह वही भारतवर्ष है जिसका सपना तिलक ने देखा था ? विवेकानन्द, रामतीर्थ, रवीन्द्रनाथ टैगोर और मदनमोहन मालवीय वाला भारत तो कहीं दिखाई ही नहीं देता जिसमें आध्यात्मिक और महान संस्कृति तथा सभ्यता थी। लेखक ने इस परिदृश्य को लक्ष्य कर तुलसीदास जी का कथन कुछ इस प्रकार से उद्धृत किया है—

सीदत साधु, साधुता शोभति,
खल विलसत, द्रुतमति भई।

इन पंक्तियों में खल विलसति अर्थात् दुष्ट प्रवृत्तियों का बोल-बाला, यह बताता है कि आज से चार सौ साल पहले भी ऐसा ही माहौल था। उस समय जैसे खल प्रवृत्तियाँ बढ़ी वैसे ही साधुता भी बढ़ी थी तभी तो तुलसीदास जी ने उस समय उन विषम परिस्थितियों में भी महान मूल्यों में आस्था नहीं छोड़ी थी। उनके समकालीन अधिकांश व्यक्तियों ने भी उस आस्था को नहीं छोड़ा, आज भी हमें उस आस्था को छोड़ने की जरूरत नहीं है।

इस समय लोगों के मन में उन महान मूल्यों और उनकी प्रासंगिकता को लेकर प्रश्न उठने लगा है। जिसने लोगों की आस्था पर प्रश्न चिह्न लगा दिया है।

इस प्रकार के वातावरण में जबकि नकारात्मक प्रवृत्तियों का विकास हो रहा है ऐसी स्थिति में जीवन के महान मूल्यों के बारे में लोगों की आस्था ही हिलने लगी है। मानवता के मूल्य दया, ईमानदारी, परोपकार आदि भावनाओं से मनुष्यों का भरोसा कम होने लगा है। लेकिन यह नहीं समझना चाहिए कि मनुष्यता का लोप हो गया है। जीवन में तमाम ऐसे उदाहरण मिलेंगे जिनसे यह प्रमाणित हो जाता है कि मनुष्यता अब भी जीवित है। जरूरत उन घटनाओं को उजागर करने की है।

प्रश्न 4. निबन्धकार ने किन दो घटनाओं के माध्यम से यह बताने का प्रयास किया है कि मनुष्यता अब भी पूरी तरह से समाप्त नहीं हुई है ? उन घटनाओं का संक्षिप्त वर्णन कीजिए।

उत्तर— मनुष्यता अब भी पूरी तरह से समाप्त नहीं हुई है। इसे समझाने के लिए निबन्धकार ने दो घटनाओं का उदाहरण दिया है, जिनमें से पहली घटना में लेखक के अनुसार—मैंने रेलवे स्टेशन से टिकट लेने के दौरान गलती से दस की जगह सौ का नोट दे दिया और जल्दी से गाड़ी में आकर बैठ गया। थोड़ी ही देर में वही टिकट बाबू गाड़ी में आकर हर आदमी का चेहरा पहचानता हुआ उपस्थित हुआ और बाकी के नब्बे रुपये देते हुए बोला कि बहुत बड़ी गलती हो गई थी न मैंने देखा न आपने। यह देख लेखक चकित हो गया।

लेखक के अनुसार यह ईमानदारी की एक घटना ठगी और वंचना की अनेक घटनाओं से अधिक शक्तिशाली है।

लेखक के अनुसार दूसरी घटना इस प्रकार हुई—एक बार लेखक अपनी पत्नी और तीनों बच्चों के साथ बस में यात्रा कर रहा था। बस गंतव्य से आठ किलोमीटर पहले ही एक सुनसान स्थान पर खराब हो गई। रात के दस बज रहे थे। कंडक्टर ऊपर गया और एक साइकिल उतारकर चलता बना। जिससे यात्रियों को यह सन्देह हुआ कि उन्हें धोखा दिया जा रहा है। बच्चे प्यास से व्याकुल हैं और बड़े डकैती आदि के बारे में बातें करने लगे। बात यहाँ तक आ गयी कि नौजवानों ने ड्राइवर को मारने का निश्चय तक कर लिया। डर तो लेखक के मन में भी था पर किसी तरह लेखक ने ड्राइवर को बचाया। उसी समय देखा कि एक खाली बस चली आ रही है और उस पर हमारे बस का कंडक्टर बैठा हुआ था। उसने बताया कि वह बच्चों के लिए दूध और पानी भी लाया है। अन्त में सबने ड्राइवर से माफी माँगी और कंडक्टर का धन्यवाद किया।

लेखक ने इन उदाहरणों के द्वारा यह समझाना चाहा है कि इन उदाहरणों को देखकर यह कैसे कहा जा सकता है कि मानवता एकदम समाप्त हो गई है।

प्रश्न 5. महान भारतवर्ष के पाने की सम्भावना बनी हुई है, बनी रहेगी। लेखक ने किस आधार पर यह कथन कहा है ? यह बताते हुए कथन का सन्दर्भ स्पष्ट कीजिए।

उत्तर—निबन्धकार हजारी प्रसाद द्विवेदी जी ने 'महान भारत के पाने की सम्भावना बनी हुई है' यह कथन उस आशा के आधार पर कहा है जिसमें उन्होंने यह माना है कि ये जो भी कोलाहल दिखाई दे रहा है। यह सब मनुष्यों के द्वारा बनाई गई नीतियों की त्रुटियों का परिणाम है।

मनुष्य ने नई-नई परिस्थितियों का सामना करने के लिए भिन्न-भिन्न नीतियाँ बनायी हैं जिनके सही साबित न होने पर उनमें अनेकों संशोधन किये जाते हैं। ये नियम कानून सबके लिए बनाये जाते हैं। इस प्रकार मनुष्य समाज जटिल प्रक्रियाओं से गुजरकर और भी जटिल हो जाता है, क्योंकि सभी के लिए एक ही नियम सुखकर नहीं होते हैं। मनुष्य की उन्नति के लिए जितने विदान बने उतनी ही मात्रा में लोभ, मोह जैसे विकार भी बढ़े। इसका परिणाम चाहे जो हो लेकिन इससे भारतवर्ष के पुराने आदर्श और भी महान और उपयोगी प्रतीत होने लगे।

आज आरोप-प्रत्यारोप के वातावरण में ऐसा लगता है कि मानों देश में कोई ईमानदार आदमी ही नहीं रह गया है। आज लोगों के दोषों को बढ़ा-चढ़ाकर दिखाया जा रहा है और गुणों की तरफ तो किसी का ध्यान ही नहीं जा रहा है। यही कारण है कि आज हर आदमी दोषी दिख रहा है। यह समस्या पहले भी थी, तब भी लोगों ने जीवन-मूल्यों में आस्था नहीं छोड़ी और आज इन विपरीत परिस्थितियों के बीच भी उस आस्था को छोड़ने की जरूरत नहीं है।

इस प्रकार से से लेखक ने बताया है कि पुराने आदर्शों और उनकी उपयोगिता को नजरंदाज नहीं किया जा सकता है, उनके प्रति जो आस्था है उसे छोड़ने की जरूरत नहीं है। लेखक ने उद्धाहरणों द्वारा यह सिद्ध किया है की मनुष्यता एकदम समाप्त हो गई है, ऐसा नहीं कहा जा सकता। यहीं आशा की वह किरण है जिसके कारण महान भारतवर्ष को पाने की सम्भावना बनी हुई है और बनी रहेगी।

प्रश्न 6. निबन्ध के आधार पर आचार्य हजारी प्रसाद द्विवेदी जी की भाषा शैली पर प्रकाश डालिए।

उत्तर—प्रस्तुत निबन्ध में द्विवेदी जी की भाषा परिमार्जित खड़ी बोली है। उन्होंने भाव और विषय के अनुसार भाषा का चयनित प्रयोग किया है। इस प्रकार की भाषा में उर्दू और अंग्रेजी के शब्दों का भी समावेश

हुआ है। द्विवेदी जी की विषय प्रतिपादन की शैली अध्यापकीय है। शास्त्रीय भाषा होने पर रचना रचने के दौरान भी प्रवाह खण्डित नहीं होता। द्विवेदी जी के इस निबन्ध में कुछ भाषागत विशेषताएँ निम्नवत् हैं—

सहज स्वाभाविक भाषा—आचार्य हजारी प्रसाद द्विवेदी जी ने सरल, स्वाभाविक और सहज रूप में बोधगम्य भाषा का प्रयोग किया है। उन्होंने ऐसी भाषा का प्रयोग नहीं किया जो कृत्रिम हो उन्होंने सहज व जनसामान्य की भाषा द्वारा गम्भीर तथ्यों को भी बड़ी सरलता से प्रस्तुत कर दिया है। भावानुकूल सहज शैली का उदाहरण दृष्टव्य है—''मेरा मन कभी -कभी बैठ जाता है।''

संस्कृत की तत्सम शब्दावली—प्रस्तुत निबन्ध में द्विवेदी जी ने संस्कृत शब्दावली को प्राय: तत्सम रूप में ही स्वीकर किया है—जैसे—अचंचल, ग्रहण-त्याग, निकृष्ट, निर्जन, ज्योति आदि अनेक तत्सम शब्दों का बड़ी ही सफलता से प्रयोग किया गया है।

सूक्तियों का प्रयोग—द्विवेदी जी ने अभिव्यक्ति को गहनता के साथ प्रस्तुत करने, भाषा को लोकप्रिय, सरस एवं मनोरंजक बनाने के साथ-साथ अपने मत का समर्थन करने के हेतु हिन्दी, बाँग्ला आदि भाषा की सूक्तियों का प्रयोग किया गया है। जैसे—

संसारेते लभिले क्षति, पाइले सुधु वंचना
तोमाके जेन करि संशय।

भावानुकूल शब्द चयन—द्विवेदी जी की भाषा कि एक बानगी देखी जा सकती है जो उनके अनुकूल शब्द चयन को प्रदर्शित करती है।

''उसके चेहरे पर विचित्र सन्तोष की गरिमा थी। मैं चकित रह गया।''

अन्य भाषा के प्रचलित शब्दों का प्रयोग—आचार्य हजारी प्रसाद द्विवेदी जी के स्मृति कोश में शब्दों का असीम भण्डार है। उन्होंने इस निबन्ध में कई स्थलों पर प्रचलित भाषा के शब्दों का प्रयोग भी किया है जैसे—गुमराह, कायदे, पर्दाफाश आदि।

इस प्रकार भाषा निबन्ध के प्रवाहमयता में सहायक है तथा विषयानुकूल है जो निबन्ध की विषयवस्तु को पूरी तरह से प्रस्तुत करने में महत्वपूर्ण योगदान देती है। भाषा की प्रांजलता से द्विवेदी जी के इस निबन्ध में विचारों की गहनता, निरीक्षण की नवीनता और विश्लेषण की सूक्ष्मता है।

प्रश्न 7. यह सही है, कि इन दिनों कुछ ऐसा माहौल बना है कि ईमानदारी से मेहनत करके जीविका चलाने वाले विरोह और भोले-भाले श्रमजीवी पिस रहे हैं, झूठ और फरेब का रोजगार करने वाले फल-फूल रहे हैं।

(i) इन पंक्तियों का क्या तात्पर्य है ?

(ii) क्या हमें आज के हालात देखकर निराश होना चाहिए ?

(iii) अधिकांश लोगों को क्या छोड़ने की आवश्यकता नहीं है ?

(iv) जो आज दिखाई दे रहा है वह क्या है ?

उत्तर—(i) इन पंक्तियों का तात्पर्य यह है कि जो लोग ईमानदारी से परिश्रम करते हैं, वे दु:खी हैं और जो झूठ और फरेब का धन्धा करते हैं वे सुखी हैं तथा आराम में हैं।

(ii) हमें आज के हालात देखकर निराश नहीं होना चाहिए। यदि हम आज के हालात देखकर निराश होते हैं तो समाज में उदासीनता फैल जायेगी, कोई काम नहीं करना चाहेगा। हमें तो उत्साह के साथ बाधाओं पर सफलता प्राप्त कर आगे बढ़ना चाहिए।

(iii) अधिकांश लोगों को अपना धैर्य और साहस के साथ कार्य करने का हौसला छोड़ने की आवश्यकता नहीं है। माहौल कैसा भी हो कर्मशील मनुष्य उस माहौल को अपने अनुसार बनाकर कार्य पथ पर आगे बढ़कर सफलता प्राप्त करता है। अपने हृदय में आशा का संचार करते रहना चाहिए ताकि अपने कार्यपक्ष पर मनुष्य आगे बढ़ता रहे।

(iv) आज जो दिखाई दे रहा है वह है झूठ और फरेब। मेहनत करने वाले लोग दु:ख पा रहे हैं और झूठ और फरेब से काम करने वाले लोग फल-फूल रहे हैं। लेकिन यह हमेशा के लिए नहीं है। ऐसे लोग अल्प

समय के लिए सुखी और फलते-फूलते दिखाई देते हैं स्थायी रूप से नहीं। थोड़े समय बाद वे अपने पथ से गिर जाते हैं। ईमानदार और परिश्रमी व्यक्ति ही स्थायी-लाभ प्राप्त करता है।

जीवन में कभी भी निराशा तो आनी ही नहीं चाहिए।

क्या निराश हुआ जाये ?

प्रश्न 8. मनुष्य आज भी वह मनुष्य से प्रेम करता है, महिलाओं का सम्मान करता है, झूठ और चोरी को गलत समझता है, दूसरे को पीड़ा पहुँचाने को पाप समझता है और कठिनाई में पड़े हुए बेवस लोगों की सहायता करने में अपने को कृत कृत्य अनुभव करता है।

(i) धर्म किससे बड़ा है ? कैसे ?

(ii) मनुष्य की सोच आज क्या है ?

(iii) समाचार पत्रों में हम क्या पढ़ते हैं ?

(iv) किसमें रस लेना बुरा है ?

उत्तर—(i) धर्म कानून से बड़ा है। धर्म को धोखा नहीं दिया जा सकता, कानून को दिया जा सकता है। जो लोग धर्म-भीरू रूढ़िग्रस्त हैं, वे कानून की त्रुटियों से लाभ उठा लेते हैं। अधिकतर लोग यह अनुभव करते हैं कि धर्म कानून से बड़ी चीज है।

(ii) मनुष्य की सोच आज यह है कि वह गलत काम से बचे। समाज में परोपकार, न्याय और ईमानदारी का व्यवहार करे। महिलाओं का सम्मान करे। दूसरों को कष्ट न पहुँचाकर बेबस लोगों की सहायता करे। आज मनुष्य सेवा, ईमानदारी, सच्चाई और आध्यात्मिकता के मूल्य को समझने का प्रयास करता है।

(iii) समाचार पत्रों में भ्रष्टाचार, ठगी, डकैती, चोरी, तस्करी आदि के समाचार भरे रहते हैं। इससे यह पता चलता है कि ईमानदारी, परोपकार तो मानो समाज से लुप्त ही हो गये हैं। जो हम समाचार-पत्रों में पढ़ते हैं वैसी ही धारणा मन में बन जाती है भलाई भले ही दबी हुई सी दिखाई देती है, पर वह समाप्त नहीं हुई है। वह बुराई से ऊपर ही है।

(iv) किसी मनुष्य की बुराई में रस लेना बुरा है। किसी की बुराई करना पापपूर्ण कार्य है। किसी की बुराई कभी नहीं करनी चाहिए। किसी की अच्छाई को उद्घाटित न करना भी बुरी बात है। अच्छाई को बताने से लोकचित्त में अच्छाई के प्रति भावना जागती है।

प्रश्न 9. मनुष्य की बनाई विधियाँ गलत नतीजे तक पहुँच रही हैं, तो उन्हें बदलना होगा। वस्तुतः आये दिन इन्हें बदला ही जा रहा है, लेकिन अब भी आशा की ज्योति बुझी नहीं है।

(i) लेखक ने भगवान से क्या चाहा है ?

(ii) मनुष्य की गलत नीतियों का क्या करना चाहिए ?

(iii) लेखक के अनुसार जीवन कब कष्टकर हो जाता है ?

(iv) बस खराब होने पर यात्री क्या सोचने लगे और उन्होंने क्या योजना बनायी ?

उत्तर—(i) लेखक ने भगवान से यह चाहा है कि संसार में केवल नुकसान ही उठाना पड़े, धोखा ही खाना पड़े तो ऐसे अवसरों पर भी उसे ऐसी शक्ति दे कि वह उस (ईश्वर) पर संदेह न कर सके।

(ii) मनुष्य की बनाई गलत नीतियों को बदलना चाहिए। वैसे तो आये दिन उन्हें बदला ही जा रहा है, लेकिन अब भी आशा की ज्योति बुझी नहीं है। भारत को और महान बनाने की सम्भावना कम नहीं हुई हैं।

(iii) लेखक ने बताया है कि वह संसार में ठगा भी गया है, धोखा भी खाया है और कई स्थानों पर विश्वासघात भी उसने झेला है। यदि वह केवल उन्हीं चीजों का हिसाब रखे जिनमें उसे विश्वासघात मिला है या उसने धोखा खाया है तो उसका जीवन कष्टकर हो जायेगा।

(iv) रात के समय सुनसान रास्ते पर यात्रियों की बस खराब हो गयी, उसी बस में लेखक अपने परिवार के साथ बैठा था। तब कण्डक्टर साइकिल लेकर दूसरी बस लेने चला गया। उस समय यात्री यह सोचने लगे कि बस का कण्डक्टर बस लुटवाने के लिए डाकुओं को बुलाने चला गया है। तब उन्होंने ड्राइवर को मारने-पीटने की योजना बनायी।

●●

8. भक्तिन

—महादेवी वर्मा

लेखिका परिचय— भारत के साहित्य आकाश में महादेवी वर्मा का नाम ध्रुव तारे की भाँति प्रकाशमान है। आधुनिक हिन्दी की सबसे सशक्त कवयित्रियों में से एक होने के कारण उन्हें आधुनिक मीरा के नाम से भी जाना जाता है। गत शताब्दी की सर्वाधिक लोकप्रिय महिला साहित्यकार के रूप में वे जीवन भर पूज्यनीय बनी रहीं। उन्होंने मन की पीड़ा को इतने स्नेह और शृंगार से सजाया कि दीपशिखा में वह जन-जन की पीड़ा के रूप में स्थापित हुई और उसने केवल पाठकों को ही नहीं, समीक्षकों को भी गहराई तक प्रभावित किया।

महादेवी का जन्म 26 मार्च, 1907 को फरुखाबाद, उत्तर प्रदेश में हुआ था। उनके परिवार में लगभग 200 वर्षों या सात पीढ़ियों के बाद पहली बार पुत्री का जन्म हुआ था। अत: बाबा बाबू बाँके बिहारी जी हर्ष से झूम उठे और इन्हें घर की देवी—महादेवी मानते हुए पुत्री का नाम महादेवी रखा। उनके पिता श्री गोविन्द प्रसाद वर्मा भागलपुर के एक कॉलेज में प्राध्यापक थे। उनकी माता का नाम हेमरानी देवी था। महादेवी वर्मा के मानस बन्धुओं में सुमित्रानन्दन पन्त एवं निराला का नाम लिया जा सकता है, जो उनसे जीवन पर्यन्त राखी बँधवाते रहे। निराला जी से उनकी अत्यधिक निकटता थी। उनका बाल-विवाह हुआ परन्तु उन्होंने अविवाहित की भाँति जीवन-यापन किया।

उन्होंने अपने जीवन का अधिकांश समय उत्तर प्रदेश के इलाहाबाद नगर में बिताया। 11 सितम्बर, 1987 को इलाहाबाद में उनका देहान्त हो गया।

महादेवी जी की रचनाओं में प्रमुख हैं- 'नीहार' , 'नीरजा' , 'रश्मि' , 'सांध्यगीत' , 'यामा', 'दीप-शिखा' और 'सप्तपर्णा' । गद्य-काव्य संग्रह हैं- 'अतीत के चलचित्र' , 'श्रृंखला की कड़ियाँ' , 'स्मृति की रेखाएँ' तथा 'विवेचनात्मक-लेख' ।

शब्दार्थ—**जिज्ञासु** = जानने की इच्छा रखने वाला, **दुर्वह** = भारी, **विरोधाभास** = विपरीत, **विमाता** = सौतेली माँ, **अगाध** = अथाह, **मरणांतक** = मरने की कगार पर, **नैहर** = माँ का घर, **मर्मव्यथा** = दिल का दु:ख, **परिच्छेद** = हिस्सा, **अलगौझा** = बँटवारा, **उपार्जित** = जमा, **कोठरी** = कमरों, **परिमार्जन** = सुधार, **कर्मठता** = उद्‌योगशीलता, **निरूपाय** = बिना किसी उपाय के, **आप्लावित** = भरी, **सारगर्भित** = अर्थपूर्ण, **प्रतिद्वन्द्वियों** = प्रतिस्पर्धी।

सारांश

महादेवी वर्मा ने अपनी एक सेविका जिसका नाम भक्तिन था, उसके चरित्र को प्रस्तुत करने के लिए सर्वप्रथम उसका शब्दों से चित्र खींचा है। भक्तिन छोटे कद और दुबले शरीर वाली महिला है जो विचित्र समझदारी वाली हैं। वे काफी समय से हमारे साथ हैं, लेकिन जब भी कोई उनसे यह प्रश्न पूछता है तो वह कुछ सोचकर यह कह देती हैं कि वह पचास बरस से हमारे साथ हैं। इस आधार पर मेरी उम्र पचहत्तर की और उनकी सौ के पार हो जाती है लेकिन वे इसमें से थोड़ा भी कम नहीं करना चाहती हैं।

सेवाभाव में हनुमान जी से स्पर्धा करने वाली भक्तिन का असली नाम लक्ष्मी (लछमिन) है जिसे वे किसी को बताना नहीं चाहती। जब वे नौकरी की खोज में आई तभी उन्होंने अपना नाम बताने के साथ यह भी प्रार्थना की कि इस नाम का उपयोग न करें। लेखिका ने उसकी कंठी माला आदि को देखकर उसका नाम भक्तिन रख दिया जिस नाम को प्राप्त कर वह गद्‌गद् हो उठी।

भक्तिन के चरित्र को समझने के लिए उसके जीवन को पूरी तरह से समझना होगा। वह इलाहाबाद के नजदीक झूँसी गाँव की एक बेटी है। जिसके पिता ने पाँच वर्ष की उम्र में उसका विवाह किया और जब वह नौ वर्ष कि हुई तो उसका गौना भी कर दिया। इस प्रकार सौतेली माँ ने उसे हँडिया के गोपालक की सबसे छोटी पुत्रवधू बनाकर अपने कर्तव्य कि इति कर ली।

विवाह के बाद उसके पिता बीमार थे तो उसकी विमाता ने उसके पास कोई सूचना नहीं भेजी। वह अपने पिता से बहुत प्रेम करती थी। जब उसके पिता की मृत्यु का समाचार आया तो सास ने लछमिन को बिना कुछ बताये यह कहकर विदा कर दिया कि जाकर एक बार नैहर देख आओ। वहाँ जाकर लछमिन को सब पता चलता है जिससे वह बहुत दु:खी हो जाती है। वह उल्टे पैर ससुराल आकर सास और अपने पति को खरी-खोटी सुनाकर अपने पिता के चिर विछोह की मर्मव्यथा व्यक्त करती है।

लछमिन के जीवन में दो कन्याओं का आगमन हुआ जबकि उसकी जिठानियों को काले-कलूटे से लड़के थे फिर भी वह उच्च बन चुकी थी। घर में उसका और उसकी कन्याओं का बड़ा अपमान होता था। जहाँ लड़कों को खाने के लिए दूध-भात मिलता वहीं दूसरी ओर उसकी कन्याओं को काला गुड़ और मट्ठा मिलता है।

एक विशेष बात यह थी कि उसकी जिठानियाँ बात-बात पर पति के द्वारा पीटी-कूटी जाती पर लछमिन के पति ने कभी उस पर उँगली भी नहीं उठाई। इसी प्रेम के बल पर अलगौझी हो जाती है। परिश्रमी दम्पत्ति के परिश्रम से उनका विकास स्वाभाविक था। धूमधाम से बड़ी लड़की का विवाह करने के बाद अपनी उनत्तीस वर्षीय पत्नी को छोड़कर भक्तिन के पति ने संसार से विदा ली। मरते समय उसके पति की आयु छत्तीस के आस-पास रही होगी लेकिन वे आज भी उन्हें बुढ़ऊ कहती हैं।

भक्तिन के हरे-भरे खेत और समृद्धि को देखकर जेठ-जिठौतों के मुँह में पानी आ गया। लेकिन वह उनके चकमें में नहीं आई और दूसरा विवाह नहीं किया। उसके घरवालों ने पूर्वजों की सम्पत्ति में से सुई के नोंक के बराबर भी जमीन नहीं दी। छोटी लड़की के भी हाथ पीले कर दिये तथा पति के चुने हुए दामाद को घरजमाई बनाकर रखा।

जीवन के तीसरे हिस्से में भी उसका दु:ख कम नहीं हुआ। उसकी बड़ी बेटी विधवा हो जाती है। बड़ा जेठ अपने साले से उसकी लड़की का विवाह करना चाहता है जिसे माँ बेटी दोनों ने अस्वीकार कर दिया। अन्तत: एक दिन माँ की अनुपस्थिति में जेठ का साला बेटी की कोठरी में घुसकर अन्दर से किवाड़ बन्द कर लेता है। इस घटना पर पंचायत बैठती है और यह फैसला होता है कि वे दोनों एक कमरे से निकले हैं इसलिए इन दोनों को पति-पत्नी के रूप में रहना होगा। इस प्रकार एक ऐसा दामाद गले पड़ गया जो सिर्फ तीतर लड़ाता था। अब धीरे-धीरे उनकी हालत और खराब होती चली गई और लगान देने तक में समस्या होने लगी। तब भक्तिन कमाई के विचार से शहर आ गई।

जीवन के चौथे हिस्से में सेविका का रूप प्रारम्भ हुआ पर उसका अन्त अभी दूर है। भक्तिन की वेशभूषा देखकर लेखिका ने पूछा कि तुम खाना बनाना जानती हो जिसके जवाब में भक्तिन ने कहा कि ये कोई बड़ी बात नहीं है। दूसरे दिन जल देने तथा जप करने के बाद भक्तिन रसोई में जाकर कोयले से एक रेखा खींच देती है जिसके उस पार जाना मना था। भोजन बन जाने के उपरान्त भक्तिन ने प्रसन्नता से मेरी थाली में एक अँगुल मोटी चार रोटियाँ और थाली टेढ़ी करके दाल परोस दी। पूछने पर तरह-तरह के तर्क देती है। उसके व्याख्यान से प्रभावित होकर एक रोटी खाकर मैं यूनिवर्सिटी चली गयी। इस प्रकार इस देहाती वृद्धा ने जीवन की सरलता के प्रति जाग्रत कर दिया। इस तरह से भक्तिन का स्वभाव यह था कि वह दूसरों को अपने मन के अनुसार बना लेती है। वह देहाती खाना बनाती है। मेरे नाराज होने पर भी उसने साफ धोती पहनना नहीं सीखा।

उसमें दुर्गुणों की कमी नहीं थी। वह मेरे इधर-उधर पड़े पैसों को भण्डार के किसी मटकी में डाल देती। जिसके बारे में उनके द्वारा दिये जाने वाले तर्क से कोई पार नहीं पा सकता। जब भक्तिन को सिर घुटाने से मना किया तो उसका जवाब यह था कि यह शास्त्र में लिखा है। हर बृहस्पतिवार को वह यह संस्कार करती है।

उसे पढ़ाई-लिखाई का कोई ज्ञान न था। जब दूसरे नौकर पढ़ते तो वह कहती है कि हमारी मालकिन तो दिन-रात किताब में लगी रहती है जब हम भी पढ़ने लगेंगे तो घर गृहस्थी कौन देखेगा। लेकिन वह दूसरों पर टीका-टिप्पणी करने से नहीं चूकती थी। कोई भी मेरे काम में सहायता नहीं कर पाता था लेकिन वह तब तक जागती रहती जब तक मैं काम करती रहती। जब मैं व्यस्त रहती तो मेरे लिए चाय आदि बनाती। मेरे कुछ

भी माँगने पर वह उसे देती। इस प्रकार वह मेरे काम में हाथ बँटाती। मैं कहीं जाने के लिए प्रस्तुत होती तो भक्तिन को छाया के समान हमेशा साथ ही पाती।

उसके दामाद और बेटी उसको बुलाने आते हैं तब भी वह उनके साथ नहीं जाती पैसा भेज देती है और कभी-कभी उन्हें देख भी आती है। जब युद्ध के कारण सब पलायन करने लगे तो भक्तिन मुझसे गाँव चलने का अनुरोध करती है और सारी योजना बना देती है। जब भक्तिन के इस प्रस्ताव को स्थगित करने के लिए मैंने यह कहा कि पैसे नहीं हैं तो वह अपने पैसों के बारे में बताती है।

हमारे बीच एक अलग किस्म का सम्बन्ध हो गया था जिसमें मैं चाहकर भी उसे अपनी सेवा से नहीं हटा सकती थी। भक्तिन मेरे साहित्यिक बन्धुओं से भी परिचित है। सबका दुःख उसे प्रभावित कर सकता है। भक्तिन के संस्कार ऐसे हैं कि वह कारागार से ऐसे डरती है, जैसे वह यमलोक हो। वह बार-बार पूछती है कि क्या ले जाना है, जिससे कोई असुविधा न हो ? मेरे न जाने की कल्पना से इतनी प्रसन्न न होती जितनी कि अपने साथ मेरे न जाने की सम्भावना से अपमानित। मैं यह सोचती हूँ कि चिर विदा के अन्तिम क्षणों में यह देहातिन वृद्ध क्या करेगी ? इस तरह भक्तिन की यह कहानी अधूरी है जिसे मैं उसे खोकर पूरा नहीं करना चाहती।

अभ्यास-प्रश्न

प्रश्न 1. 'भक्तिन' कहानी के आधार पर कहानी का उद्देश्य स्पष्ट कीजिए।

उत्तर— भारत के सहित्य आकाश में महादेवी वर्मा का नाम ध्रुव तारे की भाँति प्रकाशमान है। गत शताब्दी की सर्वाधिक लोकप्रिय महिला साहित्यकार के रूप में वे जीवन भर पूज्यनीय बनी रहीं। कवि निराला ने उन्हें हिन्दी के विशाल मन्दिर की 'सरस्वती' कहा है। 'भक्तिन' कहानी महादेवी वर्मा द्वारा रचित श्रेष्ठ कहानियों में से एक है। इस कहानी में लेखिका ने यह दिखाने का प्रयास किया है कि एक ग्रामीण महिला किस प्रकार अभावों, जिम्मेदारियों व प्रतिकूल परिस्थितियों का सामना करते हुए एक भावात्मक सम्बन्ध बना लेती है। भक्तिन कहानी में भक्तिन का जल्दी विवाह, अशिक्षित होना, उसकी बेटियों के प्रति दोहरा रवैया, पंचायत में अन्यायपूर्ण तरीके से उसकी बेटी का विवाह आदि अनेक सामाजिक कुरीतियों को उद्घाटित किया गया है।

'भक्तिन' कहानी के माध्यम से लेखिका का उद्देश्य सामाजिक समस्याओं व स्त्री-पुरुष के प्रति किये जाने वाले भेदभाव को पाठकों के समक्ष रखना है। इस कहानी में लेखिका ने स्त्रियों की मुक्ति और विकास के लिए दृढ़ता से आवाज उठाई है और सामाजिक रूढ़ियों की निन्दा भी की है। तत्कालीन समाज में व्याप्त स्त्रियों के भेदभाव को व्यक्त करना ही उनका उद्देश्य है और सन्देश भी।

लेखिका यह बताना चाहती है कि जिस प्रकार किसी की सार्थकता में ही जब हमारा सुख-दुःख निहित हो जाता है तो ऐसे समय में सम्बन्ध को सीमा की परिधि में नहीं बाँधा जा सकता है। इसी को पाठकों के समक्ष प्रस्तुत करना ही लेखिका का उद्देश्य है।

प्रश्न 2. वर्मा जी ने किस प्रकार भक्तिन का चित्र खींचा है ? भक्तिन का चरित्र-चित्रण कीजिए।

उत्तर—प्रस्तुत कहानी में भक्तिन ही कहानी की प्रमुख पात्र है। कहानी में महादेवी वर्मा जी ने भक्तिन की जीवन यात्रा के माध्यम से अनेक सामाजिक कुरीतियों और विसंगतियों को प्रस्तुत करने का प्रयास किया है। इस कहानी में भक्तिन के द्वारा ही कहानी की मूल संवेदना को उत्तेजित करने का प्रयास किया गया है।

लेखिका के भक्तिन का शाब्दिक चित्र कुछ इस प्रकार से खींचा है, ''घुटी हुई चाँद को मैली धोती से ढाँके और मानों सब प्रकार की आहट सुनने के लिए कान कपड़े से बाहर निकाले हुए है भक्तिन मेरे यहाँ सेवक धर्म दीक्षित हुई।''

पूरी कहानी भक्तिन के इर्द-गिर्द ही घूमती है। यह कहानी उसी के चरित्र पर आधारित है, उसके चरित्र की अनेक विशेषताएँ हैं।

पिता से प्रेम करने वाली—भक्तिन जो कहानी में लछमिन भी है, अपने पिता से बहुत प्रेम करती है और उसके पिता भी उससे अगाध प्रेम करते हैं। इसी कारण उसकी विमाता ने उसके पास मरणांतक रोग का समाचार तब भेजा जब उसके पिता मर गये। पिता को न पाकर वह सीधे सुसराल आ जाती है। सास को खरी-खोटी सुनाकर पति के ऊपर गहने फेंककर उसने अपने पिता के चिर विछोह की मर्मव्यथा व्यक्त की।

पति की प्रिय—भक्तिन अपने पति की प्रिय थी। जहाँ एक ओर उसकी जिठानियाँ अपने पति से बात-बात पर धमा-धम पीटी-कूटी जाती थीं, वहीं दूसरी ओर लछमिन के पति ने उसे कभी उँगली भी न छुआई। इस प्रेम के बल पर ही वह अलगौझा कर लेती है।

कर्मठ—भक्तिन बहुत ही कर्मठ थी। उसने अपने पति और दामाद की मृत्यु के बाद भी अपनी बेटी के साथ मिलकर अपनी सम्पत्ति की देखभाल की। उसकी कर्मठता पर तब ठेस लगी जब वह नये दामाद के व्यवहार के कारण लगान न दे सकी और जिसके कारण उसे आधे घण्टे तक धूप में खड़ा रहना पड़ा।

आत्मविश्वासी—भक्तिन में आत्मविश्वास कूट-कूटकर भरा है। भक्तिन के चरित्र की इस विशेषता के सम्बन्ध में सिर्फ इसी बात से जाना जा सकता है कि लेखिका ने कहा कि वह दूसरों को अपने मन के अनुसार बना लेना चाहती है, पर अपने सम्बन्ध में किसी प्रकार के परिवर्तन की कल्पना तक सम्भव नहीं।

इतना ही नहीं उसके चरित्र में अंध-विश्वास, संवेदनशीलता आदि और अनेक विशेषताएँ हैं जो उसके चरित्र को प्रभावशाली बना देते हैं। इस प्रकार भक्तिन का चरित्र पूरी तरह से लेखिका के उद्देश्य की पूर्ति में सहायक है।

प्रश्न 3. महादेवी वर्मा जी के भाषिक कौशल की प्रस्तुत कहानी के आधार पर विवेचना कीजिए।

अथवा

'भक्तिन' कहानी की भाषागत विशेषताएँ लिखिए।

उत्तर—भाषा के प्रयोग की दृष्टि से प्रस्तुत कहानी एक समृद्ध कहानी है, जिसमें पात्रानुकूलता है। जिसमें प्रवाहमयता तथा बोधगम्यता है जो कहानी के उद्देश्य की सफलता में सहायक है। भाषा के प्रयोग में कहानीकार को देश, काल, वातावरण, पात्रों की पात्रता अर्थात् चरित्र की अनुकूलता का ध्यान रखना आवश्यक है। भाषा में सरलता, प्रवाहमयता और बोधगम्यता होनी चाहिए। कहीं-कहीं भाषा में काव्यात्मकता का प्रदर्शन भाषा को प्रभावशाली बनाने में सहायक होता है। शब्द-भण्डार सटीक व समृद्ध होना चाहिए। शब्दों का चयन भावों के अनुकूल होना ही कहानीकार की सफलता का रहस्य होता है।

साहित्य में महादेवी वर्मा का आर्विभाव उस समय हुआ जब खड़ीबोली का आकार परिष्कृत हो रहा था। उन्होंने हिन्दी कविता को बृजभाषा की कोमलता दी, छन्दों के नये दौर को गीतों का भण्डार दिया और भारतीय दर्शन को वेदना की हार्दिक स्वीकृति दी। समाज-सुधार और नारी स्वतन्त्रता से सम्बन्धित उनके विचारों में दृढ़ता और विकास का अनुपम सामंजस्य मिलता है। सामाजिक जीवन की गहरी परतों को छूने वाली इतनी तीव्र दृष्टि, नारी जीवन के वैषम्य और शोषण को तीखेपन से आँकने वाली इतनी जागरुक प्रतिभा और निम्न वर्ग के निरीह, साधनहीन प्राणियों के अनूठे चित्र उन्होंने ही पहली बार हिन्दी साहित्य को दिये।

'भक्तिन' कहानी में पात्रानुकूल भाषा के उदाहरण भरे पड़े हैं। भक्तिन देहाती है तो उसी के अनुरूप ही वर्मा जी भाषा का प्रयोग करती हैं जो भाषा की व्यापक समझ को प्रदर्शित करता है। जब लेखिका भक्तिन से पूछती है कि क्या उसे खाना बनाना आता है तो भक्तिन उसका जवाब इस प्रकार देती है—

"ई कउन बड़ी बात आय। रोटी बनाय जानित है दाल राँध लइत है, साग भाजी छँउक सकित है, अउर बाकी का रहा।"

इस प्रकार से यह उदाहरण स्पष्ट करता है कि महादेवी वर्मा जी की भाषा का प्रयोग अनूठा है। वे जहाँ एक ओर शुद्ध खड़ी हिन्दी का प्रयोग करती हैं तो वहीं दूसरी ओर ग्रामीण अंचल की भाषा का भी उतनी ही कुशलता से प्रयोग करती हैं। जो कि उनके भाषिक कौशल्य को प्रदर्शित करता है।

इस प्रकार यदि भाषा की दृष्टि से भी देखें तो भाषा ग्रामीण और खड़ी हिन्दी का मिश्रण है, परन्तु कहानीकार के उद्देश्य की पूर्ति में पूरी तरह से सहायक है। कहानी की भाषा में सरलता, प्रवाहमयता और बोधगम्यता है। भाषिक दृष्टि से भी यह एक सफल कहानी है।

प्रश्न 4. शीर्षक के आधार पर 'भक्तिन' कहानी के शीर्षक का औचित्य स्पष्ट कीजिए।

उत्तर— प्रस्तुत कहानी का शीर्षक 'भक्तिन' है। यदि शीर्षक के गुणों को आधार बनाकर 'भक्तिन' कहानी के शीर्षक को देखें तो यह पता चलता है कि 'भक्तिन' कहानी का शीर्षक संक्षिप्त है, साथ ही जिज्ञासावर्धक भी है। कहानी की प्रमुख पात्र 'भक्तिन' है। कहानी की सारी घटनाएँ उसके जीवन व उसी के चरित्र पर ही आधारित हैं। 'भक्तिन' ही वह चरित्र है जो कथानक का मेरूदण्ड है।

कहानी के आरम्भ में ही सबसे पहले 'भक्तिन' का वर्णन किया गया है और उसके इतिवृत्ति को बताया गया है। भक्तिन के जीवन को तीन अलग-अलग परिच्छेदों में वर्णित किया गया है। पहले परिच्छेद में उसके जीवन के प्रारम्भिक अवस्था में उसकी विमाता द्वारा किए गए अत्याचारों की गाथा है। भक्तिन के पिता के मृत्यु तक की कहानी है।

भक्तिन के जीवन के दूसरे परिच्छेद में भी सुख की अपेक्षा दु:ख ही अधिक है। इस परिच्छेद में वह दो लड़कियों को जन्म देती है। इसमें यह बताया गया है कि भक्तिन का पति उससे बहुत प्रेम करता था। अंत में वे अपने परिवार से अलगौझा (अलगाव) कर लेती है। अलग होने के बाद वह अपने पति के साथ बड़े सुख से रहती है लेकिन यह सुख अधिक समय तक नहीं रह पाता पहली बेटी के विवाह के उपरांत उसके पति की मृत्यु हो जाती है। पति की मृत्यु के बाद भक्तिन के सास-ससुर ने उसे सुई के नोक के बराबर भी जमीन नहीं दी। दुर्भाग्य ने वहाँ भी उसका पीछा नहीं छोड़ा, उसकी बड़ी बेटी विधवा हो जाती है। उस विधवा बेटी का विवाह धोखे से एक अकर्मण्य रिश्तेदार से करा दिया जाता है। जिसके कारण उसका परिवार एक बार फिर द्वेष में झुलस जाता है। वह अधिक कमाई के विचार से शहर आ जाती है। इस प्रकार वह लेखिका के सम्पर्क में आ जाती है। यहाँ उसके जीवन का एक नया अध्याय शुरू होता है।

इस प्रकार यह कहानी पूरी तरह से भक्तिन के चरित्र को आधार बनाकर लिखी गई है, अत: इस कहानी का शीर्षक सार्थक व सटीक प्रतीत होता है।

प्रश्न 5. जीवन के तीसरे परिच्छेद में भक्तिन के जीवन में कौन-सी घटना घटी जिसके कारण भक्तिन को कमाई के विचार से शहर आना पड़ा ? समझाकर लिखें।

उत्तर— पति की मृत्यु तथा बेटियों के हाथ पीले करने के बाद भक्तिन ने अपने पति द्वारा चुने हुए दामाद को घरजमाई बनाकर रखा। यहीं से उसके जीवन के तीसरे परिच्छेद का आरम्भ होता है।

इतना होने के बाद भी दुर्भाग्य ने भक्तिन का पीछा नहीं छोड़ा। किशोरी से युवती होते ही बड़ी बेटी भी विधवा हो गई। जिठौतों ने अपने तीतर लड़ाने वाले साले को बुलाया जिससे भक्तिन की बेटी की शादी उससे कराई जा सके। जिससे जायदाद पर उनका अधिकार हो सके। लेकिन भक्तिन की बेटी माँ से कम समझदार न थी, उन दोनों ने वर को नापसन्द कर दिया। अब माँ और बेटी दोनों अपनी सम्पत्ति की देखभाल करने लगी। अब परिवार वाले किसी प्रकार तीतर लड़ाने वाले साले को उसकी बेटी की पदवी तक पहुँचाने का उपाय सोचने लगे।

एक दिन माँ की अनुपस्थिति में वर महाशय बेटी की कोठरी में घुस गये और भीतर से दरवाजा बन्द कर लिया। उसके समर्थक गाँववालों को बुलाने लगे। युवती ने इस डकैत वर की मरम्मत करने के बाद कुंडी

खोली पर तब सब समस्या में पड़ गए। अन्त में पंचायत बैठी, जिसमें यह फैसला हुआ कि दोनों एक ही कोठरी से निकले इसलिए इनका पति-पत्नी के रूप में रहना ही उचित है। अन्त में पंचायत दोनों के विवाह का फैसला सुनाती है।

इस प्रकार दामाद अब सारा दिन सिर्फ तीतर लड़ाया करता। खेती-बाड़ी और गाय-ढोर सब नष्ट होने लगे। अन्त में लगान चुकाना भी भारी हो जाता है। एक बार लगान न दे पाने के कारण जमींदार ने भक्तिन को बुलाकर कड़ी धूप में खड़ा रखा। यही अपमान उसके लिए कलंक बन गया इसीलिए भक्तिन को कमाई के विचार से शहर जाना पड़ा।

प्रश्न 6. भक्तिन के जीवन का इतिवृत्त बिना जाने हुये उसके स्वभाव को पूर्णतः क्या अशतःसमझना भी कठिन होगा।

(i) भक्तिन कौन है ? उसका असली नाम क्या है ?

(ii) उसकी उम्र क्या रही होगी ?

(iii) पिता के बारे में उसकी सास ने क्या बताया ?

(iv) गाँव में जाकर उसने क्या देखा ?

उत्तर—(i) भक्तिन लेखिका की सेविका है जिसका असली नाम है लछमिन अर्थात् लक्ष्मी। लेकिन वह इस नाम को किसी को बताती नहीं है, छुपाकर रखती है। इसलिए लेखिका ने उसका नाम भक्तिन रख दिया है।

(ii) भक्तिन के कहने के अनुसार तो उसकी उम्र सौ से ऊपर निकल जाती है क्योंकि वह लेखिका के यहाँ काम करने के समय को पचास वर्ष बताती है। उसके अनुसार तो लेखिका की उम्र ही पिचहत्तर वर्ष बैठती है।

(iii) पिता का भक्तिन पर अगाध प्रेम था इसलिए बिमाता ने उसे पिता के मरणान्तक रोग का समाचार तब भेजा जब उनकी मृत्यु हो चुकी थी। भक्तिन की सास ने भी उसे कुछ नहीं बताया बस इतना कहा कि वह बहुत दिनों से नैहर नहीं गई है, एक बार जाकर देख आवे।

(iv) गाँव जाकर उसे ऐसा अनुभव हुआ कि सब लोग उसे ऐसी दृष्टि से देख रहे हैं कि वह अब आई है जब उसका पिता मर गया है। बिमाता के व्यवहार में शिष्टाचार का लेश भी नहीं था। दुःख से शिथिल और अपमान से जलती हुयी उस घर में पानी भी पिये बिना उल्टे पैरों ससुराल लौट पड़ी। सास को खरी-खोटी सुनाकर उसने विमाता पर आया हुआ क्रोध शान्त किया और पति के ऊपर गहने फेंक कर पिता के चिर विछोह की मर्मव्यथा व्यक्त की।

प्रश्न 7. पिता का उस पर अगाध प्रेम होने के कारण स्वभावतः ईर्ष्यालु और सम्पत्ति की रक्षा में सतर्क विमाता ने उसके मरणांतक रोग का समाचार तब भेजा, जब वह मृत्यु की सूचना भी बन चुका था।

(i) विमाता ने भक्तिन को पिता का समाचार कब भेजा ?

(ii) सास ने उसे क्यों नहीं बताया ?

(iii) वहाँ से भक्तिन क्यों लौट आयी ?

(iv) सास और जेठानियों ने उसकी उपेक्षा क्यों की ?

उत्तर—(i) विमाता ने भक्तिन के पास पिता के मरणान्तक रोग का समाचार नहीं भेजा। जब उनकी मृत्यु हो गयी तभी उसके पास समाचार भेजा। भक्तिन अपने पिता से बहुत प्रेम करती थी।

(ii) रोने पीटने के अपशकुन से बचने के लिए सास ने भी भक्तिन को उसके पिता की मृत्यु के बारे में कुछ नहीं बताया। बहुत दिनों से वह नैहर नहीं गयी है सो एकबार होकर आवे ऐसा कहकर उसे नैहर के लिए विदा कर दिया।

(iii) गाँव की सीमा में घुसते ही उसे अनुभव हुआ कि लोगों की निगाहें उसे इस तरह देख रही हैं कि वह अब आयी है जब पिता की मृत्यु हो चुकी है। गाँव में न पिता का चिन्ह शेष था, न विमाता के व्यवहार में शिष्टाचार का लेश था। दुःख से शिथिल और अपमान से जलती हुई वह उस घर में पानी पिये बिना ही ससुराल को लौट पड़ी।

(iv) भक्तिन की सास और जेठानियाँ भक्तिन की उपेक्षा इसलिए करती थीं क्योंकि भक्तिन के तीन पुत्रियाँ थीं जबकि उसकी जिठानियों के पास पुत्र थे। जेठानियों ने खूब कोशिश की कि भक्तिन का पति अपनी पत्नी की उपेक्षा करने लगे; लेकिन ऐसा नहीं हुआ। वह अपनी पत्नी को खूब प्यार करता था।

प्रश्न 8. भक्तिन और मेरे बीच में सेवक स्वामी का सम्बन्ध है, यह कहना कठिन है।

(i) भक्तिन और लेखिका के बीच स्वामी-सेवक का सम्बन्ध कहना कठिन क्यों है ?

(ii) भक्तिन की वेश-भूषा देखकर लेखिका को क्यों शंका हुयी ?

(iii) छात्रावास में छात्राएँ कब इकट्ठी हो जाती हैं ?

(iv) भक्तिन किन-किन से परिचित है ?

उत्तर—(i) भक्तिन ने अपने व्यवहार से यह कभी जाहिर नहीं होने दिया कि लेखिका और भक्तिन में स्वामी-सेवक का सम्बन्ध है। वह अपने को और घर को पवित्र रखने का जल छिड़क कर पवित्र रखने का उपक्रम करती थी। वह अपने को पाक-विद्या में विख्यात बताती। सूर्य और पीपल को जल देती और रसोई में कोयले से रेखा खींचकर अपने साम्राज्य की सीमा तय कर देती।

(ii) भक्तिन की वेश-भूषा देखकर लेखिका को शंका हुई क्योंकि वह वेशभूषा तो गृहस्थ और वैरागी की थी। तभी लेखिका ने उससे पूछा कि क्या वह खाना बनाना जानती है ? भक्तिन ने उत्तर दिया कि रोटी बना लेती है, साग बना लेती है और दाल राँध लेती है और साग-भाजी छौंक सकती है।

(iii) छात्रावास की बलिकाओं में से कोई अपनी चाय बनवाने के लिए देहली पर बैठी रहती है, कोई बाहर खड़ी मेरे लिए बने नास्ते को चखकर उसके स्वाद की विवेचना करती रहती है। मेरे बाहर निकलते ही बस चिड़ियों के समान उड़ जाती हैं और भीतर आते ही यथास्थान विराजमान हो जाती हैं।

(iv) लेखिका के परिचितों और साहित्यिक बन्धुओं से भी भक्तिन विशेष परिचित है, पर उनके प्रति भक्तिन के सम्मान की मात्रा लेखिका के प्रति उनके सम्मान की मात्रा पर निर्भर है और सद्भाव उनके प्रति लेखिका के सद्भाव से निश्चित होता है। इस सम्बन्ध में भक्तिन की सहजबुद्धि विस्मित कर देने वाली है।

●●

9. संस्कृति क्या है ?

— *रामधारी सिंह दिनकर*

लेखक परिचय—रामधारी सिंह 'दिनकर' हिन्दी के एक प्रमुख लेखक, कवि व निबन्धकार थे। वे आधुनिक युग के श्रेष्ठ वीर रस के कवि के रूप में स्थापित हैं। उन्होंने इतिहास, दर्शनशास्त्र और राजनीति विज्ञान की पढ़ाई पटना विश्वविद्यालय से की। उन्होंने संस्कृत, बांग्ला, अंग्रेजी और उर्दू का गहन अध्ययन किया था। 'दिनकर' स्वतन्त्रता पूर्व एक विद्रोही कवि के रूप में स्थापित हुए और स्वतन्त्रता के बाद राष्ट्रकवि के नाम से जाने गये। वे छायावादोत्तर कवियों की पहली पीढ़ी के कवि थे। एक ओर उनकी कविताओं में ओज, विद्रोह, आक्रोश और क्रान्ति की पुकार है तो दूसरी ओर कोमल शृंगारिक भावनाओं की अभिव्यक्ति है। इन्हीं दो प्रवृत्तियों का चरम उत्कर्ष हमें उनकी 'कुरूक्षेत्र' और 'उर्वशी' नामक कृतियों में मिलता है।

उर्वशी को भारतीय ज्ञानपीठ पुरस्कार जबकि कुरूक्षेत्र को विश्व के 100 सर्वश्रेष्ठ काव्यों में 74वाँ स्थान दिया गया।

दिनकर का जन्म 23 सितम्बर, 1908 को सिमरिया, मुंगेर, बिहार में हुआ था। पटना विश्वविद्यालय से बी. ए. की परीक्षा उत्तीर्ण करने के बाद वे एक विद्यालय में अध्यापक हो गये। 1934 से 1947 तक बिहार सरकार की सेवा में सब-रजिस्ट्रार और प्रचार विभाग के उपनिदेशक पदों पर कार्य किया। 1950 से 1952 तक मुजफ्फरपुर कॉलेज में हिन्दी के विभागाध्यक्ष रहे, भागलपुर विश्वविद्यालय के उपकुलपति के पद पर कार्य किया और उसके बाद भारत सरकार के हिन्दी सलाहकार बने। उन्हें पद्म विभूषण की उपाधि से भी अलंकृत किया गया। उनकी पुस्तक 'संस्कृति के चार अध्याय' के लिए साहित्य अकादमी पुरस्कार मिला। दिनकर जी अपनी लेखनी के माध्यम से सदा अमर रहेंगे।

शब्दार्थ—परिभाषा = व्याख्या, **अर्जित** = प्राप्त, **तबीयत से** = स्वभाव से, **उज्र** = परहेज, **उपकरण** = सामग्री, **स्थूल** = मोटे तौर पर, **नक्शा** = खाका, **आवेगों** = प्रवाह, **महीन** = बारीक।

सारांश

संस्कृति ऐसी चीज है जिसे जान तो सकते हैं पर उसकी परिभाषा नहीं दे सकते। जो चीज हमारे पास है वह है सभ्यता और संस्कृति। सभ्यता वस्तुओं से है और संस्कृति हमारे भीतर व्याप्त है। इस प्रकार यह नहीं कहा जा सकता कि हर सुसभ्य आदमी सुसंस्कृत ही होगा। ऐसा इसलिए नहीं कहा जा सकता क्योंकि यह आवश्यक नहीं है कि अच्छी पोशाक वाला आदमी स्वभाव से ठीक नहीं है तो वह संस्कृति के खिलाफ है। सभ्यता की पहचान ठाट-बाट है। अगर बहुत से ऐसे लोग हैं जो झोंपड़ी में रहते हैं तथा अच्छे कपड़े नहीं पहनते हैं, लेकिन उनमें विनम्रता, सदाचार आदि गुण हैं तो ऐसे लोगों को हम सभ्य तो नहीं कह सकते लेकिन उन्हें सुसंस्कृत समझने में कोई परहेज नहीं करना चाहिए।

छोटा नागपुर के लोग भी ऐसे ही हैं। प्राचीन भारत के ऋषि भी तो जंगल में रहते थे। मिट्टी के बर्तन में खाना, जीवों से प्यार करना यही उनका जीवन था। ऐसे ऋषियों ने ही संस्कृति का निर्माण किया है। संस्कृति और सभ्यता के भेद को न समझ पाने के कारण ही कठिनाइयाँ हैं। इनकी प्रगति एक साथ होती है। गृह निर्माण का उदाहरण लें—स्थूल रूप में यह सभ्यता का कार्य है लेकिन नक्शे का निर्माण संस्कृति की प्रेरणा से बनता है। इस प्रकार संस्कृति, सभ्यता का अंग बन जाती है।

प्रकृति और संस्कृति में भी अन्तर है। ईर्ष्या, लोभ, मोह, दोष, राग और कामवासना आदि प्राकृतिक गुण हैं, जो नियन्त्रण में रहकर मनुष्य को जानवरों से अलग करते हैं। जो मनुष्य इनको जितना नियन्त्रण में रखता है, वह उतना ही सुसंस्कृत है। सभ्यता के भीतर संस्कृति दूध में मक्खन और फूल में सुगन्ध की भाँति विद्यमान रहती है। सभ्यता के उकरणों को जल्दी से जुटाया जा सकता है लेकिन संस्कृति ऐसी नहीं है। कोई व्यक्ति धनी तो तुरन्त हो सकता है लेकिन धनी व्यक्ति ऊँचे पद वाली संस्कृति उतनी जल्दी नहीं सीख सकता।

जब एक समाज के लोग शताब्दियों तक जिस तरह से रहते-सहते, पढ़ते-लिखते, सोचते-समझते, राज-काज चलाते अथवा धर्म-कर्म करते हैं तब उन कार्यों से संस्कृति उत्पन्न होती है। हमारे हर कार्य में संस्कृति की झलक होती है। असल में संस्कृति जीवन जीने का एक तरीका है। जिस समाज में हमारा जन्म होता है, हम रहते हैं, उसी की संस्कृति हमारी संस्कृति है। कभी-कभी जीवन में हम कुछ और संस्कार लाते हैं, जो बाद में हमारी संस्कृति का एक अंग बन जाता है। मरने के बाद हम सम्पत्ति के साथ-साथ संस्कृति की विरासत भी सन्तानों को देकर जाते हैं। संस्कृति हमारे जीवन में व्याप्त है और इसका निर्माण भी सदियों के अनुभव से हुआ है। सभ्यता की सामग्रियाँ शरीर से जुड़ी हैं लेकिन संस्कृति आत्मा का गुण है।

आदिकाल से ही कवि दार्शनिक, कलाकार, मूर्तिकार आदि हमारी संस्कृति के रचयिता हैं। पूजा-पाठ, मकान-मन्दिर, घर-बरतन, शादी-श्राद्ध आदि जो करते आये हैं, वही संस्कृति का अंश है। संस्कृति आदान-प्रदान से बढ़ती है। संसार में शायद ही ऐसा कोई देश हो, जो यह दावा कर सके कि उस पर किसी अन्य देश की संस्कृति का प्रभाव नहीं पड़ा है।

जो संस्कृति अन्य संस्कृतियों से उनके गुणों को लेने के लिए खुली होती है उस संस्कृति का कभी नाश नहीं होता है। मुसलमानों के आगमन ने इस देश को उर्दू भाषा व कलम चित्रकारी दी। यूरोप के प्रभाव से भारत की विज्ञान के प्रति सोच बदली। संस्कृति के इसी प्रभाव ने ही राजा राममोहन राय, दयानन्द सरस्वती, रामकृष्ण परमहंस, विवेकानन्द और गाँधीजी को जन्म दिया।

सांस्कृतिक सम्पर्क का प्रभाव दर्शन और विचारों पर भी पड़ता है। इस आदान-प्रदान के कारण ही एक जाति का धार्मिक रिवाज, दूसरी जाति का रिवाज बन जाता है। एक देश की आदत दूसरे देश के लोगों की आदत में समा जाती है। भारत सांस्कृतिक दृष्टि से महान है, क्योंकि यहाँ की सामाजिक संस्कृति में अधिक जातियों की संस्कृतियाँ समायी हुई हैं।

अभ्यास-प्रश्न

प्रश्न 1. 'संस्कृति क्या है ?' निबन्ध में निबन्धकार का क्या उद्देश्य है ?

अथवा

'संस्कृति क्या है ?' निबन्ध के माध्यम से निबन्धकार कौन-सा सन्देश देना चाहता है ?

उत्तर—साहित्य जीवन के यथार्थ को प्रदर्शित करता है तथा उसके सामने आदर्श भी प्रस्तुत करता है। इस निबन्ध में भी दिनकर जी ने सभ्यता और संस्कृति के अन्तर को स्पष्ट कर पाठकों के समक्ष रखने का प्रयास किया है। उन्होंने यह स्पष्ट करने का प्रयास किया कि सभ्यता की पहचान ठाट-बाट है लेकिन संस्कृति की पहचान विचारों से होती है। जहाँ सभ्यता का सम्बन्ध शरीर से है, वहीं संस्कृति का सम्बन्ध आत्मा से है।

संस्कृति ऐसी चीज है जिसे लक्षणों से तो हम जान सकते हैं लेकिन उसको परिभाषित नहीं कर सकते हैं। सभ्यता एक ऐसी चीज है जो हमारे पास है, संस्कृति एक ऐसा गुण है, जो हममें व्याप्त है। जब हम कोई घर बनाते हैं तो वह स्थूल रूप में सभ्यता का कार्य होता है, मगर घर के नक्शे के सम्बन्ध में हमारी पसन्द-नापसन्द का निर्णय संस्कृति करती है। जो आदमी अपने दुर्गुणों पर जितना विजयी होता है, उसकी संस्कृति उतनी ही ऊँची मानी जाती है।

दिनकर जी के अनुसार संस्कृति का निर्माण शताब्दियों में होता है। असल में संस्कृति जिन्दगी का एक तरीका है और यह तरीका सदियों से एकत्र होकर समाज पर छा जाता है। एक संस्कृति हमेशा दूसरी संस्कृति को प्रभावित करती रहती है। सांस्कृतिक दृष्टि से वह देश ज्यादा शक्तिशाली होता है जिसने अपने अन्दर अनेक प्रकार की संस्कृतियों को समाहित किया है। इसीलिए भारत देश महान है, क्योंकि यहाँ की सामाजिक संस्कृति में अधिक से अधिक जातियों की संस्कृतियों ने मिलकर भारत को बनाया है। यहाँ मुसलमानों ने उर्दू लायी,

मुगलों ने चित्रकारी को एक नई दिशा दी तो वहीं यूरोपीय सम्बन्धों ने विज्ञापन विचारधारा को एक नया आयाम भी दिया है। इस प्रकार भारत की संस्कृति में इनके मिलने से एक महान संस्कृति बन जाती है।

इस प्रकार से इस निबन्ध में निबन्धकार का यही उद्देश्य है कि वह सभ्यता और संस्कृति के अन्तर को पाठकों के समक्ष रखे। साथ ही लेखक ने यह सन्देश भी देने का प्रयास किया है कि कोई व्यक्ति अचानक धनी बनकर सभ्य तो बन सकता है लेकिन उस धनी या ऊँचाई की संस्कृति को तुरन्त नहीं समझा जा सकता है। निबन्ध में संस्कृति की समझ और उसके प्रभाव को पाठकों के समक्ष बड़े ही प्रभावशाली ढंग से रखने का प्रयास किया गया है जिस उद्देश्य में लेखक को काफी सफलता मिली है।

प्रश्न 2. 'संस्कृति क्या है ?' निबन्ध के शीर्षक के औचित्य पर प्रकाश डालिए।

उत्तर—'संस्कृति क्या है ?' यह निबन्ध दिनकर जी का एक विचारात्मक निबन्ध है जिसमें दिनकर जी ने संस्कृति के सम्बन्ध में अपने विचारों की श्रृंखला को शब्दों द्वारा रूपायित कर पाठकों के समक्ष रखने का प्रयास किया है। इस निबन्ध में संस्कृति को अलग-अलग आयामों से देखने का प्रयास किया गया है।

प्रस्तुत निबन्ध में संस्कृति की उत्पत्ति, संस्कृति और सभ्यता में अन्तर, संस्कृति का महत्व, संस्कृति के आदान प्रदान का महत्व, संस्कृति की विशेषताओं के साथ ही साथ भारत की सांस्कृति विशेषताओं का भी वर्णन श्रृंखलाबद्ध रूप में करने का प्रयास दिनकर जी ने किया है।

निबन्धकार के अनुसार मोटर, महल, पोशाक और अच्छा भोजन आदि स्थूल वस्तुएँ सभ्यता के सामान है, वहीं दूसरी ओर पोशाक पहनने और भोजन करने में जो कला है, वह संस्कृति है। इस प्रकार संस्कृति और सभ्यता दोनों अलग-अलग है। यह नहीं कहा जा सकता है कि हर सभ्य आदमी सुसंस्कृत ही होगा।

इसी प्रकार संस्कृति और प्रकृति के बीच अन्तर को भी समझाया गया है। क्रोध, लोभ, मोह, राग, द्वेष आदि मनुष्य के प्रकृतिप्रदत्त गुण हैं। इनका अनियन्त्रण मनुष्य को जानवर बना देगा, इसलिए मनुष्य इन पर नियन्त्रण करने का प्रयास करता है। जो व्यक्ति इन पर जितना अच्छा नियन्त्रण रख पाता है, उसकी संस्कृति उतनी ही अच्छी है।

संस्कृति की व्यापकता के सम्बन्ध में लेखक का यह कथन दृष्टव्य है—''यह सभ्यता के भीतर उसी तरह व्याप्त रहती है जैसे दूध में मक्खन या फूलों में सुगन्ध। ''लेखक यह भी स्पष्ट करना चाहता है कि सभ्यता की सामग्रियों को बड़ी सरलता से जुटाया जा सकता है, लेकिन संस्कृति को तुरन्त नहीं सीखा जा सकता है।

इस प्रकार अन्त में यह कहा जा सकता है कि इस निबन्ध में दिनकर जी ने संस्कृति के सभी पहलुओं को दृष्टिपात किया है। विभिन्न दिशाओं से संस्कृति की महत्ता को विवेचित किया है। इसलिए इस निबन्ध का शीर्षक 'संस्कृति क्या है ?' सर्वथा, सटीक, सार्थक व समीचीन प्रतीत होता है।

प्रश्न 3. दिनकर जी के निबन्ध 'संस्कृति क्या है ?' के अनुसार संस्कृति और सभ्यता में क्या अन्तर है ?

उत्तर—दिनकर जी ने सामाजिक और आर्थिक समानता और शोषण के खिलाफ साहित्य की रचना की। एक प्रगतिवादी और मानववादी साहित्यकार के रूप में उन्होंने ऐतिहासिक पात्रों और घटनाओं को ओजस्वी और प्रखर शब्दों का तानाबना दिया। प्रसिद्ध आलोचक नामवर सिंह जी का कहना है कि दिनकर जी सचमुच अपने युग के सूर्य थे।

दिनकर जी के अनुसार संस्कृति में सभ्यता से भिन्न गुण हैं। मोटर, महल, सड़क, हवाई जहाज, पोशाक और अच्छा भोजन, ये संस्कृति नहीं सभ्यता के समान हैं। लेकिन पोशाक पहनने और भोजन करने में जो कला है वह संस्कृति है। हर सुसभ्य आदमी सुसंस्कृत ही होगा, ऐसा नहीं कहा जा सकता। छोटा नागपुर की जनता पूर्ण रूप से सभ्य तो नहीं कही जा सकती, क्योंकि सभ्यता के बड़े-बड़े उपकरण उसके पास नहीं है, लेकिन दया-माया और सदाचार की कमी नहीं है। अतः वे सुसंस्कृत कहे जा सकते हैं।

संस्कृति और सभ्यता की प्रगति एक साथ होती है। वे एक-दूसरे को प्रभावित करते हैं। जब हम घर बनाने लगते हैं तो यह सभ्यता का कार्य होता है लेकिन उस घर का नक्शा बनाने में संस्कृति निर्णय करती है। संस्कृति की प्रेरणा से हम घर बनाते हैं जो बाद में चलकर हमारी सभ्यता का अंग बन जाता है।

सभ्यता तो आसानी से नष्ट हो सकती है किन्तु संस्कृति का विनाश आसानी से नहीं किया जा सकता।

सभ्यता के सामानों को आसानी से और जल्दी से जुटाया जा सकता है, लेकिन संस्कृति आसानी से नहीं आ सकती। संस्कृति तो विरासत में मिलती है, जिसकी रचना और विकास में सदियों का अनुभव लगा हुआ है।

इस प्रकार अन्त में यह कहा जा सकता है कि इस निबन्ध के माध्यम से दिनकर जी ने सभ्यता और संस्कृति की भिन्नता को बड़ी सहजता से व्यक्त किया है। सभ्यता और संस्कृति एक-दूसरे से जुड़े होने बावजूद एक-दूसरे से पूरी तरह भिन्न हैं।

प्रश्न 4. ''संस्कृति का स्वभाव है कि वह आदान-प्रदान से बढ़ती है।'' इस कथन के आलोक में आदान-प्रदान से संस्कृति पर पढ़ने वाले प्रभाव का वर्णन कीजिए।

उत्तर—संसार में शायद ही कोई ऐसा देश हो जो यह दावा कर सके कि उस पर किसी अन्य देश की संस्कृति का प्रभाव नहीं पड़ा है। संस्कृति का यह स्वभाव ही है कि वह आदान-प्रदान से बढ़ती है। ठीक उसी प्रकार जैसे दो व्यक्तियों की संगति का प्रभाव दोनों पर पड़ता है। जब भी दो देश किसी कारण से एक-दूसरे के सम्पर्क में आते हैं, तब उनकी संस्कृतियाँ एक-दूसरे को प्रभावित करने लगती हैं।

आदान-प्रदान की प्रक्रिया संस्कृति की जान है और इसी के सहारे वह अपने को जिन्दा रखती है। जब भी दो जातियाँ मिलती हैं, उनके सम्पर्क या संघर्ष से जिन्दगी की एक नई धारा निकलती है। एक देश में जो दार्शनिक और महात्मा उत्पन्न होते हैं, उनकी आवाज दूसरे देशों में भी मिलते-जुलते दार्शनिक और महात्माओं को जन्म देती है। एक जाति का रिवाज दूसरी जाति का रिवाज बन जाता है और एक देश की आदत दूसरे देश की आदत में समा जाती है।

सांस्कृतिक दृष्टि से वह देश विशेष है, जिसने विश्व के अधिक से अधिक देशों और जातियों की संस्कृतियों को आत्मसात कर लिया है। वह संस्कृति सबसे ज्यादा फलती-फूलती है जिसमें दूसरी संस्कृतियों को अपने भीतर समाहित करने की क्षमता होती है। एक देश में जो धर्म खड़ा होता है, वह दूसरे देशों के धर्मों को भी बहुत कुछ बदल देता है। इस प्रभाव के आलोक में जब हम भारत की बात करें तो यह दृष्टव्य है कि भारतीय संस्कृति भी एक महान संस्कृति है, क्योंकि यहाँ की संस्कृति ने अनेक प्रकार की संस्कृतियों को अपनी संस्कृति में समाविष्ट कर लिया है।

प्रश्न 5. निबन्ध के आधार पर रामधारी सिंह दिनकर जी की भाषा शैली पर प्रकाश डालिए।

उत्तर—हिन्दी साहित्य के अपने युग में सूर्य के समान अपनी प्रतिभा से हिन्दी साहित्य जगत को प्रभावित करने वाले दिनकर जी का भाषा पर विशेष अधिकार था। पद्य की भाँति गद्य में भी दिनकर जी की भाषा सहज और प्रभावशाली है। दिनकर जी के निबन्धों में भावुकता, सरसता और कोमलता के साथ-साथ आवेगपूर्ण शैली भी विद्यमान है।

दिनकर जी अपनी बात को सहज और स्वाभाविक रूप से कहते थे। उन्होंने इस निबन्ध में ऐसी भाषा का प्रयोग नहीं किया, जो कृत्रिम अथवा प्रयासजन्य हो। दिनकर जी की भाषा में बोलचाल की भाषा की प्रधानता रही है। बोलचाल की भाषा के माध्यम से उन्होंने गम्भीर तथ्यों को भी बड़ी सरलता से प्रस्तुत कर दिया है। शुद्ध साहित्यिक भाषा के स्थान पर दिनकर जी ने जन-सामान्य की भाषा को अधिक तरजीह दी है।

दिनकर जी ने प्रसंग व भावानुकूल शब्दों का प्रयोग किया है जो भाषा के प्रभाव को द्विगुणित कर देता है। भाषा में उपयुक्त उदाहरणों का प्रयोग जहाँ एक ओर विषय-वस्तु को सहज बन देता है वहीं दूसरी ओर उसके प्रभाव को व्यंजित करने में भी सहायक होता है। इसका एक उदाहरण दृष्टव्य है—

''निष्कर्ष यह है कि संस्कृति सभ्यता की अपेक्षा महीन चीज होती है। यह सभ्यता के भीतर उसी तरह व्याप्त रहती है जैसे दूध में मक्खन या फूलों में सुगन्ध. . . . .।

इस उदाहरण में मक्खन और सुगन्ध का विधान संस्कृति की व्यापकता व उसके प्रभाव को बड़ी ही सरलता से व्यंजित कर देता है।

दिनकर जी की शैली इस निबन्ध में विचारात्मक है, जो विषयवस्तु के प्रस्तुतीकरण में पूर्णतया सफल सिद्ध हुई है। इस शैली के माध्यम से दिनकर जी ने गम्भीर विषय को भी बड़ी कुशलता और बोधगम्य ढंग से प्रस्तुत किया है। इस प्रकार भाषा व शैली की दृष्टि से दिनकर जी का यह निबन्ध अद्वितीय है।

प्रश्न 6. और यह भी नहीं कहा जा सकता कि हर सुसंस्कृत आदमी सभ्य ही होता है, क्योंकि सभ्यता की पहचान सुख-सुविधा और ठाट-वाट है।

(i) सभ्यता की पहचान क्या है ?

(ii) और कौन लोग भी सभ्य होते हैं ?

(iii) नागपुर आदिवासियों को लेखक ने कैसा बताया है ?

(iv) ऋषिगणों के बारे में लेखक ने क्या बताया है ?

उत्तर—(i) हर सुसंस्कृत आदमी सभ्य ही होता है, क्योंकि सभ्यता की पहचान सुख-सुविधा और ठाठ-बाट से होती है। कुछ आदमी झोंपड़ियों में रहकर भी विनय और सदाचार रखते हैं। दूसरों के दुःख से दुःखी होते हैं और उनका दुःख दूर करने का प्रयास भी करते हैं।

(ii) कुछ लोग जो सड़े-गले झोंपड़ों में रहते हैं, जिनके पास काफी कपड़े भी नहीं होते और न ही उन्हें कपड़े पहनने का ढंग ही आता है, लेकिन फिर भी उनमें विनय और सदाचार होता है। दूसरों का दुःख दूर करने के लिए स्वयं भी मुसीबत उठाने को तैयार रहते हैं।

(iii) छोटा नागपुर की आदिवासी जनता पूर्णरूप से सभ्य तो नहीं कही जा सकती; क्योंकि सभ्यता के बड़े-बड़े उपकरण उसके पास नहीं है, लेकिन दया-माया सच्चाई और सदाचार उनमें कम नहीं है। अतः उसे सुसंस्कृत समझने में कोई ऐतराज नहीं होना चाहिए।

(iv) प्राचीन भारत में ऋषिगण जंगलों में रहते थे। फूस की झोंपड़ियों में वास करना, जंगली जीवों से दोस्ती और प्यार करना, किसी भी मोटे काम को अपने हाथ से करना, पत्तों में खाना और मिट्टी के बर्तनों में रसोई पकाना, यही उनकी जिन्दगी थी। फिर भी वे ऋषिगण सुसंस्कृत नहीं थे, बल्कि वे हमारी जाति की संस्कृति का निर्माण करते थे।

प्रश्न 7. संस्कृति ऐसी चीज नहीं है जिसकी रचना दस-बीस या सौ-पचास वर्षों में की जा सकती हो। अनेक शताब्दियों तक एक समाज के लोग जिस तरह खाते पीते, रहते-सहते, पढ़ते-लिखते, सोचते-समझते और राज-काज चलाते अथवा धर्म-कर्म करते हैं, उन सभी कार्यों से संस्कृति उत्पन्न होती है।

(i) संस्कृति कैसे बनती रहती है ?

(ii) संस्कृति की पहचान कैसे होती है ?

(iii) संस्कृति क्या है ?

(iv) साधारण नियम क्या है ?

उत्तर—(i) संस्कृति ऐसी चीज नहीं जिसकी रचना दस-बीस या पचास सौ वर्षों में की जा सकती हो। अनेक शताब्दियों तक एक समाज के लोग जिस तरह खाते-पीते, रहते, पढ़ते-लिखते, सोचते-समझते और राज-काज चलाते अथवा धर्म-कर्म करते हैं, उन सभी कार्यों से उसकी संस्कृति बनती है।

(ii) हम जो भी कार्य करते हैं जैसे खाना-पीना, रहना-सहना, पढ़ना-लिखना सोचना-समझना, राजकाज चलाना अथवा धर्म-कर्म करना इससे मनुष्य की संस्कृति बनती है और इसी से उसकी पहचान होती है।

(iii) सभ्यता वह चीज है जो हमारे पास है, संस्कृति वह गुण है जो हममें व्याप्त है। मोटर, महल, सड़क, हवाई जहाज, पोशाक और अच्छा भोजन ये तथा इसके समान सारी अन्य स्थूल वस्तुएँ, संस्कृति नहीं सभ्यता के समान हैं।

(iv) साधारण नियम यह है कि संस्कृति और सभ्यता की प्रगति, अधिकतर एक साथ होती है और दोनों का एक-दूसरे पर प्रभाव भी पड़ता है। उदाहरण के लिए हम जब कोई घर बनाते हैं, तो स्थूल रूप से यह सभ्यता का कार्य होता है।

प्रश्न 8. जो जाति केवल देना ही जानती है, लेना कुछ नहीं, उसकी संस्कृति का एक-न-एक दिन दिवाला निकल जाता है।

(i) किसका दिवाला कब निकल जाता है ?

(ii) संस्कृति को क्या भाव ले डूबता है ?

(iii) आदान-प्रदान की प्रतिक्रिया क्या है ?

(iv) कौन-सी जाति अधिक महान समझी जानी चाहिए ?

उत्तर—(i) जो जाति केवल देना ही जानती है, लेना कुछ नहीं जानती, उसकी संस्कृति का दिवाला एक दिन निकल जाता है। अर्थात् एक दिन वह समाप्त हो जाती है।

(ii) कूपमंडूपता और दुनिया से रूठकर अलग बैठने का भाव संस्कृति को ले डूबता है। हम जो हैं जहाँ है वही सब कुछ है इसके अलावा दुनिया में और कुछ नहीं है ऐसा सोचना संस्कृति को महान नुकसान पहुँचाता है।

(iii) इस देश में बुद्ध और ईसा मसीह के विचार आये तथा लोगों ने उनको समझा। अन्य बाहर के देशों में कवि हुए उनकी रचनाओं का प्रभाव हमारी संस्कृति पर पड़ा। जब भी दो जातियाँ मिलती हैं, उनके सम्पर्क एवं संघर्ष से जिन्दगी की एक नई धारा फूट निकलती है जिसका प्रभाव दोनों पर पड़ता है। यही आदान-प्रदान की प्रक्रिया है। इसी के सहारे संस्कृति अपने को जिन्दा रखती है।

(iv) सांस्कृतिक दृष्टि से वह देश और जाति अधिक शक्तिशाली और महान समझी जानी चाहिए जिसने विश्व के अधिक-से-अधिक जातियों की संस्कृतियों को अपने भीतर जज्ब करके, उन्हें पचा कर के बड़े-से-बड़े समन्वय को उत्पन्न किया है। भारत देश और भारतीय जाति इस दृष्टि से संसार में सबसे महान है। क्योंकि यहाँ की सामाजिक संस्कृति में अधिक-से-अधिक जातियों की संस्कृतियाँ पची हुई हैं।

10. मजबूरी

—मन्नू भण्डारी

लेखिका परिचय—मन्नू भण्डारी का जन्म 3 अप्रैल, 1931 को मध्य प्रदेश में मंदसौर जिले के भानपुरा गाँव में हुआ था। मन्नू जी के बचपन का नाम महेन्द्र कुमारी था। लेखन के लिए उन्होंने मन्नू नाम का चुनाव किया। उन्होंने एम. ए. तक की शिक्षा पाई और वर्षों तक दिल्ली के मीरांडा हाउस में अध्यापिका रहीं। धर्मयुग में धारावाहिक रूप से प्रकाशित उपन्यास 'आपका बंटी' से लोकप्रियता प्राप्त करने वाली मन्नू भण्डारी विक्रम विश्वविद्यालय, उज्जैन में प्रेमचन्द सृजनपीठ की अध्यक्षा भी रहीं। लेखन का संस्कार उन्हें विरासत में मिला। उनके पिता सुख सम्पतराय भी जाने-माने लेखक थे।

मन्नू भण्डारी ने कहानियाँ और उपन्यास दोनों लिखे हैं। 'एक प्लेट सैलाब' (1962), 'मैं हार गई' (1957), 'तीन निगाहों की एक तस्वीर', 'यही सच है' (1966), 'त्रिशंकु' और 'आँखों देखा झूठ' उनके महत्वपूर्ण कहानी संग्रह हैं। विवाह विच्छेद की त्रासदी में पिस रहे एक बच्चे को केन्द्र में रखकर लिखा गया उनका उपन्यास 'आपका बंटी' (1971) हिन्दी के सफलतम उपन्यासों में गिना जाता है। लेखक राजेन्द्र यादव के साथ लिखा गया उनका उपन्यास 'एक इंच मुस्कान' (1962) पढ़े लिखे आधुनिक लोगों की एक दुखान्त प्रेमकथा है जिसका एक-एक अंक लेखक-द्वय ने क्रमानुसार लिखा था। आपने 'बिना दीवारों का घर' (1966) शीर्षक से एक नाटक भी लिखा है।

मन्नू भण्डारी का नौकरशाही में व्याप्त भ्रष्टाचार के बीच आम आदमी की पीड़ा और दर्द की गहराई को उद्घाटित करने वाले उनके उपन्यास 'महाभोज' (1979) पर आधारित नाटक अत्यधिक लोकप्रिय हुआ था। इसी प्रकार 'यही सच है' पर आधारित 'रजनीगंधा' नामक फिल्म अत्यन्त लोकप्रिय हुई थी और उसको 1974 की सर्वश्रेष्ठ फिल्म का पुरस्कार भी प्राप्त हुआ था।

इनकी साहित्यिक उपलब्धियों के लिए इन्हें हिन्दी अकादमी के शिखर सम्मान सहित अनेक पुरस्कार प्राप्त हो चुके हैं जिनमें भारतीय भाषा परिषद् कोलकाता, राजस्थान संगीत नाटक अकादमी तथा उत्तर प्रदेश हिन्दी संस्थान के पुरस्कार शामिल हैं।

शब्दार्थ—लोरी = बच्चों को सुलाने के लिए गीत, **ताल** = ठेका अथवा लय, **गठिया** = जोड़ों का दर्द, **पुलकित** = आनन्दित, **लहजे** = शैली, **कातर** = व्याकुल, **मायूसी** = निराशा, **औषधालय** = दवाखाना, **उपेक्षित** = अमान्य, **साध** = इच्छा, **परिहास** = मजाक, **चिरायु** = लम्बी उम्र, **सामंजस्य** = तालमेल।

सारांश

प्रस्तुत कहानी के प्रारम्भ में ही बूढ़ी अम्मा लोरी गाते हुए लाल मिट्टी से कमरा लीप रही हैं। सर्दी का समय है। जब बर्तन मलने के लिए नर्बदा आती है तो अम्मा से यह पूछती है कि आपको गठिया है फिर भी इतनी सर्दी में आँगन लीपने बैठ गईं। अम्मा कहती हैं कि मेरा बेटू आ रहा है। तब नर्बदा समझ जाती है कि अम्मा के बेटे रामेश्वर आ रहे हैं। अम्मा कहती है कि देखो कैसे छुट्टी मिलते ही वह दौड़ा चला आ रहा है। इतना बड़ा हो गया है फिर भी मेरी गोद में जरूर सोयेगा। पर इस बार मैं मना कर दूँगी कि अब तू नहीं गोद में बेटू सोयेगा। यह कहकर हँसती है और नर्बदा से यह कहती हैं कि मैंने खड़िया भिगो दी है जरा बाहर जाकर इसे लगा दो। इतना कहकर वे फिर से गाना गाने में मगन हो जाती हैं।

गाना गाते समय अम्मा कहती है कि मैं इसके आगे का गाना भूल गई। जब रामेश्वर छोटा था तभी ये सब याद थीं और रामेश्वर के बाद कोई छोटा बच्चा घर में नहीं था जिसके कारण मैं सब भूल गई। रामेश्वर को बिना लोरी सुने नींद ही न आती थी। फिर वह बेटू के बारे में कहती हैं कि जब बहू बेटू को लेकर आई थी, तब वह दो महीने का था। मैं जब पास जाकर खड़ी हो जाती तो मुझे ही देखा करता था। सूरत रामेश्वर के जैसे ही है।

अम्मा का काम समाप्त हो जाता है और अम्मा जब उठने का प्रयास करती हैं तो उनके मुँह से आह निकल जाती है। तब वह नर्बदा को बुलाकर उसकी सहायता से उठती है और नर्बदा हाथ-पैर धुलाकर उन्हें

खटिया पर लिटा देती है। नर्बदा के कहने पर कि सबके घर बेटे-बहू आते हैं, अम्मा कहती है कि मेरा बेटा तीन बरस के बाद आ रहा है।

वह नर्बदा से कहती है कि मेरे रामेश्वर को कुछ मत कहना नौकरी के कारण नहीं आ पाता। यह तो मुझे ही पता है कि मेरे बिना उसके दिन कैसे बीतते हैं। यह कहते हुए अम्मा की आँखें डबडबा जाती हैं। नर्बदा उनके यहाँ बरसों से काम करती है। हमेशा बेटे की बात पर खरी-खोटी सुना दिया करती थी लेकिन आज ऐसा नहीं हुआ। जाते समय अम्मा ने कहा कि ग्वाले को कल जल्दी दूध देने के लिए कह देना और यह भी कहना कि अब दूध ज्यादा लगेगा। इतना ही नहीं कल से तुम भी काम करने के बाद यहीं रहना तथा लेन-देन की चिन्ता मत करना।

इसके बाद अम्मा कुछ न कर सकी और लोरी गाते हुए सो गई। वह भोर होने से पहले उठ गईं। मन के उत्साह में उनकी सारी तकलीफें खो गईं। बेटे और पोते से मिलने की उमंग में ठण्ड भी जाती रही। दूध गरम करना, पानी गरम करना है, चाय की तैयारी करनी है यही सब सोचने लगीं और ठिठुरते हुए अम्मा ने बेटे-बहू को गरम करने के सारे आयोजन कर डाले। तरकारी भी काट डाली। तभी एक ताँगा आकर रुकता है, अम्मा दौड़कर जाती हैं और रामेश्वर की गोद से बच्चे को ले लेती है। रामेश्वर को भी अपनी बाहों के घेरे में ले लेती हैं। बच्चा रोने लगता है तो अम्मा यह कहते हुए बच्चे को उसकी माँ के पास दे देती हैं कि अभी मुझे नहीं पहचानता इसलिए रो रहा है।

चाय-पानी के बाद रामेश्वर नहाने चला जाता है तब अम्मा बहू से बात करती है। बहू से कहती है कि तुमने खबर ही नहीं दी कि तुम्हें बच्चा होने वाला है। तब बहू कहती है कि अम्मा जब तक मैं यहाँ हूँ आप बेटू को अपने ही पास रखिये, क्योंकि एक को सम्भालना ही बहुत मुश्किल हो जाता है।

अम्मा को तो विश्वास ही नहीं हुआ। वह बहू को आशीर्वाद देते हुए कहती हैं कि इस सूने घर में भी एक बच्चा रहेगा तो मेरा जन्म सफल हो जायेगा। रामेश्वर के जाने के बाद तो यह घर मसान जैसा लगता है। भगवान तुम्हें दूसरा भी बेटा दें, तुम उसे पाल लेना। मैं समझूँगी कि तुमने मेरा रामेश्वर वापस दे दिया। तुम अपनी बात से मुड़ना मत। तभी रामेश्वर आता है तथा अम्मा यह बात रामेश्वर को बताती हैं। तभी वैद्यराज भी आ गये, अम्मा ने उनसे भी कहा कि बहू दो-दो को नहीं सम्भाल सकेगी इसलिए बेटू यहीं पर रहेगा। अब इस खुशी मे उनको उठने-बैठने में जरा भी तकलीफ नहीं हो रही है।

दोपहर को नर्बदा से और घर में जो कोई भी आता उसे यही खबर सुना रही थी। वह इतना प्रचार इसलिए कर रही थी कि बहू का मन बदल भी जाये तो शरम के मारे वह अपना इरादा बदल न पाये। बेटू को लेकर उनके शिथिल और नीरस जीवन में उत्साह आ गया था। वह बेटू को लादे फिरती हैं और कहती हैं कि यह तो फूल जैसा हल्का है।

निश्चित समय पर शीशी में दूध भरना, शीशी साफ करना आदि सभी काम अम्मा के लिए बिल्कुल नये थे। उन्होंने औषधालय से घड़ी मँगवा ली जिससे समय-समय पर बेटू को दूध पिलाया जा सके। वे सारा काम बड़ी सतर्कता से करती थीं। कभी-कभी जब दूध भरते समय उनके हाथ से दूध गिर जाता तो वे बहू से कहती, जल्दी ही सीख लूँगी।

बीस दिन बाद जब बहू अपनी माँ के घर जाती है तब बेटू उसके साथ जाने की जिद्द नहीं करता। बेटू को दादी के असीम दुलार में रहना अच्छा लगा। महीना बीतने पर पता चला कि बहू को दूसरा लड़का हुआ। यह सुनकर उन्हें यह सन्तोष हुआ कि अब बेटू सिर्फ मेरा है। जाने से पहले रामेश्वर ने अम्मा और पिताजी के लिए बहुत सारे कपड़े बनवाये जिसे अम्मा सारे मुहल्ले को दिखाती। कहती फिरती रामेश्वर का बस चले तो सारा घर मुझ पर ही लुटा दे। अब बुढ़ापे में ये छपी साड़ियाँ पहनकर कहाँ जाऊँगी ? जाते समय रामेश्वर से कहा कि साल में एक बार तो आया करो कम से कम अपनी बूढ़ी माँ को. . . इसके आगे वे कुछ और न कह सकीं। वे रामेश्वर के ताँगे को तब तक देखती रही जब तक कि वह आँखों से ओझल नहीं हो गया।

दूसरे साल रामेश्वर नहीं आया केवल रमा आई शायद बेटू को देखने के लिए। रमा यह देखती है कि बेटू तो बहुत जिद्दी हो गया है। बिना अम्मा की लोरी सुने उसे नींद न आती। गली के गन्दे बच्चों के साथ

खेलता। ये सारी बातें रमा को अच्छी नहीं लगी। अन्त में उसने अम्मा से यह कहा कि 'अम्मा आपने तो इसे बिगाड़कर धूल कर रखा है।' दादी ने हँसते हुए जवाब दिया कि रामेश्वर भी ऐसा ही था। समय आने पर सब छूट जायेगा। बहू खून का घूँट पीकर रह गई पर पप्पू के छोटा होने के कारण बेटू को न ले जा सकी। मुम्बई पहुँचते ही बहू ने माँ को खरी भाषा में पत्र लिखा और बेटू को स्कूल में भर्ती कराने के लिए कहा। अम्मा ने कहा कि इतना छोटा बच्चा कैसे स्कूल जायेगा, बहू तो बौरा गई है।

दो साल बाद रमा, रामेश्वर अपने छोटे बेटे पप्पू के साथ आते हैं। पप्पू तो अंग्रेजी की छोटी-छोटी कविताएँ बोल लेता था। लेकिन बेटू तो दो साल बाद भी वैसा ही था सिर्फ उम्र में वह बड़ा हो गया था। रमा अब यह कहने लगी कि किसी भी हाल में बेटू को ले जाना होगा, नहीं तो यहाँ उसकी जिन्दगी चौपट हो जायेगी। ये बातें हुई कि वह अम्मा के बिना कैसे रहेगा ? अम्मा को भी तो दु:ख होगा। लेकिन रमा अम्मा के सुख के लिए अपने बेटे की जिन्दगी नहीं खराब करना चाहती थी।

अब रमा बेटू को अपने से हिलाने की कोशिश करने लगी। जब अम्मा ने यह सुना तो उनके पैरों तले जमीन खिसक गई। उन्हें अपने कानों पर विश्वास न हुआ। वह मेरे बिना पलभर भी तो नहीं रहता। अम्मा कहती है कि बहू मैं इसे खूब पढ़ाऊँगी तू चिन्ता मत कर पर इसे मत ले जा। रमा ने कहा कि यदि आप सचमुच इसे प्यार करती हैं तो इसे जाने दें। अन्त में रमा काफी बहस के बाद बेटू को ले जाने के लिए कहती है। दो दिन बाद औषधालय के एकमात्र नौकर और दोनों बच्चों के साथ रमा अपनी माँ के यहाँ चली जाती है। अम्मा सबसे यही कहती कि बच्चा नहीं सँभाला जाता था इसलिए माँ के साथ भेज दिया।

तीन दिन बाद औषधालय का नौकर आकर यह खबर देता है कि बेटू को बुखार हो गया है तो अम्मा जाकर उसे लाने के लिए तैयार होती है। और तीसरे दिन ही बेटू को ले आती हैं।

इस प्रकार एक साल फिर निकल गया, रमा ने बेटू का वही रवैया देखा। तब उसने सीधा बेटू को मुम्बई ले जाने का विचार बनाया और अम्मा के लाख मना करने पर भी बहू बेटू को लेकर चल दी। अम्मा ने सारी जमा-पूँजी खर्च कर शिब्बू को फिर से साथ कर दिया। अब जब कोई भी अम्मा के पास आता तो वह उससे यही कहती कि बेटू किसी तरह रमा के साथ रह जाये तो मैं सवा रुपये का प्रसाद चढ़ाऊँगी। शिब्बू लौटकर आता है और अम्मा को यह बताता है कि बहू जी ने बेटू को हिला लिया। बहू जी के मकान में बहुत सारे बच्चे हैं, सबसे उसकी दोस्ती हो गई है। शिब्बू कहे जा रहा था कि अम्मा अब तुम्हारी चिन्ता दूर हुई। अब तो तुम प्रसाद चढ़ाओ।

अन्त में अम्मा कहती है कि भगवान ने मेरी सुन ली। सवा रुपये देकर प्रसाद मँगाया और भर-भर आती आँखों को पोंछते हुए यही कहती रहीं कि बेटू मुझे भूल ही गया। इस तरह से कहानी समाप्त हो जाती है।

अभ्यास-प्रश्न

प्रश्न 1. 'मजबूरी' कहानी में कहानीकार का क्या उद्देश्य है ?

अथवा

'मजबूरी' कहानी के माध्यम से कहानीकार कौन-सा सन्देश देना चाहता है ?

उत्तर—हिन्दी कहानीकार मन्नू भण्डारी जी की कहानी 'मजबूरी' की जब उद्देश्य के आधार पर समीक्षा की जाती है, तो यह पाया जाता है कि आजकल माता-पिता और बच्चों के बीच में पीढ़ियों का जो अन्तराल है वह इतना बढ़ गया है कि वे एक-दूसरे को समझ तक नहीं पाते हैं। इस कहानी में बच्चे के अध्ययन की समस्या को लेकर रमा परेशान होती है जिससे अन्त में उसे यह निर्णय लेना पड़ता है कि बेटू को अपने साथ ले जाने में ही उसकी भलाई है। रमा के दोनों बच्चों को सम्भालने की समस्या, अम्मा का बेटू के प्रति दुलार और अन्त में अम्मा की मानसिक स्थिति को समझ नहीं पाता, ये सारी समस्याएँ समाज की मूलभूत समस्याएँ हैं। यहाँ अम्मा और रमा के माध्यम से इन सभी समस्याओं को पाठकों के समक्ष प्रस्तुत करना ही कहानीकार का उद्देश्य प्रतीत होता है।

कहानी में अलग-अलग स्तरों और चरण में चरित्रों की मजबूरियाँ पाठक के समक्ष उपस्थित हो जाती है। रामेश्वर का नौकरी के कारण माँ से न मिल पाना, उसकी मजबूरी है। उसी प्रकार रमा भी दो बच्चों को सँभाल पाने में स्वयं को असमर्थ पाती है, इसलिए उसका बेटू को अम्मा के पास छोड़ना मजबूरी है। इस प्रकार कहानी का प्रत्येक पात्र किसी न किसी विवशता या मजबूरी का शिकार है।

इस कहानी के माध्यम से विवशता की इस पारिवारिक गाथा को पाठकों के समक्ष प्रस्तुत करना ही कहानीकार का उद्देश्य लगता है। इस कहानी में सामाजिक, आर्थिक, पारिवारिक तथा सांस्कृतिक समस्याओं का हृदयस्पर्शी चित्रण मिलता है। कहानीकार ने अम्मा तथा रमा के रूप में नारी-जीवन एक चित्र प्रस्तुत किया है। इस कहानी में मजबूरी एक मूलभूत प्रश्न बनकर समाज तथा समाज के व्यवहार पर आघात करती है।

समाज की इन समस्याओं को दिखाना लोकमंगल का कार्य है जो समाज के हित से जुड़ा हुआ है। इसके द्वारा समाज को यह सन्देश जाता है कि हमें अपनी संवेदनाओं तथा सहानुभूति पर काबू रखना चाहिए। इस कहानी में कहानीकार का उद्देश्य सिर्फ आनन्द प्रदान करना ही नहीं बल्कि सामाजिक हित के लिए जागरूकता का सन्देश भी देना है।

प्रश्न 2. 'मजबूरी' कहानी के शीर्षक के औचित्य पर प्रकाश डालिए।

उत्तर— प्रस्तुत कहानी मजबूरियों की एक शृंखला है जिसमें प्रत्येक चरित्र किसी न किसी कारण से मजबूर है। इस कहानी में चरित्रों की मजबूरियों ने सामाजिक व पारिवारिक समस्याओं के संघर्ष का एक विकृत स्वरूप हमारे समक्ष रखा है।

कहानी के प्रारम्भ में ही रामेश्वर का तीन साल बाद माँ से मिलने आना और अम्मा का यह कथन रामेश्वर की मजबूरी को प्रकट करता है, ''देख नर्बदा, मेरे रामेश्वर के लिए कुछ मत कहना। यह तो मैं ही जानती हूँ कि तीन-तीन बरस मुझसे दूर रहकर उसके दिन कैसे बीतते हैं, पर क्या करे, नौकरी तो आखिर नौकरी है।''

इसी प्रकार रमा का दूसरा बच्चा होने को है उस समय रमा की मजबूरी है कि वह बेटू को सँभाल न सकेगी, इसीलिए वह मजबूरी में बेटू को माँ के पास छोड़ने का निर्णय लेती है। बेटू की शिक्षा भी माँ के रूप में चिंता का विषय है, उसके बार-बार कहने पर भी जब अम्मा बेटू का प्रवेश नर्सरी स्कूल में नहीं कराती हैं तो रमा, बेटू को अपने साथ ले जाने के लिए मजबूर हो जाती है। इस प्रकार रमा के चरित्र में भी कई मजबूरियाँ दिखाई देने लगती हैं।

प्रस्तुत कहानी में अम्मा की विवशता प्रमुख है। कहानी की अधिकांश घटनाएँ अम्मा की विवशता पर आधारित हैं। अम्मा की मजबूरी ही कहानी का एक महत्वपूर्ण बिन्दु है। कहानी में बेटू का आगमन और बेटू के जाने तक की बात कथानक को एक प्रवाह देती है। इन मजबूरियों के बीच अम्मा का अकेलापन बेटू से उनका प्रेम, उनकी भी मजबूरी है।

इस प्रकार से जब कहानी के कथानक व उसकी विषय-वस्तु को देखते हैं तो यह पता चलता है कि यह कहानी मजबूरियों की दास्तान हैं, जिसमें सभी विवश हैं और परिस्थितियों के अधीन हैं। यहाँ एक चरित्र की मजबूरी दूसरे चरित्र की मजबूरी से जुड़ी है। इस आधार पर यह कहा जा सकता है कि कहानी का शीर्षक कहानी की मूल संवेदना को प्रकट करता है जो शीर्षक के औचित्य को सिद्ध करता है।

प्रश्न 3. 'मजबूरी' कहानी के आधार पर मन्नू भण्डारी जी की भाषागत विशेषताओं का उल्लेख कीजिए।

उत्तर—'मजबूरी' कहानी में मानवीय संवेदनाओं को बड़ी सहजता से उभारा गया है। जब इस कहानी की भाषा का अध्ययन करते हैं तो मन्नू भंडारी जी की भाषिक कुशलता का भान हो जाता है। कहानी के भाषा की प्रमुख विशेषताएँ निम्नवत् हैं—

पात्रानुकूल भाषा—'मजबूरी' कहानी में मन्नू भंडारी जी ने पात्रों के अनुकूल ही भाषा और शब्दों का चुनाव किया है, जो उनके शब्दकोश की व्यापकता को प्रदर्शित करता है। जैसे कहानी में नर्बदा का यह कथन

ग्रामीण भाषा व नर्बदा के चरित्र के अनुकूल है, "बेटे-बहू आ रहे हैं तो ऐसी क्या नवाई हो रही है, सभी के घर आते हैं !"

भाषा की सरलता— कहानी में भाषा का बड़ा ही सरल और सहज रूप दिखाई पड़ता है जो कहानी को स्वाभाविकता प्रदान करता है। यथा—"बच्चा एकाएक इतना प्यार और शारीरिक कष्ट पाकर रो उठा और माँ के पास जाने के लिए मचलने लगा।"

ग्रामीण तथा तत्सम शब्दों का प्रयोग— कहानी में अनेक स्थलों पर भाषा में ग्रामीण पुट देने के लिए ग्रामीण अंचल में प्रयुक्त किए जाने ग्रामीण शब्दों के साथ ही तत्सम शब्दों का भी प्रयोग किया गया है। जैसे— जस, परसाद, थाती, तरकारी आदि अनेक शब्द हैं जो कहानी में ग्रामीण अंचल के प्रभाव को बनाए रखने में सहायक हैं।

मुहावरे तथा लोकोक्तियों का प्रयोग— 'मजबूरी' कहानी में भाषा की प्रवाहमयता को बनाये रखने के लिए तथा भावों के प्रदर्शन के लिए मुहावरों और लोकोक्तियों का आवश्यकतानुसार सफल संयोजन किया गया है। पाठ में प्रयुक्त कुछ प्रमुख मुहावरे इस प्रकार हैं जैसे— छाती फूलना, पैरों तले से जमीन सरकना, खून का घूँट पीना आदि। इन मुहावरों ने जहाँ एक ओर भाषा को प्रवाहमयता प्रदान की है, वहीं दूसरी ओर भावों का सटीक प्रदर्शन भी किया है। कहानी में ग्रामीण अंचल की भाषा का प्रयोग किया गया है। प्रस्तुत है भाषा की एक बानगी—

"क्या बताऊँ ? कोई अगले जन्म का संस्कार ही समझ अब जाकर लाना पड़ेगा, नहीं तो छोरा रो-रोकर प्राण दे देगा।"

इस प्रकार निष्कर्ष रूप में यह कहा जा सकता है कि 'मजबूरी' कहानी में भाषा का प्रयोग लेखक ने देश, काल, वातावरण तथा पात्रों की पात्रता अर्थात चरित्र की अनुकूलता को ध्यान में रखकर किया है। इस प्रकार अनुकूल भाषा का प्रयोग करने से पाठकों को उसी अनुभूति का आभास होगा, जिसकी लेखक ने अभिव्यक्ति करनी चाही है। प्रस्तुत कहानी भाषा की दृष्टि से एक समृद्ध कहानी है। इस कहानी में मन्नू जी की भाषा सरल, प्रवाहमय तथा बोधगम्य है। मन्नू जी के शब्दों का चयन भावों के अनुकूल है।

प्रश्न 4. 'मजबूरी' कहानी के किस पात्र ने आपको सर्वाधिक प्रभावित किया है और क्यों ?

अथवा

'मजबूरी' कहानी में अम्मा के चरित्र की कौन-कौन सी विशेषताएँ हैं ?

उत्तर—'मजबूरी' कहानी में अम्मा का चरित्र ही मुख्य चरित्र है। अम्मा के चरित्र में स्वाभाविकता है जो उनके चरित्र को विशेष बनाती है। अम्मा के चित्र में जहाँ एक ओर अनेक विशेषताएँ हैं, वहीं दूसरी ओर अनेक दुर्बलताएँ भी हैं। अम्मा के चरित्र ने कहानीकार की उद्देश्यपूर्ति में सर्वाधिक योगदान दिया है।

पुत्र-प्रेमी— माँ का यह स्वाभाविक गुण है कि वह अपने बेटे से सर्वाधिक प्रेम करती है। मजबूरी कहानी में भी अम्मा अपने बेटे रामेश्वर से बहुत प्रेम करती हैं जबकि वह अपनी माँ से उतना प्रेम नहीं करता है। आज जब वह घर आ रहा है तो अम्मा अपनी दुःख और तकलीफ को भूलकर उसके आने की व्यवस्था में लगी हुई हैं। जब वह आँगन लीपने के बाद गठिया के दर्द के कारण उठ नहीं पाती तो नर्बदा के यह कहने पर नवाई की बात नहीं है कि तुम्हारा बेटा आ रहा है। तब अम्मा उसे इस प्रकार जवाब देती हैं—

"तू भी कैसी बात करती है, नर्बदा ! तीन बरस बाद मेरा बेटा आ रहा है, और मैं आँगन भी न लीपूँ ?"

सक्रिय— अम्मा जिसकी उम्र काफी हो गई है। जोड़ों के दर्द से कराहती रहती है पर फिर भी पुत्र के आने की तैयारी के दौरान उन्होंने अधिक से अधिक काम कर डाले जैसे— गरम पानी, चाय, दूध आदि की व्यवस्था करना। लेखक इस सन्दर्भ में कहता है कि—

"उस कड़कती सर्दी में ठिठुरते-ठिठुरते अम्मा ने बेटे-बहू को गरम करने के सारे आयोजन कर डाले।"

बुद्धिमान— अम्मा का चरित्र बुद्धिमानी से भरा है। अनेक स्थलों पर उन्होंने अपनी बुद्धिमत्ता का परिचय दिया। जैसे बहू के कहते ही कि वह बेटू को छोड़कर जाना चाहती है। वह खुश हो जाती है साथ ही

उनके मन में यह भी है कि बहू कहीं बाद में अपना इरादा न बदल दे। इसलिए वह इस बात का अधिक से अधिक प्रचार कर देना चाहती थीं। लेखक के अनुसार—

"अम्मा इस बात का इतना प्रचार कर देना चाहती थीं कि यदि किसी कारण से बहू का मन फिर भी जाये तो शरम के मारे ही वह अपना इरादा बदल न पाये।"

भावुक—अम्मा बहुत ही भावुक हैं। जब रमा उनसे बेटू को ले जाने की बात करती है तो वह अनेक तर्क देती है कि वह उसे गँवार न रहने देंगी। इतना ही नहीं उन तर्कों को देते समय वे रो पड़ती हैं जो उनकी भावुकता का छोटा सा उदाहरण है—

"तू चिन्ता मत कर, बहू, इसे ले जाने की बात मत कर ! और वे फफक-फफक कर रो पड़ीं।"

इस प्रकार अम्मा के चरित्र में अनेक विशेषताएँ हैं—संवेदनशीलता, वात्सल्य जैसे अनेक गुण जो कहानीकार के उद्देश्य की पूर्ति में अपना योगदान देते हैं।

प्रश्न 5. "मैं कह नहीं रही थी कि छुट्टी मिली नहीं कि वह दौड़ा आयेगा ? अम्मा के मारे तो उसके प्राण सूखते हैं। इतना बड़ा हो गया फिर भी यहाँ आयेगा तो रात में एक बार मेरी गोदी में जरूर सोयेगा।"

(i) नर्बदा ने अम्मा से क्या कहा ?

(ii) अम्मा ने नर्बदा को क्या उत्तर दिया ?

(iii) रामेश्वर के बारे में अम्मा क्या कहती है ?

(iv) अम्मा के मुँह से एक सर्द आह-सी क्यों निकलकर रह गयी ?

उत्तर—(i) नर्बदा ने बर्तन माँजते हुए अम्मा को काम करते हुए देखा तो कहा कि कल तो अम्मा गठिया में जुड़ी पड़ी थी, दर्द के मारे तन-बदन की सुध नहीं थी और आज ऐसी सर्दी में आँगन लीपने बैठ गयी।

(ii) अम्मा ने नर्बदा से पुलकित स्वर में कहा कि उसका बेटू कल आ रहा है रामेश्वर के साथ। इसलिए वह आँगन लीप रही है।

(iii) रामेश्वर के बारे में अम्मा ने कहा कि छुट्टी मिली नहीं कि रामेश्वर दौड़ा चला आयेगा। इतना बड़ा हो गया फिर भी यहाँ आयेगा तो रात में एक बार मेरी गोदी में जरूर सोयेगा। पर इस बार वह कह देगी कि अब तो वह अपनी गोदी में बेटू को सुलायेगी।

(iv) आँगन लीपने के बाद जब अम्मा का काम समाप्त हुआ तो मिट्टी में सनी हुई दोनों हथेलियों को जमीन पर टिकाकर उन्होंने उठने का प्रयत्न किया परन्तु एक सर्द आह-सी उनके मुँह से निकलकर रह गयी और वह नहीं उठ पायी। उठने में असफल होने पर उन्होंने नर्बदा को कातर स्वर में पुकारा और कहा, "अरे नर्बदा, मुझे जरा उठा दे री, घुटने तो जैसे फिर जुड़ गये।" जिसे बाद दर्पण नर्बद ने अम्मा को सहारा देकर उठाया, उनके हाथ धुलाये तथा खटिया पर लिटा दिया।

प्रश्न 6. नर्बदा यहाँ बरसों से काम करती है, अम्मा के लिए उसके मन में अपार श्रद्धा है, पर बेटे के प्रसंग को लेकर वह जब-तब उसका मन दुःखा दिया करती है।

(i) अम्मा ने उससे क्या कहा ?

(ii) नर्बदा अम्मा के सामने आज नम्र क्यों हो गयी ?

(iii) अम्मा का उत्साह किसने तोड़ दिया ?

(iv) अम्मा भोर होने से पहले ही क्यों उठ गयी ?

उत्तर—(i) अम्मा ने नर्बदा से कहा कि कल मेरा बेटू आ रहा है। जैसे ही रामेश्वर को छुट्टी मिलते ही वह दौड़ा चला आयेगा और रात में तो मेरी गोदी में सिर रखकर ही सोयेगा।

(ii) नर्बदा अम्मा के यहाँ बरसों से काम कर रही है। वह मन से अम्मा को बहुत चाहती है। नर्बदा वैसे तो अम्मा को काम करते देखती है तो डाँट भी देती है पर आज चूँकि अम्मा के बेटे के आने की बात हो रही थी इसलिए वह नम्र थी।

(iii) अम्मा का लीपने-पोतने का काम समाप्त हुआ तो उठने का प्रयास किया लेकिन दर्द के मारे उठ नहीं पायी। उन्होंने नर्बदा से उन्हें उठाने को कहा क्योंकि उन्हें लगा कि जैसे दोनों घुटने जुड़ गये हों। नर्बदा ने उन्हें समझाया कि उसे इतना काम नहीं करना चाहिए बच्चे तो सभी के घर आते ही हैं। अम्मा का उत्साह जैसे टूट गया।

(iv) अम्मा का बेटा रामेश्वर और उनका नाती बेटू तीन साल बाद आज आ रहे थे इसलिए अम्मा भोर होने से पहले ही उठ गयी क्योंकि उन्हें घर में काम करना था। उनके आने के समाचार से अम्मा बहुत खुश थी। वह इतनी खुश थी कि बचपन में रामेश्वर को सुनाने वाली लोरी गाने लगी तथा उसके बचपन की यादों को सोचने लगी। वह रामेश्वर के बचपन से बेटू के बचपन की तुलना करने लगी, जिससे उनकी आँखों में दौड़ते-फिरते बेटू के धुँधले चित्र बनने-बिगड़ने लगे। इन सब कल्पनाओं से ही उनका शरीर रोमांचित हो उठा।

प्रश्न 7. बीस दिन बाद जब बहू ने अपनी माँ के घर प्रयाण किया तो बेटू ने न जिद की, न वह रोया ही। माँ के कड़े नियन्त्रण के बाद दादी के असीम दुलार में रहना, जहाँ कोई बन्धन नहीं, अंकुश नहीं, बेटू को बड़ा अच्छा लगा।

(i) माँ के जाने पर बेटू ने जिद क्यों नहीं की ?

(ii) महीना बीते क्या खबर आयी ? अम्मा को कैसा लगा ?

(iii) जाने से पहले रामेश्वर ने क्या किया ?

(iv) साड़ी लाने पर अम्मा रामेश्वर से क्या कहती है ?

उत्तर—(i) अपनी माँ के जाने पर उसके साथ जाने के लिए बेटू ने जिद नहीं की और वह नहीं रोया क्योंकि माँ के कड़े नियन्त्रण के बाद दादी के असीम दुलार में रहना जहाँ कोई बन्दन नहीं, अंकुश नहीं, बेटू को बड़ा अच्छा लगा।

(ii) महीना बीते यह खबर आयी कि बहू के दूसरा लड़का हुआ है। अम्मा की छाती पर से जैसे एक भारी बोझ हट गया। संशय का एक काँटा जो रमा के जाने के बाद भी उसके मन में चुभा करता था, वह भी निकल गया। अम्मा को लगा कि अब बेटू मेरा है, यह भावना उसके मन में बैठ गई कि बेटू अब उसी के पास रहेगा।

(iii) बम्बई जाने से पहले रामेश्वर ने अम्मा और पिताजी के लिए ढेर सारे कपड़े बनवाये थे। अम्मा सारे मोहल्ले की औरतों को दिखाती फिरतीं। जो कोई आता उसी से कहतीं, "अम्मा के पीछे तो बस रामेश्वर पागल है, न आगे की सोचता है न पीछे की। उसका बस चले तो सारा घर मुझ पर लुटा दे। लाख मना करती रही, पागल ने एक बात नहीं मानी।"

(iv) साड़ी लाने पर अम्मा रामेश्वर से कहती है कि उसे बुढ़ापे में छपी साड़ियाँ पहनना अच्छा नहीं लगता। फिर भी अपने लिए साड़ियाँ लाने पर उनके चेहरे पर चमक आ गई और अपने बेटे के चिरायु होने की वह कामना करने लगीं।

●●

www.ingramcontent.com/pod-product-compliance
Lightning Source LLC
Chambersburg PA
CBHW061156240926
51846CB00006B/1030